Intermediate Accounting

THIRD EDITION

J. David Spiceland
University of Memphis

James F. Sepe
Santa Clara University

Lawrence A. Tomassini
The Ohio State University

McGraw Hill **Irwin**

Boston   Burr Ridge, IL   Dubuque, IA   Madison, WI   New York   San Francisco   St. Louis
Bangkok   Bogotá   Caracas   Kuala Lumpur   Lisbon   London   Madrid   Mexico City
Milan   Montreal   New Delhi   Santiago   Seoul   Singapore   Sydney   Taipei   Toronto

Irwin

INTERMEDIATE ACCOUNTING

Published by McGraw-Hill/Irwin, a business unit of The McGraw-Hill Companies, Inc., 1221 Avenue of the Americas, New York, NY, 10020. Copyright © 2004, 2001, 1998 by The McGraw-Hill Companies, Inc. All rights reserved. No part of this publication may be reproduced or distributed in any form or by any means, or stored in a database or retrieval system, without the prior written consent of The McGraw-Hill Companies, Inc., including, but not limited to, in any network or other electronic storage or transmission, or broadcast for distance learning.

Some ancillaries, including electronic and print components, may not be available to customers outside the United States.

This book is printed on acid-free paper.

3 4 5 6 7 8 9 0 VNH/VNH 0 9 8 7 6 5 4

ISBN 0-07-246613-8 (combined edition)
ISBN 0-07-250409-9 (volume I)
ISBN 0-07-250415-3 (volume II)

Photo credits for chapter opening photos: Chapter 1: Anthony Wood/Stock Boston; Chapter 2: David Young Wolff/PhotoEdit; Chapter 4: Bob Mahoney/The Image Works; Chapter 5: Cindy Charles/PhotoEdit; Chapter 6: Nancy Richmond/The Image Works; Chapter 7: Syracuse Newspaper/The Image Works; Chapter 8: Tom Pretyman/PhotoEdit; Chapter 9: Dennis Nett/Syracuse Newspaper/The Image Works; Chapter 10: John Neubauer/PhotoEdit; Chapter 11: Bob Daemmrich/The Image Works; Chapter 12: Dennis Budd Gray/Stock Boston; Chapter 13: Gale Zucker/Stock Boston; Chapter 14: Mark Richards/PhotoEdit; Chapter 15: Spencer Grant/PhotoEdit; Chapter 16: David Young Wolff/PhotoEdit; Chapter 17: © Frozen Images/The Image Works; Chapter 18: Tony Freeman/PhotoEdit; Chapter 19: David Young Wolff/PhotoEdit; Chapter 21: Sandy Huffaker/Getty Images; Chapter 22: Michael J. Doolittle/The Image Works.

Publisher: *Brent Gordon*
Executive editor: *Stewart Mattson*
Development editor I: *Heather Sabo*
Marketing manager: *Richard Kolasa*
Senior producer, Media technology: *Ed Przyzycki*
Senior project manager: *Pat Frederickson*
Manager, new book production: *Melonie Salvati*
Director of design BR: *Keith J. McPherson*
Photo research coordinator: *Judy Kausal*
Photo researcher: *Connie Gardner*
Senior supplement producer: *Carol Loreth*
Senior digital content specialist: *Brian Nacik*
Cover designer: *Maureen McCutheon*
Interior designer: *Maureen McCutheon*
Cover and section image: *Corbis Images*
Typeface: *10.5/12 Times Roman*
Compositor: *Cenveo*
Printer: *Von Hoffman Press, Inc.*

Library of Congress Cataloging-in-Publication Data

Spiceland, J. David, 1949
    Intermediate accounting / J. David Spiceland, James F. Sepe, Lawrence A. Tomassini —
3rd ed.
        p. cm.
    Includes bibliographical references and index.
    ISBN 0-07-246613-8 (alk. paper)
    1. Accounting. I. Sepe, James F. II. Tomassini, Lawrence A. III. Title.
HF5635 .S7838 2004
657.044—dc21

www.mhhe.com

Dear Colleagues,

As we finalize the preface to the third edition of our *Intermediate Accounting* textbook, we would like to thank each of you who adopted the second edition and the updated second edition. As fellow intermediate accounting instructors, we appreciate the importance of selecting the right book for your students. That's why we were honored that over 300 of you entrusted your intermediate accounting course to our text and its accompanying learning system. With your help, McGraw-Hill/Irwin selected the second edition for the Outstanding Revision of the Year award for 2001.

For the third edition, our goal for the revision has been to listen to our colleagues to ensure that our book continues to meet the changing needs of your students. In pursuit of that goal, we received feedback from our intermediate accounting colleagues in a variety of ways. Over 150 intermediate instructors provided us input through surveys, another 50 attended one of five focus groups held around the country in 2001, and 30 instructors participated in two reviewer panels. We thank you who participated for your generosity with your time and for your insight and many excellent suggestions.

We continue our commitment to provide you and your students with the most readable, accurate, and up-to-date intermediate text available. We also pledge to continue to write ourselves the major ancillary materials that accompany the text, including the website materials. Last, we will continue to listen to you, our colleagues, in developing our text to help prepare your students for the challenges of the 21st century.

Sincerely,

J. David Spiceland   James F. Sepe   Lawrence A. Tomassini

About the Authors

David Spiceland

David Spiceland is Professor of Accounting at the University of Memphis, where he teaches intermediate accounting and other financial accounting courses at the undergraduate, masters, and doctoral levels. He received his BS degree in finance from the University of Tennessee, his MBA from Southern Illinois University, and his PhD in accounting from the University of Arkansas.

Professor Spiceland's primary research interests are in earnings management and educational research. He has published articles in a variety of journals including *The Accounting Review, Accounting and Business Research, Journal of Financial Research,* and *Journal of Accounting Education.* David has received university and college awards and recognition for his teaching, research, and technological innovations in the classroom.

Jim Sepe

Jim Sepe is an Associate Professor of Accounting at Santa Clara University where he teaches primarily intermediate accounting in both the undergraduate and graduate programs. He previously taught at California Poly State University–San Luis Obispo and the University of Washington, and has visited at Stanford University and the Rome campus of Loyola University of Chicago.

Professor Sepe received his BS from Santa Clara University, MBA from the University of California–Berkeley, and PhD from the University of Washington. His research interests concern financial reporting issues and the use of financial information by capital markets. He has published in *The Accounting Review,* the *Journal of Business Finance and Accounting, Financial Management,* the *Journal of Forensic Accounting,* and the *Journal of Accounting Education.* He is a past recipient of the American Accounting Association's Competitive Manuscript Award and has served as a member of the editorial board of *The Accounting Review.*

Jim has received numerous awards for his teaching excellence and innovations in the classroom, including Santa Clara University's Brutocao Award for Excellence in Curriculum Innovation.

Lawrence Tomassini

Larry Tomassini is Professor of Accounting & MIS at The Ohio State University. He has held several endowed chair positions during his academic career, including the Ernst & Young Distinguished Professor at the University of Illinois and the Peat Marwick Mitchell Centennial Professorship in Accounting at the University of Texas.

His research has been widely published in scholarly journals, including *The Accounting Review, Accounting Horizons, Journal of Accounting Research,* and *Contemporary Accounting Research.* Dr. Tomassini is a reviewer for the *Journal of Financial Statement Analysis* and *Issues in Accounting Education.*

He teaches financial accounting courses at the undergraduate and master's levels. Recently, he has been Director of the Ohio State Master of Accounting Program and Vice President for Publications of the American Accounting Association.

Larry has been a pioneer in the use of Internet technology to support the teaching of accounting courses. He has been listed in *Who's Who in America* and *Who's Who in Finance and Industry.*

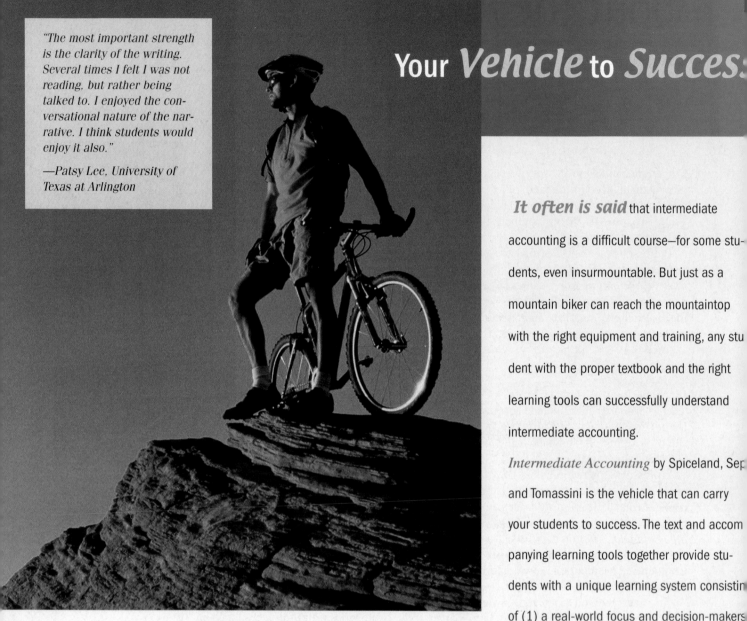

Your *Vehicle* to *Success*

> "The most important strength is the clarity of the writing. Several times I felt I was not reading, but rather being talked to. I enjoyed the conversational nature of the narrative. I think students would enjoy it also."
>
> —Patsy Lee, University of Texas at Arlington

> "Very well written and quite enjoyable for an Intermediate book. It's the best reading book I've seen."
>
> —Jeff Jones, Auburn University

It often is said that intermediate accounting is a difficult course—for some students, even insurmountable. But just as a mountain biker can reach the mountaintop with the right equipment and training, any student with the proper textbook and the right learning tools can successfully understand intermediate accounting.

Intermediate Accounting by Spiceland, Sepe and Tomassini is the vehicle that can carry your students to success. The text and accompanying learning tools together provide students with a unique learning system consisting of (1) a real-world focus and decision-makers perspective on accounting's financial reporting function, (2) end-of-chapter resources designed to reinforce concepts and to develop the problem-solving skills essential for the new CPA exam, and (3) additional integrated tools to help students master the material regardless of their preferred learning style.

Learning System

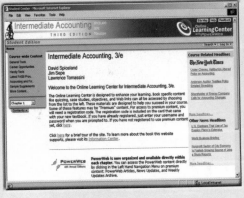

ONLINE LEARNING CENTER (OLC)

Professors and students agree that this is the #1 intermediate accounting website—perhaps even the #1 accounting website. Students love this website because it is full of assessment material and other interesting tools that help them test their knowledge and understand important intermediate accounting concepts. Unlike other accounting websites where the content is outsourced, our Online Learning Center is written by the authors. So, the flashcards, online quizzes, practice exams, and other valuable resources use consistent terminology and place the same emphasis on topics. Visit Spiceland online at www.mhhe.com/spiceland3e.

ALTERNATE EXERCISES AND PROBLEMS MANUAL

Back by popular demand and expanded! Students loved the extra problem material with solutions that they could use for practice before an exam or just to learn the concept. Faculty loved having additional problem material they could use as worked examples in class.

POWERWEB

Keeping your accounting course timely can be a job in itself, and now McGraw-Hill does that job for you. PowerWeb is a site from which you can access articles on all the latest developments pertinent to your course, without all the clutter and dead links of a typical online search. In light of the developments to the accounting profession due to Enron, McGraw-Hill created an Enron PowerWeb site that is packaged FREE with Spiceland. With PowerWeb for Enron, your students also get access to PowerWeb for Financial Accounting. Go to the Spiceland OLC to access PowerWeb.

GRADESUMMIT

GradeSummit is a practice exam bank that tells your students everything they need to know in order to study effectively. And it provides the instructor with valuable insight into which of your students are struggling and which course topics give them the most trouble. You can try out a chapter of GradeSummit for FREE. You can continue using GradeSummit with *Intermediate Accounting* for an additional fee. Go to the Spiceland Online Learning Center and click on the link to GradeSummit to get set up!

Net Tutor ™

See the back cover to learn about NetTutor's live online tutoring— FREE with this textbook!

Can a Learning System really make a difference to your students?

Net Tutor™

Listen to what some current and future Spiceland users are saying:

"I happened to mention in my intermediate class that I was looking into different texts for next year and that I liked the Spiceland book. When I mentioned the Spiceland name, a student raised her hand and said that she had been using the Spiceland website in order to understand the material. She said she would review the PowerPoint slides, the flashcards and the practice tests for every chapter we covered in class. She thought that it was excellent. I was so surprised that a student found it all on her own! Three students even went so far as to purchase the Spiceland text online. After hearing that, I was convinced that Spiceland would be the right choice." **Michelle Randall—Schoolcraft Community College**

Janice Stoudemire, a Spiceland user at Midlands Technical college submitted some comments from her students:

"… the book was like having Mrs. Stoudemire talk to us in class."

"I failed Accounting 201 last semester and I think it had a lot to do with the old book. That book was hard to read, so I really didn't read it. This one cost a lot, but it was easier to read. I like the (Coach) CD thing too. I used it a lot."

"This textbook was easier to read than the principles textbook."

"The Coach CD was awesome. It was fun to use the Coach to help with the chapters. Why doesn't my textbook for Not-for-Profit have a Coach CD?"

GradeSummit™

A Service of McGraw Hill Education

OLC

with POWERWEB

in *Intermediate Accounting*

Intermediate Accounting's learning system features:

Clarity:
Reviewers, instructors, and student users of Spiceland have enthusiastically embraced the readability of the text and its ability to clearly explain not just the simple topics, but more importantly the complex ones. The authors achieve this by using a relaxed, conversational writing style that engages students and helps to boost their confidence.

A Decision Making Perspective:
Recent events have focused public attention on the role of accounting in providing information useful to decision makers. The CPA Exam, too, is redirecting its focus to emphasize the skills needed to critically evaluate accounting method alternatives. This text provides a decision maker's perspective to emphasize the professional judgment and critical thinking skills required of accountants today.

"Decision Makers' Perspective adds realism and relevance to the role of the accountant in the organization."

—Myrtle W. Clark, University of Kentucky

Flexibility:
Not all students learn the same way, so *Intermediate Accounting* provides a toolset suitable for a variety of learning needs. The Coach CD, which is integrated with the text, provides students with an interactive multimedia environment in which to learn critical concepts. Accounting's preeminent textbook website combined with the other supplements noted in this preface provide your students with a flexible selection of tools to succeed.

Consistent Quality:
Quite often, a text's ancillary materials are written by persons other than the textbook authors. This leads to inconsistency in terminology, content, and style and consequently confuses both students and instructors. An important feature of our learning system is that the authors themselves created each major component of the system with quality and consistency in mind. The Coach CD, end-of-chapter materials, solutions manual, study guide, instructor's resource manual, test bank, and website tools all were written by the text authors.

"The three most significant strengths of this text over my current text are a focus on the theory underlying the accounting for the transactions, the attempt to couch the discussion in terms of how firms actually operate, and the careful use of well-constructed examples to illustrate the accounting."

—Marlene Plumlee, University of Utah

Intermediate Accounting, 3/e, has the quality, flexibility, and attention to detail your students need to master a challenging range of topics. In short, it's their vehicle to success.

What makes *Intermediate Accounting* such a *powerful* learning tool?

DECISION MAKERS' PERSPECTIVE

These boxes appear throughout the text to illustrate how accounting information is put to work in today's firms. With the CPA exam placing greater focus on application of skills in realistic work settings, these boxes help your students gain an edge that will remain with them as they enter the workplace.

EARNINGS QUALITY/ EARNINGS MANAGEMENT COVERAGE

Earnings Quality/Earnings Management is covered early in the text in Chapter 4 and integrated where appropriate.

AUTHOR-WRITTEN SUPPLEMENTS

In contrast to other author teams, Spiceland, Sepe, and Tomassini write all of *Intermediate Accounting's* primary supplements themselves. This ensures a perfect fit between text and supplement, cutting down on student confusion and making their study time more productive. For more on *Intermediate Accounting's* supplements package, see pages (xviii-xix).

CHAPTER 15 Leases **747**

DECISION MAKERS' PERSPECTIVE—Financial Statement Impact

As indicated in the Decision Makers' Perspective at the beginning of the chapter, leasing can allow a firm to conserve assets, to avoid some risks of owning assets, and to obtain favorable tax benefits. These advantages are desirable. It also was pointed out earlier that some firms try to obscure the realities of their financial position through off-balance-sheet financing or by avoiding violating terms of contracts that limit the amount of debt a company can have. Accounting guidelines are designed to limit the ability of firms to hide financial realities. Nevertheless, investors and creditors should be alert to the impact leases can have on a company's financial position and on its risk. ■

BALANCE SHEET AND INCOME STATEMENT

Lease transactions identified as nonoperating impact several of a firm's financial ratios. Because we record liabilities for capital leases, the debt-equity ratio (liabilities divided by shareholders' equity) is immediately impacted. Because we also record leased assets, the immediate impact on the rate of return on assets (net income divided by assets) is negative, but the lasting effect depends on how leased assets are utilized to enhance future net income. As illustrated in this chapter, the financial statement impact of a capital lease is no different from that of an installment purchase.

Even operating leases, though, can significantly affect risk. Operating leases represent long-term commitments that can become a problem if business declines and cash inflows drop off. For example, long-term lease commitments became a big problem for Businessland in the early 1990s. The company's revenues declined but it was saddled with lease commitments for numerous facilities the company no longer occupied. Its stock's market price declined from $11.88 to $.88 in one year.

Whether leases are capitalized or treated as operating leases affects the income statement as well as the balance sheet. However, the impact generally is not significant. Over the life of a lease, total expenses are equal regardless of the accounting treatment of a lease. If the lease is capitalized, total expenses comprise interest and depreciation. The total of these equals the total amount of rental payments, which would constitute rent expense if not capitalized. There is, however, a timing difference between lease capitalization and operating lease treatment, but the timing difference usually isn't great.

The more significant difference between capital leases and operating leases is the impact on the balance sheet. As mentioned above, a c... side of the balance sheet; operating leases do n... ternal financial statement users adjust their an... ences between capital and operating leases? A... all noncancelable lease commitments, includi... nancial analysts, in fact, do this on their own t... position.

To illustrate, refer to Graphic 15–16, which... closed by **Wal-Mart Stores**. If these lease arran... payments would be capitalized (reported at t... making some reasonable assumptions, we ca... ments to be made on existing operating leases... Mart to discount rental payments on capital le... approximate average rate of 10%, and make ce... debt equivalent of the operating lease commit...

If capitalized, these operating lease commit... liabilities and approximately $4,210 to the co...

[*If these operating leases were capitalized, both assets and liabili... lease. However, in later years, the leased asset account balance a... leased asset account is reduced by depreciation and the lease liab... fective interest method.]

---

748 SECTION 3 Finan...

GRAPHIC 15–17
Estimating the Debt
Equivalent of
Operating Lease
Commitments

Lease liab...
the debt-...
and the r...
on assets.

Do opera...
create lon...
commitm...
equivalen...

The net i...
difference...
treating a...
capital lea...
operating lease
generally is not
significant.

> *"This pedagogical framework was one of the reasons we selected this textbook."*
>
> *-Gary K. Taylor, University of Alabama*

4
The Income Statement and Statement of Cash Flows

CHAPTER

OVERVIEW

The purpose of the income statement is to summarize the profit-generating activities that occurred during a particular reporting period. The purpose of the statement of cash flows is to provide information about the cash receipts and cash disbursements of an enterprise that occurred during the period.

This chapter has a twofold purpose: (1) to consider important issues dealing with income statement content, presentation, and disclosure and (2) to provide an *overview* of the statement of cash flows, which is covered in depth in Chapter 22.

> *"I love the stuff on earnings quality/ earnings management. This is a very nice differentiator; while other books mention the topic, they do little else."*
>
> —Edward Ketz, Penn State

...ce between net income
...income and how we report
...difference.

...nce of income from continuing
...cribe its components.

...quality and how it is impacted by
...ces to manipulate earnings.

...ents of operating and nonoperating
...lationship to earnings quality.

...utes discontinued operations and
describe the appropriate income statement presentation
for these transactions.

LO6   Define extraordinary items and describe the appropriate
income statement presentation for these transactions.

...quality.

Before we investigate separately reported items, let's take a closer look at the components
of both operating and nonoperating income and their relationship to earnings quality.

Earnings Quality

Financial analysts are concerned with more than just the bottom line of the income statement—net income. The presentation of the components of net income and the related supplemental disclosures provide clues to the user of the statement in an assessment of *earnings quality*. Earnings quality is used as a framework for more in-depth discussions of operating and nonoperating income.

Earnings quality refers to the ability of reported earnings (income) to predict a company's future earnings.

The term **earnings quality** refers to the ability of reported earnings (income) to predict a company's future earnings. After all, an income statement simply reports on events that already have occurred. The relevance of any historical-based financial statement hinges on its predictive value. To enhance predictive value, analysts try to separate a company's *transitory earnings* effects from its *permanent earnings*. Transitory earnings effects result from transactions or events that are not likely to occur again in the foreseeable future, or that are likely to have a different impact on earnings in the future. Later in the chapter we address three items that, because of their transitory nature, are required to be reported separately in

Intermediate Accounting is full of pedagogy designed to make studying productive and hassle free. On the following pages, you will see the engaging, helpful pedagogical features that enable your students, regardless of academic major or preferred learning style, to master the fundamentals of intermediate accounting.

Operating Leases	PV Factor 10%	Present Value
$ 623	.909	$ 566
602	.826	497
586	.751	440
565	.683	386
547	.621	340
5,131	.386*	1,981
$8,054		$4,210

...alent of Wal-Mart's Operating Leases

...ich treats payments after 2007 as occurring in 2012, an assumption due to not ...after 2007.

...t to equity ratio and its return on assets ratio using selected ...ken from Wal-Mart's annual report for the fiscal year end-...w:

	($ in millions)
	$83,451
	48,349
...ders' equity	35,102
	6,671

...on assets ratios are calculated in Graphic 15–18 without ...operating leases and then again after adding $4,210 million ...ities. In the calculation of return on assets, we use only the ...e average total assets for the year. Also, we assume no im-

...effective interest each period is more than the cash paid, and the underpayment of interest adds to the amount owed.

ADDITIONAL CONSIDERATION

The preceding illustrations describe bonds sold at a discount and at a premium. The same concepts apply to bonds sold at face amount. But some of the procedures would be unnecessary. For instance, calculating the present value of the interest and the principal always will give us the face amount when the effective rate and the stated rate are the same:

Calculation of the Price of the Bonds

			Present Values
Interest	$42,000 × 4.91732*	=	$206,528
Principal	$700,000 × 0.70496†	=	493,472
Present value (price) of the bonds			$700,000

*Present value of an ordinary annuity of $1: n = 6, i = 6%.
†Present value of $1: n = 6, i = 6%.

WHEN FINANCIAL STATEMENTS ARE PREPARED BETWEEN INTEREST DATES

ETHICAL DILEMMA

The Precision Parts Corporation manufactures automobile parts. The company has reported a profit every year since the company's inception in 1977. Management prides itself on this accomplishment and believes one important contributing factor is the company's incentive plan that rewards top management a bonus equal to a percentage of operating income *if the operating income goal for the year is achieved*. However, 2003 has been a tough year, and prospects for attaining the income goal for the year are bleak.

Tony Smith, the company's chief financial officer, has determined a way to increase December sales by an amount sufficient to boost operating income over the goal for the year and earn bonuses for all top management. A reputable customer ordered $120,000 of parts to be shipped on January 15, 2004. Tony told the rest of top management "I know we can get that order ready by December 31 even though it will require some production line overtime. We can then just leave the order on the loading dock until shipment. I see nothing wrong with recognizing the sale in 2003, since the parts will have been manufactured and we do have a firm order from a reputable customer." The company's normal procedure is to ship goods f.o.b. destination and to recognize sales revenue when the customer receives the parts.

FINANCIAL REPORTING CASE

Hallib...

...We now turn our a... ...are more obviously not part of a company's permanent earnings and, appropriately, are excluded from continuing operations.

Separately Reported Items

The information in the income statement is useful if it can help users predict the future. Toward this end, users should be made aware of events reported in the income statement that are not likely to occur again in the foreseeable future.

There are three types of events that, if they have a material effect[21] on the income statement, require separate reporting and disclosure: (1) discontinued operations, (2) extraordinary items, and (3) the cumulative effect of a change in accounting principle.[22] In fact, these are the only three events that are allowed to be reported below continuing operations. Although a company has considerable flexibility in reporting income from *continuing operations*, the presentation order of these three is mandated as follows:[23]

Income from continuing operations	$xxx
Discontinued operations, net of $xx in taxes	xx
Extraordinary items, net of $xx in taxes[24]	xx
Cumulative effect of a change in accounting principle, net of $xx in taxes	xx
Net income	$xxx

The objective is to separately report all of the income effects of these items. Therefore, their income tax effects also are included in the separate presentation rather than as part of the amount reported as income tax expense. The process of associating income tax effects with income statement components that create those effects is referred to as *intraperiod tax allocation*. We address this process before defining the separately reported items more precisely.

FINANCIAL REPORTING CASE Q2, p. 167

GAAP require that certain transactions be reported separately in the income statement, below income from continuing operations.

...in my introductory accounting course," says Be... ...erations? And how about *restructuring costs*? ...about? And why is there a negative $47 millio... ...last item in the income statement *cumulative e...* You agree to try to help.

HALL... In... Year...

Revenues	
Operating costs and expenses:	
Cost of services	
Cost of sales	
General and administrative	
Restructuring costs	
Total operating costs and expenses	
Operating income	
Other income (expense):	
Interest expense	
Interest income	
Gain on sale of vessels	
Other	
Income before taxes	
Provision for income taxes	
Income (loss) from continuing operations	
Discontinued operations, net of tax	
Cumulative effect of a change in account...	
Net income (loss)	

11,570	11,91...	
374	401	170
(146)	(141)	(134)

| Cash and cash equivalents, January 1 | | 130,000 |
| Cash and cash equivalents, December 31 | | $304,000 |

FINANCIAL REPORTING CASE SOLUTION

1. **How would you explain restructuring costs to Becky? Are they necessarily a negative? What is the likely explanation for the negative expense in 1999?** (p. 177) Restructuring costs include employee severance and termination benefits plus other costs associated with the shutdown or relocation of facilities or downsizing of operations. It's not necessarily bad. In fact, the objective is to make operations more efficient. The costs are incurred now in hopes of better earnings later. When a company restructures its operations, it estimates the future costs associated with the restructuring and expenses the costs in the period in which the decision to restructure is made. An offsetting liability is recorded. Later expenditures are charged against this liability as they occur. In 1999, Halliburton lowered its estimate of the total costs associated with the 1998 restructuring and recorded an adjustment that increased

Intermediate accounting is a difficult, challenging topic. To help students learn the material covered and be able to use it in practice, the authors focus their efforts in helping students build problem-solving skills.

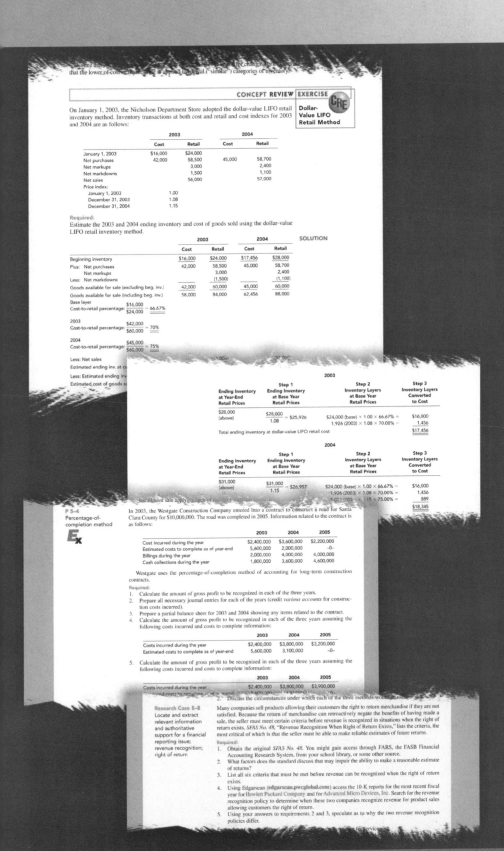

CONCEPT REVIEW EXERCISES

Included within each chapter for each core issue discussed, the Concept Review Exercises with solutions allow students to reinforce their understanding and practice applying the procedures learned in the chapter before attempting homework assignments.

What's *new* about the *Third Edition?*

Chapter 1

The political process section has been updated to include a discussion of the recent debate that occurred on the issue of accounting for business combinations.

Chapter 2

Revised material

Chapters 3, 4, and 5

The order of these three chapters has been changed. The new sequence is as follows:

Chapter 3   The balance sheet and financial disclosures

Chapter 4   The income statement and statement of cash flows

Chapter 5   Income measurement and profitability analysis

The reasons for this revision include:

The basic financial statements are now presented contiguously in chapters 3 and 4.

The balance sheet is now covered before presenting the material on the balance sheet treatment of long-term contract accounting (in the chapter on income measurement).

As with the second edition, the topic of revenue recognition (Chapter 5) again follows immediately after the income statement coverage (Chapter 4).

Chapter 3

Revised material

Chapter 4

Part A of this chapter, the income statement, has been restructured by framing the discussion of income statement presentation within the context of earnings quality/earnings management. The restructure provides an appropriate and interesting way to walk students through the income statement. In most chapters that follow, the issue of earnings quality/earnings management is revisited, in most cases within the context of Decision Makers' Perspectives.

The discontinued operations section has been revised to reflect the impact of SFAS No. 144, "Accounting for the Impairment or Disposal of Long-Lived Assets," on accounting for discontinued operations, and the section on restructuring costs has been updated to reflect SFAS No. 146, "Accounting for Costs Associated with Exit or Disposal."

Chapter 5

The two main headings within Part A are now:

1. Revenue Recognition at a Point in Time

2. Revenue Recognition over Time

We believe this is a much more logical way to present the information to students. Any specific revenue recognition issue falls nicely into one of these two logical categories.

The revised chapter includes a discussion of the *SEC's Staff Accounting Bulletin No. 101,* "Revenue Recognition in Financial Statements," and the impact this pronouncement has had on company revenue recognition policies.

Chapter 6

The chapter has been updated to include a discussion of SFAC No. 7, "Using Cash Flow Information and Present Value in Accounting Measurements."

Chapter 7

The entire section on financing with receivables has been revised and updated to incorporate SFAS No. 140, "Accounting for Transfers and Servicing of Financial Assets and Extinguishments of Liabilities." We believe this revision provides a better flow to the material. In addition, we have added some real world examples to increase the relevance of the material.

A Decision Makers' Perspective section on cash management has been added.

Chapter 8

A Decision Makers' Perspective section on inventory management has been added.

Chapter 9

The introduction to Part A, The Lower of Cost or Market, has been revised to provide increased real-world relevance to the topic.

Chapters 10 and 11

These two chapters cover accounting for operational assets. We have changed the title of Chapter 10 to "Acquisition and Disposition" and Chapter 11 to "Utilization and Impairment." A new Part B has been added to Chapter 10 entitled "Dispositions and Exchanges." The small section on disposition through sale or abandonment has been moved from Chapter 11 to this part of Chapter 10 along with all of the material on exchanges.

These chapters have been updated to include the following new pronouncements:

SFAS No. 141, "Business Combinations"

SFAS No. 142, "Goodwill and Other Intangible Assets"

SFAS No. 143, "Accounting for Asset Retirement Obligations"

SFAS No. 144, "Accounting for the Impairment or Disposal of Long-Lived Assets"

Chapter 12

Part A: Graphic 12–1 was added to provide an overview of the six approaches to accounting for investments.

Accounting for held-to-maturity securities has been expanded.

We revisit our discussion of investments in debt securities to be held to maturity in Chapter 14, "Bonds and Long-Term Notes" in order to more readily see that accounting by the company that issues bonds and by the company that invests in those bonds is opposite but parallel. However, an illustration was added to the discussion in this chapter to help students understand what it means to report these securities at amortized cost in the balance sheet and to contrast that with accounting for available-for-sale and trading securities at fair value. When we resume our discussion of bond investments in Chapter 14, we continue the same numerical illustration we began in this chapter.

A T-account analysis to reinforce the effect of the accounting treatment on the accounts affected was added.

We added numerical demonstrations of the effects on the balance sheet, income statement, and SCF.

An expanded discussion of comprehensive income is added, particularly as it relates to available-for-sale securities.

Part B: We modified our discussion, illustrations, and end-of-chapter materials pertaining to the equity method to conform with the new FASB standards eliminating the amortization of goodwill and thus the effects of that elimination on previously required adjustments in the equity method.

Introduction to financial instruments and investment derivatives has been moved to follow the Decision Makers' Perspective.

Chapter 13

In Chapter 6, we described a framework for taking into account any uncertainty concerning the amounts and timing of the cash flows. We added a demonstration of that approach in this chapter as it relates to measuring a warranty obligation and compare it with the traditional way of measuring a warranty obligation.

We expanded the Decision Makers' Perspective section to consider the possibility of management efforts to manipulate the ratios that measure liquidity, including timing strategies that manipulate the timing of revenue and expense recognition in order to "smooth" income over time.

Chapter 14

We reorganized the topics in this chapter to create a more logical flow and to provide instructors greater flexibility in the choice of topics to be covered. One result is apportioning the material into three parts rather than the two parts in the second edition.

Part A: Bonds

Part B: Notes

Part C: Debt Retired Early, Convertible into Stock, or Providing an Option to Buy Stock

We moved the primary Derivatives coverage from this chapter to an Addendum to the text, complete with typical end of chapter material. The topic is introduced in Chapter 12.

In the aftermath of Enron and other financial losses that have grabbed headlines in recent years, we expanded the Decision Makers'

Perspective section to consider risks associated with off balance sheet financing and other commitments that don't show up on the face of financial statements but nevertheless expose a company to risk, along with attempts to actively manage the risk associated with these and other obligations.

Chapter 15

We reorganized the topics in this chapter to create a more logical flow and to provide instructors greater flexibility in the choice of topics to be covered. One result is apportioning the material into four parts rather than the two parts in the second edition.

Part A: Accounting by the Lessor and Lessee

Part B: Residual Value and Bargain Purchase Options

Part C: Other Lease Accounting Issues

Part D: Special Leasing Arrangements

We clarified and expanded our discussion of the cash flow impact of each type of lease.

Chapter 16

Based on reviewer input, we eliminated our coverage of the tax effects of accounting changes and error correction and the Appendix "Investment Revenue from Equity Method Investees."

Chapter 17

We expanded the Decision Makers' Perspective section to consider the implications for earnings quality assessment of amounts reported in pension disclosures.

Chapter 18

We reorganized the topics in this chapter to create a more logical flow and to provide instructors greater flexibility in the choice of topics to be covered. One result is apportioning the material into three parts rather than the two parts in the second edition.

Part A: Postretirement Benefits Other than Pensions

Part B: Stock-Based Compensation Plans

Part C: Other Compensation Prior to Retirement

Employee Stock Ownership Plans has been moved to an appendix.

We expanded two Decision Makers' Perspective sections to consider:

1. The effect on ratio computations (such as the debt to equity ratio or return on assets) of the postretirement benefit obligation not being part of the balance sheet and how investment analysts can modify their analysis.

2. The stock-based compensation plans we discuss in this chapter as another motive managers sometimes have to manipulate income.

Chapter 19

An expanded discussion of comprehensive income is added. The discussion and illustrations focus on (a) comprehensive income created during the reporting reported as part of the statement of shareholders' equity and (b) comprehensive income accumulated over the current and prior periods reported as a separate component of shareholders' equity.

Chapter 20

We expanded the Decision Makers' Perspective section to consider the recent and controversial practice of companies reporting pro forma earnings per share and the possibility that companies judiciously use share buybacks to enhance the appearance of EPS numbers.

Chapter 21

We expanded the section on accounting errors using Enron's error correction experience as the backdrop for the discussion.

Chapters 22

We reorganized the topics in this chapter into three parts:

Part A: The Content and Value of the Statement of Cash Flows

Part B: The Direct Method of Reporting Cash Flows from Operating Activities

Part C: The Indirect Method of Reporting Cash Flows from Operating Activities

A key advantage of this division is to provide instructors greater flexibility in the choice of topics to be covered, particularly in the relative focus on the direct and indirect methods of reporting operating activities.

Can *technology* really help *students* and *professors* in the learning process?

Today, nearly 200,000 college instructors use the Internet in their respective courses. Some are just getting started, while others are ready to embrace the very latest advances in educational content delivery and course management.

That's why we at McGraw-Hill/Irwin offer you a complete range of digital solutions. Your students can use Intermediate Accounting's complete Online Learning Center, NetTutor, and PowerWeb on their own, or we can help you create your own course Website using McGraw-Hill's PageOut.

In addition to Web-based assets, *Intermediate Accounting* boasts Coach, a CD-ROM that offers special chapter-by-chapter assistance for the most demanding intermediate accounting topics. Coach breaks down each chapter or theme into four simple components: The Big Picture, Ask the Expert, Coaching Illustrations, and Show the Coach What You Know.

McGraw-Hill is a leader in bringing helpful technology into the classroom. And with *Intermediate Accounting,* your class gets all the benefits of the digital age.

"Based on my experience with giving computerized exams in our MBA program, I suggest that you don't want the first time your students take an exam on a computer to be the new uniform CPA exam. There is clearly a learning curve that can be mastered in a less risky environment that will serve your students well."

—Jan Williams, University of Tennessee–Knoxville

How can *students that are visual learners* find help?

Coach is an exciting, multimedia vehicle designed to be used in concert with the textbook to enhance the intermediate accounting learning experience. Students access the multimedia content from either of two perspectives. A Chapter Enhancement perspective provides access chapter by chapter. Alternatively, the Accounting Theme perspective brings together topics from diverse chapters that share relationships within four themes: (1) Standard Setting and the Politics of Accounting, (2) Earnings Management and Accounting Choices, (3) Financial Statement Relationships, and (4) Accounting Disclosures and Decision Making. Either way—chapter-by-chapter or by theme—multimedia content is available through four menus: The Big Picture, Ask the Expert, Coaching Illustrations, and Show the Coach What You Know.

- The Big Picture provides a summary of each accounting theme or chapter enhancement.

- Ask the Expert presents accounting questions that are answered by leading experts in industry and academia via video clips or articles on the Internet.

- Coaching Illustrations are illustrations and examples from the text brought to life with multimedia animation to walk students through important concepts.

- Show the Coach What You Know allows students to test themselves with (a) interactive questions in the Coach's Challenge component and (b) with real-world, real time electronic cases in the Web Cases component.

- Other Features: The Coach CD also has a Quick Jump feature that allows students to access a coaching illustration by simply typing in the page number from the text. An Overview feature orients the student to the navigation and context found on the CD. Also, the CD has a Bookmark feature so that when students exit the program, the next time they use the CD they will be brought back to that place on the CD.

How can I *easily integrate Web resources* into my course?

How can my *students* use their *study time* more effectively?

ONLINE LEARNING CENTER (OLC)

More and more students are studying online. That's why we offer an Online Learning Center (OLC) that follows *Intermediate Accounting* chapter by chapter. It doesn't require any building or maintenance on your part. It's ready to go the moment you and your students type in the URL.

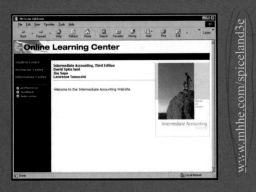

As your students study, they can refer to the OLC Website for such benefits as:

- E-learning sessions
- Self-grading quizzes
- Electronic flash cards
- Communication tools
- PowerPoint tutorial
- Articles
- Real-world electronic cases
- Online tutoring (NetTutor)
- Class activities and projects
- Alternate exercises and problems
- Check figures
- Career opportunities
- Practice exams
- Ethics Issues
- Handy tools
- FASB pronouncements
- Accounting and financial information
- International accounting resources
- FASB updates

A secured Instructor Resource Center stores your essential course materials to save you prep time before class. The Instructor's Manual, Solutions, PowerPoint, and sample syllabi are now just a couple of clicks away. You will also find useful packaging information and transition notes.

The OLC Website also serves as a doorway to other technology solutions like PageOut, which is free to Intermediate Accounting adopters.

HOMEWORK MANAGER

Homework Manager is an exciting new web-based supplement available with Intermediate Accounting by Spiceland, Sepe, and Tomassini.

Homework Manager will help your students learn intermediate accounting by allowing them to work through selected problem structures pulled from the text and powered by algorithms. Providing a wealth of these textbook-quality questions enables students to work on fresh problems with the same problem structure until they master the topics covered. Each student also receives immediate scoring and feedback from the program to guide their studies.

The problem structures available in Homework Manager can be easily identified in the text by the Homework Manager icon found in the margin.

Homework Manager to accompany Intermediate Accounting also includes problem material that will require your students to build the research, analysis, judgment, communication, and spreadsheet skills that will be required on the new Uniform CPA Exam. This provides faculty with an easy solution for ensuring that your students are prepared to sit the new exam.

Homework Manager may be used in practice, homework, or exam mode, as well a variety of other standard assignment modes. In the practice mode, students receive feedback and work as many iterations of each problem as they like without entering a record in the class grade book. In the homework mode, students receive a customized level of feedback, and their grades and individual responses are recorded in the class grade book. In the exam mode, faculty can create an online exam. Homework Manager will then record all the individual responses, grade the exams, and record the grades in the online grade book. So, you not only know how your class performed on the exam, but also, which topics or learning objectives your students struggled with.

Homework Manager is powered by Brownstone Learning.

What's the best way for my students to *brush up* their *Financial Accounting skills*?

What *help* can I rely on from McGraw-Hill for setting up my *online course*?

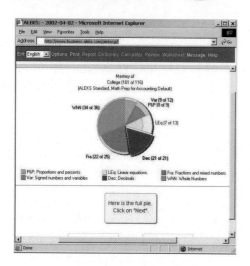

ALEKS (Assessment and LEarning in Knowledge Spaces) is an artificial intelligence-based system for individualized learning, available from McGraw-Hill over the World Wide Web.

ALEKS delivers precise, qualitative diagnostic assessments of students' knowledge, guides them in the selection of appropriate new study material, and records their progress toward mastery of curricular goals in a robust classroom management system.

ALEKS interacts with the student much as a skilled human tutor would, moving between explanation and practice as needed, correcting and analyzing errors, defining terms, and changing topics on request. By sophisticated modeling of a student's knowledge state for a given subject, ALEKS can focus clearly on what the student is most ready to learn next. When students focus on exactly what they are ready to learn, they build confidence and a learning momentum that fuels success.

ALEKS has two products for accounting students. The first is Math Prep for Accounting that provides students with business math skills. The other is ALEKS for Financial Accounting (available Spring 2003). ALEKS for Financial Accounting applies the ALEKS model to financial accounting. Visit the ALEKS website at http://www.business.aleks.com for more information.

ALEKS® Math Prep for Accounting
ISBN 0072846011

ALEKS® for Financial Accounting
(COMING SPRING 2003) ISBN 0072841966

Developed with the help of our partner, Eduprise, the McGraw-Hill Knowledge Gateway is an all-purpose service and resource center for instructors teaching online. While training programs from WebCT and Blackboard will help teach you their software, only McGraw-Hill has services to help you actually manage and teach your online course, as well as run and maintain the software. Knowledge Gateway offers an online library full of articles and insights that focus on how online learning differs from a traditional class environment.

To see how these platforms can assist your online course, visit www.mhhe.com/solutions.

PAGEOUT & SERVICE

PageOut is McGraw-Hill/Irwin's custom Website service. Now you can put your course online without knowing a word of HTML, selecting from a variety of prebuilt Website templates. And if none of our ideas suit you, we'll be happy to work with your ideas.

If you want a custom site but don't have time to build it yourself, we offer a team of product specialists ready to help. Just call 1-800-634-3963, press 0, and ask to speak with a PageOut specialist. You will be asked to send in your course materials and then participate in a brief telephone consultation. Once we have your information, we build your Website for you, from scratch.

INSTRUCTOR ADVANTAGE AND INSTRUCTOR ADVANTAGE PLUS

Instructor Advantage is a special level of service McGraw-Hill offers in conjunction with WebCT and Blackboard. A team of platform specialists is always available, either by toll-free phone or e-mail, to ensure everything runs smoothly through the life of your adoption. Instructor Advantage is available free to all McGraw-Hill customers.

Instructor Advantage Plus is available to qualifying McGraw-Hill adopters (see your representative for details). IA Plus guarantees you a full day of on-site training by a Blackboard or WebCT specialist, for yourself and up to nine colleagues. Thereafter, you will enjoy the benefits of unlimited telephone and e-mail support throughout the life of your adoption. IA Plus users also have the opportunity to access the McGraw-Hill Knowledge Gateway (see above).

How can I *easily create an online course*?

PAGEOUT—McGRAW-HILL'S COURSE MANAGEMENT SYSTEM

For the instructor needing to educate students online, we offer Intermediate Accounting content for complete online courses. To make this possible, we have joined forces with the most popular delivery platforms currently available. These platforms are designed for instructors who want complete control over course content and how it is presented to students. You can customize the Intermediate Accounting Online Learning Center content and author your own course materials. It's entirely up to you.

Products like WebCT, Blackboard, eCollege, and TopClass (a product of WBT) all expand the reach of your course. Online discussion and message boards will now complement your office hours. Thanks to a sophisticated tracking system, you will know which students need more attention—even if they don't ask for help. That's because online testing scores are recorded and automatically placed in your grade book, and if a student is struggling with coursework, a special alert message lets you know.

Remember, *Intermediate Accounting's* content is flexible enough to use with any platform currently available. If your department or school is already using a platform, we can help. For information on McGraw-Hill/Irwin's course management supplements, including Instructor Advantage and Knowledge Gateway, see "Knowledge Gateway" on the previous page.

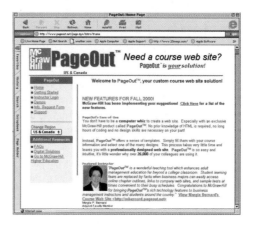

PageOut is the easiest way to create a Website for your accounting course.

There's no need for HTML coding, graphic design, or a thick how-to book. Just fill in a series of boxes with simple English and click on one of our professional designs. In no time, your course is online with a Website that contains your syllabus!

Should you need assistance in preparing your Website, we can help. Our team of product specialists is ready to take your course materials and build a custom Website to your specifications. You simply need to call a McGraw-Hill/Irwin PageOut specialist to start the process. (For information on how to do this, see "PageOut & Service" on the previous page.) Best of all, PageOut is free when you adopt *Intermediate Accounting*! To learn more, please visit www.pageout.net.

INSTRUCTOR SUPPLEMENTS

Instructor's Resource Manual
Volume 1 ISBN 0072534699
Volume 2 ISBN 0072534702

This manual is written by the authors and provides for each chapter (a) a chapter overview, (b) comprehensive lecture outline, (c) extensive teaching transparency masters that can be used as they are or modified to suit an instructor's particular needs or preferences, (d) a variety of suggested class activities (research, Internet, group, communication, eithics, FedEx, real world, and others), and (e) an assignment chart indicating topic, learning objective, and estimated completion time for every question, exercise, problem, and case.

Case Implementation Manual
ISBN 0072534745

Most accounting instructors are not trained specifically to teach ethics, international accounting, group interaction techniques, Internet techniques, and writing. To assist instructors in adding one or more of these dimensions to their courses, our Case Implementation Manual is designed to provide instructional support in teaching cases in these areas. The manual is prepared in concert with our Board of Advisors that includes recognized experts in each of these fields. Their expertise enables them to provide background material necessary to give students the perspective they need to derive maximum benefit from these cases, as well as to suggest how instructors can incorporate these cases to their best advantage. The Solutions Manual includes detailed solutions to every case.

Solutions Manual
Volume 1 ISBN 0072534729
Volume 2 ISBN 0072534710

Written by the text authors, the Solutions Manual includes detailed solutions for every question, exercise, problem, and case.

Online Learning Center (OLC)
www.mhhe.com/spiceland3e

Solutions Transparencies
Volume 1 ISBN 0072534672
Volume 2 ISBN 0072564512

Acetate overhead transparencies for every question, exercise, problem, and case are provided in a large, readable typeface.

Instructor CD-ROM
ISBN 0072534818

This all-in-one resource contains the Instructor's Resource Manual, Solutions Manual, PowerPoint® slides, Instructor Excel Templates, Computerized Testbank, and Video Clips.

Testbank
Volume 1 ISBN 0072534664
Volume 2 ISBN 0072534834

Written by the authors, this comprehensive testbank contains over 1,500 problems and true/false, multiple-choice, and essay questions.

Computerized Testbank
ISBN 0072534737

This computerized version of the printed testbank by Brownstone is a user-friendly testing system that allows faculty to easily generate exams. It will create different versions of the same test, change the answer order, edit or add questions, and even conduct online testing.

PowerPoint® Slides

The PowerPoint® slides are created by Jon Booker, Charles Caldwell, and Richard S. Rand, Jr. of Tennessee Technological University, and Susan Galbreath of David Lipscomb University. They are available on the OLC and Instructor CD-ROM and provide an easy way of including multimedia in the intermediate accounting course.

"By having the authors actually create and write the assignments you have ensured consistency in the material presented as well as the terms and jargon used. One can easily match up the assignment to the learning objective presented in the chapter. This is even carried one step further—the solutions. When I use the solution in class, I have no fear that the computation will be in a different format than what was illustrated in the textbook."—Janice Stoudemire, Midlands Technical College

STUDENT SUPPLEMENTS

Study Guide
Volume 1: ISBN 0072504110
Volume 2: ISBN 0072504129

The Study Guide, written by the text authors, provides chapter summaries, detailed illustrations, and a wide variety of self-study questions, exercises, and multiple-choice problems (with solutions).

Working Papers
ISBN 0072534680

Students use formatted solutions templates to aid them in doing homework assignments.

Excel Templates

Selected end-of-chapter exercises and problems, marked in the text with an EX icon, can be solved using these Microsoft Excel templates, located on the Online Learning Center.

Check Figures

Available on the Online Learning Center (Website), this supplement provides solutions to key end-of-chapter assignments.

Understanding Corporate Annual Reports: A Financial Analysis Project, Fourth Edition, by William R. Pasework
ISBN 0072387149

This project provides students with instruction for obtaining an annual report from a publicly traded corporation and for making an industry or competitor comparison.

MBA Survival Kit—Accounting Interactive
ISBN 0072511990

Copublished with Graduate Management Admissions Council (GMAC), facilitators of GMAT Exam, this software provides six hours of interactive overview of the basic accounting cycle.

Alternate Exercises and Problems
ISBN 0072534826

Also part of the Learning System, this manual includes additional exercises and problems for each chapter in the text.

PowerWeb

Keeping your course current can be a job in itself, and now McGraw-Hill does that job for you. Through PowerWeb, McGraw-Hill/Irwin has taken the initiative in providing a comprehensive library about the Enron accounting controversy. This site will be updated numerous times throughout the semester, ensuring your course easy access to the freshest information about this crucial topic.

Visit the PowerWeb site at www.dushkin.com/powerweb and see firsthand what PowerWeb can mean to your course.

Coach CD-ROM

This exciting, multimedia CD-ROM is packaged free with the textbook to help students better understand intermediate accounting topics.

Practice Sets:

Granite Bay Jet Ski Inc., Level 1

Instructor ISBN 0072426896
Student ISBN 0072426942

Granite Bay Jet Ski Inc., Level 2

Instructor ISBN 0072426209
Student ISBN 0072426950

Intermediate Accounting Packages:

Intermediate Accounting comes packaged with the Learning System: The Coach CD-ROM, PowerWeb: Enron, Alternate Exercises & Problems Manual, and NetTutor.

ISBN: 0072836865

The Learning System is FREE with the Intermediate Accounting SPLITS, too!

Intermediate Accounting Vol. 1 w/ Coach CD-ROM, PowerWeb: Enron, Alternate Exercises & Problems Manual, and NetTutor.

ISBN: 0072836873

Intermediate Accounting Vol. 2 w/ Coach CD-ROM, PowerWeb: Enron, and NetTutor.

ISBN: 0072836881

Online Learning Center (OLC)
www.mhhe.com/spiceland3e

ACKNOWLEDGMENTS

Many of our colleagues offered suggestions for improving *Intermediate Accounting*. This is vital feedback that we rely on in each edition. Each of those who have offered comments and suggestions has our thanks.

The efforts of many people are needed to develop and improve a text. Among these people are the reviewers and survey respondents who point out areas of concern, cite areas of strength, and make recommendations for change. In this regard, the following professors provided feedback that was enormously helpful in preparing the Third Edition of *Intermediate Accounting:*

Noel D. Addy, Jr., *Mississippi State University*

Elsie Ameen, *Sam Houston State University*

Anthony J. Amoruso, *Virginia Tech*

Matthew J. Anderson, *Michigan State University*

Joseph N. Antenucci, *Youngtown State University*

Paul Bahnson, *Boise State University*

Bruce Billings, *Florida State University*

Robert Bloom, *John Carroll University*

L. Charles Bokemeier, *Michigan State University*

Laura D. Bolding, *University of Texas at Dallas*

Joseph F. Brazel III, *Drexel University*

Richard C. Brooks, *West Virginia University*

Michael H. Brown, *Abilene Christian University*

Philip G. Buchanan, *George Mason University*

Albert R. Bundons, *Johnson County Community College*

David Burgstahler, *University of Washington*

Jane E. Campbell, *Kennesaw State University*

Nandini Chandar, *Rutgers University*

Kwang-Hyun Chung, *Pace University*

Anna Cianci, *University of Florida*

Myrtle W. Clark, *University of Kentucky*

Stan Clark, *University of Southern Mississippi*

Karen M. Collins, *Lehigh University*

Edward J. Conrad, *University of Akron*

Ronald J. Daigle, *Texas Tech University*

David B. Davidson, *California State University at Long Beach*

Denise de la Rosa, *Central Connecticut State University*

Marinus DeBruine, *Grand Valley State University*

Lee Dexter, *Minnesota State University at Moorhead*

Orapin Duangploy, *University of Houston—Downtown*

David Eichelberger, *Austin Peay State University*

Susan W. Eldridge, *University of Texas at Austin*

Daniel J. Flaherty, *Southwest Texas State University*

Richard K. Fleischman, Jr., *John Carroll University*

Mary M. Fleming, *California State University at Fullerton*

Albert H. Frakes, *Washington State University*

Diana Franz, *University of Toledo*

Robert N. Freeman, *University of Texas at Austin*

Lucille Genduso, *Nova Southeastern University*

Tae Ghil Ryu, *Metropolitan State College of Denver*

Sid Glandon, *University of Texas at El Paso*

Janet L. Grange, *Chicago State University*

Sharron M. Graves, *Stephen F. Austin State University*

Wayne R. Guay, *University of Pennsylvania*

Daryl Guffey, *Clemson University*

Abo Habib, *Minnesota State University at Mankato*

Marcia L. Halvorsen, *University of Cincinnati*

John G. Hamer, *University of Massachusetts at Lowell*

Coby J. Harmon, *University of California at Santa Barbara*

Donald R. Herrmann, *Oregon State University*

Julia Higgs, *Florida Atlantic University*

Inam Hussain, *Purdue University*

Constance M. Hylton, *George Mason University*

Marianne L. James, *California State University at Los Angeles*

Jefferson P. Jones, *Auburn University*

Kwangok Kim, *University of Southern Indiana*

Jerry G. Kreuze, *Western Michigan University*

Kenneth Lambert, *University of Memphis*

Ellen L. Landgraf, *Loyola University at Chicago*

E. John Larsen, *University of Southern California*

Doug Laufer, *Metropolitan State College of Denver*

Dave Law, *Youngstown State University*

Patsy L. Lee, *University of Texas at Arlington*

Craig Lefanowicz, *Michigan State University*

Charles Leflar, *University of Arkansas*

Chao-Shin Liu, *University of Notre Dame*

Carolyn L. Lousteau, *University of New Orleans*

Heidemarie Lundblad, *California State University at Northridge*

Gary A. Luoma, *University of South Carolina*

Wilda F. Meixner, *Southwest Texas State University*

Robert S. Milbrath, *University of Houston*

John R. Mills, *University of Nevada at Reno*

George S. Minmier, *University of Memphis*

Louella J. Moore, *Arkansas State University*

Kimberly K. Moreno, *Virginia Tech*

Jan Morris, *University of Houston at Clear Lake*

Paula H. Morris, *Kennesaw State University*

Richard M. Morton, *Florida State University*

Charles W. Murphy, *Bunker Hill Community College*

John D. Neill III, *Abilene Christian University*

Stephen Ostlund, *Minnesota State University at Moorhead*

Linda S. Perry, *Texas A&M University*

Marlene Plumlee, *University of Utah*

Kevin Poirier, *Johnson and Wales University*

Mary Ann Prater, *Clemson University*

Donald Putnam, *California Polytechnic University at Pomona*

Atul Rai, *Florida State University*

K. K. Raman, *University of North Texas*

Randall Rentfro, *Florida Atlantic University*

Vernon J. Richardson, *University of Kansas*

Richard A. Riley, Jr., *West Virginia University*

Mark Ross, *Western Kentucky University*

Pamela Roush, *University of Central Florida*

Marc A. Rubin, *Miami University*

John A. Rude, *Bloomsburg University*

Clayton Sager, *University of Wisconsin at Whitewater*

Maria Sanchez, *Drexel University*

Susan W. Scholz, *University of Kansas*

Paul Schwinghammer, *Minnesota State University at Mankato*

Richard J. Shepherd, *University of California at Santa Cruz*

Rebecca Shortridge, *Ball State University*

Joel Siegel, *Queens College*

John Sneed, *University of Nebraska at Kearney*

Julie S. Sobery, *Southern Illinois University at Carbondale*

Vic Stanton, *California State University at Hayward*

William D. Stout, *University of Louisville*

Paulette R. Tandy, *University of Nevada at Las Vegas*

Diane Tanner, *University of North Florida*

Gary K. Taylor, *University of Alabama*

Peter Theuri, *Northern Kentucky University*

Wayne Thomas, *University of Oklahoma*

Shobha Venkataraman, *Drexel University*

Larry Walther, *University of Texas at Arlington*

Andrea B. Weickgenannt, *Northern Kentucky University*

Thomas R. Weirich, *Central Michigan University*

Mike S. Wilkins, *Texas A&M University*

Arlette Wilson, *Auburn University*

Joni Young, *University of New Mexico*

Nat R. Briscoe, *Northwestern State University*

Helen Brubeck, *San Jose State University*

James Chiu, *California State University at Northridge*

Joanne Duke, *San Francisco State University*

Joseph L. Morris, *Southeastern Louisiana University*

Linda Nichols, *Texas Tech University*

Robert W. Parry, Jr., *Indiana University*

Paul J. Robertson, *New Mexico State University*

Marie Archambault, *Marshall University*

Florence Atiase, *University of Texas at Austin*

Jane Baldwin, *Baylor University*

Anne Beatty, *Pennsylvania State University*

Lisa Bryant, *Ohio State University*

Howard Bunsis, *Eastern Michigan University*

Suzanne Busch, *California State University at Hayward*

Raymond Chen, *California State University at Northridge*

Janice Cobb, *Texas Christian University*

Elizabeth Conner, *University of Colorado at Denver*

Richard Cross, *Bentley College*

Andrea Drake, *University of Cincinnati*

Richard Elmendorf, *Metropolitan State College of Denver*

J. Edward Ketz, *Pennsylvania State University*

Jacquelyn Moffitt, *Louisiana State University*

Henry Norton, *Metropolitan State College of Denver*

Emeka Ofobike, *University of Akron*

Hong Pak, *California State Polytechnic University at Pomona*

William H. Parrott, *University of South Florida*

Kirk Philipich, *Ohio State University*

Janice Stoudemire, *Midlands Technical College*

Laurel Franzen, *University of Texas—Dallas*

Richard Townsend, *University of Tennessee*

Ralph J. McQuade, *Bentley College*

Focus groups provided detailed feedback that we have found invaluable in preparing this revision, and we thank all of our focus group participants:

Elsie Ameen, *Sam Houston State University*

Matthew J. Anderson, *Michigan State University*

Maria Bullen, *Georgia State University*

Orapin Duangploy, *University of Houston—Downtown*

Laurel Franzen, *University of Texas at Dallas*

Sid Glandon, *University of Texas at El Paso*

Daryl Guffey, *Clemson University*

Gary A. Louma, *University of South Carolina*

Robert S. Milbrath, *University of Houston—Main*

Kimberly K. Moreno, *Virginia Polytechnic University*

Paula H. Morris, *Kennesaw State University*

John Neill, *Abilene Christian University*

Linda Nichols, *Texas Technological University*

Robert Parry, *Indiana University*

Atul Rai, *Florida State University*

K. K. Raman, *University of North Texas*

Richard Riley, *West Virginia University*

Mark Ross, *Western Kentucky University*

William D. Stout, *University of Louisiana*

Paulette R. Tandy, *University of Nevada at Las Vegas*

Gary Taylor, *University of Alabama*

Peter Theuri, *Northern Kentucky University*

Daisy Beck, *Louisiana State University at Baton Rouge*

Nat R. Briscoe, *Northwestern State University*

Joseph Legoria, *Mississippi State University*

Carolyn Lousteau, *University of New Orleans*

Cecily Raiborn, *Loyola University at New Orleans*

Charles Bruce Swindle, *McNesse State University*

Bruce Wampler, *University of Louisiana at Monroe*

Weimin Wang, *Tulane University*

Paul Bahnson, *Boise State University*

Thomas Black, *San Jose State University*

Suzanne Busch, *California State University at Hayward*

Alan Cherry, *Loyola Marymount University*

Jodi Duke, *San Francisco State University*

Hassan Hefzi, *California State Polytechnic University at Pomona*

Wallace Leese, *California State University at Chico*

Marc Massoud, *Claremont McKenna*

Will Snyder, *San Diego State University*

Ronald Stone, *California State University at Northridge*

Richard Fern, *Eastern Kentucky University*

Julia Higgs, *Florida Atlantic University*

Jefferson P. Jones, *Auburn University*

Barbara Lippincott, *University of South Florida*

Randy Rentfro, *Florida Atlantic University*

Pamela Roush, *University of Central Florida*

Diane Tanner, *University of North Florida*

We Are Grateful

We would like to acknowledge the following individuals for their help with the Case Implementation Manual, PowerPoint® Slides, and Excel Templates. The Case Implementation Manual was created with help from Maurice Hirsch, Jr., Southern Illinois University, James A. Schweikart, Rhode Island College, Mary E. Harston, St. Mary's University, Timothy J. Louwers, Louisiana State University, and Williams R. Pasewark, Texas Technological University. John A. Booker, Charles W. Caldwell, and Richard S. Rand, Jr., all of Tennessee Technological University, and Susan C. Galbreath, David Lipscomb University, created the PowerPoint Slides; and Jack E. Terry, ComSource Associates, developed the Excel Templates.

Thank you to Glenn and Meg Turner, Karen Nein, and the Burrston House team for all of your hard work and the wealth of market feedback you gathered for us to use as a guide while writing this edition.

Also, Alice Sineath and Barbara Schnathorst made significant contributions to the accuracy of the text, end-of-chapter material, and solutions manual.

In addition, we appreciate the help and guidance received from Gary Meek, Oklahoma State University, for his contribution to the to the Global Perspective Boxes and the Global Marketplace section in Chapter 1, and Jim Lynch, partner, KPMG, for help with the new FASB standards.

We are most grateful for the talented assistance and support from the many people at McGraw-Hill/Irwin. We would particularly like to thank Brent Gordon, publisher, Stewart Mattson, executive editor, Heather Sabo, developmental editor, Richard Kolasa, marketing manager, Greg Patterson, regional sales manager, Ed Przyzycki, senior media tech producer, Pat Frederickson, senior project manager, Melonie Salvati, manager of new book production, Keith McPherson, director of design, Jeremy Cheshareck, photo research coordinator, Carol Loreth, senior supplement producer, and Dan Wiencek and Erwin Llereza, advertising.

Finally, our thanks also goes to Federal Express Corporation for allowing us to use its Annual Report in the appendix to Chapter 1 and throughout the text. We also acknowledge permission from the AICPA to adapt material from the Uniform CPA Examination and Dow Jones & Co., Inc. for permission to excerpt material from *The Wall Street Journal*.

David Spiceland   Jim Sepe   Larry Tomassini

Contents in Brief

Contents

1
SECTION

The Role of Accounting as an Information System

1 CHAPTER
Environment and Theoretical Structure of Financial Accounting, 2

2 CHAPTER
Review of the Accounting Process, 60

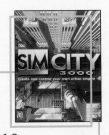

Economic Resources

9 CHAPTER
Inventories: Additional Issues, 412

10 CHAPTER
Operational Assets: Acquisition and Disposition, 460

11 CHAPTER
Operational Assets: Utilization and Impairment, 518

Financial Instruments

SECTION 3

CHAPTER 12
Investments, 570

CHAPTER 13
Current Liabilities and Contingencies, 616

14 CHAPTER
Bonds and Long-Term Notes, 664

15 CHAPTER
Leases, 714

16 CHAPTER
Accounting for Income Taxes, 776

17 CHAPTER
Pensions, 832

18 CHAPTER
Employee Benefit Plans, 882

19 CHAPTER
Shareholders' Equity, 936

4 SECTION
Additional Topics

20 CHAPTER
Earnings per Share, 994

21 CHAPTER
Accounting Changes and Error Corrections, 1034

22 CHAPTER
The Statement of Cash Flows Revisited, 1076

The Role of Accounting as an Information System

1

Environment and Theoretical Structure of Financial Accounting

After studying this chapter,
you should be able to:

LO1   Describe the function and primary focus of financial accounting.

LO2   Explain the difference between cash and accrual accounting.

LO3   Define generally accepted accounting principles (GAAP) and discuss the historical development of accounting standards.

LO4   Explain why the establishment of accounting standards is characterized as a political process.

LO5   Explain the purpose of the FASB's conceptual framework.

LO6   Identify the objectives of financial reporting, the qualitative characteristics of accounting information, and the elements of financial statements.

LO7   Describe the four basic assumptions underlying GAAP.

LO8   Describe the four broad accounting principles that guide accounting practice.

OVERVIEW

The primary function of financial accounting is to provide relevant and reliable financial information to users external to the business enterprise. The focus of financial accounting is on the information needs of investors and creditors. These users make critical resource allocation decisions that affect the nation's economy. The primary means of conveying financial information to external users is through financial statements and related notes.

In this chapter you explore important topics such as the FASB's Conceptual Framework that serve as a foundation for a more detailed study of financial statements, the way the statement elements are measured, and the concepts underlying these measurements and related disclosures.

FINANCIAL REPORTING CASE

Misguided Marketing Major

During a class break in your investments class, a marketing major tells the following story to you and some friends:

The chief financial officer of a large company is interviewing three candidates for the top accounting position with his firm. He asks each the same question:

CFO:	What is two plus two?
First candidate:	Four.
CFO:	What is two plus two?
Second candidate:	Four.
CFO:	What is two plus two?
Third candidate:	What would you like it to be?
CFO:	You're hired.

After you take some good-natured ribbing from the nonaccounting majors, your friend says, "Seriously, though, there must be ways the accounting profession prevents that kind of behavior. Aren't there some laws, or rules, or something? Are they based on some sort of theory, or are they just arbitrary?"

> By the time you finish this chapter, you should be able to respond appropriately to the questions posed in this case. Compare your response to the solution provided at the end of the chapter.

QUESTIONS

1. What should you tell your friend about the presence of accounting standards in the United States? Who has the authority for standard setting? Who has the responsibility? (page 9)

2. What is the economic and political environment in which standard setting occurs? (page 12)

3. What is the relationship among management, auditors, investors, and creditors that tends to preclude the "What would you like it to be?" attitude? (page 16)

4. In general, what is the conceptual framework that underlies accounting principles? (page 18)

PART

FINANCIAL ACCOUNTING ENVIRONMENT

Have you ever received a C grade on a paper and thought you deserved better? In 1965 Fred Smith did. His term paper for an economics class proposed a revolutionary air freight delivery method that revolved around a "hub and spokes" system. The hub would be located in a middle-America location (Memphis was eventually chosen) with spokes radiating out to cities across the country. A package from Los Angeles, destined for New York, would be flown in on the Los Angeles spoke in a few hours to the hub location in Memphis. There it would be sorted and routed out on the return flight of the plane that had just brought in shipments from New York, arriving before dawn. Los Angeles to New York overnight!

> "The concept is interesting and well formed, but in order to earn better than a 'C,' the idea must be feasible."
> —quote from a Yale University professor in response to Federal Express founder Fred Smith's paper proposing reliable overnight delivery service.

FedEx Corporation

Fred Smith had so much confidence in his idea that in 1971 he created a company called Federal Express. On April 17, 1973, when operations officially began, the company served 25 cities and delivered 186 packages. The company struggled at first, and it wasn't until three years later that it reported its first profit of $3.6 million. A quarter of a century later, Federal Express Corporation's annual profit exceeded $580 million and annual revenue topped $19 billion. Average package volume reached approximately 3.2 million daily worldwide.[1]

Many factors contributed to the success of Federal Express. The company's founder was visionary in terms of his package delivery system. The hub and spokes concept is now used throughout the air freight industry. A key factor contributing to the growth and success of Federal Express was its access to external capital (resources). At various times in the company's brief history, the ability to raise external capital from investors and creditors was critical to its phenomenal growth. For example, several bank loans provided financing in the early years, and in 1978, an initial public offering of the company's stock provided over $17 million in equity financing.

Investors and creditors use information to assess risk and return.

Investors and creditors use many different kinds of information before supplying capital to business enterprises like Federal Express. The information is used to assess the future risk and return of their potential investments in the enterprise.[2] For example, information about the enterprise's products and its management is of vital importance to this assessment. In addition, various kinds of financial information are extremely important to investors and creditors.

The primary focus of *financial accounting* is on the information needs of investors and creditors.

You might think of accounting as a special "language" used to communicate financial information about a business to those who wish to use the information to make decisions. **Financial accounting,** in particular, is concerned with providing relevant financial information to various *external* users. The chart in Graphic 1–1 illustrates a number of financial information supplier groups as well as several external user groups. Of these groups, the primary focus of financial accounting is on the financial information provided by *profit-oriented companies to their present and potential investors and creditors.* The reason for this focus is discussed in a later section of this chapter. One external user group, often referred to as *financial intermediaries,* includes financial analysts, stockbrokers, mutual fund managers, and credit rating organizations. These users provide advice to investors and creditors and/or make investment-credit decisions on their behalf. The collapse of Enron Corporation in 2001 and other high profile accounting failures made immensely clear the importance of reporting reliable financial information.

On the other hand, **managerial accounting** deals with the concepts and methods used to provide information to an organization's *internal* users, that is, its managers. You study managerial accounting elsewhere in your curriculum.

Financial statements convey financial information to external users.

The primary means of conveying financial information to investors, creditors, and other external users is through financial statements and related disclosure notes. The financial

---

[1]Vance Trimble, *Overnight Success* (New York: Crown Publishers, Inc., 1993).

[2]Risk refers to the variability of possible outcomes from an investment. Return is the amount received over and above the investment and usually is expressed as a percentage.

GRAPHIC 1–1
Financial Information
Supplier Groups and
External User Groups

PROVIDERS OF FINANCIAL INFORMATION	EXTERNAL USER GROUPS
• Profit-oriented companies	• Investors
	• Creditors (banks, bondholders, other lenders)
	• Employees
	• Labor unions
• Not-for-profit entities (e.g., government entities, charitable organizations, schools)	• Customers
	• Suppliers
	• Government regulatory agencies (e.g., Internal Revenue Service, Securities and Exchange Commission)
• Households	• Financial intermediaries (e.g., financial analysts, stockbrokers, mutual fund managers, credit-rating organizations)

statements most frequently provided are (1) the balance sheet or statement of financial position, (2) the income statement or statement of operations, (3) the statement of cash flows, and (4) the statement of shareholders' equity. As you progress through this text, you will review and expand your knowledge of the information in these financial statements, the way the elements in these statements are measured, and the concepts underlying these measurements and related disclosures. We use the term **financial reporting** to refer to the process of providing this information to external users. Keep in mind, though, that external users receive important financial information in a variety of other formats as well, including news releases and management forecasts, prospectuses, reports filed with regulatory agencies, and the president's letter.

The appendix to this chapter contains recent financial statements, including related disclosure notes, for FedEx Corporation, now the parent company of Federal Express. We occasionally refer to the FedEx financial statements in this chapter and others to illustrate certain points. You also can refer to these statements as new topics are introduced in later chapters.

FedEx Corporation

The Economic Environment and Financial Reporting

In the United States, we have a highly developed free-enterprise economy with the majority of productive resources privately owned rather than government owned. It's important in this type of system that a mechanism exists to allocate the scarce resources of our society, both natural resources and labor, in an efficient manner. Resources should be allocated to private enterprises that will use them best to provide goods and services desired by society and not to enterprises that will waste them. The mechanisms that foster this efficient allocation of resources are the **capital markets.** We can think of the capital markets simply as a composite of all investors and creditors.

The three primary forms of business organization are the sole proprietorship, the partnership, and the corporation. In the United States, sole proprietorships and partnerships outnumber corporations. However, the dominant form of business organization, in terms of the ownership of productive resources, is the **corporation.** The corporate form makes it easier for an enterprise to acquire resources through the capital markets. Investors provide resources, usually cash, to a corporation in exchange for evidence of ownership interest, that

The capital markets provide a mechanism to help our economy allocate resources efficiently.

Corporations acquire capital from investors in exchange for ownership interest and from creditors by borrowing.

is, shares of stock. Creditors such as banks lend cash to the corporation. Also, creditors can lend the corporation cash through the medium of bonds. Stocks and bonds usually are traded on organized security markets such as the New York Stock Exchange and the American Stock Exchange. The advantages and disadvantages of the corporate form are discussed at greater length in Chapter 19.

The transfers of these stocks and bonds among individuals and institutions are referred to as **secondary market** transactions. Corporations receive no new cash from secondary market transactions. New cash is provided in *primary* market transactions in which the shares or bonds are sold by the corporation to the initial owners. Nevertheless, secondary market transactions are extremely important to the efficient allocation of resources in our economy. These transactions help establish market prices for additional shares and for bonds that corporations may wish to issue in the future to acquire additional capital. Also, many shareholders and bondholders might be unwilling to initially provide resources to corporations if there were no available mechanism for the future sale of their stocks and bonds to others.

What information do investors and creditors need to decide which companies will be provided capital? We explore that question next.

Secondary market transactions provide for the transfer of stocks and bonds among individuals and institutions.

THE INVESTMENT-CREDIT DECISION—A CASH FLOW PERSPECTIVE

Investors and creditors both are interested in earning a fair return on the resources provided.

While the decisions made by investors and by creditors are somewhat different, they are similar in at least one important way. They both are concerned with providing resources to companies, usually cash, with the expectation of receiving more cash in return at some time in the future. A corporation's shareholders will receive cash from their investment through the ultimate sale of the ownership shares of stock. In addition, many corporations distribute cash to their shareholders in the form of periodic dividends. For example, if an investor provides a company with $10,000 cash (that is, purchases ownership shares) at the end of 2002, receives $400 in dividends from the company during 2003, and sells the ownership interest (shares) at the end of 2003 for $10,600 ($600 share price appreciation), the investment would have generated a **rate of return** of 10% for 2003, calculated as follows:

$$\frac{\$400 \text{ dividends} + \$600 \text{ share price appreciation}}{\$10,000 \text{ initial investment}} = 10\%$$

The expected rate of return and uncertainty, or risk, of that return are key variables in the investment decision.

Investors always are faced with more than one investment opportunity. There are many factors to consider before one of these opportunities is chosen. Two extremely important variables are the *expected rate of return* from each investment option, and the *uncertainty,* or *risk,* of that expected return. For example, consider the following two investment options:

1. Invest $10,000 in a savings account insured by the U.S. government that will generate a 5% rate of return.
2. Invest $10,000 in a profit-oriented company.

While the rate of return from option 1 is known with virtual certainty, the return from option 2 is uncertain. The amount and timing of the cash to be received in the future from option 2 are unknown. Investors require information about the company that will help them estimate the unknown return.

A company will be able to provide a return to investors and creditors only if it can generate a profit from selling its products or services.

In the long run, a company will be able to provide investors with a return only if it can generate a profit. That is, it must be able to use the resources provided by investors and creditors to generate cash receipts from selling a product or service that exceed the cash disbursements necessary to provide that product or service. If this excess can be generated, the marketplace is implicitly saying that society's resources have been efficiently allocated. The marketplace is assigning a value to the product or service that exceeds the value assigned to the resources used to produce that product or service.

The objective of financial accounting is to provide investors and creditors with useful information for decision making.

In summary, the primary objective of financial accounting is to provide investors and creditors with information that will help them make investment and credit decisions. More specifically, the information should help investors and creditors evaluate the *amounts, timing,* and *uncertainty* of the enterprise's future cash receipts and disbursements. The better this information is, the more efficient will be investor and creditor resource allocation decisions. Financial accounting, in providing key elements of the information set used by capital market participants, plays a vital societal role in the resource allocation process. The importance of this role to society explains why the primary focus of financial accounting is on the information needs of investors and creditors.

The Financial Accounting Standards Board, the current private sector body responsible for setting accounting standards in the United States, has published a conceptual framework for financial reporting (discussed later in this chapter). The first concept statement of the framework describes the specific objectives of external financial reporting. These objectives affirm the importance of the cash flow information needs of investors and creditors.

Throughout this text, you will be reminded of this cash flow perspective. For example, Chapter 4 describes certain events that are reported separately in the income statement due to the fact that these historical events have implications for future cash flows that are different from the normal operating activities. Separation of these events from normal operating activities provides financial statement users with information to more easily predict an enterprise's future cash flows.

CASH VERSUS ACCRUAL ACCOUNTING

Even though predicting future cash flows is the primary objective, the model best able to achieve that objective is the **accrual accounting** model. A competing model is **cash basis accounting.** Each model produces a periodic measure of performance that could be used by investors and creditors for predicting future cash flows.

Cash Basis Accounting.   Cash basis accounting produces a measure called **net operating cash flow.** This measure is the difference between cash receipts and cash disbursements during a reporting period from transactions related to providing goods and services to customers.

Net operating cash flow is the difference between cash receipts and cash disbursements from providing goods and services.

Net operating cash flow is very easy to understand and all information required to measure it is factual. Also, it certainly relates to a variable of critical interest to investors and creditors. What could be better in helping to predict future cash flows from selling products and services than current cash flows from these activities? Remember, a company will be able to provide a return to investors and creditors only if it can use the capital provided to generate a positive net operating cash flow. However, there is a major drawback to using the current period's operating cash flow to predict future operating cash flows. Over the life of the company, net operating cash flow definitely is the variable of concern. However, over short periods of time, *operating cash flows may not be indicative of the company's long-run cash-generating ability* (that is, its ability to generate positive net operating cash flows in the future).

To demonstrate this, consider the following example. In Illustration 1–1 net operating cash flows are determined for the Carter Company during its first three years of operations.

Over the three-year period, Carter generated a positive net operating cash flow of $60,000. At the end of this three-year period, Carter has no outstanding debts. Because total sales and cash receipts over the three-year period were each $300,000, nothing is owed to Carter by customers. Also, at the beginning of the first year, Carter prepaid $60,000 for three years' rent on

	Year 1	Year 2	Year 3	Total
Sales (on credit)	$100,000	$100,000	$100,000	$300,000
Net Operating Cash Flows				
Cash receipts from customers	$ 50,000	$125,000	$125,000	$300,000
Cash disbursements:				
Prepayment of three years' rent	(60,000)	–0–	–0–	(60,000)
Salaries to employees	(50,000)	(50,000)	(50,000)	(150,000)
Utilities	(5,000)	(15,000)	(10,000)	(30,000)
Net cash flow	$ (65,000)	$ 60,000	$ 65,000	$ 60,000

ILLUSTRATION 1–1

Cash Basis Accounting

the facilities. There are no uncompleted transactions at the end of the three-year period. In that sense, we can view this three-year period as a micro version of the entire life of a company.

The company incurred utility costs of $10,000 per year over the period. However, during the first year only $5,000 actually was paid, with the remainder being paid the second year. Employee salary costs of $50,000 were paid in full each year.

Is net operating cash flow for year 1 (negative $65,000) an accurate indicator of future cash-generating ability?[3] Obviously, it is not a good predictor of the positive net cash flows that occur in the next two years. Is the three-year pattern of net operating cash flows indicative of the company's year-by-year performance? No. But, if we measure the same activities by the accrual accounting model, we get a more accurate prediction of future operating cash flows and a more reasonable portrayal of the balanced operating performance of the company over the three years.

Accrual Accounting.   The accrual accounting model measures the entity's accomplishments and resource sacrifices during the period, regardless of when cash is received or paid. The accrual accounting model's measure of periodic accomplishments is called *revenues,* and the periodic measure of resource sacrifices is called *expenses.* The difference between revenues and expenses is *net income,* or net loss if expenses are greater than revenues.[4]

How would we measure revenues and expenses in this very simplistic situation? Illustration 1–2 offers a possible solution.

ILLUSTRATION 1–2 Accrual Accounting The accrual accounting model provides a measure of periodic performance called *net income,* the difference between revenues and expenses.	CARTER COMPANY Income Statements			
	Year 1	Year 2	Year 3	Total
Revenues	$100,000	$100,000	$100,000	$300,000
Expenses:				
Rent	20,000	20,000	20,000	60,000
Salaries	50,000	50,000	50,000	150,000
Utilities	10,000	10,000	10,000	30,000
Total expenses	80,000	80,000	80,000	240,000
Net Income	$ 20,000	$ 20,000	$ 20,000	$ 60,000

Net income of $20,000 for year 1 appears to be a reasonable predictor of the company's cash-generating ability as total net operating cash flow for the three-year period is a positive $60,000. Also, compare the three-year pattern of net operating cash flows in Illustration 1–1 to the three-year pattern of net income in Illustration 1–2. The net income pattern is more representative of the steady operating performance over the three-year period.[5]

While this example is somewhat simplistic, it allows us to see the motivation for using the accrual accounting model. Accrual income attempts to measure the accomplishments and sacrifices that occurred during the year, which may not correspond to cash inflows and outflows. For example, revenue for year 1 is the $100,000 in sales. This is a better measure of the company's accomplishments during year 1 than the $50,000 cash collected from customers.

---

[3]A negative cash flow is possible only if invested capital (i.e., owners contributed cash to the company in exchange for ownership interest) is sufficient to cover the cash deficiency. Otherwise, the company would have to either raise additional external funds or go bankrupt.

[4]Net income also includes gains and losses, which are discussed later in the chapter.

[5]Empirical evidence that accrual accounting provides a better measure of short-term performance than cash flows is provided by Patricia DeChow, "Accounting Earnings and Cash Flows as Measures of Firm Performance: The Role of Accrual Accounting," *Journal of Accounting and Economics* 18 (1994), pp. 3–42.

Does this mean that information about cash flows from operating activities is not useful? No. Indeed, when combined with information about cash flows from investing and financing activities, this information provides valuable input into decisions made by investors and creditors. In fact, collectively, this cash flow information constitutes the statement of cash flows—one of the basic financial statements.[6]

The Development of Financial Accounting and Reporting Standards

Accrual accounting is the financial reporting model used by the majority of profit-oriented companies and by many not-for-profit companies. The fact that companies use the same model is important to financial statement users. Investors and creditors use financial information to make their resource allocation decisions. It's critical that they be able to *compare* financial information among companies. To facilitate these comparisons, financial accounting employs a body of standards known as **generally accepted accounting principles**, often abbreviated as **GAAP** (and pronounced *gap*). GAAP are a dynamic set of both broad and specific guidelines that companies should follow when measuring and reporting the information in their financial statements and related notes. The more important broad principles or standards are discussed in a subsequent section of this chapter and revisited throughout the text in the context of accounting applications for which they provide conceptual support.[7] More specific standards, such as how to measure and report a lease transaction, receive more focused attention in subsequent chapters.

FINANCIAL
REPORTING CASE

Q1, p. 3

HISTORICAL PERSPECTIVE AND STANDARDS

Pressures on the accounting profession to establish uniform accounting standards began to surface after the stock market crash of 1929. Some feel that insufficient and misleading financial statement information led to inflated stock prices and that this contributed to the stock market crash and the subsequent depression.

The 1933 Securities Act and the 1934 Securities Exchange Act were designed to restore investor confidence. The 1933 act sets forth accounting and disclosure requirements for initial offerings of securities (stocks and bonds). The 1934 act applies to secondary market transactions and mandates reporting requirements for companies whose securities are publicly traded on either organized stock exchanges or in over-the-counter markets.[8] The 1934 act also created the **Securities and Exchange Commission (SEC).**

In the 1934 act, *Congress gave the SEC both the power and responsibility for setting accounting and reporting standards for companies whose securities are publicly traded.* However, the SEC, a government appointed body, always has delegated the responsibility for setting accounting standards to the private sector. It is important to understand that the SEC delegated only the responsibility, not the authority, to set standards. The power still lies with the SEC. If the SEC does not agree with a particular standard issued by the private sector, it can force a change in the standard. In fact, it has done so in the past.

The SEC does issue its own accounting standards in the form of *Financial Reporting Releases (FRRs),* which regulate what must be reported by companies to the SEC itself. These standards usually agree with those previously issued by the private sector. To learn more about the SEC, consult its Internet site at **www.sec.gov.**[9]

The *Securities and Exchange Commission (SEC)* was created by Congress with the 1934 Securities Exchange Act.

The SEC has the authority to set accounting standards for companies, but always has delegated the responsibility to the accounting profession.

---

[6]The statement of cash flows is discussed in detail in Chapters 4 and 22.

[7]The terms *standards* and *principles* sometimes are used interchangeably.

[8]Reporting requirements for SEC registrants include Form 10-K, the annual report form, and Form 10-Q, the report that must be filed for the first three quarters of each fiscal year.

[9]In 2000, the SEC issued regulation FD (Fair Disclosure) which redefined how companies interact with analysts and the public in disclosing material information. Prior to regulation FD, companies often disclosed important information to a select group of analysts before disseminating the information to the general public. Now, this type of selective disclosure is prohibited. The initial disclosure of market-sensitive information must be made available to the general public.

Early Standard Setting.   The first private sector body to assume the task of setting accounting standards was the **Committee on Accounting Procedure (CAP).** The CAP was a committee of the **American Institute of Accountants (AIA).** The AIA, which was renamed the **American Institute of Certified Public Accountants (AICPA)** in 1957, is the national organization of professional public accountants. From 1938 to 1959, the CAP issued 51 *Accounting Research Bulletins (ARBs)* which dealt with specific accounting and reporting problems. No theoretical framework for financial accounting was established. This approach of dealing with individual issues without a framework led to stern criticism of the accounting profession.

The *Accounting Principles Board (APB)* followed the CAP.

In 1959 the **Accounting Principles Board (APB)** replaced the CAP. Members of the APB also belonged to the AICPA. The APB operated from 1959 through 1973 and issued 31 *Accounting Principles Board Opinions (APBOs),* various *Interpretations,* and four *Statements.* The *Opinions* also dealt with specific accounting and reporting problems. Many *ARBs* and *APBOs* have not been superseded and still represent authoritative GAAP.

The APB's main effort to establish a theoretical framework for financial accounting and reporting was *APB Statement No. 4,* "Basic Concepts and Accounting Principles Underlying Financial Statements of Business Enterprises." Unfortunately, the effort was not successful.

The APB was composed of members of the accounting profession and was supported by their professional organization. Members participated in the activities of the board on a voluntary, part-time basis. The APB was criticized by industry and government for its inability to establish an underlying framework for financial accounting and reporting and for its inability to act quickly enough to keep up with financial reporting issues as they developed. Perhaps the most important flaw of the APB was a perceived lack of independence. Composed almost entirely of public accountants, the board was subject to the criticism that the clients of the represented public accounting firms were exerting self-interested pressure on the board and influencing their decisions. Other interest groups were underrepresented in the standard-setting process.

The *FASB* currently sets accounting standards.

Current Standard Setting.   Criticism of the APB led to the creation in 1973 of the **Financial Accounting Standards Board (FASB)** and its supporting structure. The FASB differs from its predecessor in many ways. There are seven full-time members of the FASB, compared to 18–21 part-time members of the APB. While all of the APB members belonged to the AICPA, FASB members represent various constituencies concerned with accounting standards. Members have included representatives from the accounting profession, profit-oriented companies, accounting educators, and government. The APB was supported financially by the AICPA, while the FASB is supported by its parent organization, the **Financial Accounting Foundation (FAF).** The FAF is responsible for selecting the members of the FASB and its Advisory Council, raising funds to support the activities of the FASB and exercising general oversight of the FASB's activities.[10] The FASB is, therefore, an independent, private sector body whose members represent a broad constituency of interest groups.[11]

The *Emerging Issues Task Force (EITF)* identifies financial reporting issues and attempts to resolve them without involving the FASB.

In 1984, the FASB's **Emerging Issues Task Force (EITF)** was formed to provide more timely responses to emerging financial reporting issues. The EITF membership includes 15 individuals from public accounting and private industry, along with a representative from the FASB and an SEC observer. The membership of the task force is designed to include individuals who are in a position to be aware of emerging financial reporting issues. The task force considers these emerging issues and attempts to reach a consensus on how to account for them. If consensus can be reached, generally no FASB action is required. The task force

---

[10]The FAF's primary sources of funding are contributions and the sales of the FASB's publications. The FAF is governed by trustees, the majority of whom are appointed from the membership of eight sponsoring organizations. These organizations represent important constituencies involved with the financial reporting process. For example, one of the founding organizations is the Association of Investment Management and Research (formerly known as the Financial Analysts Federation) which represents financial information *users,* and another is the Financial Executives Institute which represents financial information *preparers.* The FAF also raises funds to support the activities of the Government Accounting Standards Board (GASB).

[11]The FASB organization also includes the **Financial Accounting Standards Advisory Council** (FASAC). The major responsibility of the FASAC is to advise the FASB on the priorities of its projects, including the suitability of new projects that might be added to its agenda.

HIERARCHY OF STANDARD-SETTING AUTHORITY

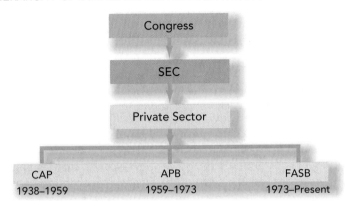

SOURCES OF GAAP

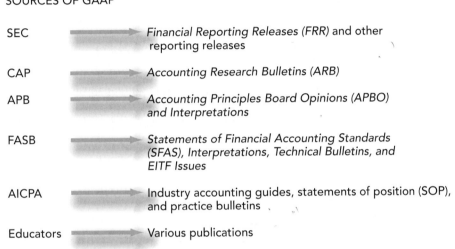

disseminates its rulings in the form of *EITF Issues*. These pronouncements are considered part of generally accepted accounting principles.

If a consensus can't be reached, FASB involvement may be necessary. The EITF plays an important role in the standard-setting process by identifying potential problem areas and then acting as a filter for the FASB. This speeds up the standard-setting process and allows the FASB to focus on pervasive long-term problems.

One of the FASB's most important activities has been the formulation of a **conceptual framework.** The conceptual framework project, discussed in more depth later in this chapter, deals with theoretical and conceptual issues and provides an underlying structure for current and future accounting and reporting standards. The FASB has issued seven *Statements of Financial Accounting Concepts (SFACs)* to describe its conceptual framework. The board also has issued over 140 specific accounting standards, called *Statements of Financial Accounting Standards (SFASs),* as well as numerous FASB *Interpretations and Technical Bulletins.*[12]

In addition to issuing specific accounting standards, the FASB has formulated a conceptual framework to provide an underlying theoretical and conceptual structure for accounting standards.

Graphic 1–2 summarizes this discussion on accounting standards. The top of the graphic shows the hierarchy of standard-setting authority. Congress gave the SEC the responsibility and authority to set accounting standards, specifically for companies whose securities are publicly traded. The SEC has delegated the task to various private sector bodies (currently the FASB) while retaining its legislated authority.

The bottom of the graphic summarizes the various sources of GAAP. Generally accepted accounting principles include the authoritative pronouncements of the SEC, CAP, APB, and

---

[12]For more information, go to the FASB's Internet site at www.fasb.org.

FASB. Some specific accounting transactions are not covered by an authoritative pronouncement issued by one of these bodies. In these cases, accountants look to other sources, such as various bulletins, industry guides, and statements of position (SOPs) published by the AICPA as well as publications of accounting educators. These publications also are included as sources of GAAP.[13]

ADDITIONAL CONSIDERATION

Accounting standards and the standard-setting process discussed above relate to standards governing the measurement and reporting of information for profit-oriented organizations. In 1984, the Government Accounting Standards Board (GASB) was created to develop accounting standards for governmental units such as states and cities. The GASB operates under the oversight of the Financial Accounting Foundation and the Governmental Accounting Standards Advisory Council.

CHECK WITH THE **COACH**

To get off to a good start in intermediate accounting, check with the Coach as a regular part of your study routine. Understanding the FASB conceptual framework and the process of setting U.S. and international financial reporting standards is important for anyone involved in business. Coach has video clips, featuring FASB members and other key people, to help you understand this important process. Come and see the Coach! You will be glad that you did. ■

THE ESTABLISHMENT OF ACCOUNTING STANDARDS— A POLITICAL PROCESS

LO4

The setting of accounting and reporting standards often has been characterized as a *political process*. Standards, particularly changes in standards, can have significant differential effects on companies, investors and creditors, and other interest groups. A change in an accounting standard or the introduction of a new standard can result in a substantial redistribution of wealth within our economy.

FINANCIAL REPORTING CASE

Q2, p. 3

The FASB must consider potential economic consequences of a change in an accounting standard or the introduction of a new standard.

The role of the FASB in setting accounting standards is a complex one. Sound accounting principles can provide significant guidance in determining the appropriate method to measure and report an economic transaction. However, the FASB must gauge the potential economic consequences of a change in a standard to the various interest groups as well as to society as a whole. One obvious desired consequence is that the new standard will provide a better set of information to external users and thus improve the resource allocation process.

An example of possible adverse economic consequences is the issue of accounting for postretirement employee health care benefits. Many corporations guarantee to pay the health care and life insurance costs of their employees after retirement. Traditionally, these companies accounted for these benefits as expenses in the period in which they made payments to or on behalf of retired employees. In 1989, the FASB proposed that these costs be accounted for by recognizing expenses over the period of employment rather than after retirement.

Companies feared that the new standard would seriously depress their annual income, and as a result, they would be forced to reduce their health care costs for retirees to soften the effect of the new standard. A survey of 992 large companies found that during the two years following the adoption of the new standard, 79% of the companies surveyed changed their retiree medical plans. Of those, 78% increased retirees' share of costs and 1% eliminated all coverage.[14] As a specific example, American Telephone and Telegraph Co. in 1989 negotiated with its union to pay health care benefits to retirees only up to a maximum fixed amount, as opposed to unlimited medical benefits offered by many companies. Of course,

---

[13]The FASB's concept statements do not constitute GAAP but provide a structure for evaluating current standards and for issuing new standards.

[14]Rod Coddington, "USA Snapshots," Hewitt Associates Survey of 992 Large Employers, *USA Today* (November 8, 1991).

AT&T's decision to limit retiree medical benefits may have been purely a business decision unrelated to the new reporting requirements.[15] Or, the new accounting standard may have caused companies like AT&T to reevaluate the costs and benefits of their postretirement packages. This issue is covered in depth in Chapter 18.

CARL LANDEGGER

If this becomes GAAP [generally accepted accounting principles], it will cause pain. It will cause evil. People will literally lose their health care benefits.[16]

Carl Landegger, chairman of The Black Clawson Company, expressed his fear of the new accounting standard in open hearings before the FASB in 1989. The FASB reacted to these fears by modifying their originally proposed accounting treatment to ease possible adverse economic consequences to current and future retirees covered by these postretirement health care plans. The resulting standard, *SFAS 106*, "Employers' Accounting for Postretirement Benefits Other Than Pensions," was issued in 1990.

Another example of the effect of economic consequences on standard setting is the highly controversial debate surrounding accounting for executive stock options. Key executives often are given the option to buy shares in the future at a preset price as an integral part of their total compensation package. The accounting objective for any form of compensation is to report compensation expense during the period of service for which the compensation is given. At issue is the amount of compensation to be recognized as expense for stock options.

Historically, options have been measured at their intrinsic value, which is the simple difference between the market price of the shares and the option price at which they can be acquired. For instance, an option that permits an employee to buy $60 stock for $42 has an intrinsic value of $18. The problem is that plans in which the exercise price equals the market value of the underlying stock at the date of grant (which describes most plans) have no intrinsic value and thus result in zero compensation when measured this way, even though the fair value of the options can be quite substantial. To the FASB and many others, it seems counterintuitive to not record any compensation expense for arrangements that routinely provide a large part of the total compensation of executives.

The FASB issued an exposure draft of a new standard in 1993 that would have required companies to measure options at their *fair values* at the time they are granted and to expense that amount over the appropriate service period. After lengthy debate, the FASB bowed to public pressure and consented to encourage, rather than require, that the fair value of options be recognized as expense. This debate is discussed at greater length in Chapter 18.

The most recent example of the political process at work in standard setting is the heated debate that occurred on the issue of accounting for business combinations. Back in 1996, the FASB added to its agenda a project to consider a possible revision in the practice of allowing two separate and distinct methods of accounting for business combinations, the pooling of interests method and the purchase method. A thorough explanation of the differences between these methods is beyond the scope of this text. For our discussion here, just note that a key issue in the debate related to goodwill, an intangible asset that arises only in business combinations accounted for using the purchase method. Under the then-existing standards, goodwill, like any other intangible asset, was amortized (expensed) over its estimated useful life thus reducing reported net income for several years following the acquisition. It was that negative impact on earnings that motivated many companies involved in a business combination to take whatever steps necessary to structure the transaction as a pooling of interests, thereby avoiding goodwill, its amortization to expense, and the resulting reduction in earnings.

Public pressure sometimes prevails over conceptual merit in the standard-setting arena.

---

[15]A change in an accounting standard does not directly affect the cash flow of a company. For example, changing from the cash to the accrual method of accounting for postretirement health care benefits does not *directly* change the amounts and timing of the cash payments the company has to make to retirees. However, real cash flow effects could result for a number of reasons. As a result of the change in a standard, (1) a company could alter the way it operates, (2) income tax payments could change, or (3) the new standard could cause the violation of a debt agreement thus increasing financing costs.

[16]Carl Landegger, reprinted in *Accounting Today* (October 23, 1989), p. 1.

As you might guess, when the FASB initially proposed eliminating the pooling method, many companies that were actively engaged in business acquisitions vigorously opposed the elimination of this means of avoiding goodwill. To support their opposition these companies argued that if they were required to use purchase accounting, many business combinations important to economic growth would prove unattractive due to the negative impact on earnings caused by goodwill amortization and would not be undertaken.

> **DENNIS POWELL—CISCO SYSTEMS, INC. VP**
> Clearly the FASB listened and responded to extensive comments from the public and the financial community to make the purchase method of accounting more effective and realistic.[17]

To satisfy opposition to its proposal, the FASB suggested several modifications over the years, but it wasn't until the year 2000 that a satisfactory compromise was reached. Specifically, under the new accounting standards issued in 2001[18], only the purchase method is acceptable, but to soften the impact, the resulting goodwill is *not* amortized. We discuss goodwill and its measurement in Chapters 10 and 11.

The FASB undertakes a series of information-gathering steps before issuing a substantive accounting standard.

The FASB's dilemma is to balance accounting considerations and political considerations resulting from perceived possible adverse economic consequences. To help solve this dilemma, the board undertakes a series of elaborate information-gathering steps before issuing a substantive accounting standard involving alternative accounting treatments for an economic transaction. These steps include open hearings, deliberations, and requests for written comments from interested parties. For example, 467 comment letters were received on the 1989 proposal concerning accounting for postretirement employee health care benefits. Graphic 1–3 outlines the FASB's standard-setting process.

GRAPHIC 1–3
The FASB's Standard-Setting Process

Step	Explanation
1. Identification of problem	A measurement or reporting issue is identified by the Emerging Issues Task Force and placed on the FASB's agenda.
2. The task force	A task force of approximately 15 knowledgeable persons is appointed to advise the Board on various matters.
3. Research and analysis	The FASB's technical staff investigates the issue.
4. *Discussion memorandum (DM)*	The DM, a detailed analysis of the problem along with alternative solutions, is prepared and disseminated to interested parties.
5. Public response	Public hearings are held to discuss the issue and letters of response are sent to the FASB which then analyzes this feedback.
6. *Exposure draft (ED)*	A preliminary draft of a proposed statement, called an exposure draft, is issued. The ED details the proposed treatment for the problem.
7. Public response	Written responses to the ED are accepted and analyzed. The ED is revised, if necessary, depending on the board's analysis.
8. *Statement* issued	An *SFAS* is issued if four of the seven FASB members support the revised ED.

These steps are the FASB's attempt to acquire consensus as to the preferred method of accounting, as well as to anticipate adverse economic consequences. The board's process is similar to that of an elected political representative, a U.S. congresswoman for example, trying to

---

[17]Jonathan Weil, "FASB Backs Down on Goodwill-Accounting Rules," *The Wall Street Journal* (December 7, 2000).
[18]"Business Combinations," *Statement of Financial Accounting Standards No. 141* (Norwalk, Conn.: FASB, 2001), and "Goodwill and Other Intangible Assets," *Statement of Financial Accounting Standards No. 142* (Norwalk, Conn.: FASB, 2001).

determine consensus among her constituency before voting on a bill on the floor of the House of Representatives. For this reason, accounting standard setting is a political process.

OUR GLOBAL MARKETPLACE

Advances in communication and transportation systems continue to expand the marketplace in which companies operate. The world economy is more integrated than ever, and many of the larger U.S. corporations are truly multinational in nature. These multinational corporations have their home in the United States but operate and perhaps raise capital in other countries. For example, Coca-Cola, IBM, Colgate-Palmolive, Gillette, and many other companies generate more than 50% of their revenue from foreign sales. It is not uncommon for even relatively small companies to transact business in many different countries.

> Many U.S. and foreign companies operate and raise capital in more than one country.

Of course, many foreign corporations operate in the United States as well. In fact, companies such as CBS Records, Firestone Tire & Rubber, and Tropicana Products are owned by companies that reside in other countries. The financial marketplace also has taken on a global dimension, with many companies crossing geographic boundaries to raise capital. For example, more than 500 companies have their securities listed on at least one stock exchange outside their home country. This expanded marketplace requires that company management understand the laws, customs, regulations, *and* accounting and reporting standards of many different countries.

Toward Global Accounting Standards.   Most industrialized countries have organizations responsible for determining accounting and reporting standards. In some countries, the United Kingdom for instance, the responsible organization is a private sector body similar to the FASB in the United States. In other countries, such as France, the organization is a governmental body.

Accounting standards prescribed by these various groups are not the same. Standards differ from country to country for many reasons, including different legal systems, levels of inflation, culture, degrees of sophistication and use of capital markets, and political and economic ties with other countries. These differences can cause problems for multinational corporations. A company doing business in more than one country may find it difficult to comply with more than one set of accounting standards if there are important differences among the sets. It has been argued that different national accounting standards impair the ability of companies to raise capital in international markets.

In response to this problem, the **International Accounting Standards Committee (IASC)** was formed in 1973 to develop global accounting standards. The IASC recently reorganized itself and created a new standard-setting body called the **International Accounting Standards Board (IASB).** The IASC now acts as an umbrella organization similar to the Financial Accounting Foundation (FAF) in the United States. This new global standard-setting structure is consistent with a recent FASB vision report attempting to identify an optimal standard-setting environment.[19] The IASB's objectives are (1) to develop a single set of high-quality, understandable global accounting standards, (2) to promote the use of those standards, and (3) to bring about the convergence of national accounting standards and International Accounting Standards.

> The *International Accounting Standards Committee (IASC)* was formed to alleviate the problem faced by multinational companies of having to comply with multiple sets of accounting standards.

The IASC issued 41 International Accounting Standards. The IASB endorsed these standards but, at the time this text was published, had not yet issued any standards of its own. IASB standards will be called **International Financial Reporting Standards.** Compliance with these standards is voluntary, since the IASB has no authority to enforce them. However, more and more countries are basing their national accounting standards on international accounting standards.[20] The International Organisation of Securities Commissions (IOSCO) recently approved a resolution permitting its members to use these standards to prepare their financial statements for cross-border offerings and listings. The European Union (EU) has

> International Accounting Standards are gaining support around the globe.

---

[19]*International Accounting Standard Setting: A Vision for the Future* (Norwalk, Conn.: FASB, 1998).
[20]Helen Gernon and Gary Meek, *Accounting: An International Perspective* (New York: The McGraw-Hill Companies, 2001).

proposed that by 2005 all member countries prepare their consolidated financial statements using these standards and many companies in the EU already state that they prepare their financial reports in accordance with International Accounting Standards.

In the United States, the move toward convergence of accounting standards began in earnest with the cooperation of the FASB and the IASC on the earnings per share (EPS) issue. In 1994, the FASB and the IASC began working on projects leading toward the issuance of new standards for the computation of EPS. The intent of the FASB's project was to issue an EPS standard that would be compatible with the new international standard and, at the same time, simplify U.S. GAAP. Chapter 20 describes this standard. The two organizations worked together to achieve compatibility.

Global Perspectives are included throughout the text to emphasize that our economy does not operate in isolation and to introduce you to some of the differences and similarities in accounting and reporting practices around the world. In addition, your instructor may assign end-of-chapter international cases to further explore these differences and similarities.

THE ROLE OF THE AUDITOR

FINANCIAL REPORTING CASE

Q3, p. 3

Auditors express an opinion on the compliance of financial statements with GAAP.

FedEx Corporation

Auditors offer credibility to financial statements.

Certified public accountants (CPAs) are licensed by states to provide audit services.

It is the responsibility of management to apply accounting standards when communicating with investors and creditors through financial statements. Another group, **auditors,** serves as an independent intermediary to help ensure that management has in fact appropriately applied GAAP in preparing the company's financial statements. Auditors examine (audit) financial statements to express a professional, independent opinion. The opinion reflects the auditors' assessment of the statements' "fairness," which is determined by the extent to which they are prepared in compliance with GAAP.

The report of the independent auditors for FedEx Corporation's financial statements is in the appendix. The first two paragraphs explain the scope of the audit, and the third states the auditors' opinion. After conducting its audit, the accounting firm Arthur Andersen LLP stated that "In our opinion, the financial statements referred to above present fairly, . . . , in conformity with accounting principles generally accepted in the United States." This is known as a *clean opinion.* If there had been any material departures from GAAP or other problems that caused the auditors to question the fairness of the statements, the report would have been modified to inform readers. In 2002, Ernst & Young LLP replaced Arthur Andersen as the company's auditor.

The auditor adds credibility to the financial statements, increasing the confidence of capital market participants who rely on the information. Auditors, therefore, play an important role in the resource allocation process.

In most states, only individuals licensed as **certified public accountants (CPAs)** in the state can represent that the financial statements have been audited in accordance with generally accepted auditing standards. Requirements to be licensed as a CPA vary from state to state, but all states specify education, testing, and experience requirements. The testing requirement is to pass the Uniform CPA Examination.

FINANCIAL REPORTING REFORM

The dramatic collapse of Enron in 2001 and the dismantling of the international public accounting firm of Arthur Andersen in 2002 severely shook U.S. capital markets. The credibility of the accounting profession itself as well as of corporate America was called into question. Public outrage over accounting scandals at high-profile companies like WorldCom, Xerox, Merck, Adelphia Communications, and others increased the pressure on lawmakers to pass measures that would restore credibility and investor confidence in the financial reporting process.

Driven by these pressures, Congress acted swiftly and passed the *Public Company Accounting Reform and Investor Protec-*

> **PAUL SARBANES—U.S. SENATOR**
> We confront an increasing crisis of confidence with the public's trust in our markets. If this continues, I think it poses a real threat to our economic health.[21]

---

[21]James Kuhnhenn, "Bush Vows to Punish Corporate Lawbreakers," *San Jose Mercury News* (July 9, 2002), p. 8A..

tion ACT of 2002. The legislation is comprehensive in its inclusion of the key players in the financial reporting process. The law provides for the regulation of auditors and the types of services they furnish to clients, increases accountability of corporate executives, addresses conflicts of interest for securities analysts, and provides for stiff criminal penalties for violators. Graphic 1–4 outlines the key provisions of the Act.

The changes imposed by the legislation are dramatic in scope and pose a significant challenge for the public accounting profession. At the same time, many maintain the changes were necessary to lessen the likelihood of corporate and accounting fraud and to restore investor confidence in the U.S. capital markets.

GRAPHIC 1–4
Public Company Accounting Reform and Investor Protection Act of 2002

Key Provisions of the Act:

- **Oversight board.**   The five-member (two accountants) Public Company Accounting Oversight Board has the authority to establish standards dealing with auditing, quality control, ethics, independence and other activities relating to the preparation of audit reports, or can choose to delegate these responsibilities to the AICPA. Prior to the act, the AICPA set auditing standards. The SEC has oversight and enforcement authority.

- **Corporate executive accountability.**   Corporate executives must personally certify the financial statements and company disclosures with severe financial penalties and the possibility of imprisonment for fraudulent misstatement.

- **Non-audit services.**   The law makes it unlawful for the auditors of public companies to perform a variety of non-audit services for audit clients. Prohibited services include bookkeeping, internal audit outsourcing, appraisal or valuation services, and various other consulting services. Other non-audit services, including tax services, require pre-approval by the audit committee of the company being audited.

- **Retention of work papers.**   Auditors of public companies must retain all audit or review work papers for five years or face the threat of a prison term for willful violations.

- **Auditor rotation.**   Lead audit partners are required to rotate every five years. Mandatory rotation of audit firms came under consideration.

- **Conflicts of interest.**   Audit firms are not allowed to audit public companies whose chief executives worked for the audit firm and participated in that company's audit during the preceding year.

- **Hiring of auditor.**   Audit firms are hired by the audit committee of the board of directors of the company, not by company management.

THE CONCEPTUAL FRAMEWORK

PART
b

The increasing complexity of our business world creates growing pressure on the FASB to delicately balance the many constituents of the accounting standard-setting process. The task of the FASB is made less complex if there exists a set of cohesive objectives and fundamental concepts on which financial accounting and reporting can be based. A number of years after coming into existence in 1973, the FASB's efforts resulted in the establishment of these objectives and concepts.

The **conceptual framework** has been described as a constitution, a coherent system of interrelated objectives and fundamentals that can lead to consistent

---

[22]Albert B. Crenshaw, "Congress Sends Corporate-Reform Bill to Bush," *Washingtonpost.com* (July 25, 2002).

FINANCIAL REPORTING CASE

Q4, p. 3

LO5

The conceptual framework does not prescribe GAAP. It provides an underlying foundation for accounting standards.

LO6

SFAC 1 establishes the objectives of financial reporting.

SFAC 1 affirms that investors and creditors are the primary external users of financial information.

standards and that prescribe the nature, function, and limits of financial accounting and reporting. The fundamentals are the underlying concepts of accounting, concepts that guide the selection of events to be accounted for, the measurement of those events, and the means of summarizing and communicating them to interested parties.[23]

The FASB has disseminated this framework through seven *Statements of Financial Accounting Concepts. SFAC 4* deals with the objectives of financial reporting for nonprofit organizations, and *SFAC 3* was superseded by *SFAC 6*, which, with the other four statements, is discussed below. It is important to realize that the conceptual framework provides structure and direction to financial accounting and reporting and does not directly prescribe GAAP.

The financial statements and their elements are most informative when they possess specific qualitative characteristics, subject to the constraints of materiality, cost effectiveness, and conservatism. Proper recognition and measurement of financial information rely on several assumptions and principles that underlie the financial reporting process.

> **FASB**
> The *Concepts Statements* will guide the Board in developing accounting standards by providing the Board with a common foundation and basic reasoning on which to consider merits of alternatives.[24]

The remainder of this chapter is devoted to discussions of the components of the conceptual framework that bear on financial statements as depicted in Graphic 1–5, beginning with the objectives of financial reporting.

Objectives of Financial Reporting

In specifying the overriding objectives of financial reporting, the board considered the economic, legal, political, and social environment in the United States. The objectives would be quite different in a socialist economy where the majority of productive resources are government owned.

Implicit in the objectives is an overall societal goal of serving the public interest by providing evenhanded financial and other information that, together with information from other sources, facilitates efficient functioning of capital markets and otherwise assists in promoting efficient capital allocation of scarce resources in the economy.[25]

The importance to our economy of providing capital market participants with information was discussed previously, as were the specific cash flow information needs of investors and creditors. *SFAC 1* articulates this importance and investor and creditor needs through three basic financial reporting objectives listed in Graphic 1–6.

The first objective specifies a focus on investors and creditors. In addition to the importance of investors and creditors as key users, information to meet their needs is likely to have general utility to other groups of external users who are interested in essentially the same financial aspects of a business as are investors and creditors.

The second objective refers to the specific cash flow information needs of investors and creditors. The third objective emphasizes the need for information about economic resources and claims to those resources. This information would include not only the amount of resources and claims at a particular point in time but also changes in resources and claims that occur over periods of time. This information is key to predicting future cash flows.

---

[23]"Conceptual Framework for Financial Accounting and Reporting: Elements of Financial Statements and Their Measurement," *Discussion Memorandum* (Stamford, Conn.: FASB, 1976), p. 2.

[24]Introduction to "Objectives of Financial Reporting by Nonbusiness Organizations," *Statement of Financial Accounting Concepts No. 4* (Stamford, Conn.: FASB, 1980).

[25]Introduction to "Objectives of Financial Reporting for Business Enterprises," *Statement of Financial Accounting Concepts No. 1* (Stamford, Conn.: FASB, 1978).

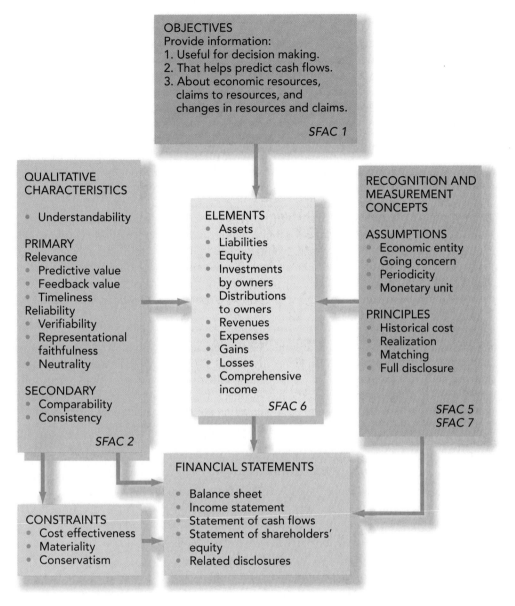

GRAPHIC 1–6
Financial Reporting
Objectives

The primary objective
of financial reporting is
to provide useful
information for
decision making.

1. Financial reporting should provide information that is useful to present and potential investors and creditors and other users in making rational investment, credit, and similar decisions.
   The information should be comprehensible to those who have a reasonable understanding of business and economic activities and are willing to study the information with reasonable diligence.
2. Financial reporting should provide information to help present and potential investors and creditors and other users to assess the amounts, timing, and uncertainty of prospective cash receipts.
   Since investors' and creditors' cash flows are related to enterprise cash flows, financial reporting should provide information to help assess the amounts, timing, and uncertainty of prospective net cash inflows to the related enterprise.
3. Financial reporting should provide information about the economic resources of an enterprise; the claims to those resources (obligations); and the effects of transactions, events, and circumstances that cause changes in resources and claims to those resources.
   These are sources, direct or indirect, of future cash inflows and cash outflows.

Qualitative Characteristics of Accounting Information

LO6

To satisfy the stated objectives, information should possess certain characteristics. The purpose of *SFAC 2* is to outline the desired qualitative characteristics of accounting information.

Graphic 1–7 indicates these qualitative characteristics, presented in the form of a hierarchy of their perceived importance. Notice that the main focus, as stated in the first concept statement is on **decision usefulness**—the ability to be useful in decision making. **Understandability** means that users must understand the information within the context of the decision being made. This is a user-specific quality because users will differ in their ability to comprehend any set of information. The first stated financial reporting objective of *SFAC 1* is to provide comprehensible information to those who have a reasonable understanding of business and economic activities and are willing to study the information.

> To be useful, information must make a difference in the decision process.

PRIMARY QUALITATIVE CHARACTERISTICS

The primary decision-specific qualities that make accounting information useful are **relevance** and **reliability.** Both are critical. No matter how reliable, if information is not relevant to the decision at hand, it is useless. Conversely, relevant information is of little value if it cannot be relied on. Let's look closer at each of these two characteristics, including the components that make those qualities desirable. We also consider two secondary qualities—comparability and consistency.

> To be decision useful, accounting information should be *relevant* and *reliable.*

Relevance.   To make a difference in the decision process, information must possess **predictive value** and/or **feedback value.** Generally, useful information will possess both qualities. For example, if net income and its components confirm investor expectations about future cash-generating ability, then net income has feedback value for investors. This confirmation can also be useful in predicting future cash-generating ability as expectations are revised.

This predictive ability is central to the concept of "earnings quality," the ability of reported earnings (income) to predict a company's future earnings. This is a concept we revisit frequently throughout this textbook in order to explore the impact on earnings quality of various topics under discussion. For instance, in Chapter 4 we discuss the contents of the income statement and certain classifications used in the statement from the perspective of helping analysts separate a company's transitory earnings effects from its permanent earnings. This separation is critical to a meaningful prediction of future earnings. In later chapters, we look at how various financial reporting decisions affect earnings quality.

GRAPHIC 1–7   Hierarchy of Desirable Characteristics of Accounting Information

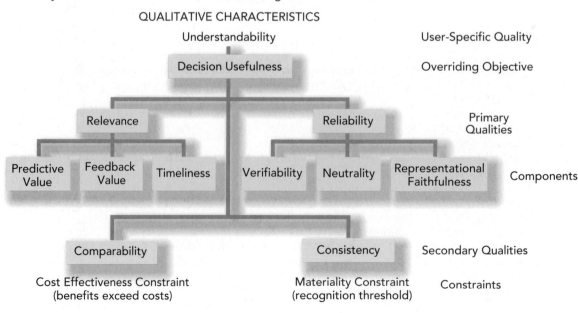

Timeliness also is an important component of relevance. Information is timely when it is available to users early enough to allow its use in the decision process. The need for timely information requires that companies provide information to external users on a periodic basis. The SEC requires its registrants to submit financial statement information not only on an annual basis, but also quarterly for the first three quarters of each fiscal year.

Information is timely *if it is available to users before a decision is made.*

Reliability.   Reliability is the extent to which information is *verifiable, representationally faithful,* and *neutral.* **Verifiability** implies a consensus among different measurers. For example, the historical cost of a piece of land to be reported in the balance sheet of a company is usually highly verifiable. The cost can be traced to an exchange transaction, the purchase of the land. However, the market value of that land is much more difficult to verify. Appraisers could differ in their assessment of market value. The term *objectivity* often is linked to verifiability. The historical cost of the land is objective but the land's market value is subjective, influenced by the measurer's past experience and prejudices. A measurement that is subjective is difficult to verify, which makes it more difficult for users to rely on.

Representational faithfulness exists when there is agreement between a measure or description and the phenomenon it purports to represent. For example, assume that the term *inventory* in a balance sheet of a retail company is understood by external users to represent items that are intended for sale in the ordinary course of business. If inventory includes, say, machines used to produce inventory, then it lacks representational faithfulness.

Representational faithfulness means agreement between a measure and a real-world phenomenon that the measure is supposed to represent.

Several years ago, accountants used the term *reserve for doubtful accounts* to describe anticipated bad debts related to accounts receivable. For many, the term *reserve* means that a sum of money has been set aside for future bad debts. Because this was not the case, this term lacked representational faithfulness. The description "reserve . . . " now has been changed to "allowance for uncollectible accounts" or "allowance for doubtful accounts." In FedEx Corporation's financial statements, the balance sheet in the appendix reports *Receivables, less allowances of $95,815,000 and $85,972,000* at the end of 2001 and 2000, respectively.

FedEx Corporation

Reliability assumes the information being relied on is neutral with respect to parties potentially affected. In that regard, **neutrality** is highly related to the establishment of accounting standards. You learned earlier that changes in accounting standards can lead to adverse economic consequences to certain companies, their investors and creditors, and other interest groups. Accounting standards should be established with overall societal goals and specific objectives in mind and should try not to favor particular groups or companies.

Accounting standards should not favor any particular groups or companies nor influence behavior in any specific way.

> **DONALD KIRK**
> If financial reporting is to be credible, there must be public confidence that the standard-setting system is credible, that selection of board members is based on merit and not the influence of special interests, and that standards are developed neutrally with the objective of relevant and reliable information, not purposeful manipulation.[26]

The FASB faces a difficult task in balancing neutrality and the consideration of economic consequences. A new accounting standard may favor one group of companies over others, but the FASB must convince the financial community that this was a consequence of the standard and not an objective used to set the standard. Donald Kirk, one of the members of the first group to serve on the FASB, stressed the importance of neutrality in the standard-setting process.

The qualities of relevance and reliability often clash. For example, a net income forecast provided by the management of a company may possess a high degree of relevance to investors and creditors trying to predict future cash flows. However, a forecast necessarily contains subjectivity in the estimation of future events. GAAP presently do not require companies to provide forecasts of any financial variables.

A trade-off often is required between various degrees of relevance and reliability.

SECONDARY QUALITATIVE CHARACTERISTICS

Graphic 1–7 identifies two secondary qualitative characteristics important to decision usefulness—comparability and consistency. **Comparability** is the ability to help users see

---

[26]Donald J. Kirk, chairman of the FASB, quoted in *Status Report,* December 23, 1986.

similarities and differences among events and conditions. We already have discussed the importance of the ability of investors and creditors to compare information across companies to make their resource allocation decisions. Closely related to comparability is the notion that **consistency** of accounting practices over time permits valid comparisons between different periods. The predictive and feedback value of information is enhanced if users can compare the performance of a company over time.[27] In the FedEx financial statements in the appendix, notice on page 38 that disclosure Note 1 includes a summary of significant accounting policies. A change in one of these policies would require disclosure in the financial statements and notes to restore comparability between periods.

Practical Boundaries (Constraints) to Achieving Desired Qualitative Characteristics

Most of us learn early in life that we can't get everything we desire. The latest electronic gadget may have all the qualitative characteristics that current technology can provide, but limited resources may lead us to purchase a fully functional model with fewer bells and whistles. **Cost effectiveness** also constrains the accounting choices we make. Specifically, it's important that the benefits of endowing accounting information with all the qualitative characteristics we've discussed exceed the costs of doing so.

A related constraint on the type of information we provide is the concept of **materiality.** For an additional $20 you can add the latest enhancement to that electronic gadget you're considering. However, despite the higher specs, if you feel it will provide no discernible improvement in the performance of the product as you will use it, why pay the extra $20? In an accounting context, if a more costly way of providing information is not expected to have a material effect on decisions made by those using the information, the less costly method may be acceptable.

Cost effectiveness and materiality impart practical constraints on each of the qualitative characteristics of accounting information. Both suggest that a certain accounting treatment might be different from that dictated solely by consideration of desired qualities of information.

COST EFFECTIVENESS

The costs of providing accounting information include those of gathering, processing, and disseminating information. There also are costs to users when interpreting information. In addition, costs include possible adverse economic consequences of implementing accounting standards. These costs in particular are difficult, if not impossible, to quantify.

An example of this is the standard that requires companies operating in more than one operating segment to disclose certain disaggregated financial information.[28] In addition to information gathering, processing, and dissemination costs, many companies feel that this reporting requirement imposes what could be called *competitive disadvantage costs*. These companies do not want their competitors to have the disaggregated data.

The perceived benefit from this or any accounting standard is increased *decision usefulness* of the information provided, which, hopefully, improves the resource allocation process. It is inherently impossible to quantify this benefit. The elaborate information-gathering process undertaken by the FASB in setting accounting standards is an attempt to assess both costs and benefits of a proposed accounting standard, even if in a subjective, nonquantifiable manner. In the case of reporting disaggregated information, the FASB decided that the perceived benefits of disclosing this information exceeded the costs of providing it.

MATERIALITY

Materiality is another pervasive constraint. Information is material if it can have an effect on a decision made by users. One consequence of considering materiality is that GAAP need not

---

[27]Companies occasionally do change their accounting practices, which makes it difficult for users to make comparisons among different reporting periods. Chapter 4 and Chapter 21 describe the disclosures that a company makes in this situation to restore consistency among periods.

[28]"Disclosures about Segments of an Enterprise and Related Information," *Statement of Financial Accounting Standards No. 131* (Norwalk, Conn.: FASB, 1997). The contents of this standard are described in the appendix to Chapter 3.

be followed if an item is immaterial. For example, GAAP requires that receivables be measured at their net realizable value. If bad debts are anticipated, they should be estimated and subtracted from the face amount of receivables for balance sheet measurement. This is called the *allowance method* of accounting for bad debts. However, if the amount of anticipated bad debts is not considered to be large enough to affect decisions made by users, the *direct write-off method* of accounting for bad debts can be used even though it is not a generally accepted technique. This method does not require estimation of bad debts for existing receivables.

The threshold for materiality will depend principally on the *relative* dollar amount of the transaction. For example, $10,000 in total anticipated bad debts for a multibillion dollar company like FedEx would not be considered material. The method used to account for these anticipated bad debts will not affect the decisions made by FedEx Corporation's financial statement users. This same $10,000 amount, however, could easily be material for a neighborhood pizza parlor. The FASB has been reluctant to establish any quantitative materiality guidelines. The threshold for materiality has been left to the subjective judgment of the company preparing the financial statements and its auditors.

Materiality is concerned not only with the dollar amount of an item but with the nature of the item as well. In 1999, the SEC issued *Staff Accounting Bulletin No. 99.*[29] The bulletin expresses the SEC's view that exclusive reliance on quantitative benchmarks to assess materiality in preparing financial statements is inappropriate. A number of other factors, including whether the item in question involves an unlawful transaction, should also be considered when determining materiality. For example, an activity such as the illegal payment of $10,000 to an official of a foreign government to secure a valuable contract would probably be considered material even if the amount is small relative to the size of the company.

> Information is *material* if it has an effect on decisions.

> Professional judgment determines what amount is material in each situation.

CONSERVATISM

Conservatism is a practice followed in an attempt to ensure that uncertainties and risks inherent in business situations are adequately considered. It is a frequently cited characteristic of accounting information. Conservatism is not, however, a desired qualitative characteristic but a practical justification for some accounting choices. In that sense, conservatism serves as a third constraint on the achievement of various qualitative characteristics.[30]

The need for conservatism often is discussed in conjunction with the estimates required to comply with GAAP. For example, assume that a company estimated that its anticipated bad debts on existing receivables could be any number between $20,000 and $30,000, with the most likely amount being $25,000, and that these amounts are material. A conservative estimate would be $30,000, thus showing the lowest amount (of a range of possible values) in the balance sheet for net receivables and the highest expense so the lowest net income in the income statement.

However, financial accounting information users could just as easily be misled by a conservative estimate as by an optimistic one. If $25,000 is the best estimate of anticipated bad debts, then that is the number that should be used. Conservatism is *not* a desirable characteristic nor is it an accounting principle. Nevertheless, there seem to be some accounting practices, such as the lower-of-cost-or-market method for measuring inventory (Chapter 9), that appear to be generated by a desire to be conservative. However, these practices are motivated by other accounting principles such as the realization principle as discussed later in this chapter. They also are influenced by practical realities of our legal system. Investors and creditors who lose money from stock purchases or loans are less likely to sue when bad news is exaggerated and good news is underestimated. While recognizing the role that conservatism plays in how information is reported, we also need to emphasize that it is not a desired characteristic from a qualitative standpoint. Instead, conservatism is a practical constraint on the extent to which other qualitative characteristics are instilled in accounting information.

> *Conservatism* is a justification for some accounting practices, *not* a desired qualitative characteristic of accounting information.

---

[29]"Materiality," *Staff Accounting Bulletin No. 99* (Washington, DC: SEC, August 1999).
[30]The FASB's hierarchy of qualitative characteristics does not specifically identify conservatism as a constraint. Most theorists include conservatism as one of the underlying accounting principles that guide accounting practice. Our classification recognizes its very real role in accounting choices as well as the practical motivation for those choices.

Now that we've discussed the qualities that the elements of financial statements should possess, let's look more closely at the elements themselves.

Elements of Financial Statements

SFAC 6 defines 10 elements of financial statements. These elements are "the building blocks with which financial statements are constructed—the classes of items that financial statements comprise."[31] They focus directly on items related to measuring performance and to reporting financial position. The definitions of these elements operationalize the resources, claims, and changes identified in the third objective of financial reporting in *SFAC 1*.[32] The *accrual accounting* model actually is embodied in the element definitions. The FASB recognized that accrual accounting produces information that is more successful in predicting future cash flows than is cash flow accounting.

The 10 elements are: (1) assets, (2) liabilities, (3) equity, (4) investments by owners, (5) distributions to owners, (6) revenues, (7) expenses, (8) gains, (9) losses, and (10) comprehensive income.

> **The 10 elements of financial statements defined in *SFAC 6* describe financial position and periodic performance.**

You probably already know in general terms what most of these elements mean. But as you will see when they are discussed, it is helpful to have a deeper understanding of their meaning. You may recognize the first three elements—assets, liabilities, and equity—as those that portray the financial position of an enterprise.

Assets are probable future economic benefits obtained or controlled by a particular entity as a result of past transactions or events.

> **Assets represent probable future economic benefits controlled by the enterprise.**

A key characteristic of this definition is that an asset represents *probable* future economic benefits. A receivable is an asset only if it is probable that future benefits will result, that cash will be collected. The *controlled by* aspect of the definition also is important. The employees of a company certainly represent future economic benefits to a company. However, they are not owned or controlled by the company and do not qualify as assets.

Liabilities are probable future sacrifices of economic benefits arising from present obligations of a particular entity to transfer assets or provide services to other entities in the future as a result of past transactions or events.[33]

> **Liabilities represent obligations to other entities.**

Most liabilities require the future payment of cash, the amount and timing of which are specified by a legally enforceable contract. Actually, though, a liability need not be payable in cash. Instead, it may require the company to transfer other assets or to provide services. For example, a warranty liability is created for the seller when a product is sold and the seller guarantees to fix or replace the product if it proves defective and it is probable that a material amount of product sold will, in fact, prove defective. A liability also need not be represented by a written agreement, nor be legally enforceable. For example, a company might choose to pay a terminated employee's salary for a period of time after termination even though not legally required to do so. The commitment creates a liability at the date of termination.

Equity or net assets, called **shareholders' equity** or **stockholders' equity** for a corporation, is the residual interest in the assets of an entity that remains after deducting liabilities.

Assets and liabilities are measured directly; equity is not. Equity is simply a residual amount. The accounting equation illustrates financial position.

---

[31]"Elements of Financial Statements," *Statement of Financial Accounting Concepts No. 6* (Stamford, Conn.: FASB, 1985), par. 5.
[32]Graphic 1–6.
[33]In 2000, the FASB issued an exposure draft proposing a revision to the *Concept Statement No. 6* definition of a liability. The proposed amendment would expand the definition to also include as liabilities certain obligations that require or permit settlement by issuance of the issuer's equity shares and that do not establish an ownership interest. At the time this text was written, a final pronouncement had not been issued.

$$\underbrace{\textbf{Assets} - \textbf{Liabilities}}_{\textit{Net Assets}} = \textbf{Equity}$$

Equity is a residual amount, the owners' interest in assets after subtracting liabilities.

For a corporation, equity arises primarily from two sources: (1) amounts *invested* by shareholders in the corporation and (2) amounts *earned* by the corporation on behalf of its shareholders. These two sources are reported as (1) **paid-in capital** and (2) **retained earnings.** We discuss this classification of shareholders' equity in more depth in Chapter 19.

The next two elements defined in *SFAC 6* deal with changes in equity from owner transactions.

Investments by owners are increases in equity resulting from transfers of resources (usually cash) to a company in exchange for ownership interest.

A corporation's issuance of ownership shares of stock in exchange for cash represents an investment by owners.

Investments by owners and *distributions to owners* are transactions describing any owner contribution to and withdrawal from the company.

Distributions to owners are decreases in equity resulting from transfers *to* owners.

A cash dividend paid by a corporation to its shareholders is the most common distribution to owners.

Revenues, gains, expenses, and losses describe changes in equity due to profit-generating transactions.

Revenues are inflows or other enhancements of assets or settlements of liabilities from delivering or producing goods, rendering services, or other activities that constitute the entity's ongoing major, or central, operations.

Revenues are gross inflows resulting from providing goods or services to customers.

A key characteristic is that revenues are inflows. The enterprise is acquiring something in exchange for providing goods and services to customers. Also, providing these goods and services represents a major operation of the enterprise.

On the other hand, if selling the item is not part of the central operations of the business but instead is only an incidental result of those operations, the inflow of assets would produce a gain rather than a revenue.

Gains are increases in equity from peripheral, or incidental, transactions of an entity.

FedEx earns revenue by providing a service, delivering packages, to its customers. If FedEx sold a piece of machinery used to deliver packages for an amount greater than its book value (original cost less depreciation recorded up to the date of sale), a gain would result. Gains are net inflows, the difference between the amount received and book value. Revenues are gross inflows, measured as the amount received or to be received for the goods or services without regard to the cost of providing the goods or services.

Expenses are outflows or other using up of assets or incurrences of liabilities during a period from delivering or producing goods, rendering services, or other activities that constitute the entity's ongoing major, or central, operations.

Expenses are gross outflows incurred in generating revenues.

A key characteristic is that expenses represent outflows of resources incurred in the process of generating revenues.

Losses represent decreases in equity arising from peripheral, or incidental, transactions of the entity.

If FedEx sold that piece of machinery used to deliver packages for *less* than its book value, a loss would result. So, losses are the opposite of gains—they are net *outflows* rather than net inflows. They differ from expenses by being net rather than gross outflows and by being peripheral, or incidental, transactions rather than major, or central, operations. Revenues plus gains less expenses and losses for a period equals **net income** or **net loss,** the so-called bottom line of the income statement.[34]

You should note that the definitions of these nine elements are in basic agreement with those used in practice. But, *SFAC 6* also introduced a new term, the 10th element, called *comprehensive income.*

> **Comprehensive income** is the change in equity of a business enterprise during a period from transactions and other events and circumstances from nonowner sources. It includes all changes in equity during a period except those resulting from investments by owners and distributions to owners.

Comprehensive income often does not equal net income.

Under present GAAP, net income as reported in the income statement often doesn't equal comprehensive income. The difference is the treatment of certain changes in assets and liabilities *not* included in the determination of net income for the period in which they are recognized but instead reported collectively as a separate component of shareholders' equity in the balance sheet called accumulated other comprehensive income. For example, in your study of investments in Chapter 12, you will learn that for certain types of investments valued at fair values in the balance sheet, the changes in those values are not included in net income but rather in a separate component of shareholders' equity. Comprehensive income is discussed in Chapter 4.

FedEx Corporation

In the FedEx Corporation financial statements in the appendix, the income statement for the most recent fiscal year reports net income of $584,371,000. The balance sheet for the most recent fiscal year shows accumulated other comprehensive income of $(55,833,000), and the statement of changes in stockholders' investment and comprehensive income provides the details of the change in this figure from the prior year.

Recognition and Measurement Concepts

Now that the various elements of financial statements have been identified, we discuss when they should be recognized (recorded) and how they should be measured. *SFAC 5* addresses these issues. **Recognition** refers to the process of admitting information into the basic financial statements. **Measurement** is the process of associating numerical amounts to the elements. For example, a revenue was previously defined as an inflow of assets from selling a good or providing a service. But, *when* should the revenue event be recorded, and at *what* amount?

RECOGNITION

According to *SFAC 5,* an item should be recognized in the basic financial statements when it meets the following four criteria, subject to a cost effectiveness constraint and materiality threshold:

Recognition criteria.

1. *Definition.* The item meets the definition of an element of financial statements.
2. *Measurability.* The item has a relevant attribute measurable with sufficient reliability.
3. *Relevance.* The information about it is capable of making a difference in user decisions.
4. *Reliability.* The information is representationally faithful, verifiable, and neutral.[35]

These obviously are very general guidelines. The concept statement does not address *specific* recognition issues.

MEASUREMENT

The question of measurement involves two choices: (1) the choice of a unit of measurement, and (2) the choice of an attribute to be measured. *SFAC 5* essentially confirmed existing

---

[34]Some companies use the term *net earnings* instead of net income. If earnings are negative, the term used is *net loss.*
[35]"Recognition and Measurement in Financial Statements," *Statement of Financial Accounting Concepts No. 5* (Stamford, Conn.: FASB, 1984), par. 63.

practice in both of these areas. The monetary unit or measurement scale used in financial statements is nominal units of money without any adjustment for changes in purchasing power. In addition, the board acknowledged that different attributes such as historical cost, net realizable value, and present value of future cash flows are presently used to measure different financial statement elements, and that they expect that practice to continue. For example, property, plant, and equipment are measured at historical cost; accounts receivable are measured at their net realizable value; and most long-term liabilities, such as bonds, are measured at the present value of future cash payments.

Present value measurements have long been associated with accounting valuation. However, because of its increased prominence, present value is the focus of a recent FASB concept statement that provides a framework for using future cash flows as the basis for accounting measurement and also asserts that the objective in valuing an asset or liability using present value is to approximate the fair value of that asset or liability.[36] We explore this objective in more depth in Chapter 6.

SFAC No. 7 provides a framework for using future cash flows in accounting measurements.

Answers to the recognition and measurement questions are imbedded in generally accepted accounting principles. *SFAC 5* confirmed some of the more important of these principles used in present practice. GAAP consist of broad principles and specific standards. The accrual accounting model is an example of a broad principle. Before addressing additional key broad principles, we look at some important assumptions that underlie those fundamental principles.

UNDERLYING ASSUMPTIONS

The four basic assumptions underlying GAAP are (1) the economic entity assumption, (2) the going concern assumption, (3) the periodicity assumption, and (4) the monetary unit assumption.

Economic Entity Assumption.

An essential assumption is that all economic events can be identified with a particular economic entity. Investors desire information about an economic entity that corresponds to their ownership interest. For example, if you were considering buying some ownership stock in FedEx, you would want information on the various operating units that constitute FedEx. You would need information not only about their United States operations but also about their European and other international operations. Also, you would not want the information about FedEx combined with that of United Parcel Service (UPS), another air freight company. These would be two separate *economic entities.* The financial information for the various companies (subsidiaries) in which FedEx owns a controlling interest (greater than 50% ownership of voting stock) should be combined with that of FedEx (the parent). The parent and its subsidiaries are separate *legal* entities but one *accounting* entity.

The economic entity assumption presumes that economic events can be identified specifically with an economic entity.

Another key aspect of this assumption is the distinction between the economic activities of owners and those of the company. For example, the economic activities of a sole proprietorship, Uncle Jim's Restaurant, should be separated from the activities of its owner, Uncle Jim. Uncle Jim's personal residence, for instance, is not an asset of the business.

Going Concern Assumption.

Another necessary assumption is that, in the absence of information to the contrary, it is anticipated that a business entity will continue to operate indefinitely. Accountants realize that the going concern assumption does not always hold since there certainly are many business failures. However, companies are begun with the hope of a long life, and many achieve that goal.

Financial statements of a company presume the business is a going concern.

This assumption is critical to many broad and specific accounting principles. For example, the assumption provides justification for measuring many assets based on their historical costs. If it were known that an enterprise was going to cease operations in the near future, assets and liabilities would not be measured at their historical costs but at their current liquidation values.

---

[36]"Using Cash Flow Information and Present Value in Accounting Measurements," *Statement of Financial Accounting Concepts No. 7* (Norwalk, Conn.: FASB, 2000).

Similarly, depreciation of a building over an estimated life of 40 years presumes the business will operate that long.

Periodicity Assumption. The periodicity assumption relates to the qualitative characteristic of *timeliness.* External users need *periodic* information to make decisions. This need for periodic information requires that the economic life of an enterprise (presumed to be indefinite) be divided into artificial time periods for financial reporting. Corporations whose securities are publicly traded are required to provide financial information to the SEC on a quarterly and annual basis.[37] Financial statements often are prepared on a monthly basis for banks and others that might need more timely information.

For many companies, the annual time period (the fiscal year) used to report to external users is the calendar year. However, other companies have chosen a fiscal year that does not correspond to the calendar year. The accounting profession and the Securities and Exchange Commission advocate that companies adopt a fiscal year that corresponds to their natural business year. A natural business year is the 12-month period that ends when the business activities of a company reach their lowest point in the annual cycle. For example, many retailers, Wal-Mart for example, have adopted a fiscal year ending on January 31. Business activity in January generally is quite slow following the very busy Christmas period. We can see from the FedEx financial statements that the company's fiscal year ends on May 31. The Campbell Soup Company's fiscal year ends in July; Clorox's in June; and Kmart's in January.

> The *periodicity assumption* allows the life of a company to be divided into artificial time periods to provide timely information.

> **FedEx Corporation**

> The *monetary unit assumption* states that financial statement elements should be measured in terms of the dollar.

Monetary Unit Assumption. Recall that to *measure* financial statement elements, a unit or scale of measurement must be chosen. Information would be difficult to use if, for example, assets were listed as "three machines, two trucks, and a building." A common denominator is needed to measure all elements. The dollar in the United States is the most appropriate common denominator to express information about financial statement elements and changes in those elements.

One problem is that this monetary unit concept assumes that the monetary unit is stable over time. That is, the value of the dollar, in terms of its ability to purchase certain goods and services, is constant over time. This obviously does not strictly hold. The U.S. economy has experienced periods of rapidly changing prices. To the extent that prices are unstable, and those machines, trucks and building were purchased at different times, the monetary unit used to measure them is not the same. The effect of changing prices on financial information generally is discussed elsewhere in your accounting curriculum, often in an advanced accounting course.

ACCOUNTING PRINCIPLES

There are four important broad accounting principles that provide significant guidance for accounting practice: (1) the historical cost principle, (2) the realization principle (also known as the *revenue recognition principle*), (3) the matching principle, and (4) the full-disclosure principle. These principles deal with the critical issues of recognition and measurement. The accrual accounting model is embodied in each of the principles.

> The *historical cost principle* states that asset and liability measurements should be based on the amount given or received in the exchange transaction.

Historical Cost Principle. The FASB recognized in *SFAC 5* that elements in financial statements currently are measured by different attributes. In general, however, GAAP measure assets and liabilities based on their *original transaction value,* that is, their historical costs. For an asset, this is the fair value of what is given in exchange (usually cash) for the asset at its initial acquisition. For liabilities, it is the current cash equivalent received in exchange for assuming the liability. For example, if a company borrowed $1 million cash and signed an interest-bearing note promising to repay the cash in the future, the liability would be valued at $1 million, the cash received in exchange.[38]

---

[37]The report that must be filed for the first three quarters of each fiscal year is Form 10-Q and the annual report is Form 10-K.
[38]This current cash equivalent for many liabilities also will equal the present value of future cash payments. This is illustrated in a subsequent chapter.

Why base measurement on historical costs? After all, the current value of a company's manufacturing plant might seem more relevant than its original cost. First, historical cost provides important cash flow information as it represents the cash or cash equivalent paid for an asset or received in exchange for the assumption of a liability. Second, because historical cost valuation is the result of an exchange transaction between two independent parties, the agreed on exchange value is objective and highly *verifiable*. Alternatives such as measuring an asset at its current market value involve *estimating* a selling price. An example given earlier in the chapter concerned the valuation of a parcel of land. Appraisers could easily differ in their assessment of current market value.

> **Historical cost measurement provides relevant cash flow information and also is highly verifiable.**

There are occasions where a departure from measuring an asset based on its historical cost is warranted. Some assets, for instance, are measured at their *net realizable value*. For example, if customers purchased goods or services on account for $10,000, the asset, accounts receivable, would initially be valued at $10,000, the original transaction value. Subsequently, if $2,000 in bad debts were anticipated, net receivables should be valued at $8,000, the net realizable value. Departures from historical cost measurement such as this provide more appropriate information in terms of the overall objective of providing information to aid in the prediction of future cash flows.

> **A departure from historical cost valuation sometimes is appropriate.**

Realization Principle.   Determining accounting income by the accrual accounting model is a challenging task. When to recognize revenue is critical to this determination. Revenues are inflows of assets resulting from providing a product or service to a customer. At what point is this event recognized by an increase in assets? The **realization principle** requires that two criteria be satisfied before revenue can be recognized:

> **Revenue should be recognized when the earnings process is virtually complete and collection is reasonably assured.**

1. The earnings process is judged to be complete or virtually complete.
2. There is reasonable certainty as to the collectibility of the asset to be received (usually cash).

These criteria help ensure that a revenue event is not recorded until an enterprise has performed all or most of its earnings activities for a financially capable buyer. The primary earnings activity that triggers the recognition of revenue is known as the *critical event*. The critical event for many businesses occurs at the **point-of-sale.** This usually takes place when the goods or services sold to the buyer are *delivered* (i.e., title is transferred).

> **Both revenue recognition criteria usually are met at the *point-of-sale*.**

The *timing* of revenue recognition is a key element of earnings measurement. An income statement should report the results of all operating activities for the time period specified in the financial statements. A one-year income statement should report the company's accomplishments only for that one-year period. Revenue recognition criteria help ensure that a proper cut-off is made each reporting period and that exactly one year's activity is reported in that income statement. Not adhering to revenue recognition criteria could result in overstating revenue and hence net income in one reporting period and, consequently, understating revenue and net income in a subsequent period. Notice that revenue recognition criteria allow for the implementation of the accrual accounting model. Revenue should be recognized in the period it is earned, *not necessarily in the period in which cash is received.*

> **Revenue is recognized when *earned*, regardless of when cash actually is received.**

Some revenue-producing activities call for revenue recognition over time, rather than at one particular point in time. For example, revenue recognition could take place *during* the earnings process for long-term construction contracts. We discuss revenue recognition in considerable depth in Chapter 5. That chapter also describes in more detail the concept of an earnings process and how it relates to performance measurement.

Matching Principle.   When are expenses recognized? The **matching principle** states that expenses are recognized in the same period as the related revenues. There is a cause-and-effect relationship between revenue and expense recognition implicit in this definition. In a given period, revenue is recognized according to the realization principle. The matching principle then requires that all expenses incurred in generating that same revenue also be recognized. The net result is a measure—net income—that matches current period accomplishments and sacrifices. This accrual-based measure provides a good indicator of future cash-generating ability.

> **Expenses are recognized in the same reporting period as the related revenues.**

Although the concept is straightforward, its implementation can be difficult. The difficulty arises in trying to identify cause-and-effect relationships. Many expenses are not incurred *directly* because of a revenue event. Instead, the expense is incurred to generate the revenue, but the association is indirect.

The matching principle is implemented by one of four different approaches, depending on the nature of the specific expense. Only the first approach involves an actual cause-and-effect relationship between revenue and expense. In the other three approaches, the relationship is indirect.

An expense can be recognized:

1. Based on an exact cause-and-effect relationship between a revenue and expense event.
2. By associating an expense with the revenues recognized in a specific time period.
3. By a systematic and rational allocation to specific time periods.
4. In the period incurred, without regard to related revenues.

There is a direct relationship between some expenses and revenues.

The first approach is appropriate for *cost of goods sold.* There is a definite cause-and-effect relationship between Dell Computer's revenue from the sale of personal computers and the costs to produce those computers. Commissions paid to salespersons for obtaining revenues also is an example of an expense recognized based on this approach.

Some expenses are associated indirectly with revenues of a particular period.

Unfortunately, for most expenses there is no obvious cause-and-effect relationship between a revenue and expense event. In other words, the revenue event does not directly *cause* expenses to be incurred. Many expenses, however, can be related to periods of time during which revenue is earned. For example, the monthly salary paid to an office worker is not directly related to any specific revenue event. The employee provides services during the month. The asset used to pay the employee, cash, provides benefits to the company only for that one month and *indirectly* relates to the revenue recognized in that same period.

Some expenses are allocated to specific time periods.

Some costs are incurred to acquire assets that provide benefits to the company for more than one reporting period. Refer again to the Carter Company example in Illustration 1–1 on page 7. At the beginning of year 1, $60,000 in rent was paid covering a three-year period. This asset, prepaid rent, helps generate revenues for more than one reporting period. In that example, we chose to "systematically and rationally" allocate rent expense equally to each of the three one-year periods rather than to charge the expense to year 1.

Some expenses are recognized in the period incurred, without regard to related revenues.

The fourth approach to expense recognition is called for in situations when costs are incurred but it is impossible to determine in which period or periods, if any, revenues will occur. For example, consider the cost of advertising. Advertising expenditures are made with the presumption that incurring that expense will generate incremental revenues. Let's say FedEx spends $1 million for a series of television commercials. It's difficult to determine when, how much, or even whether additional revenues occur as a result of that particular series of ads. Because of this difficulty, advertising expenditures are recognized as expense in the period incurred, with no attempt made to match them with revenues.

The Full-Disclosure Principle.

Any information useful to decision makers should be provided in the financial statements, subject to the cost effectiveness constraint.

Remember, the purpose of accounting is to provide information that is useful to decision makers. So, naturally, if there is accounting information not included in the primary financial statements that would benefit users, that information should be provided too. The **full-disclosure principle** means that the financial reports should include any information that could affect the decisions made by external users. Of course, the benefits of that information, as noted earlier, should exceed the costs of providing the information. Supplemental information is disclosed in a variety of ways, including:

1. **Parenthetical comments** or **modifying comments** placed on the face of the financial statements.
2. **Disclosure notes** conveying additional insights about company operations, accounting principles, contractual agreements, and pending litigation.
3. **Supplemental financial statements** that report more detailed information than is shown in the primary financial statements.

We find examples of these disclosures in the FedEx financial statements in the appendix. A parenthetical or modifying comment is provided in the common stockholders' investment section of the balance sheet with disclosure of the number of shares of stock authorized, issued, and outstanding. The statements include several notes as well as a supplemental statement disclosing information about the company's quarterly operating results. Notice that the FedEx Corporation financial statements include the following statement: "The accompanying notes are an integral part of these consolidated financial statements." We discuss and illustrate disclosure requirements as they relate to specific financial statement elements in later chapters as those elements are discussed.

FedEx Corporation

Graphic 1–8 provides a summary of the accounting assumptions and principles that guide the recognition and measurement of accounting information.

GRAPHIC 1–8
Summary of Recognition and Measurement Concepts

Assumptions	Description
Economic entity	All economic events can be identified with a particular economic entity.
Going concern	In the absence of information to the contrary, it is anticipated that a business entity will continue to operate indefinitely.
Periodicity	The life of a company can be divided into artificial time periods to provide timely information to external users.
Monetary unit	In the United States, financial statement elements should be measured in terms of the U.S. dollar.
Principles	
Historical cost	Asset and liability measurements should be based on the amount given or received in an exchange transaction.
Realization	Revenue should be recognized only after the earnings process is virtually complete and there is reasonable certainty of collecting the asset to be received from the customer.
Matching	Expenses should be recognized in the same reporting period as the related revenues.
Full disclosure	Any information that could change the decisions made by external users should be provided in the financial statements, subject to the cost effectiveness constraint.

Ethics in Accounting

Ethics is a term that refers to a code or moral system that provides criteria for evaluating right and wrong. An ethical dilemma is a situation in which an individual or group is faced with a decision that tests this code. Many of these dilemmas are simple to recognize and resolve. For example, have you ever been tempted to call your professor and ask for an extension on the due date of an assignment by claiming a fictitious illness? Temptation like this will test your personal ethics.

Ethics deals with the ability to distinguish right from wrong.

Accountants, like others operating in the business world, are faced with many ethical dilemmas, some of which are complex and difficult to resolve. For instance, the capital markets' focus on periodic profits may tempt a company's management to bend or even break accounting rules to inflate reported net income. In these situations, technical competence is not enough to resolve the dilemma.

ETHICS AND PROFESSIONALISM

One of the elements that many believe distinguishes a profession from other occupations is the acceptance by its members of a responsibility for the interests of those it serves. A high standard of ethical behavior is expected of those engaged in a profession. These standards often are articulated in a code of ethics. For example, law and medicine are professions that have their own codes of professional ethics. These codes provide guidance and rules to members in the performance of their professional responsibilities.

Public accounting has achieved widespread recognition as a profession. The AICPA, the national organization of certified professional public accountants, has its own Code of Professional Conduct which prescribes the ethical conduct members should strive to achieve. Similarly, the **Institute of Management Accountants (IMA)**—the primary national organization of accountants working in industry and government—has its own code of ethics, as does the **Institute of Internal Auditors**—the national organization of accountants providing internal auditing services for their own organizations.

ANALYTICAL MODEL FOR ETHICAL DECISIONS

Ethical codes are informative and helpful. However, the motivation to behave ethically must come from within oneself and not just from the fear of penalties for violating professional codes. Presented below is a sequence of steps that provide a framework for analyzing ethical issues. These steps can help you apply your own sense of right and wrong to ethical dilemmas:[39]

Step 1.   Determine the facts of the situation. This involves determining the who, what, where, when, and how.

Step 2.   Identify the ethical issue and the stakeholders. Stakeholders may include shareholders, creditors, management, employees, and the community.

Step 3.   Identify the values related to the situation. For example, in some situations confidentiality may be an important value that may conflict with the right to know.

Step 4.   Specify the alternative courses of action.

Step 5.   Evaluate the courses of action specified in step 4 in terms of their consistency with the values identified in step 3. This step may or may not lead to a suggested course of action.

Step 6.   Identify the consequences of each possible course of action. If step 5 does not provide a course of action, assess the consequences of each possible course of action for all of the stakeholders involved.

Step 7.   Make your decision and take any indicated action.

ETHICAL DILEMMA

You have recently been employed by a large retail chain that sells sporting goods. One of your tasks is to help prepare periodic financial statements for external distribution. The chain's largest creditor, National Savings & Loan, requires quarterly financial statements, and you are currently working on the statements for the three-month period ending June 30, 2003.

During the months of May and June, the company spent $1,200,000 on a large radio and TV advertising campaign. The $1,200,000 included the costs of producing the commercials as well as the radio and TV time purchased to run the commercials. All of the costs were charged to advertising expense. The company's chief financial officer (CFO) has asked you to prepare a June 30 adjusting entry to remove the costs from advertising expense and to set up an asset called *prepaid advertising* that will be expensed in July. The CFO explained that "This advertising campaign has produced significant sales in May and June and I think it will continue to bring in customers through the month of July. By recording the ad costs as an asset, we can match the cost of the advertising with the additional July sales. Besides, if we expense the advertising in May and June, we will show an operating loss on our income statement for the quarter. The bank requires that we continue to show quarterly profits in order to maintain our loan in good standing."

---

[39]Adapted from Harold Q. Langenderfer and Joanne W. Rockness, "Integrating Ethics into the Accounting Curriculum: Issues, Problems, and Solutions," *Issues in Accounting Education* (Spring 1989). These steps are consistent with those provided by the American Accounting Association's Advisory Committee on Professionalism and Ethics in their publication *Ethics in the Accounting Curriculum: Cases and Readings, 1990.*

Ethical dilemmas are presented throughout the text. These dilemmas are designed to raise your consciousness on accounting issues with ethical ramifications. The analytical steps outlined above provide a framework with which to evaluate these situations. In addition, your instructor may assign end-of-chapter ethics cases for further discussion and application.

FINANCIAL REPORTING CASE **SOLUTION**

1. **What should you tell your friend about the presence of accounting standards in the United States? Who has the authority for standard setting? Who has the responsibility?** *(p. 9)*   In the United States we have a set of standards known as generally accepted accounting principles. GAAP are a dynamic set of both broad and specific guidelines that companies should follow when measuring and reporting the information in their financial statements and related notes. The Securities and Exchange Commission has the authority to set accounting standards for companies whose securities are publicly traded but always has delegated the responsibility to the accounting profession. At present, the Financial Accounting Standards Board is the private sector body responsible for standard setting.

2. **What is the economic and political environment in which standard setting occurs?** *(p. 12)*   The setting of accounting and reporting standards often has been characterized as a *political process*. Standards, particularly changes in standards, can have significant differential effects on companies, investors and creditors, and other interest groups. A change in an accounting standard or the introduction of a new standard can result in a substantial redistribution of wealth within our economy. The FASB must consider potential economic consequences of a change in an accounting standard or the introduction of a new standard.

3. **What is the relationship among management, auditors, investors, and creditors that tends to preclude the "What would you like it to be?" attitude?** *(p. 16)*   It is the responsibility of management to apply accounting standards when communicating with investors and creditors through financial statements. Auditors serve as independent intermediaries to help ensure that the management-prepared statements are presented fairly in accordance with GAAP. In providing this assurance, the auditor precludes the "What would you like it to be?" attitude.

4. **In general, what is the conceptual framework that underlies accounting principles?** *(p. 18)*   The conceptual framework is a coherent system of interrelated objectives and fundamentals that can lead to consistent standards and that prescribe the nature, function, and limits of financial accounting and reporting. The fundamentals are the underlying concepts of accounting, concepts that guide the selection of events to be accounted for, the measurement of those events, and the means of summarizing and communicating them to interested parties. ■

THE BOTTOM LINE

1. Financial accounting is concerned with providing relevant financial information to various external users. However, the primary focus is on the financial information provided by profit-oriented companies to their present and potential investors and creditors.

2. Cash basis accounting provides a measure of periodic performance called *net operating cash flow,* which is the difference between cash receipts and cash disbursements from transactions related to providing goods and services to customers. Accrual accounting provides a measure of performance called *net income,* which is the difference between revenues and expenses. Periodic net income is considered a better indicator of future operating cash flows than is current net operating cash flows.

3. Generally accepted accounting principles (GAAP) comprise a dynamic set of both broad and specific guidelines that companies follow when measuring and reporting the information in their financial statements and related notes. The Securities and Exchange Commission (SEC) has both the authority and responsibility to set accounting standards. However, the SEC has always delegated the responsibility to a private sector body, at this time the Financial Accounting Standards Board (FASB).

4. Accounting standards can have significant differential effects on companies, investors, creditors, and other interest groups. For this reason, the setting of accounting standards often has been characterized as a political process.

5. The FASB's conceptual framework is a set of cohesive objectives and fundamental concepts on which financial accounting and reporting standards will be based.

6. The objectives of financial reporting are concerned with providing information to help investors and creditors predict future cash flows. The primary decision-specific qualities that make accounting information useful are relevance and reliability. To be relevant, information must possess predictive value and/or feedback value and must be provided in a timely manner. The characteristics of reliable information are verifiability, representational faithfulness, and neutrality. The 10 elements of financial statements are assets, liabilities, equity, investments by owners, distributions to owners, revenues, expenses, gains, losses, and comprehensive income.

7. The four basic assumptions underlying GAAP are (1) the economic entity assumption, (2) the going concern assumption, (3) the periodicity assumption, and (4) the monetary unit assumption.

8. The four broad accounting principles that guide accounting practice are (1) the historical cost principle, (2) the realization principle, (3) the matching principle, and (4) the full-disclosure principle. ■

APPENDIX

1

FEDEX CORPORATION FINANCIAL STATEMENTS

FEDEX CORPORATION
Consolidated Statements of Income

Years ended May 31,

	2001	2000	1999
	(in thousands, except per share amounts)		
REVENUES	$19,629,040	$18,256,945	$16,773,470
OPERATING EXPENSES			
Salaries and employee benefits	8,263,413	7,597,964	7,087,728
Purchased transportation	1,713,027	1,674,854	1,537,785
Rentals and landing fees	1,650,048	1,538,713	1,396,694
Depreciation and amortization	1,275,774	1,154,863	1,035,118
Fuel	1,142,741	918,513	604,929
Maintenance and repairs	1,170,103	1,101,424	958,873
Other	3,343,044	3,049,540	2,989,257
	18,558,150	17,035,871	15,610,384
OPERATING INCOME	1,070,890	1,221,074	1,163,086
OTHER INCOME (EXPENSE)			
Interest, net	(143,953)	(106,060)	(98,191)
Other, net	636	22,726	(3,831)
	(143,317)	(83,334)	(102,022)
INCOME BEFORE INCOME TAXES	927,573	1,137,740	1,061,064
PROVISION FOR INCOME TAXES	343,202	449,404	429,731
NET INCOME	$ 584,371	$ 688,336	$ 631,333
EARNINGS PER COMMON SHARE			
Basic	$ 2.02	$ 2.36	$ 2.13
Assuming dilution	$ 1.99	$ 2.32	$ 2.10

The accompanying notes are an integral part of these consolidated financial statements.

FEDEX CORPORATION
Consolidated Balance Sheets

	May 31,	
	2001	**2000**
	(in thousands, except shares)	
ASSETS		
CURRENT ASSETS		
Cash and cash equivalents	$ 121,302	$ 67,959
Receivables, less allowances of $95,815 and $85,972	2,506,044	2,547,043
Spare parts, supplies and fuel	269,269	255,291
Deferred income taxes	435,406	317,784
Prepaid expenses and other	117,040	96,667
Total current assets	3,449,061	3,284,744
PROPERTY AND EQUIPMENT, AT COST		
Flight equipment	5,312,853	4,960,204
Package handling and ground support equipment and vehicles	4,620,894	4,203,927
Computer and electronic equipment	2,637,350	2,416,666
Other	3,840,899	3,161,746
	16,411,996	14,742,543
Less accumulated depreciation and amortization	8,311,941	7,659,016
Net property and equipment	8,100,055	7,083,527
OTHER ASSETS		
Goodwill	1,082,223	500,547
Equipment deposits and other assets	708,673	658,293
Total other assets	1,790,896	1,158,840
	$13,340,012	$11,527,111
LIABILITIES AND STOCKHOLDERS' INVESTMENT		
CURRENT LIABILITIES		
Current portion of long-term debt	$ 221,392	$ 6,537
Accrued salaries and employee benefits	699,906	755,747
Accounts payable	1,255,298	1,120,855
Accrued expenses	1,072,920	1,007,887
Total current liabilities	3,249,516	2,891,026
LONG-TERM DEBT, LESS CURRENT PORTION	1,900,119	1,776,253
DEFERRED INCOME TAXES	455,591	344,613
OTHER LIABILITIES	1,834,366	1,729,976
COMMITMENTS AND CONTINGENCIES (Notes 5, 13 and 14)		
COMMON STOCKHOLDERS' INVESTMENT		
Common Stock, $.10 par value; 800,000,000 shares authorized; 298,573,387 shares issued	29,857	29,857
Additional paid-in capital	1,120,627	1,079,462
Retained earnings	4,879,647	4,295,041
Accumulated other comprehensive income	(55,833)	(36,074)
	5,974,298	5,368,286
Less treasury stock, at cost, and deferred compensation	73,878	583,043
Total common stockholders' investment	5,900,420	4,785,243
	$13,340,012	$11,527,111

The accompanying notes are an integral part of these consolidated financial statements.

FEDEX CORPORATION
Consolidated Statements of Cash Flows

	Years ended May 31		
	2001	2000 (in thousands)	1999
OPERATING ACTIVITIES			
Net income	$ 584,371	$ 688,336	$ 631,333
Adjustments to reconcile net income to cash provided by operating activities:			
Depreciation and amortization	1,275,774	1,154,863	1,035,118
Provision for uncollectible accounts	112,264	71,107	55,649
Aircraft related impairment charges	102,000	—	—
Deferred income taxes and other noncash items	(16,024)	(7,363)	(34,037)
Gain from disposals of property and equipment	(4,440)	(17,068)	(2,330)
Changes in operating assets and liabilities, net of the effects of businesses acquired:			
Decrease (increase) in receivables	61,702	(404,511)	(294,121)
(Increase) decrease in other current assets	(112,476)	70,720	(155,720)
Increase in accounts payable and other operating liabilities	102,390	107,543	555,565
Other, net	(61,755)	(38,385)	(19,337)
Cash provided by operating activities	2,043,806	1,625,242	1,772,120
INVESTING ACTIVITIES			
Purchases of property and equipment, including deposits on aircraft of $7,900, $1,500 and $1,200	(1,893,384)	(1,627,418)	(1,769,946)
Proceeds from dispositions of property and equipment:			
Sale-leaseback transactions	237,000	—	80,995
Reimbursements of A300 and MD11 deposits	—	24,377	67,269
Other dispositions	37,444	165,397	195,641
Business acquisitions, net of cash acquired	(476,992)	(257,095)	—
Other, net	(16,783)	(13,378)	(22,716)
Cash used in investing activities	(2,112,715)	(1,708,117)	(1,448,757)
FINANCING ACTIVITIES			
Principal payments on debt	(650,280)	(115,090)	(269,367)
Proceeds from debt issuances	743,522	517,664	—
Proceeds from stock issuances	28,654	15,523	49,932
Purchase of treasury stock	—	(606,506)	(8,168)
Other, net	356	13,920	(2)
Cash provided by (used in) financing activities	122,252	(174,489)	(227,605)
CASH AND CASH EQUIVALENTS			
Net increase (decrease) in cash and cash equivalents	53,343	(257,364)	95,758
Balance at beginning of year	67,959	325,323	229,565
Balance at end of year	$ 121,302	$ 67,959	$ 325,323

The accompanying notes are an integral part of these consolidated financial statements.

FEDEX CORPORATION
Consolidated Statements of Changes in Stockholders' Investment and Comprehensive Income

In thousands, except shares	Common Stock	Additional Paid-in Capital	Retained Earnings	Accumulated Other Comprehensive Income	Treasury Stock	Deferred Compensation	Total
BALANCE AT MAY 31, 1998	$14,741	$ 992,821	$ 2,999,354	$ (27,277)	$ —	$(18,409)	$ 3,961,230
Net income	—	—	631,333	—	—	—	631,333
Foreign currency translation adjustment, net of deferred tax benefit of $959	—	—	—	(611)	—	—	(611)
Unrealized gain on available-for-sale securities, net of deferred taxes of $2,100	—	—	—	3,200	—	—	3,200
Total comprehensive income							**633,922**
Purchase of treasury stock	—	—	—	—	(8,168)	—	(8,168)
Two-for-one stock split by FedEx Corporation in the form of a 100% stock dividend (148,931,996 shares)	14,890	—	(14,890)	—	—	—	—
Employee incentive plans and other (1,770,626 shares issued)	168	68,491	—	—	6,887	(7,766)	67,780
Amortization of deferred compensation	—	—	—	—	—	8,928	8,928
BALANCE AT MAY 31, 1999	29,799	1,061,312	3,615,797	(24,688)	(1,281)	(17,247)	4,663,692
Net income	—	—	688,336	—	—	—	688,336
Foreign currency translation adjustment, net of deferred tax benefit of $1,881	—	—	—	(9,021)	—	—	(9,021)
Unrealized loss on available-for-sale securities, net of deferred tax benefit of $1,513	—	—	—	(2,365)	—	—	(2,365)
Total comprehensive income							**676,950**
Shares issued for acquisition (175,644 shares)	—	—	191	—	6,626	—	6,817
Purchase of treasury stock	—	—	—	—	(606,506)	—	(606,506)
Employee incentive plans and other (1,539,941 shares issued)	58	18,150	(9,283)	—	37,067	(13,880)	32,112
Amortization of deferred compensation	—	—	—	—	—	12,178	12,178
BALANCE AT MAY 31, 2000	29,857	1,079,462	4,295,041	(36,074)	(564,094)	(18,949)	4,785,243
Net income	—	—	584,371	—	—	—	584,371
Foreign currency translation adjustment, net of deferred tax benefit of $6,849	—	—	—	(18,944)	—	—	(18,944)
Unrealized loss on available-for-sale securities, net of deferred tax benefit of $574	—	—	—	(815)	—	—	(815)
Total comprehensive income							**564,612**
Shares issued for acquisition (11,042,965 shares)	—	41,675	27,131	—	437,584	—	506,390
Employee incentive plans and other (1,841,543 shares issued)	—	(510)	(26,896)	—	73,020	(12,865)	32,749
Amortization of deferred compensation	—	—	—	—	—	11,426	11,426
BALANCE AT MAY 31, 2001	**$29,857**	**$1,120,627**	**$4,879,647**	**$(55,833)**	**$(53,490)**	**$(20,388)**	**$5,900,420**

The accompanying notes are an integral part of these consolidated financial statements.

FEDEX CORPORATION
Notes to Consolidated Financial Statements

NOTE 1: DESCRIPTION OF BUSINESS AND SUMMARY OF SIGNIFICANT ACCOUNTING POLICIES

Description of business. FedEx Corporation ("FedEx") is a premier global provider of transportation, e-commerce and supply chain management services, whose operations are primarily represented by Federal Express Corporation ("FedEx Express"), the world's largest express transportation company; FedEx Ground Package System, Inc. ("FedEx Ground"), North America's second largest provider of small-package ground delivery service; and FedEx Freight System, Inc. ("FedEx Freight"), a leading provider of regional less-than-truckload ("LTL") freight services. Other operating companies included in the FedEx portfolio are FedEx Custom Critical, Inc. ("FedEx Custom Critical"), a critical-shipment carrier; FedEx Trade Networks, Inc. ("FedEx Trade Networks"), a global trade services company; and FedEx Supply Chain Services, Inc. ("FedEx Supply Chain Services"), a contract logistics provider.

FedEx Freight was formed in the third quarter of 2001 in conjunction with our acquisition of American Freightways, Inc. ("American Freightways"). FedEx Freight includes the results of operations of American Freightways, a multi-regional LTL carrier from January 1, 2001 and Viking Freight, Inc. ("Viking"), an LTL carrier operating principally in the western United States, from December 1, 2000.

Principles of consolidation. The consolidated financial statements include the accounts of FedEx and its subsidiaries. All significant intercompany accounts and transactions have been eliminated.

Subsidiary guarantors. Certain long-term debt contains subsidiary guarantees. The guarantees provided by our subsidiaries are full and unconditional, joint and several, and any subsidiaries which are not guarantors are minor as defined by Securities and Exchange Commission ("SEC") regulations. FedEx, as the parent company issuer of this debt, has no independent assets or operations. There are no significant restrictions on our ability or the ability of any guarantor to obtain funds from its subsidiaries by means of dividend or loan.

Credit risk. Credit risk in trade receivables is substantially mitigated by our credit evaluation process, short collection terms, and sales to a large number of customers, as well as the low revenue per transaction for most of our transportation services. Allowances for potential credit losses are determined based on historical experience, current evaluation of the composition of accounts receivable and expected credit trends.

Revenue recognition. Revenue is recognized upon delivery of shipments. For shipments in transit, revenue is recorded based on the percentage of service completed at the balance sheet date.

Advertising. Generally, advertising costs are expensed as incurred and are classified in other operating expenses. Advertising expenses were $236,559,000, $221,511,000 and $202,104,000 in 2001, 2000 and 1999, respectively.

Cash equivalents. Cash equivalents in excess of current operating requirements are invested in short-term, interest-bearing instruments with maturities of three months or less at the date of purchase and are stated at cost, which approximates market value. Interest income was $11,197,000, $15,116,000 and $12,399,000 in 2001, 2000 and 1999, respectively.

Marketable securities. Marketable securities are classified as available-for-sale securities and are reported at fair value. Unrealized gains and losses are reported, net of related deferred income taxes, as a component of accumulated other comprehensive income.

Spare parts, supplies, and fuel. Spare parts are stated principally at weighted-average cost. Supplies and fuel are stated principally at standard cost, which approximates actual cost on a first-in, first-out basis. Neither method values inventory in excess of current replacement cost.

Property and equipment. Expenditures for major additions, improvements, flight equipment modifications and certain overhaul costs are capitalized. Maintenance and repairs are charged to expense as incurred. The cost and accumulated depreciation of property and equipment disposed of are removed from the related accounts, and any gain or loss is reflected in the results of operations.

For financial reporting purposes, depreciation and amortization of property and equipment is provided on a straight-line basis over the asset's service life or related lease term as follows:

Flight equipment	5 to 20 years
Package handling and ground support equipment and vehicles	3 to 30 years
Computer and electronic equipment	3 to 10 years
Other	2 to 30 years

Aircraft airframes and engines are assigned residual values ranging up to 20% of asset cost. All other property and equipment have no material residual values. Vehicles are depreciated on a straight-line basis over five to 10 years. Depreciation expense was $1,241,493,000, $1,132,129,000, and $1,017,950,000 in 2001, 2000 and 1999, respectively.

For income tax purposes, depreciation is generally computed using accelerated methods.

Capitalized interest. Interest on funds used to finance the acquisition and modification of aircraft, construction of certain facilities, and development of certain software up to the date the asset is placed in service is capitalized and included in the cost of the asset. Capitalized interest was $26,536,000, $34,823,000 and $38,880,000 for 2001, 2000 and 1999, respectively.

Impairment of long-lived assets. Long-lived assets including goodwill are reviewed for impairment when circumstances indicate the carrying value of an asset may not be recoverable. For assets that are to be held and used, an impairment is recognized when the estimated undiscounted cash flows associated with the asset or group of assets is less than their carrying value. If impairment exists, an adjustment is made to write the asset down to its fair value, and a loss is recorded as the difference between the carrying value and fair value. Fair values are determined based on quoted market values, discounted cash flows or internal and external appraisals, as applicable. Assets to be disposed of are carried at the lower of carrying value or estimated net realizable value. See Notes 15 and 16 for information concerning the impairment charges recognized in 2001.

Goodwill. Goodwill is recognized for the excess of the purchase price over the fair value of tangible and identifiable intangible net assets of businesses acquired. It is amortized over the estimated period of benefit on a straight-line basis over periods generally ranging from 15 to 40 years. Accumulated amortization was $201,766,000 and $165,624,000 at May 31, 2001 and 2000, respectively.

Income taxes. Deferred income taxes are provided for the tax effect of temporary differences between the tax basis of assets and liabilities and their reported amounts in the financial statements. The liability method is used to account for income taxes, which requires deferred taxes to be recorded at the statutory rate expected to be in effect when the taxes are paid.

We have not provided for U.S. federal income taxes on foreign subsidiaries' earnings deemed to be permanently reinvested and any related taxes associated with such earnings are not material.

Self-insurance reserves. We are self-insured up to certain levels for workers' compensation, employee health care and vehicle liabilities. Accruals are based on the actuarially estimated undiscounted cost of claims. Included in other liabilities at May 31, 2001 and 2000, were $363,664,000 and $324,869,000, respectively, representing the long-term portion of self-insurance accruals for workers' compensation and vehicle liabilities.

Deferred lease obligations. While certain aircraft and facility leases contain fluctuating or escalating payments, the related rent expense is recorded on a straight-line basis over the lease term. Included in other liabilities at May 31, 2001 and 2000, were $398,298,000 and $354,566,000, respectively, representing the cumulative difference between rent expense and rent payments.

Deferred gains. Gains on the sale and leaseback of aircraft and other property and equipment are deferred and amortized ratably over the life of the lease as a reduction of rent expense. Included in other liabilities at May 31, 2001 and 2000 were deferred gains of $511,932,000 and $533,371,000, respectively.

Derivative instruments. Through the period ending May 31, 2001, jet fuel forward contracts were accounted for as hedges under Statement of Financial Accounting Standards ("SFAS") No. 80, "Accounting for Futures Contracts." At June 1, 2001, we adopted SFAS 133, "Accounting for Derivative Instruments and Hedging Activities." See Recent Pronouncements.

Foreign currency translation. Translation gains and losses of foreign operations that use local currencies as the functional currency are accumulated and reported, net of applicable deferred income taxes, as a component of accumulated other comprehensive income within common stockholders' investment. Transaction gains and losses that arise from exchange rate fluctuations on transactions denominated in a currency other than the local functional currency are included in the results of operations. Balances for foreign currency translation in accumulated other comprehensive income were ($55,853,000), ($36,909,000) and ($27,888,000) at May 31, 2001, 2000 and 1999, respectively.

Recent pronouncements. We adopted SFAS 133, "Accounting for Derivative Instruments and Hedging Activities" (as amended by SFAS 137 and SFAS 138) at the beginning of 2002. The adoption of this Statement will not have a material effect on our financial position or results of operations for 2002.

Reclassifications. Certain prior year amounts have been reclassified to conform to the 2001 presentation.

Use of estimates. The preparation of the consolidated financial statements in conformity with accounting principles generally accepted in the United States requires the use of estimates and assumptions that affect the reported amounts of assets and liabilities and disclosure of contingent assets and liabilities at the date of the financial statements and the reported amounts of revenues and expenses during the reporting period. Actual results could differ from those estimates.

NOTE 2: BUSINESS COMBINATIONS

On February 9, 2001, we completed the acquisition of American Freightways, a multiregional less-than-truckload motor carrier, for approximately $978,000,000, including $471,000,000 in cash, 11.0 million shares of FedEx common stock and options to purchase 1.5 million shares of FedEx common stock. The acquisition was completed in a two-step transaction that included a cash tender offer and a merger that resulted in the acquisition of all outstanding shares of American Freightways. The first step of the transaction was completed on December 21, 2000 by acquiring for cash 50.1% of the outstanding shares of American Freightways, or 16,380,038 shares at a price of $28.13 per share. On February 9, 2001, American Freightways was merged into a newly-created subsidiary of FedEx and each remaining outstanding share of American Freightways common stock was converted into 0.6639 shares of common stock of FedEx. The excess purchase price over the estimated fair value of the net assets acquired (approximately $600 million) has been recorded as goodwill and is being amortized ratably over 40 years.

The following unaudited pro forma consolidated results of operations are presented as if the acquisition of American Freightways had been made at the beginning of the periods presented:

May 31,
In thousands,

except per share amounts	2001	2000
Revenues	**$20,493,991**	$19,541,425
Net income	**601,825**	710,119
Basic earnings per share	**2.03**	2.35
Diluted earnings per share	**2.00**	2.31

The pro forma consolidated results of operations include adjustments to give effect to the amortization of goodwill, interest expense on acquisition-related debt and certain other purchase accounting adjustments. The pro forma information is not necessarily indicative of the results of operations that would have occurred had the purchase been made at the beginning of the periods presented or the future results of the combined operations.

On March 31, 2000, the common stock of World Tariff, Limited ("World Tariff") was acquired for approximately $8,400,000 in cash and stock. World Tariff is a source of customs duty and tax information around the globe. This business is operating as a subsidiary of FedEx Trade Networks. The excess of purchase price over the estimated fair value of the net assets acquired ($8,300,000) has been recorded as goodwill and is being amortized ratably over 25 years.

On February 29, 2000, the common stock of Tower Group International, Inc. ("Tower") was acquired for approximately $140,000,000 in cash. Tower primarily provides international customs clearance services. This business is operating as a subsidiary of FedEx Trade Networks. The excess of purchase price over the estimated fair value of the net assets acquired ($30,000,000) has been recorded as goodwill and is being amortized ratably over 25 years.

On September 10, 1999, the assets of GeoLogistics Air Services, Inc. were acquired for approximately $116,000,000 in cash. This business operates under the name Caribbean Transportation Services, Inc. ("CTS"), and is a subsidiary of FedEx Trade Networks. CTS is an airfreight forwarder servicing freight shipments primarily between the United States and Puerto Rico. The excess of purchase price over the estimated fair value of the net assets acquired ($103,000,000) has been recorded as goodwill and is being amortized ratably over 15 years.

The operating results of these acquired companies are included in consolidated operations from the date of acquisition. For American Freightways, the results of operations are included from January 1, 2001, which was the date of acquisition for financial reporting purposes. Pro forma results including these acquisitions, except American Freightways, would not differ materially from reported results in any of the periods presented.

NOTE 3: ACCRUED SALARIES AND EMPLOYEE BENEFITS AND ACCRUED EXPENSES

The components of accrued salaries and employee benefits and accrued expenses were as follows:

May 31,

In thousands	2001	2000
Salaries	$ **192,892**	$ 168,582
Employee benefits	**152,979**	260,063
Compensated absences	**354,035**	327,102
Total accrued salaries and employee benefits	$ **699,906**	$ 755,747
Insurance	$ **427,685**	$ 363,899
Taxes other than income taxes	**239,718**	237,342
Other	**405,517**	406,646
Total accrued expenses	**$1,072,920**	$1,007,887

NOTE 4: LONG-TERM DEBT AND OTHER FINANCING ARRANGEMENTS

May 31,
In thousands

	2001	2000
Unsecured debt	**$1,836,616**	$ 975,862
Commercial paper, weighted-average interest rate of 6.73%	**—**	521,031
Capital lease obligations and tax exempt bonds, interest rates of 5.35% to 7.88%, due through 2017, less bond reserves of $9,024	**247,227**	244,545
Other debt, interest rates of 9.68% to 11.12%	**37,668**	41,352
	2,121,511	1,782,790
Less current portion	**221,392**	6,537
	$1,900,119	$1,776,253

We have a $1,000,000,000 revolving credit agreement with domestic and foreign banks. The revolving credit agreement comprises two parts. The first part provides for a commitment of $800,000,000 through January 27, 2003. The second part provides for a 364-day commitment for $200,000,000 through September 30, 2001. Interest rates on borrowings under this agreement are generally determined by maturities selected and prevailing market conditions. The revolving credit agreement contains certain covenants and restrictions, none of which are expected to significantly affect our operations or ability to pay dividends.

As of May 31, 2001, approximately $2,655,000,000 was available for the payment of dividends under the restrictive covenant of the revolving credit agreement. Commercial paper borrowings are backed by unused commitments under the revolving credit agreement and reduce the amount available under the agreement. As of May 31, 2001, no commercial paper borrowings were outstanding and the entire credit facility was available.

The components of unsecured debt (net of discounts) were as follows:

May 31
In thousands

	2001	2000
Senior debt:		
Interest rates of 6.63% to 7.25%, due through 2011	**$ 745,844**	$ —
Interest rates of 9.65% to 9.88%, due through 2013	**474,161**	473,970
Interest rate of 7.80%, due 2007	**200,000**	200,000
Interest rates of 6.92% to 8.91%, due through 2012	**117,701**	—
Bonds, interest rate of 7.60%, due in 2098	**239,389**	239,382
Medium term notes:		
Interest rates of 9.95% to 10.57%, due through 2007	**59,054**	62,510
Other	**467**	—
	$1,836,616	$975,862

On February 12, 2001, senior unsecured notes were issued in the amount of $750,000,000. These notes are guaranteed by all of our subsidiaries that are not considered minor as defined by SEC regulations. Net proceeds from the borrowings were used to repay indebtedness, principally borrowings under the commercial paper program, and for general corporate purposes. The notes were issued in three tranches, with the following terms and interest rates:

Amount	Maturity	Rate
$250,000,000	2004	6.625%
$250,000,000	2006	6.875%
$250,000,000	2011	7.250%

In conjunction with the American Freightways acquisition on February 9, 2001, debt of $240,000,000 was assumed, a portion of which was refinanced subsequent to the acquisition. As of May 31, 2001, $117,701,000 of the assumed debt had not been refinanced and remained outstanding. This debt matures through 2012 and bears interest at rates of 6.92% to 8.91%.

Scheduled annual principal maturities of long-term debt for the five years subsequent to May 31, 2001, are as follows: $221,400,000 in 2002; $18,400,000 in 2003; $287,300,000 in 2004; $17,600,000 in 2005; and $273,400,000 in 2006.

Long-term debt, exclusive of capital leases, had carrying values of $1,919,000,000 and $1,063,000,000 at May 31, 2001 and 2000, respectively, compared with fair values of approximately $1,999,000,000 and $1,055,000,000 at those dates. The estimated fair values were determined based on quoted market prices or on the current rates offered for debt with similar terms and maturities.

NOTE 5: LEASE COMMITMENTS

We utilize certain aircraft, land, facilities and equipment under capital and operating leases that expire at various dates through 2038. In addition, supplemental aircraft are leased under agreements that generally provide for cancellation upon 30 days' notice.

The components of property and equipment recorded under capital leases were as follows:

May 31
In thousands

	2001	2000
Package handling and ground support equipment and vehicles	**$196,900**	$226,580
Facilities	**136,178**	134,442
Computer and electronic equipment and other	**2,858**	6,852
	335,936	367,874
Less accumulated amortization	**236,921**	260,526
	$ 99,015	$107,348

Rent expense under operating leases for the years ended May 31 was as follows:

In thousands	2001	2000	1999
Minimum rentals	**$1,398,620**	$1,298,821	$1,246,259
Contingent rentals	**91,230**	98,755	59,839
	$1,489,850	$1,397,576	$1,306,098

Contingent rentals are based on hours flown under supplemental aircraft leases.

A summary of future minimum lease payments under capital leases and noncancellable operating leases (principally aircraft and facilities) with an initial or remaining term in excess of one year at May 31, 2001, is as follows:

In thousands	Capital Leases	Operating Leases
2002	$ 15,416	$ 1,246,936
2003	15,279	1,134,413
2004	15,132	1,043,549
2005	15,044	981,777
2006	15,040	916,084
Thereafter	274,665	9,040,570
	$350,576	$14,363,329

At May 31, 2001, the present value of future minimum lease payments for capital lease obligations, including certain tax-exempt bonds, was $202,107,000.

FedEx Express makes payments under certain leveraged operating leases that are sufficient to pay principal and interest on certain pass-through certificates. The pass-through certificates are not direct obligations of, or guaranteed by, us or FedEx Express.

NOTE 6: PREFERRED STOCK

The Certificate of Incorporation authorizes the Board of Directors, at its discretion, to issue up to 4,000,000 shares of Series Preferred Stock. The stock is issuable in series, which may vary as to certain rights and preferences, and has no par value. As of May 31, 2001, none of these shares had been issued.

NOTE 7: COMMON STOCKHOLDERS' INVESTMENT

Treasury Shares

During 2000, we purchased 15,208,356 treasury shares. Of these shares, 15,000,000, or approximately 5% of our outstanding shares of common stock, were purchased under a stock repurchase program at an average cost of $39.75 per share. Approximately 11,000,000 of the shares held in treasury were reissued February 9, 2001, for the acquisition of American Freightways. During 2001 and 2000, treasury shares were also utilized for issuances under the stock compensation plans discussed below. At May 31,

2001, and 2000, respectively, 1,244,490 and 14,128,998 shares remained in treasury.

Stock Compensation Plans

Options and awards outstanding under stock-based compensation plans at May 31, 2001 are described below. As of May 31, 2001, 25,880,128 shares of common stock were reserved for issuance under these plans. The Board of Directors has authorized the repurchase of common stock necessary for grants or option exercises under these stock plans.

Accounting Principles Board Opinion No. 25, "Accounting for Stock Issued to Employees," and related interpretations is applied to measure compensation expense for stock-based compensation plans. If compensation cost for stock-based compensation plans had been determined under SFAS 123, "Accounting for Stock-Based Compensation," net income and earnings per share would have been the pro forma amounts indicated below:

In thousands, except per share amounts	2001	2000	1999
Net income:			
As reported	**$584,371**	$688,336	$631,333
Pro forma	**553,033**	659,601	609,960
Earnings per share, assuming dilution:			
As reported	**$ 1.99**	$ 2.32	$ 2.10
Pro forma	**1.89**	2.23	2.03

Fixed Stock Option Plans

Under the provisions of our stock incentive plans, options may be granted to certain key employees (and, under the 1997 plan, to directors who are not employees) to purchase shares of common stock at a price not less than its fair market value at the date of grant. Options granted have a maximum term of 10 years. Vesting requirements are determined at the discretion of the Compensation Committee of the Board of Directors. Presently, option vesting periods range from one to eight years. At May 31, 2001, there were 7,218,032 shares available for future grants under these plans.

Beginning with the grants made on or after June 1, 1995, the fair value of each option grant was estimated on the grant date using the Black-Scholes option-pricing model with the following assumptions for each option grant:

	2001	2000	1999
Dividend yield	**0%**	0%	0%
Expected volatility	**35%**	30%	25%
Risk-free interest rate	**4.3%–6.5%**	5.6%–6.8%	4.2%–5.6%
Expected lives	**2.5–5.5 years**	2.5–9.5 years	2.5–5.5 years

The following table summarizes information about our fixed stock option plans for the years ended May 31:

	2001		2000		1999	
	Shares	**Weighted-Average Exercise Price**	**Shares**	**Weighted-Average Exercise Price**	**Shares**	**Weighted-Average Exercise Price**
Outstanding at beginning of year	**15,010,651**	**$29.12**	13,399,532	$23.11	13,388,452	$19.74
Granted and assumed	**4,267,753**[1]	**31.19**	3,218,450	50.79	3,377,500	31.80
Exercised	**(1,465,684)**	**20.02**	(1,232,699)	18.81	(3,135,640)	17.86
Forfeited	**(314,162)**	**37.25**	(374,632)	33.81	(230,780)	26.59
Outstanding at end of year	**17,498,558**	**30.24**	15,010,651	29.12	13,399,532	23.11
Exercisable at end of year	**8,704,009**	**25.09**	5,781,855	21.44	4,404,146	18.57

(1) Includes 1,479,016 options assumed upon acquisition of American Freightways in 2001.

The weighted-average fair value of options granted during the year was $13.19, $16.63 and $9.12 for the years ended May 31, 2001, 2000, and 1999, respectively.

The following table summarizes information about fixed stock options outstanding at May 31, 2001:

Range of Exercise Prices	Options Outstanding			Options Exercisable	
	Number Outstanding	**Weighted-Average Remaining Contractual Life**	**Weighted-Average Exercise Price**	**Number Exercisable**	**Weighted-Average Exercise Price**
$ 8.63–$12.00	157,274	0.6 years	$10.13	157,274	$10.13
12.19– 17.70	2,261,561	3.9 years	15.69	1,899,134	15.59
18.45– 25.19	4,687,294	4.8 years	20.44	3,023,630	20.48
26.44– 37.25	7,018,067	7.4 years	32.41	2,860,491	30.24
38.69– 55.94	3,374,362	8.3 years	50.04	763,480	50.75
8.63– 55.94	17,498,558	6.4 years	30.24	8,704,009	25.09

Restricted Stock Plans

Under the terms of our Restricted Stock Plans, shares of common stock are awarded to key employees. All restrictions on the shares expire over periods varying from two to five years from their date of award. Shares are valued at the market price at the date of award. Compensation related to these plans is recorded as a reduction of common stockholders' investment and is being amortized to expense as restrictions on such shares expire. In March 2001, the Board of Directors approved an additional restricted stock plan, which authorized the issuance of up to 1,000,000 common shares. The following table summarizes information about restricted stock awards for the years ended May 31:

	2001		2000		1999	
	Shares	**Weighted-Average Fair Value**	**Shares**	**Weighted-Average Fair Value**	**Shares**	**Weighted-Average Fair Value**
Awarded	**330,250**	**$39.89**	283,750	$51.90	252,000	$32.71
Forfeited	**8,438**	**40.92**	20,000	37.71	16,900	44.38

At May 31, 2001, there were 1,163,538 shares available for future awards under these plans. Compensation cost for the restricted stock plans was $11,426,000, $12,178,000 and $8,928,000 for 2001, 2000, and 1999, respectively.

NOTE 8: COMPUTATION OF EARNINGS PER SHARE

The calculation of basic earnings per share and earnings per share, assuming dilution, for the years ended May 31 was as follows:

In thousands, except per share amounts	2001	2000	1999
Net income applicable to common stockholders	$584,371	$688,336	$631,333
Weighted-average common shares outstanding	288,745	291,727	295,983
Basic earnings per share	$ 2.02	$ 2.36	$ 2.13
Weighted-average common shares outstanding	288,745	291,727	295,983
Common equivalent shares:			
Assumed exercise of outstanding dilutive options	14,690	12,735	13,090
Less shares repurchased from proceeds of assumed exercise of options	(10,256)	(8,136)	(8,430)
Weighted-average common and common equivalent shares outstanding	293,179	296,326	300,643
Earnings per share, assuming dilution	$ 1.99	$ 2.32	$ 2.10

NOTE 9: INCOME TAXES

The components of the provision for income taxes for the years ended May 31 were as follows:

In thousands	2001	2000	1999
Current provision:			
Domestic			
Federal	$310,408	$365,137	$385,164
State and local	42,788	48,837	49,918
Foreign	36,152	39,844	22,730
	389,348	453,818	457,812
Deferred provision (credit):			
Domestic			
Federal	(43,043)	(3,444)	(21,773)
State and local	(3,088)	469	(4,437)
Foreign	(15)	(1,439)	(1,871)
	(46,146)	(4,414)	(28,081)
	$343,202	$449,404	$429,731

Income taxes have been provided for foreign operations based upon the various tax laws and rates of the countries in which operations are conducted. There is no direct relationship between our overall foreign income tax provision and foreign pretax book income due to the different methods of taxation used by countries throughout the world.

A reconciliation of the statutory federal income tax rate to the effective income tax rate for the years ended May 31 is as follows:

	2001	2000	1999
Statutory U.S. income tax rate	35.0%	35.0%	35.0%
Increase resulting from:			
State income taxes, net of federal benefit	2.8	2.8	2.8
Other, net	(0.8)	1.7	2.7
Effective tax rate	37.0%	39.5%	40.5%

The significant components of deferred tax assets and liabilities as of May 31 were as follows:

In thousands	2001		2000	
	Deferred Tax Assets	Deferred Tax Liabilities	Deferred Tax Assets	Deferred Tax Liabilities
Property, equipment and leases	$ 268,696	$ 815,504	$206,239	$686,547
Employee benefits	225,931	118,104	207,297	127,784
Self-insurance accruals	276,886	—	245,923	—
Other	241,587	99,677	224,615	96,572
	$1,013,100	$1,033,285	$884,074	$910,903

NOTE 10: EMPLOYEE BENEFIT PLANS

Pension plans. We sponsor defined benefit pension plans covering a majority of employees. The largest plan covers certain U.S. employees age 21 and over, with at least one year of service, and provides benefits based on average earnings and years of service. Plan funding is actuarially determined, and is also subject to certain tax law limitations. International defined benefit pension plans provide bene-

fits primarily based on final earnings and years of service and are funded in accordance with local laws and income tax regulations. Plan assets consist primarily of marketable equity securities and fixed income instruments.

In 2001, we changed the actuarial valuation measurement date for certain of our pension plans from May 31 to February 28 to conform to the measurement date used for our postretirement health care plans and to facilitate our planning and budgeting process. Additionally, in connection with the 2001 valuation, we changed to the calculated value method of valuing plan assets. These changes had no impact on our 2001 financial position or results of operations.

The Federal Express Corporation Employees' Pension Plan and the FedEx Ground Package System, Inc. and Certain Affiliates Career Reward Pension Plan were merged effective May 31, 2001. The name of the newly merged plan is the FedEx Corporation Employees' Pension Plan. No pension benefit formulas were changed as a result of the merger.

Postretirement health care plans. FedEx Express and FedEx Corporate Services, Inc. ("FedEx Services") offer medical and dental coverage to eligible U.S. retirees and their eligible dependents. Vision coverage is provided for retirees, but not their dependents. Substantially all FedEx Express and FedEx Services U.S. employees become eligible for these benefits at age 55 and older, if they have permanent, continuous service of at least 10 years after attainment of age 45 if hired prior to January 1, 1988, or at least 20 years after attainment of age 35, if hired on or after January 1, 1988. Life insurance benefits are provided only to retirees of the former Tiger International, Inc. who retired prior to acquisition. FedEx Ground offers similar benefits to its eligible retirees.

The following table provides a reconciliation of the changes in the pension and postretirement health care plans' benefit obligations and fair value of assets over the two-year period ended May 31, 2001 and a statement of the funded status as of May 31, 2001 and 2000:

In thousands	Pension Plans		Postretirement Health Care Plans	
	2001	2000	2001	2000
CHANGE IN BENEFIT OBLIGATION				
Benefit obligation at beginning of year	$4,493,745	$4,385,519	$ 257,007	$ 246,186
Service cost	325,371	337,780	25,021	26,450
Interest cost	382,391	336,143	22,929	19,579
Amendments and benefit enhancements	39,254	12,853	371	1,420
Actuarial loss (gain)	210,692	(510,132)	(12,141)	(28,607)
Plan participant contributions	—	—	1,722	1,112
Curtailment gain	—	—	(1,232)	—
Foreign currency exchange rate changes	(10,666)	(618)	—	—
Benefits paid	(56,879)	(67,800)	(8,044)	(9,133)
Benefit obligation at end of year	$5,383,908	$4,493,745	$ 285,633	$ 257,007
CHANGE IN PLAN ASSETS				
Fair value of plan assets at beginning of year	$5,727,416	$4,952,431	$ —	$ —
Actual return on plan assets	(142,537)	630,706	—	—
Foreign currency exchange rate changes	(2,689)	(5,192)	—	—
Company contributions	96,723	217,271	6,322	8,021
Plan participant contributions	—	—	1,722	1,112
Benefits paid	(56,879)	(67,800)	(8,044)	(9,133)
Fair value of plan assets at end of year	$5,622,034	$5,727,416	$ —	$ —
FUNDED STATUS OF THE PLANS	$ 238,126	$1,233,671	$(285,633)	$(257,007)
Unrecognized actuarial gain	(159,958)	(1,173,903)	(60,099)	(49,286)
Unrecognized prior service cost	144,003	121,697	952	254
Unrecognized transition amount	(9,511)	(10,529)	—	—
Prepaid (accrued) benefit cost	$ 212,660	$ 170,936	$(344,780)	$(306,039)
AMOUNTS RECOGNIZED IN THE BALANCE SHEET AT MAY 31:				
Prepaid benefit cost	$ 365,340	$ 302,935	$ —	$ —
Accrued benefit liability	(152,680)	(131,999)	(344,780)	(306,039)
Minimum pension liability	(19,848)	(12,662)	—	—
Intangible asset	19,848	12,662	—	—
Prepaid (accrued) benefit cost	$ 212,660	$ 170,936	$(344,780)	$(306,039)

Net periodic benefit cost for the years ended May 31 was as follows:

In thousands	Pension Plans			Postretirement Health Care Plans		
	2001	**2000**	**1999**	**2001**	**2000**	**1999**
Service cost	**$325,371**	$337,780	$331,005	**$25,021**	$26,450	$23,676
Interest cost	**382,391**	336,143	288,221	**22,929**	19,579	16,962
Expected return on plan assets	**(623,735)**	(546,169)	(483,709)	**—**	—	—
Net amortization and deferral	**(23,702)**	5,977	(1,948)	**(1,267)**	(93)	(211)
Curtailment gain	**—**	—	—	**(1,620)**	—	—
	$ 60,325	$133,731	$133,569	**$45,063**	$45,936	$40,427

WEIGHTED-AVERAGE ACTUARIAL ASSUMPTIONS

	Pension Plans			Postretirement Health Care Plans		
	2001	**2000**	**1999**	**2001**	**2000**	**1999**
Discount rate	**7.7%**	8.5%	7.5%	**8.2%**	8.3%	7.3%
Rate of increase in future compensation levels	**4.0**	5.0	4.6	**—**	—	—
Expected long-term rate of return on assets	**10.9**	10.9	10.9	**—**	—	—

The projected benefit obligation, accumulated benefit obligation and fair value of plan assets for the pension plans with benefit obligations in excess of plan assets were $258,700,000, $211,700,000 and $57,100,000, respectively, as of May 31, 2001, and $177,900,000, $126,300,000 and $2,700,000, respectively, as of May 31, 2000.

Future medical benefit costs are estimated to increase at an annual rate of 8.0% during 2002, decreasing to an annual growth rate of 6.0% in 2007 and thereafter. Future dental benefit costs were estimated to increase at an annual rate of 7.3% during 2002, decreasing to an annual growth rate of 6.0% in 2007 and thereafter. Our cost is capped at 150% of the 1993 employer cost and, therefore, is not subject to medical and dental trends after the capped cost is attained. A 1% change in these annual trend rates would not have a significant impact on the accumulated postretirement benefit obligation at May 31, 2001, or 2001 benefit expense. Claims are paid as incurred.

Defined contribution plans. Profit sharing and other defined contribution plans are in place covering a majority of U.S. employees age 21 and over, with at least one year of service as of the contribution date. Profit sharing plans provide for discretionary employer contributions, which are determined annually by the Board of Directors. Other plans provide matching funds based on employee contributions to 401(k) plans. Expense under these plans was

$99,400,000 in 2001, $125,300,000 in 2000 and $137,500,000 in 1999. Included in these expense amounts are cash distributions made directly to employees of $44,800,000, $39,100,000 and $46,800,000 in 2001, 2000 and 1999, respectively.

NOTE 11: BUSINESS SEGMENT INFORMATION

We have determined our reportable operating segments to be FedEx Express, FedEx Ground and FedEx Freight, each of which operates in a single line of business. Segment financial performance is evaluated based on operating income.

Certain segment assets associated with the sales, marketing and information technology departments previously recorded at FedEx Express and FedEx Ground were transferred to FedEx Services in conjunction with its formation effective June 1, 2000. The related depreciation and amortization for those assets is now allocated to these operating segments as "Intercompany charges." Consequently, 2001 depreciation and amortization expense, assets and capital expenditure segment information presented is not comparable to prior periods. We believe the total amounts allocated to the business segments reasonably reflect the cost of providing such services. Our Other segment also includes the operations of Viking through November 30, 2000, certain unallocated corporate items and eliminations.

The following table provides a reconciliation of reportable segment revenues, depreciation and amortization, operating income and segment assets to consolidated financial statement totals:

In thousands	2001	2000	1999
Revenues			
FedEx Express	**$15,533,567**	$15,068,338	$13,979,277
FedEx Ground	**2,236,562**	2,032,570	1,878,107
FedEx Freight	**835,298**	—	—
Other	**1,023,613**	1,156,037	916,086
Consolidated total	**$19,629,040**	$18,256,945	$16,773,470
Depreciation and amortization			
FedEx Express	**$ 796,517**	$ 997,735	$ 912,002
FedEx Ground	**110,934**	99,140	82,640
FedEx Freight	**43,693**	—	—
Other	**324,630**	57,988	40,476
Consolidated total	**$ 1,275,774**	$ 1,154,863	$ 1,035,118
Operating income (loss)			
FedEx Express	**$ 847,401**[1] $	899,610	$ 871,476[3]
FedEx Ground	**175,150**	225,812	231,010
FedEx Freight	**55,032**	—	—
Other	**(6,693)**[2]	95,652	60,600
Consolidated total	**$ 1,070,890**	$ 1,221,074	$ 1,163,086
Segment assets			
FedEx Express	**$ 9,570,621**	$ 9,740,539	
FedEx Ground	**1,157,988**	1,057,519	
FedEx Freight	**1,703,121**	—	
Other	**908,282**	729,053	
Consolidated total	**$13,340,012**	$11,527,111	

(1) Includes $93,000,000 charge for impairment of certain assets related to the MD10 aircraft program and $9,000,000 charge related to the Ayres program.
(2) Includes $22,000,000 of FedEx Supply Chain Services reorganization costs.
(3) Includes $81,000,000 of strike contingency costs.

The following table provides a reconciliation of reportable segment capital expenditures to consolidated totals for the years ended May 31:

In thousands	2001	2000	1999
FedEx Express	**$1,233,051**	$1,330,904	$1,550,161
FedEx Ground	**212,415**	244,073	179,969
FedEx Freight	**62,276**	—	—
Other	**385,642**	52,441	39,816
Consolidated total	**$1,893,384**	$1,627,418	$1,769,946

The following table presents revenue by service type and geographic information for the years ended or as of May 31:

In thousands	2001	2000	1999
REVENUE BY SERVICE TYPE			
FedEx Express:			
Package:			
U.S. overnight box[1]	**$ 5,829,972**	$ 5,683,663	$ 5,409,036
U.S. overnight envelope[2]	**1,870,881**	1,854,181	1,776,426
U.S. deferred	**2,492,522**	2,428,002	2,271,151
Total domestic package revenue	**10,193,375**	9,965,846	9,456,613
International priority	**3,939,612**	3,551,593	3,018,828
Total package revenue	**14,132,987**	13,517,439	12,475,441
Freight:			
U.S.	**650,779**	566,259	439,855
International	**424,216**	492,280	530,759
Other	**325,585**	492,360	533,222
Total FedEx Express	**15,533,567**	15,068,338	13,979,277
FedEx Ground	**2,236,562**	2,032,570	1,878,107
FedEx Freight	**835,298**	—	—
Other	**1,023,613**	1,156,037	916,086
	$19,629,040	$18,256,945	$16,773,470
GEOGRAPHIC INFORMATION[3]			
Revenues:			
U.S.	**$14,857,625**	$13,804,849	$12,910,107
International	**4,771,415**	4,452,096	3,863,363
	$19,629,040	$18,256,945	$16,773,470
Long-lived assets:			
U.S.	**$ 8,637,458**	$ 7,224,219	
International	**1,253,493**	1,018,148	
	$ 9,890,951	$ 8,242,367	

(1) The U.S. overnight box category includes packages exceeding eight ounces in weight.
(2) The U.S. overnight envelope category includes envelopes weighing eight ounces or less.
(3) International revenue includes shipments that either originate in or are destined to locations outside the United States. Long-lived assets include property and equipment, goodwill and other long-term assets. Flight equipment is allocated between geographic areas based on usage.

NOTE 12: SUPPLEMENTAL CASH FLOW INFORMATION

Cash paid for interest expense and income taxes for the years ended May 31 was as follows:

In thousands	2001	2000	1999
Interest (net of capitalized interest)	**$155,860**	$124,964	$114,326
Income taxes	**444,850**	354,614	437,340

Noncash investing and financing activities for the years ended May 31 were as follows:

In thousands	2001	2000	1999
Fair value of assets surrendered under exchange agreements (with two airlines)	$ —	$19,450	$48,248
Fair value of assets acquired under exchange agreements	**4,868**	28,018	34,580
Fair value of assets surrendered (under) over fair value of assets acquired	**$ (4,868)**	$ (8,568)	$13,668
Fair value of treasury stock and common stock options issued in business acquisition	**$506,390**	$ 6,817	$ —

NOTE 13: COMMITMENTS AND CONTINGENCIES

Annual purchase commitments under various contracts as of May 31, 2001, were as follows:

In thousands	Aircraft	Aircraft-Related[1]	Other[2]	Total
2002	$425,100	$611,200	$359,400	$1,395,700
2003	411,500	610,300	13,200	1,035,000
2004	231,500	525,000	8,000	764,500
2005	261,500	254,300	7,600	523,400
2006	228,700	189,700	7,600	426,000

(1) Primarily aircraft modifications, rotables, spare parts and engines.
(2) Primarily facilities, vehicles, computer and other equipment.

FedEx Express is committed to purchase 27 MD11s, nine DC10s, seven A300s, seven A310s and 75 Ayres ALM 200s to be delivered through 2007. See Note 15 for additional information regarding the Ayres program. Deposits and progress payments of $8,300,000 have been made toward these purchases and other planned aircraft transactions. Because Ayres Corporation filed for Chapter 11 bankruptcy protection in November 2000, we believe it is unlikely that any of the ALM 2000 aircraft will be delivered to FedEx Express. The purchase commitment amounts related to these aircraft are $35,100,000, $96,100,000 and $75,800,000 in 2004, 2005 and 2006, respectively, and are included in the above table.

FedEx Express has entered into agreements with two airlines to acquire 53 DC10 aircraft (49 of which had been received as of May 31, 2001), spare parts, aircraft engines and other equipment, and maintenance services in exchange for a combination of aircraft engine noise reduction kits and cash. Delivery of these aircraft began in 1997 and will continue through 2002. Additionally, these airlines may exercise put options through December 31, 2003, requiring FedEx Express to purchase up to 10 additional DC10s along with additional aircraft engines and equipment.

In January 2001, FedEx Express entered into a memorandum of understanding to acquire 10 A380 aircraft from Airbus Industrie. The acquisition of these aircraft is subject to the execution of a definitive purchase agreement, which is currently under negotiation.

During most of 2001 and 2000, we entered into jet fuel hedging contracts on behalf of our subsidiary FedEx Express, which were designed to limit exposure to fluctuations in jet fuel prices. Under those jet fuel hedging contracts, payments were made (or received) based on the difference between a fixed price and the market price of jet fuel, as determined by an index of spot market prices representing various geographic regions. The difference was recorded as an increase or decrease in fuel expense. Under jet fuel hedging contracts, we received $92,206,000 in 2001 and $18,512,000 in 2000. All outstanding jet fuel hedging contracts were effectively closed at May 31, 2001 by entering into offsetting jet fuel hedging contracts, resulting in a deferred charge of approximately $15,000,000, which will be recognized in 2002 as fuel is purchased. At May 31, 2000, the fair value of jet fuel hedging contracts, which had no carrying value, was an asset of approximately $51,060,000.

NOTE 14: LEGAL PROCEEDINGS

We are subject to legal proceedings and claims that arise in the ordinary course of our business. In our opinion, the aggregate liability, if any, with respect to these actions will not materially adversely affect our financial position or results of operations.

NOTE 15: ASSET IMPAIRMENTS

Asset impairment adjustments of $102,000,000 at FedEx Express were recorded in the fourth quarter of 2001. Impaired assets were adjusted to fair value based on estimated fair market values. All charges relating to asset impairments were reflected as other operating expenses in the Consolidated Statements of Income. The asset impairment charge was comprised of two parts:

Certain assets related to the MD10 aircraft program	$ 93,000,000
Ayres Loadmaster program deposits and other	9,000,000
	$102,000,000

These aircraft procurement programs were in place to ensure adequate aircraft capacity for future volume growth. Due to lowered capacity requirements, it became evident during the fourth quarter of 2001 that FedEx Express had more aircraft capacity commitments than required. Certain aircraft awaiting modification under the MD10 program and the purchase commitments for the Ayres aircraft were evaluated and determined to be impaired.

The MD10 program curtailment charge is comprised primarily of the write down of impaired DC10 airframes, engines and parts to a nominal estimated salvage value. Costs relating to the disposal of the assets were also recorded. These assets are expected to be disposed of primarily during 2002. The Ayres Loadmaster program charge is comprised primarily of the write-off of deposits for aircraft purchases. Capitalized interest and other costs estimated to be unrecoverable in connection with the bankruptcy of Ayres Corporation were also expensed.

NOTE 16: OTHER EVENTS

On April 24, 2001, FedEx Supply Chain Services committed to a plan to reorganize certain of its unprofitable, non-strategic logistics business and reduce overhead. Total 2001 costs of $22,000,000 were incurred in connection with this plan, primarily comprising costs for estimated contractual settlements ($8,000,000), asset impairment charges ($5,000,000) and severance and employee separation ($5,000,000). Asset impairment charges were recognized to reduce the carrying value of long-lived assets (primarily software) to estimated fair values, and an accrual of $17,000,000 was recorded for the remaining reorganization costs. The accrual had a balance of approximately $12,000,000 remaining at May 31, 2001, reflecting primarily the payment of severance costs and contractual settlements. Approximately 120 principally administrative positions were eliminated under the plan. The reorganization will be completed in 2002.

On January 10, 2001, FedEx Express and the U.S. Postal Service entered into two service contracts: one for domestic air transportation of postal express shipments, and the other for placement of FedEx Drop Boxes at U.S. Post Offices.

In 2000, FedEx Express recorded nonoperating gains of approximately $11,000,000 from the sale of securities and approximately $12,000,000 from the insurance settlement for a leased MD11 aircraft destroyed in October 1999.

NOTE 17: SUMMARY OF QUARTERLY OPERATING RESULTS (UNAUDITED)

In thousands	First Quarter	Second Quarter	Third Quarter	Fourth Quarter[1]
2001				
Revenues	$4,778,736	$4,894,921	$4,838,780	$5,116,603
Operating income	310,967	345,412	191,305	223,206
Income before income taxes	274,245	315,128	158,489	179,711
Net income	168,660	193,804	108,689	113,218
Earnings per common share	.59	.68	.38	.38
Earnings per common share—assuming dilution	.58	.67	.37	.38
2000				
Revenues	$4,319,977	$4,570,104	$4,518,057	$4,848,807
Operating income	283,807	304,535	206,472	426,260
Income before income taxes	262,880	282,928	186,998	404,934
Net income	159,034	171,183	113,128	244,991
Earnings per common share	.53	.58	.39	.86
Earnings per common share—assuming dilution	.52	.57	.39	.85

(1) Fourth quarter of 2001 includes a $102,000,000 charge for impairment of certain assets related to aircraft programs at FedEx Express and a $22,000,000 reorganization charge at FedEx Supply Chain Services.

To the Stockholders of FedEx Corporation:

We have audited the accompanying consolidated balance sheets of FedEx Corporation (a Delaware corporation) and subsidiaries as of May 31, 2001 and 2000, and the related consolidated statements of income, changes in stockholders' investment and comprehensive income and cash flows for each of the three years in the period ended May 31, 2001. These financial statements are the responsibility of FedEx's management. Our responsibility is to express an opinion on these financial statements based on our audits.

We conducted our audits in accordance with auditing standards generally accepted in the United States. Those standards require that we plan and perform the audit to obtain reasonable assurance about whether the financial statements are free of material misstatement. An audit includes examining, on a test basis, evidence supporting the amounts and disclosures in the financial statements. An audit also includes assessing the accounting principles used and significant estimates made by management, as well as evaluating the overall financial statement presentation. We believe that our audits provide a reasonable basis for our opinion.

In our opinion, the financial statements referred to above present fairly, in all material respects, the financial position of FedEx Corporation as of May 31, 2001 and 2000, and the results of its operations and its cash flows for each of the three years in the period ended May 31, 2001, in conformity with accounting principles generally accepted in the United States.

Arthur Andersen LLP
Memphis, Tennessee
July 27, 2001 ■

QUESTIONS FOR REVIEW OF KEY TOPICS

Q 1–1 What is the function and primary focus of financial accounting?

Q 1–2 What is meant by the phrase *efficient allocation of resources*? What mechanism fosters the efficient allocation of resources in the United States?

Q 1–3 Identify two important variables to be considered when making an investment decision.

Q 1–4 What must a company do in the long run to be able to provide a return to investors and creditors?

Q 1–5 What is the primary objective of financial accounting?

Q 1–6 Define net operating cash flows. Briefly explain why periodic net operating cash flows may not be a good indicator of future operating cash flows.

Q 1–7 What is meant by GAAP? Why is it important that all companies follow GAAP in reporting to external users?

Q 1–8 Explain the roles of the SEC and the FASB in the setting of accounting standards.

Q 1–9 Explain the role of the auditor in the financial reporting process.

Q 1–10 Explain what is meant by *adverse economic consequences* of new accounting standards or changes in standards.

Q 1–11 Why does the FASB undertake a series of elaborate information-gathering steps before issuing a substantive accounting standard?

Q 1–12 What is the purpose of the FASB's conceptual framework project?

Q 1–13 Discuss the terms *relevance* and *reliability* as they relate to financial accounting information.

Q 1–14 What are the components of relevant information? What are the components of reliable information?

Q 1–15 Explain what is meant by: The benefits of accounting information must exceed the costs.

Q 1–16 What is meant by the term *materiality* in financial reporting?

Q 1–17 Briefly define the financial accounting elements: (1) assets, (2) liabilities, (3) equity, (4) investments by owners, (5) distributions to owners, (6) revenues, (7) expenses, (8) gains, (9) losses, and (10) comprehensive income.

Q 1–18 What are the four basic assumptions underlying GAAP?

Q 1–19 What is the going concern assumption?

Q 1–20   Explain the periodicity assumption.

Q 1–21   What are the four key broad accounting principles that guide accounting practice?

Q 1–22   What are two important reasons to base the valuation of assets and liabilities on their historical cost?

Q 1–23   Describe the two criteria that must be satisfied before revenue can be recognized.

Q 1–24   What are the four different approaches to implementing the matching principle? Give an example of an expense that is recognized under each approach.

Q 1–25   In addition to the financial statement elements arrayed in the basic financial statements, what are some other ways to disclose financial information to external users?

EXERCISES

E 1–1
Accrual accounting

Listed below are several transactions that took place during the first two years of operations for the law firm of Pete, Pete, and Roy.

	Year 1	Year 2
Amounts billed to customers for services rendered	$170,000	$220,000
Cash collected from customers	160,000	190,000
Cash disbursements:		
Purchase of insurance policy.....................................	60,000	–0–
Salaries paid to employees for services rendered during the year	90,000	100,000
Utilities	30,000	40,000

In addition, you learn that the company incurred utility costs of $35,000 in year one, that there were no liabilities at the end of year two, no anticipated bad debts on receivables, and that the insurance policy covers a three-year period.

Required:
1.   Calculate the net operating cash flow for years 1 and 2.
2.   Prepare an income statement for each year similar to Illustration 1–2 on page 8 according to the accrual accounting model.
3.   Determine the amount of receivables from customers that the company would show in its year 1 and year 2 balance sheets prepared according to the accrual accounting model.

E 1–2
Sources of GAAP

Different organizations historically and currently have issued various pronouncements that constitute the body of generally accepted accounting principles. Presented below are some of these organizations as well as various authoritative pronouncements. Match each organization with the one or more pronouncement(s) with which it is associated.

Organization	Pronouncements
1. Accounting Principles Board	a. *Statements of Financial Accounting Concepts*
2. Financial Accounting Standards Board	b. *Financial Reporting Releases*
3. Securities and Exchange Commission	c. *Accounting Research Bulletins*
4. Committee on Accounting Procedure	d. *Statements of Financial Accounting Standards*
5. AICPA	e. *APBOs*
	f. *Industry Accounting Guides*
	g. *Technical Bulletins*

E 1–3
Participants in establishing GAAP

Three groups that participate in the process of establishing GAAP are users, preparers, and auditors. These groups are represented by various organizations. For each organization listed below, indicate which of these groups it primarily represents.
1.   Securities and Exchange Commission
2.   Financial Executives Institute
3.   American Institute of Certified Public Accountants
4.   Institute of Management Accountants
5.   Association of Investment Management and Research

E 1–4
Financial statement elements

For each of the items listed below, identify the appropriate financial statement element or elements.
1.   Obligation to transfer cash or other resources as a result of a past transaction.
2.   Dividends paid by a corporation to its shareholders.
3.   Inflow of an asset from providing a good or service.

4. The financial position of a company.
5. Increase in equity during a period from nonowner transactions.
6. Increase in equity from peripheral or incidental transaction.
7. Sale of an asset used in the operations of a business for less than the asset's book value.
8. The owners' residual interest in the assets of a company.
9. An item owned by the company representing probable future benefits.
10. Revenues plus gains less expenses and losses.
11. An owner's contribution of cash to a corporation in exchange for ownership shares of stock.
12. Outflow of an asset related to the production of revenue.

E 1–5
Concepts; terminology; conceptual framework

Listed below are several terms and phrases associated with the FASB's conceptual framework. Pair each item from List A (by letter) with the item from List B that is most appropriately associated with it.

List A	List B
____ 1. Predictive value	a. Decreases in equity resulting from transfers to owners.
____ 2. Relevance	b. Requires consideration of the costs and value of information.
____ 3. Timeliness	c. Important for making interfirm comparisons.
____ 4. Distribution to owners	d. Applying the same accounting practices over time.
____ 5. Feedback value	e. Along with relevance, a primary decision-specific quality.
____ 6. Reliability	f. Agreement between a measure and the phenomenon it purports to represent.
____ 7. Gain	g. Information is available prior to the decision.
____ 8. Representational faithfulness	h. Pertinent to the decision at hand.
____ 9. Comprehensive income	i. Implies consensus among different measurers.
____ 10. Materiality	j. Information confirms expectations.
____ 11. Comparability	k. The change in equity from nonowner transactions.
____ 12. Neutrality	l. The process of admitting information into financial statements.
____ 13. Recognition	m. Accounting information should not favor a particular group.
____ 14. Consistency	n. Results if an asset is sold for more than its book value.
____ 15. Cost effectiveness	o. Information is useful in predicting the future.
____ 16. Verifiability	p. Concerns the relative size of an item and its effect on decisions.

E 1–6
Multiple choice; conceptual framework

The following questions dealing with the FASB's conceptual framework are adapted from questions that appeared on recent CPA examinations. Determine the response that best completes the statements or questions.

1. According to the FASB conceptual framework, which of the following situations violates the concept of reliability?
   a. Data on segments having the same expected risk and growth rates are reported to analysts estimating future profits.
   b. Financial statements are issued nine months late.
   c. Management reports to stockholders regularly refer to new projects undertaken, but the financial statements never report project results.
   d. Financial statements include property with a carrying amount increased to management's estimate of market value.

2. According to *Statements of Financial Accounting Concepts*, neutrality is an ingredient of

	Reliability	Relevance
a.	Yes	Yes
b.	Yes	No
c.	No	Yes
d.	No	No

3. According to the FASB conceptual framework, predictive value is an ingredient of

	Relevance	Reliability
a.	No	No
b.	Yes	Yes
c.	No	Yes
d.	Yes	No

4. According to the FASB conceptual framework, earnings
    a. Are the same as comprehensive income.
    b. Exclude certain gains and losses that are included in comprehensive income.
    c. Include certain gains and losses that are excluded from comprehensive income.
    d. Include certain losses that are excluded from comprehensive income.
5. According to the FASB conceptual framework, which of the following relates to both relevance and reliability?

	Consistency	Verifiability
a.	Yes	Yes
b.	Yes	No
c.	No	Yes
d.	No	No

E 1–7

Basic assumptions, principles, and constraints

Listed below are several terms and phrases associated with basic assumptions, underlying principles, and constraints. Pair each item from List A (by letter) with the item from List B that is most appropriately associated with it.

List A	List B
____ 1. Matching principle	a. The enterprise is separate from its owners and other entities.
____ 2. Periodicity	b. A common denominator is the dollar.
____ 3. Historical cost principle	c. The entity will continue indefinitely.
____ 4. Materiality	d. Record expenses in the period the related revenue is recognized.
____ 5. Realization principle	e. The original transaction value upon acquisition.
____ 6. Going concern assumption	f. All information that could affect decisions should be reported.
____ 7. Monetary unit assumption	g. The life of an enterprise can be divided into artificial time periods.
____ 8. Economic entity assumption	h. Criteria usually satisfied at point of sale.
____ 9. Full-disclosure principle	i. Concerns the relative size of an item and its effect on decisions.

E 1–8

Basic assumptions and principles

Listed below are several statements that relate to financial accounting and reporting. Identify the basic assumption, broad accounting principle, or pervasive constraint that applies to each statement.

1. Jim Marley is the sole owner of Marley's Appliances. Jim borrowed $100,000 to buy a new home to be used as his personal residence. This liability was not recorded in the records of Marley's Appliances.
2. Apple Computer, Inc., distributes an annual report to its shareholders.
3. Hewlett-Packard Corporation depreciates machinery and equipment over their useful lives.
4. The Crosby Company lists land on its balance sheet at $120,000, its original purchase price, even though the land has a current market value of $200,000.
5. The Honeywell Corporation records revenue when products are delivered to customers, even though the cash has not yet been received.
6. Liquidation values are not normally reported in financial statements even though many companies do go out of business.
7. IBM Corporation, a multibillion dollar company, purchased some small tools at a cost of $800. Even though the tools will be used for a number of years, the company recorded the purchase as an expense.

E 1–9

Basic assumptions and principles

Identify the basic assumption or broad accounting principle that was violated in each of the following situations.

1. The Pastel Paint Company purchased land two years ago at a price of $250,000. Because the value of the land has appreciated to $400,000, the company has valued the land at $400,000 in its most recent balance sheet.
2. The Atwell Corporation has not prepared financial statements for external users for over three years.
3. The Klingon Company sells farm machinery. Revenue from a large order of machinery from a new buyer was recorded the day the order was received.
4. Don Smith is the sole owner of a company called Hardware City. The company recently paid a $150 utility bill for Smith's personal residence and recorded a $150 expense.
5. The Golden Book Company purchased a large printing machine for $1,000,000 (a material amount) and recorded the purchase as an expense.

6.   The Ace Appliance Company is involved in a major lawsuit involving injuries sustained by some of its employees in the manufacturing plant. The company is being sued for $2,000,000, a material amount, and is not insured. The suit was not disclosed in the most recent financial statements because no settlement had been reached.

E 1–10

Basic assumptions and principles

For each of the following situations, indicate whether you agree or disagree with the financial reporting practice employed and state the basic assumption, pervasive constraint, or accounting principle that is applied (if you agree) or violated (if you disagree).

1.   The Wagner Corporation adjusted the valuation of all assets and liabilities to reflect changes in the purchasing power of the dollar.
2.   The Spooner Oil Company changed its method of accounting for oil and gas exploration costs from successful efforts to full cost. No mention of the change was included in the financial statements. The change had a material effect on Spooner's financial statements.
3.   The Cypress Manufacturing Company purchased machinery having a five-year life. The cost of the machinery is being expensed over the life of the machinery.
4.   The Rudeen Corporation purchased equipment for $180,000 at a liquidation sale of a competitor. Because the equipment was worth $230,000, Rudeen valued the equipment in its subsequent balance sheet at $230,000.
5.   The Davis Bicycle Company received a large order for the sale of 1,000 bicycles at $100 each. The customer paid Davis the entire amount of $100,000 on March 15. However, Davis did not record any revenue until April 17, the date the bicycles were delivered to the customer.
6.   The Gigantic Corporation purchased two small calculators at a cost of $32.00. The cost of the calculators was expensed even though they had a three-year estimated useful life.
7.   The Esquire Company provides financial statements to external users every three years.

E 1–11

Basic assumptions, principles, and constraints

Listed below are the basic assumptions, underlying principles, and constraints discussed in this chapter.

a. Economic entity assumption g. Matching principle
b. Going concern assumption h. Full-disclosure principle
c. Periodicity assumption i. Cost effectiveness
d. Monetary unit assumption j. Materiality
e. Historical cost principle k. Conservatism
f. Realization principle

Identify by letter the assumption, principle, or constraint that relates to each statement or phrase below.

____ 1. Revenue is recognized only after certain criteria are satisfied.
____ 2. Information that could affect decision making should be reported.
____ 3. Cause-and-effect relationship between revenues and expenses.
____ 4. The basis for measurement of many assets and liabilities.
____ 5. Relates to the qualitative characteristic of timeliness.
____ 6. All economic events can be identified with a particular entity.
____ 7. The benefits of providing accounting information should exceed the cost of doing so.
____ 8. A consequence is that GAAP need not be followed in all situations.
____ 9. Not a qualitative characteristic, but a practical justification for some accounting choices.
____ 10. Assumes the entity will continue indefinitely.
____ 11. Inflation causes a violation of this assumption.

E 1–12

Multiple choice; concept statements, basic assumptions, principles

Determine the response that best completes the following statements or questions.

1.   The primary objective of financial reporting is to provide information
    a.   About a firm's economic resources and obligations.
    b.   Useful in predicting future cash flows.
    c.   Concerning the changes in financial position resulting from the income-producing efforts of the entity.
    d.   About a firm's financing and investing activities.

2.   *Statements of Financial Accounting Concepts* issued by the FASB
    a.   Represent GAAP.
    b.   Have been superseded by *SFAS*s.
    c.   Are subject to approval of the SEC.
    d.   Identify the conceptual framework within which accounting standards are developed.

3. In general, revenue is recognized as earned when the earning process is virtually complete and
   a. The sales price has been collected.
   b. A purchase order has been received.
   c. There is reasonable certainty as to the collectibility of the asset to be received.
   d. A contract has been signed.
4. In depreciating the cost of an asset, accountants are most concerned with
   a. Conservatism.
   b. The realization principle.
   c. Full disclosure.
   d. The matching principle.
5. The primary objective of the matching principle is to
   a. Provide full disclosure.
   b. Record expenses in the period that related revenues are recognized.
   c. Provide timely information to decision makers.
   d. Promote comparability between financial statements of different periods.
6. The separate entity assumption states that, in the absence of contrary evidence, all entities will survive indefinitely.
   a. True
   b. False

BROADEN YOUR PERSPECTIVE

Apply your critical-thinking ability to the knowledge you've gained. These cases will provide you an opportunity to develop your research, analysis, judgment, and communication skills. You will also work with other students, integrate what you've learned, apply it in real-world situations, and consider its global and ethical ramifications. This practice will broaden your knowledge and further develop your decision-making abilities.

Judgment Case 1–1
The development of accounting standards

In 1934, Congress created the Securities and Exchange Commission (SEC) and gave the commission both the power and responsibility for setting accounting and reporting standards in the United States.

Required:
1. Explain the relationship between the SEC and the various private sector standard-setting bodies that have, over time, been delegated the responsibility for setting accounting standards.
2. Can you think of any reasons why the SEC has delegated this responsibility rather than set standards directly?

Research Case 1–2
Accessing SEC information through the Internet

Internet access to the World Wide Web has provided a wealth of information accessible with our personal computers. Many chapters in this text contain Real World Cases that require you to access the web to research an accounting issue. The purpose of this case is to introduce you to the Internet home page of the Securities and Exchange Commission (SEC) and its EDGAR database.

Required:
1. Access the SEC home page on the Internet. The web address is www.sec.gov.
2. Choose the subaddress "About the SEC" and answer the following questions:
   a. What are the two basic objectives of the 1933 Securities Act?
   b. The Securities Act Amendments of 1964 extended disclosure and reporting provisions of the 1934 Securities Exchange Act to include equity securities in the over-the-counter market. What is the "size test" for determining which over-the-counter companies must file registration forms with the SEC?
3. Return to the SEC home page and access EDGAR. Describe the contents of the database.

Research Case 1–3
Accessing FASB information through the Internet

The purpose of this case is to introduce you to the information available on the website of the Financial Accounting Standards Board (FASB).

Required:
Access the FASB home page on the Internet. The web address is www.fasb.org. Answer the following questions.
1. Describe the mission of the FASB.
2. Who are the current Board members? Briefly describe their backgrounds.
3. How are topics added to the FASB's technical agenda?

4. How many standards have been issued by the FASB? What topic is addressed in the most recently issued standard?
5. How many Exposure Drafts are currently outstanding? What topics do they address?

Research Case 1–4
Accounting standards in China

Economic reforms in the People's Republic of China are moving that nation toward a market-driven economy. China's accounting practices must also change to accommodate the needs of potential investors. In an article entitled "Institutional Factors Influencing China's Accounting Reforms and Standards," Professor Bing Xiang analyzes the changes in the accounting environment of China during the recent economic reforms and their implications for the development of accounting reforms.

Required:
1. In your library or from some other source, locate the indicated article in *Accounting Horizons*, June 1998.
2. Briefly describe the economic reforms that led to the need for increased external financial reporting in China.
3. Conformity with International Accounting Standards was specified as an overriding objective in formulating China's accounting standards. What is the author's opinion of this objective?

Communication Case 1–5
Relevance and reliability

Some theorists contend that companies that create pollution should report the social cost of that pollution in income statements. They argue that such companies are indirectly subsidized as the cost of pollution is borne by society while only production costs (and perhaps minimal pollution fines) are shown in the income statement. Thus, the product sells for less than would be necessary if all costs were included.

Assume that the FASB is considering a standard to include the social costs of pollution in the income statement. The process would require considering both relevance and reliability of the information produced by the new standard. Your instructor will divide the class into two to six groups depending on the size of the class. The mission of your group is to explain how the concepts of relevance and reliability relate to this issue.

Required:
Each group member should consider the question independently and draft a tentative answer prior to the class session for which the case is assigned.

In class, each group will meet for 10 to 15 minutes in different areas of the classroom. During that meeting, group members will take turns sharing their suggestions for the purpose of arriving at a single group treatment.

After the allotted time, a spokesperson for each group (selected during the group meetings) will share the group's solution with the class. The goal of the class is to incorporate the views of each group into a consensus answer to the question.

Communication Case 1–6
Accounting standard setting

One of your friends is a financial analyst for a major stock brokerage firm. Recently she indicated to you that she had read an article in a weekly business magazine that alluded to the political process of establishing accounting standards. She had always assumed that accounting standards were established by determining the approach that conceptually best reflected the economics of a transaction.

Required:
Write a one to two page article for a business journal explaining what is meant by the political process for establishing accounting standards. Be sure to include in your article a discussion of the need for the FASB to balance accounting considerations and economic consequences.

Ethics Case 1–7
The auditors' responsibility

It is the responsibility of management to apply accounting standards when communicating with investors and creditors through financial statements. Another group, auditors, serves as an independent intermediary to help ensure that management has in fact appropriately applied GAAP in preparing the company's financial statements. Auditors examine (audit) financial statements to express a professional, independent opinion. The opinion reflects the auditors' assessment of the statements' fairness, which is determined by the extent to which they are prepared in compliance with GAAP.

Some feel that it is impossible for an auditor to give an independent opinion on a company's financial statements because the auditors' fees for performing the audit are paid by the company. In addition to the audit fee, quite often the auditor performs other services for the company such as preparing the company's income tax returns.

Required:
How might an auditor's ethics be challenged while performing an audit?

Judgment Case 1–8
Qualitative characteristics

Generally accepted accounting principles do not require companies to disclose forecasts of any financial variables to external users. A friend, who is a finance major, is puzzled by this and asks you to explain why such relevant information is not provided to investors and creditors to help them predict future cash flows.

Required:

Explain to your friend why this information is not routinely provided to investors and creditors.

Judgment Case 1–9
GAAP, comparability, and the role of the auditor

Mary McQuire is trying to decide how to invest her money. A friend recommended that she buy the stock of one of two corporations and suggested that she should compare the financial statements of the two companies before making a decision.

Required:

1. Do you agree that Mary will be able to compare the financial statements of the two companies?
2. What role does the auditor play in ensuring comparability of financial statements between companies?

Judgment Case 1–10
Cost effectiveness

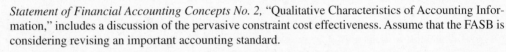

Statement of Financial Accounting Concepts No. 2, "Qualitative Characteristics of Accounting Information," includes a discussion of the pervasive constraint cost effectiveness. Assume that the FASB is considering revising an important accounting standard.

Required:

1. What is the desired benefit from revising an accounting standard?
2. What are some of the possible costs that could result from a revision of an accounting standard?
3. What does the FASB do in order to assess possible benefits and costs of a proposed revision of an accounting standard?

Judgment Case 1–11
The realization principle

A new client, the Wolf Company, asks your advice concerning the point in time that the company should recognize revenue from the rental of its office buildings. Renters usually pay rent on a quarterly basis at the beginning of the quarter. The owners contend that the critical event that motivates revenue recognition should be the date the cash is received from renters. After all, the money is in hand and is very seldom returned.

Required:

1. Describe the two criteria that must be satisfied before revenue can be recognized.
2. Do you agree or disagree with the position of the owners of Wolf Company? Support your answer.

Analysis Case 1–12
The matching principle

Revenues measure the accomplishments of a company during the period. Expenses are then matched with revenues to produce a periodic measure of performance called *net income*.

Required:

1. Explain what is meant by the phrase *matched with revenues*.
2. Describe the four approaches used to implement the matching principle and label them 1 through 4.
3. For each of the following, identify which matching approach should be used to recognize the cost as expense.
   a. The cost of producing a product.
   b. The cost of advertising.
   c. The cost of monthly rent on the office building.
   d. The salary of an office employee.
   e. Depreciation on an office building.

Real World Case 1–13
Elements; disclosures; Dell Computer Corporation

Selected financial statements from a recent annual report of Dell Computer Corporation follow. Use these statements to answer the following questions.

Required:

1. The company's fiscal year ends on what date?
2. What amounts did Dell report for the following items for the fiscal year ended February 2, 2001?
   a. Total net revenues
   b. Total operating expenses
   c. Net income
   d. Total assets
   e. Total shareholders' equity
3. How many shares of common stock did the company have issued and outstanding on February 2, 2001?
4. Why do you think Dell reports more than one year of data in its financial statements?

DELL COMPUTER CORPORATION
Consolidated Balance Sheets
($ in millions)

	February 2, 2001	January 28, 2000
Assets		
Current assets:		
Cash and cash equivalents	$ 4,910	$ 3,809
Short-term investments	528	323
Accounts receivable, net	2,895	2,608
Inventories	400	391
Other	758	550
Total current assets	9,491	7,681
Property, plant and equipment, net	996	765
Investments	2,418	2,721
Other noncurrent assets	530	304
Total assets	$13,435	$11,471
Liabilities and Stockholders' Equity		
Current liabilities:		
Accounts payable	$ 4,286	$ 3,538
Accrued and other	2,257	1,654
Total current liabilities	6,543	5,192
Long-term debt	509	508
Other	761	463
Total liabilities	7,813	6,163
Stockholders' equity:		
Preferred stock and capital in excess of $.01 par value; shares issued and outstanding: none	—	—
Common stock and capital in excess of $.01 par value; shares issued and outstanding: 2,601 and 2,575, respectively	4,795	3,583
Retained earnings	839	1,260
Other comprehensive income	62	533
Other	(74)	(68)
Total stockholders' equity	5,622	5,308
Total liabilities and stockholders' equity	$13,435	$11,471

Consolidated Statements of Income
($ in millions, except per share amounts)

	Fiscal Year Ended	
	February 2, 2001	January 28, 2000
Net revenue	$31,888	$25,265
Cost of revenue	25,445	20,047
Gross margin	6,443	5,218
Operating expenses:		
Selling, general and administrative	3,193	2,387
Research, development and engineering	482	374
Special charges	105	194
Total operating expenses	3,780	2,955
Operating income	2,663	2,263
Investment and other income, net	531	188
Income before income taxes and cumulative effect	3,194	2,451
Provision for income taxes	958	785
Income before cumulative effect of change in accounting principle	2,236	1,666
Cumulative effect of change in accounting principle, net of taxes	59	—
Net income	$ 2,177	$ 1,666
Earnings per common share:		
Before cumulative effect of change in accounting principle:		
Basic	$ 0.87	$ 0.66
Diluted	$ 0.81	$ 0.61
After cumulative effect of change in accounting principle:		
Basic	$ 0.84	$ 0.66
Diluted	$ 0.79	$ 0.61

2

Review of the Accounting Process

OVERVIEW

Chapter 1 explained that the primary means of conveying financial information to investors, creditors, and other external users is through financial statements and related notes. The purpose of this chapter is to review the fundamental accounting process used to produce the financial statements. This review establishes a framework for the study of the concepts covered in intermediate accounting.

Actual accounting systems differ significantly from company to company. This chapter focuses on the many features that tend to be common to any accounting system.

LEARNING OBJECTIVES

After studying this chapter, you should be able to:

LO1 Analyze routine economic events—transactions—and record their effects on a company's financial position using the accounting equation format.

LO2 Record transactions using the general journal format.

LO3 Post the effects of journal entries to T-accounts and prepare an unadjusted trial balance.

LO4 Identify and describe the different types of adjusting journal entries.

LO5 Determine the required adjustments, record adjusting journal entries in general journal format, and prepare an adjusted trial balance.

LO6 Describe the four basic financial statements.

LO7 Explain the closing process.

FINANCIAL REPORTING CASE

Engineering Profits

After graduating from college last year, two of your engineering-major friends started an Internet consulting practice. They began operations on July 1 and felt they did quite well during their first year. Now they would like to borrow $20,000 from a local bank to buy new computing equipment and office furniture. To support their loan application, the friends presented the bank with the following income statement for their first year of operations ending June 30:

Consulting revenue		$96,000
Operating expenses:		
Salaries	$32,000	
Rent	9,000	
Supplies	4,800	
Utilities	3,000	
Advertising	1,200	(50,000)
Net income		$46,000

The bank officer noticed that there was no depreciation expense in the income statement and has asked your friends to revise the statement after making year-end adjustments. After agreeing to help, you discover the following information:

a. The friends paid $80,000 for equipment when they began operations. They think the equipment will be useful for five years.

b. They pay $500 a month to rent office space. In January, they paid a full year's rent in advance. This is included in the $9,000 rent expense.

c. Included in consulting revenue is $13,000 they received from a customer in June as a deposit for work to be performed in August.

> By the time you finish this chapter, you should be able to respond appropriately to the questions posed in this case. Compare your response to the solution provided at the end of the chapter.

QUESTIONS

1. What purpose do adjusting entries serve? (page 76)

2. What year-end adjustments are needed to revise the income statement? Did your friends do as well their first year as they thought? (page 77)

A solid foundation is vital to a sound understanding of intermediate accounting. So, we review the fundamental accounting process here to serve as a framework for the new concepts you will learn in this course.

Chapter 1 introduced the theoretical structure of financial accounting and the environment within which it operates. The primary function of financial accounting—to provide relevant and reliable financial information to external users—is accomplished by periodically disseminating financial statements and related notes. In this chapter we review the *process* used to identify, analyze, record, summarize, and then report the economic events affecting a company's financial position.

Keep in mind as you study this chapter that the accounting information systems businesses actually use are quite different from company to company. Larger companies generally use more complex systems than smaller companies use. The types of economic events affecting companies also cause differences in systems. We focus on the many features that tend to be common to all accounting systems.

It is important to understand that this chapter and its appendixes are not intended to describe actual accounting systems. In most business enterprises, the sheer volume of data that must be processed precludes a manual accounting system. Fortunately, the computer provides a solution. *We describe and illustrate a manual accounting information system to provide an overview of the basic model that underlies the computer software programs actually used to process accounting information.*

Electronic data processing is fast, accurate, and affordable. Many large and medium-sized companies own or rent their own mainframe computers and company-specific data processing systems. Smaller companies can take advantage of technology with relatively inexpensive micro- and minicomputers and generalized data software packages such as QuickBooks and Peachtree Accounting Software. Enterprise Resource Planning (ERP) systems are now being installed in companies of all sizes. The objective of ERP is to create a customized software program that integrates all departments and functions across a company onto a single computer system that can serve the information needs of those different departments, including the accounting department.

> **Computers are used to process accounting information. In this chapter we provide an overview of the basic model that underlies computer software programs.**

The Basic Model

> **Economic events cause changes in the financial position of the company.**

The first objective of any accounting system is to identify the **economic events** that can be expressed in financial terms by the system.[1] An economic event is any event that *directly* affects the financial position of the company. Recall from Chapter 1 that financial position comprises assets, liabilities, and owners' equity. Broad and specific accounting principles determine which events should be recorded, when the events should be recorded, and the dollar amount at which they should be measured.

> **External events involve an exchange between the company and another entity.**

Economic events can be classified as either external events or internal events. **External events** involve an exchange between the company and a separate economic entity. Examples are purchasing merchandise inventory for cash, borrowing cash from a bank, and paying salaries to employees. In each instance, the company receives something (merchandise, cash, and services) in exchange for something else (cash, assumption of a liability, and cash).

> **Internal events do not involve an exchange transaction but do affect the company's financial position.**

On the other hand, **internal events** directly affect the financial position of the company but don't involve an exchange transaction with another entity. Examples are the depreciation of machinery and the use of supplies. As we will see later in the chapter, these events must be recorded to properly reflect a company's financial position and results of operations in accordance with the accrual accounting model.

---

[1]There are many economic events that affect a company *indirectly* and are not recorded. For example, when the Federal Reserve changes its discount rate, it is an important economic event that can affect the company in many ways, but it is not recorded by the company.

THE ACCOUNTING EQUATION

The **accounting equation** underlies the process used to capture the effect of economic events.

$$\text{Assets} = \text{Liabilities} + \text{Owners' Equity}$$

The elements of the equation were defined in Chapter 1.

This general expression portrays the equality between the total economic resources of an entity (its assets)—shown on the left side of the equation—and the total claims to those resources (liabilities and equity)—shown on the right side. In other words, the resources of an enterprise are provided by creditors or owners.

The equation also implies that each economic event affecting this equation will have a dual effect because resources always must equal claims to those resources. For illustration, consider the events (we refer to these throughout the text as **transactions**) in Illustration 2–1.

Each transaction is analyzed to determine its effect on the equation and on the specific financial position elements.

> Each event, or *transaction*, has a dual effect on the accounting equation.

ILLUSTRATION 2–1

Transaction Analysis

1. An attorney invested $50,000 to open a law office.
An investment by the owner causes both assets and owners' equity to increase.

Assets	=	Liabilities	+	Owners' Equity
+$50,000 (cash)				+$50,000 (investment by owner)

2. $40,000 was borrowed from a bank and a note payable was signed.
This transaction causes assets and liabilities to increase. A bank loan increases cash and creates an obligation to repay it.

Assets	=	Liabilities	+	Owners' Equity
+$40,000 (cash)		+$40,000 (note payable)		

3. Supplies costing $3,000 were purchased on account.
Buying supplies on credit also increases both assets and liabilities.

Assets	=	Liabilities	+	Owners' Equity
+$3,000 (supplies)		+$3,000 (accounts payable)		

4. Services were performed on account for $10,000.
Transactions 4, 5, and 6 are revenue and expense transactions. Revenues and expenses (and gains and losses) are events that cause owners' equity to change. Revenues and gains describe inflows of assets, causing owners' equity to increase. Expenses and losses describe outflows of assets (or increases in liabilities), causing owners' equity to decrease.

Assets	=	Liabilities	+	Owners' Equity
+$10,000 (receivables)				+$10,000 (revenue)

5. Salaries of $5,000 were paid to employees.

Assets	=	Liabilities	+	Owners' Equity
−$5,000 (cash)				−$5,000 (expense)

6. $500 of supplies were used.

Assets	=	Liabilities	+	Owners' Equity
−$500 (supplies)				−$500 (expense)

7. $1,000 was paid on account to the supplies vendor.
This transaction causes assets and liabilities to decrease.

Assets	=	Liabilities	+	Owners' Equity
−$1,000 (cash)		−$1,000 (accounts payable)		

The accounting equation can be expanded to include a column for each type of asset and liability and for each type of change in owners' equity.

As discussed in Chapter 1, owners of a corporation are its shareholders, so owners' equity for a corporation is referred to as shareholders' equity. Shareholders' equity for a corporation arises primarily from two sources: (1) amounts *invested* by shareholders in the corporation and (2) amounts *earned* by the corporation (on behalf of its shareholders). These are reported as (1) **paid-in capital** and (2) **retained earnings.** Retained earnings equals net income less distributions to shareholders (primarily dividends) since the inception of the corporation.

> Owners' equity for a corporation, called *shareholders' equity,* is classified by source as either *paid-in capital* or *retained earnings.*

GRAPHIC 2–1   Accounting Equation for a
                Corporation

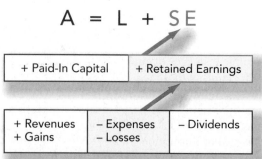

Graphic 2–1 shows the basic accounting equation for a corporation with shareholders' equity expanded to highlight its composition. We use the corporate format throughout the remainder of the chapter.

ACCOUNT RELATIONSHIPS

All transactions could be recorded in columnar fashion as increases or decreases to elements of the accounting equation. However, even for a very small company with few transactions, this would become cumbersome. So, most companies use a process called the **double-entry system.** The term *double-entry* refers to the dual effect that each transaction has on the accounting equation.

Elements of the accounting equation are represented by **accounts** which are contained in a **general ledger.** Increases and decreases in each element of a company's financial position are recorded in these accounts. A separate account is maintained for individual assets and liabilities, retained earnings, and paid-in capital. Also, to accumulate information needed for the income statement, we use separate accounts to keep track of the changes in retained earnings caused by revenues, expenses, gains, and losses. The number of accounts depends on the complexity of the company's operations.

An account includes the account title, an account number to aid the processing task, and columns or fields for increases, decreases, the cumulative balance, and the date. For instructional purposes we use **T-accounts** instead of formal ledger accounts. A T-account has space at the top for the account title and two sides for recording increases and decreases.

The *double-entry system* is used to process transactions.

A *general ledger* is a collection of storage areas, called *accounts,* used to keep track of increases and decreases in financial position elements.

Account Title

For centuries, accountants have effectively used a system of **debits** and **credits** to increase and decrease account balances in the ledger. Debits merely represent the *left* side of the account and credits the *right* side, as shown below.

In the double-entry system, *debit* means *left* side of an account and *credit* means *right* side of an account.

Account Title	
debit side	credit side

Whether a debit or a credit represents an increase or a decrease depends on the type of account. Accounts on the left side of the accounting equation (assets) are *increased* (+) by *debit* entries and *decreased* (−) by *credit* entries. Accounts on the right side of the accounting equation (liabilities and shareholders' equity) are *increased* (+) by *credit* entries and *decreased* (−) by *debit* entries. This arbitrary, but effective, procedure ensures that for each transaction the net impact on the left sides of accounts always equals the net impact on the right sides of accounts.

For example, consider the bank loan in our earlier illustration. An asset, cash, increased by $40,000. Increases in assets are *debits*. Liabilities also increased by $40,000. Increases in liabilities are *credits*.

Asset *increases* are entered on the *debit* side of accounts and *decreases* are entered on the *credit* side. Liability and equity account *increases* are *credits* and *decreases* are *debits.*

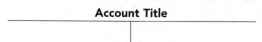

Assets		=	Liabilities	+	Owners' Equity

Cash			Note Payable	
debit	credit	debit		credit
40,000			40,000	
+				+

The debits equal the credits in every transaction (dual effect), so both before and after a transaction the accounting equation is in balance.

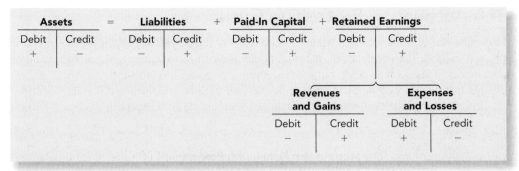

Prior exposure to the terms debit and credit probably comes from your experience with a bank account. For example, when a bank debits your checking account for service charges, it decreases your account balance. When you make a deposit, the bank credits your account, increasing your account balance. You must remember that from the bank's perspective, your bank account balance is a liability—it represents the amount that the bank owes you. Therefore, when the bank debits your account, it is decreasing its liability. When the bank credits your account, its liability increases.

Graphic 2–2 illustrates the relationship among the accounting equation, debits and credits, and the increases and decreases in financial position elements.

Notice that increases and decreases in retained earnings are recorded *indirectly*. For example, an expense represents a decrease in retained earnings, which requires a debit. That debit, however, is recorded in an appropriate expense account rather than in retained earnings itself. This allows the company to maintain a separate record of expenses incurred during an accounting period. The debit to retained earnings for the expense is recorded in a closing entry (reviewed later) at the end of the period, only after the expense total is reflected in the income statement. Similarly, an increase in retained earnings due to a revenue is recorded indirectly with a credit to a revenue account, which is later reflected as a credit to retained earnings.

The general ledger accounts serve as control accounts. Subsidiary accounts associated with a particular general ledger control account are maintained in separate subsidiary ledgers. For example, a subsidiary ledger for accounts receivable contains individual account receivable accounts for each of the company's credit customers. Subsidiary ledgers are discussed in more detail in Appendix 2C.

Each general ledger account can be classified as either *permanent* or *temporary*. **Permanent accounts** represent assets, liabilities, and shareholders' equity at a point in time. **Temporary accounts** represent changes in the retained earnings component of shareholders' equity for a corporation caused by revenue, expense, gain, and loss transactions. It would be cumbersome to record each revenue/expense, gain/loss transaction directly into the retained earnings account. The different types of events affecting retained earnings should be kept separate to facilitate the preparation of the financial statements. The balances in these temporary accounts are periodically, usually once a year, closed or zeroed out, and the net effect is recorded in the permanent retained earnings account. The temporary accounts need to be zeroed out to measure income on an annual basis. This closing process is discussed in a later section of this chapter.

Permanent accounts represent the basic financial position elements of the accounting equation.

Temporary accounts keep track of the changes in the retained earnings component of shareholders' equity.

CHECK WITH THE **COACH**

It's review time. The Coach is ready to help you review the accounting process. On the court or playing field, practicing the fundamentals makes you a winner. Understanding accounting fundamentals is vital to you for tackling the new challenges ahead in intermediate accounting. So work with the Coach to practice and reinforce your knowledge. ■

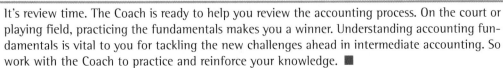

The Accounting Processing Cycle

Now that we've reviewed the basics of the double-entry system, let's look closer at the process used to identify, analyze, record, and summarize transactions and prepare financial statements. This section deals only with *external transactions,* those that involve an exchange transaction with another entity. Internal transactions are discussed in a later section.

The 10 steps in the accounting processing cycle are listed in Graphic 2–3:

GRAPHIC 2–3
The Accounting
Processing Cycle

The Steps of the Accounting Processing Cycle
1. Obtain information about external transactions from **source documents.**
2. **Analyze the transaction.**
3. Record the transaction in a **journal.**
4. **Post** from the journal to the general ledger.
5. Prepare an **unadjusted trial balance.**
6. Record **adjusting entries** and post to the general ledger accounts.
7. Prepare an **adjusted trial balance.**
8. Prepare **financial statements.**
9. **Close** the temporary accounts to retained earnings (at year-end only).
10. Prepare a **post-closing trial balance** (at year-end only).

We now discuss these steps in order.

STEP 1: Obtain information about transactions from *source documents.*

The first step in the process is to *identify* external transactions affecting the accounting equation. An accountant usually does not directly witness business transactions. A mechanism is needed to relay the essential information about each transaction to the accountant. **Source documents** such as sales invoices, bills from suppliers, and cash register tapes serve this need.

These source documents usually identify the date and nature of each transaction, the participating parties, and the monetary terms. For example, a sales invoice identifies the date of sale, the customer, the specific goods sold, the dollar amount of the sale, and the payment terms. With this information, the second step in the processing cycle, **transaction analysis,** can be accomplished. Transaction analysis is the process of reviewing the source documents to determine the dual effect on the accounting equation and the specific elements involved.

STEP 2: Analyze the transaction.

This process is summarized in Illustration 2–2 for the seven transactions described previously in Illustration 2–1.

STEP 3: Record the transaction in a *journal.*

The third step in the process is to record the transaction in a **journal.** Journals provide a chronological record of all economic events affecting a firm. Each journal entry is expressed in terms of equal debits and credits to accounts affected by the transaction being recorded. Debits and credits represent increases or decreases to specific accounts, depending on the type of account, as explained earlier. For example, for credit sales, a debit to accounts receivable and a credit to sales revenue is recorded in a sales journal.

A sales journal is an example of a **special journal** used to record a repetitive type of transaction. Appendix 2C discusses the use of special journals in more depth. In this chapter and throughout the text, we use the **general journal** format to record all transactions.

Any type of transaction can be recorded in a general journal. It has a place for the date of the transaction, a place for account titles, account numbers, and supporting explanations, a place for debit entries, and a place for credit entries. A simplified journal entry is used throughout the text that lists the account titles to be debited and credited and the dollar amounts. A common convention is to list the debited accounts first, indent the credited accounts, and use the first of two columns for the debit amounts and the second column for the credit amounts. For example, the **journal entry** for the bank loan in Illustration 2–1, which requires a debit to cash and a credit to note payable, is recorded as follows:

To record the borrowing of cash and the signing of a note payable.

Cash.	40,000	
Note payable.		40,000

ILLUSTRATION 2–2   Transaction Analysis, the Accounting Equation, and Debits and Credits

Transaction	Transaction Analysis	Accounting Equation			Account Entry
		Assets	= Liabilities +	Owners' Equity	

1. An attorney invested $50,000 to open a law office.

Assets (cash) and owners' equity each increased by $50,000.

Assets	= Liabilities +	Owners' Equity
+50,000		+50,000

Cumulative balances

50,000	=	50,000

Account Entry:

Cash		Owners' Equity	
50,000			50,000

2. $40,000 was borrowed from a bank and a note payable was signed.

Assets (cash) and liabilities (note payable) each increased by $40,000.

+40,000	+40,000	

Cumulative balances

90,000	= 40,000 +	50,000

Account Entry:

Cash		Note Payable	
50,000			40,000
40,000			

3. Supplies costing $3,000 were purchased on account.

Assets (supplies) and liabilities (accounts payable) each increased by $3,000.

+3,000	+3,000	

Cumulative balances

93,000	= 43,000 +	50,000

Account Entry:

Supplies		Accounts Payable	
3,000			3,000

4. Services were performed on account for $10,000.

Assets (accounts receivable) and owners' equity (revenue) each increased by $10,000.

+10,000		+10,000

Cumulative balances

103,000	= 43,000 +	60,000

Account Entry:

Accounts Receivable		Owners' Equity (Revenue)	
10,000			10,000

5. Salaries of $5,000 were paid to employees.

Assets (cash) and owners' equity decreased (salaries expense increased) by $5,000.

−5,000		−5,000

Cumulative balances

98,000	= 43,000 +	55,000

Account Entry:

Cash		Owners' Equity (Salaries Expense)	
40,000	5,000	5,000	
50,000			

6. $500 of supplies were used.

Assets (supplies) decreased and owners' equity decreased (supplies expense increased) by $500.

−500		−500

Cumulative balances

97,500	= 43,000 +	54,500

Account Entry:

Supplies		Owners' Equity (Supplies Expense)	
3,000	500	500	

7. $1,000 was paid on account to the supplies vendor.

Assets (cash) and liabilities (accounts payable) each decreased by $1,000.

−1,000	−1,000	

Cumulative balances

96,500	= 42,000 +	54,500

Account Entry:

Cash		Accounts Payable	
40,000	5,000	1,000	3,000
50,000	1,000		

STEP 4: *Post* from the
journal to the general
ledger accounts.

Step 4 is to periodically transfer or *post* the debit and credit information from the journal to individual ledger accounts. Recall that a ledger is simply a collection of all of the company's various accounts. Each account provides a summary of the effects of all events and transactions on that individual account. This process is called **posting.** Posting involves transferring debits and credits recorded in individual journal entries to the specific accounts affected. As discussed earlier in the chapter, most accounting systems today are computerized, with the journal and ledger kept on disk. For these systems, the journal input information is automatically and instantly posted to the ledger accounts.

These first four steps in the processing cycle are illustrated using the external transactions in Illustration 2–3 which occurred during the month of July 2003, the first month of operations for Dress Right Clothing Corporation. The company operates a retail store that sells men's and women's clothing. Dress Right is organized as a corporation so owners' equity is classified by source as either paid-in capital or retained earnings.

ILLUSTRATION 2–3			
External Transactions for July 2003	July	1	Two individuals each invested $30,000 in the corporation. Each investor was issued 3,000 shares of common stock.
		1	Borrowed $40,000 from a local bank and signed two notes. The first note for $10,000 requires payment of principal and 10% interest in six months. The second note for $30,000 requires the payment of principal in two years. Interest at 10% is payable each year on July 1, 2004, and July 1, 2005.
		1	Paid $24,000 in advance for one year's rent on the store building.
		1	Purchased furniture and fixtures from Acme Furniture for $12,000 cash.
		3	Purchased $60,000 of clothing inventory on account from the Birdwell Wholesale Clothing Company.
		6	Purchased $2,000 of supplies for cash.
		4–31	Sold merchandise costing $20,000 for $35,000 cash.
		9	Sold clothing on account to St. Jude's School for Girls for $3,500. The clothing cost $2,000.
		16	Subleased a portion of the building to a jewelry store. Received $1,000 in advance for the first two months' rent beginning on July 16.
		20	Paid Birdwell Wholesale Clothing $25,000 on account.
		20	Paid salaries to employees for the first half of the month, $5,000.
		25	Received $1,500 on account from St. Jude's.
		30	The corporation paid its shareholders a cash dividend of $1,000.

The local bank requires that Dress Right furnish financial statements on a monthly basis. The transactions listed in the illustration are used to demonstrate the accounting processing cycle for the month of July 2003.

For each transaction, a source document provides the necessary information to complete steps two and three in the processing cycle, transaction analysis and recording the appropriate journal entry. Each transaction listed in Illustration 2–3 is analyzed below, preceded by the necessary journal entry.

July 1		
Cash.	60,000	
Common stock		60,000

This first transaction is an investment by owners that increases an asset, cash, and also increases shareholders' equity. Increases in assets are recorded as debits and increases in shareholders' equity are recorded as credits. We use the paid-in capital account called common stock because stock was issued in exchange for cash paid in.[2]

---

[2]The different types of stock are discussed in Chapter 19.

July 1

Cash..	40,000	
Notes payable		40,000

This transaction causes increases in both cash and the liability, notes payable. Increases in assets are debits and increases in liabilities are credits. The notes require payment of $40,000 in principal and $6,500 ([$10,000 × 10% × 6/12 = $500] + [$30,000 × 10% × 2 years = $6,000]) in interest. However, at this point we are concerned only with the external transaction that occurs when the cash is borrowed and the notes are signed. Later we discuss how the interest is recorded.

July 1

Prepaid rent...	24,000	
Cash..		24,000

This transaction decreased cash (a credit) and increased an asset called prepaid rent, which is debited. Dress Right acquired the right to use the building for one full year. This is an asset because it represents a future benefit to the company. As we will see later, this asset expires over the one-year rental period.

July 1

Furniture and fixtures	12,000	
Cash..		12,000

This transaction increases one asset, furniture and fixtures, and decreases another, cash.

July 3

Inventory..	60,000	
Accounts payable		60,000

This purchase of merchandise on account is recorded by a debit to inventory, an asset, and a credit to accounts payable, a liability. Increases in assets are debits, and increases in liabilities are credits.

The Dress Right Clothing Company uses the *perpetual inventory system* to keep track of its merchandise inventory. This system requires that the cost of merchandise purchased be recorded in inventory, an asset account. When inventory is sold, the inventory account is decreased by the cost of the item sold. The alternative method, the periodic system, is briefly discussed on the next page, and Chapters 8 and 9 cover the topic of inventory in depth.

July 6

Supplies..	2,000	
Cash..		2,000

The acquisition of supplies is recorded as a debit to the asset account supplies (an increase) and a credit to the asset cash (a decrease). Supplies are recorded as an asset because they represent future benefits.

July 4–31

Cash..	35,000	
Sales revenue...		35,000
Cost of goods sold (expense)	20,000	
Inventory		20,000

During the month of July, cash sales to customers totaled $35,000. The company's assets (cash) increase by this amount as does shareholders' equity. This increase in equity is recorded by a credit to the temporary account sales revenue.

At the same time, an asset, inventory, decreases and retained earnings decreases. Recall that expenses are outflows or using up of assets from providing goods and services. Dress Right incurred an expense equal to the cost of the inventory sold. The temporary account cost of goods sold increases. However, this increase in an expense represents a *decrease* in shareholders' equity—retained earnings—and accordingly the account is debited. Both of these transactions are *summary* transactions. Each sale made during the month requires a separate and similar entry.

To record a credit sale and the cost of that sale.

July 9		
Accounts receivable	3,500	
Sales revenue		3,500
Cost of goods sold	2,000	
Inventory		2,000

This transaction is similar to the cash sale above. The only difference is that the asset acquired in exchange for merchandise is accounts receivable rather than cash.

ADDITIONAL CONSIDERATION

Periodic Inventory System

The principal alternative to the perpetual inventory system is the periodic system. This system requires that the cost of merchandise purchased be recorded in a temporary account called *purchases*. When inventory is sold, the inventory account is not decreased and cost of goods sold is not recorded. Cost of goods sold for a period is determined and the inventory account is adjusted only at the end of a reporting period.

For example, the purchase of $60,000 of merchandise on account by Dress Right Clothing is recorded as follows:

Purchases	60,000	
Accounts payable		60,000

No cost of goods sold entry is recorded when sales are made in the periodic system.

At the end of July, the amount of ending inventory is determined (either by means of a physical count of goods on hand or by estimation) to be $38,000 and cost of goods sold for the month is determined as follows:

Beginning inventory	-0-
Plus: Purchases	60,000
Less: Ending inventory	(38,000)
Cost of goods sold	22,000

The following journal entry records cost of goods sold for the period and adjusts the inventory account to the actual amount on hand (in this case from zero to $38,000):

Cost of goods sold	22,000	
Inventory	38,000	
Purchases		60,000

Inventory is discussed in depth in Chapters 8 and 9.

To record the receipt of rent in advance.

July 16		
Cash	1,000	
Unearned rent revenue (liability)		1,000

Cash increases by $1,000 so the cash account is debited. At this point, Dress Right does not recognize revenue even though cash has been received. Recall that the first criterion required for revenue recognition as stated in the realization principle is that the "earnings process is judged to be complete or virtually complete." Dress Right does not earn the revenue until it has provided the jewelry store with the use of facilities; that is, the revenue is earned as the rental period expires. On receipt of the cash, a liability called *unearned rent revenue* increases and is credited. This liability represents Dress Right's obligation to provide the use of facilities to the jewelry store.

July 20		
Accounts payable	25,000	
Cash.		25,000

To record the payment of accounts payable.

This transaction decreases both an asset (cash) and a liability (accounts payable). Decreases in assets are credits, and decreases in liabilities are debits.

July 20		
Salaries expense	5,000	
Cash.		5,000

To record the payment of salaries for the first half of the month.

Employees were paid for services rendered during the first half of the month. The cash expenditure did not create an asset since no future benefits result. Cash decreases and is credited; shareholders' equity decreases and is debited. The debit is recorded in the temporary account salaries expense.

July 25		
Cash.	1,500	
Accounts receivable		1,500

To record receipt of cash on account.

This transaction is an exchange of one asset, accounts receivable, for another asset, cash.

July 30		
Retained earnings	1,000	
Cash.		1,000

To record the payment of a cash dividend.

The payment of a cash dividend reduces both cash and retained earnings. An alternative is to debit a temporary account—dividends—that is closed to retained earnings at the end of the fiscal year along with the other temporary accounts.

Illustration 2–4 summarizes each of the transactions just discussed as they would appear in a general journal. In addition to the date, account titles, debit and credit columns, the journal also has a column titled Post Ref. (Posting Reference). This usually is a number assigned to the general ledger account that is being debited or credited. For purposes of this illustration, all asset accounts have been assigned numbers in the 100s, all liabilities are 200s, permanent shareholders' equity accounts are 300s, revenues are 400s, and expenses are 500s.

The ledger accounts also contain a posting reference, usually the page number of the journal in which the journal entry was recorded. This allows for easy cross-referencing between the journal and the ledger. Page 1 is used for Illustration 2–4.

Step 4 in the processing cycle is to transfer the debit/credit information from the journal to the general ledger accounts. Illustration 2–5 contains the ledger accounts (in T-account form) for Dress Right *after* all of the general journal transactions have been posted. The reference GJ1 next to each of the posted amounts indicates that the source of the entry is page 1 of the general journal.

Before financial statements are prepared and before adjusting entries are recorded (internal transactions) at the end of an accounting period, an **unadjusted trial balance** usually is

STEP 5: Prepare an unadjusted trial balance.

ILLUSTRATION 2–4					

		General Journal			Page 1
Date 2003		**Account Title and Explanation**	**Post Ref.**	**Debit**	**Credit**
July	1	Cash	100	60,000	
		Common stock	300		60,000
		To record the issuance of common stock.			
	1	Cash	100	40,000	
		Notes payable	220		40,000
		To record the borrowing of cash and the signing of notes payable.			
	1	Prepaid rent	130	24,000	
		Cash	100		24,000
		To record the payment of one year's rent in advance.			
	1	Furniture and fixtures	150	12,000	
		Cash	100		12,000
		To record the purchase of furniture and fixtures.			
	3	Inventory	140	60,000	
		Accounts payable	210		60,000
		To record the purchase of merchandise inventory.			
	6	Supplies	125	2,000	
		Cash	100		2,000
		To record the purchase of supplies.			
	4–31	Cash	100	35,000	
		Sales revenue	400		35,000
		To record cash sales for the month.			
	4–31	Cost of goods sold	500	20,000	
		Inventory	140		20,000
		To record the cost of cash sales.			
	9	Accounts receivable	110	3,500	
		Sales revenue	400		3,500
		To record credit sale.			
	9	Cost of goods sold	500	2,000	
		Inventory	140		2,000
		To record the cost of a credit sale.			
	16	Cash	100	1,000	
		Unearned rent revenue	230		1,000
		To record the receipt of rent in advance.			
	20	Accounts payable	210	25,000	
		Cash	100		25,000
		To record the payment of accounts payable.			
	20	Salaries expense	510	5,000	
		Cash	100		5,000
		To record the payment of salaries for the first half of the month.			
	25	Cash	100	1,500	
		Accounts receivable	110		1,500
		To record the receipt of cash on account.			
	30	Retained earnings	310	1,000	
		Cash	100		1,000
		To record the payment of a cash dividend.			

The General Journal

prepared—step 5. A trial balance is simply a list of the general ledger accounts and their balances at a particular date. Its purpose is to check for completeness and to prove that the sum of the accounts with debit balances equals the sum of the accounts with credit balances, that is, the accounting equation is in balance. The fact that the debits and credits are equal does not necessarily mean that the equal balances are correct. The trial balance could contain off-

ILLUSTRATION 2–5

General Ledger Accounts

Balance Sheet Accounts

Cash — 100

July 1 GJ1	60,000	24,000	July 1 GJ1
1 GJ1	40,000	12,000	1 GJ1
4–31GJ1	35,000	2,000	6 GJ1
16 GJ1	1,000	25,000	20 GJ1
25 GJ1	1,500	5,000	20 GJ1
		1,000	30 GJ1
July 31 Bal.	**68,500**		

Prepaid Rent — 130

July 1 GJ1	24,000		
July 31 Bal.	**24,000**		

Accounts Receivable — 110

July 9 GJ1	3,500	1,500	July 25 GJ1
July 31 Bal.	**2,000**		

Inventory — 140

July 3 GJ1	60,000	20,000	July 4–31
		2,000	9 GJ1
July 31 Bal.	**38,000**		

Supplies — 125

July 6 GJ1	2,000		
July 31 Bal.	**2,000**		

Furniture and Fixtures — 150

July 1 GJ1	12,000		
July 31 Bal.	**12,000**		

Accounts Payable — 210

July 20 GJ1	25,000	60,000	July 3 GJ1
		35,000	**July 31 Bal.**

Notes Payable — 220

		40,000	July 1 GJ1
		40,000	**July 31 Bal.**

Unearned Rent Revenue — 230

		1,000	July 16 GJ1
		1,000	**July 31 Bal.**

Common Stock — 300

		60,000	July 1 GJ1
		60,000	**July 31 Bal.**

Retained Earnings — 310

July 30 GJ1	1,000		
July 31 Bal.	**1,000**		

Income Statement Accounts

Sales Revenue — 400

		35,000	July 4–31
		3,500	9 GJ1
		38,500	**July 31 Bal.**

Cost of Goods Sold — 500

July 4–31GJ1	20,000		
July 9 GJ1	2,000		
July 31 Bal.	**22,000**		

Salaries Expense — 510

July 20 GJ1	5,000		
July 31 Bal.	**5,000**		

setting errors. As we will see later in the chapter, this trial balance also facilitates the preparation of adjusting entries.

The unadjusted trial balance at July 31, 2003, for the Dress Right Clothing Corporation appears in Illustration 2–6. Notice that retained earnings has a debit balance of $1,000. This reflects the payment of the cash dividend to shareholders. The increases and decreases in retained earnings from revenue, expense, gain and loss transactions are recorded indirectly in temporary accounts. Before the start of the next year, these increases and decreases are transferred to the retained earnings account.

ILLUSTRATION 2–6		
Unadjusted Trial Balance		

DRESS RIGHT CLOTHING CORPORATION
Unadjusted Trial Balance
July 31, 2003

Account Title	Debits	Credits
Cash	68,500	
Accounts receivable	2,000	
Supplies	2,000	
Prepaid rent	24,000	
Inventory	38,000	
Furniture and fixtures	12,000	
Accounts payable		35,000
Notes payable		40,000
Unearned rent revenue		1,000
Common stock		60,000
Retained earnings	1,000	
Sales revenue		38,500
Cost of goods sold	22,000	
Salaries expense	5,000	
Totals	174,500	174,500

At any time, the total of all debit balances should equal the total of all credit balances.

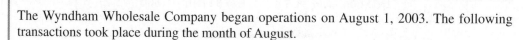

CONCEPT REVIEW EXERCISE

Journal Entries for External Transactions

The Wyndham Wholesale Company began operations on August 1, 2003. The following transactions took place during the month of August.

a. Owners invested $50,000 cash in the corporation in exchange for 5,000 shares of common stock.
b. Equipment is purchased for $20,000 cash.
c. On the first day of August, $6,000 rent on a building is paid for the months of August and September.
d. Merchandise inventory costing $38,000 is purchased on account. The company uses the perpetual inventory system.
e. $30,000 is borrowed from a local bank, and a note payable is signed.
f. Credit sales for the month are $40,000. The cost of merchandise sold is $22,000.
g. $15,000 is collected on account from customers.
h. $20,000 is paid on account to suppliers of merchandise.
i. Salaries of $7,000 are paid to employees for August.
j. A bill for $2,000 is received from the local utility company for the month of August.
k. $20,000 cash was loaned to another company, evidenced by a note receivable.
l. The corporation paid its shareholders a cash dividend of $1,000.

Required:
1. Prepare a journal entry for each transaction.
2. Prepare an unadjusted trial balance as of August 31, 2003.

1. Prepare a journal entry for each transaction.

    a. The issuance of common stock for cash increases both cash and shareholders' equity (common stock).

Cash.	50,000	
Common Stock		50,000

    b. The purchase of equipment increases equipment and decreases cash.

Equipment.	20,000	
Cash.		20,000

    c. The payment of rent in advance increases prepaid rent and decreases cash.

Prepaid rent.	6,000	
Cash.		6,000

    d. The purchase of merchandise on account increases both inventory and accounts payable.

Inventory	38,000	
Accounts payable		38,000

    e. Borrowing cash and signing a note increases both cash and note payable.

Cash.	30,000	
Note payable.		30,000

    f. The sale of merchandise on account increases both accounts receivable and sales revenue. Also, cost of goods sold increases and inventory decreases.

Accounts receivable	40,000	
Sales revenue.		40,000
Cost of goods sold	22,000	
Inventory		22,000

    g. The collection of cash on account increases cash and decreases accounts receivable.

Cash.	15,000	
Accounts receivable		15,000

    h. The payment of suppliers on account decreases both accounts payable and cash.

Accounts payable	20,000	
Cash.		20,000

    i. The payments of salaries for the period increases salaries expense (decreases retained earnings) and decreases cash.

Salaries expense	7,000	
Cash.		7,000

    j. The receipt of a bill for services rendered increases both an expense (utilities expense) and accounts payable.

| Utilities expense . . . . | 2,000 | |
| Accounts payable . . . . | | 2,000 |

k. The lending of cash to another entity and the signing of a note increases note receivable and decreases cash.

| Note receivable. . . . . | 20,000 | |
| Cash. . . . . | | 20,000 |

l. Cash dividends paid to shareholders reduce both retained earnings and cash.

| Retained earnings[3] . . . . | 1,000 | |
| Cash. . . . . | | 1,000 |

2. Prepare an unadjusted trial balance as of August 31, 2003.

Account Title	Debits	Credits
Cash	21,000	
Accounts receivable	25,000	
Prepaid rent	6,000	
Inventory	16,000	
Note receivable	20,000	
Equipment	20,000	
Accounts payable		20,000
Note payable		30,000
Common stock		50,000
Retained earnings	1,000	
Sales revenue		40,000
Cost of goods sold	22,000	
Salaries expense	7,000	
Utilities expense	2,000	
Totals	140,000	140,000

Adjusting Entries

STEP 6: Record *adjusting entries* and post to the ledger accounts.

FINANCIAL REPORTING CASE

Q1, p. 61

Step 6 in the processing cycle is to record in the general journal and post to the ledger accounts the effect of *internal events* on the accounting equation. These transactions do not involve an exchange transaction with another entity and, therefore, are not initiated by a source document. They are recorded *at the end of any period when financial statements must be prepared.* These transactions are commonly referred to as **adjusting entries.**

Even when all transactions and events are analyzed, corrected, journalized, and posted to appropriate ledger accounts, some account balances will require updating. Adjusting entries are required to implement the *accrual accounting model.* More specifically, these entries are required to satisfy the *realization principle* and the *matching principle.* Adjusting entries help ensure that all revenues earned in a period are recognized in that period, regardless of when the cash payment is received. Also, they enable a company to recognize all expenses incurred during a period, regardless of when cash payment is made. As a result, a period's income statement provides a more complete measure of a company's operating performance and a better measure for predicting future operating cash flows. The balance sheet also pro-

---

[3]An alternative is to debit a temporary account—dividends—that is closed to retained earnings at the end of the fiscal year along with the other temporary accounts.

vides a more complete assessment of assets and liabilities as sources of future cash receipts and disbursements. You might think of adjusting entries as a method of bringing the company's financial information up to date before preparing the financial statements.

Adjusting entries are necessary for three situations:

1. **Prepayments,** sometimes referred to as *deferrals*.
2. **Accruals.**
3. **Estimates.**

FINANCIAL REPORTING CASE

Q2, p. 61

LO4

PREPAYMENTS

Prepayments occur when the cash flow *precedes* either expense or revenue recognition. For example, a company may buy supplies in one period but use them in a later period. The cash outflow creates an asset (supplies) which then must be expensed in a future period as the asset is used up. Similarly, a company may receive cash from a customer in one period but provide the customer with a good or service in a future period. For instance, magazine publishers usually receive cash in advance for magazine subscriptions. The cash inflow creates a liability (unearned revenue) that is recognized as revenue in a future period when it is earned.

Prepayments are transactions in which the cash flow precedes expense or revenue recognition.

Prepaid Expenses. **Prepaid expenses** are the costs of assets acquired in one period and expensed in a future period. Whenever cash is paid, and it is not to (1) satisfy a liability or (2) pay a dividend or return capital to owners, it must be determined whether or not the payment creates future benefits or whether the payment benefits only the current period. The purchase of machinery, equipment, or supplies or the payment of rent in advance are examples of payments that create future benefits and should be recorded as assets. The benefits provided by these assets expire in future periods and their cost is expensed in future periods as related revenues are recognized.

Prepaid expenses represent assets recorded when a cash disbursement creates benefits beyond the current reporting period.

To illustrate this concept, assume that a company paid a radio station $2,000 in July for advertising. If that $2,000 were for advertising provided by the radio station during the month of July, the entire $2,000 would be expensed in the same period as the cash disbursement. If, however, the $2,000 was a payment for advertising to be provided in a future period, say the month of August, then the cash disbursement creates an asset called *prepaid advertising*. An adjusting entry is required at the end of August to increase advertising expense (decrease shareholders' equity) and to decrease the asset prepaid advertising by $2,000. Assuming that the cash disbursement records a debit to an asset, as in this example, the adjusting entry for a prepaid expense is, therefore, a *debit to an expense* and a *credit to an asset.*

The adjusting entry required for a prepaid expense is a debit to an expense and a credit to an asset.

The unadjusted trial balance can provide a starting point for determining which adjusting entries are required for a period, particularly for prepayments. Review the July 31, 2003, unadjusted trial balance for the Dress Right Clothing Corporation in Illustration 2–6 on page 74 and try to anticipate the required adjusting entries for prepaid expenses.

The first asset that requires adjustment is supplies, $2,000 of which were purchased during July. This transaction created an asset as the supplies will be used in future periods. The company could either track the supplies used or simply count the supplies at the end of the period and determine the dollar amount of supplies remaining. Assume that Dress Right determines that at the end of July, $1,200 of supplies remain. The following adjusting journal entry is required.

LO5

July 31		
Supplies expense	800	
Supplies.		800

To record the cost of supplies used during the month of July.

After this entry is recorded and posted to the ledger accounts, the supplies (asset) account is reduced to a $1,200 debit balance, and the supplies expense account will have an $800 debit balance.

The next prepaid expense requiring adjustment is rent. Recall that at the beginning of July, the company paid $24,000 to its landlord representing one year's rent in advance. As it

Supplies		
Beg. bal.	0	
	2,000	800
Bal.	1,200	

is reasonable to assume that the rent services provided each period are equal, the monthly rent is $2,000. At the end of July 2003, one month's prepaid rent has expired and must be recognized as expense.

To record the cost of expired rent for the month of July.

July 31		
Rent expense ($24,000 ÷ 12)...............................	2,000	
Prepaid rent...		2,000

Prepaid Rent		
Beg. bal. 0		
24,000	2,000	
Bal. 22,000		

After this entry is recorded and posted to the ledger accounts, the prepaid rent account will have a debit balance of $22,000, representing 11 remaining months at $2,000 a month, and the rent expense account will have a $2,000 debit balance.

The final prepayment involves the asset represented by furniture and fixtures that was purchased for $12,000. This asset has a long life but nevertheless will expire over time. For the previous two adjusting entries, it was fairly straightforward to determine the amount of the asset that expired during the period.

However, it is difficult, if not impossible, to determine how much of the benefits from using the furniture and fixtures expired during any particular period. Recall from Chapter 1 that one approach to implementing the matching principle is to "recognize an expense by a systematic and rational allocation to specific time periods."

Assume that the furniture and fixtures have a useful life of five years or 60 months and will be worthless at the end of that period, and that we choose to allocate the cost equally over the period of use. The amount of monthly expense, called *depreciation expense,* is $200 ($12,000 ÷ 60 months = $200), and the following adjusting entry is recorded.

To record depreciation of furniture and fixtures for the month of July.

July 31		
Depreciation expense.....................................	200	
Accumulated depreciation—furniture and fixtures.............		200

The entry reduces an asset, furniture and fixtures, by $200. However, the asset account is not reduced directly. Instead, the credit is to an account called *accumulated depreciation.* This is a contra account to furniture and fixtures. The normal balance in a contra asset account will be a credit, that is, "contra," or opposite, to the normal debit balance in an asset account. The purpose of the contra account is to keep the original cost of the asset intact while reducing it indirectly. In the balance sheet, furniture and fixtures is reported net of accumulated depreciation. This topic is covered in depth in Chapter 11.

After this entry is recorded and posted to the ledger accounts, the accumulated depreciation account will have a credit balance of $200 and the depreciation expense account will have a $200 debit balance. If a required adjusting entry for a prepaid expense is not recorded, net income, assets, and shareholders' equity (retained earnings) will be overstated.

Unearned revenues represent liabilities recorded when cash is received from customers in advance of providing a good or service.

Unearned Revenues. **Unearned revenues** are created when a company receives cash from a customer in one period for goods or services that are to be provided in a future period. The cash receipt, an external transaction, is recorded as a debit to cash and a credit to a liability. This liability reflects the company's obligation to provide goods or services in the future.

To illustrate an unearned revenue transaction, assume that during the month of June a magazine publisher received $24 in cash for a 24-month subscription to a monthly magazine. The subscription begins in July. On receipt of the cash, the publisher records a liability, unearned subscription revenue, of $24. Subsequently, revenue of $1 is earned as each monthly magazine is published and mailed to the customer. An adjusting entry is required each month to increase shareholders' equity (revenue) to recognize the $1 in revenue earned and to decrease the liability. Assuming that the cash receipt records a credit to a liability, the adjusting entry for unearned revenues, therefore, is a *debit to a liability,* in this case unearned subscription revenue, and a *credit to revenue.*

The adjusting entry required when unearned revenues are earned is a debit to a liability and a credit to revenue.

Once again, the unadjusted trial balance provides information concerning unearned revenues. For Dress Right Clothing Corporation, the only unearned revenue in the trial balance is unearned rent revenue. Recall that the company subleased a portion of its building to a jewelry store for $500 per month. On July 16, the jewelry store paid Dress Right $1,000 in advance for the first two months' rent. The transaction was recorded as a debit to cash and a credit to unearned rent revenue.

At the end of July, how much of the $1,000 has been earned? Approximately one-half of one month's rent has been earned, or $250, requiring the following adjusting journal entry.

July 31

Unearned rent revenue..	250	
Rent revenue...		250

To record the amount of unearned rent revenue earned during July.

Unearned Rent Revenue

		0 Beg. bal.
250	1,000	
		750 End bal.

After this entry is recorded and posted to the ledger accounts, the unearned rent revenue account is reduced to a credit balance of $750 for the remaining one and one-half months' rent, and the rent revenue account will have a $250 credit balance. If this entry is not recorded, net income and shareholders' equity (retained earnings) will be understated, and liabilities will be overstated.

Alternative Approach to Record Prepayments. The same end result can be achieved for prepayments by recording the external transaction directly into an expense or revenue account. In fact, many companies prefer this approach. For simplicity, bookkeeping instructions may require all cash payments for expenses to be debited to the appropriate expense account and all cash receipts for revenues to be credited to the appropriate revenue account. The adjusting entry then records the *unexpired* prepaid expense (asset) or *unearned* revenue (liability) as of the end of the period.

For example, on July 1, 2003, Dress Right paid $24,000 in cash for one year's rent on its building. The entry included a debit to prepaid rent. The company could have debited rent expense instead.

Alternative Approach:

July 1

Rent expense	24,000	
Cash.......................................		24,000

Rent Expense

Beg. bal.	0	
	24,000	22,000
End bal.	2,000	

The adjusting entry then records the amount of prepaid rent as of the end of July, $22,000, and reduces rent expense to $2,000, the cost of rent for the month of July.

Alternative Approach:

July 31

Prepaid rent.......................................	22,000	
Rent expense.......................................		22,000

Prepaid Rent

Beg. bal.	0	
	22,000	
End bal.	22,000	

The net effect of handling the transactions in this manner is the same as the previous treatment. Either way, the prepaid rent account will have a debit balance at the end of July of $22,000, and the rent expense account will have a debit balance of $2,000. What's important is that an adjusting entry is recorded to ensure the appropriate amounts are reflected in both the expense and asset *before financial statements are to be prepared.*

Similarly, the July 16 cash receipt from the jewelry store representing an advance for two months' rent could have been recorded by Dress Right as a credit to rent revenue instead of unearned rent revenue (a liability).

Alternative approach:

July 16

Cash.......................................	1,000	
Rent revenue		1,000

If Dress Right records the entire $1,000 as rent revenue in this way, it would then use the adjusting entry to record the amount of unearned revenue as of the end of July, $750, and reduce rent revenue to $250, the amount of revenue earned during the month of July.

Alternative approach:

July 31

Rent revenue..	750	
Unearned rent revenue		750

ACCRUALS

Accruals involve transactions where the cash outflow or inflow takes place in a period subsequent to expense or revenue recognition.

Accruals occur when the cash flow comes *after* either expense or revenue recognition. For example, a company often uses the services of another entity in one period and pays for them in a subsequent period. An expense must be recognized in the period incurred and an accrued liability recorded. Also, goods and services often are provided to customers on credit. In such instances, a revenue is recognized in the period earned and an asset, a receivable, is recorded.

Many accruals involve external transactions that automatically are recorded from a source document. For example, a sales invoice for a credit sale provides all the information necessary to record the debit to accounts receivable and the credit to sales revenue. However, there are some accruals that involve internal transactions and thus require adjusting entries. Because accruals involve recognition of expense or revenue before cash flow, the unadjusted trial balance will not be as helpful in identifying required adjusting entries as with prepayments.

Accrued liabilities represent liabilities recorded when an expense has been incurred prior to cash payment.

Accrued Liabilities. For **accrued liabilities,** we are concerned with expenses incurred but not yet paid. Dress Right Clothing Corporation requires two adjusting entries for accrued liabilities at July 31, 2003.

The first entry is for employee salaries for the second half of July. Recall that on July 20 the company paid employees $5,000 for salaries for the first half of the month. Salaries for the second half of July will probably be paid in early August. Nevertheless, the company incurred an expense in July for services provided to it by its employees. Also, there exists an obligation at the end of July to pay the salaries earned by employees. An adjusting entry is required to increase salaries expense (decrease shareholders' equity) and to increase liabilities for the salaries payable. The adjusting entry for an accrued liability always includes a *debit to an expense,* and a *credit to a liability.* Assuming that salaries for the second half of July are $5,500, the following adjusting entry is recorded.

The adjusting entry required to record an accrued liability is a debit to an expense *and a* credit to a liability.

To record accrued salaries at the end of July.

July 31

Salaries expense	5,500	
Salaries payable..		5,500

After this entry is recorded and posted to the general ledger, the salaries expense account will have a debit balance of $10,500 ($5,000 + 5,500), and the salaries payable account will have a credit balance of $5,500.

The unadjusted trial balance does provide information about the second required accrued liability entry. In the trial balance we can see a balance in the notes payable account of $40,000. The company borrowed this amount on July 1, 2003. Both notes require the payment of 10% interest. Whenever the trial balance reveals interest-bearing debt, and interest is not paid on the last day of the period, an adjusting entry is required for the amount of interest that has built up (accrued) since the last payment date or the last date interest was accrued. In this case, we calculate interest as follows:

Salaries Payable

	0 Beg. bal.
	5,500
	5,500 End bal.

$$\text{Principal} \times \text{Interest rate} \times \text{Time} = \text{Interest}$$
$$\$40,000 \times \quad 10\% \quad \times \quad \tfrac{1}{12} \; = \$333 \text{ (rounded)}$$

Interest rates always are stated as the annual rate. Therefore, the above calculation uses this annual rate multiplied by the principal amount multiplied by the amount of time outstanding, in this case one month or one-twelfth of a year.

July 31
Interest expense   333
   Interest payable.   333

After this entry is recorded and posted to the ledger accounts, the interest expense account will have a debit balance $333, and the interest payable account will have a credit balance of $333.[4] Failure to record a required adjusting entry for an accrued liability will cause net income and shareholders' equity (retained earnings) to be overstated, and liabilities to be understated.

Accrued Receivables.   Accrued receivables involve the recognition of revenue earned before cash is received. An example of an internal accrued revenue event is the recognition of interest earned on a loan to another entity. For example, assume that Dress Right loaned another corporation $30,000 at the beginning of August, evidenced by a note receivable. Terms of the note call for the payment of principal, $30,000, and interest at 8% in three months. An external transaction records the cash disbursement—a debit to note receivable and a credit to cash of $30,000.

Accrued receivables involve situations when the revenue is earned in a period prior to the cash receipt.

What adjusting entry would be required at the end of August? Dress Right needs to record the interest revenue earned but not yet received and the corresponding receivable. Interest receivable increases and interest revenue (shareholders' equity) also increases. The adjusting entry for accrued receivables always includes a *debit to an asset,* a receivable, and a *credit to revenue.* In this case, at the end of August Dress Right recognizes $200 in interest revenue ($30,000 $\times$ 8% $\times$ $\frac{1}{12}$) and makes the following adjusting entry. If this entry is not recorded, net income, assets, and shareholders' equity (retained earnings) will be understated.

The adjusting entry required to record an accrued revenue is a debit to an asset, a receivable, and a credit to revenue.

August 31
Interest receivable.   200
   Interest revenue.   200

There are no accrued revenue adjusting entries required for Dress Right at the end of July.

The required adjusting entries for prepayments and accruals are recapped in Graphic 2–4. Each case involves recognizing an expense or revenue in a period that differs from the period in which cash was paid or received. These entries are necessary to properly measure operating performance and financial position according to the accrual accounting model.

GRAPHIC 2–4
Adjusting Entries

	Adjusting Entries			
	Expenses		**Revenues**	
Prepayments	Debit	Expense	Debit	Liability
(initially recorded as assets or liabilities)	Credit	Asset	Credit	Revenue
Prepayments	Debit	Asset	Debit	Revenue
(initially recorded as expenses or revenues)	Credit	Expense	Credit	Liability
Accruals	Debit	Expense	Debit	Asset
	Credit	Liability	Credit	Revenue

---

[4]Dress Right Clothing is a corporation. Corporations are income-tax-paying entities. Income taxes—federal, state and local— are assessed on an annual basis and payments are made throughout the year. An additional adjusting entry would be required for Dress Right to accrue the amount of estimated income taxes payable that are applicable to the month of July. Accounting for income taxes is introduced in Chapter 4 and covered in depth in Chapter 16.

ESTIMATES

A third classification of adjusting entries is **estimates.** Accountants often must make estimates of future events to comply with the accrual accounting model. For example, the calculation of depreciation expense requires an estimate of expected useful life of the asset being depreciated as well as its expected residual value. We discussed the adjusting entries for depreciation expense in the context of its being a prepayment, but it also could be thought of as an estimate.

One situation involving an estimate that does not fit neatly into either the prepayment or accrual classification is **bad debt expense.** Chapter 1 introduced briefly the allowance method of accounting for bad debts. This method requires an estimate of the amount of accounts receivable that will ultimately prove to be uncollectible. This estimate is required to properly match the bad debt expense with the revenue it helps generate as well as reflect the collectible portion of the receivable on the balance sheet.

The July 31, 2003, unadjusted trial balance for Dress Right shows a balance in accounts receivable of $2,000. Assume that the company's management felt that of this amount, only $1,500 would ultimately be collected. An adjusting entry is required to decrease accounts receivable and increase bad debt expense (decrease shareholders' equity) by $500. The adjusting entry is:

July 31		
Bad debt expense.	500	
Allowance for uncollectible accounts		500

Notice that the accounts receivable account is not reduced directly. A contra account, called *allowance for uncollectible accounts,* is credited. After this entry is recorded and posted to the ledger accounts, bad debt expense will have a debit balance of $500 and the allowance for uncollectible accounts account will have a credit balance of $500.[5]

The contra account is used to keep intact in the accounts receivable account the total amount of receivables that are still outstanding. The allowance account will always have a credit balance equal to estimated bad debts on existing accounts receivable. Only when the account is actually written off as uncollectible would accounts receivable be reduced. At this point, the $500 is just an estimate. In the balance sheet, accounts receivable is shown net of the allowance account, in this case $1,500. Chapter 7 addresses the topics of accounts receivable and bad debts in more depth.

Illustration 2–7 recaps the July 31, 2003, adjusting entries for Dress Right Clothing Corporation as they would appear in a general journal.

After the adjusting entries are posted to the general ledger accounts, the next step—step 7—in the processing cycle is to prepare an **adjusted trial balance.** The term adjusted refers to the fact that adjusting entries have now been posted to the accounts. Recall that the column titled Post Ref. (Posting Reference) is the number assigned to the general ledger account that is being debited or credited. Illustration 2–8 shows the July 31, 2003, adjusted trial balance for Dress Right Clothing Corporation.

---

[5]If the allowance for uncollectible accounts had a credit balance before the adjusting entry, say $150, then the adjusting entry would have required only a $350 debit to bad debt expense and credit to the allowance account.

ILLUSTRATION 2–7

The General Journal—Adjusting Entries

DRESS RIGHT CLOTHING CORPORATION

General Journal — Page 2

Date 2003	Account Title and Explanation	Post Ref.	Debit	Credit
July 31	Supplies expense	520	800	
	Supplies	125		800
	To record the cost of supplies used during the month of July.			
31	Rent expense	530	2,000	
	Prepaid rent	130		2,000
	To record the cost of expired rent for the month of July.			
31	Depreciation expense	540	200	
	Accumulated depreciation—furniture and fixtures	155		200
	To record depreciation for furniture and fixtures for the month of July.			
31	Unearned rent revenue	230	250	
	Rent revenue	410		250
	To record the amount of unearned rent revenue earned during July.			
31	Salaries expense	510	5,500	
	Salaries payable	230		5,500
	To record accrued salaries at the end of July.			
31	Interest expense	550	333	
	Interest payable	240		333
	To accrue interest expense for July on notes payable.			
31	Bad debt expense	560	500	
	Allowance for uncollectible accounts	115		500
	To record bad debt expense for July.			

DRESS RIGHT CLOTHING CORPORATION
Adjusted Trial Balance
July 31, 2003

Account Title	Debits	Credits
Cash	68,500	
Accounts receivable	2,000	
Allowance for uncollectible accounts		500
Supplies	1,200	
Prepaid rent	22,000	
Inventory	38,000	
Furniture and fixtures	12,000	
Accumulated depreciation—furniture and fixtures		200
Accounts payable		35,000
Notes payable		40,000
Unearned rent revenue		750
Salaries payable		5,500
Interest payable		333
Common stock		60,000
Retained earnings	1,000	
Sales revenue		38,500
Rent revenue		250
Cost of goods sold	22,000	
Salaries expense	10,500	
Supplies expense	800	
Rent expense	2,000	
Depreciation expense	200	
Interest expense	333	
Bad debt expense	500	
Totals	181,033	181,033

CONCEPT REVIEW EXERCISE

Adjusting
Entries

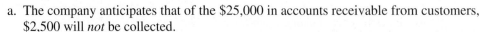

The Wyndham Wholesale Company needs to prepare financial statements at the end of August 2003 for presentation to its bank. An unadjusted trial balance as of August 31, 2003, was presented in a previous concept review exercise on page 76.

The following information also is available:

a. The company anticipates that of the $25,000 in accounts receivable from customers, $2,500 will *not* be collected.

b. The note payable requires the entire $30,000 in principal plus interest at 10% to be paid on July 31, 2004. The date of the loan is August 1, 2003.

c. Depreciation on the equipment for the month of August is $500.

d. The note receivable is dated August 16, 2003. The note requires the entire $20,000 in principal plus interest at 12% to be repaid in four months (the loan was outstanding for one-half month during August).

e. The prepaid rent of $6,000 represents rent for the months of August and September.

Required:

1. Prepare any necessary adjusting entries at August 31, 2003.
2. Prepare an adjusted trial balance as of August 31, 2003.
3. What is the total net effect on income (overstated or understated) if the adjusting entries are not made?

SOLUTION

1. Prepare any necessary adjusting entries at August 31, 2003.

a. An adjusting entry is required to adjust allowance for uncollectible accounts to $2,500. Because there is no balance in the allowance account before adjustment, the adjusting entry must record a bad debt expense of $2,500.

Bad debt expense..	2,500	
Allowance for uncollectible accounts		2,500

b. An adjusting entry is required to accrue the interest expense on the note payable for the month of August. Accrued interest is calculated as follows:

$$\$30,000 \times 10\% \times 1/12 = \$250$$

Interest expense	250	
Interest payable...		250

c. Depreciation expense on the equipment must be recorded.

Depreciation expense......................................	500	
Accumulated depreciation—equipment....................		500

d. An adjusting entry is required for the one-half month of accrued interest revenue earned on the note receivable. Accrued interest is calculated as follows:

$$\$20,000 \times 12\% \times 1/12 \times 1/2 = \$100$$

Interest receivable..	100	
Interest revenue..		100

e. An adjusting entry is required to recognize the amount of prepaid rent that expired during August.

Rent expense	3,000	
Prepaid rent.		3,000

2. Prepare an adjusted trial balance as of August 31, 2003.

Account Title	Debits	Credits
Cash	21,000	
Accounts receivable	25,000	
Allowance for uncollectible accounts		2,500
Prepaid rent	3,000	
Inventory	16,000	
Interest receivable	100	
Note receivable	20,000	
Equipment	20,000	
Accumulated depreciation—equipment		500
Accounts payable		20,000
Interest payable		250
Note payable		30,000
Common stock		50,000
Retained earnings	1,000	
Sales revenue		40,000
Interest revenue		100
Cost of goods sold	22,000	
Salaries expense	7,000	
Utilities expense	2,000	
Bad debt expense	2,500	
Interest expense	250	
Depreciation expense	500	
Rent expense	3,000	
Totals	143,350	143,350

3. What is the effect on income (overstated or understated), if the adjusting entries are not made?

Adjusting Entry	Income Overstated (understated)
Bad debt expense	$2,500
Interest expense	250
Depreciation expense	500
Interest revenue	(100)
Rent expense	3,000
Net effect, income overstated by	$6,150

We now turn our attention to the preparation of financial statements.

Preparing the Financial Statements

The purpose of each of the steps in the processing cycle to this point is to provide information for step 8—preparation of the **financial statements.** The adjusted trial balance contains the necessary information. After all, the financial statements are the primary means of communicating financial information to external parties.

LO6

STEP 8: Preparation of
financial statements.

The *income statement* is a *change* statement that summarizes the profit-generating transactions that caused shareholders' equity (retained earnings) to change during the period.

THE INCOME STATEMENT

The purpose of the **income statement** is to summarize the profit-generating activities of a company that occurred during a particular period of time. It is a *change* statement in that it reports the changes in shareholders' equity (retained earnings) that occurred during the period as a result of revenues, expenses, gains, and losses. Illustration 2–9 shows the income statement for Dress Right Clothing Corporation for the month of July 2003.

ILLUSTRATION 2–9

Income Statement

DRESS RIGHT CLOTHING CORPORATION
Income Statement
For the Month of July, 2003

Sales revenue		$38,500
Cost of goods sold		22,000
Gross profit		16,500
Operating expenses:		
Salaries expense	$10,500	
Supplies expense	800	
Rent expense	2,000	
Depreciation expense	200	
Bad debt expense	500	
Total operating expenses		14,000
Operating income		2,500
Other income (expense):		
Rent revenue	250	
Interest expense	(333)	(83)
Net income		$ 2,417

The income statement indicates a profit for the month of July of $2,417. During the month, the company was able to increase its net assets (equity) from activities related to selling its product. Dress Right is a corporation and subject to the payment of income tax on its profits. We ignore this required accrual here and address income taxes in a later chapter.

The components of the income statement usually are classified, that is, grouped according to common characteristics. A common classification scheme is to separate operating items from nonoperating items, as we do in Dress Right's income statement. Operating items include revenues and expenses directly related to the principal revenue-generating activities of the company. For example, operating items for a manufacturing company include sales revenues from the sale of products and all expenses related to this activity. Companies that sell products like Dress Right often report a subtotal within operating income, sales less cost of goods sold, called *gross profit.* Nonoperating items include gains and losses and revenues and expenses from peripheral activities. For Dress Right Clothing, rent revenue and interest expense are nonoperating items because they do not relate to the principal revenue-generating activity of the company, selling clothes. In Chapter 4 we discuss the format and content of the income statement in more depth.

The *balance sheet* is a position statement that presents an organized list of assets, liabilities and equity at a particular point in time.

THE BALANCE SHEET

The purpose of the **balance sheet** is to present the financial position of the company on a particular date. Unlike the income statement, which is a change statement reporting events that occurred *during a period of time,* the balance sheet is a statement that presents an organized list of assets, liabilities, and shareholders' equity *at a point in time.* To provide a quick overview, Illustration 2–10 shows the balance sheet for Dress Right Clothing at July 31, 2003.

As we do in the income statement, we group the balance sheet elements into meaningful categories. For example, most balance sheets include the classifications of **current assets** and **current liabilities.** Current assets are those assets that are cash, will be converted into cash, or will be used up within one year or the operating cycle, whichever is longer. Current liabilities are those liabilities that will be satisfied within one year or the operating cycle,

DRESS RIGHT CLOTHING CORPORATION		

ILLUSTRATION 2–10

Balance Sheet

DRESS RIGHT CLOTHING CORPORATION
Balance Sheet
At July 31, 2003

Assets

Current assets:		
Cash		$ 68,500
Accounts receivable	$ 2,000	
Less: Allowance for uncollectible accounts	500	1,500
Supplies		1,200
Inventory		38,000
Prepaid rent		22,000
Total current assets		131,200
Property and equipment:		
Furniture and fixtures	12,000	
Less: Accumulated depreciation	200	11,800
Total assets		$143,000

Liabilities and Shareholders' Equity

Current liabilities:		
Accounts payable		$ 35,000
Salaries payable		5,500
Unearned rent revenue		750
Interest payable		333
Note payable		10,000
Total current liabilities		51,583
Long-term liabilities:		
Note payable		30,000
Shareholders' equity:		
Common stock, 6,000 shares issued and outstanding	$60,000	
Retained earnings	1,417*	
Total shareholders' equity		61,417
Total liabilities and shareholders' equity		$143,000

*Beginning retained earnings + Net income − Dividends
        0   + $2,417   −   1,000   = $1,417

whichever is longer. For a manufacturing company, the operating cycle refers to the period of time necessary to convert cash to raw materials, raw materials to a finished product, the finished product to receivables, and then finally receivables back to cash. For most companies, this period is less than a year.

Balance sheet items usually are classified (grouped) according to common characteristics.

Examples of assets not classified as current include property and equipment and long-term receivables and investments. The only noncurrent asset that Dress Right has at July 31, 2003, is furniture and fixtures, which is classified under the property and equipment category.

All liabilities not classified as current are listed as long term. Dress Right's liabilities at July 31, 2003, include the $30,000 note payable due to be paid in 23 months. This liability is classified as long term.

Shareholders' equity lists the *paid-in capital* portion of equity—common stock—and *retained earnings*. Notice that the income statement we looked at in Illustration 2–9 ties in to the balance sheet through retained earnings. Specifically, the revenue, expense, gain, and loss transactions that make up net income in the income statement ($2,417) become the major components of retained earnings. Later in the chapter we discuss the closing process we use to transfer, or close, these *temporary* income statement accounts to the *permanent* retained earnings account.

During the month, retained earnings, which increased by the amount of net income, also decreased by the amount of the cash dividend paid to shareholders, $1,000. The net effect of these two changes is an increase in retained earnings from zero at the beginning of the period to $1,417 ($2,417 − 1,000) at the end of the period and is also reported in the statement of shareholders' equity in Illustration 2–12 on page 89.

THE STATEMENT OF CASH FLOWS

The purpose of the *statement of cash flows* is to summarize the transactions that caused cash to change during the period.

Similar to the income statement, the **statement of cash flows** also is a change statement, disclosing the events that caused cash to change during the period. The statement classifies all transactions affecting cash into one of three categories: (1) **operating activities,** (2) **investing activities,** and (3) **financing activities.** Operating activities are inflows and outflows of cash related to transactions entering into the determination of net income. Investing activities involve the acquisition and sale of (1) long-term assets used in the business and (2) nonoperating investment assets. Financing activities involve cash inflows and outflows from transactions with creditors and owners.

The statement of cash flows for Dress Right for the month of July 2003 is shown in Illustration 2–11. As this is the first period of operations for Dress Right, the cash balance at the beginning of the period is zero. The net increase in cash of $68,500, therefore, equals the ending balance of cash disclosed in the balance sheet.

ILLUSTRATION 2–11 Statement of Cash Flows	**DRESS RIGHT CLOTHING CORPORATION** **Statement of Cash Flows** **For the Month of July 2003**

DRESS RIGHT CLOTHING CORPORATION
Statement of Cash Flows
For the Month of July 2003

Cash Flows from Operating Activities		
Cash inflows:		
From customers	$36,500	
From rent	1,000	
Cash outflows:		
For rent	(24,000)	
For supplies	(2,000)	
To suppliers of merchandise	(25,000)	
To employees	(5,000)	
Net cash used by operating activities		$(18,500)
Cash Flows from Investing Activities		
Purchase of furniture and fixtures		(12,000)
Cash Flows from Financing Activities		
Issue of common stock	$60,000	
Increase in notes payable	40,000	
Payment of cash dividend	(1,000)	
Net cash provided by financing activities		99,000
Net increase in cash		$68,500

There are two generally accepted formats that can be used to report operating activities, the direct method and the indirect method. In Illustration 2–11 we use the direct method. These two methods are discussed and illustrated in subsequent chapters.

THE STATEMENT OF SHAREHOLDERS' EQUITY

The *statement of shareholders' equity* discloses the sources of changes in the permanent shareholders' equity accounts.

The final statement, the **statement of shareholders' equity,** also is a change statement. It discloses the sources of the changes in the various permanent shareholders' equity accounts that occurred during the period. Illustration 2–12 shows the statement of shareholders' equity for Dress Right for the month of July 2003.[6]

---

[6]Some companies choose to disclose the changes in the retained earnings component of shareholders' equity in a separate statement or in a combined statement of income and retained earnings.

ILLUSTRATION 2–12

Statement of
Shareholders' Equity

DRESS RIGHT CLOTHING CORPORATION
Statement of Shareholders' Equity
For the Month of July 2003

	Common Stock	Retained Earnings	Total Shareholders' Equity
Balance at July 1, 2003	-0-	-0-	-0-
Issue of common stock	$60,000		$60,000
Net income for July 2003		$2,417	2,417
Less: Dividends		(1,000)	(1,000)
Balance at July 31, 2003	$60,000	$1,417	$61,417

The individual profit-generating transactions causing retained earnings to change are summarized in the income statement. Therefore, the statement of shareholders' equity only shows the net effect of these transactions on retained earnings, in this case an increase of $2,417. In addition, the company paid its shareholders a cash dividend that reduced retained earnings.

The Closing Process

At the end of any interim reporting period, the accounting processing cycle is now complete. An interim reporting period is any period when financial statements are produced other than at the end of the fiscal year. However, at the end of the fiscal year, two final steps are necessary, closing the temporary accounts—step 9—and preparing a post-closing trial balance—step 10.

The **closing process** serves a *dual purpose:* (1) the temporary accounts (revenues, expenses, gains and losses) are reduced to *zero balances,* ready to measure activity in the upcoming accounting period, and (2) these temporary account balances are *closed (transferred) to retained earnings* to reflect the changes that have occurred in that account during the period. Often, an intermediate step is to close revenues and expenses to **income summary**; then income summary is closed to retained earnings. The use of the income summary account is just a bookkeeping convenience that provides a check that all temporary accounts have been properly closed (that is, the balance equals net income or loss).

To illustrate the closing process, assume that the fiscal year-end for Dress Right Clothing Corporation is July 31. Using the adjusted trial balance in Illustration 2–8, we can prepare the following general journal entries.

STEP 9: *Close the temporary accounts to retained earnings (at year-end only).*

LO7

July 31

Sales revenue	38,500	
Rent revenue	250	
Income summary		38,750

To close the revenue accounts to income summary.

The first closing entry transfers the revenue account balances to income summary. Because revenue accounts have credit balances, they are debited to bring them to zero. After this entry is posted to the accounts, both revenue accounts have a zero balance.

July 31

Income summary	36,333	
Cost of goods sold		22,000
Salaries expense		10,500
Supplies expense		800
Rent expense		2,000
Depreciation expense		200
Interest expense		333
Bad debt expense		500

To close the expense accounts to income summary.

The second closing entry transfers the expense account balances to income summary. As expense accounts have debit balances, they are credited to bring them to zero. After this entry is posted to the accounts, the expense accounts have a zero balance and the income summary account has a credit balance equal to net income for the period, in this case $2,417.

Income Summary

Expenses	36,333	38,750	Revenues
		2,417	Net

To close the income summary account to retained earnings.

July 31

Income summary	2,417	
Retained earnings		2,417

After this entry is posted to the accounts, the temporary accounts have zero balances and retained earnings has increased by the amount of the net income. It is important to remember that the temporary accounts are closed only at year-end and not at the end of any interim period. Closing the temporary accounts during the year would make it difficult to prepare the annual income statement.

Step 10: Prepare a *post-closing trial balance* (at year-end only).

After the closing entries are posted to the ledger accounts, a **post-closing trial balance** is prepared. The purpose of this trial balance is to verify that the closing entries were prepared and posted correctly and that the accounts are now ready for next year's transactions. Illustration 2–13 shows the post-closing trial balance for Dress Right at July 31, 2003, assuming a July 31 fiscal year-end.

ILLUSTRATION 2–13

Post-Closing Trial Balance

DRESS RIGHT CLOTHING CORPORATION
Post-Closing Trial Balance
July 31, 2003

Account Title	Debits	Credits
Cash	68,500	
Accounts receivable	2,000	
Allowance for uncollectible accounts		500
Supplies	1,200	
Prepaid rent	22,000	
Inventory	38,000	
Furniture and fixtures	12,000	
Accumulated depreciation—furniture and fixtures		200
Accounts payable		35,000
Notes payable		40,000
Unearned rent revenue		750
Salaries payable		5,500
Interest payable		333
Common stock		60,000
Retained earnings		1,417
Totals	143,700	143,700

Refer to the August 31, 2003, adjusted trial balance of the Wyndham Wholesale Company presented in a previous concept review exercise on page 85.

Required:
1. Prepare an income statement and a statement of shareholders' equity for the month ended August 31, 2003, and a classified balance sheet as of August 31, 2003.
2. Assume that August 31 is the company's fiscal year-end. Prepare the necessary closing entries and a post-closing trial balance.

SOLUTION

1. Prepare an income statement and a statement of shareholders' equity for the month ended August 31, 2003, and a classified balance sheet as of August 31, 2003.

WYNDHAM WHOLESALE COMPANY
Income Statement
For the Month of August 2003

Sales revenue		$40,000
Cost of goods sold		22,000
Gross profit		18,000
Operating expenses:		
Salaries expense	$7,000	
Utilities expense	2,000	
Bad debt expense	2,500	
Depreciation expense	500	
Rent expense	3,000	
Total operating expenses		15,000
Operating income		3,000
Other income (expense):		
Interest revenue	100	
Interest expense	(250)	(150)
Net income		$ 2,850

WYNDHAM WHOLESALE COMPANY
Statement of Shareholders' Equity
For the Month of August 2003

	Common Stock	Retained Earnings	Total Shareholders' Equity
Balance at August 1, 2003	-0-	-0-	-0-
Issue of common stock	$50,000		$50,000
Net income for August 2003		$2,850	2,850
Less: Dividends		(1,000)	(1,000)
Balance at August 31, 2003	$50,000	$1,850	$51,850

WYNDHAM WHOLESALE COMPANY
Balance Sheet
At August 31, 2003

Assets

Current assets:		
Cash		$ 21,000
Accounts receivable	$25,000	
Less: Allowance for uncollectible accounts	2,500	22,500
Inventory		16,000
Interest receivable		100
Note receivable		20,000
Prepaid rent		3,000
Total current assets		82,600
Property and equipment:		
Equipment	20,000	
Less: Accumulated depreciation	500	19,500
Total assets		$102,100

Liabilities and Shareholders' Equity

Current liabilities:		
Accounts payable		$ 20,000
Interest payable		250
Note payable		30,000
Total current liabilities		50,250
Shareholders' equity:		
Common stock, 5,000 shares issued and outstanding	$50,000	
Retained earnings	1,850	
Total shareholders' equity		51,850
Total liabilities and shareholders' equity		$102,100

2. Assume that August 31 is the company's fiscal year-end. Prepare the necessary closing entries and a post-closing trial balance.

To close the revenue accounts to income summary.	**August 31**		
	Sales revenue	40,000	
	Interest revenue	100	
	Income summary		40,100
To close the expense accounts to income summary.	**August 31**		
	Income summary	37,250	
	Cost of goods sold		22,000
	Salaries expense		7,000
	Utilities expense		2,000
	Bad debt expense		2,500
	Interest expense		250
	Depreciation expense		500
	Rent expense		3,000
To close the income summary account to retained earnings.	**August 31**		
	Income summary	2,850	
	Retained earnings		2,850

Post-Closing Trial Balance

Account Title	Debits	Credits
Cash	21,000	
Accounts receivable	25,000	
Allowance for uncollectible accounts		2,500
Prepaid rent	3,000	
Inventory	16,000	
Interest receivable	100	
Note receivable	20,000	
Equipment	20,000	
Accumulated depreciation—equipment		500
Accounts payable		20,000
Interest payable		250
Note payable		30,000
Common stock		50,000
Retained earnings		1,850
Totals	105,100	105,100

Conversion from Cash Basis to Accrual Basis

In Chapter 1, we discussed and illustrated the differences between cash and accrual accounting. Cash basis accounting produces a measure called *net operating cash flow*. This measure is the difference between cash receipts and cash disbursements during a reporting period from transactions related to providing goods and services to customers. On the other hand, the accrual accounting model measures an entity's accomplishments and resource sacrifices during the period, regardless of when cash is received or paid. At this point, you might wish to review the material in Chapter 1 on pages 7 to 9 to reinforce your understanding of the motivation for using the accrual accounting model.

Adjusting entries, for the most part, are conversions from cash to accrual. Prepayments and accruals occur when cash flow precedes or follows expense or revenue recognition.

Accountants sometimes are called upon to convert cash basis financial statements to accrual basis financial statements, particularly for small businesses. You now have all of the tools you need to make this conversion. For example, if a company paid $20,000 cash for insurance during the fiscal year and you determine that there was $5,000 in prepaid insurance at the beginning of the year and $3,000 at the end of the year, then you can determine (accrual basis) *insurance expense* for the year. Prepaid insurance decreased by $2,000 during the year, so insurance expense must be $22,000 ($20,000 in cash paid *plus* the decrease in prepaid insurance). You can visualize as follows:

Prepaid Insurance

Balance, beginning of year	$ 5,000
Plus: Cash paid	20,000
Less: Insurance expense	?
Balance, end of year	$ 3,000

Insurance expense of $22,000 completes the explanation of the change in the balance of prepaid insurance. Prepaid insurance of $3,000 is reported as an asset in an accrual basis balance sheet.

Using T-accounts is a convenient approach for converting from cash to accrual. For example, if the amount of cash collected from customers during the year was $220,000, and you know that accounts receivable at the beginning of the year was $45,000 and $33,000 at the end of the year, you can use T-accounts to determine that sales revenue for the year must have been $208,000.

Accounts Receivable				Sales Revenue	
Beg. balance	45,000				
Credit sales	?			?	Credit sales
		220,000	Cash collections		
End balance	33,000				

Illustration 2–14 provides an example of a conversion from cash basis net income to accrual basis net income.

ILLUSTRATION 2–14

Cash to Accrual

The Krinard Cleaning Services Company maintains its records on the cash basis, with one exception. The company reports equipment as an asset and records depreciation expense on the equipment. During 2003, Krinard collected $165,000 from customers, paid $92,000 in operating expenses, and recorded $10,000 in depreciation expense, resulting in net income of $63,000. The owner has asked you to convert this $63,000 in net income to full accrual net income. You are able to determine the following information about accounts receivable, prepaid expenses, and accrued liabilities:

	January 1, 2003	December 31, 2003
Accounts receivable	$16,000	$25,000
Prepaid expenses	7,000	4,000
Accrued liabilities (for operating expenses)	2,100	1,400

Accrual net income is $69,700, determined as follows:

Cash basis net income	$63,000
Add: Increase in accounts receivable	9,000
Deduct: Decrease in prepaid expenses	(3,000)
Add: Decrease in accrued liabilities	700
Accrual basis net income	$69,700

When converting from cash to accrual income, we add increases and deduct decreases in assets. For example, an increase in accounts receivable means that the company earned more revenue than cash collected, requiring the addition to cash basis income. Conversely, we add decreases and deduct increases in accrued liabilities. For example, a decrease in interest payable means that the company incurred less interest expense than the cash interest it paid, requiring the addition to cash basis income.

FINANCIAL REPORTING CASE **SOLUTION**

1. **What purpose do adjusting entries serve?** *(p. 76)*   Adjusting entries help ensure that only revenues actually earned in a period are recognized in that period, regardless of when cash is received. In this instance, for example, $13,000 cash has been received for services that haven't yet been performed. Also, adjusting entries enable a company to recognize all expenses incurred during a period, regardless of when cash is paid. Without depreciation, the friends' cost of using the equipment is not taken into account. Conversely, without adjustment, the cost of rent is overstated by $3,000 paid in advance for part of next year's rent.

With adjustments, we get an accrual income statement that provides a more complete measure of a company's operating performance and a better measure for predicting future operating cash flows. Similarly, the balance sheet provides a more complete assessment of assets and liabilities as sources of future cash receipts and disbursements.

2. **What year-end adjustments are needed to revise the income statement? Did your friends do as well their first year as they thought?** *(p. 77)*   Three year-end adjusting entries are needed:

1. Depreciation expense ($80,000 ÷ 5 years)	16,000	
Accumulated depreciation—equipment		16,000
2. Prepaid rent ($500 × 6 months [July–Dec.])	3,000	
Rent expense		3,000
3. Consulting revenue	13,000	
Unearned consulting revenue		13,000

No, your friends did not fare as well as their cash based statement would have indicated. With appropriate adjustments, their net income is actually only $20,000:

Consulting revenue ($96,000 − 13,000)		$83,000
Operating expenses:		
Salaries	$32,000	
Rent ($9,000 − 3,000)	6,000	
Supplies	4,800	
Utilities	3,000	
Advertising	1,200	
Depreciation	16,000	63,000
Net income		$20,000

THE BOTTOM LINE

1. The accounting equation underlies the process used to capture the effect of economic events. The equation (Assets = Liabilities + Owners' Equity) implies an equality between the total economic resources of an entity (its assets) and the total claims to those resources (liabilities and equity). It also implies that each economic event affecting this equation will have a dual effect because resources always must equal claims to those resources.

2. After determining the dual effect of external events on the accounting equation, the transaction is recorded in a journal. A journal is a chronological list of transactions in debit/credit form.

3. The next step in the processing cycle is to periodically transfer, or *post*, the debit and credit information from the journal to individual general ledger accounts. A general ledger is simply a collection of all of the company's various accounts. Each account provides a summary of the effects of all events and transactions on that individual account. This process is called *posting*. An unadjusted trial balance is then prepared.

4. The next step in the processing cycle is to record in the general journal and post to the ledger accounts the effect of *internal events* on the accounting equation. These transactions do not involve an exchange transaction with another entity. They are recorded at the end of any period when financial statements must be prepared for external use. These transactions are commonly referred to as *adjusting entries*. After these entries are posted to the general ledger accounts, an adjusted trial balance is prepared.

5. Adjusting entries can be classified into three types: (1) prepayments, (2) accruals, and (3) estimates. Prepayments are transactions in which the cash flow *precedes* expense or revenue recognition. Accruals involve transactions where the cash outflow or inflow takes place in a period *subsequent* to expense or revenue recognition. Estimates for items such as future bad debts on receivables often are required to comply with the accrual accounting model.

6. The adjusted trial balance is used to prepare the financial statements. The four basic financial statements are: (1) the income statement, (2) the balance sheet, (3) the statement of cash flows, and (4) the statement of shareholders' equity. The purpose of the income statement is to summarize the profit-generating activities of the company that occurred during a particular period of time. The balance sheet presents the financial position of the company on a particular date. The statement of cash flows discloses the events that caused cash to change during the reporting period. The statement of shareholders' equity discloses the sources of the changes in the various permanent shareholders' equity accounts that occurred during the period.

7. At the end of the fiscal year, a final step in the accounting processing cycle, closing, is required. The closing process serves a *dual purpose:* (1) the temporary accounts (revenues and expenses) are reduced to *zero balances,* ready to measure activity in the upcoming accounting period, and (2) these temporary account balances are *closed (transferred) to retained earnings* to reflect the changes that have occurred in that account during the period. Often, an intermediate step is to close revenues and expenses to *income summary;* then *income summary* is closed to *retained earnings.* ▪

APPENDIX
2A

A *worksheet* can be used as a tool to facilitate the preparation of adjusting and closing entries and the financial statements.

The first step is to enter account titles in column 1 and the unadjusted account balances in columns 2 and 3.

The second step is to determine end-of-period adjusting entries and enter them in columns 4 and 5.

The third step adds or deducts the effects of the adjusting entries on the account balances.

The fourth step is to transfer the temporary retained earnings account balances to columns 8 and 9.

USE OF A WORKSHEET

A **worksheet** often is used to organize the accounting information needed to prepare adjusting and closing entries and the financial statements. It is an informal tool only and is not part of the accounting system. There are many different ways to design and use worksheets. We will illustrate a representative method using the financial information for the Dress Right Clothing Corporation presented in the chapter. Computerized programs such as Lotus 1-2-3 and Excel facilitate the use of worksheets.

Illustration 2A–1 presents the completed worksheet. The worksheet is utilized after and instead of step 5 in the processing cycle, preparation of an unadjusted trial balance.

Step 1. The account titles as they appear in the general ledger are entered in column 1 and the balances of these accounts are copied onto columns 2 and 3, entitled Unadjusted Trial Balance. The accounts are copied in the same order as they appear in the general ledger, which usually is assets, liabilities, shareholders' equity permanent accounts, revenues, and expenses. The debit and credit columns are totaled to make sure that they balance. This procedure is repeated for each set of columns in the worksheet to check for accuracy.

Step 2. The end-of-period adjusting entries are determined and entered directly on the worksheet in columns 4 and 5, entitled Adjusting Entries. The adjusting entries for Dress Right Clothing Corporation were discussed in detail in the chapter and exhibited in general journal form in Illustration 2–7 on page 83. You should refer back to this illustration and trace each of the entries to the worksheet. For worksheet purposes, the entries have been numbered from (1) to (7) for easy referencing.

For example, entry (1) records the cost of supplies used during the month of July with a debit to supplies expense and a credit to supplies for $800. A (1) is placed next to the $800 in the debit column in the supplies expense row as well as next to the $800 in the credit column in the supplies row. This allows us to more easily reconstruct the entry for general journal purposes and locate errors if the debit and credit columns do not balance.

Step 3. The effects of the adjusting entries are added to or deducted from the account balances listed in the Unadjusted Trial Balance columns and copied across to columns 6 and 7, entitled Adjusted Trial Balance. For example, supplies had an unadjusted balance of $2,000. Adjusting entry (1) credited this account by $800, reducing the balance to $1,200.

Step 4. The balances in the temporary retained earnings accounts, revenues and expenses, are transferred to columns 8 and 9, entitled Income Statement. The difference between the total debits and credits in these columns is equal to net income or net loss. In this case, because credits (revenues) exceed debits (expenses), a net income of $2,417 results. To balance the debits and credits in this set of columns, a $2,417 debit entry is made in the line labeled Net income.

ILLUSTRATION 2A-1   Worksheet, Dress Right Clothing Corporation, July 2003

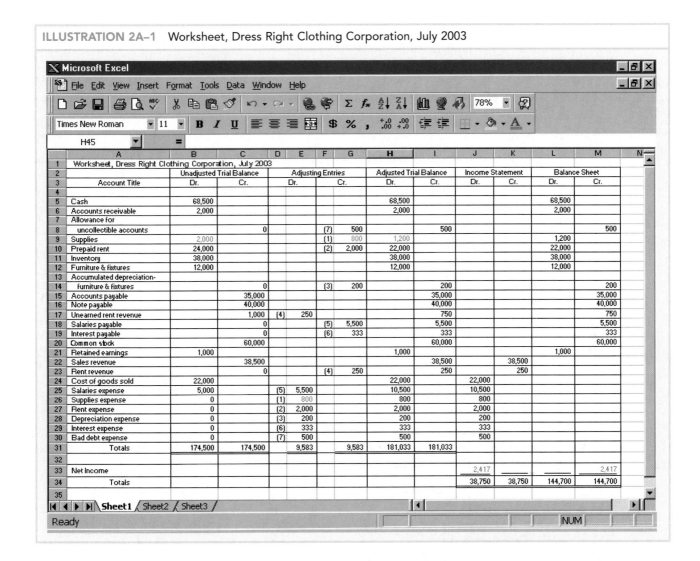

Step 5. The balances in the permanent accounts are transferred to columns 10 and 11, entitled Balance Sheet. To keep the debits and credits equal in the worksheet, a $2,417 credit must be recorded to offset the $2,417 debit recorded in step 4 and labeled as net income. This credit represents the fact that when the temporary accounts are closed out to retained earnings, a $2,417 credit to retained earnings will result. The credit in column 11, therefore, represents an increase in retained earnings for the period, that is, net income.

> The fifth step is to transfer the balances in the permanent accounts to columns 10 and 11.

After the worksheet is completed, the financial statements can be prepared directly from columns 8–11. The financial statements for Dress Right Clothing Corporation are shown in Illustrations 2–9 through 2–12. The accountant must remember to then record the adjusting entries in the general journal and post them to the general ledger accounts. An adjusted trial balance should then be prepared which should be identical to the one in the worksheet. At fiscal year-end, the income statement columns can then be used to prepare closing entries. ■

REVERSING ENTRIES

APPENDIX

2B

Accountants sometimes use **reversing entries** at the beginning of a reporting period. These optional entries remove the effects of some of the adjusting entries made at the end of the previous reporting period for the sole purpose of simplifying journal entries made during the new period. If the accountant does use reversing entries, these entries are recorded in the general journal and posted to the general ledger accounts on the first day of the new period.

Reversing entries are used most often with accruals. For example, the following adjusting entry for accrued salaries was recorded at the end of July 2003 for the Dress Right Clothing Corporation in the chapter:

To record accrued salaries at the end of July.

July 31		
Salaries expense	5,500	
Salaries payable.		5,500

If reversing entries are not used, when the salaries actually are paid in August, the accountant needs to remember to debit salaries payable and not salaries expense.

The account balances before and after salary payment can be seen below with the use of T-accounts.

Salaries Expense		Salaries Payable	
Bal. July 31 10,500		5,500 Bal. July 31	
		(Cash Payment) 5,500	
		-0- Balance	

If the accountant for Dress Right employs reversing entries, the following entry is made on August 1, 2003:

To reverse accrued salaries expense recorded at the end of July.

August 1		
Salaries payable	5,500	
Salaries expense		5,500

This entry reduces the salaries payable account to zero and reduces the salary expense account by $5,500. When salaries actually are paid in August, the debit is to salaries expense, thus increasing the account by $5,500.

Salaries Expense		Salaries Payable	
Bal. July 31 10,500	5,500 (Reversing entry)	5,500 Bal. July 31	
(Cash payment) 5,500			
Balance 10,500		-0- Balance	

We can see that balances in the accounts after cash payment is made are identical. The use of reversing entries for accruals, which is optional, simply allows cash payments or cash receipts to be entered directly into the temporary expense or revenue accounts without regard to the accruals made at the end of the previous period. ■

APPENDIX

2C

SUBSIDIARY LEDGERS AND SPECIAL JOURNALS

Subsidiary Ledgers

Accounting systems employ a *subsidiary ledger* which contains a group of subsidiary accounts associated with particular general ledger control accounts.

The general ledger contains what are referred to as *control accounts*. In addition to the general ledger, a subsidiary ledger contains a group of subsidiary accounts associated with a particular general ledger control account. For example, there will be a subsidiary ledger for accounts receivable that keeps track of the increases and decreases in the account receivable balance for each of the company's customers purchasing goods or services on credit. After all of the postings are made from the appropriate journals, the balance in the accounts receivable control account should equal the sum of the balances in the accounts receivable subsidiary ledger accounts. Subsidiary ledgers also are used for accounts payable, plant and equipment, investments, and other accounts.

Special Journals

An actual accounting system employs many different types of journals. The purpose of each journal is to record, in chronological order, the dual effect of a transaction in debit/credit form. The chapter used the general journal format to record each transaction. However, even for small companies with relatively few transactions, the general journal is used to record only a few types of transactions.[7]

The majority of transactions are recorded in **special journals.** These journals capture the dual effect of *repetitive* types of transactions. For example, cash receipts are recorded in a **cash receipts journal,** cash disbursements in a **cash disbursements journal,** credit sales in a **sales journal,** and the purchase of merchandise on account in a **purchases journal.**

Special journals simplify the recording process in the following ways:

1. Journalizing the effects of a particular transaction is made more efficient through the use of specifically designed formats.
2. Individual transactions are not posted to the general ledger accounts but are accumulated in the special journals and a summary posting is made on a periodic basis.
3. The responsibility for recording journal entries for the repetitive types of transactions is placed on individuals who have specialized training in handling them.

The concepts of subsidiary ledgers and special journals are illustrated using the *sales journal* and the *cash receipts journal.*

For most external transactions, special journals are used to capture the dual effect of the transaction in debit/credit form.

Sales Journal

The purpose of the **sales journal** is to record all credit sales. Cash sales are recorded in the cash receipts journal. Every entry in the sales journal has exactly the same effect on the accounts; the sales revenue account is credited and the accounts receivable control account is debited. Therefore, there is only one column needed to record the debit/credit effect of these transactions. Other columns are needed to capture information for updating the accounts receivable subsidiary ledger. Illustration 2C–1 presents the sales journal for Dress Right Clothing Corporation for the month of August 2003.

All credit sales are recorded in the sales journal.

				Page 1
Date	Accounts Receivable Subsidiary Account No.	Customer Name	Sales Invoice No.	Cr. Sales Revenue (400) Dr. Accounts Receivable (110)
2003				
Aug. 5	801	Leland High School	10-221	1,500
9	812	Mr. John Smith	10-222	200
18	813	Greystone School	10-223	825
22	803	Ms. Barbara Jones	10-224	120
29	805	Hart Middle School	10-225	650
				3,295

ILLUSTRATION 2C–1

Sales Journal, Dress Right Clothing Corporation, August 2003

During the month of August, the company made five credit sales, totaling $3,295. This amount is posted as a debit to the accounts receivable control account, account number 110, and a credit to the sales revenue account, account number 400. The T-accounts for accounts receivable and sales revenue appear below. The reference SJ1 refers to page 1 of the sales journal.

---

[7]For example, end-of-period adjusting entries would be recorded in the general journal.

General Ledger

Accounts Receivable	110		Sales Revenue	400
July 31 Balance 2,000				
Aug. 31 SJ1 3,295			3,295 Aug. 31 SJ1	

In a computerized accounting system, as each transaction is recorded in the sales journal, the subsidiary ledger accounts for the customer involved will automatically be updated. For example, the first credit sale of the month is to Leland High School for $1,500. The sales invoice number for this sale is 10-221 and the customer's subsidiary account number is 801. As this transaction is entered, the subsidiary account 801 for Leland High School is debited for $1,500.

Accounts Receivable Subsidiary Ledger

Leland High School	801
August 5 SJ1 1,500	

As cash is collected from this customer, the cash receipts journal records the transaction with a credit to the accounts receivable control account and a debit to cash. At the same time, the accounts receivable subsidiary ledger account number 801 also is credited. After the postings are made from the special journals, the balance in the accounts receivable control account should equal the sum of the balances in the accounts receivable subsidiary ledger accounts.

Cash Receipts Journal

All cash receipts are recorded in the *cash receipts journal*.

The purpose of the **cash receipts journal** is to record all cash receipts, regardless of the source. Every transaction recorded in this journal produces a debit entry to the cash account with the credit to various other accounts. Illustration 2C–2 shows a cash receipts journal using transactions of the Dress Right Clothing Corporation for the month of August 2003.

ILLUSTRATION 2C–2							Page 1
Cash Receipts Journal, Dress Right Clothing Corporation, August 2003	Date	Explanation or Account Name	Dr. Cash (100)	Cr. Accounts Receivable (110)	Cr. Sales Revenue (400)	Cr. Other	Other Accounts
	2003						
	Aug. 7	Cash sale	500		500		
	11	Borrowed cash	10,000			10,000	Note payable (220)
	17	Leland High School	750	750			
	20	Cash sale	300		300		
	25	Mr. John Smith	200	200			
			11,750	950	800	10,000	

Because every transaction results in a debit to the cash account, No. 100, a column is provided for that account. At the end of August, an $11,750 debit is posted to the general ledger cash account with the source labeled CR1, cash receipts journal, page 1.

Because cash and credit sales are common, separate columns are provided for these accounts. At the end of August, a $950 credit is posted to the accounts receivable general ledger account, No. 110, and an $800 credit is posted to the sales revenue account, No. 400. Two additional credit columns are provided for uncommon cash receipt transactions, one for the credit amount and one for the account being credited. We can see that in August, Dress Right borrowed $10,000 requiring a credit to the note payable account, No. 220.

In addition to the postings to the general ledger control accounts, each time an entry is recorded in the accounts receivable column, a credit is posted to the accounts receivable subsidiary ledger account for the customer making the payment. For example, on August 17, Leland High School paid $750 on account. The subsidiary ledger account for Leland High School is credited for $750. ■

Accounts Receivable Subsidiary Ledger

Leland High School		801	
August 5 SJ1	1,500		
		750	August 17 CR1

QUESTIONS FOR REVIEW OF KEY TOPICS

Q 2–1   Explain the difference between external events and internal events. Give an example of each type of event.

Q 2–2   Each economic event or transaction will have a dual effect on financial position. Explain what is meant by this dual effect.

Q 2–3   What is the purpose of a journal? What is the purpose of a general ledger?

Q 2–4   Explain the difference between permanent accounts and temporary accounts. Why does an accounting system include both types of accounts?

Q 2–5   Describe how debits and credits affect assets, liabilities, and permanent owners' equity accounts.

Q 2–6   Describe how debits and credits affect temporary owners' equity accounts.

Q 2–7   What is the first step in the accounting processing cycle? What role do source documents fulfill in this step?

Q 2–8   Describe what is meant by transaction analysis.

Q 2–9   Describe what is meant by posting, the fourth step in the processing cycle.

Q 2–10   Describe the events that correspond to the following two journal entries:

1. Inventory	20,000	
Accounts payable.		20,000
2. Accounts receivable	30,000	
Sales revenue.		30,000
Cost of goods sold	18,000	
Inventory		18,000

Q 2–11   What is an unadjusted trial balance? An adjusted trial balance?

Q 2–12   Define adjusting entries and discuss their purpose.

Q 2–13   Define closing entries and their purpose.

Q 2–14   Define prepaid expenses and provide at least two examples.

Q 2–15   Unearned revenues represent liabilities recorded when cash is received from customers in advance of providing a good or service. What adjusting journal entry is required at the end of a period to recognize the amount of unearned revenues that were earned during the period?

Q 2–16   Define accrued liabilities. What adjusting journal entry is required to record accrued liabilities?

Q 2–17   Describe the purpose of each of the four primary financial statements.

Q 2–18   [based on Appendix 2A] What is the purpose of a worksheet? In an 11-column worksheet similar to Illustration 2A–1, what would be the result of incorrectly transferring the balance in a liability account to column 9, the credit column under income statement?

Q 2–19   [based on Appendix 2B] Define reversing entries and discuss their purpose.

Q 2–20   [based on Appendix 2C] What is the purpose of special journals? In what ways do they simplify the recording process?

Q 2–21   [based on Appendix 2C] Explain the difference between the general ledger and a subsidiary ledger.

EXERCISES

E 2–1
Transaction analysis

The following transactions occurred during March 2003 for the Wainwright Corporation. The company owns and operates a wholesale warehouse.
1. Issued 20,000 shares of common stock in exchange for $200,000 in cash.
2. Purchased equipment at a cost of $40,000. $10,000 cash was paid and a note payable was signed for the balance owed.
3. Purchased inventory on account at a cost of $90,000. The company uses the perpetual inventory system.
4. Credit sales for the month totaled $120,000. The cost of the goods sold was $70,000.
5. Paid $5,000 in rent on the warehouse building for the month of March.
6. Paid $6,000 to an insurance company for fire and liability insurance for a one-year period beginning April 1, 2003.
7. Paid $60,000 on account for the merchandise purchased in 3.
8. Collected $55,000 from customers on account.
9. Recorded depreciation expense of $1,000 for the month on the equipment.

Required:
Analyze each transaction and show the effect of each on the accounting equation for a corporation.

Example:

Assets   = Liabilities + Paid-In Capital + Retained Earnings
1.   +200,000 (cash)   +200,000 (common stock)

E 2–2
Journal entries

Prepare journal entries to record each of the transactions listed in Exercise 2–1.

E 2–3
T-accounts and trial balance

Post the journal entries prepared in Exercise 2–2 to T-accounts. Assume that the opening balances in each of the accounts is zero. Prepare a trial balance from the ending account balances.

E 2–4
Journal entries

The following transactions occurred during the month of June 2003 for the Stridewell Corporation. The company owns and operates a retail shoe store.
1. Issued 100,000 shares of common stock in exchange for $500,000 cash.
2. Purchased furniture and fixtures at a cost of $100,000. $40,000 was paid and a note payable was signed for the balance owed.
3. Purchased inventory on account at a cost of $200,000. The company uses the perpetual inventory system.
4. Credit sales for the month totaled $180,000. The cost of the goods sold was $90,000.
5. Paid $6,000 in rent on the store building for the month of June.
6. Paid $3,000 to an insurance company for fire and liability insurance for a one-year period beginning June 1, 2003.
7. Paid $120,000 on account for the merchandise purchased in 3.
8. Collected $55,000 from customers on account.
9. Paid shareholders a cash dividend of $5,000.
10. Recorded depreciation expense of $2,000 for the month on the furniture and fixtures.
11. Recorded the amount of prepaid insurance that expired for the month.

Required:
Prepare journal entries to record each of the transactions listed above.

E 2–5
The accounting processing cycle

Listed below are several terms and phrases associated with the accounting processing cycle. Pair each item from List A (by letter) with the item from List B that is most appropriately associated with it.

List A	List B
_____ 1. Source documents	a. Records the dual effect of a transaction in debit/credit form.
_____ 2. Transaction analysis	b. Internal events recorded at the end of a reporting period.
_____ 3. Journal	c. Primary means of disseminating information to external decision makers.
_____ 4. Posting	
_____ 5. Unadjusted trial balance	d. To zero out the temporary owners' equity accounts.
_____ 6. Adjusting entries	e. Determine the dual effect on the accounting equation.
_____ 7. Adjusted trial balance	f. List of accounts and their balances before recording adjusting entries.
_____ 8. Financial statements	g. List of accounts and their balances after recording closing entries.
_____ 9. Closing entries	h. List of accounts and their balances after recording adjusting entries.
_____ 10. Post-closing trial balance	i. A means of organizing information: not part of the formal accounting system.
_____ 11. Worksheet	
	j. Transferring balances from the journal to the ledger.
	k. Used to identify and process external transactions.

E 2–6
Debits and credits

Indicate whether a debit will increase (I) or decrease (D) each of the following accounts:

Increase (I) or Decrease (D)	Account
1. _____	Inventory
2. _____	Depreciation expense
3. _____	Accounts payable
4. _____	Prepaid rent
5. _____	Sales revenue
6. _____	Common stock
7. _____	Wages payable
8. _____	Cost of goods sold
9. _____	Utility expense
10. _____	Equipment
11. _____	Accounts receivable
12. _____	Allowance for uncollectible accounts
13. _____	Bad debt expense
14. _____	Interest expense
15. _____	Interest revenue
16. _____	Gain on sale of equipment

E 2–7
Transaction analysis; debits and credits

Some of the ledger accounts for the Sanderson Hardware Company are numbered and listed below. For each of the October 2003 transactions numbered 1 through 12 below, indicate by account number which accounts should be debited and credited. The company uses the perpetual inventory system. Assume that appropriate adjusting entries were made at the end of September.

(1) Accounts payable	(2) Equipment	(3) Inventory
(4) Accounts receivable	(5) Cash	(6) Supplies
(7) Supplies expense	(8) Prepaid rent	(9) Sales revenue
(10) Retained earnings	(11) Note payable	(12) Common stock
(13) Unearned revenue	(14) Rent expense	(15) Wages payable
(16) Cost of goods sold	(17) Wage expense	(18) Interest expense

	Account(s) Debited	Account(s) Credited
Example: Purchased inventory for cash	3	5

1. Paid a cash dividend.
2. Paid rent for the next three months.
3. Sold goods to customers on account.
4. Purchased inventory on account.
5. Purchased supplies for cash.
6. Paid employees wages for September.
7. Issued common stock in exchange for cash.
8. Collected cash from customers for goods sold in 3.
9. Borrowed cash from a bank and signed a note.
10. At the end of October, recorded the amount of supplies that had been used during the month.

11. Received cash for advance payment from customer.
12. Accrued employee wages for October.

E 2–8
Adjusting entries

Prepare the necessary adjusting entries at December 31, 2003, for the Falwell Company for each of the following situations. Assume that no financial statements were prepared during the year and no adjusting entries were recorded.

1. A three-year fire insurance policy was purchased on July 1, 2003, for $6,000. The company debited insurance expense for the entire amount.
2. Depreciation on equipment totaled $15,000 for the year.
3. The company determined that accounts receivable in the amount of $6,500 will probably not be collected. The allowance for uncollectible accounts account has a credit balance of $2,000 before any adjustment.
4. Employee salaries of $18,000 for the month of December will be paid in early January 2004.
5. On November 1, 2003, the company borrowed $100,000 from a bank. The note requires principal and interest at 12% to be paid on April 30, 2004.
6. On December 1, 2003, the company received $3,000 in cash from another company that is renting office space in Falwell's building. The payment, representing rent for December and January, was credited to unearned rent revenue.

E 2–9
Adjusting entries

Prepare the necessary adjusting entries at December 31, 2003, for the Microchip Company for each of the following situations. Assume that no financial statements were prepared during the year and no adjusting entries were recorded.

1. On October 1, 2003, Microchip lent $60,000 to another company. A note was signed with principal and 10% interest to be paid on September 30, 2004.
2. On November 1, 2003, the company paid its landlord $6,000 representing rent for the months of November through January. Prepaid rent was debited.
3. On August 1, 2003, collected $12,000 in advance rent from another company that is renting a portion of Microchip's factory. The $12,000 represents one year's rent and the entire amount was credited to rent revenue.
4. Depreciation on machinery is $4,500 for the year.
5. Vacation pay for the year that had been earned by employees but not paid to them or recorded is $7,000.
6. Microchip began the year with $2,000 in its asset account, supplies. During the year, $6,500 in supplies were purchased and debited to supplies. At year-end, supplies costing $3,250 remain on hand.

E 2–10
Financial statements and closing entries

The December 31, 2003, adjusted trial balance for the Blueboy Cheese Corporation is presented below.

Account Title	Debits	Credits
Cash	21,000	
Accounts receivable	300,000	
Allowance for uncollectible accounts		20,000
Prepaid rent	10,000	
Inventory	50,000	
Equipment	600,000	
Accumulated depreciation—equipment		250,000
Accounts payable		40,000
Note payable (due in six months)		60,000
Salaries payable		8,000
Interest payable		2,000
Common stock		400,000
Retained earnings		100,000
Sales revenue		800,000
Cost of goods sold	480,000	
Salaries expense	120,000	
Rent expense	30,000	
Depreciation expense	60,000	
Interest expense	4,000	
Bad debt expense	5,000	
Totals	1,680,000	1,680,000

Required:
1. Prepare an income statement for the year ended December 31, 2003, and a classified balance sheet as of December 31, 2003.
2. Prepare the necessary closing entries at December 31, 2003.

E 2–11
Closing entries

The American Chip Corporation's fiscal year-end is December 31. The following is a partial adjusted trial balance as of December 31, 2003.

Account Title	Debits	Credits
Retained earnings		80,000
Sales revenue		650,000
Interest revenue		3,000
Cost of goods sold	320,000	
Salaries expense	100,000	
Rent expense	15,000	
Depreciation expense	20,000	
Interest expense	5,000	
Insurance expense	6,000	

Required:
Prepare the necessary closing entries at December 31, 2003.

E 2–12
Cash versus accrual accounting; adjusting entries

The Righter Shoe Store Company prepares monthly financial statements for its bank. The November 30 and December 31, 2003, trial balances contained the following account information:

	Nov. 30 Dr.	Nov. 30 Cr.	Dec. 31 Dr.	Dec. 31 Cr.
Supplies	1,000		3,000	
Prepaid insurance	6,000		4,250	
Wages payable		10,000		15,000
Unearned rent revenue		2,000		1,000

The following information also is known:
a. The December income statement reported $2,000 in supplies expense.
b. No insurance payments were made in December.
c. $10,000 was paid to employees during December for wages.
d. On November 1, 2003, a tenant paid Righter $3,000 in advance rent for the period November through January. Unearned rent revenue was credited.

Required:
1. What was the cost of supplies purchased during December?
2. What was the adjusting entry recorded at the end of December for prepaid insurance?
3. What was the adjusting entry recorded at the end of December for accrued wages?
4. What was the amount of rent revenue earned in December? What adjusting entry was recorded at the end of December for unearned rent?

E 2–13
External transactions and adjusting entries

The following transactions occurred during 2003 for the Beehive Honey Corporation:

Feb. 1	Borrowed $12,000 from a bank and signed a note. Principal and interest at 10% will be paid on January 31, 2004.
Apr. 1	Paid $3,600 to an insurance company for a two-year fire insurance policy.
July 17	Purchased supplies costing $2,800 on account. The company records supplies purchased in an asset account. At the December 31, 2003, year-end, supplies costing $1,250 remained on hand.
Nov. 1	A customer borrowed $6,000 and signed a note requiring the customer to pay principal and 8% interest on April 30, 2004.

Required:
1. Record each transaction in general journal form. Omit explanations.
2. Prepare any necessary adjusting entries at the December 31, 2003, year-end. No adjusting entries were made during the year for any item.

E 2–14
Accrual accounting income determination

During the course of your examination of the financial statements of the Hales Corporation for the year ended December 31, 2003, you discover the following:

a. An insurance policy covering three years was purchased on January 1, 2003, for $3,000. The entire amount was debited to insurance expense and no adjusting entry was made for this item.

b. During 2003, the company received a $1,000 cash advance from a customer for merchandise to be manufactured and shipped in 2004. The $1,000 was credited to sales revenue. No entry was made for the cost of merchandise.

c. There were no supplies listed in the balance sheet under assets. However, you discover that supplies costing $750 were on hand at December 31.

d. Hales borrowed $20,000 from a local bank on October 1, 2003. Principal and interest at 12% will be paid on September 30, 2004. No accrual was made for interest.

e. Net income reported in the 2003 income statement is $30,000 before reflecting any of the above items.

Required:
Determine the proper amount of net income for 2003.

E 2–15
Worksheet
[based on
Appendix 2A]

The December 31, 2003, unadjusted trial balance for the Wolkstein Drug Company is presented below. December 31 is the company's fiscal year-end.

Account Title	Debits	Credits
Cash	20,000	
Accounts receivable	35,000	
Allowance for uncollectible accounts		2,000
Prepaid rent	5,000	
Inventory	50,000	
Equipment	100,000	
Accumulated depreciation—equipment		30,000
Accounts payable		23,000
Wages payable		-0-
Common stock		100,000
Retained earnings		29,000
Sales revenue		323,000
Cost of goods sold	180,000	
Wage expense	71,000	
Rent expense	30,000	
Depreciation expense	-0-	
Utility expense	12,000	
Bad debt expense	4,000	
Totals	507,000	507,000

The following year-end adjusting entries are required:
a. Depreciation expense for the year on the equipment is $10,000.
b. The company has determined that the allowance for uncollectible accounts should be $5,000.
c. Accrued wages payable at year-end should be $4,000.

Required:
1. Prepare and complete a worksheet similar to Illustration 2A–1.
2. Prepare an income statement for 2003 and a balance sheet as of December 31, 2003.

E 2–16
Reversing entries
[based on
Appendix 2B]

The employees of Xitrex, Inc., are paid each Friday. The company's fiscal year-end is June 30, which falls on a Wednesday for the current year. Wages are earned evenly throughout the five-day workweek, and $10,000 will be paid on Friday, July 2.

Required:
1. Prepare an adjusting entry to record the accrued wages as of June 30, a reversing entry on July 1, and an entry to record the payment of wages on July 2.
2. Prepare journal entries to record the accrued wages as of June 30 and the payment of wages on July 2 assuming a reversing entry is not made.

E 2–17
Special journals
[based on
Appendix 2C]

The White Company's accounting system consists of a general journal (GJ), a cash receipts journal (CR), a cash disbursements journal (CD), a sales journal (SJ), and a purchases journal (PJ). For each of the following, indicate which journal should be used to record the transaction.

Transaction	Journal
1. Purchased merchandise on account.	_____
2. Collected an account receivable.	_____
3. Borrowed $20,000 and signed a note.	_____
4. Recorded depreciation expense.	_____
5. Purchased equipment for cash.	_____
6. Sold merchandise for cash (the sale only, not the cost of the merchandise).	_____
7. Sold merchandise on credit (the sale only, not the cost of the merchandise).	_____
8. Recorded accrued wages payable.	_____
9. Paid employee wages.	_____
10. Sold equipment for cash.	_____
11. Sold equipment on credit.	_____
12. Paid a cash dividend to shareholders.	_____
13. Issued common stock in exchange for cash.	_____
14. Paid accounts payable.	_____

PROBLEMS

P 2–1

Accounting cycle through unadjusted trial balance

The Halogen Laminated Products Company began business on January 1, 2003. During January, the following transactions occurred:

Jan.	1	Issued common stock in exchange for $100,000 cash.
	2	Purchased inventory on account for $35,000 (the perpetual inventory system is used).
	4	Paid an insurance company $2,400 for a one-year insurance policy.
	10	Sold merchandise on account for $12,000. The cost of the merchandise was $7,000.
	15	Borrowed $30,000 from a local bank and signed a note. Principal and interest at 10% is to be repaid in six months.
	20	Paid employees $6,000 wages for the first half of the month.
	22	Sold merchandise for $10,000 cash. The cost of the merchandise was $6,000.
	24	Paid $15,000 to suppliers for the merchandise purchased on January 2.
	26	Collected $6,000 on account from customers.
	28	Paid $1,000 to the local utility company for January gas and electricity.
	30	Paid $4,000 rent for the building. $2,000 was for January rent, and $2,000 for February rent.

Required:
1. Prepare general journal entries to record each transaction. Omit explanations.
2. Post the entries to T-accounts.
3. Prepare an unadjusted trial balance as of January 30, 2003.

P 2–2

Accounting cycle through unadjusted trial balance

The following is the post-closing trial balance for the Whitlow Manufacturing Corporation as of December 31, 2002.

Account Title	Debits	Credits
Cash	5,000	
Accounts receivable	2,000	
Inventory	5,000	
Equipment	11,000	
Accumulated depreciation—equipment		3,500
Accounts payable		3,000
Common stock		10,000
Retained earnings		6,500
Sales revenue		-0-
Cost of goods sold	-0-	
Wage expense	-0-	
Rent expense	-0-	
Advertising expense	-0-	
Totals	23,000	23,000

The following transactions occurred during January 2003:

Jan. 1 Sold merchandise for cash, $3,500. The cost of the merchandise was $2,000. The company uses the perpetual inventory system.

2 Purchased equipment on account for $5,500 from the Strong Company.

4 Received a $150 bill from the local newspaper for an advertisement that appeared in the paper on January 2.

8 Sold merchandise on account for $5,000. The cost of the merchandise was $2,800.

10 Purchased merchandise on account for $9,500.

13 Purchased equipment for cash, $800.

16 Paid the entire amount due to the Strong Company.

18 Received $4,000 from customers on account.

20 Paid $800 to the owner of the building for January's rent.

30 Paid employees $3,000 for salaries for the month of January.

31 Paid a cash dividend of $1,000 to shareholders.

Required:
1. Set up T-accounts and enter the beginning balances as of January 1, 2003.
2. Prepare general journal entries to record each transaction. Omit explanations.
3. Post the entries to T-accounts.
4. Prepare an unadjusted trial balance as of January 31, 2003.

P 2–3
Adjusting entries

The Pastina Company manufactures and sells various types of pasta to grocery chains as private label brands. The company's fiscal year-end is December 31. The unadjusted trial balance as of December 31, 2003, appears below.

Account Title	Debits	Credits
Cash	30,000	
Accounts receivable	40,000	
Allowance for uncollectible accounts		3,000
Supplies	1,500	
Inventory	60,000	
Note receivable	20,000	
Interest receivable	-0-	
Prepaid rent	2,000	
Prepaid insurance	-0-	
Equipment	80,000	
Accumulated depreciation—equipment		30,000
Accounts payable		28,000
Wages payable		-0-
Note payable		50,000
Interest payable		-0-
Unearned revenue		-0-
Common stock		60,000
Retained earnings		24,500
Sales revenue		148,000
Interest revenue		-0-
Cost of goods sold	70,000	
Wage expense	18,900	
Rent expense	11,000	
Depreciation expense	-0-	
Interest expense	-0-	
Supplies expense	1,100	
Insurance expense	6,000	
Bad debt expense	3,000	
Totals	343,500	343,500

Information necessary to prepare the year-end adjusting entries appears below.
1. Depreciation on the equipment for the year is $10,000.
2. The company estimates that of the $40,000 in accounts receivable outstanding at year-end, $5,500 probably will not be collected.

3. Employee wages are paid twice a month, on the 22nd for wages earned from the 1st through the 15th, and on the 7th of the following month for wages earned from the 16th through the end of the month. Wages earned from December 16 through December 31, 2003, were $1,500.

4. On October 1, 2003, Pastina borrowed $50,000 from a local bank and signed a note. The note requires interest to be paid annually on September 30 at 12%. The principal is due in 10 years.

5. On March 1, 2003, the company lent a supplier $20,000 and a note was signed requiring principal at 8% to be paid on February 28, 2004.

6. On April 1, 2003, the company paid an insurance company $6,000 for a two-year fire insurance policy. The entire $6,000 was debited to insurance expense.

7. $800 of supplies remained on hand at December 31, 2003.

8. A customer paid Pastina $2,000 in December for 1,500 pounds of spaghetti to be manufactured and delivered in January 2004. Pastina credited sales revenue.

9. On December 1, 2003, $2,000 rent was paid to the owner of the building. The payment represented rent for December and January 2004, at $1,000 per month.

Required:
Prepare the necessary December 31, 2003, adjusting journal entries.

P 2–4
Accounting cycle;
adjusting entries
through post-closing
trial balance

Refer to Problem 2–3 and complete the following steps:

1. Enter the unadjusted balances from the trial balance into T-accounts.
2. Post the adjusting entries prepared in Problem 2–3 to the accounts.
3. Prepare an adjusted trial balance.
4. Prepare an income statement and a statement of shareholders' equity for the year ended December 31, 2003, and a classified balance sheet as of December 31, 2003. Assume that no common stock was issued during the year and that $4,000 in cash dividends were paid to shareholders during the year.
5. Prepare closing entries and post to the accounts.
6. Prepare a post-closing trial balance.

P 2–5
Adjusting entries

The Howarth Company's fiscal year-end is December 31. Below are the unadjusted and adjusted trial balances for December 31, 2003.

Account Title	Unadjusted		Adjusted	
	Debits	Credits	Debits	Credits
Cash	50,000		50,000	
Accounts receivable	35,000		35,000	
Allowance for uncollectible accounts		2,000		3,500
Prepaid rent	2,000		1,200	
Supplies	1,500		800	
Inventory	60,000		60,000	
Note receivable	30,000		30,000	
Interest receivable	-0-		1,500	
Equipment	45,000		45,000	
Accumulated depreciation—equipment		15,000		20,000
Accounts payable		32,000		32,000
Wages payable		-0-		6,200
Note payable		50,000		50,000
Interest payable		-0-		2,500
Unearned rent revenue		-0-		2,000
Common stock		46,000		46,000
Retained earnings		20,000		20,000
Sales revenue		244,000		244,000
Rent revenue		6,000		4,000
Interest revenue		-0-		1,500
Cost of goods sold	126,000		126,000	
Wage expense	45,000		51,200	
Rent expense	11,000		11,800	
Depreciation expense	-0-		5,000	
Supplies expense	1,100		1,800	
Interest expense	5,400		7,900	
Bad debt expense	3,000		4,500	
Totals	415,000	415,000	431,700	431,700

Required:

Prepare the adjusting journal entries that were made at December 31, 2003.

P 2–6
Accounting cycle

The general ledger of the Karlin Company, a consulting company, at January 1, 2003, contained the following account balances:

Account Title	Debits	Credits
Cash	30,000	
Accounts receivable	15,000	
Allowance for uncollectible accounts		500
Equipment	20,000	
Accumulated depreciation		6,000
Salaries payable		9,000
Common stock		40,000
Retained earnings		9,500
Total	65,000	65,000

The following is a summary of the transactions for the year:
a. Sales of services, $100,000, of which $30,000 was on credit.
b. Collected on accounts receivable, $27,300.
c. Issued shares of common stock in exchange for $10,000 in cash.
d. Paid salaries, $50,000 (of which $9,000 was for salaries payable).
e. Paid miscellaneous expenses, $24,000.
f. Purchased equipment for $15,000 in cash.
g. Paid $2,500 in cash dividends to shareholders.

Required:
1. Set up the necessary T-accounts and enter the beginning balances from the trial balance.
2. Prepare a general journal entry for each of the summary transactions listed above.
3. Post the journal entries to the accounts.
4. Prepare an unadjusted trial balance.
5. Prepare and post adjusting journal entries. Accrued salaries at year-end amounted to $1,000. Depreciation for the year on the equipment is $2,000. The allowance for uncollectible accounts is estimated to be $1,500.
6. Prepare an adjusted trial balance.
7. Prepare an income statement for 2003 and a balance sheet as of December 31, 2003.
8. Prepare and post closing entries.
9. Prepare a post-closing trial balance.

P 2–7
Adjusting entries and
income effects

The information necessary for preparing the 2003 year-end adjusting entries for Vito's Pizza Parlor appears below. Vito's fiscal year-end is December 31.
a. On July 1, 2003, purchased $10,000 of IBM Corporation bonds at face value. The bonds pay interest twice a year on January 1 and July 1. The annual interest rate is 12%.
b. Vito's depreciable equipment has a cost of $30,000, a five-year life, and no salvage value. The equipment was purchased in 2001. The straight-line depreciation method is used.
c. On November 1, 2003, the bar area was leased to Jack Donaldson for one year. Vito's received $6,000 representing the first six months' rent and credited unearned rent revenue.
d. On April 1, 2003, the company paid $2,400 for a two-year fire and liability insurance policy and debited insurance expense.
e. On October 1, 2003, the company borrowed $20,000 from a local bank and signed a note. Principal and interest at 12% will be paid on September 30, 2004.
f. At year-end there is a $1,800 debit balance in the supplies (asset) account. Only $700 of supplies remain on hand.

Required:
1. Prepare the necessary adjusting journal entries at December 31, 2003.
2. Determine the amount by which net income would be misstated if Vito's failed to make these adjusting entries. (Ignore income tax expense.)

P 2–8
Adjusting entries

The Excalibur Corporation manufactures and sells video games for personal computers. The unadjusted trial balance as of December 31, 2003, appears below. December 31 is the company's fiscal year-end. The company uses the perpetual inventory system.

Account Title	Debits	Credits
Cash	23,300	
Accounts receivable	32,500	
Allowance for uncollectible accounts		100
Supplies	-0-	
Prepaid rent	-0-	
Inventory	65,000	
Equipment	75,000	
Accumulated depreciation—equipment		10,000
Accounts payable		26,000
Wages payable		3,000
Note payable		30,000
Common stock		80,000
Retained earnings		16,050
Sales revenue		180,000
Cost of goods sold	95,000	
Interest expense	-0-	
Wage expense	32,350	
Rent expense	14,000	
Supplies expense	2,000	
Utility expense	6,000	
Bad debt expense	-0-	
Totals	345,150	345,150

Information necessary to prepare the year-end adjusting entries appears below.
1. The equipment was purchased in 2001 and is being depreciated using the straight-line method over an eight-year useful life with no salvage value.
2. Accrued wages at year-end should be $4,500.
3. The company estimates that 2% of all year-end accounts receivable will probably not be collected.
4. The company borrowed $30,000 on September 1, 2003. The principal is due to be repaid in 10 years. Interest is payable twice a year on each August 31 and February 28 at an annual rate of 10%.
5. The company debits supplies expense when supplies are purchased. Supplies on hand at year-end cost $500.
6. Prepaid rent at year-end should be $1,000.

Required:
Prepare the necessary December 31, 2003, adjusting entries.

P 2–9
Cash versus accrual accounting

Selected balance sheet information for the Wolf Company at November 30, and December 31, 2003, is presented below. The company uses the perpetual inventory system and all sales to customers are made on credit.

	Nov. 30		Dec. 31	
	Dr.	Cr.	Dr.	Cr.
Accounts receivable	10,000		3,000	
Prepaid insurance	5,000		7,500	
Inventory	7,000		6,000	
Accounts payable		12,000		15,000
Wages payable		5,000		3,000

The following cash flow information also is available:
a. Cash collected from credit customers—$80,000.
b. Cash paid for insurance—$5,000.
c. Cash paid to suppliers of inventory—$60,000 (the entire accounts payable amounts relate to inventory purchases).
d. Cash paid to employees for wages—$10,000.

Required:
1. Determine the following for the month of December:
   a. Sales revenue
   b. Cost of goods sold

c.   Insurance expense
d.   Wage expense

2.   Prepare a summary journal entry to record the month's sales and cost of those sales.

P 2–10

Accounting cycle; unadjusted trial balance through closing

The unadjusted trial balance as of December 31, 2003, for the Bagley Consulting Company appears below. December 31 is the company's fiscal year-end.

Account Title	Debits	Credits
Cash	8,000	
Accounts receivable	9,000	
Allowance for uncollectible accounts		50
Prepaid insurance	3,000	
Land	200,000	
Buildings	50,000	
Accumulated depreciation—buildings		20,000
Equipment	100,000	
Accumulated depreciation—equipment		40,000
Accounts payable		35,000
Salaries payable		-0-
Unearned rent revenue		-0-
Common stock		200,000
Retained earnings		56,450
Sales revenue		90,000
Interest revenue		3,000
Rent revenue		7,500
Salaries expense	37,000	
Bad debt expense	-0-	
Depreciation expense	-0-	
Insurance expense	-0-	
Utility expense	30,000	
Maintenance expense	15,000	
Totals	452,000	452,000

Required:

1.   Enter the account balances in T-accounts.
2.   From the trial balance and information given, prepare adjusting entries and post to the accounts.
    a.   The buildings have an estimated useful life of 50 years with no salvage value. The company uses the straight-line depreciation method.
    b.   The equipment is depreciated at 10 percent of original cost per year.
    c.   Prepaid insurance expired during the year, $1,500.
    d.   It is estimated that 10% of the accounts receivable balance will be uncollectible.
    e.   Accrued salaries at year-end, $1,500.
    f.   Unearned rent revenue at year-end should be $1,200.
3.   Prepare an adjusted trial balance.
4.   Prepare closing entries.
5.   Prepare a post-closing trial balance.

P 2–11

Accrual accounting; financial statements

The McGuire Corporation began operations in 2003. The company purchases computer equipment from manufacturers and then sells to retail stores. During 2003, the bookkeeper used a check register to record all cash receipts and cash disbursements. No other journals were used. The following is a re-cap of the cash receipts and disbursements made during the year.

Cash receipts:	
Sale of common stock	$ 50,000
Collections from customers	320,000
Borrowed from local bank on April 1, note signed requiring principal and interest at 12% to be paid on March 31, 2004	40,000
Total cash receipts	$410,000

Cash disbursements:	
Purchase of merchandise	$220,000
Payment of salaries	80,000
Purchase of equipment	30,000
Payment of rent on building	14,000
Miscellaneous expenses	10,000
Total cash disbursements	$354,000

You are called in to prepare financial statements at December 31, 2003. The following additional information was provided to you:

1. Customers owed the company $22,000 at year-end. Of this amount, it was anticipated that $3,000 would probably not be collected. There were no actual bad debt write-offs in 2003.
2. At year-end, $30,000 was still due to suppliers of merchandise purchased on credit.
3. At year-end, merchandise inventory costing $50,000 still remained on hand.
4. Salaries owed to employees at year-end amounted to $5,000.
5. On December 1, $3,000 in rent was paid to the owner of the building used by McGuire. This represented rent for the months of December through February.
6. The equipment, which has a 10-year life and no salvage value, was purchased on January 1, 2003. Straight-line depreciation is used.

Required:
Prepare an income statement for 2003 and a balance sheet as of December 31, 2003.

P 2–12
Worksheet
[based on
Appendix 2A]

Using the information from Problem 2–8, prepare and complete a worksheet similar to Illustration 2A–1. Use the information in the worksheet to prepare an income statement and a statement of shareholders' equity for 2003 and a balance sheet as of December 31, 2003. Cash dividends paid to shareholders during the year amounted to $6,000. Also prepare the necessary closing entries assuming that adjusting entries have been correctly posted to the accounts.

BROADEN YOUR PERSPECTIVE

Judgment Case 2–1
Cash versus accrual
accounting; adjusting
entries; Chapters 1
and 2

Apply your critical-thinking ability to the knowledge you've gained. These cases will provide you an opportunity to develop your research, analysis, judgment, and communication skills. You also will work with other students, integrate what you've learned, apply it in real world situations, and consider its global and ethical ramifications. This practice will broaden your knowledge and further develop your decision-making abilities.

You have recently been hired by David & Company, a small public accounting firm. One of the firm's partners, Alice Davis, has asked you to deal with a disgruntled client, Mr. Sean Pitt, owner of the city's largest hardware store. Mr. Pitt is applying to a local bank for a substantial loan to remodel his store. The bank requires accrual based financial statements but Mr. Pitt has always kept the company's records on a cash basis. He does not see the purpose of accrual based statements. His most recent outburst went something like this: "After all, I collect cash from customers, pay my bills in cash, and I am going to pay the bank loan with cash. And, I already show my building and equipment as assets and depreciate them. I just don't understand the problem."

Required:
1. Explain the difference between a cash basis and an accrual basis measure of performance.
2. Why, in most cases, does accrual basis net income provide a better measure of performance than net operating cash flow?
3. Explain the purpose of adjusting entries as they relate to the difference between cash and accrual accounting.

Judgment Case 2–2
Cash versus accrual
accounting

Refer to Case 2–1 above. Mr. Pitt has relented and agrees to provide you with the information necessary to convert his cash basis financial statements to accrual basis statements. He provides you with the following transaction information for the fiscal year ending December 31, 2003:

1. A comprehensive insurance policy requires a payment every year for the upcoming year. The last payment of $12,000 was made on September 1, 2003.
2. Mr. Pitt allows customers to pay using a credit card. At the end of the current year, various credit card companies owed Mr. Pitt $6,500. At the end of last year, customer credit card charges outstanding were $5,000.

3. Employees are paid once a month, on the 10th of the month following the work period. Cash disbursements to employees were $8,200 and $7,200 for January 10, 2003, and January 10, 2002, respectively.

4. Utility bills outstanding totaled $1,200 at the end of 2003 and $900 at the end of 2002.

5. A physical count of inventory is always taken at the end of the fiscal year. The merchandise on hand at the end of 2003 cost $35,000. At the end of 2002, inventory on hand cost $32,000.

6. At the end of 2002, Mr. Pitt did not have any bills outstanding to suppliers of merchandise. However, at the end of 2003, he owed suppliers $4,000.

Required:

1. Mr. Pitt's 2003 cash basis net income (including depreciation expense) is $26,000. Determine net income applying the accrual accounting model.

2. Explain the effect on Mr. Pitt's balance sheet of converting from cash to accrual. That is, would assets, liabilities, and owner's equity be higher or lower and by what amounts?

Communication Case 2–3
Adjusting entries

"I don't understand," complained Chris, who yesterday answered your bulletin board posting for a tutor. The complaint was in response to your statements that recording adjusting entries is a critical step in the accounting processing cycle, and the two major classifications of adjusting entries are prepayments and accruals.

Required:

Respond to Chris.

1. When do prepayments occur? Accruals?

2. Describe the appropriate adjusting entry for prepaid expenses and for unearned revenues. What is the effect on net income, assets, liabilities, and shareholders' equity of not recording a required adjusting entry for prepayments?

3. Describe the required adjusting entry for accrued liabilities and for accrued receivables. What is the effect on net income, assets, liabilities, and shareholders' equity of not recording a required adjusting entry for accruals?

Analysis Case 2–4
Financial statement information

FedEx Corporation

Refer to the financial statements and related disclosure notes of FedEx Corporation in the appendix to Chapter 1.

Required:

1. Determine the amount of cash paid to or in behalf of employees for salaries and benefits during the 2001 fiscal year.

2. Assuming that spare parts and supplies are used for maintenance and repairs, determine the combined amount of cash paid for maintenance and repairs and spare parts, supplies, and fuel purchased during the 2001 fiscal year.

3. What is the amount of depreciation and amortization recorded during the 2001 fiscal year?

3

The Balance Sheet and Financial Disclosures

CHAPTER

OVERVIEW

Chapter 1 stressed the importance of the financial statements in helping investors and creditors predict future cash flows. The balance sheet, along with accompanying disclosures, provides relevant information useful in helping investors and creditors not only to predict future cash flows, but also to make the related assessments of liquidity and long-term solvency.

The purpose of this chapter is to provide an overview of the balance sheet and financial disclosures and to explore how this information is used by decision makers.

LEARNING OBJECTIVES

After studying this chapter, you should be able to:

LO1 Describe the purpose of the balance sheet and understand its usefulness and limitations.

LO2 Distinguish among current and noncurrent assets and liabilities.

LO3 Identify and describe the various balance sheet asset classifications.

LO4 Identify and describe the two balance sheet liability classifications.

LO5 Explain the purpose of financial statement disclosures.

LO6 Explain the purpose of the management discussion and analysis disclosure.

LO7 Explain the purpose of an audit and describe the content of the audit report.

LO8 Describe the techniques used by financial analysts to transform financial information into forms more useful for analysis.

LO9 Identify and calculate the common liquidity and financing ratios used to assess risk.

What's It Worth?

"I can't believe it. Why don't you accountants prepare financial statements that are relevant?" Your friend Jerry is a finance major and is constantly badgering you about what he perceives to be a lack of relevance of financial statements prepared according to generally accepted accounting principles. "For example, take a look at this balance sheet for Electronic Arts that I just downloaded off the Internet. Electronic Arts is the company in California that produces all those cool video games like NASCAR, NBA Street, and Madden NFL. Anyway, the shareholders' equity of the company according to the 2001 balance sheet is $1,034,347,000. But if you multiply the number of outstanding shares by the most recent stock price per share, the company's market value is almost nine times that amount. I thought financial statements were supposed to help investors and creditors value a company." You decide to look at the company's balance sheet and try to set Jerry straight.

By the time you finish this chapter, you should be able to respond appropriately to the questions posed in this case. Compare your response to the solution provided at the end of the chapter.

QUESTIONS

1. Respond to Jerry's criticism that shareholders' equity does not represent the market value of the company. What information does the balance sheet provide? (page 119)

2. The usefulness of the balance sheet is enhanced by classifying assets and liabilities according to common characteristics. What are the classifications used in Electronic Arts' balance sheet and what elements do those categories include? (page 120)

ELECTRONIC ARTS
Balance Sheets
As of March 31
($ in 000s except share data)

	2001	2000
Assets		
Current assets:		
Cash and cash equivalents	$ 466,492	$ 339,804
Marketable securities	10,022	236
Receivables, less allowances of $89,833		
and $65,067 respectively	174,449	234,087
Inventories	15,686	22,986
Other current assets	152,078	108,210
Total current assets	818,727	705,323
Property and equipment, net	337,199	285,466
Long-term investments	8,400	8,400
Investment in affiliates	19,052	22,601
Intangible assets	136,764	117,236
Other assets	58,776	53,286
Total assets	$1,378,918	$1,192,312
Liabilities and Shareholders' Equity		
Current liabilities:		
Accounts payable	$ 73,061	$ 97,703
Accrued liabilities	266,965	167,599
Total current liabilities	340,026	265,302
Minority interest in consolidated joint venture	4,545	3,617
Shareholders' equity:		
Preferred stock, $.01 par value. Authorized		
10,000,000 shares	—	—
Common stock, $.01 par value. Authorized		
500,000,000 shares; issued and outstanding		
140,964,464 and 134,869,088, respectively	1,410	1,348
Paid-in capital in excess of par	540,354	412,038
Retained earnings	505,286	516,368
Accumulated other comprehensive loss	(12,703)	(6,361)
Total shareholders' equity	1,034,347	923,393
Total liabilities and shareholders' equity	$1,378,918	$1,192,312

The balance sheet, along with accompanying disclosures, provides a wealth of information to external decision makers. The information provided is useful not only in the prediction of future cash flows but also in the related assessments of liquidity and long-term solvency.

This chapter begins our discussion of the financial statements by providing an overview of the balance sheet and the financial disclosures that accompany the financial statements. The first part of the chapter describes the usefulness and limitations of the balance sheet and illustrates the content of the statement. The second part illustrates financial statement disclosures presented to external users in addition to the basic financial statements. In the third part we discuss how this information can be used by decision makers to assess business risk. That discussion introduces some common financial ratios used to assess liquidity and long-term solvency.

Chapter 4 continues this discussion of the financial statements with its coverage of the income statement and the statement of cash flows.

THE BALANCE SHEET

The purpose of the **balance sheet** is to report a company's financial position on a particular date. Unlike the income statement, which is a change statement reporting events that occurred *during a period of time,* the balance sheet presents an organized array of assets, liabilities, and shareholders' equity *at a point in time.* It is a freeze frame or snapshot of financial position at the end of a particular day marking the end of an accounting period.

Usefulness and Limitations

LO1

Carter Hawley Hale Stores (CHHS), Inc., was one of the largest department store retailers in the United States. In 1991, the company operated over 100 stores in the sunbelt regions of the country. The company's divisions included The Broadway and Emporium. During the 1980s, the company struggled financially and in February of 1991 declared bankruptcy. CHHS's February 2, 1991, quarterly balance sheet, filed with the SEC and made publicly available, disclosed the information in Graphic 3–1.

The negative shareholders' equity includes negative retained earnings of nearly $1 billion resulting from operating losses incurred over a number of years.

By the summer of 1991, the company's stock price had dropped to $1 per share from a 1989 high of $8. In June 1991, the following (condensed) balance sheet information was reported to the bankruptcy court:

GRAPHIC 3–1   Quarterly Balance Sheet—Carter Hawley Hale Stores, Inc.

Balance Sheet (condensed)
At February 2, 1991
($ in 000s)

Assets	
Current assets	$1,154,064
Property and equipment, net	511,690
Other assets	89,667
Total assets	$1,755,421
Liabilities	
Current liabilities	$ 175,982
Long-term liabilities	1,852,066
Total liabilities	2,028,048
Shareholders' equity	(272,627)
Total liabilities and shareholders' equity	$1,755,421

	($ in 000s)
Property	$1,596,312
Debts	1,112,989
Excess of property over debts	$ 483,323

Has the financial position changed this dramatically from February to June? No. Differences in reporting requirements by the SEC and the bankruptcy court cause the apparent discrepancy. First, the property (assets) disclosed to the bankruptcy court does not include accounts receivable and debts do not include the related liabilities for which the receivables had been pledged as collateral. This accounts for the smaller asset and debt figures as compared to those disclosed in the February statement provided to the SEC.

But the striking difference is that the *negative equity* of $272,627,000 disclosed in the SEC report becomes a *positive equity* (excess of assets over liabilities) of $483,323,000 in the information disclosed to the bankruptcy court. This positive equity, divided by the number of common shares outstanding, results in a per share value of nearly $16. Why the discrepancy? The answer relates to the valuation of property. In the balance sheet submitted to the SEC, these assets are valued based on their original cost. However, the bankruptcy court requires assets to be reported at market value.[1] The market value of CHHS's property, which

**FINANCIAL
REPORTING** CASE

Q1, p. 117

---

[1]The bankruptcy court requires market value information in order to assess, among other things, the ability of the company to pay its creditors if assets were liquidated.

includes some valuable land in locations like San Francisco, was significantly higher than its original cost.

This example illustrates an important limitation of the balance sheet. *The balance sheet does not portray the market value of the entity* as a going concern, nor, as in the CHHS example, its liquidation value. Many assets, like land and buildings for example, are measured at their historical costs rather than their market values. Relatedly, many company resources including its trained employees, its experienced management team, and its reputation are not recorded as assets at all. Also, many items and amounts reported in the balance sheet are heavily reliant on estimates rather than determinable amounts. For example, companies estimate the amount of receivables they will be able to actually collect and the amount of warranty costs they will eventually incur for products already sold. For these and other reasons, a company's **book value**, its assets minus its liabilities as shown in the balance sheet, usually will not directly measure the company's market value.

Consider for example that in 2001, the average ratio for the 30 companies comprising the Dow Jones Industrial Average of their market value to their book value was approximately 5.5. The ratio for Merck, one of the world's largest pharmaceutical companies, was 11.2. Can you think of an important reason why Merck's market value would be over 11 times higher than its book value? One reason is that Merck spends significant amounts, over $2.4 billion in 2001 alone, on research and development of new drugs. Many of the drugs the company has developed have been successful, and yet the costs to discover and develop these drugs are not represented in the balance sheet. Research and development costs are expensed in the period incurred, and not capitalized as an asset.

Despite these limitations, the balance sheet does have significant value. An important feature of the statement is that it describes many of the resources a company has available for generating future cash flows. Another way the statement's content is informative is in combination with income statement items. For example, the relation between net income and assets provides a measure of return that is useful in predicting future profitability. In fact, many of the amounts reported in either of the two statements are more informative when viewed relative to an amount from the other statement.[2]

The balance sheet does not simply list assets and liabilities. Instead, assets and liabilities are classified (grouped) according to common characteristics. These classifications, which we explore in the next section, along with related disclosure notes, help the balance sheet to provide additional important information about liquidity and long-term solvency. **Liquidity** refers to the period of time before an asset is converted to cash or until a liability is paid. This information is useful in assessing a company's ability to pay its *current* obligations. **Long-term solvency** refers to the riskiness of a company with regard to the amount of liabilities in its capital structure. Other things being equal, the risk to an investor or creditor increases as the percentage of liabilities, relative to equity, increases.

Solvency also provides information about *financial flexibility*—the ability of a company to alter cash flows in order to take advantage of unexpected investment opportunities and needs. For example, the higher the percentage of a company's liabilities to its equity, the more difficult it typically will be to borrow additional funds either to take advantage of a promising investment opportunity or to meet obligations. In general, the lower the financial flexibility, the higher the risk is that the enterprise will fail. In a subsequent section of this chapter, we introduce some common ratios used to assess liquidity and long-term solvency.

In summary, even though the balance sheet does not *directly measure* the market value of the entity, it provides valuable information that can be used to help *judge* market value.

Classifications

The usefulness of the balance sheet is enhanced when assets and liabilities are grouped according to common characteristics. *The broad distinction made in the balance sheet is the current versus noncurrent classification of both assets and liabilities.* The remainder of Part

---

[2]We explore some of these relationships in Chapter 5.

A provides an overview of the balance sheet. We discuss each of the three primary elements of the balance sheet (assets, liabilities, and shareholders' equity) in the order they are reported in the statement as well as the classifications typically made within the elements. The balance sheet elements were defined in Chapter 1 as follows:

> **Assets** are probable future economic benefits obtained or controlled by a particular entity as a result of past transactions or events.
>
> **Liabilities** are probable future sacrifices of economic benefits arising from present obligations of a particular entity to transfer assets or provide services to other entities in the future as a result of past transactions or events.
>
> **Equity** (or net assets), called **shareholders' equity** or **stockholders' equity** for a corporation, is the residual interest in the assets of an entity that remains after deducting liabilities.

The key classification of assets and liabilities in the balance sheet is the current versus noncurrent distinction.

Graphic 3–2 lists the balance sheet elements along with their subclassifications.

We intentionally avoid detailed discussion of the question of valuation in order to focus on an overview of the balance sheet. In later chapters we look closer at the nature and valuation of the specific assets and liabilities.

GRAPHIC 3–2   Classification of Elements within a Balance Sheet

> **Assets**
> Current assets
> Investments and funds
> Property, plant, and equipment
> Intangible assets
> Other assets
>
> **Liabilities**
> Current liabilities
> Long-term liabilities
>
> **Shareholders' Equity**
> Paid-in capital
> Retained earnings

ASSETS

Current Assets.   Current assets include cash and other assets that are reasonably expected to be converted to cash or consumed within the coming year, or within the normal operating cycle of the business if that's longer than one year. The **operating cycle** for a typical manufacturing company refers to the period of time necessary to convert cash to raw materials, raw materials to a finished product, the finished product to receivables, and then finally receivables back to cash. This concept is illustrated in Graphic 3–3.

Current assets include cash and all other assets expected to become cash or be consumed within one year or the *operating cycle*, whichever is longer.

In some businesses, such as shipbuilding or distilleries, the operating cycle extends far beyond one year. For example, if it takes two years to build an oil-carrying supertanker, then the shipbuilder will classify as current those assets that will be converted to cash or consumed within two years. But for most businesses the operating cycle will be shorter than one year. In these situations the one-year convention is used to classify both assets and liabilities. Where a company has no clearly defined operating cycle, the one-year convention is used.

Graphic 3–4 presents the current asset section of FedEx Corporation's 2001 and 2000 balance sheets that also appears in the appendix to Chapter 1. In keeping with common practice, the individual current assets are listed in the order of their liquidity (nearness to cash).

GRAPHIC 3–3   Operating Cycle of a Typical Manufacturing Company

Cash and cash equivalents.   The most liquid asset, cash, is listed first. Cash includes cash on hand and in banks that is available for use in the operations of the business and such items as bank drafts, cashier's checks, and money orders. **Cash equivalents** frequently include certain negotiable items such as commercial paper, money market funds, and U.S. treasury bills. These are highly liquid investments that can be quickly converted into cash. Most companies draw a distinction between investments classified as cash equivalents and the next category of current assets, short-term investments, according to the scheduled maturity

GRAPHIC 3–4
Current Assets—FedEx
Corporation

FedEx Corporation

(In thousands)	May 31	
	2001	**2000**
Assets		
Current Assets		
Cash and cash equivalents	$ 121,302	$ 67,959
Receivables, less allowances of $95,815 and $85,972	2,506,044	2,547,043
Spare parts, supplies and fuel	269,269	255,291
Deferred income taxes	435,406	317,784
Prepaid expenses and other	117,040	96,667
Total current assets	3,449,061	3,284,744

of the investment. It is common practice to classify investments that have a maturity date of three months or less from the date of purchase as cash equivalents. FedEx Corporation's policy follows this practice and is disclosed in the summary of significant accounting policies disclosure note. The portion of the note from the company's 2001 financial statements is shown in Graphic 3–5.

GRAPHIC 3–5
Disclosure of Cash
Equivalents—FedEx
Corporation

FedEx Corporation

Summary of Significant Accounting Policies (in part)
Cash Equivalents. Cash equivalents in excess of current operating requirements are invested in short-term, interest-bearing instruments with maturities of three months or less at the date of purchase and are stated at cost, which approximates market value.

Cash that is restricted for a special purpose and not available for current operations should not be classified as a current asset. For example, if cash is being accumulated to repay a debt due in five years, the cash is classified as investments and funds, a noncurrent asset.[3]

CHECK WITH THE **COACH**

Creditors and other users of financial statements depend on meaningful accounting disclosures to make good decisions. The Coach shows you how lenders and others rely on balance sheet classifications, ratios, and other disclosures. How do you know if a company is a good credit risk? The Coach is waiting to show you. ■

Investments are classified as current if management intends to liquidate the investment in the near term.

Short-term investments. Liquid investments not classified as cash equivalents are reported as **short-term investments,** sometimes called *temporary investments* or *short-term marketable securities,* or investments and funds, a noncurrent asset. Investments in stock and debt securities of other corporations are included as short-term investments *if* the company intends to sell those securities within the next 12 months or operating cycle, whichever is longer. If, for example, a company owns 1,000 shares of IBM Corporation stock and intends to hold those shares for several years, the stock is a long-term investment and should be classified as investments and funds.

For reporting purposes, investments in debt and equity securities are classified in one of three categories: (1) held to maturity, (2) trading securities, or (3) securities available for sale. We discuss these different categories and their accounting treatment in Chapter 12.

---

[3]If the debt is due in the next year and classified as a current liability, then the cash also would be classified as current.

Accounts receivable. Accounts receivable result from the sale of goods or services on credit. Notice in Graphic 3–4 that the FedEx receivables are valued less allowance, that is, net of the amount not expected to be collected. Accounts receivable often are referred to as *trade receivables* because they arise in the course of a company's normal trade. *Nontrade receivables* result from loans or advances by the company to other entities. When receivables are supported by a formal agreement or note that specifies payment terms they are called **notes receivable.**

FedEx Corporation

Accounts receivable usually are due in 30 to 60 days, depending on the terms offered to customers and are, therefore, classified as current assets. Any receivable, regardless of the source, not expected to be collected within one year or the operating cycle, whichever is longer, is classified as investments and funds, a noncurrent asset.

Inventories. Inventories include goods awaiting sale (finished goods), goods in the course of production (work in process), and goods to be consumed directly or indirectly in production (raw materials). Inventory for a wholesale or retail company consists only of finished goods, but the inventory of a manufacturer will include all three types of goods. Occasionally, a manufacturing company will report all three types of inventory directly in the balance sheet. More often, only the total amount of inventories is shown in the balance sheet and the balances of each type are shown in a disclosure note. For example, the note shown in Graphic 3–6 appears in the 2001 financial statements of IBM Corporation.

Inventories **consist of assets that a retail or wholesale company acquires for resale or goods that manufacturers produce for sale.**

E. Inventories **($ in millions)**		
	At Dec. 31	
	2001	**2000**
Finished goods	$1,259	$1,446
Work in process and raw materials	3,045	3,319
	$4,304	$4,765

GRAPHIC 3–6
Inventories
Disclosure—IBM
Corporation

Inventories are reported as current assets because they normally are sold within the operating cycle.

FedEx Corporation earns revenue by providing services to its customers rather than by selling goods. That is why there are no merchandise inventories listed in the company's balance sheet. Instead, the company shows an inventory of "spare parts, supplies and fuel." These assets will be *used* during the coming year in the process of earning service revenues.

FedEx Corporation

Prepaid expenses. Recall from Chapter 2 that a **prepaid expense** represents an asset recorded when an expense is paid in advance, creating benefits beyond the current period. Examples are prepaid rent and prepaid insurance. Even though these assets are not converted to cash, they would involve an outlay of cash if not prepaid.

Whether a prepaid expense is current or noncurrent depends on when its benefits will be realized. For example, if rent on an office building were prepaid for one year, then the entire prepayment is classified as a current asset. However, if rent were prepaid for a period extending beyond the coming year, a portion of the prepayment is classified as an other asset, a noncurrent asset.[4] FedEx Corporation combines prepaid expenses with other current assets in its balance sheet. Presumably, the "other" current asset category includes assets—such as short-term investments and nontrade receivables—that, because their amounts are not material, did not warrant separate disclosure.

FedEx Corporation

FedEx lists one other current asset in its balance sheet, "Deferred income taxes." This asset is discussed in Chapter 16.

---

[4]Companies often include prepayments for benefits extending beyond one year as current assets when the amounts are not material.

When assets are expected to provide economic benefits beyond the next year, or operating cycle, they are reported as *noncurrent assets.* Typical classifications of noncurrent assets are (1) investments and funds, (2) property, plant, and equipment, and (3) intangible assets.

Investments and funds are nonoperating assets not used directly in operations.

Investments and Funds.   Most companies occasionally acquire assets that are not used directly in the operations of the business. These "nonoperating" assets include investments in equity and debt securities of other corporations, land held for speculation, noncurrent receivables, and cash set aside for special purposes (such as for future plant expansion). These assets are classified as noncurrent because management does not intend to convert the assets into cash in the next year (or the operating cycle if that's longer).

Tangible, long-lived assets used in the operations of the business are classified as property, plant, and equipment.

Property, Plant, and Equipment.   Virtually all companies own assets classified as **property, plant, and equipment.** The common characteristics these assets share are that they are *tangible, long-lived, and used in the operations of the business.* Property, plant, and equipment, along with intangible assets, generally are referred to as **operational assets.** They often are the primary revenue-generating assets of the business.

Property, plant, and equipment includes land, buildings, equipment, machinery, and furniture, as well as natural resources, such as mineral mines, timber tracts, and oil wells. These various assets usually are reported as a single amount in the balance sheet, with details provided in a note. They are reported at original cost less accumulated depreciation (or depletion for natural resources) to date. Land often is listed as a separate item in this classification because it has an unlimited useful life and thus is not depreciated.

Intangible assets generally represent exclusive rights that a company can use to generate future revenues.

Intangible Assets.   Some assets used in the operations of a business have no physical substance. These are appropriately called **intangible assets.** Generally, these represent the ownership of an exclusive right to something such as a product, a process, or a name. This right can be a valuable resource in generating future revenues. Patents, copyrights, and franchises are examples. They are reported in the balance sheet net of accumulated amortization. Some companies include intangible assets as part of property, plant, and equipment, while others report them either in a separate intangible asset classification or as other noncurrent assets.

Quite often, much of the value of intangibles is not reported in the balance sheet. For example, it would not be unusual for the historical cost of a patent to be significantly lower than its market value. As we discuss in Chapter 10, for internally developed intangibles, the costs that are included as part of historical cost are limited. Specifically, none of the research and development costs incurred in developing the intangible are included in cost.

Other Assets.   Balance sheets often include a catch-all classification of noncurrent assets called **other assets.** This classification includes long-term prepaid expenses, called *deferred charges,* and any noncurrent asset not falling in one of the other classifications. For instance, if a company's noncurrent investments are not material in amount, they might be reported in the other asset classification rather than in a separate investments and funds category.

Graphic 3–7 reproduces the noncurrent asset section of FedEx Corporation's 2001 and 2000 balance sheets.

Quite often, a company will present only the net amount of property, plant, and equipment in the balance sheet and provide details in a disclosure note.

For FedEx, all other noncurrent assets are reported as other assets. This includes the intangible asset goodwill, equipment deposits, and other noncurrent assets.

We've seen how assets are grouped into current and noncurrent categories and that noncurrent assets always are subclassified further. Let's now turn our attention to liabilities. These, too, are separated into current and noncurrent (long-term) categories.

LIABILITIES

Liabilities represent obligations to other entities. The information value of reporting these amounts is enhanced by classifying them as current liabilities and long-term liabilities. Graphic 3–8 shows the liability section of FedEx Corporation's 2001 and 2000 balance sheets.

GRAPHIC 3–7
Property, Plant, and Equipment and Other Assets—FedEx Corporation

FedEx Corporation

(In thousands)	May 31	
	2001	2000
Assets		
Property and equipment, at cost:		
Flight equipment	$ 5,312,853	$ 4,960,204
Package handling and ground support equipment and vehicles	4,620,894	4,203,927
Computer and electronic equipment	2,637,350	2,416,666
Other	3,840,899	3,161,746
	16,411,996	14,742,543
Less accumulated depreciation and amortization	8,311,941	7,659,016
Net property and equipment	8,100,055	7,083,527
Other assets:		
Goodwill	1,082,223	500,547
Equipment deposits and other assets	708,673	658,293
Total other assets	$ 1,790,896	$ 1,158,840

GRAPHIC 3–8
Liabilities—FedEx Corporation

FedEx Corporation

(In thousands)	May 31	
	2001	2000
Liabilities		
Current liabilities		
Current portion of long-term debt	$ 221,392	$ 6,537
Accrued salaries and employee benefits	699,906	755,747
Accounts payable	1,255,298	1,120,855
Accrued expenses	1,072,920	1,007,887
Total current liabilities	3,249,516	2,891,026
Long-term debt, less current portion	1,900,119	1,776,253
Deferred income taxes	455,591	344,613
Other liabilities	1,834,366	1,729,976

Current Liabilities.   Current liabilities are those obligations that are expected to be satisfied through the use of current assets or the creation of other current liabilities. So, this classification includes all liabilities that are expected to be satisfied within one year or the operating cycle, whichever is longer. An exception is a liability that management intends to refinance on a long-term basis. For example, if management intends to refinance a six-month note payable by substituting a two-year note payable and has the ability to do so, then the liability would not be classified as current even though it's due within the coming year. This exception is discussed in more detail in Chapter 13.

The most common current liabilities are accounts payable, notes payable (short-term borrowings), unearned revenues, accrued liabilities, and the currently maturing portion of long-term debt. **Accounts payable** are obligations to suppliers of merchandise or of services purchased on *open account,* with payment usually due in 30 to 60 days. **Notes payable** are written promises to pay cash at some future date (I.O.U.s). Unlike accounts payable, notes usually require the payment of explicit interest in addition to the original obligation amount. Notes maturing in the next year or operating cycle, whichever is longer, will be classified as current liabilities. **Unearned revenues** represent cash received from a customer for goods or services to be provided in a future period.

Current liabilities are expected to be satisfied within one year or the operating cycle, whichever is longer.

Current liabilities usually include accounts and notes payable, unearned revenues, accrued liabilities, and the current maturities of long-term debt.

Accrued liabilities represent obligations created when expenses have been incurred but will not be paid until a subsequent reporting period. Examples are accrued salaries payable, accrued interest payable, and accrued taxes payable. FedEx Corporation reported accrued liabilities at the end of 2001 in two categories: (1) accrued salaries and benefits of $699,906,000, and (2) accrued expenses of $1,072,920,000. In the disclosure note, shown in Graphic 3–9, the company provided the details.

GRAPHIC 3–9
Accrued Expenses
Disclosure—FedEx
Corporation

FedEx Corporation

Note 3: Accrued Salaries and Employee Benefits and Accrued Expenses
The components of accrued salaries and employee benefits and accrued expenses were as follows:
(In thousands)

	May 31	
	2001	**2000**
Salaries	$ 192,892	$ 168,582
Employee benefits	152,979	260,063
Compensated absences	354,035	327,102
Total accrued salaries and employee benefits	$ 699,906	$ 755,747
Insurance	$ 427,685	$ 363,899
Taxes other than income taxes	239,718	237,342
Other	405,517	406,646
Total accrued expenses	$1,072,920	$1,007,887

Current liabilities include the *current maturities of long-term debt.*

Long-term notes, loans, mortgages, and bonds payable usually are reclassified and reported as current liabilities as they become payable within the next year (or operating cycle if that's longer).[5] Likewise, when long-term debt is payable in installments, the installment payable currently is reported as a current liability. For example, a $1,000,000 note payable requiring $100,000 in principal payments to be made in each of the next 10 years is classified as a $100,000 current liability—**current maturities of long-term debt**—and a $900,000 long-term liability.

Chapter 13 provides a more detailed analysis of current liabilities.

Noncurrent, or long-term liabilities, usually are those payable beyond the current year.

Long-Term Liabilities. Long-term liabilities are obligations that will *not* be satisfied in the next year or operating cycle, whichever is longer. They do not require the use of current assets or the creation of current liabilities for payment. Examples are long-term notes, bonds, pension obligations, and lease obligations.

But simply classifying a liability as long-term doesn't provide complete information to external users. For instance, long-term could mean anything from 2 to 20, 30, or 40 years. Payment terms, interest rates, and other details needed to assess the impact of these obligations on future cash flows and long-term solvency are reported in a disclosure note.

At the end of its 2001 fiscal year, FedEx Corporation reported long-term debt, deferred income taxes, and other liabilities. A disclosure note indicated that long-term debt consisted of notes payable, bonds payable, and capital lease obligations. Each of these liabilities, as well as deferred income taxes, is discussed in later chapters. The long-term liability category called *other liabilities* relates primarily to deferred gains on certain lease transactions. This topic also is addressed in a later chapter.

---

[5]Payment can be with current assets or the creation of other current liabilities.

GLOBAL PERSPECTIVE

Balance Sheet

There are significant differences from country to country in the accounting methods used to measure balance sheet items. These differences, of course, also affect income statement amounts. For example, differences in inventory measurement methods affect the calculation of cost of goods sold as well as the inventory balance reported in the balance sheet. Many of these measurement differences are highlighted in the specific chapters that deal with the specific issues.

In terms of balance sheet presentation, the classification of assets and liabilities into current and noncurrent categories is prevalent globally. However, significant differences do exist, particularly with respect to terminology. In the United Kingdom, the term *stocks* refers to inventory. A U.S. investor would interpret stocks to mean investments in equity securities of other companies. In the United States, shareholders' equity is composed of paid-in capital and retained earnings. In many other countries, shareholders' equity is divided into capital and reserves. For example, in Germany, equity is divided into share capital, capital reserves, and revenue reserves. In India, liabilities whose existence is certain but whose value must be estimated, are called *provisions* and are listed separately.

Balance sheet presentation differences also exist. For example, a typical U.K. balance sheet begins with noncurrent assets, called *fixed assets.* Current assets are listed next and current liabilities are subtracted to arrive at net current assets, which is added to fixed assets. Long-term debt is then subtracted from this subtotal to arrive at net assets. The net assets total is equal to shareholders' interest, which is the last item reported in the balance sheet.

SHAREHOLDERS' EQUITY

Shareholders' equity is composed of *paid-in capital* (invested capital) and *retained earnings* (earned capital).

Recall from our discussions in Chapters 1 and 2 that owners' equity is simply a residual amount derived by subtracting liabilities from assets. For that reason, it's also sometimes called net assets. Also recall that owners of a corporation are its shareholders, so owners' equity for a corporation is referred to as shareholders' equity or stockholders' equity. Shareholders' equity for a corporation arises primarily from two sources: (1) amounts *invested* by shareholders in the corporation, and (2) amounts *earned* by the corporation (on behalf of its shareholders). These are reported as (1) **paid-in capital** and (2) **retained earnings.** Retained earnings represents the accumulated net income earned since the inception of the corporation and not (yet) paid to shareholders as dividends.

Graphic 3–10 presents the shareholders' equity section of FedEx Corporation's 2001 and 2000 balance sheets. The company calls this section common stockholders' investment.

GRAPHIC 3–10
Shareholders' Equity—FedEx Corporation

FedEx Corporation

(In thousands, except shares)	**May 31**	
	2001	**2000**
Common Stockholders' Investment:		
Common Stock, $.10 par value; 800,000,000 shares authorized; 298,573,387 shares issued	29,857	29,857
Additional paid-in capital	1,120,627	1,079,462
Retained earnings	4,879,647	4,295,041
Accumulated other comprehensive income	(55,833)	(36,074)
	5,974,298	5,368,286
Less treasury stock, at cost, and deferred compensation	73,878	583,043
Total common stockholders' investment	5,900,420	4,785,243

From the inception of the corporation through May 31, 2001, FedEx has accumulated net income, less dividends, of $4,879,647,000, which is reported as *retained earnings*. The company's *paid-in capital* is represented by common stock and additional paid-in capital which collectively represent cash invested by shareholders in exchange for ownership interests. Information about the number of shares the company has authorized and how many shares have been issued also must be disclosed.

In addition to paid-in capital and retained earnings, shareholders' equity may include a few other equity components. For example, FedEx lists accumulated other comprehensive income, treasury stock, and deferred compensation. Accumulated other comprehensive income is discussed in Chapter 4. Other equity components are addressed in later chapters, Chapter 19 in particular. We also discuss the concept of par value in Chapter 19.

CONCEPT REVIEW EXERCISE

CRE

Balance Sheet Classification

The following is a post-closing trial balance for the Sepia Paint Corporation at December 31, 2003, the end of the company's fiscal year:

Account Title	Debits	Credits
Cash	80,000	
Accounts receivable	200,000	
Allowance for uncollectible accounts		20,000
Inventories	300,000	
Prepaid expenses	30,000	
Note receivable (due in one month)	60,000	
Investments	50,000	
Land	120,000	
Buildings	550,000	
Machinery	500,000	
Accumulated depreciation—buildings and machinery		450,000
Patent (net of amortization)	50,000	
Accounts payable		170,000
Salaries payable		40,000
Interest payable		10,000
Note payable		100,000
Bonds payable (due in 10 years)		500,000
Common stock, no par		400,000
Retained earnings		250,000
Totals	1,940,000	1,940,000

The $50,000 balance in the investment account consists of marketable equity securities of other corporations. The company's intention is to hold the securities for at least three years. The $100,000 note payable is an installment loan. $10,000 of the principal, plus interest, is due on each July 1 for the next 10 years. At the end of the year, 100,000 shares of common stock were issued and outstanding. The company has 500,000 shares of common stock authorized.

Required:
Prepare a classified balance sheet for the Sepia Paint Corporation at December 31, 2003.

SEPIA PAINT CORPORATION
Balance Sheet
At December 31, 2003

Assets

Current assets:

Cash		$ 80,000
Accounts receivable	$ 200,000	
Less: Allowance for uncollectible amounts	(20,000)	180,000
Note receivable		60,000
Inventories		300,000
Prepaid expenses		30,000
Total current assets		650,000
Investments		50,000

Property, plant, and equipment:

Land	120,000	
Buildings	550,000	
Machinery	500,000	
	1,170,000	
Less: Accumulated depreciation	(450,000)	
Net property, plant, and equipment		720,000

Intangibles:

Patent		50,000
Total assets		$1,470,000

Liabilities and Shareholders' Equity

Current liabilities:

Accounts payable		$ 170,000
Salaries payable		40,000
Interest payable		10,000
Current maturities of long-term debt		10,000
Total current liabilities		230,000

Long-term liabilities:

Note payable	$ 90,000	
Bonds payable	500,000	
Total long-term liabilities		590,000

Shareholders' equity:

Common stock, no par, 500,000 shares authorized,		
100,000 shares issued and outstanding	400,000	
Retained earnings	250,000	
Total shareholders' equity		650,000
Total liabilities and shareholders' equity		$1,470,000

The usefulness of the balance sheet, as well as the other financial statements, is significantly enhanced by financial statement disclosures. We now turn our attention to these disclosures.

FINANCIAL DISCLOSURES

Financial statements are included in the annual report a company mails to its shareholders. They are, though, only part of the information provided. Critical to understanding the financial statements and to evaluating the firm's performance and financial health are disclosure notes and other information included in the annual report.

Disclosure Notes

LO5

The full-disclosure principle requires that financial statements provide all material, relevant information concerning the reporting entity.

Disclosure notes typically span several pages and explain or elaborate on the data presented in the financial statements themselves. Throughout this text you will encounter examples of items that usually are disclosed this way. For instance, information providing details of pension plans, leases, debt, and several assets is disclosed in the notes. Disclosures must include certain specific notes such as a summary of significant accounting policies, descriptions of subsequent events, and related-party transactions, but many notes are fashioned to suit the disclosure needs of the particular reporting enterprise. Actually, any explanation that contributes to investors' and creditors' understanding of the results of operations, financial position, or cash flows of the company should be included. Some common disclosures are made by some companies in the form of notes, while other companies disclose the same information as separate schedules or in other formats within the annual report. The specific format of disclosure is not important, only that the information is, in fact, disclosed. Let's take a look at just a few disclosure notes.

SUMMARY OF SIGNIFICANT ACCOUNTING POLICIES

The *summary of significant accounting policies* conveys valuable information about the company's choices from among various alternative accounting methods.

FedEx Corporation

There are many areas where management chooses from among equally acceptable alternative accounting methods. For example, management chooses whether to use accelerated or straight-line depreciation, whether to use FIFO, LIFO, or average cost to measure inventories, and whether the completed contract or percentage-of-completion method best reflects the performance of construction operations. It also defines which securities it considers to be cash equivalents and its policies regarding the timing of recognizing revenues. Typically, the first disclosure note consists of a summary of significant accounting policies that discloses the choices the company makes.[6] Graphic 3–11 shows you a portion of a typical summary note from a recent annual report of the Ralston Purina Company. FedEx Corporation reports the summary in its Note 2, shown in the appendix to Chapter 1.

GRAPHIC 3–11 Summary of Significant Accounting Policies—Ralston Purina Company

Summary of Accounting Policies (in part)
Ralston Purina Company's (the Company) significant accounting policies, which conform to generally accepted accounting principles and are applied on a consistent basis among years, except as indicated, are described below:
Principles of Consolidation—The consolidated financial statements include the accounts of the Company and its majority-owned subsidiaries. All significant intercompany transactions are eliminated. Investments in affiliated companies, 20% through 50%-owned, are carried at equity.
Financial Instruments (in part)—The Company uses financial and commodities derivatives in the management of foreign currency, commodities pricing and interest rate risks that are inherent to its business operations. Such instruments are not held or issued for trading purposes.
Cash Equivalents for purposes of the statement of cash flows are considered to be all highly liquid investments with a maturity of three months or less when purchased.
Inventories are valued generally at the lower of average cost or market.
Depreciation is generally provided on the straight-line basis by charges to costs or expenses at rates based on the estimated useful lives of the properties. Estimated useful lives range from 3 to 25 years for machinery and equipment and 10 to 50 years for buildings.
Revenue Recognition—Revenue is recognized upon shipment of product to customers. Sales discounts, returns and allowances are included in net sales, and the provision for doubtful accounts is included in selling, general and administrative expenses in the consolidated statement of earnings.

Studying this note is an essential step in analyzing financial statements. Obviously, knowing which methods were used to derive certain accounting numbers is critical to assessing the adequacy of those amounts.

---

[6]"Disclosure of Accounting Policies," *Accounting Principles Board Opinion No. 22* (New York: AICPA, 1972).

SUBSEQUENT EVENTS

When an event that has a material effect on the company's financial position occurs after the fiscal year-end but before the financial statements actually are issued, the event is disclosed in a **subsequent event** disclosure note. Examples include the issuance of debt or equity securities, a business combination or the sale of a business, the sale of assets, an event that sheds light on the outcome of a loss contingency, or any other event having a material effect on operations. Graphic 3–12 illustrates the required disclosure by showing a note that International Paper Company included in its December 31, 2000, financial statements, announcing both the sale of certain businesses and an agreement to sell forestlands.

> A *subsequent event* is a significant development that takes place after the company's fiscal year-end but before the financial statements are issued.

> **GRAPHIC 3–12**
> Subsequent Events— International Paper Company

19 Subsequent Events

As of March 1, 2001, the dispositions of certain businesses discussed in Note 7—Businesses Held for Sale were completed. Zanders, the Argentine businesses and the Hamilton mill were sold for approximately $130 million. In addition, the oil and gas interests were conveyed to a third party for approximately $260 million.

On February 15, 2001, International Paper announced that an agreement was reached to sell approximately 265,000 acres of forestlands in the state of Washington for approximately $500 million.

We cover subsequent events in more depth in Chapter 13.

NOTEWORTHY EVENTS AND TRANSACTIONS

Some transactions and events occur only occasionally, but when they do occur are potentially important to evaluating a company's financial statements. In this category are related-party transactions, errors and irregularities, and illegal acts. The more frequent of these is related-party transactions.

Sometimes a company will engage in transactions with owners, management, families of owners or management, affiliated companies, and other parties that can significantly influence or be influenced by the company. The potential problem with **related-party transactions** is that their economic substance may differ from their legal form. For instance, borrowing or lending money at an interest rate that differs significantly from the market interest rate is an example of a transaction that could result from a related-party involvement. As a result of the potential for misrepresentation, financial statement users are particularly interested in more details about these transactions.

When related-party transactions occur, companies must disclose the nature of the relationship, provide a description of the transactions, and report the dollar amounts of transactions and any amounts due from or to related parties.[7] Graphic 3–13 shows a disclosure note from a recent annual report of GAP Inc. The note describes the company's relationship with Fisher Development, Inc., a general contractor wholly owned by the brother of GAP's chairman and his immediate family.

> The economic substance of *related-party* transactions should be disclosed, including dollar amounts involved.

More infrequent are errors, irregularities, and illegal acts; however, when they do occur, their disclosure is important. The distinction between errors and **irregularities** is that errors are unintentional while irregularities are *intentional* distortions of financial statements.[8] Obviously, management fraud might cause a user to approach financial analysis from an entirely different and more cautious viewpoint.

Closely related to irregularities are **illegal acts** such as bribes, kickbacks, illegal contributions to political candidates, and other violations of the law. Accounting for illegal practices has been influenced by the Foreign Corrupt Practices Act passed by Congress in 1977. The Act is intended to discourage illegal business practices through tighter controls and also

---

[7]"Related Party Disclosures," *Statement of Financial Accounting Standards No. 57* (Stamford, Conn.: FASB, 1982).
[8]"The Auditor's Responsibility to Detect and Report Errors and Irregularities," *Statement on Auditing Standards No. 53* (New York: AICPA, 1988).

GRAPHIC 3–13
Related-Party
Transactions
Disclosure—GAP Inc.

Note I: Related Party Transactions (in part)
We have an agreement with Fisher Development, Inc. (FDI), a company wholly owned by the brother of our chairman and the brother's immediate family, setting forth the terms under which FDI may act as one of our general contractors in connection with our construction activities. FDI acted as general contractor for 282, 675, and 547 new store concepts' leasehold improvements and fixtures during fiscal 2001, 2000 and 1999, respectively. In the same respective years, FDI supervised construction of 171, 262 and 123 store concept expansions, remodels and relocations as well as headquarters facilities. . . . The agreement with FDI is reviewed annually by the Audit and Finance Committee of the Board of Directors.

encourage better disclosure of those practices when encountered. The nature of such disclosures should be influenced by the materiality of the impact of illegal acts on amounts disclosed in the financial statements.[9] However, the SEC in *Staff Accounting Bulletin No. 99*,[10] expressed its view that exclusive reliance on quantitative benchmarks to assess materiality in preparing financial statements is inappropriate. A number of other factors, including whether the item in question involves an unlawful transaction, should also be considered when determining materiality.

As you might expect, any disclosures of related-party transactions, irregularities, and illegal acts can be quite sensitive. Although auditors must be considerate of the privacy of the parties involved, that consideration cannot be subordinate to users' needs for full disclosure.

We've discussed only a few of the disclosure notes most frequently included in annual reports. Other common disclosures include details concerning earnings per share calculations, income taxes, property and equipment, contingencies, long-term debt, leases, pensions, stock options, changes in accounting methods, fair values of financial instruments, and exposure to market risk and credit risk. We discuss and illustrate these in later chapters in the context of related financial statement elements.

> Disclosure notes for some financial statement elements are required. Others are provided when required by specific situations in the interest of full disclosure.

Management Discussion and Analysis

> **LO6**
>
> The management discussion and analysis provides a biased but informed perspective of a company's (a) operations, (b) liquidity, and (c) capital resources.

Each annual report includes a fairly lengthy discussion and analysis provided by the company's management. In this section, management provides its views on significant events, trends, and uncertainties pertaining to the company's (a) operations, (b) liquidity, and (c) capital resources. Although the **management discussion and analysis (MDA)** section may embody management's biased perspective, it can offer an informed insight that might not be available elsewhere. Graphic 3–14 contains part of the liquidity and capital resources portion of the Walt Disney Company's MDA that followed a discussion of operations in its 2000 annual report.

Management's Responsibilities

Auditors examine financial statements and the internal control procedures designed to support the content of those statements. Their role is to attest to the fairness of the financial statements based on that examination. However, management prepares and is responsible for the financial statements and other information in the annual report. To enhance the awareness of the users of financial statements concerning the relative roles of management and the auditor, annual reports include a management's responsibilities section that asserts the responsibility of management for the information contained in the annual report as well as an assessment of the company's internal control procedures. Wording of this section is fairly standard. A typical disclosure is provided in Graphic 3–15.

---

[9]"Illegal Acts by Clients," *Statement on Auditing Standards No. 54* (New York: AICPA, 1988).
[10]"Materiality," *Staff Accounting Bulletin No. 99* (Washington, DC: SEC, August 1999).

Management Discussion and Analysis of Financial Condition and Results of Operations
(In part: Liquidity and Capital Resources only)

During the year, strong operating and other cash flows enable the Company to reduce its borrowings by $2.2 billion, even after investing approximately $4.7 billion in film and television projects and parks, resorts and other properties, and after paying dividends totaling $434 million and repurchasing $166 million of its common stock.

Cash provided by operations increased 15%, or $846 million, to $6.4 billion, driven by higher income before amortization of intangible assets and noncash gains and higher amortization of television broadcast rights relative to cash payments, partially offset by higher income tax payments.

In 2000, the Company invested $2.7 billion to develop, produce and acquire rights to film and television properties, a decrease of $341 million compared to the prior year. The decrease was primarily due to a $310 million payment related to the acquisition of a film library in the prior year.

During the year, the Company invested $2.0 billion in parks, resorts and other properties. These expenditures reflected continued expansion activities related to Disney's California Adventure and certain resort facilities at the Walt Disney World Resort. The decrease of $121 million from the prior year reflects the final payment for the second cruise ship, the Disney Wonder, in the prior year, partially offset by increased spending on Disney's California Adventure in the current year.

The Company believes that its financial condition is strong and that its cash, other liquid assets, operating cash flows, access to equity capital markets and borrowing capacity, taken together, provide adequate resources to fund ongoing operating requirements and future capital expenditures related to the expansion of existing businesses and development of new projects.

GRAPHIC 3–14
Management Discussion and Analysis—Walt Disney Company

Responsibility for Financial Statements
Hershey Foods Corporation is responsible for the financial statements and other financial information contained in this report. The Corporation believes that the financial statements have been prepared in conformity with generally accepted accounting principles appropriate under the circumstances to reflect in all material respects the substance of applicable events and transactions. In preparing the financial statements, it is necessary that management make informed estimates and judgments. The other financial information in this annual report is consistent with the financial statements.

The Corporation maintains a system of internal accounting controls designed to provide reasonable assurance that financial records are reliable for purposes of preparing financial statements and that assets are properly accounted for and safeguarded. The concept of reasonable assurance is based on the recognition that the cost of the system must be related to the benefits to be derived. The Corporation believes its system provides an appropriate balance in this regard. The Corporation maintains an Internal Audit Department that reviews the adequacy and tests the application of internal accounting controls.

The financial statements have been audited by Arthur Andersen LLP, independent public accountants, whose appointment was ratified by stockholder vote at the stockholders' meeting held on April 24, 2001. Their report expresses an opinion that the Corporation's financial statements are fairly stated in conformity with generally accepted accounting principles, and they have indicated to us that their examination was performed in accordance with generally accepted auditing standards that are designed to obtain reasonable assurance about whether the financial statements are free of material misstatement.

The Audit Committee of the Board of Directors of the Corporation, consisting solely of outside directors, meets regularly with the independent public accountants, internal auditors and management to discuss, among other things, the audit scopes and results. Arthur Andersen LLP and the internal auditors both have full and free access to the Audit Committee, with and without the presence of management.

GRAPHIC 3–15
Management's Responsibilities—Hershey Foods Corporation

The management's responsibilities section avows the responsibility of management for the company's financial statements and internal control system.

GRAPHIC 3–16
Auditors' Report—
Microsoft Corporation

The *auditors' report* provides the analyst with an independent and professional opinion about the fairness of the representations in the financial statements.

Independent Auditors' Report

We have audited the accompanying balance sheets of Microsoft Corporation and subsidiaries as of June 30, 2000 and 2001, and the related statements of income, cash flows, and stockholders' equity for each of the three years ended June 30, 2001. These financial statements are the responsibility of the Company's management. Our responsibility is to express an opinion on these financial statements based on our audits.

We conducted our audits in accordance with generally accepted auditing standards. Those standards require that we plan and perform the audit to obtain reasonable assurance about whether the financial statements are free of material misstatement. An audit includes examining, on a test basis, evidence supporting the amounts and disclosures in the financial statements. An audit also includes assessing the accounting principles used and significant estimates made by management, as well as evaluating the overall financial statement presentation. We believe that our audits provide a reasonable basis for our opinion.

In our opinion, such financial statements present fairly, in all material respects, the financial position of Microsoft Corporation and subsidiaries as of June 30, 2000 and 2001, and the results of their operations and their cash flows for each of the three years ended June 30, 2001, in conformity with accounting principles generally accepted in the United States of America.

As discussed in the notes to the financial statements, the Company was required to adopt *Statement of Financial Accounting Standards No. 133,* "Accounting for Derivative Instruments and Hedging Activities," effective July 1, 2000.

Seattle, Washington
July 19, 2001

Deloitte & Touche LLP

Auditors' Report

LO7

One step in financial analysis should be an examination of the **auditors' report.** This is the report issued by the CPAs who audit the financial statements that informs users of the audit findings. Every audit report looks similar to the one prepared by Deloitte & Touche LLP for the financial statements of Microsoft Corporation, as shown in Graphic 3–16.

The reason for the similarities is that auditors' reports must be in exact compliance with the specifications of the AICPA.[11] In most cases, including the report for Microsoft, the auditors will be satisfied that the financial statements "present fairly" the financial position, results of operations, and cash flows and are "in conformity with generally accepted accounting principles." These situations prompt an **unqualified opinion.** Sometimes circumstances cause the auditors' report to include an explanatory paragraph in addition to the standard wording, even though the report is unqualified. Most notably, these include:

a. *Lack of consistency* due to a change in accounting principle such that comparability is affected even though the auditor concurs with the desirability of the change.

b. *Uncertainty* as to the ultimate resolution of a contingency for which a loss is material in amount but not necessarily probable or probable but not estimable.

c. *Emphasis* of a matter concerning the financial statements that does not affect the existence of an unqualified opinion but relates to a significant event such as a related-party transaction.

The auditors' report calls attention to problems that might exist in the financial statements.

Some audits result in the need to issue other than an unqualified opinion, in which case the auditor will issue a (an):

a. *Qualified opinion* This contains an exception to the standard unqualified opinion but not of sufficient seriousness to invalidate the financial statements as a whole.

---

[11]"Reports on Audited Financial Statements," *Statements on Auditing Standards No. 58* (New York: AICPA, 1988), as amended by "Omnibus Statement on Auditing Standards—2000," *Statements on Auditing Standards No. 93* (New York: AICPA, 2000).

Examples of exceptions are (a) nonconformity with generally accepted accounting principles, (b) inadequate disclosures, and (c) a limitation or restriction of the scope of the examination.

  b. *Adverse opinion* This is necessary when the exceptions are so serious that a qualified opinion is not justified. Adverse opinions are rare because auditors usually are able to persuade management to rectify problems to avoid this undesirable report.

  c. *Disclaimer* An auditor will disclaim an opinion if insufficient information has been gathered to express an opinion.

During the course of each audit, the auditor is required to evaluate the company's ability to continue as a going concern for a reasonable time. If the auditor determines there is significant doubt, an explanation of the potential problem must be included in the auditors' report.[12]

Obviously, the auditors' report is most informative when any of these deviations from the standard unqualified opinion are present. These departures from the norm should raise a red flag to a financial analyst and prompt additional search for information.

The auditors' report of Covad Communications Group, Inc., a provider of broadband communications services, exhibited in Graphic 3–17, included a fourth paragraph after the standard first three paragraphs.

> **The auditor should assess the firm's ability to continue as a going concern.**

The accompanying consolidated financial statements have been prepared assuming that Covad Communications Group, Inc. will continue as a going concern. As more fully described in Note 1 to the consolidated financial statements, the company has incurred recurring operating losses and negative cash flows from operating and investing activities and it has a stockholders' deficit as of December 31, 2000. In addition, a number of the Company's customers have experienced financial difficulties and certain of them have filed for bankruptcy protection. Furthermore, several of the Company's stockholders and purchasers of its convertible notes have filed lawsuits against the Company and certain of its current and former officers alleging violations of federal and state securities laws. The relief sought in these lawsuits includes rescission of certain convertible note sales completed by the Company in September 2000 and unspecified damages. Additionally, subsequent to December 31, 2000, the Company has received two notices of default relating to its lack of compliance with a covenant contained in one of its senior note indentures. These conditions raise substantial doubt about the Company's ability to continue as a going concern.

> **GRAPHIC 3–17**
> Going Concern Paragraph—Covad Communications Group, Inc.

Compensation of Directors and Top Executives

In the early 1990s, the compensation large U.S. corporations pay their top executives became an issue of considerable public debate and controversy. Shareholders, employees, politicians, and the public in general began to question the huge pay packages received by company officials at the same time that more and more rank and file employees were being laid off as a result of company cutbacks. Contributing to the debate was the realization that the compensation gap between executives and lower level employees was much wider than in Japan and most other industrial countries. During this time, it also became apparent that discovering exactly how much compensation corporations paid their top people was nearly impossible.

Part of the problem stemmed from the fact that disclosures of these amounts were meager; but a large part of the problem was that a substantial portion of executive pay often is in the form of stock options. Executive stock options give their holders the right to buy stock at a specified price, usually equal to the market price when the options are granted. When stock prices rise, executives can exercise their options and realize a profit. In some cases, options have made executive compensation seem extremely high. Stock options are discussed in depth in Chapter 18.

---

[12]"The Auditor's Consideration of an Entity's Ability to Continue as a Going Concern," *Statement on Auditing Standards No. 59* (New York: AICPA, 1988).

To help shareholders and others sort out the content of executive pay packages and better understand the commitments of the company in this regard, recent SEC requirements now provide for more disclosures on compensation to directors and executives, and in particular, concerning stock options. The **proxy statement** which must be sent each year to all shareholders, usually in the same mailing with the annual report, previously served primarily to invite shareholders to the meeting to elect board members and to vote on issues before the shareholders or to vote using an enclosed proxy card. Beginning with 1992 financial statements, the proxy statement assumed a larger role. Graphic 3–18 lists the information that the statement now also reports.

The *proxy statement*, which is sent each year to all shareholders, contains disclosures on compensation to directors and executives.

GRAPHIC 3–18
Proxy Statement Information

A summary compensation table that outlines how much directors and top executives are paid and what retirement benefits they will receive.

A table of options granted that reports information about options given to individually identified executives in the most recent year, including:
- The number of options and dates granted.
- The percentage of total options given to each top executive.
- The exercise price and expiration date of options.
- The company's estimate of the options' values.

A table of options holdings that reports information about all options currently held by individually identified executives, including:
- The number of options each executive owns and their value.
- The number of shares acquired in the most recent year by exercising options.
- The amount of profit realized from exercising options.

GLOBAL PERSPECTIVE

Disclosure Practices around the World

Most countries require specific disclosures by companies operating within their borders. Many of these disclosures are similar. However, the amount and types of required and voluntary disclosures differ from country to country. For example, in Israel, companies whose securities are publicly traded are required to disclose any receivable that exceeds 5 percent of total current assets. In Mexico, a disclosure reports the separate identification of long-term liabilities into the following categories: suppliers, affiliates, income tax, employees' profit sharing, and bank loans.

Several supplemental disclosures are uniquely European. These include information about shares and shareholders, certain employee disclosures, and environmental disclosures. An example of an environmental disclosure would be a discussion of safety measures adopted by the company in their manufacturing plants. In France, many enterprises are required to publish an annual social balance sheet. This report covers matters such as employment, training, health and safety conditions, employee benefits, and environmental issues. In general, European companies consider the full-disclosure concept to include a much broader set of information than do U.S. companies.

PART

C

RISK ANALYSIS

Using Financial Statement Information

The overriding objective of financial reporting is providing information that investors and creditors can use to make decisions. Nevertheless, it's sometimes easy to lose sight of that objective while dealing with the intricacies that specific concepts and procedures can involve. In this part of the chapter we provide an overview of financial statement analysis and then demonstrate the use of ratios, a popular financial statement analysis technique, to analyze risk.

LO8

Investors, creditors, and others use information that companies provide in corporate financial reports to make decisions. Although the financial reports focus primarily on the past performance and the present financial condition of the reporting company, information users are most interested in the outlook for the future. Trying to gain a glimpse of the future from past and present data entails using various tools and techniques to formulate predictions. This is the goal of financial statement analysis.

Financial statements are not presented in isolation. Every financial statement issued is accompanied by the corresponding financial statement of the preceding year, and often the previous two years. These are called **comparative financial statements.** They enable investors, creditors, and other users to compare year-to-year financial position, results of operations, and cash flows. These comparative data help an analyst detect and predict trends. Because operations often expand and contract in a cyclical fashion, analysis of any one year's data may not provide an accurate picture of a company.

Comparative financial statements allow financial statement users to compare year-to-year financial position, results of operations, and cash flows.

Some analysts enhance their comparison by expressing each item as a percentage of that same item in the financial statements of another year (base amount) in order to more easily see year-to-year changes. This is referred to as **horizontal analysis.** Similarly, **vertical analysis** involves expressing each item in the financial statements as a percentage of an appropriate corresponding total, or base amount, but within the same year. For example, cash, inventory, and other assets can be restated as a percentage of total assets; net income and each expense can be restated as a percentage of revenues.

Regardless of the specific technique used, the essential point is that accounting numbers are virtually meaningless in isolation. Their value derives from comparison with other numbers. The most common way of comparing accounting numbers to evaluate the performance and risk of a firm is **ratio analysis.**

No accounting numbers are meaningful in and of themselves.

We use ratios every day. Batting averages indicate how well our favorite baseball players are performing. We evaluate basketball players by field goal percentage and rebounds per game. Speedometers measure the speed of our cars in terms of miles per hour. We compare grocery costs on the basis of price per pound or ounce. In each of these cases, the ratio is more meaningful than a single number by itself. Do 45 hits indicate satisfactory performance? It depends on the number of at-bats. Is $2 a good price for cheese? It depends on how many ounces the $2 buys. Ratios make these measurements meaningful.

Likewise, we can use ratios to help evaluate a firm's performance and financial position. Is net income of $4 million a cause for shareholders to celebrate? Probably not if shareholders' equity is $10 billion. But if shareholders equity is $10 million, that's a 40% return on equity! Although ratios provide more meaningful information than absolute numbers alone, the ratios are most useful when analyzed relative to some standard of comparison. That standard of comparison may be previous performance of the same company, the performance of a competitor company, or an industry average for the particular ratio.

Evaluating information in ratio form allows analysts to control for size differences over time and among firms.

Accountants should be conversant with ratio analysis for at least three reasons. First, when preparing financial statements, accountants should be familiar with the ways users will use the information provided to make better decisions concerning what and how to report. Second, when accountants participate in company decisions concerning operating and financing alternatives, they may find ratio analysis helpful in evaluating available choices. Third, during the planning stages of an audit, independent auditors often use ratio analysis to identify potential audit problems and determine the specific audit procedures that should be performed.

We introduce ratios related to risk analysis in this chapter and ratios related to profitability analysis in Chapter 5. You will also employ ratios in Decision Makers' Perspective sections of many of the chapters in this text. Analysis cases that benefit from ratio analysis are included in many of these chapters as well.

Investors and creditors use financial information to assess the future risk and return of their investments in business enterprises. The balance sheet provides information useful to this assessment. A key element of risk analysis is investigating a company's ability to pay its obligations when they come due. This type of risk often is referred to as **default risk.** Another aspect of risk is **operational risk** which relates more to how adept a company is at withstanding various events and circumstances that might impair its ability to earn profits. Obviously, these two types of risk are not completely independent of one another. Inability to earn profits certainly increases a company's chances of defaulting on its obligations. Conversely, regardless of a company's long-run prospects for generating profits, if it can't meet its obligations, the company's operations are at risk.

Assessing risk necessarily involves consideration of a variety of economywide risk factors such as inflation, interest rates, and the general business climate. Industrywide influences including competition, labor conditions, and technological forces also affect a company's risk profile. Still other risk factors are specific to the company itself. Financial ratios often are used in risk analysis to investigate a company's **liquidity** and **long-term solvency.** As we discuss some of the more common ratios in the following paragraphs, keep in mind the inherent relationship between risk and return and thus between our risk analysis in this chapter and our profitability analysis in Chapter 5.

LIQUIDITY RATIOS

LO9

Liquidity refers to the readiness of assets to be converted to cash. By comparing a company's liquid assets with its short-term obligations, we can obtain a general idea of the firm's ability to pay its short-term debts as they come due. Usually, current assets are thought of as the most liquid of a company's assets. Obviously, though, some are more liquid than others, so it's important also to evaluate the specific makeup of current assets. Two common measures of liquidity are (1) the current ratio and (2) the acid-test ratio (or quick ratio) calculated as follows:

$$\text{Current ratio} = \frac{\text{Current assets}}{\text{Current liabilities}}$$

$$\text{Acid-test ratio (or quick ratio)} = \frac{\text{Quick assets}}{\text{Current liabilities}}$$

Working capital, the difference between current assets and current liabilities, is a popular measure of a company's ability to satisfy its short-term obligations.

Current Ratio.   Implicit in the definition of a current liability is the relationship between current assets and current liabilities. The difference between current assets and current liabilities is called **working capital.** By comparing a company's obligations that will shortly become due with the company's cash and other assets that, by definition, are expected to shortly be converted to cash, the ratio offers some indication as to ability to pay those debts. Although used in a variety of decisions, it is particularly useful to those considering whether to extend short-term credit. The **current ratio** is computed by dividing current assets by current liabilities. A current ratio of 2 indicates that the company has twice as many current assets available as current liabilities.

FedEx Corporation

FedEx Corporation's working capital (in thousands) at the end of its 2001 fiscal year is $199,545 consisting of current assets of $3,449,061 (Graphic 3–4 on page 122) minus current liabilities of $3,249,516 (Graphic 3–8 on page 125). The current ratio can be computed as follows:

$$\text{Current ratio} = \frac{\$3,449,061}{\$3,249,516} = 1.06$$

Working capital may not present an accurate or complete picture of a company's liquidity.

Care should be taken, however, in assessing liquidity based solely on working capital. Liabilities usually are paid with cash, not other components of working capital. A company could have difficulty paying its liabilities even with a current ratio significantly greater than 1.0. For example, if a significant portion of current assets consisted of inventories, and inventories usually are not converted to cash for several months, there could be a problem in paying accounts payable due in 30 days. On the other hand, a current ratio of less than 1.0 doesn't necessarily mean the company will have difficulty meeting its current obligations. A line of credit, for instance, which the company can use to borrow funds, provides financial flexibility. FedEx Corporation's 2001 annual report discloses a $1 billion credit agreement with banks. That also must be considered in assessing liquidity.

ETHICAL DILEMMA

The Raintree Cosmetic Company has several loans outstanding with a local bank. The debt agreements all contain a covenant stipulating that Raintree must maintain a current ratio of at least .9. Jackson Phillips, company controller, estimates that the 2003 year-end current assets and current liabilities will be $2,100,000 and $2,400,000, respectively. These estimates provide a current ratio of only .875. Violation of the debt agreement will increase Raintree's borrowing costs as the loans are renegotiated at higher rates.

Jackson proposes to the company president that Raintree purchase inventory of $600,000 on credit before year-end. This will cause both current assets and current liabilities to increase by the same amount, but the current ratio will increase to .9. The extra $600,000 in inventory will be used over the later part of 2004. However, the purchase will cause warehousing costs and financing costs to increase.

Jackson is concerned about the ethics of his proposal. What do you think?

Acid-Test Ratio (or Quick Ratio).   Some analysts like to modify the current ratio to consider only current assets that are readily available to pay current liabilities. One such variation in common use is the **acid-test ratio.** This ratio excludes inventories and prepaid items from current assets before dividing by current liabilities. The numerator, then, consists of cash, short-term investments, and accounts receivable, the "quick assets." By eliminating current assets less readily convertible into cash, the acid-test ratio provides a more rigorous indication of liquidity than does the current ratio.

> The *acid-test ratio* provides a more stringent indication of a company's ability to pay its current obligations.

FedEx Corporation's quick assets at the end of its 2001 fiscal year (in thousands) total $2,627,346 ($121,302 + 2,506,044). The acid-test ratio can be computed as follows:

> **FedEx Corporation**

$$\text{Acid-test ratio} = \frac{\$2,627,346}{\$3,249,516} = .81$$

Are these liquidity ratios adequate? It's difficult to say without some point of comparison. As indicated previously, common standards for such comparisons are industry averages for similar ratios or ratios of the same company in prior years. Industry averages for the above two ratios are as follows:

Industry Average

Current ratio = 1.23

Acid-test ratio = .95

FedEx Corporation's ratios are less than the industry average. Is this an indication that liquidity is a problem for FedEx? Not necessarily, but it certainly would raise a red flag that calls for caution in analyzing other areas. Remember, each ratio is but one piece of the entire puzzle. For instance, profitability is perhaps the best indication of liquidity in the long run. We discuss ratios that measure profitability in Chapter 5.

Also, management may be very efficient in managing current assets so that, for example, receivables are collected faster than normal or inventory is sold faster than normal, making those assets more liquid than they otherwise would be. Higher turnover ratios, relative to that of a competitor or the industry, generally indicate a more liquid position for a given level of the current ratio. We discuss these turnover ratios in Chapter 5.

> Liquidity ratios should be assessed in the context of both profitability and efficiency of managing assets.

FINANCING RATIOS

Investors and creditors, particularly long-term creditors, are vitally interested in a company's long-term solvency and stability. Financing ratios provide some indication of the riskiness of a company with regard to its ability to pay its long-term debts. Two common financing ratios are (1) the debt to equity ratio and (2) the times interest earned ratio. These ratios are calculated as follows:

$$\text{Debt to equity ratio} = \frac{\text{Total liabilities}}{\text{Shareholders' equity}}$$

$$\text{Times interest earned ratio} = \frac{\text{Net income} + \text{Interest expense} + \text{Taxes}}{\text{Interest expense}}$$

The *debt to equity ratio* indicates the extent of reliance on creditors, rather than owners, in providing resources.

Debt to Equity Ratio. The **debt to equity ratio** compares resources provided by creditors with resources provided by owners. It is calculated by dividing total liabilities (current and noncurrent) by total shareholders' equity (including retained earnings).[13]

The ratio provides a measure of creditors' protection in the event of insolvency. Other things being equal, the higher the ratio, the higher the risk. The higher the ratio, the greater the creditor claims on assets, so the higher the likelihood an individual creditor would not be paid in full if the company is unable to meet its obligations. Relatedly, a high ratio indicates not only more fixed interest obligations, but probably a higher *rate* of interest as well because lenders tend to charge higher rates as the level of debt increases.

FedEx Corporation

FedEx Corporation's total liabilities at the end of its 2001 fiscal year (in thousands) are $7,439,592 (current liabilities, $3,249,516 + long-term debt, $1,900,119 + deferred income taxes, $455,591 + other liabilities, $1,834,366—Graphic 3–8 on page 125), and shareholders' equity totals $5,900,420 (Graphic 3–10 on page 127). The debt to equity ratio can be computed as follows:

$$\text{Debt to equity ratio} = \frac{\$7,439,592}{\$5,900,420} = 1.26$$

As with all ratios, the debt to equity ratio is more meaningful if compared to some standard such as an industry average or a competitor. For example, the debt to equity ratio for United Parcel Service, Inc. (UPS), a major competitor, is 1.23—very similar to FedEx Corporation's ratio. On the other hand, the ratio for Microsoft Corporation is only .25, indicating that Microsoft has significantly less debt in its capital structure than does FedEx. Does this mean Microsoft's default risk is less than that of FedEx? Other things equal—yes. Is that good? Not necessarily. As discussed in the next section, it may be that debt is being underutilized by Microsoft. More debt might increase the potential for return, but the price would be higher risk. This is a fundamental tradeoff faced by virtually all firms when trying to settle on the optimal capital structure.

Relationship between risk and profitability. The proportion of debt in the capital structure also is of interest to shareholders. After all, shareholders receive no return on their investments until after all creditor claims are paid. Therefore, the higher the debt to equity ratio, the higher the risk to shareholders. On the other hand, by earning a return on borrowed funds that exceeds the cost of borrowing the funds, a company can provide its shareholders with a total return higher than it could achieve by employing equity funds alone. This is referred to as favorable **financial leverage**.

The debt to equity ratio indicates the extent of trading on the equity or *financial leverage*.

For illustration, consider a newly formed corporation attempting to determine the appropriate mix of debt and equity. The initial capitalization goal is $50 million. The capitalization mix alternatives have been narrowed to two: (1) $10 million in debt and $40 million in equity and (2) $30 million in debt and $20 million in equity.

Also assume that regardless of the capitalization mix chosen, the corporation will be able to generate a 16% annual return, *before payment of interest and income taxes,* on the $50 million in assets acquired. In other words, income before interest and taxes will be $8 million (16% × $50 million). If the interest rate on debt is 8% and the income tax rate is 40%, comparative net income for the first year of operations for the two capitalization alternatives can be calculated as follows:

---

[13]A commonly used variation of the debt to equity ratio is found by dividing total liabilities by *total assets* (or total equities), rather than by shareholders' equity only. Of course, in this configuration the ratio measures precisely the same attribute of the firm's capital structure but can be interpreted as the percentage of a company's total assets provided by funds from creditors, rather than by owners.

	Alternative 1	**Alternative 2**
Income before interest and taxes	$8,000,000	$8,000,000
Less: Interest expense	(800,000)[a]	(2,400,000)[b]
Income before taxes	$7,200,000	$5,600,000
Less: Income tax expense (40%)	(2,880,000)	(2,240,000)
Net income	$4,320,000	$3,360,000

[a]8% × $10,000,000
[b]8% × $30,000,000

Choose Alternative 1? Probably not. Although alternative 1 provides a higher net income, the return on the shareholders' equity (net income divided by shareholders' equity) is higher for alternative 2. Here's why:

	Alternative 1	**Alternative 2**
Return on shareholders' equity[14] =	$\dfrac{\$4,320,000}{\$40,000,000}$	$\dfrac{\$3,360,000}{\$20,000,000}$
	= 10.8%	16.8%

Favorable financial leverage means earning a return on borrowed funds that exceeds the cost of borrowing the funds.

Alternative 2 generated a higher return for each dollar invested by shareholders. This is because the company leveraged its $20 million equity investment with additional debt. Because the cost of the additional debt (8%) is less than the return on assets invested (16%), the return to shareholders is higher. This is the essence of favorable financial leverage.

Be aware, though, leverage is not always favorable; the cost of borrowing the funds might exceed the returns they provide. If the return on assets turned out to be less than expected, the additional debt could result in a lower return on equity for alternative 2. If, for example, the return on assets invested (before interest and taxes) had been 6%, rather than 16%, alternative 1 would have provided the better return on equity:

	Alternative 1	**Alternative 2**
Income before interest and taxes	$3,000,000	$3,000,000
Less: Interest expense	(800,000)[a]	(2,400,000)[b]
Income before taxes	$2,200,000	$ 600,000
Less: Income tax expense (40%)	(880,000)	(240,000)
Net income	$1,320,000	$ 360,000

[a]8% × $10,000,000
[b]8% × $30,000,000

	Alternative 1	**Alternative 2**
Return on shareholders' equity[15] =	$\dfrac{\$1,320,000}{\$40,000,000}$	$\dfrac{\$360,000}{\$20,000,000}$
	= 3.3%	1.8%

---

[14]If return is calculated on *average* shareholders' equity, we're technically assuming that all income is paid to shareholders in cash dividends, so that beginning, ending, and average shareholders' equity are the same. On the other hand, if we assume *no* dividends are paid, rates of return would be:

	Alternative 1	**Alternative 2**
Return on shareholders' equity =	$\dfrac{\$4,320,000}{(\$44,320,000 + 40,000,000)/2}$	$\dfrac{\$3,360,000}{(\$20,000,000 + 23,360,000)/2}$
	= 10.25%	15.50%

In any case our conclusions are the same.

[15]If we assume *no* dividends are paid, rates of return would be:

	Alternative 1	**Alternative 2**
Return on shareholders' equity =	$\dfrac{\$1,320,000}{(\$41,320,000 + 40,000,000)/2}$	$\dfrac{\$360,000}{(\$20,000,000 + 20,360,000)/2}$
	= 3.25%	1.78%

In any case, our conclusions are the same.

So, shareholders typically are faced with a tradeoff between the risk that high debt denotes and the potential for a higher return from having the higher debt. In any event, the debt to equity ratio offers a basis for making the choice.

Times Interest Earned Ratio.   Another way to gauge the ability of a company to satisfy its fixed debt obligations is by comparing interest charges with the income available to pay those charges. The **times interest earned ratio** is designed to do this. It is calculated by dividing income before subtracting either interest expense or income taxes by interest expense.

The **times interest earned ratio** *indicates the margin of safety provided to creditors.*

Bondholders, noteholders, and other creditors can measure the margin of safety they are accorded by a company's earnings. If income is many times greater than interest expense, creditors' interests are more protected than if income just barely covers this expense. For this purpose, income should be the amount available to pay interest which is income before subtracting either interest or income taxes, calculated by adding back to net income the interest and taxes that were deducted.

FedEx Corporation

As an example, FedEx Corporation's 2001 financial statements report the following items:

	($ in 000s)
Net income	$ 584,371
Interest expense*	143,953
Income taxes	343,202
Income before interest and taxes	$1,071,526

*This amount actually is interest expense net of interest income. No separate disclosure of the components is provided in the financial statements.

The times interest earned ratio can be computed as follows:

$$\text{Times interest earned ratio} = \frac{\$1,071,526}{\$143,953} = 7.4 \text{ times}$$

The ratio of 7.4 times indicates a considerable margin of safety for creditors. Income could decrease many times and the company would still be able to meet its interest payment obligations.[16] In comparison, UPS's times interest earned ratio for 2001 is 22 times. UPS has more interest-bearing debt in its capital structure than does FedEx but it earned higher income.

Especially when viewed alongside the debt-equity ratio, the coverage ratio seems to indicate a comfortable safety cushion for creditors. It also indicates a degree of financial mobility if the company were to decide to raise new debt funds to "trade on the equity" and attempt to increase the return to shareholders through favorable financial leverage.

FINANCIAL REPORTING CASE SOLUTION

1. **Respond to Jerry's criticism that shareholders' equity does not represent the market value of the company. What information does the balance sheet provide?** *(p. 119)*   Jerry is correct. The financial statements are supposed to help investors and creditors value a company. However, the balance sheet is not intended to portray the market value of the entity. The assets of a company minus its liabilities as shown in the balance sheet (shareholders' equity) usually will not equal the company's market value for several reasons. For example, many assets are measured at their historical costs rather than their market values. Also, many company resources including its trained employees, its experienced management team, and its reputation are not recorded as assets at all. The balance sheet must be used in conjunction with other financial statements, disclosure notes, and other publicly available information.

---

[16]Of course, interest is paid with cash, not with "income." The times interest earned ratio often is calculated by using cash flow from operations before subtracting either interest payments or tax payments as the numerator and interest payments as the denominator.

The balance sheet does, however, provide valuable information that can be used by investors and creditors to help determine market value. After all, it is the balance sheet that describes many of the resources a company has available for generating future cash flows. The balance sheet also provides important information about liquidity and long-term solvency.

2. **The usefulness of the balance sheet is enhanced by classifying assets and liabilities according to common characteristics. What are the classifications used in Electronic Arts' balance sheet and what elements do those categories include?** *(p. 120)*

Electronic Arts' balance sheet contains the following asset and liability classifications:

Assets:
- *Current assets* include cash and several other assets that are reasonably expected to be converted to cash or consumed within the coming year, or within the normal operating cycle of the business if that's longer than one year.
- *Property and equipment* are the tangible long-lived assets used in the operations of the business. This category includes land, buildings, equipment, machinery, and furniture, as well as natural resources.
- *Long-term investments* represent investments in debt and equity securities of other corporations that management does not intend to convert into cash in the next year or operating cycle if that's longer.
- *Investment in affiliates* are investments in debt and equity securities of affiliated companies.
- *Intangible assets* generally represent exclusive rights to something such as a product, a process, or a name. Patents, copyrights, and franchises are examples.
- *Other assets* is a "catch-all" classification of noncurrent assets and could include long-term prepaid expenses and any noncurrent asset not included in one of the other categories.

Liabilities:

Current liabilities are those obligations that are expected to be satisfied through the use of current assets or the creation of other current liabilities. Usually, this means liabilities that are expected to be paid within one year or the operating cycle, whichever is longer. ∎

THE BOTTOM LINE

1. The balance sheet is a position statement that presents an organized array of assets, liabilities, and shareholders' equity at a particular point in time. The statement does not portray the market value of the entity. However, the information in the statement can be useful in assessing market value, as well as in providing important information about liquidity and long-term solvency.

2. Current assets include cash and other assets that are reasonably expected to be converted to cash or consumed during one year, or within the normal operating cycle of the business if the operating cycle is longer than one year. All other assets are classified as various types of noncurrent assets. Current liabilities are those obligations that are expected to be satisfied through the use of current assets or the creation of other current liabilities. All other liabilities are classified as long term.

3. In addition to cash and cash equivalents, current assets include short-term investments, accounts receivable, inventories, and prepaid expenses. Other asset classifications include investments and funds; property, plant, and equipment; intangible assets; and other assets.

4. Current liabilities include notes and accounts payable, unearned revenues, accrued liabilities, and the current maturities of long-term debt. Long-term liabilities include long-term notes, loans, mortgages, bonds, pension and lease obligations, as well as deferred income taxes.

5. Financial disclosures are used to convey additional information about the account balances in the basic financial statements as well as to provide supplemental information. This information is disclosed parenthetically in the basic financial statements or in notes or supplemental financial statements.

6. Annual financial statements will include management's discussion and analysis of key aspects of the company's business. The purpose of this disclosure is to provide external parties with management's insight into certain transactions, events, and circumstances that affect the enterprise, including their financial impact.

7. The purpose of an audit is to provide a professional, independent opinion as to whether or not the financial statements are prepared in conformity with GAAP. The audit report contains three paragraphs; the first two deal with the scope of the audit and the third paragraph states the auditors' opinion.

8. Financial analysts use various techniques to transform financial information into forms more useful for analysis. Horizontal analysis and vertical analysis provide a useful way of analyzing year-to-year changes. Ratio analysis allows analysts to control for size differences over time and among firms while investigating important relationships among financial variables.

9. The balance sheet provides information that can be useful in assessing risk. A key element of risk analysis is investigating a company's ability to pay its obligations when they come due. Liquidity ratios and financing ratios provide information about a company's ability to pay its obligations. ■

APPENDIX
3

Many companies operate in several business segments as a strategy to achieve growth and to reduce operating risk through diversification.

REPORTING SEGMENT INFORMATION

Financial analysis of diversified companies is especially difficult. Consider, for example, a company that operates in several distinct business segments including computer peripherals, home health care systems, textiles, and consumer food products. The results of these distinctly different activities will be aggregated into a single set of financial statements, making difficult an informed projection of future performance. It may well be that the five-year outlook differs greatly among the areas of the economy represented by the different segments. To make matters worse for an analyst, the integrated financial statements do not reveal the relative investments in each of the business segments nor the success the company has had within each area. Given the fact that so many companies these days have chosen to balance their operating risks through diversification, aggregated financial statements pose a widespread problem for analysts, lending and credit officers, and other financial forecasters.

Reporting by Operating Segment

To address the problem, the accounting profession requires companies engaged in more than one significant line of business to provide supplemental information concerning individual operating segments. The supplemental disaggregated data does not include complete financial statements for each reportable segment, only certain specified items.

Segment reporting facilitates the financial statement analysis of diversified companies.

Prior to 1997, *SFAS 14,* "Financial Reporting for Segments of a Business Enterprise," provided the specific reporting requirements for segment reporting.[17] *SFAS 14* applied the industry approach in determining reportable segments. The standard was the subject of much criticism because it allowed for inconsistent definitions of the term *industry* demonstrated by companies applying the standard. This inconsistency reduced the relevance and comparability of segment disclosures. In June 1997, the Financial Accounting Standards Board issued *SFAS 131* to replace *SFAS 14.*

WHAT IS A REPORTABLE OPERATING SEGMENT?

The new standard employs a *management approach* in determining which segments of a company are reportable. This approach is based on the way that management organizes the segments within the enterprise for making operating decisions and assessing performance. The segments are, therefore, evident from the structure of the enterprise's internal organization.

---

[17]"Financial Reporting for Segments of a Business Enterprise," *Statement of Financial Accounting Standards No. 14* (Stamford, CT: FASB, 1976).

More formally, the following characteristics define an **operating segment:**[18]
An operating segment is a component of an enterprise:

• That engages in business activities from which it may earn revenues and incur expenses (including revenues and expenses relating to transactions with other components of the same enterprise).
• Whose operating results are regularly reviewed by the enterprise's chief operating decision maker to make decisions about resources to be allocated to the segment and assess its performance.
• For which discrete financial information is available.

The FASB hopes that this new approach provides insights into the risk and opportunities management sees in the various areas of company operations. Also, reporting information based on the enterprise's internal organization should reduce the incremental cost to companies of providing the data. In addition, the board added quantitative thresholds to the definition of an operating segment to limit the number of reportable segments. Only segments of certain size (10% or more of total company revenues, assets, or net income) must be disclosed. However, a company must account for at least 75% of consolidated revenue through segment disclosures.

WHAT AMOUNTS ARE REPORTED BY AN OPERATING SEGMENT?
For areas determined to be reportable operating segments, the following disclosures are required:

a. General information about the operating segment.
b. Information about reported segment profit or loss, including certain revenues and expenses included in reported segment profit or loss, segments assets, and the basis of measurement.
c. Reconciliations of the totals of segment revenues, reported profit or loss, assets, and other significant items to corresponding enterprise amounts.
d. Interim period information.[19]

Graphic 3A–1 shows the business segment information reported by Minnesota Mining & Manufacturing Company (3M) in its 2000 annual report.

REPORTING BY GEOGRAPHIC AREA
In today's global economy it is sometimes difficult to distinguish domestic and foreign companies. Most large U.S. firms conduct significant operations in other countries in addition to having substantial export sales from this country. Differing political and economic environments from country to country means risks and associated rewards sometimes vary greatly among the various operations of a single company. For instance, manufacturing facilities in a South American country embroiled in political unrest pose different risks from having a plant in Vermont, or even Canada. Without disaggregated financial information, these differences cause problems for analysts.

SFAS 131 requires an enterprise to report certain geographic information unless it is impracticable to do so. This information includes:

a. Revenues from external customers (1) attributed to the enterprise's country of domicile and (2) attributed to all foreign countries in total from which the enterprise derives revenues, and
b. Long-lived assets other than financial instruments, long-term customer relationships of a financial institution, mortgage and other servicing rights, deferred policy acquisition costs, and deferred tax assets (1) located in the enterprise's country of domicile and (2) located in all foreign countries in total in which the enterprise holds assets.[20]

[18]"Disclosures about Segments of an Enterprise and Related Information," *Statement of Financial Accounting Standards No. 131* (Norwalk, CT: FASB, 1997), par. 10.
[19]Ibid., par. 25.
[20]Ibid., par. 38.

GRAPHIC 3A–1
Business Segment
Information
Disclosure—Minnesota
Mining &
Manufacturing
Company

Business Segment Information ($ in millions)

		Net Sales	Operating Income	Assets	Depr. and Amort.	Capital Expendit.
Industrial	2000	$ 3,525	$ 641	$ 2,392	$ 213	$ 214
	1999	3,409	612	2,357	220	202
	1998	3,372	561	2,394	199	281
Transportation, Graphics & Safety	2000	3,518	783	2,741	186	239
	1999	3,234	675	2,673	140	199
	1998	3,025	532	2,652	170	336
Health Care	2000	3,135	675	2,025	188	189
	1999	3,138	680	2,076	203	189
	1998	3,102	571	2,168	161	225
Consumer and Office	2000	2,848	434	1,711	101	134
	1999	2,705	401	1,589	118	123
	1998	2,624	398	1,614	136	182
Electro and Communications	2000	2,467	404	1,961	158	208
	1999	2,017	402	1,359	130	194
	1998	1,743	263	1,177	111	225
Specialty Material	2000	1,197	57	1,230	144	131
	1999	1,194	185	1,323	79	143
	1998	1,133	194	1,112	66	188
Corporate and Unallocated	2000	34	64	2,462	35	—
	1999	51	1	2,519	10	—
	1998	95	(480)	3,036	23	16
Total Company	2000	$16,724	$3,058	$14,522	$1,025	$1,115
	1999	15,748	2,956	13,896	900	1,050
	1998	15,094	2,039	14,153	866	1,453

3M reported its geographic area information separately in a table reproduced in Graphic 3A–2. Notice that both the business segment (Graphic 3A–1) and geographic information disclosures include a reconciliation to company totals. For example, in both graphics, year 2000 net sales of both the segments and the geographic areas are reconciled to the company's total net sales of $16,724 ($ in millions).

For another example of both business segment and geographic area disclosures, see the FedEx Corporation segment information in the appendix to Chapter 1.

INFORMATION ABOUT MAJOR CUSTOMERS

Revenues from major
customers must be
disclosed.

Some companies in the defense industry derive substantial portions of their revenues from contracts with the Defense Department. When cutbacks occur in national defense or in specific defense systems, the impact on a company's operations can be considerable. Obviously, financial analysts are extremely interested in information concerning the extent to which a company's prosperity depends on one or more major customers such as in the situation described here. For this reason, if 10% or more of the revenue of an enterprise is derived from transactions with a single customer, the enterprise must disclose that fact, the total amount of revenue from each such customer, and the identity of the operating segment or segments earning the revenue. The identity of the major customer or customers need not be disclosed, although companies routinely provide that information. In its 2000 annual report, 3M did not

GRAPHIC 3A–2   Geographic Area Information Disclosure—Minnesota Mining & Manufacturing Company

Geographic Area Information ($ in millions)

		United States	Europe & Middle East	Asia Pacific	Latin America, Africa and Canada	Eliminations and Other	Total Company
Net sales to	2000	$7,858	$3,946	$3,329	$1,564	$ 27	$16,724
customers	1999	7,559	3,808	2,887	1,467	27	15,748
	1998	7,297	3,863	2,375	1,539	20	15,094
Operating Income	2000	1,160	589	961	376	(28)	3,058
	1999	1,198	574	768	348	68	2,956
	1998	1,185	515	512	339	(512)	2,039
Property, plant	2000	3,699	1,046	711	367	—	5,823
and equipment	1999	3,647	1,017	757	355	—	5,776
	1998	3,504	1,116	718	376	—	5,714

report any major customer information. As an example of this type of disclosure, Procter & Gamble Company's business segment disclosure included information on its largest customer, Wal-Mart, as shown in Graphic 3A–3. ∎

GRAPHIC 3A–3
Major Customer Disclosure—Procter & Gamble Company

Note 12. Segment Information (in part)
The Company's largest customer, Wal-Mart Stores, Inc. and its affiliates, accounted for 15%, 14% and 12% of consolidated net sales in 2001, 2000, and 1999, respectively. These sales occurred primarily in the United States.

GLOBAL   PERSPECTIVE

There is more international uniformity regarding disaggregated disclosures than with many other accounting issues. Many countries adopted *International Accounting Standard No. 14*, "Reporting Financial Information by Segment," issued in 1981 by the International Accounting Standards Committee. Under this standard, companies report revenues, identifiable assets and capital expenditures for both industry segments and geographic segments.

QUESTIONS FOR REVIEW OF KEY TOPICS

Q 3–1   Describe the purpose of the balance sheet.

Q 3–2   Explain why the balance sheet does not portray the market value of the entity.

Q 3–3   Define current assets and list the typical asset categories included in this classification.

Q 3–4   Define current liabilities and list the typical liability categories included in this classification.

Q 3–5   Describe what is meant by an operating cycle for a typical manufacturing company.

Q 3–6   Explain the difference(s) between investments in equity securities classified as current assets versus those classified as noncurrent assets.

Q 3–7   Describe the common characteristics of assets classified as property, plant, and equipment and identify some assets included in this classification.

Q 3–8   Distinguish between property, plant, and equipment and intangible assets.

Q 3–9   Explain how each of the following liabilities would be classified in the balance sheet:

- A note payable of $100,000 due in five years.
- A note payable of $100,000 payable in annual installments of $20,000 each, with the first installment due next year.

Q 3–10   Define the terms paid-in-capital and retained earnings.

Q 3–11   Disclosure notes are an integral part of the information provided in financial statements. In what ways are the notes critical to understanding the financial statements and to evaluating the firm's performance and financial health?

Q 3–12   A summary of the company's significant accounting policies is a required disclosure. Why is this disclosure important to external financial statement users?

Q 3–13   Define a subsequent event.

Q 3–14   Every annual report includes an extensive discussion and analysis provided by the company's management. Specifically, which aspects of the company must this discussion address? Isn't management's perspective too biased to be of use to investors and creditors?

Q 3–15   The auditors' report provides the analyst with an independent and professional opinion about the fairness of the representations in the financial statements. What are the four main types of opinion an auditor might issue? Describe each.

Q 3–16   What is a proxy statement? What information does it provide?

Q 3–17   Define the terms working capital, current ratio, and acid-test ratio (or quick ratio).

Q 3–18   Show the calculation of the following financing ratios: (1) the debt to equity ratio, and (2) the times interest earned ratio.

Q 3–19   (based on Appendix 3) Segment reporting facilitates the financial statement analysis of diversified companies. What determines whether an operating segment is a reportable segment for this purpose?

Q 3–20   (based on Appendix 3) For segment reporting purposes, what amounts are reported by each operating segment?

EXERCISES

E 3–1
Balance sheet; missing elements

The following December 31, 2003, fiscal year-end account balance information is available for the Stonebridge Corporation:

Cash and cash equivalents	$ 5,000
Accounts receivable (net)	20,000
Inventories	60,000
Property, plant, and equipment (net)	120,000
Accounts payable	44,000
Wages payable	15,000
Paid-in-capital	100,000

The only asset not listed is short-term investments. The only liabilities not listed are a $30,000 note payable due in two years and related accrued interest of $1,000 due in four months. The current ratio at year-end is 1.5:1.

Required:
Determine the following at December 31, 2003:
1. Total current assets
2. Short-term investments
3. Retained earnings

E 3–2
Balance sheet classification

The following are the typical classifications used in a balance sheet:
a.   Current assets
b.   Investments and funds
f.   Current liabilities
g.   Long-term liabilities

c. Property, plant, and equipment   h. Paid-in-capital
d. Intangible assets   i. Retained earnings
e. Other assets

Required:
For each of the following balance sheet items, use the letters above to indicate the appropriate classification category. If the item is a contra account, place a minus sign before the chosen letter.

1. ____	Equipment	10. ____	Inventories
2. ____	Accounts payable	11. ____	Patent
3. ____	Allowance for uncollectible accounts	12. ____	Land, in use
4. ____	Land, held for investment	13. ____	Accrued liabilities
5. ____	Note payable, due in 5 years	14. ____	Prepaid rent
6. ____	Unearned rent revenue	15. ____	Common stock
7. ____	Note payable, due in 6 months	16. ____	Building, in use
8. ____	Income less dividends, accumulated	17. ____	Cash
9. ____	Investment in XYZ Corp., long-term	18. ____	Taxes payable

E 3–3
Balance sheet
classification

The following are the typical classifications used in a balance sheet:

a. Current assets   f. Current liabilities
b. Investments and funds   g. Long-term liabilities
c. Property, plant, and equipment   h. Paid-in-capital
d. Intangible assets   i. Retained earnings
e. Other assets

Required:
For each of the following 2003 balance sheet items, use the letters above to indicate the appropriate classification category. If the item is a contra account, place a minus sign before the chosen letter.

1. ____	Accrued interest payable	10. ____	Supplies
2. ____	Franchise	11. ____	Machinery
3. ____	Accumulated depreciation	12. ____	Land, in use
4. ____	Prepaid insurance, for 2005	13. ____	Unearned revenue
5. ____	Bonds payable, due in 10 years	14. ____	Copyrights
6. ____	Current maturities of long-term debt	15. ____	Preferred stock
7. ____	Note payable, due in three months	16. ____	Land, held for speculation
8. ____	Long-term receivables	17. ____	Cash equivalents
9. ____	Bond sinking fund, will be used to retire bonds in 10 years	18. ____	Wages payable

E 3–4
Balance sheet
preparation

The following is a December 31, 2003, post-closing trial balance for the Jackson Corporation.

Account Title	Debits	Credits
Cash	30,000	
Accounts receivable	34,000	
Inventories	75,000	
Prepaid rent	6,000	
Marketable securities (short term)	10,000	
Machinery	145,000	
Accumulated depreciation—machinery		11,000
Patent (net of amortization)	83,000	
Accounts payable		8,000
Wages payable		4,000
Taxes payable		32,000
Bonds payable (due in 10 years)		200,000
Common stock		100,000
Retained earnings		28,000
Totals	383,000	383,000

Required:
Prepare a classified balance sheet for Jackson Corporation at December 31, 2003.

E 3–5
Balance sheet
preparation

The following is a December 31, 2003, post-closing trial balance for the Valley Pump Corporation.

Account Title	Debits	Credits
Cash	25,000	
Accounts receivable	62,000	
Inventories	81,000	
Interest payable		5,000
Marketable securities	38,000	
Land	120,000	
Buildings	300,000	
Accumulated depreciation—buildings		100,000
Equipment	75,000	
Accumulated depreciation—equipment		25,000
Copyright (net of amortization)	12,000	
Prepaid expenses	32,000	
Accounts payable		65,000
Unearned revenues		20,000
Notes payable		250,000
Allowance for uncollectible accounts		5,000
Common stock		200,000
Retained earnings		75,000
Totals	745,000	745,000

Additional information:
1. The $120,000 balance in the land account consists of $100,000 for the cost of land where the plant and office buildings are located. The remaining $20,000 represents the cost of land being held for speculation.
2. The $38,000 in the marketable securities account represents an investment in the common stock of another corporation. Valley intends to sell one-half of the stock within the next year.
3. The notes payable account consists of a $100,000 note due in six months and a $150,000 note due in three annual installments of $50,000 each, with the first payment due in August of 2004.

Required:
Prepare a classified balance sheet for the Valley Pump Corporation at December 31, 2003.

E 3–6
Balance sheet
preparation; errors

The following balance sheet for the Los Gatos Corporation was prepared by a recently hired accountant. In reviewing the statement you notice several errors.

LOS GATOS CORPORATION
Balance Sheet
At December 31, 2003

Assets

Cash	$ 40,000
Accounts receivable	80,000
Inventories	65,000
Machinery (net)	120,000
Franchise (net)	20,000
Total assets	$325,000

Liabilities and Shareholders' Equity

Accounts payable	$ 60,000
Allowance for uncollectible accounts	5,000
Note payable	55,000
Bonds payable	100,000
Shareholders' equity	105,000
Total liabilities and shareholders' equity	$325,000

Additional information:
1. Cash includes a $20,000 bond sinking fund to be used for repayment of the bonds payable in 2007.
2. The cost of the machinery is $190,000.

3. Accounts receivable includes a $20,000 note receivable from a customer due in 2006.
4. The note payable includes accrued interest of $5,000. Principal and interest are both due on February 1, 2004.
5. The company began operations in 1998. Income less dividends since inception of the company totals $35,000.
6. 50,000 shares of no par common stock were issued in 1998. 100,000 shares are authorized.

Required:
Prepare a corrected, classified balance sheet.

E 3–7

Balance sheet; current versus noncurrent classification

The Cone Corporation is in the process of preparing its December 31, 2003, balance sheet. There are some questions as to the proper classification of the following items:
a. $50,000 in cash set aside in a savings account to pay bonds payable. The bonds mature in 2007.
b. Prepaid rent of $24,000, covering the period January 1, 2004, through December 31, 2005.
c. Note payable of $200,000. The note is payable in annual installments of $20,000 each, with the first installment payable on March 1, 2004.
d. Accrued interest payable of $12,000 related to the note payable.
e. Investment in marketable securities of other corporations, $60,000. Cone intends to sell one-half of the securities in 2004.

Required:
Prepare a partial classified balance sheet to show how each of the above items should be reported.

E 3–8

Financial disclosures

The following are typical disclosures that would appear in the notes accompanying financial statements. For each of the items listed, indicate where the disclosure would likely appear—either in (A) the significant accounting policies note or (B) a separate note.
1. Inventory costing method   ___A___
2. Information on related party transactions   _____
3. Composition of property, plant, and equipment   _____
4. Depreciation method   _____
5. Subsequent event information   _____
6. Basis of revenue recognition on long-term contracts   _____
7. Important merger occurring after year-end   _____
8. Composition of receivables   _____

E 3–9

Disclosure notes

The Hallergan Company produces car and truck batteries that it sells primarily to auto manufacturers. Dorothy Hawkins, the company's controller, is preparing the financial statements for the year ended December 31, 2003. Hawkins asks for your advice concerning the following information that has not yet been included in the statements. The statements will be issued on February 28, 2004.
1. Hallergan leases its facilities from the brother of the chief executive officer.
2. On January 8, 2004, Hallergan entered into an agreement to sell a tract of land that it had been holding as an investment. The sale, which resulted in a material gain, was completed on February 2, 2004.
3. Hallergan uses the straight-line method to determine depreciation on all of the company's depreciable assets.
4. On February 8, 2004, Hallergan completed negotiations with its bank for a $10,000,000 line of credit.
5. Hallergan uses the first-in, first-out (FIFO) method to value inventory.

Required:
For each of the above items, discuss any additional disclosures that Hawkins should include in Hallergan's financial statements.

E 3–10

Multiple choice; financial disclosures

The following questions dealing with disclosures are adapted from questions that appeared on recent CPA examinations. Determine the response that best completes the statements or questions.
1. What is the purpose of information presented in notes to the financial statements?
    a. To provide disclosure required by generally accepted accounting principles.
    b. To correct improper presentation in the financial statements.
    c. To provide recognition of amounts not included in the totals of the financial statements.
    d. To present management's responses to auditor comments.
2. Which of the following information should be disclosed in the summary of significant accounting policies?
    a. Refinancing of debt subsequent to the balance sheet date.
    b. Guarantees of indebtedness of others.

c. Criteria for determining which investments are treated as cash equivalents.
d. Adequacy of pension plan assets relative to vested benefits.
3. Which of the following facts concerning fixed assets should be included in the summary of significant accounting policies?

	Depreciation Method	Composition
a.	No	Yes
b.	Yes	Yes
c.	Yes	No
d.	No	No

E 3–11

Concepts; terminology

Listed below are several terms and phrases associated with the balance sheet and financial disclosures. Pair each item from List A (by letter) with the item from List B that is most appropriately associated with it.

List A	List B
____ 1. Balance sheet	a. Will be satisfied through the use of current assets.
____ 2. Liquidity	b. Items expected to be converted to cash or consumed within one year or the operating cycle.
____ 3. Current assets	c. The statements are presented fairly in conformity with GAAP.
____ 4. Operating cycle	
____ 5. Current liabilities	
____ 6. Cash equivalent	d. An organized array of assets, liabilities and equity.
____ 7. Intangible asset	e. Important to a user in comparing financial information across companies.
____ 8. Working capital	
____ 9. Accrued liabilities	f. Scope limitation or a departure from GAAP.
____ 10. Summary of significant accounting policies	g. Recorded when an expense is incurred but not yet paid.
____ 11. Subsequent events	h. Relates to the amount of time before an asset is converted to cash or a liability is paid.
____ 12. Unqualified opinion	i. Occurs after the fiscal year-end but before the statements are issued.
____ 13. Qualified opinion	j. Cash to cash.
	k. One-month U.S. treasury bill.
	l. Current assets minus current liabilities.
	m. Lacks physical existence.

E 3–12

Calculating ratios

The 2003 balance sheet for Hallbrook Industries, Inc. is shown below.

HALLBROOK INDUSTRIES, INC.
Balance Sheet
December 31, 2003
($ in 000s)

Assets

Cash	$ 100
Short-term investments	150
Accounts receivable	200
Inventories	400
Property, plant, and equipment (net)	1,000
Total assets	$1,850

Liabilities and Shareholders' Equity

Current liabilities	$ 400
Long-term liabilities	350
Paid-in capital	700
Retained earnings	400
Total liabilities and shareholders' equity	$1,850

The company's 2003 income statement reported the following amounts ($ in 000s):

Net sales	$4,600
Interest expense	20
Income tax expense	100
Net income	160

Required:
Determine the following ratios for 2003:
1.   Current ratio
2.   Acid-test ratio
3.   Debt to equity ratio
4.   Times interest earned ratio

E 3–13
Calculating ratios;
solve for unknowns

The current asset section of the Excalibur Tire Company's balance sheet consists of cash, marketable securities, accounts receivable, and inventories. The December 31, 2003, balance sheet revealed the following:

Inventories	$ 420,000
Total assets	$2,800,000
Current ratio	2.25
Acid-test ratio	1.2
Debt to equity ratio	1.8

Required:
Determine the following 2003 balance sheet items:
1.   Current assets
2.   Shareholders' equity
3.   Noncurrent assets
4.   Long-term liabilities

E 3–14
Effect of management
decisions on ratios

Most decisions made by management impact the ratios analysts use to evaluate performance. Indicate (by letter) whether each of the actions listed below will immediately increase (I), decrease (D), or have no effect (N) on the ratios shown. Assume each ratio is less than 1.0 before the action is taken.

Action	Current Ratio	Acid-Test Ratio	Debt to Equity Ratio
1. Issuance of long-term bonds	____	____	____
2. Issuance of short-term notes	____	____	____
3. Payment of accounts payable	____	____	____
4. Purchase of inventory on account	____	____	____
5. Purchase of inventory for cash	____	____	____
6. Purchase of equipment with a 4-year note	____	____	____
7. Retirement of bonds	____	____	____
8. Sale of common stock	____	____	____
9. Write-off of obsolete inventory	____	____	____
10. Purchase of short-term investment for cash	____	____	____
11. Decision to refinance on a long-term basis some currently maturing debt	____	____	____

E 3–15
Multiple choice; ratio
analysis

The following questions dealing with ratio analysis are adapted from questions that appeared on recent CPA examinations. Determine the response that best completes the statements or questions.
1.   At December 30, 2003, Vida Co. had cash of $200,000, a current ratio of 1.5:1 and a quick ratio of .5:1. On December 31, 2003, all cash was used to reduce accounts payable. How did these cash payments affect the ratios?

	Current Ratio	**Quick Ratio**
a.	Increased	Decreased
b.	Increased	No Effect
c.	Decreased	Increased
d.	Decreased	No Effect

2.   In analyzing a company's financial statements, which financial statement would a potential investor primarily use to assess the company's liquidity and financial flexibility?
   a.   Balance sheet.
   b.   Income statement.
   c.   Statement of retained earnings.
   d.   Statement of cash flows.

PROBLEMS

P 3–1
Balance sheet
preparation

Presented below is a list of balance sheet accounts presented in alphabetical order.

Accounts payable
Accounts receivable
Accumulated depreciation—buildings
Accumulated depreciation—equipment
Allowance for uncollectible accounts
Bond sinking fund
Bonds payable (due in 10 years)
Buildings
Cash
Common stock
Copyright
Equipment
Interest receivable (due in three months)

Inventories
Land (in use)
Long-term investments
Notes payable (due in 6 months)
Notes receivable (due in 2 years)
Patent
Preferred stock
Prepaid expenses
Rent payable (current)
Retained earnings
Short-term investments
Taxes payable
Wages payable

Required:
Prepare a classified balance sheet ignoring monetary amounts.

P 3–2
Balance sheet
preparation; missing
elements

The data listed below are taken from a recent balance sheet of Amdahl Corporation. Some amounts, indicated by question marks, have been intentionally omitted.

	($ in 000s)
Cash and cash equivalents	$ 239,186
Short-term investments	353,700
Accounts receivable (net of allowance)	504,944
Inventories	?
Prepaid expenses (current)	83,259
Total current assets	1,594,927
Long-term receivables	110,800
Property and equipment (net)	?
Total assets	?
Notes payable and short-term debt	31,116
Accounts payable	?
Accrued liabilities	421,772
Other current liabilities	181,604
Total current liabilities	693,564
Long-term debt and deferred taxes	?
Total liabilities	956,140
Shareholders' equity	1,370,627

Required:
1. Determine the missing amounts.
2. Prepare Amdahl's classified balance sheet.

P 3–3
Balance sheet
preparation

The following is a December 31, 2003, post-closing trial balance for Almway Corporation.

Account Title	Debits	Credits
Cash	45,000	
Investments	110,000	
Accounts receivable	60,000	
Inventories	200,000	
Prepaid insurance	9,000	
Land	90,000	
Buildings	420,000	
Accumulated depreciation—buildings		100,000
Equipment	110,000	
Accumulated depreciation—equipment		60,000
Patents (net of amortization)	10,000	

Accounts payable		75,000
Notes payable		130,000
Interest payable		20,000
Bonds payable		240,000
Common stock		300,000
Retained earnings		129,000
Totals	1,054,000	1,054,000

Additional information:
1. The investment account includes an investment in common stock of another corporation of $30,000 which management intends to hold for at least three years.
2. The land account includes land which cost $25,000 that the company has not used and is currently listed for sale.
3. The cash account includes $15,000 set aside in a fund to pay bonds payable that mature in 2006 and $23,000 set aside in a three-month treasury bill.
4. The notes payable account consists of the following:
   a. a $30,000 note due in six months.
   b. a $50,000 note due in six years.
   c. a $50,000 note due in five annual installments of $10,000 each, with the next installment due February 15, 2004.
5. The $60,000 balance in accounts receivable is net of an allowance for uncollectible accounts of $8,000.
6. The common stock account represents 100,000 shares of no par value common stock issued and outstanding. The corporation has 500,000 shares authorized.

Required:
Prepare a classified balance sheet for the Almway Corporation at December 31, 2003.

P 3–4
Balance sheet preparation

The following is a December 31, 2003, post-closing trial balance for the Weismuller Publishing Company.

Account Title	Debits	Credits
Cash	65,000	
Accounts receivable	160,000	
Inventories	285,000	
Prepaid expenses	148,000	
Machinery and equipment	320,000	
Accumulated depreciation—equipment		110,000
Investments	140,000	
Accounts payable		60,000
Interest payable		20,000
Unearned revenue		80,000
Taxes payable		30,000
Notes payable		200,000
Allowance for uncollectible accounts		16,000
Common stock		400,000
Retained earnings		202,000
Totals	1,118,000	1,118,000

Additional information:
1. Prepaid expenses include $120,000 paid on December 31, 2003, for a two-year lease on the building that houses both the administrative offices and the manufacturing facility.
2. Investments include $30,000 in treasury bills purchased on November 30, 2003. The bills mature on January 30, 2004. The remaining $110,000 includes investments in marketable equity securities that the company intends to sell in the next year.
3. Unearned revenue represents customer prepayments for magazine subscriptions. Subscriptions are for periods of one year or less.
4. The notes payable account consists of the following:
   a. a $40,000 note due in six months.
   b. a $100,000 note due in six years.

    c.   a $60,000 note due in three annual installments of $20,000 each, with the next installment due August 31, 2004.

5. The common stock account represents 400,000 shares of no par value common stock issued and outstanding. The corporation has 800,000 shares authorized.

Required:
Prepare a classified balanced sheet for the Weismuller Publishing Company at December 31, 2003.

P 3–5
Balance sheet
preparation

The following is a June 30, 2003, post-closing trial balance for Excell Company.

Account Title	Debits	Credits
Cash	83,000	
Short-term investments	65,000	
Accounts receivable	280,000	
Prepaid expenses	32,000	
Land	75,000	
Buildings	320,000	
Accumulated depreciation—buildings		160,000
Equipment	265,000	
Accumulated depreciation—equipment		120,000
Accounts payable		173,000
Accrued expenses		45,000
Notes payable		100,000
Mortgage payable		250,000
Common stock		100,000
Retained earnings		172,000
Totals	1,120,000	1,120,000

Additional information:

1. The short-term investments account includes $18,000 in U.S. treasury bills purchased in May. The bills mature in July.
2. The accounts receivable account consists of the following:

a.	Amounts owed by customers	$225,000
b.	Allowance for uncollectible accounts—trade customers	(15,000)
c.	Nontrade note receivable (due in three years)	65,000
d.	Interest receivable on note (due in four months)	5,000
	Total	$280,000

3. The notes payable account consists of two notes of $50,000 each. One note is due on September 30, 2003, and the other is due on November 30, 2004.
4. The mortgage payable is payable in *semiannual* installments of $5,000 each plus interest. The next payment is due on October 31, 2003. Interest has been properly accrued and is included in accrued expenses.
5. Five hundred thousand shares of no par common stock are authorized, of which 200,000 shares have been issued and are outstanding.
6. The land account includes $50,000 representing the cost of the land on which the company's office building resides. The remaining $25,000 is the cost of land that the company is holding for investment purposes.

Required:
Prepare a classified balance sheet for the Excell Company at June 30, 2003.

P 3–6
Balance sheet
preparation; errors

The following balance sheet for the Hubbard Corporation was prepared by the company:

HUBBARD CORPORATION
Balance Sheet
At December 31, 2003

Assets

Buildings	$ 750,000
Land	250,000
Cash	60,000
Accounts receivable (net)	120,000
Inventories	240,000
Machinery	280,000

Patent (net)	100,000
Investment in marketable equity securities	60,000
Total assets	$1,860,000

Liabilities and Shareholders' Equity

Accounts payable	$ 215,000
Accumulated depreciation	255,000
Notes payable	500,000
Appreciation of inventories	80,000
Common stock, authorized and issued	
100,000 shares of no par stock	430,000
Retained earnings	380,000
Total liabilities and shareholders' equity	$1,860,000

Additional information:

1. The buildings, land, and machinery are all stated at cost except for a parcel of land that the company is holding for future sale. The land originally cost $50,000 but, due to a significant increase in market value, is listed at $120,000. The increase in the land account was credited to retained earnings.
2. Marketable equity securities consist of stocks of other corporations and are recorded at cost, $20,000 of which will be sold in the coming year. The remainder will be held indefinitely.
3. Notes payable are all long-term. However, a $100,000 note requires an installment payment of $25,000 due in the coming year.
4. Inventories are recorded at current resale value. The original cost of the inventories is $160,000.

Required:
Prepare a corrected classified balance sheet for the Hubbard Corporation at December 31, 2003.

P 3–7
Balance sheet
preparation

Presented below is the balance sheet for HHD, Inc., at December 31, 2003.

Current assets	$ 600,000	Current liabilities	$ 400,000
Investments	500,000	Long-term liabilities	1,100,000
Property, plant, and equipment	2,000,000	Shareholders' equity	1,800,000
Intangible assets	200,000		
Total assets	$3,300,000	Total liabilities and shareholders' equity	$3,300,000

The captions shown in the summarized statement above include the following:

a. Current assets: cash, $150,000; accounts receivable, $200,000; inventories, $225,000; and prepaid insurance, $25,000.
b. Investments: investments in common stock, short term, $90,000, and long term, $160,000; and bond sinking fund, $250,000.
c. Property, plant, and equipment: buildings, $1,500,000 less accumulated depreciation, $600,000; equipment, $500,000 less accumulated depreciation, $200,000; and land, $800,000.
d. Intangible assets: patent, $110,000; and copyright, $90,000.
e. Current liabilities: accounts payable, $100,000; notes payable, short term, $150,000, and long term, $90,000; and taxes payable, $60,000.
f. Long-term liabilities: bonds payable due 2008.
g. Shareholders' equity: preferred stock, $450,000; common stock, $1,000,000; retained earnings, $350,000.

Required:
Prepare a corrected classified balance sheet for HHD, Inc., at December 31, 2003.

P 3–8
Balance sheet
preparation

The Melody Lane Music Company was started by John Ross early in 2003. Initial capital was acquired by issuing shares of common stock to various investors and by obtaining a bank loan. The company operates a retail store that sells records, tapes, and compact discs. Business was so good during the first year of operations that John is considering opening a second store on the other side of town. The funds necessary for expansion will come from a new bank loan. In order to approve the loan, the bank requires financial statements.

John asks for your help in preparing the balance sheet and presents you with the following information for the year ending December 31, 2003:

a. Cash receipts consisted of the following:

From customers	$360,000
From issue of common stock	100,000
From bank loan	100,000

b. Cash disbursements were as follows:

Purchase of inventory	$300,000
Rent	15,000
Salaries	30,000
Utilities	5,000
Insurance	3,000
Purchase of equipment and furniture	40,000

c. The bank loan was made on March 31, 2003. A note was signed requiring payment of interest and principal on March 31, 2004. The interest rate is 12%.

d. The equipment and furniture were purchased on January 3, 2003, and have an estimated useful life of 10 years with no anticipated salvage value. Depreciation per year is $4,000.

e. Inventories on hand at the end of the year cost $100,000.

f. Amounts owed at December 31, 2003, were as follows:

To suppliers of inventory	$20,000
To the utility company	1,000

g. Rent on the store building is $1,000 per month. On December 1, 2003, four months' rent was paid in advance.

h. Net income for the year was $76,000. Assume that the company is not subject to federal, state, or local income tax.

Required:
Prepare a balance sheet at December 31, 2003.

BROADEN YOUR PERSPECTIVE

Apply your critical-thinking ability to the knowledge you've gained. These cases will provide you an opportunity to develop your research, analysis, judgment, and communication skills. You also will work with other students, integrate what you've learned, apply it in real world situations, and consider its global and ethical ramifications. This practice will broaden your knowledge and further develop your decision-making abilities.

Communication Case 3–1
Current versus noncurrent classification

A first-year accounting student is confused by a statement made in a recent class. Her instructor stated that the assets listed in the balance sheet of the IBM Corporation include computers that are classified as current assets as well as computers that are classified as noncurrent assets. In addition, the instructor stated that investments in marketable securities of other corporations could be classified in the balance sheet as either current or noncurrent assets.

Required:
Explain to the student the distinction between current and noncurrent assets pertaining to the IBM computers and the investments in marketable securities.

Analysis Case 3–2
Current versus noncurrent classification

The usefulness of the balance sheet is enhanced when assets and liabilities are grouped according to common characteristics. The broad distinction made in the balance sheet is the current versus noncurrent classification of both assets and liabilities.

Required:
1. Discuss the factors that determine whether an asset or liability should be classified as current or noncurrent in a balance sheet.
2. Identify six items that under different circumstances could be classified as either current or noncurrent. Indicate the factors that would determine the correct classification.

Communication Case 3–3
Inventory or property, plant, and equipment

The Red Hen Company produces, processes, and sells fresh eggs. The company is in the process of preparing financial statements at the end of its first year of operations and has asked for your help in determining the appropriate treatment of the cost of its egg-laying flock. The estimated life of a laying hen is approximately two years, after which they are sold to soup companies.

The controller considers the company's operating cycle to be two years and wants to present the cost of the egg-producing flock as inventory in the current asset section of the balance sheet. He feels that the hens are "goods awaiting sale." The chief financial officer does not agree with this treatment. He thinks that the cost of the flock should be classified as property, plant, and equipment because the hens are used in the production of product—the eggs.

The focus of this case is the balance sheet presentation of the cost of the egg-producing flock. Your instructor will divide the class into two to six groups depending on the size of the class. The mission of your group is to reach consensus on the appropriate presentation.

Required:

1. Each group member should deliberate the situation independently and draft a tentative argument prior to the class session for which the case is assigned.

2. In class, each group will meet for 10 to 15 minutes in different areas of the classroom. During that meeting, group members will take turns sharing their suggestions for the purpose of arriving at a single group treatment.

3. After the allotted time, a spokesperson for each group (selected during the group meetings) will share the group's solution with the class. The goal of the class is to incorporate the views of each group into a consensus approach to the situation.

Judgment Case 3–4
Balance sheet; errors

You recently joined the internal auditing department of Marcus Clothing Corporation. As one of your first assignments, you are examining a balance sheet prepared by a staff accountant.

MARCUS CLOTHING CORPORATION
Balance Sheet
At December 31, 2003
Assets

Current assets:		
Cash		$137,000
Accounts receivable, net		80,000
Note receivable		53,000
Inventories		240,000
Investments		66,000
Total current assets		576,000
Other assets:		
Land	$200,000	
Equipment, net	320,000	
Prepaid expenses	27,000	
Patent	22,000	
Total other assets		569,000
Total assets		$1,145,000

Liabilities and Shareholders' Equity

Current liabilities:		
Accounts payable		$ 125,000
Salaries payable		32,000
Total current liabilities		157,000
Long-term liabilities:		
Note payable	$100,000	
Bonds payable	300,000	
Interest payable	20,000	
Total long-term liabilities		420,000
Shareholders' equity:		
Common stock	500,000	
Retained earnings	68,000	
Total shareholders' equity		568,000
Total liabilities and shareholders' equity		$1,145,000

In the course of your examination you uncover the following information pertaining to the balance sheet:

1. The company rents its facilities. The land that appears in the statement is being held for future sale.

2. The note receivable is due in 2005. The balance of $53,000 includes $3,000 of accrued interest. The next interest payment is due in July 2004.

3. The note payable is due in installments of $20,000 per year. Interest on both the notes and bonds is payable annually.

4. The company's investments consist of marketable equity securities of other corporations. Management does not intend to liquidate any investments in the coming year.

Required:

Identify and explain the deficiencies in the statement prepared by the company's accountant. Include in your answer items that require additional disclosure, either on the face of the statement or in a note.

Judgment Case 3–5
Financial disclosures

You recently joined the auditing staff of Best, Best, and Krug, CPAs. You have been assigned to the audit of Clearview, Inc., and have been asked by the audit senior to examine the balance sheet prepared by Clearview's accountant.

CLEARVIEW, INC.
Balance Sheet
At December 31, 2003
($ in millions)

Assets

Current assets:		
Cash		$10.5
Accounts receivable		112.1
Inventories		220.6
Prepaid expenses		5.5
Total current assets		348.7
Investments		22.0
Property, plant, and equipment, net		486.9
Total assets		$857.6

Liabilities and Shareholders' Equity

Current liabilities:		
Accounts payable		$ 83.5
Accrued taxes and interest		25.5
Current maturities of long-term debt		20.0
Total current liabilities		129.0
Long-term liabilities:		420.0
Total liabilities		549.0
Shareholders' equity:		
Common stock	$100.0	
Retained earnings	208.6	
Total shareholders' equity		308.6
Total liabilities and shareholders' equity		$857.6

Required:

Identify the items in the statement that most likely would require further disclosure either on the face of the statement or in a note. Further identify those items that would require disclosure in the significant accounting policies note.

Real World Case 3–6
Balance sheet and significant accounting policies disclosure

The balance sheet and disclosure of significant accounting policies taken from the 2000 annual report of International Business Machines Corporation (IBM) appear below. Use this information to answer the following questions:

1. What are the asset classifications contained in IBM's balance sheet?
2. What amounts did IBM report for the following items for 2000:
   a. Total assets
   b. Current assets
   c. Current liabilities
   d. Total shareholders' equity
   e. Retained earnings
   f. Inventories
3. What is the par value of IBM's common stock? How many shares of common stock are authorized and issued at the end of 2000?

4. Compute IBM's current ratio for 2000.
5. Identify the following items:
   a. The company's inventory valuation method.
   b. The company's depreciation method.
   c. The definition of cash equivalents.

CONSOLIDATED STATEMENT OF FINANCIAL POSITION
INTERNATIONAL BUSINESS MACHINES CORPORATION
and Subsidiary Companies
($ in millions)

	Notes	At December 31: 2000	1999
Assets			
Current assets:			
Cash and cash equivalents		$ 3,563	$ 5,043
Marketable securities	K	159	788
Notes and accounts receivable—trade, net of allowances		10,447	9,103
Short-term financing receivables	F	18,705	17,156
Other accounts receivable		1,574	1,359
Inventories	E	4,765	4,868
Deferred taxes	O	2,701	2,907
Prepaid expenses and other current assets		1,966	1,931
Total current assets		43,880	43,155
Plant, rental machines and other property	G	38,455	39,616
Less: Accumulated depreciation		21,741	22,026
Plant, rental machines and other property—net		16,714	17,590
Long-term financing receivables	F	13,308	13,078
Investments and sundry assets	H	14,447	13,672
Total assets		$88,349	$87,495
Liabilities and Stockholders' Equity			
Current liabilities:			
Taxes	G	$ 4,827	$ 4,792
Short-term debt	J & K	10,205	14,230
Accounts payable		8,192	6,400
Compensation and benefits		3,801	3,840
Deferred income		4,516	4,529
Other accrued expenses and liabilities		4,865	5,787
Total current liabilities		36,406	39,578
Long-term debt	J & K	18,371	14,124
Other liabilities	L	12,948	13,282
Total liabilities		67,725	66,984
Contingencies	N		
Stockholders' equity:	M		
Preferred stock, par value $.01 per share—			
shares authorized: 150,000,000			
shares issued and outstanding: 2,546,011		247	247
Common stock, par value $.20 per share—			
shares authorized: 4,687,500,000			
shares issued: 2000—1,893,940,595;			
1999—1,876,665,245	C	12,400	11,762
Retained earnings		23,784	16,878
Treasury stock, at cost (shares: 2000—131,041,411;			
1999—72,449,015)		(13,800)	(7,375)
Employee benefits trust, at cost (20,000,000 shares)		(1,712)	(2,162)
Accumulated gains and losses not affecting			
retained earnings		(295)	1,161
Total stockholders' equity		20,624	20,511
Total liabilities and stockholders' equity		$88,349	$87,495

NOTES TO CONSOLIDATED FINANCIAL STATEMENTS
INTERNATIONAL BUSINESS MACHINES CORPORATION
AND SUBSIDIARY COMPANIES

A. Significant accounting policies (in part)

Revenue

The company recognized revenue when it is realized or realizable and earned. The company considers revenue realized or realizable and earned when it has persuasive evidence of an arrangement, the product has been shipped or the services provided to the customer, the sales price is fixed or determinable and collectibility is reasonably assured. The company reduces revenue for estimated customer returns.

Cash Equivalents

All highly liquid investments with a maturity of three months or less at date of purchase are carried at fair value and considered to be cash equivalents.

Inventories

Raw materials, work in process, and finished goods are stated at the lower of average cost or market.

Depreciation

Plant, rental machines and other property are carried at cost, and depreciated over their estimated useful lives using the straight-line method.

Judgment Case 3–7
Post fiscal year-end events

The fiscal year-end for the Northwest Distribution Corporation is December 31. The company's 2003 financial statements were issued on March 15, 2004. The following events occurred between December 31, 2003, and March 15, 2004.

1. On January 22, 2004, the company negotiated a major merger with Blandon Industries. The merger will be completed by the middle of 2004.
2. On February 3, 2004, Northwest negotiated a $10 million long-term note with the Credit Bank of Ohio. The amount of the note is material.
3. On February 25, 2004, a flood destroyed one of the company's manufacturing plants causing $600,000 of uninsured damage.

Required:

Determine the appropriate treatment of each of these events in the 2003 financial statements of Northwest Distribution Corporation.

Research Case 3–8
Related party disclosures; locate and extract relevant information and authoritative support for a financial reporting issue; Enron Corporation

Enron Corporation provides products and services related to natural gas, electricity, and communications to wholesale and retail customers. The company was a darling in the energy-provider arena and in January of 2001 its stock price rose above $100 per share. A collapse of investor confidence in 2001 and revelations of accounting irregularities led to one of the largest bankruptcies in U.S. history. By the end of the year, its stock price had plummeted to less than $1 per share. Investigations and lawsuits followed. One problem area concerned transactions with related parties that were not adequately disclosed in the company's financial statements. Critics stated that the lack of information about these transactions made it difficult for analysts following Enron to identify problems the company was experiencing.

Required:

1. Consult the Summaries of FASB pronouncements at **www.fasb.org** or access the pronouncements from some other source. What authoritative pronouncement requires the disclosure of related-party transactions? When did the requirement become effective?
2. Describe the disclosures required for related-party transactions.
3. Use Edgarscan (**edgarscan.pwcglobal.com**) or another method to locate the December 31, 2000, financial statements of Enron. Search for the related-party disclosure. Briefly describe the relationship central to the numerous transactions described.
4. Why is it important that companies disclose related-party transactions? Use the Enron disclosure of the sale of dark fiber inventory in your answer.

Research Case 3–9
Disclosure of debt covenants

Classifying a liability as short or long term provides useful cash flow information to financial statement users. Additional cash flow information is contained in a disclosure note that provides information about the payment terms, interest rates, collateral, and scheduled maturity amounts of long-term debt. Quite often, debt agreements contain certain constraints placed by the lender on the borrower in order to protect the lender's investment. Many of these constraints, called *debt covenants*, are based on accounting information. Professors Press and Weintrop in "Financial Statement Disclosure of Accounting-Based Debt Covenants" investigate the adequacy of debt covenant disclosures in financial statements.

Required:

1. In your library or from some other source, locate the indicated article in *Accounting Horizons*, March 1991.

2. Describe the two types of accounting-based debt covenants—affirmative covenants and negative covenants—discussed by the authors.

3. What is the authors' conclusion about the adequacy of disclosure of accounting-based covenants in financial statements?

International Case 3–10

Comparison of audit reports in the U.K. and the United States

British Airways PLc is the largest international passenger airline in the world. The following is the Report of the Auditors accompanying the company's 2000 financial statements:

Report of the Auditors to the Members of British Airways PLc

We have audited the accounts, which have been prepared under the historical cost convention as modified by the revaluation of certain fixed assets and on the basis of the accounting policies set out here.

Respective responsibilities of directors and auditors (in part)

The directors are responsible for preparing the annual report. As described above, this includes responsibility for preparing the accounts in accordance with applicable United Kingdom law and accounting standards. Our responsibilities, as independent auditors, are established in the United Kingdom by statute, the Auditing Practices Board, the Listing Rules of the Financial Services Authority and by our profession's ethical guidance. We report to you our opinion as to whether the accounts give a true and fair view and are properly prepared in accordance with the Companies Act.

Basis of audit opinion

We conducted our audit in accordance with Auditing Standards issued by the Auditing Practices Board. An audit includes examination, on a test basis, of evidence relevant to the amounts and disclosures in the accounts. It also includes an assessment of the significant estimates and judgments made by the directors in the preparation of the accounts and of whether the accounting policies are appropriate to the group's circumstances, consistently applied and adequately disclosed.

We planned and performed our audit so as to obtain all the information and explanations which we considered necessary in order to provide us with sufficient evidence to give reasonable assurance that the accounts are free from material misstatement, whether caused by fraud or other irregularity or error. In forming our opinion we also evaluated the overall adequacy of the presentation of information in the accounts.

Opinion

In our opinion the accounts give a true and fair view of the state of affairs of the Company and of the Group at March 31, 2000 and of the loss of the group for the year then ended and have been properly prepared in accordance with the Companies Act of 1985.

Ernst & Young

Registered Auditor

London

May 23, 2000

Required:

Compare the auditors' report in the United Kingdom with that of the United States.

Real World Case 3–11

Disclosures; proxy statement

EDGAR, the Electronic Data Gathering, Analysis, and Retrieval system, performs automated collection, validation, indexing, and forwarding of submissions by companies and others who are required by law to file forms with the SEC. All publicly traded domestic companies use EDGAR to make the majority of their filings. (Some foreign companies file voluntarily.) Form 10-K or 10-KSB, which includes the annual report, is required to be filed on EDGAR. The SEC makes this information available on the Internet.

Required:

1. Access EDGAR on the Internet. The web address is **www.sec.gov**. Edgarscan (**edgarscan. pwcglobal.com**) from Pricewaterhouse Cooper makes the process of accessing data from EDGAR easier.

2. Search for the Calpine Corporation, a company engaged in the generation of electricity in the United States. Access the 10-K filing for the fiscal year ended December 31, 2000. Search or scroll to find the disclosure notes and audit report.

3. Answer the following questions:
   a. Describe the subsequent events disclosed by the company.
   b. Which firm is the company's auditor? What type of opinion did the auditor render? Does the audit report contain any explanatory paragraphs?

4. Search for Microsoft Corporation. Access the proxy statement filed with the SEC on October 12, 2001 (the proxy statement designation is Def 14A) and answer the following questions:
   a. What is the principal position of William Gates?
   b. What was the annual compensation paid to Mr. Gates?

Judgment Case 3–12
Debt versus equity

A common problem facing any business entity is the debt versus equity decision. When funds are required to obtain assets, should debt or equity financing be used? This decision also is faced when a company is initially formed. What will be the mix of debt versus equity in the initial capital structure? The characteristics of debt are very different from those of equity as are the financial implications of using one method of financing as opposed to the other.

Cherokee Plastics Corporation is formed by a group of investors to manufacture household plastic products. Their initial capitalization goal is $50,000,000. That is, the incorporators have decided to raise $50,000,000 to acquire the initial operating assets of the company. They have narrowed down the financing mix alternatives to two:

1. All equity financing.
2. $20,000,000 in debt financing and $30,000,000 in equity financing.

No matter which financing alternative is chosen, the corporation expects to be able to generate a 10% annual return, before payment of interest and income taxes, on the $50,000,000 in assets acquired. The interest rate on debt would be 8%. The effective income tax rate will be approximately 50%.

Alternative 2 will require specified interest and principal payments to be made to the creditors at specific dates. The interest portion of these payments (interest expense) will reduce the taxable income of the corporation and hence the amount of income tax the corporation will pay. The all-equity alternative requires no specified payments to be made to suppliers of capital. The corporation is not legally liable to make distributions to its owners. If the board of directors does decide to make a distribution, it is not an expense of the corporation and does not reduce taxable income and hence the taxes the corporation pays.

Required:

1. Prepare abbreviated income statements that compare first-year profitability for each of the two alternatives.
2. Which alternative would be expected to achieve the highest first-year profits? Why?
3. Which alternative would provide the highest rate of return on shareholders' equity? Why?
4. What other related implications of the decision should be considered?

Analysis Case 3–13
Obtain and critically evaluate an actual annual report

Financial reports are the primary means by which corporations report their performance and financial condition. Financial statements are one component of the annual report mailed to their shareholders and to interested others.

Required:

Obtain an annual report from a corporation with which you are familiar. Using techniques you learned in this chapter and any analysis you consider useful, respond to the following questions:

1. Do the firm's auditors provide a clean opinion on the financial statements?
2. Has the company made changes in any accounting methods it uses?
3. Have there been any subsequent events, errors and irregularities, illegal acts, or related-party transactions that have a material effect on the company's financial position?
4. What are two trends in the company's operations or capital resources that management considers significant to the company's future?
5. Is the company engaged in more than one significant line of business? If so, compare the relative profitability of the different segments.
6. How stable are the company's operations?
7. Has the company's situation deteriorated or improved with respect to liquidity, solvency, asset management, and profitability?

Note: You can obtain a copy of an annual report from a local company, from a friend who is a shareholder, from the investor relations department of the corporation, from a friendly stockbroker, or from EDGAR (Electronic Data Gathering, Analysis, and Retrieval) on the Internet (**www.sec.gov** or through Edgarscan at **edgarscan.pwcglobal.com**).

Analysis Case 3–14
Obtain and compare annual reports from companies in the same industry

Insight concerning the performance and financial condition of a company often comes from evaluating its financial data in comparison with other firms in the same industry.

Required:

Obtain annual reports from three corporations in the same primary industry. Using techniques you learned in this chapter and any analysis you consider useful, respond to the following questions:

1. Are there differences in accounting methods that should be taken into account when making comparisons?
2. How do earnings trends compare in terms of both the direction and stability of income?
3. Which of the three firms had greater earnings relative to resources available?
4. Which corporation has made most effective use of financial leverage?

5. Of the three firms, which seems riskiest in terms of its ability to pay short-term obligations? Long-term obligations?

    Note: You can obtain copies of annual reports from friends who are shareholders, from the investor relations department of the corporations, from a friendly stockbroker, or from EDGAR (Electronic Data Gathering, Analysis, and Retrieval) on the Internet (**www.sec.gov** or through Edgarscan at **edgarscan.pwcglobal.com**).

Analysis Case 3–15
Balance sheet information
FedEx Corporation

Refer to the financial statements and related disclosure notes of FedEx Corporation in the appendix to Chapter 1.

Required:
1. What categories does the company use to classify its assets? Its liabilities?
2. Why are "Spare parts, supplies and fuel" shown as a current asset?
3. Explain the current liability "current portion of long-term debt."
4. What purpose do the disclosure notes serve?
5. What method does the company use to depreciate its property and equipment?
6. Does the company report any subsequent events or related party transactions in its disclosure notes?

Analysis Case 3–16
[based on Appendix 3]
Segment reporting concepts

Levens Co. operates in several distinct business segments. The company does not have any reportable foreign operations or major customers.

Required:
1. What is the purpose of operating segment disclosures?
2. Define an operating segment.
3. List the amounts to be reported by operating segment.

Ethics Case 3–17
[based on Appendix 3]
Segment reporting

You are in your third year as an accountant with McCarver-Lynn Industries, a multidivisional company involved in the manufacturing, marketing, and sales of surgical prosthetic devices. After the fiscal year-end, you are working with the controller of the firm to prepare supplemental business segment disclosures. Yesterday you presented her with the following summary information:

($ in millions)

	Domestic	Union of South Africa	Egypt	France	Denmark	Total
Revenues	$ 845	$222	$265	$343	$311	$1,986
Capital expenditures	145	76	88	21	42	372
Assets	1,005	301	290	38	285	1,919

Upon returning to your office after lunch, you find the following memo:

Nice work. Let's combine the data this way

($ in millions)

	Domestic	Africa	Europe	Total
Revenues	$ 845	$487	$654	$1,986
Capital expenditures	145	164	63	372
Assets	1,005	591	323	1,919

Some of our shareholders might react unfavorably to our recent focus on South African operations.

Required:
Do you perceive an ethical dilemma? What would be the likely impact of following the controller's suggestions? Who would benefit? Who would be injured?

4

The Income Statement and Statement of Cash Flows

CHAPTER

OVERVIEW

The purpose of the income statement is to summarize the profit-generating activities that occurred during a particular reporting period. The purpose of the statement of cash flows is to provide information about the cash receipts and cash disbursements of an enterprise that occurred during the period. This chapter has a twofold purpose: (1) to consider important issues dealing with income statement content, presentation, and disclosure and (2) to provide an *overview* of the statement of cash flows, which is covered in depth in Chapter 22.

LEARNING OBJECTIVES

After studying this chapter, you should be able to:

LO1 Explain the difference between net income and comprehensive income and how we report components of the difference.

LO2 Discuss the importance of income from continuing operations and describe its components.

LO3 Describe earnings quality and how it is impacted by management practices to manipulate earnings.

LO4 Discuss the components of operating and nonoperating income and their relationship to earnings quality.

LO5 Define what constitutes discontinued operations and describe the appropriate income statement presentation for these transactions.

LO6 Define extraordinary items and describe the appropriate income statement presentation for these transactions.

LO7 Describe and illustrate the measurement and reporting requirements for the cumulative effect of a change in accounting principle.

LO8 Explain the accounting treatments of changes in estimates and correction of errors.

LO9 Define earnings per share (EPS) and explain required disclosures of EPS for certain income statement components.

LO10 Describe the purpose of the statement of cash flows.

LO11 Identify and describe the various classifications of cash flows presented in a statement of cash flows.

Halliburton Company

Your friend Becky Morgan, has just received a generous gift from her grandfather. Accompanying a warm letter were 200 shares of stock in the Halliburton Company, a large energy services company, along with the most recent financial statements of the company. Becky knows that you are an accounting major and pleads with you to explain some items in the company's income statement. "I remember studying the income statement in my introductory accounting course," says Becky, "but I am still confused. What is this item *discontinued operations?* And how about *restructuring costs?* These don't sound good. Are these something I should worry about? And why is there a negative $47 million expense in 1999? How can you have a negative expense? The last item in the income statement *cumulative effect of a change in accounting principle* also makes no sense." You agree to try to help.

HALLIBURTON COMPANY
Income Statements
Years Ended December 31
($ in millions)

	2000	1999	1998
Revenues	$11,944	$12,313	$14,504
Operating costs and expenses:			
Cost of services	9,755	10,368	11,127
Cost of sales	1,463	1,240	1,895
General and administrative	352	351	437
Restructuring costs	—	(47)	875
Total operating costs and expenses	11,570	11,912	14,334
Operating income	374	401	170
Other income (expense):			
Interest expense	(146)	(141)	(134)
Interest income	25	74	26
Gain on sale of vessels	88	—	—
Other	(24)	(44)	(27)
Income before taxes	317	290	35
Provision for income taxes	129	116	155
Income (loss) from continuing operations	188	174	(120)
Discontinued operations, net of tax	313	283	105
Cumulative effect of a change in accounting principle, net of tax	—	(19)	—
Net income (loss)	501	438	(15)

(continued)

(concluded)

By the time you finish this chapter, you should be able to respond appropriately to the questions posed in this case. Compare your response to the solution provided at the end of the chapter.

QUESTIONS

1. How would you explain restructuring costs to Becky? Are they necessarily a negative? What is the likely explanation for the negative expense in 1999? (page 178)

2. In addition to discontinued operations and the cumulative effect of a change in accounting principle, what other events sometimes are reported separately in the income statement that you might tell Becky about? Why are these items reported separately? (page 182)

3. Explain to Becky what is meant by a discontinued operation and describe to her how one is reported in an income statement. (page 184)

4. Explain how to measure the cumulative effect of a change in accounting principle. (page 190)

In Chapter 1 we discussed the critical role of financial accounting information in allocating resources within our economy. Ideally, resources should be allocated to private enterprises that will (1) provide the goods and services our society desires and (2) at the same time provide a fair rate of return to those who supply the resources. A company will be able to achieve these goals only if it can use the resources society provides to generate revenues from selling products and services that exceed the expenses necessary to provide those products and services (that is, generate a profit).

The income statement displays a company's operating performance, that is, its net profit or loss, during the reporting period.

The purpose of the **income statement**, sometimes called the **statement of operations** or **statement of earnings,** is to summarize the profit-generating activities that occurred during a particular reporting period. Many investors and creditors perceive it as the statement most useful for predicting future profitability (future cash-generating ability).

The purpose of the **statement of cash flows** is to provide information about the cash receipts and cash disbursements of an enterprise that occurred during a period. In describing cash flows, the statement provides valuable information about the operating, investing, and financing activities that occurred during the period.

The *income statement* and *statement of cash flows* report changes that occurred during a particular reporting period.

Unlike the balance sheet, which is a position statement, the income statement and the statement of cash flows are *change* statements. The income statement reports the changes in shareholders' equity (retained earnings) that occurred during the reporting period as a result of revenues, expenses, gains, and losses. The statement of cash flows also is a change statement, disclosing the events that caused cash to change during the period.

This chapter is divided into two parts. The first part describes the content and presentation of the income statement and related disclosure issues. The second part provides an overview of the statement of cash flows.

THE INCOME STATEMENT

Before we discuss the specific components of an income statement in much depth, let's take a quick look at the general makeup of the statement. Graphic 4–1 offers a comprehensive statement for a hypothetical manufacturing company that you can refer to as we proceed through the chapter. At this point, our objective is only to gain a general perspective of the items reported and classifications contained in corporate income statements.

We'll look closer at the components of net income, but first we should consider the notion of net income itself and how it fits within the concept of comprehensive income.

Comprehensive Income

Accounting professionals have engaged in an ongoing debate concerning which transactions should be included as components of periodic income. For instance, some argue that certain

GRAPHIC 4–1
Income Statement

Income Statements
(in millions, except earnings per share)

Section		Years Ended June 30 2003	2002
Income from Continuing Operations	Sales revenue	$1,450.6	$1,380.0
	Cost of goods sold	832.6	800.4
	Gross profit	618.0	579.6
	Operating expenses:		
	Selling	123.5	110.5
	General and administrative	147.8	139.1
	Research and development	55.0	65.0
	Restructuring costs	125.0	—
	Total operating expenses	451.3	314.6
	Operating income	166.7	265.0
	Other income (expense):		
	Interest income	12.4	11.1
	Interest expense	(25.9)	(24.8)
	Gain on sale of investments	18.0	19.0
	Income before income taxes	171.2	270.3
	Income tax expense	59.9	94.6
	Income from continuing operations	111.3	175.7
Separately Reported Items	Discontinued operations:		
	Loss from operations of discontinued component (including gain on disposal in 2003 of $47)	(7.6)	(45.7)
	Income tax benefit	2.0	13.0
	Loss on discontinued operations	(5.6)	(32.7)
	Income before extraordinary gain and the cumulative effect of a change in accounting principle	105.7	143.0
	Extraordinary gain, net of $11 in tax expense	—	22.0
	Cumulative effect of a change in accounting principle, net of $12 tax benefit	(32.8)	—
	Net income	$ 72.9	$ 165.0
Earnings per Share	**Earnings per common share—basic:**		
	Income from continuing operations	$ 2.14	$ 3.38
	Discontinued operations	(.11)	(.62)
	Extraordinary gain	—	.42
	Cumulative effect of a change in accounting principle	(.63)	—
	Net income	$ 1.40	$ 3.18
	Earnings per common share—diluted:		
	Income from continuing operations	$ 2.06	$ 3.25
	Discontinued operations	(.11)	(.62)
	Extraordinary gain	—	.42
	Cumulative effect of a change in accounting principle	(.63)	—
	Net income	$ 1.32	$ 3.05

Comprehensive income is the total change in equity for a reporting period other than from transactions with owners.

changes in shareholders' equity besides those attributable to traditional net income should be included in the determination of income. In what might be viewed as a compromise, the FASB has decided to maintain the traditional view of net income, but to require companies also to report an expanded version of income called **comprehensive income** that includes not only traditional net income but other nonowner changes in equity as well. Let's consider what that means.

Recall that equity refers to the ownership interest in a company's net assets (assets − liabilities = equity). Remember, too, that a company's equity, or net assets, changes primarily as a result of (a) transactions with owners of the company (for example, the sale or purchase of shares of the company's stock) as well as (b) the company earning additional net assets on behalf of its owners (that is, net income). These two types of changes are reflected in a balance sheet as changes in (a) paid-in capital or (b) retained earnings. We explore these distinctions in detail in Chapter 19. Here, though, our concern is with those few *nonowner* changes in equity (not type a) that traditionally are not part of net income (that is, not part of type b changes). Under the concept, then, of comprehensive income consisting of all changes in equity other than from transactions with owners, we can refer to these few nonowner changes in equity outside the realm of traditional net income as *other comprehensive income.*

OTHER COMPREHENSIVE INCOME

As we just discussed, the calculation of net income omits certain transactions that are included in comprehensive income. As one example, in Chapter 12 you will learn that certain investments are reported in the balance sheet at their fair values, but the net unrealized holding gains and losses resulting from changes in fair values of those investments are *not* included in net income. Instead, they are reported as a separate component of shareholders' equity, **other comprehensive income** (loss).

To convey the relationship between the two measures, companies must report both net income and comprehensive income and reconcile the difference between the two.[1] Be sure to realize that net income is actually a part of comprehensive income. The reconciliation simply extends net income to include other comprehensive income items, reported net of tax, as shown in Illustration 4–1.

ILLUSTRATION 4–1		($ in millions)
Comprehensive Income	Net income	$135
	Other comprehensive income:	
	Net unrealized holding gains (losses) on investments (net of tax)* $22	
	Minimum pension liability adjustment (net of tax)† (3)	
	Deferred gain (loss) from derivatives (net of tax)‡ 5	
	Foreign currency translation adjustments (net of tax)§ 16	40
	Comprehensive income	$175

*Changes in the market value of securities available for sale (described in Chapter 12).
†Reporting a pension liability sometimes requires a reduction in shareholders' equity (described in Chapter 17).
‡When a derivative designated as a cash flow hedge is adjusted to fair value, the gain or loss is deferred as a component of comprehensive income and included in earnings later, at the same time as earnings are affected by the hedged transaction (described in Chapter 14).
§Gains or losses from changes in foreign currency exchange rates. The amount could be an addition to or reduction in shareholders' equity. (This item is discussed elsewhere in your accounting curriculum.)

FLEXIBILITY IN REPORTING

The presentation shown in Illustration 4–1 can be (a) included as an extension to the income statement, (b) reported (exactly the same way) as a separate statement of comprehensive in-

---

[1]"Reporting Comprehensive Income," *Statement of Financial Accounting Standards No. 130* (Norwalk, Conn: FASB, 1997).

come, often included in the financial statements as a disclosure note, or (c) included in the statement of changes in shareholders' equity (Chapter 19). Each component of other comprehensive income can be displayed net of tax, as in Illustration 4–1, or alternatively, before tax with one amount shown for the aggregate income tax expense (or benefit). In either case, the amount of income tax expense (or benefit) allocated to each component of other comprehensive income must be disclosed either on the face of the statement in which those components are displayed or in a disclosure note.[2] A recent survey of reporting practices of 600 large public companies indicates that of those companies that had other comprehensive income items, 81% chose to include the presentation of comprehensive income in their statements of changes in shareholders' equity.[3]

Many, though, such as Fairchild Corporation for its fiscal year ended June 30, 2001, choose to present comprehensive income as an extension to their income statements. Fairchild's income statements, beginning with income from continuing operations, are shown in Graphic 4–2.

Reporting comprehensive income can be accomplished with a separate statement or by including the information in either the income statement or the statement of changes in shareholders' equity.

GRAPHIC 4–2
Comprehensive Income Presented as an Extension to the Income Statement—Fairchild Corporation

FAIRCHILD CORPORATION
Consolidated Statements of Income (in part)
($ in thousands)
Years Ended June 30

	2001	2000	1999
Income (loss) from continuing operations	$(15,000)	$21,764	$(23,507)
Loss from discontinued operations, net	—	(12,006)	(31,349)
Extraordinary items, net	—	—	(4,153)
Net income (loss)	$(15,000)	$ 9,758	$(59,009)
Other comprehensive income (loss), net of tax:			
Foreign currency translation adjustments	(24,452)	(10,098)	(2,545)
Derivative financial instrument adjustments	(478)	—	—
Unrealized periodic holding gains on securities	(1,028)	(3,961)	(16,544)
Total other comprehensive income (loss)	(25,958)	(14,059)	(19,089)
Comprehensive income (loss)	$(40,958)	$ (4,301)	$(78,098)

On the other hand, in its 2001 financial statements, Solectron Corporation chose to use the separate statement approach. Graphic 4–3 shows its statements of comprehensive income that were reported directly below the income statements. The FedEx Corporation statements of changes in stockholders' investment and comprehensive income in the Appendix to Chapter 1 provides an example of a presentation of comprehensive income in that statement.

FedEx Corporation

In a balance sheet, the retained earnings component of shareholders' equity includes only the net income portion of comprehensive income. The total of other comprehensive income (or comprehensive loss) is reported as a component of shareholders' equity that is displayed separately from retained earnings and additional paid-in capital as demonstrated in Graphic 4–4 for Solectron Corporation.

Net income and comprehensive income are identical for an enterprise that has no other comprehensive income items. Our focus in the remainder of this chapter is on the measurement and reporting of net income in an income statement. Components of other comprehensive income are described in subsequent chapters.

---

[2]The standard does not require the reporting of comprehensive earnings per share.
[3]*Accounting Trends and Techniques—2001* (New York: AICPA, 2001), p. 401.

GRAPHIC 4–3
Comprehensive
Income Presented as a
Separate Statement—
Solectron Corporation

SOLECTRON CORPORATION
Consolidated Statements of Comprehensive Income (Loss)
($ in millions)
Years Ended August 31

	2001	2000	1999
Net income (loss)	$(123.5)	$497.2	$350.3
Other comprehensive income (loss):			
Foreign currency translation adjustments, net of income tax expense of $13.5 in 2001, income tax benefits of $15.9 in 2000 and $0.4 in 1999	(139.8)	(32.8)	(78.6)
Unrealized gain (loss) on investments, net of income tax benefit of $3.1 in 2001, income tax expense of $3.8 in 2000, and income tax benefit of $0.6 in 1999	(5.0)	6.3	(1.1)
Comprehensive income (loss)	$(268.3)	$470.7	$270.6

GRAPHIC 4–4
Shareholders' Equity—
Solectron Corporation

SOLECTRON CORPORATION
Consolidated Balance Sheets (in part)
($ in millions)
Years Ended August 31

	2001	2000
Shareholders' equity:		
Common stock, $.001 par value; 1,600 shares authorized; 658.2 and 605.0 shares issued and outstanding, respectively	0.7	0.6
Additional paid-in capital	3,877.6	2,259.1
Retained earnings	1,531.6	1,656.8
Accumulated other comprehensive losses	(259.2)	(114.4)
Total shareholders' equity	5,150.7	3,802.1

Income from Continuing Operations

LO2

Income from continuing
operations includes the
revenues, expenses,
gains and losses that
will probably continue
in future periods.

The need to provide information to help analysts predict future cash flows emphasizes the importance of properly reporting the amount of income from the entity's continuing operations. Clearly, it is the operating transactions that probably will continue into the future that are the best predictors of future cash flows. The components of **income from continuing operations** are revenues, expenses (including income taxes), gains, and losses, excluding those related to discontinued operations, extraordinary items, and the cumulative effect of changes in accounting principles.[4]

REVENUES, EXPENSES, GAINS, AND LOSSES

Revenues are inflows of resources resulting from providing goods or services to customers. For merchandising companies like Wal-Mart, the main source of revenue is sales revenue derived from selling merchandise. Service firms such as FedEx and State Farm Insurance generate revenue by providing services.

---

[4]These three separately reported items are addressed in a subsequent section.

Expenses are outflows of resources incurred while generating revenue. They represent the costs of providing goods and services. The *matching principle* is a key player in the way we measure expenses. We attempt to establish a causal relationship between revenues and expenses. If causality can be determined, expenses are reported in the same period that the related revenue is recognized. If a causal relationship cannot be established, we either relate the expense to a particular period, allocate it over several periods, or expense it as incurred.

Gains and losses are increases or decreases in equity from peripheral or incidental transactions of an entity. In general, these gains and losses are those changes in equity that do not result directly from operations but nonetheless are related to those activities. For example, gains and losses from the routine sale of equipment, buildings, or other operating assets and from the sale of investment assets normally would be included in income from continuing operations. Later in the chapter we discuss certain gains and losses that are excluded from continuing operations.

INCOME TAX EXPENSE

Income taxes represent a major expense to a corporation, and accordingly, income tax expense is given special treatment in the income statement. Income taxes are levied on taxpayers in proportion to the amount of taxable income that is reported to taxing authorities. Like individuals, corporations are income-tax-paying entities.[5] Because of the importance and size of **income tax expense** (sometimes called *provision for income taxes*), it always is reported as a separate expense in corporate income statements.

> *Income tax expense* is shown as a separate expense in the income statement.

Federal, state, and sometimes local taxes are assessed annually and usually are determined by first applying a designated percentage (or percentages), the tax rate (or rates), to **taxable income.** Taxable income comprises revenues, expenses, gains, and losses as measured according to the regulations of the appropriate taxing authority.

Many of the components of taxable income and income reported in the income statement coincide. But sometimes tax rules and GAAP differ with respect to when and even whether a particular revenue or expense is included in income. When tax rules and GAAP differ regarding the timing of revenue or expense recognition, the actual payment of taxes may occur in a period different from when income tax expense is reported in the income statement. A common example is when a corporation takes advantage of tax laws by legally deducting more depreciation in the early years of an asset's life in its federal income tax return than it reports in its income statement. The amount of tax actually paid in the early years is less than the amount that is found by applying the tax rate to the reported GAAP income before taxes. We discuss this and other issues related to accounting for income taxes in Chapter 16. At this point, consider income tax expense to be simply a percentage of income before taxes.

> While the actual measurement of income tax expense can be complex, at this point we can consider income tax expense to be a simple percentage of income before taxes.

OPERATING VERSUS NONOPERATING INCOME

Many corporate income statements distinguish between **operating** income and **nonoperating** income within continuing operations. Operating income includes revenues and expenses directly related to the principal revenue-generating activities of the company. For example, operating income for a manufacturing company includes sales revenues from the sale of products and all expenses related to this activity. Nonoperating income includes gains and losses and revenues and expenses related to peripheral or incidental activities of the company. For example, income from investments, gains and losses from the sale of operating assets and from investments, interest and dividend revenue, and interest expense are included in nonoperating income.[6] *Other income (expense)* often is used in income statements as the classification heading for nonoperating items. A financial institution like a bank considers interest revenue and interest expense to be a part of operating income because they relate to the principal revenue-generating activities for that type of business.

> A distinction often is made between *operating* and *nonoperating* income.

---

[5]Partnerships are not tax-paying entities. Their taxable income or loss is included in the taxable income of the individual partners.
[6]Even though these activities are nonoperating, they are still included in continuing operations because they *generally* are expected to continue in future periods.

Graphic 4–5 presents the 2001, 2000, and 1999 income statements for FedEx Corporation. Notice that FedEx distinguishes between operating and nonoperating income. Nonoperating revenues, expenses, gains and losses, and income tax expense (called provision for income taxes) are added to or subtracted from operating income to arrive at net income. As FedEx has no separately reported items, *income from continuing operations equals net income.*[7]

GRAPHIC 4–5
Income Statements—
FedEx Corporation

FedEx Corporation

Income Statements
(In thousands, except per share amounts)

	Year Ended May 31		
	2001	**2000**	**1999**
Revenues	$19,629,040	$18,256,945	$16,773,470
Operating expenses:			
Salaries and employee benefits	8,263,413	7,597,964	7,087,728
Purchased transportation	1,713,027	1,674,854	1,537,785
Rentals and landing fees	1,650,048	1,538,713	1,396,694
Depreciation and amortization	1,275,774	1,154,863	1,035,118
Fuel	1,142,741	918,513	604,929
Maintenance and repairs	1,170,103	1,101,424	958,873
Other	3,343,044	3,049,540	2,989,257
	18,558,150	17,035,871	15,610,384
Operating income	1,070,890	1,221,074	1,163,086
Other income (expense):			
Interest, net	(143,953)	(106,060)	(98,191)
Other, net	636	22,726	(3,831)
	(143,317)	(83,334)	(102,022)
Income before income taxes	927,573	1,137,740	1,061,064
Provision for income taxes	343,202	449,404	429,731
Net income	$ 584,371	$ 688,336	$ 631,333
Earnings per Common Share			
Basic	$2.02	$2.36	$2.13
Assuming dilution	$1.99	$2.32	$2.10

Now let's consider the formats used to report the components of income.

INCOME STATEMENT FORMATS

No specific standards dictate how income from continuing operations must be displayed, so companies have considerable latitude in how they present the components of income from continuing operations. This flexibility has resulted in a considerable variety of income statement presentations. However, we can identify two general approaches, the single-step and the multiple-step formats, that might be considered the two extremes, with the income statements of most companies falling somewhere in between.

A *single-step* income statement format groups all revenues and gains together and all expenses and losses together.

The **single-step** format first lists all the revenues and gains included in income from continuing operations. Then, expenses and losses are grouped, subtotaled, and subtracted—in a single step—from revenues and gains to derive income from continuing operations. Operating and nonoperating items are not separately classified. Illustration 4–2 shows an example of a single-step income statement for a hypothetical manufacturing company, Maxwell Gear Corporation.

---

[7]In a later section we discuss items that are reported separately from continuing operations—discontinued operations, extraordinary items, and the cumulative effect of a change in accounting principle.

MAXWELL GEAR CORPORATION		ILLUSTRATION 4–2
Income Statement		
For the Year Ended December 31, 2003		Single-Step Income Statement

Revenues and gains:

Sales		$573,522
Interest and dividends		26,400
Gain on sale of operating assets		5,500
Total revenues and gains		$605,422

Expenses and losses:

Cost of goods sold	$302,371	
Selling	47,341	
General and administrative	24,888	
Research and development	16,300	
Interest	6,200	
Loss on sale of investments	8,322	
Income taxes	80,000	
Total expenses and losses		485,422
Net income		$120,000

The **multiple-step** format reports a series of intermediate subtotals such as gross profit, operating income, and income before taxes. The overview income statements presented in Graphic 4–1 and the FedEx Corporation income statements in Graphic 4–5 are variations of the multiple-step format. Illustration 4–3 presents a multiple-step income statement for the Maxwell Gear Corporation.

A *multiple-step* income statement format includes a number of intermediate subtotals before arriving at income from continuing operations.

MAXWELL GEAR CORPORATION		ILLUSTRATION 4–3
Income Statement		
For the Year Ended December 31, 2003		Multiple-Step Income Statement

Sales revenue		$573,522
Cost of goods sold		302,371
Gross profit		$271,151
Operating expenses:		
Selling	$47,341	
General and administrative	24,888	
Research and development	16,300	
Total operating expenses		88,529
Operating income		$182,622
Other income (expense):		
Interest and dividend revenue	$26,400	
Gain on sale of operating assets	5,500	
Interest expense	(6,200)	
Loss on sale of investments	(8,322)	
Total other income, net		$ 17,378
Income before income taxes		$200,000
Income tax expense		80,000
Net income		$120,000

An advantage of the single-step format is its simplicity. Revenues and expenses are not classified or prioritized. A primary advantage of the multiple-step format is that, by separately classifying operating and nonoperating items, it provides information that might be useful in

In addition to net income, the components of the income statement and their presentation also are important to financial statement users in their assessment of earnings quality.

analyzing trends. Similarly, the classification of expenses by function also provides useful information. For example, reporting gross profit for merchandising companies highlights the important relationship between sales revenue and cost of goods sold. It is important to note that this issue is one of presentation. The bottom line, net income, is the same regardless of the format used. A recent survey of income statements of 600 large public companies indicates that the multiple-step format is used more than three times as often as the single-step format.[8] We use the multiple-step format for illustration purposes throughout the remainder of this chapter.

Before we investigate separately reported items, let's take a closer look at the components of both operating and nonoperating income and their relationship to earnings quality.

Earnings Quality

Financial analysts are concerned with more than just the bottom line of the income statement—net income. The presentation of the components of net income and the related supplemental disclosures provide clues to the user of the statement in an assessment of *earnings quality*. Earnings quality is used as a framework for more in-depth discussions of operating and nonoperating income.

Earnings quality refers to the ability of reported earnings (income) to predict a company's future earnings.

The term **earnings quality** refers to the ability of reported earnings (income) to predict a company's future earnings. After all, an income statement simply reports on events that already have occurred. The relevance of any historical-based financial statement hinges on its predictive value. To enhance predictive value, analysts try to separate a company's *transitory earnings* effects from its *permanent earnings*. Transitory earnings effects result from transactions or events that are not likely to occur again in the foreseeable future, or that are likely to have a different impact on earnings in the future. Later in the chapter we address three items that, because of their transitory nature, are required to be reported separately in the bottom of the income statement. Analysts begin their assessment of permanent earnings with income before these three items, that is, income from continuing operations.

It would be a mistake, though, to assume income from continuing operations reflects permanent earnings entirely. In other words, there may be transitory earnings effects included in income from continuing operations. In a sense, the phrase *continuing* may be misleading.

MANIPULATING INCOME AND INCOME SMOOTHING

A recent *Fortune* magazine article "Hocus-Pocus: How IBM Grew 27% a Year" contained a subtitle "Do you want to believe in the IBM miracle? Then don't look too closely at the numbers."[10] The article is highly critical of IBM's earnings management practices that allowed the company to report earnings per share growth of 27% per year from 1994 through 1999 with only minimal growth in revenues. The article's author attributes the increase in earnings per share to share buybacks, the sale of assets, and gains in pension fund assets, not a growth in permanent earnings.

An often-debated contention is that, within GAAP, managers have the power, to a limited degree, to manipulate reported company income. And the manipulation is not always in the direction of higher income. One author states that "Most executives prefer to report earnings that follow a smooth, regular, upward path. They hate to report declines, but they also want to avoid increases that vary wildly from year to year; it's better to have two years of 15% earnings increases than a 30% gain one year and none the next. As a result, some companies 'bank' earnings by understating them in particularly good years and use the banked profits to polish results in bad years."[11]

> **KEN SCHAPIRO—CONDOR CAPITAL MANAGEMENT**
> IBM has run out of easy things to do to generate earnings growth. Now they have to do the hard stuff.[9]

---

[8]*Accounting Trends and Techniques-2001* (New York: AICPA, 2001), p. 289.
[9]Bethany McLean, "Hocus-Pocus: How IBM Grew 27% a Year," *Fortune*, June 26, 2000, p. 168.
[10]Ibid.
[11]Ford S. Worthy, "Manipulating Profits: How It's Done," *Fortune*, June 25, 1984, p. 50.

ARTHUR LEVITT, JR.
While the problem of earnings management is not new, it has swelled in a market that is unforgiving of companies that miss their estimates. I recently read of one major U.S. company that failed to meet its so-called numbers by one penny and lost more than six percent of its stock value in one day.[12]

Many believe that manipulating income reduces earnings quality because it can mask permanent earnings. A recent *BusinessWeek* issue was devoted entirely to the topic of earnings management. The issue, entitled "Corporate Earnings: Who Can You Trust," contains articles that are highly critical of corporate America's earnings manipulation practices. Arthur Levitt, Jr., former Chairman of the Securities and Exchange Commission, has been outspoken in his criticism of corporate earnings management practices and their effect on earnings quality. In an article appearing in the *CPA Journal*, he states,

> Increasingly, I have become concerned that the motivation to meet Wall Street earnings expectations may be overriding common-sense business practices. Too many corporate managers, auditors, and analysts are participants in a game of nods and winks. In the zeal to satisfy consensus earnings estimates and project a smooth earnings path, wishful thinking may be winning the day over faithful representation. As a result, I fear that we are witnessing an erosion in the *quality of earnings*, and therefore, the quality of financial reporting. Managing may be giving way to manipulation; integrity may be losing out to illusion. (emphasis added)[13]

How do managers manipulate income? Two major methods are (1) income shifting and (2) income statement classification. Income shifting is achieved by accelerating or delaying the recognition of revenues or expenses. For example, a practice called "channel stuffing" accelerates revenue recognition by persuading distributors to purchase more of your product than necessary near the end of a reporting period. The most common income statement classification manipulation involves the inclusion of recurring operating expenses in "special charge" categories such as restructuring costs (discussed below).[14] This practice sometimes is referred to as "big bath" accounting, a reference to cleaning up company balance sheets. Asset reductions, or the incurrence of liabilities, for these restructuring costs result in large reductions in income that might otherwise appear as normal operating expenses either in the current or future years.

Mr. Levitt would like to see various rule changes by standard setters to improve the transparency of financial statements. He does not want to eliminate necessary flexibility in financial reporting, but would like to make it easier for financial statement users to "see through the numbers" to the future. A key to a meaningful assessment of a company's future profitability is to understand the events reported in the income statement and their relationship with future earnings. Let's now revisit the components of operating income.

Many believe that corporate earnings management practices reduce the quality of reported earnings.

CHECK WITH THE **COACH**

Every day, news stories in the business and financial press mention company earnings (income) reports. Throughout the intermediate accounting course, you will study both important and controversial issues that affect the quality of earnings information. Check with the Coach to get a head start on these issues. There you will see recent articles about earnings quality, listen to experts discuss the use of earnings and cash flow statement information, and review an illustration of an earnings disclosure. ∎

---

[12]Arthur Levitt, Jr., "The Numbers Game," *The CPA Journal*, December 1998, p. 16.
[13]Ibid, p. 14.
[14]John J. Wild, Leopold A. Bernstein, and K.R. Subramanyam, *Financial Statement Analysis*, Seventh Edition, 2001, McGraw-Hill/Irwin, Burr Ridge, Illinois, p. 123.

OPERATING INCOME AND EARNINGS QUALITY

LO4

Should all items of revenue and expense included in operating income be considered indicative of a company's permanent earnings? No, not necessarily. Sometimes, for example, operating expenses include some unusual items that may or may not continue in the future. Look closely at the 2000, 1999, and 1998 partial income statements of Burlington Industries, the world's largest manufacturer of softgoods for apparel and interior furnishings, presented in Graphic 4–6. What items appear unusual? The items "Provision for restructuring" and "Write-off of goodwill" certainly require further investigation. Let's first discuss restructuring costs.

GRAPHIC 4–6
Partial Income
Statements—
Burlington Industries,
Inc.

Income Statements (in part)
($ in thousands)

For the 52 weeks ended September 30, 2000, and October 2, 1999,
and the 53 weeks ended October 3, 1998

	2000	1999	1998
Net sales	$1,620,247	$1,651,689	$2,010,414
Cost of sales	1,434,867	1,426,311	1,659,485
Gross profit	185,380	225,378	350,929
Operating expenses:			
Selling, general, and administrative	138,725	143,171	148,383
Provision for doubtful accounts	4,380	5,482	1,677
Provision for restructuring	67,003	62,069	—
Amortization of intangibles	16,715	17,810	18,100
Write-off of goodwill	463,247	—	—
Operating income (loss)	(504,690)	(3,154)	182,769

FINANCIAL REPORTING CASE

Q1, p. 168

Restructuring costs
include costs associated
with shutdown or
relocation of facilities
or downsizing of
operations.

GRAPHIC 4–7
Disclosure of
Restructuring Costs—
Burlington Industries,
Inc.

Restructuring Costs. When a company reorganizes its operations to attain greater efficiency, it often incurs significant associated costs. For instance, let's consider our Burlington Industries example. A disclosure note accompanying the company's financial statements indicates a 1999 reorganization related to its apparel fabrics business and various moves in 2000 to strengthen its interior furnishing products business. In both cases, facility closings and asset write-downs were important components of the restructurings. Facility closings and related employee layoffs translate into costs incurred for severance pay and relocation costs. For example, Graphic 4–7 reports a portion of the disclosure note related to the 2000 restructuring.

Restructuring and Impairment Charges (in part)
The closings and overhead reductions outlined above will result in the elimination of approximately 2,450 jobs in the United States and 950 jobs in Mexico, with severance benefit payments to be paid over periods of up to 12 months from the termination date depending on the employee's length of service.

Prior to 2003,
restructuring costs
were recognized
(expensed) in the
period the decision to
restructure was made,
not in the period or
periods in which the
actual activities took
place.

Notice that the severance benefit payments were "to be paid over periods of up to 12 months from the termination date . . ." This means that a portion of the restructuring activities and related cash outflows will occur during the following fiscal year. Prior to 2003, when a company restructured its operations, it estimated the future costs associated with the restructuring and expensed the costs in the period in which the decision to restructure was made. An offsetting liability was recorded. Later expenditures were charged against this liability as they occurred. The rationale for expensing now an estimate of future expenditures was to match the restructuring costs with the decision to restructure and not with the period or periods in which the actual activities take place or when the benefits (if any) are realized.

What if the estimates turned out to be incorrect?

Levi Strauss & Co., the famous jeans manufacturer, reported the following item as part of operating expenses in its 2000 and 1999 income statements ($ in thousands):

	2000	**1999**
Restructuring costs	$(33,144)	$497,683

Why the negative expense in 2000? A review of the disclosure note that accompanied Levi's financial statements reveals that in 1998 and 1999 the company recorded restructuring costs that included estimated employee-related expenses and estimated facilities expenses associated with a plan to reduce capacity. However, in 2000, Levi lowered its estimate of the total costs associated with the restructuring and recorded an adjustment that increased income. As we discuss later in this chapter and throughout the text, when an estimate is changed in a reporting period after the period the estimate was made, the company should record the effect of the change in the current period rather than restate prior years' financial statements to correct the estimate.

The appearance of restructuring costs in corporate income statements increased significantly in the 1980s and 1990s. Many U.S. companies reacted to increased competition by streamlining their operations. The popular term heard often is *downsizing*. The SEC became concerned about the frequency with which companies were accruing restructuring costs in the manner described above. One of the chief concerns was that some companies purposely expensed large costs currently in an effort to manipulate future income. For example, employee relocation costs incurred in conjunction with a restructuring may produce future benefits to a company through greater operating efficiency. If so, accrual prior to any action may result in premature expense recognition of these costs.

The FASB responded to the SEC's concern in June 2002 with *SFAS No. 146.*[15] The Standard prohibits management from recognizing a liability for a cost associated with an exit or disposal activity unless and until a liability actually *has been incurred.* No longer can a company accrue restructuring costs in the period the company commits to an exit plan, unless the costs actually have been incurred. As an example, suppose terminated employees are to receive termination benefits, but only after they remain with the employer beyond a minimum retention period. In that case, a liability for termination benefits, and corresponding expense, should be accrued in the period(s) the employees render their service. On the other hand, if future service beyond a minimum retention period is not required, the benefits are recognized at the time the company communicates the arrangement to employees. In either case, the liability and expense are recorded at the point they are deemed incurred. Similarly, costs associated with closing facilities and relocating employees are recognized when goods or services associated with those activities are received and not accrued at the commitment date.

> A new standard requires that restructuring costs be recognized only in the period incurred.

The Standard also establishes that fair value is the objective for initial measurement of the liability, and that a liability's fair value often will be measured by determining the present value of future estimated cash outflows. We discuss such present value calculations at length in later chapters, particularly in Chapters 6 and 14.

> Fair value is the objective for the initial measurement of a liability associated with restructuring costs.

A major benefit of the new requirements is that liabilities accrued as a result of restructuring activities now comply with the definition of a liability in *Statement of Financial Concepts 6* and therefore are accounted for consistent with other liabilities. The new Standard also significantly

> **BUSINESS WEEK**
>
> Of course, companies have always taken write-offs and restructuring charges. But nervous regulators and investors fear that such multiyear write-offs are increasingly distorting corporate earnings—so much so, in fact, that some question whether the underlying meaning of profit numbers and their value as a true reflection of corporate performance is getting trampled.[16]

---

[15]"Accounting for Costs Associated with Exit or Disposal Activities," *Statement of Financial Accounting Standards No. 146* (Norwalk, Conn.: FASB, 2002).

[16]Nanette Byrnes, Richard A. Melcher, and Debra Sparks, "Earnings Hocus-Pocus: How Companies Come Up with the Numbers They Want," *BusinessWeek*, October 5, 1998, p. 135.

Should restructuring costs be considered part of a company's permanent earnings stream?

reduces the possibility that restructuring costs can be used as a method to manipulate earnings.

Now that we understand the nature of restructuring costs, we can address the important question: Should financial statement users consider these costs part of a company's permanent earnings stream, or are they transitory in nature? There is no easy answer. Burlington incurred restructuring costs in both 1999 and 2000. Will the company incur these costs again in the near future? Consider the following facts. During the nine-year period from 1991 through 1999, the Dow Jones Industrial 30 companies reported 62 restructuring charges in their collective income statements. That is an average of approximately two per company. But the average is deceiving. Nine of the 30 companies reported no restructuring charges during that period. However, DuPont incurred restructuring charges in seven of the nine years, and Alcoa and Eastman Kodak reported restructuring charges in six of their nine income statements. An analyst must interpret restructuring charges in light of a company's past history in this area. Information in disclosure notes describing the restructuring and management plans related to the business involved also can be helpful.

A second questionable expense included in Burlington's income statement for 2000 is the *write-off of goodwill*. This item involves what is referred to as an *asset impairment* loss or charge. Any operational asset, not just goodwill, should be written down if there has been a significant and permanent impairment of value. We explore operational assets in Chapters 10 and 11. After discussing this topic in more depth in those chapters, we will revisit this concept of earnings quality as it relates to impairment of goodwill. It is interesting to note that were it not for these two "unusual" items, Burlington would have reported operating income rather than operating losses in both 1999 and 2000.

Is it possible that financial analysts might look favorably at a company in the year it incurs a substantial restructuring charge or other unusual expense such as an asset write-off, even if it causes an operating loss as in the case of Burlington? Perhaps so, if they view management as creating higher profits in future years through operating efficiencies. Would analysts then reward that company again in future years when those operating efficiencies materialize? Certainly, this double halo effect might provide an attractive temptation to the management of some companies.

There are other operating expenses that also call into question this issue of earnings quality. For example, in Chapter 9 we discuss the write-down of inventory to comply with the lower-of-cost-or-market rule. A very controversial expense called *in-process research and development* is addressed in Chapter 10. Earnings quality also is influenced by the way income from investments is recorded (Chapter 12) and in the manner companies account for their pension plans (Chapter 17). In each case, after discussing these issues, we revisit this concept of earnings quality.

Earnings quality is affected by revenue issues as well. As an example, suppose that toward the end of its fiscal year, a company loses a major customer that can't be replaced. That would mean the current year's revenue figures contain a transitory component equal to the revenue generated from sales to that customer. Of course, in addition to its effect on revenues, losing the customer would have implications for the transitory/permanent nature of expenses and the bottom line net income. And the pressure on companies to meet their earnings numbers often has

ARTHUR LEVITT, JR.
When a company decides to restructure, management and employees, investors and creditors, customers and suppliers all want to understand the expected effects. We need, of course, to ensure that financial reporting provides this information. But this should not lead to flushing all the associated costs—and maybe a little extra—through the financial statements.[17]

LUCENT TECHNOLOGIES
Citing unidentified people familiar with the investigation, the report said SEC enforcement division investigators are probing whether the troubled telecom equipment maker improperly booked $679 million in revenue during its 2000 fiscal year.[18]

---

[17]Arthur Levitt, Jr., "The Numbers Game," *The CPA Journal*, December, 1998, p. 16.
[18]"SEC Probes Lucent Accounting," *CBS.MarketWatch.com*, February 9, 2001.

led to premature revenue recognition, reducing the quality of the current period's earnings. Accelerating revenue recognition has caused problems for many companies. For example, Lucent Technologies' revenue recognition practices recently attracted the attention of the SEC. Of particular concern was sales revenue for equipment that Lucent shipped to distributor partners but that had not been sold to end user customers by the end of the reporting period. We save these issues for Chapter 5 in which we discuss revenue recognition in considerable depth. Now, though, let's discuss earnings quality issues related to *nonoperating* items.

NONOPERATING INCOME AND EARNINGS QUALITY

Most of the components of earnings in an income statement relate directly to the ordinary, continuing operations of the company. Some, though, such as interest and gains or losses are only tangentially related to normal operations. These we refer to as nonoperating items. Some nonoperating items have generated considerable discussion with respect to earnings quality, notably gains and losses generated either from the sale of operational assets or from the sale of investments. For example, as the stock market boom reached its height late in the year 2000, many companies recorded large gains from sale of investments that had appreciated significantly in value. How should those gains be interpreted in terms of their relationship to future earnings? Are they transitory or permanent? Let's consider an example.

> **Gains and losses from the sale of operational assets and investments often can significantly inflate or deflate current earnings.**

Intel Corporation is the world's largest manufacturer of semiconductors. Graphic 4–8 shows the nonoperating section of Intel's income statements for the nine months ended September 30, 2000 and September 25, 1999. In 2000, income before taxes for the nine months increased by approximately 48% from the prior year's comparable nine-month period. But notice that the *gains on investments, net* (net means net of losses) increased from $556 million to over $3.3 billion accounting for a large portion of the increase in income. Some analysts questioned the quality of Intel's earnings for the period ending Sept. 30, 2000 because of these large gains.

> **GRAPHIC 4–8**
> Income Statements (in part)—Intel Corporation

Income Statements (in part)
(in millions)

	Nine Months Ended	
	Sept. 30, 2000	Sept. 25, 1999
Operating income	$ 7,819	$7,013
Gains on investments, net	3,309	556
Interest expense	(26)	(28)
Interest income and other, net	664	425
Income before taxes	11,766	7,966

Consider also Citicorp's fourth quarter 1997 earnings of $1.67 billion. This figure included $733 million of capital gains from the sale of securities and other assets. Some analysts considered these gains as transitory in nature. Coca-Cola Company has been criticized for manipulating its profits through the timely sale of bottling companies. The company often invests in weaker bottlers, enhances their operations, and then sells them for a profit. Are these gains an integral part of the soft-drink business or are they transitory blips in earnings? There are no easy answers to these questions.

Companies often voluntarily provide a **pro forma earnings** number when they announce annual or quarterly earnings calculated according to GAAP. These pro forma earnings numbers are management's view of permanent earnings. For example, Sun Microsystems, Inc., a leading provider of hardware, software, and services that power enterprises and network computing, announced on April 19, 2001, that its income for the quarter ended April 1, 2001, was

> **Many companies voluntarily provide *pro forma earnings*—management's assessment of permanent earnings.**

$136 million. The company also announced that its "pro forma net income (which excludes realized gains/losses on Sun's venture equity portfolio, the effects of acquisition-related charges, any unusual one-time items, and the cumulative tax effects) for the third quarter was $263 million."[19] These pro forma earnings numbers are controversial as they represent management's biased view of permanent earnings and should be interpreted in that light. Nevertheless, these disclosures do provide additional information to the financial community.

Standard setters are concerned with the issue of reporting multiple earnings figures and the potential for investor confusion. In August 2001, the FASB disseminated a proposal for a new project entitled "Reporting Information About the Financial Performance of Business Enterprises." One of the principal reasons cited for the project was the increase in the reporting of pro forma earnings.[20] At the time this text was published, no new pronouncements had resulted from the project.

We now turn our attention to three income statement items that, because of their nature, are more obviously not part of a company's permanent earnings and, appropriately, are excluded from continuing operations.

Separately Reported Items

FINANCIAL REPORTING CASE

Q2, p. 168

GAAP require that certain transactions be reported separately in the income statement, below income from continuing operations.

The information in the income statement is useful if it can help users predict the future. Toward this end, users should be made aware of events reported in the income statement that are not likely to occur again in the foreseeable future.

There are three types of events that, if they have a material effect[21] on the income statement, require separate reporting and disclosure: (1) discontinued operations, (2) extraordinary items, and (3) the cumulative effect of a change in accounting principle.[22] In fact, these are the only three events that are allowed to be reported below continuing operations. Although a company has considerable flexibility in reporting income from *continuing operations*, the presentation order of these three is mandated as follows:[23]

Income from continuing operations	$xxx
Discontinued operations, net of $xx in taxes	xx
Extraordinary items, net of $xx in taxes[24]	xx
Cumulative effect of a change in accounting principle, net of $xx in taxes	xx
Net income	$xxx

The objective is to separately report all of the income effects of these items. Therefore, their income tax effects also are included in the separate presentation rather than as part of the amount reported as income tax expense. The process of associating income tax effects with the income statement components that create those effects is referred to as *intraperiod tax allocation*. We address this process before defining the separately reported items more precisely.

INTRAPERIOD INCOME TAX ALLOCATION

Intraperiod tax allocation associates (allocates) income tax expense (or income tax benefit if there is a loss) with each major component of income that causes it.[25] More specifically,

---

[19]"Sun Microsystems Reports Third Quarter Revenues and Earnings," *PR Newswire*, April 19, 2001.

[20]"Reporting Information About the Financial Performance of Business Enterprises," *Proposal for a New Agenda Project*, (Norwalk, Conn.: FASB, 2001).

[21]The concept of materiality was discussed in Chapter 1. If the effect on the income statement is not material, these items are included in income from continuing operations.

[22]"Reporting Results of Operations," *Accounting Principles Board Opinion No. 30* (New York: AICPA, 1973).

[23]The presentation of these separately reported items is the same for single-step and multiple-step income statement formats. The single-step versus multiple-step distinction applies to items included in income from continuing operations.

[24]Companies that report discontinued operations and one of the other separately reported items often show a subtotal after discontinued operations. This is not required. However, due to its frequency of use, we use this convention in examples and illustrations in the remainder of this chapter.

[25]*Intraperiod* tax allocation concerns the association of income tax with income statement components. *Interperiod* tax allocation, covered in Chapter 16, addresses the problem created when taxable income does not equal income before taxes as determined by GAAP because of differences in the timing of revenue or expense recognition.

income tax is allocated to income from continuing operations and each of the three separately reported items. For example, assume a company experienced an extraordinary gain during the year.[26] The amount of income tax expense deducted from income from continuing operations is the amount of income tax expense that the company would have incurred *if there were no extraordinary gain*. The effect on income taxes caused by the extraordinary item is deducted from the extraordinary gain itself in the income statement. Illustration 4–4 demonstrates this concept.

The Maxwell Gear Corporation had income from continuing operations before income tax expense of $200,000 and an extraordinary gain of $60,000 in 2003. The income tax rate is 40% on all items of income or loss. Therefore, the company's total income tax expense is $104,000 (40% × $260,000).	**ILLUSTRATION 4–4** Intraperiod Tax Allocation

How should the company allocate the tax expense between income from continuing operations and the extraordinary gain? A partial income statement, beginning with income from continuing operations before income tax expense, *ignoring* intraperiod tax allocation, is shown in Illustration 4–4A.

Income from continuing operations before income taxes	$200,000	**ILLUSTRATION 4–4A**
Income tax expense	(104,000)	Income Statement Presented
Income before extraordinary gain	96,000	*Incorrectly*—No
Extraordinary gain (gross)	60,000	Intraperiod Tax
Net income	$156,000	Allocation (extraordinary gain)

The deficiency of this presentation is that the apparent contribution to net income of (a) income before the extraordinary gain (that is, income from continuing operations) and (b) the extraordinary gain, is misleading. If the extraordinary gain had not occurred, income tax expense would not have been $104,000 but rather $80,000 (40% × $200,000). Similarly, the net benefit of the extraordinary gain is not $60,000, but rather $36,000 ($60,000 minus 40% × $60,000). The total tax expense of $104,000 must be *allocated*, $80,000 to continuing operations and $24,000 (40% × $60,000) to the extraordinary gain. The appropriate income statement presentation appears in Illustration 4–4B.

Income from continuing operations before income taxes	$200,000	**ILLUSTRATION 4–4B**
Income tax expense	(80,000)	Income Statement—
Income before extraordinary gain	120,000	Intraperiod Tax
Extraordinary gain, net of $24,000 tax expense	36,000	Allocation (extraordinary gain)
Net income	$156,000	

Net income is $156,000 either way. Intraperiod tax allocation is not an issue of measurement but an issue of presentation. The $120,000 income before extraordinary gain properly reflects income from continuing operations *including* the appropriate tax effects. Also, notice that income tax expense represents taxes that relate to the total of all of the revenue, expense, gain, and loss items included in continuing operations. Each of the items following

The three items reported separately below income from continuing operations are presented net of the related income tax effect.

---

[26]The criteria for classifying gains and losses as extraordinary are discussed in a later section of this chapter.

continuing operations (discontinued operations, extraordinary items, and cumulative effect of a change in accounting principle) are presented *net of their tax effect*. No items included in the computation of income from continuing operations are reported net of tax.

In the illustration, the extraordinary gain caused additional income tax expense to be incurred. What if the company had experienced an extraordinary loss of $60,000 instead of an extraordinary gain? In that case, rather than creating additional tax, the loss actually decreases tax due to its reducing taxable income by $60,000. The company's total income tax expense would be $56,000 [40% × ($200,000 − 60,000)].

The extraordinary loss *decreased* the amount of tax the company otherwise would have had to pay by $24,000. This is commonly referred to as a *tax benefit*. A partial income statement, beginning with income from continuing operations before income tax expense, *ignoring* intraperiod tax allocation is shown in Illustration 4–4C.

ILLUSTRATION 4–4C		
Income Statement Presented *Incorrectly*—No Intraperiod Tax Allocation (extraordinary loss)	Income from continuing operations before income taxes	$200,000
	Income tax expense	(56,000)
	Income before extraordinary loss	144,000
	Extraordinary loss (gross)	(60,000)
	Net income	$ 84,000

Once again, income before the extraordinary loss (that is, income from continuing operations) is misleading. If the extraordinary loss had not occurred, income tax expense would not have been $56,000 but rather $80,000 (40% × $200,000). The total tax expense of $56,000 must be *allocated*, $80,000 tax expense to continuing operations and $24,000 tax benefit to the extraordinary loss. The appropriate income statement presentation appears in Illustration 4–4D.

ILLUSTRATION 4–4D		
Income Statement— Intraperiod Tax Allocation (extraordinary loss)	Income from continuing operations before income taxes	$200,000
	Income tax expense	(80,000)
	Income before extraordinary loss	120,000
	Extraordinary loss, net of $24,000 tax benefit	(36,000)
	Net income	$ 84,000

Now that we have seen how to report items net of their related tax effects, let's look closer at all three items reported net of tax below income from continuing operations: discontinued operations, extraordinary items, and changes in accounting principle.

DISCONTINUED OPERATIONS

LO5

FINANCIAL
REPORTING CASE

Q3, p. 168

Bausch & Lomb Inc. is a world leader in the development, manufacture and marketing of health care products for the eye. The company is perhaps best known for its contact lenses. Prior to 2000, the company's businesses also included a sunglass unit, a hearing aid business, and a skin care business. In 1999, though, Bausch & Lomb decided to discontinue its sunglass, hearing aid, and skin care lines of business and accordingly sold them.[27] These are examples of **discontinued operations.**

---

[27]The primary reason companies discontinue operations often is that the line of business is no longer profitable. This was not the case with Bausch & Lomb's various lines sold in 1999 that had been generating a profit.

SFAS NO. 144

. . . a component of an entity comprises operations and cash flows that can be clearly distinguished, operationally and for financial reporting purposes, from the rest of the entity.[28]

What Constitutes an Operation?   For many years *APB Opinion No. 30*[29] provided authoritative guidance for accounting and reporting of discontinued operations. This Opinion defined an operation as a "segment of a business." A segment could be either a separate line of business or a separate class of customer. *SFAS No. 144,* issued in 2001, replaces the term segment of a business with *component of an entity.* A component of an entity comprises operations and cash flows that can be clearly distinguished, operationally and for financial reporting purposes, from the rest of the entity.

SFAS No. 144 considers an operation to be a component of an entity whose operations and cash flows can be clearly distinguished from the rest of the entity.

If a component of an entity has either been disposed of or classified as held for sale, we report the results of its operations separately in discontinued operations if two conditions are met:

1. The operations and cash flows of the component have been (or will be) eliminated from the ongoing operations.
2. The entity will not have any significant continuing involvement in the operations of the component after the disposal transaction.

Notice that the definition of an operation is significantly broadened with *SFAS No. 144.* A component of an entity may be a reportable segment or operating segment, a reporting unit, a subsidiary, or an asset group. For example, suppose Chadwick Industries operates a chain of 12 restaurants in the Southeast and also has a division that engages in the production of canned goods sold to retailers. Previously, either the restaurant chain or the canned goods division would qualify as an operation for purposes of reporting discontinued operations, but an individual restaurant within the chain or a manufacturing plant in the canned goods division would not qualify. Now, though, under *SFAS No. 144,* it could if it represents a component of the company with "operations and cash flows that can be clearly distinguished, operationally and for financial reporting purposes," from the rest of the restaurants or plants.

Remember, too, that the second condition for being reported separately as a discontinued operation is that the entity will not have any significant continuing involvement in the operations of the component after the disposal transaction. As an example, let's say Scooter's Barbecue franchises restaurants to independent owners but also has several company-owned restaurants. If Scooter's commits to a plan to sell its company-owned restaurants to an existing franchisee, the way it reports the transaction would depend on the terms of the agreement. If the franchise agreement requires Scooter's to maintain significant continuing involvement in the operations of the restaurants after they are sold, Scooter's will not report this transaction as a discontinued operation. On the other hand, if no continuing involvement is indicated, Scooter's will report the transaction separate from its franchising operations as a discontinued operation.[30] We see how in the next section.

Reporting Discontinued Operations.   By definition, the income or loss stream from an identifiable discontinued operation no longer will continue. If Bausch & Lomb had not separately reported the results of discontinuing its businesses, its 2000 and 1999 comparative income statements (in condensed form) would have appeared as in Illustration 4–5A.

The company generated net income of 83.4 million and $444.8 million in 2000 and 1999, respectively. However, an analyst concerned with Bausch & Lomb's future profitability is more interested in the 2000 and 1999 results after separating the effects of the discontinued operations from the results of operations that will continue. This information might have a significant impact on the analyst's assessment of future profitability.

Now let's compare these with the actual income statements (in condensed form) adjusted to reflect the reporting format of *SFAS No. 144* as presented in Illustration 4–5B. The income tax effect of the discontinued operations was disclosed in a note.

---

[28]"Accounting for the Impairment or Disposal of Long-Lived Assets," *Statement of Financial Accounting Standards No. 144* (Norwalk, Conn.: FASB, 2001), par. 41.

[29]"Reporting Results of Operations," *Accounting Principles Board Opinion No. 30* (New York: AICPA, 1973).

[30]"Accounting for the Impairment or Disposal of Long-Lived Assets," *Statement of Financial Accounting Standards No. 144* (Norwalk, Conn: FASB, 2001), par. A25 and A27.

ILLUSTRATION 4–5A

Income Statements Presented Incorrectly *without* Separate Reporting of Discontinued Operations

BAUSCH & LOMB, INC.
Income Statements
Years Ended December 31

	($ in millions)	
	2000	**1999**
Net sales..................................	$1,772.4	$2,258.0
Costs and expenses	1,623.5	1,726.0
Income before income taxes	148.9	532.0
Income tax expense.......................	65.5	87.2
Net income.............................	$ 83.4	$ 444.8

ILLUSTRATION 4–5B

Income Statements *with* Separate Reporting of Discontinued Operations

BAUSCH & LOMB, INC.
Income Statements
Years Ended December 31

	($ in millions)	
	2000	**1999**
Net sales	$1,772.4	$1,764.3
Costs and expenses	1,623.5	1,595.0
Income before income taxes	148.9	169.3
Income tax expense	65.5	66.6
Income from continuing operations	83.4	102.7
Discontinued operations:		
Income from discontinued operations (including gain on disposal of $308), net of taxes	—	342.1
Net income	$ 83.4	$ 444.8

The net-of-tax income effects of a discontinued operation are reported separately in the income statement, below income from continuing operations.

Compare the two income statements for their ability to predict future profitability. The income statements in Illustration 4–5B separate the net-of-tax income effects of the discontinued operation. The 1999 revenues, expenses, gains, losses, and income tax related to the *discontinued* operations have been removed from *continuing* operations and reported separately.[31] Otherwise, as in Illustration 4–5A, it would appear that the company's profitability decreased by 81%, from $444.8 to $83.4 million, and its revenue decreased by 22%, from $2,258.0 to $1,772.4 million. However, a key in the assessment of profitability is the comparison of the company's performance from *continuing* operations. That comparison reveals a slight *increase* in revenue of $8 million and a drop in income of only 19% ($102.7 to $83.4). This provides a significantly different picture of Bausch & Lomb's future profitability.

Sometimes a discontinued component actually has been sold as of the end of a reporting period. In other situations, though, the component is being held for sale but the disposal transaction has not been completed before the end of the reporting period. We consider these two possibilities next.

When the component has been sold.   When its reporting period ended in 1999, Bausch & Lomb had sold its sunglass, hearing aid, and skin care businesses. In such situations, when the discontinued component is sold before the end of the reporting period, the reported income effects of a discontinued operation will include two elements:

---

[31]Even though the operations were discontinued in 1999, it is important for comparative purposes to separate the effects for any prior years presented. This allows an apples-to-apples comparison of income from *continuing* operations. So, in comparative income statements reporting three years, the 1998 income statement would be reclassified and the income from discontinued operations presented as a separately reported item.

1. Operating income or loss (revenues, expenses, gains, and losses) of the component from the beginning of the reporting period to the disposal date.
2. Gain or loss on disposal.

These two elements can be combined or reported separately, net of their tax effects. If combined, the gain or loss on disposal must be disclosed. In our illustrations, we combine the income effects. We consider this situation in Illustration 4–6.

<table>
<tr><td>

The Duluth Holding Company has several operating divisions. In October 2003, management decided to sell one of its divisions that qualifies as a separate component according to *SFAS No. 144.* The division was sold on December 18, 2003, for a net selling price of $14,000,000. On that date, the assets of the division had a book value of $12,000,000. For the period January 1 through disposal, the division reported a pretax operating loss of $4,200,000. The company's income tax rate is 40% on all items of income or loss. Duluth generated after-tax profits of $22,350,000 from its continuing operations.

Duluth's income statement for the year 2003, beginning with income from continuing operations, would be reported as follows:
</td><td>

ILLUSTRATION 4–6

Discontinued Operations—Gain on Disposal
</td></tr>
</table>

Income from continuing operations	$22,350,000
Discontinued operations:	
Loss from operations of discontinued component (including gain on disposal of $2,000,000*) $(2,200,000)†	
Income tax benefit 880,000‡	
Loss on discontinued operations	(1,320,000)
Net income	$21,030,000

*Net selling price of $14 million less book value of $12 million
†Operating loss of $4.2 million less gain on disposal of $2 million
‡$2,200,000 × 40%

Notice that a tax *benefit* occurs because a *loss* reduces taxable income, saving the company $880,000. On the other hand, had there been *income* from operations of $2,200,000, the $880,000 income tax effect would have represented additional income tax expense.

For comparison purposes, the net of tax operating income or loss of the discontinued component for any prior years included in the comparative income statements also are separately reported as discontinued operations.

When the component is considered held for sale.   What if a company has decided to discontinue a component but, when the reporting period ends, the component has not yet been sold? If the situation indicates that the component is likely to be sold within a year, the component is considered "held for sale."[32] In that case, the income effects of the discontinued operation still are reported, but the two components of the reported amount are modified as follows:

If a component to be discontinued has not yet been sold, its income effects, including any impairment loss, usually still are reported separately as discontinued operations.

1. Operating income or loss (revenues, expenses, gains and losses) of the component from the beginning of the reporting period *to the end of the reporting period.*
2. An "impairment loss" if the carrying value of the assets of the component is more than fair value minus cost to sell.

The balance sheet is affected, too. The assets of the component considered held for sale are reported at the lower of their carrying amount (book value) or fair value minus cost to

[32]There are six criteria designed to determine whether the component is likely to be sold and therefore considered "held for sale." "Accounting for the Impairment or Disposal of Long-Lived Assets," *Statement of Financial Accounting Standards No. 144* (Norwalk, Conn.: FASB, 2001). In Chapter 11 we discuss this standard and the held for sale criteria in the context of accounting for the impairment of operational assets.

sell. And, because it's not in use, an operational asset classified as held for sale is not depreciated or amortized.

The two income elements can be combined or reported separately, net of their tax effects. In addition, if the amounts are combined and there is an impairment loss, the loss must be disclosed, either parenthetically on the face of the statement or in a disclosure note. Consider the example in Illustration 4–7.

ILLUSTRATION 4–7	
Discontinued Operations— Impairment Loss	The Duluth Holding Company has several operating divisions. In October 2003, management decided to sell one of its divisions that qualifies as a separate component according to *SFAS No. 144.* On December 31, 2003, the end of the company's fiscal year, the division had not yet been sold. On that date, the assets of the division had a book value of $12,000,000 and a fair value, minus anticipated costs to sell, of $9,000,000. For the year, the division reported a pre-tax operating loss of $4,200,000. The company's income tax rate is 40% on all items of income or loss. Duluth generated after-tax profits of $22,350,000 from its continuing operations.

Duluth's income statement for 2003, beginning with income from continuing operations, would be reported as follows:

Income from continuing operations		$22,350,000
Discontinued operations:		
Loss from operations of discontinued component (including impairment loss of $3,000,000)	$(7,200,000)*	
Income tax benefit	2,880,000†	
Loss on discontinued operations		(4,320,000)
Net income		$18,030,000

*Operating loss of $4.2 million plus impairment loss of $3 million
†$7,200,000 × 40%

A disclosure note would provide additional details about the discontinued component, including the identity of the component, the major classes of assets and liabilities of the component, the reason for the discontinuance, and the expected manner of disposition. Also, the net-of-tax operating income or loss of the component being discontinued is also reported separate from continuing operations for any prior year that is presented for comparison purposes along with the 2003 income statement.

In the above illustration, if the fair value of the division's assets minus cost to sell exceeded the book value of $12,000,000, there is no impairment loss and the income effects of the discontinued operation would include only the operating loss of $4,200,000, less the income tax benefit.[33]

Interim reporting. Remember that companies whose ownership shares are publicly traded in the United States must file quarterly reports with the Securities and Exchange Commission. If a component of an entity is considered held for sale at the end of a quarter, the income effects of the discontinued component must be separately reported in the quarterly income statement. These effects would include the operating income or loss for the quarter as well as an impairment loss if the component's assets have a book value less than fair value minus cost to sell. If the assets are impaired and written down, any gain or loss on disposal in a subsequent quarter is determined relative to the new, written-down book value.

Let's now turn our attention to the second separately reported item, extraordinary gains and losses.

---

[33]In the following year when the component is sold, the income effects must also be reported as a discontinued operation. Prior to SFAS No. 144, operating results for the subsequent period were estimated and considered in determining the income effect for the year the segment was deemed held for sale. This is no longer the case.

EXTRAORDINARY ITEMS

Occasionally, an unusual event may occur that materially affects the current year's income but is highly unlikely to occur again in the foreseeable future. If such an item is allowed to simply alter net income without pointing out its extraordinary nature, earnings quality is seriously compromised and investors and creditors may be misled into basing predictions of future income on current income that includes the nonrecurring event. For that reason, **extraordinary items** are "red flagged" in an income statement by being reported separately, net of tax, and appropriately labeled. Extraordinary items are material events and transactions that are both:

1. Unusual in nature.
2. Infrequent in occurrence.[34]

These criteria must be considered in light of the environment in which the entity operates. There obviously is a considerable degree of subjectivity involved in the determination. The concepts of unusual and infrequent require judgment. In making these judgments, an accountant should keep in mind the overall objective of the income statement. The key question is how the event relates to a firm's future profitability. If it is judged that the event, because of its unusual nature and infrequency of occurrence, *is not likely to occur again*, separate reporting is warranted.

Extraordinary items are material gains and losses that are both unusual in nature and infrequent in occurrence.

Companies often experience *unexpected* events that are not considered extraordinary items. The loss of a major customer or the death of the company president are unexpected events that likely will affect a company's future but are both normal risks of operating a business that could recur in the future. Other gains and losses from unexpected events that are *not* considered extraordinary include the effects of a strike, including those against competitors and major suppliers, and the adjustment of accruals on long-term contracts.[35]

A key point in the definition of an extraordinary item is that determining whether an event satisfies *both* criteria depends on the environment in which the firm operates. The environment includes factors such as the type of products or services sold and the geographical location of the firm's operations. What is extraordinary for one firm may not be extraordinary for another firm. For example, a loss caused by a hurricane in Florida may not be judged to be extraordinary. However, hurricane damage in New York may indeed be unusual and infrequent.

The determination of whether an item is unusual and infrequent should consider the environment in which the company operates.

Companies frequently sell subsidiary companies. Generally, the gain or loss is reported as a nonoperating item in the income statement or as a discontinued operation if the subsidiary is considered a component of the entity according to *SFAS No. 144*. In contrast, though, consider the disclosure note from El Paso Energy Corporation's 2000 financial statements shown in Graphic 4–9.

3. Extraordinary Gain
During the first quarter of 2000, we sold East Tennessee Natural Gas and Sea Robin Pipeline Company to comply with an FTC order related to our merger with Sonat. Net proceeds from the sales were $457 million and we recognized an extraordinary gain of $89 million, net of income taxes of $60 million.

GRAPHIC 4–9
Extraordinary Gain Disclosure—El Paso Energy Corporation

Why was the gain on sale of two subsidiary companies considered an extraordinary item? We can only speculate as to the company's reasoning, but it seems likely that the unusual nature of the sale, to comply with an order from the Federal Trade Commission, resulted in the conclusion by the company that such a gain was unlikely to occur again in the foreseeable future.

Logic and reasoning must be applied to the determination of whether or not an event is extraordinary. Keep in mind that the income statement should be a guide to predicting the

[34]"Reporting Results of Operations," *Accounting Principles Board Opinions No. 30* (New York: AICPA, 1973), par. 20.
[35]Ibid, par. 23.

future. If it is extremely unlikely that a material gain or loss will occur again in the future, the quality of earnings is improved and the usefulness of the income statement in predicting the future is enhanced if the income effects of that gain or loss are reported separately.

As shown previously in the table on page 182, the net-of-tax effects of extraordinary gains and losses are presented in the income statement below discontinued operations. In addition, a disclosure note is necessary to describe the nature of the event and the tax effects, if they are not indicated on the face of the income statement.[36]

Unusual or Infrequent Items.   If the income effect of an event is material and the event is either unusual or infrequent—but not both—the item should be *included in continuing operations* but reported as a separate income statement component. Recall the Burlington Industries, Inc. example in Graphic 4–6 on page 178. Restructuring costs and the write-off of goodwill included in that company's continuing operations, are two examples of this type of event. The events may be unusual or infrequent, but, by their nature, they could occur again in the foreseeable future. However, rather than include these items with other gains and losses or with other expenses, they are reported as a separate line item in the income statement.[37] This method of reporting, including note disclosure, enhances earnings quality by providing information to the statement user to help assess the events' relationship with future profitability.

CUMULATIVE EFFECT OF A CHANGE IN ACCOUNTING PRINCIPLE

The third item reported separately after income from continuing operations is the **cumulative effect of a change in accounting principle.** A change in accounting principle refers to a change from one acceptable accounting method to another. There are many situations in which there are alternative treatments for similar transactions. Common examples of these situations include the choice among FIFO, LIFO, and average cost for the measurement of inventory and between straight-line and other depreciation methods for plant and equipment.

Occasionally, a company will change from one generally accepted treatment to another. When these changes in accounting principles occur, information lacks consistency, hampering the ability of external users to compare financial information over reporting periods. If, for example, depreciation expense is measured in one reporting period using an accelerated depreciation method and the straight-line method in a subsequent period, depreciation expense and hence net income for the two periods are not comparable. Difficulties created by inconsistency and lack of comparability are alleviated somewhat by the way we report accounting changes.

There is more than one approach that could be used to account for a change in accounting principle. The method used most frequently requires that the effects of the change be reflected in the statements in the year the change is made rather than by retroactively restating prior years' comparative financial statements as if the new accounting principle had been in use. The cumulative effect of a change in accounting principle should be reflected in the financial statements of the change year.[38] Previous financial statements included for comparative purposes should be presented as previously reported.

The cumulative effect of a change in accounting principle is the cumulative effect on the income of previous years from having used the previous method rather than the new method. Stated differently, it's the difference between the balance in retained earnings at the beginning of the period of the change and what that balance would have been if the new method had been applied all along.

Illustration 4–8 provides an example.

Extraordinary gains and losses are presented, net of tax, in the income statement below discontinued operations.

The income effect of an event that is either unusual or infrequent should be reported as a separate component of continuing operations.

LO7

FINANCIAL REPORTING CASE

Q4, p. 168

The most frequently used accounting treatment for a change in accounting principle is to show the cumulative effect of the change in the income statement below extraordinary items.

---

[36]For several years the FASB required companies to report material gains and losses from the early extinguishment of debt as extraordinary items. This is no longer the case and now these gains and losses are subject to the same criteria as other gains and losses for such treatment; namely, that they be both (a) unusual in nature and (b) infrequent in occurrence.

[37]These items are *not* reported net of tax. Only the three separately reported items—discontinued operations, extraordinary items, and the cumulative effect of a change in accounting principle—are reported net of tax.

[38]"Accounting Changes," *Accounting Principles Board Opinion No. 20* (New York: AICPA, 1971).

ILLUSTRATION 4–8

Change in Accounting Principle

The Maxwell Gear Corporation uses the double-declining balance (DDB) depreciation method for most of its equipment. In 2003, the company switched from the DDB method to straight-line depreciation for a large group of equipment purchased at the beginning of 2001. This equipment was purchased at a cost of $50 million. The machinery has an expected useful life of five years and no estimated salvage value.

Before-Tax Cumulative Effect of the Change:

	($ in millions)	
	DDB	**Straight Line**
2001 depreciation	$20 ($50 × 40%)	$10 ($50 ÷ 5)
2002 depreciation	12 ([$50 − 20] × 40%)	10 ($50 ÷ 5)
Accumulated depreciation and 2001–02 reduction in income	$32	$20

difference

$12

The cumulative income effect is reported—net of the tax effect of the change—in the income statement as a separate item of income, between extraordinary items and net income, as shown here:

Reported as a Separate Component of Income:

	($ in millions)	
	2003	**2002**
Income before extraordinary item and accounting change	$xxx	$xxx
Extraordinary gain (loss), net of tax	xx	xx
Cumulative effect of a change in accounting principle, net of $3.6 tax expense	8.4	—
Net income	$xxx	$xxx

The cumulative after-tax effect on prior years' income is reported as a separate item of income between extraordinary items and net income.

Reporting the income effect net of tax is consistent with the way we report the other two separately reported income statement items: extraordinary gains and losses and discontinued operations.

The before-tax cumulative effect of the change in Maxwell Gear's depreciation method is $12 million. If Maxwell Gear's tax rate is 30%, the cumulative tax effect of the depreciation change is $3.6 million ($12 million × 30%). This is because, under straight-line depreciation, the reduction of income for depreciation is $12 million less, causing tax expense to be higher by that amount times the tax rate. The higher tax expense partially offsets the lower depreciation expense when determining the net, after-tax, cumulative effect of the change.

Of course, the asset side of the balance sheet also is adjusted for the depreciation change. In our illustration, accumulated depreciation is reduced by $12 million.

If the switch had been from straight-line to DDB depreciation rather than from DDB to straight-line, the effects would have been reversed. The cumulative effect of the change would have been a negative component of net income. That is, income (and therefore retained earnings) would have been $8.4 million less ($12 million − 3.6 million) in prior years if DDB depreciation had been used rather than straight-line.

To assist interyear comparisons, additional disclosure is required for various pro forma (as if) amounts for each period presented. Specifically, income statements should include pro forma restatement of (a) income before extraordinary items, (b) net income, and (c) earnings per share. In other words, these specific items, calculated as if the new method had been in effect in those prior years, are reported as supplemental information. In addition, a disclosure note is required that describes the change, the justification for the change, and the effect of the change on the current period's income.[39]

Graphic 4–10 describes an accounting change made by Geron Corporation, a large bio-pharmaceutical company, in response to the FASB's *Emerging Issues Task Force Issue No. 00-27*. The Issue addresses accounting for certain convertible securities.

GRAPHIC 4–10
Disclosure of Change in Accounting Principle—Geron Corporation

Summary of Significant Accounting Policies (in part)

Recent Accounting Pronouncements (in part)

The Company has presented the effect of adopting the new accounting principle as a cumulative effect of a change in accounting principle as allowed for in *EITF 00-27*. Accordingly, the Company has recognized an additional $13,259,000 in imputed noncash interest expense. Prior year financial statements have not been restated to reflect the change in accounting principle. Had the company adopted the new accounting principle in 1999, the effect of the change on the Company's Consolidated Statement of Operations would have been to increase the net loss by approximately $2,732,000 for the year ended December 31, 1999, and $10,527,000 for the year ended December 31, 2000.

Because of their unique nature, some changes in accounting principles are more appropriately accounted for *retroactively* rather than by the usual approach described above. For these exceptions to the general manner of treating a change in accounting principle, prior years' financial statements are *restated* to reflect the use of the new accounting method. For example, in Chapter 9 you will learn that a change from the LIFO method of valuing inventory to any other inventory method is treated this way. Chapter 21 provides more detailed coverage of the measurement and disclosure requirements for a change in accounting principle.

Accounting changes fall into one of three categories: (1) a change in an accounting principle, (2) a change in estimate, or (3) a change in reporting entity. We just discussed changes in accounting principles. A brief overview of each of the other two changes is provided here. We cover accounting changes in detail in Chapter 21.

Change in Accounting Estimate.   Estimates are a necessary aspect of accounting. Some common accounting estimates are the estimation of the amount of future bad debts on existing accounts receivable, the estimation of the useful life and residual (salvage) value of a depreciable asset, and the estimation of future warranty expenses.

A change in accounting estimate is reflected in the financial statements of the current period and future periods.

Because estimates require the prediction of future events, it's not unusual for them to turn out wrong. When an estimate is revised as new information comes to light, accounting for the change in estimate is quite straightforward. We do not restate prior years' financial statements to reflect the new estimate; nor do we include the cumulative effect of the change in current income. Instead, we merely incorporate the new estimate in any related accounting determinations from there on.[40]

Consider the example in Illustration 4–9.

If the after-tax income effect of the change in estimate is material, the effect on net income and earnings per share must be disclosed in a note, along with the justification for the change. In this example, assuming a 40% tax rate, the after-tax effect of the change is a decrease in income of $48,000 [$80,000 ($280,000 revised depreciation − $200,000 old depreciation) multiplied by 60% (1 − 40% tax rate)].

NationsRent, Inc., operates a nationwide network of equipment rental locations offering a broad selection of equipment primarily to the construction and industrial segments of the equipment rental industry. Graphic 4–11 shows the disclosure note included in the com-

---

[39]These disclosures are discussed and illustrated in Chapter 21.
[40]If the original estimate had been based on erroneous information or calculations or had not been made in good faith, the revision of that estimate would constitute the correction of an error.

ILLUSTRATION 4–9

Change in Accounting Estimate

The Maxwell Gear Corporation purchased machinery in 2000 for $2 million. The useful life of the machinery was estimated to be 10 years with no salvage value. The straight-line depreciation method was used in 2000 through 2002, with a full-year of depreciation taken in 2000. In 2003, the company revised the useful life of the machinery to eight years.

Neither depreciation expense nor accumulated depreciation reported in prior years is restated. No account balances are adjusted. The cumulative effect of the estimate change is not included in current income. Rather, in 2003 and later years, the adjusting entry to record depreciation expense simply will reflect the new useful life. In 2003, the entry is:

Depreciation expense (below)................................ 280,000
    Accumulated depreciation 280,000

	$2,000,000	Cost
$200,000		Old annual depreciation ($2,000,000 ÷ 10 years)
× 3 years	600,000	Depreciation to date (2000–2002)
	$1,400,000	Book value as of 1/1/03
	÷ 5	Estimated remaining life (8 years − 3 years)
	$ 280,000	New annual depreciation

pany's year 2000 annual report that described a change in the useful life and residual values for certain of its rental assets.

GRAPHIC 4–11
Change in Estimate—
NationsRent, Inc.

2. Change in Depreciation Estimate
Effective July 1, 2000, the Company revised the estimated service lives and residual values for certain of its rental assets to better allocate depreciation expense over the time that such assets are in its rental fleet. This change decreased the estimated service lives and increased the residual values for certain rental assets. The change in estimate resulted in a decrease in rental equipment depreciation expense of approximately $9,800,000 and a decrease in net loss of approximately $6,000,000 or $0.10 per diluted share for the 12 months ended December 31, 2000.

Change in Reporting Entity.   A third type of change—the **change in reporting entity**—involves the preparation of financial statements for an accounting entity other than the entity that existed in the previous period.[41] For example, if Company A acquired Company B during 2003, consolidated financial statements are generally required that combine the statements of the two companies as if they were a single reporting entity. The combined financial statements for A and B for 2003 would not be comparable to the financial statements of the separate companies for 2002.[42]

A change in reporting entity is reported by restating all previous periods' financial statements presented for comparative purposes as if the new reporting entity existed in those periods. In other words, in our example, the financial statements are presented as if A and B had been combined in prior years. In addition, in the first set of financial statements issued after the change, a disclosure note is required that describes the nature of the change, the reason it occurred, and the effect of the change on net income, income before extraordinary items, and related per share amounts for all periods presented.

A change in reporting entity requires that financial statements of prior periods be retroactively restated.

[41]In Chapter 21 we discuss the different types of situations that result in a change in accounting entity.
[42]The issuance of *SFAS 94*, "Consolidation of All Majority-Owned Subsidiaries," resulted in hundreds of reporting entities being altered to include previously unconsolidated finance subsidiaries.

Correction of Accounting Errors

Errors occur when transactions are either recorded incorrectly or not recorded at all. We briefly discuss the correction of errors here as an overview and in later chapters in the context of the effect of errors on specific chapter topics. In addition, Chapter 21 provides comprehensive coverage of the correction of errors.

Accountants employ various control mechanisms to ensure that transactions are accounted for correctly. In spite of this, errors occur. When errors do occur, they can affect any one or several of the financial statement elements on any of the financial statements a company prepares. In fact, many kinds of errors simultaneously affect more than one financial statement. When errors are discovered, they should be corrected.

Most errors are discovered in the same year that they are made. These errors are simple to correct. The original erroneous journal entry is reversed and the appropriate entry is recorded. If an error is discovered in a year subsequent to the year the error is made, accounting treatment depends on whether or not the error is material with respect to its effect on the financial statements. In practice, the vast majority of errors are not material and are, therefore, simply corrected in the year discovered.

PRIOR PERIOD ADJUSTMENTS

After its financial statements are published and distributed to shareholders', Roush Distribution Company discovers an error in the statements. What does it do? *Material* errors discovered after the year the error is made are rare. The correction of these errors is considered to be a **prior period adjustment**.[43] A prior period adjustment refers to an addition to or reduction in the beginning retained earnings balance in a statement of shareholders' equity (or statement of retained earnings if that's presented instead).

When it's discovered that the ending balance of retained earnings in the period prior to the discovery of an error was incorrect as a result of that error, the balance is corrected. However, simply reporting a corrected amount might cause misunderstanding for someone familiar with the previously reported amount. Explicitly reporting a prior period adjustment on the statement of shareholders' equity (or statement of retained earnings) avoids this confusion.

In addition to reporting the prior period adjustment to retained earnings, previous years' financial statements that are incorrect as a result of the error are retroactively restated to reflect the correction. Also, a disclosure note communicates the impact of the error on income.

Earnings per Share Disclosures

As we discussed in Chapter 3, financial statement users often use summary indicators, called *ratios,* to more efficiently make comparisons among different companies and over time for the same company. Besides highlighting important relationships among financial statement variables, ratios also accommodate differences in company size.

One of the most widely used ratios is **earnings per share (EPS)**, which shows the amount of income earned by a company expressed on a per share basis. Companies report both **basic** and **diluted** EPS. Basic EPS is computed by dividing income available to common stockholders (net income less any preferred stock dividends) by the weighted-average number of common shares outstanding for the period. Diluted EPS reflects the potential dilution that could occur for companies that have certain securities outstanding that are convertible into common shares or stock options that could create additional common shares if the options were exercised. These items could cause EPS to decrease (become diluted). Because of the complexity of the calculation and the importance of EPS to investors, we devote

---

[43]"Prior Period Adjustments," *Statement of Financial Accounting Standards No. 16* (Stamford, Conn: FASB, 1977).

an entire chapter (Chapter 20) to this topic. At this point, we focus on the financial statement presentation of EPS.

All corporations whose common stock is publicly traded must report EPS on the face of the income statement. In Graphic 4–5 on page 174, FedEx Corporation discloses both basic ($2.02 in 2001) and diluted ($1.99 in 2001) EPS in its income statements for all years presented.

When the income statement includes one or more of the separately reported items below income from continuing operations, EPS data is reported separately for both income from continuing operations and net income. Per share amounts for discontinued operations, extraordinary items, and the cumulative effect of a change in accounting principle would be disclosed on the face of the income statement.

Lucent Technologies, Inc., designs, develops, manufactures, and services systems and software that enable network operators and other service providers to provide wireline and wireless access, local, long distance, data, and other services. The company's fiscal year ends on September 30. During the quarter ended December 31, 1999, the company discontinued an operation. In its income statement for the quarter ended December 31, 2000, the company also reported both an extraordinary gain and the cumulative effect of a change in accounting principle, and accordingly reported corresponding per share amounts as shown in Graphic 4–12, a partial income statement for the three months ended December 31, 2000, and 1999.

All corporations whose common stock is publicly traded must disclose EPS.

FedEx Corporation

The EPS for income from continuing operations, and for each item below continuing operations, must be disclosed.

GRAPHIC 4–12
EPS Disclosures—Lucent Technologies, Inc.

LUCENT TECHNOLOGIES, INC.
Consolidated Statements of Income (in part)
For the Three Months Ended December 31
($ in millions, except per share amounts)

	2000	1999
Income (loss) from continuing operations	$(1,579)	$1,124
Income from discontinued operations, net of tax expense of $67	—	125
Income before extraordinary items and cumulative effect of change in accounting principle	(1,579)	1,249
Extraordinary gain, net of tax expense of $762	1,154	—
Cumulative effect of change in accounting principle, net of tax expense of $17	30	—
Net income (loss)	$ (395)	$1,249
Earnings (loss) per share—basic		
Income (loss) from continuing operations	$ (0.47)	$ 0.36
Income from discontinued operations	—	0.04
Extraordinary gain	0.34	—
Cumulative effect of change in accounting principle	0.01	—
Net income (loss)	$ (0.12)	$ 0.40
Earnings (loss) per share—diluted		
Income (loss) from continuing operations	$ (0.47)	$ 0.34
Income from discontinued operations	—	0.04
Extraordinary gain	0.34	—
Cumulative effect of change in accounting principle	0.01	—
Net income (loss)	$ (0.12)	$ 0.38

GLOBAL   PERSPECTIVE

The Income Statement

There are significant differences from country to country in the presentation and content of the income statement as well as in the accounting methods used to measure income statement amounts. Many of the measurement differences are highlighted in the specific chapters that deal with the specific issues. For example, differences in inventory measurement methods, differences in the treatment of goodwill, and differences in the method used to value and depreciate property and equipment are but three of the areas where global practices differ widely.

There also are many differences in the presentation and content of the income statement. Here are just a few examples:

1. *The title of the statement.* For example, in the United Kingdom (U.K.) it's called the Group Profit and Loss Account.
2. *Revenue terminology.* In a number of countries (e.g., the U.K. and Denmark), sales revenue is referred to as *turnover.*
3. *The treatment of extraordinary gains and losses.* In some countries, such as The Netherlands, certain extraordinary gains and losses are not included in the income statement, but are shown as direct adjustments to shareholders' equity. In other countries, extraordinary gains and losses are shown in the income statement at their gross amounts, not net of tax. In Korea, accounting principles specify certain transactions that must be reported as extraordinary.
4. *The treatment of a change in accounting principle.* For example, in Australia, a change in accounting principle is treated as an adjustment to retained earnings. No cumulative effect is shown in the income statement.

 **CONCEPT | REVIEW EXERCISE**

Income Statement Presentation

The Lippincott Construction Company builds office buildings. It also owns and operates a chain of motels throughout the Northwest. On September 30, 2003, the company decided to sell the entire motel business for $40 million. The sale was completed on December 15, 2003. Income statement information for 2003 is provided below for the two components of the company.

	($ in millions)	
	Construction Component	**Motel Component**
Sales revenue	$450.0	$200.0
Operating expenses	226.0	210.0
Other income (loss)*	16.0	(30.0)
Income (loss) before income taxes	$240.0	$ (40.0)
Income tax expense (benefit)†	96.0	(16.0)
Net income (loss)	$144.0	$ (24.0)

*For the motel component, the entire Other income (loss) amount represents the loss on sale of assets of the component for $40 million when their book value was $70 million.
†A 40% tax rate applies to all items of income or loss.

In addition to the revenues and expenses of the construction and motel components, the following material events also occurred during the year:

1. Lippincott experienced a before-tax loss of $20 million to its construction business from damage to buildings and equipment caused by volcanic activity at Mount St. Helens. The event was considered unusual and infrequent.

2. The company changed its method of depreciation for operational assets of the construction business from the double-declining balance method to the straight-line method. Depreciation expense for 2003 has been correctly computed using the straight-line method. Cumulative prior years' depreciation expense would have been $5 million lower had the straight-line method been employed in prior years.

Required:

Prepare a 2003 income statement for the Lippincott Construction Company including EPS disclosures. There were 100 million shares of common stock outstanding throughout 2003. The company had no potential common shares outstanding.

SOLUTION

LIPPINCOTT CONSTRUCTION COMPANY
Income Statement
For the Year Ended December 31, 2003
($ in millions, except per share amounts)

Sales revenue		$450.0
Operating expenses		226.0
Operating income		224.0
Other income		16.0
Income from continuing operations before income taxes		240.0
Income tax expense		96.0
Income from continuing operations		144.0
Discontinued operations:		
Loss from operations of discontinued motel component		
(including loss on disposal of $30)	$(40)	
Income tax benefit	16	
Loss on discontinued operations		(24.0)
Income before extraordinary item and accounting change		120.0
Extraordinary loss from volcano damage, net of $8.0 tax benefit		(12.0)
Cumulative effect of a change in accounting principle,		
net of $2.0 tax expense		3.0
Net income		$111.0
Earnings per share:		
Income from continuing operations		$1.44
Discontinued operations		(.24)
Extraordinary gain		(.12)
Cumulative effect of a change in accounting principle		.03
Net income		$1.11

Now that we have discussed the presentation and content of the income statement, we turn our attention to the statement of cash flows.

THE STATEMENT OF CASH FLOWS

PART

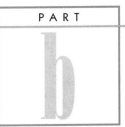

LO10

In addition to the income statement and the balance sheet, a **statement of cash flows (SCF)** is an essential component within the set of basic financial statements.[44] Specifically, when a balance sheet and an income statement are presented, a statement of cash flows is required for each income statement period. The purpose of the SCF is to provide information about the cash receipts and cash disbursements of an enterprise that occurred during a period. Similar to the income statement, it is a *change* statement, summarizing the transactions that caused cash to change during a reporting period. The term *cash* refers to *cash plus cash*

---

[44]"Statement of Cash Flows," *Statement of Financial Accounting Standards No. 95* (Stamford, Conn.: FASB, 1987).

A *statement of cash flows* is presented for each period for which results of operations are provided.

equivalents. Cash equivalents, discussed in Chapter 3, include highly liquid (easily converted to cash) investments such as treasury bills. Chapter 22 is devoted exclusively to the SCF. A brief overview is provided here.

Usefulness of the Statement of Cash Flows

We discussed the difference between cash and accrual accounting in Chapter 1. It was pointed out and illustrated that over short periods of time, operating cash flows may not be indicative of the company's long-run cash-generating ability, and that accrual-based net income provides a more accurate prediction of future operating cash flows. Nevertheless, information about cash flows from operating activities, when combined with information about cash flows from other activities, can provide information helpful in assessing future profitability, liquidity, and long-term solvency. After all, a company must pay its debts with cash, not with income.

Of particular importance is the amount of cash generated from operating activities. In the long run, a company must be able to generate positive cash flow from activities related to selling its product or service. These activities must provide the necessary cash to pay debts, provide dividends to shareholders, and provide for future growth.

Classifying Cash Flows

A list of cash flows is more meaningful to investors and creditors if they can determine the type of transaction that gave rise to each cash flow. Toward this end, the statement of cash flows classifies all transactions affecting cash into one of three categories: (1) operating activities, (2) investing activities, and (3) financing activities.

OPERATING ACTIVITIES

The inflows and outflows of cash that result from activities reported in the income statement are classified as cash flows from **operating activities.** In other words, this classification of cash flows includes the elements of net income reported on a cash basis rather than an accrual basis.[45]

Operating activities are inflows and outflows of cash related to the transactions entering into the determination of net operating income.

Cash inflows include cash received from:

1. Customers from the sale of goods or services.
2. Interest and dividends from investments.

These amounts may differ from sales and investment income reported in the income statement. For example, sales revenue measured on the accrual basis reflects revenue earned during the period, not necessarily the cash actually collected. Revenue will not equal cash collected from customers if receivables from customers or unearned revenue changed during the period.

Cash outflows include cash paid for:

1. The purchase of inventory.
2. Salaries, wages, and other operating expenses.
3. Interest on debt.
4. Income taxes.

Likewise, these amounts may differ from the corresponding accrual expenses reported in the income statement. Expenses are reported when incurred, not necessarily when cash is actually paid for those expenses. Also, some revenues and expenses, like depreciation expense, don't affect cash at all and aren't reported in the statement of cash flows.

The difference between the inflows and outflows is called *net cash flows from operating activities.* This is equivalent to net income if the income statement had been prepared on a cash basis rather than an accrual basis.

---

[45]Cash flows related to gains and losses from the sale of assets shown in the income statement are reported as investing activities in the SCF.

The Statement of Cash Flows

Many other countries also require either the presentation of a statement of cash flows or a similar statement based on funds flows (for example, working capital). The international trend, however, is moving toward the U.S. practice of requiring cash flow statements.

In many countries, companies are not required to present either a statement of cash flows or a statement of funds flows. This is the case in Italy and Finland.

Direct and Indirect Methods of Reporting.   Two generally accepted formats can be used to report operating activities, the direct method and the indirect method. Under the **direct method,** the cash effect of each operating activity is reported directly in the statement. For example, *cash received from customers* is reported as the cash effect of sales activities. Income statement transactions that have no cash flow effect, such as depreciation, are simply not reported.

The **indirect method,** on the other hand, arrives at net cash flow from operating activities indirectly by starting with reported net income and working backwards to convert that amount to a cash basis. For example, depreciation expense would be added back to net income because this expense reduces net income but does not entail a cash disbursement. Also, adjustments are necessary for changes in certain current assets and liabilities. For instance, if accounts receivable increased during the period, credit sales revenue exceeded cash collected from customers. This increase in accounts receivable must be deducted from net income to arrive at cash flow from operating activities. Both methods produce the same net cash flows from operating activities; they are merely alternative approaches to reporting the cash flows. The FASB, in *SFAS 95,* stated its preference for the direct method. However, while either method is acceptable and both are used in practice, the indirect method is used much more frequently.

The choice of presentation method for cash flow from operating activities has no effect on how investing activities and financing activities are reported. We now look at how cash flows are classified into those two categories.

By the direct method, the cash effect of each operating activity is reported directly in the SCF.

By the indirect method, cash flows from operating activities are derived indirectly by starting with reported net income and adding and subtracting items to convert that amount to a cash basis.

INVESTING ACTIVITIES

Cash flows from **investing activities** include inflows and outflows of cash related to the acquisition and disposition of long-term assets used in the operations of the business (such as property, plant, and equipment) and investment assets (except those classified as cash equivalents). The purchase and sale of inventories are not considered investing activities. Inventories are purchased for the purpose of being sold as part of the company's operations, so their purchase and sale are included with operating activities rather than investing activities.

Cash outflows from investing activities include cash paid for:

1. The purchase of long-term assets used in the business.
2. The purchase of investment securities like stocks and bonds of other entities (other than those classified as cash equivalents).
3. Loans to other entities.

Later, when the assets are disposed of, cash inflow from the sale of the assets (or collection of loans and notes) also is reported as cash flows from investing activities. As a result, cash inflows from these transactions are considered investing activities:

1. The sale of long-term assets used in the business.
2. The sale of investment securities (other than cash equivalents).
3. The collection of a nontrade receivable (excluding the collection of interest, which is an operating activity).

Net cash flows from investing activities represents the difference between the inflows and outflows.

Investing activities involve the acquisition and sale of (1) long-term assets used in the business and (2) nonoperating investment assets.

FINANCING ACTIVITIES

Financing activities relate to the external financing of the company. Cash inflows occur when cash is borrowed from creditors or invested by owners. Cash outflows occur when cash is paid back to creditors or distributed to owners. The payment of interest to a creditor, however, is classified as an operating activity.

Cash inflows include cash received from:

1. Owners when shares are sold to them.
2. Creditors when cash is borrowed through notes, loans, mortgages, and bonds.

Cash outflows include cash paid to:

1. Owners in the form of dividends or other distributions.
2. Owners for the reacquisition of shares previously sold.
3. Creditors as repayment of the principal amounts of debt (excluding trade payables that relate to operating activities).

Net cash flows from financing activities is the difference between the inflows and outflows.

NONCASH INVESTING AND FINANCING ACTIVITIES

As we just discussed, the statement of cash flows provides useful information about the investing and financing activities in which a company is engaged. Even though these primarily result in cash inflows and cash outflows, there may be significant investing and financing activities occurring during the period that do not involve cash flows at all. In order to provide complete information about these activities, the SCF shows any significant *noncash* investing and financing activities (that is, noncash exchanges). An example is the acquisition of equipment (an investing activity) by issuing either a long-term note payable or equity securities (a financing activity). These noncash activities are reported either in a separate schedule or in a note.

An illustration of a statement of cash flows is provided in the following concept review exercise.

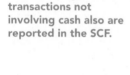

CONCEPT | REVIEW EXERCISE

Statement of Cash Flows

The following are summary transactions that occurred during 2003 for the Lashlee Parts Company:

Cash Received from:	
Customers	$660,000
Interest on note receivable	12,000
Sale of investments	20,000
Proceeds from note payable	100,000
Sale of equipment	40,000
Issuance of common stock	200,000
Cash Paid for:	
Purchase of investments (not cash equivalents)	100,000
Interest on note payable	18,000
Purchase of equipment	120,000
Operating expenses	440,000
Principal on note payable	150,000
Payment of dividends to shareholders	30,000

The balance of cash and cash equivalents is $130,000 at the *beginning* of 2003 and $304,000 at the *end* of 2003.

Required:
Prepare a statement of cash flows for 2003 for the Lashlee Parts Company. Use the direct method for reporting operating activities.

LASHLEE PARTS COMPANY
Statement of Cash Flows
For the Year Ended December 31, 2003

Cash Flows from Operating Activities

Collections from customers	$660,000	
Interest on note receivable	12,000	
Interest on note payable	(18,000)	
Payment of operating expenses	(440,000)	
Net cash inflows from operating activities		$214,000

Cash Flows from Investing Activities

Purchase of investments	(100,000)	
Sale of investments	20,000	
Purchase of equipment	(120,000)	
Sale of equipment	40,000	
Net cash outflows from investing activities		(160,000)

Cash Flows from Financing Activities

Proceeds from note payable	100,000	
Payment of note payable	(150,000)	
Issuance of common stock	200,000	
Payment of dividends	(30,000)	
Net cash inflows from financing activities		120,000
Net increase in cash		174,000
Cash and cash equivalents, January 1		130,000
Cash and cash equivalents, December 31		$304,000

FINANCIAL REPORTING CASE **SOLUTION**

1. **How would you explain restructuring costs to Becky? Are they necessarily a negative? What is the likely explanation for the negative expense in 1999?** *(p. 178)*   Restructuring costs include employee severance and termination benefits plus other costs associated with the shutdown or relocation of facilities or downsizing of operations. It's not necessarily bad. In fact, the objective is to make operations more efficient. The costs are incurred now in hopes of better earnings later. Prior to 2003, when a company restructured its operations, it estimated the future costs associated with the restructuring and expensed the costs in the period in which the decision to restructure was made. An offsetting liability was recorded. Later expenditures were charged against this liability as they occurred. In 1999, Halliburton lowered its estimate of the total costs associated with the 1998 restructuring and recorded an adjustment that increased income, resulting in a negative expense. SFAS No. 146 now requires that restructuring costs be expensed in the period(s) incurred.

2. **In addition to discontinued operations and the cumulative effect of a change in accounting principle, what other events sometimes are reported separately in the income statement that you might tell Becky about? Why are these items reported separately?** *(p. 182)*   In addition to discontinued operations and the cumulative effect of a change in accounting principle, extraordinary items also are reported separately in the income statement when they are present. The predictive ability of an income statement is significantly enhanced if normal and recurrent transactions are separated from unusual and nonrecurrent items. The income statement is a historical report, summarizing the most recent profit-generating activities of a company. The information in the statement is useful if it can help users predict the future. Toward this end, users should be made aware of events reported in the income statement that are not likely to occur again in the foreseeable future.

3. **Explain to Becky what is meant by a discontinued operation and describe to her how one is reported in an income statement.** *(p. 184)*   A discontinued operation occurs when a company decides to discontinue a separate component. A component of an entity comprises

operations and cash flows that can be clearly distinguished, operationally and for financial reporting purposes, from the rest of the entity. The net-of-tax effect of discontinued operations is separately reported below income from continuing operations. If the component has been disposed of by the end of the reporting period, the income effects include: (1) income or loss from operations of the discontinued component from the beginning of the reporting period through the disposal date and (2) gain or loss on disposal of the component's assets. If the component has not been disposed of by the end of the reporting period, the income effects include: (1) income or loss from operations of the discontinued component from the beginning of the reporting period through the end of the reporting period, and (2) an impairment loss if the fair value minus cost to sell of the component's assets is less than their carrying amount (book value).

4. **Explain how to measure the cumulative effect of a change in accounting principle.** *(p. 190)* The cumulative effect of a change in accounting principle is the cumulative effect on the income of previous years from having used the previous method rather than the new method. Stated differently, it's the difference between the balance in retained earnings at the beginning of the period of the change and what that balance would have been if the new method had been applied all along. ■

THE BOTTOM LINE

1. The FASB's Concept Statement 6 defines the term *comprehensive income* as the change in equity from nonowner transactions. The calculation of net income, however, excludes certain transactions that otherwise would be included in comprehensive income. To convey the relationship between the two measures, companies must report both net income and comprehensive income and reconcile the difference between the two. The presentation can be (a) included as an extension to the income statement, (b) reported (exactly the same way) as a separate statement of comprehensive income, or (c) included in the statement of changes in shareholders' equity.

2. The components of income from continuing operations are revenues, expenses (including income taxes), gains, and losses, excluding those related discontinued operations, extraordinary items, and the cumulative effect of changes in accounting principles. Companies often distinguish between operating and nonoperating income within continuing operations.

3. The term *earnings quality* refers to the ability of reported earnings (income) to predict a company's future earnings. The relevance of any historical-based financial statement hinges on its predictive value. To enhance predictive value, analysts try to separate a company's *transitory earnings* effects from its *permanent earnings*. Many believe that manipulating income reduces earnings quality because it can mask permanent earnings. Two major methods used by managers to manipulate earnings are (1) income shifting and (2) income statement classification.

4. Analysts begin their assessment of permanent earnings with income from continuing operations. It would be a mistake to assume income from continuing operations reflects permanent earnings entirely. In other words, there may be transitory earnings effects included in both operating and nonoperating income.

5. A discontinued operation refers to the disposal or a planned disposal of a component of the entity. A component of an entity comprises operations and cash flows that can be clearly distinguished, operationally and for financial reporting purposes, from the rest of the company. The net-of-tax effects of discontinued operations are separately reported below income from continuing operations.

6. Extraordinary items are material gains and losses that are both unusual in nature and infrequent in occurrence. The net-of-tax effects of extraordinary items are presented in the income statement below discontinued operations, if any.

7. The accounting treatment for most changes in accounting principle is to report the net-of-tax cumulative effect of the change in the income statement of the year of the change below extraordinary items. In addition, disclosure reports various pro forma (as if)

amounts for each period presented and also describes the change, the justification for the change, and the effect of the change on the current period's income.

8. A change in accounting estimate is treated currently and prospectively, rather than by restating prior years' financial statements to correct the estimate, or by including the cumulative effect of the change in current income. In other words, the new estimate merely is used from that point on. Most errors are discovered in the same year that they are made. These errors are simple to correct. However, material errors discovered in a year subsequent to the year the error was made are considered prior period adjustments. The correction of the error is accounted for by restating prior years' financial statements, causing an adjustment to beginning of period retained earnings.

9. Earnings per share (EPS) is the amount of income achieved during a period expressed per share of common stock outstanding. The EPS must be disclosed for income from continuing operations and for each item below continuing operations.

10. When a company provides a set of financial statements that reports both financial position and results of operations, a statement of cash flows is reported for each period for which results of operations are provided. The purpose of the statement is to provide information about the cash receipts and cash disbursements that occurred during the period.

11. To enhance the usefulness of the information, the statement of cash flows classifies all transactions affecting cash into one of three categories: (1) operating activities, (2) investing activities, or (3) financing activities.

QUESTIONS FOR REVIEW OF KEY TOPICS

Q 4–1   The income statement is a change statement. Explain what is meant by this.

Q 4–2   Define comprehensive income. What are the three ways companies can present the reconciliation between net income and comprehensive income?

Q 4–3   What transactions are included in income from continuing operations? Briefly explain why it is important to segregate income from continuing operations from other transactions affecting net income.

Q 4–4   Distinguish between operating and nonoperating income in relation to the income statement.

Q 4–5   Briefly explain the difference between the single-step and multiple-step income statement formats.

Q 4–6   Explain what is meant by the term earnings quality.

Q 4–7   What are restructuring costs and where are they reported in the income statement?

Q 4–8   Define intraperiod tax allocation. Why is the process necessary?

Q 4–9   Define what is meant by a component of an entity in the context of reporting the results of discontinued operations. How are discontinued operations reported in the income statement?

Q 4–10   Define extraordinary items.

Q 4–11   How should extraordinary gains and losses be reported in the income statement?

Q 4–12   What is meant by a change in accounting principle? Describe the income statement presentation for a change in accounting principle.

Q 4–13   Define earnings per share (EPS). For which income statement items must EPS be disclosed?

Q 4–14   Accountants very often are required to make estimates, and very often those estimates prove incorrect. In what period(s) is the effect of a change in an accounting estimate reported?

Q 4–15   The correction of a material error discovered in a year subsequent to the year the error was made is considered a prior period adjustment. Briefly describe the accounting treatment for prior period adjustments.

Q 4–16   Describe the purpose of the statement of cash flows.

Q 4–17   Identify and briefly describe the three categories of cash flows reported in the statement of cash flows.

Q 4–18   Explain what is meant by noncash investing and financing activities pertaining to the statement of cash flows. Give an example of one of these activities.

Q 4–19   Distinguish between the direct method and the indirect method for reporting the results of operating activities in the statement of cash flows.

EXERCISES

E 4–1
Comprehensive income

The Massoud Consulting Group reported net income of $1,354,000 for its fiscal year ended December 31, 2003. In addition, during the year the company experienced a foreign currency translation adjustment gain of $210,000 and had unrealized losses on investment securities of $80,000. The company's effective tax rate on all items effecting comprehensive income is 30%. Each component of other comprehensive income is displayed net of tax.

Required:
1. Prepare a combined statement of income and comprehensive income for 2003, beginning with net income.
2. Prepare a separate statement of comprehensive income for 2003.

E 4–2
Income statement format; single step and multiple step

The following is a partial trial balance for the Green Star Corporation as of December 31, 2003:

Account Title	Debits	Credits
Sales revenue		1,200,000
Interest revenue		30,000
Gain on sale of equipment		50,000
Cost of goods sold	720,000	
Salaries expense	110,000	
Depreciation expense	50,000	
Interest expense	40,000	
Rent expense	25,000	
Income tax expense	100,000	

100,000 shares of common stock were outstanding throughout 2003.

Required:
1. Prepare a single-step income statement for 2003, including EPS disclosures.
2. Prepare a multiple-step income statement for 2003, including EPS disclosures.

E 4–3
Income statement format; single step and multiple step

The following is a partial trial balance for General Lighting Corporation as of December 31, 2003:

Account Title	Debits	Credits
Sales revenue		2,350,000
Rental revenue		80,000
Loss on sale of equipment	22,500	
Loss from flood damage (event is both unusual and infrequent)	120,000	
Cost of goods sold	1,200,300	
Loss from write-down of inventory due to obsolescence	200,000	
Salaries expense	300,000	
Depreciation expense	100,000	
Interest expense	90,000	
Rent expense	50,000	

300,000 shares of common stock were outstanding throughout 2003. Income tax expense has not yet been accrued, The income tax rate is 40%.

Required:
1. Prepare a single-step income statement for 2003, including EPS disclosures.
2. Prepare a multiple-step income statement for 2003, including EPS disclosures.

E 4–4
Multiple-step statement of income and comprehensive income

The trial balance for Lindor Corporation, a manufacturing company, for the year ended December 31, 2003, included the following comprehensive income accounts:

Account Title	Debits	Credits
Sales revenue		2,300,000
Gain on early debt extinguishment (unusual and infrequent)		300,000
Cost of goods sold	1,400,000	
Cumulative effect of a change in accounting principle	115,000	
Selling and administrative expenses	420,000	
Interest expense	40,000	
Unrealized holding gains on investment securities		80,000

The trial balance does not include the accrual for income taxes. Lindor's income tax rate is 30%. One million shares of common stock were outstanding throughout 2003.

Required:
Prepare a combined multiple-step statement of income and comprehensive income for 2003, including appropriate EPS disclosures.

E 4–5
Income statement presentation; intraperiod tax allocation

The following *incorrect* income statement was prepared by the accountant of the Axel Corporation:

AXEL CORPORATION
Income Statement
For the Year Ended December 31, 2003

Revenues and gains:		
Sales		$592,000
Interest and dividends		32,000
Gain from early extinguishment of debt		86,000
Total revenues and gains		710,000
Expenses and losses:		
Cost of goods sold	$295,000	
Selling expenses	67,000	
Administrative expenses	87,000	
Interest	26,000	
Restructuring costs	55,000	
Income taxes	72,000	
Total expenses and losses		602,000
Net Income		$108,000
Earnings per share		$ 1.08

Required:
Prepare a multiple-step income statement for 2003 applying generally accepted accounting principles. The income tax rate is 40%. The gain from early extinguishment of debt is considered an unusual and infrequent event.

E 4–6
Discontinued operations

The Chance Company had two operating divisions, one manufacturing farm equipment and the other office supplies. Both divisions are considered separate components as defined by *SFAS No. 144*. The farm equipment component had been unprofitable, and on September 1, 2003, the company adopted a plan to sell the assets of the division. The actual sale was effected on December 15, 2003, at a price of $600,000. The book value of the division's assets was $1,000,000, resulting in a before-tax loss of $400,000 on the sale.

The division incurred before-tax operating losses of $130,000 from the beginning of the year through December 15. The income tax rate is 40%. Chance's after-tax income from its continuing operations is $350,000.

Required:
Prepare an income statement for 2003 beginning with income from continuing operations. Include appropriate EPS disclosures assuming that 100,000 shares of common stock were outstanding throughout the year.

E 4–7
Income statement presentation; change in accounting method; discontinued operations; restructuring charges

The Esquire Comic Book Company had income before tax of $1,000,000 in 2003 *before* considering the following material items:
1. The company switched from the sum-of-the-years' digits method to the straight-line method of depreciation for all of its equipment. Depreciation expense for 2003 has been correctly computed using the straight-line method. The before-tax cumulative effect of the change on prior years' income was a $120,000 increase.
2. Esquire sold one of its operating divisions, which qualified as a separate component according to *SFAS No. 144*. The before-tax loss on disposal was $350,000. The division generated before-tax operating income from the beginning of the year through disposal of $500,000. Neither the loss on disposal nor the operating income are included in the $1,000,000 before-tax income the company generated from its other divisions.
3. The company incurred restructuring costs of $70,000 during the year.

Required:
Prepare a 2003 income statement for Esquire beginning with income from continuing operations. Assume an income tax rate of 40%. Ignore EPS disclosures.

E 4–8
Discontinued operations; disposal in subsequent year

Kandon Enterprises, Inc. has two operating divisions, one manufactures machinery and the other breeds and sells horses. Both divisions are considered separate components as defined by *SFAS No. 144*. The horse division has been unprofitable, and on November 15, 2003, Kandon adopted a formal plan to sell the division. The sale was completed on April 30, 2004. At December 31, 2003, the component was considered held for sale.

On December 31, 2003, the company's fiscal year-end, the book value of the assets of the horse division was $250,000. On that date, the fair value of the assets, less costs to sell, was $200,000. The before-tax operating loss of the division for the year was $140,000. The company's effective tax rate is 40%. The after-tax income from continuing operations for 2003 was $400,000.

Required:
1. Prepare a partial income statement for 2003 beginning with income from continuing operations. Ignore EPS disclosures.
2. Repeat requirement 1 assuming that the estimated net sales price of the horse division's assets was $400,000, instead of $200,000.

E 4–9
Accounting change

The Canliss Milling Company purchased machinery on January 2, 2001, for $800,000. A five-year life was estimated and no salvage value was anticipated. Canliss decided to use the straight-line depreciation method and recorded $160,000 in depreciation in 2001 and 2002. Early in 2003, the company revised the *total* estimated life of the machinery to eight years.

Required:
1. What type of accounting change is this?
2. Briefly describe the accounting treatment for this change.
3. Determine depreciation for 2003.

E 4–10
Accounting change

[This is a variation of the previous exercise]
The Canliss Milling Company purchased machinery on January 2, 2001, for $800,000. A five-year life was estimated and no salvage value was anticipated. Canliss decided to use the straight-line depreciation method and recorded $160,000 in depreciation in 2001 and 2002. Early in 2003, the company changed its depreciation method to the double-declining-balance (DDB) method. DDB depreciation for 2001, 2002, and 2003 is $320,000, $192,000, and $115,200, respectively.

Required:
1. What type of accounting change is this?
2. What would appear in the 2003 income statement related to this change? Assume an income tax rate of 40%. Ignore EPS disclosures.

E 4–11
Earnings per share

The Esposito Import Company had 1 million shares of common stock outstanding during 2003. Its income statement reported the following items: income from continuing operations, $5 million; loss from discontinued operations, $1.6 million; extraordinary gain, $2.2 million; cumulative effect of a change in accounting principle, $700,000. All of these amounts are net of tax.

Required:
Prepare the 2003 EPS presentation for the Esposito Import Company.

E 4–12
Multiple choice; income statement presentation

The following questions dealing with income statement presentation are adapted from questions that appeared in recent CPA examinations. Determine the response that best completes the statements or questions.
1. In Baer Food Co.'s 2003 single-step income statement, the section titled Revenues consisted of the following:

Net sales revenue	$187,000
Results from discontinued operations:	
Income from discontinued component, net of tax	12,000
Interest revenue	10,200
Gain on sale of equipment	4,700
Cumulative change in 2001 and 2002 income due to	
change in depreciation method (net of $750 tax effect)	1,500
Total revenues	$215,400

In the revenues section of the 2003 income statement, Baer Food should have reported total revenues of:
a. $216,300
b. $215,400
c. $203,700
d. $201,900

2. A transaction that is unusual but *not* infrequent should be reported separately as a(an)
    a. Extraordinary item, net of applicable income taxes.
    b. Extraordinary item, but *not* net of applicable income taxes.
    c. Component of income from continuing operations, net of applicable income taxes.
    d. Component of income from continuing operations, but *not* net of applicable income taxes.
3. The cumulative effect of changing to a new accounting principle on the amount of retained earnings at the beginning of the period in which the change is made should be included in net income of:

	Future Periods	**Period of Change**
a.	No	No
b.	Yes	No
c.	Yes	Yes
d.	No	Yes

E 4–13
Statement of cash flows; classifications

The statement of cash flows classifies all cash inflows and outflows into one of the three categories shown below and lettered from a through c. In addition, certain transactions that do not involve cash are reported in the statement as noncash investing and financing activities, labeled d.
a. Operating activities
b. Investing activities
c. Financing activities
d. Noncash investing and financing activities

Required:
For each of the following transactions, use the letters above to indicate the appropriate classification category.
1. ____ Purchase of equipment for cash.
2. ____ Payment of employee salaries.
3. ____ Collection of cash from customers.
4. ____ Cash proceeds from a note payable.
5. ____ Purchase of common stock of another corporation for cash.
6. ____ Issuance of common stock for cash.
7. ____ Sale of machinery for cash.
8. ____ Payment of interest on note payable.
9. ____ Issuance of bonds payable in exchange for land and building.
10. ____ Payment of cash dividends to shareholders.
11. ____ Payment of principal on note payable.

E 4–14
Statement of cash flows preparation

The following summary transactions occurred during 2003 for Bluebonnet Bakers:

Cash Received from:	
Customers	$380,000
Interest on note receivable	6,000
Principal on note receivable	50,000
Sale of investments	30,000
Proceeds from note payable	100,000
Cash Paid for:	
Purchase of inventory	160,000
Interest on note payable	5,000
Purchase of equipment	85,000
Salaries to employees	90,000
Principal on note payable	25,000
Payment of dividends to shareholders	20,000

The balance of cash and cash equivalents at the beginning of 2003 was $17,000.

Required:
Prepare a statement of cash flows for 2003 for Bluebonnet Bakers. Use the direct method for reporting operating activities.

E 4–15
Statement of cash flows directly from transactions

The following transactions occurred during March 2003 for the Wainwright Corporation. The company owns and operates a wholesale warehouse. [These are the same transactions analyzed in Exercise 2–1, when we determined their effect on elements of the accounting equation.]
1. Issued 20,000 shares of capital stock in exchange for $200,000 in cash.
2. Purchased equipment at a cost of $40,000. $10,000 cash was paid and a note payable was signed for the balance owed.

3. Purchased inventory on account at a cost of $90,000. The company uses the perpetual inventory system.
4. Credit sales for the month totaled $120,000. The cost of the goods sold was $70,000.
5. Paid $5,000 in rent on the warehouse building for the month of March.
6. Paid $6,000 to an insurance company for fire and liability insurance for a one-year period beginning April 1, 2003.
7. Paid $60,000 on account for the merchandise purchased in 3.
8. Collected $55,000 from customers on account.
9. Recorded depreciation expense of $1,000 for the month on the equipment.

Required:
1. Analyze each transaction and classify each as a financing, investing and/or operating activity (a transaction can represent more than one type of activity). In doing so, also indicate the cash effect of each, if any. If there is no cash effect, simply place a check mark (✓) in the appropriate column(s).

Example:

Financing	Investing	Operating
1. $200,000		

2. Prepare a statement of cash flows. Assume the cash balance at the beginning of the month was $40,000.

E 4–16
Multiple choice;
statement of cash flows

The following questions dealing with the statement of cash flows are adapted from questions that appeared in recent CPA examinations. Determine the response that best completes the statements or questions.
1. The primary purpose of a statement of cash flows is to provide relevant information about
   a. Differences between net income and associated cash receipts and disbursements.
   b. An enterprise's ability to generate future positive net cash flows.
   c. The cash receipts and cash disbursements of an enterprise during a period.
   d. An enterprise's ability to meet cash operating needs.
2. In a statement of cash flows, proceeds from issuing equity instruments should be classified as cash inflows from
   a. Lending activities.
   b. Operating activities.
   c. Investing activities.
   d. Financing activities.
3. In a statement of cash flows, payments to acquire debt instruments of other entities (other than cash equivalents) should be classified as cash outflows for
   a. Operating activities.
   b. Investing activities.
   c. Financing activities.
   d. Lending activities.

E 4–17
Concepts; terminology

Listed below are several terms and phrases associated with income statement presentation and the statement of cash flows. Pair each item from List A (by letter) with the item from List B that is most appropriately associated with it.

List A	List B
____ 1. Intraperiod tax allocation	a. Unusual, infrequent, and material gains and losses.
____ 2. Comprehensive income	b. Starts with net income and works backwards to convert to cash.
____ 3. Extraordinary items	c. Reports the cash effects of each operating activity directly on the statement.
____ 4. Operating income	d. Correction of a material error of a prior period.
____ 5. An operation (according to SFAS 144)	e. Related to the external financing of the company.
____ 6. Earnings per share	f. Associates tax with income statement item.
____ 7. Prior period adjustment	g. Total nonowner change in equity.
____ 8. Financing activities	h. Related to the transactions entering into the determination of net income.
____ 9. Operating activities (SCF)	i. Related to the acquisition and disposition of long-term assets.
____ 10. Investing activities	j. Required disclosure for publicly traded corporation.
____ 11. Direct method	k. A component of an entity.
____ 12. Indirect method	l. Directly related to principal revenue-generating activities.

PROBLEMS

P 4–1
Multiple-step
statement of income
and comprehensive
income

The Duke Company's records show the following account balances at December 31, 2003:

Sales..................................	$15,000,000
Cost of goods sold	9,000,000
General and administrative expenses......	1,000,000
Selling expenses	500,000
Interest expense	700,000

Income tax expense has not yet been determined. The following events also occurred during 2003:
1. $300,000 in restructuring costs were incurred in connection with plant closings.
2. The company operates a factory in South America. During the year, the foreign government took over (expropriated) the factory and paid Duke $1,000,000, which was one-fourth of the book value of the assets involved.
3. Inventory costing $400,000 was written off as obsolete. Material losses of this type were incurred twice in the last 10 years.
4. It was discovered that depreciation expense for 2002 was understated by $50,000 due to a mathematical error.
5. The depreciation method used for the office building was changed from the double-declining balance to the straight-line method. The cumulative effect of the change on prior years' income is an increase of $60,000. Depreciation expense for 2003, included in general and administrative expenses, has been correctly computed using the straight-line method.
6. The company experienced a foreign currency translation adjustment loss of $300,000 and had unrealized gains on investment securities of $180,000.

Required:
Prepare a combined multiple-step statement of income and comprehensive income for 2003. The company's effective tax rate on all items affecting comprehensive income is 40%. Each component of other comprehensive income should be displayed net of tax. Ignore EPS disclosures.

P 4–2
Comparative income
statements; multiple-
step format

Selected information about income statement accounts for the Reed Company are presented below (the company's fiscal year ends on December 31):

	2003	2002
Sales	$4,400,000	$3,500,000
Cost of goods sold	2,860,000	2,000,000
Administrative expenses	800,000	675,000
Selling expenses	360,000	312,000
Interest revenue	150,000	140,000
Interest expense	200,000	200,000
Loss on sale of assets of discontinued component	50,000	—

On July 1, the company adopted a plan to discontinue a division that qualifies as a component of an entity as defined in *SFAS No. 144*. The assets of the component were sold on September 30 for $50,000 less than their book value. Results of operations for the component (*included* in the above account balances) were as follows:

	1/1/03–9/30/03	2002
Sales	$400,000	$500,000
Cost of goods sold	(290,000)	(320,000)
Administrative expenses	(50,000)	(40,000)
Selling expenses	(20,000)	(30,000)
Operating income before taxes	$ 40,000	$110,000

In addition to the account balances above, several events occurred during 2003 that have *not* yet been reflected in the above accounts:
1. A fire caused $50,000 in uninsured damages to the main office building. The fire was considered to be an infrequent but not unusual event.
2. $5 million face value of bonds payable were re-purchased (paid off) prior to maturity resulting in a loss of $100,000. The amount of the loss is material and the event is considered unusual and infrequent.

3. Inventory that had cost $40,000 had become obsolete because a competitor introduced a better product. The inventory was sold as scrap for $5,000.
4. Income taxes have not yet been accrued.

Required:

Prepare a multiple-step income statement for the Reed Company for 2003, showing 2002 information in comparative format, including income taxes computed at 40% and EPS disclosures assuming 300,000 shares of common stock.

P 4–3
Discontinued operations

The following condensed income statements of the Jackson Holding Company are presented for the two years ended December 31, 2003 and 2002:

	2003	2002
Sales	$15,000,000	$9,600,000
Cost of goods sold	9,200,000	6,000,000
Gross profit	5,800,000	3,600,000
Operating expenses	3,200,000	2,600,000
Operating income	2,600,000	1,000,000
Gain on sale of division	600,000	—
	3,200,000	1,000,000
Income tax expense	1,280,000	400,000
Net income	$ 1,920,000	$ 600,000

On October 15, 2003, Jackson entered into a tentative agreement to sell the assets of one of its divisions. The division comprises operations and cash flows that can be clearly distinguished, operationally and for financial reporting purposes, from the rest of the company. The division was sold on December 31, 2003, for $5,000,000. Book value of the division's assets was $4,400,000. The division's contribution to Jackson's operating income before-tax for each year was as follows:

2003	$400,000 loss
2002	$300,000 loss

Assume an income tax rate of 40%.

Required:

1. Prepare revised income statements according to generally accepted accounting principles, beginning with income from continuing operations before income taxes. Ignore EPS disclosures.
2. Assume that by December 31, 2003, the division had not yet been sold but was considered held for sale. The fair value of the division's assets on December 31 was $5,000,000. How would the presentation of discontinued operations be different from your answer to requirement 1?
3. Assume that by December 31, 2003, the division had not yet been sold but was considered held for sale. The fair value of the division's assets on December 31 was $3,900,000. How would the presentation of discontinued operations be different from your answer to requirement 1?

P 4–4
Income statement presentation

For the year ending December 31, 2003, Micron Corporation had income from continuing operations before taxes of $1,200,000 before considering the following transactions and events. All of the items described below are before taxes and the amounts should be considered material.

1. During 2003, Micron decided to call in an outstanding issue of bonds. As a result, the firm recognized a gain on the early extinguishment of bonds of $400,000. The event is considered unusual and infrequent.
2. In November of 2003, Micron sold its Waffle House restaurant chain that qualified as a component of an entity. The company had adopted a plan to sell the chain in May of 2003. The operating income of the chain from January 1, 2003, through November was $160,000 and the loss on sale of the chain's assets was $300,000.
3. In 2003, Micron sold one of its six factories for $1,200,000. At the time of the sale, the factory had a carrying value of $1,100,000. The factory was not considered a component of the entity.
4. In 2001, Micron's accountant omitted the annual adjustment for patent amortization expense of $120,000. The error was not discovered until December, 2003.

Required:

1. Prepare Micron's income statement, beginning with income from continuing operations before taxes, for the year ended December 31, 2003. Assume an income tax rate of 30%. Ignore EPS disclosures.

2. Briefly explain the motivation for segregating certain income statement events from income from continuing operations.

P 4–5
Statement of cash flows

The Diversified Portfolio Corporation provides investment advice to customers. A condensed income statement for the year ended December 31, 2003, appears below:

Service revenue	$900,000
Operating expenses	700,000
Income before income taxes	200,000
Income tax expense	80,000
Net income	$120,000

The following balance sheet information also is available:

	12/31/03	12/31/02
Cash	$275,000	$70,000
Accounts receivable	120,000	100,000
Accounts payable (operating expenses)	70,000	60,000
Income taxes payable	10,000	15,000

In addition, the following transactions took place during the year:
1. Common stock was issued for $100,000 in cash.
2. Long-term investments were sold for $50,000 in cash. The original cost of the investments also was $50,000.
3. $80,000 in cash dividends was paid to shareholders.
4. The company has no outstanding debt, other than those payables listed above.
5. Operating expenses include $30,000 in depreciation expense.

Required:
Prepare a statement of cash flows for 2003 for the Diversified Portfolio Corporation. Use the direct method for reporting operating activities.

P 4–6
Income statement presentation; unusual items

The preliminary 2003 income statement of Alexian Systems, Inc., is presented below:

ALEXIAN SYSTEMS, INC.
Income Statement
For the Year Ended December 31, 2003
($ in millions, except earnings per share)

Revenues and gains:	
Net sales	$425
Interest	3
Other income	126
Total revenues and gains	554
Expenses:	
Cost of goods sold	270
Selling and administrative	154
Income taxes	52
Total expenses	476
Net Income	$ 78
Earnings per share	$3.90

Additional facts:
1. Selling and administrative expenses include $26 million in restructuring costs.
2. Included in other income is an extraordinary gain of $120 million. The remaining $6 million is from the gain on sale of operating assets.
3. Cost of goods sold was increased by $5 million to correct an error in the calculation of 2002's ending inventory. The amount is material.

Required:
For each of the three additional facts listed above, discuss the appropriate presentation of the item described. Do not prepare a revised statement.

P 4–7
Income statement
presentation; unusual
items

P 4–8
Income statement—
comprehensive

[This is a variation of the previous problem focusing on income statement presentation.]

Required:

Refer to the information presented in Problem 4–6. Prepare a revised income statement for 2003 reflecting the additional facts. Use a multiple-step format. Assume that an income tax rate of 40% applies to all income statement items, and that 20 million shares of common stock were outstanding throughout the year.

The Rembrandt Paint Company had the following income statement items for the year ended December 31, 2003 ($ in 000s):

Net sales	$18,000	Cost of goods sold	$10,500
Interest income	200	Selling and administrative	
Interest expense	350	expenses	2,500
Extraordinary gain	3,000	Restructuring costs	800

In addition, during the year the company completed the disposal of its plastics business and incurred a loss from operations of $1.6 million and a gain on disposal of the component's assets of $2 million. Also, early in the year Rembrandt switched its method of computing depreciation. The cumulative effect of the change is $(600,000). 500,000 shares of common stock were outstanding throughout 2003. Income tax expense has not yet been accrued. The income tax rate is 30% on all items of income (loss).

Required:

Prepare a multiple-step income statement for 2003, including EPS disclosures.

BROADEN YOUR PERSPECTIVE

Apply your critical-thinking ability to the knowledge you've gained. These cases will provide you an opportunity to develop your research, analysis, judgment, and communication skills. You also will work with other students, integrate what you've learned, apply it in real world situations, and consider its global and ethical ramifications. This practice will broaden your knowledge and further develop your decision-making abilities.

Judgment Case 4–1
Earnings quality

The financial community in the United States has become increasingly concerned with the quality of reported company earnings.

Required:
1. Define the term *earnings quality*.
2. Explain the distinction between permanent and transitory earnings as it relates to the concept of earnings quality.
3. How do earnings management practices affect the quality of earnings?
4. Assume that a manufacturing company's annual income statement included a large gain from the sale of investment securities. What factors would you consider in determining whether or not this gain should be included in an assessment of the company's permanent earnings?

Judgment Case 4–2
Restructuring costs

The appearance of restructuring costs in corporate income statements increased significantly in the 1980s and 1990s.

Required:
1. What types of costs are included in restructuring costs?
2. When are restructuring costs recognized?
3. How would you classify restructuring costs in a multi-step income statement?
4. What factors would you consider in determining whether or not restructuring costs should be included in an assessment of a company's permanent earnings?

Judgment Case 4–3
Earnings management

Companies often are under pressure to meet or beat Wall Street earnings projections in order to increase stock prices and also to increase the value of stock options. Some resort to earnings management practices to artificially create desired results.

Required:
Is *earnings management* always intended to produce higher income? Explain.

Real World Case 4–4

Earnings quality and pro forma earnings

[The solution to this case requires access to company data via the Internet.]

Cisco Systems, Inc., the world's largest networking products company, announced on May 8, 2001, that its *pro forma earnings* for the quarter ended April 28, 2001, were $230 million. They also disclosed that actual earnings for the quarter, determined according to generally accepted accounting principles, were a *loss* of $2.69 billion.

Required:

1. What is meant by the term *pro forma earnings* in this context?
2. How do pro forma earnings relate to the concept of earnings quality?
3. Access the company's 10Q (quarterly report) for the quarter ended April 28, 2001. You can go to the company's Internet site, EDGAR, or Edgarscan (**edgarscan.pwcglobal.com**). Using the company's income statement for the quarter and disclosure notes, reconcile the GAAP loss of $2.69 billion to the pro forma earnings figure of $230 million. Remember that both of these earnings (loss) figures are net of tax.

Communication Case 4–5

Income statement presentation of gain

McMinville Corporation manufactures paper products. In 1999, the company purchased several large tracts of timber for $22 million with the intention of harvesting the timber rather than buying this critical raw material from outside suppliers. However, in 2003, McMinville abandoned the idea and all of the timber tracts were sold for $31 million. Net income for 2003, before considering this event, is $17.5 million and the company's effective tax rate is 30%.

The focus of this case is the income statement presentation of the gain on the sale of the timber tracts. Your instructor will divide the class into two to six groups depending on the size of the class. The mission of your group is to reach consensus on the appropriate income statement presentation of the gain.

Required:

Each group member should deliberate the situation independently and draft a tentative argument prior to the class session for which the case is assigned.

In class, each group will meet for 10 to 15 minutes in different areas of the classroom. During that meeting, group members will take turns sharing their suggestions for the purpose of arriving at a single group treatment.

After the allotted time, a spokesperson for each group (selected during the group meetings) will share the group's solution with the class. The goal of the class is to incorporate the views of each group into a consensus approach to the situation.

Communication Case 4–6

Income statement presentation

Carter Hawley Hale Stores (CHHS), Inc. was one of the largest department store retailers in the United States. At the end of fiscal 1989, the company operated 113 stores in the sunbelt regions of the country. The company's divisions included The Broadway, with 43 stores in Southern California and 11 stores in the southwest, and Emporium, with 22 stores in the greater San Francisco Bay Area.

On October 17, 1989, a 7.1 Richter scale earthquake caused significant amounts of monetary damage to the San Francisco Bay Area. This was the largest earthquake to hit the Bay Area since the quake of 1906 destroyed much of San Francisco. California is lined with many active earthquake faults. Hundreds of small earthquakes occur each year throughout the state.

The Emporium division of CHHS suffered extensive damage as a result of the October 17 earthquake. Twelve of the twenty-two stores were closed for varying periods of time, with the Oakland store hardest hit. In total, uninsured damage was $27.5 million ($16.5 million after tax benefits).

For the fiscal year ending August 4, 1990, CHHS reported an after-tax loss of $9.47 million *before* considering the earthquake loss. Total revenues for the year were $2.857 billion.

Required:

Assume that you are the CHHS controller. The chief financial officer of CHHS has asked you to prepare a short report (1–2 pages) in memo form giving your recommendation as to the proper reporting of the earthquake damage costs in the income statement for the year ending August 4, 1990. Explain why your recommendation is appropriate. Be sure to include in your report any references to authoritative pronouncements that support your recommendation.

Ethics Case 4–7

Income statement presentation of unusual loss

After a decade of consistent income growth, the Cranor Corporation sustained a before-tax loss of $8.4 million in 2003. The loss was primarily due to $10 million in expenses related to a product recall. Cranor manufactures medical equipment, including x-ray machines. The recall was attributable to a design flaw in the manufacture of the company's new line of machines.

The company controller, Jim Dietz, has suggested that the loss should be included in the 2003 income statement as an extraordinary item. "If we report it as an extraordinary item, our income from continuing operations will actually show an increase from the prior year. The stock market will appreciate the continued growth in ongoing profitability and will discount the one-time loss. And our bonuses are tied to income from continuing operations, not net income."

The chief executive officer asked Jim to justify this treatment. "I know we have had product recalls before and, of course, they do occur in our industry," Jim replied, "but we have never had a recall of this magnitude, and we fixed the design flaw and upgraded our quality control procedures."

Required:
Discuss the ethical dilemma faced by Jim Dietz and the company's chief executive officer.

Research Case 4–8
Locate and extract relevant information and authoritative support for a financial reporting issue; treatment of losses from terrorist attacks

Yesterday you watched a TV special on the terrorist attacks of September 11, 2001. Those attacks resulted in a tragic loss of life and property. Today in your intermediate accounting class, your professor discussed the measurement and reporting of separately reported items, including extraordinary gains and losses. A classmate asked her if companies that sustained significant losses as a result of the attacks reported those losses as extraordinary items in their income statements. She asked the class to think about it and to formulate an answer for the next class period. She also mentioned that there is an Emerging Issues Task Force Issue that addresses this question and suggested you do some research.

Required:

1. Do you think that the terrorist attacks of September 11 constitute an "extraordinary" event?
2. Obtain the EITF Issue on accounting for the impact of the terrorist attacks. You might gain access through FARS, the FASB Financial Accounting Research System, from your school library, or some other source. The Issue also is available online. You can navigate to the issue from the FASB's website at **www.fasb.org.**
3. Why did the EITF address this issue and not the FASB itself?
4. What did your research reveal? What reasons did the EITF provide for its conclusion?

Judgment Case 4–9
Income statement presentation

Each of the following situations occurred during 2003 for one of your audit clients:

1. The write-off of inventory due to obsolescence.
2. Discovery that depreciation expenses were omitted by accident from 2002's income statement.
3. The useful lives of all machinery were changed from eight to five years.
4. The depreciation method used for all equipment was changed from the declining-balance to the straight-line method.
5. Ten million dollars face value of bonds payable were repurchased (paid off) prior to maturity resulting in a material loss of $500,000. The company considers the event unusual and infrequent.
6. Restructuring costs were incurred.
7. The Stridewell Company, a manufacturer of shoes, sold all of its retail outlets. It will continue to manufacture and sell its shoes to other retailers. A loss was incurred in the disposition of the retail stores. The retail stores are considered components of the entity.

Required:

1. For each situation, identify the appropriate reporting treatment from the list below (consider each event to be material):

   a. As an extraordinary item.
   b. As an unusual or infrequent gain or loss.
   c. As a prior period adjustment.
   d. As a change in accounting principle.
   e. As a discontinued operation.
   f. As a change in accounting estimate.

2. Indicate whether each situation would be included in the income statement in continuing operations (CO) or below continuing operations (BC), or if it would appear as an adjustment to retained earnings (RE). Use the format shown below to answer requirements 1 and 2.

Situation	Treatment (a–f)	Financial Statement Presentation (CO, BC, or RE)
1.		
2.		
3.		
4.		
5.		
6.		
7.		

Judgment Case 4–10
Income statement presentation

The following events occurred during 2003 for various audit clients of your firm. Consider each event to be independent and the effect of each event to be material.

1. A manufacturing company recognized a loss on the sale of equipment used in its manufacturing operations.
2. An automobile manufacturer sold all of the assets related to its financing component. The operations of the financing business can be clearly distinguished from the rest of the entity.
3. A company changed its depreciation method from the double-declining-balance method to the straight-line method.
4. Due to obsolescence, a company engaged in the manufacture of high-technology products incurred a loss on the write-down of inventory.
5. One of your clients discovered that 2002's depreciation expense was overstated. The error occurred because of a miscalculation of depreciation for the office building.
6. A cosmetics company decided to discontinue the manufacture of a line of women's lipstick. Other cosmetic lines will be continued. A loss was incurred on the sale of assets related to the lipstick product line. The operations of the discontinued line cannot be distinguished from the rest of the cosmetics business.

Required:
Discuss the 2003 financial statement presentation of each of the above events. Do not consider earnings per share disclosures.

International Case 4–11
Comparison of income statement presentation in the U.K. and the United States

Cadbury Schweppes is a major global manufacturer of beverages and confectionery located in Great Britain whose products are sold in over 170 countries. Presented below is a recent company income statement:

CADBURY SCHWEPPES PLC
Group Profit and Loss Account
For the 52 Weeks Ended 31 December 2000
(in millions of pounds, except earnings per ordinary share)

	2000	1999
Turnover		
Continuing operations	4,575	4,234
Discontinued operations	—	67
	4,575	4,301
Operating costs		
Trading expenses	(3,813)	(3,603)
Major restructuring costs	(49)	(64)
	(3,862)	(3,667)
Trading profit		
Continuing operations	713	618
Discontinued operations	—	16
	713	634
Share of operating profit in associates	65	35
Operating profit	778	669
Profit on sale of subsidiaries and investments	27	350
Profit on ordinary activities before interest	805	1,019
Net interest	(49)	(61)

Profit on ordinary activities before taxation	756	958
Tax on profit on ordinary activities		
On operating profit, associates and interest	(224)	(181)
On profit on sale of subsidiaries and investments	—	(34)
Profit on ordinary activities after taxation	532	743
Equity minority interests	(12)	(79)
Nonequity minority interests	(24)	(22)
Profit for the financial year	496	642
Dividends to ordinary shareholders	(209)	(202)
Profit retained for the financial year	287	440
Earnings per ordinary share of 12.5 p		
Basic	24.8 p	31.7 p
Diluted	24.5 p	31.3 p

Required:

Describe the differences between income statement presentation in the United Kingdom with that of the United States.

Judgment Case 4–12
Management incentives for change

It has been suggested that not all accounting choices are made by management in the best interest of fair and consistent financial reporting.

Required:

What motivations can you think of for management's choice of accounting methods?

Research Case 4–13
Changes in accounting principles

When a company changes an accounting principle, justification for the change is required in a disclosure note. Quite often, the stated justification is that the new accounting method is a more appropriate way to measure the related economic transaction. However, there are those that feel management makes accounting changes in order to manipulate earnings. Professors Pincus and Wasley in "The Incidence of Accounting Changes and Characteristics of Firms Making Accounting Changes" investigate accounting changes and possible motivations for making them.

Required:

1. In your library or from some other source, locate the indicated article in *Accounting Horizons*, June 1994.
2. What is the most frequent type of voluntary accounting change?
3. What inferences do the authors make about the use of voluntary accounting changes to manipulate earnings and what conclusion do they reach?

Integrating Case 4–14
Balance sheet and income statement; Chapters 3 and 4

The Rice Corporation is negotiating a loan for expansion purposes and the bank requires financial statements. Before closing the accounting records for the year ended December 31, 2003, Rice's controller prepared the following financial statements:

RICE CORPORATION
Balance Sheet
At December 31, 2003
($ in 000s)

Assets

Cash	$ 275
Marketable securities	78
Accounts receivable	487
Inventories	425
Allowance for uncollectible accounts	(50)
Property and equipment, net	160
Total assets	$1,375

Liabilities and Shareholders' Equity

Accounts payable and accrued liabilities	$ 420
Notes payable	200
Common stock	260
Retained earnings	495
Total liabilities and shareholders' equity	$1,375

RICE CORPORATION
Income Statement
For the Year Ended December 31, 2003
($ in 000s)

Net sales		$1,580
Expenses:		
Cost of goods sold	$755	
Selling and administrative	385	
Miscellaneous	129	
Income taxes	100	
Total expenses		1,369
Net income		$ 211

Additional information:

1. The company's common stock is traded on an organized stock exchange.
2. The investment portfolio consists of short-term investments valued at $57,000. The remaining investments will not be sold until the year 2005.
3. Miscellaneous expense represents the before-tax loss from damages caused by an earthquake. The event is considered to be both unusual and infrequent.
4. Notes payable consist of two notes:
   Note 1: $80,000 face value dated September 30, 2003. Principal and interest at 10% are due on September 30, 2004.
   Note 2: $120,000 face value dated April 30, 2003. Principal is due in two equal installments of $60,000 plus interest on the unpaid balance. The two payments are scheduled for April 30, 2004, and April 30, 2005.
   Interest on both loans has been correctly accrued and is included in accrued liabilities on the balance sheet and selling and administrative expenses on the income statement.
5. Selling and administrative expenses include a $90,000 charge incurred by the company in restructuring some of its operations. The amount of the charge is material.

Required:

Identify and explain the deficiencies in the presentation of the statements prepared by the company's controller. Do not prepare corrected statements. Include in your answer a list of items which require additional disclosure, either on the face of the statement or in a note.

Analysis Case 4–15
Income statement information

Refer to the income statements of FedEx Corporation in the appendix to Chapter 1.

Required:

1. What was the percentage increase or decrease in the company's net income from 2000 to 2001? From 1999 to 2000?
2. Using 2001 data, what is the company's approximate income tax rate?
3. Using 2001 data, what is the percentage of net income relative to revenue dollars?

Real World Case 4–16
Income statement information

EDGAR, the Electronic Data Gathering, Analysis, and Retrieval system, performs automated collection, validation, indexing, and forwarding of submissions by companies and others who are required by law to file forms with the U.S. Securities and Exchange Commission (SEC). All publicly traded domestic companies use EDGAR to make the majority of their filings. (Some foreign companies file voluntarily.) Form 10-K or 10-KSB, which include the annual report, is required to be filed on EDGAR. The SEC makes this information available on the Internet.

Required:

1. Access EDGAR on the Internet. The web address is **www.sec.gov**. Edgarscan (**edgarscan.pwcglobal.com**) from PricewaterhouseCoopers makes the process of accessing data from EDGAR easier.
2. Search for a public company with which you are familiar. Access the most recent 10-K filing. Search or scroll to find the financial statements and related notes.
3. Answer the following questions related to the company's income statement:
   a. Does the company use the single-step or multiple-step format, or a variation?
   b. Does the income statement contain any separately reported items in any year presented (discontinued operation, extraordinary item, cumulative effect of a change in accounting principle)? If it does, describe the event that caused the item. (Hint: there should be a related disclosure note.)
   c. Describe the trend in net income over the years presented.
4. Repeat requirements 2 and 3 for two additional companies.

5

Income Measurement and Profitability Analysis

OVERVIEW

Key to income measurement is the timing of revenue and expense recognition. The matching principle states that we recognize expenses in the period we recognize the related revenues. The timing of revenue recognition, therefore, is critical to income measurement. The focus of this chapter is revenue recognition. We also continue our discussion of financial statement analysis.

LEARNING OBJECTIVES

After studying this chapter, you should be able to:

LO1 Discuss the general objective of the timing of revenue recognition, list the two general criteria that must be satisfied before revenue can be recognized, and explain why these criteria usually are satisfied at a specific point in time.

LO2 Describe the installment sales and cost recovery methods of recognizing revenue for certain installment sales and explain the unusual conditions under which these methods might be used.

LO3 Discuss the implications for revenue recognition of allowing customers the right of return.

LO4 Identify situations that call for the recognition of revenue over time and distinguish between the percentage-of-completion and completed contract methods of recognizing revenue for long-term contracts.

LO5 Discuss the revenue recognition issues involving software and franchise sales.

LO6 Identify and calculate the common ratios used to assess profitability.

You Don't Have to Be a Rocket Scientist

"Good news! I got the job," she said, closing the door behind her.

Your sister, an aerospace engineer, goes on to explain that she accepted a position at Lockheed Martin Corporation, a world leader in the design, development, manufacture, and servicing of aircraft, spacecraft and launch vehicles, missiles, electronics, and information and telecommunication systems. She will supervise a long-term government contract beginning Tuesday.

"I got the salary I was asking for too," she continued. "Mr. Watson, my supervisor, also said I'll be getting a bonus tied to the gross profit on the project. It didn't hit me until I left his office, though, that this project will take two and a half years to complete. I hope I don't have to wait that long to get my bonus." Pointing to a page where she's circled part of a disclosure note, your sister hands you Lockheed's annual report. "I can't believe they wait that long to record income on all these multiyear projects. You're the accountant in the family; is that what this note is telling us?"

Sales and earnings (in part)
Sales and anticipated profits under long-term fixed-price production contracts are recorded on a percentage of completion basis . . .

> By the time you finish this chapter, you should be able to respond appropriately to the questions posed in this case. Compare your response to the solution provided at the end of the chapter.

QUESTIONS

1. Does your sister have to wait two and a half years to get her bonus? Explain. (page 232)

2. How are gross profits recognized using the percentage-of-completion method? (page 233)

3. Are there other situations in which revenue is recognized at times other than when a product is delivered? (page 225)

Revenue recognition criteria help ensure that an income statement reflects the actual accomplishments of a company for the period.

REVENUE RECOGNITION

In Chapter 4 we discussed the *nature of income* and its presentation in the income statement. In this chapter we turn our attention to the *measurement* of periodic accounting income. Of primary interest here is the timing of revenue recognition. This is an important issue not only in its own right but also because the matching principle states that expenses should be recognized in the period in which the related revenues are recognized.

Why is the timing of revenue recognition so important? An income statement should report the results of operations only for the time period specified in the report. That is, a one-year income statement should report the company's accomplishments and sacrifices (revenues and expenses) only for that one-year period.[1] Revenue recognition criteria help ensure that a proper cutoff is made each period and that no more than one year's activity is reported in the annual income statement. Revenues reflect positive inflows from activities, activities that generate cash flows. By comparing these activity levels period to period, a user can better assess future activities and thus future cash flows.

Our objective, then, is to recognize revenue in the period or periods that the revenue-generating activities of the company are performed. But we also must consider that recognizing revenue presumes that an asset (usually cash) has been received or will be received in exchange for the goods or services sold. Our judgment as to the collectibility of the cash from the sale of a product or service will, therefore, impact the timing of revenue recognition. These two concepts of performance and collectibility are captured by the general guidelines for revenue recognition in the realization principle.

The **realization principle** requires that two criteria be satisfied before revenue can be recognized (recorded):[2]

1. The earnings process is judged to be complete or virtually complete *(the earnings process refers to the activity or activities performed by the company to generate revenue).*
2. There is reasonable certainty as to the collectibility of the asset to be received (usually cash).

The first criterion indicates that revenue is recognized at a point in time at or near the end of the earnings process. We sometimes encounter situations when strictly adhering to this criterion would violate our overriding objective of recognizing revenue in the period or periods that the revenue-generating activities of the company are performed. Later in this chapter we discuss situations when revenue is recognized over time, rather than at one particular point in time.

Even with this guideline, revenue recognition continues to be a controversial issue. For instance, Former SEC Chairman Arthur Levitt identified revenue recognition as a popular way for companies to manage their earnings, primarily prematurely.

Premature revenue recognition reduces the quality of reported earnings, particularly if those revenues never materialize. Many sad stories have surfaced involving companies forced to revise earnings numbers due to a restatement of revenues. Consider the case of Critical Path, Inc., a provider of messaging and collaboration solutions for Internet service providers and telecommunication companies. In January 2001, the company announced a net loss of $11.5 million for the quarter ended December 31, 2000. In February 2001, this loss was revised to

Premature revenue recognition reduces the quality of reported earnings and can cause serious problems for the reporting company.

CBS MARKETWATCH
If corporate information is no longer reliable, investors are left twisting in the wind. Suddenly, the financial assumptions you've used to calculate a stock's value become bogus.[3]

---

[1]In addition to reporting on an annual basis, companies often provide information quarterly and, on occasion, monthly. The SEC requires its registrants to provide information on a quarterly and annual basis. This information, referred to as *interim financial statements*, pertains to any financial report covering a period of less than one year. The key accounting issues related to the presentation of interim statements are discussed in Appendix 5.

[2]These criteria are addressed in SFAC 5, "Recognition and Measurement in Financial Statements," *Statement of Financial Accounting Concepts No. 5* (Stamford, Conn.: FASB, 1984).

[3]Deborah Adamson, "What Investors Should Fear the Most," *CBS.MarketWatch.com*, April 30, 2001.

ARTHUR LEVITT, JR.
Lastly, companies try to boost earnings by manipulating the recognition of revenue. Think about a bottle of fine wine. You wouldn't pop the cork on that bottle before it was ready. But some companies are doing this with their revenue . . .[4]

over $19 million, primarily a result of an $8 million decrease in previously reported revenues. Of that amount, the company indicated that over $4 million would never result in revenue, while the rest "may" be realized in 2001. Wall Street is extremely sensitive to revisions in earnings. On the day of the announced revision, Critical Path's stock price dropped nearly 70% in value!

As part of its crackdown on earnings management, the SEC issued *Staff Accounting Bulletin No. 101*,[5] summarizing the SEC's views on revenue. The Bulletin provides additional criteria for judging whether or not the realization principle is satisfied:

1. Persuasive evidence of an arrangement exists.
2. Delivery has occurred or services have been rendered.
3. The seller's price to the buyer is fixed or determinable.
4. Collectibility is reasonably assured.

***SEC Staff Accounting Bulletin (SAB) No. 101* provides general and specific guidelines for revenue recognition.**

Soon after *SAB No. 101* was issued, many companies changed their revenue recognition methods. In most cases, the changes resulted in a deferral of revenue recognition. As a case in point, consider the change made by Brown & Sharpe Manufacturing Company, a multinational manufacturer of metrology products, described in a disclosure note, displayed in Graphic 5–1.

GRAPHIC 5–1
Disclosure of Change in Revenue Recognition Policy—Brown & Sharpe Manufacturing Company

2. Accounting Change (in part)
In 2000, the Company adopted *SEC Staff Accounting Bulletin No. 101 (SAB 101)*. As a result of adopting *SAB 101*, the Company changed the way it recognizes revenue for machines sold to customers. Prior to the adoption of *SAB 101*, the Company recognized revenue when the machines were shipped and title passed to the customer. Effective as of January 1, 2001, the Company recognizes revenue for machines sold to customers once the performance of machines is accepted by the customers.

In requiring customer acceptance as part of the agreement, revenue recognition is delayed until this part of the earnings process is completed. Many of the changes in revenue recognition companies made in response to *SAB No. 101* are related to service revenue. We discuss some of these later in the chapter.

The central issue in most decisions concerning when to record revenue is judging when the earnings process is substantially complete and whether it is reasonably certain that a determinable amount of cash is collectible. Sometimes this decision is straightforward, as when Intel Corporation sells Dell Computer a microprocessor. Other times, though, consideration must be given to whether (a) a customer in a risky transaction will actually pay, (b) a customer will exercise its right to return a purchased product, (c) it is reasonable to wait several years to recognize revenue on a long-term project, or (d) other atypical situations should justify altering the timing of revenue recognition. We'll discuss these variations on the timing decision in Part a of this chapter. First, though, it might be helpful to look at the overview of the variations provided in Graphic 5–2.

In January 2002, the FASB disseminated a proposal for a new project addressing revenue recognition.[6] The objective of the project would be the issuance of a new standard on revenue recognition that enhanced the authoritative and conceptual guidance for recognizing revenues. At the time this text was published, no new pronouncements had resulted from the project.

[4]Arthur Levitt, Jr., "The Numbers Game," *The CPA Journal*, December 1998, p. 18.
[5]"Revenue Recognition in Financial Statements," *Staff Accounting Bulletin No. 101* (Washington, DC: SEC, December 1999).
[6]"Revenue Recognition," *Proposal for a New Agenda Project* (Norwalk, Conn.: FASB, 2002).

GRAPHIC 5–2
Revenue Recognition

We usually recognize revenue at or near the completion of the earnings process unless collectibility is an issue.

Sometimes, it is more meaningful to recognize revenue over time in proportion to the performance of the activity.

Nature of the Revenue	Usually Recognize Revenue for:	
	Sale of a Product	Sale of a Service
Substantive completion of the earnings process can be identified with a specific point in time within a single reporting period:		
Collectibility of cash is reasonably certain.	When product is delivered (title transfers)	When the key activity is performed
Collectibility of cash is *not* reasonably certain:		
• Because payments are significantly uncertain	When cash is collected (installment sales or cost recovery method)	When cash is collected (installment sales or cost recovery method)
• Because reliable estimates of product returns are unavailable	When critical event occurs that reduces product return uncertainty	Not applicable
• Because the product sold is out on consignment	When the consignee sells the product to the ultimate consumer	Not applicable
Substantive completion of the earnings process occurs over more than one reporting period:		
Reasonably dependable estimates of progress are available.	Each period during the earning process (e.g., long-term construction contract) in proportion to its percentage of completion—usually the fraction of costs incurred to date	Each period during the earning process (e.g., rental period) in proportion to its percentage of performance—usually the fraction of time transpired
Dependable estimates of progress are not available.	At the completion of the project	Not applicable
Industry-specific revenue:		
Franchise sales:		
• Initial franchise fee	Not applicable	When initial services are "substantially performed"
• Continuing franchise fees	Not applicable	As services are performed
Computer software sales	As each product component (e.g., initial product; upgrade) is delivered	As each service component (e.g., customer support) is delivered

CHECK WITH THE **COACH**

Analyzing a company's profitability and forecasting its future success is an important challenge for investors and management alike. Revenue recognition is a particularly important element that affects the usefulness of income statement data. For Chapter 5, check with the Coach to strengthen your grip on revenue recognition and ratios used by the experts to assess the operating performance of a business. Make your investment of practice time with the Coach now, and it will pay off throughout the course. ■

ETHICAL   DILEMMA

The Precision Parts Corporation manufactures automobile parts. The company has reported a profit every year since the company's inception in 1977. Management prides itself on this accomplishment and believes one important contributing factor is the company's incentive plan that rewards top management a bonus equal to a percentage of operating income *if the operating income goal for the year is achieved.* However, 2003 has been a tough year, and prospects for attaining the income goal for the year are bleak.

Tony Smith, the company's chief financial officer, has determined a way to increase December sales by an amount sufficient to boost operating income over the goal for the year and earn bonuses for all top management. A reputable customer ordered $120,000 of parts to be shipped on January 15, 2004. Tony told the rest of top management "I know we can get that order ready by December 31 even though it will require some production line overtime. We can then just leave the order on the loading dock until shipment. I see nothing wrong with recognizing the sale in 2003, since the parts will have been manufactured and we do have a firm order from a reputable customer." The company's normal procedure is to ship goods f.o.b. destination and to recognize sales revenue when the customer receives the parts.

Revenue Recognition at a Point in Time

WHEN COLLECTIBILITY IS REASONABLY CERTAIN

Consider the timing of revenue recognition for a typical manufacturing company that sells its products on credit. Usually the buyer is given a length of time, say 30 days, to pay for the goods after they have been delivered. Graphic 5–3 shows several alternative points in time during the earnings process that could be considered the critical event for revenue recognition. It should be pointed out that revenue actually is earned *throughout* the earnings process. The critical event is the point in time when the realization principle is satisfied.[7]

> While revenue usually is earned during a period of time, revenue often is recognized at one specific point in time when both revenue recognition criteria are satisfied.

| Materials purchased | Production begins | Production in process | Production ends | Product delivered | Cash is collected |

> **GRAPHIC 5–3**
> Earnings Process for a Typical Manufacturing Company

The product delivery date occurs when legal title to the goods passes from seller to buyer. This occurs either on the date the product is shipped from the seller's facility or when the goods actually are received by the buyer, depending on the terms of the sales agreement. If the goods are shipped *f.o.b. (free on board) shipping point,* then legal title to the goods changes hands at the point of shipment when the seller delivers the goods to the common carrier (for example, a trucking company) and the purchaser is responsible for shipping costs and transit insurance. On the other hand, if the goods are shipped *f.o.b. destination,* the seller is responsible for shipping and legal title does not pass until the goods arrive at the customer's location.[8]

> The point of delivery refers to the date legal title to the product passes from seller to buyer.

Let's consider the date production ends. At that point, it might be said that the earnings process is virtually complete. After all, the majority of the costs that must be expended to generate revenue have been incurred. The product has been produced and the remaining tasks are to sell the product and collect the cash.

---

[7]As you will learn later in this chapter, revenue often is not only earned throughout an earnings process, but also is recognized during the process rather than at one particular point in time.
[8]We discuss this aspect of title transfer in Chapter 7.

Revenue from the sale of products usually is recognized at the point of product delivery.

However, at this point there usually exists significant uncertainty as to the collectibility of the asset to be received. We don't know if the product will be sold or the selling price or the buyer if eventually sold. Because of these uncertainties, revenue recognition usually is delayed until the point of product delivery. At that point we know the product has been sold, the price, and the buyer. The only remaining uncertainty involves the ultimate cash collection, which usually can be accounted for by estimating and recording allowances for possible return of the product and for uncollectibility of the cash, that is, bad debts. Both of these estimates are discussed in Chapter 7. As we discuss in the next section, significant uncertainty at point of product delivery related to either collectibility or product return causes a delay in revenue recognition.

In addition, at the point of delivery, legal title to the goods is transferred. A critical element of the contract between buyer and seller—product delivery—is now fulfilled and the earnings process normally is virtually complete.

Sometimes, a sales agreement requires additional, important performance steps to be performed by the seller. In this case, the earnings process is not virtually complete until those steps are performed. Graphic 5–1 on page 221 illustrates a situation where the seller, Brown & Sharpe, delays revenue recognition beyond delivery of machines until the performance of the machines has been accepted by the buyer. Customer acceptance is an important part of the agreement between buyer and seller.

For service revenue, if there is one final service that is critical to the earnings process, revenues and costs are deferred and recognized after this service has been performed.

FedEx Corporation

Service revenue, too, often is recognized at a point in time if there is one final activity that is deemed critical to the earnings process. In this case, all revenue and costs are deferred until this final activity has been performed. For example, a moving company will pack, load, transport, and deliver household goods for a fixed fee. Although packing, loading, and transporting all are important to the earning process, delivery is the culminating event of the earnings process. So, the entire service fee is recognized as revenue after the goods have been delivered. FedEx recognizes revenue in this manner. The Company's Summary of Significant Accounting Policies disclosure note indicates that "Revenue is generally recognized upon delivery of shipments." As with the sale of product, estimates of uncollectible amounts must be made for service revenue provided to customers on a credit basis.

United Airlines (and other major airlines) provide another example. Do you ever add miles to your frequent flyer mileage program by accumulating miles with a credit card or long-distance phone services? For example, you can obtain a Citibank credit card and earn one frequent flyer mile on United Airlines for every $1 charged on the card. Or if you use MCI long-distance, you can earn one mile for every $1 in long-distance charges. When you accumulate enough miles, you earn a free flight on United. Citibank and MCI must pay United Airlines for the frequent flyer miles it gives its customers. So, when does United Airlines recognize revenue for the miles it provides to customers of Citibank and MCI?

Until recently, United recognized revenue as the miles were sold. But, is United actually selling a product—miles? No, it is providing a service by flying customers of Citibank and MCI. The SEC's *Staff Accounting Bulletin No. 101*, discussed earlier, motivated United to change its revenue recognition policy for the sale of mileage. Graphic 5–4 shows a disclosure describing the change in policy.

GRAPHIC 5–4
Disclosure of Change in Revenue Recognition Policy— United Airlines, Inc.

Accounting Changes (in part)
During the first quarter of 2000, United changed its method of accounting for the sale of mileage to participating partners in its Mileage Plus program, in accordance with *Staff Accounting Bulletin No. 101*, "Revenue Recognition in Financial Statements." Under the new accounting method, a portion of revenue from the sale of mileage (previously recognized in other revenue) is deferred and recognized as passenger revenue when the transportation is provided.

United is recognizing "a portion of revenue" (probably a significant portion) when the final critical activity takes place, specifically "when the transportation is provided." While not specifically mentioned, the nondeferred portion of the revenue is recognized earlier to coincide with, and offset, the costs of administering the program.

SIGNIFICANT UNCERTAINTY OF COLLECTIBILITY

Recognizing revenue at a specific point in time as described in the previous section assumes we are able to make reasonable estimates of amounts due from customers that potentially might be uncollectible. For product sales, this also includes amounts not collectible due to customers returning the products they purchased. Otherwise, we would violate one of the requirements of the revenue realization principle we discussed earlier that there must be reasonable certainty as to the collectibility of cash from the customer. Now, in this section, we address a few situations when uncertainties could cause a delay in recognizing revenue from a sale of a product or service. One such situation occasionally occurs when products (or services) are sold on an installment basis.

Installment Sales.   Customers sometimes are allowed to pay for purchases in installments over a long period of time. Many large retail stores, for instance, such as Sears and J.C. Penney sell certain products on an installment plan. Increasing the length of time allowed for payment usually increases the inevitable uncertainty about whether the store actually will collect a receivable. Is the uncertainty sufficient in an installment sale to cause Sears to delay recognizing revenue and related expenses beyond the point of sale? Usually, it's not.

In most situations, the increased uncertainty concerning the collection of cash from installment sales can be accommodated satisfactorily by estimating uncollectible amounts. If, however, the installment sale creates significant uncertainty concerning cash collection, making impossible a reasonable assessment of future bad debts, then revenue and expense recognition should be delayed. For example, real estate sales often are made on an installment basis with relatively small down payments and long payment periods, perhaps 25 years or more. These payment characteristics, combined with the general speculative nature of many of these transactions, may translate into significant uncertainty concerning the collectibility of the installment receivable.[9] In fact, *SFAS No. 66* requires that the installment sales method (discussed below) be applied to a retail land sale that meets certain criteria.[10]

When extreme uncertainty exists regarding the ultimate collectibility of cash, we delay recognizing revenue and related expenses using one of two accounting techniques, the **installment sales method** or the **cost recovery method.** *We emphasize that these methods should be used only in situations involving exceptional uncertainty.* As an example, Rouse Company acquires, develops, and manages income-producing properties throughout the United States and develops and sells land for residential, commercial, and other uses. Graphic 5–5 shows the company's revenue recognition disclosure note included with recent annual financial statements. The note indicates that the preferred method is to recognize revenue upon delivery (full accrual method), but that in certain circumstances, one of these two alternative methods could be used.

FINANCIAL REPORTING CASE

Q3, p. 219

At times, revenue recognition is delayed due to a high degree of uncertainty related to ultimate cash collection.

The installment sales and cost recovery methods are only used in unusual circumstances.

(d) Sales of property (in part)
Gains from sales of operating properties and revenues from land sales are recognized using the full accrual method provided that various criteria relating to the terms of the transactions and any subsequent involvement by the Company with the properties sold are met. Gains or revenues relating to transactions that do not meet the established criteria are deferred and recognized when the criteria are met or using the installment or cost recovery methods, as appropriate in the circumstances.

GRAPHIC 5–5
Disclosure of Revenue Recognition Policy— Rouse Company

---

[9]For income tax purposes, the installment sales method applies only to gains from the sale of certain types of properties. The tax law requires the use of the installment sales method for these transactions unless a taxpayer elects not to use the method.
[10]"Accounting for Sales of Real Estate," *Statement of Financial Accounting Standards No. 66* (Stamford, Conn.: FASB, 1982).

The *installment sales method* recognizes the gross profit by applying the gross profit percentage on the sale to the amount of cash actually received.

Installment Sales Method.   To deal with the uncertainty of collection, the **installment sales method** recognizes revenue and costs only when cash payments are received. Each payment is assumed to be composed of two components: (1) a partial recovery of the cost of the item sold and (2) a gross profit component. These components are determined by the gross profit percentage applicable to the sale. For example, if the gross profit percentage (gross profit ÷ sales price) is 40%, then 60% of each dollar collected represents cost recovery and the remaining 40% is gross profit. Consider the example in Illustration 5–1.

ILLUSTRATION 5–1 Installment Sales Method	On November 1, 2003, the Belmont Corporation, a real estate developer, sold a tract of land for $800,000. The sales agreement requires the customer to make four equal annual payments of $200,000 plus interest on each November 1, beginning November 1, 2003. The land cost $560,000 to develop. The company's fiscal year ends on December 31.

Gross profit recognition, installment sales method

The gross profit of $240,000 ($800,000 − 560,000) represents 30% of the sales price ($240,000 ÷ $800,000). The collection of cash and the recognition of gross profit under the installment method are summarized below. We ignore the collection of interest charges and the recognition of interest revenue to concentrate on the collection of the $800,000 sales price and the recognition of gross profit on the sale.

Date	Cash Collected	Cost Recovery (70%)	Gross Profit (30%)
Nov. 1, 2003	$200,000	$140,000	$ 60,000
Nov. 1, 2004	200,000	140,000	60,000
Nov. 1, 2005	200,000	140,000	60,000
Nov. 1, 2006	200,000	140,000	60,000
Totals	$800,000	$560,000	$240,000

This illustrates that the gross profit recognized in a period will be equal to the gross profit percentage multiplied by the period's cash collection. The following journal entries are recorded (interest charges ignored):

Inventory is credited for the portion of the receivable that represents the cost of the land sold. The difference is deferred gross profit.

November 1, 2003
Installment receivables	800,000	
Inventory		560,000
Deferred gross profit.....................................		240,000
To record installment sale.		

The first entry records the installment receivable and the reduction of inventory. The difference between the $800,000 selling price and the $560,000 cost of sales represents the gross profit on the sale of $240,000. As it will be recognized only as collections are made, it is recorded in an account called *deferred gross profit*. This is a contra account to the installment receivable. It will be reduced to zero as the payments are received.[11]

---

[11]Accountants sometimes record installment sales in the following manner:

Installment sales receivable................	800,000	
Installment sales......................		800,000
To record installment sales.		
Cost of installment sales	560,000	
Inventory		560,000
To record the cost of installment sales.		

Then at the end of the period, the following adjusting/closing entry is recorded:

Installment sales........................	800,000	
Cost of installment sales		560,000
Deferred gross profit on installment sales ...		240,000

The text entries concentrate on the effect of the transactions and avoid this unnecessary procedural complexity.

November 1, 2003

Cash..	200,000	
Installment receivables		200,000
To record cash collection from installment sale.		
Deferred gross profit.....................................	60,000	
Realized gross profit		60,000
To recognize gross profit from installment sale.		

When payments are received, gross profit is recognized, calculated by applying the gross profit percentage to the cash collected (30% × $200,000).

The second set of entries records the collection of the first installment and recognizes the gross profit component of the payment, $60,000. Journal entries to record the remaining three payments are identical.

At the end of 2003, the balance sheet would report the following:

Installment receivables	$600,000
Less: Deferred gross profit	(180,000)
Installment receivables (net)	$420,000

The net amount of the receivable reflects the portion of the remaining payments that represents cost recovery (70% × $600,000). The installment receivables are classified as current assets if they will be collected within one year (or within the company's operating cycle, if longer); otherwise, they are classified as noncurrent assets.

The income statement for 2003 would report a gross profit from installment sales of $60,000. Sales and cost of goods sold usually are not reported in the income statement, just the resulting gross profit. But if installment sales are significant, the 2003 income statement in this illustration would report sales of $200,000 and cost of goods sold of $140,000.

ADDITIONAL CONSIDERATION

We discuss the problem of accounting for bad debts in significant depth in Chapter 7. However, bad debts related to receivables on sales accounted for using the installment method create a unique problem. Assume that in the example described in Illustration 5–1, the Belmont Corporation collected the first payment but the customer was unable to make the remaining payments. Typically, the seller would repossess the item sold and make the following journal entry:

Repossessed inventory	420,000	
Deferred gross profit..................................	180,000	
Installment receivable		600,000

This entry removes the receivable and the remaining deferred gross profit and records the repossessed land in an inventory account. The entry assumes that the land's current fair value is equal to the net receivable of $420,000. If the land's fair value at the date of repossession is less than $420,000, a loss on repossession is recorded (debited).

GLOBAL PERSPECTIVE

Many countries follow the U.S. practice of recognizing revenue on installment sales at date of sale, unless the installment sale creates a situation where there is significant uncertainty concerning cash collection, in which case revenue and expense recognition are delayed.

There are, however, some countries where accounting procedures do not differentiate between installment and other credit sales. Italy, Spain, Norway, the Netherlands, France, and Belgium are examples of countries that fall into this category.

The *cost recovery method* defers all gross profit recognition until cash equal to the cost of the item sold has been received.

Cost Recovery Method. In situations where there is an extremely high degree of uncertainty regarding the ultimate cash collection on an installment sale, an even more conservative approach, the **cost recovery method,** can be used. This method defers all gross profit recognition until the cost of the item sold has been recovered. The gross profit recognition pattern applying the cost recovery method to the Belmont Corporation situation used in Illustration 5–1 to demonstrate the installment sales method is shown below.

Gross profit recognition, cost recovery method

Date	Cash Collected	Cost Recovery	Gross Profit
Nov. 1, 2003	$200,000	$200,000	$ –0–
Nov. 1, 2004	200,000	200,000	–0–
Nov. 1, 2005	200,000	160,000	40,000
Nov. 1, 2006	200,000	–0–	200,000
Totals	$800,000	$560,000	$240,000

The journal entries using this method are similar to those by the installment sales method except that $40,000 in gross profit is recognized in 2005 and $200,000 in 2006.

The cost recovery initial journal entry is identical to the installment sales method.

November 1, 2003
Installment receivables 800,000
   Inventory 560,000
   Deferred gross profit. 240,000
To record installment sale.

November 1, 2003, 2004, 2005, and 2006
Cash. 200,000
   Installment receivables 200,000
To record cash collection from installment sale.

When payments are received, gross profit is recognized only after cost has been fully recovered.

November 1, 2003 and 2004
No entry for gross profit.

November 1, 2005
Deferred gross profit. 40,000
   Realized gross profit 40,000
To recognize gross profit from installment sale.

November 1, 2006
Deferred gross profit. 200,000
   Realized gross profit 200,000
To recognize gross profit from installment sale.

CONCEPT REVIEW EXERCISE

Installment Sales

Boatwright Implements, Inc., manufactures and sells farm machinery. For most of its sales, revenue and cost of sales are recognized at the delivery date. In 2003, it sold a cotton baler to a new customer for $100,000. The cost of the machinery was $60,000. Payment will be made in five annual installments of $20,000 each, with the first payment due in 2003. Boatwright usually does not allow its customers to pay in installments. Due to the unusual nature of the payment terms and the uncertainty of collection of the installment payments, Boatwright is considering alternative methods of recognizing profit on this sale.

Required:
Ignoring interest charges, prepare a table showing the gross profit to be recognized from 2003 through 2007 on the sale using the following three methods:

1. Point of delivery revenue recognition.
2. The installment sales method.

3. The cost recovery method.

	Point of Delivery	Installment Sales Method (40% × cash collection)	Cost Recovery Method
2003	$40,000	$ 8,000	$ –0–
2004	–0–	8,000	–0–
2005	–0–	8,000	–0–
2006	–0–	8,000	20,000
2007	–0–	8,000	20,000
Totals	$40,000	$40,000	$40,000

Right of Return. Retailers usually give their customers the right to return merchandise if they are not satisfied. In most situations, even though the right to return merchandise exists, revenues and expenses can be appropriately recognized at point of delivery. Based on past experience, a company usually can estimate the returns that will result for a given volume of sales. These estimates are used to reduce both sales and cost of goods sold in anticipation of returns. The purpose of the estimates is to avoid overstating gross profit in the period of sale and understating gross profit in the period of return. The specific accounting treatment for sales returns is illustrated in Chapter 7 in conjunction with discussing the valuation of accounts receivable.

Because the return of merchandise can retroactively negate the benefits of having made a sale, the seller must meet certain criteria before revenue is recognized in situations when the right of return exists. The most critical of these criteria is that the seller must be able to make reliable estimates of future returns.[12] In certain situations, these criteria are not satisfied at the point of delivery of the product. For example, manufacturers of semiconductors like Intel Corporation and Motorola Corporation usually sell their products through independent distributor companies. Economic factors, competition among manufacturers, and rapid obsolescence of the product motivate these manufacturers to grant the distributors the right of return if they are unable to sell the semiconductors. So, revenue recognition often is deferred beyond the delivery point to the date the products actually are sold by the distributor to an end user.

As an example, the disclosure note shown in Graphic 5–6 appeared in a recent annual report of Intel Corporation.

Notes: Revenue Recognition
Certain of Intel's sales are made to distributors under agreements allowing right of return and price protection on merchandise unsold by the distributors. Because of rapid technological obsolescence and frequent sales price reductions in the industry, Intel defers recognition of such sales until the merchandise is sold by the distributors.

GRAPHIC 5–6
Disclosure of Revenue Recognition Policy— Intel Corporation

For Intel, the event critical to revenue recognition is *not* the delivery of the product to the buyer but the ultimate sale of the product by the buyer (the distributor company) to an end user.

Any time a company recognizes revenue at a point other than the point of delivery, the revenue recognition method used is disclosed in the summary of significant accounting policies. Intel's disclosure note is an example. Graphic 5–7, a disclosure note from a recent financial statement of Amdahl Corporation, a manufacturer of mainframe computers, provides another example.

---

[12]Other, less critical criteria are listed in "Revenue Recognition When Right of Return Exists, " *Statement of Financial Accounting Standards No. 48* (Stamford, Conn.: FASB, 1981).

GRAPHIC 5–7
Disclosure of Revenue
Recognition Policy—
Amdahl Corporation

Notes: Revenue Recognition (in part)
Revenue from equipment sales is generally recognized when equipment has been shipped, installed, and financing arrangements have been completed.

As the note indicates, revenue is delayed beyond the point of product delivery. Amdahl waits until the product has been properly installed and financing has been arranged by the buyer. Why does Amdahl delay revenue recognition? Until the product has been installed and financing arranged, there is a high degree of uncertainty concerning the possibility the product might be returned. Also, installation is an important part of the agreement between Amdahl and its customers.

Consignment Sales. Sometimes a company arranges for another company to sell its product under **consignment.** The "consignor" physically transfers the goods to the other company (the consignee), but the consignor retains legal title. If the consignee can't find a buyer within an agreed-upon time, the consignee returns the goods to the consignor. However, if a buyer is found, the consignee remits the selling price (less commission and approved expenses) to the consignor.

Because the consignor retains the risks and rewards of ownership of the product and title does not pass to the consignee, the consignor does not record a sale (revenue and related expenses) until the consignee sells the goods and title passes to the eventual customer. Of course, that means goods on consignment are still part of the consignor's inventory. As an example, Cypress Semiconductor Corporation designs, develops, and manufactures a broad range of high-performance integrated circuits. Some of the company's product is sold using consignment arrangements. Graphic 5–8 shows a portion of their revenue recognition disclosure note that was included in a recent annual report.

GRAPHIC 5–8
Disclosure of Revenue
Recognition Policy—
Cypress
Semiconductor
Corporation

Revenue Recognition (in part)
The Company also has inventory at certain customers on a consignment basis. Revenue is not recorded until the time the title transfers per the consignment arrangement.

Up until now, we've focused on revenue-generating activities in which some specific event (e.g., delivery, collection, product performance, and resale) indicates that the earnings process is substantially completed and significant uncertainties have been alleviated, prompting us to recognize revenue and related expenses. We now turn our attention to situations in which it's desirable to recognize revenue over more than one reporting period—before a specific event indicates the earnings process is substantially completed.

Revenue Recognition over Time

Revenue recognition at a single point in time, when an earnings process is virtually complete, is inappropriate for certain types of service revenue activities and also, usually, for long-term contracts.

SERVICE REVENUE EARNED OVER TIME

Service revenue often is recognized over time, in proportion to the amount of service performed.

In a previous section we saw that many service activities encompass some final activity that is deemed critical to the earnings process. In these cases, we recognize revenue when that activity occurs. However, in many instances, service revenue activities occur over extended periods and recognizing revenue at any single date within that period would be inappropriate. Instead, it's more meaningful to recognize revenue over time in proportion to the performance of the activity.

As an example, consider the revenue a property owner earns when renting office space. If a landlord charges a tenant $12,000 in rent for the upcoming year, it would seem logical to recognize $1,000 of rent revenue each month over the one-year period (i.e., straight-line method) since services performed are similar over the period. The landlord recognizes rent revenue in proportion to the passage of time. Likewise, Gold's Gym will recognize revenue from a two-year membership ratably over the 24-month membership period.

A similar situation occurs if you buy a season pass to Disney World. When would Walt Disney Co. recognize revenue for the $350 it collects for the sale of a 365-day pass? Rationalizing that a pass can be used any number of times during the season, thus making it difficult to determine when service is provided, many companies once recognized all revenue from the sale of season passes on the date of sale. However, the SEC's *Staff Accounting Bulletin No. 101*, discussed earlier in the chapter, motivated most of these companies to change their revenue recognition policy. For example, Graphic 5–9 provides a disclosure note Six Flags, Inc. included in a recent annual report. Notice that the company now recognizes revenue *over time*, based on the anticipated usage of the season pass over the operating season.

Revenue Recognition (in part)

. . . the provisions of *SAB No 101* did change the accounting policies that the Company uses to recognize revenue from multi-admission tickets and season passes during the year. The Company's accounting policy as of January 1, 2000, recognizes the revenue from multi-admission tickets and season passes over the operating season on a usage basis rather than upon receipt.

GRAPHIC 5–9
Disclosure of Revenue Recognition Policy— Six Flags, Inc.

LONG-TERM CONTRACTS

Another activity in which it is desirable to recognize revenue over time is one involving a long-term contract. The types of companies that make use of long-term contracts are many and varied. A recent survey of reporting practices of 600 large public companies indicates that one in every six companies engages in long-term contracts.[13] And they are not just construction companies. In fact, even services such as research, installation, and consulting often are contracted for on a long-term basis. Graphic 5–10 lists just a sampling of companies that use long-term contracts, many of which you might recognize.

LO4

GRAPHIC 5–10
Companies Engaged in Long-Term Contracts

Company	Type of Industry or Product
Oracle Corp.	Computer software, license and consulting fees
Lockheed Martin Corporation	Aircraft, missiles, and spacecraft
Datatec Systems, Inc.	Integrated computer systems design
Newport News Shipbuilding, Inc.	Shipbuilding
Nortel Networks Corp.	Networking solutions and services to support the Internet
Hamilton McGregor International Inc.	Construction, medical facilities
SBA Communications Corp.	Telecommunications
Layne Christensen Company	Water supply services and geotechnical construction
Kaufman & Broad Home Corp.	Commercial and residential construction
Raytheon Company	Defense electronics
Foster Wheeler Corp.	Construction, petroleum and chemical facilities
Halliburton	Construction, energy services
Morrison Knudsen Corp.	Construction, facilities including electric utilities
Allied Products Corp.	Large metal stamping presses

[13]*Accounting Trends and Techniques—2001* (New York: AICPA, 2001), p. 382.

The *completed contract method* recognizes revenue at a point in time when the earnings process is complete.

FINANCIAL REPORTING CASE

Q1, p. 219

The general revenue recognition criteria described in the realization principle suggest that revenue should be recognized when a long-term project is finished (that is, when the earnings process is virtually complete). This is known as the **completed contract method** of revenue recognition. The problem with this method is that all revenues, expenses, and resulting income from the project are recognized in the period in which the project is completed; no revenues or expenses are reported in the income statements of earlier reporting periods in which much of the work may have been performed. Net income should provide a measure of periodic accomplishment to help predict future accomplishments. Clearly, income statements prepared using the completed contract method do not fairly report each period's accomplishments when a project spans more than one reporting period. Much of the earnings process is far removed from the point of delivery.

The **percentage-of-completion method** of revenue recognition for long-term projects is designed to help address this problem. This method recognizes revenue (and expenses) over time by allocating a share of the project's expected revenues and expenses to each period in which the earnings process occurs, that is, the contract period. Although the contract usually specifies total revenues, the project's expenses are not known until completion. Consequently, it is necessary for a company to estimate the project's future costs at the end of each reporting period to estimate total gross profit to be earned on the project.

Illustration 5–2 provides information to compare accounting for long-term contracts using the completed contract and percentage-of-completion methods.

The *percentage-of-completion method* allocates a share of a project's revenues and expenses to each reporting period during the contract period.

ILLUSTRATION 5–2 Completed Contract and Percentage-of-Completion Methods Compared	At the beginning of 2003, the Harding Construction Company received a contract to build an office building for $5 million. The project is estimated to take three years to complete. According to the contract, Harding will bill the buyer in installments over the construction period according to a prearranged schedule. Information related to the contract is as follows:		

	2003	2004	2005
Construction costs incurred during the year	$1,500,000	$1,000,000	$1,600,000
Construction costs incurred in prior years	–0–	1,500,000	2,500,000
Cumulative construction costs	1,500,000	2,500,000	4,100,000
Estimated costs to complete at end of year	2,250,000	1,500,000	–0–
Total estimated and actual construction costs	$3,750,000	$4,000,000	$4,100,000
Billings made during the year	$1,200,000	$2,000,000	$1,800,000
Cash collections during year	1,000,000	1,400,000	2,600,000

Construction costs include the labor, materials, and overhead costs directly related to the construction of the building. Notice how the total of estimated and actual construction costs changes from period to period. Cost revisions are typical in long-term contracts where costs are estimated over long periods of time.

Completed Contract Method. With both the completed contract and percentage-of-completion methods, all costs of construction are recorded in an asset account called **construction in progress**. This account is equivalent to the asset work-in-process inventory in a manufacturing company. For the completed contract method, *no revenues or expenses related to this project are recognized in 2003 and 2004*. Construction in progress will show a balance of $1,500,000 and $2,500,000 at the end of 2003 and 2004, respectively, and $4,100,000 when the project is completed in 2005. This asset is then "sold" and revenue of $5,000,000 and cost of construction (similar to cost of goods sold) of $4,100,000 (gross profit of $900,000) are recognized in 2005.

The completed contract method recognizes no income until project completion.

The completed contract method does not properly portray a company's performance over the construction period.

Does this solution capture the reality of the situation? To the contrary, it seems to suggest that the construction company was idle or unproductive for two years and then produced a sizable profit the third year. For this reason, the percentage-of-completion method is preferable, and the completed contract method should be used only "when lack of dependable estimates or inherent hazards cause forecasts to be doubtful . . ."[14]

Percentage-of-Completion Method.

The percentage-of-completion method recognizes a portion of the estimated gross profit each period based on progress to date. Progress to date depends on three factors:

FINANCIAL REPORTING CASE

Q2, p. 219

1. The costs incurred to date.
2. The most recent estimate of the project's total cost.
3. The most recent gross profit estimate.

Let's first focus on the calculation of periodic gross profit for each of the three years of construction. We then address the gross profit components—revenue and cost of construction. Progress to date usually is assumed to be the *proportion of the project's cost incurred to date divided by total estimated costs.* This fraction, the estimated percentage of completion, is assumed to be a measure of progress. It should be mentioned that this measure is based on costs and could differ significantly from an estimate of physical progress made by an engineer or architect. Companies use this method, often referred to as the cost-to-cost method of estimating a percentage-of-completion, more frequently than estimates of physical progress. In a recent disclosure note shown in Graphic 5–11, SBA Communications indicates it uses the cost-to-cost method "because management considers total cost to be the best available measure of progress . . . "

Progress to date can be estimated as the proportion of the project's cost incurred to date divided by total estimated costs, or by relying on an engineer's or architect's estimate.

GRAPHIC 5–11
Disclosure of Revenue Recognition Policy— SBA Communications Corp.

Revenue Recognition (in part)
Revenue from construction projects is recognized on the percentage-of-completion method of accounting, determined by the percentage of cost incurred to date compared to management's estimated total anticipated cost for each contract. This method is used because management considers total cost to be the best available measure of progress on the contracts.

The objective of determining a percentage of completion is to measure activity or project accomplishment to date. If the cost-to-cost approach does not properly parallel this accomplishment, then another method should be used. For example, the construction of a road might encounter a particularly difficult section of terrain requiring abnormal costs to be incurred without much progress being made on the road. In such a case, the cost-to-cost method might not adequately reflect how much of the project has actually been completed.

Illustration 5–2A shows the calculation of gross profit for each of the years for our Harding Construction Company example.

At the end of each period, the revised project gross profit estimate is multiplied by the revised estimate of the percentage of completion. The result is the estimated gross profit earned from inception to date. The current period's gross profit is calculated by subtracting from this amount the gross profit recognized in previous periods.

Income statements are more informative if the sales revenue and cost components of gross profit are reported rather than the net figure alone. So, the income statement for each year will report the appropriate revenue and cost of construction amounts. For example, in 2003 the gross profit of $500,000 consists of revenue of $2,000,000 (40% multiplied by the $5,000,000 contract price) and $1,500,000 in cost of construction. In subsequent periods, revenue is calculated by multiplying the percentage of completion by the contract price and then subtracting revenue recognized in prior periods. The cost of construction is the difference between

---

[14]"Long-Term Construction-Type Contracts," *Accounting Research Bulletin No. 45* (New York: AICPA 1955).

ILLUSTRATION 5–2A		**2003**	**2004**	**2005**
Percentage-of-Completion Method—Allocation of Gross Profit to Each Period	Contract price	$5,000,000	$5,000,000	$5,000,000
	Actual costs to date	1,500,000	2,500,000	4,100,000
	Estimated costs to complete	2,250,000	1,500,000	–0–
	Total project cost	3,750,000	4,000,000	4,100,000
	Total gross profit (estimated for 2003 and 2004, actual in 2005)—Contract price minus total costs	$1,250,000	$1,000,000	$ 900,000
	Percentage-of-completion—actual costs to date	$1,500,000	$2,500,000	(project is complete)
	divided by the estimated total project cost	$3,750,000	$4,000,000	
		= 40%	= 62.5%	100%
	Total project gross profit	$1,250,000	$1,000,000	$ 900,000
	Multiplied by the estimated % of completion	40%	62.5%	100%
	Gross profit earned to date	$ 500,000	$ 625,000	$ 900,000
	Less gross profit recognized in previous periods	–0–	(500,000)	(625,000)
	Gross profit recognized currently	$ 500,000	$ 125,000	$ 275,000

revenue and gross profit. In most cases, cost of construction also equals the construction costs incurred during the period.[15] The table in Illustration 5–2B shows the revenue and cost of construction recognized in each of the three years of our example.

ILLUSTRATION 5–2B			
Percentage-of-Completion Method—Allocation of Revenue and Cost of Construction to Each Period	**2003**		
	Revenue recognized ($5,000,000 × 40%)		$2,000,000
	Cost of construction		1,500,000
	Gross profit		$ 500,000
	2004		
	Revenue recognized to date ($5,000,000 × 62.5%)	$3,125,000	
	Less: Revenue recognized in 2003	(2,000,000)	
	Revenue recognized		$1,125,000
	Cost of construction		1,000,000
	Gross profit		$ 125,000
	2005		
	Revenue recognized to date ($5,000,000 × 100%)	$5,000,000	
	Less: Revenue recognized in 2003 and 2004	(3,125,000)	
	Revenue recognized		$1,875,000
	Cost of construction		1,600,000
	Gross profit		$ 275,000

---

[15]Cost of construction does not equal the construction costs incurred during the year when a loss is projected on the entire project. This case is illustrated later in the chapter.

A COMPARISON OF THE TWO METHODS—INCOME RECOGNITION

A period-by-period comparison of the gross profit patterns produced by each method of revenue recognition is presented below:

	Percentage-of-Completion	Completed Contract
Gross profit recognized		
2003	$500,000	–0–
2004	125,000	–0–
2005	275,000	$900,000
Total gross profit	$900,000	$900,000

Although both methods yield identical gross profit of $900,000 for the entire three-year period, the timing differs. The completed contract method defers all gross profit to 2005, when the project is completed. Obviously, the percentage-of-completion method provides a better measure of the company's economic activity and progress over the three-year period. That's why the percentage-of-completion method is preferred, and, as mentioned above, the completed contract method should be used only in situations where the company is unable to make dependable estimates of future costs necessary to apply the percentage-of-completion method.[16]

> The percentage-of-completion method provides a more realistic measure of a project's periodic profitability, and is almost always used.

Our discussion to this point has concentrated on income recognition. Notice that *the amount billed and the cash actually received have no effect on income recognition.* We now turn our attention to the balance sheet effect of accounting for long-term construction contracts.

Balance Sheet Effects Compared.   Summary journal entries for *both* the percentage-of-completion and completed contract methods are shown in Illustration 5–2C for construction costs, billings, and cash receipts.

ILLUSTRATION 5–2C   Journal Entries—Costs, Billings, and Receipts

	2003		2004		2005	
Construction in progress	1,500,000		1,000,000		1,600,000	
Cash, materials, etc.		1,500,000		1,000,000		1,600,000
To record construction costs.						
Accounts receivable	1,200,000		2,000,000		1,800,000	
Billings on construction contract. . . .		1,200,000		2,000,000		1,800,000
To record progress billings.						
Cash	1,000,000		1,400,000		2,600,000	
Accounts receivable		1,000,000		1,400,000		2,600,000
To record cash collections.						

Notice that periodic billings are credited to **billings on construction contract.** This account is a contra account to the asset construction in progress. At the end of each period, the balances in these two accounts are compared. If the net amount is a debit, it is reported in the balance sheet as an asset. Conversely, if the net amount is a credit, it is reported as a liability.[17]

> **Billings on construction contract** is subtracted from construction in progress to determine balance sheet presentation.

---

[16]For income tax purposes, the completed contract method may be used for home construction contracts and certain other real estate construction contracts. All other contracts must use the percentage-of-completion method.

[17]If the company is engaged in more than one long-term contract, all contracts for which construction in progress exceeds billings are grouped together and all contracts for which billings exceed construction in progress also are grouped. This could result in the presentation of both an asset and a liability in the balance sheet.

A debit balance essentially represents an unbilled receivable. The construction company is incurring construction costs (and recognizing gross profit using the percentage-of-completion method) for which it will be paid by the buyer. If the construction company bills the buyer an amount exactly equal to these costs (and profits recognized) then the accounts receivable balance properly reflects the claims of the construction company. If, however, the amount billed is less than the costs incurred (plus profits recognized) the difference represents the remaining claim to cash.

On the other hand, if the amount billed exceeds the costs incurred (plus profits recognized), then the overbilled accounts receivable overstate the amount of the claim to cash earned to that date and must be reported as a liability. This is similar to the situation when a customer pays for a product or service in advance. The advance is properly shown as a liability representing the obligation to provide the good or service in the future.

Accounting under each of the methods is precisely the same to this point. But, as explained earlier, gross profit (revenue less cost of construction) is recognized differently by the two approaches. The entries shown in Illustration 5–2D are the additional journal entries required using the percentage-of-completion method to recognize periodic revenue and cost of construction and to close the construction contract accounts (construction in progress and billings on construction contracts) and for the completed contract method at the end of the project to recognize revenue and cost of construction and to close the construction contract accounts.

> **Under the completed contract method, profit is recognized only at the completion of the project.**

ILLUSTRATION 5–2D   Journal Entries—Profit Recognition and Closing

	2003		2004		2005	
Percentage-of-Completion						
Construction in progress (gross profit).	500,000		125,000		275,000	
Cost of construction	1,500,000		1,000,000		1,600,000	
Revenue from long-term contracts . .		2,000,000		1,125,000		1,875,000
To record gross profit.						
Billings on construction contract					5,000,000	
Construction in progress.						5,000,000
To close accounts.						
Completed Contract						
Construction in progress (gross profit).					900,000	
Cost of construction					4,100,000	
Revenue from long-term contracts . .						5,000,000
To record gross profit.						
Billings on construction contract					5,000,000	
Construction in progress.						5,000,000
To close accounts.						

Why debit construction in progress for the amount of gross profit recognized? In the typical manufacturing situation, inventory prior to sale is stated at cost. The difference between the historical cost of the inventory and its sales price (the gross profit) is not recognized until product delivery. In other words, assets are not increased until the inventory is sold.

The percentage-of-completion method departs from historical cost and recognizes a portion of the markup between the cost and the selling price of inventory prior to delivery. In our illustration, at the end of 2003 the total estimated cost is $3,750,000 and the estimated markup to sales price is $1,250,000. The inventory is increased by $500,000 which represents 40% of this total markup. The completed contract method recognizes the actual markup when the project is completed.

The construction in progress account and the billings on construction contracts account before closing entries are illustrated on the next page for both methods using T-accounts:

Percentage-of-Completion

Construction in Progress

2003 construction costs	1,500,000
2003 gross profit	500,000
End balance, 2003	2,000,000
2004 construction costs	1,000,000
2004 gross profit	125,000
End balance, 2004	3,125,000
2005 construction costs	1,600,000
2005 gross profit	275,000
Balance, before closing	5,000,000

Completed Contract

Construction in Progress

2003 construction costs	1,500,000
End balance, 2003	1,500,000
2004 construction costs	1,000,000
End balance, 2004	2,500,000
2005 construction costs	1,600,000
2005 gross profit	900,000
Balance, before closing	5,000,000

Construction in progress includes periodic profit by the percentage-of-completion method.

Billings on Construction Contract

1,200,000	2003 billings
2,000,000	2004 billings
1,800,000	2005 billings
5,000,000	Balance, before closing

Billings on Construction Contract

1,200,000	2003 billings
2,000,000	2004 billings
1,800,000	2005 billings
5,000,000	Balance, before closing

Billings are the same by either method.

The balance sheet presentation for the construction-related accounts by both methods is shown in Illustration 5–2E.

Balance Sheet (End of Year)	2003	2004
Percentage-of-Completion:		
Current assets:		
Accounts receivable	$200,000	$800,000
Costs and profit ($2,000,000) in excess of billings ($1,200,000)	800,000	
Current liabilities:		
Billings ($3,200,000) in excess of costs and profit ($3,125,000)		$ 75,000
Completed Contract:		
Current assets:		
Accounts receivable	$200,000	$800,000
Costs ($1,500,000) in excess of billings ($1,200,000)	$300,000	
Current liabilities:		
Billings ($3,200,000) in excess of costs ($2,500,000)		$700,000

ILLUSTRATION 5–2E

Balance Sheet Presentation

GLOBAL PERSPECTIVE

There are significant differences among countries in the method used to recognize profit on long-term contracts. Practices in many countries, such as the U.K., Norway, Brazil, and Japan are similar to the United States. The percentage-of-completion method is preferred and the completed contract method can be used only in unusual situations. In Germany, the completed contract method is used in almost all cases and recognizing gross profit prior to contract completion is rare. In Switzerland, Denmark, and Belgium, companies can use either method.

Disclosure of the method used to account for long-term contracts will appear in the summary of significant accounting policies.

GRAPHIC 5–12
Disclosure of Revenue Recognition Policy for Construction Contracts—Fluor Corporation

The first disclosure note to any set of financial statements usually is a summary of significant accounting policies. This note discloses the method the company uses to account for its long-term contracts. As an example of this, Graphic 5–12 shows the disclosure note that appeared in a recent annual report of Fluor Corporation.

> **Notes: Engineering and Construction Contracts (in part)**
> The company recognizes engineering and construction contract revenues using the percentage-of-completion method, based primarily on contract costs incurred to date compared with total estimated contract costs. . . . Changes to total estimated contract costs or losses, if any, are recognized in the period in which they are determined. Revenues recognized in excess of amounts billed are classified as current assets under contract work in progress. Amounts billed to clients in excess of revenues recognized to date are classified as current liabilities under advance billings on contracts.

Long-Term Contract Losses. The Harding Construction Company example above involves a situation in which a profit was realized on the construction contract. Unfortunately, losses sometimes occur on long-term contracts. As a prelude to the following discussion, notice in Graphic 5–12 that Fluor Corporation recognizes losses "in the period in which they are determined."

Periodic loss occurs for profitable project. At times, a loss must be recognized in at least one period over the life of the project even though the project as a whole is profitable. We determine the loss in precisely the same way we determined the profit in profitable years. For example, assume the same $5 million contract for Harding Construction Company described in Illustration 5–2 but with the following cost information:

	2003	2004	2005
Construction costs incurred during the year	$1,500,000	$1,260,000	$1,840,000
Construction costs incurred in prior years	–0–	1,500,000	2,760,000
Cumulative construction costs	1,500,000	2,760,000	4,600,000
Estimated costs to complete at end of year	2,250,000	1,840,000	–0–
Total estimated and actual construction costs	$3,750,000	$4,600,000	$4,600,000

At the end of 2003, gross profit of $500,000 (revenue of $2,000,000 less cost of construction of $1,500,000) is recognized as previously determined.

At the end of 2004, the company still forecasts a profit of $400,000 ($5,000,000 − $4,600,000) on the project and, at that time, the project is estimated to be 60% complete ($2,760,000 ÷ $4,600,000). Applying this percentage to the anticipated gross profit of $400,000 results in a gross profit *to date* of $240,000. But remember, a gross profit of $500,000 was recognized in 2003.

This situation is treated as a *change in accounting estimate* because it resulted from a change in the estimation of costs to complete at the end of 2003. Costs to complete—$4,600,000—were much higher than the end of 2003 estimate of $3,750,000. Recall from our discussion of changes in accounting estimates in Chapter 4 that we don't go back and restate the prior year's gross profit. Instead, the 2004 income statement would report *a loss of $260,000* ($500,000 − 240,000). The loss consists of revenue of $1,000,000 ($5,000,000 × 60% = $3,000,000 less 2003 revenue of $2,000,000) less cost of construction of $1,260,000 (cost incurred in 2004). The following journal entry records the loss:

Recognized losses on long-term contracts reduce the construction in progress account.

Cost of construction	1,260,000	
Revenue from long-term contracts		1,000,000
Construction in progress (loss)		260,000

The 2005 income statement would report a gross profit of $160,000 determined as follows:

Project gross profit	$400,000
Less: Gross profit recognized	
in prior periods ($500,000 − 260,000)	(240,000)
2005 gross profit	$160,000

The 2005 gross profit comprises $2,000,000 in revenue ($5,000,000 less revenue of $3,000,000 recognized in 2003 and 2004) and $1,840,000 in cost of construction (cost incurred in 2005).

Of course, by the completed contract method, no profit or loss is recorded in 2003 or 2004. Instead, a $400,000 gross profit (revenue of $5,000,000 and cost of construction of $4,600,000) is recognized in 2005.

Loss is projected on the entire project.   A more conservative approach is indicated when a loss actually is projected on the entire contract. Again consider the Harding Construction Company example but with the following cost information:

	2003	2004	2005
Construction costs incurred during the year	$1,500,000	$1,260,000	$2,440,000
Construction costs incurred in prior years	–0–	1,500,000	2,760,000
Cumulative construction costs	1,500,000	2,760,000	5,200,000
Estimated costs to complete at end of year	2,250,000	2,340,000	–0–
Total estimated and actual construction costs	$3,750,000	$5,100,000	$5,200,000

At the end of 2004, revised costs indicate a loss of $100,000 for the entire project ($5,000,000 − 5,100,000). In this situation, the *total* anticipated loss must be recognized in 2004 for both the percentage-of-completion method and the completed contract method. As a gross profit of $500,000 was recognized in 2003 using the percentage-of-completion method, *a $600,000 loss is recognized in 2004.* Once again, this situation is treated as a change in accounting estimate with no restatement of 2003 income. If the completed contract method is used, because no gross profit is recognized in 2003 the $100,000 loss for the project is recognized in 2004.

If the loss is not recognized in 2004, construction in progress would be valued at an amount greater than the company expects to realize from the contract. The construction in progress account is reduced to $2,660,000 ($2,760,000 in costs to date less $100,000 loss recognized to date). This amount combined with the estimated costs to complete of $2,340,000 equals the realizable contract price of $5,000,000. Recognizing losses on long-term projects in the period the losses become known is equivalent to measuring inventory at the lower of cost or market.

> An estimated loss on a long-term contract is fully recognized in the first period the loss is anticipated, regardless of the revenue recognition method used.

Comparison of Periodic Gross Profit (Loss), Loss on Entire Contract.   The pattern of gross profit (loss) over the contract period for the two methods is summarized in the following table. Notice that an unanticipated increase in costs of $100,000 causes a further loss of $100,000 to be recognized in 2005.

	Percentage-of-Completion	Completed Contract
Gross profit (loss) recognized:		
2003	$ 500,000	–0–
2004	(600,000)	$(100,000)
2005	(100,000)	(100,000)
Total project loss	$(200,000)	$(200,000)

The table in Illustration 5–2F shows the revenue and cost of construction recognized in each of the three years using the percentage-of-completion method.

ILLUSTRATION 5–2F	**2003**	
Percentage-of-Completion Method: Allocation of Revenue and Cost of Construction to Each Period—Loss on Entire Project	Revenue recognized ($5,000,000 × 40%)	$2,000,000
	Costs of construction	1,500,000
	Gross profit	$ 500,000
	2004	
	Revenue recognized to date ($5,000,000 × 54.12%)* $2,706,000	
	Less: Revenue recognized in 2003 (2,000,000)	
	Revenue recognized	$ 706,000
	Cost of construction†	1,306,000
	Loss	$ (600,000)
	2005	
	Revenue recognized to date ($5,000,000 × 100%) $5,000,000	
	Less: Revenue recognized in 2003 and 2004 (2,706,000)	
	Revenue recognized	$2,294,000
	Cost of construction†	2,394,000
	Loss	$ (100,000)

*$2,760,000 ÷ $5,100,000 = 54.12%
†The difference between revenue and loss

Revenue is recognized in the usual way by multiplying a percentage of completion by the total contract price. In situations where a loss is expected on the entire project, cost of construction for the period will no longer be equal to cost incurred during the period. The easiest way to compute cost of construction is to add the amount of the recognized loss to the amount of revenue recognized. For example, in 2004 revenue recognized of $706,000 is added to the loss of $600,000 to arrive at the cost of construction of $1,306,000.[18]

The journal entries to record the losses in 2004 and 2005 are as follows:

Recognized losses on long-term contracts reduce the construction in progress account.

2004		
Cost of construction	1,306,000	
Revenue from long-term contracts		706,000
Construction in progress (loss).		600,000
2005		
Cost of construction	2,394,000	
Revenue from long-term contracts		2,294,000
Construction in progress (loss).		100,000

---

[18]The cost of construction also can be determined as follows:

Loss to date (100% recognized)		$ 100,000
Add:		
Remaining total project cost, not including the loss ($5,100,000 − 100,000)	$5,000,000	
Multiplied by the percentage of completion	× .5412*	2,706,000
Total		2,806,000
Less: Cost of construction recognized in 2003		(1,500,000)
Cost of construction recognized in 2004		$1,306,000

*$2,760,000 ÷ $5,100,000

Using the completed contract method, no revenue or cost of construction is recognized until the contract is complete. In 2004, a loss on long-term contracts (an income statement account) of $100,000 is recognized. In 2005, the income statement will report revenue of $5,000,000 and cost of construction of $5,100,000, thus reporting the additional loss of $100,000. The journal entries to record the losses in 2004 and 2005 are as follows:

2004

Loss on long-term contracts	100,000	
Construction in progress (loss).		100,000

2005

Cost of construction	5,100,000	
Revenue from long-term contracts		5,000,000
Construction in progress (loss))		100,000

You can see from this that use of the percentage-of-completion method in this case produces a large overstatement of income in 2003 and a large understatement in 2004 caused by a change in the estimation of future costs. Recall that if a company feels that it is unable to make dependable forecasts of future costs, the completed contract method should be used.

CONCEPT **REVIEW** EXERCISE

Long-Term Construction Contracts

During 2003, the Samuelson Construction Company began construction on an office building for the City of Gernon. The contract price is $8,000,000 and the building will take approximately 18 months to complete. Completion is scheduled for early in 2005. The company's fiscal year ends on December 31.

The following is a year-by-year recap of construction costs incurred and the estimated costs to complete the project as of the end of each year. Progress billings and cash collections also are indicated.

	2003	2004	2005
Construction costs incurred during the year	$1,500,000	$4,500,000	$1,550,000
Construction costs incurred in prior years	–0–	1,500,000	6,000,000
Cumulative construction costs	1,500,000	6,000,000	7,550,000
Estimated costs to complete at end of year	4,500,000	1,500,000	–0–
Total estimated and actual construction costs	$6,000,000	$7,500,000	$7,550,000
Billings made during the year	$1,400,000	$5,200,000	$1,400,000
Cash collections during year	1,000,000	4,000,000	3,000,000

Required:

1. Determine the amount of gross profit or loss to be recognized in each of the three years applying both the percentage-of-completion and completed contract methods.
2. Prepare the necessary summary journal entries for each of the three years to account for construction costs incurred, recognized revenue and cost of construction, contract billings, and cash collections and to close the construction accounts in 2005 using the percentage-of-completion method only.
3. Prepare a partial balance sheet for 2003 and 2004 to include all construction-related accounts using the percentage-of-completion method.

1. Determine the amount of gross profit or loss to be recognized in each of the three years   SOLUTION
   applying both the percentage-of-completion and completed contract methods.

	Percentage-of-Completion Method		
	2003	**2004**	**2005**
Contract price	$8,000,000	$8,000,000	$8,000,000
Less: costs to complete	6,000,000	$7,500,000	7,550,000
Total estimated gross profit to date	2,000,000	500,000	450,000
Multiplied by % of completion*	25%	80%	100%
Gross profit recognized to date	500,000	400,000	450,000
Less gross profit recognized in prior years	–0–	(500,000)	(400,000)
Gross profit (loss) recognized	$ 500,000	$ (100,000)	$ 50,000

*Estimates of percentage-of-completion:

2003	**2004**	**2005**
$\dfrac{1,500,000}{6,000,000} = 25\%$	$\dfrac{6,000,000}{7,500,000} = 80\%$	Project complete

	Completed Contract Method		
	2003	**2004**	**2005**
Gross profit recognized	–0–	–0–	$450,000

2. Prepare the necessary summary journal entries for each of the three years to account for construction costs incurred, recognized revenue and cost of construction, contract billings, and cash collections and to close the construction accounts in 2005 using the percentage-of-completion method only.

	2003		**2004**		**2005**	
Construction in progress	1,500,000		4,500,000		1,550,000	
Cash, materials, etc.		1,500,000		4,500,000		1,550,000
To record construction costs.						
Construction in progress						
(gross profit)	500,000				50,000	
Cost of construction	1,500,000				1,550,000	
Revenue from long-term						
contracts (below)		2,000,000				1,600,000
To record gross profit.						
Cost of construction			4,500,000			
Revenue from long-term						
contracts (below)				4,400,000		
Construction in progress (loss)				100,000		
To record loss.						
Accounts receivable	1,400,000		5,200,000		1,400,000	
Billings on construction contract. . . .		1,400,000		5,200,000		1,400,000
To record progress billings.						
Cash	1,000,000		4,000,000		3,000,000	
Accounts receivable		1,000,000		4,000,000		3,000,000
To record cash collections.						
Billings on construction contract					8,000,000	
Construction in progress.						8,000,000
To close accounts.						

Revenue recognized:

2003:	$8,000,000 × 25% =		$2,000,000
2004:	$8,000,000 × 80% =		$6,400,000
	Less: Revenue recognized in 2003		(2,000,000)
	Revenue recognized in 2004		$4,400,000
2005:	$8,000,000 × 100% =		$8,000,000
	Less: Revenue recognized in 2003 and 2004		(6,400,000)
	Revenue recognized in 2005		$1,600,000

3. Prepare a partial balance sheet for 2003 and 2004 to include all construction related accounts using the percentage-of-completion method.

Balance Sheet
(End of Year)

	2003	2004
Current assets:		
Accounts receivable	$400,000	$1,600,000
Costs and profit ($2,000,000) in excess of billings ($1,400,000)	600,000	
Current liabilities:		
Billings ($6,600,000) in excess of costs and profit ($6,400,000)		200,000

Industry-Specific Revenue Issues

The previous sections addressed situations when revenue is recognized either at a point in time after the earnings process is virtually complete or over time during the earnings process. We now look at two industry-specific situations, software and franchise sales, that require revenue recognition using a combination of the two approaches.

SOFTWARE REVENUE RECOGNITION

We all know how important personal computers and the software to run them have become in our daily lives. The software industry is a key economic component of our economy. Microsoft alone reported revenues in excess of $25 billion for its 2001 fiscal year.

The recognition of software revenues was a controversial issue throughout the 1990s. The controversy stemmed from the way software vendors typically package their products. It is not unusual for these companies to sell multiple software deliverables in a bundle for a lump-sum contract price. The bundle often includes product, upgrades, postcontract customer support, and other services. The critical accounting question concerns the timing of revenue recognition.

The American Institute of Certified Public Accountants (AICPA) issued a Statement of Position (SOP) in 1991 providing guidance in this area. However, inconsistencies in practice led to a new SOP in 1997.[19] *SOP 97-2* indicates that if an arrangement includes multiple elements, the revenue from the arrangement should be allocated to the various elements based on the relative fair values of the individual elements, "regardless of any separate prices stated within the contract for each element."[20]

For example, suppose that a vendor sold software to a customer for $100,000. As part of the contract, the vendor promises to provide technical support over the next six months. Prior to the issuance of *SOP 97-2,* some vendors were recognizing the entire $100,000 as revenue when the initial software was delivered. Now, the $100,000 contract price must be allocated based on fair values. So, the seller might recognize $80,000 in revenue initially and defer the remaining $20,000 and recognize it ratably over the next six months. In its 2001 balance sheet, Microsoft reported a liability for unearned (deferred) software revenue of $5.614 billion.

In 1998, *SOP 98-9*[21] amended certain paragraphs of *SOP 97-2* related to the methodology used to allocate the contract price in certain circumstances. Graphic 5–13 contains a portion of Microsoft Corporation's unearned revenue disclosure note explaining the changes it made in the allocation of revenue from the sale of its Windows and Office operating systems to comply with *SOP 98-9.*

Generally, a portion of the proceeds received from the sale of software is deferred and recognized as revenue in future periods.

---

[19]"Software Revenue Recognition," *Statement of Position 97-2* (New York: AICPA, 1997).
[20]Ibid, p. 14.
[21]"Modification of SOP 97-2, Software Revenue Recognition With Respect to Certain Transactions," *Statement of Position 98-9* (New York: AICPA, 1998).

Unearned Revenue (in part)

End users receive certain elements of the Company's products over a period of time. These elements include items such as browser technologies and technical support. Consequently, Microsoft's earned revenue reflects the recognition of fair value of these elements over the product's life cycle. Upon adoption of *SOP 98-9* during the fourth quarter of fiscal 1999, the Company was required to change the methodology of attributing fair value to undelivered elements. The percentages of undelivered elements in relation to the total arrangement decreased, reducing the amount of Windows and Office revenue treated as unearned, and increasing the amount of revenue recognized upon shipment. The percentage of revenue recognized ratably decreased from a range of 20% to 35% to a range of approximately 15% to 25% of Windows desktop operating systems.

It is interesting to note that some analysts questioned the quality of Microsoft's earnings because of their revenue recognition policy. Specifically, Microsoft was criticized for deferring excessive amounts of revenue. As you can see in the disclosure note, it now recognizes more revenue currently and defers less than it had in the past.

The accounting treatment of the cost of developing computer software is discussed in Chapter 10.

FRANCHISE SALES

The use of franchise arrangements has become increasingly popular in the United States over the past 30 years. Many retail outlets for fast food, restaurants, motels, and auto rental agencies are operated as franchises. In the franchise arrangements, the **franchisor**, for example McDonald's Corporation, grants to the **franchisee**, quite often an individual, the right to sell the franchisor's products and use its name for a specified period of time. The restaurant where you ate your last Big Mac was probably owned and operated by an individual under a franchise agreement, not by McDonald's Corporation.

The fees to be paid by the franchisee to the franchisor usually comprise (1) the *initial franchise fee* and (2) *continuing franchise fees*. The services to be performed by the franchisor in exchange for the initial franchise fee, in addition to the right to use its name and sell its products, might include assistance in finding a location, constructing the facilities, and training employees. The initial franchise fee usually is a fixed amount, but it may be payable in installments.

The continuing franchise fees are paid to the franchisor for continuing rights as well as for advertising and promotion and other services provided over the life of the franchise agreement. These fees sometimes are a fixed annual or monthly amount, a percentage of the volume of business done by the franchise, or a combination of both.

Continuing franchise fees are recognized over time as the services are performed.

The continuing franchise fees usually do not present any accounting difficulty and are recognized by the franchisor as revenue *over time* in the periods the services are performed by the franchisor, which generally corresponds to the periods they are received. The challenging revenue recognition issue pertains to the initial franchise fee. In the early 1960s and 1970s, many franchisors recognized the entire initial franchise fee as revenue in the period in which the contract was signed. In many cases, there were significant services to be performed and the fee was collectible in installments over an extended period of time creating uncertainty as to cash collection.

Initial franchise fees generally are recognized at a point in time when the earnings process is virtually complete.

Specific guidelines for revenue recognition of the initial franchise fee are provided by *SFAS 45*. You should notice the similarity of these specific guidelines with those of the general revenue

FASB

Franchise fee revenue from an individual franchise sale ordinarily shall be recognized, with an appropriate provision for estimated uncollectible amounts, when all material services or conditions relating to the sale have been substantially performed or satisfied by the franchisor.[22]

---

[22]"Accounting for Franchise Fee Revenue," *Statement of Financial Accounting Standards No. 45* (Stamford, Conn.: FASB, 1981).

recognition guidelines we've discussed previously. A key to these conditions is the concept of *substantial performance.* It requires that substantially all of the initial services of the franchisor required by the franchise agreement have been performed before the initial franchise fee can be recognized as revenue. The term *substantial* requires professional judgment on the part of the accountant. In situations when the initial franchise fee is collectible in installments, even after substantial performance has occurred, the installment sales or cost recovery methods should be used for profit recognition, if a reasonable estimate of uncollectibility cannot be made.

Consider the example in Illustration 5–3.

On March 31, 2003, the Red Hot Chicken Wing Corporation entered into a franchise agreement with Thomas Keller. In exchange for an initial franchise fee of $50,000, Red Hot will provide initial services to include the selection of a location, construction of the building, training of employees, and consulting services over several years. $10,000 is payable on March 31, 2003, with the remaining $40,000 payable in annual installments which include interest at an appropriate rate. In addition, the franchisee will pay continuing franchise fees of $1,000 per month for advertising and promotion provided by Red Hot, beginning immediately after the franchise begins operations. Thomas Keller opened his Red Hot franchise for business on September 30, 2003.	**ILLUSTRATION 5–3** Franchise Sales

Initial Franchise Fee.   Assuming that the initial services to be performed by Red Hot subsequent to the contract signing are substantial but that collectibility of the installment receivable is reasonably certain, the following journal entry is recorded:

> *Revenue from initial franchise services is deferred until the services are rendered.*

March 31, 2003
Cash.	10,000	
Note receivable.	40,000	
Unearned franchise fee revenue		50,000

To record franchise agreement and down payment.

The unearned franchise fee revenue would then be recognized when the initial services have been performed. This could occur in increments or at one point in time, depending on the circumstances.[23] For example, in our illustration, if substantial performance was deemed to have occurred when the franchise began operations, the following entry would be recorded:

Sept. 30, 2003
Unearned franchise fee revenue	50,000	
Franchise fee revenue		50,000

To recognize franchise fee revenue.

If collectibility of the installment receivable is uncertain and there is no basis for estimating uncollectible amounts, the initial entry would record a credit to deferred franchise fee revenue which is then recognized as being earned using either the installment sales or cost recovery methods.

Continuing Franchise Fees.   Continuing franchise fee revenue is recognized on a monthly basis as follows:

Cash (or accounts receivable)	1,000	
Service revenue		1,000

To recognize continuing franchise fee revenue.

---

[23]Franchise agreements sometimes require that any payments made to the franchisor will be refunded if the franchise fails to open. If this condition is present, it would be an important factor in deciding whether to recognize revenue before the franchise opens.

Expenses incurred by the franchisor in providing these continuing franchise services should be recognized in the same periods as the service revenue.

Other unique industry-specific revenue recognition situations exist besides those we have discussed. The FASB and AICPA have issued detailed revenue recognition standards for such industries as insurance, record and music, cable television, and motion pictures.[24] These industry standards are beyond the scope of this text. However, in each case, the objective is the same: to recognize revenue in the period or periods that the revenue-generating activities of the company are performed.

ADDITIONAL CONSIDERATION

In certain circumstances, revenue is recognized at the completion of the production process (before delivery). This approach generally is used by companies that deal in precious metals, and ". . . agricultural, mineral, and other products, units of which are interchangeable and have an immediate marketability at quoted prices. . . ."[25] This is called the *production basis* of recognizing revenue and is accomplished by writing inventory up from cost to market value.

Recall that in a typical manufacturing situation, revenue is not recognized at the completion of the production process due to significant uncertainty as to the collectibility of the asset to be received. We don't know if the product will be sold, nor the selling price, nor the buyer if eventually sold. These uncertainties are not significant when there is immediate marketability at quoted market prices for products like precious metals.

In cases when the production basis of recognizing revenue is used, full disclosure of the fact is required.

PART

b

LO6

Activity ratios measure a company's efficiency in managing its assets.

PROFITABILITY ANALYSIS

Chapter 3 provided an overview of financial statement analysis and introduced some of the common ratios used in risk analysis to investigate a company's liquidity and long-term solvency. We now introduce ratios related to profitability analysis.

ACTIVITY RATIOS

One key to profitability is how well a company manages and utilizes its assets. Some ratios are designed to evaluate a company's effectiveness in managing assets. Of particular interest is the activity, or turnover ratios, of certain assets; that is, the frequency with which those assets are replaced. The greater the number of times an asset turns over—the higher the ratio—the less cash a company must devote to that asset, and the more cash it can commit to other purposes. In other words, if these turnover ratios increase, fewer assets are required to maintain a given level of activity (revenue). Activity ratios do not measure profitability directly. However, they are important factors affecting profitability.

Although, in concept, the activity or turnover can be measured for any asset, activity ratios are most frequently calculated for accounts receivable, inventory, and total assets. These ratios are calculated as follows:

$$\text{Receivables turnover ratio} = \frac{\text{Net sales}}{\text{Average accounts receivable (net)}}$$

---

[24]"Accounting and Reporting by Insurance Enterprises," *Statement of Financial Accounting Standards No. 60* (Stamford, Conn.: FASB, 1982), "Financial Reporting in the Record and Music Industry," *Statement of Financial Accounting Standards No. 50* (Stamford, Conn.: FASB, 1981), "Financial Reporting by Cable Television Companies," *Statement of Financial Accounting Standards No. 51* (Stamford, Conn.: FASB, 1981), "Accounting by Producers or Distributors of Films," *Statement of Position 00-2* (New York: AICPA, 2000).

[25]"Restatement and Revision of Accounting Research Bulletins," *Accounting Research Bulletin No. 43* (New York: AICPA, 1953), chapter 4, par. 16.

$$\text{Inventory turnover ratio} = \frac{\text{Cost of goods sold}}{\text{Average inventory}}$$

$$\text{Asset turnover ratio} = \frac{\text{Net sales}}{\text{Average total assets}}$$

Receivables Turnover.   The **receivables turnover ratio** is calculated by dividing a period's net credit sales by the average net accounts receivable. Because income statements seldom distinguish between cash sales and credit sales, this ratio usually is computed using total net sales as the numerator. The denominator, average accounts receivable, is determined by adding beginning and ending net accounts receivable (gross accounts receivable less allowance for uncollectible accounts) and dividing by two.

The receivables turnover ratio provides an indication of a company's efficiency in collecting receivables. The ratio shows the number of times during a period that the average accounts receivable balance is collected. The higher the ratio, the shorter the average time between credit sales and cash collection.

A convenient extension is the **average collection period.** This measure is computed simply by dividing 365 days by the receivables turnover ratio. The result is an approximation of the number of days the average accounts receivable balance is outstanding.

> *The receivables turnover ratio offers an indication of how quickly a company is able to collect its accounts receivable.*

> *The average collection period indicates the average age of accounts receivable.*

$$\text{Average collection period} = \frac{365}{\text{Receivables turnover ratio}}$$

Monitoring the receivables turnover ratio (and average collection period) over time can provide useful information about a company's future prospects. For example, a decline in the receivables turnover ratio (an increase in the average collection period) could be an indication of customer dissatisfaction with the company's products. Another possible explanation is that the company has changed its credit policy and is granting extended credit terms in order to maintain customers. Ratio analysis does not explain what might be wrong. It does provide information that highlights areas for further investigation.

Inventory Turnover.   An important activity measure for a merchandising company (a retail, wholesale, or manufacturing company) is the **inventory turnover ratio.** The ratio shows the number of times the average inventory balance is sold during a reporting period. It indicates how quickly inventory is sold. The more frequently a business is able to sell, or turn over, its inventory, the lower its investment in inventory must be for a given level of sales. The ratio is computed by dividing the period's cost of goods sold by the average inventory balance. The denominator, average inventory, is determined by adding beginning and ending inventory and dividing by two.[26]

> *The inventory turnover ratio measures a company's efficiency in managing its investment in inventory.*

A relatively high ratio, say compared to a competitor, usually is desirable. A high ratio indicates comparative strength, perhaps caused by a company's superior sales force, the existence of highly popular products, or maybe a successful advertising campaign. However, it might also be caused by a relatively low inventory level, which could mean stockouts and lost sales in the future. As with any ratio, care must be taken in evaluating this ratio.

On the other hand, a relatively low ratio, or a decrease in the ratio over time, usually is perceived to be unfavorable. Too much capital may be tied up in inventory. A relatively low ratio may result from overstocking, the presence of obsolete items, or poor marketing and sales efforts.

Similar to the receivables turnover, we can divide the inventory turnover ratio into 365 days to compute the **average days in inventory.** This measure indicates the number of days it normally takes to sell inventory.

---

[26]Notice the consistency in the measure used for the numerator and denominator of the two turnover ratios. For the receivables turnover ratio, both numerator and denominator are based on sales dollars, whereas they are both based on cost for the inventory turnover ratio.

$$\text{Average days in inventory} = \frac{365}{\text{Inventory turnover ratio}}$$

Asset Turnover. A broad measure of asset efficiency is the **asset turnover ratio.** The ratio is computed by dividing a company's net sales or revenues by the average total assets available for use during a period. The denominator, average assets, is determined by adding beginning and ending total assets and dividing by two. The asset turnover ratio provides an indication of how efficiently a company utilizes all of its assets to generate revenue.

> The *asset turnover ratio* measures a company's efficiency in using assets to generate revenue.

Industry standards are particularly important when evaluating asset turnover. Some industries are characterized by low turnover but typically make up for it with higher profit margins. Others have low profit margins but compensate with high turnover. Grocery stores typically have relatively low profit margins but relatively high asset turnover. In comparison, a manufacturer of specialized equipment will have a higher profit margin but a lower asset turnover ratio. But again, this ratio is best evaluated in conjunction with profit margin on sales. We do this in the next section.

PROFITABILITY RATIOS

A fundamental element of an analyst's task is to develop an understanding of a firm's profitability. Profitability ratios attempt to measure a company's ability to earn an adequate return relative to sales or resources devoted to operations. Resources devoted to operations can be defined as total assets or only those assets provided by owners, depending on the evaluation objective.

Three common profitability measures are (1) the profit margin on sales, (2) the return on assets, and (3) the return on shareholders' equity. These ratios are calculated as follows:

> Profitability ratios assist in evaluating various aspects of a company's profit-making activities.

$$\text{Profit margin on sales} = \frac{\text{Net income}}{\text{Net sales}}$$

$$\text{Return on assets} = \frac{\text{Net income}}{\text{Average total assets}}$$

$$\text{Return on shareholders' equity} = \frac{\text{Net income}}{\text{Average shareholders' equity}}$$

Notice that for all of the profitability ratios, our numerator is net income. Recall our discussion in Chapter 4 on earnings quality. The relevance of any historical-based financial statement hinges on its predictive value. To enhance predictive value, analysts try to separate a company's *transitory earnings* effects from its *permanent earnings*. Analysts begin their assessment of permanent earnings with income from continuing operations. Then, adjustments are made for transitory income effects, if any, included in income from continuing operations. It is this adjusted number that we use as the numerator in these ratios.

> When calculating profitability ratios, analysts adjust net income for any transitory income effects.

Profit Margin on Sales. The **profit margin on sales** is simply net income divided by net sales. The ratio measures an important dimension of a company's profitability. It indicates the portion of each dollar of revenue that is available to cover expenses. It offers a measure of the company's ability to withstand either higher expenses or lower revenues.

> The *profit margin on sales* measures the amount of net income achieved per sales dollar.

As we discussed in the previous section, what is considered to be a desirable profit margin is highly sensitive to the nature of the business activity. For instance, you would expect a specialty shop to have a higher profit margin than, say, Wal-Mart. A low profit margin can be compensated for by a high asset turnover rate, and vice versa.

Return on Assets. The **return on assets (ROA)** indicates a company's overall profitability. The ratio expresses income as a percentage of the average total assets available to generate that income. Because total assets are partially financed with debt and partially by equity funds, this is an inclusive way of measuring earning power that ignores specific sources of financing.

Recall from our previous discussion that a company's return on assets is related to both profit margin and asset turnover. Specifically, profitability can be achieved by either a high profit margin, high turnover, or a combination of the two.[27] In fact, the return on assets can actually be calculated by multiplying the profit margin ratio by the asset turnover ratio.

$$\text{Return on assets} = \text{Profit margin on sales} \times \text{Asset turnover}$$

$$= \frac{\text{Net income}}{\text{Net sales}} \times \frac{\text{Net sales}}{\text{Average total assets}}$$

The decomposition of return on assets illustrates why some companies with relatively small profit margins can be very profitable if they have high asset turnover. Alternatively, companies with relatively low asset turnover ratios can be profitable if they are able to sustain large profit margins.

ADDITIONAL CONSIDERATION

The return on assets ratio often is computed as follows:

$$\text{Return on assets} = \frac{\text{Net income} + \text{Interest expense} (1 - \text{Tax rate})}{\text{Average total assets}}$$

The reason for adding back interest expense (net of tax) is that interest represents a return to suppliers of debt capital and should not be deducted in the computation of net income when computing the return on total assets. In other words, the numerator is the total amount of income available to both debt and equity capital.

Return on Shareholders' Equity.   One measure of profitability is the ability of management to generate net income from the resources owners provide. Sometimes viewed by shareholders as the key criterion of profitability, the ratio is obtained by dividing net income by average shareholders' equity.

When the **return on shareholders' equity** is greater than the return on assets, management is using assets funded by debt to increase the income available for shareholders. This concept, known as *financial leverage,* was discussed in Chapter 3.

> The *return on shareholders' equity* measures the return to suppliers of equity capital.

ADDITIONAL CONSIDERATION

Sometimes when this ratio is calculated, shareholders' equity is viewed more narrowly to include only common shareholders. In that case, preferred stock is excluded from the denominator, and preferred dividends are deducted from net income in the numerator. The resulting rate of return on common shareholders' equity focuses on profits generated on resources provided by common shareholders.

Graphic 5–14 provides a recap of the activity and profitability ratios.

Profitability Analysis—An Illustration

To illustrate the computation of the activity and profitability ratios, we analyze two well-known pharmaceutical companies, Bristol-Myers Squibb (BMS) and Merck & Co., Inc. The operations of these two companies are similar in terms of their involvement in pharmaceutical and other health care products. Illustration 5–4A presents selected financial statement information for the two companies.

---

[27]This notion is sometimes referred to as the Du Pont analysis because the Du Pont Company was a pioneer in emphasizing this relationship.

GRAPHIC 5–14
Activity and
Profitability Ratios

Activity ratios

$$\text{Receivables turnover} = \frac{\text{Net sales}}{\text{Average accounts receivable (net)}}$$

$$\text{Average collection period} = \frac{365}{\text{Receivables turnover ratio}}$$

$$\text{Inventory turnover} = \frac{\text{Cost of goods sold}}{\text{Average inventory}}$$

$$\text{Average days in inventory} = \frac{365}{\text{Inventory turnover ratio}}$$

$$\text{Asset turnover} = \frac{\text{Net sales}}{\text{Average total assets}}$$

Profitability ratios

$$\text{Profit margin on sales} = \frac{\text{Net income}}{\text{Net sales}}$$

$$\text{Return on assets} = \frac{\text{Net income}}{\text{Average total assets}}$$

$$\text{Return on shareholders' equity} = \frac{\text{Net income}}{\text{Average shareholders' equity}}$$

ILLUSTRATION 5–4A

Selected Financial
Information for
Bristol-Myers Squibb
and Merck & Co., Inc.

	($ in millions)			
Balance Sheet	**BMS**		**Merck**	
	2000	**1999**	**2000**	**1999**
Accounts receivable (net)	$ 3,662	$ 3,272	$ 5,018	$ 4,089
Inventories	1,831	2,126	3,022	2,847
Total assets	17,578	17,114	39,910	35,635
Total liabilities	8,398	8,469	25,078	22,211
Total shareholders' equity	9,180	8,645	14,832	13,242
Two-year averages:				
Accounts receivable (net)	$ 3,467.0		$ 4,553.5	
Inventories	1,978.5		2,934.5	
Total assets	17,346.0		37,772.5	
Total shareholders' equity	8,912.5		14,037.0	
Income Statement—2000				
Net sales	$18,216		$40,363	
Cost of goods sold	4,759		22,444	
Net income	4,711*		6,822	

*Includes $605 in income from discontinued operations

On the surface, it appears that Merck was more profitable than BMS. Merck's 2000 net income was $6.822 billion compared to $4.711 billion for BMS. But that's not the whole story. Even though both are very large companies, Merck is larger than BMS in terms of total assets. Illustration 5–4B presents a comparison of the various activity and profitability ratios for 2000. Notice that net income for BMS includes $605 million in income from

ILLUSTRATION 5–4B

Activity and
Profitability Ratios—
Bristol-Myers Squibb
(BMS) and Merck &
Co., Inc.

	BMS	Merck	Industry Average*
Activity ratios:			
Receivables turnover	$=\dfrac{18,216}{3,467.5}=$ **5.25**	$\dfrac{40,363}{4,553.5}=$ **8.86**	**6.36**
Average collection period	$=\dfrac{365}{5.25}=$ **70 days**	$\dfrac{365}{8.86}=$ **41 days**	**57 days**
Inventory turnover	$=\dfrac{4,759}{1,978.5}=$ **2.41**	$\dfrac{22,444}{2,934.5}=$ **7.65**	**3.35**
Average days in inventory	$=\dfrac{365}{2.41}=$ **151 days**	$\dfrac{365}{7.65}=$ **48 days**	**109 days**
Asset turnover	$=\dfrac{18,216}{17,346}=$ **1.05**	$\dfrac{40,363}{37,772.5}=$ **1.07**	**.90**
Profitability ratios			
Profit margin on sales	$=\dfrac{4,106}{18,216}=$ **.225**	$\dfrac{6,822}{40,363}=$ **.169**	**.168**
Return on assets	$=\dfrac{4,106}{17,346}=$ **.237**	$\dfrac{6,822}{37,772.5}=$ **.181**	**.158**
Return on shareholders' equity	$=\dfrac{4,106}{8,912.5}=$ **.461**	$\dfrac{6,822}{14,037}=$ **.486**	**.30**

*Source: Multex Investor

discontinued operations. The profitability ratios in our illustration are calculated using income from continuing operations of $4,106 million ($4,711 − 605).

Merck's receivables and inventory turnover ratios are significantly higher than BMS's. A possible cause is the different mix of products sold by the two companies. BMS is more diversified than Merck in terms of its product lines and markets that it serves. BMS's receivables and inventory turnovers are also less than the industry average.

The return on shareholders' equity ratios are similar. However, BMS has a higher return on assets and profit margin. Both companies' profitability ratios exceed the industry average. As shown below, BMS's higher return on assets can be attributed to higher profit margin.

	Profit Margin	×	Asset Turnover		Return on Assets
BMS:	.225	×	1.05	=	23.7%
Merck:	.169	×	1.07	=	18.1%

Both companies produced a higher return on shareholders' equity than return on assets. This means that they were both able to use assets funded by debt to increase the income available for shareholders. This is an example of favorable financial leverage to which we referred earlier.

The essential point of our discussion here, and in Part C of Chapter 3, is that raw accounting numbers alone mean little to decision makers. The numbers gain value when viewed in relation to other numbers. Similarly, the financial ratios formed by those relationships provide even greater perspective when compared with similar ratios of other companies, or relatedly, with averages for several companies in the same industry. Accounting information is useful in making decisions. Financial analysis that includes comparisons of financial ratios enhances the value of that information.

FINANCIAL REPORTING CASE **SOLUTION**

1. **Does your sister have to wait two and a half years to get her bonus? Explain.** *(p. 232)* No. The *general* revenue recognition criteria would suggest that revenue and costs should be recognized when a project is finished. The difficulty this would create is that all revenues, expenses, and resulting profit from the project are recognized when the project is completed; no revenues or expenses would be reported in the income statements of earlier reporting periods in which much of the work may have been performed. The percentage-of-completion method of revenue recognition for long-term projects addresses this problem. A share of the project's profit is allocated to each period in which the earnings process occurs. This is two and a half years in this instance.

2. **How are gross profits recognized using the percentage-of-completion method?** *(p. 233)* The percentage-of-completion method recognizes part of the estimated gross profit each period. The amount recognized is based on progress to date which is estimated as the fraction of the project's cost incurred to date divided by total estimated costs. The estimated percentage of completion is multiplied by the revised project gross profit estimate. This yields the estimated gross profit earned from the beginning of the project. The gross profit recognized is calculated by subtracting from this amount the gross profit recognized in previous periods.

3. **Are there other situations in which revenue is recognized at times other than when a product is delivered?** *(p. 225)* Yes, revenue recognition sometimes is delayed until after the product is delivered. These situations involve either the possibility of product returns or bad debts. In most cases, product returns and bad debt are estimated and revenues are recognized when a product is delivered. However, in situations involving an abnormal degree of uncertainty about cash collection caused by potential returns or bad debts, revenue recognition *after* delivery sometimes is appropriate. ■

THE BOTTOM LINE

1. The objective of revenue recognition is to recognize revenue in the period or periods that the revenue-generating activities of the company are performed. Also, judgment as to the collectibility of the cash from the sale of a product or service will impact the timing of revenue recognition. These two concepts of performance and collectibility are captured by the general guidelines for revenue recognition in the realization principle which requires that revenue should be recognized only after (1) the earnings process is virtually complete and (2) there is reasonable certainty of collecting the asset to be received (usually cash) from the customer. For the sale of product, these criteria usually are satisfied at the point of product delivery. At that point, the majority of the productive activities have taken place and any remaining uncertainty concerning asset collection can be accounted for by estimating possible returns and bad debts. Also, service revenue often is recognized at a point in time if there is one final activity that is deemed critical to the earnings process.

2. The installment sales method recognizes gross profit in collection periods by applying the gross profit percentage on the sale to the amount of cash actually received. The cost recovery method defers all gross profit recognition until cash has been received equal to the cost of the item sold. These methods of recognizing revenue should only be used in situations where there is an unusually high degree of uncertainty regarding the ultimate cash collection on an installment sale.

3. In most situations, even though the right to return merchandise exists, revenues and expenses can be appropriately recognized at point of delivery. Based on past experience, a company usually can estimate the returns that will result for a given volume of sales. These estimates reduce both sales and cost of goods sold in anticipation of returns. Revenue cannot be recognized at the point of delivery unless the seller is able to make reliable estimates of future returns. Otherwise, revenue recognition is deferred beyond the delivery point.

4. Revenue recognition at a single point in time when the earnings process is virtually complete is inappropriate for certain types of service revenue activities and also, usually, for long-term contracts. The completed contract method recognizes revenues and expenses on long-term construction and other long-term contracts at a point in time when the project is complete. This method is only used in unusual situations. The preferable method for recognizing revenues and expenses for long-term contracts is the percentage-of-completion method, which recognizes revenues over time by assigning a share of the project's revenues and costs to each reporting period during the project.

5. Industry guidelines require that the lump-sum contract price for software be allocated to the various elements of the package based on the relative fair values of the individual elements. Generally, this results in a deferral of a portion of the proceeds that are then recognized as revenue in future periods. The use of franchise arrangements has become increasingly popular. The fees to be paid by the franchisee to the franchisor usually are composed of (1) the initial franchise fee and (2) continuing franchise fees. *SFAS 45* requires that the franchisor has substantially performed the services promised in the franchise agreement and that the collectibility of the initial franchise fee is reasonably assured before the initial fee can be recognized as revenue. The continuing franchise fees are recognized by the franchisor as revenue over time in the periods the services are performed by the franchisor.

6. Activity and profitability ratios provide information about a company's profitability. Activity ratios include the receivables turnover ratio, the inventory turnover ratio, and the asset turnover ratio. Profitability ratios include the profit margin on sales, the return on assets, and the return on shareholders' equity.

INTERIM REPORTING

APPENDIX

5

Financial statements covering periods of less than a year are called *interim reports.* Companies registered with the SEC, which includes most public companies, must submit quarterly reports.[28] Though there is no requirement to do so, most also mail quarterly reports to their shareholders and typically include abbreviated, unaudited interim reports as supplemental information within their annual reports. For instance, Graphic 5A–1 shows the quarterly information disclosed in the 2000 annual report of Delta Air Lines, Inc.

For accounting information to be useful to decision makers, it must be available on a timely basis. One of the objectives of interim reporting is to enhance the timeliness of financial information. In addition, quarterly reports provide investors and creditors with additional insight on the seasonality of business operations that might otherwise get lost in annual reports.

However, the downside to the benefits is the relative unreliability of interim reporting. With a shorter reporting period, questions associated with estimation and allocation are magnified. For example, certain expenses often benefit an entire year's operations and yet are incurred primarily within a single interim period. Similarly, should smaller companies use lower tax rates in the earlier quarters and higher rates in later quarters as higher tax brackets are reached? Another result of shorter reporting periods is the intensified effect of major events such as discontinued operations or extraordinary items. A second quarter casualty loss, for instance, that would reduce annual profits by 10% might reduce second quarter profits by 40% or more. Is it more realistic to allocate such a loss over the entire year? These and similar questions tend to hinge on the way we view an interim period in relation to the fiscal year. More specifically, should each interim period be viewed as a *discrete* reporting period or as an *integral part* of the annual period?

Interim reports are issued for periods of less than a year, typically as quarterly financial statements.

Interim reporting serves to enhance the timeliness of financial information.

The fundamental debate regarding interim reporting centers on the choice between the *discrete* and *integral part* approaches.

---

[28]Quarterly reports are filed with the SEC on form 10-Q. Annual reports to the SEC are on form 10-K.

20. Quarterly Financial Data (Unaudited)
The following table summarizes our unaudited quarterly results of operations for
2000 and 1999
($ in millions, except per share data):

	Three Months Ended			
2000	**Mar. 31**	**June 30**	**Sept. 30**	**Dec. 31**
Operating revenues	$3,911	$4,469	$4,345	$4,016
Operating income	343	606	510	178
Net income	217	460	133	18
Basic earnings per share*	1.68	3.73	1.05	.12
Diluted earnings per share*	1.61	3.51	1.01	.12

	Three Months Ended			
1999	**Mar. 31**	**June 30**	**Sept. 30**	**Dec. 31**
Operating revenues	$3,469	$3,907	$3,829	$3,678
Operating income	350	630	336	2
Net income	159	357	344	348
Basic earnings per share*	1.10	2.53	2.46	2.60
Diluted earnings per share*	1.03	2.35	2.33	2.48

*The sum of the quarterly earnings per share does not equal the annual earnings per share due to changes in average shares outstanding. The results presented are net of the cumulative effect of changes in accounting principles.

Reporting Revenues and Expenses

Existing practice and current reporting requirements for interim reporting generally follow the viewpoint that interim reports are an integral part of annual statements, although the discrete approach is applied to some items. Most revenues and expenses are recognized using the same accounting principles applicable to annual reporting. Some modifications are necessary to help cause interim statements to relate better to annual statements. This is most evident in the way costs and expenses are recognized. Most are recognized in interim periods as incurred. But when an expenditure clearly benefits more than just the period in which it is incurred, the expense should be allocated among the periods benefited on an allocation basis consistent with the company's annual allocation procedures. For example, annual repair expenses, property tax expense, and advertising expenses incurred in the first quarter that clearly benefit later quarters are assigned to each quarter through the use of accruals and deferrals. Costs and expenses subject to year-end adjustments, such as depreciation and bad debt expense, are estimated and allocated to interim periods in a systematic way. Similarly, income tax expense at each interim date should be based on estimates of the effective tax rate for the whole year. This would mean, for example, that if the estimated effective rate has changed since the previous interim period(s), the tax expense that period would be determined as the new rate times the cumulative pretax income to date, less the total tax expense reported in previous interim periods.

> With only a few exceptions, the same accounting principles applicable to annual reporting are used for interim reporting.

Reporting Unusual Items

> Discontinued operations and extraordinary items are reported entirely within the interim period in which they occur.

On the other hand, major events such as discontinued operations or extraordinary items should be reported separately in the interim period in which they occur. That is, these amounts should not be allocated among individual quarters within the fiscal year. The same is true for items that are unusual or infrequent but not both. Notice that treatment of these items is more consistent with the discrete view than the integral part view.

Earnings Per Share

A second item that is treated in a manner consistent with the discrete view is earnings per share. EPS calculations for interim reports follow the same procedures as annual calculations that you will study in Chapter 20. The calculations are based on conditions actually existing during the particular interim period rather than on conditions estimated to exist at the end of the fiscal year.

Quarterly EPS calculations follow the same procedures as annual calculations.

Reporting Accounting Changes

Recall from Chapter 4 that when most accounting changes are adopted, the cumulative effect of the change on retained earnings must be determined and reported in earnings of the change period. For interim reporting, the cumulative effect should be reported in the *first* interim period of the fiscal year in which the change is made, even if the change actually is made in a later interim period. So, it is the cumulative effect on the income of previous years from using the new method rather than the previous method *as of the beginning of that fiscal year.*[29] Also, if the change occurs in an interim period other than the first, financial statement information for prechange interim periods is restated to reflect the new accounting method when those prior statements are presented again.[30]

The cumulative effect of changes in accounting principle are reflected in the *first* interim period.

Minimum Disclosures

Complete financial statements are not required for interim period reporting, but certain minimum disclosures are required as follows:[31]

- Sales, income taxes, extraordinary items, cumulative effect of accounting principle changes, and net income.
- Earnings per share.
- Seasonal revenues, costs, and expenses.
- Significant changes in estimates for income taxes.
- Discontinued operations, extraordinary items, and unusual or infrequent items.
- Contingencies.
- Changes in accounting principles or estimates.
- Significant changes in financial position.

When fourth quarter results are not separately reported, material fourth quarter events, including year-end adjustments, should be reported in disclosure notes to annual statements.

QUESTIONS FOR REVIEW OF KEY TOPICS

Q 5–1   What are the two general criteria that must be satisfied before a company can recognize revenue?

Q 5–2   Explain why, in most cases, a seller recognizes revenue when it delivers its product rather than when it produces the product.

Q 5–3   Revenue recognition for most installment sales occurs at the point of delivery of the product or service. Under what circumstances would a seller delay revenue recognition for installment sales beyond the delivery date?

Q 5–4   Distinguish between the installment sales method and the cost recovery method of accounting for certain installment sales.

---

[29]Stated differently, the cumulative effect is the difference between the balance in retained earnings at the beginning of the period of the change and what the balance would have been if the new method had been applied all along.

[30]"Reporting Accounting Changes in Interim Financial Statements," *Statement of Financial Accounting Standards No. 3* (Stamford, Conn.: FASB, 1974), par. 9–10.

[31]"Interim Financial Reporting," *Accounting Principles Board Opinion No 28* (New York: AICPA, 1973).

Q 5–5   How does a company report deferred gross profit resulting from the use of the installment sales method in its balance sheet?

Q 5–6   Revenue recognition for most product sales that allow the right of return occurs at the point of product delivery. Under what circumstances would revenue recognition be delayed?

Q 5–7   Describe a consignment sale. When does a consignor recognize revenue for a consignment sale?

Q 5–8   Service revenue is recognized either at one point in time or over extended periods. Explain the rationale for recognizing revenue using these two approaches.

Q 5–9   Distinguish between the percentage-of-completion and completed contract methods of accounting for long-term contracts with respect to income recognition. Under what circumstances should a company use the completed contract method?

Q 5–10   Periodic billings to the customer for a long-term construction contract are recorded as billings on construction contract. How is this account reported in the balance sheet?

Q 5–11   When is an estimated loss on a long-term contract recognized using the percentage-of-completion method? The completed contract method?

Q 5–12   Briefly describe the guidelines provided by SOPs 97-2 and 98-9 for recognizing revenue from the sale of software.

Q 5–13   Briefly describe the guidelines provided by SFAS 45 for the recognition of revenue by a franchisor for an initial franchise fee.

Q 5–14   Show the calculation of the following activity ratios: (1) the receivables turnover ratio, (2) the inventory turnover ratio, and (3) the asset turnover ratio. What information about a company do these ratios offer?

Q 5–15   Show the calculation of the following profitability ratios: (1) the profit margin on sales, (2) the return on assets, and (3) the return on shareholders' equity. What information about a company do these ratios offer?

Q 5–16   [Based on Appendix 5] Interim reports are issued for periods of less than a year, typically as quarterly financial statements. Should these interim periods be viewed as separate periods or integral parts of the annual period?

EXERCISES

E 5–1
Installment sales method

The Charter Corporation, which began business in 2003, appropriately uses the installment sales method of accounting for its installment sales. The following data were obtained for sales made during 2003 and 2004:

	2003	2004
Installment sales	$360,000	$350,000
Cost of installment sales	216,000	245,000
Cash collections on installment sales during:		
2003	150,000	100,000
2004	—	120,000

Required:
1.   How much gross profit should Charter recognize in 2003 and 2004 from installment sales?
2.   What should be the balance in the deferred gross profit account at the end of 2003 and 2004?

E 5–2
Installment sales method; journal entries

[This is a variation of the previous exercise focusing on journal entries.]
    The Charter Corporation, which began business in 2003, appropriately uses the installment sales method of accounting for its installment sales. The following data were obtained for sales during 2003 and 2004.

	2003	2004
Installment sales	$360,000	$350,000
Cost of installment sales	216,000	245,000
Cash collections on installment sales during:		
2003	150,000	100,000
2004	—	120,000

Required:
Prepare summary journal entries for 2003 and 2004 to account for the installment sales and cash collections. The company uses the perpetual inventory system.

E 5–3
Installment sales; alternative recognition methods

On July 1, 2003, the Foster Company sold inventory to the Slate Corporation for $300,000. Terms of the sale called for a down payment of $75,000 and three annual installments of $75,000 due on each July 1, beginning July 1, 2004. Each installment also will include interest on the unpaid balance applying an appropriate interest rate. The inventory cost Foster $120,000. The company uses the perpetual inventory system.

Required:
1. Compute the amount of gross profit to be recognized from the installment sale in 2003, 2004, 2005, and 2006 using point of delivery revenue recognition. Ignore interest charges.
2. Repeat requirement 1 applying the installment sales method.
3. Repeat requirement 1 applying the cost recovery method.

E 5–4
Journal entries; point of delivery, installment sales, and cost recovery methods

[This is a variation of the previous exercise focusing on journal entries.]
On July 1, 2003, the Foster Company sold inventory to the Slate Corporation for $300,000. Terms of the sale called for a down payment of $75,000 and three annual installments of $75,000 due on each July 1, beginning July 1, 2004. Each installment also will include interest on the unpaid balance applying an appropriate interest rate. The inventory cost Foster $120,000. The company uses the perpetual inventory system.

Required:
1. Prepare the necessary journal entries for 2003 and 2004 using point of delivery revenue recognition. Ignore interest charges.
2. Repeat requirement 1 applying the installment sales method.
3. Repeat requirement 1 applying the cost recovery method.

E 5–5
Installment sales and cost recovery methods; solve for unknowns

The Wolf Computer Company began operations in 2003. The company allows customers to pay in installments for many of its products. Installment sales for 2003 were $1,000,000. If revenue is recognized at the point of delivery, $600,000 in gross profit would be recognized in 2003. If the company instead uses the cost recovery method, $100,000 in gross profit would be recognized in 2003.

Required:
1. What was the amount of cash collected on installment sales in 2003?
2. What amount of gross profit would be recognized if the company uses the installment sales method?

E 5–6
Real estate sales; gain recognition

On April 1, 2003, the Apex Corporation sold a parcel of underdeveloped land to the Applegate Construction Company for $2,400,000. The book value of the land on Apex's books was $600,000. Terms of the sale required a down payment of $120,000 and 19 annual payments of $120,000 plus interest at an appropriate interest rate due on each April 1 beginning in 2004. Apex has no significant obligations to perform services after the sale.

Required:
1. Prepare the necessary entries for Apex to record the sale, receipt of the down payment, and receipt of the first installment assuming that Apex is able to make a reliable estimate of possible uncollectible amounts (that is, point of delivery profit recognition is used). Ignore interest charges.
2. Repeat requirement 1 assuming that Apex cannot make a reliable estimate of possible uncollectible amounts and decides to use the installment sales method for profit recognition.

E 5–7
Long-term contract; percentage-of-completion and completed contract methods

Nortel Networks contracted to provide a customer with Internet infrastructure for $2,000,000. The project began in 2003 and was completed in 2004. Data relating to the contract are summarized below:

	2003	2004
Costs incurred during the year	$ 300,000	$1,575,000
Estimated costs to complete as of 12/31	1,200,000	–0–
Billings during the year	360,000	1,640,000
Cash collections during the year	250,000	1,750,000

Required:
1. Compute the amount of gross profit or loss to be recognized in 2003 and 2004 using the percentage-of-completion method.
2. Compute the amount of gross profit or loss to be recognized in 2003 and 2004 using the completed contract method.
3. Prepare a partial balance sheet to show how the information related to this contract would be presented at the end of 2003 using the percentage-of-completion method.
4. Prepare a partial balance sheet to show how the information related to this contract would be presented at the end of 2003 using the completed contract method.

E 5–8
Percentage-of-completion method; loss projected on entire project

On February 1, 2003, Arrow Construction Company entered into a three-year construction contract to build a bridge for a price of $8,000,000. During 2003, costs of $2,000,000 were incurred with estimated costs of $4,000,000 yet to be incurred. Billings of $2,500,000 were sent and cash collected was $2,250,000.

In 2004, costs incurred were $2,500,000 with remaining costs estimated to be $3,600,000. 2004 billings were $2,750,000 and $2,475,000 cash was collected. The project was completed in 2005 after additional costs of $3,800,000 were incurred. The company's fiscal year-end is December 31. Arrow uses the *percentage-of-completion* method.

Required:
1. Calculate the amount of gross profit or loss to be recognized in each of the three years.
2. Prepare journal entries for 2003 and 2004 to record the transactions described (credit various accounts for construction costs incurred).
3. Prepare a partial balance sheet to show the presentation of the project as of December 31, 2003 and 2004.

E 5–9
Completed contract method; loss projected on entire project

[This is a variation of the previous exercise focusing on the completed contract method.]

On February 1, 2003, Arrow Construction Company entered into a three-year construction contract to build a bridge for a price of $8,000,000. During 2003, costs of $2,000,000 were incurred with estimated costs of $4,000,000 yet to be incurred. Billings of $2,500,000 were sent and cash collected was $2,250,000.

In 2004, costs incurred were $2,500,000 with remaining costs estimated to be $3,600,000. 2004 billings were $2,750,000 and $2,475,000 cash was collected. The project was completed in 2005 after additional costs of $3,800,000 were incurred. The company's fiscal year-end is December 31. Arrow uses the *completed contract* method.

Required:
1. Calculate the amount of gross profit or loss to be recognized in each of the three years.
2. Prepare journal entries for 2003 and 2004 to record the transactions described (credit various accounts for construction costs incurred).
3. Prepare a partial balance sheet to show the presentation of the project as of December 31, 2003 and 2004.

E 5–10
Income (loss) recognition; percentage-of-completion and completed contract methods compared

The Brady Construction Company contracted to build an apartment complex for a price of $5,000,000. Construction began in 2003 and was completed in 2005. The following are a series of independent situations, numbered 1 through 6, involving differing costs for the project. All costs are stated in thousands of dollars.

Situation	Costs Incurred During Year			Estimated Costs to Complete (As of the End of the Year)		
	2003	2004	2005	2003	2004	2005
1	1,500	2,100	900	3,000	900	—
2	1,500	900	2,400	3,000	2,400	—
3	1,500	2,100	1,600	3,000	1,500	—
4	500	3,000	1,000	3,500	875	—
5	500	3,000	1,300	3,500	1,500	—
6	500	3,000	1,800	4,600	1,700	—

Required:
Copy and complete the following table.

	Gross Profit (Loss) Recognized					
	Percentage-of-Completion			Completed Contract		
Situation	2003	2004	2005	2003	2004	2005
1						
2						
3						
4						
5						
6						

E 5–11
Percentage-of-completion method; solve for unknowns

In 2003, Long Construction Corporation began construction work under a three-year contract. The contract price is $1,600,000. Long uses the percentage-of-completion method for financial reporting purposes. The financial statement presentation relating to this contract at December 31, 2003, is as follows:

Balance Sheet

Accounts receivable (from construction progress billings)		$30,000
Construction in progress	$100,000	
Less: Billings on construction contract	(94,000)	
Cost of uncompleted contracts in excess of billings		6,000

Income Statement

Income (before tax) on the contract recognized in 2003	$20,000

Required:
1. What was the cost of construction actually incurred in 2003?
2. How much cash was collected in 2003 on this contract?
3. What was the estimated cost to complete as of the end of 2003?
4. What was the estimated percentage of completion used to calculate income in 2003?

(AICPA adapted)

E 5–12
Revenue recognition; software

The Easywrite Software Company shipped software to a customer on July 1, 2003. The arrangement with the customer also requires the company to provide technical support over the next 12 months and to ship an expected software upgrade on January 1, 2004. The total contract price is $243,000, and Easywrite estimates that the individual fair values of the components of the arrangement if sold separately would be:

Software	$210,000
Technical support	30,000
Upgrade	30,000

Required:
1. Determine the timing of revenue recognition for the $243,000.
2. Assume that the $243,000 contract price was paid in advance on July 1, 2003. Prepare a journal entry to record the cash receipt. Do not worry about the cost of the items sold.

E 5–13
Franchise sales; revenue recognition

On October 1, 2003, the Submarine Sandwich Company entered into a franchise agreement with an individual. In exchange for an initial franchise fee of $200,000, Submarine will provide initial services to the franchisee to include assistance in design and construction of the building, help in training employees, help in obtaining financing, and management advice over the first five years of the 10-year franchise agreement.

10% of the initial franchise fee is payable on October 1, 2003, with the remaining $180,000 payable in nine equal annual installments beginning on October 1, 2004. These installments will include interest at an appropriate rate. The franchise opened for business on January 15, 2004.

Required:
Assume that the initial services to be performed by Submarine Sandwich subsequent to October 1, 2003, are substantial and that collectibility of the installment receivable is reasonably certain. Substantial performance of the initial services is deemed to have occurred when the franchise opened. Prepare the necessary journal entries for the following dates (ignoring interest charges):
1. October 1, 2003
2. January 15, 2004

E 5–14
Multiple choice; revenue recognition

The following questions dealing with revenue recognition are adapted from questions that appeared on recent CPA examinations. Determine the response that best completes the statements or questions.
1. Drew Co. produces expensive equipment for sale on installment contracts. When there is doubt about eventual collectibility, the income recognition method *least* likely to overstate income is
   a. At the time the equipment is completed.
   b. The installment method.
   c. The cost recovery method.
   d. At the time of delivery.
2. Hill Company began operations on January 1, 2003, and appropriately uses the installment method of accounting. Data available for 2003 are as follows:

Installment accounts receivable	$500,000
Installment sales	900,000
Cost of goods sold, as a percentage of sales	60%

Using the installment method, Hill's realized gross profit for 2003 would be

a. $360,000
b. $240,000
c. $200,000
d. $160,000

Questions 3 and 4 are based on the following data pertaining to Pell Co.'s construction jobs, which commenced during 2003:

	Project 1	Project 2
Contract price	$420,000	$300,000
Cost incurred during 2003	240,000	280,000
Estimated costs to complete	120,000	40,000
Billed to customers during 2003	150,000	270,000
Received from customers during 2003	90,000	250,000

3.   If Pell used the completed contract method, what amount of gross profit (loss) would Pell report in its 2003 income statement?

a. $(20,000)
b. $0
c. $340,000
d. $420,000

4.   If Pell used the percentage-of-completion method, what amount of gross profit (loss) would Pell report in its 2003 income statement?

a. $(20,000)
b. $20,000
c. $22,500
d. $40,000

E 5–15
Concepts; terminology

Listed below are several terms and phrases associated with revenue recognition and profitability analysis. Pair each item from List A (by letter) with the item from List B that is most appropriately associated with it.

List A	List B
____ 1. Inventory turnover	a. Net income divided by net sales.
____ 2. Return on assets	b. Defers recognition until cash collected equals cost.
____ 3. Return on shareholders' equity	c. Defers recognition until project is complete.
____ 4. Profit margin on sales	d. Net income divided by assets.
____ 5. Cost recovery method	e. Risks and rewards of ownership retained by seller.
____ 6. Percentage-of-completion method	f. Contra account to construction in progress.
____ 7. Completed contract method	g. Net income divided by shareholders' equity.
____ 8. Asset turnover	h. Cost of goods sold divided by inventory.
____ 9. Receivables turnover	i. Recognition is in proportion to work completed.
____ 10. Right of return	j. Recognition is in proportion to cash received.
____ 11. Billings on construction contract	k. Net sales divided by assets.
____ 12. Installment sales method	l. Net sales divided by accounts receivable.
____ 13. Consignment sales	m. Could cause the deferral of revenue recognition beyond delivery point.

E 5–16
Inventory turnover; calculation and evaluation

The following is a portion of the condensed income statement for Rowan, Inc., a manufacturer of plastic containers:

Net sales		$2,460,000
Less: Cost of goods sold:		
Inventory, January 1	$ 630,000	
Net purchases	1,800,000	
Inventory, December 31	(690,000)	1,740,000
Gross profit		$ 720,000

Required:
1. Determine Rowan's inventory turnover.
2. What information does this ratio provide?

E 5–17
Evaluating efficiency of asset management

The 2003 income statement of Anderson Medical Supply Company reported net sales of $8 million, cost of goods sold of $4.8 million, and net income of $800,000. The following table shows the company's comparative balance sheets for 2003 and 2002:

	($ in 000s)	
	2003	**2002**
Assets		
Cash	$ 300	$ 380
Accounts receivable	700	500
Inventory	900	700
Property, plant, and equipment (net)	2,400	2,120
Total assets	$4,300	$3,700
Liabilities and Shareholders' Equity		
Current liabilities	$ 960	$ 830
Bonds payable	1,200	1,200
Paid-in capital	1,000	1,000
Retained earnings	1,140	670
Total liabilities and shareholders' equity	$4,300	$3,700

Some industry averages for Anderson's line of business are

Inventory turnover	5 times
Average collection period	25 days
Asset turnover	1.8 times

Required:
Assess Anderson's asset management relative to its industry.

E 5–18
Profitability ratios

The following condensed information was reported by Peabody Toys, Inc., for 2003 and 2002:

	($ in 000s)	
	2003	**2002**
Income statement information		
Net sales	$5,400	$4,200
Net income	150	124
Balance sheet information		
Current assets	$ 800	$ 750
Property, plant, and equipment (net)	1,100	950
Total assets	$1,900	$1,700
Current liabilities	$ 600	$ 450
Long-term liabilities	750	750
Paid-in capital	400	400
Retained earnings	150	100
Liabilities and shareholders' equity	$1,900	$1,700

Required:
1. Determine the following ratios for 2003:
   a. Profit margin on sales
   b. Return on assets
   c. Return on shareholders' equity
2. Determine the amount of dividends paid to shareholders during 2003.

E 5–19
Interim financial
statements; income tax
expense
[Based on Appendix 5]

Joplin Laminating Corporation reported income before income taxes during the first three quarters and management's estimates of the annual effective tax rate at the end of each quarter as shown below:

	Quarter		
	First	**Second**	**Third**
Income before income taxes	$50,000	$40,000	$100,000
Estimated annual effective tax rate	34%	30%	36%

Required:
Determine the income tax expense to be reported in the income statement in each of the three quarterly reports.

E 5–20
Interim reporting;
recognizing expenses
[Based on Appendix 5]

Security-Rand Corporation determines executive incentive compensation at the end of its fiscal year. At the end of the first quarter, management estimated that the amount will be $300 million. Depreciation expense for the year is expected to be $60 million. Also during the quarter, the company realized a gain of $23 million from selling two of its manufacturing plants.

Required:
What amounts for these items should be reported in the first quarter's income statement?

E 5–21
Interim financial
statements; reporting
expenses
[Based on Appendix 5]

Shields Company is preparing its interim report for the second quarter ending June 30. The following payments were made during the first two quarters:

Expenditure	**Date**	**Amount**
Annual advertising	January	$800,000
Property tax for the fiscal year	February	350,000
Annual equipment repairs	March	260,000
Extraordinary casualty loss	April	185,000
Research and development	May	96,000

Required:
For each expenditure indicate the amount that would be reported in the quarterly income statements for the periods ending March 31, June 30, September 30, and December 31.

PROBLEMS

P 5–1
Income statement
presentation;
installment sales
method (Chapters 4
and 5)

The Reagan Corporation computed income from continuing operations before income taxes of $4,200,000 for 2003. The following material items have not yet been considered in the computation of income:

1. The company sold equipment and recognized a gain of $50,000. The equipment had been used in the manufacturing process and was replaced by new equipment.
2. In December, the company received a settlement of $1,000,000 for a lawsuit it had filed based on antitrust violations of a competitor. The settlement was considered to be an unusual and infrequent event.
3. Inventory costing $400,000 was written off as obsolete. Material losses of this type were incurred twice in the last eight years.
4. It was discovered that depreciation expense on the office building of $50,000 per year was not recorded in either 2002 or 2003.

In addition, you learn that *included* in revenues is $400,000 from installment sales made during the year. The cost of these sales is $240,000. At year-end, $100,000 in cash had been collected on the related installment receivables. Because of considerable uncertainty regarding the collectibility of receivables from these sales, the company's accountant should have used the installment sales method to recognize revenue and gross profit on these sales.

Also, the company's income tax rate is 40% and there were 1 million shares of common stock outstanding throughout the year.

Required:
Prepare an income statement for 2003 beginning with income from continuing operations before income taxes. Include appropriate EPS disclosures.

P 5–2
Installment sales and
cost recovery methods

The Ajax Company appropriately accounts for certain sales using the installment sales method. The perpetual inventory system is used. Information related to installment sales for 2003 and 2004 is as follows:

	2003	2004	
Sales	$300,000	$400,000	
Cost of sales	180,000	280,000	
Customer collections on:			
2003 sales	120,000	100,000	220,000
2004 sales		150,000	180,—
			40,—

GP = 0

Required:
1. Calculate the amount of gross profit that would be recognized each year from installment sales.
2. Prepare all necessary journal entries for each year.
3. Repeat requirements 1 and 2 assuming that Ajax uses the cost recovery method to account for its installment sales.

P 5–3
Installment sales;
alternative recognition
methods

On August 31, 2003, the Silva Company sold merchandise to the Bendix Corporation for $500,000. Terms of the sale called for a down payment of $100,000 and four annual installments of $100,000 due on each August 31, beginning August 31, 2004. Each installment also will include interest on the unpaid balance applying an appropriate interest rate. The book value of the merchandise on Silva's books on the date of sale was $300,000. The perpetual inventory system is used. The company's fiscal year-end is December 31.

Required:
1. Prepare a table showing the amount of gross profit to be recognized in each of the five years of the installment sale applying each of the following methods:
    a.   Point of delivery revenue recognition.
    b.   Installment sales method.
    c.   Cost recovery method.
2. Prepare journal entries for each of the five years applying the three revenue recognition methods listed in requirement 1. Ignore interest charges.
3. Prepare a partial balance sheet as of the end of 2003 and 2004 listing the items related to the installment sale applying each of the three methods listed in requirement 1.

P 5–4
Percentage-of-
completion method

In 2003, the Westgate Construction Company entered into a contract to construct a road for Santa Clara County for $10,000,000. The road was completed in 2005. Information related to the contract is as follows:

	2003	2004	2005
Cost incurred during the year	$2,400,000	$3,600,000	$2,200,000
Estimated costs to complete as of year-end	5,600,000	2,000,000	–0–
Billings during the year	2,000,000	4,000,000	4,000,000
Cash collections during the year	1,800,000	3,600,000	4,600,000

Westgate uses the percentage-of-completion method of accounting for long-term construction contracts.

Required:
1. Calculate the amount of gross profit to be recognized in each of the three years.
2. Prepare all necessary journal entries for each of the years (credit *various accounts* for construction costs incurred).
3. Prepare a partial balance sheet for 2003 and 2004 showing any items related to the contract.
4. Calculate the amount of gross profit to be recognized in each of the three years assuming the following costs incurred and costs to complete information:

	2003	2004	2005
Costs incurred during the year	$2,400,000	$3,800,000	$3,200,000
Estimated costs to complete as of year-end	5,600,000	3,100,000	–0–

5. Calculate the amount of gross profit to be recognized in each of the three years assuming the following costs incurred and costs to complete information:

	2003	2004	2005
Costs incurred during the year	$2,400,000	$3,800,000	$3,900,000
Estimated costs to complete as of year-end	5,600,000	4,100,000	–0–

P 5–5

Completed contract method

P 5–6

Construction accounting; loss projected on entire project

E**x**

[This is a variation of the previous problem modified to focus on the completed contract method.]

Required:

Complete the requirements of Problem 5–4 assuming that Westgate Construction uses the completed contract method.

Curtiss Construction Company, Inc. entered into a fixed-price contract with Axelrod Associates on July 1, 2003, to construct a four-story office building. At that time, Curtiss estimated that it would take between two and three years to complete the project. The total contract price for construction of the building is $4,000,000. Curtiss appropriately accounts for this contract under the completed contract method in its financial statements. The building was completed on December 31, 2005. Estimated percentage of completion, *accumulated* contract costs incurred, estimated costs to complete the contract, and *accumulated* billings to Axelrod under the contract were as follows:

	At 12-31-03	At 12-31-04	At 12-31-05
Percentage of completion	10%	60%	100%
Costs incurred to date	$ 350,000	$2,500,000	$4,250,000
Estimated costs to complete	3,150,000	1,700,000	–0–
Billings to Axelrod, to date	720,000	2,170,000	3,600,000

Required:

1. Prepare schedules to compute gross profit or loss to be recognized as a result of this contract for each of the three years.
2. Assuming Curtiss uses the percentage-of-completion method of accounting for long-term construction contracts, compute gross profit or loss to be recognized in each of the three years.
3. Assuming the percentage-of-completion method, compute the amount to be shown in the balance sheet at the end of 2003 and 2004 as either cost in excess of billings or billings in excess of costs.

(AICPA adapted)

P 5–7

Franchise sales; installment sales method

The Olive Branch Restaurant Corporation sells franchises throughout the western states. On January 30, 2003, the company entered into the following franchise agreement with Jim and Tammy Masters:

1. The initial franchise fee is $1.2 million. $200,000 is payable immediately and the remainder is due in 10, $100,000 installments plus 10% interest on the unpaid balance each January 30, beginning January 30, 2004. The 10% interest rate is an appropriate market rate.
2. In addition to allowing the franchisee to use the franchise name for the 10-year term of the agreement, in exchange for the initial fee Olive Branch agrees to assist the franchisee in selecting a location, obtaining financing, designing and constructing the restaurant building, and training employees.
3. All of the initial down payment of $200,000 is to be refunded by Olive Branch and the remaining obligation canceled if, for any reason, the franchisee fails to open the franchise.
4. In addition to the initial franchise fee, the franchisee is required to pay a monthly fee of 3% of franchise sales for advertising, promotion, menu planning, and other continuing services to be provided by Olive Branch over the life of the agreement. This fee is payable on the 10th of the following month.

Substantial performance of the initial services provided by Olive Branch, which are significant, is deemed to have occurred when the franchise opened on September 1, 2003. Franchise sales for the month of September 2003 were $40,000.

Required:

1. Assuming that collectibility of the installment receivable is reasonably certain, prepare the necessary journal entries for Olive Branch on the following dates (ignore interest charges on the installment receivable and the costs of providing franchise services):
   a. January 30, 2003
   b. September 1, 2003
   c. September 30, 2003
   d. January 30, 2004
2. Assume that significant uncertainty exists as to the collection of the installment receivable and that Olive Branch elects to recognize initial franchise fee revenue using the installment sales method. Prepare the necessary journal entries for the dates listed in requirement 1 (ignore interest charges on the installment receivable and the costs of providing franchise services).

P 5–8
Calculating activity and
profitability ratios

Financial statements for Askew Industries for 2003 are shown below:

2003 Income Statement
($ in 000s)

Sales	$9,000
Cost of goods sold	(6,300)
Gross profit	2,700
Operating expenses	(2,000)
Interest expense	(200)
Tax expense	(200)
Net income	$ 300

Comparative Balance Sheets

	Dec. 31	
	2003	**2002**
Assets		
Cash	$ 600	$ 500
Accounts receivable	600	400
Inventory	800	600
Property, plant, and equipment (net)	2,000	2,100
	$4,000	$3,600
Liabilities and Shareholders' Equity		
Current liabilities	$1,100	$ 850
Bonds payable	1,400	1,400
Paid-in capital	600	600
Retained earnings	900	750
	$4,000	$3,600

Required:
Calculate the following ratios for 2003.
1. Inventory turnover ratio
2. Average days in inventory
3. Receivables turnover ratio
4. Average collection period
5. Asset turnover ratio
6. Profit margin on sales
7. Return on assets
8. Return on shareholders' equity

P 5–9
Use of ratios to
compare two
companies in the
same industry

Presented below are condensed financial statements adapted from those of two actual companies competing in the pharmaceutical industry—Johnson and Johnson (J&J) and Pfizer, Inc. ($ in millions, except per share amounts).

Required:
Evaluate and compare the two companies by responding to the following questions.
  Note: Because two-year comparative statements are not provided, you should use year-end balances in place of average balances as appropriate.
1. Which of the two companies appears more efficient in collecting its accounts receivable and managing its inventory?
2. Which of the two firms had greater earnings relative to resources available?
3. Have the two companies achieved their respective rates of return on assets with similar combinations of profit margin and turnover?
4. From the perspective of a common shareholder, which of the two firms provided a greater rate of return?

Balance Sheets

	J&J	Pfizer
Assets:		
Cash	$ 3,411	$ 1,099
Short-term investments	2,333	5,764
Accounts receivable (net)	4,464	5,489

Inventories	2,842	2,702
Other current assets	2,400	2,133
Current assets	$15,450	$17,187
Property, plant, and equipment (net)	6,971	9,425
Intangibles and other assets	8,900	6,898
Total assets	$31,321	$33,510
Liabilities and Shareholders' Equity:		
Accounts payable	$ 2,083	$ 1,719
Short-term notes	1,479	4,289
Other current liabilities	3,578	5,973
Current liabilities	7,140	11,981
Long-term debt	2,037	1,123
Other long-term liabilities	3,336	4,330
Total liabilities	12,513	17,434
Common stock (par and additional paid-in capital)	1,535	9,232
Retained earnings	18,812	19,599
Accumulated other comprehensive income (loss)	(470)	(1,515)
Less: treasury stock and other equity adjustments	(1,069)	(11,240)
Total shareholders' equity	18,808	16,076
Total liabilities and shareholders' equity	$31,321	$33,510

Income Statements

Net sales	$29,139	$29,574
Cost of goods sold	8,861	4,907
Gross profit	20,278	24,667
Operating expenses	13,822	19,134
Other (income) expense—net	(166)	(234)
Income before taxes	6,622	5,767
Tax expense	1,822	2,049
Net income	$ 4,800	$ 3,718*
Basic net income per share	$ 3.45	$ 0.60

*This is before income from discontinued operations. There were no other separately reported items for either company.

P 5–10
Creating a balance sheet from ratios;
Chapters 3 and 5

The Cadux Candy Company's income statement for the year ended December 31, 2003, reported interest expense of $2 million and income tax expense of $12 million. Current assets listed in its balance sheet include cash, accounts receivable, and inventories. Property, plant, and equipment is the company's only noncurrent asset. Financial ratios for 2003 are listed below. Profitability and turnover ratios with balance sheet items in the denominator were calculated using year-end balances rather than averages.

Debt to equity ratio	1.0
Current ratio	2.0
Acid-test ratio	1.0
Times interest earned ratio	17 times
Return on assets	10%
Return on shareholders' equity	20%
Profit margin on sales	5%
Gross profit margin	
(gross profit divided by net sales)	40%
Inventory turnover	8 times
Receivables turnover	20 times

Required:
Prepare a December 31, 2003, balance sheet for the Cadux Candy Company.

P 5–11

Compare two companies in the same industry; Chapters 3 and 5

Presented below are condensed financial statements adapted from those of two actual companies competing as the primary players in a specialty area of the food manufacturing and distribution industry. ($ in millions, except per share amounts.)

Balance Sheets

Assets	Metropolitan	Republic
Cash	$ 179.3	$ 37.1
Accounts receivable (net)	422.7	325.0
Short-term investments	—	4.7
Inventories	466.4	635.2
Prepaid expenses and other current assets	134.6	476.7
Current assets	$1,203.0	$1,478.7
Property, plant, and equipment (net)	2,608.2	2,064.6
Intangibles and other assets	210.3	464.7
Total assets	$4,021.5	$4,008.0
Liabilities and Shareholders' Equity		
Accounts payable	$ 467.9	$ 691.2
Short-term notes	227.1	557.4
Accruals and other current liabilities	585.2	538.5
Current liabilities	$1,280.2	$1,787.1
Long-term debt	535.6	542.3
Deferred tax liability	384.6	610.7
Other long-term liabilities	104.0	95.1
Total liabilities	$2,304.4	$3,035.2
Common stock (par and additional paid-in capital)	144.9	335.0
Retained earnings	2,476.9	1,601.9
Less: treasury stock	(904.7)	(964.1)
Total liabilities and shareholders' equity	$4,021.5	$4,008.0

Income Statements

	Metropolitan	Republic
Net sales	$5,698.0	$7,768.2
Cost of goods sold	(2,909.0)	(4,481.7)
Gross profit	$2,789.0	$3,286.5
Operating expenses	(1,743.7)	(2,539.2)
Interest expense	(56.8)	(46.6)
Income before taxes	$ 988.5	$ 700.7
Tax expense	(394.7)	(276.1)
Net income	$ 593.8	$ 424.6
Net income per share	$ 2.40	$ 6.50

Required:

Evaluate and compare the two companies by responding to the following questions.

Note: Because comparative statements are not provided you should use year-end balances in place of average balances as appropriate.

1. Which of the two firms had greater earnings relative to resources available?
2. Have the two companies achieved their respective rates of return on assets with similar combinations of profit margin and turnover?
3. From the perspective of a common shareholder, which of the two firms provided a greater rate of return?
4. Which company is most highly leveraged and which has made most effective use of financial leverage?
5. Of the two companies, which appears riskier in terms of its ability to pay short-term obligations?
6. How efficiently are current assets managed?
7. From the perspective of a creditor, which company offers the most comfortable margin of safety in terms of its ability to pay fixed interest charges?

P 5–12
Interim financial
reporting
(Based on Appendix 5)

Branson Electronics Company is a small, publicly traded company preparing its first quarter interim report to be mailed to shareholders. The following information for the quarter has been compiled:

Revenues		$180,000
Cost of goods sold		35,000
Operating expenses:		
Fixed	$59,000	
Variable	48,000	107,000

Fixed operating expenses include payments of $50,000 to an advertising firm to promote the firm through various media throughout the year. The income tax rate for the firm's level of operations in the first quarter is 30%, but management estimates the effective rate for the entire year will be 36%.

Required:
Prepare the income statement to be included in Branson's first quarter interim report.

BROADEN YOUR PERSPECTIVE

Apply your critical-thinking ability to the knowledge you've gained. These cases will provide you an opportunity to develop your research, analysis, judgment, and communication skills. You also will work with other students, integrate what you've learned, apply it in real world situations, and consider its global and ethical ramifications. This practice will broaden your knowledge and further develop your decision-making abilities.

Real World Case 5–1
Chainsaw Al; Revenue
recognition and
earnings management

In May 2001, the Securities and Exchange Commission sued the former top executives at Sunbeam, charging the group with financial reporting fraud that allegedly cost investors billions in losses. Sunbeam Corporation is a recognized designer, manufacturer, and marketer of household and leisure products, including Coleman, Eastpak, First Alert, Grillmaster, Mixmaster, Mr. Coffee, Oster, Powermate, and Campingaz. In the mid-1990s, Sunbeam needed help: its profits had declined by over 80% percent, and in 1996, its stock price was down over 50% from its high. To the rescue: Albert Dunlap, also known as "Chainsaw Al" based on his reputation as a ruthless executive known for his ability to restructure and turn around troubled companies, largely by eliminating jobs.

The strategy appeared to work. In 1997, Sunbeam's revenues had risen by 18 percent. However, in April 1998, the brokerage firm of Paine Webber downgraded Sunbeam's stock recommendation. Why the downgrade? Paine Webber had noticed unusually high accounts receivable, massive increases in sales of electric blankets in the third quarter 1997, which usually sell best in the fourth quarter, as well as unusually high sales of barbeque grills for the fourth quarter. Soon after, Sunbeam announced a first quarter loss of $44.6 million, and Sunbeam's stock price fell 25 percent.

It eventually came to light that Dunlap and Sunbeam had been using a "bill and hold" strategy with retail buyers. This involved selling products at large discounts to retailers before they normally would buy and then holding the products in third-party warehouses, with delivery at a later date.

Many felt Sunbeam had deceived shareholders by artificially inflating earnings and the company's stock price. A class-action lawsuit followed, alleging that Sunbeam and Dunlap violated federal securities laws, suggesting the motivation to inflate the earnings and stock price was to allow Sunbeam to complete hundreds of millions of dollars of debt financing in order to complete some ongoing mergers. Shareholders alleged damages when Sunbeam's subsequent earnings decline caused a huge drop in the stock price.

Required:
1. How might Sunbeam's 1997 "bill and hold" strategy have contributed to artificially high earnings in 1997?
2. How would the strategy have led to the unusually high accounts receivable Paine Webber noticed?
3. How might Sunbeam's 1997 "bill and hold" strategy have contributed to a 1998 earnings decline?
4. How does earnings management of this type affect earnings quality?

Judgment Case 5–2
Revenue recognition

Revenue earned by a business enterprise is recognized for accounting purposes at different times, according to the circumstances. In some situations revenue is recognized approximately as it is earned in the economic sense. In other situations revenue is recognized at point of delivery.

Required:

1. Explain and justify why revenue often is recognized as earned at point of delivery.
2. Explain in what situations it would be useful to recognize revenue as the productive activity takes place.
3. At what times, other than those included in (1) and (2) above, may it be appropriate to recognize revenue?

Judgment Case 5–3
Revenue recognition; trade-ins

The Apex Computer Company manufactures and sells large, mainframe computers. The computers range in price from $1 to $3 million and gross profit averages 40% of sales price. The company has a liberal trade-in policy. Customers are allowed to trade in their computers for a new generation machine anytime within three years of sale. The trade-in allowance granted will vary depending on the number of years between original sale and trade-in. However, in all cases, the allowance is expected to be approximately 25% higher than the prevailing market price of the computer.

As an example, in 2003 a customer who purchased a computer in 2001 for $2 million (the computer cost Apex $1,200,000 to manufacture) decided to trade it in for a new computer. The sales price of the new computer was $2.5 million and a trade-in allowance of $600,000 was granted on the old machine. As a result of the trade-in allowance, the customer had to pay only $1.9 million ($2.5 million less $600,000) for the new computer. The old computer taken back by Apex had a resale value of $480,000. The new computer cost $1.5 million to manufacture. The company accounted for the trade-in by recognizing revenue of $2,380,000 ($1.9 million received in cash + $480,000 value of old computer).

Required:
Does the company's revenue recognition policy for trade-ins seem appropriate? If not, describe the problem created by the liberal trade-in policy.

Communication Case 5–4
Revenue recognition

Jerry's Ice Cream Parlor is considering a marketing plan to increase sales of ice cream cones. The plan will give customers a free ice cream cone if they buy 10 ice cream cones at regular prices. Customers will be issued a card that will be punched each time an ice cream cone is purchased. After 10 punches, the card can be turned in for a free cone.

Jerry Donovan, the company's owner, is not sure how the new plan will affect accounting procedures. He realizes that the company will be incurring costs each time a free ice cream cone is awarded, but there will be no corresponding revenue or cash inflow.

The focus of this case is the matching of revenues and expenses related to the free ice cream cones that will be awarded if the new plan is adopted. Your instructor will divide the class into two to six groups depending on the size of the class. The mission of your group is to reach consensus on the appropriate accounting treatment for the new plan.

Required:

1. Each group member should deliberate the situation independently and draft a tentative argument prior to the class session for which the case is assigned.
2. In class, each group will meet for 10–15 minutes in different areas of the classroom. During that meeting, group members will take turns sharing their suggestions for the purpose of arriving at a single group treatment.
3. After the allotted time, a spokesperson for each group (selected during the group meetings) will share the group's solution with the class. The goal of the class is to incorporate the views of each group into a consensus approach to the situation.

Research Case 5–5
Revenue recognition

An article in *BusinessWeek* entitled "Numbers Game at Bausch & Lomb?" questions the company's method of recognizing revenue resulting from a 1993 change in sales strategy. The article considers the possibility that the company ". . . may have used dubious methods to inflate year-end sales."

Required:

1. In your library or from some other source, locate the indicated article in *BusinessWeek*, December 19, 1994.
2. Describe the change in sales strategy in question and the revenue recognition controversy it created.
3. What alternative method might Bausch & Lomb have used to recognize revenue from the controversial sales?

Ethics Case 5–6
Revenue recognition

The Horizon Corporation manufactures personal computers. The company began operations in 1996 and reported profits for the years 1998 through 2001. Due primarily to increased competition and price slashing in the industry, 2002's income statement reported a loss of $20 million. Just before the end of the 2003 fiscal year, a memo from the company's chief financial officer to Jim Fielding, the company controller, included the following comments:

If we don't do something about the large amount of unsold computers already manufactured, our auditors will require us to write them off. The resulting loss for 2003 will cause a violation of our debt covenants and force the company into bankruptcy. I suggest that you ship half of our inventory to J.B. Sales, Inc., in Oklahoma City. I know the company's president and he will accept the merchandise and acknowledge the shipment as a purchase. We can record the sale in 2003 which will boost profits to an acceptable level. Then J.B. Sales will simply return the merchandise in 2004 after the financial statements have been issued.

Required:
Discuss the ethical dilemma faced by Jim Fielding.

Judgment Case 5–7
Revenue recognition; installment sale

On October 1, 2003, the Marshall Company sold a large piece of machinery to the Hammond Construction Company for $80,000. The cost of the machine was $40,000. Hammond made a down payment of $10,000 and agreed to pay the remaining balance in seven equal monthly installments of $10,000, plus interest at 12% on the unpaid balance, beginning November 1.

Required:
1. Identify three alternative methods for recognizing revenue and costs for the situation described and compute the amount of gross profit that would be recognized in 2003 using each method.
2. Discuss the circumstances under which each of the three methods would be used.

Research Case 5–8
Locate and extract relevant information and authoritative support for a financial reporting issue; revenue recognition; right of return

Many companies sell products allowing their customers the right to return merchandise if they are not satisfied. Because the return of merchandise can retroactively negate the benefits of having made a sale, the seller must meet certain criteria before revenue is recognized in situations when the right of return exists. *SFAS No. 48,* "Revenue Recognition When Right of Return Exists," lists the criteria, the most critical of which is that the seller must be able to make reliable estimates of future returns.

Required:
1. Obtain the original *SFAS No. 48.* You might gain access through FARS, the FASB Financial Accounting Research System, from your school library, or some other source.
2. What factors does the standard discuss that may impair the ability to make a reasonable estimate of returns?
3. List all six criteria that must be met before revenue can be recognized when the right of return exists.
4. Using Edgarscan (**edgarscan.pwcglobal.com**) access the 10-K reports for the most recent fiscal year for Hewlett Packard Company and for Advanced Micro Devices, Inc. Search for the revenue recognition policy to determine when these two companies recognize revenue for product sales allowing customers the right of return.
5. Using your answers to requirements 2 and 3, speculate as to why the two revenue recognition policies differ.

Judgment Case 5–9
Revenue recognition; service sales

Each of the following situations concerns revenue recognition for services.
1. Delta Airlines books a reservation for a roundtrip flight to Orlando for Ming Tsai on April 12. Delta charges the $425 to Tsai's Visa card on April 13 and receives the cash from Visa on May 1. The roundtrip flight commences on May 15. The ticket is nonrefundable.
2. Highlife Ski Resort in Colorado sells a season pass to Larry Werner on October 15. Highlife usually opens its season just after Thanksgiving and stays open until approximately April 30.
3. Dixon Management requires tenants to sign a three-year lease and charges $5,000 per month for one floor in its midtown high-rise. In addition to the monthly fee, payable at the beginning of each month, tenants pay a nonrefundable fee of $12,000 to secure the lease.
4. Janora Hawkins, attorney, agrees to accept an accident victim's case. Hawkins will be paid on a contingency basis. That is, if she wins the case, she will receive 30% of the total settlement. The case commences on July 15 and is settled successfully on August 28. On September 15 Hawkins receives her contingency payment of $60,000.

Required:
For each of the above situations, determine the appropriate timing of revenue recognition.

Judgment Case 5–10
Revenue recognition; long-term construction contracts

Two accounting students were discussing the alternative methods of accounting for long-term construction contracts. The discussion focused on which method was most like the typical revenue recognition method of recognizing revenue at point of product delivery. Bill argued that the completed contract method was preferable because it was analogous to recognizing revenue at the point of delivery. John disagreed and supported the percentage-of-completion method, stating that it was analogous to accruing revenue during the earnings process, that is, as the work was performed.

Required:
Discuss the arguments made by both students. Which argument do you support? Why?

Communication Case 5–11
Percentage-of-completion and completed contract methods

Willingham Construction is in the business of building high-priced, custom, single-family homes. The company, headquartered in Anaheim, California, operates throughout the Southern California area. The construction period for the average home built by Willingham is six months, although some homes have taken as long as nine months.

You have just been hired by Willingham as the assistant controller and one of your first tasks is to evaluate the company's revenue recognition policy. The company presently uses the completed contract method for all of its projects and management is now considering a switch to the percentage-of-completion method.

Required:
Write a 1- to 2-page memo to Virginia Reynolds, company controller, describing the differences between the percentage-of-completion and completed contract methods. Be sure to include references to GAAP as they pertain to the choice of method. Do not address the differential effects on income taxes nor the effect on the financial statements of switching between methods.

International Case 5–12
Comparison of revenue recognition in Sweden and the United States

Electrolux, headquartered in Sweden, is the European leader in food-service equipment and the second largest producer in the world. The revenue recognition disclosure, included in a recent financial statement, is reproduced below.

Other Accounting and Valuation Principles (in part)
Revenue recognition
Sales of products and services are recorded as of the date of shipment. Sales include the sales value less VAT (Value-Added Tax), individual sales taxes, returns and trade discounts.

In most cases, sales of projects are not reported as operating income until the project has been fully invoiced. In certain exceptional cases referring to particularly large projects extending over several accounting years, revenue is recognized while the project is in progress, on condition that revenue can be computed for the part of the project that has been completed and that this contributes to a more accurate timing of group income and expense.

Required:
On the basis of the information the disclosures provide, compare revenue recognition in Sweden with that in the United States.

Trueblood Accounting Case 5–13
Revenue recognition; license agreement

The following Trueblood case is recommended for use with this chapter. The case provides an excellent opportunity for class discussion, group projects, and writing assignments. The case, along with Professor's Discussion Material, can be obtained from the Deloitte Foundation at its website: www.deloitte.com/more/DTF/cases_subj.htm.

Case 01-5: *The Daily Grind*

This case concerns the appropriate timing of revenue recognition for a license agreement.

Real World Case 5–14
Revenue recognition; franchise sales

EDGAR, the Electronic Data Gathering, Analysis, and Retrieval system, performs automated collection, validation, indexing, and forwarding of submissions by companies and others who are required by law to file forms with the U.S. Securities and Exchange Commission (SEC). All publicly traded domestic companies use EDGAR to make the majority of their filings. (Some foreign companies file voluntarily.) Form 10-K or 10-KSB, which include the annual report, is required to be filed on EDGAR. The SEC makes this information available on the Internet.

Required:
1. Access EDGAR on the Internet. The web address is www.sec.gov. Edgarscan (edgarscan.pwcglobal.com) from PricewaterhouseCoopers makes the process of accessing data from EDGAR easier.
2. Search for Jack in the Box, Inc. Access the most recent 10-K filing. Search or scroll to find the financial statements and related notes.
3. Answer the following questions related to the company's revenue recognition policies:
   a. How much is the usual initial franchise license fee per restaurant?
   b. When does the company recognize this initial franchise license fee revenue?
   c. How are continuing fees determined?
4. Repeat requirements 2 and 3 for two additional companies that you suspect also earn revenues through the sale of franchise rights. Compare their revenue recognition policies with the policies of Jack in the Box.

Analysis Case 5–15
Evaluating profitability and asset management; obtain and compare annual reports from companies in the same industry

Performance and profitability of a company often are evaluated using the financial information provided by a firm's annual report in comparison with other firms in the same industry. Ratios are useful in this assessment.

Required:

Obtain annual reports from two corporations in the same primary industry. Using techniques you learned in this chapter and any analysis you consider useful, respond to the following questions:

1. How do earnings trends compare in terms of both the direction and stability of income?
2. Which of the two firms had greater earnings relative to resources available?
3. How efficiently are current assets managed?
4. Has each of the companies achieved its respective rate of return on assets with similar combinations of profit margin and turnover?
5. Are there differences in accounting methods that should be taken into account when making comparisons?

   Note: You can obtain copies of annual reports from friends who are shareholders, the investor relations department of the corporations, from a friendly stockbroker, or from EDGAR (Electronic Data Gathering, Analysis, and Retrieval) on the Internet (**www.sec.gov** or through Edgarscan at **edgarscan.pwcglobal.com**).

Judgment Case 5–16
Relationships among ratios; Chapters 3 and 5

You are a part-time financial advisor. A client is considering an investment in common stock of a waste recycling firm. One motivation is a rumor the client heard that the company made huge investments in a new fuel creation process. Unable to confirm the rumor, your client asks you to determine whether the firm's assets had recently increased significantly.

   Because the firm is small, information is sparse. Last quarter's interim report showed total assets of $324 million, approximately the same as last year's annual report. The only information more current than that is a press release last week in which the company's management reported "record net income for the year of $21 million, representing a 14.0% return on shareholders' equity. Performance was enhanced by the Company's judicious use of financial leverage on a debt/equity ratio of 2 to 1."

Required:

Use the information available to provide your client with an opinion as to whether the waste recycling firm invested in the new fuel creation process during the last quarter of the year.

Integrating Case 5–17
Using ratios to test reasonableness of data; Chapters 3 and 5

You are a new staff accountant with a large regional CPA firm, participating in your first audit. You recall from your auditing class that CPAs often use ratios to test the reasonableness of accounting numbers provided by the client. Since ratios reflect the relationships among various account balances, if it is assumed that prior relationships still hold, prior years' ratios can be used to estimate what current balances should approximate. However, you never actually performed this kind of analysis until now. The CPA in charge of the audit of Covington Pike Corporation brings you the list of ratios shown below and tells you these reflect the relationships maintained by Covington Pike in recent years.

profit margin on sales = 5%
return on assets = 7.5%
gross profit margin = 40%
inventory turnover ratio = 6 times
receivables turnover ratio = 25
acid-test ratio = .9
current ratio = 2 to 1
return on shareholders' equity = 10%
debt to equity ratio = 1/3
times interest earned ratio = 12 times

Jotted in the margins are the following notes:

- Net income $15,000
- Only one short-term note ($5,000); all other current liabilities are trade accounts
- Property, plant, and equipment are the only noncurrent assets
- Bonds payable are the only noncurrent liabilities
- The effective interest rate on short-term notes and bonds is 8%
- No investment securities
- Cash balance totals $15,000

Required:

You are requested to approximate the current year's balances in the form of a balance sheet and income statement, to the extent the information allows. Accompany those financial statements with the calculations you use to estimate each amount reported.

Analysis Case 5–18
Revenue recognition; profitability analysis

FedEx Corporation

Refer to the financial statements and related disclosure notes of FedEx Corporation in the appendix to Chapter 1.

Required:

1. What method does the company use to recognize revenue?
2. What percentage of total 2001 revenues was generated by international operations? (Hint: see Note 11.)
3. Compute the following ratios for 2001:
    a.   Receivables turnover ratio
    b.   Profit margin on sales
    c.   Return on assets
    d.   Return on shareholders' equity

6

Time Value of Money Concepts

CHAPTER

OVERVIEW

Time value of money concepts, specifically future value and present value, are essential in a variety of accounting situations. These concepts and the related computational procedures are the subjects of this chapter. Present values and future values of *single amounts* and present values and future values of *annuities* (series of equal periodic payments) are described separately but shown to be interrelated.

LEARNING OBJECTIVES

After studying this chapter, you should be able to:

LO1 Explain the difference between simple and compound interest.

LO2 Compute the future value of a single amount.

LO3 Compute the present value of a single amount.

LO4 Solve for either the interest rate or the number of compounding periods when present value and future value of a single amount are known.

LO5 Explain the difference between an ordinary annuity and an annuity due situation.

LO6 Compute the future value of both an ordinary annuity and an annuity due.

LO7 Compute the present value of an ordinary annuity, an annuity due, and a deferred annuity.

LO8 Solve for unknown values in annuity situations involving present value.

LO9 Briefly describe how the concept of the time value of money is incorporated into the valuation of bonds, long-term leases, and pension obligations.

John Smiley's Settlement[1]

On a rainy afternoon two years ago, John Smiley left work early to attend a family birthday party. Eleven minutes later, a careening truck slammed into his station wagon on the freeway causing John to spend two months in a coma. Now he can't hold a job or make everyday decisions and is in need of constant care. Last week, the 40-year old Smiley won an out-of-court settlement from the truck driver's company. He was given payment for all medical costs and attorney fees, plus a lump-sum settlement of $2,330,716. At the time of the accident, John was president of his family's business and earned approximately $200,000 per year. He had anticipated working 25 more years before retirement.

John's sister, an acquaintance of yours from college, has asked you to explain to her how the attorneys came up with the settlement amount. "They said it was based on his lost future income and a 7% rate of some kind," she explained. "But it was all 'legal-speak' to me."

> By the time you finish this chapter, you should be able to respond appropriately to the questions posed in this case. Compare your response to the solution provided at the end of the chapter.

QUESTIONS

1. How was the amount of the lump-sum settlement determined? Create a calculation that John's sister can look at. (page 288)

2. What are some of the accounting applications that also take into account the time value of money? (page 297)

---

[1]This case is adapted from an actual situation. Names are changed.

BASIC CONCEPTS

Time Value of Money

The *time value of money* means that money can be invested today to earn interest and grow to a larger dollar amount in the future.

The key to solving the problem described in the financial reporting case is an understanding of the concept commonly referred to as the **time value of money.** This concept means that money invested today will grow to a larger dollar amount in the future. For example, $100 invested in a savings account at your local bank yielding 6% annually will grow to $106 in one year. The difference between the $100 invested now—the present value of the investment—and its $106 future value represents the time value of money.

This concept has nothing to do with the worth or buying power of those dollars. Prices in our economy can change. If the inflation rate were higher than 6%, then the $106 you would have in the savings account actually would be worth less than the $100 you had a year earlier. The time value of money concept concerns only the growth in the dollar amounts of money.

Time value of money concepts are useful in valuing several assets and liabilities.

The concepts you will learn in this chapter are useful in solving many business decisions such as, for example, the determination of the accident settlement award presented in the financial reporting case. More important, the concepts also are necessary when valuing assets and liabilities for financial reporting purposes. As you will see in this and subsequent chapters, most accounting applications that incorporate the time value of money involve the concept of present value. The valuation of leases, bonds, pension obligations, and certain notes receivable and payable are a few prominent examples. It is important that you master the concepts and tools we review here. This knowledge is essential to the remainder of your accounting education.

SIMPLE VERSUS COMPOUND INTEREST

LO1

Interest is the "rent" paid for the use of money for some period of time. In dollar terms, it is the amount of money paid or received in excess of the amount of money borrowed or lent. If you lent the bank $100 today and "received" $106 a year from now, your interest earned would be $6. Interest also can be expressed as a rate at which money will grow. In this case, that rate is 6%. It is this interest that gives money its time value.

Interest is the amount of money paid or received in excess of the amount borrowed or lent.

Simple interest is computed by multiplying an initial investment times both the applicable interest rate and the period of time for which the money is used. For example, simple interest earned each year on a $1,000 investment paying 10% is $100 ($1,000 × 10%).

Compound interest includes interest not only on the initial investment but also on the accumulated interest in previous periods.

Compound interest results in increasingly larger interest amounts for each period of the investment. The reason is that interest is now being earned not only on the initial investment amount but also on the accumulated interest earned in previous periods.

For example, Cindy Johnson invested $1,000 in a savings account paying 10% interest *compounded* annually. How much interest will she earn each year, and what will be her investment balance after three years?

Date	Interest (Interest rate × Outstanding balance = Interest)	Balance
Initial deposit		$1,000
End of year 1	10% × $1,000 = $100	$1,100
End of year 2	10% × $1,100 = $110	$1,210
End of year 3	10% × $1,210 = $121	$1,331

With compound interest at 10% annually, the $1,000 investment would grow to $1,331 at the end of the three-year period. Of course, if Cindy withdrew the interest earned each year, she would earn only $100 in interest each year, that is, the amount of simple interest. If the investment period had been 20 years, 20 individual calculations would be needed. However, calculators, computer programs, and compound interest tables make these calculations much easier.

Most banks compound interest more frequently than once a year. Daily compounding is common for savings accounts. More rapid compounding has the effect of increasing the actual rate, which is called the **effective rate,** at which money grows per year. It is important to note that interest is typically stated as an annual rate regardless of the length of the compounding period involved. In situations when the compounding period is less than a year, the interest rate per compounding period is determined by dividing the annual rate by the number of periods. Assuming an annual rate of 12%:

Interest rates are typically stated as annual rates.

Compounded	Interest Rate Per Compounding Period
Semiannually	12% ÷ 2 = 6%
Quarterly	12% ÷ 4 = 3%
Monthly	12% ÷ 12 = 1%

As an example, now let's assume Cindy Johnson invested $1,000 in a savings account paying 10% interest *compounded* twice a year. There are two six-month periods paying interest at 5% (the annual rate divided by two periods). How much interest will she earn the first year, and what will be her investment balance at the end of the year?

The *effective yield* is the rate at which money actually will grow during a full year.

Date	Interest (Interest rate × Outstanding balance = Interest)	Balance
Initial deposit		$1,000.00
After six months	5% × $1,000 = $50.00	$1,050.00
End of year 1	5% × $1,050 = $52.50	$1,102.50

The $1,000 would grow by $102.50, the interest earned, to $1,102.50, $2.50 more than if interest were compounded only once a year. The effective annual interest rate, often referred to as the annual *yield,* is 10.25% ($102.50 ÷ $1,000).

Valuing a Single Cash Flow Amount

FUTURE VALUE OF A SINGLE AMOUNT

In the first Cindy example, in which $1,000 was invested for three years at 10% compounded annually, the $1,331 is referred to as the **future value (FV).** A time diagram is a useful way to visualize this relationship, with 0 indicating the date of the initial investment.

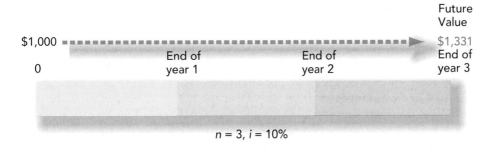

Future value of a single amount.

The future value after one year can be calculated as $1,000 × 1.10 (1.00 + .10) = $1,100. After three years, the future value is $1,000 × 1.10 × 1.10 × 1.10 = $1,331. In fact, the future value of any invested amount can be determined as follows:

$$FV = I\,(1 + i)^n$$

where: FV = Future value of the invested amount
  I = Amount invested at the beginning of the period
  i = Interest rate
  n = Number of compounding periods

The *future value* of a single amount is the amount of money that a dollar will grow to at some point in the future.

GRAPHIC 6–1
Future Value of $1
(excerpt from Table
6A–1, Appendix 6)

Periods (*n*)	Interest Rates (*i*)					
	7%	**8%**	**9%**	**10%**	**11%**	**12%**
1	1.07000	1.08000	1.09000	1.10000	1.11000	1.12000
2	1.14490	1.16640	1.18810	1.21000	1.23210	1.25440
3	1.22504	1.25971	1.29503	1.33100	1.36763	1.40493
4	1.31080	1.36049	1.41158	1.46410	1.51807	1.57352
5	1.40255	1.46933	1.53862	1.61051	1.68506	1.76234
6	1.50073	1.58687	1.67710	1.77156	1.87041	1.97382
7	1.60578	1.71382	1.82804	1.94872	2.07616	2.21068
8	1.71819	1.85093	1.99256	2.14359	2.30454	2.47596

The future value can be determined by using Table 6A–1, Future Value of $1, in Appendix 6 on page 302. The table contains the future value of $1 invested for various periods of time, *n,* and at various rates, *i.*

With this table, it's easy to determine the future value of any invested amount simply by multiplying it by the table value at the *intersection* of the column for the desired rate and the row for the number of compounding periods. Graphic 6–1 contains an excerpt from Table 6A–1.

The table shows various values of $(1 + i)^n$ for different combinations of *i* and *n*. From the table you can find the future value factor for three periods at 10% to be 1.331. This means that $1 invested at 10% compounded annually will grow to approximately $1.33 in three years. So, the future value of $1,000 invested for three years at 10% is $1,331:

$$FV = I \times FV \text{ factor}$$
$$FV = \$1,000 \times 1.331^* = \$1,331$$
*Future value of $1; n = 3, i = 10%

The future value function in financial calculators or in computer spreadsheet programs calculates future values in the same way. Determining future values (and present values) electronically avoids the need for tables such as those in the chapter appendix. It's important to remember that the *n* in the future value formula refers to the number of compounding periods, not necessarily the number of years. For example, suppose you wanted to know the future value *two* years from today of $1,000 invested at 12% with *quarterly* compounding. The number of periods is therefore eight and the compounding rate is 3% (12% annual rate divided by four, the number of quarters in a year). The future value factor from Table 6A–1 is 1.26677, so the future value is $1,266.77 ($1,000 × 1.26677).[2]

PRESENT VALUE OF A SINGLE AMOUNT

LO3

The *present value* of a single amount is today's equivalent to a particular amount in the future.

The example used to illustrate future value reveals that $1,000 invested today is equivalent to $1,100 received after one year, $1,210 after two years, or $1,331 after three years, assuming 10% interest compounded annually. Thus, the $1,000 investment (I) is the **present value (PV)** of the single sum of $1,331 to be received at the end of three years. It is also the present value of $1,210 to be received in two years and $1,100 in one year.

Remember that the future value of a present amount is the present amount *times* $(1 + i)^n$. Logically, then, that computation can be reversed to find the *present value* of a future amount

---

[2]When interest is compounded more frequently than once a year, the effective annual interest rate, or yield, can be determined using the following equation:

$$\text{Yield} = (1 + \frac{i}{p})^p - 1$$

with *i* being the annual interest rate and *p* the number of compounding periods per year. In this example, the annual yield would be 12.55%, calculated as follows:

$$\text{Yield} = (1 + \frac{.12}{4})^4 - 1 = 1.1255 - 1 = .1255$$

Determining the yield is useful when comparing returns on investment instruments with different compounding period length.

to be the future amount *divided* by $(1 + i)^n$. We substitute PV for I (invested amount) in the future value formula above.

$$FV = PV (1 + i)^n$$

$$PV = \frac{FV}{(1 + i)^n}$$

In our example,

$$PV = \frac{\$1,331}{(1 - .10)^3} = \frac{\$1,331}{1.331} = \$1,000$$

Of course, dividing by $(1 + i)^n$ is the same as multiplying by its reciprocal, $1/(1 + i)^n$.

$$PV = \$1,331 \times \frac{1}{(1 + .10)^3} = \$1,331 \times .75131 = \$1,000$$

As with future value, these computations are simplified by using calculators, computer programs, or present value tables. Table 6A–2, Present Value of $1, on page 303 in Appendix 6 provides the solutions of $1/(1 + i)^n$ for various interest rates (i) and compounding periods (n). These amounts represent the present value of $1 to be received at the *end* of the different periods. The table can be used to find the present value of any single amount to be received in the future by *multiplying* that amount by the value in the table that lies at the *intersection* of the column for the appropriate rate and the row for the number of compounding periods.[3] Graphic 6–2 contains an excerpt from Table 6A–2.

Periods (n)	7%	8%	9%	10%	11%	12%
			Interest Rates (i)			
1	.93458	.92593	.91743	.90909	.90090	.89286
2	.87344	.85734	.84168	.82645	.81162	.79719
3	.81630	.79383	.77218	.75131	.73119	.71178
4	.76290	.73503	.70843	.68301	.65873	.63552
5	.71299	.68058	.64993	.62092	.59345	.56743
6	.66634	.63017	.59627	.56447	.53464	.50663
7	.62275	.58349	.54703	.51316	.48166	.45235
8	.58201	.54027	.50187	.46651	.43393	.40388

GRAPHIC 6–2
Present Value of $1 (excerpt from Table 6A–2, Appendix 6)

Notice that the farther into the future the $1 is to be received, the less valuable it is now. This is the essence of the concept of the time value of money. Given a choice between $1,000 now and $1,000 three years from now, you would choose to have the money now. If you have it now, you could put it to use. But the choice between, say, $740 now and $1,000 three years from now would depend on your time value of money. If your time value of money is 10%, you would choose the $1,000 in three years, because the $740 invested at 10% for three years would grow to only $984.94 [$740 × 1.331 (FV of $1, i = 10%, n = 3)]. On the other hand, if your time value of money is 11% or higher, you would prefer the $740 now. Presumably, you would invest the $740 now and have it grow to $1,012.05 ($740 × 1.36763) in three years.

Using the present value table above, the present value of $1,000 to be received in three years assuming a time value of money of 10% is $751.31 [$1,000 × .75131 (PV of $1, i = 10% and n = 3)]. Because the present value of the future amount, $1,000, is higher than

---

[3]The factors in Table 6A–1 are the reciprocals of those in Table 6A–1. For example, the future value factor for 10%, three periods is 1.331, while the present value factor is .75131. $1 ÷ 1.331 = $.75131, and $1 ÷ .75131 = $1.331.

$740 we could have today, we again determine that with a time value of money of 10%, the $1,000 in three years is preferred to the $740 now.

In our earlier example, $1,000 now is equivalent to $1,331 in three years, assuming the time value of money is 10%. Graphically, the relation between the present value and the future value can be viewed this way:

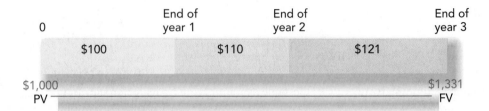

While the calculation of future value of a single sum invested today requires the *inclusion* of compound interest, present value problems require the *removal* of compound interest. The process of computing present value *removes* the $331 of interest earned over the three-year period from the future value of $1,331, just as the process of computing future value *adds* $331 of interest to the present value of $1,000 to arrive at the future value of $1,331.

> **The calculation of future value requires the addition of interest, while the calculation of present value requires the removal of interest.**

CHECK WITH THE **COACH**

Need help understanding how to apply the time value of money concept? If so, you are not alone. Many business students struggle with this. Check with the Coach and get in some quality practice time now. You will be a winner come test time. ■

SOLVING FOR OTHER VALUES WHEN FV AND PV ARE KNOWN

There are four variables in the process of adjusting single cash flow amounts for the time value of money: the present value (PV), the future value (FV), the number of compounding periods (n), and the interest rate (i). If you know any three of these, the fourth can be determined. Illustration 6–1 solves for an unknown interest rate and Illustration 6–2 determines an unknown number of periods.

Determining the Unknown Interest Rate

ILLUSTRATION 6–1 Determining *i* When PV, FV, and *n* Are Known	Suppose a friend asks to borrow $500 today and promises to repay you $605 two years from now. What is the annual interest rate you would be agreeing to?

The following time diagram illustrates the situation:

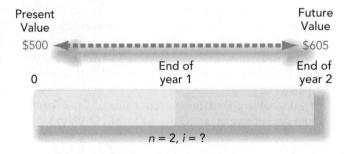

The interest rate is the discount rate that will provide a present value of $500 when discounting $605 to be received in two years:

$500 (present value) = $605 (future value) × ?*
*Present value of $1: $n = 2$, $i = ?$

Rearranging algebraically, we find that the present value table factor is .82645.

$500 (present value) ÷ $605 (future value) = .82645*
*Present value of $1: $n = 2$, $i = ?$

When you consult the present value table, Table 6A–2, you search row two ($n = 2$) for this value and find it in the 10% column. So the effective interest rate is 10%. Notice that the computed factor value exactly equals the table factor value.[4]

Determining the Unknown Number of Periods

You want to invest $10,000 today to accumulate $16,000 for graduate school. If you can invest at an interest rate of 10% compounded annually, how many years will it take to accumulate the required amount?

ILLUSTRATION 6–2
Determining n When PV, FV, and i Are Known

The following time diagram illustrates the situation:

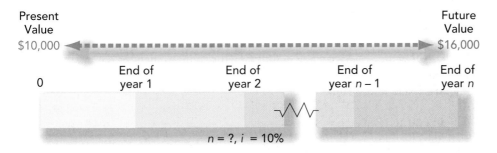

The number of years is the value of n that will provide a present value of $10,000 when discounting $16,000 at a rate of 10%:

$10,000 (present value) = $16,000 (future value) × ?*
*Present value of $1; $n = ?$, $i = 10\%$

Rearranging algebraically, we find that the present value table factor is .625.

$10,000 (present value) ÷ $16,000 (future value) = .625*
*Present value of $1: $n = ?$, $i = 10\%$

When you consult the present value table, Table 6A–2, you search the 10% column ($i = 10\%$) for this value and find .62092 in row five. So it would take approximately five years to accumulate $16,000 in the situation described.

ADDITIONAL CONSIDERATION

Solving for the unknown factor in either of these examples could just as easily be done using the future value tables. The number of years is the value of n that will provide a present value of $10,000 when discounting $16,000 at a discount rate of 10%.

---

[4]If the calculated factor lies between two table factors, interpolation is useful in finding the unknown value. For example, if the future value in our example is $600, instead of $605, the calculated PV factor is .83333 ($500 ÷ $600). This factor lies between the 9% factor of .84168 and the 10% factor of .82645. The total difference between these factors is .01523 (.84168 − .82645). The difference between the calculated factor of .83333 and the 10% factor of .82645 is .00688. This is 45% of the difference between the 9% and 10% factors:

$$\frac{.00688}{.01523} = .45$$

Therefore, the interpolated interest rate is 9.55% (10 − .45).

$16,000 (future value) = $10,000 (present value) × ?*
*Future value of $1: n = ?, i = 10%

Rearranging algebraically, the future value table factor is 1.6.

$16,000 (future value) ÷ $10,000 (present value) = 1.6*
*Future value of $1: n = ?, i = 10%

When you consult the future value table, Table 6A–1, you search the 10% column ($i =$ 10%) for this value and find 1.61051 in row five. So it would take approximately five years to accumulate $16,000 in the situation described.

CONCEPT REVIEW EXERCISE

Valuing a Single Cash Flow Amount

Using the appropriate table in Appendix 6, answer each of the following independent questions.

1. What is the future value of $5,000 at the end of six periods at 8% compound interest?
2. What is the present value of $8,000 to be received eight periods from today assuming a compound interest rate of 12%?
3. What is the present value of $10,000 to be received two *years* from today assuming an annual interest rate of 24% and *monthly* compounding?
4. If an investment of $2,000 grew to $2,520 in three periods, what is the interest rate at which the investment grew? Solve using both present and future value tables.
5. Approximately how many years would it take for an investment of $5,250 to accumulate to $15,000, assuming interest is compounded at 10% annually? Solve using both present and future value tables.

SOLUTION

1. FV = $5,000 × 1.58687* = $7,934
   *Future value of $1: n = 6, i = 8% (from Table 6A–1)

2. PV = $8,000 × .40388* = $3,231
   *Present value of $1: n = 8, i = 12% (from Table 6A–2)

3. PV = $10,000 × .62172* = $6,217
   *Present value of $1: n = 24, i = 2% (from Table 6A–2)

4. Using present value table,
   $$\frac{\$2,000}{\$2,520} = .7937*$$
   *Present value of $1: n = 3, i = ? (from Table 6A–2, i = approximately **8%**)

   Using future value table,
   $$\frac{\$2,520}{\$2,000} = 1.260*$$
   *Future value of $1: n = 3, i = ? (from Table 6A–1, i = approximately **8%**)

5. Using present value table,
   $$\frac{\$5,250}{\$15,000} = .35*$$
   *Present value of $1: n = ?, i = 10% (from Table 6A–2, n = approximately **11 years**)

   Using future value table,
   $$\frac{\$15,000}{\$5,250} = 2.857*$$
   *Future value of $1: n = ?. i = 10% (from Table 6A–1, n = approximately **11 years**)

Preview of Accounting Applications of Present Value Techniques—Single Cash Amount

Kile Petersen switched off his television set immediately after watching the Super Bowl game and swore to himself that this would be the last year he would watch the game on his 10-year-old 20-inch TV set. "Next year, a big screen TV," he promised himself. Soon after, he saw an advertisement in the local newspaper from Slim Jim's TV and Appliance offering a Philips 60-inch large screen television on sale for $1,800. And the best part of the deal was that Kile could take delivery immediately but would not have to pay the $1,800 for one whole year! "In a year, I can easily save the $1,800," he thought.

In the above scenario, the seller, Slim Jim's TV and Appliance, records a sale when the TV is delivered to Kile. How should the company value its receivable and corresponding sales revenue? We provide a solution to this question at the end of this section on page 284. The following discussion will help you to understand that solution.

Many assets and most liabilities are monetary in nature. **Monetary assets** include money and claims to receive money, the amount of which is fixed or determinable. Examples include cash and most receivables. **Monetary liabilities** are obligations to pay amounts of cash, the amount of which is fixed or determinable. Most liabilities are monetary. For example, if you borrow money from a bank and sign a note payable, the amount of cash to be repaid to the bank is fixed. Monetary receivables and payables are valued based on the fixed amount of cash to be received or paid in the future with proper reflection of the time value of money. In other words, we value most receivables and payables at the present value of future cash flows, reflecting an appropriate time value of money.[5]

Monetary assets and *monetary liabilities* **are valued at the present value of future cash flows.**

The example in Illustration 6–3 demonstrates this concept.

Explicit Interest

The Stridewell Wholesale Shoe Company manufactures athletic shoes for sale to retailers. The company recently sold a large order of shoes to Harmon Sporting Goods for $50,000. Stridewell agreed to accept a note in payment for the shoes requiring payment of $50,000 in one year plus interest at 10%.

ILLUSTRATION 6–3

Valuing a Note: One Payment, Explicit Interest

How should Stridewell value the note receivable and corresponding sales revenue earned? How should Harmon value the note payable and corresponding inventory purchased? As long as the interest rate explicitly stated in the agreement properly reflects the time value of money, the answer is $50,000, the face value of the note. It's important to realize that this amount also equals the present value of future cash flows at 10%. Future cash flows equal $55,000, $50,000 in note principal plus $5,000 in interest ($50,000 × 10%). Using a time diagram:

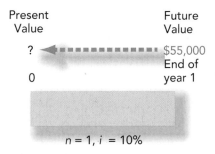

$$n = 1, i = 10\%$$

In equation form, we can solve for present value as follows:

$55,000 (future value) × .90909* = $50,000 (present value)
*Present value of $1: $n = 1, i = 10\%$

By calculating the present value of $55,000 to be received in one year, the interest of $5,000 is removed from the future value, resulting in a proper note receivable/sales revenue value of $50,000 for Stridewell and a $50,000 note payable/inventory value for Harmon.

While most notes, loans, and mortgages explicitly state an interest rate that will properly reflect the time value of money, there can be exceptions. Consider the example in Illustration 6–4.

---

[5]"Interest on Receivables and Payables," *Accounting Principles Board Opinion No. 21* (New York: AICPA, 1971).

ILLUSTRATION 6–4	**No Explicit Interest**
Valuing a Note: One Payment, No Explicit Interest	The Stridewell Wholesale Shoe Company recently sold a large order of shoes to Harmon Sporting Goods. Terms of the sale require Harmon to sign a noninterest-bearing note of $60,500 with payment due in two years.

How should Stridewell and Harmon value the note receivable/payable and corresponding sales revenue/inventory? Even though the agreement states a noninterest-bearing note, the $60,500 does, in fact, include interest for the two-year period of the loan. We need to remove the interest portion of the $60,500 to determine the portion that represents the sales price of the shoes. We do this by computing the present value. The following time diagram illustrates the situation assuming that a rate of 10% reflects the appropriate interest rate for a loan of this type:

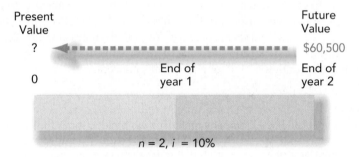

Again, using the present value of $1 table,

$60,500 (future value) × .82645* = $50,000 (present value)
*Present value of $1: n = 2, i = 10%

Both the note receivable for Stridewell and the note payable for Harmon initially will be valued at $50,000. The difference of $10,500 ($60,500 − 50,000) represents interest revenue/expense to be recognized over the life of the note. The appropriate journal entries are illustrated in later chapters.

Now can you answer the question posed in the scenario at the beginning of this section? Assuming that a rate of 10% reflects the appropriate interest rate in this situation, Slim Jim's TV and Appliance records a receivable and sales revenue of $1,636 which is the present value of the $1,800 to be received from Kile Petersen one year from the date of sale.

$1,800 (future value) × .90909* = $1,636 (present value)
*Present value of $1: n = 1, i = 10% (from Table 6A–2)

Expected Cash Flow Approach

SFAC No. 7

SFAC No. 7 provides a framework for using future cash flows in accounting measurements.

Present value measurement has long been integrated with accounting valuation and is specifically addressed in several accounting standards. Because of its increased importance, the FASB in 2000 issued *Statement of Financial Accounting Concepts No. 7,* "Using Cash Flow Information and Present Value in Accounting Measurements."[6] This statement provides a framework for using future cash flows as the basis for accounting measurement and asserts that the objective in valuing an asset or liability using present value is to approximate the fair value of that asset or liability. Key to that objective is determining the present value of future cash flows associated with the asset or liability, *taking into account any uncertainty concerning the amounts and timing of the cash flows.* Although future cash flows in many instances are contractual and certain, the amounts and timing of cash flows are less certain in other situations.

For example, lease payments are provided in the contract between lessor and lessee. On the other hand, the future cash flows to be paid to settle a pending lawsuit may be highly un-

---

[6]"Using Cash Flow Information and Present Value in Accounting Measurements," *Statement of Financial Accounting Concepts No. 7* (Norwalk, Conn.: FASB, 2000). Recall that Concept Statements do not directly prescribe GAAP, but instead provide structure and direction to financial accounting.

certain. Traditionally, the way uncertainty has been considered in present value calculations has been by discounting the "best estimate" of future cash flows applying a discount rate that has been adjusted to reflect the uncertainty or risk of those cash flows. With the approach described by *SFAC No. 7,* though, the adjustment for uncertainty or risk of cash flows is applied to the cash flows, not the discount rate. This new *expected cash flow approach* incorporates specific probabilities of cash flows into the analysis. Consider Illustration 6–5.

LDD Corporation faces the likelihood of having to pay an uncertain amount in five years in connection with an environmental cleanup. The future cash flow estimate is in the range of $100 million to $300 million with the following estimated probabilities:

Loss amount	Probability
$100 million	10%
$200 million	60%
$300 million	30%

The expected cash flow, then, is $220 million:

$100 × 10% = $ 10 million
200 × 60% = 120 million
300 × 30% =   90 million
            $220 million

If the risk-free rate of interest is 5%, LDD will report a liability of $172,376,600, the present value of the expected cash outflow:

$220,000,000
× .78353*
$172,376,600
*Present value of $1, n = 5, i = 5% (from Table 6A–2)

ILLUSTRATION 6–5
Expected Cash Flow Approach

Compare the approach described in Illustration 6–5 to the traditional approach that uses the present value of the most likely estimate of $200 million and ignores information about cash flow probabilities.

The discount rate used to determine present value when applying the expected cash flow approach should be the *risk-free rate of interest.* Other elements of uncertainty are incorporated into the determination of the probability-weighted expected cash flows. In the traditional approach, elements of uncertainty are incorporated into a risk-adjusted discount rate.

The FASB expects that the traditional approach to calculating present value will continue to be used in many situations, particularly those where future cash flows are contractual. The Board also believes that the expected cash flow approach is more appropriate in more complex situations. In fact, the Board has incorporated the concepts developed in *SFAC No. 7* into recent standards on asset retirement obligations, impairment losses, and business combinations. In Chapter 10 we illustrate the use of the expected cash flow approach as it would be applied to the measurement of an asset retirement obligation. In Chapter 13, we use the approach to measure the liability associated with a loss contingency.

The risk-free rate of interest is used when applying the expected cash flow approach to the calculation of present value.

[7]Ibid., para. 48.

PART

LO5

BASIC ANNUITIES

The previous examples involved the receipt or payment of a single future amount. Financial instruments frequently involve multiple receipts or payments of cash. If the same amount is to be received or paid each period, the cash flows are referred to as an **annuity.** A common annuity encountered in practice is a loan on which periodic interest is paid in equal amounts. For example, bonds typically pay interest semiannually in an amount determined by multiplying a stated rate by a fixed principal amount. Some loans and most leases are paid in equal installments during a specified period of time.

In an *ordinary annuity* cash flows occur at the *end* of each period.

An agreement that creates an annuity can produce either an **ordinary annuity** or an **annuity due** (sometimes referred to as an annuity in advance) situation. The first cash flow (receipt or payment) of an ordinary annuity is made one compounding period *after* the date on which the agreement begins. The final cash flow takes place on the *last* day covered by the agreement. For example, an installment note payable dated December 31, 2003, might require the debtor to make three equal annual payments, with the first payment due on December 31, 2004, and the last one on December 31, 2006. The following time diagram illustrates an ordinary annuity:

Ordinary annuity.

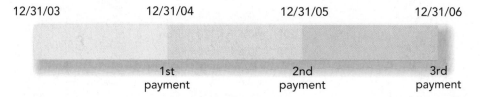

In an *annuity due* cash flows occur at the *beginning* of each period.

The first payment of an annuity due is made on the *first* day of the agreement, and the last payment is made one period *before* the end of the agreement. For example, a three-year lease of a building that begins on December 31, 2003, and ends on December 31, 2006, may require the first year's lease payment in advance on December 31, 2003. The third and last payment would take place on December 31, 2005, the beginning of the third year of the lease. The following time diagram illustrates this situation:

Annuity due.

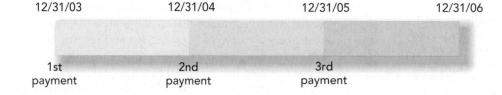

Future Value of an Annuity

FUTURE VALUE OF AN ORDINARY ANNUITY
Let's first consider the future value of an ordinary annuity in Illustration 6–6.

ILLUSTRATION 6–6	Sally Rogers wants to accumulate a sum of money to pay for graduate school. Rather than investing a single amount today that will grow to a future value, she decides to invest $10,000 a year over the next three years in a savings account paying 10% interest compounded annually. She decides to make the first payment to the bank one year from today.
Future Value of an Ordinary Annuity	

The following time diagram illustrates this ordinary annuity situation. Time 0 is the start of the first period.

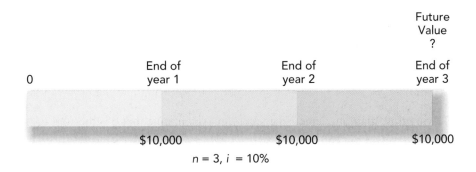

$n = 3, i = 10\%$

Using the FV of $1 factors from Table 6A–1, we can calculate the future value of this annuity by calculating the future value of each of the individual payments as follows:

	Payment		FV of $1 $i = 10\%$		Future Value (at the end of year 3)	n
First payment	$10,000	×	1.21	=	$12,100	2
Second payment	10,000	×	1.10	=	11,000	1
Third payment	10,000	×	1.00	=	10,000	0
Total			3.31		$33,100	

From the time diagram, we can see that the first payment has two compounding periods to earn interest. The factor used, 1.21, is the FV of $1 invested for two periods at 10%. The second payment has one compounding period and the last payment does not earn any interest because it is invested on the last day of the three-year annuity period. Therefore, the factor used is 1.00.

In the future value of an ordinary annuity, the last cash payment will not earn any interest.

This illustration shows that it's possible to calculate the future value of the annuity by separately calculating the FV of each payment and then adding these amounts together. Fortunately, that's not necessary. Table 6A–3, Future Value of an Ordinary Annuity, in Appendix 6 on page 304 simplifies the computation by summing the individual FV of $1 factors for various factors of n and i. Graphic 6–3 contains an excerpt from Table 6A–3.

	Interest Rates (i)					
Periods (n)	**7%**	**8%**	**9%**	**10%**	**11%**	**12%**
1	1.0000	1.0000	1.0000	1.0000	1.0000	1.0000
2	2.0700	2.0800	2.0900	2.1000	2.1100	2.1200
3	3.2149	3.2464	3.2781	3.3100	3.3421	3.3744
4	4.4399	4.5061	4.5731	4.6410	4.7097	4.7793
5	5.7507	5.8666	5.9847	6.1051	6.2278	6.3528
6	7.1533	7.3359	7.5233	7.7156	7.9129	8.1152
7	8.6540	8.9228	9.2004	9.4872	9.7833	10.0890
8	10.2598	10.6366	11.0285	11.4359	11.8594	12.2997

GRAPHIC 6–3
Future Value of an Ordinary Annuity of $1 (excerpt from Table 6A–3, Appendix 6)

The future value of $1 at the end of each of three periods invested at 10% is shown in Table 6A–3 to be $3.31. We can simply multiply this factor by $10,000 to derive the FV of our ordinary annuity (FVA):

$$FVA = \$10,000 \text{ (annuity amount)} \times 3.31^* = \$33,100$$
*Future value of an ordinary annuity of $1: n = 3, i = 10%

FUTURE VALUE OF AN ANNUITY DUE

Let's modify the previous illustration to create an annuity due in Illustration 6–7.

ILLUSTRATION 6–7	Sally Rogers wants to accumulate a sum of money to pay for graduate school. Rather than in-
Future Value of an Annuity Due	vesting a single amount today that will grow to a future value, she decides to invest $10,000 a year over the next three years in a savings account paying 10% interest compounded annu- ally. She decides to make the first payment to the bank immediately. How much will Sally have available in her account at the end of three years?

The following time diagram depicts the situation. Again, note that 0 is the start of the first period.

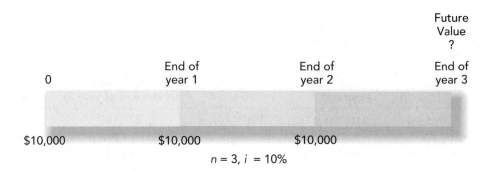

The future value can be found by separately calculating the FV of each of the three pay-ments and then summing those individual future values:

	Payment		FV of $1 i = 10%		Future Value (at the end of year 3)	n
First payment	$10,000	×	1.331	=	$13,310	3
Second payment	10,000	×	1.210	=	12,100	2
Third payment	10,000	×	1.100	=	11,000	1
Total			3.641		$36,410	

> In the future value of an annuity due, the last cash payment will earn interest.

And, again, this same future value can be found by using the future value of an annuity due (FVAD) factor from Table 6A–5, Future Value of an Annuity Due, in Appendix 6 on page 306, as follows:

$$\text{FVAD} = \$10,000 \text{ (annuity amount)} \times 3.641^* = \$36,410$$
*Future value of an annuity due of $1: n = 3, i = 10%

Of course, if *unequal* amounts are invested each year, we can't solve the problem by us-ing the annuity tables. The future value of each payment would have to be calculated separately.

Present Value of an Annuity

PRESENT VALUE OF AN ORDINARY ANNUITY

● LO7

You will learn in later chapters that liabilities and receivables, with the exception of certain trade receivables and payables, are reported in financial statements at their present values. Most of these financial instruments specify equal periodic interest payments or installment payments. As a result, the most common accounting applications of the time value of money involve determining present value of annuities. As in the future value applications we dis-cussed above, an annuity can be either an ordinary annuity or an annuity due. Let's look at an ordinary annuity first.

FINANCIAL REPORTING CASE

Q1, p. 275

On page 287, we determined that Sally Rogers could accumulate $33,100 for graduate school by investing $10,000 at the end of each of three years at 10%. The $33,100 is the fu-ture value of the ordinary annuity described. Another alternative is to invest one single amount at the beginning of the three-year period. (See Illustration 6–8.) This single amount will equal the present value at the beginning of the three-year period of the $33,100 future value. It will also equal the present value of the $10,000 three-year annuity.

Sally Rogers wants to accumulate a sum of money to pay for graduate school. She wants to invest a single amount today in a savings account earning 10% interest compounded annually that is equivalent to investing $10,000 at the end of each of the next three years.	**ILLUSTRATION 6–8** Present Value of an Ordinary Annuity

The present value can be found by separately calculating the PV of each of the three payments and then summing those individual present values:

	Payment		PV of $1 $i = 10\%$		Future Value (at the beginning of year 1)	n
First payment	$10,000	×	.90909	=	$ 9,091	1
Second payment	10,000	×	.82645	=	8,264	2
Third payment	10,000	×	.75131	=	7,513	3
Total			2.48685		$24,868	

A more efficient method of calculating present value is to use Table 6A–4, Present Value of an Ordinary Annuity, in Appendix 6 on page 305. Graphic 6–4 contains an excerpt from Table 6A–4.

	Interest Rates (i)					
Periods (n)	**7%**	**8%**	**9%**	**10%**	**11%**	**12%**
1	0.93458	0.92583	0.91743	0.90909	0.90090	0.89286
2	1.80802	1.78326	1.75911	1.73554	1.71252	1.69005
3	2.62432	2.57710	2.53129	2.48685	2.44371	2.40183
4	3.38721	3.31213	3.23972	3.16987	3.10245	3.03735
5	4.10020	3.99271	3.88965	3.79079	3.69590	3.60478
6	4.76654	4.62288	4.48592	4.35526	4.23054	4.11141
7	5.38929	5.20637	5.03295	4.86842	4.71220	4.56376
8	5.97130	5.74664	5.53482	5.33493	5.14612	4.96764

GRAPHIC 6–4
Present Value of an Ordinary Annuity of $1 (excerpt from Table 6A–4, Appendix 6)

Using Table 6A–4, we calculate the PV of the ordinary annuity (PVA) as follows:

PVA = $10,000 (annuity amount) × 2.48685* = $24,868
*Present value of an ordinary annuity of $1: $n = 3$, $i = 10\%$

The relationship between the present value and the future value of the annuity can be depicted graphically as follows:

Present Value $24,868   Future Value $33,100   **Relationship between present value and future value—ordinary annuity**

0	End of year 1	End of year 2	End of year 3
	$10,000	$10,000	$10,000

$n = 3$, $i = 10\%$

This can be interpreted in several ways:

1. $10,000 invested at 10% at the end of each of the next three years will accumulate to $33,100 at the end of the third year.
2. $24,868 invested at 10% now will grow to $33,100 after three years.
3. Someone whose time value of money is 10% would be willing to pay $24,868 now to receive $10,000 at the end of each of the next three years.
4. If your time value of money is 10%, you should be indifferent with respect to paying/receiving (a) $24,868 now, (b) $33,100 three years from now, or (c) $10,000 at the end of each of the next three years.

ADDITIONAL CONSIDERATION

We also can verify that these are the present value and future value of the same annuity by calculating the present value of a single cash amount of $33,100 three years hence:

$$PV = \$33,100 \text{ (future value)} \times .75131^* = \$24,868$$

*Present value of $1: $n = 3$, $i = 10\%$

PRESENT VALUE OF AN ANNUITY DUE

ILLUSTRATION 6–9

Present Value of an Annuity Due

In the previous illustration, suppose that the three equal payments of $10,000 are to be made at the *beginning* of each of the three years. Recall from the illustration on page 288 that the future value of this annuity is $36,410. What is the present value?

The following time diagram depicts this situation:

Present value of an annuity due.

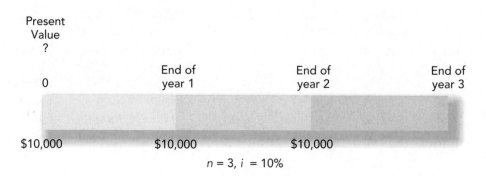

Present
Value
?

| 0 | End of year 1 | End of year 2 | End of year 3 |

$10,000 $10,000 $10,000

$n = 3$, $i = 10\%$

Once again, using individual PV factors of $1 from Table 6A–2, the PV of the annuity due can be calculated as follows:

	Payment		PV of $1 $i = 10\%$		Present Value (at the beginning of year 1)	n
First payment	$10,000	×	1.00000	=	$10,000	0
Second payment	10,000	×	.90909	=	9,091	1
Third payment	10,000	×	.82645	=	8,264	2
Total			2.73554		$27,355	

In the present value of an annuity due, no interest needs to be removed from the first cash payment.

The first payment does not contain any interest since it is made on the first day of the three-year annuity period. Therefore, the factor used is 1.00. The second payment has one compounding period and the factor used of .90909 is the PV factor of $1 for one period and 10%, and we need to remove two compounding periods of interest from the third payment. The factor used of .82645 is the PV factor of $1 for two periods and 10%.

The relationship between the present value and the future value of the annuity can be depicted graphically as follows:

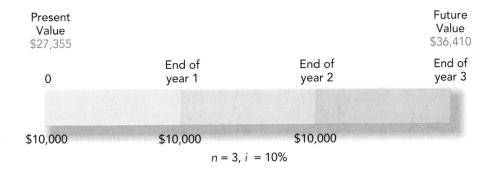

Relationship between present value and future value—annuity due.

Using Table 6A–6, Present Value of an Annuity Due, in Appendix 6 on page 307, we can more efficiently calculate the PV of the annuity due (PVAD):

$$PVAD = \$10,000 \text{ (annuity amount)} \times 2.73554^* = \$27,355$$

*Present value of an annuity due of $1: n = 3, i = 10%

To better understand the relationship between Tables 6A–4 and 6A–6, notice that the PVAD factor for three periods, 10%, from Table 6A–6 is 2.73554. This is simply the PVA factor for two periods, 10%, of 1.73554, plus 1.0. The addition of 1.0 reflects the fact that the first payment does not require the removal of any interest.

PRESENT VALUE OF A DEFERRED ANNUITY

Accounting valuations often involve the present value of annuities in which the first cash flow is expected to occur more than one time period after the date of the agreement. As the inception of the annuity is deferred beyond a single period, this type of annuity is referred to as a **deferred annuity**.[8]

A deferred annuity exists when the first cash flow occurs more than one period after the date the agreement begins.

ILLUSTRATION 6–10
At January 1, 2003, you are considering acquiring an investment that will provide three equal payments of $10,000 each to be received at the end of three consecutive years. However, the first payment is not expected until *December 31, 2005*. The time value of money is 10%. How much would you be willing to pay for this investment?

ILLUSTRATION 6–10
Deferred Annuity

The following time diagram depicts this situation:

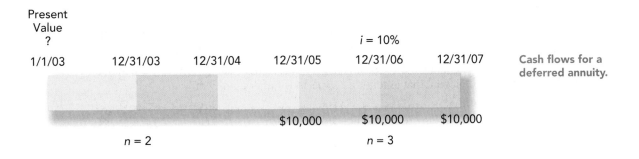

Cash flows for a deferred annuity.

---

[8]The future value of a deferred annuity is the same as the future amount of an annuity not deferred. That is because there are no interest compounding periods prior to the beginning of the annuity period.

The present value of the annuity can be calculated by summing the present values of the three individual cash flows, each discounted to today's PV:

	Payment		PV of $1 i = 10%		Present Value	n
First payment	$10,000	×	.75131	=	$ 7,513	3
Second payment	10,000	×	.68301	=	6,830	4
Third payment	10,000	×	.62092	=	6,209	5
					$20,552	

A more efficient way of calculating the present value of a deferred annuity involves a two-step process:

1. Calculate the PV of the annuity as of the beginning of the annuity period.
2. Discount the single amount calculated in (1) to its present value *as of today.*

In this case, we compute the present value of the annuity as of December 31, 2004, by multiplying the annuity amount by the three-period ordinary annuity factor:

$$PVA = \$10,000 \text{ (annuity amount)} \times 2.48685^* = \$24,868$$
*Present value of an ordinary annuity of $1: n = 3, i = 10%

This is the present value as of December 31, 2004. This single amount is then reduced to present value as of January 1, 2003, by making the following calculation:

$$PV = \$24,868 \text{ (future amount)} \times .82645^* = \$20,552$$
*Present value of $1: n = 2, i = 10%

The following time diagram illustrates this two-step process:

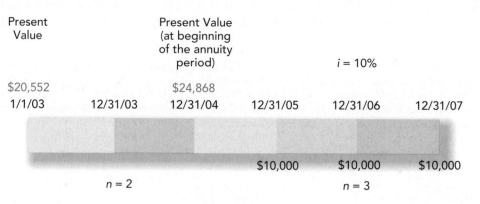

If you recall the concepts you learned in this chapter, you might think of other ways the present value of a deferred annuity can be determined. Among them:

1. Calculate the PV of an annuity due, rather than an ordinary annuity, and then discount that amount three periods rather than two:

$$PVAD = \$10,000 \text{ (annuity amount)} \times 2.73554^* = \$27,355$$
*Present value of an annuity due of $1: n = 3, i = 10%

This is the present value as of December 31, 2005. This single amount is then reduced to present value as of January 1, 2003 by making the following calculation:

$$PV = \$27,355 \times .75131^* = \$20,552$$
*Present value of $1: n = 3, i = 10%

2. From Table 6A–4, subtract the two-period PVA factor (1.73554) from the five-period PVA factor (3.79079) and multiply the difference (2.05525) by $10,000 to get $20,552.

Solving for Unknown Values in Present Value Situations

In present value problems involving annuities, there are four variables: (1) present value of an ordinary annuity (PVA) or present value of an annuity due (PVAD), (2) the amount of each annuity payment, (3) the number of periods, *n*, and (4) the interest rate, *i*. If you know any three of these, the fourth can be determined.

Assume that you borrow $700 from a friend and intend to repay the amount in four equal annual installments beginning one year from today. Your friend wishes to be reimbursed for the time value of money at an 8% annual rate. What is the required annual payment that must be made (the annuity amount), to repay the loan in four years?	**ILLUSTRATION 6–11** Determining the Annuity Amount When Other Variables Are Known

The following time diagram illustrates the situation:

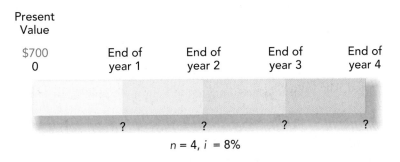

Determining the unknown annuity amount—ordinary annuity

The required payment is the annuity amount that will provide a present value of $700 when discounting that amount at a discount rate of 8%:

$$\$700 \text{ (present value)} = 3.31213^* \times \text{annuity amount}$$

The unknown variable is the annuity amount.

Rearranging algebraically, we find that the annuity amount is $211.34.

$$\$700 \text{ (present value)} \div 3.31213^* = \$211.34 \text{ (annuity amount)}$$
*Present value of an ordinary annuity of $1: *n* = 4, *i* = 8%

You would have to make four annual payments of $211.34 to repay the loan. Total payments of $845.36 (4 × $211.34) would include $145.36 in interest ($845.36 − 700.00).

Assume that you borrow $700 from a friend and intend to repay the amount in equal installments of $100 per year over a period of years. The payments will be made at the end of each year beginning one year from now. Your friend wishes to be reimbursed for the time value of money at a 7% annual rate. How many years would it take before you repaid the loan?	**ILLUSTRATION 6–12** Determining *n* When Other Variables Are Known

Once again, this is an ordinary annuity situation because the first payment takes place one year from now. The following time diagram illustrates the situation:

Determining the unknown number of periods—ordinary annuity

Present
Value

| $700
0 | End of
year 1 | End of
year 2 | End of
year *n* − 1 | End of
year *n* |

n = ?, *i* = 7%

The number of years is the value of n that will provide a present value of $700 when discounting $100 at a discount rate of 7%:

The unknown variable is the number of periods.

$700 (present value) = $100 (annuity amount) × ?*

*Present value of an ordinary annuity of $1: $n = ?$, $i = 7\%$

Rearranging algebraically, we find that the PVA table factor is 7.0.

$700 (present value) ÷ $100 (annuity amount) = 7.0*

*Present value of an ordinary annuity of $1: $n = ?$, $i = 7\%$

When you consult the PVA table, Table 6A–4, you search the 7% column ($i = 7\%$) for this value and find 7.02358 in row 10. So it would take approximately 10 years to repay the loan in the situation described.

ILLUSTRATION 6–13

Determining *i* When Other Variables Are Known

Suppose that a friend asked to borrow $331 today (present value) and promised to repay you $100 (the annuity amount) at the end of each of the next four years. What is the annual interest rate implicit in this agreement?

First of all, we are dealing with an ordinary annuity situation as the payments are at the end of each period. The following time diagram illustrates the situation:

Determining the unknown interest rate—ordinary annuity.

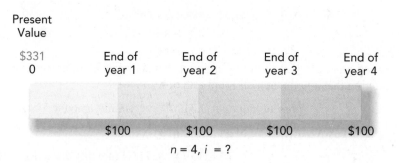

Present Value

| $331 | End of | End of | End of | End of |
| 0 | year 1 | year 2 | year 3 | year 4 |

$100 $100 $100 $100

$n = 4, i = ?$

The interest rate is the discount rate that will provide a present value of $331 when discounting the $100 four-year ordinary annuity:

The unknown variable is the interest rate.

$331 (present value) = $100 (annuity amount) × ?*

*Present value of an ordinary annuity of $1: $n = 4$, $i = ?$

Rearranging algebraically, we find that the PVA table factor is 3.31.

$331 (present value) ÷ $100 (annuity amount) = 3.31*

*Present value of an ordinary annuity of $1: $n = 4$, $i = ?$

When you consult the PVA table, Table 6A–4, you search row four ($n = 4$) for this value and find it in the 8% column. So the effective interest rate is 8%.

ILLUSTRATION 6–14

Determining *i* When Other Variables Are Known—Unequal Cash Flows

Suppose that you borrowed $400 from a friend and promised to repay the loan by making three annual payments of $100 at the end of each of the next three years plus a final payment of $200 at the end of year four. What is the interest rate implicit in this agreement?

The following time diagram illustrates the situation:

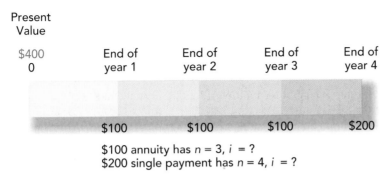

$100 annuity has $n = 3$, i = ?
$200 single payment has $n = 4$, i = ?

The interest rate is the discount rate that will provide a present value of $400 when discounting the $100 three-year ordinary annuity plus the $200 to be received in four years:

$400 (present value) = $100 (annuity amount) × ?* + $200 (single payment) × ?†
*Present value of an ordinary annuity of $1: $n = 3$, i = ?
†Present value of $1: $n = 4$, i = ?

This equation involves two unknowns and is not as easily solved as the two previous examples. One way to solve the problem is to trial-and-error the answer. For example, if we assumed i to be 9%, the total PV of the payments would be calculated as follows:

$$PV = \$100 \,(2.53129^*) + \$200 \,(.70843^†) = \$395$$

*Present value of an ordinary annuity of $1: $n = 3$, $i = 9\%$
†Present value of $1: $n = 4$, $i = 9\%$

Because the present value computed is less than the $400 borrowed, using 9% removes too much interest. Recalculating PV with $i = 8\%$ results in a PV of $405. This indicates that the interest rate implicit in the agreement is between 8% and 9%.

ADDITIONAL CONSIDERATION

As previously mentioned, financial calculators can be used to solve future and present value problems. For example, a Texas Instruments model BA-35 has the following pertinent keys:

    PMT

These keys are defined as follows:

 N = Number of periods
% i = Interest rate
PV = Present value
FV = Future value
PMT = Annuity payments
CPT = Compute button

To illustrate its use, assume that you need to determine the present value of a 10-period ordinary annuity of $200 using a 10% interest rate. You would enter 10 = N, 10 = % i, 200 = PMT, then press CPT and PV to obtain the answer of $1,229.

Many professionals choose to use spreadsheet software, such as Excel, to solve time value of money problems. These spreadsheets can be used in a variety of ways. A template can be created using the formulas shown in Graphic 6–5 on page 300. An alternative is to use the software's built-in financial functions. For example, Excel has a function called PV that calculates the present value of an ordinary annuity. To use the function, you would select the pull-down menu for "insert," click on "function" and choose the category called "financial." Scroll down to PV and double click. You will then be asked to input the necessary variables—interest rate, the number of periods, and the payment amount.

CONCEPT REVIEW EXERCISE

CRE Annuities

Using the appropriate table in Appendix 6, answer each of the following independent questions.

1. What is the future value of an annuity of $2,000 invested at the *end* of each of the next six periods at 8% interest?
2. What is the future value of an annuity of $2,000 invested at the *beginning* of each of the next six periods at 8% interest?
3. What is the present value of an annuity of $6,000 to be received at the *end* of each of the next eight periods assuming an interest rate of 10%?
4. What is the present value of an annuity of $6,000 to be received at the *beginning* of each of the next eight periods assuming an interest rate of 10%?
5. Jane bought a $3,000 audio system and agreed to pay for the purchase in 10 equal annual installments of $408 beginning one year from today. What is the interest rate implicit in this agreement?
6. Jane bought a $3,000 audio system and agreed to pay for the purchase in 10 equal annual installments beginning one year from today. The interest rate is 12%. What is the annual installment that must be made?
7. Jane bought a $3,000 audio system and agreed to pay for the purchase by making nine equal annual installments beginning one year from today plus a lump-sum payment of $1,000 at the end of 10 periods. The interest rate is 10%. What is the required annual installment?
8. Jane bought an audio system and agreed to pay for the purchase by making four equal annual installments of $800 beginning one year from today plus a lump-sum payment of $1,000 at the end of five years. The interest rate is 12%. What was the cost of the audio system? (Hint: What is the present value of the cash payments?)
9. Jane bought an audio system and agreed to pay for the purchase by making five equal annual installments of $1,100 beginning four years from today. The interest rate is 12%. What was the cost of the audio system? (Hint: What is the present value of the cash payments?)

SOLUTION

1. FVA = $2,000 × 7.3359* = $14,672
   *Future value of an ordinary annuity of $1: n = 6, i = 8% (from Table 6A–3)

2. FVAD = $2,000 × 7.9228* = $15,846
   *Future value of an annuity due of $1: n = 6, i = 8% (from Table 6A–5)

3. PVA = $6,000 × 5.33493* = $32,010
   *Present value of ordinary annuity of $1: n = 8, i = 10% (from Table 6A–4)

4. PVAD = $6,000 × 5.86842* = $35,211
   *Present value of an annuity due of $1: n = 8, i = 10% (from Table 6A–6)

5. $\dfrac{\$3.000}{\$408} = 7.35*$
   *Present value of an ordinary annuity of $1: n = 10, i = ? (from Table 6A–4, i = approximately **6%**)

6. Each annuity payment $= \dfrac{\$3,000}{5.65022*} = \$531$
   *Present value of an ordinary annuity of $1: n = 10, i = 12% (from Table 6A–4)

7. Each annuity payment $= \dfrac{\$3,000 - [\text{PV of } \$1,000 \ (n = 10, i = 10\%)]}{5.75902*}$

   Each annuity payment $= \dfrac{\$3,000 - (\$1,000 \times .38554^{\dagger})}{5.75902*}$

   Each annuity payment $= \dfrac{\$2,614}{5.75902*} = \$454$

   *Present value of an ordinary annuity of $1: n = 9, i = 10% (from Table 6A–4)
   †Present value of $1: n = 10, i = 10% (from Table 6A–2)

8. $PV = \$800 \times 3.03735^* + \$1,000 \times .56743^\dagger = \$2,997$
   *Present value of an ordinary annuity of $1: $n = 4$, $i = 12\%$ (from Table 6A–4)
   †Present value of $1: $n = 5$, $i = 12\%$ (from Table 6A–2)

9. $PVA = \$1,100 \times 3.60478^* = \$3,965$
   *Present value of an ordinary annuity of $1: $n = 5$, $i = 12\%$ (from Table 6A–4)

This is the present value three years from today (the beginning of the five-year annuity). This single amount is then reduced to present value as of today by making the following calculation:

$PV = \$3,965 \times .71178^\dagger = \$2,822$
†Present value of $1: $n = 3$, $i = 12\%$, (from Table 6A–2)

Preview of Accounting Applications of Present Value Techniques—Annuities

The time value of money has many applications in accounting. Most of these applications involve the concept of present value. Because financial instruments typically specify equal periodic payments, these applications quite often involve annuity situations. For example, let's consider one accounting situation using both an ordinary annuity and the present value of a single amount (long-term bonds), one using an annuity due (long-term leases), and a third using a deferred annuity (pension obligations).

VALUATION OF LONG-TERM BONDS

You will learn in Chapter 14 that a long-term bond usually requires the issuing (borrowing) company to repay a specified amount at maturity and make periodic stated interest payments over the life of the bond. The *stated* interest payments are equal to the contractual stated rate multiplied by the face value of the bonds. At the date the bonds are issued (sold), the marketplace will determine the price of the bonds based on the *market* rate of interest for investments with similar characteristics. The market rate at date of issuance may not equal the bonds' stated rate in which case the price of the bonds (the amount the issuing company actually is borrowing) will not equal the bonds' face value. Bonds issued at more than face value are said to be issued at a premium, while bonds issued at less than face value are said to be issued at a discount. Consider the example in Illustration 6–15.

FINANCIAL REPORTING CASE
Q2, p. 275

On June 30, 2003, Fumatsu Electric issued 10% stated rate bonds with a face amount of $200 million. The bonds mature on June 30, 2023 (20 years). The market rate of interest for similar issues was 12%. Interest is paid semiannually (5%) on June 30 and December 31, beginning December 31, 2003. The interest payment is $10 million (5% × $200 million). What was the price of the bond issue?

ILLUSTRATION 6–15
Valuing a Long-Term Bond Liability

To determine the price of the bonds, we calculate the present value of the 40-period annuity (40 semiannual interest payments of $10 million) and the lump-sum payment of $200 million paid at maturity using the semiannual market rate of interest of 6%. In equation form,

$$PVA = \$10 \text{ million (annuity amount)} \times 15.04630^* = \$150,463,000$$
$$PV = \$200 \text{ million (lump sum)} \times .09722^\dagger = \underline{19,444,000}$$
$$\text{Price of the bond issue} = \underline{\underline{\$169,907,000}}$$

*Present value of an ordinary annuity of $1: $n = 40$, $i = 6\%$
†Present value of $1: $n = 40$, $i = 6\%$

The bonds will sell for $169,907,000, which represents a discount of $30,093,000 ($200,000,000 − 169,907,000). The discount results from the difference between the semiannual stated rate of 5% and the market rate of 6%. Fumatsu records a $169,907,000 increase in cash and a corresponding liability for bonds payable. We discuss and illustrate the specific accounts used to record this transaction in Chapter 14.

VALUATION OF LONG-TERM LEASES

Companies frequently acquire the use of assets by leasing rather than purchasing them. Leases usually require the payment of fixed amounts at regular intervals over the life of the lease. You will learn in Chapter 15 that certain long-term, noncancelable leases are treated in a manner similar to an installment sale by the lessor and an installment purchase by the lessee. In other words, the lessor records a receivable and the lessee records a liability for the several installment payments. For the lessee, this requires that the leased asset and corresponding lease liability be valued at the present value of the lease payments. Consider the example in Illustration 6–16.

ILLUSTRATION 6–16 Valuing a Long-Term Lease Liability	On January 1, 2003, the Stridewell Wholesale Shoe Company signed a 25-year noncancelable lease agreement for an office building. Terms of the lease call for Stridewell to make annual lease payments of $10,000 at the *beginning* of each year, with the first payment due on January 1, 2003. Assuming an interest rate of 10% properly reflects the time value of money in this situation, how should Stridewell value the asset acquired and the corresponding lease liability if it is to be treated in a manner similar to an installment purchase?

Certain long-term leases require the recording of an asset and corresponding liability at the present value of future lease payments.

Once again, by computing the present value of the lease payments, we remove the portion of the payments that represents interest, leaving the portion that represents payment for the asset itself. Because the first payment is due immediately, as is common for leases, this is an annuity due situation. In equation form:

$$\text{PVAD} = \$10,000 \text{ (annuity amount)} \times 9.98474^* = \$99,847$$
*Present value of an annuity due of $1: $n = 25$, $i = 10\%$

Stridewell initially will value the leased asset and corresponding lease liability at $99,847.

Journal entry at the inception of a lease

Leased office building.	99,847	
Lease payable		99,847

The difference between this amount and total future cash payments of $250,000 ($10,000 × 25) represents the interest that is implicit in this agreement. That difference is recorded as interest over the life of the lease.

VALUATION OF PENSION OBLIGATIONS

Pension plans are important compensation vehicles used by many U.S. companies. These plans are essentially forms of deferred compensation as the pension benefits are paid to employees after they retire. You will learn in Chapter 17 that some pension plans create obligations during employees' service periods that must be paid during their retirement periods. These obligations are funded during the employment period. This means companies contribute cash to pension funds annually with the intention of accumulating sufficient funds to pay employees the retirement benefits they have earned. The amounts contributed are determined using estimates of retirement benefits. The actual amounts paid to employees during retirement depend on many factors including future compensation levels and length of life. Consider Illustration 6–17.

ILLUSTRATION 6–17 Valuing a Pension Obligation	On January 1, 2003, the Stridewell Wholesale Shoe Company hired Sammy Sossa. Sammy is expected to work for 25 years before retirement on December 31, 2027. Annual retirement payments will be paid at the end of each year during his retirement period, expected to be 20 years. The first payment will be on December 31, 2028. During 2003 Sammy earned an annual retirement benefit estimated to be $2,000 per year. The company plans to contribute cash to a pension fund that will accumulate to an amount sufficient to pay Sammy this benefit. Assuming that Stridewell anticipates earning 6% on all funds invested in the pension plan, how much would the company have to contribute at the end of 2003 to pay for pension benefits earned in 2003?

To determine the required contribution, we calculate the present value on December 31, 2003, of the deferred annuity of $2,000 that begins on December 31, 2028, and is expected to end on December 31, 2047.

The following time diagram depicts this situation:

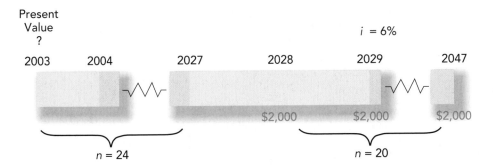

We can calculate the present value of the annuity using a two-step process. The first step computes the present value of the annuity as of December 31, 2027, by multiplying the annuity amount by the 20-period ordinary annuity factor:

$$\text{PVA} = \$2,000 \text{ (annuity amount)} \times 11.46992^* = \$22,940$$
*Present value of an ordinary annuity of $1: $n = 20$, $i = 6\%$

This is the present value as of December 31, 2027. This single amount is then reduced to present value as of December 31, 2003, by a second calculation:

$$\text{PV} = \$22,940 \text{ (future amount)} \times .24698^* = \$5,666$$
*Present value of $1: $n = 24$, $i = 6\%$

Stridewell would have to contribute $5,666 at the end of 2003 to fund the estimated pension benefits earned by its employee in 2003. Viewed in reverse, $5,666 invested now at 6% will accumulate a fund balance of $22,940 at December 31, 2027. If the fund balance remains invested at 6%, $2,000 can be withdrawn each year for 20 years before the fund is depleted.

Among the other situations you'll encounter using present value techniques are valuing notes (Chapters 10 and 14) and postretirement benefits (Chapter 18).

Summary of Time Value of Money Concepts

Graphic 6–5 summarizes the time value of money concepts discussed in this chapter.

FINANCIAL REPORTING CASE **SOLUTION**

1. **How was the amount of the lump-sum settlement determined? Create a calculation that John's sister can look at.** *(p. 288)*   The settlement was determined by calculating the present value of lost future income ($200,000 per year)[9] discounted at a rate that is expected to approximate the time value of money. In this case, the discount rate, *i*, apparently is 7% and the number of periods, *n*, is 25 (the number of years to John's retirement). John's settlement was calculated as follows:

$$\$200,000 \text{ (annuity amount)} \times 11.65358^* = \$2,330,716$$
*Present value of an ordinary annuity of $1: $n = 25$, $i = 7\%$ (from Table 6A–4)

---

[9]In the actual case, John's present salary was increased by 3% per year to reflect future salary increases.

GRAPHIC 6–5
Summary of Time
Value of Money
Concepts

Concept	Summary	Formula	Table
Future value (FV) of $1	The amount of money that a dollar will grow to at some point in the future.	$FV = \$1 (1 + i)^n$	6A–1
Present value (PV) of $1	The amount of money today that is equivalent to a given amount to be received or paid in the future.	$PV = \dfrac{\$1}{(1 + i)^n}$	6A–2
Future value of an ordinary annuity (FVA) of $1	The future value of a series of equal-sized cash flows with the first payment taking place at the end of the first compounding period.	$FVA = \dfrac{(1 + i)^n - 1}{i}$	6A–3
Present value of an ordinary annuity (PVA) of $1	The present value of a series of equal-sized cash flows with the first payment taking place at the end of the first compounding period.	$PVA = \dfrac{1 - \dfrac{1}{(1 + i)^n}}{i}$	6A–4
Future value of an annuity due (FVAD) of $1	The future value of a series of equal-sized cash flows with the first payment taking place at the beginning of the annuity period.	$FVAD = \left[\dfrac{(1 + i)^n - 1}{i}\right] \times (1 + i)$	6A–5
Present value of an annuity due (PVAD) of $1	The present value of a series of equal-sized cash flows with the first payment taking place at the beginning of the annuity period.	$PVAD = \left[\dfrac{1 - \dfrac{1}{(1 + i)^n}}{i}\right] \times (1 + i)$	6A–6

2. **What are some of the accounting applications that also take into account the time value of money?** *(p. 297)* Accounting applications that use annuity techniques include the valuation of long-term notes receivable and various long-term liabilities that include bonds, notes, leases, pension obligations, and postretirement benefits other than pensions. We study these in detail in later chapters. ∎

THE BOTTOM LINE

1. A dollar today is worth more than a dollar to be received in the future. The difference between the present value of cash flows and their future value represents the time value of money. Interest is the rent paid for the use of money over time.

2. The future value of a single amount is the amount of money that a dollar will grow to at some point in the future. It is computed by *multiplying* the single amount by $(1 + i)^n$, where i is the interest rate and n the number of compounding periods. The Future Value of $1 table allows for the calculation of future value for any single amount by providing the factors for various combinations of i and n.

3. The present value of a single amount is the amount of money today that is equivalent to a given amount to be received or paid in the future. It is computed by *dividing* the future amount by $(1 + i)^n$. The Present Value of $1 table simplifies the calculation of the present value of any future amount.

4. There are four variables in the process of adjusting single cash flow amounts for the time value of money: present value (PV), future value (FV), i and n. If you know any three of these, the fourth can be computed easily.

5. An annuity is a series of equal-sized cash flows occurring over equal intervals of time. An ordinary annuity exists when the cash flows occur at the end of each period. An annuity due exists when the cash flows occur at the beginning of each period.

6. The future value of an ordinary annuity (FVA) is the future value of a series of equal-sized cash flows with the first payment taking place at the end of the first compounding period. The last payment will not earn any interest since it is made at the end of the annuity period. The future value of an annuity due (FVAD) is the future value of a series of equal-sized cash flows with the first payment taking place at the beginning of the annuity period (the beginning of the first compounding period).

7. The present value of an ordinary annuity (PVA) is the present value of a series of equal-sized cash flows with the first payment taking place at the end of the first compounding period. The present value of an annuity due (PVAD) is the present value of a series of equal-sized cash flows with the first payment taking place at the beginning of the annuity period. The present value of a deferred annuity is the present value of a series of equal-sized cash flows with the first payment taking place more than one time period after the date of the agreement.

8. In present value problems involving annuities, there are four variables: PVA or PVAD, the annuity amount, the number of compounding periods (n) and the interest rate (i). If you know any three of these, you can determine the fourth.

9. Most accounting applications of the time value of money involve the present values of annuities. The initial valuation of long-term bonds is determined by calculating the present value of the periodic stated interest payments and the present value of the lump-sum payment made at maturity. Certain long-term leases require the lessee to compute the present value of future lease payments to value the leased asset and corresponding lease obligation. Also, pension plans require the payment of deferred annuities to retirees. ■

PRESENT AND FUTURE VALUE TABLES

This table shows the future value of $1 at various interest rates (*i*) and time periods (*n*). It is used to calculate the future value of any single amount.

TABLE 6A–1 Future Value of $1
$FV = \$1 (1 + i)^n$

n/i	1.0%	1.5%	2.0%	2.5%	3.0%	3.5%	4.0%	4.5%	5.0%	5.5%	6.0%	7.0%	8.0%	9.0%	10.0%	11.0%	12.0%	20.0%
1	1.01000	1.01500	1.02000	1.02500	1.03000	1.03500	1.04000	1.04500	1.05000	1.05500	1.06000	1.07000	1.08000	1.09000	1.10000	1.11000	1.12000	1.20000
2	1.02010	1.03022	1.04040	1.05063	1.06090	1.07123	1.08160	1.09203	1.10250	1.11303	1.12360	1.14490	1.16640	1.18810	1.21000	1.23210	1.25440	1.44000
3	1.03030	1.04568	1.06121	1.07689	1.09273	1.10872	1.12486	1.14117	1.15763	1.17424	1.19102	1.22504	1.25971	1.29503	1.33100	1.36763	1.40493	1.72800
4	1.04060	1.06136	1.08243	1.10381	1.12551	1.14752	1.16986	1.19252	1.21551	1.23882	1.26248	1.31080	1.36049	1.41158	1.46410	1.51807	1.57352	2.07360
5	1.05101	1.07728	1.10408	1.13141	1.15927	1.18769	1.21665	1.24618	1.27628	1.30696	1.33823	1.40255	1.46933	1.53862	1.61051	1.68506	1.76234	2.48832
6	1.06152	1.09344	1.12616	1.15969	1.19405	1.22926	1.26532	1.30226	1.34010	1.37884	1.41852	1.50073	1.58687	1.67710	1.77156	1.87041	1.97382	2.98598
7	1.07214	1.10984	1.14869	1.18869	1.22987	1.27228	1.31593	1.36086	1.40710	1.45468	1.50363	1.60578	1.71382	1.82804	1.94872	2.07616	2.21068	3.58318
8	1.08286	1.12649	1.17166	1.21840	1.26677	1.31681	1.36857	1.42210	1.47746	1.53469	1.59385	1.71819	1.85093	1.99256	2.14359	2.30454	2.47596	4.29982
9	1.09369	1.14339	1.19509	1.24886	1.30477	1.36290	1.42331	1.48610	1.55133	1.61909	1.68948	1.83846	1.99900	2.17189	2.35795	2.55804	2.77308	5.15978
10	1.10462	1.16054	1.21899	1.28008	1.34392	1.41060	1.48024	1.55297	1.62889	1.70814	1.79085	1.96715	2.15892	2.36736	2.59374	2.83942	3.10585	6.19174
11	1.11567	1.17795	1.24337	1.31209	1.38423	1.45997	1.53945	1.62285	1.71034	1.80209	1.89830	2.10485	2.33164	2.58043	2.85312	3.15176	3.47855	7.43008
12	1.12683	1.19562	1.26824	1.34489	1.42576	1.51107	1.60103	1.69588	1.79586	1.90121	2.01220	2.25219	2.51817	2.81266	3.13843	3.49845	3.89598	8.91610
13	1.13809	1.21355	1.29361	1.37851	1.46853	1.56396	1.66507	1.77220	1.88565	2.00577	2.13293	2.40985	2.71962	3.06580	3.45227	3.88328	4.36349	10.69932
14	1.14947	1.23176	1.31948	1.41297	1.51259	1.61869	1.73168	1.85194	1.97993	2.11609	2.26090	2.57853	2.93719	3.34173	3.79750	4.31044	4.88711	12.83918
15	1.16097	1.25023	1.34587	1.44830	1.55797	1.67535	1.80094	1.93528	2.07893	2.23248	2.39656	2.75903	3.17217	3.64248	4.17725	4.78459	5.47357	15.40702
16	1.17258	1.26899	1.37279	1.48451	1.60471	1.73399	1.87298	2.02237	2.18287	2.35526	2.54035	2.95216	3.42594	3.97031	4.59497	5.31089	6.13039	18.48843
17	1.18430	1.28802	1.40024	1.52162	1.65285	1.79468	1.94790	2.11338	2.29202	2.48480	2.69277	3.15882	3.70002	4.32763	5.05447	5.89509	6.86604	22.18611
18	1.19615	1.30734	1.42825	1.55966	1.70243	1.85749	2.02582	2.20848	2.40662	2.62147	2.85434	3.37993	3.99602	4.71712	5.55992	6.54355	7.68997	26.62333
19	1.20811	1.32695	1.45681	1.59865	1.75351	1.92250	2.10685	2.30786	2.52695	2.76565	3.02560	3.61653	4.31570	5.14166	6.11591	7.26334	8.61276	31.94800
20	1.22019	1.34686	1.48595	1.63862	1.80611	1.98979	2.19112	2.41171	2.65330	2.91776	3.20714	3.86968	4.66096	5.60441	6.72750	8.06231	9.64629	38.33760
21	1.23239	1.36706	1.51567	1.67958	1.86029	2.05943	2.27877	2.52024	2.78596	3.07823	3.39956	4.14056	5.03383	6.10881	7.40025	8.94917	10.80385	46.00512
25	1.28243	1.45095	1.64061	1.85394	2.09378	2.36324	2.66584	3.00543	3.38635	3.81339	4.29187	5.42743	6.84848	8.62308	10.83471	13.58546	17.00006	95.39622
30	1.34785	1.56308	1.81136	2.09757	2.42726	2.80679	3.24340	3.74532	4.32194	4.98395	5.74349	7.61226	10.06266	13.26768	17.44940	22.89230	29.95992	237.37631
40	1.48886	1.81402	2.20804	2.68506	3.26204	3.95926	4.80102	5.81636	7.03999	8.51331	10.28572	14.97446	21.72452	31.40942	45.25926	65.00087	93.05097	1469.77160

This table shows the present value of $1 at various interest rates (*i*) and time periods (*n*). It is used to calculate the present value of any single amount.

TABLE 6A–2 Present Value of $1

$$PV = \frac{\$1}{(1+i)^n}$$

n/i	1.0%	1.5%	2.0%	2.5%	3.0%	3.5%	4.0%	4.5%	5.0%	5.5%	6.0%	7.0%	8.0%	9.0%	10.0%	11.0%	12.0%	20.0%
1	0.99010	0.98522	0.98039	0.97561	0.97087	0.96618	0.96154	0.95694	0.95238	0.94787	0.94340	0.93458	0.92593	0.91743	0.90909	0.90090	0.89286	0.83333
2	0.98030	0.97066	0.96117	0.95181	0.94260	0.93351	0.92456	0.91573	0.90703	0.89845	0.89000	0.87344	0.85734	0.84168	0.82645	0.81162	0.79719	0.69444
3	0.97059	0.95632	0.94232	0.92860	0.91514	0.90194	0.88900	0.87630	0.86384	0.85161	0.83962	0.81630	0.79383	0.77218	0.75131	0.73119	0.71178	0.57870
4	0.96098	0.94218	0.92385	0.90595	0.88849	0.87144	0.85480	0.83856	0.82270	0.80722	0.79209	0.76290	0.73503	0.70843	0.68301	0.65873	0.63552	0.48225
5	0.95147	0.92826	0.90573	0.88385	0.86261	0.84197	0.82193	0.80245	0.78353	0.76513	0.74726	0.71299	0.68058	0.64993	0.62092	0.59345	0.56743	0.40188
6	0.94205	0.91454	0.88797	0.86230	0.83748	0.81350	0.79031	0.76790	0.74622	0.72525	0.70496	0.66634	0.63017	0.59627	0.56447	0.53464	0.50663	0.33490
7	0.93272	0.90103	0.87056	0.84127	0.81309	0.78599	0.75992	0.73483	0.71068	0.68744	0.66506	0.62275	0.58349	0.54703	0.51316	0.48166	0.45235	0.27908
8	0.92348	0.88771	0.85349	0.82075	0.78941	0.75941	0.73069	0.70319	0.67684	0.65160	0.62741	0.58201	0.54027	0.50187	0.46651	0.43393	0.40388	0.23257
9	0.91434	0.87459	0.83676	0.80073	0.76642	0.73373	0.70259	0.67290	0.64461	0.61763	0.59190	0.54393	0.50025	0.46043	0.42410	0.39092	0.36061	0.19381
10	0.90529	0.86167	0.82035	0.78120	0.74409	0.70892	0.67556	0.64393	0.61391	0.58543	0.55839	0.50835	0.46319	0.42241	0.38554	0.35218	0.32197	0.16151
11	0.89632	0.84893	0.80426	0.76214	0.72242	0.68495	0.64958	0.61620	0.58468	0.55491	0.52679	0.47509	0.42888	0.38753	0.35049	0.31728	0.28748	0.13459
12	0.88745	0.83639	0.78849	0.74356	0.70138	0.66178	0.62460	0.58966	0.55684	0.52598	0.49697	0.44401	0.39711	0.35553	0.31863	0.28584	0.25668	0.11216
13	0.87866	0.82403	0.77303	0.72542	0.68095	0.63940	0.60057	0.56427	0.53032	0.49856	0.46884	0.41496	0.36770	0.32618	0.28966	0.25751	0.22917	0.09346
14	0.86996	0.81185	0.75788	0.70773	0.66112	0.61778	0.57748	0.53997	0.50507	0.47257	0.44230	0.38782	0.34046	0.29925	0.26333	0.23199	0.20462	0.07789
15	0.86135	0.79985	0.74301	0.69047	0.64186	0.59689	0.55526	0.51672	0.48102	0.44793	0.41727	0.36245	0.31524	0.27454	0.23939	0.20900	0.18270	0.06491
16	0.85282	0.78803	0.72845	0.67362	0.62317	0.57671	0.53391	0.49447	0.45811	0.42458	0.39365	0.33873	0.29189	0.25187	0.21763	0.18829	0.16312	0.05409
17	0.84438	0.77639	0.71416	0.65720	0.60502	0.55720	0.51337	0.47318	0.43630	0.40245	0.37136	0.31657	0.27027	0.23107	0.19784	0.16963	0.14564	0.04507
18	0.83602	0.76491	0.70016	0.64117	0.58739	0.53836	0.49363	0.45280	0.41552	0.38147	0.35034	0.29586	0.25025	0.21199	0.17986	0.15282	0.13004	0.03756
19	0.82774	0.75361	0.68643	0.62553	0.57029	0.52016	0.47464	0.43330	0.39573	0.36158	0.33051	0.27651	0.23171	0.19449	0.16351	0.13768	0.11611	0.03130
20	0.81954	0.74247	0.67297	0.61027	0.55368	0.50257	0.45639	0.41464	0.37689	0.34273	0.31180	0.25842	0.21455	0.17843	0.14864	0.12403	0.10367	0.02608
21	0.81143	0.73150	0.65978	0.59539	0.53755	0.48557	0.43883	0.39679	0.35894	0.32486	0.29416	0.24151	0.19866	0.16370	0.13513	0.11174	0.09256	0.02174
24	0.78757	0.69954	0.62172	0.55288	0.49193	0.43796	0.39012	0.34770	0.31007	0.27666	0.24698	0.19715	0.15770	0.12640	0.10153	0.08170	0.06588	0.01258
25	0.77977	0.68921	0.60953	0.53939	0.47761	0.42315	0.37512	0.33273	0.29530	0.26223	0.23300	0.18425	0.14602	0.11597	0.09230	0.07361	0.05882	0.01048
28	0.75684	0.65910	0.57437	0.50088	0.43708	0.38165	0.33348	0.29157	0.25509	0.22332	0.19563	0.15040	0.11591	0.08955	0.06934	0.05382	0.04187	0.00607
29	0.74934	0.64936	0.56311	0.48866	0.42435	0.36875	0.32065	0.27902	0.24295	0.21168	0.18456	0.14056	0.10733	0.08215	0.06304	0.04849	0.03738	0.00506
30	0.74192	0.63976	0.55207	0.47674	0.41199	0.35628	0.30832	0.26700	0.23138	0.20064	0.17411	0.13137	0.09938	0.07537	0.05731	0.04368	0.03338	0.00421
31	0.73458	0.63031	0.54125	0.46511	0.39999	0.34423	0.29646	0.25550	0.22036	0.19018	0.16425	0.12277	0.09202	0.06915	0.05210	0.03935	0.02980	0.00351
40	0.67165	0.55126	0.45289	0.37243	0.30656	0.25257	0.20829	0.17193	0.14205	0.11746	0.09722	0.06678	0.04603	0.03184	0.02209	0.01538	0.01075	0.00068

This table shows the future value of an ordinary annuity of $1 at various interest rates (*i*) and time periods (*n*). It is used to calculate the future value of any series of equal payments made at the *end* of each compounding period.

TABLE 6A–3 Future Value of an Ordinary Annuity of $1

$$FVA = \frac{(1+i)^n - 1}{i}$$

n/i	1.0%	1.5%	2.0%	2.5%	3.0%	3.5%	4.0%	4.5%	5.0%	5.5%	6.0%	7.0%	8.0%	9.0%	10.0%	11.0%	12.0%	20.0%
1	1.0000	1.0000	1.0000	1.0000	1.0000	1.0000	1.0000	1.0000	1.0000	1.0000	1.0000	1.0000	1.0000	1.0000	1.0000	1.0000	1.0000	1.0000
2	2.0100	2.0150	2.0200	2.0250	2.0300	2.0350	2.0400	2.0450	2.0500	2.0550	2.0600	2.0700	2.0800	2.0900	2.1000	2.1100	2.1200	2.2000
3	3.0301	3.0452	3.0604	3.0756	3.0909	3.1062	3.1216	3.1370	3.1525	3.1680	3.1836	3.2149	3.2464	3.2781	3.3100	3.3421	3.3744	3.6400
4	4.0604	4.0909	4.1216	4.1525	4.1836	4.2149	4.2465	4.2782	4.3101	4.3423	4.3746	4.4399	4.5061	4.5731	4.6410	4.7097	4.7793	5.3680
5	5.1010	5.1523	5.2040	5.2563	5.3091	5.3625	5.4163	5.4707	5.5256	5.5811	5.6371	5.7507	5.8666	5.9847	6.1051	6.2278	6.3528	7.4416
6	6.1520	6.2296	6.3081	6.3877	6.4684	6.5502	6.6330	6.7169	6.8019	6.8881	6.9753	7.1533	7.3359	7.5233	7.7156	7.9129	8.1152	9.9299
7	7.2135	7.3230	7.4343	7.5474	7.6625	7.7794	7.8983	8.0192	8.1420	8.2669	8.3938	8.6540	8.9228	9.2004	9.4872	9.7833	10.0890	12.9159
8	8.2857	8.4328	8.5830	8.7361	8.8923	9.0517	9.2142	9.3800	9.5491	9.7216	9.8975	10.2598	10.6366	11.0285	11.4359	11.8594	12.2997	16.4991
9	9.3685	9.5593	9.7546	9.9545	10.1591	10.3685	10.5828	10.8021	11.0266	11.2563	11.4913	11.9780	12.4876	13.0210	13.5795	14.1640	14.7757	20.7989
10	10.4622	10.7027	10.9497	11.2034	11.4639	11.7314	12.0061	12.2882	12.5779	12.8754	13.1808	13.8164	14.4866	15.1929	15.9374	16.7220	17.5487	25.9587
11	11.5668	11.8633	12.1687	12.4835	12.8078	13.1420	13.4864	13.8412	14.2068	14.5835	14.9716	15.7836	16.6455	17.5603	18.5312	19.5614	20.6546	32.1504
12	12.6825	13.0412	13.4121	13.7956	14.1920	14.6020	15.0258	15.4640	15.9171	16.3856	16.8699	17.8885	18.9771	20.1407	21.3843	22.7132	24.1331	39.5805
13	13.8093	14.2368	14.6803	15.1404	15.6178	16.1130	16.6268	17.1599	17.7130	18.2868	18.8821	20.1406	21.4953	22.9534	24.5227	26.2116	28.0291	48.4966
14	14.9474	15.4504	15.9739	16.5190	17.0863	17.6770	18.2919	18.9321	19.5986	20.2926	21.0151	22.5505	24.2149	26.0192	27.9750	30.0949	32.3926	59.1959
15	16.0969	16.6821	17.2934	17.9319	18.5989	19.2957	20.0236	20.7841	21.5786	22.4087	23.2760	25.1290	27.1521	29.3609	31.7725	34.4054	37.2797	72.0351
16	17.2579	17.9324	18.6393	19.3802	20.1569	20.9710	21.8245	22.7193	23.6575	24.6411	25.6725	27.8881	30.3243	33.0034	35.9497	39.1899	42.7533	87.4421
17	18.4304	19.2014	20.0121	20.8647	21.7616	22.7050	23.6975	24.7417	25.8404	26.9964	28.2129	30.8402	33.7502	36.9737	40.5447	44.5008	48.8837	105.9306
18	19.6147	20.4894	21.4123	22.3863	23.4144	24.4997	25.6454	26.8551	28.1324	29.4812	30.9057	33.9990	37.4502	41.3013	45.5992	50.3959	55.7497	128.1167
19	20.8109	21.7967	22.8406	23.9460	25.1169	26.3572	27.6712	29.0636	30.5390	32.1027	33.7600	37.3790	41.4463	46.0185	51.1591	56.9395	63.4397	154.7400
20	22.0190	23.1237	24.2974	25.5447	26.8704	28.2797	29.7781	31.3714	33.0660	34.8683	36.7856	40.9955	45.7620	51.1601	57.2750	64.2028	72.0524	186.6880
21	23.2392	24.4705	25.7833	27.1833	28.6765	30.2695	31.9692	33.7831	35.7193	37.7861	39.9927	44.8652	50.4229	56.7645	64.0025	72.2651	81.6987	225.0256
30	34.7849	37.5387	40.5681	43.9027	47.5754	51.6227	56.0849	61.0071	66.4388	72.4355	79.0582	94.4608	113.2832	136.3075	164.4940	199.0209	241.3327	1181.8816
40	48.8864	54.2679	60.4020	67.4026	75.4013	84.5503	95.0255	107.0303	120.7998	136.6056	154.7620	199.6351	259.0565	337.8824	442.5926	581.8261	767.0914	7343.8578

This table shows the present value of an ordinary annuity of $1 at various interest rates (i) and time periods (n). It is used to calculate the present value of any series of equal payments made at the *end* of each compounding period.

TABLE 6A–4 Present Value of an Ordinary Annuity of $1

$$PVA = \frac{1 - \dfrac{1}{(1+i)^n}}{i}$$

n/i	1.0%	1.5%	2.0%	2.5%	3.0%	3.5%	4.0%	4.5%	5.0%	5.5%	6.0%	7.0%	8.0%	9.0%	10.0%	11.0%	12.0%	20.0%
1	0.99010	0.98522	0.98039	0.97561	0.97087	0.96618	0.96154	0.95694	0.95238	0.94787	0.94340	0.93458	0.92583	0.91743	0.90909	0.90090	0.89286	0.83333
2	1.97040	1.95588	1.94156	1.92742	1.91347	1.89969	1.88609	1.87267	1.85941	1.84632	1.83339	1.80802	1.78326	1.75911	1.73554	1.71252	1.69005	1.52778
3	2.94099	2.91220	2.88388	2.85602	2.82861	2.80164	2.77509	2.74896	2.72325	2.69793	2.67301	2.62432	2.57710	2.53129	2.48685	2.44371	2.40183	2.10648
4	3.90197	3.85438	3.80773	3.76197	3.71710	3.67308	3.62990	3.58753	3.54595	3.50515	3.46511	3.38721	3.31213	3.23972	3.16987	3.10245	3.03735	2.58873
5	4.85343	4.78264	4.71346	4.64583	4.57971	4.51505	4.45182	4.38998	4.32948	4.27028	4.21236	4.10020	3.99271	3.88965	3.79079	3.69590	3.60478	2.99061
6	5.79548	5.69719	5.60143	5.50813	5.41719	5.32855	5.24214	5.15787	5.07569	4.99553	4.91732	4.76654	4.62288	4.48592	4.35526	4.23054	4.11141	3.32551
7	6.72819	6.59821	6.47199	6.34939	6.23028	6.11454	6.00205	5.89270	5.78637	5.68297	5.58238	5.38929	5.20637	5.03295	4.86842	4.71220	4.56376	3.60459
8	7.65168	7.48593	7.32548	7.17014	7.01969	6.87396	6.73274	6.59589	6.46321	6.33457	6.20979	5.97130	5.74664	5.53482	5.33493	5.14612	4.96764	3.83716
9	8.56602	8.36052	8.16224	7.97087	7.78611	7.60769	7.43533	7.26879	7.10782	6.95220	6.80169	6.51523	6.24689	5.99525	5.75902	5.53705	5.32825	4.03097
10	9.47130	9.22218	8.98259	8.75206	8.53020	8.31661	8.11090	7.91272	7.72173	7.53763	7.36009	7.02358	6.71008	6.41766	6.14457	5.88923	5.65022	4.19247
11	10.36763	10.07112	9.78685	9.51421	9.25262	9.00155	8.76048	8.52892	8.30641	8.09254	7.88687	7.49867	7.13896	6.80519	6.49506	6.20652	5.93770	4.32706
12	11.25508	10.90751	10.57534	10.25776	9.95400	9.66333	9.38507	9.11858	8.86325	8.61852	8.38384	7.94269	7.53608	7.16073	6.81369	6.49236	6.19437	4.43922
13	12.13374	11.73153	11.34837	10.98319	10.63496	10.30274	9.98565	9.68285	9.39357	9.11708	8.85268	8.35765	7.90378	7.48690	7.10336	6.74987	6.42355	4.53268
14	13.00370	12.54338	12.10625	11.69091	11.29607	10.92052	10.56312	10.22283	9.89864	9.58965	9.29498	8.74547	8.24424	7.78615	7.36669	6.98187	6.62817	4.61057
15	13.86505	13.34323	12.84926	12.38138	11.93794	11.51741	11.11839	10.73955	10.37966	10.03758	9.71225	9.10791	8.55948	8.06069	7.60608	7.19087	6.81086	4.67547
16	14.71787	14.13126	13.57771	13.05500	12.56110	12.09412	11.65230	11.23402	10.83777	10.46216	10.10590	9.44665	8.85137	8.31256	7.82371	7.37916	6.97399	4.72956
17	15.56225	14.90765	14.29187	13.71220	13.16612	12.65132	12.16567	11.70719	11.27407	10.86461	10.47726	9.76322	9.12164	8.54363	8.02155	7.54879	7.11963	4.77463
18	16.39827	15.67256	14.99203	14.35336	13.75351	13.18968	12.65930	12.15999	11.68959	11.24607	10.82760	10.05909	9.37189	8.75563	8.20141	7.70162	7.24967	4.81219
19	17.22601	16.42617	15.67846	14.97889	14.32380	13.70984	13.13394	12.59329	12.08532	11.60765	11.15812	10.33560	9.60360	8.95011	8.36492	7.83929	7.36578	4.84350
20	18.04555	17.16864	16.35143	15.58916	14.87747	14.21240	13.59033	13.00794	12.46221	11.95038	11.46992	10.59401	9.81815	9.12855	8.51356	7.96333	7.46944	4.86958
21	18.85698	17.90014	17.01121	16.18455	15.41502	14.69797	14.02916	13.40472	12.82115	12.27524	11.76408	10.83553	10.01680	9.29224	8.64869	8.07507	7.56200	4.89132
25	22.02316	20.71961	19.52346	18.42438	17.41315	16.48151	15.62208	14.82821	14.09394	13.41393	12.78336	11.65358	10.67478	9.82258	9.07704	8.42174	7.84314	4.94759
30	25.80771	24.01584	22.39646	20.93029	19.60044	18.39205	17.29203	16.28889	15.37245	14.53375	13.76483	12.40904	11.25778	10.27365	9.42691	8.69379	8.05518	4.97894
40	32.83469	29.91585	27.35548	25.10278	23.11477	21.35507	19.79277	18.40158	17.15909	16.04612	15.04630	13.33171	11.92461	10.75736	9.77905	8.95105	8.24378	4.99660

This table shows the future value of an annuity due of $1 at various interest rates (i) and time periods (n). It is used to calculate the future value of any series of equal payments made at the *beginning* of each compounding period.

TABLE 6A–5 Future Value of an Annuity Due of $1

$$FVAD = \left[\frac{(1+i)^n - 1}{i}\right] \times (1+i)$$

n/i	1.0%	1.5%	2.0%	2.5%	3.0%	3.5%	4.0%	4.5%	5.0%	5.5%	6.0%	7.0%	8.0%	9.0%	10.0%	11.0%	12.0%	20.0%
1	1.0100	1.0150	1.0200	1.0250	1.0300	1.0350	1.0400	1.0450	1.0500	1.0550	1.0600	1.0700	1.0800	1.0900	1.1000	1.1100	1.1200	1.2000
2	2.0301	2.0452	2.0604	2.0756	2.0909	2.1062	2.1216	2.1370	2.1525	2.1680	2.1836	2.2149	2.2464	2.2781	2.3100	2.3421	2.3744	2.6400
3	3.0604	3.0909	3.1216	3.1525	3.1836	3.2149	3.2465	3.2782	3.3101	3.3423	3.3746	3.4399	3.5061	3.5731	3.6410	3.7097	3.7793	4.3680
4	4.1010	4.1523	4.2040	4.2563	4.3091	4.3625	4.4163	4.4707	4.5256	4.5811	4.6371	4.7507	4.8666	4.9847	5.1051	5.2278	5.3528	6.4416
5	5.1520	5.2296	5.3081	5.3877	5.4684	5.5502	5.6330	5.7169	5.8019	5.8881	5.9753	6.1533	6.3359	6.5233	6.7156	6.9129	7.1152	8.9299
6	6.2135	6.3230	6.4343	6.5474	6.6625	6.7794	6.8983	7.0192	7.1420	7.2669	7.3938	7.6540	7.9228	8.2004	8.4872	8.7833	9.0890	11.9159
7	7.2857	7.4328	7.5830	7.7361	7.8923	8.0517	8.2142	8.3800	8.5491	8.7216	8.8975	9.2598	9.6366	10.0285	10.4359	10.8594	11.2997	15.4991
8	8.3685	8.5593	8.7546	8.9545	9.1591	9.3685	9.5828	9.8021	10.0266	10.2563	10.4913	10.9780	11.4876	12.0210	12.5795	13.1640	13.7757	19.7989
9	9.4622	9.7027	9.9497	10.2034	10.4639	10.7314	11.0061	11.2882	11.5779	11.8754	12.1808	12.8164	13.4866	14.1929	14.9374	15.7220	16.5487	24.9587
10	10.5668	10.8633	11.1687	11.4835	11.8078	12.1420	12.4864	12.8412	13.2068	13.5835	13.9716	14.7836	15.6455	16.5603	17.5312	18.5614	19.6546	31.1504
11	11.6825	12.0412	12.4121	12.7956	13.1920	13.6020	14.0258	14.4640	14.9171	15.3856	15.8699	16.8885	17.9771	19.1407	20.3843	21.7132	23.1331	38.5805
12	12.8093	13.2368	13.6803	14.1404	14.6178	15.1130	15.6268	16.1599	16.7130	17.2868	17.8821	19.1406	20.4953	21.9534	23.5227	25.2116	27.0291	47.4966
13	13.9474	14.4504	14.9739	15.5190	16.0863	16.6770	17.2919	17.9321	18.5986	19.2926	20.0151	21.5505	23.2149	25.0192	26.9750	29.0949	31.3926	58.1959
14	15.0969	15.6821	16.2934	16.9319	17.5989	18.2957	19.0236	19.7841	20.5786	21.4087	22.2760	24.1290	26.1521	28.3609	30.7725	33.4054	36.2797	71.0351
15	16.2579	16.9324	17.6393	18.3802	19.1569	19.9710	20.8245	21.7193	22.6575	23.6411	24.6725	26.8881	29.3243	32.0034	34.9497	38.1899	41.7533	86.4421
16	17.4304	18.2014	19.0121	19.8647	20.7616	21.7050	22.6975	23.7417	24.8404	25.9964	27.2129	29.8402	32.7502	35.9737	39.5447	43.5008	47.8837	104.9306
17	18.6147	19.4894	20.4123	21.3863	22.4144	23.4997	24.6454	25.8551	27.1324	28.4812	29.9057	32.9990	36.4502	40.3013	44.5992	49.3959	54.7497	127.1167
18	19.8109	20.7967	21.8406	22.9460	24.1169	25.3572	26.6712	28.0636	29.5390	31.1027	32.7600	36.3790	40.4463	45.0185	50.1591	55.9395	62.4397	153.7400
19	21.0190	22.1237	23.2974	24.5447	25.8704	27.2797	28.7781	30.3714	32.0660	33.8683	35.7856	39.9955	44.7620	50.1601	56.2750	63.2028	71.0524	185.6880
20	22.2392	23.4705	24.7833	26.1833	27.6765	29.2695	30.9692	32.7831	34.7193	36.7861	38.9927	43.8652	49.4229	55.7645	63.0025	71.2651	80.6987	224.0256
21	23.4716	24.8376	26.2990	27.8629	29.5368	31.3289	33.2480	35.3034	37.5052	39.8643	42.3923	48.0057	54.4568	61.8733	70.4027	80.2143	91.5026	270.0307
25	28.5256	30.5140	32.6709	35.0117	37.5530	40.3131	43.3117	46.5706	50.1135	53.9660	58.1564	67.6765	78.9544	92.3240	108.1818	126.9988	149.3339	566.3773
30	35.1327	38.1018	41.3794	45.0003	49.0027	53.4295	58.3283	63.7524	69.7608	76.4194	83.8017	101.0730	122.3459	148.5752	180.9434	220.9132	270.2926	1418.2579
40	49.3752	55.0819	61.6100	69.0876	77.6633	87.5095	98.8265	111.8467	126.8398	144.1189	164.0477	213.6096	279.7810	368.2919	486.8518	645.8269	859.1424	8812.6294

This table shows the present value of an ordinary annuity of $1 at various interest rates (i) and time periods (n). It is used to calculate the present value of any series of equal payments made at the *beginning* of each compounding period.

TABLE 6A–6 Present Value of an Annuity Due of $1

$$PVAD = \left[\frac{1 - \dfrac{1}{(1+i)^n}}{i}\right] \times (1+i)$$

n/i	1.0%	1.5%	2.0%	2.5%	3.0%	3.5%	4.0%	4.5%	5.0%	5.5%	6.0%	7.0%	8.0%	9.0%	10.0%	11.0%	12.0%	20.0%
1	1.00000	1.00000	1.00000	1.00000	1.00000	1.00000	1.00000	1.00000	1.00000	1.00000	1.00000	1.00000	1.00000	1.00000	1.00000	1.00000	1.00000	1.00000
2	1.99010	1.98522	1.98039	1.97561	1.97087	1.96618	1.86154	1.95694	1.95238	1.94787	1.94340	1.93458	1.92593	1.91743	1.90909	1.90090	1.89286	1.83333
3	2.97040	2.95588	2.94156	2.92742	2.91347	2.89969	2.88609	2.87267	2.85941	2.84632	2.83339	2.80802	2.78326	2.75911	2.73554	2.71252	2.69005	2.52778
4	3.94099	3.91220	3.88388	3.85602	3.82861	3.80164	3.77509	3.74896	3.72325	3.69793	3.67301	3.62432	3.57710	3.53129	3.48685	3.44371	3.40183	3.10648
5	4.90197	4.85438	4.80773	4.76197	4.71710	4.67308	4.62990	4.58753	4.54595	4.50515	4.46511	4.38721	4.31213	4.23972	4.16987	4.10245	4.03735	3.58873
6	5.85343	5.78264	5.71346	5.64583	5.57971	5.51505	5.45182	5.38998	5.32948	5.27028	5.21236	5.10020	4.99271	4.88965	4.79079	4.69590	4.60478	3.99061
7	6.79548	6.69719	6.60143	6.50813	6.41719	6.32855	6.24214	6.15787	6.07569	5.99553	5.91732	5.76654	5.62288	5.48592	5.35526	5.23054	5.11141	4.32551
8	7.72819	7.59821	7.47199	7.34939	7.23028	7.11454	7.00205	6.89270	6.78637	6.68238	6.58238	6.38929	6.20637	6.03295	5.86842	5.71220	5.56376	4.60459
9	8.65168	8.48593	8.32548	8.17014	8.01969	7.87396	7.73274	7.59589	7.46321	7.33457	7.20979	6.97130	6.74664	6.53482	6.33493	6.14612	5.96764	4.83716
10	9.56602	9.36052	9.16224	8.97087	8.78611	8.60769	8.43533	8.26879	8.10782	7.95220	7.80169	7.51523	7.24689	6.99525	6.75902	6.53705	6.32825	5.03097
11	10.47130	10.22218	9.98259	9.75206	9.53020	9.31661	9.11090	8.91272	8.72173	8.53763	8.36009	8.02358	7.71008	7.41766	7.14457	6.88923	6.65022	5.19247
12	11.36763	11.07112	10.78685	10.51421	10.25262	10.00155	9.76048	9.52892	9.30641	9.09254	8.88687	8.49867	8.13896	7.80519	7.49506	7.20652	6.93770	5.32706
13	12.25508	11.90751	11.57534	11.25776	10.95400	10.66333	10.38507	10.11858	9.86325	9.61852	9.38384	8.94269	8.53608	8.16073	7.81369	7.49236	7.19437	5.43922
14	13.13374	12.73153	12.34837	11.98318	11.63496	11.30274	10.98565	10.68285	10.39357	10.11708	9.85268	9.35765	8.90378	8.48690	8.10336	7.74987	7.42355	5.53268
15	14.00370	13.54338	13.10625	12.69091	12.29607	11.92052	11.56312	11.22283	10.89864	10.58965	10.29498	9.74547	9.24424	8.78615	8.36669	7.98187	7.62817	5.61057
16	14.86505	14.34323	13.84926	13.38138	12.93794	12.51741	12.11839	11.73955	11.37966	11.03758	10.71225	10.10791	9.55948	9.06069	8.60608	8.19087	7.81086	5.67547
17	15.71787	15.13126	14.57771	14.05500	13.56110	13.09412	12.65230	12.23402	11.83777	11.46216	11.10590	10.44665	9.85137	9.31256	8.82371	8.37916	7.97399	5.72956
18	16.56225	15.90765	15.29187	14.71220	14.16612	13.65132	13.16567	12.70719	12.27407	11.86461	11.47726	10.76322	10.12164	9.54363	9.02155	8.54879	8.11963	5.77463
19	17.39827	16.67256	15.99203	15.35336	14.75351	14.18968	13.65930	13.15999	12.68959	12.24607	11.82760	11.05909	10.37189	9.75563	9.20141	8.70162	8.24967	5.81219
20	18.22601	17.42617	16.67846	15.97889	15.32380	14.70984	14.13394	13.59329	13.08532	12.60765	12.15812	11.33560	10.60360	9.95011	9.36492	8.83929	8.36578	5.84350
21	19.04555	18.16864	17.35143	16.58916	15.87747	15.21240	14.59033	14.00794	13.46221	12.95038	12.46992	11.59401	10.81815	10.12855	9.51356	8.96333	8.46944	5.86958
25	22.24339	21.03041	19.91393	18.88499	17.93554	17.05837	16.24696	15.49548	14.79864	14.15070	13.55036	12.46933	11.52876	10.70661	9.98474	9.34814	8.78432	5.93710
30	26.06579	24.37608	22.84438	21.45355	20.18845	19.03577	17.98371	17.02189	16.14107	15.33310	14.59072	13.27767	12.15841	11.19828	10.36961	9.65011	9.02181	5.97472
40	33.16303	30.36458	27.90259	25.73034	23.80822	22.10250	20.58448	19.22966	18.01704	16.92866	15.94907	14.26493	12.87858	11.72552	10.75696	9.93567	9.23303	5.99592

QUESTIONS FOR REVIEW OF KEY TOPICS

Q 6–1   Define interest.

Q 6–2   Explain compound interest.

Q 6–3   What would cause the annual interest rate to be different from the annual effective rate or yield?

Q 6–4   Identify the three items of information necessary to calculate the future value of a single amount.

Q 6–5   Define the present value of a single amount.

Q 6–6   Explain the difference between monetary and nonmonetary assets and liabilities.

Q 6–7   What is an annuity?

Q 6–8   Explain the difference between an ordinary annuity and an annuity due.

Q 6–9   Explain the relationship between Table 6A–2, Present Value of $1, and Table 6A–4, Present Value of an Ordinary Annuity.

Q 6–10   Prepare a time diagram for the present value of a four-year ordinary annuity of $200. Assume an interest rate of 10% per year.

Q 6–11   Prepare a time diagram for the present value of a four-year annuity due of $200. Assume an interest rate of 10% per year.

Q 6–12   What is a deferred annuity?

Q 6–13   Assume that you borrowed $500 from a friend and promised to repay the loan in five equal annual installments beginning one year from today. Your friend wants to be reimbursed for the time value of money at an 8% annual rate. Explain how you would compute the required annual payment.

Q 6–14   Compute the required annual payment in Question 6–13.

Q 6–15   Explain how the time value of money concept is incorporated into the valuation of long-term leases.

EXERCISES

E 6–1
Future value; single amount

Determine the future value of the following single amounts:

	Invested Amount	Interest Rate	No. of Periods
1.	$10,000	6%	12
2.	20,000	8	10
3.	30,000	12	20
4.	50,000	10	12

E 6–2
Present value; single amount

Determine the present value of the following single amounts:

	Future Amount	Interest Rate	No. of Periods
1.	$20,000	7%	10
2.	10,000	8	12
3.	25,000	12	20
4.	40,000	10	12

E 6–3
Present value; multiple, unequal amounts

Determine the combined present value as of December 31, 2003, of the following four payments to be received at the *end* of each of the designated years, assuming an annual interest rate of 8%.

Payment	Year Received
$5,000	2004
6,000	2005
8,000	2007
7,000	2009

E 6–4
Future value; single amounts

Determine the future value of $10,000 under each of the following sets of assumptions:

	Annual Rate	Period Invested	Interest Compounded
1.	10%	10 years	Semiannually
2.	12	5 years	Quarterly
3.	24	30 months	Monthly

E 6–5
Future value; annuities

Wiseman Video plans to make four annual deposits of $2,000 each to a special building fund. The fund's assets will be invested in mortgage instruments expected to pay interest at 12% on the fund's balance. Using the appropriate annuity table, determine how much will be accumulated in the fund on December 31, 2006, under each of the following situations:
1. The first deposit is made on December 31, 2003, and interest is compounded annually.
2. The first deposit is made on December 31, 2002, and interest is compounded annually.
3. The first deposit is made on December 31, 2002, and interest is compounded quarterly.
4. The first deposit is made on December 31, 2002, interest is compounded annually, *and* interest earned is withdrawn at the end of each year.

E 6–6
Present value; annuities

Using the appropriate present value table and assuming a 12% annual interest rate, determine the present value on December 31, 2003, of a five-period annual annuity of $5,000 under each of the following situations:
1. The first payment is received on December 31, 2004, and interest is compounded annually.
2. The first payment is received on December 31, 2003, and interest is compounded annually.
3. The first payment is received on December 31, 2004, and interest is compounded quarterly.

E 6–7
Solving for unknowns; single amounts

For each of the following situations involving single amounts, solve for the unknown (?). Assume that interest is compounded annually. (i = interest rate, and n = number of years)

	Present Value	Future Value	i	n
1.	?	$ 30,000	10%	5
2.	$36,289	65,000	?	10
3.	15,884	40,000	8	?
4.	46,651	100,000	?	8
5.	15,376	?	7	20

E 6–8
Solve for unknowns; annuities

For each of the following situations involving annuities, solve for the unknown (?). Assume that interest is compounded annually and that all annuity amounts are received at the *end* of each period. (i = interest rate, and n = number of years)

	Present Value	Annuity Amount	i	n
1.	?	$ 3,000	8%	5
2.	$242,980	75,000	?	4
3.	161,214	20,000	9	?
4.	500,000	80,518	?	8
5.	250,000	?	10	4

E 6–9
Future value; solving for annuities and single amount

John Rider wants to accumulate $100,000 to be used for his daughter's college education. He would like to have the amount available on December 31, 2008. Assume that the funds will accumulate in a certificate of deposit paying 8% interest compounded annually.

Required:
Answer each of the following independent questions.
1. If John were to deposit a single amount, how much would he have to invest on December 31, 2003?
2. If John were to make five equal deposits on each December 31, beginning on December 31, 2004, what is the required deposit?
3. If John were to make five equal deposits on each December 31, beginning on December 31, 2003, what is the required deposit?

E 6–10
Future and present value

Answer each of the following independent questions.
1. Alex Meir recently won a lottery and has the option of receiving one of the following three prizes: (1) $50,000 cash immediately, (2) $20,000 cash immediately and a five-period annuity of $8,000 beginning one year from today, or (3) a five-period annuity of $13,000 beginning one year from today. Assuming an interest rate of 6%, which option should Alex choose?
2. The Weimer Corporation wants to accumulate a sum of money to repay certain debts due on December 31, 2012. Weimer will make annual deposits of $100,000 into a special bank account at the end of each of 10 years beginning December 31, 2003. Assuming that the bank account pays 7% interest compounded annually, what will be the fund balance after the last payment is made on December 31, 2012?

E 6–11
Noninterest-bearing
note; single payment

The Field Detergent Company sold merchandise to the Abel Company on June 30, 2003. Payment was made in the form of a noninterest-bearing note requiring Abel to pay $85,000 on June 30, 2005. Assume that a 9% interest rate properly reflects the time value of money in this situation.

Required:
Calculate the amount at which Field should record the note receivable and corresponding sales revenue on June 30, 2003.

E 6–12
Solving for unknown
annuity payment

Don James purchased a new automobile for $20,000. Don made a cash down payment of $6,000 and agreed to pay the remaining balance in 30 monthly installments, beginning one month from the date of purchase. Financing is available at a 24% *annual* interest rate.

Required:
Calculate the amount of the required monthly payment.

E 6–13
Solving for unknown
interest rate

Lang Warehouses borrowed $100,000 from a bank and signed a note requiring 20 annual payments of $13,388 beginning one year from the date of the agreement.

Required:
Determine the interest rate implicit in this agreement.

E 6–14
Solving for unknown
annuity amount

Sandy Kupchack just graduated from State University with a bachelors degree in history. During her four years at the U, Sandy accumulated $10,000 in student loans. She asks for your help in determining the amount of the *quarterly* loan payment. She tells you that the loan must be paid back in five years and that the annual interest rate is 6%. Payments begin in three months.

Required:
Determine Sandy's quarterly loan payment.

E 6–15
Price of a bond

On September 30, 2003, the San Fillipo Corporation issued 8% stated rate bonds with a face amount of $300 million. The bonds mature on September 30, 2023 (20 years). The market rate of interest for similar bonds was 10%. Interest is paid semiannually on March 31 and September 30.

Required:
Determine the price of the bonds on September 30, 2003.

E 6–16
Deferred annuities

The Lincoln Company purchased merchandise from Grandville Corp. on September 30, 2003. Payment was made in the form of a noninterest-bearing note requiring Lincoln to make six annual payments of $5,000 on each September 30, beginning on September 30, 2006.

Required:
Calculate the amount at which Lincoln should record the note payable and corresponding purchases on September 30, 2003, assuming that an interest rate of 10% properly reflects the time value of money in this situation.

E 6–17
Deferred annuities;
solving for annuity
amount

On April 1, 2003, John Vaughn purchased appliances from the Acme Appliance Company for $1,200. In order to increase sales, Acme allows customers to pay in installments and will defer any payments for six months. John will make 18 equal monthly payments, beginning October 1, 2003. The annual interest rate implicit in this agreement is 24%.

Required:
Calculate the monthly payment necessary for John to pay for his purchases.

E 6–18
Lease payments

On June 30, 2003, Fly-By-Night Airlines leased a jumbo jet from Boeing Corporation. The terms of the lease require Fly-By-Night to make 20 annual payments of $250,000 on each June 30. Accounting standards require this lease to be recorded as a liability for the present value of scheduled payments. Assume that a 7% interest rate properly reflects the time value of money in this situation.

Required:
1. At what amount should Fly-By-Night record the lease liability on June 30, 2003, assuming that the first payment will be made on June 30, 2004.
2. At what amount should Fly-By-Night record the lease liability on June 30, 2003, *before* any payments are made, assuming that the first payment will be made on June 30, 2003.

E 6–19
Concepts; terminology

Listed below are several terms and phrases associated with concepts discussed in the chapter. Pair each item from List A (by letter) with the item from List B that is most appropriately associated with it.

List A	List B
____ 1. Interest	a. First cash flow occurs one period after agreement begins.
____ 2. Monetary asset	b. The rate at which money will actually grow during a year.
____ 3. Compound interest	c. First cash flow occurs on the first day of the agreement.
____ 4. Simple interest	d. The amount of money that a dollar will grow to.
____ 5. Annuity	e. Amount of money paid/received in excess of amount borrowed/lent.
____ 6. Present value of a single amount	f. Obligation to pay a sum of cash, the amount of which is fixed.
____ 7. Annuity due	
____ 8. Future value of a single amount	g. Money can be invested today and grow to a larger amount.
____ 9. Ordinary annuity	h. No fixed dollar amount attached.
____ 10. Effective rate or yield	i. Computed by multiplying an invested amount by the interest rate.
____ 11. Nonmonetary asset	j. Interest calculated on invested amount plus accumulated interest.
____ 12. Time value of money	k. A series of equal-sized cash flows.
____ 13. Monetary liability	l. Amount of money required today that is equivalent to a given future amount.
	m. Claim to receive a fixed amount of money.

PROBLEMS

P 6–1
Analysis of alternatives

The Esquire Company needs to acquire a molding machine to be used in its manufacturing process. Two types of machines that would be appropriate are presently on the market. The company has determined the following:

> Machine A could be purchased for $48,000. It will last 10 years with annual maintenance costs of $1,000 per year. After 10 years the machine can be sold for $5,000.
> Machine B could be purchased for $40,000. It also will last 10 years and will require maintenance costs of $4,000 in year three, $5,000 in year six, and $6,000 in year eight. After 10 years, the machine will have no salvage value.

Required:
Determine which machine Esquire should purchase. Assume an interest rate of 8% properly reflects the time value of money in this situation and that maintenance costs are paid at the end of each year. Ignore income tax considerations.

P 6–2
Present and future value

The Johnstone Company is facing several decisions regarding investing and financing activities. Address each decision independently.

1. On June 30, 2003, the Johnstone Company purchased equipment from Genovese Corp. Johnstone agreed to pay Genovese $10,000 on the purchase date and the balance in five annual installments of $8,000 on each June 30 beginning June 30, 2004. Assuming that an interest rate of 10% properly reflects the time value of money in this situation, at what amount should Johnstone value the equipment?

2. Johnstone needs to accumulate sufficient funds to pay a $400,000 debt that comes due on December 31, 2008. The company will accumulate the funds by making five equal annual deposits to an account paying 6% interest compounded annually. Determine the required annual deposit if the first deposit is made on December 31, 2003.

3. On January 1, 2003, Johnstone leased an office building. Terms of the lease require Johnstone to make 20 annual lease payments of $120,000 beginning on January 1, 2003. A 10% interest rate is implicit in the lease agreement. At what amount should Johnstone record the lease liability on January 1, 2003, *before* any lease payments are made?

P 6–3

Analysis of alternatives

The Harding Company is in the process of purchasing several large pieces of equipment from Danning Machine Corporation. Several financing alternatives have been offered by Danning:
1. Pay $1,000,000 in cash immediately.
2. Pay $420,000 immediately and the remainder in 10 annual installments of $80,000, with the first installment due in one year.
3. Make 10 annual installments of $135,000 with the first payment due immediately.
4. Make one lump-sum payment of $1,500,000 five years from date of purchase.

Required:
Determine the best alternative for Harding, assuming that Harding can borrow funds at an 8% interest rate.

P 6–4

Investment analysis

John Wiggins is contemplating the purchase of a small restaurant. The purchase price listed by the seller is $800,000. John has used past financial information to estimate that the net cash flows (cash inflows less cash outflows) generated by the restaurant would be as follows:

Years	Amount
1–6	$80,000
7	70,000
8	60,000
9	50,000
10	40,000

If purchased, the restaurant would be held for 10 years and then sold for an estimated $700,000.

Required:
Assuming that John desires a 10% rate of return on this investment, should the restaurant be purchased? (Assume that all cash flows occur at the end of the year.)

P 6–5

Investment decision; varying rates

John and Sally Claussen are contemplating the purchase of a hardware store from John Duggan. The Claussens anticipate that the store will generate cash flows of $70,000 per year for 20 years. At the end of 20 years, they intend to sell the store for an estimated $400,000. The Claussens will finance the investment with a variable rate mortgage. Interest rates will increase twice during the 20-year life of the mortgage. Accordingly, the Claussens' desired rate of return on this investment varies as follows:

Years 1–5	8%
Years 6–10	10%
Years 11–20	12%

Required:
What is the maximum amount the Claussens should pay John Duggan for the hardware store? (Assume that all cash flows occur at the end of the year.)

P 6–6

Solving for unknowns

The following situations should be considered independently.
1. John Jamison wants to accumulate $60,000 for a down payment on a small business. He will invest $30,000 today in a bank account paying 8% interest compounded annually. Approximately how long will it take John to reach his goal?
2. The Jasmine Tea Company purchased merchandise from a supplier for $28,700. Payment was a noninterest-bearing note requiring Jasmine to make five annual payments of $7,000 beginning one year from the date of purchase. What is the interest rate implicit in this agreement?
3. Sam Robinson borrowed $10,000 from a friend and promised to pay the loan in 10 equal annual installments beginning one year from the date of the loan. Sam's friend would like to be reimbursed for the time value of money at a 9% annual rate. What is the annual payment Sam must make to pay back his friend?

P 6–7

Solving for unknowns

The Lowlife Company defaulted on a $250,000 loan that was due on December 31, 2003. The bank has agreed to allow Lowlife to repay the $250,000 by making a series of equal annual payments beginning on December 31, 2004.

Required:
1. Calculate the required annual payment if the bank's interest rate is 10% and four payments are to be made.
2. Calculate the required annual payment if the bank's interest rate is 8% and five payments are to be made.

3. If the bank's interest rate is 10%, how many annual payments of $51,351 would be required to repay the debt?
4. If three payments of $104,087 are to be made, what interest rate is the bank charging Lowlife?

P 6–8

Deferred annuities

On January 1, 2003, the Montgomery company agreed to purchase a building by making six payments. The first three are to be $25,000 each, and will be paid on December 31, 2003, 2004, and 2005. The last three are to be $40,000 each and will be paid on December 31, 2006, 2007, and 2008. Montgomery borrowed other money at a 10% annual rate.

Required:
1. At what amount should Montgomery record the note payable and corresponding cost of the building on January 1, 2003?
2. How much interest expense on this note will Montgomery recognize in 2003?

P 6–9

Deferred annuities

John Roberts is 55 years old and has been asked to accept early retirement from his company. The company has offered John three alternative compensation packages to induce John to retire:
1. $180,000 cash payment to be paid immediately.
2. A 20-year annuity of $16,000 beginning immediately.
3. A 10-year annuity of $50,000 beginning at age 65.

Required:
Which alternative should John choose assuming that he is able to invest funds at a 7% rate?

P 6–10

Noninterest-bearing note; annuity and lump-sum payment

On January 1, 2003, The Barrett Company purchased merchandise from a supplier. Payment was a noninterest-bearing note requiring five annual payments of $20,000 on each December 31 beginning on December 31, 2003, and a lump-sum payment of $100,000 on December 31, 2007. A 10% interest rate properly reflects the time value of money in this situation.

Required:
Calculate the amount at which Barrett should record the note payable and corresponding merchandise purchased on January 1, 2003.

P 6–11

Solving for unknown lease payment

The Benning Manufacturing Company is negotiating with a customer for the lease of a large machine manufactured by Benning. The machine has a cash price of $800,000. Benning wants to be reimbursed for financing the machine at an 8% annual interest rate.

Required:
1. Determine the required lease payment if the lease agreement calls for 10 equal annual payments beginning immediately.
2. Determine the required lease payment if the first of 10 annual payments will be made one year from the date of the agreement.
3. Determine the required lease payment if the first of 10 annual payments will be made immediately and Benning will be able to sell the machine to another customer for $50,000 at the end of the 10-year lease.

P 6–12

Solving for unknown lease payment; compounding periods of varying length

(This is a variation of the previous problem focusing on compounding periods of varying length.)

The Benning Manufacturing Company is negotiating with a customer for the lease of a large machine manufactured by Benning. The machine has a cash price of $800,000. Benning wants to be reimbursed for financing the machine at a 12% annual interest rate over the five-year lease term.

Required:
1. Determine the required lease payment if the lease agreement calls for 10 equal semiannual payments beginning six months from the date of the agreement.
2. Determine the required lease payment if the lease agreement calls for 20 equal quarterly payments beginning immediately.
3. Determine the required lease payment if the lease agreement calls for 60 equal monthly payments beginning one month from the date of the agreement. The present value of an ordinary annuity factor for $n = 60$ and $i = 1\%$ is 44.9550.

P 6–13

Lease vs. buy alternatives

The Kiddy Toy Corporation needs to acquire the use of a machine to be used in its manufacturing process. The machine needed is manufactured by Lollie Corp. The machine can be used for 10 years and then sold for $10,000 at the end of its useful life. Lollie has presented Kiddy with the following options:
1. *Buy machine.* The machine could be purchased for $160,000 in cash. All maintenance and insurance costs, which approximate $5,000 per year, would be paid by Kiddy.
2. *Lease machine.* The machine could be leased for a 10-year period for an annual lease payment of $25,000 with the first payment due immediately. All maintenance and insurance costs will be paid for by the Lollie Corp. and the machine will revert back to Lollie at the end of the 10-year period.

Required:

Assuming that a 12% interest rate properly reflects the time value of money in this situation and that all maintenance and insurance costs are paid at the end of each year, determine which option Kiddy should choose. Ignore income tax considerations.

P 6–14
Deferred annuities;
pension obligation

Three employees of the Horizon Distributing Company will receive annual pension payments from the company when they retire. The employees will receive their annual payments for as long as they live. Life expectancy for each employee is 15 years beyond retirement. Their names, the amount of their annual pension payments, and the date they will receive their first payment are shown below:

Employee	Annual Payment	Date of First Payment
Tinkers	$20,000	12/31/06
Evers	25,000	12/31/07
Chance	30,000	12/31/08

Required:

1. Compute the present value of the pension obligation to these three employees as of December 31, 2003. Assume an 11% interest rate.
2. The company wants to have enough cash invested at December 31, 2006, to provide for all three employees. To accumulate enough cash, they will make three equal annual contributions to a fund that will earn 11% interest compounded annually. The first contribution will be made on December 31, 2003. Compute the amount of this required annual contribution.

BROADEN YOUR PERSPECTIVE

Real World Case 6–1
Lottery winnings

Apply your critical-thinking ability to the knowledge you've gained. These cases will provide you an opportunity to develop your research, analysis, judgment, and communication skills. You also will work with other students, integrate what you've learned, apply it in real world situations, and consider its global and ethical ramifications. This practice will broaden your knowledge and further develop your decision-making abilities.

Al Castellano had been buying California State lottery tickets for 15 years at his neighborhood liquor store. On Sunday, June 24, 2001, he awoke, opened the local newspaper, and compared his lottery ticket numbers with Saturday night's winning numbers. He couldn't believe his eyes as all of the numbers on his ticket matched the winning numbers. He went outside for a walk, came back into the kitchen and checked the numbers again. He woke his wife, Carmen, told her what had happened, and they started dancing. Al, a 66-year-old retired supermarket clerk, and Carmen, a 62-year-old semire-tired secretary, had won the richest lottery in California's history, $141 million!

On Thursday of the following week, Al and Carmen claimed their prize. They were informed that they would soon be receiving a check for approximately $43 million. The Castellanos chose to receive their lottery winnings in one lump-sum payment immediately rather than in 26 equal annual installments beginning immediately. The State of California is required to withhold 31% of lottery winnings for federal income tax purposes.

Required:

1. Explain why the Castellanos received $43 million rather than the $141 million lottery prize.
2. Determine the approximate interest rate the State of California used to calculate the $43 million lump-sum payment.
3. Did the Castellanos actually win $141 million?

Analysis Case 6–2
Bonus alternatives;
present value analysis

Sally Hamilton has performed well as the chief financial officer of the Maxtech Computer Company and has earned a bonus. She has a choice among the following three bonus plans:

1. A $50,000 cash bonus paid now.
2. A $10,000 annual cash bonus to be paid each year over the next six years, with the first $10,000 paid now.
3. A three-year $22,000 annual cash bonus with the first payment due three years from now.

Required:

Evaluate the three alternative bonus plans. Sally can earn a 6% annual return on her investments.

Communication Case 6–3
Present value of annuities

Harvey Alexander, an all-league professional football player, has just declared free agency. Two teams, the San Francisco 49ers and the Dallas Cowboys, have made Harvey the following offers to obtain his services:

49ers: $1 million signing bonus payable immediately and an annual salary of $1.5 million for the five-year term of the contract.

Cowboys: $2.5 million signing bonus payable immediately and an annual salary of $1 million for the five-year term of the contract.

With both contracts, the annual salary will be paid in one lump-sum at the end of the football season.

Required:
You have been hired as a consultant to Harvey's agent, Phil Marks, to evaluate the two contracts. Write a short letter to Phil with your recommendation including the method you used to reach your conclusion. Assume that Harvey has no preference between the two teams and that the decision will be based entirely on monetary considerations. Also assume that Harvey can invest his money and earn an 8% annual return.

Ethics Case 6–4
Rate of return

The Damon Investment Company manages a mutual fund composed mostly of speculative stocks. You recently saw an ad claiming that investments in the funds have been earning a rate of return of 21%. This rate seemed quite high so you called a friend who works for one of Damon's competitors. The friend told you that the 21% return figure was determined by dividing the two-year appreciation on investments in the fund by the average investment. In other words, $100 invested in the fund two years ago would have grown to $121 ($21 ÷ $100 = 21%).

Required:
Discuss the ethics of the 21% return claim made by the Damon Investment Company.

Judgment Case 6–5
Replacement decision

The Hughes Corporation is considering replacing a machine used in the manufacturing process with a new, more efficient model. The purchase price of the new machine is $150,000 and the old machine can be sold for $100,000. Output for the two machines is identical; they will both be used to produce the same amount of product for five years. However, the annual operating costs of the old machine are $18,000 compared to $10,000 for the new machine. Also, the new machine has a salvage value of $25,000, but the old machine will be worthless at the end of the five years.

Required:
Should the company sell the old machine and purchase the new model? Assume that an 8% rate properly reflects the time value of money in this situation and that all operating costs are paid at the end of the year. Ignore the effect of the decision on income taxes.

Real World Case 6–6
Zero-coupon notes

The 1997 financial statements of Hewlett-Packard Company included the following information in the long-term debt disclosure note:

	($ in millions)	
	1997	**1996**
Zero-coupon subordinated notes, due 2017	$968	—

Zero-coupon notes pay no interest. The disclosure stated that notes totaling $1.8 billion in maturity value were issued in October of 1997. The maturity value indicates the amount that the company will have to pay noteholders in 2017. Each individual note has a maturity value of $1,000. The company is accreting the issue price to maturity value using the note's effective interest rate.

Required:
1. Determine the approximate effective interest rate on the notes (round to the nearest whole %).
2. Determine the issue price of one $1,000 maturity value note.

Analysis Case 6–7
Time value of money applications
FedEx Corporation

Refer to the financial statements and related disclosure notes of FedEx Corporation in the appendix to Chapter 1.

Required:
1. Identify the various liabilities that are valued by applying the time value of money concept.
2. What rate is used to value pension obligations?

Economic Resources

2

7

CHAPTER

Cash and Receivables

OVERVIEW

We begin our study of assets by looking at cash and receivables—the two assets typically listed first in a balance sheet. Internal control and classification in the balance sheet are key issues we address in consideration of cash. For receivables, the key issues are valuation and the related income statement effects of transactions involving accounts receivable and notes receivable.

LEARNING OBJECTIVES

After studying this chapter, you should be able to:

LO1 Define what is meant by internal control and describe some key elements of an internal control system for cash receipts and disbursements.

LO2 Explain the possible restrictions on cash and their implications for classification in the balance sheet.

LO3 Distinguish between the gross and net methods of accounting for cash discounts.

LO4 Describe the accounting treatment for merchandise returns.

LO5 Describe the accounting treatment of anticipated uncollectible accounts receivable.

LO6 Describe the two approaches to estimating bad debts.

LO7 Describe the accounting treatment of short-term notes receivable.

LO8 Differentiate between the use of receivables in financing arrangements accounted for as a secured borrowing and those accounted for as a sale.

What Does It All Mean?

Your roommate, Todd Buckley, was surfing the net looking for information about his future employer, Cisco Systems. Todd, an engineering major, recently accepted a position with Cisco, the world's largest provider of hardware, software, and services that drive the Internet. He noticed an article on TheStreet.com entitled "Cisco Triples Bad-Account Provision." "This doesn't look good," Todd grumbled. "The article says that my new employer's deadbeat account column has more than tripled in the span of a year. I guess all those dot-com companies are not paying their bills. But this sentence is confusing. 'For the fiscal first quarter Cisco moved $275 million from operating cash to cover potential nonpayments from failed customers.' Did they actually move cash and if so, where did they move it and why?"

You studied accounting for bad debts in your intermediate accounting class and are confident you can help. After reading the article, you comfort Todd. "First of all, the term *provision* just means expense, and no, Cisco didn't move any cash. The company uses what is called the *allowance method* to account for its bad debts, and it looks like it simply recorded $275 million in expense for the quarter and increased the allowance for uncollectible accounts." Todd was not happy with your answer. "Provisions! allowance method! uncollectible accounts! I want you to help me understand, not make things worse." "Okay," you offer, "let's start at the beginning."

> By the time you finish this chapter, you should be able to respond appropriately to the questions posed in this case. Compare your response to the solution provided at the end of the chapter.

QUESTIONS:

1. Explain the allowance method of accounting for bad debts. (page 327)

2. What approaches might Cisco have used to arrive at the $275 million bad debt provision? (page 328)

3. Are there any alternatives to the allowance method? (page 331)

In the earlier chapters of this text, we studied the underlying measurement and reporting concepts for the basic financial statements presented to external decision makers. Now we turn our attention to the elements of those financial statements. Specifically, we further explore the elements of the balance sheet including the income statement effects of transactions involving these elements. We first address assets, then liabilities, and finally shareholders' equity. This chapter focuses on the current assets **cash and cash equivalents** and **receivables.**

PART

a

CASH AND CASH EQUIVALENTS

Cash includes currency and coins, balances in checking accounts, and items acceptable for deposit in these accounts, such as checks and money orders received from customers. These forms of cash represent amounts readily available to pay off debt or to use in operations without any legal or contractual restriction.

Managers typically invest temporarily idle cash to earn interest on those funds rather than keep an unnecessarily large checking account. These amounts are essentially equivalent to cash because they can quickly become available for use as cash. So, short-term, highly liquid investments that can be readily converted to cash with little risk of loss are viewed as cash equivalents. For financial reporting we make no distinction between cash in the form of currency or bank account balances and amounts held in cash equivalent investments.

A company's policy concerning which short-term, highly liquid investments it classifies as cash equivalents should be described in a disclosure note.

Cash equivalents include such things as certain money market funds, treasury bills, and commercial paper. To be classified as cash equivalents, these investments must have a maturity date no longer than three months *from the date of purchase.* Companies are permitted flexibility in designating cash equivalents and must establish individual policies regarding which short-term, highly liquid investments are classified as cash equivalents. A company's policy should be consistent with the usual motivation for acquiring certain types of investments. The policy should be disclosed in the notes to the financial statements. Graphic 7–1 shows a note from a recent annual report of the Colgate-Palmolive Company that provides a description of the company's cash equivalents.

GRAPHIC 7–1
Disclosure of Cash Equivalents—Colgate-Palmolive Company

> **2. Summary of Significant Accounting Policies (in part)**
> **Cash and Cash Equivalents**
> The company considers all highly liquid investments with maturities of three months or less when purchased to be cash equivalents. Investments in securities that do not meet the definition of cash equivalents are classified as marketable securities.

The measurement and reporting of cash and cash equivalents are largely straightforward because cash generally presents no measurement problems. It is the standard medium of exchange and the basis for measuring assets and liabilities. Cash and cash equivalents usually are combined and reported as a single amount in the balance sheet. However, cash that is not available for use in current operations because it is restricted for a special purpose usually is classified in one of the noncurrent asset categories. Restricted cash is discussed later in this chapter.

All assets must be safeguarded against possible misuse. However, cash is the most liquid asset and the asset most easily expropriated. As a result, a system of internal control of cash is a key accounting issue.

Internal Control of Cash

The success of any business enterprise depends on an effective system of **internal control.** Internal control refers to a company's plan to (a) encourage adherence to company policies and procedures, (b) promote operational efficiency, (c) minimize errors and theft, and (d) enhance the reliability and accuracy of accounting data. From a financial accounting perspective, the focus is on controls intended to improve the accuracy and reliability of accounting information and to safeguard the company's assets.

A critical aspect of an internal control system is the *separation of duties.* Individuals who have physical responsibility for assets should not also have access to accounting records. For example, if the same individual has control of both the supplies inventory and the accounting records, the theft of supplies could be concealed by a reduction of the supplies account.

As cash is the most liquid of all assets, a well-designed and functioning system of internal control must surround all cash transactions. Separation of duties is critical. Ideally, those who handle cash should not be involved in or have access to accounting records nor be involved in the reconciliation of cash book balances to bank balances.

> **Employees involved in recordkeeping should not also have physical access to the assets.**

INTERNAL CONTROL PROCEDURES—CASH RECEIPTS

Consider the cash receipt process. Most nonretail businesses receive payment for goods by checks received through the mail. An approach to internal control over cash receipts might include the following steps:

1. Employee A opens the mail each day and prepares a multicopy listing of all checks including the amount and payor's name.
2. Employee B takes the checks, along with one copy of the listing, to the person responsible for depositing the checks in the company's bank account.
3. A second copy of the check listing is sent to the accounting department where the receipts are entered into the records.

The amount received should equal the amount deposited as verified by comparison with the bank-generated deposit slip and the amount recorded in the accounting records. This helps ensure accuracy as well as safeguard cash against theft.

INTERNAL CONTROL PROCEDURES—CASH DISBURSEMENTS

Proper controls for cash disbursements should be designed to prevent any unauthorized payments and ensure that disbursements are recorded in the proper general ledger and subsidiary ledger accounts. Important elements of a cash disbursement control system include:

1. All disbursements, other than very small disbursements from petty cash, should be made by check. This provides a permanent record of all disbursements.
2. All expenditures should be *authorized* before a check is prepared. For example, a vendor invoice for the purchase of inventory should be compared with the purchase order and receiving report to ensure the accuracy of quantity, price, part numbers, and so on. This process should include verification of the proper ledger accounts to be debited.
3. Checks should be signed only by authorized individuals.

Responsibilities for check signing, check writing, check mailing, cash disbursement documentation, and recordkeeping ideally should be separated whenever possible.

An important part of any system of internal control of cash is the periodic reconciliation of book balances and bank balances to the correct balance. In addition, a petty cash system is employed by many business enterprises. We cover these two topics in Appendix 7 beginning on page 346.

Restricted Cash and Compensating Balances

We discussed the classification of assets and liabilities in Chapter 3. You should recall that only cash available for current operations or to satisfy current liabilities is classified as a current asset. Cash that is restricted in some way and not available for current use usually is reported as *investments and funds* or *other assets.*

Restrictions on cash can be informal, arising from management's intent to use a certain amount of cash for a specific purpose. For example, a company may set aside funds for future plant expansion. This cash, if material, should be classified as investments and funds or other assets. Sometimes restrictions are contractually imposed. Debt instruments, for instance, frequently require the borrower to set aside funds (often referred to as a sinking fund) for the future payment of a debt. In these instances, the restricted cash is classified as investments and funds or other assets if the debt is classified as noncurrent. On the other hand, if the liability is current, the restricted cash also is classified as current. Disclosure notes should describe any material restrictions of cash.

> **The effect of a *compensating balance* is a higher effective interest rate on the debt.**

Banks frequently require cash restrictions in connection with loans or loan commitments (lines of credit). Typically, the borrower is asked to maintain a specified balance in a low-interest or noninterest-bearing account at the bank (creditor). The required balance usually is some percentage of the committed amount (say 2% to 5%). These are known as **compensating balances** because they compensate the bank for granting the loan or extending the line of credit.

A compensating balance results in the borrower's paying an effective interest rate higher than the stated rate on the debt. For example, suppose that a company borrows $10,000,000 from a bank at an interest rate of 12%. If the bank requires a compensating balance of $2,000,000 to be held in a noninterest-bearing checking account, the company really is borrowing only $8,000,000 (the loan less the compensating balance). This means an effective interest rate of 15% ($1,200,000 interest divided by $8,000,000 cash available for use).

> **A material compensating balance must be disclosed regardless of the classification of the cash.**

The classification and disclosure of a compensating balance depends on the nature of the restriction and the classification of the related debt.[1] If the restriction is legally binding, the cash is classified as either current or noncurrent (investments and funds or other assets) depending on the classification of the related debt. In either case, note disclosure is appropriate.

If the compensating balance arrangement is informal with no contractual agreement that restricts the use of cash, the compensating balance can be reported as part of cash and cash equivalents, with note disclosure of the arrangement. Graphic 7–2 provides an example of a note disclosure of a compensating balance for Rag Shops, Inc., a company that operates a chain of retail craft and fabric stores in a number of eastern states.

GRAPHIC 7–2
Disclosure of Compensating Balances—Rag Shops, Inc.

> **Note 3. Note Payable—Bank (in part)**
> The Company maintains a credit facility with a bank. The credit facility is renewable annually on or before each December 31 and currently consists of a discretionary unsecured line of credit for direct borrowings and the issuance and refinance of letters of credit. The line of credit was increased from $8,000,000 to $10,000,000 on August 31, 1999. There were no direct borrowings outstanding under the line of credit at both September 1, 2001, and September 2, 2000, and the unused line of credit for direct borrowings and the issuance of letters of credit at September 1, 2001, was $9,803,146. The facility requires the Company to maintain a compensating balance of $400,000 . . .

DECISION MAKERS' PERSPECTIVE

Cash often is referred to as a *nonearning* asset because it earns no interest. For this reason, managers invest idle cash in either cash equivalents or short-term investments, both of which provide a return. Management's goal is to hold the minimum amount of cash necessary to conduct normal business operations, meet its obligations, and take advantage of opportuni-

---

[1]"Amendments to Regulations S-X and Related Interpretations and Guidelines Regarding the Disclosure of Compensating Balances and Short-Term Borrowing Arrangements," *Accounting Series Release No. 148,* Securities and Exchange Commission (November 13, 1973).

ties. Too much cash reduces profits through lost returns, while too little cash increases risk. This tradeoff between risk and return is an ongoing choice made by internal decision makers. Whether the choice made is appropriate is an ongoing assessment made by investors and creditors.

A company must have cash available for the compensating balances we discussed in the previous section as well as for planned disbursements related to normal operating, investing, and financing cash flows. However, because cash inflows and outflows can vary from planned amounts, a company needs an additional cash cushion as a precaution against that contingency. The size of the cushion depends on the company's ability to convert cash equivalents and short-term investments into cash quickly, along with its short-term borrowing capacity.

Liquidity is a measure of a company's cash position and overall ability to obtain cash in the normal course of business. A company is assumed to be liquid if it has sufficient cash or is capable of converting its other assets to cash in a relatively short period of time so that current needs can be met. Frequently, liquidity is measured with respect to the ability to pay currently maturing debt. The current ratio is one of the most common ways of measuring liquidity and is calculated by dividing current assets by current liabilities. By comparing liabilities that must be satisfied in the near term with assets that either are cash or will be converted to cash in the near term we have a base measure of a company's liquidity. We can refine the measure by adjusting for the implicit assumption of the current ratio that all current assets are equally liquid. In the acid-test or quick ratio, the numerator consists of "quick assets," which include only cash and cash equivalents, short-term investments, and accounts receivable. By eliminating inventories and prepaid expenses, the current assets that are less readily convertible into cash, we get a more precise indication of a company's short-term solvency than with the current ratio. We discussed and illustrated these liquidity ratios in Chapter 3.

We should evaluate the adequacy of any ratio in the context of the industry in which the company operates and other specific circumstances. Bear in mind, though, that industry averages are only one indication of acceptability and any ratio is but one indication of liquidity. Profitability, for instance, is perhaps the best long-run indication of liquidity. And a company may be very efficient in managing its current assets so that, say, receivables are more liquid than they otherwise would be. The receivables turnover ratio we discuss in Part b of this chapter offers a measure of management's efficiency in this regard.

There are many techniques that a company can use to manage cash balances. A discussion of these techniques is beyond the scope of this text. However, it is sufficient here to understand that management must make important decisions related to cash that have a direct impact on a company's profitability and risk. Because the lack of prudent cash management can lead to the failure of an otherwise sound company, it is essential that managers as well as outside investors and creditors maintain close vigil over this facet of a company's health. ■

Companies hold cash to pay for planned and unplanned transactions and to satisfy compensating balance requirements.

A liquidity ratio is but one indication of a company's liquidity.

A manager should actively monitor the company's cash position.

CURRENT RECEIVABLES

P A R T

b

Receivables represent a company's claims to the future collection of cash, other assets, or services. Receivables resulting from the sale of goods or services on account are called **accounts receivable** and often are referred to as *trade receivables*. *Nontrade receivables* are those other than trade receivables and include tax refund claims, interest receivable, and loans by the company to other entities including stockholders and employees. When a receivable, trade or nontrade, is accompanied by a formal promissory note, it is referred to as a note receivable. We consider notes receivable after first discussing accounts receivable.

As you study receivables, realize that one company's claim to the future collection of cash corresponds to another company's (or individual's) obligation to pay cash. One company's account receivable will be the mirror image of another company's account payable—the measurement issues are identical. Chapter 13 addresses accounts payable and other current liabilities.

An account receivable and an account payable are two sides of the same coin.

CHECK WITH THE **COACH**

Managing a company's liquidity is a key to its survival. Lenders and suppliers are especially concerned with liquidity when evaluating the creditworthiness of a company. The Coach will help you understand why accounting information is critical in assessing credit risks. Use the Coach to hear what lenders and managers have to say about what the numbers mean to them and to gain an understanding of the judgments involved in accounting for receivables. ■

Accounts Receivable

Accounts receivable are current assets because, by definition, they will be converted to cash within the normal operating cycle.

Most businesses provide credit to their customers, either because it's not practical to require immediate cash payment or to encourage customers to purchase the company's product or service. Accounts receivable are *informal* credit arrangements supported by an invoice and normally are due in 30 to 60 days after the sale. They almost always are classified as *current* assets because their normal collection period, even if longer than a year, is part of, and therefore less than, the operating cycle.

Typically, revenue and related accounts receivable are recognized at the point of delivery of the product or service.

The point at which accounts receivable are recognized depends on the earnings process of the company. We discussed the realization principle in Chapter 5 and the criteria that must be met before revenue can be recognized. Recall that revenue can be recognized only after the earnings process is *virtually complete* and *collection* from the customer is *reasonably certain.* For the typical credit sale, these criteria are satisfied at the point of delivery of the product or service, so revenue and the related receivable are recognized at that time.

INITIAL VALUATION OF ACCOUNTS RECEIVABLE

We know from prior discussions that receivables should be recorded at the present value of future cash receipts using a realistic interest rate. So, a $10,000 sale on credit due in 30 days should result in a receivable valued at the present value of the $10,000. In other words, the interest portion of the $10,000 due in 30 days should be removed and recognized as interest revenue over the 30-day period, not as sales revenue at date of delivery of the product. If the monthly interest rate is 2%, the receivable would be valued at $9,804, calculated by multiplying the future cash payment of $10,000 by the present value of $1 factor for one period at 2% (.98039).

The typical account receivable is valued at the amount expected to be received, not the present value of that amount.

However, because the difference between the future and present values of accounts receivable often is immaterial, *APB Opinion 21* specifically excludes accounts receivable from the general rule that receivables be recorded at present value.[2] Therefore, accounts receivable initially are valued at the exchange price agreed on by the buyer and seller. In our example, both the account receivable and sales revenue would be recorded at $10,000. Let's discuss two aspects of accounts receivable related to their initial valuation—trade discounts and cash discounts.

Trade Discounts. Companies frequently offer **trade discounts** to customers, usually a percentage reduction from the list price. Trade discounts can be a way to change prices without publishing a new catalog or to disguise real prices from competitors. They also are used to give quantity discounts to large customers. For example, a manufacturer might list a machine part at $2,500 but sell it to a customer at list less a 10% discount. The trade discount of $250 is not recognized directly when recording the transaction. The discount is recognized indirectly by recording the sale at the net of discount price of $2,250, not at the list price.

Cash discounts reduce the amount to be paid if remittance is made within a specified short period of time.

Cash Discounts. Be careful to distinguish a *trade* discount from a *cash* discount. **Cash discounts,** often called *sales discounts,* represent reductions not in the selling price of a good or service but in the amount to be paid by a credit customer if paid within a specified period of time. It is a discount intended to provide incentive for quick payment.

---

[2]"Interest on Receivables and Payables," *Accounting Principles Board Opinion No. 21* (New York: AICPA, 1971).

The amount of the discount and the time period within which it's available usually are conveyed by cryptic terms like 2/10, n/30 (meaning a 2% discount if paid within 10 days, otherwise full payment within 30 days). There are two ways to record cash discounts, the gross method and the net method. Conceptually, the **gross method** views a discount not taken by the customer as part of sales of revenue. On the other hand, the **net method** considers sales revenue to be the net amount, after discount, and any discounts not taken by the customer as interest revenue. The discounts are viewed as compensation to the seller for providing financing to the customer. With both methods, discounts *taken* reduce sales revenue. Consider the example in Illustration 7–1.

The Hawthorne Manufacturing Company offers credit customers a 2% cash discount if the sales price is paid within 10 days. Any amounts not paid within 10 days are due in 30 days. These repayment terms are stated as 2/10, n/30. On October 5, 2003, Hawthorne sold merchandise at a price of $20,000. The customer paid $13,720 ($14,000 less the 2% cash discount) on October 14 and the remaining balance of $6,000 on November 4.

The appropriate journal entries to record the sale and cash collection, comparing the gross and net methods are as follows:

Gross Method			Net Method		
October 5, 2003					
Accounts receivable	20,000		Accounts receivable	19,600	
Sales revenue		20,000	Sales revenue		19,600
October 14, 2003					
Cash	13,720		Cash	13,720	
Sales discounts	280		Accounts receivable		13,720
Accounts receivable . . .		14,000			
November 4, 2003					
Cash	6,000		Cash	6,000	
Accounts receivable . . .		6,000	Accounts receivable		5,880
			Interest revenue		120

ILLUSTRATION 7–1
Cash Discounts

By either method, net sales is reduced by discounts *taken*.

Discounts *not* taken are included in sales revenue using the gross method and interest revenue using the net method.

Notice that by using the gross method, we record the revenue and related receivable at the full $20,000 price. On remittance within the discount period, the $280 discount is recorded as a debit to an account called *sales discounts*. This is a contra account to sales revenue and is deducted from sales revenue to derive the net sales reported in the income statement. For payments made after the discount period, cash is simply increased and accounts receivable decreased by the gross amount originally recorded.

Under the net method, we record revenue and the related accounts receivable at the agreed on price *less* the 2% discount applied to the entire price. Payments made within the discount period are recorded as debits to cash and credits to accounts receivable for the amount received. If a customer loses a discount by failing to pay within the discount period, the discount not taken is recorded as interest revenue. In this case, $120 in cash (2% × $6,000) is interest.

Total revenue in the 2003 income statement would be the same by either method:

The *gross method* views cash discounts *not* taken as part of sales revenue.

The *net method* considers cash discounts *not* taken as interest revenue.

	Gross Method	Net Method
Sales	$20,000	$19,600
Less: Sales discounts	(280)	-0-
Net sales revenue	19,720	19,600
Interest revenue	0	120
Total revenue	$19,720	$19,720

Revenue comparison of the gross method and the net method

Which is correct? Conceptually, the net method usually reflects the reality of the situation—the real price is $19,600 and $120 is an interest penalty for not paying promptly. The net price usually is the price expected by the seller because the discount usually reflects a hefty interest cost that prudent buyers are unwilling to bear. Consider Illustration 7–1. Although the discount rate is stated as 2%, the effective rate really is 36.5%. The buyer must pay 2% of the price to delay payment an additional 20 days beyond the 10-day discount period. To convert this 20-day rate to an annual rate, we multiply by 365/20:

$$2\% \times 365/20 = 36.5\% \text{ effective rate}$$

Understandably, most buyers try to take the discount if at all possible.

The difference between the two methods, in terms of the effect of the transactions on income, is in the timing of the recognition of any discounts not taken. The gross method recognizes discounts not taken as revenue when the sale is made. The net method recognizes them as revenue after the discount period has passed and the cash is collected. These two measurement dates could be in different reporting periods.

From a practical standpoint, the effect on the financial statements of the difference between the two methods usually is immaterial. As a result, most companies use the gross method because it's easier and doesn't require adjusting entries for discounts not taken.

SUBSEQUENT VALUATION OF ACCOUNTS RECEIVABLE

Following the initial valuation of an account receivable, two situations possibly could cause the cash ultimately collected to be less than the initial valuation of the receivable: (1) the customer could return the product, or (2) the customer could default and not pay the agreed on sales price. When accounting for sales and accounts receivable, we anticipate these possibilities.

LO4

Sales Returns.   Customers frequently are given the right to return the merchandise they purchase if they are not satisfied. We discussed how this policy affects revenue recognition in Chapter 5. We now discuss it from the perspective of asset valuation.

When merchandise is returned for a refund or for credit to be applied to other purchases the situation is called a **sales return.** When practical, a dissatisfied customer might be given a special price reduction as an incentive to keep the merchandise purchased.[3] Returns are common and often substantial in some industries such as food products, publishing, and retailing. In these cases, recognizing returns and allowances only as they occur could cause profit to be overstated in the period of the sale and understated in the return period. For example, assume merchandise is sold to a customer for $10,000 in December 2003, the last month in the selling company's fiscal year, and that the merchandise cost $6,000. If all of the merchandise is returned in 2004 after financial statements for 2003 are issued, gross profit will be overstated in 2003 and understated in 2004 by $4,000. Assets at the end of 2003 also will be overstated by $4,000 because a $10,000 receivable would be recorded instead of $6,000 in inventory.

Recognizing sales returns when they occur could result in an overstatement of income in the period of the related sale.

To avoid misstating the financial statements, when amounts are material, returns should be anticipated by subtracting an allowance for estimated returns. For an example, refer to Illustration 7–2.

The allowance for sales returns is a contra account to accounts receivable. When returns actually occur in the following reporting period, the allowance for sales returns is debited. In this way, income is not reduced in the return period but in the period of the sales revenue.[4]

The perpetual inventory system records increases (debits) and decreases (credits) in the inventory account as they occur. The inventory of $78,000 in the first set of entries represents merchandise actually returned and on hand, while the inventory of $42,000 in the second set of entries represents an estimate of the cost of merchandise expected to be returned.

---

[3]Price reductions sometimes are referred to as *sales allowances* and are distinguished from situations when the products actually are returned for a refund or credit (sales returns).

[4]Of course, if the allowance for sales returns is estimated incorrectly, income in both the period of the sale and the return will be misstated.

During 2003, its first year of operations, the Hawthorne Manufacturing Company sold merchandise on account for $2,000,000. This merchandise cost $1,200,000 (60% of the selling price). Industry experience indicates that 10% of all sales will be returned. Customers returned $130,000 in sales during 2003, prior to making payment.

The entries to record sales and merchandise returned during the year, *assuming that a perpetual inventory system is used,* are as follows:

Sales

Accounts receivable	2,000,000	
Sales revenue		2,000,000
Cost of goods sold (60% × $2,000,000)	1,200,000	
Inventory		1,200,000

Returns

Sales returns (actual returns)	130,000	
Accounts receivable		130,000
Inventory	78,000	
Cost of goods sold (60% × $130,000)		78,000

At the end of 2003, the company would anticipate the remaining estimated returns using the following adjusting entries:

Adjusting entries

Sales returns ([10% × $2,000,000] − $130,000)	70,000	
Allowance for sales returns		70,000
Inventory—estimated returns	42,000	
Cost of goods sold (60% × $70,000)		42,000

ILLUSTRATION 7–2

Sales Returns

If sales returns are material, they should be estimated and recorded in the same period as the related sales.

This later amount is included in the period-end inventory in the company's balance sheet even though the actual merchandise belongs to other entities.

Quite often, a customer will return merchandise because it has been damaged during shipment or is defective. This possibility must be anticipated in a company's estimate of returns. As you will study in Chapter 9, inventory is valued at the lower-of-cost-or-market. Therefore, damaged or defective merchandise returned from a customer must be written down to market value.

Assuming that the estimates of future returns are correct, the following (summary) journal entry would be recorded in 2004:

Allowance for sales returns	70,000	
Accounts receivable		70,000

In some industries, returns are typically small and infrequent. Companies in these industries usually simply record returns in the period they occur because the effect on income measurement and asset valuation is immaterial. In a few situations, significant uncertainty as to future collection is created by the right of return. In those cases, revenue recognition is deferred until the uncertainty is resolved. We discussed this possibility in Chapter 5.

If sales returns are immaterial, they can be recorded as they occur.

Uncollectible Accounts Receivable.   Companies that extend credit to customers know that it's unlikely that all customers will fully pay their accounts. **Bad debt expense** is an inherent cost of granting credit. It's an operating expense incurred to boost sales. As a result, even when specific customer accounts haven't been proven uncollectible by the end of the reporting period, the expense properly should be matched with sales revenue in the income statement for that period.[5] Likewise, as it's not expected that all accounts receivable will be collected, the balance sheet should report only the expected net realizable value of the asset, that is, the amount of cash the company expects to actually collect from customers. An

FINANCIAL REPORTING CASE

Q1, p. 319

---

[5]Some consider bad debts to be a contra (reduction) to revenue rather than an operating expense.

The use of the *allowance method* is an attempt to satisfy the matching principle in accounting for bad debts.

estimate is therefore needed to record bad debt expense and the related reduction of accounts receivable. In an adjusting entry, we record bad debt expense and reduce accounts receivable indirectly by crediting a contra account (allowance for uncollectible accounts) to accounts receivable for an estimate of the amount that eventually will prove uncollectible. This approach to accounting for bad debts is known as the **allowance method.**

There are two ways commonly used to arrive at this estimate of future bad debts—the income statement approach and the balance sheet approach. Illustration 7–3 is used to demonstrate both approaches. As you proceed through the illustration, remember that the two approaches represent alternative ways to estimate the *amount* of future bad debts. Except for the amounts, the accounting entries are identical.

ILLUSTRATION 7–3

Bad Debts

The Hawthorne Manufacturing Company sells its products offering 30 days' credit to its customers. During 2003, its first year of operations, the following events occurred:

Sales on credit	$1,200,000
Cash collections from credit customers	(895,000)
Accounts receivable, end of year	$ 305,000

There were no specific accounts determined to be uncollectible in 2003. The company anticipates that 2% of all credit sales will ultimately become uncollectible.

Bad debt expense is estimated as a percentage of net credit sales.

FINANCIAL REPORTING CASE

Q2, p. 319

Income statement approach.   Using the **income statement approach,** we estimate bad debt expense as a percentage of each period's net credit sales. This percentage usually is determined by reviewing the company's recent history of the relationship between credit sales and actual bad debts. For a relatively new company, this percentage may be obtained by referring to other sources such as industry averages.

Under the income statement approach, the Hawthorne Manufacturing Company would make the following adjusting journal entry at the end of 2003:

Bad debt expense (2% × $1,200,000)	24,000	
Allowance for uncollectible accounts		24,000

Allowance for uncollectible accounts is a contra account to accounts receivable. In the current asset section of the 2003 balance sheet, accounts receivable would be reported *net* of the allowance, as follows:

Accounts receivable	$305,000
Less: Allowance for uncollectible accounts	(24,000)
Net accounts receivable	$281,000

Quite often, companies report the allowance for uncollectible accounts (sometimes called *allowance for doubtful accounts*) parenthetically or alongside the accounts receivable account title separated by a dash or a comma. For example, FedEx Corporation reported the following under current assets in its comparative balance sheets for 2001 and 2000:

FedEx Corporation

	($ in thousands)	
	2001	**2000**
Receivables—less allowances of $95,815 and $85,972	$2,506,044	$2,547,043

The $2,506,044,000 figure at the end of 2001 is the company's estimate of the net realizable value of accounts receivable. Actual (gross) accounts receivable at the end of 2001 were $2,601,859,000 ($2,506,044,000 + 95,815,000).

ETHICAL DILEMMA

The management of the Auto Parts Division of the Santana Corporation receives a bonus if the division's income achieves a specific target. For 2003 the target will be achieved by a wide margin. Mary Beth Williams, the controller of the division, has been asked by Philip Stanton, the head of the division's management team, to try to reduce this year's income and "bank" some of the profits for future years. Mary Beth suggests that the division's bad debt expense as a percentage of net credit sales for 2003 be increased from 3% to 5%. She believes that 3% is the more accurate estimate but knows that both the corporation's internal auditors as well as the external auditors allow some flexibility when estimates are involved. Does Mary Beth's proposal present an ethical dilemma?

It's important to notice that the income statement approach focuses on the current year's credit sales. The effect on the balance sheet—the allowance for uncollectible accounts and hence net accounts receivable—is an incidental result of estimating the expense. An alternative is to focus on the balance sheet amounts instead. We look at this approach next.

> Using the *income statement approach*, the balance sheet amount is an indirect outcome of estimating bad debt expense.

Balance sheet approach. Using the **balance sheet approach** to estimate future bad debts, we determine bad debt expense by estimating the net realizable value of accounts receivable to be reported in the balance sheet. In other words, the allowance for uncollectible accounts is determined. Bad debt expense is an indirect outcome of adjusting the allowance account to the desired balance.

> Using the *balance sheet approach*, bad debt expense is an incidental result of estimating the net realizable value of accounts receivable.

For the Hawthorne Manufacturing Company example in Illustration 7–3, the company would estimate the amount of uncollectible accounts that will result from the $305,000 in accounts receivable outstanding at the end of 2003. This could be done by analyzing each customer account, by applying a percentage to the entire outstanding receivable balance, or by applying different percentages to accounts receivable balances depending on the length of time outstanding. This latter approach normally employs an **accounts receivable aging schedule.** For example, the aging schedule for Hawthorne's 2003 year-end accounts receivable is shown in Illustration 7–3A.

Customer	Accounts Receivable 12/31/03	0–60 Days	61–90 Days	91–120 Days	Over 120 Days
Axel Manufacturing Co.	$ 20,000	$ 14,000	$ 6,000		
Banner Corporation	33,000		20,000	$10,000	$ 3,000
Dando Company	60,000	50,000	10,000		
` ` ` `	` `	` `	` `	` `	` `
` ` ` `	` `	` `	` `	` `	` `
Xicon Company	18,000	10,000	4,000	3,000	1,000
Totals	$305,000	$220,000	$50,000	$25,000	$10,000

ILLUSTRATION 7–3A

Accounts Receivable Aging Schedule

The schedule assumes older accounts are more likely to prove uncollectible.

Summary

Age Group	Amount	Estimated Percent Uncollectible	Estimated Allowance
0–60 days	$220,000	5%	$11,000
61–90 days	50,000	10%	5,000
91–120 days	25,000	20%	5,000
Over 120 days	10,000	45%	4,500
Allowance for uncollectible accounts			$25,500

Higher estimated default percentages are applied to groups of older receivables.

The schedule classifies the year-end receivable balances according to their length of time outstanding. Presumably, the longer an account has been outstanding the more likely it will prove uncollectible. Based on past experience or other sources of information, a percentage is applied to age group totals.

The 2003 entry to record bad debts adjusts the balance in the allowance for uncollectible accounts to this required amount of $25,500. Because it is the first year of operations for Hawthorne and the beginning balance in the allowance account is zero, the adjusting entry would *debit* bad debt expense and *credit* allowance for uncollectible accounts for $25,500.

To illustrate the concept further, let's suppose that this was not the first year of operations and the allowance account prior to the adjusting entry had a *credit* balance of $4,000. Then the amount of the entry would be $21,500—the amount necessary to adjust a credit balance of $4,000 to a credit balance of $25,500. Similarly, if the allowance account prior to the adjusting entry had a *debit* balance[6] of $4,000, then the amount of the entry would be $29,500.

Some companies use a combination of approaches in estimating bad debts. For example, Hawthorne could decide to accrue bad debts on a monthly basis using the income statement approach and then employ the balance sheet approach at the end of the year based on an aging of receivables. Each month an adjusting entry would record a debit to bad debt expense and a credit to allowance for uncollectible accounts equal to 2% of credit sales. In our illustration, the monthly accruals for 2003 would result in the following account balances at the end of 2003:

Allowance	
Beg. bal.	4,000
Adj. entry	21,500
Bal.	25,500

Accounts Receivable		Bad Debt Expense	
305,000		24,000	

Allowance for Uncollectible Accounts	
	24,000

At the end of the year, if the aging revealed a required allowance of $25,500, the following adjusting entry would be recorded:

Bad debt expense...	1,500	
Allowance for uncollectible accounts		1,500

This entry adjusts the allowance account to the required amount.

In the 2003 balance sheet, accounts receivable would be reported net of the allowance, as follows:

Accounts receivable	$305,000
Less: Allowance for uncollectible accounts	(25,500)
Net accounts receivable	$279,500

When accounts are deemed uncollectible.   The actual write-off of a receivable occurs when it is determined that all or a portion of the amount due will not be collected. Using the allowance method, the write-off is recorded as a debit to allowance for uncollectible accounts and a credit to accounts receivable. In our illustration, assume that actual bad debts in 2004 were $25,000. These write-offs would be recorded (in a summary journal entry) as follows:

Allowance for uncollectible accounts	25,000	
Accounts receivable		25,000

---

[6]A debit balance could result if the amount of receivables actually written off (discussed below) during the period exceeds the beginning credit balance in the allowance account.

Net realizable value is not affected directly by the write-offs.

Accounts receivable	$280,000
Less: Allowance for uncollectible accounts	(500)
Net accounts receivable	$279,500

Of course, actual bad debts will tend to differ from estimates. However, the year in which the estimate is made, 2003 in this case, is unaffected by the incorrect estimate. If the prior year's estimate of bad debts is too low, then, using the balance sheet approach, bad debt expense in the subsequent year will be increased. If the estimate is too high, then bad debt expense in the subsequent year will be decreased. For example, in our illustration, the allowance at the end of 2003 is $25,500. Actual bad debts related to 2003 receivables are $25,000. 2003's financial information cannot be changed. Instead, the $500 credit balance in allowance for uncollectible accounts will cause 2004's bad debt expense to be less than if 2003's estimate of bad debts had been correct.

When previously written-off accounts are collected.   Occasionally, a receivable that has been written off will be collected in part or in full. When this happens, the receivable and the allowance should be reinstated. In other words, the entry to write off the account simply is reversed. The collection is then recorded the usual way as a debit to cash and a credit to accounts receivable. This process ensures that the company will have a complete record of the payment history of the customer. For example, assume that in our illustration, $1,200 that was previously written off is collected. The following journal entries record the event:

Accounts receivable	1,200	
Allowance for uncollectible accounts		1,200
Cash.	1,200	
Accounts receivable		1,200

Direct write-off of uncollectible accounts.   If uncollectible accounts are not anticipated or are immaterial, or if it's not possible to reliably estimate uncollectible accounts, an allowance for uncollectible accounts is not appropriate. In these few cases, adjusting entries are not recorded and any bad debts that do arise simply are written off as bad debt expense. A $750 uncollectible account would be recorded as follows:

Bad debt expense.	750	
Accounts receivable		750

This approach is known as the **direct write-off method**. Of course, if the sale that generated this receivable occurred in a previous reporting period, the matching principle is violated. Operating expenses would have been understated and assets overstated in that period. This is why the direct write-off method of accounting for uncollectible accounts is not permitted by GAAP except in limited circumstances. Specifically, the allowance method must be used if it is probable that a material amount of receivables will not be collected and the amount can be reasonably estimated.[7] For federal income tax purposes, however, the direct write-off method is the required method for most companies and the allowance method is not permitted.

Graphic 7–3 summarizes the key issues involving measuring and reporting accounts receivable.

---

[7] "Accounting for Contingencies," *Statement of Financial Accounting Standards No. 5* (Stamford, Conn.: FASB, 1975), par. 8.

Recognition	Depends on the earnings process; for most credit sales, revenue and the related receivables are recognized at the point of delivery.
Initial valuation	Initially recorded at the exchange price agreed upon by the buyer and seller.
Subsequent valuation	Initial valuation reduced by: 1. Allowance for sales returns 2. Allowance for uncollectible accounts: —The income statement approach —The balance sheet approach
Classification	Almost always classified as a current asset.

GLOBAL PERSPECTIVE

In the United States, bad debts are estimated and the allowance for uncollectibles is deducted from the face amount of receivables. Globally, the practice of estimating bad debts is standard. Most countries also establish an allowance, or reserve for bad debts that reduces receivables to net realizable value. However, differences do exist. For example, in Germany estimated bad debts are deducted directly from the receivables.

CONCEPT REVIEW EXERCISE

Uncollectible Accounts Receivable

The Hawthorne Manufacturing Company sells its products, offering 30 days' credit to its customers. Uncollectible amounts are estimated by accruing a monthly charge to bad debt expense equal to 2% of credit sales. At the end of the year, the allowance for uncollectible accounts is adjusted based on an aging of accounts receivable. The company began 2004 with the following balances in its accounts:

Accounts receivable	$305,000
Allowance for uncollectible accounts	(25,500)

During 2004, sales on credit were $1,300,000, cash collections from customers were $1,250,000, and actual write-offs of accounts were $25,000. An aging of accounts receivable at the end of 2004 indicates a required allowance of $30,000.

Required:
1. Determine the balances in accounts receivable and allowance for uncollectible accounts at the end of 2004.
2. Determine bad debt expense for 2004.
3. Prepare journal entries for the monthly accrual of bad debts (in summary form), the write-off of receivables, and the year-end adjusting entry for bad debts.

SOLUTION

1. Determine the balances in accounts receivable and allowance for uncollectible accounts at the end of 2004.

Accounts receivable:	
Beginning balance	$ 305,000
Add: Credit sales	1,300,000
Less: Cash collections	(1,250,000)
Write-offs	(25,000)
Ending balance	$ 330,000

Allowance for uncollectible accounts:

Beginning balance	$ 25,500
Add: Bad debt expense recorded monthly (2% × $1,300,000)	26,000 ✓
Less: Write-offs	(25,000)
Balance before year-end adjustment	26,500
Year-end adjustment	3,500*
Ending balance	$ 30,000

*Required allowance of $30,000 less $26,500 already in allowance account.

2. Determine bad debt expense for 2004.

Bad debt expense would be $29,500 (monthly accrual of $26,000 plus year-end adjustment of an additional $3,500).

3. Prepare journal entries for the monthly accrual of bad debts (in summary form), the write-off of receivables, and the year-end adjusting entry for bad debts.

Bad debt expense (2% × $1,300,000)	26,000	
Allowance for uncollectible accounts		26,000
Monthly accrual of 2% of credit sales—summary entry.		
Allowance for uncollectible accounts	25,000	
Accounts receivable		25,000
Write-off of accounts receivable as they are determined uncollectible.		
Bad debt expense.	3,500	
Allowance for uncollectible accounts		3,500
Year-end adjusting entry for bad debts.		

Notes Receivable

Notes receivable are formal credit arrangements between a creditor (lender) and a debtor (borrower). Notes arise from loans to other entities including affiliated companies and to stockholders and employees, from the extension of the credit period to trade customers, and occasionally from the sale of merchandise, other assets, or services. Notes receivable are classified as either current or noncurrent depending on the expected payment date(s).

Our examples below illustrate short-term notes. When the term of a note is longer than a year, it is reported as a long-term note. Long-term notes receivable are discussed in conjunction with long-term notes payable in Chapter 14.

INTEREST-BEARING NOTES

The typical note receivable requires the payment of a specified face amount, also called *principal,* at a specified maturity date or dates. In addition, interest is paid at a stated percentage of the face amount. Interest on notes is calculated as:

LO7

Face amount × Annual rate × Fraction of the annual period

For an example, consider Illustration 7–4.

ILLUSTRATION 7–4	The Stridewell Wholesale Shoe Company manufactures athletic shoes that it sells to retailers. On May 1, 2003, the company sold shoes to Harmon Sporting Goods. Stridewell agreed to accept a $700,000, 6-month, 12% note in payment for the shoes. Interest is payable at maturity. Stridewell would account for the note as follows:*
Note Receivable	

May 1, 2003

Note receivable...	700,000	
Sales revenue..		700,000
To record the sale of goods in exchange for a note receivable.		

November 1, 2003

Cash ($700,000 + $42,000)............................	742,000	
Interest revenue ($700,000 × 12% × $6/12$)............		42,000
Note receivable......................................		700,000
To record the collection of the note at maturity.		

*To focus on recording the note we intentionally omit the entry required for the cost of the goods sold if the perpetual inventory system is used.

If the sale in the illustration occurs on August 1, 2003, and the company's fiscal year-end is December 31, a year-end adjusting entry accrues interest earned.

December 31, 2003

Interest receivable....................................	35,000	
Interest revenue ($700,000 × 12% × $5/12$).............		35,000

The February 1 collection is then recorded as follows:

February 1, 2004

Cash ($700,000 + [$700,000 × 12% × $6/12$])....................	742,000	
Interest revenue ($700,000 × 12% × $1/12$)....................		7,000
Interest receivable (accrued at December 31).................		35,000
Note receivable..		700,000

NONINTEREST-BEARING NOTES

Sometimes a receivable assumes the form of a so-called **noninterest-bearing note.** The name is a misnomer, though. Noninterest-bearing notes actually do bear interest, but the interest is deducted (or discounted) from the face amount to determine the cash proceeds made available to the borrower at the outset. For example, the preceding note could be packaged as a $700,000 noninterest-bearing note, with a 12% discount rate. In that case, the $42,000 interest would be discounted at the outset rather than explicitly stated. As a result, the selling price of the shoes would have been only $658,000. Assuming a May 1, 2003 sale, the transaction is recorded as follows:[8]

---

[8]The entries shown assume the note is recorded by the gross method. By the net method, the interest component is netted against the face amount of the note as follows:

May 1, 2003

Note receivable..	658,000	
Sales revenue..		658,000

November 1, 2003

Cash..	700,000	
Note receivable..		658,000
Interest revenue ($700,000 × 12% × $6/12$)......................		42,000

May 1, 2003

Note receivable (face amount)...........................	700,000	
Discount on note receivable ($700,000 × 12% × ⁶⁄₁₂)		42,000
Sales revenue (difference)		658,000

The discount becomes interest revenue in a noninterest-bearing note.

November 1, 2003

Discount on note receivable.............................	42,000	
Interest revenue.......................................		42,000
Cash..	700,000	
Note receivable (face amount)		700,000

The discount on note receivable is a contra account to the note receivable account. That is, the note receivable would be reported in the balance sheet net (less) any remaining discount. The discount represents future interest revenue that will be recognized as it is earned over time. The sales revenue under this arrangement is only $658,000, but the interest is calculated as the discount rate times the $700,000 face amount. This causes the *effective* interest rate to be higher than the 12% stated rate.

When interest is discounted from the face amount of a note, the effective interest rate is higher than the stated discount rate.

$ 42,000	Interest for 6 months
÷$658,000	Sales price
= 6.38%	Rate for 6 months
× 2*	To annualize the rate
= 12.76%	Effective interest rate

*Two 6-month periods

If the sale occurs on August 1, the December 31, 2003, adjusting entry and the entry to record the cash collection on February 1, 2004, are recorded as follows:

December 31, 2003

Discount on note receivable	35,000	
Interest revenue ($700,000 × 12% × ⁵⁄₁₂)		35,000

February 1, 2004

Discount on note receivable.............................	7,000	
Interest revenue ($700,000 × 12% × ¹⁄₁₂)		7,000
Cash..	700,000	
Note receivable (face amount)		700,000

In the December 31, 2003, balance sheet, the note receivable is shown at $693,000, face amount ($700,000) less remaining discount ($7,000).

Metro-Goldwyn-Mayer, Inc., (MGM) is engaged in the production and distribution of motion picture and television programs. The company licenses its television programs to networks. The disclosure note shown in Graphic 7–4 describes the company's revenue recognition policy for its license agreements and the use of noninterest-bearing notes.

Revenue Recognition (in part)
Revenues from television licensing, together with related costs, are recognized when the feature film or television program is available to the licensee for telecast. . . . noninterest-bearing receivables arising from licensing agreements are discounted to present value.

GRAPHIC 7–4
Disclosure of Revenue Recognition for License Agreements— Metro-Goldwyn-Mayer, Inc.

Notes Received Solely for Cash.   If a note with an unrealistic interest rate—even a noninterest-bearing note—is received *solely* in exchange for cash, the cash paid to the issuer

When a noninterest-bearing note is received solely in exchange for cash, the amount of cash exchanged is the basis for valuing the note.

is considered to be its present value.[9] Even if this means recording interest at a ridiculously low or zero rate, the amount of cash exchanged is the basis for valuing the note. When a non-cash asset is exchanged for a note with a low stated rate, we can argue that its real value is less than it's purported to be, but we can't argue that the present value of a sum of cash currently exchanged is less than that sum. If the noninterest-bearing note in the previous example had been received solely in exchange for $700,000 cash, the transaction would be recorded as follows:

Note receivable (face amount)	700,000	
Cash (given)		700,000

SUBSEQUENT VALUATION OF NOTES RECEIVABLE

Similar to accounts receivable, if a company anticipates bad debts on short-term notes receivable, it uses an allowance account to reduce the receivable to net realizable value. The process of recording bad debt expense is the same as with accounts receivable.

Long-term notes present a more significant measurement problem. The longer the duration of the note, the more likely are bad debts. One of the more difficult measurement problems facing banks and other lending institutions is the estimation of bad debts on their long-term notes (loans). As an example, Wells Fargo & Company, a large bank holding company, reported the following in the asset section of a recent balance sheet:

	December 31 (in millions)	
	2001	**2000**
Loans	$172,499	$161,124
Allowance for loan losses	(3,761)	(3,719)
Net loans	$168,738	$157,405

A disclosure note, reproduced in Graphic 7–5, describes Wells Fargo's loan loss policy.

GRAPHIC 7–5
Disclosure of Allowance for Loan Losses—Wells Fargo & Company

> **Allowance for Loan Losses (in part)**
> The Company's determination of the level of the allowance and correspondingly the provision for loan losses rests upon various judgments and assumptions, including general economic conditions, loan portfolio composition, prior loan loss experience and the Company's ongoing examination process and that of its regulators.

When it becomes probable that a creditor will be unable to collect all amounts due according to the contractual terms of a note, the receivable is considered **impaired.** When a creditor's investment in a note receivable becomes impaired for any reason, the receivable is remeasured as the discounted present value of currently expected cash flows at the loan's original effective rate. Impairments of receivables are discussed in Appendix 12B.

Financing with Receivables

LO8

Receivables, like any other asset, can be sold or used as collateral for debt. In fact, many companies avoid the difficulties of servicing (billing and collecting) receivables by transfer-

---

[9]This assumes that no other present or future considerations are included in the agreement. For example, a noninterest-bearing note might be given to a vendor in exchange for cash *and* a promise to provide future inventories at prices lower than anticipated market prices. The issuer values the note at the present value of cash payments using a realistic interest rate, and the difference between present value and cash payments is recognized as interest revenue over the life of the note. This difference also increases future inventory purchases to realistic market prices.

ring them to financial institutions. This practice also shortens those companies' operating cycles by providing cash to the companies immediately rather than having them wait until credit customers pay the amounts due. Of course, the financial institution will require compensation for providing this service, usually interest and/or a finance charge.

Responding to these desires, financial institutions have developed a wide variety of ways for companies to use their receivables to obtain immediate cash. The methods differ with respect to which rights and risks are retained by the *transferor* (the original holder of the receivables) and those passed on to the *transferee* (the new holder, the financial institution). Despite this diversity, any of these methods can be described as either:

1. A secured borrowing
2. A sale of receivables.

When a company chooses between a borrowing or a sale, the critical element is the extent to which it (the transferor) is willing to *surrender control over the assets transferred*. The distinction for some arrangements is not always obvious. For such situations the FASB has provided guidelines. Specifically, the transferor is determined to have surrendered control over the receivables if and only if all of the following conditions are met:[10]

a. The transferred assets have been isolated from the transferor—put presumptively beyond the reach of the transferor and its creditors, even in bankruptcy or other receivership.
b. Each transferee has the right to pledge or exchange the assets it received.
c. The transferor does not maintain effective control over the transferred assets through either (1) an agreement that the transferor repurchase or redeem them before their maturity or (2) the ability to cause the transferee to return specific assets.

If all of the above conditions are *not* met, the transferor treats the transaction as *a secured borrowing*. In that case the company records a liability with the receivables serving as collateral.

On the other hand, if each of the three conditions is met, the transferor treats the transaction as a *sale* and accounts for it in the same manner as the sale of any other asset. That is, the transferor "derecognizes" (removes) the receivables from its books, records the proceeds received (usually cash), and recognizes the difference as either a gain or loss (usually a loss) on the sale. On the other side of the transaction, the transferee recognizes the receivables obtained and measures them at their fair value. Let's now look in more detail at these two possibilities.

> If the transferor is deemed to have surrendered control over the receivables, the arrangement is accounted for as a sale; otherwise as a secured borrowing.

SECURED BORROWING

As defined in the previous section, companies sometimes use receivables as collateral for loans. You may already be familiar with the concept of **assigning** or **pledging** receivables as collateral if you or someone you know has a mortgage on a home. The bank or other financial institution holding the mortgage will require that, if the homeowner defaults on the mortgage payments, the home be sold and the proceeds used to pay off the mortgage debt. Similarly, in the case of an assignment of receivables, nonpayment of a debt will require the proceeds from collecting the assigned receivables to go directly toward repayment of the debt.

Usually, the amount borrowed is less than the amount of receivables assigned. The difference provides some protection for the lender to allow for possible uncollectible accounts. Also, the assignee (transferee) usually charges the assignor an up-front finance charge in addition to stated interest on the collateralized loan. The receivables might be collected either by the assignor or the assignee, depending on the details of the arrangement. Illustration 7–5 provides an example.

---

[10]"Accounting for Transfers and Servicing of Financial Assets and Extinguishments of Liabilities," *Statement of Financial Accounting Standards No. 140* (Norwalk, Conn.: FASB, 2000). The standard replaces *SFAS 125.*

ILLUSTRATION 7–5 Assignment of Accounts Receivable	At the end of November 2003, Santa Teresa Glass Company had outstanding accounts receivable of $750,000. On December 1, 2003, the company borrowed $500,000 from Finance Affiliates and signed a promissory note. Interest at 12% is payable monthly. The company assigned $620,000 of its receivables as collateral for the loan. Finance Affiliates charges a finance fee equal to 1.5% of the accounts receivable assigned. Santa Teresa Glass records the borrowing as follows:

Cash (difference)	490,700	
Finance charge expense* (1.5% × $620,000)	9,300	
Liability—financing arrangement.		500,000

Santa Teresa will continue to collect the receivables, record any discounts, sales returns, and bad debt write-offs, but will remit the cash to Finance Affiliates, usually on a monthly basis. When $400,000 of the receivables assigned are collected in December, Santa Teresa Glass records the following entries:

Cash.	400,000	
Accounts receivable.		400,000
Interest expense ($500,000 × 12% × $\frac{1}{12}$)	5,000	
Liability—financing arrangement	400,000	
Cash.		405,000

*In theory, this fee should be allocated over the entire period of the loan rather than recorded as an expense in the initial period. However, amounts usually are small and the loan period usually is short. For expediency, then, we expense the entire fee immediately.

In Santa Teresa's December 31, 2003, balance sheet, the company would report the receivables and note payable together as follows:

Current assets:	
Accounts receivable assigned ($620,000 − 400,000)	$220,000
Less: Liability—financing arrangement ($500,000 − 400,000)	(100,000)
Equity in accounts receivable assigned	$120,000

Netting a liability against a related asset usually is not allowed by GAAP. However, in this case, we deduct the note payable from the accounts receivable assigned because, by contractual agreement, the note will be paid with cash collected from the receivables. In Santa Teresa's financial statements, the arrangement also is described in a disclosure note.

A variation of assigning specific receivables occurs when trade receivables in general rather than specific receivables are pledged as collateral. The responsibility for collection of the receivables remains solely with the company. This variation is referred to as a **pledging** of accounts receivable. No special accounting treatment is needed and the arrangement is simply described in a disclosure note. For example, Graphic 7–6 shows a portion of the long-term debt disclosure note included in recent financial statements of Smithfield Foods, Inc., the world's largest hog producer and pork processor.

GRAPHIC 7–6 Disclosure of Receivables Used as Collateral—Smithfield Foods, Inc.	**Note 4 Debt (in part)** The company has a five-year $650,000 revolving credit facility as its primary short-term financing source. . . . The $650,000 credit facility is secured by substantially all of the Company's U.S. inventories and accounts receivable.

SALE OF RECEIVABLES

In recent years, the sale of accounts receivable has become an increasingly popular method of financing. Traditionally a technique used by companies in a few industries or with poor credit ratings, the sale of receivables is now a common occurrence for many different types of companies. For example, Boise Cascade, Delta Airlines, Phillips Petroleum, Unocal, IBM, Sears, and Raytheon all sell receivables. The two most common types of selling arrangements are **factoring** and **securitization.** We'll now discuss each type.

Two popular arrangements used for the sale of receivables are *factoring* and *securitization.*

A **factor** is a financial institution that buys receivables for cash, handles the billing and collection of the receivables, and charges a fee for this service. Actually, credit cards like VISA and Mastercard are forms of factoring arrangements. The seller relinquishes all rights to the future cash receipts in exchange for cash from the buyer (the *factor*).

As an example, Graphic 7–7 shows an excerpt from a recent advertisement of Bankers Mutual Capital Corporation, a financial institution that offers factoring as one of its services.

Accounts Receivable Factoring

Accounts receivable factoring is the selling of your invoices (accounts receivable) for cash versus waiting 30–60 days to be paid by your customer. Factoring will get you the working capital you need now and improve your cash flow. Bankers Mutual will advance 65%–80% against the invoice you generate and pay you the balance less our fee (typically 3%–6%) when the invoice is paid.

GRAPHIC 7–7
Advertisement of Factoring Service— Bankers Mutual Capital Corporation

Notice that the factor, Bankers Mutual, advances only between 65%–80% of the factored receivables. The remaining balance is retained as security until all of the receivables are collected and then remitted to the transferor, net of the factor's fee. The fee charged by this factor ranges from 3%–6%. The range depends on, among other things, the quality of the receivables and the length of time before payment is required.

Another popular arrangement used to sell receivables is a **securitization**. In a typical accounts receivable securitization, the company creates a special purpose entity (SPE), usually a trust or a subsidiary. The SPE buys a pool of trade receivables, credit card receivables, or loans from the company, and then sells related securities, for example bonds or commercial paper, that are backed (collateralized) by the receivables.

As an example of a securitization, Graphic 7–8 shows a portion of the disclosure note included in recent financial statements of Sears Roebuck Company describing its securitization of credit card receivables.

Note 3—Credit Card Securitizations (in part)

The Company utilizes credit card securitizations as a part of its overall funding strategy. Under generally accepted accounting principles, if the structure of the securitization meets certain requirements, these are accounted for as sales of receivables.

. . . the Company transfers credit card receivable balances to a Master Trust ("Trust") in exchange . . .

The Trust securitizes balances by issuing certificates representing undivided interests in the Trust's receivables to outside investors.

GRAPHIC 7–8
Disclosure of Credit Card Securitizations— Sears Roebuck Company

The specific accounting treatment for the sale of receivables using factoring and securitization arrangements depends on the amount of risk the factor assumes, in particular whether it buys the receivables **without recourse** or **with recourse.**

Sale without Recourse.   When a company sells accounts receivable **without recourse**, the buyer assumes the risk of uncollectibility. This means the buyer has no *recourse* to the seller if customers don't pay the receivables. In that case, the seller simply accounts for the transaction as a sale of an asset. As we discussed above, the buyer charges a fee for providing this service, usually a percentage of the book value of receivables. Because the fee reduces the proceeds the seller receives from selling the asset, the seller records a loss on sale of assets. The typical factoring arrangement is made without recourse. Illustration 7–6 provides an example.

The buyer assumes the risk of uncollectibility when accounts receivable are sold *without recourse.*

ILLUSTRATION 7–6	At the end of November 2003, the Santa Teresa Glass Company had outstanding accounts receivable of $750,000. In December 2003, the company factored $600,000 of accounts receivable to Finance Affiliates. The transfer was made without recourse. Finance Affiliates remits 90% of the factored receivables to Santa Teresa and retains the remaining 10%. When Finance Affiliates collects the receivables, it remits to Santa Teresa the retained amount, less a 4% fee (4% of the total factored amount).
Accounts Receivable Factored without Recourse	
	Santa Teresa Glass records the transfer as follows:
The factor's fee is recorded as a loss.	

Cash (90% × $600,000)...	540,000	
Loss on sale of receivables (4% × $600,000)	24,000	
Receivable from factor (10% × $600,000 = $60,000 − 24,000 fee).....	36,000	
Accounts receivable (balance sold)............................		600,000

deposit

Sale with Recourse. When a company sells accounts receivable **with recourse**, the seller retains the risk of uncollectibility. In effect, the seller guarantees that the buyer will be paid even if some receivables prove to be uncollectible. In Illustration 7–6, even if the receivables were sold with recourse, as long as the three conditions for sale treatment are met, Santa Teresa Glass would still account for the transfer as a sale. The only difference would be the additional requirement that Santa Teresa record the estimated fair value of the recourse obligation as a liability. The recourse obligation is the estimated amount that Santa Teresa will have to pay Finance Affiliates as a reimbursement for uncollectible receivables. Assuming that this amount is estimated at $5,000, the entry recorded by Santa Teresa would be as follows:

Cash (90% × $600,000)	540,000	
Loss on sale of receivables (4% × $600,000 + 5,000).............	29,000	
Receivable from factor (10% × $600,000 = $60,000 − 24,000 fee) ..	36,000	
Recourse liability		5,000
Accounts receivable (balance sold)		600,000

Notice that the estimated recourse liability increases the loss on sale. If the factor collects all of the receivables, Santa Teresa eliminates the recourse liability and increases income (reduces the loss).

DISCOUNTING A NOTE

Similar to accounts receivable, a note receivable can be used to obtain immediate cash from a financial institution either by pledging the note as collateral for a loan or by selling the note. The transfer of a note is referred to as **discounting**. The financial institution accepts the note and gives the seller cash equal to the maturity value of the note reduced by a discount. The discount is computed by applying a discount rate to the maturity value and represents the financing fee the financial institution charges for the transaction. Illustration 7–7 provides an example of the calculation of the proceeds received by the transferor.

ILLUSTRATION 7–7	On December 31, 2003, the Stridewell Wholesale Shoe Company sold land in exchange for a nine-month, 10% note. The note requires the payment of $200,000 *plus* interest on September 30, 2004. The company's fiscal year-end is December 31. The 10% rate properly reflects the time value of money for this type of note. On March 31, 2004, Stridewell discounted the note at the Bank of the East. The bank's discount rate is 12%.
Discounting a Note Receivable	
	Because the note had been outstanding for three months before it's discounted at the bank, Stridewell first records the interest that has accrued prior to being discounted:
STEP 1: Accrue interest earned on the note receivable prior to its being discounted.	**March 31, 2004**

Interest receivable..	5,000	
Interest revenue ($200,000 × 10% × $\frac{3}{12}$)		5,000

Next, the value of the note if held to maturity is calculated. Then the discount for the time remaining to maturity is deducted to determine the cash proceeds from discounting the note:

$200,000	Face amount
15,000	Interest to maturity ($200,000 × 10% × 9/12)
215,000	Maturity value
(12,900)	Discount ($215,000 × 12% × 6/12)
$202,100	Cash proceeds

ILLUSTRATION 7–7

(concluded)

STEP 2: Add interest to maturity to calculate maturity value.

STEP 3: Deduct discount to calculate cash proceeds.

Similar to accounts receivable, if the three conditions for sale treatment are met, Stridewell would account for the transfer as a sale. If the conditions are not met, it is treated as a secured borrowing. For example, if the sale conditions are met, Illustration 7–7a shows the appropriate journal entries.

Cash (proceeds determined above).	202,100	
Loss on sale of note receivable (difference).	2,900	
Note receivable (face amount)		200,000
Interest receivable (accrued interest determined above).		5,000

ILLUSTRATION 7–7a

Discounted Note Treated as a Sale

Record a loss (or gain) for difference between the cash proceeds and the note's book value.

CONCEPT REVIEW EXERCISE

Financing with Receivables

The Hollywood Lumber Company obtains financing from the Midwest Finance Company by factoring (or discounting) its receivables. During June 2003, the company factored $1,000,000 of accounts receivable to Midwest. The transfer was made *without* recourse. The factor, Midwest Finance, remits 80% of the factored receivables and retains 20%. When the receivables are collected by Midwest, the retained amount, less a 3% fee (3% of the total factored amount), will be remitted to Hollywood Lumber.

In addition, on June 30, 2003, Hollywood discounted a note receivable without recourse. The note, which originated on March 31, 2003, requires the payment of $150,000 *plus* interest at 8% on March 31, 2004. Midwest's discount rate is 10%. The company's fiscal year-end is December 31.

Required:
Prepare journal entries for Hollywood Lumber for the factoring of accounts receivable and the note receivable discounted on June 30. Assume that the required criteria are met and the transfers are accounted for as sales.

SOLUTION

The Factoring of Receivables		
Cash (80% × $1,000,000)	800,000	
Loss on sale of receivables (3% × $1,000,000)	30,000	
Receivable from factor (20% × $1,000,000 − 30,000 fee)	170,000	
Accounts receivable (balance sold)		1,000,000
The Note Receivable Discounted		
Interest receivable.	3,000	
Interest revenue ($150,000 × 8% × 3/12)		3,000

Cash (proceeds determined below)	149,850	
Loss on sale of note receivable (difference).	3,150	
Note receivable (face amount)		150,000
Interest receivable (accrued interest determined above)		3,000

Add interest to maturity to calculate maturity value.

Deduct discount to calculate cash proceeds.

$150,000	Face amount
12,000	Interest to maturity ($150,000 × 8%)
162,000	Maturity value
(12,150)	Discount ($162,000 × 10% × %12)
$149,850	Cash proceeds

In summary, there are several ways receivables can be used as a method of financing. However, each of these arrangements can be categorized as either a secured borrowing or as an outright sale of the receivables. Graphic 7–9 provides a visual summary of the possibilities.

GRAPHIC 7–9
Accounting for the Financing of Receivables

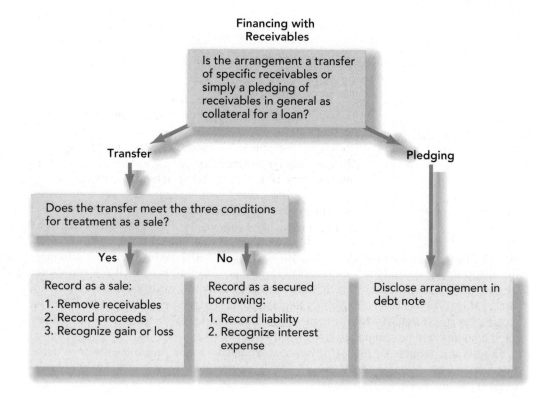

Financing with Receivables

Is the arrangement a transfer of specific receivables or simply a pledging of receivables in general as collateral for a loan?

Transfer — Does the transfer meet the three conditions for treatment as a sale?

Pledging

Yes — Record as a sale:
1. Remove receivables
2. Record proceeds
3. Recognize gain or loss

No — Record as a secured borrowing:
1. Record liability
2. Recognize interest expense

Disclose arrangement in debt note

DECISION MAKERS' PERSPECTIVE

RECEIVABLES MANAGEMENT

A company's investment in receivables is influenced by several variables, including the level of sales, the nature of the product or service sold, and credit and collection policies. These variables are, of course, related. For example, a change in credit policies could affect sales. In fact, more liberal credit policies—allowing customers a longer time to pay or offering cash discounts for early payment—often are initiated with the specific objective of increasing sales volume.

Management's choice of credit and collection policies often involves trade-offs. For example, offering cash discounts may increase sales volume, accelerate customer payment, and reduce bad debts. These benefits are not without cost. The cash discounts reduce the amount of cash collected from customers who take advantage of the discounts. Extending payment terms also may increase sales volume. However, this creates an increase in the required investment in receivables and may increase bad debts.

The ability to use receivables as a method of financing also offers management alternatives. Assigning, factoring, and discounting receivables are alternative methods of financing operations that must be evaluated relative to other financing methods such as lines of credit or other types of short-term borrowing.

Investors, creditors, and financial analysts can gain important insights by monitoring a company's investment in receivables. Chapter 5 introduced the receivables turnover ratio and the related average collection period, ratios designed to monitor receivables. Recall that these ratios are calculated as follows:

> Management must evaluate the costs and benefits of any change in credit and collection policies.

$$\text{Receivables turnover ratio} = \frac{\text{Net sales}}{\text{Average accounts receivable (net)}}$$

$$\text{Average collection period} = \frac{365 \text{ days}}{\text{Receivables turnover ratio}}$$

The turnover ratio shows the number of times during a period that the average accounts receivable balance is collected, and the average collection period is an approximation of the number of days the average accounts receivable balance is outstanding.

As a company's sales grow, receivables also will increase. If the percentage increase in receivables is greater than the percentage increase in sales, the receivables turnover ratio will decline (the average collection period will increase). This could indicate customer dissatisfaction with the product or that the company has extended too generous payment terms in order to attract new customers, which, in turn, could increase sales returns and bad debts.

These ratios also can be used to compare the relative effectiveness of companies in managing the investment in receivables. Of course, it would be meaningless to compare the receivables turnover ratio of a computer products company such as IBM with that of, say, a food products company like Hershey. A company selling high-priced, low-volume products like mainframe computers generally will grant customers longer payment terms than a company selling lower priced, higher volume food products. Graphic 7–10 lists the 2001 receivables turnover ratio for some well-known companies. The differences are as expected, given the nature of the companies' products.

Let's compute the 2001 receivables turnover ratio and the average collection period for two companies in the same industry, Maytag and Whirlpool.

GRAPHIC 7–10 Receivables Turnover Ratios

Company	2001 Receivables Turnover Ratio
Johnson & Johnson	7.15
Caterpillar	7.32
IBM	8.79
Sara Lee	10.75
Hershey	12.29
Dell Computer	13.29

($ in millions)

	Maytag		Whirlpool	
	2001	2000	2001	2000
Accounts receivable (net)	$618	$476	$1,515	$1,748
Two-year averages	$ 547		$ 1,631.5	
Net sales—2001	$4,324		$10,343.0	

> Balance sheet and income statement information—Maytag and Whirlpool

	Maytag	Whirlpool	Industry Average
Receivables turnover	$=\dfrac{4{,}324}{547}=7.9$	$\dfrac{10{,}343}{1{,}631.5}=6.3$	5.6
Average collection period	$=\dfrac{365}{7.9}=46$ **days**	$\dfrac{365}{6.3}=58$ **days**	65 days

> Receivables turnover and average collection period—Maytag and Whirlpool

On average, it takes Whirlpool 12 days longer than Maytag to collect its receivables. Both companies take less time to collect receivables than the industry average

Academic research also has shown receivables information to be useful in financial statement analysis. Professors Lev and Thiagarajan empirically demonstrated the importance of a set of 12 fundamental variables in valuing companies' common stock. The set of variables included accounts receivable (change in accounts receivable minus change in sales) and allowance for uncollectible accounts (change in accounts receivable minus change in the allowance). Motivation for the receivables variable was that disproportionate increases in accounts receivable (relative to sales increases) can indicate difficulties in selling products, reflected in more lenient credit policies. The allowance variable was expected to indicate inadequate bad debt provisions. Both were found to be significant indicators of stock returns during high inflation years.[11]

EARNINGS QUALITY

In May 2001 the Securities and Exchange Commission sued the former top executives at Sunbeam, charging the company with financial reporting fraud that allegedly cost investors billions in losses. In the mid-1990s, Sunbeam needed help: its profits had declined significantly as did its stock price, and in 1996, the company reported a loss from continuing operations of $198 million. To the rescue comes Albert Dunlap, also known as "Chainsaw Al," based on his reputation as a ruthless executive known for his ability to restructure and turn around troubled companies, largely by eliminating jobs.

The strategy appeared to work. In 1997, Sunbeam's revenues had risen by 18% and profits were back in the black with income from continuing operations of $123 million. However, in April 1998, PaineWebber Inc. downgraded Sunbeam's stock recommendation. Why the downgrade? PaineWebber had noticed unusually high accounts receivable, massive increases in sales of electric blankets in the third quarter 1997, which usually sell best in the fourth quarter, as well as unusually high sales of barbecue grills for the fourth quarter. Soon after, Sunbeam announced a first quarter loss of $44.6 million, and Sunbeam's stock price fell 25%.

It eventually came to light that Dunlap and Sunbeam had been using a "bill and hold" strategy with retail buyers. This involved selling products at large discounts to retailers before they normally would buy and then holding the products in third-party warehouses, with delivery at a later date. According to an article in *Barron's*, much of the variation in Sunbeam's income from 1996 to 1997 reflected *a discretionary use of accruals* to accelerate expenses to 1996.[12]

> **Bad debt expense is one of a variety of discretionary accruals that provide management with the opportunity to manipulate income.**

Bad debt expense, and the corresponding allowance for uncollectible accounts, is one of several so-called discretionary accruals that directly impact a company's income. Other discretionary accruals include warranty expenses, discretionary compensation expenses such as bonuses, sales returns, and restructuring costs. Each of these accruals requires estimates of future events, thus providing management the opportunity to shift income among reporting periods. For example, if management overestimates bad debt expense in one period, a company will report lower profit that period and higher profit in a later period.

Recall our discussion in Chapter 4 concerning earnings quality. We learned that managers have the ability, to a limited degree, to manipulate reported income and that many observers believe this practice diminishes earnings quality because it can mask permanent earnings. Former SEC Chairman Arthur Levitt

> **ARTHUR LEVITT, JR.**
> A third illusion played by some companies is using unrealistic assumptions to estimate . . . such items as sales returns, loan losses or warranty costs. In doing so, they stash accruals in cookie jars during good times and reach into them when needed in the bad times.[13]

---

[11]B. Lev and S. R. Thiagarajan, "Fundamental Information Analysis," *Journal of Accounting Research* 31, no. 2 (Autumn 1993). The main conclusion of the study was that fundamental variables, not just earnings, are useful in firm valuation, particularly when examined in the context of macroeconomic conditions such as inflation.

[12]Jonathan Laing, "Dangerous Games," *Barron's* (June 8, 1998).

[13]Arthur Levitt, Jr., "The Numbers Game," *The CPA Journal*, December, 1998, p. 16.

listed discretionary accruals, which he called "Miscellaneous Cookie Jar Reserves," as one of the most popular methods companies use to manipulate income.

Financial analysts must be alert to the effect of discretionary accruals on income. Abnormal fluctuations in these items should raise a red flag, motivating further investigation. In the Sunbeam example, for instance, red flags in the 1996 income statement included a variety of unusual expenses and a large increase in general and administrative expenses. The balance sheet reported an increase of 44% in current liabilities from the prior year. This increase was caused by activities that included a significant accrual for restructuring costs and a large increase in the accrued warranty liability. The allowance for uncollectible accounts also increased by 30%. The marketplace was less than vigilant in noting and interpreting these signs. ■

FINANCIAL REPORTING CASE **SOLUTION**

1. **Explain the allowance method of accounting for bad debts.** *(p. 327)*   The allowance method estimates future bad debts in order to (1) match bad debt expense with related revenues and (2) report accounts receivable in the balance sheet at net realizable value. In an adjusting entry, we record bad debt expense and reduce accounts receivable indirectly by crediting a contra account to accounts receivable for an estimate of the amount that eventually will prove uncollectible.

2. **What approaches might Cisco have used to arrive at the $275 million bad debt provision?** *(p. 328)*   There are two ways commonly used to arrive at an estimate of future bad debts, the income statement approach and the balance sheet approach. Using the income statement approach, we estimate bad debt expense as a percentage of each period's net credit sales. The balance sheet approach determines bad debt expense by estimating the net realizable value of accounts receivable. In other words, the allowance for uncollectible accounts is determined and bad debt expense is an indirect outcome of adjusting the allowance account to the desired balance.

3. **Are there any alternatives to the allowance method?** *(p. 331)*   An alternative to the allowance method is the direct write-off method. Using this method, adjusting entries are not recorded and any bad debt that does arise simply is written off as bad debt expense. Of course, if the sale that generated this receivable occurred in a previous reporting period, this violates the matching principle. Operating expenses would have been understated and assets overstated that period. This is why the direct write-off method is not permitted by GAAP except in limited circumstances. ■

THE BOTTOM LINE

1. Internal control refers to the plan designed to encourage adherence to company policies and procedures; promote operational efficiency; minimize irregularities, errors, thefts or fraud; and maximize the reliability and accuracy of accounting data. Key elements of an internal control system for cash receipts and disbursements include separation of record-keeping from control of cash duties and the periodic preparation of a bank reconciliation.

2. Cash can be informally restricted by management for a particular purpose. Restrictions also can be contractually imposed. If restricted cash is available for current operations or to pay current liabilities, it's classified as a current asset; otherwise, it's classified as investments and funds or other assets.

3. The gross method of accounting for cash discounts considers a discount not taken as part of sales revenue. The net method considers a discount not taken as interest revenue.

4. When merchandise returns are anticipated, an allowance for sales returns should be recorded as a contra account to accounts receivable and sales revenue also should be reduced by the anticipated sales returns.

5. Uncollectible accounts receivable should be anticipated in order to match bad debt expense with revenues generated. Likewise, accounts receivable should be reduced by an allowance for uncollectible accounts to report accounts receivable at net realizable value.

6. There are two approaches to estimating future bad debts. The income statement approach estimates bad debt expense based on the notion that a certain percentage of each period's credit sales will prove to be uncollectible. The balance sheet approach to estimating future bad debts indirectly determines bad debt expense by directly estimating the net realizable value of accounts receivable at the end of the period.

7. Notes receivable are formal credit arrangements between a creditor (lender) and a debtor (borrower). The typical note receivable requires the payment of a specified face amount, also called principal, at a specified maturity date or dates. In addition, interest is paid at a stated percentage of the face amount. Interest on notes is calculated by multiplying the face amount by the annual rate by the fraction of the annual period.

8. A wide variety of methods exist for companies to use their receivables to obtain immediate cash. These methods can be described as either:
   a. A secured borrowing
   b. A sale of receivables
   If three conditions indicating surrender of control are met, the transferor accounts for the transfer of receivables as a sale; otherwise as a secured borrowing. ▪

APPENDIX
7

CASH CONTROLS

Bank Reconciliation

One of the most important tools used in the control of cash is the **bank reconciliation.** Since all cash receipts are deposited into the bank account and cash disbursements are made by check, the bank account provides a separate record of cash. It's desirable to periodically compare the bank balance with the balance in the company's own records and reconcile any differences.

From your own personal experience, you know that the ending balance in your checking account reported on the monthly bank statement you receive rarely equals the balance you have recorded in your checkbook. Differences arise from two types of items: timing differences and errors.

Differences between the cash book and bank balance occur due to differences in the timing of recognition of certain transactions and errors.

Timing differences occur when the company and the bank record transactions at different times. At any point in time the company may have adjusted the cash balance for items of which the bank is not yet aware. Likewise, the bank may have adjusted its record of that balance by items of which the company is not yet aware. For example, checks written and cash deposits are not all processed by the bank in the same month that they are recorded by the company. Also, the bank may adjust the company's account for items such as service charges that the company is not aware of until the bank statement is received.

Errors can be made either by the company or the bank. For example, a check might be written for $210 but recorded on the company's books as a $120 disbursement; a deposit of $500 might be processed incorrectly by the bank as a $50 deposit. In addition to serving as a safeguard of cash, the bank reconciliation also uncovers errors such as these and helps ensure that the proper cash balance is reported in the balance sheet.

STEP 1: Adjust the bank balance to the corrected cash balance.

Bank reconciliations include adjustments to the balance per bank for timing differences involving transactions already reflected in the company's accounting records that have not yet been processed by the bank. These adjustments usually include *checks outstanding* and *deposits outstanding*. In addition, the balance per bank would be adjusted for any bank errors discovered. These adjustments produce an adjusted bank balance that represents the corrected cash balance.

STEP 2: Adjust the book balance to the corrected cash balance.

The balance per books is similarly adjusted for timing differences involving transactions already reflected by the bank of which the company is unaware until the bank statement is

GRAPHIC 7A–1
Bank Reconciliation—
Reconciling Items

Step 1: Adjustments to Bank Balance:
1. *Add deposits outstanding.* These represent cash amounts received by the company and debited to cash that have not been deposited in the bank by the bank statement cutoff date and cash receipts deposited in the bank near the end of the period that are not recorded by the bank until after the cutoff date.
2. *Deduct checks outstanding.* These represent checks written and recorded by the company as credits to cash that have not yet been processed by the bank before the cutoff date.
3. *Bank errors.* These will either be increases or decreases depending on the nature of the error.

Step 2: Adjustments to Book Balance:
1. *Add collections made by the bank* on the company's behalf and other increases in cash that the company is unaware of until the bank statement is received.
2. *Deduct service and other charges* made by the bank that the company is unaware of until the bank statement is received.
3. *Deduct NSF* (nonsufficient funds) *checks.* These are checks previously deposited for which the payors do not have sufficient funds in their accounts to cover the amount of the checks. The checks are returned to the company whose responsibility it is to seek payment from payors.
4. *Company errors.* These will either be increases or decreases depending on the nature of the error.

Bank balance
+ Deposits outstanding
− Checks outstanding
± Errors
_____
Corrected balance

Book balance
+ Collections by bank
− Service charges
− NSF checks
± Errors
_____
Corrected balance

The two corrected balances must equal.

received. These would include service charges, charges for NSF (nonsufficient funds) checks, and collections made by the bank on the company's behalf. In addition, the balance per books is adjusted for any company errors discovered, resulting in an adjusted book balance that will also represent the corrected cash balance. *Each of these adjustments requires a journal entry to correct the book balance.* Only adjustments to the book balance require journal entries. Graphic 7A–1 recaps these reconciling items.

To demonstrate the bank reconciliation process, consider Illustration 7A–1.

The next step is to prepare adjusting journal entries to reflect each of the adjustments to the balance per books. These represent amounts the company was not previously aware of. No adjusting entries are needed for the adjustments to the balance per bank because the company has already recorded these items. However, the bank needs to be notified of any errors discovered.

Cash.	1,120	
Notes receivable		1,000
Interest revenue.		120

To record the receipt of principal and interest on note collected directly by the bank.

Miscellaneous expense (bank service charges).	80	
Accounts receivable (NSF checks)	2,187	
Accounts payable (error in check to supplier).	1,000	
Cash.		3,267

To record credits to cash revealed by the bank reconciliation.

After these entries are posted, the general ledger cash account will equal the corrected balance of $33,129.

Petty Cash

Most companies keep a small amount of cash on hand to pay for low-cost items such as postage, office supplies, delivery charges, and entertainment expenses. It would be inconvenient, time consuming, and costly to process a check each time these small payments are made. A petty cash fund provides a more efficient way to handle these payments.

ILLUSTRATION 7A–1 Bank Reconciliation	The Hawthorne Manufacturing Company maintains a general checking account at the First Pacific Bank. First Pacific provides a bank statement and canceled checks once a month. The cutoff date is the last day of the month. The bank statement for the month of May is summarized as follows:

Balance, May 1, 2003	$32,120
Deposits	82,140
Checks processed	(78,433)
Service charges	(80)
NSF checks	(2,187)
Note payment collected by bank (includes $120 interest)	1,120
Balance, May 31, 2003	$34,680

The company's general ledger cash account has a balance of $35,276 at the end of May. A review of the company records and the bank statement reveals the following:

1. Cash receipts not yet deposited totaled $2,965.
2. A deposit of $1,020 was made on May 31 that was not credited to the company's account until June.
3. All checks written in April have been processed by the bank. Checks written in May that had not been processed by the bank total $5,536.
4. A check written for $1,790 was incorrectly recorded by the company as a $790 disbursement. The check was for payment to a supplier of raw materials.

The bank reconciliation prepared by the company appears as follows:

Step 1: Bank Balance to Corrected Balance

Balance per bank statement	$34,680
Add: Deposits outstanding	3,985*
Deduct: Checks outstanding	(5,536)
Corrected cash balance	$33,129

Step 2: Book Balance to Corrected Balance

Balance per books	$35,276
Add: Note collected by bank	1,120
Deduct:	
Service charges	(80)
NSF checks	(2,187)
Error—understatement of check	(1,000)
Corrected cash balance	$33,129

*$2,965 + 1,020 = $3,985

The petty cash fund always should have cash and receipts that together equal the amount of the fund.

A petty cash fund is established by transferring a specified amount of cash from the company's general checking account to an employee designated as the petty cash custodian. The amount of the fund should approximate the expenditures made from the fund during a relatively short period of time (say a week or a month). The custodian disburses cash from the fund when the appropriate documentation is presented, such as a receipt for the purchase of office supplies. At any point in time, the custodian should be in possession of cash and appropriate receipts that sum to the amount of the fund. The receipts serve as the basis for recording appropriate expenses each time the fund is replenished. Consider the example in Illustration 7A–2.

On May 1, 2003, the Hawthorne Manufacturing Company established a $200 petty cash fund. John Ringo is designated as the petty cash custodian. The fund will be replenished at the end of each month. On May 1, 2003, a check is written for $200 made out to John Ringo, petty cash custodian. During the month of May, John paid bills totaling $160 summarized as follows:

Postage	$ 40
Office supplies	35
Delivery charges	55
Entertainment	30
Total	$160

ILLUSTRATION 7A–2

Petty Cash Fund

In journal entry form, the transaction to establish the fund would be recorded as follows:

May 1, 2003

Petty Cash.	200	
Cash (checking account)		200

A petty cash fund is established by writing a check to the custodian.

No entries are recorded at the time the actual expenditures are made from the fund. The expenditures are recorded when reimbursement is requested at the end of the month. At that time, a check is written to John Ringo, petty cash custodian, for the total of the fund receipts, $160 in this case. John cashes the check and replenishes the fund to $200. In journal entry form, replenishing the fund would be recorded as follows:

May 31, 2003

Postage expense.	40	
Office supplies expense	35	
Delivery expense.	55	
Entertainment expense.	30	
Cash (checking account)		160

The appropriate expense accounts are debited when the petty cash fund is reimbursed.

The petty cash account is not debited when replenishing the fund. If, however, the size of the fund is increased at time of replenishment, the account is debited for the increase. Similarly, petty cash would be credited if the size of the fund is decreased.

To maintain the control objective of separation of duties, the petty cash custodian should not be involved in the process of writing or approving checks, nor in recordkeeping. In addition, management should arrange for surprise counts of the fund. ∎

QUESTIONS FOR REVIEW OF KEY TOPICS

Q 7–1   Define cash equivalents.

Q 7–2   Explain the primary functions of internal controls procedures in the accounting area. What is meant by separation of duties?

Q 7–3   Define a compensating balance. How are compensating balances reported in financial statements?

Q 7–4   Explain the difference between a trade discount and a cash discount.

Q 7–5   Distinguish between the gross and net methods of accounting for cash discounts.

Q 7–6   Briefly explain the accounting treatment for sales returns.

Q 7–7   Explain the typical way companies account for uncollectible accounts receivable (bad debts). When is it permissible to record bad debt expense only when receivables actually prove uncollectible?

Q 7–8   Briefly explain the difference between the income statement approach and the balance sheet approach to estimating bad debts.

Q 7–9 Is any special accounting treatment required for the assigning of accounts receivable in general as collateral for debt?

Q 7–10 Explain any possible differences between accounting for accounts receivable factored without recourse and those factored with recourse.

Q 7–11 What is meant by the discounting of a note receivable? Describe the four-step process used to account for discounted notes.

Q 7–12 (Based on Appendix 7) In a two-step bank reconciliation, identify the items that might be necessary to adjust the bank balance to the corrected cash balance. Identify the items that might be necessary to adjust the book balance to the corrected cash balance.

Q 7–13 (Based on Appendix 7) How is a petty cash fund established? How is the fund replenished?

EXERCISES

E 7–1
Cash and cash equivalents; restricted cash

The controller of the Red Wing Corporation is in the process of preparing the company's 2003 financial statements. She is trying to determine the correct balance of cash and cash equivalents to be reported as a current asset in the balance sheet. The following items are being considered:

a. Balances in the company's accounts at the First National Bank; checking $13,500, savings $22,100.
b. Undeposited customer checks of $3,200.
c. Currency and coins on hand of $580.
d. Savings account at the East Bay Bank with a balance of $400,000. This account is being used to accumulate cash for future plant expansion (in 2005).
e. $20,000 in a checking account at the East Bay Bank. The balance in the account represents a 20% compensating balance for a $100,000 loan with the bank. Red Wing may not withdraw the funds until the loan is due in 2006.
f. U.S. treasury bills; 2-month maturity bills totaling $15,000, and 7-month bills totaling $20,000.

Required:
1. Determine the correct balance of cash and cash equivalents to be reported in the current asset section of the 2003 balance sheet.
2. For each of the items not included in your answer to requirement 1, explain the correct classification of the item.

E 7–2
Cash and cash equivalents

The Delta Automotive Corporation has the following assets listed in its 12/31/03 trial balance:

Cash in bank—checking account	$22,500
U.S. Treasury bills (mature in 30 days)*	5,000
Cash on hand (currency and coins)	1,350
U.S Treasury bills (mature in six months)*	10,000
Undeposited customer checks	1,840

*Purchased on 11/30/03

Required:
1. Determine the correct balance of cash and cash equivalents to be reported in the current asset section of the 2003 balance sheet.
2. For each of the items not included in your answer to requirement 1, explain the correct classification of the item.

E 7–3
Trade and cash discounts; the gross method and the net method compared

Tracy Company, a manufacturer of air conditioners, sold 100 units to Thomas Company on November 17, 2003. The units have a list price of $500 each, but Thomas was given a 30% trade discount. The terms of the sale were 2/10, n/30.

Required:
1. Prepare the journal entries to record the sale on November 17 (ignore cost of goods) and payment on November 26, 2003, assuming that the gross method of accounting for cash discounts is used.
2. Prepare the journal entries to record the sale on November 17 (ignore cost of goods) and payment on December 15, 2003, assuming that the gross method of accounting for cash discounts is used.
3. Repeat requirements 1 and 2 assuming that the net method of accounting for cash discounts is used.

E 7–4
Cash discounts; the gross method

Harwell Company manufactures automobile tires. On July 15, 2003, the company sold 1,000 tires to the Nixon Car Company for $50 each. The terms of the sale were 2/10, n/30. Harwell uses the gross method of accounting for cash discounts.

Required:
1. Prepare the journal entries to record the sale on July 15 (ignore cost of goods) and payment on July 23, 2003.
2. Prepare the journal entries to record the sale on July 15 (ignore cost of goods) and payment on August 15, 2003.

E 7–5
Cash discounts; the net method

[This is a variation of the previous exercise modified to focus on the net method of accounting for cash discounts.]

Harwell Company manufactures automobile tires. On July 15, 2003, the company sold 1,000 tires to the Nixon Car Company for $50 each. The terms of the sale were 2/10, n/30. Harwell uses the net method of accounting for cash discounts.

Required:
1. Prepare the journal entries to record the sale on July 15 (ignore cost of goods) and payment on July 23, 2003.
2. Prepare the journal entries to record the sale on July 15 (ignore cost of goods) and payment on August 15, 2003.

E 7–6
Uncollectible accounts; allowance method vs. direct write-off method

The Johnson Company uses the allowance method to account for uncollectible accounts receivable. Bad debt expense is established as a percentage of credit sales. For 2003, net credit sales totaled $4,500,000, and the estimated bad debt percentage is 1.2%. The allowance for uncollectible accounts had a credit balance of $32,000 at the beginning of 2003 and $40,000, after adjusting entries, at the end of 2003.

Required:
1. What is bad debt expense for 2003?
2. Determine the amount of accounts receivable written off during 2003.
3. If the company uses the direct write-off method, what would bad debt expense be for 2003?

E 7–7
Uncollectible accounts; allowance method; balance sheet approach

The Colorado Rocky Cookie Company offers credit terms to its customers. At the end of 2003, accounts receivable totaled $625,000. The allowance method is used to account for uncollectible accounts. The allowance for uncollectible accounts had a credit balance of $32,000 at the beginning of 2003 and $21,000 in receivables were written off during the year as uncollectible. Also, $1,200 in cash was received in December from a customer whose account previously had been written off. The company estimates bad debts by applying a percentage of 10% to accounts receivable at the end of the year.

Required:
1. Prepare journal entries to record the write-off of receivables, the collection of $1,200 for previously written off receivables, and the year-end adjusting entry for bad debt expense.
2. How would accounts receivable be shown in the 2003 year-end balance sheet?

E 7–8
Uncollectible accounts; allowance method and direct write-off method compared; solving for unknown

The Castle Company provides estimates for its uncollectible accounts. The allowance for uncollectible accounts had a credit balance of $17,280 at the beginning of 2003 and a $22,410 credit balance at the end of 2003 (after adjusting entries). If the direct write-off method had been used to account for uncollectible accounts (bad debt expense equals actual write-offs), the income statement for 2003 would have included bad debt expense of $14,800 and revenue of $2,200 from the collection of previously written off bad debts.

Required:
Determine bad debt expense for 2003 according to the allowance method.

E 7–9
Note receivable

On June 30, 2003, the Esquire Company sold some merchandise to a customer for $30,000. In payment, Esquire agreed to accept an 8% note requiring the payment of interest and principal on March 31, 2004. The 8% rate is appropriate in this situation.

Required:
Prepare journal entries to record the sale of merchandise (omit any entry that might be required for the cost of the goods sold), the December 31, 2003, interest accrual, and the March 31 collection.

E 7–10
Noninterest-bearing note receivable

[This is a variation of the previous exercise modified to focus on a noninterest-bearing note.]

On June 30, 2003, the Esquire Company sold some merchandise to a customer for $30,000 and agreed to accept as payment a noninterest-bearing note with an 8% discount rate requiring the payment of $30,000 on March 31, 2004. The 8% rate is appropriate in this situation.

Required:
1. Prepare journal entries to record the sale of merchandise (omit any entry that might be required for the cost of the goods sold), the December 31, 2003, interest accrual, and the March 31 collection.
2. What is the *effective* interest rate on the note?

E 7–11 Interest-bearing note receivable; solving for unknown rate	On January 1, 2003, the Apex Company exchanged some shares of common stock it had been holding as an investment for a note receivable. The note principal plus interest is due on January 1, 2004. The 2003 income statement reported $2,200 in interest revenue from this note and a $6,000 gain on sale of investment in stock. The stock's book value was $16,000. The company's fiscal year ends on December 31.

Required:
1. What is the note's effective interest rate?
2. Reconstruct the journal entries to record the sale of the stock on January 1, 2003, and the adjusting entry to record interest revenue at the end of 2003. The company records adjusting entries only at year-end.

E 7–12 Multiple choice; accounts receivable	The following questions dealing with accounts receivable are adapted from questions that appeared on recent CPA examinations. Determine the response that best completes the statements or questions.

1. When the allowance method of recognizing uncollectible accounts is used, the entry to record the write-off of a specific account:
   - a. Decreases both accounts receivable and the allowance for uncollectible accounts.
   - b. Decreases accounts receivable and increases the allowance for uncollectible accounts.
   - c. Increases the allowance for uncollectible accounts and decreases net income.
   - d. Decreases both accounts receivable and net income.
2. The following information pertains to Tara Co.'s accounts receivable at December 31, 2003:

Days Outstanding	Amount	Estimated % Uncollectible
0–60	$120,000	1%
61–120	90,000	2
Over 120	100,000	6
	$310,000	

During 2003, Tara wrote off $7,000 in receivables and recovered $4,000 that had been written off in prior years. Tara's December 31, 2002, allowance for uncollectible accounts was $22,000. Under the aging method, what amount of allowance for uncollectible accounts should Tara report at December 31, 2003?
   - a. $9,000
   - b. $10,000
   - c. $13,000
   - d. $19,000
3. Mill Co.'s allowance for uncollectible accounts was $100,000 at the end of 2003 and $90,000 at the end of 2002. For the year ended December 31, 2003, Mill reported bad debt expense of $16,000 in its income statement. What amount did Mill debit to the appropriate account in 2003 to write off actual bad debts?
   - a. $6,000
   - b. $10,000
   - c. $16,000
   - d. $26,000
4. At January 1, 2003, Jamin Co. had a credit balance of $260,000 in its allowance for uncollectible accounts. Based on past experience, 2% of Jamin's credit sales have been uncollectible. During 2003, Jamin wrote off $325,000 of uncollectible accounts. Credit sales for 2003 were $9,000,000. In its December 31, 2003, balance sheet, what amount should Jamin report as allowance for uncollectible accounts?
   - a. $115,000
   - b. $180,000
   - c. $245,000
   - d. $440,000

E 7–13 Assigning of specific accounts receivable	On June 30, 2003, the High Five Surfboard Company had outstanding accounts receivable of $600,000. On July 1, 2003, the company borrowed $400,000 from the Equitable Finance Corporation and signed a promissory note. Interest at 10% is payable monthly. The company assigned specific receivables totaling $500,000 as collateral for the loan. Equitable Finance charges a finance fee equal to 1.5% of the accounts receivable assigned.

Required:
Prepare the journal entries to record the borrowing on the books of High Five Surfboard.

E 7–14
Factoring of accounts receivable without recourse

The Mountain High Ice Cream Company transferred $50,000 of accounts receivable to the Prudential Bank. The transfer was made *without recourse.* Prudential remits 90% of the factored amount to Mountain High and retains 10%. When the bank collects the receivables, it will remit to Mountain High the retained amount less a 2% fee (2% of the total factored amount).

Required:
Prepare the journal entry to record the transfer on the books of Mountain High assuming that the sale criteria are met.

E 7–15
Factoring of accounts receivable with recourse

[This is a variation of the previous exercise modified to focus on factoring with recourse.]

The Mountain High Ice Cream Company transferred $50,000 of accounts receivable to the Prudential Bank. The transfer was made *with recourse.* Prudential remits 90% of the factored amount to Mountain High and retains 10%. When the bank collects the receivables, it will remit to Mountain High the retained amount less a 2% fee (2% of the total factored amount). Mountain High anticipates a $3,000 recourse obligation.

Required:
Prepare the journal entry to record the transfer on the books of Mountain High assuming that the sale criteria are met.

E 7–16
Discounting a note receivable

The Selkirk Company obtained a $10,000 note receivable from a customer on January 1, 2003. The note, along with interest at 12%, is due on July 1, 2003. On February 28, 2003, Selkirk discounted the note at Unionville Bank. The bank's discount rate is 14%.

Required:
Prepare the journal entries required on February 28, 2003, to accrue interest and to record the discounting (round all calculations to the nearest dollar) for Selkirk. Assume that the discounting is accounted for as a sale.

E 7–17
Multiple choice; financing with receivables

The following questions dealing with financing with receivables are adapted from questions that appeared on recent CPA examinations. Determine the response that best completes the statements or questions.

1. Gar Co. factored its receivables without recourse with Ross Bank. Gar received cash as a result of this transaction, which is best described as a:
    a. Loan from Ross collateralized by Gar's accounts receivable.
    b. Loan from Ross to be repaid by the proceeds from Gar's accounts receivable.
    c. Sale of Gar's accounts receivable to Ross, with the risk of uncollectible accounts retained by Gar.
    d. Sale of Gar's accounts receivable to Ross, with the risk of uncollectible accounts transferred to Ross.

2. Roth, Inc. received from a customer a one-year, $500,000 note bearing annual interest of 8%. After holding the note for six months, Roth discounted the note at Regional Bank at an effective interest rate of 10%. What amount of cash did Roth receive from the bank?
    a. $540,000
    b. $523,810
    c. $513,000
    d. $495,238

E 7–18
Concepts; terminology

Listed below are several terms and phrases associated with cash and receivables. Pair each item from List A (by letter) with the item from List B that is most appropriately associated with it.

List A	List B
____ 1. Internal control	a. Restriction on cash.
____ 2. Trade discount	b. Cash discount not taken is sales revenue.
____ 3. Cash equivalents	c. Includes separation of duties.
____ 4. Allowance for uncollectibles	d. Bad debt expense a % of credit sales.
____ 5. Cash discount	e. Recognizes bad debts as they occur.
____ 6. Balance sheet approach	f. Sale of receivables to a financial institution.
____ 7. Income statement approach	g. Include highly liquid investments.
____ 8. Net method	h. Estimate of bad debts.
____ 9. Compensating balance	i. Reduction in amount paid by credit customer.
____ 10. Discounting	j. Reduction below list price.
____ 11. Gross method	k. Cash discount not taken is interest revenue.
____ 12. Direct write-off method	l. Bad debt expense determined by estimating realizable value.
____ 13. Factoring	m. Sale of note receivable to a financial institution.

E 7–19
Receivables;
transaction analysis

The Weldon Corporation's fiscal year ends December 31. The following is a list of transactions involving receivables that occurred during 2003:

Mar. 17   Accounts receivable of $1,700 were written off as uncollectible. The company uses the allowance method.

30   Loaned an officer of the company $20,000 and received a note requiring principal and interest at 7% to be paid on March 30, 2004.

May 30   Discounted the $20,000 note at a local bank. The bank's discount rate is 8%. The note was discounted without recourse and the sale criteria are met.

June 30   Sold merchandise to the Blankenship Company for $12,000. Terms of the sale are 2/10, n/30. Weldon uses the gross method to account for cash discounts.

July 8   The Blankenship Company paid its account in full.

Aug. 31   Sold stock in a nonpublic company with a book value of $5,000 and accepted a $6,000 noninterest-bearing note with a discount rate of 8%. The $6,000 payment is due on February 28, 2004. The stock has no ready market value.

Dec. 31   Bad debt expense is estimated to be 2% of credit sales for the year. Credit sales for 2003 were $700,000.

Required:
1.   Prepare journal entries for each of the above transactions (round all calculations to the nearest dollar).
2.   Prepare any additional year-end adjusting entries indicated.

E 7–20
Ratio analysis

Cisco Systems is the world's largest provider of hardware, software, and services that drive the Internet. The company reported the following information in its financial statements for three successive quarters during the 2001 fiscal year ($ in millions):

| | Three Months Ended | | |
	4/28/01 (Q3)	1/27/01 (Q2)	10/28/00 (Q1)
Balance sheets:			
Accounts receivable, net	$1,983	$3,512	$2,887
Income statements:			
Sales revenue	$4,728	$6,748	$6,519

Required:
1.   Compute the receivables turnover ratio and the average collection period for the second and third quarters. Assume that each quarter consists of 91 days.
2.   Speculate as to the reasons that might have caused the increase in the average collection period from the second to the third quarter.

E 7–21
Ratio analysis; solve for unknown

The current asset section of the Moorcroft Outboard Motor Company's balance sheet reported the following amounts:

	12/31/03	12/31/02
Accounts receivable, net	$400,000	$300,000

The average collection period for 2003 is 50 days.

Required:
Determine net sales for 2003.

E 7–22
Petty cash
(Based on Appendix 7)

The Loucks Company established a $200 petty cash fund on October 2, 2003. The fund is replenished at the end of each month. At the end of October 2003, the fund contained $37 in cash and the following receipts:

Office supplies	$76
Lunch with client	48
Postage	20
Miscellaneous	19

Required:
Prepare the necessary general journal entries to establish the petty cash fund on October 2 and to replenish the fund on October 31.

E 7–23
Bank reconciliation
(Based on Appendix 7)

The Jansen Company's general ledger showed a checking account balance of $23,820 at the end of May 2003. The May 31 cash receipts of $2,340, included in the general ledger balance, were placed in the night depository at the bank on May 31 and were processed by the bank on June 1. The bank statement dated May 31, 2003, showed bank service charges of $38. All checks written by the company had been processed by the bank by May 31 and were listed on the bank statement except for checks totaling $1,890.

Required:

Prepare a bank reconciliation as of May 31, 2003. [*Hint:* You will need to compute the balance that would appear on the bank statement.]

E 7–24
Bank reconciliation and adjusting entries (Based on Appendix 7)

The Harrison Company maintains a checking account at the First National City Bank. The bank provides a bank statement along with canceled checks on the last day of each month. The July 2003 bank statement included the following information:

Balance, July 1, 2003	$ 55,678
Deposits	179,500
Checks processed	(192,610)
Service charges	(30)
NSF checks	(1,200)
Monthly loan payment deducted directly by bank from account (includes $320 in interest)	(3,320)
Balance, July 31, 2003	$ 38,018

The company's general ledger account had a balance of $38,918 at the end of July. Deposits outstanding totaled $6,300 and all checks written by the company were processed by the bank except for those totaling $8,420. In addition, a $2,000 July deposit from a credit customer was recorded as a $200 debit to cash and credit to accounts receivable, and a check correctly recorded by the company as a $30 disbursement was incorrectly processed by the bank as a $300 disbursement.

Required:
1. Prepare a bank reconciliation for the month of July.
2. Prepare the necessary journal entries at the end of July to adjust the general ledger cash account.

PROBLEMS

P 7–1
Uncollectible accounts; allowance method; income statement and balance sheet approach

The Swathmore Clothing Corporation grants its customers 30 days' credit. The company uses the allowance method for its uncollectible accounts receivable. During the year, a monthly bad debt accrual is made by multiplying 3% times the amount of credit sales for the month. At the fiscal year-end of December 31, an aging of accounts receivable schedule is prepared and the allowance for uncollectible accounts is adjusted accordingly.

At the end of 2002, accounts receivable were $574,000 and the allowance account had a credit balance of $54,000. Accounts receivable activity for 2003 was as follows:

Beginning balance	$ 574,000
Credit sales	2,620,000
Collections	(2,483,000)
Write-offs	(68,000)
Ending balance	$ 643,000

The company's controller prepared the following aging summary of year-end accounts receivable:

	Summary		
Age Group	Amount	Percent Uncollectible	
0–60 days	$430,000	4%	17,200
61–90 days	98,000	15	14,700
91–120 days	60,000	25	15,000
Over 120 days	55,000	40	22,000
Total	$643,000		68,900

Required:
1. Prepare a summary journal entry to record the monthly bad debt accrual and the write-offs during the year.

2. Prepare the necessary year-end adjusting entry for bad debt expense.
3. What is total bad debt expense for 2003? How would accounts receivable appear in the 2003 balance sheet?

P 7–2
Uncollectible accounts

The Amdahl Corporation manufactures large-scale, high performance computer systems. In a recent annual report, the balance sheet included the following information (dollars in thousands):

	Current Year	Previous Year
Current assets:		
Receivables, net of allowances of $5,042 and $6,590 in the previous year	$504,944	$580,640

In addition, the income statement reported sales revenue of $2,158,755 (dollars in thousands) for the current year. All sales are made on a credit basis. The statement of cash flows indicates that cash collected from customers during the current year was $2,230,065 (dollars in thousands). There were no recoveries of accounts receivable previously written off.

Required:
1. Compute the following (dollar amounts in thousands):
   a. The amount of uncollectibles written off by Amdahl during the current year.
   b. The amount of bad debt expense that Amdahl would include in its income statement for the current year.
   c. The approximate percentage that Amdahl used to estimate uncollectibles for the current year, assuming that it uses the income statement approach.
2. Suppose that Amdahl had used the direct write-off method to account for uncollectibles. Compute the following (dollars in thousands):
   a. The accounts receivable information that would be included in the year-end balance sheet.
   b. The amount of bad debt expense that Amdahl would include in its income statement for the current year.

P 7–3
Uncollectible accounts

The Raintree Cosmetic Company sells its products to customers on a credit basis. An adjusting entry for bad debt expense is recorded only at December 31, the company's fiscal year-end. The 2002 balance sheet disclosed the following:

Current assets:
Receivables, net of allowance for uncollectible accounts of $30,000 $432,000

During 2003, credit sales were $1,750,000, cash collections from customers $1,830,000, and $35,000 in accounts receivable were written off. In addition, $3,000 was collected from a customer whose account was written off in 2002. An aging of accounts receivable at December 31, 2003, reveals the following:

Age Group	Percentage of Year-End Receivables in Group	Percent Uncollectible
0–60 days	65%	4%
61–90 days	20	15
91–120 days	10	25
Over 120 days	5	40

Required:
1. Prepare summary journal entries to account for the 2003 write-offs and the collection of the receivable previously written off.
2. Prepare the year-end adjusting entry for bad debts according to each of the following situations:
   a. Bad debt expense is estimated to be 3% of credit sales for the year.
   b. Bad debt expense is estimated by computing net realizable value of the receivables. The allowance for uncollectible accounts is estimated to be 10% of the year-end balance in accounts receivable.
   c. Bad debt expense is estimated by computing net realizable value of the receivables. The allowance for uncollectible accounts is determined by an aging of accounts receivable.
3. For situations (a)–(c) in requirement 2 above, what would be the net amount of accounts receivable reported in the 2003 balance sheet?

P 7–4

Notes receivable; solving for unknowns

The Cypress Oil Company's December 31, 2003, balance sheet listed $645,000 of notes receivable and $16,000 of interest receivable included in current assets. The following notes make up the notes receivable balance:

Note 1   Dated 8/31/03, principal of $300,000 and interest at 10% due on 2/28/04.
Note 2   Dated 6/30/03, principal of $150,000 and interest due 3/31/04.
Note 3 $200,000 face value noninterest-bearing note dated 9/31/03, due 3/31/04. Note was issued in exchange for merchandise.

The company records adjusting entries only at year-end. There were no other notes receivable outstanding during 2003.

Required:
1.   Determine the rate used to discount the noninterest-bearing note.
2.   Determine the explicit interest rate on Note 2.
3.   What is the amount of interest revenue that appears in the company's 2003 income statement related to these notes?

P 7–5

Factoring versus assigning of accounts receivable

The Lonergan Company occasionally uses its accounts receivable to obtain immediate cash. At the end of June 2003, the company had accounts receivable of $780,000. Lonergan needs approximately $500,000 to capitalize on a unique investment opportunity. On July 1, 2003, a local bank offers Lonergan the following two alternatives:
a.   Borrow $500,000, sign a note payable, and assign the entire receivable balance as collateral. At the end of each month, a remittance will be made to the bank that equals the amount of receivables collected plus 12% interest on the unpaid balance of the note at the beginning of the period.
b.   Transfer $550,000 of specific receivables to the bank without recourse. The bank will charge a 2% finance charge on the amount of receivables transferred. The bank will collect the receivables directly from customers. The sale criteria are met.

Required:
1.   Prepare the journal entries that would be recorded on July 1 for each of the alternatives.
2.   Assuming that 80% of all June 30 receivables are collected during July, prepare the necessary journal entries to record the collection and the remittance to the bank.
3.   For each alternative, explain any required note disclosures that would be included in the July 31, 2003, financial statements.

P 7–6

Factoring of accounts receivable; with and without recourse

The Samson Wholesale Beverage Company regularly factors its accounts receivable with the Milpitas Finance Company. On April 30, 2003, the company transferred $800,000 of accounts receivable to Milpitas. The transfer was made without recourse. Milpitas remits 90% of the factored amount and retains 10%. When Milpitas collects the receivables, it remits to Samson the retained amount less a 4% fee (4% of the total factored amount).

Required:
Prepare journal entries for Samson Wholesale Beverage for the transfer of accounts receivable on April 30 assuming the sale criteria are met.

P 7–7

Miscellaneous receivable transactions

The Evergreen Company sells lawn and garden products to wholesalers. The company's fiscal year-end is December 31. During 2003, the following transactions related to receivables occurred:

Feb. 28   Sold merchandise to Lennox, Inc. for $10,000 and accepted a 10%, 7-month note. 10% is an appropriate rate for this type of note.
Mar. 31   Sold merchandise to Maddox Co. and accepted a noninterest-bearing note with a discount rate of 10%. The $8,000 payment is due on March 31, 2004.
Apr.   3   Sold merchandise to Carr Co. for $7,000 with terms 2/10, n/30. Evergreen uses the gross method to account for cash discounts.
      11   Collected the entire amount due from Carr Co.
      17   A customer returned merchandise costing $3,200. Evergreen reduced the customer's receivable balance by $5,000, the sales price of the merchandise. Sales returns are recorded by the company as they occur.
      30   Transferred receivables of $50,000 to a factor without recourse. The factor charged Evergreen a 1% finance charge on the receivables transferred. The sale criteria are met.
June 30   Discounted the Lennox, Inc., note at the bank. The bank's discount rate is 12%. The note was discounted without recourse.
Aug. 31   Lennox, Inc., paid the note amount plus interest to the bank.

Required:

1. Prepare the necessary journal entries for Evergreen for each of the above dates. For transactions involving the sale of merchandise, ignore the entry for the cost of goods sold (round all calculations to the nearest dollar).
2. Prepare any necessary adjusting entries at December 31, 2003. Adjusting entries are only recorded at year-end (round all calculations to the nearest dollar).
3. Prepare a schedule showing the effect of the journal entries in requirements 1 and 2 on 2003 income before taxes.

P 7–8

Discounting a note receivable

Descriptors are provided below for six situations involving notes receivable being discounted at a bank. In each case, the maturity date of the note is December 31, 2003, and the principal and interest are due at maturity. For each, determine the proceeds received from the bank on discounting the note.

Note	Note Face Value	Date of Note	Interest Rate	Date Discounted	Discount Rate
1	$50,000	3/31/00	8%	6/30/03	10%
2	50,000	3/31/00	8	9/30/03	10
3	50,000	3/31/00	8	9/30/03	12
4	80,000	6/30/00	6	10/31/03	10
5	80,000	6/30/00	6	10/31/03	12
6	80,000	6/30/00	6	11/30/03	10

P 7–9

Bank reconciliation and adjusting entries; cash and cash equivalents (Based on Appendix 7)

The bank statement for the checking account of Management Systems, Inc. (MSI) showed a December 31, 2003, balance of $14,632.12. Information that might be useful in preparing a bank reconciliation is as follows:

a. Outstanding checks were $1,320.25.
b. The December 31, 2003, cash receipts of $575 were not deposited in the bank until January 2, 2004.
c. One check written in payment of rent for $246 was correctly recorded by the bank but was recorded by MSI as a $264 disbursement.
d. In accordance with prior authorization, the bank withdrew $450 directly from the checking account as payment on a mortgage note payable. The interest portion of that payment was $350. MSI has made no entry to record the automatic payment.
e. Bank service charges of $14 were listed on the bank statement.
f. A deposit of $875 was recorded by the bank on December 13, but it did not belong to MSI. The deposit should have been made to the checking account of MSI, Inc.
g. The bank statement included a charge of $85 for an NSF check. The check was returned with the bank statement and the company will seek payment from the customer.
h. MSI maintains a $200 petty cash fund that was appropriately reimbursed at the end of December.
i. According to instructions from MSI on December 30, the bank withdrew $10,000 from the account and purchased U.S. Treasury bills for MSI. MSI recorded the transaction in its books on December 31 when it received notice from the bank. Half of the treasury bills mature in two months and the other half in six months.

Required:

1. Prepare a bank reconciliation for the MSI checking account at December 31, 2003. You will have to compute the balance per books.
2. Prepare any necessary adjusting journal entries indicated.
3. What amount would MSI report as cash and cash equivalents in the current asset section of the December 31, 2003, balance sheet?

P 7–10

Bank reconciliation and adjusting entries (Based on Appendix 7)

The El Gato Painting Company maintains a checking account at American Bank. Bank statements are prepared at the end of each month. The November 30, 2003, reconciliation of the bank balance is as follows:

Balance per bank, November 30		$3,231
Add: Deposits outstanding		1,200
Less: Checks outstanding		
#363	$123	
#365	201	
#380	56	
#381	86	
#382	340	(806)
Adjusted balance per bank, November 30		$3,625

The company's general ledger checking account showed the following for December:

Balance, December 1	$ 3,625
Receipts	42,650
Disbursements	(41,853)
Balance, December 31	$ 4,422

The December bank statement contained the following information:

Balance, December 1	$ 3,231
Deposits	43,000
Checks processed	(41,918)
Service charges	(22)
NSF checks	(440)
Balance, December 31	$ 3,851

The checks that were processed by the bank in December include all of the outstanding checks at the end of November except for check #365. In addition, there are some December checks that had not been processed by the bank by the end of the month. Also, you discover that check #411 for $320 was correctly recorded by the bank but was incorrectly recorded on the books as a $230 disbursement for advertising expense. Included in the bank's deposits is a $1,300 deposit incorrectly credited to the company's account. The deposit should have been posted to the credit of the Los Gatos Company. The NSF checks have not been redeposited and the company will seek payment from the customers involved.

Required:
1. Prepare a bank reconciliation for the El Gato checking account at December 31, 2003.
2. Prepare any necessary adjusting journal entries indicated.

BROADEN YOUR PERSPECTIVE

Apply your critical-thinking ability to the knowledge you've gained. These cases will provide you an opportunity to develop your research, analysis, judgment, and communication skills. You also will work with other students, integrate what you've learned, apply it in real world situations, and consider its global and ethical ramifications. This practice will broaden your knowledge and further develop your decision-making abilities.

Judgment Case 7–1
Accounts and notes receivable

Magrath Company has an operating cycle of less than one year and provides credit terms for all of its customers. On April 1, 2003, the company factored, without recourse, some of its accounts receivable.

Magrath uses the allowance method to account for uncollectible accounts. During 2003, some accounts were written off as uncollectible and other accounts previously written off as uncollectible were collected.

Required:
1. How should Magrath account for and report the accounts receivable factored on April 1, 2003? Why is this accounting treatment appropriate?
2. How should Magrath account for the collection of the accounts previously written off as uncollectible?
3. What are the two basic approaches to estimating uncollectible accounts under the allowance method? What is the rationale for each approach?

(AICPA adapted)

Communication Case 7–2
Uncollectible accounts

You have been hired as a consultant by a parts manufacturing firm to provide advice as to the proper accounting methods the company should use in some key areas. In the area of receivables, the company president does not understand your recommendation to use the allowance method for uncollectible accounts. She stated, "Financial statements should be based on objective data rather than the guesswork required for the allowance method. Besides, since my uncollectibles are fairly constant from period to period, with significant variations occurring infrequently, the direct write-off method is just as good as the allowance method."

Required:

Draft a one-page response in the form of a memo to the president in support of your recommendation for the company to use the allowance method.

Judgment Case 7–3
Accounts receivable

Hogan Company uses the net method of accounting for sales discounts. Hogan offers trade discounts to various groups of buyers.

On August 1, 2003, Hogan factored some accounts receivable on a without recourse basis. Hogan incurred a finance charge.

Hogan also has some notes receivable bearing an appropriate rate of interest. The principal and total interest are due at maturity. The notes were received on October 1, 2003, and mature on September 30, 2004. Hogan's operating cycle is less than one year.

Required:

1. a.   Using the net method, how should Hogan account for the sales discounts at the date of sale? What is the rationale for the amount recorded as sales under the net method?
    b.   Using the net method, what is the effect on Hogan's sales revenues and net income when customers do not take the sales discounts?
2.   What is the effect of trade discounts on sales revenues and accounts receivable? Why?
3.   How should Hogan account for the accounts receivable factored on August 1, 2003? Why?
4.   How should Hogan report the effects of the interest-bearing notes receivable in its December 31, 2003, balance sheet and its income statement for the year ended December 31, 2003? Why?

(AICPA adapted)

Ethics Case 7–4
Uncollectible accounts

You have recently been hired as the assistant controller for Stanton Industries, a large, publicly held manufacturing company. Your immediate superior is the controller who, in turn, is responsible to the vice president of finance.

The controller has assigned you the task of preparing the year-end adjusting entries. In the receivables area, you have prepared an aging of accounts receivable and have applied historical percentages to the balances of each of the age categories. The analysis indicates that an appropriate balance for the allowance for uncollectible accounts is $180,000. The existing balance in the allowance account prior to any adjusting entry is a $20,000 credit balance.

After showing your analysis to the controller, he tells you to change the aging category of a large account from over 120 days to current status and to prepare a new invoice to the customer with a revised date that agrees with the new aging category. This will change the required allowance for uncollectible accounts from $180,000 to $135,000. Tactfully, you ask the controller for an explanation for the change and he tells you "We need the extra income, the bottom line is too low."

Required:

1.   What is the effect on income before taxes of the change requested by the controller?
2.   Discuss the ethical dilemma you face. Consider your options and responsibilities along with the possible consequences of any action you might take.

Judgment Case 7–5
Internal control

For each of the following independent situations, indicate the apparent internal control weaknesses and suggest alternative procedures to eliminate the weaknesses.

1.   John Smith is the petty cash custodian. John approves all requests for payment out of the $200 fund which is replenished at the end of each month. At the end of each month, John submits a list of all accounts and amounts to be charged and a check is written to him for the total amount. John is the only person ever to tally the fund.
2.   All of the company's cash disbursements are made by check. Each check must be supported by an approved voucher which is in turn supported by the appropriate invoice and, for purchases, a receiving document. The vouchers are approved by Dean Leiser, the chief accountant, after reviewing the supporting documentation. Betty Hanson prepares the checks for Leiser's signature. Leiser also maintains the company's check register (the cash disbursements journal) and reconciles the bank account at the end of each month.
3.   Fran Jones opens the company's mail and makes a listing of all checks and cash received from customers. A copy of the list is sent to Jerry McDonald who maintains the general ledger accounts. Fran prepares and makes the daily deposit at the bank. Fran also maintains the subsidiary ledger for accounts receivable which is used to generate monthly statements to customers.

Real World Case 7–6
Bad debts

Cirrus Logic, Inc. is a leading designer and manufacturer of advanced integrated circuits that integrate algorithms and mixed-signal processing for mass storage, communications, consumer electronics, and industrial markets. The company's 2001 financial statements contained the following information:

	($ in thousands)	
Balance Sheets	**2001**	**2000**
Current assets:		
Accounts receivable, less allowance for doubtful accounts of $2,200 in 2001 and $3,870 in 2000	$136,102	$94,672
Income Statements	**2001**	**2000**
Net sales	$778,673	$564,400

In addition, the statement of cash flows disclosed that accounts receivable increased during 2001 by $43,397 (in thousands). This indicates that cash received from customers was $43,397 (in thousands) less than accrual sales revenue.

Required:
1. What is the amount of accounts receivable due from customers at the end of 2001 and 2000?
2. Assuming that all sales are made on a credit basis, determine the amount of bad debt expense for 2001 and the amount of actual bad debt write-offs made in 2001.

Real World Case 7–7
Receivables; bad debts

EDGAR, the Electronic Data Gathering, Analysis, and Retrieval system, performs automated collection, validation, indexing, and forwarding of submissions by companies and others who are required by law to file forms with the U.S. Securities and Exchange Commission (SEC). All publicly traded domestic companies use EDGAR to make the majority of their filings. (Some foreign companies file voluntarily.) Form 10-K or 10-KSB, which include the annual report, is required to be filed on EDGAR. The SEC makes this information available on the Internet.

Required:
1. Access EDGAR on the Internet. The web address is **www.sec.gov**. Edgarscan (**edgarscan. pwcglobal.com**) from Pricewaterhouse Coopers makes the process of accessing data from EDGAR easier.
2. Search for Avon Products, Inc. Access the 10-K filing for the most recent fiscal year. Search or scroll to find the financial statements.
3. Answer the following questions related to the company's accounts receivable and bad debts:
   a. What is the amount of gross trade accounts receivable at the end of the year?
   b. What is the amount of bad debt expense for the year? (*Hint:* check the statement of cash flows.)
   c. Determine the amount of actual bad debt write-offs made during the year. Assume that all bad debts relate only to trade accounts receivable.
   d. Using only information from the balance sheets, income statements, and your answer to requirement 3.c., determine the amount of cash collected from customers during the year. Assume that all sales are made on a credit basis, that the company provides no allowances for sales returns, that no previously written-off receivables were collected, and that all sales relate to trade accounts receivable.

Integrating Case 7–8
Change in estimate of bad debts

The McLaughlin Corporation uses the allowance method to account for bad debts. At the end of the company's fiscal year, accounts receivable are analyzed and the allowance for uncollectible accounts is adjusted. At the end of 2003, the company reported the following amounts:

Accounts receivable	$10,850,000
Less: Allowance for uncollectible accounts	(450,000)
Accounts receivable, net	$10,400,000

In 2004, it was determined that $1,825,000 of year-end 2003 receivables had to be written off as uncollectible. This was due in part to the fact that Hughes Corporation, a long-standing customer that had always paid its bills, unexpectedly declared bankruptcy in 2004. Hughes owed McLaughlin $1,400,000. At the end of 2003, none of the Hughes receivable was considered uncollectible.

Required:
Describe the appropriate accounting treatment and required disclosures for McLaughlin's underestimation of bad debts at the end of 2003.

Analysis Case 7–9
Financing with receivables

Financial institutions have developed a wide variety of methods for companies to use their receivables to obtain immediate cash. The methods differ with respect to which rights and risks are retained by the transferor (the original holder of the receivable) and those passed on to the transferee (the new holder, usually a financial institution).

Required:

1. Describe the alternative methods available for companies to use their receivables to obtain immediate cash.
2. Discuss the alternative accounting treatments for these methods.

Research Case 7–10
Locate and extract relevant information and authoritative support for a financial reporting issue; financing with receivables

You are spending the summer working for a local wholesale furniture company, Samson Furniture, Inc. The company is considering a proposal from a local financial institution, Old Reliant Financial, to factor Samson's receivables. The company controller is unfamiliar with the most recent FASB pronouncement that deals with accounting for the transfer of assets and has asked you to do some research. The controller wants to make sure the arrangement with the financial institution is structured in such a way as to allow the factoring to be accounted for as a sale.

Old Reliant has offered to factor all of the company's receivables on a "without recourse" basis. Old Reliant will remit to Samson 90% of the factored amount, collect the receivables from Samson's customers, and retain the remaining 10% until all of the receivables have been collected. When Old Reliant collects all of the receivables, it will remit to Samson the retained amount, less a 4% fee (4% of the total factored amount).

Required:

1. Explain the meaning of the term *without recourse.*
2. Obtain the FASB standard on accounting for the transfer or assets. You might gain access through FARS, the FASB Financial Accounting Research System, from your school library, or some other source.
3. What conditions must be met for a transfer of receivables to be accounted for as a sale? What is the specific citation that Samson would rely on in applying that accounting treatment?
4. Assuming that the conditions for treatment as a sale are met, prepare Samson's journal entry to record the factoring of $400,000 of receivables.
5. An agreement that both entitles and obligates the transferor, Samson, to repurchase or redeem transferred assets from the transferee, Old Reliant, maintains the transferor's effective control over those assets and the transfer is accounted for as a secured borrowing, not a sale, if and only if what conditions are met?

Analysis Case 7–11
Compare receivables management using ratios

The table below contains selected financial information included in the 2001 financial statements of Sara Lee Corporation and Tyson Foods, Inc.

	($ in millions)			
	Sara Lee		Tyson Foods	
	2001	**2000**	**2001**	**2000**
Balance sheet:				
Accounts receivable, net	$ 1,538	$ 1,764	$ 1,199	$ 508
Income statement:				
Net sales	17,747	17,511	10.751	7,410

Required:

1. Calculate the 2001 receivables turnover ratio and average collection period for both companies. Evaluate the management of each company's investment in receivables.
2. Obtain annual reports from three corporations in the same primary industry and compare the management of each company's investment in receivables.

Note: You can obtain copies of annual reports from your library, from friends who are shareholders, from the investor relations department of the corporations, from a friendly stockbroker, or from EDGAR (Electronic Data Gathering, Analysis, and Retrieval) on the Internet (www.sec.gov or through Edgarscan at edgarscan.pwcglobal.com).

Analysis Case 7–12
Reporting cash and receivables

FedEx Corporation

Refer to the financial statements and related disclosure notes of FedEx Corporation in the appendix to Chapter 1.

Required:

1. What is FedEx's policy for designating investments as cash equivalents?
2. Determine the gross amount of receivables outstanding at May 31, 2001, and May 31, 2000.
3. What amount of receivables were written off during the 2001 fiscal year? Assume that no previously written-off receivables were collected during the year and that allowances relate only to allowances for uncollectible accounts. (*Hint:* check the statement of cash flows.)

8

CHAPTER

Inventories: Measurement

OVERVIEW

The next two chapters continue our study of assets by investigating the measurement and reporting issues involving inventories and the related expense—cost of goods sold. Inventory refers to the assets a company (1) intends to sell in the normal course of business, (2) has in production for future sale, or (3) uses currently in the production of goods to be sold.

LEARNING OBJECTIVES

After studying this chapter, you should be able to:

LO1 Explain the difference between a perpetual inventory system and a periodic inventory system.

LO2 Explain which physical quantities of goods should be included in inventory.

LO3 Determine the expenditures that should be included in the cost of inventory.

LO4 Differentiate between the specific identification, FIFO, LIFO, and average cost methods used to determine the cost of ending inventory and cost of goods sold.

LO5 Discuss the factors affecting a company's choice of inventory method.

LO6 Determine ending inventory using the dollar-value LIFO inventory method.

Inventory Measurement at Ford Motor Company

A recent article in the financial section of your local newspaper reported on the labor negotiations between Ford Motor Company and the United Auto Workers. When you showed the article to a friend, he said, "I'll bet Ford uses LIFO to value its inventories. That way they can report lower profits and give them an edge in the negotiations." This aroused your curiosity and led you to download from the Internet Ford's most recent financial statements, which contained the following disclosure note:

Note 6. Inventories

Inventories at December 31 were as follows (in millions):

	2000	1999
Raw materials, work in process, and supplies	$2,798	$2,035
Finished products	4,716	3,649
Total inventories	$7,514	$5,684

Inventories are stated at the lower of cost or market. The cost of most U.S. inventories is determined by the last-in, first-out ("LIFO") method. The cost of the remaining inventories is determined primarily by the first-in, first-out ("FIFO") method.

If the FIFO method had been used instead of the LIFO method, inventories would have been higher by $1.1 billion and $1.0 billion at December 31, 2000 and 1999, respectively.

> By the time you finish this chapter, you should be able to respond appropriately to the questions posed in this case. Compare your response to the solution provided at the end of the chapter.

QUESTIONS

1. What inventory methods does Ford use to value its inventories? Is this permissible according to GAAP? (page 381)

2. What is the purpose of the disclosure information that reports what LIFO inventories would have been if valued at FIFO? (page 383)

3. Is your friend correct in his assertion that by using LIFO, Ford was able to report lower profits in 2000? (page 388)

PART

a

RECORDING AND MEASURING INVENTORY

Inventory refers to the assets a company (1) intends to sell in the normal course of business, (2) has in production for future sale, or (3) uses currently in the production of goods to be sold (raw materials). The computers produced by Apple Computer that are intended for sale to customers are inventory, as are partially completed components in the assembly lines of Apple's Cupertino facility, and the computer chips and memory modules that will go into computers produced later. The computers *used* by Apple to maintain its accounting system, however, are classified and accounted for as plant and equipment. Similarly, the stocks and bonds a securities dealer holds for sale are inventory, whereas Apple would classify the securities it holds as investments.

Proper accounting for inventories is essential for manufacturing, wholesale, and retail companies (enterprises that earn revenue by selling goods). Inventory usually is one of the most valuable assets listed in the balance sheet for these firms. Cost of goods sold—the expense recorded when inventory is sold—typically is the largest expense in the income statement. For example, a recent balance sheet for Sara Lee Corporation reported inventories of $2.582 billion, which represented 25% of total assets. The company's income statement reported cost of goods sold of $10 billion representing 64% of all expenses.

In this and the following chapter we discuss the measurement and reporting issues involving **inventory**, an asset, and the related expense, **cost of goods sold**. Inventory represents *quantities* of goods acquired, manufactured, or in the process of being manufactured. The inventory amount in the balance sheet at the end of an accounting period represents the cost of the inventory still on hand, and cost of goods sold in the income statement represents the cost of the inventory sold during the period. The historical cost principle and matching principle offer guidance for measuring inventory and cost of goods sold, but as we will see in this and the next chapter, it's usually difficult to measure inventory (cost of goods sold) at the exact cost of the actual physical quantities on hand (sold). Fortunately, accountants can use one of several techniques to approximate the desired result and satisfy our measurement objectives.

Inventories consist of assets that a retail or wholesale company acquires for resale or goods that manufacturers produce for sale.

An important objective in inventory accounting is to match the appropriate cost of goods sold with sales revenue.

Types of Inventory

MERCHANDISING INVENTORY

Wholesale and retail companies purchase goods that are primarily in finished form. These companies are intermediaries in the process of moving goods from the manufacturer to the end-user. They often are referred to as merchandising companies and their inventory as merchandise inventory. *The cost of merchandise inventory includes the purchase price plus any other costs necessary to get the goods in condition and location for sale.* We discuss the concept of condition and location and the types of costs that typically constitute inventory later in this chapter.

MANUFACTURING INVENTORIES

Inventory for a manufacturing company consists of raw materials, work in process, and finished goods.

Unlike merchandising companies, manufacturing companies actually produce the goods they sell to wholesalers, retailers, or other manufacturers. Inventory for a manufacturer consists of (1) raw materials, (2) work in process, and (3) finished goods. **Raw materials** represent the cost of components purchased from other manufacturers that will become part of the finished product. For example, Apple's raw materials inventory includes semiconductors, circuit boards, plastic, and glass that go into the production of personal computers.

The cost of work in process and finished goods includes the cost of raw materials, direct labor, and an allocated portion of manufacturing overhead.

Work-in-process inventory refers to the products that are not yet complete. The cost of work in process includes the cost of raw materials used in production, the cost of labor that can be directly traced to the goods in process, and an allocated portion of other manufacturing costs, called *manufacturing overhead.* Overhead costs include electricity and other utility costs to operate the manufacturing facility, depreciation of manufacturing equipment, and many other manufacturing costs that cannot be directly linked to the production of specific goods. Once the manufacturing process is completed, these costs that have accumulated in work in process are transferred to **finished goods.**

Manufacturing companies generally disclose, either in a note or directly in the balance sheet, the dollar amount of each inventory category. For example, IBM Corporation's note disclosure of inventory category was shown on page 123. Sara Lee Corporation reports inventory categories directly in the balance sheet, as illustrated in Graphic 8–1.

The inventory accounts and the cost flows for a typical manufacturing company are shown using T-accounts in Graphic 8–2. The costs of raw materials used, direct labor applied, and manufacturing overhead applied, flow into work in process and then to finished goods. When the goods are sold, the cost of those goods flows to cost of goods sold.

GRAPHIC 8–1 Inventories Disclosure—Sara Lee Corporation

Balance Sheet

	($ in millions)	
	2001	**2000**
Current assets:		
Inventories		
Finished goods	$1,715	$1,941
Work in process	454	529
Materials and supplies	413	481
Total	$2,582	$2,951

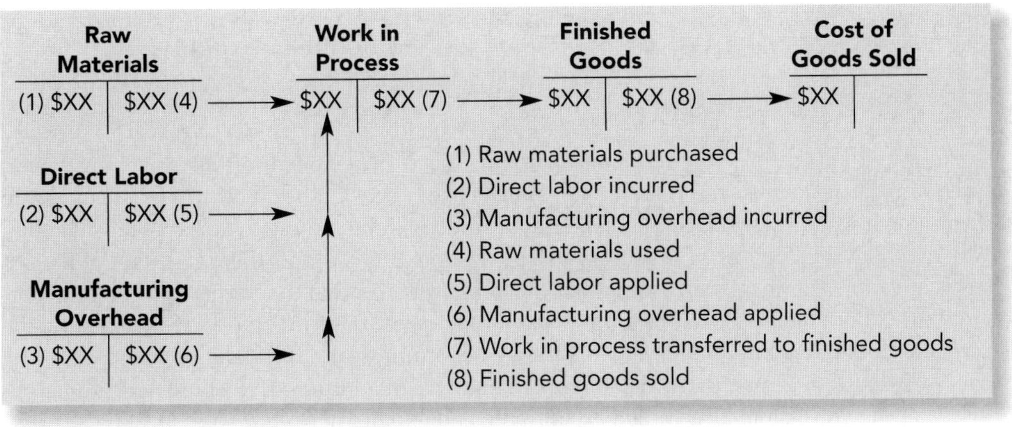

GRAPHIC 8–2
Inventory Components and Cost Flow for a Manufacturing Company

The costs of inventory units follow their physical movement from one stage of activity to another.

We focus here primarily on merchandising companies (wholesalers and retailers). Still, most of the accounting principles and procedures discussed here also apply to manufacturing companies. The unique problems involved with accumulating the direct costs of raw materials and labor and with allocating manufacturing overhead are addressed in managerial and cost accounting textbooks.

Perpetual Inventory System

Two accounting systems are used to record transactions involving inventory: the **perpetual inventory system** and the **periodic inventory system.** The perpetual system was introduced in Chapter 2. The system is aptly termed perpetual because the account *inventory* is continually adjusted for each change in inventory, whether it's caused by a purchase, a sale, or a return of merchandise by the company to its supplier (a *purchase return* for the buyer, a *sales return* for the seller).[1] The cost of goods sold account, along with the inventory account, is adjusted each time goods are sold or are returned by a customer. This concept is applied to the Lothridge Wholesale Beverage Company for which inventory information is provided in Illustration 8–1. This hypothetical company also will be used in the next several illustrations.

A perpetual inventory system continuously records both changes in inventory quantity and inventory cost.

---

[1] We discussed accounting for sales returns in Chapter 7.

The Lothridge Wholesale Beverage Company purchases soft drinks from producers and then sells them to retailers. The company begins 2003 with merchandise inventory of $120,000 on hand. During 2003 additional merchandise is purchased on account at a cost of $600,000. Sales for the year, all on account, totaled $820,000. The cost of the soft drinks sold is $540,000. Lothridge uses the perpetual inventory system to keep track of both inventory quantities and inventory costs.

The following summary journal entries record the inventory transactions for the Lothridge Company:

2003

Inventory	600,000	
Accounts payable		600,000

To record the purchase of merchandise inventory.

2003

Accounts receivable	820,000	
Sales revenue		820,000

To record sales on account.

Cost of goods sold	540,000	
Inventory		540,000

To record the cost of sales.

An important feature of a perpetual system is that it is designed to track inventory quantities from their acquisition to their sale. If the system is accurate, it allows management to determine how many goods are on hand on any date without having to take a physical count. However, physical counts of inventory usually are made anyway, either at the end of the fiscal year or on a sample basis throughout the year, to verify that the perpetual system is correctly tracking quantities. Differences between the quantity of inventory determined by the physical count and the quantity of inventory according to the perpetual system could be caused by system errors, theft, breakage, or spoilage. In addition to keeping up with inventory, a perpetual system also directly determines how many items are sold during a period.

You are probably familiar with the scanning mechanisms used at grocery store checkout counters. The scanners not only record the sale on the cash register but also can be used to track the sale of merchandise for inventory management purposes. For a company to use the perpetual inventory system to record inventory and cost of goods sold transactions, merchandise cost data also must be included on the system. That is, when merchandise is purchased/sold, the system must be able to record not only the addition/reduction in inventory quantity but also the addition/reduction in the *cost* of inventory.

A perpetual inventory system tracks both inventory quantities and inventory costs.

Periodic Inventory System

A **periodic inventory system** is not designed to track either the quantity or cost of merchandise. The merchandise inventory account balance is not adjusted as purchases and sales are made but only periodically at the end of a reporting period. A physical count of the period's ending inventory is made and costs are assigned to the quantities determined. Merchandise purchases, purchase returns, purchase discounts, and freight-in (purchases plus freight-in less returns and discounts equals net purchases) are recorded in temporary accounts and the period's cost of goods sold is determined at the end of the period by combining the temporary accounts with the inventory account:

A *periodic inventory system* adjusts inventory and records cost of goods sold only at the end of each reporting period.

Cost of goods sold equation

Beginning inventory + Net purchases − Ending inventory = Cost of goods sold

The cost of goods sold equation assumes that all inventory quantities not on hand at the end of the period were sold. This may not be the case if inventory items were either damaged or stolen. If damaged and stolen inventory are identified, they must be removed from beginning inventory or purchases before calculating cost of goods sold and then classified as a separate expense item.

Illustration 8–2 looks at the periodic system using the Lothridge Wholesale Beverage Company example.

The Lothridge Wholesale Beverage Company purchases soft drinks from producers and then sells them to retailers. The company began 2003 with merchandise inventory of $120,000 on hand. During 2003 additional merchandise was purchased on account at a cost of $600,000. Sales for the year, all on account, totaled $820,000. Lothridge uses a periodic inventory system. A physical count determined the cost of inventory at the end of the year to be $180,000. The following journal entries summarize the inventory transactions for 2003. Of course, each individual transaction would actually be recorded as incurred:	**ILLUSTRATION 8–2** Periodic Inventory System

2003

Purchases.	600,000	
Accounts payable.		600,000

To record the purchase of merchandise inventory.

2003

Accounts receivable	820,000	
Sales revenue.		820,000

To record sales on account.

No entry is recorded for the cost of inventory sold.

Because cost of goods sold isn't determined automatically and continually by the periodic system, it must be determined indirectly after a physical inventory count. Cost of goods sold for 2003 is determined as follows:

Beginning inventory	$120,000
Plus: Purchases	600,000
Cost of goods available for sale	720,000
Less: Ending inventory (per physical count)	(180,000)
Cost of goods sold	$540,000

The following journal entry combines the components of cost of goods sold into a single expense account and updates the balance in the inventory account:

December 31, 2003

Cost of goods sold	540,000	
Inventory (ending).	180,000	
Inventory (beginning)		120,000
Purchases.		600,000

To adjust inventory, close the purchases account, and record cost of goods sold.

This entry adjusts the inventory account to the correct period-end amount, closes the temporary purchases account, and records the residual as cost of goods sold. Now let's compare the two inventory accounting systems.

A Comparison of the Perpetual and Periodic Inventory Systems

Beginning inventory plus net purchases during the period is the cost of goods available for sale. The main difference between a perpetual and a periodic system is that the periodic system allocates cost of goods available for sale between ending inventory and cost of goods sold (periodically) *at the end of the period.* In contrast, the perpetual system performs this allocation by decreasing inventory and increasing cost of goods sold (perpetually) *each time goods are sold.*

The impact on the financial statements of choosing one system over the other generally is not significant. The choice between the two approaches usually is motivated by management control considerations as well as the comparative costs of implementation. Perpetual systems can provide more information about the dollar amounts of inventory levels on a continuous basis. They also facilitate the preparation of interim financial statements by providing fairly accurate information without the necessity of a physical count of inventory.

On the other hand, a perpetual system may be more expensive to implement than a periodic system. This is particularly true for inventories consisting of large numbers of low-cost items. Perpetual systems are more workable with inventories of high-cost items such as construction equipment or automobiles. However, with the help of computers and electronic sales devices such as cash register scanners, the perpetual inventory system is now available to many small businesses that previously could not afford them and is economically feasible for a broader range of inventory items than before.

The periodic system is less costly to implement during the period but requires a physical count before ending inventory and cost of goods sold can be determined. This makes the preparation of interim financial statements more costly unless an inventory estimation technique is used.[2] And, perhaps most importantly, the inventory monitoring features provided by a perpetual system are not available. However, it is important to remember that a perpetual system involves the tracking of both inventory quantities *and* costs. Many companies that determine costs only periodically employ systems to constantly monitor inventory quantities.

> A perpetual system provides more timely information but generally is more costly.

What Is Included in Inventory?

PHYSICAL QUANTITIES INCLUDED IN INVENTORY

LO2

Regardless of the system used, the measurement of inventory and cost of goods sold starts with determining the physical quantities of goods. Typically, determining the physical quantity that should be included in inventory is a simple matter because it consists of items in the possession of the company. However, in some situations the identification of items that should be included in inventory is more difficult. Consider, for example, goods in transit, goods on consignment, and sales returns.

Goods in Transit. At the end of a reporting period, it's important to ensure a proper inventory cutoff. This means determining the ownership of goods that are in transit between the company and its customers as well as between the company and its suppliers. For example, in December 2003, the Lothridge Wholesale Beverage Company sold goods to the Jabbar Company. The goods were shipped on December 29, 2003, and arrived at Jabbar's warehouse on January 3, 2004. The fiscal year-end for both companies is December 31.

Should the merchandise shipped to Jabbar be recorded as a sale by Lothridge and a purchase by Jabbar in 2003 and thus included in Jabbar's 2003 ending inventory? Should recording the sale/purchase be delayed until 2004 and the merchandise be included in Lothridge's 2003 ending inventory? The answer depends on who owns the goods at December 31. Ownership depends on the terms of the agreement between the two companies. If the goods are shipped **f.o.b. (free on board) shipping point,** then legal title to the goods changes hands at the point of shipment when the seller delivers the goods to the common carrier (for example, a trucking company), and the purchaser is responsible for shipping costs and transit insurance. In that case, Lothridge records the sale and inventory reduction in 2003 and Jabbar records a 2003 purchase and includes the goods in 2003 ending inventory even though the company is not in physical possession of the goods on the last day of the fiscal year.

> Inventory shipped *f.o.b. shipping point* is included in the purchaser's inventory as soon as the merchandise is shipped.

---

[2]In Chapter 9 we discuss inventory estimation techniques that avoid the necessity of a physical count to determine ending inventory and cost of goods sold.

On the other hand, if the goods are shipped **f.o.b. destination,** the seller is responsible for shipping and legal title does not pass until the goods arrive at their destination (the customer's location). In our example, Lothridge includes the merchandise in its 2003 ending inventory and the sale is recorded in 2004. Jabbar records the purchase in 2004.

Goods on Consignment.   Sometimes a company arranges for another company to sell its product under **consignment.** The goods are physically transferred to the other company (the consignee), but the transferor (consignor) retains legal title. If the consignee can't find a buyer, the goods are returned to the consignor. If a buyer is found, the consignee remits the selling price (less commission and approved expenses) to the consignor.

As we discussed in Chapter 5, because risk is retained by the consignor, the sale is not complete (revenue is not recognized) until an eventual sale to a third party occurs. As a result, goods held on consignment generally are not included in the consignee's inventory. While in stock, they belong to the consignor and should be included in inventory of the consignor even though not in the company's physical possession. A sale is recorded by the consignor only when the goods are sold by the consignee and title passes to the customer.

Sales Returns.   Recall from our discussions in Chapters 5 and 7 that when the right of return exists, a seller must be able to estimate those returns before revenue can be recognized. The adjusting entry for estimated sales returns reduces sales revenue and accounts receivable. At the same time, cost of goods sold is reduced and inventory is increased (See Illustration 7–2 on page 327). As a result, a company includes in inventory the cost of merchandise it anticipates will be returned.

Now that we've considered which goods are part of inventory, let's examine the types of costs that should be associated with those inventory quantities.

EXPENDITURES INCLUDED IN INVENTORY

As mentioned earlier, the cost of inventory includes all necessary expenditures to acquire the inventory and bring it to its desired condition and location for sale or for use in the manufacturing process. Obviously, the cost includes the purchase price of the goods. But usually the cost of acquiring inventory also includes freight charges on incoming goods borne by the buyer,[3] insurance costs incurred by the buyer while the goods are in transit (if shipped f.o.b. shipping point), and the costs of unloading, unpacking, and preparing merchandise inventory for sale or raw materials inventory for use. The costs included in inventory are called **product costs.** They are associated with products and expensed as cost of goods sold only when the related products are sold.

For practical reasons, though, some of these expenditures often are not included in inventory cost and are treated as **period costs.** They often are immaterial or it is impractical to associate the expenditures with particular units of inventory (for example, unloading and unpacking costs). Period costs are not associated with products and are expensed in the *period* incurred.

Freight-In on Purchases.   Freight-in on purchases is commonly included in the cost of inventory. These costs clearly are necessary to get the inventory in location for sale or use and can generally be associated with particular goods. Freight costs are added to the inventory account in a perpetual system. In a periodic system, freight costs generally are added to a temporary account called **freight-in** or **transportation-in,** which is added to purchases in determining net purchases. The account is closed to cost of goods sold along with purchases and other components of cost of goods sold at the end of the reporting period. (See Illustration 8–4 on page 373.) From an accounting system perspective, freight-in also could be added to the purchases account. From a control perspective, by recording freight-in as a separate item, management can more easily track its freight costs. The same perspectives pertain to purchases returns and purchase discounts, which are discussed below.

<div class="margin-notes">

Inventory shipped *f.o.b. destination* is included in the purchaser's inventory only after it reaches the purchaser's destination.

Goods held on *consignment* are included in the inventory of the consignor until sold by the consignee.

Expenditures necessary to bring inventory to its condition and location for sale or use are included in its cost.

The cost of *freight-in* paid by the purchaser generally is part of the cost of inventory.

</div>

---

[3]Shipping charges on outgoing goods are related to the selling activity and are reported as a selling expense when incurred, not as part of inventory cost.

Purchase Returns.   In Chapter 7 we discussed merchandise returns from the perspective of the selling company. We now address returns from the buyer's point of view. You may recall that the seller views a return as a reduction of net sales. Likewise, a buyer views a return as a reduction of net purchases. When the buyer returns goods to the seller, a **purchase return** is recorded. In a perpetual inventory system, this means a reduction in both inventory and accounts payable (if the account has not yet been paid) at the time of the return. In a periodic system an account called *purchase returns* temporarily accumulates these amounts. Purchase returns are subtracted from purchases when determining net purchases. The account is closed to cost of goods sold at the end of the reporting period.

A purchase return represents a reduction of net purchases.

Purchase Discounts.   Cash discounts also were discussed from the seller's perspective in Chapter 7. These discounts really are quick-payment discounts because they represent reductions in the amount to be paid by the buyer in the event payment is made within a specified period of time. The amount of the discount and the time period within which it's available are conveyed by cryptic terms like 2/10, n/30 (meaning a 2% discount if paid within 10 days, otherwise full payment within 30 days). As with the seller, the purchaser can record these **purchase discounts** using either the **gross method** or the **net method.** Consider Illustration 8–3 which is similar to the cash discount illustration in Chapter 7.

Purchase discounts represent reductions in the amount to be paid if remittance is made within a designated period of time.

ILLUSTRATION 8–3 Purchase Discounts	On October 5, 2003, the Lothridge Wholesale Beverage Company purchased merchandise at a price of $20,000. The repayment terms are stated as 2/10, n/30. Lothridge paid $13,720 ($14,000 less the 2% cash discount) on October 14 and the remaining balance of $6,000 on November 4. Lothridge employs a periodic inventory system.

The gross and net methods of recording the purchase and cash payment are compared as follows:

	Gross Method			**Net Method**		
October 5, 2003						
Purchases*.............	20,000		Purchases*.............	19,600		
Accounts payable.....		20,000	Accounts payable......		19,600	
October 14, 2003						
Accounts payable.......	14,000		Accounts payable	13,720		
Purchase discounts* ...		280	Cash		13,720	
Cash		13,720				
November 4, 2003						
Accounts payable.......	6,000		Accounts payable	5,880		
Cash		6,000	Interest expense	120		
			Cash		6,000	

By either method, net purchases is reduced by discounts taken.

Discounts not taken are included as purchases using the gross method and as interest expense using the net method.

*The inventory account is used in a perpetual system.

Conceptually, the gross method views a discount not taken as part of the cost of inventory. The net method considers the cost of inventory to include the net, after-discount amount, and any discounts not taken are reported as *interest expense.*[4] The discount is viewed as compensation to the seller for providing financing to the buyer.

The gross method views discounts not taken as part of inventory cost.

Purchase discounts recorded under the gross method are subtracted from purchases when determining net purchases. The account is a temporary account that is closed to cost of goods sold at the end of the reporting period. Under the perpetual inventory system, purchase discounts are treated as a reduction in the inventory account.

The net method considers discounts not taken as interest expense.

The effect on the financial statements of the difference between the two methods usually is immaterial. Net income over time will be the same using either method. There will,

---

[4]An alternative treatment is to debit an expense account called *purchase discounts lost* rather than interest expense. This enables a company to more easily identify the forgone discounts.

however, be a difference in gross profit between the two methods equal to the amount of discounts not taken. In the preceding illustration, $120 in discounts not taken is included as interest expense using the net method and cost of goods sold using the gross method.

Illustration 8–4 compares the perpetual and periodic inventory systems, using the net method.

The Lothridge Wholesale Beverage Company purchases soft drinks from producers and then sells them to retailers. The company began 2003 with merchandise inventory of $120,000 on hand. During 2003 additional merchandise is purchased on account at a cost of $600,000. Lothridge's suppliers offer credit terms of 2/10, n/30. All discounts were taken. Lothridge uses the net method to record purchase discounts. All purchases are made f.o.b. shipping point. Freight charges paid by Lothridge totaled $16,000. Merchandise costing $20,000 (net of discounts) was returned to suppliers for credit. Sales for the year, all on account, totaled $830,000. The cost of the soft drinks sold is $550,000. $154,000 of inventory remained on hand at the end of 2003.

The above transactions are recorded in summary form according to both the perpetual and periodic inventory systems as follows:

ILLUSTRATION 8–4

Inventory Transactions— Perpetual and Periodic Systems

($ in 000s)

Perpetual System			Periodic System		
Purchases					
Inventory ($600 × 98%) ..	588		Purchases ($600 × 98%)...	588	
Accounts payable		588	Accounts payable		588
Freight					
Inventory	16		Freight-in	16	
Cash		16	Cash................		16
Returns					
Accounts payable	20		Accounts payable	20	
Inventory		20	Purchase returns		20
Sales					
Accounts receivable	830		Accounts receivable	830	
Sales revenue		830	Sales revenue		830
Cost of goods sold	550		No entry		
Inventory		550			
			End of period		
No Entry			Cost of goods sold (below)	550	
			Inventory (ending)	154	
			Purchase returns.........	20	
			Inventory (beginning) ...		120
			Purchases		588
			Freight-in.............		16

Supporting Schedule:

Cost of goods sold:		
Beginning inventory		$120
Purchases	$588	
Less: Returns..........	(20)	
Plus: Freight-in	16	
Net purchases...........		584
Cost of goods available ...		704
Less: Ending inventory ..		(154)
Cost of goods sold.......		$550

Inventory Cost Flow Assumptions

Regardless of whether the perpetual or periodic system is used, it's necessary to assign dollar amounts to the physical quantities of goods sold and goods remaining in ending inventory. Unless each item of inventory is specifically identified and traced through the system, assigning dollars is accomplished by making an assumption regarding how goods (and their associated costs) flow through the system. We examine the common cost flow assumptions next. In previous illustrations, dollar amounts of the cost of goods sold and the cost of ending inventory were assumed known. However, if various portions of inventory are acquired at different costs, we need a way to decide which units were sold and which remain in inventory. Illustration 8–5 will help explain.

ILLUSTRATION 8–5	The Browning Company began 2003 with $22,000 of inventory. The cost of beginning inventory (BI) is composed of 4,000 units purchased for $5.50 each. Merchandise transactions during 2003 were as follows:
Cost Flow	

Purchases

	Date of Purchase	Units	Unit Cost*	Total Cost
Goods available for sale include beginning inventory plus purchases.	Jan.17	1,000	$6.00	$ 6,000
	Mar. 22	3,000	7.00	21,000
	Oct. 15	3,000	7.50	22,500
	Totals	7,000		$49,500

Sales

Date of Sale	Units
Jan. 10	2,000
Apr. 15	1,500
Nov. 20	3,000
Total	6,500

*includes purchase price and cost of freight.

As the data show, 7,000 units were purchased during 2003 at various prices and 6,500 units were sold. What is the cost of the 6,500 units sold? If all units, including beginning inventory, were purchased at the same price, then the answer would be simple. However, that rarely is the case.

The year started with 4,000 units, 7,000 units were purchased, and 6,500 units were sold. This means 4,500 units remain in ending inventory. This allocation of units available for sale is depicted in Graphic 8–3.

If a periodic system is used, what is the cost of the 4,500 units in ending inventory? In other words, which of the 11,000 (4,000 + 7,000) units available for sale were sold? Are they the more expensive ones bought toward the end of the year, or the less costly ones acquired before prices increased? Using the numbers given, let's consider the question as follows:

Beginning inventory (4,000 units @ $5.50)	$22,000
Plus: Purchases (7,000 units @ various prices)	49,500
Cost of goods available for sale (11,000 units)	$71,500
Less: Ending inventory (4,500 units @ ?)	?
Cost of goods sold (6,500 units @ ?)	?

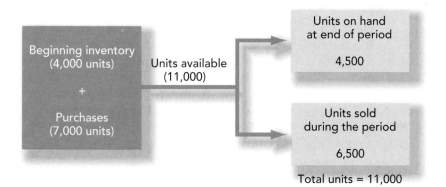

The $71,500 in cost of goods available for sale must be allocated to ending inventory and cost of goods sold. The allocation decision is depicted in Graphic 8–4.

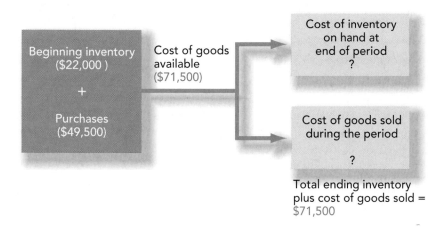

Let's turn our attention now to the various inventory methods that can be used to achieve this allocation.

SPECIFIC IDENTIFICATION

It's sometimes possible for each unit sold during the period or each unit on hand at the end of the period to be matched with its actual cost. Actual costs can be determined by reference to the invoice representing the purchase of the item. This method is used frequently by companies selling unique, expensive products with low sales volume which makes it relatively easy and economically feasible to associate each item with its actual cost. For example, automobiles have unique serial numbers that can be used to match a specific auto with the invoice identifying the actual purchase price.

The **specific identification method,** however, is not feasible for many types of products either because items are not uniquely identifiable or because it is too costly to match a specific purchase price with each item sold or each item remaining in ending inventory. Most companies use cost flow methods to determine cost of goods sold and ending inventory. Cost flow methods are based on assumptions about how inventory might flow in and out of a company. However, it's important to note that the actual flow of a company's inventory does not have to correspond to the cost flow assumed. The various motivating factors that influence management's choice among alternative methods are discussed later in this chapter. We now explore the three most common cost flow methods: average cost, first-in, first-out (FIFO) and last-in, first-out (LIFO).

AVERAGE COST

The *average cost method* assumes that items sold and items in ending inventory come from a mixture of all the goods available for sale.

The **average cost method** assumes that cost of goods sold and ending inventory consist of a mixture of all the goods available for sale. The average unit cost applied to goods sold or to ending inventory is not simply an average of the various unit costs of purchases during the period but an average unit cost *weighted* by the number of units acquired at the various unit costs.

Periodic Average Cost.   In a periodic inventory system, this weighted average is calculated at the end of the period as follows:

$$\text{Weighted-average unit cost} = \frac{\text{Cost of goods available for sale}}{\text{Quantity available for sale}}$$

The calculation of average cost is demonstrated in Illustration 8–5A using data from Illustration 8–5.

ILLUSTRATION 8–5A		
Average Cost— Periodic Inventory System	Beginning inventory (4,000 units @ $5.50)	$22,000
	Plus: Purchases (7,000 units @ various prices)	49,500
	Cost of goods available for sale (11,000 units)	71,500
	Less: Ending inventory (determined below)	(29,250)
	Cost of goods sold (6,500 units)	$42,250
	Cost of Ending Inventory:	
	Weighted-average unit cost $= \dfrac{\$71,500}{11,000 \text{ units}} = \$6.50$	
	4,500 units $\times$ $6.50 = $29,250	

Cost of goods sold also could be determined directly by multiplying the weighted-average unit cost of $6.50 by the number of units sold ($6.50 $\times$ 6,500 = $42,250).

In a perpetual inventory system, the average cost method is applied by computing a moving-average unit cost each time additional inventory is purchased.

Perpetual Average Cost.   The weighted-average unit cost in a perpetual inventory system becomes a moving-average unit cost. A new weighted-average unit cost is calculated each time additional units are *purchased*. The new average is determined after each purchase by (1) summing the cost of the previous inventory balance and the cost of the new purchase, and (2) dividing this new total cost (cost of goods available for sale) by the number of units on hand (the inventory units that are available for sale). This average is then used to cost any units sold before the next purchase is made. The moving-average concept is applied in Illustration 8–5B.

On January 17 the new average of $5.667 (rounded) is calculated by dividing the $17,000 cost of goods available ($11,000 from beginning inventory + $6,000 purchased on January 17) by the 3,000 units available (2,000 units from beginning inventory + 1,000 units acquired on January 17). The average is updated to $6.333 (rounded) with the March 22 purchase. The 1,500 units sold on April 15 are then costed at the average cost of $6.333.

Periodic average cost and perpetual average cost generally produce different allocations to cost of goods sold and ending inventory.

FIRST-IN, FIRST-OUT (FIFO)

The *first-in, first-out (FIFO) method* assumes that items sold are those that were acquired first.

The **first-in, first-out (FIFO) method** assumes that units sold are the first units acquired. Beginning inventory is sold first, followed by purchases during the period in the chronological order of their acquisition. In our illustration, 6,500 units were sold during 2003. Applying FIFO, these would be the 4,000 units in beginning inventory, the 1,000 units purchased on January 17, and 1,500 of the 3,000 units from the March 22 purchase. By default,

Date	Purchased	Sold	Balance
ILLUSTRATION 8–5B Average Cost—Perpetual Inventory System			

Date	Purchased	Sold	Balance
Beginning inventory	4,000 @ $5.50 = $22,000		4,000 @ $5.50 = $22,000
Jan. 10		2,000 @ $5.50 = $11,000	2,000 @ $5.50 = $11,000
Jan. 17	1,000 @ $6.00 = $6,000		$11,000 + $6,000 = $17,000
			2,000 + 1,000 = 3,000 units
	$\left[\dfrac{\$17,000}{3,000 \text{ units}} = \$5.667/\text{unit}\right]$		
Mar. 22	3,000 @ $7.00 = $21,000		$17,000 + $21,000 = $38,000
	$\left[\dfrac{\$38,000}{6,000 \text{ units}} = \$6.333/\text{unit}\right]$		3,000 + 3,000 = 6,000 units
Apr. 15		1,500 @ $6.333 = $ 9,500	4,500 @ $6.333 = $28,500
Oct. 15	3,000 @ $7.50 = $22,500		$28,500 + $22,500 = $51,000
	$\left[\dfrac{\$51,000}{7,500 \text{ units}} = \$6.80/\text{unit}\right]$		4,500 + 3,000 = 7,500 units
Nov. 20		3,000 @ $6.80 = $20,400	4,500 @ $6.80 = **$30,600**
	Total cost of goods sold	= **$40,900**	

ending inventory consists of the most recently acquired units. In this case, the 4,500 units in ending inventory consist of the 3,000 units purchased on October 15, and 1,500 of the 3,000 units purchased on March 22. Graphically, the flow is as follows:

Ending inventory applying FIFO consists of the most recently acquired items.

Units Available		
BI	4,000	
Jan. 17	1,000	6,500 units sold
Mar. 22	1,500	
Mar. 22	1,500	
		4,500 units in ending inventory
Oct. 15	3,000	
Total	11,000	

FIFO flow

Periodic FIFO.   Recall that we determine physical quantities on hand in a periodic inventory system by taking a physical count. Costing the 4,500 units in ending inventory this way automatically gives us the cost of goods sold as well. Using the numbers from our illustration, we determine cost of goods sold to be $38,500 by subtracting the $33,000 ending inventory from $71,500 cost of goods available for sale as shown in Illustration 8–5C.

Of course, the 6,500 units sold could be costed directly as follows:

Date of Purchase	Units	Unit Cost	Total Cost
Beg. inv.	4,000	$5.50	$22,000
Jan. 17	1,000	6.00	6,000
Mar. 22	1,500	7.00	10,500
Total	6,500		$38,500

ILLUSTRATION 8–5C	Beginning inventory (4,000 units @ $5.50)			$22,000
FIFO—Periodic Inventory System	Plus: Purchases (7,000 units @ various prices)			49,500
	Cost of goods available for sale (11,000 units)			71,500
	Less: Ending inventory (determined below)			(33,000)
	Cost of goods sold (6,500 units)			$38,500

Cost of Ending Inventory:

Date of Purchase	Units	Unit Cost	Total Cost
Mar. 22	1,500	$7.00	$10,500
Oct. 15	3,000	7.50	22,500
Total	4,500		$33,000

Perpetual FIFO.   The same ending inventory and cost of goods sold amounts are always produced in a perpetual inventory system as in a periodic inventory system when FIFO is used. This is because the same units and costs are first in and first out whether cost of goods sold is determined as each sale is made or at the end of the period as a residual amount. The application of FIFO in a perpetual system is shown in Illustration 8–5D.

ILLUSTRATION 8–5D	Date	Purchased	Sold	Balance
FIFO—Perpetual Inventory System	Beginning inventory	4,000 @ $5.50 = $22,000		4,000 @ $5.50 = $22,000
	Jan. 10		2,000 @ $5.50 = $11,000	2,000 @ $5.50 = $11,000
	Jan. 17	1,000 @ $6.00 = $ 6,000		$2,000 @ $5.50 ⎫ $17,000 1,000 @ $6.00 ⎭
	Mar. 22	3,000 @ $7.00 = $21,000		2,000 @ $5.50 ⎫ 1,000 @ $6.00 ⎬ $38,000 3,000 @ $7.00 ⎭
	Apr. 15		1,500 @ $5.50 = $ 8,250	500 @ $5.50 ⎫ 1,000 @ $6.00 ⎬ $29,750 3,000 @ $7.00 ⎭
	Oct. 15	3,000 @ $7.50 = $22,500		500 @ $5.50 ⎫ 1,000 @ $6.00 ⎪ $52,250 3,000 @ $7.00 ⎬ 3,000 @ $7.50 ⎭
	Nov. 20		500 @ $5.50 + 1,000 @ $6.00 + 1,500 @ $7.00 = $19,250	1,500 @ $7.00 ⎫ $33,000 3,000 @ $7.50 ⎭
		Total cost of goods sold	= $38,500	

LAST-IN, FIRST-OUT (LIFO)

The last-in, first-out (LIFO) method assumes that items sold are those that were most recently acquired.

The **last-in, first-out (LIFO) method** assumes that the units sold are the most recent units purchased. In our illustration, the 6,500 units assumed sold would be the 6,500 units acquired most recently: the 3,000 units acquired on October 15, the 3,000 units acquired on March 22, and 500 of the 1,000 units purchased on January 17. Ending inventory, then, consists of the units acquired first; in this case, the 4,000 units from beginning inventory and 500 of the 1,000 units purchased on January 17. Graphically, the flow is as follows:

Units Available

BI	4,000
Jan. 17	500
Jan. 17	500
Mar. 22	3,000
Oct. 15	3,000
Total	11,000

4,500 units in ending inventory

6,500 units sold

Ending inventory applying LIFO consists of the items acquired first.

LIFO flow

Periodic LIFO.   The cost of ending inventory determined to be $25,000 (calculated below) by the LIFO assumption and using a periodic system is subtracted from cost of goods available for sale to arrive at the cost of goods sold of $46,500 as shown in Illustration 8–5E.

Beginning inventory (4,000 units @ $5.50)			$22,000
Plus: Purchases (7,000 units @ various prices)			49,500
Cost of goods available for sale (11,000 units)			71,500
Less: Ending inventory (determined below)			(25,000)
Cost of goods sold (6,500 units)			$46,500
Cost of Ending Inventory:			
Date of Purchase	**Units**	**Unit Cost**	**Total Cost**
Beginning inventory	4,000	$5.50	$22,000
Jan. 17	500	6.00	3,000
Total	4,500		$25,000

ILLUSTRATION 8–5E

LIFO—Periodic Inventory System

The 6,500 sold could be costed directly as follows:

Date of Purchase	**Units**	**Unit Cost**	**Total Cost**
Jan. 17	500	$6.00	$ 3,000
Mar. 22	3,000	7.00	21,000
Oct. 15	3,000	7.50	22,500
Total	6,500		$46,500

Perpetual LIFO.   The application of LIFO in a perpetual system is shown in Illustration 8–5F. Each time inventory is purchased or sold, the LIFO layers are adjusted. For example, after the March 22 purchase, we have three layers of inventory at different unit costs listed in the chronological order of their purchase. When 1,500 units are sold on April 15, we assume they come from the most recent layer of 3,000 units purchased at $7.00.

Notice that $44,000 of the cost of goods available for sale is allocated to cost of goods sold by LIFO and $27,500 to ending inventory (the balance after the last transaction), which is different from the periodic LIFO result of $46,500 and $25,000. Unlike FIFO, applying LIFO in a perpetual inventory system will generally result in an ending inventory and cost of goods sold different from the allocation arrived at applying LIFO in a periodic system. Periodic LIFO applies the last-in, first-out concept to total sales and total purchases only at the conclusion of the reporting period. Perpetual LIFO applies the same concept, but several times during the period—every time a sale is made.

For example, when 2,000 units are sold on January 10, perpetual LIFO costs those units at $5.50, the beginning inventory unit cost. Periodic LIFO, by contrast, would be applied at year-end. By the end of the year, enough purchases have been made that the beginning

Perpetual LIFO generally results in cost of goods sold and inventory amounts that are different from those obtained by applying periodic LIFO.

ILLUSTRATION 8–5F	Date	Purchased	Sold	Balance
LIFO—Perpetual Inventory System	Beginning inventory	4,000 @ $5.50 = $22,000		4,000 @ $5.50 = $22,000
	Jan. 10		2,000 @ $5.50 = $11,000	2,000 @ $5.50 = $11,000
	Jan. 17	1,000 @ $6.00 = $6,000		2,000 @ $5.50 1,000 @ $6.00 } $17,000
	Mar. 22	3,000 @ $7.00 = $21,000		2,000 @ $5.50 1,000 @ $6.00 3,000 @ $7.00 } $38,000
	Apr. 15		1,500 @ $7.00 = $10,500	2,000 @ $5.50 1,000 @ $6.00 1,500 @ $7.00 } $27,500
	Oct. 15	3,000 @ $7.50 = $22,500		2,000 @ $5.50 1,000 @ $6.00 1,500 @ $7.00 3,000 @ $7.50 } $50,000
	Nov. 20		3,000 @ $7.50 = $22,500	2,000 @ $5.50 1,000 @ $6.00 1,500 @ $7.00 } $27,500
		Total cost of goods sold	= $44,000	

inventory would be assumed to remain intact, and the January 10 units sold would be costed at a more recent price.

CHECK WITH THE **COACH**

This is the first of two chapters concerning the interplay between measuring inventory and the cost of goods sold. Check with the Coach to help you focus on the key points involving inventory measurement and to build your confidence in tackling the more challenging elements of inventory accounting. The Coach will help you understand dollar-value LIFO, a method that puzzles many intermediate accounting students. You also hear from managers and analysts about the ratios they use to assess a company's operating efficiency. ■

COMPARISON OF COST FLOW METHODS

The three cost flow methods are compared below assuming a periodic inventory system.

Comparison of cost flow methods

	Average	FIFO	LIFO
Cost of goods sold	$42,250	$38,500	$46,500
Ending inventory	29,250	33,000	25,000
Total	$71,500	$71,500	$71,500

Notice that the average cost method in this example produces amounts that fall in between the FIFO and LIFO amounts for both cost of goods sold and ending inventory. This will usually be the case. Whether it will be FIFO or LIFO that produces the highest or lowest value of cost of goods sold and ending inventory depends on the pattern of the actual unit cost changes during the period.

If unit costs are increasing, LIFO will result in a higher cost of goods sold and lower ending inventory than FIFO.

During periods of generally rising costs, as in our example, FIFO results in a lower cost of goods sold than LIFO because the lower costs of the earliest purchases are assumed sold. LIFO cost of goods sold will include the more recent higher cost purchases. On the other hand, FIFO ending inventory includes the most recent higher cost purchases which results in a higher ending inventory than LIFO. LIFO ending inventory includes the lower costs of the earliest purchases. Conversely, if costs are declining, then FIFO will result in a higher cost of goods sold and lower ending inventory than LIFO.[5]

Each of the three methods is permissible according to generally accepted accounting principles and frequently is used. Also, a company need not use the same method for all of its inventory. For example, International Paper Company uses LIFO for its raw materials and finished pulp and paper products, and both the FIFO and average cost methods for other inventories. Because of the importance of inventories and the possible differential effects of different methods on the financial statements, a company must identify in a disclosure note the method(s) it uses. The chapter's opening case included an example of this disclosure for Ford Motor Company, and you will encounter additional examples later in the chapter.

Graphic 8–5 shows the results of a survey of inventory methods used by 600 large public companies in 2000 and 1973.[6] FIFO is the most popular method in both periods, but there has been a dramatic increase in the use of LIFO since the earlier period. Notice that the column total for the number of companies is greater than 600, indicating that many companies included in this sample do use multiple methods.

FINANCIAL REPORTING CASE

Q1, p. 365

A company must disclosure the inventory method(s) it uses.

	2000		1973	
	# of Companies	**% of Companies**	**# of Companies**	**% of Companies**
FIFO	386	44%	394	43%
LIFO	283	32	150	16
Average	180	20	235	25
Other*	38	4	148	16
Total	887	100%	927	100%

GRAPHIC 8–5
Inventory Cost Flow Methods Used in Practice

*"Other" includes the specific identification method and miscellaneous less popular methods.

DECISION MAKERS' PERSPECTIVE—Factors Influencing Method Choice

What factors motivate companies to choose one method over another? What factors have caused the increased popularity of LIFO? Choosing among alternative accounting methods is a complex issue. Often such choices are not made in isolation but in such a way that the combination of inventory cost flow assumptions, depreciation methods, pension assumptions, and other choices meet a particular objective. Also, many believe managers sometimes

LO5

---

[5]The differences between the various methods also hold when a perpetual inventory system is used.
[6]*Accounting Trends and Techniques—2001* and *1974* (New York, New York: AICPA, 2001 and 1974)

make these choices to maximize their own personal benefits rather than those of the company or its external constituents. But regardless of the motive, the impact on reported numbers is an important consideration in each choice of method. The inventory choice determines (a) how closely reported costs reflect the actual physical flow of inventory, (b) the timing of reported income and income tax expense, and (c) how well costs are matched with associated revenues.

Physical Flow.   If a company wanted to choose a method that most closely approximates specific identification, then the actual physical flow of inventory in and out of the company would motivate the choice of method.

For example, companies often attempt to sell the oldest goods in inventory first for some of their products. This certainly is the case with perishable goods such as many grocery items. The FIFO method best mirrors the physical flow in these situations. The average cost method might be used for liquids such as chemicals where items sold are taken from a mixture of inventory acquired at different times and different prices. There are very few inventories that actually flow in a LIFO manner. It is important for you to understand that there is no requirement that companies choose an inventory method that approximates actual physical flow and few companies make the choice on this basis. In fact, as we discuss next, the effect of inventory method on income and income taxes is the primary motivation that influences method choice.

> A company is not required to choose an inventory method that approximates actual physical flow.

Income Taxes and Net Income.   If the unit cost of inventory changes during a period, the inventory method chosen can have a significant effect on the amount of income reported by the company to external parties and also on the amount of income taxes paid to the Internal Revenue Service (IRS) and state and local taxing authorities. Over the entire life of a company, cost of goods sold for all years will equal actual costs of items sold regardless of the inventory method used. However, as we have discussed, different inventory methods can produce significantly different results in each particular year.

When prices rise and inventory quantities are not decreasing, LIFO produces a higher cost of goods sold and therefore lower net income than the other methods. The company's income tax returns will report a lower taxable income using LIFO and lower taxes will be paid currently. Taxes are not reduced permanently, only deferred. The reduced amount will be paid to the taxing authorities when either the unit cost of inventory or the quantity of inventory subsequently declines. However, we know from our discussion of the time value of money that it is advantageous to save a dollar today even if it must be paid back in the future. Recall from the recent survey results exhibited earlier that the popularity of LIFO increased significantly between 1973 and 2000. The main reason for this increased popularity is attributable to high inflation (increasing prices) during the 1970s which motivated many companies to switch to LIFO in order to gain this tax benefit.

> Many companies choose LIFO in order to reduce income taxes in periods when prices are rising.

A corporation's taxable income comprises revenues, expenses (including cost of goods sold), gains, and losses measured according to the regulations of the appropriate taxing authority. Income before tax as reported in the income statement does not always equal taxable income. In some cases, differences are caused by the use of different measurement methods.[7]

GLOBAL PERSPECTIVE

In the United States, if a company uses LIFO for tax purposes, the same method must be used for financial reporting, but differences might exist for other accounting choices. Other countries require much closer conformity of accounting practice and tax laws. In fact, in Germany all financial accounting must be consistent with tax laws.

---

[7]For example, a corporation can take advantage of incentives offered by Congress by deducting more depreciation in the early years of an asset's life in its federal income tax return than it reports in its income statement.

However, IRS regulations, which determine federal taxable income, require that if a company uses LIFO to measure taxable income, the company also must use LIFO for external financial reporting. This is known as the **LIFO conformity rule** with respect to inventory methods.

Because of the LIFO conformity rule, to obtain the tax advantages of using LIFO in periods of rising prices, lower net income is reported to shareholders, creditors, and other external parties. The income tax motivation for using LIFO may be offset by a desire to report higher net income. Reported net income could have an effect on a corporation's share price,[8] on bonuses paid to management, or on debt agreements with lenders. For example, research has indicated that the managers of companies with bonus plans tied to income measures are more likely to choose accounting methods that maximize their bonuses (often those that increase net income).[9]

In 1981, the LIFO conformity rule was liberalized to permit LIFO users to present designated supplemental disclosures, allowing a company to report in a note the effect of using another method on inventory valuation rather than LIFO. For example, Graphic 8–6 shows the note disclosure provided by the Sara Lee Corporation included in the summary of significant accounting policies in its 2001 financial statements.[10]

> **Inventory Valuation**
> ($ in millions)
>
> Inventories are stated at the lower of cost or market. Cost is determined by the first-in, first-out (FIFO) method for 94% of the corporation's inventories at June 30, 2001, and by the last-in, first-out (LIFO) method for the remainder. Had the FIFO method been used for the valuation of all inventories, the book value of this asset would have been higher by $7 at June 30, 2001, $12 at July 1, 2000, and $1 at July 3, 1999.

LIFO Liquidations.   Earlier in the text, we demonstrated the importance of matching revenues and expenses in creating an income statement that is useful in predicting future cash flows. If prices change during a period, then LIFO generally will provide a better match of revenues and expenses. Sales reflect the most recent selling prices, and cost of goods sold includes the costs of the most recent purchases. Graphic 8–7 shows the General Mills, Inc. disclosure that was included in its summary of significant accounting policies.

> **(C) Inventories (in part)**
> Inventories are valued at the lower of cost or market. We generally use LIFO as the preferred method of valuing inventory because we believe that it is a better match with current revenues.

If a company uses LIFO to measure its taxable income, IRS regulations require that LIFO also be used to measure income reported to investors and creditors (the *LIFO conformity rule*).

FINANCIAL REPORTING CASE
Q2, p. 365

GRAPHIC 8–6
Inventories Disclosure—Sara Lee Corporation

Proponents of LIFO argue that it results in a better match of revenues and expenses.

GRAPHIC 8–7
Inventory Policy Disclosure—General Mills, Inc.

---

[8]The concept of capital market efficiency has been debated for many years. In an efficient capital market, the market is not fooled by differences in accounting method choice that do not translate into real cash flow differences. The only apparent cash flow difference caused by different inventory methods is the amount of income taxes paid currently. In an efficient market, we would expect the share price of a company that switched its method to LIFO and saved tax dollars to increase even though it reported lower net income than if LIFO had not been adopted. Research on this issue is mixed. For example, see William E. Ricks, "Market's Response to the 1974 LIFO Adoptions," *Journal of Accounting Research* (Autumn 1982), and Robert Moren Brown, "Short-Range Market Reaction to Changes to LIFO Using Preliminary Earnings Announcement Dates," *Journal of Accounting Research* (Spring 1980).

[9]For example, see P. M. Healy, "The Effect of Bonus Schemes on Accounting Decisions," *Journal of Accounting and Economics* (April 1985), and D. Dhaliwal, G. Salamon, and E. Smith, "The Effect of Owner Versus Management Control on the Choice of Accounting Methods," *Journal of Accounting and Economics* (July 1982).

[10]Sara Lee uses both the LIFO and FIFO inventory methods. Earlier in the chapter we pointed out that a company need not use the same inventory method for all of its inventory.

For the same reason, though, inventory costs in the balance sheet with LIFO generally are out of date because they reflect old purchase transactions. It is not uncommon for a company's LIFO inventory balance to be based on unit costs actually incurred several years earlier.

This distortion sometimes carries over to the income statement as well. When inventory quantities decline during a period, then these out-of-date inventory layers are liquidated and the cost of goods sold will partially match noncurrent costs with current selling prices. If costs have been increasing (decreasing), LIFO liquidations produce higher (lower) net income than would have resulted if the liquidated inventory were included in cost of goods sold at current costs. The paper profits (losses) caused by including out of date, low (high) costs in cost of goods sold is referred to as the effect on income of liquidations of LIFO inventory.

To illustrate this problem, consider the example in Illustration 8–6.

A LIFO liquidation occurs when inventory quantity declines during the period.

ILLUSTRATION 8–6

LIFO Liquidation

National Distributors, Inc., uses the LIFO inventory method. The company began 2003 with inventory of 10,000 units that cost $20 per unit. During 2003, 30,000 units were purchased for $25 each and 35,000 units were sold.

National's LIFO cost of goods sold for 2003 consists of:

30,000 units @ $25 per unit =	$750,000
5,000 units @ $20 per unit =	$100,000
35,000	$850,000

Included in cost of goods sold are 5,000 units from beginning inventory that have now been liquidated. If the company had purchased at least 35,000 units, no liquidation would have occurred. Then cost of goods sold would have been $875,000 (35,000 units × $25 per unit) instead of $850,000. The difference between these two cost of goods sold figures is $25,000 ($875,000 − 850,000). This is the before tax income effect of the LIFO liquidation. Assuming a 40% income tax rate, the net effect of the liquidation is to increase net income by $15,000 [$25,000 × (1 − .40)]. The lower the costs of the units liquidated, the more severe the effect on income.

A company must disclose in a note any material effect of **LIFO liquidation** on income. For example, Graphic 8–8 shows the disclosure that accompanies recent financial statements of Ethyl Corporation, a manufacturer of fuels and lubricants.

A material effect on net income of LIFO layer liquidation must be disclosed in a note.

GRAPHIC 8–8

LIFO Liquidation Disclosure—Ethyl Corporation

6. Inventories (in part)
During 2000 and 1999, TEL inventory quantities were reduced resulting in a liquidation of LIFO layers. The effect of these liquidations increased net income by $1 million in 2000 and $500 thousand in 1999.

In our illustration, National Distributors, Inc. would disclose that LIFO liquidations increased income by $15,000 in 2003, assuming that this effect on income is considered material.

We've discussed several factors that influence companies in their choice of inventory method. A company could be influenced by the actual physical flow of its inventory, by the effect of inventory method on reported net income and the amount of income taxes payable currently, or by a desire to provide a better match of expenses with revenues. You've seen that the direction of the change in unit costs determines the effect of using different methods on net income and income taxes. While the United States has experienced persistent inflation for many years (increases in the general price-level), the prices of many goods and services have experienced periods of declining prices (for example, personal computers). ■

ADDITIONAL CONSIDERATION

LIFO Reserves

Many companies use LIFO for external reporting and income tax purposes but maintain their internal records using FIFO or average cost. The reasons for doing this might include: (1) the high recordkeeping costs of the LIFO method, (2) the existence of contractual agreements such as bonus or profit sharing plans that prohibit the use of LIFO in the calculation of net income, and (3) the need for FIFO or average cost information for pricing decisions.

Generally, the conversion to LIFO is performed at the end of the period and not entered into the company's records. However, some companies enter the results of the conversion—the difference between the internal method and LIFO—directly into the accounts as a contra account to inventory. This contra account is called either the LIFO reserve or the LIFO allowance.

Occasionally, such companies report ending inventory valued using the internal method less the LIFO reserve or allowance to arrive at LIFO inventory reported in the balance sheet. For example, General Motors recently reported the following in a note:

Inventories ($ in millions)	2001	2000
Total inventories at FIFO	$11,848	$12,801
Less LIFO allowance	1,814	1,856
Total inventories, at LIFO cost	$10,034	$10,945

Note that this is merely another way of presenting the supplemental non-LIFO disclosures discussed previously.

CONCEPT REVIEW EXERCISE

Inventory Cost Flow Methods

The Rogers Company began 2003 with an inventory of 10 million units of its principal product. These units cost $5 each. The following inventory transactions occurred during the first six months of 2003.

Date	Transaction
Feb. 15	Purchased, on account, 5 million units at a cost of $6.50 each.
Mar. 20	Sold, on account, 8 million units at a selling price of $12 each.
Apr. 30	Purchased, on account, 5 million units at a cost of $7 each.

On June 30, 2003, 12 million units were on hand.

Required:
1. Prepare journal entries to record the above transactions. The company uses a periodic inventory system.
2. Prepare the required adjusting entry on June 30, 2003, applying each of the following inventory methods:
   a. Average
   b. FIFO
   c. LIFO
3. Repeat requirement 1 assuming that the company uses a perpetual inventory system.

SOLUTION

1. Prepare journal entries to record the above transactions. The company uses a periodic inventory system.

February 15	($ in millions)	
Purchases (5 million × $6.50)	32.5	
Accounts payable		32.5
To record the purchase of inventory.		
March 20		
Accounts receivable (8 million × $12)	96	
Sales revenue..		96
To record sales on account.		
No entry is recorded for the cost of inventory sold.		
April 30		
Purchases (5 million × $7)	35	
Accounts payable		35
To record the purchase of inventory.		

2. Prepare the required adjusting entry on June 30, 2003, applying each method.

		($ in millions)				
Date	**Journal entry**	**Average**		**FIFO**		**LIFO**
June 30	Cost of goods sold (determined below)	47.0		40.0		54.5
	Inventory (ending—determined below)	70.5		77.5		63.0
	Inventory (beginning − [10 million @ $5])		50.0		50.0	50.0
	Purchases ($32.5 million + 35 million)		67.5		67.5	67.5

Calculation of Ending Inventory and Cost of Goods Sold:

a. Average:

	($ in millions)
Beginning inventory (10 million units @ $5.00)	$ 50.0
Plus: Purchases (10 million units @ various prices)	67.5
Cost of goods available for sale (20 million units)	117.5
Less: Ending inventory (determined below)	(70.5)
Cost of goods sold	$ 47.0

Cost of ending inventory:

$$\text{Weighted average unit cost} = \frac{\$117.5}{20 \text{ million units}} = \$5.875$$

$$12 \text{ million units} \times \$5.875 = \$70.5 \text{ million}$$

b. FIFO:

Cost of goods available for sale (20 million units)	$117.5
Less: Ending inventory (determined below)	(77.5)
Cost of goods sold	$ 40.0

Cost of ending inventory:

Date of Purchase	Units	Unit Cost	Total Cost
April 30	5 million	$7.00	$35.0
Feb. 15	5 million	6.50	32.5
Beg. inv.	2 million	5.00	10.0
Total	12 million		$77.5

c. LIFO:

Cost of goods available for sale (20 million units)	$117.5
Less: Ending inventory (determined below)	(63.0)
Cost of goods sold	$ 54.5

Cost of ending inventory:

Date of Purchase	Units	Unit Cost	Total Cost
Beg. inv.	10 million	$5.00	$50.0
Feb. 15	2 million	6.50	13.0
Total	12 million		$63.0

3. Repeat requirement 1 assuming that the company uses a perpetual inventory system.

	($ in millions)
February 15	
Inventory (5 million units × $6.50)	32.5
Accounts payable	32.5
To record the purchase of inventory.	
April 30	
Inventory (5 million units × $7.00)	35.0
Accounts payable	35.0
To record the purchase of inventory.	

	($ in millions)					
Journal Entries—March 20	**Average**		**FIFO**		**LIFO**	
Accounts receivable (8 million × $12)	96.0		96.0		96.0	
Sales revenue		96.0		96.0		96.0
To record sales on account.						
Cost of goods sold (determined below)	44.0		40.0		47.5	
Inventory (determined below)		44.0		40.0		47.5
To record cost of goods sold.						

Calculation of Cost of Goods Sold:

a. Average:
    Cost of goods sold:

		($, except unit costs, in millions)	
Date	**Purchased**	**Sold**	**Balance**
Beg. inv.	10 million @ $5.00		10 million @ $5.00 = $50.0
Feb. 15	5 million @ $6.50		$50 + 32.5 = $82.5
	$\frac{\$82.5}{15 \text{ million units}} = \$5.50/\text{unit}$		
Mar. 20		8 million @ $5.50 = $44.0	

b. FIFO:
    Cost of goods sold:

Units Sold	Cost of Units Sold	Total Cost
8 million (from BI)	$5.00	$40.0

c. LIFO:

Cost of goods sold:

Units Sold	Cost of Units Sold	Total Cost
5 million (from Feb. 15 purchase)	$6.50	$32.5
3 million (from beg. inventory)	5.00	15.0
8 million		$47.5

A company should maintain sufficient inventory quantities to meet customer demand while at the same time minimizing inventory ordering and carrying costs.

DECISION MAKERS' PERSPECTIVE

INVENTORY MANAGEMENT

Managers closely monitor inventory levels to (1) ensure that the inventories needed to sustain operations are available, and (2) hold the cost of ordering and carrying inventories to the lowest possible level.[11] Unfortunately, these objectives often conflict with one another. Companies must maintain sufficient quantities of inventory to meet customer demand. However, maintaining inventory is costly. Fortunately, a variety of tools are available, including computerized inventory control systems and the outsourcing of inventory component production, to help balance these conflicting objectives.[12]

A **just-in-time (JIT) system** is another valuable technique that many companies have adopted to assist them with inventory management. JIT is a system used by a manufacturer to coordinate production with suppliers so that raw materials or components arrive just as they are needed in the production process. Have you ever ordered a personal computer from Dell Computer Corporation? If so, the PC you received was not manufactured until you placed your order, and many of the components used in the production of your PC were not even acquired by Dell until then as well. This system enables Dell to maintain relatively low inventory balances. At the same time, the company's efficient production techniques, along with its excellent relationships with suppliers ensuring prompt delivery of components, enables Dell to quickly meet customer demand. In its February 1, 2002, fiscal year-end financial statements, Dell reported an inventory balance of $278 million. With this relatively low investment in inventory, Dell was able to generate over $31 billion in sales revenue. To appreciate the advantage this provides, compare these numbers with Hewlett Packard (HP), a company that includes PCs among its wide variety of technology products. For its fiscal year ended October 31, 2001, HP reported product revenue of $37 billion. However, to achieve this level of sales, HP's investment in inventory was over $5 billion.

It is important for a financial analyst to evaluate a company's effectiveness in managing its inventory. As we discussed in Chapter 5, one key to profitability is how well a company utilizes its assets. This evaluation is influenced by the company's inventory method choice. The choice of inventory method is an important and complex management decision. The many factors affecting this decision were discussed in a previous section. The inventory method also affects the analysis of a company's liquidity and profitability by investors, creditors, and financial analysts. Analysts must make adjustments when evaluating companies that use different inventory methods. During periods of rising prices, we would expect a company using FIFO to report higher income than a LIFO or average cost company. If one of the companies being analyzed uses LIFO, precise adjustments can often be made using the supplemental disclosures provided by many LIFO companies. Recall that the LIFO conformity rule was liberalized to permit LIFO users to report in a note the effect of using a method other than LIFO for inventory valuation.

For example, the disclosure note exhibited on page 383 reveals that Sara Lee Corporation uses both the FIFO and LIFO inventory methods with 6% of its inventories valued using LIFO. Tyson Foods, Inc., values all of its inventory using FIFO. Both of these companies

FINANCIAL REPORTING CASE

Q3, p. 365

---

[11]The cost of carrying inventory includes the possible loss from the write-down of obsolete inventory. We discuss inventory write-downs in Chapter 9. There are analytical models available to determine the appropriate amount of inventory a company should maintain. A discussion of these models is beyond the scope of this text.

[12]Eugene Brigham and Joel Houston, *Fundamentals of Financial Management,* 8th Edition, 1998, The Dryden Press, Orlando, Florida, p. 632.

derive a significant portion of their revenues from the sale of food products. Financial statement values for the two companies for 2001 are as follows:

	($ in millions)			
	Sara Lee Corporation		**Tyson Foods, Inc.**	
	2001	**2000**	**2001**	**2000**
Balance sheet:				
Inventories	$ 2,582	$2,951	$ 1,911	$965
	2001		**2001**	
Income statement:				
Net sales	$17,747		$10,751	
Cost of goods sold	10,264		9,661	

We can convert Sara Lee's inventory and cost of goods sold to a 100% FIFO basis before comparing the two companies by using the information provided in Graphic 8–6 on page 383. Inventories recorded at LIFO were lower by approximately $7 million at June 30, 2001, and $12 million at July 1, 2000, than if they had been valued at FIFO:

Supplemental LIFO disclosures can be used to convert LIFO inventory and cost of goods sold amounts.

	2001	**2000**
Inventories (as reported)	$2,582	$2,951
Add: conversion to FIFO	7	12
Inventories (100% FIFO)	$2,589	$2,963

Cost of goods sold for 2001 would have been $5 million higher had Sara Lee used FIFO instead of LIFO. While beginning inventory would have been $12 million higher, ending inventory also would have been higher by $7 million. An increase in beginning inventory causes an increase in cost of goods sold, but an increase in ending inventory causes a decrease in cost of goods sold. Purchases for 2001 are the same regardless of the inventory valuation method used. Cost of goods sold for 2001 would have been $10,269 million ($10,264 + 5) if FIFO had been used for all inventories.

We can now use the 100% FIFO amounts to compare the two companies. Since cost of goods sold is higher by $5 million, income taxes and net income require adjustment before calculating any profitability ratio. Also, the converted inventory amounts can be used to compute liquidity ratios.

One important profitability indicator using cost of goods sold is **gross profit** or **gross margin**, which highlights the important relationship between net sales revenue and cost of goods sold. The **gross profit ratio** is computed as follows:

$$\text{Gross profit ratio} = \frac{\text{Gross profit}}{\text{Net sales}}$$

The higher the ratio, the higher is the markup a company is able to achieve on its products. For example, a product that costs $100 that is sold for $150 provides a gross profit of $50 ($150 − 100) and a gross profit ratio of 33% ($50 ÷ $150). If that same product can be sold for $200, the gross profit increases to $100 and the gross profit ratio increases to 50% ($100 ÷ $200) and more dollars are available to cover expenses other than cost of goods sold.

The *gross profit ratio* indicates the percentage of each sales dollar available to cover other expenses and provide a profit.

The 2001 gross profit ($ in millions), for Sara Lee, using the 100% FIFO amounts, is $7,478 ($17,747 − 10,269) and the gross profit ratio is 42% ($7,478 ÷ $17,747). The ratio for Tyson Foods is 10% ([$10,751 − 9,661] = $1,090 ÷ $10,751), indicating that Sara Lee is able to sell its products at significantly higher markups than Tyson Foods. Sara Lee's percentage of each sales dollar available to cover other expenses and provide a profit is over four times as much as that of Tyson Foods. Sara Lee's gross profit ratio also is slightly higher than the industry average of 40%.

Monitoring this ratio over time can provide valuable insights. For example, a declining ratio could indicate that the company is unable to offset rising costs with corresponding increases in sales price, or that sales prices are declining without a commensurate reduction in costs. In either case, the decline in the ratio has important implications for future profitability.

Chapter 5 introduced an important ratio, the **inventory turnover ratio**, which is designed to evaluate a company's effectiveness in managing its investment in inventory. The ratio shows the number of times the average inventory balance is sold during a reporting period. The more frequently a business is able to sell or turn over its inventory, the lower its investment in inventory must be for a given level of sales. Usually, the higher the ratio, the more profitable a company will be. Monitoring the inventory turnover ratio over time can highlight potential problems. A declining ratio generally is unfavorable and could be caused by the presence of obsolete or slow-moving products, or poor marketing and sales efforts.

Recall that the ratio is computed as follows:

$$\text{Inventory turnover ratio} = \frac{\text{Cost of goods sold}}{\text{Average inventory}}$$

We can divide the inventory turnover ratio into 365 days to compute the **average days in inventory**, which indicates the average number of days it normally takes to sell inventory.

For Sara Lee, the inventory turnover ratio for 2001 is 3.70 ($10,269 ÷ [($2,589 + 2,963) ÷ 2]) and the average days inventory is 99 days (365 ÷ 3.70). This compares to a turnover 6.72 ($9,661 ÷ [($1,911 + 965) ÷ 2]) and an average days inventory of 54 days (365 days ÷ 6.72) for Tyson Foods. It takes nearly twice as long for Sara Lee to turn over its inventory. Sara Lee's products command a higher markup (higher gross profit ratio) but take longer to sell (lower inventory turnover ratio) than the products of Tyson Foods. Tyson Food's inventory turnover ratio is approximately equal to the industry average of 6.7.

Inventory increases that outrun increases in cost of goods sold might indicate difficulties in generating sales. These inventory buildups may also indicate that a company has obsolete or slow-moving inventory. This proposition was tested in an important academic research study. Professors Lev and Thiagarajan empirically demonstrated the importance of a set of 12 fundamental variables in valuing companies' common stock. The set of variables included inventory (change in inventory minus change in sales). The inventory variable was found to be a significant indicator of stock returns, particularly during high and medium inflation years.[13]

EARNINGS QUALITY

Changes in the ratios we discussed above often provide information about the quality of a company's current period earnings. For example, a slowing turnover ratio combined with higher than normal inventory levels may indicate the potential for decreased production, obsolete inventory, or a need to decrease prices to sell inventory (which will then decrease gross profit ratios and net income).

The choice of which inventory method to use also affects earnings quality, particularly in times of rapidly changing prices. Earlier in this chapter we discussed the effect of a LIFO liquidation on company profits. A LIFO liquidation profit (or loss) reduces the quality of current period earnings. Fortunately for analysts, companies must disclose these profits or losses, if material. In addition, LIFO cost of goods sold determined using a periodic inventory system is more susceptible to manipulation than is FIFO. Year-end purchases can have a dramatic effect on LIFO cost of goods sold in rapid cost-change environments. Recall again our discussion in Chapter 4 concerning earnings quality. Many believe that manipulating income reduces earnings quality because it can mask permanent earnings. Inventory write-downs and changes in inventory method are two additional inventory-related techniques a company could use to manipulate earnings. We discuss these issues in the next chapter. ■

[13]B. Lev and S. R. Thiagarajan, "Fundamental Information Analysis," *Journal of Accounting Research* (Autumn 1993). The main conclusion of the study was that fundamental variables, not just earnings, are useful in firm valuation, particularly when examined in the context of macroeconomic conditions such as inflation.

METHODS OF SIMPLIFYING LIFO

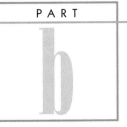

The LIFO method described and illustrated to this point is called *unit LIFO*[14] because the last-in, first-out concept is applied to individual units of inventory. One problem with unit LIFO is that it can be very costly to implement. It requires records of each unit of inventory. The costs of maintaining these records can be significant, particularly when a company has numerous individual units of inventory and when unit costs change often during a period.

In the previous section, a second disadvantage of unit LIFO was identified—the possibility that LIFO layers will be liquidated if the quantity of a particular inventory unit declines below its beginning balance. Even if a company's total inventory quantity is stable or increasing, if the quantity of any particular inventory unit declines, unit LIFO will liquidate all or a portion of a LIFO layer of inventory. When inventory quantity declines in a period of rising costs, noncurrent lower costs will be included in cost of goods sold and matched with current selling prices, resulting in LIFO liquidation profit.

This part of the chapter discusses techniques that can be used to significantly reduce the recordkeeping costs of LIFO and to minimize the probability of LIFO inventory layers being liquidated. Specifically, we discuss the use of inventory pools and the dollar-value LIFO method.

> The recordkeeping costs of unit LIFO can be significant.
>
> Another disadvantage of unit LIFO is the possibility of LIFO liquidation.

LIFO Inventory Pools

The objectives of using **LIFO inventory pools** are to simplify recordkeeping by grouping inventory units into pools based on physical similarities of the individual units and to reduce the risk of LIFO layer liquidation. For example, a glass company might group its various grades of window glass into a single window pool. Other pools might be auto glass and sliding door glass. A lumber company might pool its inventory into hardwood, framing lumber, paneling, and so on.

This allows a company to account for a few inventory pools rather than every specific type of inventory separately. Within pools, all purchases during a period are considered to have been made at the same time and at the same cost. Individual unit costs are converted to an average cost for the pool. If the quantity of ending inventory for the pool increases, then ending inventory will consist of the beginning inventory plus a single layer added during the period at the average acquisition cost for that pool.

Here's an example. Let's say Diamond Lumber Company has a rough-cut lumber inventory pool that includes three types: oak, pine, and maple. The beginning inventory consisted of the following:

> A pool consists of inventory units grouped according to natural physical similarities.
>
> The average cost for all of the pool purchases during the period is applied to the current year's LIFO layer.

	Quantity (Board Feet)	Cost (Per Foot)	Total Cost
Oak	16,000	$2.20	$35,200
Pine	10,000	3.00	30,000
Maple	14,000	2.40	33,600
	40,000		$98,800

The average cost for this pool is $2.47 per board foot ($98,800 ÷ 40,000 board feet). Now assume that during the next reporting period Diamond sold 46,000 board feet of lumber and purchased 50,000 board feet as follows:

	Quantity (Board Feet)	Cost (Per Foot)	Total Cost
Oak	20,000	$2.25	$45,000
Pine	14,000	3.00	42,000
Maple	16,000	2.50	40,000
	50,000		$127,000

---

[14]Unit LIFO sometimes is called *specific goods LIFO*.

The average cost for this pool is $2.54 per board foot ($127,000 ÷ 50,000 board feet). Because the quantity of inventory for the pool increased by 4,000 board feet (50,000 purchased less 46,000 sold), ending inventory will include the beginning inventory and a LIFO layer consisting of the 4,000 board feet increase. We would add this LIFO layer at the average cost of purchases made during the period, $2.54. The ending inventory of $108,960 now consists of two layers:

	Quantity (Board Feet)	Cost (Per Foot)	Total Cost
Beginning inventory	40,000	$2.47	$ 98,800
LIFO layer added	4,000	2.54	10,160
Ending inventory	44,000		$108,960

Despite the advantages of LIFO inventory pools, it's easy to imagine situations in which its benefits are not achieved. Suppose, for instance, that a company discontinues a certain product included in one of its pools. The old costs that existed in prior layers of inventory would be recognized as cost of goods sold and produce LIFO liquidation profit. Even if the product is replaced with another product, the replacement may not be similar enough to be included in the same inventory pool. In fact, the process itself of having to periodically redefine pools as changes in product mix occur, can be expensive and time consuming. The **dollar-value LIFO** approach helps overcome these problems.

Dollar-Value LIFO

LO6

Dollar-value LIFO (DVL) gained such widespread popularity during the 1960s and 1970s that most LIFO applications are now based on this approach. DVL extends the concept of inventory pools by allowing a company to combine a large variety of goods into one pool. Physical units are not used in calculating ending inventory. Instead, the inventory is viewed as a quantity of value instead of a physical quantity of goods. Instead of layers of units from different purchases, the DVL inventory pool is viewed as comprising layers of dollar value from different years.

A DVL pool is made up of items that are likely to face the same cost change pressures.

Because the physical characteristics of inventory items are not relevant to DVL, an inventory pool is identified in terms of economic similarity rather than physical similarity. Specifically, a pool should consist of those goods that are likely to be subject to the same cost change pressures.

ADVANTAGES OF DVL

The DVL method has important advantages. First, it simplifies the recordkeeping procedures compared to unit LIFO because no information is needed about unit flows. Second, it minimizes the probability of the liquidation of LIFO inventory layers, even more so than the use of pools alone, through the aggregation of many types of inventory into larger pools. In addition, the method can be used by firms that do not replace units sold with new units of the same kind. For firms whose products are subject to annual model changes, for example, the items in one year's inventory are not the same as the prior year's. Under pooled LIFO, the new replacement items must be substantially identical to previous models to be included in the same pool. Under DVL, no distinction is drawn between the old and new merchandise on the basis of their physical characteristics, so a much broader range of goods can be included in the pool. That is, the acquisition of the new items is viewed as replacement of the dollar value of the old items. Because the old layers are maintained, this approach retains the benefits of LIFO by matching the most recent acquisition cost of goods with sales measured at current selling prices.

COST INDEXES

In either the unit LIFO approach or the pooled LIFO approach, we determine whether a new LIFO layer was added by comparing the ending quantity with the beginning quantity. The focus is on *units* of inventory. Under DVL, we determine whether a new LIFO layer was added by comparing the ending dollar amount with the beginning dollar amount. The focus is on inventory *value*, not units. However, if the price level has changed, we need a way to determine whether an observed increase is a real increase (an increase in the quantity of inventory) or one caused by an increase in prices. So before we compare the beginning and ending inventory amounts, we need to deflate inventory amounts by any increase in prices so that both the beginning and ending amounts are measured in terms of the same price level. We accomplish this by using cost indexes. A cost index for a particular layer year is determined as follows:

$$\text{Cost index in layer year} = \frac{\text{Cost in layer year}}{\text{Cost in base year}}$$

The base year is the year in which the DVL method is adopted and the layer year is any subsequent year in which an inventory layer is created. The cost index for the base year is set at 1.00. Subsequent years' indexes reflect cost changes relative to the base year. For example, if a "basket" of inventory items cost $120 at the end of the current year, and $100 at the end of the base year, the cost index for the current year would be: $120 ÷ $100 = 120%, or 1.20. This index simply tells us that costs in the layer year are 120% of what they were in the base year (i.e., costs increased by 20%).

> The cost index for the base year (the year DVL is initially adopted) is set at 1.00.

There are several techniques that can be used to determine an index for a DVL pool. An external index like the Consumer Price Index or the Producer Price Index can be used. However, in most cases these indexes would not properly reflect cost changes for any individual DVL pool. Instead, most companies use an internally generated index. These indexes can be calculated using one of several techniques such as the *double-extension method* or the *link-chain method*. A discussion of these methods is beyond the scope of this text. In our examples and illustrations, we assume cost indexes are given.

THE DVL INVENTORY ESTIMATION TECHNIQUE

DVL estimation begins with the determination of the current year's ending inventory valued in terms of year-end costs. It's not necessary for a company using DVL to track the item-by-item cost of purchases during the year. All that's needed is to take the physical quantities of goods on hand at the end of the year and apply year-end costs. Let's say the Hanes Company adopted the dollar-value LIFO method on January 1, 2003, when the inventory value was $400,000. The 2003 ending inventory valued at year-end costs is $441,000, and the cost index for the year is 1.05 (105%).

> The starting point in DVL is determining the current year's ending inventory valued at year-end costs.

What is the 2003 ending inventory valued at DVL cost? The first step is to convert the ending inventory from year-end costs to base year costs so we can see if there was a real increase in inventory rather than an illusory one caused by price increases. We divide the ending inventory by the year's cost index to get an amount that can be compared directly with beginning inventory.

> STEP 1: Convert ending inventory valued at year-end cost to base year cost.

$$\text{Ending inventory at } \textit{base year} \text{ cost} = \frac{\$441,000}{1.05} = \$420,000$$

The $420,000 reflects the 2003 ending inventory deflated to base year cost.

Next we compare the $420,000 ending inventory at base year cost to the beginning inventory, also at base year cost, of $400,000. The $20,000 increase in base-year dollars signifies a real increase in inventory quantity during the year. Applying the LIFO concept, ending inventory at base year cost consists of the beginning inventory layer of $400,000 plus a $20,000 2003 layer. These are the hypothetical costs of the layers as if each was acquired at base year prices.

> STEP 2: Identify the layers of ending inventory and the years they were created.

Once the layers are identified, each is restated to prices existing when the layers were acquired. Each layer is multiplied by the cost index for the year it was acquired. The costs are totaled to obtain ending inventory at DVL cost.[15]

---

[15]It is important to note that the costs of the year's layer are only an approximation of actual acquisition cost. DVL assumes that all inventory quantities added during a particular year were acquired at a single cost.

STEP 3: Convert each layer's base year cost to layer year cost using the cost index for the year it was acquired.

Date	Ending Inventory at Base Year Cost	×	Cost Index	=	Ending Inventory at DVL Cost
1/1/03	$400,000		1.00		$400,000
2003 layer	20,000		1.05		21,000
Totals	$420,000				$421,000

If we determined that inventory quantity had decreased during the year, then there would have been no 2003 layer added. The most recently added layer, in this case the beginning inventory layer, would be decreased to the inventory valuation determined in step 1. Once a layer of inventory or a portion of a layer is used (that is, sold) it cannot be replaced. In our example, if the base year layer is reduced to $380,000, it will never be increased. Future increases in inventory quantity will result in new layers being added. This situation is illustrated in the concept review exercise that follows.

CONCEPT REVIEW EXERCISE

Dollar-Value LIFO

On January 1, 2003, the Johnson Company adopted the dollar-value LIFO method. The inventory value on this date was $500,000. Inventory data for 2003 through 2006 is as follows:

Date	Ending Inventory at Year-End Costs	Cost Index
12/31/03	$556,500	1.05
12/31/04	596,200	1.10
12/31/05	615,250	1.15
12/31/06	720,000	1.25

Required:
Calculate Johnson's ending inventory for the years 2003 through 2006.

SOLUTION

JOHNSON COMPANY

Date	Ending Inventory at Year-End Cost	Step 1 — Ending Inventory at Base Year Cost	Step 2 — Inventory Layers at Base Year Cost	Step 3 — Inventory Layers Converted to Acquisition Year Cost	Ending Inventory At DVL Cost
1/1/03	$500,000 (base year)	$\frac{\$500,000}{1.00} = \$500,000$	$500,000 (base)	$500,000 × 1.00 = $500,000	**$500,000**
12/31/03	556,500	$\frac{\$556,500}{1.05} = \$530,000$	$500,000 (base) 30,000 (2003)	$500,000 × 1.00 = $500,000 30,000 × 1.05 = 31,500	**531,500**
12/31/04	596,200	$\frac{\$596,200}{1.10} = \$542,000$	$500,000 (base) 30,000 (2003) 12,000 (2004)	$500,000 × 1.00 = $500,000 30,000 × 1.05 = 31,500 12,000 × 1.10 = 13,200	**544,700**
12/31/05	615,250	$\frac{\$615,250}{1.15} = \$535,000^*$	$500,000 (base) 30,000 (2003) 5,000 (2004)	$500,000 × 1.00 = $500,000 30,000 × 1.05 = 31,500 5,000 × 1.10 = 5,500	**537,000**
12/31/06	720,000	$\frac{\$720,000}{1.25} = \$576,000$	$500,000 (base) 30,000 (2003) 5,000 (2004) 41,000 (2006)	$500,000 × 1.00 = $500,000 30,000 × 1.05 = 31,500 5,000 × 1.10 = 5,500 41,000 × 1.25 = 51,250	**588,250**

*Since inventory declined during 2005 (from $542,000 to $535,000 at base year costs), no new layer is added. Instead the most recently acquired layer, 2004, is reduced to arrive at the $535,000 ending inventory at base year cost.

FINANCIAL REPORTING CASE **SOLUTION**

1. **What inventory methods does Ford use to value its inventories? Is this permissible according to GAAP?** *(p. 381)*   Ford uses the LIFO inventory method to value most of its U.S. inventories. The cost of the remaining inventories is determined primarily by the FIFO method. Yes, both of these methods are permissible according to generally accepted accounting principles.

2. **What is the purpose of the disclosure information that reports what LIFO inventories would have been if valued at FIFO?** *(p. 383)*   The LIFO conformity rule requires that if a company uses LIFO to measure taxable income, it also must use LIFO for external financial reporting. Ford does this. However, in 1981, the LIFO conformity rule was liberalized to allow LIFO users to provide supplemental disclosure of the effect on inventories of using another method on inventory valuation rather than LIFO. Ford's disclosure note offers this additional information.

3. **Is your friend correct in his assertion that by using LIFO, Ford was able to report lower profits in 2000?** *(p. 388)*   Yes. If Ford had used FIFO instead of LIFO for its LIFO inventories, income before taxes in all prior years, including 2000, would have been higher by $1.1 billion (the increase in 2000 ending inventory). In 2000 alone, income before taxes would have been *higher* by $.1 billion. Here's why. The increase in ending inventory of $1.1 billion *decreases* cost of goods sold, but the increase in beginning inventory of $1.0 billion *increases* cost of goods sold, resulting in a net decrease in cost of goods sold of $.1 billion. ■

THE BOTTOM LINE

1. In a perpetual inventory system, inventory is continually adjusted for each change in inventory. Cost of goods sold is adjusted each time goods are sold or returned by a customer. A periodic inventory system adjusts inventory and records cost of goods sold only at the end of a reporting period.

2. Generally, determining the physical quantity that should be included in inventory is a simple matter, because it consists of items in the possession of the company. However, at the end of a reporting period it's important to determine the ownership of goods that are in transit between the company and its customers as well as between the company and its suppliers. Also, goods on consignment should be included in inventory of the consignor even though the company doesn't have physical possession of the goods. In addition, a company anticipating sales returns includes in inventory the cost of merchandise it estimates will be returned.

3. The cost of inventory includes all expenditures necessary to acquire the inventory and bring it to its desired condition and location for sale or use. Generally, these expenditures include the purchase price of the goods reduced by any returns and purchase discounts, plus freight-in charges.

4. Once costs are determined, the cost of goods available for sale must be allocated between cost of goods sold and ending inventory. Unless each item is specifically identified and traced through the system, the allocation requires an assumption regarding the flow of costs. First-in, first-out (FIFO) assumes that units sold are the first units acquired. Last-in, first-out (LIFO) assumes that the units sold are the most recent units purchased. The average cost method assumes that cost of goods sold and ending inventory consist of a mixture of all the goods available for sale.

5. A company's choice of inventory method will be influenced by (a) how closely cost flow reflects the actual physical flow of its inventory, (b) the timing of income tax expenses, and (c) how costs are matched with revenues.

6. The dollar-value LIFO method converts ending inventory at year-end cost to base year cost using a cost index. After identifying the layers in ending inventory with the years they were created, each year's base year cost measurement is converted to layer year cost measurement using the layer year's cost index. The layers are then summed to obtain total ending inventory at cost.

QUESTIONS FOR REVIEW OF KEY TOPICS

Q 8–1 Describe the three types of inventory of a manufacturing company.

Q 8–2 What is the main difference between a perpetual inventory system and a periodic inventory system?

Q 8–3 The Cloud Company employs a perpetual inventory system and the McKenzie Corporation uses a periodic system. Describe the differences between the two systems in accounting for the following events: (1) purchase of merchandise, (2) sale of merchandise, (3) return of merchandise to supplier, and (4) payment of freight charge on merchandise purchased. Indicate which accounts would be debited and credited for each event.

Q 8–4 The Bockner Company shipped merchandise to Laetner Corporation on December 28, 2003. Laetner received the shipment on January 3, 2004. December 31 is the fiscal year-end for both companies. The merchandise was shipped f.o.b. shipping point. Explain the difference in the accounting treatment of the merchandise if the shipment had instead been designated f.o.b. destination.

Q 8–5 What is a consignment arrangement? Explain the accounting treatment of goods held on consignment.

Q 8–6 Distinguish between the gross and net methods of accounting for purchase discounts.

Q 8–7 The Esquire Company employs a periodic inventory system. Indicate the effect (increase or decrease) of the following items on cost of goods sold:
1. Beginning inventory
2. Purchases
3. Ending inventory
4. Purchase returns
5. Freight-in

Q 8–8 Identify four methods of assigning cost to ending inventory and cost of goods sold and briefly explain the difference in the methods.

Q 8–9 It's common in the electronics industry for unit costs of raw materials inventories to decline over time. In this environment, explain the difference between LIFO and FIFO, in terms of the effect on income and financial position. Assume that inventory quantities remain the same for the period.

Q 8–10 Explain why proponents of LIFO argue that it provides a better match of revenue and expenses. In what situation would it not provide a better match?

Q 8–11 Explain what is meant by the Internal Revenue Service conformity rule with respect to inventory method choice.

Q 8–12 What is a LIFO inventory pool? How is the cost of ending inventory determined when pools are used?

Q 8–13 Identify two advantages of dollar-value LIFO compared with unit LIFO.

Q 8–14 The Austin Company uses the dollar-value LIFO inventory method with internally developed price indexes. Assume that ending inventory at year-end cost has been determined. Outline the remaining steps used in the dollar-value LIFO computations.

EXERCISES

E 8–1
Perpetual inventory system; journal entries

John's Specialty Store uses a perpetual inventory system. The following are some inventory transactions for the month of May, 2003:
1. John's purchased merchandise on account for $4,000. Freight charges of $300 were paid in cash.
2. John's returned some of the merchandise purchased in (1). The cost of the merchandise was $600 and John's account was credited by the supplier.
3. Merchandise costing $2,800 was sold for $5,000 in cash.

Required:
Prepare the necessary journal entries to record these transactions.

E 8–2
Periodic inventory system; journal entries

[This is a variation of the previous exercise modified to focus on the periodic inventory system.]
    John's Specialty Store uses a periodic inventory system. The following are some inventory transactions for the month of May, 2003:
1. John's purchased merchandise on account for $4,000. Freight charges of $300 were paid in cash.
2. John's returned some of the merchandise purchased in (1). The cost of the merchandise was $600 and John's account was credited by the supplier.
3. Merchandise costing $2,800 was sold for $5,000 in cash.

Required:
Prepare the necessary journal entries to record these transactions.

E 8–3
Determining cost of goods sold; periodic inventory system

The Askew Company uses a periodic inventory system. The June 30, 2003, year-end trial balance for the company contained the following information:

Account	Debit	Credit
Merchandise inventory, 7/1/02	32,000	
Sales		380,000
Sales returns	12,000	
Purchases	230,000	
Purchase discounts		6,000
Purchase returns		8,000
Freight-in	16,000	
Freight-out	13,000	

In addition, you determine that the June 30, 2003, inventory balance is $40,000.

Required:
1. Calculate the cost of goods sold for the Askew Company for the year ending June 30, 2003.
2. Prepare the year-end adjusting entry to record cost of goods sold.

E 8–4
Perpetual and periodic inventory systems compared

The following information is available for the Johnson Corporation for 2003:

Beginning inventory	$ 25,000
Merchandise purchases (on account)	150,000
Freight charges on purchases (paid in cash)	10,000
Merchandise returned to supplier (for credit)	12,000
Ending inventory	30,000
Sales (on account)	250,000
Cost of merchandise sold	143,000

Required:
Applying both a perpetual and a periodic inventory system, prepare the journal entries that summarize the transactions that created these balances. Include all end-of-period adjusting entries indicated.

E 8–5
Periodic inventory system; missing data

The Playa Company uses a periodic inventory system. The following information is taken from Playa's records. Certain data have been intentionally omitted. ($ in thousands)

	2003	2004	2005
Beginning inventory	?	?	225
Cost of goods sold	627	621	?
Ending inventory	?	225	216
Cost of goods available for sale	876	?	800
Purchases (gross)	630	?	585
Purchase discounts	18	15	?
Purchase returns	24	30	14
Freight-in	13	32	16

Required:
Determine the missing numbers. Show computations where appropriate.

E 8–6
Purchase discounts; the gross method

On July 15, 2003, the Nixon Car Company purchased 1,000 tires from the Harwell Company for $50 each. The terms of the sale were 2/10, n/30. Nixon uses a periodic inventory system and the *gross* method of accounting for purchase discounts.

Required:
1. Prepare the journal entries to record the purchase on July 15 and payment on July 23, 2003.
2. Prepare the journal entries to record the purchase on July 15 and payment on August 15, 2003.
3. If Nixon instead uses a perpetual inventory system, explain any changes to the journal entries created in requirements 1 and 2.

E 8–7
Purchase discounts; the net method

[This is a variation of the previous exercise modified to focus on the net method of accounting for purchase discounts.]

On July 15, 2003, the Nixon Car Company purchased 1,000 tires from the Harwell Company for $50 each. The terms of the sale were 2/10, n/30. Nixon uses a periodic inventory system and the *net* method of accounting for purchase discounts.

Required:
1. Prepare the journal entries to record the purchase on July 15 and payment on July 23, 2003.
2. Prepare the journal entries to record the purchase on July 15 and payment on August 15, 2003.
3. If Nixon instead uses a perpetual inventory system, explain any changes to the journal entries created in requirements 1 and 2.

E 8–8

Trade and purchase discounts; the gross method and the net method compared

Tracy Company, a manufacturer of air conditioners, sold 100 units to Thomas Company on November 17, 2003. The units have a list price of $500 each, but Thomas was given a 30% trade discount. The terms of the sale were 2/10, n/30. Thomas uses a periodic inventory system.

Required:
1. Prepare the journal entries to record the purchase by Thomas on November 17 and payment on November 26, 2003, using the gross method of accounting for purchase discounts.
2. Prepare the journal entries to record the purchase on November 17 and payment on December 15, 2003, using the gross method of accounting for purchase discounts.
3. Repeat requirements 1 and 2 using the net method of accounting for purchase discounts.

E 8–9

Goods in transit

The Kwok Company's inventory balance on December 31, 2003, was $165,000 (based on a 12/31/03 physical count) *before* considering the following transactions:
1. Goods shipped to Kwok f.o.b. destination on December 20, 2003, were received on January 4, 2004. The invoice cost was $30,000.
2. Goods shipped to Kwok f.o.b. shipping point on December 28, 2003, were received on January 5, 2004. The invoice cost was $17,000.
3. Goods shipped from Kwok to a customer f.o.b. destination on December 27, 2003, were received by the customer on January 3, 2004. The sales price was $40,000 and the merchandise cost $22,000.
4. Goods shipped from Kwok to a customer f.o.b. destination on December 26, 2003, were received by the customer on December 30, 2003. The sales price was $20,000 and the merchandise cost $13,000.
5. Goods shipped from Kwok to a customer f.o.b. shipping point on December 28, 2003, were received by the customer on January 4, 2004. The sales price was $25,000 and the merchandise cost $12,000.

Required:
Determine the correct inventory amount to be reported in Kwok's 2003 balance sheet.

E 8–10

Goods in transit; consignment

The December 31, 2003, year-end inventory balance of the Raymond Corporation is $220,000. You have been asked to review the following transactions to determine if they have been correctly recorded.
1. Goods shipped to Raymond f.o.b. destination on December 26, 2003, were received on January 2, 2004. The invoice cost of $30,000 *is* included in the preliminary inventory balance.
2. At year-end, Raymond held $12,000 of merchandise on consignment from the Harrison Company. This merchandise *is* included in the preliminary inventory balance.
3. On December 29, merchandise costing $6,000 was shipped to a customer f.o.b. shipping point and arrived at the customer's location on January 3, 2004. The merchandise is *not* included in the preliminary inventory balance.
4. At year-end, Raymond had merchandise costing $15,000 on consignment with the Joclyn Corporation. The merchandise is *not* included in the preliminary inventory balance.

Required:
Determine the correct inventory amount to be reported in Raymond's 2003 balance sheet.

E 8–11

Inventory cost flow methods; periodic system

Altira Corporation uses a periodic inventory system. The following information related to its merchandise inventory during the month of August 2003 is available:

Aug. 1   Inventory on hand—2,000 units; cost $6.10 each.
     8   Purchased 10,000 units for $5.50 each.
   14   Sold 8,000 units for $12.00 each.
   18   Purchased 6,000 units for $5.00 each.
   25   Sold 7,000 units for $11.00 each.
   31   Inventory on hand—3,000 units.

Required:
Determine the inventory balance Altira would report in its August 31, 2003, balance sheet and the cost of goods sold it would report in its August 2003 income statement using each of the following cost flow methods:

1. First-in, first-out (FIFO)
2. Last-in, first-out (LIFO)
3. Average cost

E 8–12
Inventory cost flow methods; perpetual system

[This is a variation of the previous exercise modified to focus on the perpetual inventory system and alternative cost flow methods.]

Altira Corporation uses a perpetual inventory system. The following transactions affected its merchandise inventory during the month of August 2003:

Aug. 1 Inventory on hand—2,000 units; cost $6.10 each.
      8 Purchased 10,000 units for $5.50 each.
     14 Sold 8,000 units for $12.00 each.
     18 Purchased 6,000 units for $5.00 each.
     25 Sold 7,000 units for $11.00 each.
     31 Inventory on hand—3,000 units.

Required:
Determine the inventory balance Altira would report in its August 31, 2003, balance sheet and the cost of goods sold it would report in its August 2003 income statement using each of the following cost flow methods:
1. First-in, first-out (FIFO)
2. Last-in, first-out (LIFO)
3. Average cost

E 8–13
Comparison of FIFO and LIFO; periodic system

Alta Ski Company's inventory records contained the following information regarding its latest ski model. The company uses a periodic inventory system.

Beginning inventory, January 1, 2003	600 units @ $80 each
Purchases:	
January 15	1,000 units @ $90 each
January 21	800 units @ $100 each
Sales:	
January 5	400 units @ $120 each
January 22	800 units @ $130 each
January 29	400 units @ $135 each
Ending inventory, January 31, 2003	800 units

Required:
1. Which method, FIFO or LIFO, will result in the highest cost of goods sold figure for January 2003? Why? Which method will result in the highest ending inventory balance? Why?
2. Compute cost of goods sold for January and the ending inventory using both the FIFO and LIFO methods.

E 8–14
Average cost method; periodic and perpetual systems

The following information is taken from the inventory records of the CNB Company:

Beginning inventory, 9/1/03	5,000 units @ $10.00
Purchases:	
9/7	3,000 units @ $10.40
9/25	8,000 units @ $10.75
Sales:	
9/10	4,000 units
9/29	5,000 units
7,000 units were on hand at the end of September.	

Required:
1. Assuming that CNB uses a periodic inventory system and employs the average cost method, determine cost of goods sold for September and September's ending inventory.
2. Repeat requirement 1 assuming that the company uses a perpetual inventory system.

E 8–15
FIFO, LIFO, and average cost methods

The Causwell Company began 2003 with 10,000 units of inventory on hand. The cost of each unit was $5.00. During 2003 an additional 30,000 units were purchased at a single unit cost, and 20,000 units remained on hand at the end of 2003 (20,000 units therefore were sold during 2003). Causwell uses a periodic inventory system. Cost of goods sold for 2003, applying the average cost method, is $115,000. The company is interested in determining what cost of goods sold would have been if the FIFO or LIFO methods were used.

Required:

1. Determine the cost of goods sold for 2003 using the FIFO method. [*Hint:* Determine the cost per unit of 2003 purchases.]
2. Determine the cost of goods sold for 2003 using the LIFO method.

E 8–16
Multiple choice;
inventory measurement

The following questions dealing with inventory measurement are adapted from questions that appeared on recent CPA examinations. Determine the response that best completes the statements or questions.

1. Herc Co.'s inventory at December 31, 2003, was $1,500,000 based on a physical count priced at cost, and before any adjustment for the following:
   - Merchandise costing $90,000, shipped f.o.b. shipping point from a vendor on December 30, 2003, was received and recorded on January 5, 2004.
   - Goods in the shipping area were excluded from inventory although shipment was not made until January 4, 2004. The goods, billed to the customer f.o.b. shipping point on December 30, 2003, had a cost of $120,000.

   What amount should Herc report as inventory in its December 31, 2003, balance sheet?
   a. $1,500,000
   b. $1,590,000
   c. $1,620,000
   d. $1,710,000

Items 2 and 3 are based on the following:

During 2003, Metro Co., which maintains a perpetual inventory system, recorded the following information pertaining to its inventory:

	Units	Unit Cost	Total Cost	Units on Hand
Balance on 1/1/03	1,000	$1	$1,000	1,000
Purchased on 1/7/03	600	3	1,800	1,600
Sold on 1/20/03	900			700
Purchased on 1/25/03	400	5	2,000	1,100

2. Under the moving-average inventory method, what amount should Metro report as inventory at January 31, 2003?
   a. $2,640
   b. $3,225
   c. $3,300
   d. $3,900
3. Under the LIFO method, what amount should Metro report as inventory at January 31, 2003?
   a. $1,300
   b. $2,700
   c. $3,900
   d. $3,400
4. According to the net method, which of the following items would be included in the cost of inventory?

	Freight Costs	Purchase Discounts Not Taken
a.	Yes	No
b.	Yes	Yes
c.	No	Yes
d.	No	No

E 8–17
LIFO liquidation

The Reuschel Company began 2003 with inventory of 10,000 units at a cost of $7 per unit. During 2003, 50,000 units were purchased for $9 each. Sales for the year totaled 56,000 units leaving 4,000 units on hand at the end of 2003. Reuschel uses a periodic inventory system and the LIFO inventory cost method.

Required:

1. Calculate cost of goods sold for 2003.
2. From a financial reporting perspective, what problem is created by the use of LIFO in this situation? Describe the disclosure required to report the effects of this problem.

E 8–18
Ratio analysis

The table below contains selected financial information from the 2000 financial statements of Maytag Corporation and Whirlpool Corporation (dollars in millions):

	Maytag		**Whirlpool**	
	2000	**1999**	**2000**	**1999**
Net sales	$4,248	$4,324	$10,325	$10,511
Cost of goods sold	3,102	3,072	7,838	7,852
Year-end inventory	409	404	1,119	1,065

Required:
Calculate and compare the 2000 gross profit ratio, the inventory turnover ratio, and the average days in inventory for the two companies.

E 8–19
Dollar-value LIFO

On January 1, 2003, the Haskins Company adopted the dollar-value LIFO method for its one inventory pool. The pool's value on this date was $660,000. The 2003 and 2004 ending inventory valued at year-end costs were $690,000 and $770,000, respectively. The appropriate cost indexes are 1.03 for 2003 and 1.10 for 2004:

Required:
Calculate the inventory value at the end of 2003 and 2004 using the dollar-value LIFO method.

E 8–20
Dollar-value LIFO

The Mercury Company has only one inventory pool. On December 31, 2003, Mercury adopted the dollar-value LIFO inventory method. The inventory on that date using the dollar-value LIFO method was $200,000. Inventory data are as follows:

Year	Inventory at Year-End Costs	Inventory at Base Year Costs
2004	$231,000	$220,000
2005	299,000	260,000
2006	300,000	250,000

Required:
Compute the inventory at December 31, 2004, 2005, and 2006, using the dollar-value LIFO method.

(AICPA adapted)

E 8–21
Multiple choice; dollar-value LIFO

The following questions dealing with dollar-value LIFO are adapted from questions that appeared on recent CPA examinations. Determine the response that best completes the statements or questions.

1. Walt Co. adopted the dollar-value LIFO inventory method as of January 1, 2003, when its inventory was valued at $500,000. Walt's entire inventory constitutes a single pool. Using a relevant cost index of 1.10, Walt determined that its December 31, 2003, inventory was $577,500 at current year cost, and $525,000 at base year cost. What was Walt's dollar-value LIFO inventory at December 31, 2003?
   a. $525,000
   b. $527,500
   c. $552,500
   d. $577,500

2. Brock Co. adopted the dollar-value LIFO inventory method as of January 1, 2002. A single inventory pool and an internally computed cost index are used to compute Brock's LIFO inventory layers. Information about Brock's dollar value inventory follows:

	Inventory		
Date	**At Base Year Cost**	**At Current Year Cost**	**At Dollar-Value LIFO**
1/1/02	$40,000	$40,000	$40,000
2002 layer	5,000	14,000	6,000
12/31/02	45,000	54,000	46,000
2003 layer	15,000	26,000	?
12/31/03	$60,000	$80,000	?

What was Brock's dollar-value LIFO inventory at December 31, 2003?
   a. $80,000
   b. $74,000
   c. $66,000
   d. $60,000

E 8–22
Concepts; terminology

Listed below are several terms and phrases associated with inventory measurement. Pair each item from List A (by letter) with the item from List B that is most appropriately associated with it.

List A	List B
____ 1. Perpetual inventory system	a. Legal title passes when goods are delivered to common carrier.
____ 2. Periodic inventory system	b. Goods are transferred to another company but title remains with transferor.
____ 3. F.o.b. shipping point	c. Purchase discounts not taken are included in inventory cost.
____ 4. Gross method	d. If LIFO is used for taxes, it must be used for financial reporting.
____ 5. Net method	e. Items sold are those acquired first.
____ 6. Cost index	f. Items sold are those acquired last.
____ 7. F.o.b. destination	g. Purchase discounts not taken are considered interest expense.
____ 8. FIFO	h. Used to convert ending inventory at year-end cost to base year cost.
____ 9. LIFO	i. Continuously records changes in inventory.
____ 10. Consignment	j. Items sold come from a mixture of goods acquired during the period.
____ 11. Average cost	k. Legal title passes when goods arrive at location.
____ 12. IRS conformity rule	l. Adjusts inventory at the end of the period.

PROBLEMS

P 8–1
Various inventory
transactions; journal
entries

The James Company began the month of October with inventory of $15,000. The following inventory transactions occurred during the month:

a. The company purchased merchandise on account for $22,000 on October 12, 2003. Terms of the purchase were 2/10, n/30. James uses the net method to record purchases. The merchandise was shipped f.o.b. shipping point and freight charges of $500 were paid in cash.

b. On October 18 the company returned merchandise costing $3,000. The return reduced the amount owed to the supplier. The merchandise returned came from beginning inventory, not from the October 12 purchase.

c. On October 31, James paid for the merchandise purchased on October 12.

d. During October merchandise costing $18,000 was sold on account for $28,000.

e. It was determined that inventory on hand at the end of October cost $16,060.

Required:

1. Assuming that the James Company uses a periodic inventory system, prepare journal entries for the above transactions including the adjusting entry at the end of October to record cost of goods sold.

2. Assuming that the James Company uses a perpetual inventory system, prepare journal entries for the above transactions.

P 8–2
Items to be included in
inventory

The following inventory transactions took place near December 31, 2003, the end of the Rasul Company's fiscal year-end:

1. On December 27, 2003, merchandise costing $2,000 was shipped to the Myers Company on consignment. The shipment arrived at Myers's location on December 29, but none of the merchandise was sold by the end of the year. The merchandise was *not* included in the 2003 ending inventory.

2. On January 5, 2004, merchandise costing $8,000 was received from a supplier and recorded as a purchase on that date and *not* included in the 2003 ending inventory. The invoice revealed that the shipment was made f.o.b. shipping point on December 28, 2003.

3. On December 29, 2003, the company shipped merchandise costing $12,000 to a customer f.o.b. destination. The goods, which arrived at the customer's location on January 4, 2004, were *not* included in Rasul's 2003 ending inventory. The sale was recorded in 2003.

4. Merchandise costing $4,000 was received on December 28, 2003, on consignment from the Aborn Company. A purchase was *not* recorded and the merchandise was *not* included in 2003 ending inventory.

5. Merchandise costing $6,000 was received and recorded as a purchase on January 8, 2004. The invoice revealed that the merchandise was shipped from the supplier on December 28, 2003, f.o.b. destination. The merchandise was *not* included in 2003 ending inventory.

Required:

State whether the company correctly accounted for each of the above transactions. Give the reason for your answer.

P 8–3

Costs included in inventory

The Reagan Corporation is a wholesale distributor of truck replacement parts. Initial amounts taken from Reagan's records are as follows:

Inventory at December 31 (based on a physical count
  of goods in Reagan's warehouse on December 31) $1,250,000
Accounts payable at December 31:

Vendor	Terms	Amount
Baker Company	2%, 10 days, net 30	$ 265,000
Charlie Company	Net 30	210,000
Dolly Company	Net 30	300,000
Eagler Company	Net 30	225,000
Full Company	Net 30	—
Greg Company	Net 30	—
		$1,000,000
Sales for the year		$9,000,000

Additional information:

1. Parts held by Reagan on consignment from Charlie, amounting to $155,000, were included in the physical count of goods in Reagan's warehouse and in accounts payable at December 31.
2. Parts totaling $22,000, which were purchased from Full and paid for in December, were sold in the last week of the year and appropriately recorded as sales of $28,000. The parts were included in the physical count of goods in Reagan's warehouse on December 31 because the parts were on the loading dock waiting to be picked up by customers.
3. Parts in transit on December 31 to customers, shipped f.o.b. shipping point on December 28, amounted to $34,000. The customers received the parts on January 6 of the following year. Sales of $40,000 to the customers for the parts were recorded by Reagan on January 2.
4. Retailers were holding goods on consignment from Reagan, which had a cost of $210,000 and a retail value of $250,000.
5. Goods were in transit from Greg to Reagan on December 31. The cost of the goods was $25,000, and they were shipped f.o.b. shipping point on December 29.
6. A freight bill in the amount of $2,000 specifically relating to merchandise purchased in December, all of which was still in the inventory at December 31, was received on January 3. The freight bill was not included in either the inventory or in accounts payable at December 31.
7. All the purchases from Baker occurred during the last seven days of the year. These items have been recorded in accounts payable and accounted for in the physical inventory at cost before discount. Reagan's policy is to pay invoices in time to take advantage of all discounts, adjust inventory accordingly, and record accounts payable net of discounts.

Required:

Prepare a schedule of adjustments to the initial amounts using the format shown below. Show the effect, if any, of each of the transactions separately and if the transactions would have no effect on the amount shown, state *none*.

	Inventory	Accounts Payable	Sales
Initial amounts	$1,250,000	$1,000,000	$9,000,000
Adjustments—increase (decrease):			
1.			
2.			
3.			
4.			
5.			
6.			
7.			
Total adjustments			
Adjusted amounts	$	$	$

(AICPA adapted)

P 8–4

Various inventory transactions; determining inventory and cost of goods

The Johnson Corporation began 2003 with inventory of 10,000 units of its only product. The units cost $8 each. The company uses a periodic inventory system and the LIFO cost method. The following transactions occurred during 2003:

a. Purchased 50,000 additional units at a cost of $10 per unit. Terms of the purchases were 2/10, n/30, and 60% of the purchases were paid for within the 10-day discount period. The company uses the gross method to record purchase discounts. The merchandise was purchased f.o.b. shipping point and freight charges of $.50 per unit were paid by Johnson.

b. 1,000 units purchased during the year were returned to suppliers for credit. Johnson was also given credit for the freight charges of $.50 per unit it had paid on the original purchase. The units were defective and were returned two days after they were received.

c. Sales for the year totaled 45,000 units at $18 per unit.

d. On December 28, 2003, Johnson purchased 5,000 additional units at $10 each. The goods were shipped f.o.b. destination and arrived at Johnson's warehouse on January 4, 2004.

e. 14,000 units were on hand at the end of 2003.

Required:

1. Determine ending inventory and cost of goods sold for 2003.

2. Assuming that operating expenses other than those indicated in the above transactions amounted to $150,000, determine income before income taxes for 2003.

P 8–5

Various inventory costing methods

The Ferris Company began 2003 with 6,000 units of its principal product. The cost of each unit is $8. Merchandise transactions for the month of January 2003 are as follows:

	Purchases		
Date of Purchase	Units	Unit Cost*	Total Cost
Jan. 10	5,000	$ 9	$ 45,000
Jan. 18	6,000	10	60,000
Totals	11,000		$105,000

*Includes purchase price and cost of freight.

Sales	
Date of Sale	Units
Jan. 5	3,000
Jan. 12	2,000
Jan. 20	4,000
Total	9,000

8,000 units were on hand at the end of the month.

Required:

Calculate January's ending inventory and cost of goods sold for the month using each of the following alternatives:

1. FIFO, periodic system
2. LIFO, periodic system
3. LIFO, perpetual system
4. Average cost, periodic system
5. Average cost, perpetual system

P 8–6

Various inventory costing methods; gross profit ratio

The Topanga Group began operations early in 2003. Inventory purchase information for the quarter ended March 31, 2003, for Topanga's only product is provided below. The unit costs include the cost of freight. The company uses a periodic inventory system.

Date of Purchase	Units	Unit Cost	Total Cost
Jan. 7	5,000	$4.00	$ 20,000
Feb. 16	12,000	4.50	54,000
March 22	17,000	5.00	85,000
Totals	34,000		$159,000

Sales for the quarter, all at $7.00 per unit, totaled 20,000 units leaving 14,000 units on hand at the end of the quarter.

Required:
1. Calculate the Topanga's gross profit ratio for the first quarter using:
   a. FIFO
   b. LIFO
   c. Average cost
2. Comment on the relative effect of each of the three inventory methods on the gross profit ratio.

P 8–7
Various inventory
costing methods

Carlson Auto Dealers Inc. sells a handmade automobile as its only product. Each automobile is identical; however, they can be distinguished by their unique ID number. At the beginning of 2003, Carlson had three cars in inventory, as follows:

Car ID	Cost
203	$60,000
207	60,000
210	63,000

During 2003, each of the three autos sold for $90,000. Additional purchases (listed in chronological order) and sales for the year were as follows:

Car ID	Cost	Selling Price
211	$63,000	$ 90,000
212	63,000	93,000
213	64,500	not sold
214	66,000	96,000
215	69,000	100,500
216	70,500	not sold
217	72,000	105,000
218	72,300	106,500
219	75,000	not sold

Required:
1. Compute 2003 ending inventory and cost of goods sold assuming the company uses the specific identification inventory method.
2. Compute ending inventory and cost of goods sold assuming FIFO and a periodic inventory system.
3. Compute ending inventory and cost of goods sold assuming LIFO and a periodic inventory system.
4. Compute ending inventory and cost of goods sold assuming the average cost method and a periodic inventory system.

P 8–8
Supplemental LIFO
disclosures

Caterpillar, Inc. is one of the world's largest manufacturers of construction, mining, agricultural, and forestry machinery. The following disclosure note is included in the company's 2000 financial statements:

D. Inventories ($ in millions)
Inventories are stated at the lower of cost or market. Cost is principally determined using the last-in, first-out, (LIFO) method. The value of inventories on the LIFO basis represented about 80% of total inventories at December 31, 2000, 1999, and 85% at December 31, 1998.

If the FIFO (first-in, first-out) method had been in use, inventories would have been $2,065, $2,000, and $1,978 higher than reported at December 31, 2000, 1999, and 1998, respectively.

If inventories valued at LIFO cost had been valued at FIFO cost, net income would have increased by approximately $46.0 million and $15.6 million, respectively, for the year ended December 31, 2000 and 1999.

Required:
1. Approximate the company's effective income tax rate for the year ended December 31, 2000.
2. Why might the information contained in the disclosure note be useful to a financial analyst?

3. Using the income tax rate calculated in 1, how much higher (lower) would retained earnings have been at the end of 2000 if Caterpillar had used the FIFO inventory method for all of its inventory?

P 8–9
LIFO liquidation

The Taylor Corporation has used a periodic inventory system and the LIFO cost method since its inception in 2003. The company began 2003 with the following inventory layers (listed in chronological order of acquisition):

10,000 units @ $15	$150,000
15,000 units @ $20	300,000
Beginning inventory	$450,000

During 2003, 30,000 units were purchased for $25 per unit. Due to unexpected demand for the company's product, 2003 sales totaled 40,000 units at various prices, leaving 15,000 units in ending inventory.

Required:
1. Calculate cost of goods sold for 2003.
2. Determine the amount of LIFO liquidation profit that the company must report in a disclosure note to its 2003 financial statements. Assume an income tax rate of 40%.
3. If the company decided to purchase an additional 10,000 units at $25 per unit at the end of the year, how much income tax currently payable would be saved?

P 8–10
Dollar-value LIFO

On January 1, 2003, the Taylor Company adopted the dollar-value LIFO method. The inventory value for its one inventory pool on this date was $400,000. Inventory data for 2003 through 2005 is as follows:

Date	Ending Inventory at Year-End Costs	Cost Index
12/31/03	$441,000	1.05
12/31/04	487,200	1.12
12/31/05	510,000	1.20

Required:
Calculate Taylor's ending inventory for 2003, 2004, and 2005.

P 8–11
Dollar-value LIFO

The Kingston Company uses the dollar-value LIFO method of computing inventory. An external price index is used to convert ending inventory to base year. The company began operations on January 1, 2003, with an inventory of $150,000. Year-end inventories at year-end costs and cost indexes for its one inventory pool were as follows:

Year Ended December 31	Inventory at Year-End Costs	Cost Index (Relative to Base Year)
2003	$200,000	1.08
2004	245,700	1.17
2005	235,980	1.14
2006	228,800	1.10

Required:
Compute inventory amounts at the end of each year.

BROADEN YOUR PERSPECTIVE

Judgment Case 8–1
Riding the
Merry-Go-Round

Apply your critical-thinking ability to the knowledge you've gained. These cases will provide you an opportunity to develop your research, analysis, judgment, and communication skills. You also will work with other students, integrate what you've learned, apply it in real world situations, and consider its global and ethical ramifications. This practice will broaden your knowledge and further develop your decision-making abilities.

Merry-Go-Round Enterprises, the clothing retailer for dedicated followers of young men's and women's fashion, was looking natty as a company. It was March 1993, and the Joppa, Maryland-based outfit had just announced the acquisition of Chess King, a rival clothing chain, a move that would give it the biggest share of the young men's clothing market. Merry-Go-Round told brokerage firm analysts that the purchase would add $13 million, or 15 cents a share, to profits for the year. So some Wall Street analysts raised their earnings estimates for Merry-Go-Round. The company's stock rose $2.25, or 15 percent, to $17 on the day of the Chess King news. Merry-Go-Round was hot—$100 of its stock in January 1988 was worth $804 five years later. In 1993 the chain owned 1,460 stores in 44 states, mostly under the Cignal, Chess King, and Merry-Go-Round names.

Merry-Go-Round's annual report for the fiscal year ended January 30, 1993, reported a 15% sales growth, to $877.5 million from $761.2 million. A portion of the company's balance sheet is reproduced below:

	Jan. 30, 1993	Feb. 1, 1992
Assets		
Cash and cash equivalents	$40,115,000	$29,781,000
Marketable securities	—	9,703
Receivables	6,466,000	6,195
Merchandise inventories	82,197,000	59,971,000

But Merry-Go-Round spun out. The company lost $544,000 in the first six months of 1993, compared with earnings of $13.5 million in the first half of 1992. In the fall of 1992, Leonard "Boogie" Weinglass, Merry-Go-Round's flamboyant founder and chairman who had started the company in 1968, boarded up his Merry-Go-Ranch in Aspen, Colorado, and returned to management after a 12-year hiatus. But the ponytailed, shirtsleeved entrepreneur—the inspiration for the character Boogie in the movie *Diner*—couldn't save his company from bankruptcy. In January 1994, the company filed for Chapter 11 protection in Baltimore. Shares crumbled below $3.

Required:

In retrospect, can you identify any advance warning at the date of the financial statements of the company's impending bankruptcy?
[Adapted from Jonathan Burton, "Due Diligence," *Worth,* June 1994, pp. 89–96.]

Judgment Case 8–2
The specific identification inventory method; inventoriable costs

Happlia Co. imports household appliances. Each model has many variations and each unit has an identification number. Happlia pays all costs for getting the goods from the port to its central warehouse in Des Moines. After repackaging, the goods are consigned to retailers. A retailer makes a sale, simultaneously buys the appliance from Happlia, and pays the balance due within one week.

To alleviate the overstocking of refrigerators at a Minneapolis retailer, some were reshipped to a Kansas City retailer where they were still held in inventory at December 31, 2003. Happlia paid the costs of this reshipment. Happlia uses the specific identification inventory costing method.

Required:
1. In regard to the specific identification inventory costing method:
   a. Describe its key elements.
   b. Discuss why it is appropriate for Happlia to use this method.
2. a. What general criteria should Happlia use to determine inventory carrying amounts at December 31, 2003?
   b. Give four examples of costs included in these inventory carrying amounts.
3. What costs should be reported in Happlia's 2003 income statement? Ignore lower of cost or market considerations.

(AICPA adapted)

Communication Case 8–3
LIFO versus FIFO

You have just been hired as a consultant to Tangier Industries, a newly formed company. The company president, John Meeks, is seeking your advice as to the appropriate inventory method Tangier should use to value its inventory and cost of goods sold. Mr. Meeks has narrowed the choice to LIFO and FIFO. He has heard that LIFO might be better for tax purposes, but FIFO has certain advantages for financial reporting to investors and creditors. You have been told that the company will be profitable in its first year and for the foreseeable future.

Required:
Prepare a report for the president describing the factors that should be considered by Tangier in choosing between LIFO and FIFO.

Communication Case 8–4
LIFO versus FIFO

An accounting intern for a local CPA firm was reviewing the financial statements of a client in the electronics industry. The intern noticed that the client used the FIFO method of determining ending inventory and cost of goods sold. When she asked a colleague why the firm used FIFO instead of LIFO, she was told that the client used FIFO to minimize its income tax liability. This response puzzled the intern because she thought that LIFO would minimize income tax liability.

Required:

What would you tell the intern to resolve the confusion?

Judgment Case 8–5
Goods in transit

At the end of 2003, the Biggie Company performed its annual physical inventory count. John Lawrence, the manager in charge of the physical count, was told that an additional $22,000 in inventory that had been sold and was in transit to the customer should be included in the ending inventory balance. John was of the opinion that the merchandise shipped should be excluded from the ending inventory since Biggie was not in physical possession of the merchandise.

Required:

Discuss the situation and indicate why John's opinion might be incorrect.

Ethics Case 8–6
Profit manipulation

In 2002 the Moncrief Company purchased from Jim Lester the right to be the sole distributor in the western states of a product called Zelenex. In payment, Moncrief agreed to pay Lester 20% of the gross profit recognized from the sale of Zelenex in 2003.

Moncrief uses a periodic inventory system and the LIFO inventory method. Late in 2003, the following information is available concerning the inventory of Zelenex:

Beginning inventory, 1/1/03 (10,000 units @ $30)	$ 300,000
Purchases (40,000 units @ $30)	1,200,000
Sales (35,000 units @ $60)	$2,100,000

By the end of the year, the purchase price of Zelenex had risen to $40 per unit. On December 28, 2003, three days before year-end, Moncrief is in a position to purchase 20,000 additional units of Zelenex at the $40 per unit price. Due to the increase in purchase price, Moncrief will increase the selling price in 2004 to $80 per unit. Inventory on hand before the purchase, 15,000 units, is sufficient to meet the next six months' sales and the company does not anticipate any significant changes in purchase price during 2004.

Required:

1. Determine the effect of the purchase of the additional 20,000 units on the 2003 gross profit from the sale of Zelenex and the payment due to Jim Lester.
2. Discuss the ethical dilemma Moncrief faces in determining whether or not the additional units should be purchased.

Real World Case 8–7
Effects of inventory valuation methods; LIFO and FIFO

Income statement and balance sheet information abstracted from a recent annual report of Safeway, Inc., one of the world's largest food retailers, appears below:

Balance Sheets
($ in millions)

	At Dec. 31,	
	2000	**1999**
Current assets:		
Merchandise inventories	$ 2,508	$ 2,445

Income Statements
($ in millions)

	For the Year Ended Dec. 31,	
	2000	**1999**
Net sales	$31,977	$28,860
Cost of goods sold	22,482	20,349
Gross profit	$ 9,495	$ 8,511

The significant accounting policies note disclosure contained the following:

Merchandise Inventories

Merchandise inventory of $1,846 million at year-end 2000 and $1,823 million at year-end 1999 is valued at the lower of cost on a last-in, first-out ("LIFO") basis or market value. Such LIFO inventory had a replacement or current cost of $1,926 million at year-end 2000 and $1,905 million at year-end 1999. All remaining inventory is valued at the lower of cost on a first-in, first-out ("FIFO") basis or market value. The FIFO cost of inventory approximates replacement or current cost.

Required:
1. Why is Safeway disclosing the replacement or current cost of its LIFO inventory?
2. Assuming that year-end replacement/current cost figures approximate FIFO inventory values, estimate what the beginning and ending inventory balances for the 2000 fiscal year would have been if Safeway had used FIFO for all of its inventories.
3. Estimate the effect on cost of goods sold (that is, would it have been greater or less and by how much?) for the 2000 fiscal year if Safeway had used FIFO for all of its inventories.

Real World Case 8–8
Effects of inventory valuation methods

EDGAR, the Electronic Data Gathering, Analysis, and Retrieval system, performs automated collection, validation, indexing, and forwarding of submission by companies and others who are required by law to file forms with the U.S. Securities and Exchange Commission (SEC). All publicly traded domestic companies use EDGAR to make the majority of their filings. (Some foreign companies file voluntarily.) Form 10-K or 10-KSB, which includes the annual report, is required to be filed on EDGAR. The SEC makes this information available on the Internet.

Required:
1. Access EDGAR on the Internet. The web address is www.sec.gov. Edgarscan (edgarscan.pwcglobal.com) from Pricewaterhouse Coopers makes the process of accessing data from EDGAR easier.
2. Search for Unocal Corporation. Access the 10-K filing for the most recent fiscal year. Search or scroll to find the financial statements and related notes.
3. Answer the following questions related to the company's inventories:
   a. What method(s) does the company use to value its inventories?
   b. Calculate what cost of sales would have been for the year if the company had used FIFO to value its inventories.
   c. Calculate inventory turnover for the year using the reported numbers.

Research Case 8–9
The use of LIFO inventory pools

An inventory pool consists of inventory units grouped according to natural physical similarities. The objectives of using LIFO inventory pools is to simplify recordkeeping by grouping inventory units into pools based on physical similarities of the individual units and to reduce the risk of LIFO layer liquidation. Professors Reeve and Stanga, in "The LIFO Pooling Decision: Some Empirical Results from Accounting Practice," conducted a survey to investigate the number of pools companies use in practice.

Required:
1. In your library or from some other source, locate the indicated article in *Accounting Horizons*, June 1987.
2. For the companies included in the sample, what are the median and mean number of pools used by retail and nonretail companies?
3. What are the authors' six conclusions?

International Case 8–10
Comparison of inventory valuation in Denmark and the U.S.A.

The Carlsberg Group, headquartered in Denmark, is one of the world's major international brewing groups. Carlsberg and Tuborg are two of its most famous brands. The inventory (stocks) disclosure note included in recent financial statements of the company is reproduced below:

Significant Accounting Policies (in part)
Stocks
Stocks are stated at purchase price or production cost (average method), or net realizable value, if lower. Write-down is effected for obsolete stocks. Indirect production overheads are not included in the production cost.

Required:
On the basis of the information the note provides, compare inventory valuation in Denmark with that in the United States.

Communication Case 8–11
Dollar-value LIFO method

The Maxi Corporation uses the unit LIFO inventory method. The costs of the company's products have been steadily rising since the company began operations in 1993 and cost increases are expected to continue. The chief financial officer of the company would like to continue using LIFO because of its tax advantages. However, the controller, Sally Hamel, would like to reduce the recordkeeping costs of LIFO that have steadily increased over the years as new products have been added to the company's product line. Sally suggested the use of the dollar-value LIFO method. The chief financial officer has asked Sally to describe the dollar-value LIFO procedure.

Required:
Describe the dollar-value LIFO procedure.

Research Case 8–12
Locate and extract relevant information and authoritative support for a financial reporting issue; product financing arrangement

You were recently hired to work in the controller's office of the Balboa Lumber Company. Your boss, Alfred Eagleton, took you to lunch during your first week and asked a favor. "Things have been a little slow lately, and we need to borrow a little cash to tide us over. Our inventory has been building up and the CFO wants to pledge the inventory as collateral for a short-term loan. But I have a better idea." Mr. Eagleton went on to describe his plan. "On July 1, 2003, the first day of the company's third quarter, we will sell $100,000 of inventory to the Harbaugh Corporation for $160,000. Harbaugh will pay us immediately and then we will agree to repurchase the merchandise in two months for $164,000. The $4,000 is Harbaugh's fee for holding the inventory and for providing financing. I already checked with Harbaugh's controller and he has agreed to the arrangement. Not only will we obtain the financing we need, but the third quarter's before-tax profits will be increased by $56,000, the gross profit on the sale less the $4,000 fee. Go research the issue and make sure we would not be violating any specific accounting standards related to product financing arrangements."

Required:
1. Obtain the original FASB Standard on accounting for product financing arrangements. You might gain access through FARS, the FASB Financial Accounting Research System, from your school library, or some other source. Determine the appropriate treatment of product financing arrangements like the one proposed by Mr. Eagleton.
2. Prepare the journal entry to record the "sale" of the inventory and subsequent repurchase.

Analysis Case 8–13
Compare inventory management using ratios

The table below contains selected financial information included in the 2000 financial statements of General Motors and Ford Motor Company:

	($ in millions)			
	General Motors		Ford Motor Company	
	2000	**1999**	**2000**	**1999**
Balance sheet:				
Inventories	$ 10,945	$10,638	$ 7,514	$5,684
	2000		**2000**	
Income statement:				
Net sales	$184,632		$141,230	
Cost of goods sold	145,664		126,120	

Disclosure notes reveal that both companies use the LIFO inventory method to value the majority of their inventories.
1. Calculate the 2000 gross profit ratio, inventory turnover ratio, and average days in inventory for both companies. Evaluate the management of each company's investment in inventory. Industry averages for these ratios are as follows:

Gross profit	18%
Inventory turnover	12.36
Average days in inventory	30

2. Obtain annual reports from three corporations in the same primary industry (but not autos) and compare the management of each company's investment in inventory.
Note: You can obtain copies of annual reports from your library, from friends who are shareholders, from the investor relations department of the corporations, from a friendly stockbroker, or from EDGAR (Electronic Data Gathering, Analysis, and Retrieval) on the Internet (www.sec.gov or through Edgarscan at edgarscan.pwcglobal.com).

Analysis Case 8–14
Reporting of inventories

FedEx Corporation

Refer to the financial statements and related disclosure notes of FedEx Corporation in the appendix to Chapter 1.

Required:
1. Why does merchandise inventory not appear in FedEx's balance sheet? Does the balance sheet report any type of inventory?
2. What method does FedEx use to value its inventory?

9

Inventories: Additional Issues

CHAPTER

OVERVIEW

We covered most of the principal measurement and reporting issues involving the asset inventory and the corresponding expense cost of goods sold in the previous chapter. In this chapter we complete our discussion of inventory measurement by explaining the lower-of-cost-or-market rule used to value inventories. In addition, we investigate inventory estimation techniques, methods of simplifying LIFO, changes in inventory method, and inventory errors.

LEARNING OBJECTIVES

After studying this chapter, you should be able to:

LO1 Understand and apply the lower-of-cost-or-market rule used to value inventories.

LO2 Estimate ending inventory and cost of goods sold using the gross profit method.

LO3 Estimate ending inventory and cost of goods sold using the retail inventory method, applying the various cost flow methods.

LO4 Explain how the retail inventory method can be made to approximate the lower-of-cost-or-market rule.

LO5 Determine ending inventory using the dollar-value LIFO retail inventory method.

LO6 Explain the appropriate accounting treatment required when a change in inventory method is made.

LO7 Explain the appropriate accounting treatment required when an inventory error is discovered.

Does It Count?

Today you drove over to Sears to pick up a few items. Yesterday, your accounting professor had discussed inventory measurement issues and the different methods (FIFO, LIFO, and average) used by companies to determine ending inventory and cost of goods sold. You can't imagine actually counting the inventory in all of the Sears stores around the country. "There must be some way they can avoid counting all of that inventory every time they want to produce financial statements," you tell your dog when you get home. "I think I'll go check their financial statements on the Internet to see what kind of inventory method they use." You find the following in the summary of significant accounting policies included in Sears's most recent financial statements:

Merchandise Inventories (in part):

Approximately 86% of merchandise inventories are valued at the lower of cost (using the last-in, first-out or "LIFO" method) or market using the retail method. To estimate the effects of inflation on inventories, the Company utilizes internally developed price indices.

> By the time you finish this chapter, you should be able to respond appropriately to the questions posed in this case. Compare your response to the solution provided at the end of the chapter.

QUESTIONS

1. Sears values its inventory at the lower of cost or market. What does that mean? Under what circumstances might Sears be justified in reporting its inventory at less than cost? (page 413)

2. How does Sears avoid counting all its inventory every time it produces financial statements? What are internal price indices used for? (page 431)

REPORTING—LOWER OF COST OR MARKET

In the previous chapter you learned that there are several methods a company could use to determine the cost of inventory at the end of a period and the corresponding cost of goods sold for the period. You also learned that it is important for a company to disclose the inventory method that it uses. Otherwise, investors and creditors would be unable to meaningfully compare accounting information from company to company. This disclosure typically is made in the summary of significant accounting policies accompanying the financial statements. Coca-Cola Company's inventory method disclosure is shown in Graphic 9–1.

GRAPHIC 9–1
Disclosure of Inventory
Method—Coca-Cola
Company

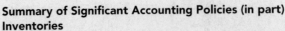

Summary of Significant Accounting Policies (in part)
Inventories
Inventories consist primarily of raw materials and supplies and are valued at the lower of cost or market. In general, cost is determined on the basis of average cost or first-in, first-out methods.

The disclosure indicates that Coca-Cola uses both the average cost and FIFO methods to determine the cost of its inventories. Notice that inventories actually are valued at the *lower of cost or market*. Assets are initially valued at their historical costs, but a departure from cost is warranted when the utility of an asset (its probable future economic benefits) is no longer as great as its cost. Accounts receivable, for example, are valued at net realizable value by reducing initial valuation with an allowance for uncollectible accounts.

The utility or benefits from inventory result from the ultimate sale of the goods. So, deterioration, obsolescence, changes in price levels, or any situation that might compromise the inventory's saleability impairs utility. The **lower-of-cost-or-market (LCM)** approach to reporting inventory was developed to avoid reporting inventory at an amount greater than the benefits it can provide. Reporting inventories at LCM causes losses to be recognized when the value of inventory declines below its cost rather than in the period that the goods ultimately are sold.

FINANCIAL REPORTING CASE

Q1, p. 413

The *lower-of-cost-or-market* approach to valuing inventory recognizes losses in the period that the value of inventory declines below its cost.

The tremendous growth of the Internet that took place during the decade of the 90s allowed companies that produced products that support the Internet to become extremely profitable. Cisco Systems, Inc., the world's largest networking products company, is one of those companies. In 1993, Cisco reported $649 million in sales revenue. By 2000, sales had reached nearly $19 billion! Growth rates of 50% year-to-year were commonplace. The company's market capitalization (price per share of common stock multiplied by the number of common shares outstanding) soared to over $500 billion. To keep pace with this growth in sales, inventories swelled from $71 million in 1993 to over $2.5 billion in 2000.

At the end of 2000, corporate spending on Internet infrastructure took a drastic downturn. Many dot-com companies went bankrupt, and companies like Cisco saw their fantastic growth rates nosedive. Early in 2001, the company reported its first-ever quarterly loss and, due to declining demand for its products, recorded an inventory write-down in excess of $2 billion. The company's once lofty market capitalization dropped to just over $100 billion.

CISCO POSTS $5BN LOSS ON HUGE WRITE-DOWNS
Technology giant Cisco Systems posted on Tuesday a third-quarter net loss of $2.69 billion, its first ever, following a write-down of inventory, restructuring costs and a sharp drop-off in corporate spending.

. . . and a write-down of over $2 billion for excess inventory.

Cisco said 80 percent of the inventory charge relates to raw materials, such as semiconductor memories, optical components, . . .

"Most of the excess inventory cannot be sold as it is custom built for Cisco," chief financial officer Mr. Larry Carter said in a conference call.[1]

---

[1]Fiona Buffini, "Cisco Posts $5bn Loss on Huge Writedowns," *Financial Review*, May 9, 2001.

DETERMINING MARKET VALUE

From the preceding discussion, you might interpret the term *market* to mean the amount that could be realized if the inventory were sold. However, *Accounting Research Bulletin No. 43* defines market for LCM purposes as the inventory's current replacement cost (by purchase or reproduction) except that market should not:

> a. Exceed the net realizable value (that is, estimated selling price in the ordinary course of business less reasonably predictable costs of completion and disposal).
> b. Be less than net realizable value reduced by an allowance for an approximately normal profit margin.

Replacement cost (RC) generally means the cost to replace the item by purchase or manufacture.

In effect, we have a ceiling and a floor between which market (that is, replacement cost) must fall. **Net realizable value (NRV)** represents the upper limit and **net realizable value less a normal profit margin (NRV − NP)** provides the lower limit. If **replacement cost (RC)** is within the range, it represents market; if it is above the ceiling or below the floor, the ceiling or the floor becomes market. As a result, the designated market value is the number that falls in the middle of the three possibilities: replacement cost, net realizable value, and net realizable value less a normal profit margin. The designated market value is compared with cost, and the lower of the two is used to value inventory.

The ceiling of net realizable value (NRV) and the floor of net realizable value less a normal profit margin (NRV − NP) establish a range within which the market must fall.

Let's see how the LCM rule is applied in Illustration 9–1 and then we will discuss its theoretical merit.

Notice that the designated market value is the middle amount of the three market possibilities. This number is then compared to cost and the lower of the two is the final inventory value. For item A, cost is lower than market. For each of the other items, the designated market is lower than cost, requiring an adjustment to the carrying value of inventory. We discuss the adjustment procedure later in the chapter. First though, let's consider the conceptual justification of the LCM rule.

GLOBAL PERSPECTIVE

The technique of valuing inventories at the lower of cost or market is fairly standard around the globe. However, differences exist in the designation of market. In the United States, market is defined as replacement cost, constrained by the ceiling of net realizable value and the floor of net realizable value less a normal profit margin. In many other countries, for example the United Kingdom, France, and New Zealand, market value is defined as net realizable value. In Sweden, inventories are carried at the lower of cost or fair value. Fair value is defined as net realizable value, but replacement cost is permissible for raw materials and semi-finished products.

Theoretical Merits.   What is the logic for designating replacement cost as the principal meaning of market value in the LCM rule? First, a change in replacement cost usually is a good indicator of the direction of change in selling price. If replacement cost declines, selling price usually will decline, or already has declined. Another reason is that if previously acquired inventory is revalued at its replacement cost, then the profit margin realized on its sale will likely approximate the profit margin realizable on the sale of newly acquired items.

The upper limit placed on replacement cost prevents inventory from being valued at an amount above what can be realized from its sale. The lower limit prevents inventory from being valued at an amount below what can be realized from its sale after considering normal profit margin. For example, consider item D in our illustration. If item D is valued at its replacement cost of $37 without considering the ceiling or floor, a loss of $53 ($90 cost less $37) would be recognized. If the item is subsequently sold at its current selling price less usual disposal costs (NRV = $76), then a gross profit of $39 ($76 less $37) would be recognized. This is much higher than its normal profit of $20 (20% × $100) and causes a shifting

ILLUSTRATION 9–1

Lower of Cost or Market

The Collins Company has five inventory items on hand at the end of 2003. The year-end unit costs (determined by applying the average cost method), current unit selling prices, and estimated disposal (selling) costs for each of the items are presented below. The gross profit ratio for each of the products is 20% of selling price.

Item	Cost	Replacement Cost	Selling Price	Estimated Disposal Costs
A	$ 50	$55	$100	$15
B	100	90	120	20
C	80	70	85	20
D	90	37	100	24
E	95	92	110	24

The determination of inventory value is a two-step process: first, determine the designated market value and second, compare the designated market value to cost. The lower of the two is the LCM inventory value.

Inventory is valued at the lower of cost or the designated market value.

	(1)	(2)	(3)	(4)	(5)	
Item	RC	NRV	NRV − NP	Designated Market Value [Middle Value of (1) − (3)]	Cost	Inventory Value [Lower of (4) or (5)]
A	$55	$ 85	$65	$65	$ 50	$50
B	90	100	76	90	100	90
C	70	65	48	65	80	65
D	37	76	56	56	90	56
E	92	86	64	86	95	86

RC = Current replacement cost.
NRV = Estimated selling price less estimated disposal costs.
NRV − NP = NRV less a normal profit margin.

Example for item B:

Selling price	$120
Less: Disposal costs	(20)
NRV	100
Less: Normal profit	(24) ($120 selling price × 20%)
NRV − NP	$ 76

of income from the period the inventory loss is recognized to the period the item is sold. The ceiling and floor prohibit this kind of profit distortion.

Some accountants complain that LCM promotes conservatism at the expense of consistency.

On the other hand, critics of LCM contend that the method causes losses to be recognized that haven't actually occurred. Others maintain that it introduces needless inconsistency in order to be conservative. Inconsistency is created because LCM recognizes decreases in market value as they occur, but not increases.

The practice of recognizing decreases but not increases is not simply an application motivated by conservatism. Recall our discussions in previous chapters on revenue recognition and the realization principle. Recognizing increases in the value of inventory prior to sale would, in most cases, violate the realization principle. Assume that merchandise costing $100 has a net realizable value of $150. Recognizing the increase in value would increase pretax income by $50. This is equivalent to recognizing revenue of $150, cost of goods sold of $100, and gross profit of $50. Either way, pretax income is increased in a period prior to sale of the product. Prior to sale, there usually exists significant uncertainty as to the collectibility of the asset to be received. We don't know if the product will be sold, nor the selling price, or the buyer if eventually sold.

ETHICAL DILEMMA

The Hartley Paper Company, owned and operated by Bill Hartley, manufactures and sells different types of computer paper. The company has reported profits in the majority of years since the company's inception in 1962 and is projecting a profit in 2003 of $65,000, down from $96,000 in 2002.

Near the end of 2003, the company is in the process of applying for a bank loan. The loan proceeds will be used to replace manufacturing equipment necessary to modernize the manufacturing operation. In preparing the financial statements for the year, the chief accountant, Don Davis, mentioned to Bill Hartley that approximately $40,000 of paper inventory has become obsolete and should be written off as a loss in 2003. Bill is worried that the write-down would lower 2003 income to a level that might cause the bank to refuse the loan. Without the loan, it would be difficult for the company to compete. This could cause decreased future business and employees might have to be laid off. Bill is considering waiting until 2004 to write down the inventory. Don Davis is contemplating his responsibilities in this situation.

ARB NO. 43

The most common practice is to apply the *lower of cost or market rule* separately to each item of the inventory. However, if there is only one end-product category the cost utility of the total stock—the inventory in its entirety—may have the greatest significance for accounting purposes.

Similarly, where more than one major product or operational category exists, the application of the *lower of cost or market, whichever is lower* rule to the total of items included in such major categories may result in the most useful determination of income.[2]

The LCM rules stated in *ARB No. 43* are intended as a guide rather than a literal rule. In practice, companies frequently define market as net realizable value. This is a number that often is easier to estimate than replacement cost. Also, assuming the NRV does not change, when the item is sold, there will be neither gross profit nor additional loss. The entire effect on income is recognized in the period the realizable value drops below cost.

APPLYING LOWER OF COST OR MARKET

Lower of cost or market can be applied to individual inventory items, to logical categories of inventory, or to the entire inventory. A major product line can be considered a logical category of inventory. For income tax purposes, the lower-of-cost-or-market rule must be applied on an individual item basis.

Let's return to our illustration and assume the unit amounts pertain to 1,000 units of each inventory item. Also, let's say items A–B and items C–E are two collections of similar items that can be considered logical categories of inventory. Illustration 9–1A compares the LCM valuation accounting to each of three possible applications.

The final LCM inventory value is different for each of the three applications. The inventory value is $347,000 if LCM is applied to each item, $357,000 if it is applied to product line categories, and $362,000 if applied to the entire inventory. Applying LCM to groups of inventory items will usually cause a higher inventory valuation than if applied on an item-by-item basis because group application permits decreases in the market value of some items to be offset by increases in others. Each approach is acceptable but should be applied consistently from one period to another.

> The LCM rule can be applied to individual inventory items, logical inventory categories, or the entire inventory.

---

[2]"Restatement and Revision of Accounting Research Bulletins," *Accounting Research Bulletin No. 43* (New York: AICPA, 1953), ch. 4, par. 11.

ILLUSTRATION 9–1A

LCM Determination—Application at Different Levels of Aggregation

Item	Cost	Designated Market Value	Lower-of-Cost-or-Market By Individual Items	By Product Line	By Total Inventory
A	$ 50,000	$ 65,000	$ 50,000		
B	100,000	90,000	90,000		
Total A + B	$150,000	$155,000		$150,000	
C	$ 80,000	$ 65,000	65,000		
D	90,000	56,000	56,000		
E	95,000	86,000	86,000		
Total C, D, & E	$265,000	$207,000		207,000	
Total	$415,000	$362,000	$347,000	$357,000	$362,000

ADJUSTING COST TO MARKET

When a company applies the LCM rule and a material write-down of inventory is required, the company has two choices of how to record the reduction. One way found in practice is to report the loss as a separate item in the income statement. An alternative is to include the loss as part of the cost of goods sold.

Loss on reduction to LCM	xx		Cost of goods sold	xx
Inventory*		xx **or**	Inventory*	xx

*Or, inventory can be reduced indirectly with a credit to an allowance account.

> **The preferable way to report a loss from an inventory write-down is as a separate item in the income statement.**

Recording the write-down as a separate item more accurately reports the event that occurred—a loss from holding inventory during a period when inventory value declined. Including this holding loss as part of cost of goods sold has the same effect on reported earnings, but distorts the relationship between sales and cost of goods sold. Conceptually, cost of goods sold should include only the cost of goods actually sold during the period. Even so, many companies do include the "holding loss" in cost of goods sold.

Recall from our introductory discussion to this chapter that Cisco Systems, Inc., recently recorded an inventory write-down in excess of $2 billion. To understand how the relationship between sales and cost of goods sold can be distorted, let's consider the top part of the company's income statements for the first quarter of 2001 and 2000 shown in Graphic 9–2.

GRAPHIC 9–2
Partial Income Statements—Cisco Systems, Inc.

INCOME STATEMENTS (IN PART)
For the Three Months Ended,
($ in millions)

	April 28, 2001	April 29, 2000
Net sales	$4,728	$4,933
Cost of sales	4,400	1,761
Gross profit	328	3,172

> **Reporting a loss from an inventory write-down as part of cost of goods sold distorts the relationship between sales and cost of goods sold.**

Using the information in the statements, the gross profit ratio dropped from 64% ($3,172 ÷ $4,933) in 2000 to 7% ($328 ÷ $4,728) in 2001. An analyst might conclude that there was a significant deterioration in the markup the company was able to achieve on its products. However, this assessment is premature. A disclosure note included in the financial statements for the first quarter of 2001 reported that during the quarter Cisco recorded "an excess inventory charge of $2.25 billion classified as cost of sales." We get a more accurate portrayal of the company's gross profit ratio if we reduce the cost of goods sold by the inventory charge (write-down):

Sales	$4,728
Adjusted cost of sales ($4,400 − 2,250)	2,150
Adjusted gross profit	2,578
Adjusted gross profit ratio	55%

Cisco's gross profit ratio did decline from the prior year, but not nearly as drastically as the reported financial statement information would lead us to believe.

Regardless of which method we use to record the write-down, the reduced inventory value becomes the new cost basis for subsequent reporting, and if the inventory value later recovers prior to its sale, we do not write it back up.[3]

ADDITIONAL CONSIDERATION

In very limited circumstances, businesses are allowed under GAAP to carry inventory at a market value above cost. *ARB 43* restricted this approach generally to companies that deal in precious metals, and ". . . agricultural, mineral, and other products, units of which are interchangeable and have an immediate marketability at quoted prices . . ."[4] Writing inventory up to market value means recognizing revenue for the increase. This is called the *production basis* of recognizing revenue. In rare cases when the method is appropriate, full disclosure of the fact that inventory is valued at market is required.

CONCEPT REVIEW EXERCISE

Lower of Cost or Market

The Strand Company sells four products that can be grouped into two major categories. Information necessary to apply the LCM rule at the end of 2003 for each of the four products is presented below. The normal profit margin for each of the products is 25% of selling price. The company records any losses from adjusting cost to market as separate income statement items and reduces inventory directly.

Product	Cost	Replacement Cost	Selling Price	Disposal Costs
101	$ 80,000	$ 85,000	$160,000	$30,000
102	175,000	160,000	200,000	25,000
201	160,000	140,000	180,000	50,000
202	45,000	20,000	60,000	22,000

Products 101 and 102 are in category A and products 201 and 202 are in category B.

Required:
1. Determine the designated market value for each of the four products according to the LCM rule.
2. Determine the amount of the loss from write-down of inventory that would be required, applying the LCM rule to:
   a. Individual items
   b. Major categories
   c. The entire inventory

---

[3]The SEC, in its *Staff Accounting Bulletin No. 100*, "Restructuring and Impairment Charges" (Washington, DC: SEC, November, 1999), paragraph B.B., reaffirmed the provisions of *Accounting Research Bulletin No. 43* on this issue. For interim reporting purposes, however, recoveries of losses on the same inventory in subsequent interim periods of the same fiscal year through market price recoveries should be recognized as gains in the later interim period, not to exceed the previously recognized losses.
[4]"Restatement and Revision of Accounting Research Bulletins," *Accounting Research Bulletin No. 43* (New York: AICPA, 1953), Ch. 4, par. 16.

SOLUTION

1. Determine the designated market value for each of the four products according to the LCM rule.

Product	(1) RC	(2) NRV (Selling Price Less Disposal Costs)	(3) NRV − NP	(4) Designated Market Value [Middle Value of (1) − (3)]
101	$ 85,000	$130,000	$ 90,000	$ 90,000
102	160,000	175,000	125,000	160,000
201	140,000	130,000	85,000	130,000
202	20,000	38,000	23,000	23,000

Calculation of NRV − NP:

Product	NRV	NP	NRV − NP
101	$130,000	$40,000 (25% × $160,000)	$ 90,000
102	175,000	50,000 (25% × $200,000)	125,000
201	130,000	45,000 (25% × $180,000)	85,000
202	38,000	15,000 (25% × $ 60,000)	23,000

2. Determine the amount of the loss from write-down of inventory that would be required.

Product	Cost	Designated Market Value	Lower-of-Cost-or-Market By Individual Products	By Category	By Total Inventory
101	$ 80,000	$ 90,000	$ 80,000		
102	175,000	160,000	160,000		
Total 101 + 102	$255,000	$250,000		$250,000	
201	$160,000	$130,000	130,000		
202	45,000	23,000	23,000		
Total 201 + 202	$205,000	$153,000		153,000	
Total	$460,000	$403,000	$393,000	$403,000	$403,000

The LCM value for both the category application and the entire inventory application are identical because, in this particular case, market is below cost for both of the categories.

Amount of loss from write-down using individual items:

$$\$460,000 - 393,000 = \textbf{\$67,000}$$

Amount of loss from write-down using categories or the entire inventory:

$$\$460,000 - 403,000 = \textbf{\$57,000}$$

PART
b

INVENTORY ESTIMATION TECHNIQUES

The Southern Wholesale Company distributes approximately 100 products throughout the state of Mississippi. Southern uses a periodic inventory system and takes a physical count of inventory once a year at its fiscal year-end. A recent fire destroyed the entire inventory in one of Southern's warehouses. How can the company determine the dollar amount of inventory destroyed when submitting an insurance claim to obtain reimbursement for the loss?

Home Improvement Stores, Inc., sells over 1,000 different products to customers in each of its 17 retail stores. The company uses a periodic inventory system and takes a physical count of inventory once a year at its fiscal year-end. Home Improvement's bank has asked for monthly financial statements as a condition attached to a recent loan. Can the company avoid the costly procedure of counting inventory at the end of each month to determine ending inventory and cost of goods sold?

These are just two examples of situations when it is either impossible or infeasible to determine the dollar amount of ending inventory by taking a count of the physical quantity of inventory on hand at the end of a period. Fortunately, companies can estimate inventory in these situations by either the gross profit method or the retail inventory method.

The Gross Profit Method

The **gross profit method,** also known as the **gross margin method,** is useful in situations where estimates of inventory are desirable. The technique is valuable in a variety of situations:

1. In determining the cost of inventory that has been lost, destroyed, or stolen.
2. In estimating inventory and cost of goods sold for interim reports, avoiding the expense of a physical inventory count.
3. In auditors' testing of the overall reasonableness of inventory amounts reported by clients.
4. In budgeting and forecasting.

However, the gross profit method provides only an approximation of inventory and is not acceptable according to generally accepted accounting principles for annual financial statements.

The gross profit method is not acceptable for the preparation of annual financial statements.

The technique relies on a relationship you learned in the previous chapter—ending inventory and cost of goods sold always equal the cost of goods available for sale. Even when inventory is unknown, we can estimate it because accounting records usually indicate the cost of goods available for sale (beginning inventory plus net purchases), and the cost of goods sold can be estimated from available information. So by subtracting the cost of goods sold estimate from the cost of goods available for sale, we obtain an estimate of ending inventory. Let's compare that with the way inventory and cost of goods sold normally are determined.

Usually, in a periodic inventory system, ending inventory is known from a physical count and cost of goods sold is *derived* as follows:

Beginning inventory	(from the accounting records)
Plus: Net purchases	(from the accounting records)
Goods available for sale	
Less: Ending inventory	(from a physical count)
Cost of goods sold	

However, when using the gross profit method, the ending inventory is *not* known. Instead, the amount of sales is known—from which we can estimate the cost of goods sold—and ending inventory is the amount calculated.

Beginning inventory	(from the accounting records)
Plus: Net purchases	(from the accounting records)
Goods available for sale	
Less: Cost of goods sold	(estimated)
Ending inventory	(estimated)

So, a first step in estimating inventory is to estimate cost of goods sold. This estimate relies on the historical relationship among (a) net sales, (b) cost of goods sold, and (c) gross profit. Gross profit, you will recall, is simply net sales minus cost of goods sold. So, if we know what net sales are, and if we know what percentage of net sales the gross profit is, we can fairly accurately estimate cost of goods sold. Companies often sell products that have similar gross profit ratios. As a result, accounting records usually provide the information necessary to estimate the cost of ending inventory, even when a physical count is impractical. Let's use the gross profit method to solve the problem of Southern Wholesale Company introduced earlier in the chapter. Suppose the company began 2003 with inventory of $600,000, and on March 17 a warehouse fire destroyed the entire inventory. Company records indicate net purchases of $1,500,000 and net sales of $2,000,000 prior to the fire. The gross profit ratio in each of the previous three years has been very close to 40%. Illustration 9–2 shows how Southern can estimate the cost of the inventory destroyed for its insurance claim.

ILLUSTRATION 9–2	Beginning inventory (from records)	$ 600,000
Gross Profit Method	Plus: Net purchases (from records)	1,500,000
	Goods available for sale	2,100,000
	Less: Cost of goods sold:	
	Net sales	$2,000,000
	Less: Estimated gross profit of 40%	(800,000)
	Estimated cost of goods sold*	(1,200,000)
	Estimated ending inventory	$ 900,000

*Alternatively, cost of goods sold can be calculated as $2,000,000 × (1 − .40) = $1,200,000.

A WORD OF CAUTION

The key to obtaining good estimates is the reliability of the gross profit ratio.

The gross profit method provides only an estimate. The key to obtaining good estimates is the reliability of the gross profit ratio. The ratio usually is estimated from relationships between sales and cost of goods sold. However, the current relationship may differ from the past. In that case, all available information should be used to make necessary adjustments. For example, the company may have made changes in the markup percentage of some of its products. Very often different products have different markups. In these situations, a blanket ratio should not be applied across the board. The accuracy of the estimate can be improved by grouping inventory into pools of products that have similar gross profit relationships rather than using one gross profit ratio for the entire inventory.

The company's cost flow assumption should be implicitly considered when estimating the gross profit ratio. For example, if LIFO is used and the relationship between cost and selling price has changed for recent acquisitions, this would suggest a ratio different from one where the average cost method was used. Another difficulty with the gross profit method is that it does not explicitly consider possible theft or spoilage of inventory. The method assumes that if the inventory was not sold, then it must be on hand at the end of the period. Suspected theft or spoilage would require an adjustment to estimates obtained using the gross profit method.

ADDITIONAL CONSIDERATION

The gross profit ratio is, by definition, a percentage of sales. Sometimes, though, information provided will state the gross profit as a percentage of cost instead. In that case, it will be referred to as the **markup on cost.** For instance, a 66⅔% markup on cost is equivalent to a gross profit ratio of 40%. Here's why:

A gross profit ratio of 40% can be formulated as:

$$\text{Sales} = \text{Cost} + \text{Gross Profit}$$
$$100\% = 60\% + 40\%$$

Now, expressing gross profit as a percentage of cost we get:

$$\text{Gross Profit} \div \text{Cost} = 40\% \div 60\% = 66\tfrac{2}{3}\%$$

As a result, it's necessary to be careful to note which way the percentage is being stated. If stated as a markup on cost, it can be converted to the gross profit ratio, and the gross profit method can be applied the usual way.

CHECK WITH THE **COACH**

Check with the Coach to reinforce your understanding of inventory accounting. Building on Chapter 8, the Coach extends the dollar-value LIFO approach to a context in which you estimate costs based on retail inventory data. A lively illustration by the Coach makes this complex technique a piece of cake. ■

The Retail Inventory Method

The **retail inventory method** is similar to the gross profit method in that it relies on the relationship between cost and selling price to estimate ending inventory and cost of goods sold. As the name implies, the method is used by many retail companies such as Kmart, Dayton Hudson, Wal-Mart, Sears Roebuck, Saks, J.C. Penney, and May Department Stores. Certain retailers like auto dealers and jewelry stores, whose inventory consists of few, high-priced items, can economically use the specific identification inventory method. However, high-volume retailers selling many different items at low unit prices find the retail inventory method ideal, although with the advent of bar coding on more and more retail merchandise, use of the method is declining. Similar to the gross profit method, its principal benefit is that a physical count of inventory is not required to estimate ending inventory and cost of goods sold.

The retail method tends to provide a more accurate estimate than the gross profit method because it's based on the current **cost-to-retail percentage** rather than on a historical gross profit ratio.

The increased reliability in the estimate of the cost percentage is achieved by comparing cost of goods available for sale with goods available for sale *at current selling prices.* So, to use the technique, a company must maintain records of inventory and purchases not only at cost, but also at current selling price. We refer to this as *retail information.* In its simplest form, the retail inventory method estimates the amount of ending inventory (at retail) by subtracting sales (at retail) from goods available for sale (at retail). This estimated ending inventory at retail is then converted to cost by multiplying it by the cost-to-retail percentage. This ratio is found by dividing goods available for sale at *cost* by goods available for sale at *retail.*

Let's use the retail inventory method to solve the problem of the Home Improvement Store introduced earlier in the chapter. Suppose the company's bank has asked for monthly financial statements as a condition attached to a loan dated May 31, 2003. To avoid a physical count of inventory, the company intends to use the retail inventory method to estimate ending inventory and cost of goods sold for the month of June. Using data available in its accounting records, Illustration 9–3 shows how Home Improvement can estimate ending inventory and cost of goods sold for June.

Unlike the gross profit method, the retail inventory method is acceptable for external financial reporting if the results of applying the method are sufficiently close to what would have been achieved using a more rigorous determination of the cost of ending inventory. Also, it's allowed by the Internal Revenue Service as a method that can be used to determine cost of goods sold for income tax purposes.[5] Another advantage of the method is that different cost flow methods can be explicitly incorporated into the estimation technique. In other words, we can modify the application of the method to estimate ending inventory and cost of goods sold to approximate average cost, lower-of-average-cost-or-market (conventional

The retail inventory method uses the cost-to-retail percentage based on a current relationship between cost and selling price.

The retail inventory method can be used for financial reporting and income tax purposes.

---

[5]The retail method is acceptable for external reporting and for tax purposes because it tends to provide a better estimate than the gross profit method. The retail method uses a current cost-to-retail percentage rather than a historical gross profit ratio.

	Cost	Retail
Beginning inventory	$ 60,000	$100,000
Plus: Net purchases	287,200	460,000
Goods available for sale	$347,200	$560,000
Cost-to-retail percentage: $\dfrac{\$347,200}{\$560,000} = 62\%$		
Less: Net sales		(400,000)
Estimated ending inventory at retail		$160,000
Estimated ending inventory at cost (62% × $160,000)	(99,200)	
Estimated cost of goods sold—goods available for sale (at cost) minus ending inventory (at cost) equals cost of goods sold	$248,000	

method) and LIFO. (The FIFO retail method is possible but used less frequently in practice.) We illustrate these variations later in the chapter.

Like the gross profit method, the retail inventory method also can be used to estimate the cost of inventory lost, stolen, or destroyed; for testing the overall reasonableness of physical counts; in budgeting and forecasting as well as in generating information for interim financial statements. Even though the retail method provides fairly accurate estimates, a physical count of inventory usually is performed at least once a year to verify accuracy and detect spoilage, theft, and other irregularities.

RETAIL TERMINOLOGY

Our example above is simplified in that we implicitly assumed that the selling prices of beginning inventory and of merchandise purchased did not change from date of acquisition to the end of the period. This frequently is an unrealistic assumption. The terms in Graphic 9–3 are associated with changing retail prices of merchandise inventory.

Initial markup	Original amount of markup from cost to selling price.
Additional markup	Increase in selling price subsequent to initial markup.
Markup cancellation	Elimination of an additional markup.
Markdown	Reduction in selling price below the original selling price.
Markdown cancellation	Elimination of a markdown.

To illustrate, assume that a product purchased for $6 is initially marked up $4 to $10. This $10 is our original selling price. If the selling price is subsequently increased to $12, the additional markup is $2. If the selling price is then subsequently decreased to $10.50, the markup cancellation is $1.50. We refer to the net effect of the changes ($2.00 − 1.50 = $.50) as the **net markup.**

Now let's say the selling price of the product, purchased for $6 and initially marked up to $10, is decreased to $7. The markdown is $3. If the selling price is later increased to $8, the markdown cancellation is $1. The net effect of the change ($3 − 1 = $2) is the **net markdown.** When applying the retail inventory method, *net markups and net markdowns must be included in the determination of ending inventory at retail.* Graphic 9–4 demonstrates the retail inventory method terminology.

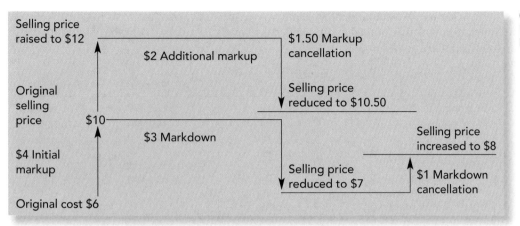

We now continue our illustration of the retail inventory method but expand it to incorporate markups and markdowns as well as to approximate cost by each of the alternative inventory cost flow methods.

COST FLOW METHODS

Let's continue the Home Improvement Stores example into July with Illustration 9–4 and see how the retail inventory method can be used to approximate different cost flow assumptions. We'll also use the same illustration to see how the retail method can be modified to approximate lower of cost or market.

ILLUSTRATION 9–4

The Retail Inventory
Method—Various
Cost Flow Methods

Home Improvement Stores, Inc., uses a periodic inventory system and the retail inventory method to estimate ending inventory and cost of goods sold. The following data are available from the company's records for the month of July 2003:

	Cost	Retail
Beginning inventory	$ 99,200	$160,000
Net purchases	305,280[1]	470,000[2]
Net markups		10,000
Net markdowns		8,000
Net sales		434,000[3]

[1]Purchases at cost less returns, plus freight-in.
[2]Original selling price of purchased goods less returns at retail.
[3]Gross sales less returns.

Approximating Average Cost.

Recall that the average cost method assumes that cost of goods sold and ending inventory each consist of a *mixture* of all the goods available for sale. So when we use the retail method to approximate average cost, the cost-to-retail percentage should be based on the weighted averages of the costs and retail amounts for *all* goods available for sale. This is achieved by calculating the cost-to-retail percentage by dividing the total cost of goods available for sale by total goods available for sale at retail. When this average percentage is applied to ending inventory at retail, we get an estimate of ending inventory at average cost. If you look back to our simplified example for the month of June, you'll notice that we used this approach there. So, our ending inventory and cost of goods sold estimates for June were estimates of average cost.[6]

To approximate average cost, the cost-to-retail percentage is determined for *all* goods available for sale.

---

[6]We also implicitly assumed no net markups or markdowns.

Now, we use the retail inventory method to approximate average costs for July. Notice in Illustration 9–5 that both markups and markdowns are included in the determination of goods available for sale at retail.

ILLUSTRATION 9–5

Retail Method—
Average Cost

	Cost	Retail
Beginning inventory	$ 99,200	$160,000
Plus: Net purchases	305,280	470,000
Net markups		10,000
Less: Net markdowns		(8,000)
Goods available for sale	404,480	632,000
Cost-to-retail percentage: $\frac{\$404,480}{\$632,000} = 64\%$		
Less: Net sales		(434,000)
Estimated ending inventory at retail		$198,000
Estimated ending inventory at cost (64% × $198,000)	(126,720)	
Estimated cost of goods sold	$277,760	

Approximating Average LCM—The Conventional Retail Method. Recall from our discussion earlier in the chapter that, however costs are determined, inventory should be reported in the balance sheet at LCM. Fortunately, we can apply the retail inventory method in such a way that LCM is approximated. This method often is referred to as the **conventional retail method.** We apply the method by *excluding markdowns from the calculation of the cost-to-retail percentage.* Markdowns still are subtracted in the retail column but only *after* the percentage is calculated. To approximate lower of average cost or market, the retail method is modified as shown in Illustration 9–6.

LO4

To approximate LCM, markdowns are not included in the calculation of the cost-to-retail percentage.

ILLUSTRATION 9–6

Retail Method—
Average Cost, LCM

	Cost	Retail
Beginning inventory	$ 99,200	$160,000
Plus: Net purchases	305,280	470,000
Net markups		10,000
		640,000
Cost-to-retail percentage: $\frac{\$404,480}{\$640,000} = 63.2\%$		
Less: Net markdowns		(8,000)
Goods available for sale	404,480	632,000
Less: Net sales		(434,000)
Estimated ending inventory at retail		$198,000
Estimated ending inventory at cost (63.2% × $198,000)	(125,136)	
Estimated cost of goods sold	$279,344	

The logic for using this approximation is that a markdown is evidence of a reduction in the utility of inventory.

Notice that by not subtracting net markdowns from the denominator, the cost-to-retail percentage is lower than it was previously (63.2% versus 64%). This always will be the case when markdowns exist. As a result, the cost approximation of ending inventory always will be less when markdowns exist. To understand why this lower amount approximates LCM, we need to realize that markdowns usually occur when obsolescence, spoilage, overstocking, price declines, or competition has lessened the utility of the merchandise. To recognize this decline in utility in the period it occurs, as LCM does, we exclude net markdowns from the calculation of the cost-to-retail (market) percentage. It should be emphasized that this approach provides only an *approximation* of what ending inventory might be as opposed to applying the LCM rule in the more exact way described earlier in the chapter.

Also notice that the ending inventory at retail is the same using both approaches ($198,000). This will be the case regardless of the cost flow method used because in all approaches this amount reflects the ending inventory at current retail prices.

The LCM variation also could be applied to the FIFO method, but it is not generally used in combination with LIFO. This does not mean that a company using LIFO ignores the LCM rule. Any obsolete or slow-moving inventory that has not been marked down by year-end can be written down to market after the estimation of inventory using the retail method. This is usually not a significant problem. If prices are rising, LIFO ending inventory includes old lower priced items whose costs are likely to be lower than current market.

The LIFO Retail Method.   The last-in, first-out (LIFO) method assumes that units sold are those most recently acquired. When there's a net increase in inventory quantity during a period, the use of LIFO results in ending inventory that includes the beginning inventory as well as one or more additional layers added during the period. When there's a net decrease in inventory quantity, LIFO layer(s) are liquidated. In applying LIFO to the retail method in the simplest way, we assume that the retail prices of goods remained stable during the period. This assumption, which is relaxed later in the chapter, allows us to look at the beginning and ending inventory in dollars to determine if inventory quantity has increased or decreased.

We'll use the numbers from our previous example to illustrate using the retail method to approximate LIFO so we can compare the results with those of the conventional retail method. Recall that beginning inventory at retail is $160,000 and ending inventory at retail is 198,000. If we assume stable retail prices, inventory quantity must have increased during the year. This means ending inventory includes the beginning inventory layer of $160,000 ($99,200 at cost) as well as some additional merchandise purchased during the period. To estimate total ending inventory at LIFO cost, we also need to determine the inventory layer added during the period. When using the LIFO retail method, we assume no more than one inventory layer is added per year if inventory increases.[7] Each layer will carry its own cost-to-retail percentage.

> If inventory at retail increases during the year, a new layer is added.

Illustration 9–7 shows how Home Improvement Stores would estimate total ending inventory and cost of goods sold for the period using the LIFO retail method. The beginning inventory layer carries a cost-to-retail percentage of 62% ($99,200 ÷ $160,000). The layer of inventory added during the period is $38,000 at retail, which is determined by subtracting beginning inventory at retail from ending inventory at retail ($198,000 − 160,000). This layer will be converted to cost by multiplying it by its own cost-to-retail percentage reflecting the *current* period's ratio of cost to retail amounts, in this case 64.68%.

The next period's (August's) beginning inventory will include the two distinct layers (June and July), each of which carries its own unique cost-to-retail percentage. Notice in the illustration that both net markups and net markdowns are included in the calculation of the current period's cost-to-retail percentage.

OTHER ISSUES PERTAINING TO THE RETAIL METHOD

To focus on the key elements of the retail method, we've so far ignored some of the details of the retail process. Fundamental elements such as returns and allowances, discounts, freight, spoilage, and shortages can complicate the retail method.

Recall that net purchases is found by adding freight-in to purchases and subtracting both purchase returns and purchase discounts. When these components are considered separately in the retail method, purchase returns are deducted from purchases on both the cost and retail side (at different amounts) and freight-in is added only to the cost side in determining net

---

[7]Of course, any number of layers at different costs can actually be added through the years. When using the regular LIFO method, rather than LIFO retail, we would keep track of each of those layers.

		Cost	Retail
ILLUSTRATION 9–7	Beginning inventory	$ 99,200	$160,000
LIFO Retail Method	Plus: Net purchases	305,280	470,000
	Net markups		10,000
Beginning inventory is excluded from the calculation of the cost-to-retail percentage.	Less: Net markdowns		(8,000)
	Goods available for sale (excluding beginning inventory)	305,280	472,000
	Goods available for sale (including beginning inventory)	404,480	632,000

July cost-to-retail percentage: $\dfrac{\$305,280}{\$472,000} = \underline{64.68\%}$

		Cost	Retail
	Less: Net sales		(434,000)
	Estimated ending inventory at retail		$198,000

Estimated ending inventory at cost:

	Retail			Cost	
Each layer has its own cost-to-retail percentage.	Beginning inventory	$160,000 × 62.00%*	=	$ 99,200	
	Current period's layer	38,000 × 64.68%	=	24,578	
	Total	$198,000		$123,778	(123,778)
	Estimated cost of goods sold				$280,702

*$99,200 ÷ $160,000 = 62%

purchases. If the gross method is used to record purchases, purchase discounts taken also are deducted in determining the cost of net purchases.

If sales are recorded net of employee discounts, the discounts are added to sales.

Likewise, net sales is found by subtracting sales returns from sales. However, sales discounts are *not* subtracted because to do so would cause the inventory to be overstated. Sales discounts do not represent an adjustment in selling price but a financial incentive for customers to pay early. On the other hand, when sales are recorded net of employee discounts, the discounts are *added* to net sales before sales are deducted in the retail column.

For example, suppose an item of merchandise purchased for $6 is initially marked up to $10. Original selling price is therefore $10. When the item is sold, we deduct sales of $10 from the retail column. But if the item is sold to an employee for $7 (a $3 employee discount) and recorded as a $7 sale, the $3 employee discount must be added back to sales so the full $10 is deducted from goods available at retail to arrive at ending inventory at retail.

We also need to consider spoilage, breakage, and theft. So far we've assumed that by subtracting goods sold from goods available for sale, we find ending inventory. It's possible, though, that some of the goods available for sale were lost to such shortages and therefore do not remain in ending inventory.

Normal shortages are deducted in the retail column *after* the calculation of the cost-to-retail percentage.

To take these shortages into account when using the retail method, we deduct the retail value of inventory lost due to spoilage, breakage, or theft in the retail column. These losses are expected for most retail ventures so they are referred to as *normal shortages* (spoilage, breakage, etc.), and are deducted in the retail column *after* the calculation of the cost-to-retail percentage. Because these losses are anticipated, they are included implicitly in the determination of selling prices. Including normal spoilage in the calculation of the percentage would distort the normal relationship between cost and retail. *Abnormal shortages* should be deducted in the retail column *before* the calculation of the cost-to-retail percentage. These losses are not anticipated and are not included in the determination of selling prices.

Abnormal shortages are deducted in the retail column *before* the calculation of the cost-to-retail percentage.

We recap the treatment of special elements in the application of the retail method in Graphic 9–5 and illustrate the use of some of them in the concept review exercise that follows.

GRAPHIC 9–5 Recap of Other Retail Method Elements

Element	Treatment
Before calculating the cost-to-retail percentage:	
Freight-in	*Added* in the cost column.
Purchase returns	*Deducted* in both the cost and retail columns.
Purchase discounts taken (if gross method used to record purchases)	*Deducted* in the cost column.
Abnormal shortages (spoilage, breakage, theft)	*Deducted* in the retail column.
After calculating the cost-to-retail percentage:	
Normal shortages (spoilage, breakage, theft)	*Deducted* in the retail column.
Employee discounts (if sales recorded net of discounts)	*Added* to net sales.

CONCEPT REVIEW EXERCISE

Retail Inventory Method

The Henderson Company uses the retail inventory method to estimate ending inventory and cost of goods sold. The following data for 2003 is available in Henderson's accounting records:

	Cost	Retail
Beginning inventory	$ 8,000	$12,000
Purchases	68,000	98,000
Freight-in	3,200	
Purchase returns	3,000	4,200
Net markups		6,000
Net markdowns		2,400
Normal spoilage		1,800
Net sales		92,000

The company records sales net of employee discounts. These discounts for 2003 totaled $2,300.

Required:
1. Estimate Henderson's ending inventory and cost of goods sold for the year using the average cost method.
2. Estimate Henderson's ending inventory and cost of goods sold for the year using the conventional retail method (LCM, average cost).
3. Estimate Henderson's ending inventory and cost of goods sold for the year using the LIFO retail method.

1. Estimate Henderson's ending inventory and cost of goods sold for the year using the average cost method.

SOLUTION

	Cost	Retail
Beginning inventory	$ 8,000	$ 12,000
Plus: Purchases	68,000	98,000
Freight-in	3,200	
Less: Purchase returns	(3,000)	(4,200)
Plus: Net markups		6,000
Less: Net markdowns		(2,400)
Goods available for sale	$76,200	$109,400

Cost-to-retail percentage: $\dfrac{\$76,200}{\$109,400} = \underline{\underline{69.65\%}}$

		Cost	Retail
Less: Normal spoilage			(1,800)
Sales:			
Net sales	$92,000		
Add back employee discounts	2,300		(94,300)
Estimated ending inventory at retail			$ 13,300
Estimated ending inventory at cost (69.65% × $13,300)		(9,263)	
Estimated cost of goods sold		$66,937	

2. Estimate Henderson's ending inventory and cost of goods sold for the year using the conventional retail method (LCM, average cost).

		Cost	Retail
Beginning inventory		$ 8,000	$ 12,000
Plus: Purchases		68,000	98,000
Freight-in		3,200	
Less: Purchase returns		(3,000)	(4,200)
Plus: Net markups			6,000
			111,800

Cost-to-retail percentage: $\dfrac{\$76,200}{\$111,800} = 68.16\%$

		Cost	Retail
Less: Net markdowns			(2,400)
Goods available for sale		76,200	109,400
Less: Normal spoilage			(1,800)
Sales:			
Net sales	$92,000		
Add back employee discounts	2,300		(94,300)
Estimated ending inventory at retail			$ 13,300
Estimated ending inventory at cost (68.16% × $13,300)		(9,065)	
Estimated cost of goods sold		$67,135	

3. Estimate Henderson's ending inventory and cost of goods sold for the year using the LIFO retail method.

		Cost	Retail
Beginning inventory		$ 8,000	$ 12,000
Plus: Purchases		68,000	98,000
Freight-in		3,200	
Less: Purchase returns		(3,000)	(4,200)
Plus: Net markups			6,000
Less: Net markdowns			(2,400)
Goods available for sale (excluding beginning inventory)		68,200	97,400
Goods available for sale (including beginning inventory)		76,200	109,400

Cost-to-retail percentage: $\dfrac{\$68,200}{\$97,400} = 70.02\%$

		Cost	Retail
Less: Normal spoilage			(1,800)
Sales:			
Net sales	$92,000		
Add back employee discounts	2,300		(94,300)
Estimated ending inventory at retail			$ 13,300

Estimated ending inventory at cost:

	Retail			Cost	
Beginning inventory	$12,000	× 66.67%* =	$8,000		
Current period's layer	1,300	× 70.02% =	910		
Total	$13,300		$8,910	(8,910)	
Estimated cost of goods sold				$67,290	

*$8,000 ÷ $12,000 = 66.67%

DOLLAR-VALUE LIFO RETAIL

PART

LO5

In our earlier illustration of the LIFO retail method, we assumed that the retail prices of the inventory remained stable during the period. If you recall, we compared the ending inventory (at retail) with the beginning inventory (at retail) to see if inventory had increased. If the dollar amount of ending inventory exceeded the beginning amount, we assumed a new LIFO layer had been added. But this isn't necessarily true. It may be that the dollar amount of ending inventory exceeded the beginning amount simply because prices increased, without an actual change in the quantity of goods. So, to see if there's been a "real" increase in quantity, we need a way to eliminate the effect of any price changes before we compare the ending inventory with the beginning inventory. Fortunately, we can accomplish this by combining two methods we've already discussed—the LIFO retail method (Part b of this chapter) and dollar-value LIFO (previous chapter). The combination is called the **dollar-value LIFO retail method.**

To illustrate, we return to the Home Improvement Stores situation (Illustration 9–7) in which we applied LIFO retail. We keep the same inventory data, but change the illustration from the month of July to the fiscal year 2003. This allows us to build into Illustration 9–7A a significant change in retail prices over the year of 10% (an increase in the retail price index from 1 to 1.10). We follow the LIFO retail procedure up to the point of comparing the ending inventory with the beginning inventory. However, because prices have risen, the apparent increase in inventory is only partly due to an additional layer of inventory and partly due to the increase in retail prices. The real increase is found by deflating the ending inventory amount to beginning of the year prices before comparing beginning and ending amounts. We did this with the dollar-value LIFO technique discussed in the previous chapter.[8]

FINANCIAL REPORTING CASE

Q2, p. 413

Using the retail method to approximate LIFO is referred to as the *dollar-value LIFO retail method.*

	Cost	Retail
Beginning inventory	$ 99,200	$160,000
Plus: Net purchases	305,280	470,000
Net markups		10,000
Less: Net markdowns		(8,000)
Goods available for sale (excluding beginning inventory)	305,280	472,000
Goods available for sale (including beginning inventory)	404,480	632,000
Base layer cost-to-retail percentage: $\frac{\$99,200}{\$160,000} = 62\%$		
2003 layer cost-to-retail percentage: $\frac{\$305,280}{\$472,000} = 64.68\%$		
Less: Net sales		(434,000)
Ending inventory at current year retail prices		$198,000
Estimated ending inventory at cost (calculated below)	(113,430)	
Estimated cost of goods sold	$291,050	

ILLUSTRATION 9–7A

The Dollar-Value LIFO Retail Method

Ending Inventory at Year-end Retail Prices	Step 1 Ending Inventory at Base Year Retail Prices	Step 2 Inventory Layers at Base Year Retail Prices	Step 3 Inventory Layers Converted to Cost
$198,000 (determined above)	$\frac{\$198,000}{1.10} = \$180,000$ → $180,000		
		160,000 (base) × 1.00 × .62	= $ 99,200
		$ 20,000 (2003) × 1.10 × .6468	= 14,230
Total ending inventory at dollar-value LIFO retail cost			$113,430

Base year retail amounts are converted to layer year retail and then to cost.

---

[8]The index used here is analogous to the cost index used in regular DVL except that it reflects the change in retail prices rather than in acquisition costs.

Each layer year carries
its unique retail price
index and its unique
cost-to-retail
percentage.

In this illustration, a $20,000 year 2003 layer is added to the base layer. Two adjustments are needed to convert this amount to LIFO cost. Multiplying by the 2003 price index (1.10) converts it from its base year retail to 2003 retail. Multiplying by the 2003 cost-to-retail percentage (.6468) converts it from its 2003 retail to 2003 cost. The two steps are combined in our illustration. The base year inventory also is converted to cost. The two layers are added to derive ending inventory at dollar-value LIFO retail cost.

When additional layers are added in subsequent years, their LIFO amounts are determined the same way. For illustration, let's assume ending inventory in 2004 is $226,200 at current retail prices and the price level has risen to 1.16. Also assume that the cost-to-retail percentage for 2004 net purchases is 63%. In Illustration 9–7B, the ending inventory is converted to base year retail (step 1). This amount is apportioned into layers, each at base year retail (step 2). Layers then are converted to layer year costs (step 3).

ILLUSTRATION 9–7B		Step 1	Step 2	Step 3
The Dollar-Value LIFO Retail Inventory Method	Ending Inventory at Year-End Retail Prices	Ending Inventory at Base Year Retail Prices	Inventory Layers at Base Year Retail Prices	Inventory Layers Converted to LIFO Cost
	$226,200 (assumed) →	$\frac{\$226,200}{1.16}$ = $195,000 →	$195,000	
Base year retail amounts are converted to layer year retail and then to cost.			160,000 (base) × 1.00 × .62 =	$ 99,200
			20,000 (2003) × 1.10 × .6468 =	14,230
			$ 15,000 (2004) × 1.16 × .63 =	10,962
	Total ending inventory at dollar-value LIFO retail cost			$124,392

Now, let's assume that ending inventory in 2004 is $204,160 at current retail prices (instead of $226,200) and the price level has risen to 1.16. Also assume that the cost-to-retail percentage for 2004 net purchases is 63%. Step 1 converts the ending inventory to a base year price of $176,000 ($204,160 ÷ 1.16). A comparison to the beginning inventory at base year prices of $180,000 ($160,000 base year layer + $20,000 2003 layer) indicates that inventory *decreased* during 2004. In this case, no 2004 layer is added and 2004 ending inventory at dollar-value LIFO retail of $110,584 is determined in Illustration 9–7C.

ILLUSTRATION 9–7C		Step 1	Step 2	Step 3
The Dollar-Value LIFO Retail Inventory Method	Ending Inventory at Year-End Retail Prices	Ending Inventory at Base Year Retail Prices	Inventory Layers at Base Year Retail Prices	Inventory Layers Converted to LIFO Cost
	$204,160 (assumed) →	$\frac{\$204,160}{1.16}$ = $176,000 →	$176,000	
			160,000 (base) × 1.00 × .62 =	$ 99,200
			16,000 (2003) × 1.10 × .6468 =	11,384
	Total ending inventory at dollar-value LIFO retail cost			$110,584

A portion of the 2003 inventory layer has been liquidated—reduced from $20,000 to $16,000 at base year prices—to reduce total inventory at base year prices to $176,000.

As we mentioned earlier in this section, many high-volume retailers selling many different items use the retail method. J.C. Penney Company, Inc., for example, uses the dollar-value LIFO variation of the retail method. Graphic 9–6 shows the inventory disclosure note included in the company's recent financial statements.

GRAPHIC 9–6
Disclosure of Inventory
Method—J.C. Penney
Company, Inc.

Summary of Significant Accounting Policies (in part)
Merchandise Inventories
Substantially all merchandise inventory is valued at the lower of cost (using the last-in, first-out, or "LIFO," method) or market, determined by the retail method. The Company determines the lower of cost or market on an aggregated basis for similar types of merchandise. To estimate the effects of inflation on inventories, the Company utilizes internally developed price indices.

Notice that J.C. Penney uses internally developed indices to adjust for changing prices and that the lower of cost or market rule is applied to logical ("similar") categories of inventory.

CONCEPT **REVIEW** EXERCISE

Dollar-Value LIFO Retail Method

On January 1, 2003, the Nicholson Department Store adopted the dollar-value LIFO retail inventory method. Inventory transactions at both cost and retail and cost indexes for 2003 and 2004 are as follows:

	2003		2004	
	Cost	Retail	Cost	Retail
January 1, 2003	$16,000	$24,000		
Net purchases	42,000	58,500	45,000	58,700
Net markups		3,000		2,400
Net markdowns		1,500		1,100
Net sales		56,000		57,000
Price index:				
January 1, 2003	1.00			
December 31, 2003	1.08			
December 31, 2004	1.15			

Required:
Estimate the 2003 and 2004 ending inventory and cost of goods sold using the dollar-value LIFO retail inventory method.

SOLUTION

	2003		2004	
	Cost	Retail	Cost	Retail
Beginning inventory	$16,000	$24,000	$17,456	$28,000
Plus: Net purchases	42,000	58,500	45,000	58,700
Net markups		3,000		2,400
Less: Net markdowns		(1,500)		(1,100)
Goods available for sale (excluding beg. inv.)	42,000	60,000	45,000	60,000
Goods available for sale (including beg. inv.)	58,000	84,000	62,456	88,000

Base layer
Cost-to-retail percentage: $\dfrac{\$16,000}{\$24,000} = 66.67\%$

2003
Cost-to-retail percentage: $\dfrac{\$42,000}{\$60,000} = 70\%$

2004
Cost-to-retail percentage: $\dfrac{\$45,000}{\$60,000} = 75\%$

	2003		2004	
Less: Net sales		(56,000)		(57,000)
Estimated ending inv. at current year retail prices		$28,000		$31,000
Less: Estimated ending inventory at cost (below)	(17,456)		(18,345)	
Estimated cost of goods sold	$40,544		$44,111	

2003

Ending Inventory at Year-End Retail Prices	Step 1 Ending Inventory at Base Year Retail Prices	Step 2 Inventory Layers at Base Year Retail Prices	Step 3 Inventory Layers Converted to Cost
$28,000 (above)	$\dfrac{\$28,000}{1.08} = \$25,926$	$24,000 \text{ (base)} \times 1.00 \times 66.67\% =$ $1,926 \text{ (2003)} \times 1.08 \times 70.00\% =$	$16,000 1,456
Total ending inventory at dollar-value LIFO retail cost			$17,456

2004

Ending Inventory at Year-End Retail Prices	Step 1 Ending Inventory at Base Year Retail Prices	Step 2 Inventory Layers at Base Year Retail Prices	Step 3 Inventory Layers Converted to Cost
$31,000 (above)	$\dfrac{\$31,000}{1.15} = \$26,957$	$24,000 \text{ (base)} \times 1.00 \times 66.67\% =$ $1,926 \text{ (2003)} \times 1.08 \times 70.00\% =$ $1,031 \text{ (2004)} \times 1.15 \times 75.00\% =$	$16,000 1,456 889
Total ending inventory at dollar-value LIFO retail cost			$18,345

CHANGE IN INVENTORY METHOD AND INVENTORY ERRORS

PART

LO6

Change in Accounting Principle

Accounting principles should be applied consistently from period to period to allow for comparability of operating results. However, changes within a company as well as changes in the external economic environment may require a company to change an accounting method. As we mentioned in Chapter 8, high inflation in the 1970s motivated many companies to switch to the LIFO inventory method.

Specific accounting treatment and disclosures are prescribed for companies that change accounting principles. Chapter 4 introduced the subject of accounting changes and Chapter 21 provides in-depth coverage of the topic. Here we provide an overview of how changes in inventory methods are reported.

CHANGES NOT INVOLVING LIFO

For changes not involving LIFO, the cumulative after-tax effect on prior years' income is reported as a separate item of income.

For most accounting changes, the effect of the change is accounted for by reporting it in the income statement in the year of change rather than by restating prior years' financial statements to the new method. Changes in inventory method that don't involve LIFO are treated this way. The amount reported is the cumulative effect of the change, which is the difference between retained earnings at the beginning of the year of the change as reported and the beginning of year retained earnings that would have resulted if the new accounting method had been used in all prior years. The cumulative after-tax effect is reported in the income statement immediately below any discontinued operations and extraordinary items. Consider Illustration 9–8.

The effect of the change on certain key income numbers is disclosed for all periods reported.

Previous financial statements are not restated. However, the effect of the change on certain key income numbers is disclosed on a pro forma (as if) basis for financial statements of all prior periods that are included for comparison purposes with the current financial statements. Specifically, income statements should include pro forma restatement of (a) income before extraordinary items, (b) net income, and (c) earnings per share for both income amounts. In addition, a disclosure note describes the change and justification for the change along with the effect of the change on the current year's income numbers. The pro forma information allows for a comparison of current and prior years' operating results using the new

In early 2003, the Xavier Company changed its method of valuing inventory from the average cost method to the FIFO cost method. At December 31, 2002, and December 31, 2001, Xavier's inventories were $46 million and $43 million, respectively. Xavier's records indicated that inventories would have totaled $58 million at December 31, 2002, and $50 million at December 31, 2001, if FIFO had been used. Xavier's financial statements include the current year and one prior year for comparative purposes.

For inventory to reflect the FIFO cost method, its balance must be increased by $12 million (from $46 million to $58 million). Prior years' cost of goods sold would have been lower and income before income tax higher by $12 million if FIFO had been used. Of course, income tax expense also would have been higher. With a 40% tax rate, the after-tax effect would be $7.2 million. The cumulative effect reported in the 2003 income statement is the net of tax effect on prior years' income. The change is reported in Xavier's income statement as follows:

	($ in millions) 2003
Income before extraordinary item and accounting change	$xxx
Extraordinary gain (loss), net of tax	xx
Cumulative effect of accounting change (net of $4.8 tax)	7.2
Net income	$xxx

ILLUSTRATION 9–8

Change in Inventory Method

method. The disclosure note information indicates the effect of the change on the current year's income numbers permitting the same comparison using the old method.

For changes that involve LIFO, reporting requirements are different from the usual way changes in accounting principles are reported. As we see next, accounting treatment depends on whether the change is *to* LIFO or *from* LIFO.

CHANGE TO THE LIFO METHOD

When a company changes to the LIFO inventory method from any other method, it usually is impossible to calculate the cumulative effect. To do so would require assumptions as to when specific LIFO inventory layers were created in years prior to the change. As a result, a company changing to LIFO does not report the cumulative income effect. Instead, the LIFO method simply is used from that point on. The base year inventory for all future LIFO determinations is the beginning inventory in the year the LIFO method is adopted.[9]

A disclosure note is needed to explain (a) the nature of and justification for the change, (b) the effect of the change on current year's income and earnings per share, and (c) why the cumulative income effect was omitted. When General Cable Corporation adopted the LIFO inventory method, it reported the change in the note shown in Graphic 9–7.

> Accounting records usually are inadequate for a company changing *to* LIFO to report the cumulative income effect.

GRAPHIC 9–7

Change in Inventory Method Disclosure— General Cable Corporation

Inventories (in part)
As of January 1, 2000, General Cable changed its accounting method for its North American non-metal inventories from the FIFO method to the LIFO method. The impact of the change was an increase in operating income of $6.4 million, or $0.12 of earnings per share on both a basic and diluted basis during the year. The cumulative effect of the change on prior years was not determinable. The Company believes that the change to the LIFO accounting method for its North American non-metal inventories more accurately reflects the impact of both volatile raw material prices and ongoing cost productivity initiatives, conforms the accounting for all North American inventories and provides a more comparable basis of accounting with direct competitors in North America who are on LIFO for the majority of their inventories.

---

[9]A change to LIFO is handled the same way for income tax purposes.

As we discussed in Chapter 8, an important motivation for using LIFO in periods of rising costs is that it produces higher cost of goods sold and lowers income and income taxes. Notice in the disclosure note that the switch to LIFO caused an *increase* in income in the year of the switch indicating an environment of decreasing costs. General Cable had reasons other than an immediate reduction in its tax bill for switching to LIFO.

Recall from Chapter 8 that inflation was extremely high in 1974 causing hundreds of companies to switch to LIFO. These companies were likely motivated by the opportunity to lower their income taxes. Graphic 9–8 lists the earnings per share (EPS) effect of the switch from FIFO to LIFO for just a few of the hundreds of companies that switched to LIFO in 1974.

GRAPHIC 9–8
Income Effect of
Change to LIFO—1974
Examples

Company	FIFO EPS	LIFO EPS	% Effect of the Switch
DuPont	$6.27	$5.10	−18.7
Eastman Kodak	1.68	1.54	− 8.3
Firestone Tire	2.40	1.53	−36.2
Florida Steel	4.61	3.96	−14.1
Marathon Oil	4.84	4.32	−10.7
Std. Oil of Ohio	2.27	2.02	−11.0
Stokely Van Camp	3.69	2.70	−26.8

CHANGE FROM THE LIFO METHOD

Because of their unique nature, some changes in accounting principle are accounted for by restating prior years' financial statements for the income effect of the change, rather than by reporting that effect as part of net income in the year the change occurs. Usually the effect of these changes is quite large. If the total effect is recognized currently, net income would be distorted in the year of the change. Also, previous financial statements would lose meaning if not restated for such large changes.

A change *from* the
LIFO method to
another inventory
method is a change in
accounting principle
requiring retroactive
restatement.

A change from the LIFO inventory method to any other inventory method is one of these changes in accounting principle that is accounted for retroactively. We *restate* financial statements for each year reported for comparative purposes to reflect the use of the new method. Each financial statement is thereby presented on a comparable basis. Also, a description of the change and justification for the change, along with the effect of the change on income for all years presented, should be provided in the disclosure notes to the financial statements.

As an example, in 2000, Varian, Inc., a major supplier of scientific instruments, changed its inventory method for certain inventories from LIFO to average cost. Graphic 9–9 shows the disclosure note that described the change.

ADDITIONAL CONSIDERATION

When changing from one generally accepted accounting principle to another, a company must justify that the change results in financial information that more properly portrays operating results and financial position. For income tax purposes, a company generally must obtain consent from the Internal Revenue Service before changing an accounting method. A special form also must be filed with the IRS when a company intends to adopt the LIFO inventory method. When a company changes from LIFO for tax purposes, it can't change back to LIFO until five tax returns have been filed using the non-LIFO method.

Note 4. Change in Method of Accounting for Inventory

The Company has accounted for all inventories using the average cost method beginning July 1, 2000, whereas in all prior years, certain inventories maintained in the U.S. were valued using the last-in, first-out (LIFO) method. The new method of accounting for inventory was adopted because the Company believes the average cost method of accounting for inventory will result in more consistent matching of product costs with revenues. The financial statements of prior years have been restated to apply the new method retroactively, and accordingly, retained earnings as of September 26, 1997, has been increased by $9.3 million to reflect the restatement. The effect of the accounting change on net income and earnings per share as previously reported for the fiscal years ended October 1, 1999, and October 2, 1998, is as follows (in thousands, except per share amounts):

	1999	1998
Net income:		
As previously reported	$7,328	$23,428
Effect of change in accounting for inventories	251	(179)
As adjusted	$7,579	$23,249

	1999	1998
Basic earnings per share:		
As previously reported	$0.24	$0.77
Effect of change in accounting for inventories	0.01	(0.01)
As adjusted	$0.25	$0.76

	1999	1998
Diluted earnings per share:		
As previously reported	$0.24	$0.77
Effect of change in accounting for inventories	—	(0.01)
As adjusted	$0.24	$0.76

GRAPHIC 9–9
Disclosure of Change in Inventory Method—Varian, Inc.

Inventory Errors

Accounting errors must be corrected when they are discovered. In Chapter 4 we briefly discussed the correction of accounting errors and Chapter 21 provides in-depth coverage. Here we provide an overview of the accounting treatment and disclosures in the context of inventory errors. Inventory errors include the over- or understatement of ending inventory due to a mistake in physical count or a mistake in pricing inventory quantities. Also, errors include the over- or understatement of purchases which could be caused by the cutoff errors described in Chapter 8.

 LO7

If an inventory error is discovered in the same accounting period it occurred, the original erroneous entry should simply be reversed and the appropriate entry recorded. This situation presents no particular reporting problem.

If a *material* inventory error is discovered in an accounting period subsequent to the period in which the error was made, any previous years' financial statements that were incorrect as a result of the error are retroactively restated to reflect the correction.[10] And, of course, any account balances that are incorrect as a result of the error are corrected by journal entry. If, due to an error affecting net income, retained earnings is one of the incorrect

Previous years' financial statements are retroactively restated.

Incorrect balances are corrected.

---

[10]If the effect of the error is not material, it is simply corrected in the year of discovery.

A correction of retained earnings is reported as a prior period adjustment.

A disclosure note describes the nature and the impact of the error.

accounts, the correction is reported as a prior period adjustment to the beginning balance on the statement of shareholders' equity.[11] In addition, a disclosure note is needed to describe the nature of the error and the impact of its correction on net income, income before extraordinary items, and earnings per share.

When analyzing inventory errors, it's helpful to visualize the way cost of goods sold, net income, and retained earnings are determined (see Graphic 9–10). Beginning inventory and net purchases are *added* in the calculation of cost of goods sold. If either of these is overstated (understated) then cost of goods sold would be overstated (understated). On the other hand, ending inventory is *deducted* in the calculation of cost of goods sold, so if ending inventory is overstated (understated) then cost of goods sold is understated (overstated). Of course, errors that affect income also will affect income taxes. In the illustration that follows, we ignore the tax effects of the errors and focus on the errors themselves rather than their tax aspects.

GRAPHIC 9–10
Visualizing the Effect of Inventory Errors

Beginning inventory
Plus: Net purchases
Less: Ending inventory   Revenues
Cost of goods sold ─────▶ Less: Cost of goods sold
                                Less: Other expenses   Beginning retained earnings
                                Net income ─────▶ Plus: Net income
                                                 Less: Dividends

                                                 Ending retained earnings

Let's look at an example in Illustration 9–9.

ILLUSTRATION 9–9

Inventory Error Correction

The Barton Company uses a periodic inventory system. At the end of 2002, a mathematical error caused an $800,000 overstatement of ending inventory. Ending inventories for 2003 and 2004 are correctly determined.

The way we correct this error depends on when the error is discovered. Assuming that the error is not discovered until after 2003, the 2002 and 2003 effects of the error, ignoring income tax effects, are shown below. The overstated and understated amounts are $800,000 in each instance.

Analysis: U = Understated   O = Overstated

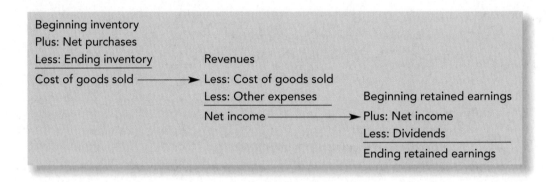

2002		2003	
Beginning inventory		Beginning inventory	O
Plus: Net purchases		Plus: Net purchases	
Less: Ending inventory	O	Less: Ending inventory	
Cost of goods sold	U	Cost of goods sold	O
Revenues		Revenues	
Less: Cost of goods sold	U	Less: Cost of goods sold	O
Less: Other expenses		Less: Other expenses	
Net income	O	Net income	U
↓		↓	
Retained earnings	O	Retained earnings	*corrected*

---

[11]The prior period adjustment is applied to beginning retained earnings for the year following the error, or for the earliest year being reported in the comparative financial statements when the error occurs prior to the earliest year presented. The retained earnings balances in years after the first year also are adjusted to what those balances would be if the error had not occurred, but a company may choose not to explicitly report those adjustments as separate line items.

WHEN THE INVENTORY ERROR IS DISCOVERED THE FOLLOWING YEAR

First, let's assume the error is discovered in 2003. The 2002 financial statements that were incorrect as a result of the error are retroactively restated to reflect the correct inventory amount, cost of goods sold, net income, and retained earnings when those statements are reported again for comparative purposes in the 2003 annual report. The following journal entry, ignoring income taxes, corrects the error.

Previous years' financial statements are retroactively restated.

Retained earnings	800,000	
Inventory		800,000

A journal entry corrects any incorrect account balance.

Because retained earnings is one of the accounts that is incorrect, when the error is discovered in 2003, the correction to that account is reported as a prior period adjustment to the 2003 beginning retained earnings balance in Barton's statement of shareholders' equity (or statement of retained earnings). Prior period adjustments do not flow through the income statement but directly adjust retained earnings. This adjustment is illustrated in Chapter 21.

When retained earnings requires correction, a prior period adjustment is made on the statement of shareholders' equity.

WHEN THE INVENTORY ERROR IS DISCOVERED SUBSEQUENT TO THE FOLLOWING YEAR

If the error isn't discovered until 2004, the 2003 financial statements also are retroactively restated to reflect the correct cost of goods sold and net income even though no correcting entry would be needed at that point. Inventory and retained earnings would not require adjustment. The error has self-corrected and no prior period adjustment is needed.

Also, a disclosure note in Barton's annual report should describe the nature of the error and the impact of its correction on each year's net income (overstated by $800,000 in 2002; understated by $800,000 in 2003), income before extraordinary items (same as net income in this case), and earnings per share.

A disclosure note describes the nature of the error and the impact of the correction on income.

CONCEPT REVIEW EXERCISE

Inventory Errors

In 2003, the controller of the Fleischman Wholesale Beverage Company discovered the following material errors related to the 2001 and 2002 financial statements:

a. Inventory at the end of 2001 was understated by $50,000.
b. Late in 2002, a $3,000 purchase was incorrectly recorded as a $33,000 purchase. The invoice has not yet been paid.
c. Inventory at the end of 2002 was overstated by $20,000.

The company uses a periodic inventory system.

Required:
1. Assuming that the errors were discovered after the 2002 financial statements were issued, analyze the effect of the errors on 2001 and 2002 cost of goods sold, net income, and retained earnings. Ignore income taxes.
2. Prepare a journal entry to correct the errors.

SOLUTION

1. **Analysis: U = Understated   O = Overstated**

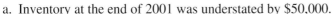

2001		2002	
Beginning inventory		Beginning inventory	U-50,000
Plus: Net purchases		Plus: Net purchases	O-30,000
Less: Ending inventory	U-50,000	Less: Ending inventory	O-20,000
Cost of goods sold	O-50,000	Cost of goods sold	U-40,000
Revenues		Revenues	
Less: Cost of goods sold	O-50,000	Less: Cost of goods sold	U-40,000
Less: Other expenses		Less: Other expenses	
Net income	U-50,000	Net income	O-40,000
↓		↓	
Retained earnings	U-50,000	Retained earnings	U-10,000

2. Prepare a journal entry to correct the errors.

Accounts payable	30,000	
Inventory		20,000
Retained earnings		10,000

Earnings Quality

A change in the accounting method a company uses to value inventory is one way managers can artificially manipulate income. However, this method of income manipulation is transparent. As we learned in a previous section, the effect on income of switching from one inventory method to another must be disclosed. That disclosure restores comparability between periods and enhances earnings quality.

On the other hand, inventory write-downs are included in the broader category of "big bath" accounting techniques some companies use to manipulate earnings. By overstating the write-down, profits are increased in future periods as the inventory is used or sold. When the demand for many high technology products decreased significantly in late 2000 and early 2001, several companies, including Sycamore Networks, Lucent Technologies, and JDS Uniphase, recorded large inventory write-offs, some in the billions of dollars. In the introduction to this chapter, we discussed the over $2 billion inventory write-off recorded by Cisco Systems. Certainly these write-offs reflected the existing economic environment. However, some analysts questioned the size of some of the write-offs. For example, William Schaff, an investment officer at Bay Isle Financial noted that Cisco's write-off was approximately equal to the balance of inventory on hand at the end of the previous quarter and about equal to the cost of goods actually sold during the quarter.

A financial analyst must carefully consider the effect of any significant asset write-down on the assessment of a company's permanent earnings.

> **Inventory write-downs often are cited as a method used to shift income between periods.**

> **WILLIAM SCHAFF—BAY ISLE FINANCIAL**
> I have nothing on which to base these theories other than the fact that writing off a whole quarter's inventory seems a bit much to just shrug off. It's very disturbing.[12]

FINANCIAL REPORTING CASE **SOLUTION**

1. **Sears values its inventory at the lower of cost or market. What does that mean? Under what circumstances might Sears be justified in reporting its inventory at less than cost?** *(p. 413)*   A departure from historical cost is warranted when the probable benefits to be received from any asset drop below the asset's cost. The benefits from inventory result from the ultimate sale of the goods. Deterioration, obsolescence, and changes in price levels are situations that might cause the benefits to be received from sale to drop below cost. The lower-of-cost-or-market approach recognizes losses in the period when the value of the inventory declines below its cost rather than in the period in which the goods ultimately are sold.

2. **How does Sears avoid counting all its inventory every time it produces financial statements? What are internal price indices used for?** *(p. 431)*   Sears uses the dollar-value LIFO retail inventory method. The retail inventory estimation technique avoids the counting of ending inventory by keeping track of goods available for sale not only at cost but also at retail prices. Each period's sales, at sales prices, are deducted from the retail amount of goods available for sale to arrive at ending inventory at retail. This amount is then converted to cost using a cost-to-retail percentage.

---

[12]William Schaff, "What Is the Definition of an Earnings Bath," *Information Week Online*, April 24, 2001.

The dollar-value LIFO retail method uses a price index to first convert ending inventory at retail to base year prices. Yearly LIFO layers are then determined and each layer is converted to that year's current year retail prices using the year's price index and then to cost using the layer's cost-to-retail percentage. For the price index, Sears uses an internally generated index rather than an external price index. ∎

THE BOTTOM LINE

1. Inventory is valued at the lower of cost or market (LCM). The designated market value in the LCM rule is the middle number of replacement cost (RC), net realizable value (NRV), and net realizable value less a normal profit margin (NRV − NP).

2. The gross profit method estimates cost of goods sold which is then subtracted from cost of goods available for sale to estimate ending inventory. The estimate of cost of goods sold is determined by subtracting an estimate of gross profit from net sales. The estimate of gross profit is determined by multiplying the historical gross profit ratio times net sales.

3. The retail inventory method determines the amount of ending inventory at retail by subtracting sales for the period from goods available for sale at retail. Ending inventory at retail is then converted to *cost* by multiplying it by the cost-to-retail percentage, which is based on a current relationship between cost and selling price.

4. By the conventional retail method, we estimate average cost at lower of cost or market. Average cost is estimated by including beginning inventory in the calculation of the cost-to-retail percentage. LCM is estimated by excluding markdowns from the calculation. Markdowns are subtracted in the retail column after the percentage is calculated.

5. By the LIFO retail method, ending inventory includes the beginning inventory plus the current year's layer. To determine layers, we compare ending inventory at retail to beginning inventory at retail and assume that no more than one inventory layer is added if inventory increases. Each layer carries its own cost-to-retail percentage which is used to convert each layer from retail to cost. The dollar-value LIFO retail inventory method combines the LIFO retail method and the dollar-value LIFO method (Chapter 8) to estimate LIFO from retail prices when the price level has changed.

6. When a company changes its inventory method, the accounting treatment depends on whether or not the LIFO method is involved. For changes not involving LIFO, the event is accounted for as a normal change in accounting principle with the cumulative effect of the change reported in the income statement in the year of the change. When a company changes to LIFO, no cumulative effect is reported. A change from the LIFO method is a change in accounting principle requiring retroactive restatement.

7. If a material inventory error is discovered in an accounting period subsequent to the period in which the error is made, previous years' financial statements that were incorrect as a result of the error are retroactively restated to reflect the correction. Account balances are corrected by journal entry. A correction of retained earnings is reported as a prior period adjustment to the beginning balance in the statement of shareholders' equity. In addition, a disclosure note is needed to describe the nature of the error and the impact of its correction on income.

PURCHASE COMMITMENTS

APPENDIX

9

Purchase commitments are contracts that obligate a company to purchase a specified amount of merchandise or raw materials at specified prices on or before specified dates. Companies enter into these agreements to make sure they will be able to obtain important inventory as well as to protect against increases in purchase price. However, if the purchase price decreases before the agreement is exercised, the commitment has the disadvantage of

Purchase commitments protect the buyer against price increases and provide a supply of product.

Purchases made pursuant to a purchase commitment are recorded at the lower of contract price or market price on the date the contract is executed.

requiring the company to purchase inventory at a higher than market price. If this happens, a loss on the purchase commitment is recorded.

Because purchase commitments create the possibility of this kind of loss, the loss occurs when the market price falls below the commitment price rather than when the inventory eventually is sold. This means recording the loss when the product is purchased or, if the commitment is still outstanding, at the end of the reporting period. In other words, purchases are recorded at market price when that price is lower than the contract price, and a loss is recognized for the difference. Also, losses are recognized for any purchase commitments outstanding at the end of a reporting period when market price is less than contract price. In effect, the LCM rule is applied to purchase commitments. This is best understood by the example in Illustration 9A–1.

ILLUSTRATION 9A–1 Purchase Commitments	In July 2003, the Lassiter Company signed two purchase commitments. The first requires Lassiter to purchase inventory for $500,000 by November 15, 2003. The second requires the company to purchase inventory for $600,000 by February 15, 2004. Lassiter's fiscal year-end is December 31. The company uses a perpetual inventory system.

CONTRACT PERIOD WITHIN FISCAL YEAR

The contract period for the first commitment is contained within a single fiscal year. Lassiter would record the purchase at the contract price if the market price at date of acquisition is at least *equal to* the contract price of $500,000.[13]

If market price is equal to or greater than the contract price, the purchase is recorded at the contract price.

Inventory (contract price)	500,000	
Cash (or accounts payable)		500,000

If the market price at acquisition is *less* than the contract price, inventory is recorded at the market price and a loss is recognized.[14] For example, if the market price is $425,000, the following entry records the purchase:

If market price is less than the contract price, the purchase is recorded at the market price.

Inventory (market price)	425,000	
Loss on purchase commitment	75,000	
Cash (or accounts payable)		500,000

The objective of this treatment is to associate the loss with the period in which the price declines rather than with the period in which the company eventually sells the inventory. This is the same objective as the LCM rule you studied in the chapter.

CONTRACT PERIOD EXTENDS BEYOND FISCAL YEAR

Now let's consider Lassiter's second purchase commitment that is outstanding at the end of the fiscal year 2003 (that is, the purchases have not yet been made). If the market price at the end of the year is at least *equal* to the contract price of $600,000, no entry is recorded. However, if the market price at year-end is *less* than the contract price, a loss must be recognized to satisfy the LCM objective of associating the loss with the period in which the price declines rather than with the period in which the company eventually sells the inventory. Let's say the year-end market price of the inventory for Lassiter's second purchase commitment is $540,000. The following adjusting entry is recorded:

---

[13]In each of the following situations, if a periodic inventory system is used *purchases* is debited instead of *inventory*.
[14]Recall from the LCM discussion in the chapter that the preferred method of recording losses from inventory write-downs is to recognize the loss as a separate item in the income statement, rather than as an increase in cost of goods sold.

December 31, 2003

Estimated loss on purchase commitment ($600,000 − 540,000). . . .	60,000	
Estimated liability on purchase commitment		60,000

If the market price at year-end is less than the contract price a loss is recorded for the difference.

At this point, the loss is an *estimated* loss. The actual loss, if any, will not be known until the inventory actually is purchased. The best estimate of the market price on date of purchase is the current market price, in this case $540,000. Because no inventory has been acquired, we can't credit inventory for the LCM loss. Instead, a liability is credited because, in a sense, the loss represents an obligation to the seller of the inventory to purchase inventory above market price.

A liability is credited for estimated losses on purchase commitments.

The entry to record the actual purchase on or before February 15, 2004, will vary depending on the market price of the inventory at date of purchase. If the market price is unchanged or has increased from the year-end price, the following entry is made:

Inventory (accounting cost)	540,000	
Estimated liability on purchase commitment	60,000	
Cash (or accounts payable)		600,000

If market price on purchase date has not declined from year-end price, the purchase is recorded at the year-end market price.

Even if the market price of the inventory increases, there is no recovery of the $60,000 loss recognized in 2003. Remember that when the LCM rule is applied, the reduced inventory value, in this case the reduced value of purchases, is considered to be the new cost and any recovery of value is ignored.

If the market price declines even further from year-end levels, an additional loss is recognized. For example, if the market price of the inventory covered by the commitment declines to $510,000, the following entry is recorded:

Inventory (market price)	510,000	
Loss on purchase commitment ($540,000 − 510,000)	30,000	
Estimated liability on purchase commitment	60,000	
Cash (or accounts payable)		600,000

If market price on purchase date declines from year-end price, the purchase is recorded at the market price.

The total loss on this purchase commitment of $90,000 is thus allocated between 2003 and 2004 according to when the decline in value of the inventory covered by the commitment occurred.

If there are material amounts of purchase commitments outstanding at the end of a reporting period, the contract details are disclosed in a note. This disclosure is required even if no loss estimate has been recorded. ■

QUESTIONS FOR REVIEW OF KEY TOPICS

Q 9–1 Explain the lower-of-cost-or-market approach to valuing inventory.

Q 9–2 What is the meaning of market in the lower-of-cost-or-market rule?

Q 9–3 What are the various ways the LCM determination can be made?

Q 9–4 Describe the preferred method of adjusting from cost to market for material inventory write-downs.

Q 9–5 Explain the gross profit method of estimating ending inventory.

Q 9–6 The Rider Company uses the gross profit method to estimate ending inventory and cost of goods sold. The cost percentage is determined based on historical data. What factors could cause the estimate of ending inventory to be overstated?

Q 9–7 Explain the retail inventory method of estimating ending inventory.

Q 9–8 Both the gross profit method and the retail inventory method provide a way to estimate ending inventory. What is the main difference between the two estimation techniques?

Q 9–9 Define each of the following retail terms: initial markup, additional markup, markup cancellation, markdown, markdown cancellation.

Q 9–10   Explain how to estimate the average cost of inventory when using the retail inventory method.

Q 9–11   What is the conventional retail method?

Q 9–12   Explain the LIFO retail inventory method.

Q 9–13   Discuss the treatment of freight-in, net markups, normal spoilage, and employee discounts in the application of the retail inventory method.

Q 9–14   Explain the difference between the retail inventory method using LIFO and the dollar-value LIFO retail method.

Q 9–15   Describe the accounting treatment of a change in inventory method that does not involve LIFO.

Q 9–16   When a company changes its inventory method to or from LIFO, an exception is made for the way accounting changes usually are reported. Explain the difference in the accounting treatment of a change *to* the LIFO inventory method and a change *from* LIFO.

Q 9–17   Explain the accounting treatment of material inventory errors discovered in an accounting period subsequent to the period in which the error is made.

Q 9–18   It is discovered in 2003 that ending inventory in 2001 was understated. What is the effect of the understatement on the following:

2001:	Cost of goods sold
	Net income
	Ending retained earnings
2002:	Net purchases
	Cost of goods sold
	Net income
	Ending retained earnings

Q 9–19   (Based on Appendix 9) Define purchase commitments. What is the advantage(s) of these agreements to buyers?

Q 9–20   (Based on Appendix 9) Explain how the lower-of-cost-or-market rule is applied to purchase commitments.

EXERCISES

E 9–1
Lower of cost or market

The Herman Company has three products in its ending inventory. Specific per unit data for each of the products is as follows:

	Product 1	Product 2	Product 3
Cost	$20	$ 90	$50
Replacement cost	18	85	40
Selling price	40	150	70
Disposal costs	6	40	10
Normal profit margin	5	30	12

Required:
What unit values should Herman use for each of its products when applying the LCM rule to ending inventory?

E 9–2
Lower of cost or market

The Tatum Company has four products in its inventory. Information about the December 31, 2003, inventory is as follows:

Product	Total Cost	Total Replacement Cost	Total Net Realizable Value
101	$120,000	$110,000	$100,000
102	90,000	85,000	110,000
103	60,000	40,000	50,000
104	30,000	28,000	50,000

The normal gross profit percentage is 25% of *cost*.

Required:
1. Determine the balance sheet inventory carrying value at December 31, 2003, assuming the LCM rule is applied to individual products.
2. Assuming that Tatum recognizes an inventory write-down as a separate income statement item, determine the amount of the loss.

E 9–3
Gross profit method

On September 22, 2003, a flood destroyed the entire merchandise inventory on hand in a warehouse owned by the Rocklin Sporting Goods Company. The following information is available from the records of the company's periodic inventory system:

Inventory, January 1, 2003	$120,000
Net purchases, January 1 through September 22	370,000
Net sales, January 1 through September 22	500,000
Gross profit ratio	20%

Required:
Estimate the cost of inventory destroyed in the flood using the gross profit method.

E 9–4
Gross profit method

On November 21, 2003, a fire at Hodge Company's warehouse caused severe damage to its entire inventory of Product Tex. Hodge estimates that all usable damaged goods can be sold for $10,000. The following information was available from the records of Hodge's periodic inventory system:

Inventory, November 1	$100,000
Net purchases from November 1, to the date of the fire	140,000
Net sales from November 1, to the date of the fire	220,000

Based on recent history, Hodge's gross profit ratio on Product Tex is 30% of net sales.

Required:
Calculate the estimated loss on the inventory from the fire, using the gross profit method.

(AICPA adapted)

E 9–5
Gross profit method

A fire destroyed a warehouse of the Goren Group, Inc., on May 4, 2003. Accounting records on that date indicated the following:

Merchandise inventory, January 1, 2003	$1,800,000
Purchases to date	5,800,000
Freight-in	400,000
Sales to date	9,200,000

The gross profit ratio has averaged 30% of sales for the past four years.

Required:
Use the gross profit method to estimate the cost of the inventory destroyed in the fire.

E 9–6
Gross profit method; solving for unknown cost percentage

The National Distributing Company uses a periodic inventory system to track its merchandise inventory and the gross profit method to estimate ending inventory and cost of goods sold for interim periods. Net purchases for the month of August were $31,000. The July 31 and August 31, 2003, financial statements contained the following information:

Income Statements
For the Months Ending

	August 31, 2003	July 31, 2003
Net sales	$50,000	$40,000

Balance Sheets
At

	August 31, 2003	July 31, 2003
Assets:		
Merchandise inventory	$28,000	$27,000

Required:
Determine the company's cost percentage.

<table>
<tr><td>E 9–7
Retail inventory
method; average cost</td><td>The San Lorenzo General Store uses a periodic inventory system and the retail inventory method to estimate ending inventory and cost of goods sold. The following data is available for the month of October 2003:</td></tr>
</table>

	Cost	Retail
Beginning inventory	$35,000	$50,000
Net purchases	20,760	31,600
Net markups		1,200
Net markdowns		800
Net sales		31,000

Required:
Estimate the average cost of ending inventory and cost of goods sold for October. Do not approximate LCM.

E 9–8
Conventional retail method

Campbell Corporation uses the retail method to value its inventory. The following information is available for the year 2003:

	Cost	Retail
Merchandise inventory, January 1, 2003	$190,000	$280,000
Purchases	600,000	840,000
Freight-in	8,000	
Net markups		20,000
Net markdowns		4,000
Net sales		800,000

Required:
Determine the December 31, 2003, inventory that approximates average cost, lower of cost or market.

E 9–9
Retail inventory method; LIFO

The Crosby Company owns a chain of hardware stores throughout the state. The company uses a periodic inventory system and the retail inventory method to estimate ending inventory and cost of goods sold. The following data is available for the three months ending March 31, 2003:

	Cost	Retail
Beginning inventory	$160,000	$280,000
Net purchases	599,200	840,000
Net markups		20,000
Net markdowns		4,000
Net sales		820,000

Required:
Estimate the LIFO cost of ending inventory and cost of goods sold for the three months ending March 31, 2003. Assume stable retail prices during the period.

E 9–10
Conventional retail method; normal spoilage

The Almaden Valley Variety Store uses the retail inventory method to estimate ending inventory and cost of goods sold. Data for 2003 is as follows:

	Cost	Retail
Beginning inventory	$ 12,000	$ 20,000
Purchases	102,600	165,000
Freight-in	3,480	
Purchase returns	4,000	7,000
Net markups		6,000
Net markdowns		3,000
Normal spoilage		4,200
Net sales		156,000

Required:
Estimate the ending inventory and cost of goods sold for 2003, applying the conventional retail method (average, LCM).

E 9–11
Conventional retail method; employee discounts

The LeMay Department Store uses the retail inventory method to estimate ending inventory for its monthly financial statements. The following data pertains to one of its largest departments for the month of March 2003:

	Cost	Retail
Beginning inventory	$ 40,000	$ 60,000
Purchases	201,000	400,000
Freight-in	10,752	
Purchase returns	4,000	6,000
Net markups		4,800
Net markdowns		3,500
Normal breakage		6,000
Net sales		270,000
Employee discounts		1,800

Sales are recorded net of employee discounts.

Required:
1. Compute estimated ending inventory and cost of goods sold for March applying the conventional retail method (average, LCM).
2. Recompute the cost-to-retail percentage using the average cost method and ignoring LCM considerations.

E 9–12
Retail inventory method; solving for unknowns

The Adams Corporation uses a periodic inventory system and the retail inventory method to estimate ending inventory and cost of goods sold. The following data is available for the month of September 2003:

	Cost	Retail
Beginning inventory	$21,000	$35,000
Net purchases	10,500	?
Net markups		4,000
Net markdowns		1,000
Net sales		?

The company used the average cost flow method and estimated inventory at the end of September to be $17,437.50. If the company had used the LIFO cost flow method, the cost-to-retail percentage would have been 50%.

Required:
Compute net purchases at retail and net sales for the month of September.

E 9–13
Multiple choice; LCM; inventory estimation techniques

The following questions dealing with the lower-of-cost-or-market rule for valuing inventory and inventory estimation techniques are adapted from questions that appeared on recent CPA examinations. Determine the response that best completes the statements or questions.

1. Which of the following statements are correct when a company applying the lower-of-cost-or-market method reports its inventory at replacement cost?
    I. The original cost is less than replacement cost.
    II. The net realizable value is greater than replacement cost.
    a. I only.
    b. II only.
    c. Both I and II.
    d. Neither I nor II.

2. Moss Co. has determined its December 31, 2003, inventory on a FIFO basis to be $400,000. Information pertaining to that inventory follows:

Estimated selling price	$408,000
Estimated cost of disposal	20,000
Normal profit margin	60,000
Current replacement cost	360,000

Moss records losses that result from applying the lower-of-cost-or-market rule. At December 31, 2003, what should be the net carrying amount of Moss's inventory?
    a. $400,000
    b. $388,000
    c. $360,000
    d. $328,000

3. Hutch, Inc. uses the conventional retail inventory method to account for inventory. The following information relates to 2003 operations:

	Cost	Retail
Beginning inventory and purchases	$600,000	$920,000
Net markups		40,000
Net markdowns		60,000
Sales		780,000

What amount should be reported as cost of goods sold for 2003?
- a. $480,000
- b. $487,500
- c. $520,000
- d. $525,000

4.   The following information is available for Cooke Company in 2003:

Net sales	$1,800,000
Freight-in	45,000
Purchase discounts	25,000
Ending inventory	120,000

The gross margin is 40% of net sales. What is the cost of goods available for sale?
- a. $840,000
- b. $960,000
- c. $1,200,000
- d. $1,220,000

E 9–14
Dollar-value LIFO retail

On January 1, 2003, the Brunswick Hat Company adopted the dollar-value LIFO retail method. The following data is available for 2003:

	Cost	Retail
Beginning inventory	$ 71,280	$132,000
Net purchases	120,000	255,000
Net markups		6,000
Net markdowns		11,000
Net sales		230,000
Retail price index, 12/31/03		1.04

Required:
Calculate the estimated ending inventory and cost of goods sold for 2003.

E 9–15
Dollar-value LIFO retail

The Canova Corporation adopted the dollar-value LIFO retail method on January 1, 2003. On that date, the cost of the inventory on hand was $15,000 and its retail value was $18,750. Information for 2003 and 2004 is as follows:

Date	Ending Inventory at Retail	Retail Price Index	Cost-to-Retail Percentage
12/31/03	$25,000	1.25	82%
12/31/04	28,600	1.30	85

Required:
1.   What is the cost-to-retail percentage for the inventory on hand at 1/1/03?
2.   Calculate the inventory value at the end of 2003 and 2004 using the dollar-value LIFO retail method.

E 9–16
Dollar-value LIFO retail

Lance-Hefner Specialty Shoppes decided to use the dollar-value LIFO retail method to value its inventory. Accounting records provide the following information:

	Cost	Retail
Merchandise inventory, January 1, 2003	$160,000	$250,000
Net purchases	360,500	510,000
Net markups		7,000
Net markdowns		2,000
Net sales		380,000

Pertinent retail price indexes are as follows:

January 1, 2003	1.00
December 31, 2003	1.10

Required:
Determine ending inventory and cost of goods sold.

E 9–17
Dollar-value LIFO retail;
solving for unknowns

The Bosco Company adopted the dollar-value LIFO retail method at the beginning of 2003. Information for 2003 and 2004 is as follows, with certain data intentionally omitted:

	Inventory			
Date	Cost	Retail	Retail Price Index	Cost-to-Retail Percentage
Inventory, 1/1/03	$21,000	$28,000	1.00	?
Inventory, 12/31/03	22,792	33,600	1.12	?
2004 net purchases	60,000	88,400		
2004 net sales		80,000		
Inventory, 12/31/04	?	?	1.20	

Required:
Determine the missing data.

E 9–18
Change in inventory
costing methods

Exercise 21–6 deals with changes in inventory costing methods.

E 9–19
Change in inventory
costing methods

Goddard Company has used the FIFO method of inventory valuation since it began operations in 2000. Goddard decided to change to the average cost method for determining inventory costs at the beginning of 2003. The following schedule shows year-end inventory balances under the FIFO and average cost methods:

Year	FIFO	Average cost
2000	$45,000	$54,000
2001	78,000	71,000
2002	83,000	78,000

Required:
1. What amount, before income taxes, should be reported in the 2003 income statement as the cumulative effect of the change in accounting principle?
2. What is the pro forma effect of the change in method on 2002's income before taxes?

(AICPA adapted)

E 9–20
Error correction;
inventory error

Exercise 21–19 deals with the correction of an inventory error.

E 9–21
Inventory errors

For each of the following inventory errors occurring in 2003, determine the effect of the error on 2003's cost of goods sold, net income, and retained earnings. Assume that the error is not discovered until 2004 and that a periodic inventory system is used. Ignore income taxes.

U = understated   O = overstated   NE = no effect

	Cost of Goods Sold	Net Income	Retained Earnings
(Example) 1. Overstatement of ending inventory	U	O	O
2. Overstatement of purchases			
3. Understatement of beginning inventory			
4. Freight-in charges are understated			
5. Understatement of ending inventory			
6. Understatement of purchases			
7. Overstatement of beginning inventory			
8. Understatement of purchases plus understatement of ending inventory by the same amount			

E 9–22
Inventory error

In 2003, the internal auditors of Development Technologies, Inc. discovered that a $3 million purchase of merchandise in 2003 was recorded in 2002 instead. The physical inventory count at the end of 2002 was correct.

Required:
Prepare the journal entry needed in 2003 to correct the error. Also, briefly describe any other measures Development Technologies would take in connection with correcting the error. (Ignore income taxes.)

E 9–23
Multiple choice; dollar-value LIFO retail, inventory errors, accounting changes

The following questions dealing with dollar-value LIFO retail, inventory errors, and changes in inventory methods are adapted from questions that appeared on recent CPA examinations. Determine the response that best completes the statements or questions.

1. On December 31, 2002, Jason Company adopted the dollar-value LIFO retail inventory method. Inventory data for 2003 are as follows:

	LIFO Cost	Retail
Inventory, 12/31/02	$360,000	$500,000
Inventory, 12/31/03	?	660,000
Increase in price level for 2003		10%
Cost to retail ratio for 2003		70%

   Under the LIFO retail method, Jason's inventory at December 31, 2003, should be
   a. $437,000
   b. $462,000
   c. $472,000
   d. $483,000

2. Bren Co.'s beginning inventory at January 1, 2003, was understated by $26,000, and its ending inventory was overstated by $52,000. As a result, Bren's cost of goods sold for 2003 was
   a. Understated by $26,000.
   b. Overstated by $26,000.
   c. Understated by $78,000.
   d. Overstated by $78,000.

3. On December 31, 2003, Rapp Co. changed inventory cost methods to FIFO from LIFO for financial statement and income tax purposes. The change will result in a $175,000 increase in the beginning inventory at January 1, 2003. Assuming a 30% income tax rate, the cumulative effect of this accounting change reported in the income statement for the year ended December 31, 2003, is
   a. $175,000
   b. $122,000
   c. $52,500
   d. $0

E 9–24
Concepts; terminology

Listed below are several terms and phrases associated with inventory measurement. Pair each item from List A (by letter) with the item from List B that is most appropriately associated with it.

List A	List B
____ 1. Gross profit ratio	a. Reduction in selling price below the original selling price.
____ 2. Cost-to-retail percentage	
____ 3. Additional markup	b. Beginning inventory is not included in the calculation of the cost-to-retail percentage.
____ 4. Markdown	c. Deducted in the retail column after the calculation of the cost-to-retail percentage.
____ 5. Net markup	
____ 6. Retail method, FIFO and LIFO	d. Requires base year retail to be converted to layer year retail and then to cost.
____ 7. Conventional retail method	
____ 8. Change from LIFO	e. Gross profit divided by net sales.
____ 9. Dollar-value LIFO retail	f. Material inventory error discovered in a subsequent year.
____ 10. Normal spoilage	
____ 11. Requires retroactive restatement	g. Must be added to sales if sales are recorded net of discounts.
____ 12. Employee discounts	
____ 13. Net markdowns	h. Deducted in the retail column to arrive at goods available for sale at retail.
____ 14. Net realizable value	
	i. Divide cost of goods available for sale by goods available at retail.
	j. Average cost, LCM.
	k. Added to the retail column to arrive at goods available for sale.
	l. Increase in selling price subsequent to initial markup.
	m. Ceiling in the determination of market.
	n. Accounting change requiring retroactive restatement.

E 9–25
Purchase commitments
(Based on Appendix 9)

On October 6, 2003, the Elgin Corporation signed a purchase commitment to purchase inventory for $60,000 on or before March 31, 2004. The company's fiscal year-end is December 31. The contract was exercised on March 21, 2004, and the inventory was purchased for cash at the contract price. On the purchase date of March 21, the market price of the inventory was $54,000. The market price of the inventory on December 31, 2003, was $56,000. The company uses a perpetual inventory system.

Required:
1. Prepare the necessary adjusting journal entry (if any is required) on December 31, 2003.
2. Prepare the journal entry to record the purchase on March 21, 2004.

E 9–26
Purchase commitments
(Based on Appendix 9)

In March 2003, the Phillips Tool Company signed two purchase commitments. The first commitment requires Phillips to purchase inventory for $100,000 by June 15, 2003. The second commitment requires the company to purchase inventory for $150,000 by August 20, 2003. The company's fiscal year-end is June 30. Phillips uses a periodic inventory system.

The first commitment is exercised on June 15, 2003, when the market price of the inventory purchased was $85,000. The second commitment was exercised on August 20, 2003, when the market price of the inventory purchased was $120,000.

Required:
Prepare the journal entries required on June 15, June 30, and August 20, 2003, to account for the two purchase commitments. Assume that the market price of the inventory related to the outstanding purchase commitment was $140,000 at June 30.

PROBLEMS

P 9–1
Lower of cost or market

The Decker Company has five products in its inventory. Information about the December 31, 2003, inventory follows.

Product	Quantity	Unit Cost	Unit Replacement Cost	Unit Selling Price
A	1,000	$10	$12	$16
B	800	15	11	18
C	600	3	2	8
D	200	7	4	6
E	600	14	12	13

The selling cost for each product consists of a 15 percent sales commission. The normal profit percentage for each product is 40 percent of the selling price.

Required:
1. Determine the balance sheet inventory carrying value at December 31, 2003, assuming the LCM rule is applied to individual products.
2. Determine the balance sheet inventory carrying value at December 31, 2003, assuming the LCM rule is applied to the entire inventory. Also, assuming that Decker recognizes an inventory write-down as a separate income statement item, determine the amount of the loss.

P 9–2
Lower of cost or market

The Almaden Hardware Store sells two distinct types of products, tools and paint products. Information pertaining to its 2003 year-end inventory is as follows:

Inventory, by Product Type	Quantity	Per Unit Cost	Designated Market
Tools:			
Hammers	100	$ 5.00	$5.50
Saws	200	10.00	9.00
Screwdrivers	300	2.00	2.60
Paint products:			
1-gallon cans	500	6.00	5.00
Paint brushes	100	4.00	4.50

Required:
1. Determine the balance sheet inventory carrying value at year-end, assuming the LCM rule is applied to (a) individual products, (b) product type, and (c) total inventory.
2. Assuming that the company recognizes an inventory write-down as a separate income statement item, for each of the LCM applications determine the amount of the loss.

P 9–3
Gross profit method

Smith Distributors, Inc., supplies ice cream shops with various toppings for making sundaes. On November 17, 2003, a fire resulted in the loss of all of the toppings stored in one section of the warehouse. The company must provide its insurance company with an estimate of the amount of inventory lost. The following information is available from the company's accounting records:

	Fruit Toppings	Marshmallow Toppings	Chocolate Toppings
Inventory, January 1, 2003	$ 20,000	$ 7,000	$ 3,000
Net purchases through Nov. 17	150,000	36,000	12,000
Net sales through Nov. 17	200,000	55,000	20,000
Historical gross profit ratio	20%	30%	35%

Required:
1. Calculate the estimated cost of each of the toppings lost in the fire.
2. What factors could cause the estimates to be over- or understated?

P 9–4
Retail inventory method; various cost methods

The Sparrow Company uses the retail inventory method to estimate ending inventory and cost of goods sold. Data for 2003 is as follows:

	Cost	Retail
Beginning inventory	$ 90,000	$180,000
Purchases	355,000	580,000
Freight-in	9,000	
Purchase returns	7,000	11,000
Net markups		16,000
Net markdowns		12,000
Normal spoilage		3,000
Abnormal spoilage		8,000
Sales		540,000
Sales returns		10,000

The company records sales net of employee discounts. Discounts for 2003 totaled $4,000.

Required:
Estimate Sparrow's ending inventory and cost of goods sold for the year using the retail inventory method and the following applications:
1. Average cost
2. Conventional (average, LCM)

P 9–5
Retail inventory method; conventional and LIFO

The Alquist Company uses the retail method to estimate its ending inventory. Selected information about its year 2003 operations is as follows:
a. January 1, 2003, beginning inventory had a cost of $100,000 and a retail value of $150,000.
b. Purchases during 2003 cost $1,387,500 with an original retail value of $2,000,000.
c. Freight costs were $10,000 for incoming merchandise and $25,000 for outgoing (sold) merchandise.
d. Net additional markups were $300,000 and net markdowns were $150,000.
e. Based on prior experience, shrinkage due to shoplifting was estimated to be $15,000 of retail value.
f. Merchandise is sold to employees at a 20% of selling price discount. Employee sales are recorded in a separate account at the net selling price. The balance in this account at the end of 2003 is $250,000.
g. Sales to customers totaled $1,750,000 for the year.

Required:
1. Estimate ending inventory and cost of goods sold using the conventional retail method (average, LCM).
2. Estimate ending inventory and cost of goods sold using the LIFO retail method. (Assume stable prices.)

P 9–6
Retail inventory
method

The Grand Department Store, Inc., uses the retail inventory method to estimate ending inventory for its monthly financial statements. The following data pertain to a single department for the month of October 2003:

Inventory, October 1, 2003:	
At cost	$ 20,000
At retail	30,000
Purchases (exclusive of freight and returns):	
At cost	100,151
At retail	146,495
Freight-in	5,100
Purchase returns:	
At cost	2,100
At retail	2,800
Additional markups	2,500
Markup cancellations	265
Markdowns (net)	800
Normal spoilage and breakage	4,500
Sales	135,730

Required:
1. Using the conventional retail method, prepare a schedule computing estimated lower-of-cost-or-market inventory for October 31, 2003.
2. A department store using the conventional retail inventory method estimates the cost of its ending inventory as $29,000. An accurate physical count reveals only $22,000 of inventory at lower of cost or market. List the factors that may have caused the difference between computed inventory and the physical count.

(AICPA adapted)

P 9–7
Retail method—
average cost and LCM

The Smith-Kline Company maintains inventory records at selling prices as well as at cost. For 2003, the records indicate the following data:

	($ in 000s)	
	Cost	**Retail**
Beginning inventory	$ 80	$ 125
Purchases	671	1,006
Freight-in on purchases	30	
Purchase returns	1	2
Net markups		4
Net markdowns		8
Net sales		916

Required:
Use the retail method to approximate cost of ending inventory in each of the following ways:
1. Average cost
2. Average (LCM) cost

P 9–8
Dollar-value LIFO retail
method

[This is a variation of the previous problem, modified to focus on the dollar-value LIFO retail method.]

The Smith-Kline Company maintains inventory records at selling prices as well as at cost. For 2003, the records indicate the following data:

	($ in 000s)	
	Cost	**Retail**
Beginning inventory	$ 80	$ 125
Purchases	671	1,006
Freight-in on purchases	30	
Purchase returns	1	2
Net markups		4
Net markdowns		8
Net sales		916

Required:
Assuming the price level increased from 1.00 at January 1 to 1.10 at December 31, 2003, use the dollar-value LIFO retail method to approximate cost of ending inventory and cost of goods sold.

P 9–9
Dollar-value LIFO retail

On January 1, 2003, the HGC Camera Store adopted the dollar-value LIFO retail inventory method. The following information was available at December 31, 2003, the company's fiscal year-end:

	Cost	Retail
Beginning inventory	$28,000	$ 40,000
Purchases (net of returns)	85,000	108,000
Freight-in	2,000	
Net markups		10,000
Net markdowns		2,000
Sales to customers		100,000
Sales to employees (net of 20% discount)		2,400

The retail prices for cameras increased by 6% from January 1 to December 31, 2003.

Required:
Estimate HGC's ending inventory at December 31 and cost of goods sold for the year using the dollar-value LIFO retail inventory method.

P 9–10
Retail inventory method; various applications

The Raleigh Department Store converted from the conventional retail method to the LIFO retail method on January 1, 2001, and is now considering converting to the dollar-value LIFO retail inventory method. Management requested, during your examination of the financial statements for the year ended December 31, 2003, that you furnish a summary showing certain computations of inventory costs for the past three years. Available information follows:
a.   The inventory at January 1, 2001, had a retail value of $45,000 and a cost of $27,500 based on the conventional retail method.
b.   Transactions during 2001 were as follows:

	Cost	Retail
Gross purchases	$282,000	$490,000
Purchase returns	6,500	10,000
Purchase discounts	5,000	
Gross sales		492,000
Sales returns		5,000
Employee discounts		3,000
Freight-in	26,500	
Net markups		25,000
Net markdowns		10,000

Sales to employees are recorded net of discounts.
c.   The retail value of the December 31, 2002, inventory was $56,100, the cost-to-retail percentage for 2002 under the LIFO retail method was 62%, and the appropriate price index was 102% of the January 1, 2002, price level.
d.   The retail value of the December 31, 2003, inventory was $48,300, the cost-to-retail percentage for 2003 under the LIFO retail method was 61%, and the appropriate price index was 105% of the January 1, 2002, price level.

Required:
1.   Prepare a schedule showing the computation of the cost of inventory at December 31, 2001, based on the conventional retail method.
2.   Prepare a similar schedule as in requirement 1 based on the LIFO retail method.
3.   Same requirement as (1) for December 31, 2002 and 2003, based on the dollar-value LIFO retail method.

(AICPA adapted)

P 9–11
Change in methods

The Rockwell Corporation uses a periodic inventory system and has used the FIFO cost method since inception of the company in 1971. In 2003, the company decided to switch to the average cost method. Data for 2003 is as follows:

Beginning inventory, FIFO (5,000 units @ $30)		$150,000
Purchases:		
5,000 units @ $36	$180,000	
5,000 units @ $40	200,000	380,000
Cost of goods available for sale		$530,000
Sales for 2003 (8,000 units @ $70)		$560,000

Additional information:

a. The company's effective income tax rate is 40% for all years.
b. If the company had used the average cost method prior to 2003, ending inventory for 2002 would have been $130,000.
c. 7,000 units remained in inventory at the end of 2003.

Required:
1. What is the cumulative effect of the change in inventory methods that will appear in the 2003 income statement?
2. What is the effect of the change in methods on 2003 income before the cumulative effect?

P 9–12
Inventory errors

You have been hired as the new controller for the Ralston Company. Shortly after joining the company in 2003, you discover the following errors related to the 2001 and 2002 financial statements:

a. Inventory at 12/31/01 was understated by $6,000.
b. Inventory at 12/31/02 was overstated by $9,000.
c. On 12/31/02, inventory was purchased for $3,000. The company did not record the purchase until the inventory was paid for early in 2003. At that time, the purchase was recorded by a debit to purchases and a credit to cash.

The company uses a periodic inventory system.

Required:
1. Assuming that the errors were discovered after the 2002 financial statements were issued, analyze the effect of the errors on 2002 and 2001 cost of goods sold, net income, and retained earnings. (Ignore income taxes.)
2. Prepare a journal entry to correct the errors.
3. What other step(s) would be taken in connection with the error?

P 9–13
Inventory errors

The December 31, 2003, inventory of Tog Company, based on a physical count, was determined to be $450,000. Included in that count was a shipment of goods that cost $50,000 received from a supplier at the end of the month. The purchase was recorded and paid for in 2004. Another supplier shipment costing $20,000 was correctly recorded as a purchase in 2003. However, the merchandise, shipped FOB shipping point, was not received until 2004 and was incorrectly omitted from the physical count. A third purchase, shipped from a supplier FOB shipping point on December 28, 2003, did not arrive until January 3, 2004. The merchandise, which cost $80,000, was not included in the physical count and the purchase has not yet been recorded.

The company uses a periodic inventory system.

Required:
1. Determine the correct December 31, 2003, inventory balance and, assuming that the errors were discovered after the 2003 financial statements were issued, analyze the effect of the errors on 2003 cost of goods sold, net income, and retained earnings. (Ignore income taxes.)
2. Prepare a journal entry to correct the errors.

P 9–14
Purchase commitments (Based on Appendix 9)

In November 2003, the Brunswick Company signed two purchase commitments. The first commitment requires Brunswick to purchase 10,000 units of inventory at $10 per unit by December 15, 2003. The second commitment requires the company to purchase 20,000 units of inventory at $11 per unit by March 15, 2004. Brunswick's fiscal year-end is December 31. The company uses a periodic inventory system. Both contracts were exercised on their expiration date.

Required:
1. Prepare the journal entry to record the December 15 purchase for cash assuming the following alternative unit market prices on that date:
   a. $10.50
   b. $9.50

2. Prepare any necessary adjusting entry at December 31, 2003, for the second purchase commitment assuming the following alternative unit market prices on that date:
    a. $12.50
    b. $10.30
3. Assuming that the unit market price on December 31 was $10.30, prepare the journal entry to record the purchase on March 15, 2004, assuming the following alternative unit market prices on that date:
    a. $11.50
    b. $10.00

BROADEN YOUR PERSPECTIVE

Apply your critical-thinking ability to the knowledge you've gained. These cases will provide you an opportunity to develop your research, analysis, judgment, and communication skills. You also will work with other students, integrate what you've learned, apply it in real world situations, and consider its global and ethical ramifications. This practice will broaden your knowledge and further develop your decision-making abilities.

Judgment Case 9–1
Inventoriable costs; lower of cost or market; retail inventory method

Hudson Company, which is both a wholesaler and a retailer, purchases its inventories from various suppliers.

Additional facts for Hudson's wholesale operations are as follows:
a. Hudson incurs substantial warehousing costs.
b. Hudson uses the lower-of-cost-or-market method. The replacement cost of the inventories is below the net realizable value and above the net realizable value less the normal profit margin. The original cost of the inventories is above replacement cost and below the net realizable value.

Additional facts for Hudson's retail operations are as follows:
a. Hudson determines the estimated cost of its ending inventories held for sale at retail using the conventional retail inventory method, which approximates lower of average cost or market.
b. Hudson incurs substantial freight-in costs.
c. Hudson has net markups and net markdowns.

Required:
1. Theoretically, how should Hudson account for the warehousing costs related to its wholesale inventories? Why?
2. a. In general, why is the lower-of-cost-or-market method used to value inventory?
    b. At which amount should Hudson's wholesale inventories be reported in the balance sheet? Explain the application of the lower-of-cost-or-market method in this situation.
3. In the calculation of the cost-to-retail percentage used to determine the estimated cost of its ending retail inventories, how should Hudson treat
    a. Freight-in costs?
    b. Net markups?
    c. Net markdowns?
4. Why does Hudson's retail inventory method approximate lower of average cost or market?

(AICPA adapted)

Communication Case 9–2
Lower of cost or market

The lower-of-cost-or-market approach to valuing inventory is a departure from the accounting principle of reporting assets at their historical costs. There are those who believe that inventory, as well as other assets, should be valued at market, regardless of whether market is above or below cost.

The focus of this case is the justification for the lower-of-cost-or-market rule for valuing inventories. Your instructor will divide the class into two to six groups depending on the size of the class. The mission of your group is to defend the lower-of-cost-or-market approach against the alternatives of valuing inventory at either historical cost or market value.

Required:
1. Each group member should consider the situation independently and draft a tentative argument prior to the class session for which the case is assigned.
2. In class, each group will meet for 10 to 15 minutes in different areas of the classroom. During that meeting, group members will take turns sharing their suggestions for the purpose of arriving at a single group argument.

3. After the allotted time, a spokesperson for each group (selected during the group meetings) will share the group's solution with the class. The goal of the class is to incorporate the views of each group into a consensus approach to the situation.

Integrating Case 9–3
Unit LIFO and LCM

York Co. sells one product, which it purchases from various suppliers. York's trial balance at December 31, 2003, included the following accounts:

Sales (33,000 units @ $16)	$528,000
Sales discounts	7,500
Purchases	368,900
Purchase discounts	18,000
Freight-in	5,000
Freight-out	11,000

York Co.'s inventory purchases during 2003 were as follows:

	Cost Units	Total per Unit	Cost
Beginning inventory	8,000	$8.20	$ 65,600
Purchases, quarter ended March 31	12,000	8.25	99,000
Purchases, quarter ended June 30	15,000	7.90	118,500
Purchases, quarter ended September 30	13,000	7.50	97,500
Purchases, quarter ended December 31	7,000	7.70	53,900
	55,000		$434,500

Additional information:

a. York's accounting policy is to report inventory in its financial statements at the lower of cost or market, applied to total inventory. Cost is determined under the last-in, first-out (LIFO) method.

b. York has determined that, at December 31, 2003, the replacement cost of its inventory was $8 per unit and the net realizable value was $8.80 per unit. York's normal profit margin is $1.05 per unit.

Required:

1. Prepare York's schedule of cost of goods sold, with a supporting schedule of ending inventory. York uses the direct method of reporting losses from market decline of inventory.

2. Explain the rule of lower of cost or market and its application in this situation.

(AICPA adapted)

Judgment Case 9–4
The dollar-value LIFO method; the retail inventory method

Huddell Company, which is both a wholesaler and retailer, purchases merchandise from various suppliers. The dollar-value LIFO method is used for the wholesale inventories.

Huddell determines the estimated cost of its retail ending inventories using the conventional retail inventory method, which approximates lower of average cost or market.

Required:

1. a. What are the advantages of using the dollar-value LIFO method as opposed to the traditional LIFO method?

    b. How does the application of the dollar-value LIFO method differ from the application of the traditional LIFO method?

2. a. In the calculation of the cost-to-retail percentage used to determine the estimated cost of its ending inventories, how should Huddell use

    -   Net markups?
    -   Net markdowns?

    b. Why does Huddell's retail inventory method approximate lower of average cost or market?

(AICPA adapted)

Communication Case 9–5
Retail inventory method

The Brenly Paint Company, your client, manufactures paint. The company's president, Mr. Brenly, decided to open a retail store to sell paint as well as wallpaper and other items that would be purchased from other suppliers. He has asked you for information about the retail method of estimating inventories at the retail store.

Required:

Prepare a report to the president explaining the retail method of estimating inventories.

Analysis Case 9–6
Change in inventory
method

Generally accepted accounting principles should be applied consistently from period to period. However, changes within a company, as well as changes in the external economic environment, may force a company to change an accounting method. The specific reporting requirements when a company changes from one generally accepted inventory method to another depend on the methods involved.

Required:
Explain the accounting treatment and disclosures required for a change in inventory method (1) not involving LIFO, (2) to the LIFO method, and (3) from the LIFO method.

Real World Case 9–7
Change in inventory
method

On January 16, 2001, Pennzoil-Quaker State Company made the following announcement:

Houston (January 16, 2001)—Pennzoil-Quaker State Company (NYSE: PZL) announced today that it has changed its inventory costing method from last-in, first-out (LIFO) to moving average cost for all products previously on the LIFO method. The new method is expected to provide a better matching of raw material costs to product selling prices, producing a more accurate measure of operating results for the Company's businesses.

   The change will require the Company to restate its historical reported earnings. Recurring earnings per share are expected to be reduced in pro forma 1998 to 24 cents from 48 cents, increased in 1999 to 61 cents from 49 cents, and increased in the first nine months of 2000 by a total of 17 cents.

Required:
1. Why does GAAP require Pennzoil-Quaker State to "restate its historical reported earnings" for this type of accounting change?
2. Assuming that the quantity of inventory remained stable during the first nine months of 2000, did the cost of Pennzoil-Quaker State's inventory move up or down during that period?

Real World Case 9–8
Change in inventory
method

EDGAR, the Electronic Data Gathering, Analysis, and Retrieval system, performs automated collection, validation, indexing, and forwarding of submissions by companies and others who are required by law to file forms with the U.S. Securities and Exchange Commission SEC. All publicly traded domestic companies use EDGAR to make the majority of their filings. (Some foreign companies file voluntarily.) Form 10-K or 10-KSB, which include the annual report, is required to be filed on EDGAR. The SEC makes this information available on the Internet.

Required:
1. Access EDGAR on the Internet. The web address is **www.sec.gov**. Edgarscan (**edgarscan. pwcglobal.com**) from Pricewaterhouse Coopers makes the process of accessing data from EDGAR easier.
2. Search for Dillard's Inc. Access the 10-K filing for the fiscal year ended February 3, 2001. Search or scroll to find the financial statements and related notes.
3. Answer the following questions related to the company's inventories:
   a. Describe the change made in the company's method of accounting for inventories.
   b. What is the net-of-tax cumulative effect of the change reported in the income statement?
   c. What is the impact of the change on fiscal 2000 income?

Communication Case 9–9
Change in inventory
method; disclosure
note

Mayfair Department Stores, Inc., operates over 30 retail stores in the Pacific Northwest. Prior to 2003, the company used the FIFO method to value its inventory. In 2003, Mayfair decided to switch to the dollar-value LIFO retail inventory method. One of your responsibilities as assistant controller is to prepare the disclosure note describing the change in method that will be included in the company's 2003 financial statements. Kenneth Meier, the controller, provided the following information:
a. Internally developed retail price indexes are used to adjust for the effects of changing prices.
b. If the change had not been made, cost of goods sold for the year would have been $22 million lower. The company's income tax rate is 40% and there were 100 million shares of common stock outstanding during 2003.
c. The cumulative effect of the change on prior years' income is not determinable.
d. The reasons for the change were (a) to provide a more consistent matching of merchandise costs with sales revenue, and (b) the new method provides a more comparable basis of accounting with competitors that also use the LIFO method.

Required:
1. Prepare for Kenneth Meier the disclosure note that will be included in the 2003 financial statements.
2. Explain why the "cumulative effect of the change on prior years' income is not determinable."

Judgment Case 9–10
Inventory errors

Some inventory errors are said to be self-correcting in that the error has the opposite financial statement effect in the period following the error, thereby correcting the original account balance errors.

Required:
Despite this self-correcting feature, discuss why these errors should not be ignored and describe the steps required to account for the error correction.

Ethics Case 9–11
Overstatement of ending inventory

Danville Bottlers is a wholesale beverage company. Danville uses the FIFO inventory method to determine the cost of its ending inventory. Ending inventory quantities are determined by a physical count. For the fiscal year-end June 30, 2003, ending inventory was originally determined to be $3,265,000. However, on July 17, 2003, John Howard, the company's controller, discovered an error in the ending inventory count. He determined that the correct ending inventory amount should be $2,600,000.

Danville is a privately owned corporation with significant financing provided by a local bank. The bank requires annual audited financial statements as a condition of the loan. By July 17, the auditors had completed their review of the financial statements which are scheduled to be issued on July 25. They did not discover the inventory error.

John's first reaction was to communicate his finding to the auditors and to revise the financial statements before they are issued. However, he knows that his and his fellow workers' profit-sharing plans are based on annual pretax earnings and that if he revises the statements, everyone's profit-sharing bonus will be significantly reduced.

Required:
1. Why will bonuses be negatively affected? What is the effect on pretax earnings?
2. If the error is not corrected in the current year and is discovered by the auditors during the following year's audit, how will it be reported in the company's financial statements?
3. Discuss the ethical dilemma John Howard faces.

Analysis Case 9–12
Purchase commitments
(Based on Appendix 9)

The management of the Esquire Oil Company believes that the wholesale price of heating oil that they sell to homeowners will increase again as the result of increased political problems in the Middle East. The company is currently paying $.80 a gallon. If they are willing to enter an agreement in November 2003 to purchase a million gallons of heating oil during the winter of 2004, their supplier will guarantee the price at $.80 per gallon. However, if the winter is a mild one, Esquire would not be able to sell a million gallons unless they reduced their retail price and thereby increased the risk of a loss for the year. On the other hand, if the wholesale price did increase substantially, they would be in a favorable position with respect to their competitors. The company's fiscal year-end is December 31.

Required:
Discuss the accounting issues related to the purchase commitment that Esquire is considering.

10

Operational Assets: Acquisition and Disposition

CHAPTER

OVERVIEW

This chapter and the one that follows address the measurement and reporting issues involving operational assets. Operational assets include tangible and intangible long-term assets that are used in the production of goods and services. This chapter covers the valuation at date of acquisition and the disposition of these assets. In Chapter 11 we discuss the allocation of the cost of operational assets to the periods benefited by their use, the treatment of expenditures made over the life of these assets to maintain and improve them, and the impairment of operational assets.

LEARNING OBJECTIVES

After studying this chapter, you should be able to:

LO1 Identify the various costs included in the initial cost of property, plant, and equipment, natural resources, and intangible assets.

LO2 Determine the initial cost of individual operational assets acquired as a group for a lump-sum purchase price.

LO3 Determine the initial cost of an operational asset acquired in exchange for a deferred payment contract.

LO4 Determine the initial cost of operational assets acquired in exchange for equity securities or through donation.

LO5 Explain how to account for dispositions and exchanges for other nonmonetary assets.

LO6 Identify the items included in the cost of a self-constructed asset and determine the amount of capitalized interest.

LO7 Explain the difference in the accounting treatment of costs incurred to purchase intangible assets versus the costs incurred to internally develop intangible assets.

FINANCIAL REPORTING CASE

A Question of Interest

"Now I'm really confused," confessed Stan, your study partner. "I thought that interest was always expensed in the income statement in the period incurred. Now you're telling me that sometimes interest is capitalized. I'm not even sure what *capitalize* means!" "That's right," you tell Stan, "and if you hadn't missed class today, we wouldn't be having this conversation. Here, take a look at this example of a disclosure note for Walt Disney Company that our professor passed out today. I'll try to explain it all to you."

"While we're at it, we can go over the rest of today's lecture," Stan added hopefully.

Borrowings (in part)
The Company capitalizes interest on assets constructed for its parks, resorts and other property, and on theatrical and television productions in process. In 2001, 2000, and 1999, respectively, total interest costs incurred were $606 million, $702 million and $826 million, of which $94 million, $132 million and $109 million were capitalized.

> By the time you finish this chapter, you should be able to respond appropriately to the questions posed in this case. Compare your response to the solution provided at the end of the chapter.

QUESTIONS

1. What does it mean to capitalize an expenditure? What is the general rule for determining which costs are capitalized when an operational asset is acquired? (page 463)

2. Describe to Stan which costs might be included in the initial cost of equipment. (page 465)

3. In what situations is interest capitalized? (page 486)

4. What is the three-step process used to determine the amount of interest capitalized? (page 487)

General Motors Corporation has significant investments in the production facilities it uses to manufacture the automobiles it sells. On the other hand, the principal revenue-producing assets of Microsoft Corporation are the copyrights on its computer software that permit it the exclusive rights to earn profits from those products. Timber reserves provide major revenues to Boise Cascade. From a reporting perspective, we classify GM's production facilities as property, plant, and equipment;[1] Microsoft's copyrights as intangible assets, and Boise Cascade's timber reserves as natural resources. Together, these three noncurrent assets constitute **operational assets,** a term used to describe the broad category of *long-term, revenue-producing assets.* Unlike manufacturers, many service firms and merchandising companies rely primarily on people or investments in inventories rather than on operational assets to generate revenues. Even nonmanufacturing firms, though, typically have at least modest investments in buildings, equipment, and other operational assets.

The measurement and reporting issues pertaining to this group of assets include valuation at date of acquisition, disposition, the treatment of expenditures made over the life of these assets to maintain and improve them, the allocation of cost to reporting periods that benefit from their use, and impairment. The allocation of asset cost over time is called *depreciation* for plant and equipment, *amortization* for intangible assets, and *depletion* for natural resources. We focus on initial valuation and disposition in this chapter, and subsequent expenditures, cost allocation, and impairment in the next chapter.

PART

VALUATION AT ACQUISITION

Types of Operational Assets

For financial reporting purposes, operational assets typically are classified in two categories:

1. **Property, plant, and equipment.** Assets in this category include land, buildings, equipment, machinery, autos, and trucks. **Natural resources** such as oil and gas deposits, timber tracts, and mineral deposits also are included.
2. **Intangible assets.** Unlike other operational assets, these lack physical substance and the extent and timing of their future benefits typically are highly uncertain. They include patents, copyrights, trademarks, franchises, and goodwill.

Of course, every company maintains its own unique mix of operational assets. The way these assets are classified and combined for reporting purposes also varies from company to company. As an example, a recent Tyson Foods, Inc., balance sheet reported net property, plant, and equipment of $4,085 million and $2,141 million at the end of fiscal 2001 and 2000, respectively. A disclosure note, shown in Graphic 10–1, provided the details.

In practice, some companies report intangibles as part of property, plant, and equipment. Some include intangible assets in the other asset category in the balance sheet, and others show intangibles as a separate balance sheet category. For example, Pepsico, Inc., reported intangibles as a separate category in a recent balance sheet:

Assets (in part)	($ in millions)	
	2001	**2000**
Intangibles, net	$4,841	$4,714

The disclosure note shown in Graphic 10–2 provided the details.

Before we examine in detail specific operational assets, you should find it helpful to study the overview provided by Graphic 10–3 on page 464.

---

[1]These are sometimes called *plant assets* or *fixed assets.*

GRAPHIC 10–1
Property, Plant, and
Equipment—Tyson
Foods, Inc.

Property, Plant, and Equipment and Depreciation (in part):
The major categories of property, plant, and equipment and accumulated depreciation, at cost, are as follows:

	($ in millions)	
	2001	**2000**
Land	$ 114	$ 61
Buildings and leasehold improvements	2,085	1,291
Machinery and equipment	3,218	2,219
Land improvements and other	174	110
Buildings and equipment under construction	379	103
	5,970	3,784
Less: accumulated depreciation	1,885	1,643
Net property, plant, and equipment	$4,085	$2,141

GRAPHIC 10–2
Intangible Assets—
Pepsico, Inc.

Note 9—Intangible Assets, net

	($ in millions)	
	2001	**2000**
Goodwill	$3,374	$3,522
Trademarks and brands	1,320	994
Other identifiable intangibles	147	198
	$4,841	$4,714

Costs to Be Capitalized

LO1

Operational assets can be acquired through purchase, exchange, lease, donation, self-construction, or a business combination. We address acquisitions through leasing in Chapter 15 and acquisitions through business combinations later in this chapter and in Chapter 12.

The initial valuation of operational assets usually is quite simple. We know from prior study that assets are valued on the basis of their original costs. In Chapter 8 we introduced the concept of condition and location in determining the cost of inventory. This concept applies to the valuation of operational assets as well. The initial cost of an operational asset includes the purchase price and all expenditures necessary to bring the asset to its desired condition and location for use.

Our objective in identifying the costs of an asset is to distinguish the expenditures that produce future benefits from those that produce benefits only in the current period. The costs in the second group are recorded as expenses, but those in the first group are *capitalized*. That is, they are recorded as an asset and expensed in future periods.[2]

The distinction is not trivial. This point was unmistakably emphasized in the summer of 2002 when WorldCom, Inc. disclosed that it had improperly capitalized nearly $4 billion in expenditures related to the company's telecom network. This massive fraud resulted in one of the largest financial statement restatements in history and triggered the collapse of the once powerful corporation. Capitalizing rather than expensing these expenditures caused a substantial overstatement of reported income for 2001 and the first quarter of 2002, in fact, producing impressive profits where losses should have been reported. If the deception had

FINANCIAL REPORTING CASE

Q1, p. 461

The initial cost of an operational asset includes the purchase price and all expenditures necessary to bring the asset to its desired condition and location for use.

---

[2]Exceptions are land and certain intangible assets that have indefinite useful lives. Costs to acquire these assets also produce future benefits and therefore are capitalized, but unlike other operational assets, their costs are not systematically expensed in future periods as depreciation or amortization.

GRAPHIC 10–3
Operational Assets and
Their Acquisition Costs

Asset	Description	Typical Acquisition Costs
Property, Plant, and Equipment	Productive assets that derive their value from long-term use in operations rather than from resale.	All expenditures necessary to get the asset in condition and location for its intended use.
Equipment	Broad term that includes machinery, computers and other office equipment, vehicles, furniture, and fixtures.	Purchase price (less discounts), taxes, transportation, installation, testing, trial runs, reconditioning.
Land	Real property used in operations (land held for speculative investment or future use is reported as investments or other assets).	Purchase price, attorney's fees, title, recording fees, commissions, back taxes, mortgages, liens, clearing, filling, draining, removing old buildings.
Land improvements	Enhancements to property such as parking lots, driveways, private roads, fences, landscaping, and sprinkler systems.	Separately identifiable costs.
Buildings	Structures that include warehouses, plant facilities, and office buildings.	Purchase price, attorney's fees, commissions, reconditioning.
Natural resources	Productive assets that are physically consumed in operations such as timber, mineral deposits, and oil and gas reserves.	Acquisition, exploration, development, and restoration costs.
Intangible Assets	Productive assets that lack physical substance and have long-term but typically uncertain benefits.	All expenditures necessary to get the asset in the location and condition for its intended use.
Patents	Exclusive 20-year right to manufacture a product or use a process.	Purchase price, legal fees, filing fees, not including internal R&D.
Copyrights	Exclusive right to benefit from a creative work such as a song, film, painting, photograph, or book.	Purchase price, legal fees, filing fees, not including internal R&D.
Trademarks (tradenames)	Exclusive right to display a word, a slogan, a symbol, or an emblem that distinctively identifies a company, product, or a service.	Purchase price, legal fees, filing fees, not including internal R&D.
Franchises	A contractual arrangement under which a franchisor grants the franchisee the exclusive right to use the franchisor's trademark or tradename.	Franchise fee plus any legal fees.
Goodwill	The unique value of the company as a whole over and above all identifiable assets.	Excess of the purchase price of the company over the fair value of the net assets acquired.

not been discovered, not only would income for 2001 and 2002 have been overstated, but income for many years into the future would have been understated as the fraudulent capitalized assets were depreciated. Of course, the balance sheet also would have overstated the assets and equity of the company.

PROPERTY, PLANT, AND EQUIPMENT

FINANCIAL REPORTING CASE

Q2, p. 461

Cost of Equipment.   Equipment is a broad term that encompasses machinery used in manufacturing, computers and other office equipment, vehicles, furniture, and fixtures. The cost of equipment includes the purchase price plus any sales tax (less any discounts received from the seller), transportation costs paid by the buyer to transport the asset to the location in which it will be used, expenditures for installation, testing, legal fees to establish title, and any other costs of bringing the asset to its condition and location for use. To the extent that these costs can be identified and measured, they should be included in the asset's initial valuation rather than expensed currently.

   Although most costs can be identified easily, others are more difficult. For example, the costs of training personnel to operate machinery could be considered a cost necessary to make the asset ready for use. However, because it is difficult to measure the amount of training costs associated with specific assets, these costs usually are expensed. Consider Illustration 10–1.

ILLUSTRATION 10–1

Initial Cost of Equipment

Central Machine Tools purchased an industrial lathe to be used in its manufacturing process. The purchase price was $62,000. Central paid a freight company $1,000 to transport the machine to its plant location plus $300 shipping insurance. In addition, the machine had to be installed and mounted on a special platform built specifically for the machine at a cost of $1,200. After installation, several trial runs were made to ensure proper operation. The cost of these trials including wasted materials was $600. At what amount should Central capitalize the lathe?

Purchase price	$62,000
Freight and handling	1,000
Insurance during shipping	300
Special foundation	1,200
Trial runs	600
	$65,100

Each of the expenditures described was necessary to bring the machine to its condition and location for use and should be capitalized and expensed in the future periods in which the asset is used.

Cost of Land.   The cost of land also should include each expenditure needed to get the land ready for its intended use. These include the purchase price plus closing costs such as fees for the attorney, real estate agent commissions, title and title search, and recording. If the property is subject to back taxes, liens, mortgages, or other obligations, these amounts are included also. In addition, any expenditures such as clearing, filling, draining, and even removing old buildings that are needed to prepare the land for its intended use are part of the land's cost. Proceeds from the sale of salvaged materials from old buildings torn down after purchase reduce the cost of land. Illustration 10–2 provides an example.

Land improvements.   It's important to distinguish between the cost of land and the cost of land improvements because land has an indefinite life and land improvements usually do not. Examples of land improvements include the cost of parking lots, driveways, and private roads and the costs of fences and lawn and garden sprinkler systems. Costs of these assets are separately identified and capitalized. We depreciate their cost over periods benefited by their use.

The costs of land improvements are capitalized and depreciated.

ILLUSTRATION 10–2	The Byers Structural Metal Company purchased a six-acre tract of land and an existing build-
Initial Cost of Land	ing for $500,000. The company plans to raze the old building and construct a new office building on the site. In addition to the purchase price, the company made the following expenditures at closing of the purchase:

Title insurance	$ 3,000
Commissions	16,000
Property taxes	6,000

Shortly after closing, the company paid a contractor $10,000 to tear down the old building and remove it from the site. An additional $5,000 was paid to grade the land. The $6,000 in property taxes included $4,000 of delinquent taxes paid by Byers on behalf of the seller and $2,000 attributable to the portion of the current fiscal year after the purchase date. What should be the capitalized cost of the land?

Capitalized cost of land:	
Purchase price of land (and building to be razed)	$500,000
Title insurance	3,000
Commissions	16,000
Delinquent property taxes	4,000
Cost of removing old building	10,000
Cost of grading	5,000
Total cost of land	$538,000

Two thousand dollars of the property taxes relate only to the current period and should be expensed. Other costs were necessary to acquire the land and are capitalized.

Cost of Buildings.   The cost of acquiring a building usually includes realtor commissions and legal fees in addition to the purchase price. Quite often a building must be refurbished, remodeled, or otherwise modified to suit the needs of the new owner. These reconditioning costs are part of the building's acquisition cost. When a building is constructed rather than purchased, unique accounting issues are raised. We discuss these in the "Self-Constructed Assets" section of this chapter.

Cost of Natural Resources.   Natural resources that provide long-term benefits are reported as property, plant, and equipment. These include timber tracts, mineral deposits, and oil and gas deposits. They can be distinguished from other assets by the fact that their benefits are derived from their physical consumption. For example, mineral deposits are physically diminishing as the minerals are extracted from the ground and either sold or used in the production process.[3] On the contrary, equipment, land, and buildings produce benefits for a company through their *use* in the production of goods and services. Unlike those of natural resources, their physical characteristics usually remain unchanged during their useful lives.

The cost of a natural resource includes the *acquisition costs* for the use of land, the *exploration* and *development costs* incurred before production begins, and *restoration costs* incurred during or at the end of extraction.

Sometimes a company buys natural resources from another company. In that case, initial valuation is simply the purchase price plus any other costs necessary to bring the asset to condition and location for use. More frequently, though, the company will develop these assets. In this situation, the initial valuation can include (a) acquisition costs, (b) exploration costs, (c) development costs, and (d) restoration costs. **Acquisition costs** are the amounts paid to acquire the rights to explore for undiscovered natural resources or to extract proven natural resources. **Exploration costs** are expenditures such as drilling a well, or excavating a mine, or any other costs of searching for natural resources. **Development costs** are incurred after the resource has been discovered but before production begins. They include a variety of costs such as expenditures for tunnels, wells, and shafts. It is not unusual for the

---

[3]Because of this characteristic, natural resources sometimes are called *wasting assets*.

cost of a natural resource, either purchased or developed, also to include estimated **restoration costs**. These are costs to restore land or other property to its original condition after extraction of the natural resource ends. Because restoration expenditures occur later—after production begins—they initially represent an obligation incurred in conjunction with an asset retirement. Restoration costs are one example of *asset retirement obligations*, the topic of the next subsection.

On the other hand, the costs of heavy equipment and other assets a company uses during drilling or excavation usually are not considered part of the cost of the natural resource itself. Instead, they are considered depreciable plant and equipment. However, if an asset used in the development of a natural resource cannot be moved and has no alternative use, its depreciable life is limited by the useful life of the natural resource.

Asset Retirement Obligations.   Sometimes a company incurs obligations associated with the disposition of an operational asset, often as a result of acquiring that asset. For example, an oil and gas exploration company might be required to restore land to its original condition after extraction is completed. Until recently, there was considerable diversity in the ways companies accounted for these obligations. Some companies recognized these **asset retirement obligations** (AROs) gradually over the life of the asset while others did not recognize the obligations until the asset was retired or sold.

SFAS No. 143 now requires that an existing legal obligation associated with the retirement of a tangible, long-lived asset be recognized as a liability and measured at fair value. When the liability is credited, the offsetting debit is to the related operational asset.[4] These retirement obligations could arise in connection with several types of operational assets. We introduce the topic here because they are most likely with natural resources. Let's consider some of the provisions of this new accounting standard.

As asset retirement obligation (ARO) is measured at fair value and is recognized as a liability and corresponding increase in asset valuation.

Scope.   AROs arise only from *legal* obligations associated with the retirement of a tangible long-lived asset that result from the acquisition, construction, or development and (or) normal operation of a long-lived asset.

Recognition.   A retirement obligation might arise at the inception of an asset's life or during its operating life. For instance, an offshore oil-and-gas production facility typically incurs its removal obligation when it begins operating. On the other hand, a landfill or a mining operation might incur a reclamation obligation gradually over the life of the asset as space is consumed with waste or as the mine is excavated.

Measurement.   A company recognizes the fair value of an ARO in the period it's incurred. The liability increases the valuation of the operational asset. Usually, the fair value is estimated by calculating the present value of estimated future cash outflows.

Present Value Calculations.   Traditionally, the way uncertainty has been considered in present value calculations has been by discounting the "best estimate" of future cash flows applying a discount rate that has been adjusted to reflect the uncertainty or risk of those cash flows. That's not the approach we take here. Instead, we follow the approach described in the FASB's Concept Statement No. 7[5] which is to adjust the cash flows, not the discount rate, for the uncertainty or risk of those cash flows. This **expected cash flow approach** incorporates specific probabilities of cash flows into the analysis. We use a discount rate equal to the *credit-adjusted risk free rate*. The higher a company's credit risk, the higher will be the discount rate. All other uncertainties or risks are incorporated into the cash flow probabilities. We first considered an illustration of this approach in Chapter 6. Illustration 10–3 demonstrates the approach in connection with the acquisition of a natural resource.

---

[4]"Accounting for Asset Retirement Obligations," *Statement of Financial Accounting Standards No. 143* (Norwalk, Conn.: FASB, 2001).

[5]"Using Cash Flow Information and Present Value in Accounting Measurements," *Statement of Financial Accounting Concepts No. 7* (Norwalk, Conn.: FASB, 2000).

ILLUSTRATION 10–3

Cost of Natural Resources

The Jackson Mining Company paid $1,000,000 for the right to explore for a coal deposit on 500 acres of land in Pennsylvania. Costs of exploring for the coal deposit totaled $800,000 and intangible development costs incurred in digging and erecting the mine shaft were $500,000. In addition, Jackson purchased new excavation equipment for the project at a cost of $600,000. After the coal is removed from the site, the equipment will be sold.

Jackson is required by its contract to restore the land to a condition suitable for recreational use after it extracts the coal. The company has provided the following three cash flow possibilities (A, B and C) for the restoration costs to be paid in three years, after extraction is completed:

	Cash Outflow	Probability
A	$500,000	30%
B	600,000	50%
C	700,000	20%

The company's credit-adjusted risk free interest rate is 8%.
Total capitalized cost for the coal deposit is:

Purchase of rights to explore	$1,000,000
Exploration costs	800,000
Development costs	500,000
Restoration costs	468,360*
Total cost of coal deposit	$2,768,360

*Present value of expected cash outflow for restoration costs (asset retirement obligation):
$500,000 × 30% = $150,000
600,000 × 50% = 300,000
700,000 × 20% = 140,000
$590,000 × .79383 = $468,360
(.79383 is the present value of $1, $n = 3$, $i = 8\%$)

Journal Entries:

Coal mine (determined above)	2,768,360	
Cash ($1,000,000 + 800,000 + 500,000)		2,300,000
Asset retirement liability (determined above)		468,360
Excavation equipment	600,000	
Cash (cost)		600,000

As we discuss in Chapter 11, the cost of the coal mine is allocated to future periods as *depletion* using a depletion rate based on the estimated amount of coal discovered. The $600,000 cost of the excavation equipment, less any anticipated residual value, is allocated to future periods as *depreciation*.

The difference between the asset retirement liability of $468,360 and the probability-weighted expected cash outflow of $590,000, represents interest. It is recognized as interest expense over the three-year excavation period. This process increases the liability to $590,000 by the end of the excavation period.

Year	Interest Expense (accretion)	Increase in Balance	Asset Retirement Obligation
			468,360
1	8% (468,360) = 37,469	37,469	505,829
2	8% (505,829) = 40,466	40,466	546,295
3	8% (546,295) = 43,705*	43,705	590,000

*rounded

If the actual restoration costs are more (less) than the $590,000, a loss (gain) on retirement of the obligation is recognized for the difference.

Sometimes, after exploration or development, it becomes apparent that continuing the project is economically infeasible. If that happens, any costs incurred are expensed rather than capitalized. An exception is in the oil and gas industry, where we have two generally accepted accounting alternatives for accounting for projects that prove unsuccessful. We discuss these alternatives in Appendix 10.

CHECK WITH THE **COACH**

This is the first of two chapters that deal with accounting for operational assets. In studying Chapter 10, the Coach will help you understand the more subtle dimensions of acquiring these assets, such as the impact of goodwill on financial statements. Using Coach, you will read about controversial reporting practices regarding research and development costs in technology companies. ■

INTANGIBLE ASSETS

Intangible assets include such items as patents, copyrights, trademarks, franchises, and goodwill. Despite their lack of physical substance, these assets can be extremely valuable resources for a company. For example, a recent edition of *Financial World* magazine estimated the value of the Coca-Cola trademark to be $43 billion.[6] In general, intangible assets refer to the ownership of exclusive rights that provide benefits to the owner in the production of goods and services.

Intangible assets generally represent exclusive rights that provide benefits to the owner.

The issues involved in accounting for intangibles are similar to those of other operational assets. One key difference, though, is that the future benefits that we attribute to intangible assets usually are much less certain than those attributed to tangible operational assets. For example, will the new toy for which a company acquires a patent be accepted by the market? If so, will it be a blockbuster like Beanie Babies or Rubik's Cube, or will it be only a moderate success? Will it have lasting appeal like Barbie dolls, or will it be a short-term fad? In short, it's often very difficult to anticipate the timing, and even the existence, of future benefits attributable to many intangible assets. In fact, this uncertainty is a discriminating characteristic of intangible assets that perhaps better distinguishes them from tangible assets than their lack of physical substance. After all, other assets, too, do not exist physically but are not considered intangible assets. Accounts receivable and prepaid expenses, for example, have no physical substance and yet are reported among tangible assets.

Companies can either (1) *purchase* intangible assets from other entities (existing patent, copyright, trademark, or franchise rights) or (2) *develop* intangible assets internally (say, develop a new product or process that is then patented). In either case, we amortize its cost, unless it has an indefinite useful life.[7] Also, just like other operational assets, intangibles are subject to asset impairment rules. We discuss amortization and impairment in Chapter 11. In this chapter, we consider the acquisition cost of intangibles.

Intangible assets with finite useful lives are amortized; intangible assets with indefinite useful lives are not amortized.

The initial valuation of purchased intangibles usually is quite simple. We value a purchased intangible at its original cost, which includes its purchase price and all other costs necessary to bring it to condition and location for intended use. For example, if a company purchases a patent from another entity, it might pay legal fees and filing fees in addition to the purchase price. We value intangible assets acquired in exchange for stock, or for other nonmonetary assets, or with deferred payment contracts exactly as we do other operational assets. Let's look briefly at the costs of purchasing some of the more common intangible assets.

Purchased intangibles are valued at their original cost.

Patents.   A **patent** is an exclusive right to manufacture a product or to use a process. This right is granted by the U.S. Patent Office for a period of 20 years. In essence, the holder of a patent has a monopoly on the use, manufacture, or sale of the product or process. If a patent is purchased from an inventor or another individual or company, the amount paid is its initial valuation. The cost might also include such other costs as legal and filing fees to secure

---

[6]This $43 billion represents an estimate of the market value to the company at the time the estimate was made, not the historical cost valuation that appears in the balance sheet of Coca-Cola.
[7]"Goodwill and Other Intangible Assets," *Statement of Financial Accounting Standards No. 142* (Norwalk, Conn.: FASB, 2001).

the patent. Holders of patents often need to defend a patent in court against infringement. Any attorney fees and other costs of successfully defending a patent are added to the patent account.

When a patent is *developed internally,* the research and development costs of doing so are expensed as incurred. We discuss research and development in more detail in a later section. We capitalize legal and filing fees to secure the patent, even if internally developed.

Copyrights. A copyright is an exclusive right of protection given to a creator of a published work, such as a song, film, painting, photograph, or book. Copyrights are protected by law and give the creator the exclusive right to reproduce and sell the artistic or published work for the life of the creator plus 70 years. Accounting for the costs of copyrights is virtually identical to that of patents.

Trademarks. A trademark, also called tradename, is an exclusive right to display a word, a slogan, a symbol, or an emblem that distinctively identifies a company, a product, or a service. The trademark can be registered with the U.S. Patent Office which protects the trademark from use by others for a period of 10 years. The registration can be renewed for an indefinite number of 10-year periods, so a trademark is an example of an intangible asset whose useful life could be indefinite.

A trademark or tradename can be very valuable. The estimated value of $43 billion for the Coca-Cola trademark mentioned previously is a good example. Note that the cost of the trademark reported in the balance sheet is far less than the estimate of its worth to the company. The Coca-Cola Company's 2001 balance sheet disclosed goodwill and other intangibles at a cost of only $2.6 billion.

Franchise **operations are among the most common ways of doing business.**

Franchises. A franchise is a contractual arrangement under which the franchisor grants the franchisee the exclusive right to use the franchisor's trademark or tradename within a geographical area, usually for a specified period of time. Many popular retail businesses such as fast food outlets, automobile dealerships, and motels are franchises. For example, the last time you ordered a hamburger at McDonald's, you were probably dealing with a franchise. The owner of that McDonald's outlet paid McDonald's Corporation a fee in exchange for the exclusive right to use the McDonald's name and to sell its products within a specified geographical area. In addition, many franchisors provide other benefits to the franchisee, such as participating in the construction of the retail outlet, training of employees, and national advertising.

Payments to the franchisor usually include an initial payment plus periodic payments over the life of the franchise agreement. The franchisee capitalizes as an intangible asset, franchise, the initial franchise fee plus any legal costs associated with the contract agreement. The asset is then amortized over the life of the franchise agreement. The periodic payments usually relate to services provided by the franchisor on a continuing basis and are expensed as incurred.

Most purchased intangibles are *specifically identifiable.* That is, cost can be directly associated with a specific intangible right. An exception is goodwill, which we discuss next.

Goodwill **can only be purchased through the acquisition of another company.**

Goodwill **is the excess of the purchase price over the fair market value of the net assets acquired.**

Goodwill. Goodwill is a unique intangible asset in that its cost can't be directly associated with any specifically identifiable right and it is not separable from the company itself. It represents the unique value of a company as a whole over and above all identifiable tangible and intangible assets. Goodwill can emerge from a company's clientele and reputation, its trained employees and management team, its favorable business location, and any other unique features of the company that can't be associated with a specific asset.

Because goodwill can't be separated from a company, it's not possible for a buyer to acquire it without also acquiring the whole company or a substantial portion of it. Goodwill will appear as an asset in a balance sheet only when it was paid for in connection with the acquisition of another company. In that case, the capitalized cost of goodwill equals the purchase price of the company less the fair value of the net assets acquired. The fair value of the net assets equals the fair value of all identifiable tangible and intangible assets less the market value of any liabilities of the selling company assumed by the buyer. Goodwill is a residual asset; it's the amount left after other assets are identified and valued. Consider Illustration 10–4.

The Smithson Corporation acquired all of the outstanding common stock of the Rider Corporation in exchange for $18 million cash.* Smithson assumed all of Rider's long-term debts which have a fair value of $12 million at the date of acquisition. The fair values of all identifiable assets of Rider are as follows ($ in millions):

ILLUSTRATION 10–4

Goodwill

Receivables	$ 5
Inventory	7
Property, plant, and equipment	9
Patent	4
Total	$25

The cost of the goodwill resulting from the acquisition is $5 million:

Purchase price		$18
Less: fair value of net assets		
Assets	$25	
Less: liabilities assumed	(12)	(13)
Goodwill		$ 5

The Smithson Corporation records the acquisition as follows:

Receivables (fair value)	5	
Inventory (fair value)	7	
Property, plant, and equipment (fair value)	9	
Patent (fair value)	4	
Goodwill (difference)	5	
Liabilities (fair value)		12
Cash (purchase price)		18

---

*Determining the amount a purchaser is willing to pay for a company in excess of the identifiable net assets is a question of determining the value of a company as a whole. This question is addressed in most introductory and advanced finance textbooks.

ADDITIONAL CONSIDERATION

It's possible for the fair value of net assets to be greater than the purchase price. The fact that the sum of the separate values of the assets is greater than their combined values indicates that bringing them together actually reduced their value. This effect is rare and often is referred to as *negative goodwill*. Some accountants have argued that this negative amount should be disclosed in the balance sheet as a deduction from other assets. GAAP generally requires the simpler treatment of recognizing the acquired assets at their combined purchase price instead of their individual fair values.

Of course, a company can develop its own goodwill through advertising, training, and other efforts. In fact, most do. However, a company must expense all such costs incurred in the internal generation of goodwill. By not capitalizing these items, accountants realize that the matching principle is violated because many of these expenditures do result in significant future benefits. Also, it's difficult to compare two companies when one has purchased goodwill and the other has not. But imagine how difficult it would be to associate these expenditures with any objective measure of goodwill. In essence, we have an example of a situation where the characteristic of reliability overshadows relevance.

Goodwill, along with other intangible assets with indefinite useful lives, is not amortized.

As we discussed in Chapter 1, recent accounting standards have significantly changed the way we account for business combinations. Before these new standards became effective in 2001, we amortized (expensed in future periods) purchased goodwill just like any other intangible asset. This no longer is the case. Now, just like other intangible assets that have indefinite useful lives, *we do not amortize goodwill.* This makes it imperative that companies make every effort to identify specific intangibles other than goodwill that they acquire in a business combination since goodwill is the amount left after other assets are identified.

SFAS 141 requires that in a business combination an intangible asset be recognized as an asset apart from goodwill if it arises from contractual or other legal rights or be separable.

In keeping with that goal, *SFAS 141* provides guidelines for determining which intangibles should be separately recognized and valued. Specifically, an intangible should be recognized as an asset apart from goodwill if it arises from contractual or other legal rights or is capable of being separated from the acquired entity. Possibilities are patents, trademarks, copyrights, and franchise agreements, and such items as customer lists, license agreements, order backlogs, employment contracts, and noncompetition agreements.[8] In past years, some of these intangibles, if present in a business combination, often were included in the cost of goodwill.[9]

GLOBAL PERSPECTIVE

In the United States, goodwill is capitalized and not amortized. Internationally, the treatment of goodwill varies widely. Countries such as Australia, Japan, and Sweden capitalize and amortize goodwill. Other countries, such as France, Germany, and Italy permit the immediate write-off of goodwill against current earnings, but as an extraordinary or nonrecurring item. The United Kingdom permits the immediate write-off of goodwill against shareholders' equity. Like the United States, Switzerland allows companies to capitalize goodwill without amortization.

Lump-Sum Purchases

It's not unusual for a group of operational assets to be acquired for a single sum. If these assets are indistinguishable, for example 10 identical delivery trucks purchased for a lump-sum price of $150,000, valuation is obvious. Each of the trucks would be valued at $15,000 ($150,000 ÷ 10). However, if the lump-sum purchase involves different assets, it's necessary to allocate the lump-sum acquisition price among the separate items. The assets acquired may have different characteristics and different useful lives. For example, the acquisition of a factory may include assets that are significantly different such as land, building, and equipment.

The allocation is made in proportion to the individual assets' relative market values. This process is best explained by an example in Illustration 10–5.

The relative market value percentages are multiplied by the lump-sum purchase price to determine the initial valuation of each of the separate assets. Notice that the lump-sum purchase includes inventories, which is not an operational asset. The procedure used here to allocate the purchase price in a lump-sum acquisition pertains to any type of asset mix, not just to operational assets.

Noncash Acquisitions

Assets acquired in noncash transactions are valued at the fair value of the assets given or the fair value of the assets received, whichever is more clearly evident.

Companies sometimes acquire operational assets without paying cash but instead by issuing debt or equity securities, receiving donated assets, or exchanging other assets. *The controlling principle in each of these situations is that in any noncash transaction (not just those dealing with operational assets), the components of the transaction are recorded at their fair values.* The first indicator of fair value is the fair value of the assets, debt, or equity securities given. Sometimes the fair value of the assets received is used when their fair value is more clearly evident than the fair value of the assets given.

---

[8]"Business Combinations," *Statement of Financial Accounting Standards No. 141* (Norwalk, Conn.: FASB, 2001).
[9]An assembled workforce is an example of an intangible that is not recognized as a separate asset. A workforce does not represent a contractual or legal right, nor is it separable from the company as a whole.

ILLUSTRATION 10–5

Lump-Sum Purchase

The Smyrna Hand & Edge Tools Company purchased an existing factory for a single sum of $2,000,000. The price included title to the land, the factory building, and the manufacturing equipment in the building, a patent on a process the equipment uses, and inventories of raw materials. An independent appraisal estimated the market values of the assets (if purchased separately) at $330,000 for the land, $550,000 for the building, $660,000 for the equipment, $440,000 for the patent and $220,000 for the inventories. The lump-sum purchase price of $2,000,000 is allocated to the separate assets as follows:

Market Values		
Land	$ 330,000	15%
Building	550,000	25
Equipment	660,000	30
Patent	440,000	20
Inventories	220,000	10
Total	$2,200,000	100%

Land	(15% × $2,000,000)	300,000
Building	(25% × $2,000,000)	500,000
Equipment	(30% × $2,000,000)	600,000
Patent	(20% × $2,000,000)	400,000
Inventories	(10% × $2,000,000)	200,000
Cash		2,000,000

The total purchase price is allocated in proportion to the relative market values of the assets acquired.

ETHICAL DILEMMA

Grandma's Cookie Company purchased a factory building. The company controller, Don Nelson, is in the process of allocating the lump-sum purchase price between land and building. Don suggests to the company's chief financial officer, Judith Prince, that they fudge a little by allocating a disproportionately higher share of the price to land. Don reasons that this will reduce depreciation expense, boost income, increase their profit-sharing bonus, and hopefully, increase the price of the company's stock. Judith has some reservations about this because the higher reported income will also cause income taxes to be higher than they would be if a correct allocation of the purchase price is made.

What are the ethical issues? What stakeholders' interests are in conflict?

DEFERRED PAYMENTS

A company can acquire an operational asset by giving the seller a promise to pay cash in the future and thus creating a liability, usually a note payable. The initial valuation of the asset is, again, quite simple as long as the note payable explicitly requires the payment of interest at a realistic interest rate. For example, suppose a machine is acquired for $15,000 and the buyer signs a note requiring the payment of $15,000 sometime in the future *plus* interest in the meantime at a realistic interest rate. The machine would be valued at $15,000 and the transaction recorded as follows:

Machine.	15,000	
Note payable.		15,000

We know from our discussion of the time value of money in Chapter 6 that most liabilities are valued at the present value of future cash payments, reflecting an appropriate time value of money. As long as the note payable explicitly contains a realistic interest rate, the present value will equal the face value of the note, $15,000 in our previous example. This also should be equal to the fair value of the machine purchased. On the other hand, when an interest rate is not specified or is unrealistic, determining the cost of the asset is less straightforward. In that case, the accountant should look beyond the form of the transaction and record its substance. Consider Illustration 10–6.

ILLUSTRATION 10–6 Deferred Payment Contract	On June 30, 2003, the Midwestern Steam Gas Corporation purchased an industrial furnace. Midwestern paid $10,000 on the purchase date and signed a noninterest-bearing note requiring the balance to be paid in five annual installments of $10,000 beginning June 30, 2004. An interest rate of 10% would be reasonable in this situation.

Some portion of the payments required by a noninterest-bearing note in reality is interest.

Noncash transactions are recorded at the fair value of the items exchanged.

On the surface, it might appear that Midwestern is paying $60,000 for the furnace, the sum of the eventual cash payments. However, when you note that the agreement specifies no interest even though the final payment won't be made for five years, it becomes obvious that a portion of the payments is not actually payment for the furnace but instead is interest on the note. At what amount should Midwestern value the furnace and the related note payable?

Midwestern could either (1) determine the fair value of the note payable by computing the present value of the cash payments at the appropriate interest rate of 10% or (2) determine the fair value of the furnace on the date of purchase. Theoretically, both alternatives should lead to the same valuation. In this case, because we can determine an appropriate interest rate for the note, we determine the fair value of the note by computing its present value. The amount actually paid for the machine is the present value of the cash flows called for by the loan agreement, discounted at the market rate—assumed in this case to be 10%.

$$PV = \$10,000 \times 3.79079^* = \$37,908$$
*Present value of an ordinary annuity of $1; $n = 5$, $i = 10\%$ (from Table 6A–4).

So the furnace should be recorded at its *real* cost, $47,908, as follows:[10]

The economic essence of a transaction should prevail over its outward appearance.

Furnace ($37,908 + 10,000)	47,908	
Cash (payment on purchase date)		10,000
Note payable (determined above)		37,908

Assuming that Midwestern's fiscal year-end is December 31 and that adjusting entries are recorded only at the end of the year, the company would record the following entries for the year-end interest accrual and the first annual note payment.

December 31, 2003		
Interest expense (10% × $37,908 × 6/12)	1,895	
Interest payable		1,895
June 30, 2004		
Interest expense (10% × $37,908 × 6/12)	1,895	
Interest payable (amount accrued)	1,895	
Note payable (difference)	6,210	
Cash		10,000

---

[10]The entry shown assumes the note is recorded by the net method. By the gross method, the note is recorded at its present value of $37,908 by using a contra account, called *discount on note payable,* to offset note payable for the difference between the face value of the note and its present value. The difference of $12,092 is recognized as interest expense over the life of the note.

Machine	47,908	
Discount on note payable	12,092	
Cash		10,000
Note payable (face amount)		50,000

Sometimes, the fair value of an asset acquired in a noncash transaction is readily available from price lists, previous purchases, or otherwise. In that case, this fair value may be more clearly evident than the fair value of the note and it would serve as the best evidence of the exchange value of the transaction. As an example, let's look at Illustration 10–7.

On January 1, 2003, Dennison, Inc., purchased a machine and signed a noninterest-bearing note in payment. The note requires the company to make five annual payments of $20,000 beginning on December 31, 2003. Dennison is not sure what interest rate appropriately reflects the time value of money. However, price lists indicate the machine could have been purchased for cash at a price of $79,854.

Dennison records the following entry on January 1:

Machine (cash price)...	79,854	
Note payable...		79,854

ILLUSTRATION 10–7

Noninterest-Bearing Note—Fair Value Known

In this situation, we infer the present value of the note from the fair value of the asset. Again, the difference between the note's $79,854 present value and the total of the cash payments to be made—$20,000 × 5 = $100,000 in this case—represents interest. We can determine the interest rate that is implicit in the agreement as follows:

$$\$79{,}854 \text{ (present value)} = \$20{,}000 \text{ (annuity amount)} \times \text{PV factor}$$

$$\frac{\$79{,}854}{\$20{,}000} = 3.9927*$$

*Present value of an ordinary annuity of $1; $n = 5$, $i = ?$ (from Table 6A–4, $i = $ **8%**)

We refer to the 8% rate as the *implicit rate of interest,* which also is the implied market rate. Dennison records interest after one year at 8% multiplied by $79,854, the balance of the liability outstanding during that first year:

December 31, 2003

Interest expense (8% × $79,854).........................	6,388	
Note payable (difference)	13,612	
Cash (annual installment payment)		20,000

> The effective interest on debt is the market rate of interest multiplied by the outstanding balance of the debt (during the interest period).

Because $6,388 of the $20,000 payment is determined to be interest, this leaves $13,612 to reduce the carrying amount of the note from $79,854 to $66,242. Interest in the second year is 8% × $66,242 = $5,299. We discuss this concept in greater depth in Chapter 14.

We now turn our attention to the acquisition of operational assets acquired in exchange for equity securities or through donation.

ISSUANCE OF EQUITY SECURITIES

The most common situation in which equity securities are issued for operational assets occurs when small companies incorporate and the owner or owners contribute assets to the new corporation in exchange for ownership securities, usually common stock. Because the common shares are not publicly traded, it's difficult to determine their fair value. In that case, the fair value of the assets received by the corporation is probably the better indicator of the transaction's exchange value. In other situations, particularly those involving corporations whose stock is actively traded, the market value of the shares is the best indication of fair value. Consider Illustration 10–8.

If the market value of the common stock had not been reliably determinable, the value of the land as determined through an independent appraisal would be used as the cost of the land and the value of the common stock.

LO4

> Assets acquired by issuing common stock are valued at the fair value of the securities or the fair value of the assets, whichever is more clearly evident.

ILLUSTRATION 10–8	On March 31, 2003, the Elcorn Company issued 10,000 shares of its nopar common stock in exchange for land. On the date of the transaction, the market value of the common stock was $20 per share. The journal entry to record this transaction is:
Asset Acquired by Issuing Equity Securities	Land... 200,000
	Common stock (10,000 shares × $20) 200,000

DONATED ASSETS

On occasion, companies acquire operational assets through donation. The donation usually is an enticement to do something that benefits the donor. For example, the developer of an industrial park might pay some of the costs of building a manufacturing facility to entice a company to locate in its park. Companies record assets donated by unrelated parties at their fair values based on either an available market price or an appraisal value. This should not be considered a departure from historical cost valuation. Instead, it is equivalent to the donor contributing cash to the company and the company using the cash to acquire the asset.

Donated assets are recorded at their fair values.

As the recipient records the asset at its fair value, what account receives the offsetting credit? Over the years, there has been disagreement over this question. Should the recipient increase its paid-in capital—the part of shareholders' equity representing investments in the firm? Or, should the donated asset be considered revenue? *SFAS 116* requires that donated assets be recorded as *revenue*.[11] Recall that revenues generally are inflows of assets from delivering or producing goods, rendering services, or from other activities that constitute the entity's ongoing major or central operations. The rationale is that the company receiving the donation is performing a service for the donor in exchange for the asset donated.

Revenue is credited for the amount paid by an unrelated party.

Corporations occasionally receive donations from governmental units. A local governmental unit might provide land or pay all or some of the cost of a new office building or manufacturing plant to entice a company to locate within its geographical boundaries. For example, the city of San Jose, California, recently paid a significant portion of the cost of a new office building for IBM Corporation. *SFAS 116 does not apply to transfers of assets from governmental units.* However, it is the opinion of the authors that this type of donation also should be accounted for as revenue by the recipient. In the IBM example, the new office building, located in downtown San Jose, brought jobs to a revitalized downtown area and increased revenues to the city. The City of San Jose did not receive an equity interest in IBM through its donation, but significantly benefited nevertheless.

Illustration 10–9 provides an example. In this illustration, we assume that, even though the donation is from a governmental unit, *SFAS 116* guidelines apply.

ILLUSTRATION 10–9	Elcorn Enterprises decided to relocate its office headquarters to the city of Westmont. The city agreed to pay 20% of the $20 million cost of building the headquarters in order to entice Elcorn to relocate. The building was completed on May 3, 2003. Elcorn paid its portion of the cost of the building in cash. Elcorn records the transaction as follows:
Asset Donation	Building 20,000,000
	Cash 16,000,000
	Revenue—donation of asset (20% × $20 million) 4,000,000

Operational assets also can be acquired in an exchange. Because an exchange transaction inherently involves a disposition of one operational asset as it is given up in exchange for another, we cover these transactions in Part B, Dispositions and Exchanges.

---

[11]"Accounting for Contributions Received and Contributions Made," *Statement of Financial Accounting Standards No. 116* (Norwalk, Conn: FASB, 1993).

DECISION MAKERS' PERSPECTIVE

The operational asset acquisition decision is among the most significant decisions that management must make. A decision to acquire a new fleet of airplanes or to build or purchase a new office building or manufacturing plant could influence a company's performance for many years.

These decisions, often referred to as **capital budgeting** decisions, require management to forecast all future net cash flows (cash inflows minus cash outflows) generated by the operational asset(s). These cash flows are then used in a model to determine if the future cash flows are sufficient to warrant the capital expenditure. One such model, the net present value model, compares the present value of future net cash flows with the required initial acquisition cost of the asset(s). If the present value is higher than the acquisition cost, the asset is acquired. You have studied or will study capital budgeting in considerable depth in a financial management course. The introduction to the time value of money concept in Chapter 6 provided you with important tools necessary to evaluate capital budgeting decisions.

A key to profitability is how well a company manages and utilizes its assets. Financial analysts often use activity, or turnover, ratios to evaluate a company's effectiveness in managing assets. This concept was illustrated with receivables and inventory in previous chapters. Operational assets—particularly property, plant, and equipment (PP&E)—usually are a company's primary revenue-generating assets. Their efficient use is critical to generating a satisfactory return to owners. One ratio analysts often use to measure how effectively managers use PP&E is the **fixed-asset turnover ratio.** This ratio is calculated as follows:

> *The **fixed-asset turnover ratio** measures a company's effectiveness in managing property, plant, and equipment.*

$$\text{Fixed-asset turnover ratio} = \frac{\text{Net sales}}{\text{Average fixed assets}}$$

The ratio indicates the level of sales generated by the company's investment in fixed assets. The denominator usually is the book value (cost less accumulated depreciation and depletion) of property, plant, and equipment.[12]

As with other turnover ratios, we can compare a company's fixed-asset turnover with that of its competitors, with an industry average, or with the same company's ratio over time. Let's compare the fixed-asset turnover ratios for Maytag and Whirlpool, the same two companies we used in Chapter 7 to illustrate accounts receivable turnover.

	($ in millions)			
	Maytag		**Whirlpool**	
	2001	**2000**	**2001**	**2000**
Property, plant, and equipment (net)	$1,036	$864	$2,052	$2,134
Net sales—2001	$4,324		$10,343	

The fixed-asset turnover ratio for 2001 for Maytag is 4.55 ($4,324 ÷ [($1,036 + 864) ÷ 2]) compared to Whirlpool's turnover of 4.93 ($10,343 ÷ [($2,052 + 2,134) ÷ 2]). Whirlpool is able to generate $.38 more than Maytag in sales dollars for each dollar of investment in fixed assets. ▪

DISPOSITIONS AND EXCHANGES

PART

b

After using operational assets, companies will sell, retire, or exchange those assets. Accounting for exchanges differs somewhat from accounting for sales and retirements because they involve both an acquisition and a disposition. So let's look first at sales and retirements

---

[12]If intangible assets are significant, their book value could be added to the denominator to produce a turnover that reflects all operational assets. The use of book value provides an approximation of the company's current investment in these assets.

and then we'll address accounting for exchanges. Be sure to note that in each case, the companies should record depreciation, depletion, or amortization up to the date of disposition or exchange.

Dispositions

When selling operational assets for monetary consideration (cash or a receivable), the seller recognizes a gain or loss for the difference between the consideration received and the book value of the asset sold. Illustration 10–10 provides an example.

ILLUSTRATION 10–10 Sale of Operational Asset **A gain or loss is recognized for the difference between the consideration received and the asset's book value.**	The Robosport Company sold for $6,000 machinery that originally cost $20,000. Depreciation of $12,000 had been recorded up to the date of sale. Since the $8,000 book value of the asset ($20,000 − 12,000) exceeds the $6,000 consideration Robosport received, the company recognizes a $2,000 loss. The sale is recorded as follows:

Cash (selling price)	6,000	
Accumulated depreciation (account balance)	12,000	
Loss on disposal of machinery (difference)	2,000	
Machinery (account balance)		20,000

Retirements (or abandonments) are treated similarly. The only difference is that there will be no monetary consideration received. A loss is recorded for the remaining book value of the asset.

Operational assets to be disposed of by sale are classified as held for sale and measured at the lower of book value or fair value less cost to sell.

When an operational asset is to be disposed of by *sale,* we classify it as "held for sale" and report it at the lower of its book value or fair value less any cost to sell.[13] If the fair value less cost to sell is below book value, we recognize an impairment loss. Operational assets classified as held for sale are not depreciated or amortized. Recall from your study of discontinued operations in Chapter 4 that this treatment is the same one we employed in accounting for a component of an entity that is held for sale. We cover this topic in more depth in the impairment section of Chapter 11.

ADDITIONAL CONSIDERATION

Involuntary Conversions

Occasionally companies dispose of operational assets unintentionally. These so-called involuntary conversions include destruction by fire, earthquake, flood, or other catastrophe and expropriation by a governmental body.

Usually, the company receives a cash settlement from an insurance company for destroyed assets or from the governmental body for expropriated assets. The company often immediately reinvests this cash in similar assets. Nevertheless, involuntary conversions are treated precisely the same as voluntary conversions. That is, the proceeds are recorded, the book value of the lost assets are removed, and a gain or loss is recognized for the difference.

Exchanges

Sometimes a company will acquire an operational asset in exchange for another operational asset. This frequently involves a trade-in by which a new asset is acquired in exchange for an old asset, and cash is given to equalize the fair values of the assets exchanged. The basic

---

[13]"Accounting for the Impairment or Disposal of Long-Lived Assets," *Statement of Financial Accounting Standards No. 144* (Norwalk, Conn.: FASB, 2001)

principle followed in these nonmonetary exchanges is to value the asset received at fair value.[14] This can be the fair value of the asset given up or the fair value of the asset received plus (or minus) any cash exchanged.[15] We first look to the fair value of the asset given up. However, in a trade-in, quite often the fair value of the new asset is more clearly evident than the second-hand value of the asset traded in.

An important exception to the fair value principle relates to certain exchanges involving similar productive assets. Assets are considered similar if the transaction does not result in the culmination of an earnings process. For these exchanges, the earnings process in which the assets are employed continues. So, if a delivery truck is exchanged for a new delivery truck that will perform the same function as the old truck, the earnings process continues and the transaction is considered a similar asset exchange. We consider this exception later in this section.

Another exception is situations when we cannot determine the fair value of either the asset given up or the asset received. In these cases, the asset received is valued at the book value of the asset given. This would apply in the unusual situation when we could not reasonably determine fair value.

> An asset received in a nonmonetary exchange generally is recorded at the cash equivalent value of the assets exchanged.

> If we cannot determine the fair value of either asset in the exchange, the asset received is valued at the book value of the asset given.

EXCHANGES OF DISSIMILAR ASSETS

When dissimilar assets are exchanged, four possibilities arise regarding whether a loss or gain is created and whether cash is paid or received. By varying the terms of a single exchange transaction, we can compare the effect of the four possibilities.

The Elcorn Company traded land it had been holding as an investment in exchange for equipment. The land had a book value of $100,000.	**ILLUSTRATION 10–11** Nonmonetary Exchange—Dissimilar Assets

If the fair value of the asset given up, the land, is determinable, it is used to value the transaction. The difference between that amount and the book value of the land would determine whether a gain or loss is indicated. The equipment is valued at the fair value of the land plus (minus) any cash paid (received) regardless of whether a gain or loss is indicated. If we cannot determine the fair value of the land, then we use the fair value of the asset received, the equipment.

The fair value of the land is $80,000, and $10,000 cash is *given*.

> **SITUATION D1:** Dissimilar assets; loss indicated; cash given.

The $10,000 cash is given to equate the fair values of the exchanged assets. In this case, because the land's fair value is $80,000, and the Elcorn Company paid $10,000 in cash to equalize the transaction, the equipment apparently has a fair value of $90,000. The equipment is recorded at this amount, and a $20,000 loss is recognized for the difference between the fair value and book value of the land.

Equipment ($80,000 + 10,000)	90,000	
Loss ($100,000 − 80,000)	20,000	
Cash (amount paid)		10,000
Land (book value)		100,000

The fair value of the land is $80,000, and $10,000 is *received*.

> **SITUATION D2:** Dissimilar assets; loss indicated; cash received.

Because cash is received in this case to equalize fair values, the new equipment's fair value must be less than the fair value of the land.

---

[14]Monetary items are assets and liabilities whose *amounts are fixed*, by contract or otherwise, in terms of a specific number of dollars. Others are considered nonmonetary.

[15]"Accounting for Nonmonetary Transactions," *Accounting Principles Board Opinion No. 29* (New York: AICPA, 1973).

Equipment ($80,000 − 10,000)	70,000	
Cash (amount received)	10,000	
Loss ($100,000 − 80,000)	20,000	
Land (book value)		100,000

Notice that in each of the first two situations the loss is the same, the $20,000 difference between the fair value and book value of the land.

The fair value of the land is $140,000, and $10,000 cash is given.

SITUATION D3:
Dissimilar assets; gain indicated; cash given.

In this situation, a gain is indicated because the fair value of the land is higher than its book value. Again, the equipment is valued at the fair value of the land plus the cash paid.

Equipment ($140,000 + 10,000)	150,000	
Cash (amount paid)		10,000
Land (book value)		100,000
Gain ($140,000 − 100,000)		40,000

SITUATION D4:
Dissimilar assets; gain indicated; cash received.

The fair value of the land is $140,000, and $10,000 cash is received.

The equipment is valued at $130,000, the fair value of the land less cash received, and the indicated gain is recognized.

Equipment ($140,000 − 10,000)	130,000	
Cash (amount received)	10,000	
Land (book value)		100,000
Gain ($140,000 − 100,000)		40,000

Notice that in situations D3 and D4, the gain is the same, the $40,000 difference between the fair value and book value of the land.

We can summarize accounting for dissimilar nonmonetary asset exchanges as follows:

- We recognize the difference between the fair value and the book value of the asset given up as a gain or loss.
- We value the asset acquired at the fair value of the asset given up plus (minus) any cash paid (received).
- If we can't determine the fair value of the asset given up, we record the asset received at its fair value.

EXCHANGES OF SIMILAR ASSETS

When an exchange involves similar assets—say an old delivery truck for a new delivery truck or old factory equipment for new factory equipment—the accounting treatment depends on (1) whether a gain or loss is indicated by the fair value of the asset given up compared to its book value and (2) whether or not cash is received. Specifically, gains are not recognized unless cash is received in the exchange. Let's consider why.

An exchange of similar assets is viewed as a continuation of the earnings process using the same operational assets rather than the culmination of an earnings process.

To record a gain implies that an earnings process has been completed. When similar assets are exchanged, the earnings process in which the assets are employed typically continues. On the contrary, in an exchange of *dissimilar* assets such as land for equipment or inventory for a computer, the transaction is considered to be the culmination of an earnings process. Stated differently, since the old asset isn't being replaced, it is viewed as having been sold. This is not the case when *similar* assets are exchanged, *unless cash is received*. Then it's assumed that part of the old asset is *traded* for the new asset and part of the old asset is *sold* for cash. In such a case, a gain is recorded on the sale portion of the transaction if the cash received exceeds the book value of the portion of the asset considered sold. This is best understood through the example provided in Illustration 10–12.

As before, we'll vary the terms of this single transaction in order to compare four different scenarios.

The Elcorn Company exchanged equipment used in the production process for new equipment to be used for a similar purpose. The old equipment has a book value of $100,000 (original cost of $140,000 less accumulated depreciation of $40,000) on the date of the exchange.	ILLUSTRATION 10–12 Exchange of Similar Assets

The fair value of the old equipment is $80,000, and $10,000 cash is *given.*

SITUATION S1: Similar assets; loss indicated; cash given.

A loss is indicated in this situation because the fair value of the old equipment ($80,000) relinquished is less than its book value ($100,000). The basic principle of using fair value of the assets given up is used to value the new equipment. The new equipment is recorded at the fair value of old equipment plus cash paid and a $20,000 loss is recognized.

Equipment—new ($80,000 + 10,000)	90,000	
Loss ($100,000 − 80,000)	20,000	
Accumulated depreciation (account balance)	40,000	
Cash (amount paid)		10,000
Equipment—old (account balance)		140,000

The fair value of the old equipment is $80,000, and $10,000 cash is *received.*

SITUATION S2: Similar assets; loss indicated; cash received.

Again, a loss is indicated. The market value of the old equipment minus the cash received is the initial valuation of the new equipment.

Equipment—new ($80,000 − 10,000)	70,000	
Cash (amount received)	10,000	
Loss ($100,000 − 80,000)	20,000	
Accumulated depreciation (account balance)	40,000	
Equipment—old (account balance)		140,000

Notice again that in situations S1 and S2 the loss is the same, the $20,000 difference between the fair value and book value of the equipment.

The fair value of the old equipment is $110,000, and $10,000 cash is *given.*

SITUATION S3: Similar assets; gain indicated; cash given.

A $10,000 gain is indicated by the excess of the fair value of old equipment of $110,000 over its book value of $100,000. As we discussed earlier, it is inappropriate to record this gain because the exchange of similar assets is considered to be a trade rather than the culmination of an earnings process. As a result, the new equipment is valued at the book value of the old asset plus the cash paid. No gain is recognized.[16]

Equipment—new ($100,000 + 10,000)	110,000	
Accumulated depreciation (account balance)	40,000	
Cash (amount paid)		10,000
Equipment—old (account balance)		140,000

To better understand the reasoning behind the nonrecognition of gain, consider the effect of the exchange. The company has exchanged similar assets and is in no better position economically than before the exchange. Whatever benefits the old asset provided, the new asset will continue to provide. That is, the new equipment replaces the old equipment in an ongoing earnings process (the production of merchandise for sale).

---

[16]*APBO 29* considers nonmonetary transactions to be those that involve little or no monetary assets. If monetary consideration is significant, the exchange is considered a monetary exchange by both parties and fair values are used to value assets and measure gains and losses. This distinction is important only in situations S3 and S4 when a departure from using fair values is otherwise appropriate. The Emerging Issues Task Force in *EITF Issue No. 86-29,* "Nonmonetary Transactions: Magnitude of Boot and the Exception to the Use of Fair Value," stated that if monetary consideration represents 25% or more of the total consideration received, the transaction is monetary. In our illustrations and concept review, cash received is less than 25% and the transactions are treated as nonmonetary.

SITUATION S4: Similar assets; gain indicated; cash received.

The fair value of the old equipment is $150,000, and $15,000 cash is *received*.

An apparent gain of $50,000 is indicated because the exchange gives Elcorn credit for the old equipment's fair value of $150,000 while its book value is only $100,000. In the previous situation, we did not recognize the gain because similar assets were exchanged. In this situation, though, in addition to receiving the *similar* asset—equipment—the company also receives a *dissimilar* asset—cash. In a sense, part of the old equipment is *sold* for cash, and part is *exchanged* for a similar asset. We can recognize a gain on the portion sold because it represents the completion of an earnings process. To do this, we need to allocate the book value of the old asset between the part that is sold and the part that is traded. The allocation is based on the proportional relationship between the fair value of the new asset and the cash received. This is the same technique we used earlier to allocate a lump-sum purchase price among the individual asset accounts.

The proportion of the asset considered sold is the proportion of the total fair value received represented by cash.

$$\frac{\text{Cash received}}{\text{Cash received} + \text{Fair value of similar asset received*}}$$

$$\frac{\$15,000}{\$15,000 + 135,000} = 10\%$$

*Indicated in this case by the fair value of the equipment surrendered ($150,000) minus the cash received ($15,000).

Calculation of the Gain:

Determine Relative Fair Values of Assets Received:	Fair Values	Relative Proportions
Cash	$ 15,000	10%
New equipment* ($150,000 − 15,000)	135,000	90
Total	$150,000	100%

10% of the fair value received is cash.

Determine Portion of Old Equipment Sold:

Portion sold (10% × $100,000)	$ 10,000
Portion traded (90% × $100,000)	90,000
Total book value ($140,000 − 40,000)	$100,000

10% of the old equipment is considered sold.

Determine Gain on Portion of Old Equipment Sold:

Cash received	$ 15,000
Portion sold (10% × $100,000)	(10,000)
Gain recognized on portion sold	$ 5,000

*Fair value of old equipment minus the cash received.

You should note that the total gain is more than the amount recognized:

A gain can be recognized only on the portion of the old equipment considered sold.

Cash received	$ 15,000
New equipment ($150,000 − 15,000)	135,000
Total received (fair value of old equipment)	150,000
Total given up (book value of old equipment)	(100,000)
Total gain	$ 50,000

Another way to calculate the portion of the gain to be recognized is by multiplying the sold percentage by the total gain:

Total gain	$50,000
Portion of old asset considered sold	× 10%
Gain recognized on portion sold	$ 5,000

The journal entry to record the exchange is as follows:

Equipment—new (to balance)	90,000	
Cash (amount received)	15,000	
Accumulated depreciation (account balance)	40,000	
Equipment—old (account balance).		140,000
Gain (determined above)		5,000

The cost of the new equipment can be calculated as the fair value of the new equipment minus the portion of the gain not recognized, as follows:

Fair value of the new equipment	$135,000
Less: Gain not recognized ($50,000 − 5,000)	(45,000)
Cost of new equipment	$ 90,000

Cost also can be determined by adding the book value of the old equipment less any cash received plus the gain recognized, as follows:

Book value of the old equipment	$100,000
Less: Cash received	(15,000)
Plus: Gain recognized	5,000
Cost of new equipment	$ 90,000

ADDITIONAL CONSIDERATION

For illustration, you might find it helpful to separate the entry into its two components:

Portion Sold:

Cash (amount received)	15,000	
Accumulated depreciation (10% × $40,000)	4,000	
Equipment—old (10% × $140,000)		14,000
Gain (difference: also calculated above).		5,000

Portion Traded:

Equipment—new (plug: book value of portion traded).	90,000	
Accumulated depreciation (90% × $40,000)	36,000	
Equipment—old (90% × $140,000)		126,000

CONCEPT REVIEW EXERCISE

Nonmonetary Exchanges

Part A:

The MD Corporation recently acquired new equipment to be used in its production process. In exchange, the company traded in an existing asset that had an original cost of $60,000 and accumulated depreciation on the date of the exchange of $45,000. In addition, MD paid $40,000 cash to the equipment manufacturer. The fair value of the old equipment is $10,000.

Required:
1. Prepare the journal entry to record the exchange transaction assuming that the old and new equipment are considered dissimilar assets.
2. Prepare the journal entry to record the exchange transaction assuming that the old and new equipment are considered similar assets.

Part B:

The MD Corporation recently acquired new equipment to be used in its production process. In exchange, the company traded in an existing asset that had an original cost of $100,000 and accumulated depreciation on the date of the exchange of $60,000. In addition, MD received $10,000 in cash from the equipment manufacturer. The fair value of the old equipment is $80,000, which means the fair value of the new equipment is $70,000 ($80,000 − cash received of $10,000).

Required:
1. Prepare the journal entry to record the exchange transaction assuming that the old and new equipment are considered dissimilar assets.
2. Prepare the journal entry to record the exchange transaction assuming that the old and new equipment are considered similar assets.

SOLUTION

Part A:
1. Prepare the journal entry to record the exchange transaction assuming that the old and new equipment are considered dissimilar assets.

Equipment—new ($10,000 + 40,000)	50,000	
Loss ($15,000 − 10,000)	5,000	
Accumulated depreciation (account balance)	45,000	
Cash (amount paid)		40,000
Equipment—old (account balance)		60,000

2. Prepare the journal entry to record the exchange transaction assuming that the old and new equipment are considered similar assets.
    Answer is the same as requirement 1.

Part B:
1. Prepare the journal entry to record the exchange transaction assuming that the old and new equipment are considered dissimilar assets.

Equipment—new ($80,000 − 10,000)	70,000	
Cash (amount received)	10,000	
Accumulated depreciation (account balance)	60,000	
Gain ($80,000 − 40,000)		40,000
Equipment—old (account balance)		100,000

2. Prepare the journal entry to record the exchange transaction assuming that the old and new equipment are considered similar assets.
    The proportion of the asset considered sold is the proportion of the total fair value received represented by cash.

$$\frac{\text{Cash received}}{\text{Cash received} + \text{Fair value of similar asset received}}$$

$$\frac{\$10,000}{\$10,000 + 70,000} = 12.5\%$$

Calculation of the gain

12.5% of the old equipment is considered sold.

Cash received	$10,000
Portion sold [12.5% × ($100,000 − 60,000)]	(5,000)
Gain recognized on portion sold	$ 5,000

Equipment—new (to balance*)	35,000	
Cash (amount received)	10,000	
Accumulated depreciation (account balance)	60,000	
Equipment—old (account balance)		100,000
Gain (determined above)		5,000

*The cost of the new equipment can also be calculated as the fair value of the new equipment minus the portion of the gain not recognized, as follows:

Fair value of the new equipment	$70,000
Less: Gain not recognized ($40,000 − 5,000)	(35,000)
Cost of new equipment	$35,000

Graphic 10–4 provides a summary of accounting for nonmonetary exchanges.

GRAPHIC 10–4   Nonmonetary Exchanges

Summary of Recording Exchanges of Nonmonetary Assets

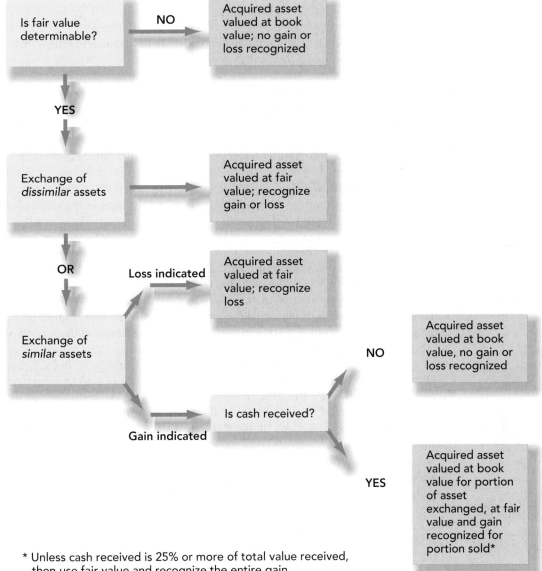

* Unless cash received is 25% or more of total value received, then use fair value and recognize the entire gain.

SELF-CONSTRUCTED ASSETS AND RESEARCH AND DEVELOPMENT

PART

C

Two types of expenditures relating to operational assets whose accounting treatment has generated considerable controversy are interest costs pertaining to self-constructed assets and amounts spent for research and development. We now consider those expenditures and why those controversies have developed.

Self-Constructed Assets

A company might decide to construct an operational asset for its own use rather than buy an existing one. For example, a retailer like Nordstrom might decide to build its own store rather than purchase an existing building. A manufacturing company like Intel could construct its own manufacturing facility. In fact, Nordstrom and Intel are just two of the many companies that self-construct assets. Other recognizable examples include Walt Disney, Sears, and Caterpillar. Quite often these companies act as the main contractor and then subcontract most of the actual construction work.

The critical accounting issue in these instances is identifying the cost of the self-constructed asset. The task is more difficult than for purchased assets because there is no external transaction to establish an exchange price. Actually, two difficulties arise in connection with assigning costs to self-constructed assets: (1) determining the amount of the company's indirect manufacturing costs (overhead) to be allocated to the construction and (2) deciding on the proper treatment of interest (actual or implicit) incurred during construction.

OVERHEAD ALLOCATION

The cost of a self-constructed asset includes identifiable materials and labor and a portion of the company's manufacturing overhead costs.

One difficulty of associating costs with self-constructed assets is the same difficulty encountered when determining cost of goods manufactured for sale. The costs of material and direct labor usually are easily identified with a particular construction project and are included in cost. However, the treatment of manufacturing overhead cost and its allocation between construction projects and normal production is a controversial issue.

Some accountants advocate the inclusion of only the *incremental* overhead costs in the total cost of construction. That is, the asset's cost would include only those additional costs that are incurred because of the decision to construct the asset. This would exclude such indirect costs as depreciation and the salaries of supervisors that would be incurred whether or not the construction project is undertaken. If, however, a new construction supervisor was hired specifically to work on the project, then that salary would be included in asset cost.

Others advocate assigning overhead on the same basis that is used for a regular manufacturing process. That is, all overhead costs are allocated both to production and to self-constructed assets based on the relative amount of a chosen cost driver (for example, labor hours) incurred. This is known as the *full-cost approach* and is the generally accepted method used to determine the cost of a self-constructed asset.

INTEREST CAPITALIZATION

FINANCIAL REPORTING CASE

Q3, p. 461

To reiterate, the cost of an asset includes all costs necessary to get the asset ready for its intended use. Unlike one purchased from another company, a self-constructed asset requires time to create it. During this construction period, the project must be financed in some way. This suggests the question as to whether interest costs during the construction period are one of the costs of acquiring the asset itself or simply costs of financing the asset. On the one hand, we might point to interest charges to finance inventories during their period of manufacture or to finance the purchase of plant assets from others and argue that construction period interest charges are merely costs of financing the asset that should be expensed as incurred like all other interest costs. On the other hand, we might argue that self-constructed assets are different in that during the construction period, they are not yet ready for their intended use for producing revenues. And, so, in keeping with both the historical cost principle and the matching concept, all costs during this period, including interest, should be capitalized and then allocated as depreciation during later periods when the assets are providing benefits.

Only assets that are constructed as discrete projects qualify for interest capitalization.

Qualifying Assets.   Generally accepted accounting principles are consistent with the second argument. Specifically, interest is capitalized during the construction period for (a) assets built for a company's own use as well as for (b) assets constructed *as discrete projects* for sale or lease (a ship or a real estate development, for example). This excludes from interest capitalization consideration inventories that are routinely manufactured in large quantities on a repetitive basis and assets that already are in use or are ready for their intended use.[17] Interest costs incurred during the productive life of the asset are expensed as incurred.

Prior to 1979, when this treatment was mandated by *SFAS 34,* many companies treated construction-period interest costs as a cost of obtaining funds and not a cost of obtaining an asset. Accordingly, interest costs were expensed rather than capitalized. In fact, prior to the early 1970s, few companies other than utilities capitalized interest. Utilities have long been motivated to do so by the desire to increase their asset bases on which regulated utility rates are determined. Nonregulated companies began to follow suit during the economic slowdown of the early 1970s as a way to decrease expenses and bolster profits. *SFAS 34* was an attempt to address the diversity of accounting practice. Now all companies capitalize interest incurred during the construction of a qualified asset.

Only interest incurred during the construction period is eligible for capitalization.

Period of Capitalization.   The capitalization period for a self-constructed asset starts with the first expenditure (materials, labor, or overhead) and ends either when the asset is substantially complete and ready for use or when interest costs no longer are being incurred. Interest costs incurred can pertain to borrowings other than those obtained specifically for the construction project. However, interest costs can't be imputed; actual interest costs must be incurred.

The interest capitalization period begins when construction begins and the first expenditure is made as long as interest costs are actually being incurred.

Average Accumulated Expenditures.   Because we consider interest to be a necessary cost of getting a self-constructed asset ready for use, the amount capitalized is only that portion of interest cost incurred during the construction period that *could have been avoided* if expenditures for the asset had not been made. In other words, if construction had not been undertaken, debt incurred for the project would not have been necessary and/or other interest-bearing debt could have been liquidated or employed elsewhere.

As a result, interest should be determined for only the construction expenditures actually incurred during the capitalization period. And unless all expenditures are made at the outset of the period, it's necessary to determine the *average* amount outstanding during the period. This is the amount of debt that would be required to finance the expenditures and thus the amount on which interest would accrue. For instance, if a company accumulated $1,500,000 of construction expenditures fairly evenly throughout the construction period, the average expenditures would be:

Average accumulated expenditures approximates the average debt necessary for construction.

Total accumulated expenditures incurred evenly throughout the period	$1,500,000
	÷2
Average accumulated expenditures	$ 750,000

At the beginning of the period, no expenditures have accumulated, so no interest has accrued (on the equivalent amount of debt). But, by the end of the period interest is accruing on the total amount, $1,500,000. On average, then, interest accrues on half the total or $750,000.

If expenditures are not incurred evenly throughout the period, a simple average is insufficient. In that case, a weighted average is determined by time-weighting individual expenditures or groups of expenditures by the number of months from their incurrence to the end of the construction period. This is demonstrated in Illustration 10–13.

The weighted-average accumulated expenditures by the end of 2003 are:

Average accumulated expenditures is determined by time-weighting individual expenditures made during the construction period.

January 3, 2003	$500,000 × $^{12}\!/_{12}$ =	$500,000
March 31, 2003	400,000 × $^{9}\!/_{12}$ =	300,000
September 30, 2003	600,000 × $^{3}\!/_{12}$ =	150,000
Average accumulated expenditures for 2003	=	$950,000

FINANCIAL REPORTING CASE

Q4, p. 461

STEP 1: Determine the average accumulated expenditures.

Again notice that the average accumulated expenditures are less than the total accumulated expenditures of $1,500,000. If Mills had borrowed exactly the amount necessary to

[17]"Capitalization of Interest Costs," *Statement of Financial Accounting Standards No. 34* (Stamford, Conn: FASB, 1979).

ILLUSTRATION 10–13 Interest Capitalization	On January 1, 2003, the Mills Conveying Equipment Company began construction of a building to be used as its office headquarters. The building was completed on June 30, 2004. Expenditures on the project, mainly payments to subcontractors, were as follows:

January 3, 2003	$ 500,000
March 31, 2003	400,000
September 30, 2003	600,000
Accumulated expenditures at December 31, 2003 (before interest capitalization)	$1,500,000
January 31, 2004	600,000
April 30, 2004	300,000

On January 2, 2003, the company obtained a $1 million construction loan with an 8% interest rate. The loan was outstanding during the entire construction period. The company's other interest-bearing debt included two long-term notes of $2,000,000 and $4,000,000 with interest rates of 6% and 12%, respectively. Both notes were outstanding during the entire construction period.

finance the project, it would not have incurred interest on a loan of $1,500,000 for the whole year but only on an average loan of $950,000. The next step is to determine the interest to be capitalized for the average accumulated expenditures.

Interest Rates.   In this situation, debt financing was obtained specifically for the construction project, and the amount borrowed is sufficient to cover the average accumulated expenditures. To determine the interest capitalized, then, we simply multiply the construction loan rate of 8% by the average accumulated expenditures.

STEP 2: Calculate the amount of interest to be capitalized.

The amount of interest capitalized is determined by multiplying an interest rate by the average accumulated expenditures.

Interest capitalized for 2003 = $950,000 × 8% = $76,000

Notice that this is the same answer we would get by assuming separate 8% construction loans were made for each expenditure at the time each expenditure was made:

Loans		Annual Rate		Portion of Year Outstanding		Interest
$500,000	×	8%	×	$^{12}/_{12}$	=	$40,000
400,000	×	8%	×	$^{9}/_{12}$	=	24,000
600,000	×	8%	×	$^{3}/_{12}$	=	12,000
Interest capitalized for 2003						$76,000

The interest of $76,000 is added to the cost of the building, bringing accumulated expenditures at December 31, 2003, to $1,576,000 ($1,500,000 + 76,000). The remaining interest cost incurred but not capitalized is expensed.

It should be emphasized that interest capitalization does not require that funds actually be borrowed for this specific purpose, only that the company does have outstanding debt. The presumption is that even if the company doesn't borrow specifically for the project, funds from other borrowings must be diverted to finance the construction. Either way—directly or indirectly—interest costs are incurred. In our illustration, for instance, even without the construction loan, interest would be capitalized because other debt was outstanding. The capitalized interest would be the average accumulated expenditures multiplied by the weighted-average rate on these other loans. The weighted-average interest rate on all debt other than the construction loan would be 10%, calculated as follows:[18]

---

[18]The same result can be obtained simply by multiplying the individual debt interest rates by the relative amount of debt at each rate. In this case, one-third of total debt is at 6% and two-thirds of the total debt is at 12% (1/3 × 6% + 2/3 × 12% = 10%).

Loans		Rate		Interest
$2,000,000	$\times$	6%	=	$120,000
4,000,000	$\times$	12%	=	480,000
$6,000,000				$600,000

$$\text{Weighted-average rate: } \frac{\$600,000}{\$6,000,000} = 10\%$$

This is a weighted average because total interest is $600,000 on total debt of $6,000,000.

ADDITIONAL CONSIDERATION

The weighted-average rate isn't used for 2003 in our illustration because the specific construction loan is sufficient to cover the average accumulated expenditures. If the specific construction loan had been insufficient to cover the average accumulated expenditures, its 8% interest rate would be applied to the average accumulated expenditures up to the amount of the specific borrowing, and any remaining average accumulated expenditures in excess of specific borrowings would be multiplied by the weighted-average rate on all other outstanding interest-bearing debt. Suppose, for illustration, that the 8% construction loan had been only $500,000 rather than $1,000,000. We would calculate capitalized interest using both the specific rate and the weighted-average rate:

	Average Accumulated Expenditures		Rate		Interest
Total	$950,000				
Specific borrowing	500,000	$\times$	8%	=	$40,000
Excess	$450,000	$\times$	10%	=	45,000
Capitalized interest					$85,000

In our illustration, it's necessary to use this approach in 2004.

It's possible that the amount of interest calculated to be capitalized exceeds the amount of interest actually incurred. If that's the case, we limit the interest capitalized to the actual interest incurred. In our illustration, total interest cost incurred during 2003 far exceeds the $76,000 of capitalized interest calculated, so it's not necessary to limit the capitalized amount.

Interest capitalized is limited to interest incurred.

Loans		Rate		Actual Interest	Calculated Interest
$1,000,000	$\times$	8%	=	$ 80,000	
2,000,000	$\times$	6%	=	120,000	
4,000,000	$\times$	12%	=	480,000	
				$680,000	$76,000

STEP 3: Compare calculated interest with actual interest incurred.

Use lower amount

Continuing the example based on the information in Illustration 10–13, let's determine the amount of interest capitalized during 2004 for the building. The total accumulated expenditures by the end of the project are:

Accumulated expenditures at the beginning of 2004 (including interest capitalization)	$1,576,000
January 31, 2004	600,000
April 30, 2004	300,000
Accumulated expenditures at June 30, 2004 (before 2004 interest capitalization)	$2,476,000

The weighted-average accumulated expenditures by the end of the project are:

STEP 1: Determine the average accumulated expenditures.

January 1, 2004	$1,576,000 × 6/6 =	$1,576,000
January 31, 2004	600,000 × 5/6 =	500,000
April 30, 2004	300,000 × 2/6 =	100,000
Average accumulated expenditures for 2004		$2,176,000

Notice that the 2004 expenditures are weighted relative to the construction period of six months because the project was finished on June 30, 2004. Interest capitalized for 2004 would be $98,800, calculated as follows:

STEP 2: Calculate the amount of interest to be capitalized.

	Average Accumulated Expenditures		Annual Rate		Fraction of Year		
	$2,176,000						
Specific borrowing	1,000,000	×	8%	×	6/12	=	$40,000
Excess	$1,176,000	×	10%	×	6/12	=	58,800
Capitalized interest							$98,800

Multiplying by six-twelfths reflects the fact that the interest rates are annual rates (12-month rates) and the construction period is only 6 months.

STEP 3: Compare calculated interest with actual interest incurred.

Loans		Annual Rate		Actual Interest	Calculated Interest
$1,000,000	×	8% × 6/12 =		$ 40,000	
2,000,000	×	6% × 6/12 =		60,000	
4,000,000	×	12% × 6/12 =		240,000	
				$340,000	$98,800

Use lower amount

For the first six months of 2004, $98,800 interest would be capitalized, bringing the total capitalized cost of the building to $2,574,800 ($2,476,000 + 98,800), and $241,200 in interest would be expensed ($340,000 − 98,800).

ADDITIONAL CONSIDERATION

To illustrate how the actual interest limitation might come into play, let's assume the nonspecific borrowings in our illustration were $200,000 and $400,000 (instead of $2,000,000 and $4,000,000). Our comparison would change as follows:

Loans		Annual Rate		Actual Interest	Calculated Interest
$1,000,000	×	8% × $^{6}/_{12}$ =		$40,000	
200,000	×	6% × $^{6}/_{12}$ =		6,000	
400,000	×	12% × $^{6}/_{12}$ =		24,000	
				$70,000	$98,800

Use lower amount

The method of determining interest to capitalize that we've discussed is called the **specific interest method** because we use rates from specific construction loans to the extent of specific borrowings before using the average rate of other debt. Sometimes, though, it's difficult to associate specific borrowings with projects. In these situations, it's acceptable to just use the weighted-average rate on all interest-bearing debt, including all construction loans. This is known as the **weighted-average method**. In our illustration, for example, if the $1,000,000, 8% loan had not been specifically related to construction, we would calculate a single weighted-average rate as shown below.

Loans		Rate		Interest
$1,000,000	×	8%	=	$ 80,000
2,000,000	×	6%	=	120,000
4,000,000	×	12%	=	480,000
$7,000,000				$680,000

Weighted-average method

$$\text{Weighted-average rate:} \quad \frac{\$680,000}{\$7,000,000} = 9.7\%$$

If we were using the weighted-average method rather than the specific interest method, we would simply multiply this single rate times the average accumulated expenditures to determine capitalizable interest.

Disclosure.   For an accounting period in which interest costs are capitalized, both the total amount of interest costs incurred and the amount that has been capitalized should be disclosed. Graphic 10–5 shows an interest capitalization disclosure note that was included in a recent annual report of IBM Corporation.

If material, the amount of interest capitalized during the period must be disclosed.

GRAPHIC 10–5
Capitalized Interest Disclosure—IBM Corporation

Interest on Debt (in part)
Interest paid and accrued on borrowings of the company and its subsidiaries was $1,449 million in 2000, $1,475 million in 1999, and $1,585 million in 1998. Of these amounts, the company capitalized $20 million in 2000, $23 million in 1999, and $28 million in 1998.

GLOBAL   PERSPECTIVE

The accounting principles of most countries permit some form of interest capitalization; Japan and Brazil are exceptions. However, differences do exist as to the situations when interest can be capitalized. For example, in Belgium and France interest can be capitalized on inventory routinely manufactured as long as the production cycle exceeds 12 months. Differences also exist as to the amount of interest to be capitalized. In Argentina imputed interest on the company's equity may be capitalized.

RESEARCH AND DEVELOPMENT (R&D)

For years the practice was to allow companies to either expense or capitalize R&D costs, but in 1974 the FASB issued *SFAS 2* which now requires all research and development costs to be charged to expense when incurred.[19] This was a controversial standard opposed by many companies who preferred delaying the recognition of these expenses until later years when presumably the expenditures bear fruit.

Most R&D costs are expensed in the periods incurred.

A company undertakes an R&D project because it believes the project will eventually provide benefits that exceed the current expenditures. Unfortunately, though, it's difficult to predict which individual research and development projects will ultimately provide benefits. In fact, only 1 in 10 actually reach commercial production. Moreover, even for those projects that pan out, a direct relationship between research and development costs and specific future revenue is difficult to establish. In other words, even if R&D costs do lead to future benefits, it's difficult to objectively determine the size of the benefits and in which periods the costs should be expensed if they are capitalized. These are the issues that prompted the FASB to require immediate expensing.

R&D costs entail a high degree of uncertainty of future benefits and are difficult to match with future revenues.

The FASB's approach is certain in most cases to understate assets and overstate current expense because at least some of the R&D expenditures will likely produce future benefits.

Determining R&D Costs.   *SFAS 2* distinguishes research and development as follows:

Research is planned search or critical investigation aimed at discovery of new knowledge with the hope that such knowledge will be useful in developing a new product or service or a new process or technique or in bringing about a significant improvement to an existing product or process.

Development is the translation of research findings or other knowledge into a plan or design for a new product or process or for a significant improvement to an existing product or process whether intended for sale or use.[20]

R&D costs include salaries, wages, and other labor costs of personnel engaged in R&D activities, the costs of materials consumed, equipment, facilities, and intangibles used in R&D projects, the costs of services performed by others in connection with R&D activities, and a reasonable allocation of indirect costs related to those activities. General and administrative costs should not be included unless they are clearly related to the R&D activity.

R&D expense includes the depreciation and amortization of operational assets used in R&D activities.

If an operational asset is purchased specifically for a single R&D project, its cost is considered R&D and expensed immediately even though the asset's useful life extends beyond the current year. However, the cost of an operational asset that has an alternative future use beyond the current R&D project is *not* a current R&D expense. Instead, the depreciation or amortization of these alternative-use assets is included as R&D expenses in the current and future periods the assets are used for R&D activities.

In general, R&D costs pertain to activities that occur prior to the start of commercial production, and costs of starting commercial production and beyond are not R&D costs. Graphic 10–6 captures this concept with a time line beginning with the start of an R&D project and ending with the ultimate sale of a developed product or the use of a developed process. The graphic also provides examples of activities typically included as R&D and examples of activities typically excluded from R&D.[21]

Costs incurred before the start of commercial production are all expensed as R&D. The costs incurred after commercial production begins would be either expensed or treated as manufacturing overhead and included in the cost of inventory. Let's look at an example in Illustration 10–14.

---

[19]"Accounting for Research and Development Costs," *Statement of Financial Accounting Standards No. 2* (Stamford, Conn: FASB, 1974), par. 12.
[20]Ibid., par. 8.
[21]Ibid., par. 9 and 10.

GRAPHIC 10–6
Research and
Development
Expenditures

Start of R & D Activity	Start of Commercial Production	Sale of Product or Process

Examples of R&D Costs:

- Laboratory research aimed at discovery of new knowledge

- Searching for applications of new research findings or other knowledge

- Design, construction, and testing of preproduction prototypes and models

- Modification of the formulation or design of a product or process

Examples of Non-R&D Costs:

- Engineering follow-through in an early phase of commercial production

- Quality control during commercial production including routine testing of products

- Routine ongoing efforts to refine, enrich, or otherwise improve on the qualities of an existing product

- Adaptation of an existing capability to a particular requirement or customer's need as a part of a continuing commercial activity

Costs incurred *before* the start of commercial production are all expensed as R&D.

Costs incurred *after* commercial production begins would be either expensed or included in the cost of inventory.

ILLUSTRATION
10–14

Research and
Development Costs

The Askew Company made the following cash expenditures during 2003 related to the development of a new industrial plastic:

R&D salaries and wages	$10,000,000
R&D supplies consumed during 2003	3,000,000
Purchase of R&D equipment	5,000,000
Patent filing and legal costs	100,000
Payments to others for services performed in connection with R&D activities	1,200,000
Total	$19,300,000

The project resulted in a new product to be manufactured in 2004. A patent was filed with the U.S. Patent Office. The equipment purchased will be employed in other projects. Depreciation on the equipment for 2003 was $500,000.

The salaries and wages, supplies consumed, and payments to others for R&D services are expensed in 2003 as R&D. The equipment is capitalized and the 2003 depreciation is expensed as R&D. Even though the costs to develop the patented product are expensed, the filing and legal costs for the patent are capitalized and amortized in future periods just as similar costs are capitalized for purchased intangibles. Amortization of the patent is discussed in Chapter 11.

Filing and legal costs for patents, copyrights, and other developed intangibles are capitalized and amortized in future periods.

The various expenditures would be recorded as follows:

R&D expense ($10,000,000 + 3,000,000 + 1,200,000)............	14,200,000	
Cash......................................		14,200,000
To record R&D expenses.		
Equipment...	5,000,000	
Cash......................................		5,000,000
To record the purchase of equipment.		
R&D expense	500,000	
Accumulated depreciation—equipment...................		500,000
To record R&D depreciation.		
Patent	100,000	
Cash......................................		100,000
To capitalize the patent filing and legal costs.		

Expenditures reconciliation:	
Recorded as R&D	$14,200,000
Capitalized as equipment	5,000,000
Capitalized as patent	100,000
Total expenditures	$19,300,000

GAAP require disclosure of total R&D expense incurred during the period.

   GAAP require that total R&D expense incurred must be disclosed either as a line item in the income statement or in a disclosure note. For example, Microsoft reported $4.379 billion of R&D expense on the face of its 2001 income statement. In our illustration, total R&D expense disclosed in 2003 would be $14,700,000 ($14,200,000 in expenditures and $500,000 in depreciation). Note that if Askew later sells this patent to another company for, say, $15 million, the buyer would capitalize the entire purchase price rather than only the filing and legal costs. Once again, the reason for the apparent inconsistency in accounting treatment of internally generated intangibles and externally purchased intangibles is the difficulty of associating costs and benefits.

R&D Performed for Others.   The requirements of *SFAS 2* do not apply to companies that perform R&D for other companies under contract. In these situations, the R&D costs are capitalized as inventory and carried forward into future years until the project is completed. Of course, justification is that the benefits of these expenditures are the contract fees that are determinable and are earned over the term of the project. Income from these contracts can be recognized using either the percentage-of-completion or completed contract method. We discussed these alternatives in Chapter 5.

   Another exception pertains to a company that develops computer software. Expenditures made after the software is determined to be technologically feasible but before it is ready for commercial production are capitalized. Costs incurred before technological feasibility is established are expensed as incurred. We discuss software development costs below.

GLOBAL   PERSPECTIVE

Unlike the United States, the capitalization of research and development costs as an intangible asset is permitted in most other industrialized countries. Germany and Mexico are two countries that do follow the U.S. treatment of expensing all R&D costs in the period incurred.

Start-Up Costs.   For its fiscal year ended January 28, 2001, Home Depot, Inc. opened 204 new stores throughout the world. The company incurred a variety of one-time pre-opening costs for salaries of employees supervising construction, training, travel, and relocation of employees totaling $142 million. In fact, whenever a company introduces a new product or service, or commences business in a new territory or with a new customer, it incurs similar **start-up costs.** As with R&D expenditures, a company must expense all the costs related to a company's start-up activities in the period incurred, rather than capitalize those costs as an asset. Start-up costs also include **organization costs** related to organizing a new entity, such as legal fees and state filing fees to incorporate.[22]

Start-up costs are expensed in the period incurred.

ADDITIONAL CONSIDERATION

Development Stage Enterprises
A development stage enterprise is a new business that has either not commenced its principal operations or has begun its principal operations but has not generated significant revenues. Prior to SFAS 7,[23] many of these companies recorded an asset for the normal operating costs incurred during the development stage. This asset was then expensed over a period of time beginning with the commencement of operations.

SFAS 7 requires that these enterprises comply with the same generally accepted accounting principles that apply to established operating companies in determining whether a cost is to be charged to expense when incurred or capitalized and expensed in future periods. Therefore, normal operating costs incurred during the development stage are expensed, not capitalized. SFAS 7 does allow development stage enterprises to provide items of supplemental information to help financial statement readers more readily assess their future cash flows.

Software Development Costs.   The computer software industry has become a large and important U.S. business over the last two decades. Relative newcomers such as Microsoft and Adobe Systems, as well as traditional hardware companies like IBM, are leaders in this multibillion dollar industry. A significant expenditure for these companies is the cost of developing software. Prior to 1985, some companies were capitalizing software development costs and expensing them in future periods and others were expensing these costs in the period incurred.

In 1985, the FASB issued *SFAS 86,* which requires all companies to expense costs incurred to develop or purchase computer software to be sold, leased, or otherwise marketed as R&D costs until **technological feasibility** of the product has been established.[24] The Statement does not address the accounting treatment of costs incurred to develop computer software to be used internally. We account for these costs in a similar manner, however. Costs incurred during the preliminary project stage are expensed as R&D. After the application development stage is reached (for example, at the coding stage or installation stage), we capitalize any further costs.[25] We generally capitalize the costs of computer software *purchased* for internal use.

Technological feasibility is established "when the enterprise has completed all planning, designing, coding, and testing activities that are necessary to establish that the product can be produced to meet its design specifications including functions, features, and technical performance requirements."[26] Costs incurred after technological feasibility but before the product is

GAAP require the capitalization of software development costs incurred after technological feasibility is established.

---

[22]"Reporting on the Costs of Start-Up Activities," *Statement of Position 98-5* (New York: AIPA, 1998).

[23]"Accounting and Reporting by Development Stage Enterprises," *Statement of Financial Accounting Standards No. 7* (Stamford, Conn.: FASB, 1975).

[24]"Accounting for the Costs of Computer Software to be Sold, Leased, or Otherwise Marketed," *Statement of Financial Accounting Standards No. 86* (Stamford, Conn.: FASB, 1985).

[25]"Accounting for the Costs of Computer Software Developed or Obtained for Internal Use," *Statement of Position 98-1* (New York: AICPA, 1998).

[26]"Accounting for the Costs of Computer Software to Be Sold, Leased, or Otherwise Marketed," *Statement of Financial Accounting Standards No. 86* (Stamford, Conn.: FASB, 1985), par. 4.

available for general release to customers are capitalized as an intangible asset. These costs include coding and testing costs and the production of product masters. Similar to the treatment of such costs under *SFAS 2*, costs incurred after the product release date usually are not R&D expenditures. Graphic 10–7 shows the R&D time line introduced earlier in the chapter and adds the point of establishment of technological feasibility. Only the costs incurred between technological feasibility and the product release date are capitalized.

GRAPHIC 10–7
Research and
Development
Expenditures—
Computer Software

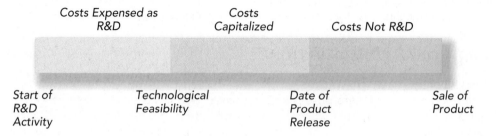

The amortization of capitalized computer software development costs begins when the product is available for general release to customers. The periodic amortization percentage is the greater of (1) the ratio of current revenues to current and anticipated revenues (percentage-of-revenue method) or (2) the straight-line percentage over the useful life of the asset, as shown in Illustration 10–15.

ILLUSTRATION 10–15

Software Development Costs

The Astro Corporation develops computer software graphics programs for sale. A new development project begun in 2002 reached technological feasibility at the end of June 2003, and the product was available for release to customers early in 2004. Development costs incurred in 2003 prior to June 30 were $1,200,000 and costs incurred from June 30 to the product availability date were $800,000. 2004 revenues from the sale of the new product were $3,000,000 and the company anticipates an additional $7,000,000 in revenues. The economic life of the software is estimated at four years.

Astro Corporation would expense the $1,200,000 in costs incurred prior to the establishment of technological feasibility and capitalize the $800,000 in costs incurred between technological feasibility and the product availability date. 2004 amortization of the intangible asset, software development costs, is calculated as follows:

1. Percentage-of-revenue method:

$$\frac{\$3,000,000}{\$3,000,000 + 7,000,000} = 30\% \times \$800,000 = \$240,000$$

2. Straight-line method:

$$\text{¼ or } 25\% \times \$800,000 = \$200,000.$$

The percentage-of-revenue method is used because it produces the greater amortization, $240,000.

Graphic 10–8 shows the software disclosure included in a recent IBM Corporation annual report. The note provides a good summary of the accounting treatment of software development costs.

Why do generally accepted accounting principles allow this exception to the general rule of expensing all R&D? We could attribute it to the political process. Software is a very important industry to our economy and perhaps its lobbying efforts resulted in the standard allowing software companies to capitalize certain R&D costs.

We could also attribute the exception to the nature of the software business. Recall that R&D costs in general are expensed in the period incurred for two reasons: (1) they entail a

GRAPHIC 10–8
Software Disclosure—
International Business
Machines Corporation

Software Costs (in part)
Costs that are related to the conceptual formulation and design of licensed programs are expensed as research and development. Also, for licensed programs, the company capitalizes costs that are incurred to produce the finished product after technological feasibility is established. The annual amortization of the capitalized amounts is the greater of the amount computed based on the estimated revenue distribution over the products' revenue-producing lives, or the straight-line method, and is applied over periods ranging up to three years.

high degree of uncertainty of future benefits, and (2) they are difficult to match with future benefits. With software, there is an important identifiable engineering milestone, technological feasibility. When this milestone is attained, the probability of the software product's success increases significantly. And because the useful life of software is fairly short (one to four years in most cases), it is much easier to determine the periods of increased revenues than for R&D projects in other industries. Compare this situation with, say, the development of a new drug. Even after the drug has been developed, it must go through extensive testing to meet FDA (Food and Drug Administration) approval, which may never be attained. If attained, the useful life of the drug could be anywhere from a few months to many years.

Purchased Research and Development and Earnings Quality.   It is not unusual for one company to buy another company in order to obtain technology developed or in the process of being developed by the acquired company. When one company buys another, we allocate the purchase price to tangible and intangible assets as well as to in-process research and development. To do this, we must distinguish between *developed* technology (an intangible asset) and *in-process* R&D. Using terminology adopted in accounting for software development costs, if *technological feasibility* has been achieved, the value of that technology is considered "developed." The amount we attribute to developed technology is capitalized and amortized. The amount we attribute to in-process R&D, though, is expensed (written off), in the period of the acquisition.

> In a business acquisition, the amount allocated to developed technology is capitalized and amortized, but the amount allocated to in-process research and development, is expensed (written off), in the period of the acquisition.

As an example, in 1999 IBM Corporation acquired 100% of the shares of Sequent Computer Systems, Inc. for $837 million. IBM allocated the purchase price as follows ($ in millions):

Net tangible assets	$382
Developed technology	87
Other identifiable intangible assets	91
In-process research and development	85
Goodwill	192
Total	$837

Note that the Sequent acquisition included an $85 million allocation, more than 10% of purchase price, to in-process R&D. Indeed, in the late 1990s, many technology-motivated acquisitions included allocations to in-process R&D that exceeded 75% of the purchase price. Graphic 10–9 shows some examples.

A profusion of large-percentage write-offs caused the SEC to scrutinize the amounts allocated to in-process R&D and, in some cases, require the write-offs to be reduced. For example, the $37 billion acquisition of MCI by WorldCom originally included a $7 billion amount allocated to in-process R&D. The SEC convinced WorldCom to reduce this amount to $3.1 billion.

Should financial statement users consider in-process R&D expenses as part of a company's permanent earnings stream, or are they transitory in nature? Consider the fact that significant in-process R&D expenses appear regularly in the income statements of Cisco, Sun Microsystems, and other high-technology companies. In a manner similar to such items as

> An analyst must decide whether to consider in-process R&D expenses as transitory in nature or as a part of permanent earnings.

GRAPHIC 10–9
Percentages of In-
Process R&D

Acquiring Company	Acquired Company	Percentage of Purchase Price Allocated to In-Process R&D
Adobe Systems	Ares Software	95%
3Com	Axon Networks	80
Sphinx Pharmaceutical	Genesis Pharmaceutical	100
Cisco Systems	Lightstream	80
H&R Block	Spry	78

restructuring costs and losses from inventory write-downs, a financial analyst must carefully consider the nature of these expenses in an assessment of a company's permanent earnings.

The immediate expensing of in-process R&D is another example of "big bath" accounting techniques some companies use to manipulate earnings. By writing off large amounts of the purchase price, companies significantly reduce earnings in the year of acquisition. However, the larger the write-off, the smaller the amount allocated to goodwill. Until 2001, goodwill was capitalized and amortized over periods ranging from 3 to 10 years for most technology companies. The immediate write-off of a portion of the purchase price increased earnings for years into the future by reducing the amount of goodwill amortization.

As you learned earlier in this chapter, recent accounting standards significantly changed the accounting treatment of goodwill, eliminating the practice of amortizing goodwill. Will this change in accounting standards reduce companies' desire to write off large amounts of purchase price as in-process R&D? There is no easy answer to this question. Even though goodwill is no longer subject to periodic amortization, it is still subject to the impairment of value rules that we discuss in Chapter 11. These rules could result in large future write-downs of the cost of goodwill. Companies may still be motivated to write-off immediately as much of the purchase price of a business acquisition as possible to avoid any future income reductions.

BUSINESSWEEK
". . . The aim of many of today's giant write-offs is to front-load expenses. Charge off three years of expenses all at once, and by definition future earnings will be better. It's akin to making three years of mortgage payments at once, then claiming your income has grown."[27]

FINANCIAL REPORTING CASE **SOLUTION**

1. **What does it mean to capitalize an expenditure? What is the general rule for determining which costs are capitalized when an operational asset is acquired?** *(p. 463)*   To capitalize an expenditure simply means to record it as an asset. All expenditures other than payments to shareholders and debt repayments are either expensed as incurred or capitalized. In general, the choice is determined by whether the expenditure benefits more than just the current period. Exceptions to this general principle are discussed in the chapter. The initial cost of an operational asset includes all expenditures necessary to bring the asset to its desired condition and location for use.

2. **Describe to Stan which costs might be included in the initial cost of equipment.** *(p. 463)*   In addition to the purchase price, the cost of equipment might include the cost of transportation, installation, testing, and legal fees to establish title.

3. **In what situations is interest capitalized?** *(p. 486)*   Interest is capitalized only for assets constructed for a company's own use or for assets constructed as discrete products for sale or lease. For example, Walt Disney capitalizes interest on assets constructed for its theme

---

[27]"Earnings Hocus-Pocus: How Companies Come Up with the Numbers They Want," *BusinessWeek* (October 5, 1998), p. 135.

parks, resorts and other property, and on theatrical and television productions in process. During the construction period, interest is considered a cost necessary to get the asset ready for its intended use.

4. **What is the three-step process used to determine the amount of interest capitalized?** *(p. 487)*   The first step is to determine the average accumulated expenditures for the period. The second step is to multiply the average accumulated expenditures by an appropriate interest rate or rates to determine the amount of interest capitalized. A final step compares the interest determined in step two with actual interest incurred. Interest capitalized is limited to the amount of interest incurred. ■

THE BOTTOM LINE

1. The initial cost of an operational asset acquired in an exchange transaction includes the purchase price and all expenditures necessary to bring the asset to its desired condition and location for use. The cost of a natural resource includes the acquisition costs for the use of land, the exploration and development costs incurred before production begins, and restoration costs incurred during or at the end of extraction. Purchased intangibles are valued at their original cost to include the purchase price and legal and filing fees.

2. If a lump-sum purchase involves different assets, it is necessary to allocate the lump-sum acquisition price among the separate items according to some logical allocation method. A widely used allocation method is to divide the lump-sum purchase price according to the individual assets' relative market values.

3. Assets acquired in exchange for deferred payment contracts are valued at their fair value or the present value of payments using a realistic interest rate.

4. Assets acquired through the issuance of equity securities are valued at the fair value of the securities if known; if not known, the fair value of the assets received is used. Donated assets are valued at their fair value.

5. When an operational asset is sold, a gain or loss is recognized for the difference between the consideration received and the asset's book value. The basic principle used for nonmonetary exchanges is to value the asset(s) received based on the fair value of the asset(s) given up. In certain situations, the valuation of the asset(s) received is based on the book value of the asset(s) given up.

6. The cost of a self-constructed asset includes identifiable materials and labor and a portion of the company's manufacturing overhead costs. In addition, GAAP provides for the capitalization of interest incurred during construction. The amount of interest capitalized is equal to the average accumulated expenditures for the period multiplied by the appropriate interest rates, not to exceed actual interest incurred.

7. Research and development costs incurred to internally develop an intangible asset are expensed in the period incurred. Filing and legal costs for developed intangibles are capitalized.

OIL AND GAS ACCOUNTING

APPENDIX
10

Chapter 1 characterized the establishment of accounting and reporting standards as a political process. Standards, particularly changes in standards, can have significant differential effects on companies, investors and creditors, and other interest groups. The FASB must consider potential economic consequences of a change in an accounting standard or the introduction of a new standard. The history of oil and gas accounting provides a good example of this political process and the effect of possible adverse economic consequences on the standard-setting process.

There are two generally accepted methods that companies can use to account for oil and gas exploration costs. The **successful efforts method** requires that exploration costs that are known *not* to have resulted in the discovery of oil or gas (sometimes referred to as *dry holes*) be included as expenses in the period the expenditures are made. The alternative, the **full-cost method,** allows costs incurred in searching for oil and gas within a large geographical area to be capitalized as assets and expensed in the future as oil and gas from the successful wells are removed from that area. Both of these methods are widely used. Illustration 10A–1 compares the two alternatives.

ILLUSTRATION 10A–1 Oil and Gas Accounting	The Shannon Oil Company incurred $2,000,000 in exploration costs for each of 10 oil wells drilled in 2003 in west Texas. Eight of the 10 wells were dry holes. The accounting treatment of the $20 million in total exploration costs will vary significantly depending on the accounting method used. The summary journal entries using each of the alternative methods are as follows:

Successful Efforts		**Full Cost**	
Oil deposit	4,000,000	Oil deposit	20,000,000
Exploration expense	16,000,000	Cash	20,000,000
Cash	20,000,000		

Using the full-cost method, Shannon would capitalize the entire $20 million which is expensed as oil from the two successful wells is depleted. On the other hand, using the successful efforts method, the cost of the unsuccessful wells is expensed in 2003, and only the $4 million cost related to the successful wells is capitalized and expensed in future periods as the oil is depleted.

In 1977 the FASB attempted to establish uniformity in the accounting treatment of oil and gas exploration costs. *SFAS 19* was issued requiring all companies to use the successful efforts method.[28]

SFAS 19 met with criticism from the oil and gas companies that were required to switch from full cost to successful efforts accounting. These companies felt that the switch would seriously depress their reported income over time. As a result, they argued, their ability to raise capital in the securities markets would be inhibited, which would result in a cutback of new exploration. The fear that the standard would cause domestic companies to significantly reduce oil and gas exploration and thus increase our dependence on foreign oil was compelling to the U.S. Congress, the SEC, and the Department of Energy.

Extensive pressure from Congress, the SEC, and affected companies forced the FASB to rescind *Standard 19.* Presently, oil and gas companies can use either the successful efforts or full-cost method to account for oil and gas exploration costs. Of course, the method used must be disclosed. For example, Graphic 10A–1 shows how Texaco, Inc., disclosed their use of the successful efforts method in a note to recent financial statements.

Many feared that the implementation of SFAS 19 would cause a significant cutback in the exploration for new oil and gas in the United States.

GRAPHIC 10A–1 Oil and Gas Accounting Disclosure— Texaco, Inc.	**Properties, Plant and Equipment and Depreciation, Depletion and Amortization (in part)** We follow the "successful efforts" method of accounting for our oil and gas exploration and producing operations.

---

[28]"Financial Accounting and Reporting by Oil and Gas Producing Companies," *Statement of Financial Accounting Standards No. 19* (Stamford, Conn.: FASB, 1977).

QUESTIONS FOR REVIEW OF KEY TOPICS

Q 10–1   Define operational assets and explain the difference between tangible and intangible operational assets.

Q 10–2   What is included in the original cost of an operational asset acquired in an exchange transaction?

Q 10–3   Identify the costs associated with the initial valuation of a developed natural resource.

Q 10–4   Briefly summarize the accounting treatment for intangible assets, explaining the difference between purchased and internally developed intangible assets.

Q 10–5   What is goodwill and how is it measured?

Q 10–6   Explain the method generally used to allocate the cost of a lump-sum purchase to the individual assets acquired.

Q 10–7   When an operational asset is acquired and a note payable is assumed, explain how acquisition cost of the asset is determined when the interest rate for the note is less than the current market rate for similar notes.

Q 10–8   Explain how operational assets acquired in exchange for equity securities are valued.

Q 10–9   Explain how operational assets acquired through donation are valued.

Q 10–10   When an operational asset is disposed of, how is gain or loss on disposal computed?

Q 10–11   What is the basic principle for valuing operational assets acquired in exchange for other nonmonetary assets?

Q 10–12   Identify the three exceptions to valuing assets acquired in nonmonetary exchanges at the fair market value of the asset(s) given up.

Q 10–13   In what situations is interest capitalized?

Q 10–14   Define average accumulated expenditures and explain how it is computed.

Q 10–15   Explain the difference between the specific interest method and the weighted-average method in determining the amount of interest to be capitalized.

Q 10–16   Define R&D according to *SFAS 2.*

Q 10–17   Explain the accounting treatment of equipment acquired for use in R&D projects.

Q 10–18   Explain the accounting treatment of costs incurred to develop computer software.

Q 10–19   Explain the difference in the accounting treatment of the cost of developed technology and the cost of in-process R&D in an acquisition.

Q 10–20   (Based on Appendix 10) Explain the difference between the successful efforts and the full-cost methods of accounting for oil and gas exploration costs.

EXERCISES

E 10–1
Acquisition costs; land and building

On March 1, 2003, Beldon Corporation purchased land as a factory site for $50,000. An old building on the property was demolished, and construction began on a new building that was completed on December 15, 2003. Costs incurred during this period are listed below:

Demolition of old building	$ 4,000
Architect's fees (for new building)	10,000
Legal fees for title investigation of land	2,000
Property taxes on land (for period beginning March 1, 2003)	3,000
Construction costs	500,000
Interest on construction loan	5,000

Salvaged materials resulting from the demolition of the old building were sold for $2,000.

Required:
Determine the amounts that Beldon should capitalize as the cost of the land and the new building.

E 10–2
Acquisition cost; machinery

The Oaktree Company purchased a new machine and made the following expenditures:

Purchase price	$40,000
Freight charges for shipment of machine	700
Insurance on the machine for the first year	800
Installation of machine	1,000

The machine was purchased on open account, with payment due in 30 days. The other expenditures listed above were paid in cash.

Required:
Prepare the necessary journal entries to record the above expenditures.

E 10–3
Cost of a natural resource

The Jackpot Mining Company operates a copper mine in central Montana. The company paid $1,000,000 in 2003 for the mining site and spent an additional $500,000 to prepare the mine for extraction of the copper. After the copper is extracted in approximately four years, the company is required to restore the land to its original condition, including repaving of roads and replacing a greenbelt. The company has provided the following three cash flow possibilities for the restoration costs:

	Cash Outflow	Probability
1	$300,000	25%
2	400,000	40%
3	500,000	35%

To aid extraction, Jackpot purchased some new equipment on July 1, 2003, for $120,000. After the copper is removed from this mine, the equipment will be sold. The credit-adjusted, risk-free rate of interest is 10%.

Required:
1. Determine the cost of the copper mine.
2. Prepare the journal entries to record the acquisition costs of the mine and the purchase of equipment.

E 10–4
Intangibles

The Freitas Corporation was organized early in 2003. The following expenditures were made during the first few months of the year:

Attorneys' fees in connection with the organization of the corporation	$ 12,000
State filing fees and other incorporation costs	3,000
Purchase of a patent	20,000
Legal and other fees for transfer of the patent	2,000
Purchase of furniture	30,000
Pre-opening salaries	40,000
Total	$107,000

Required:
Prepare a summary journal entry to record the $107,000 in cash expenditures.

E 10–5
Goodwill

On March 31, 2003, the Wolfson Corporation acquired all of the outstanding common stock of Barney Corporation for $16,000,000 in cash. The book values and fair values of Barney's assets and liabilities were as follows:

	Book Value	Fair Value
Current assets	$ 6,000,000	$ 7,500,000
Property, plant, and equipment	11,000,000	14,000,000
Other assets	1,000,000	1,500,000
Current liabilities	4,000,000	4,000,000
Long-term liabilities	6,000,000	5,500,000

Required:
Calculate the amount paid for goodwill.

E 10–6
Goodwill

The Johnson Corporation purchased all of the outstanding common stock of Smith Corporation for $11,000,000 in cash. The book value of Smith's net assets (assets minus liabilities) was $7,800,000. The fair values of all of Smith's assets and liabilities were equal to their book values with the following exceptions:

	Book Value	Fair Value
Receivables	$1,300,000	$1,100,000
Property, plant, and equipment	8,000,000	9,200,000
Intangible assets	200,000	1,200,000

Required:
Calculate the amount paid for goodwill.

E 10–7

Multiple choice; operational assets

The following questions dealing with operational assets are adapted from questions that appeared on recent CPA examinations. Determine the response that best completes the statements or questions.

1. On December 1, 2003, Boyd Co. purchased a $400,000 tract of land for a factory site. Boyd razed an old building on the property and sold the materials it salvaged from the demolition. Boyd incurred additional costs and realized salvage proceeds during December 2003 as follows:

Demolition of old building	$50,000
Legal fees for purchase contract and recording of ownership	10,000
Title guarantee insurance	12,000
Proceeds from sale of salvaged materials	8,000

In its December 31, 2003, balance sheet, Boyd should report a balance in the land account of
   a. $464,000
   b. $460,000
   c. $442,000
   d. $422,000

2. On October 1, 2003, Shaw Corp. purchased a machine for $126,000 that was placed in service on November 30, 2003. Shaw incurred additional costs for this machine, as follows:

Shipping	$3,000
Installation	4,000
Testing	5,000

In Shaw's December 31, 2003, balance sheet, the machine's cost should be reported as
   a. $126,000
   b. $129,000
   c. $133,000
   d. $138,000

3. Hy Corp. bought Patent A for $40,000 and Patent B for $60,000. Hy also paid acquisition costs of $5,000 for Patent A and $7,000 for Patent B. Both patents were challenged in legal actions. Hy paid $20,000 in legal fees for a successful defense of Patent A and $30,000 in legal fees for an unsuccessful defense of Patent B. What amount should Hy capitalize for patents?
   a. $162,000
   b. $112,000
   c. $65,000
   d. $45,000

E 10–8

Lump-sum acquisition

The Pinewood Company purchased two buildings on four acres of land. The lump-sum purchase price was $900,000. According to independent appraisals, the fair market values were $450,000 (building A) and $250,000 (building B) for the buildings and $300,000 for the land.

Required:
Determine the initial valuation of the buildings and the land.

E 10–9

Acquisition cost; noninterest-bearing note

On January 1, 2003, the Byner Company purchased a used tractor. Byner paid $5,000 down and signed a noninterest-bearing note requiring five annual installments of $5,000 to be paid on each December 31 beginning December 31, 2003. The fair value of the tractor is not determinable. An interest rate of 10% properly reflects the time value of money in this situation.

Required:
1. Prepare the journal entry to record the acquisition of the tractor. Round computations to the nearest dollar.
2. Prepare the journal entry to record the first payment on December 31, 2003. Round computations to the nearest dollar.
3. Prepare the journal entry to record the second payment on December 31, 2004. Round computations to the nearest dollar.

E 10–10

Acquisition cost; issuance of equity securities and donation

On February 1, 2003, the Xilon Corporation issued 5,000 shares of its nopar common stock in exchange for five acres of land located in the city of Monrovia. On the date of the acquisition, Xilon's common stock had a market value of $18 per share. An office building was constructed on the site by an independent contractor. The building was completed on November 2, 2003, at a cost of $600,000. Xilon paid $400,000 in cash and the remainder was paid by the city of Monrovia.

Required:
Prepare the journal entries to record the acquisition of the land and the building, assuming that *SFAS 116* guidelines apply.

E 10–11
Disposal of operational asset

Funseth Farms, Inc. purchased a tractor in 2000 at a cost of $30,000. The tractor was sold for $6,000 in 2003. Depreciation recorded through the disposal date totaled $22,000.

Required:
1. Prepare the journal entry to record the sale.
2. Assuming that the tractor was sold for $10,000, prepare the journal entry to record the sale.

E 10–12
Nonmonetary exchange; similar assets

The Cedric Company recently traded in an older model computer for a new model. The old model's book value was $180,000 (original cost of $400,000 less $220,000 in accumulated depreciation) and its fair value was $200,000. Cedric paid $50,000 to complete the exchange.

Required:
Prepare the journal entry to record the exchange.

E 10–13
Nonmonetary exchange; similar assets

[This is a variation of the previous exercise.]

Required:
Assume the same facts as in Exercise 10–12, except that the fair value of the old equipment is $170,000. Prepare the journal entry to record the exchange.

E 10–14
Nonmonetary exchange; dissimilar assets

The Bronco Corporation exchanged land for a patent. The land had a carrying value of $120,000 and a fair value of $150,000. Bronco paid the owner of the patent $10,000 to complete the exchange.

Required:
1. What is the fair value of the patent?
2. Prepare the journal entry to record the exchange.

E 10–15
Nonmonetary exchange; dissimilar assets

[This is a variation of the previous exercise.]

Required:
Assume the same facts as in Exercise 10–14 except that Bronco *received* $10,000 from the owner of the patent to complete the exchange.
1. What is the fair value of the patent?
2. Prepare the journal entry to record the exchange.

E 10–16
Nonmonetary exchange; similar assets

The Tinsley Company exchanged land that it had been holding for future plant expansion for a more suitable parcel located farther from residential areas. Tinsley carried the land at its original cost of $30,000. According to an independent appraisal, the land currently is worth $60,000. Tinsley received $10,000 in cash to complete the transaction.

Required:
1. What is the fair value of the new parcel of land received by Tinsley?
2. Prepare the journal entry to record the exchange.

E 10–17
Acquisition cost; multiple methods

The Connors Corporation acquired manufacturing equipment for use in its assembly line. Below are four *independent* situations relating to the acquisition of the equipment.
1. The equipment was purchased on account for $25,000. Credit terms were 2/10, n/30. Payment was made within the discount period and the company records the purchases of equipment net of discounts.
2. Connors gave the seller a noninterest-bearing note. The note required payment of $27,000 one year from date of purchase. The fair value of the equipment is not determinable. An interest rate of 10% properly reflects the time value of money in this situation.
3. Connors traded in old, similar equipment that had a book value of $6,000 (original cost of $14,000 and accumulated depreciation of $8,000) and paid cash of $22,000. The old equipment had a fair value of $2,500 on the date of the exchange.
4. Connors issued 1,000 shares of its nopar common stock in exchange for the equipment. The market value of the common stock was not determinable. The equipment could have been purchased for $24,000 in cash.

Required:
For each of the above situations, prepare the journal entry required to record the acquisition of the equipment. Round computations to the nearest dollar.

E 10–18
Interest capitalization

On January 1, 2003, the Marjlee Company began construction of an office building to be used as its corporate headquarters. The building was completed early in 2004. Construction expenditures for 2003, which were incurred evenly throughout the year, totaled $5,000,000. Marjlee had the following debt obligations which were outstanding during all of 2003:

Construction loan, 10%	$1,000,000
Long-term note, 9%	2,000,000
Long-term note, 6%	4,000,000

Required:
Calculate the amount of interest capitalized for the building using the specific interest method.

E 10–19
Interest capitalization

On January 2, 2003, the Shagri Company began construction on a new manufacturing facility for its own use. The building was completed in 2004. The only interest-bearing debt the company had outstanding during 2003 was long-term bonds with a carrying value of $10,000,000 and an effective interest rate of 8%. Construction expenditures incurred during 2003 were as follows:

January 2	$500,000
March 1	600,000
July 31	480,000
September 30	600,000
December 31	300,000

Required:
Calculate the amount of interest capitalized for 2003.

E 10–20
Interest capitalization

On January 2, 2003, the Highlands Company began construction on a new manufacturing facility for its own use. The building was completed in 2004. The company borrowed $1,500,000 at 10% on January 2 to help finance the construction. In addition to the construction loan, Highlands had the following debt outstanding throughout 2003:

$5,000,000, 12% bonds
$3,000,000, 8% long-term note

Construction expenditures incurred during 2003 were as follows:

January 2	$ 400,000
March 31	1,200,000
June 30	800,000
September 30	600,000
December 31	400,000

Required:
Calculate the amount of interest capitalized for 2003 using the specific interest method.

E 10–21
Research and development

In 2003, Space Technology Company modified its model Z2 satellite to incorporate a new communication device. The company made the following expenditures:

Basic research to develop the technology	$2,000,000
Engineering design work	600,000
Development of a prototype device	300,000
Acquisition of equipment	60,000
Testing and modification of the prototype	200,000
Legal and other fees for patent application on the new communication system	40,000
Legal fees for successful defense of the new patent	30,000
Total	$3,230,000

The equipment will be used on this and other research projects. Depreciation on the equipment for 2003 is $10,000.

During your year-end review of the accounts related to intangibles, you discover that the company has capitalized all of the above as costs of the patent. Management contends that the device simply represents an improvement of the existing communication system of the satellite and, therefore, should be capitalized.

Required:
Prepare correcting entries that reflect the appropriate treatment of the expenditures.

E 10–22
Research and
development

The Delaware Company incurred the following research and development costs during 2003:

Salaries and wages for lab research	$ 400,000
Materials used in R&D projects	200,000
Purchase of equipment	900,000
Fees paid to outsiders for R&D projects	320,000
Patent filing and legal costs for a developed product	65,000
Salaries, wages, and supplies for R&D work performed for another company under a contract	350,000
Total	$2,235,000

The equipment has a seven-year life and will be used for a number of research projects. Depreciation for 2003 is $120,000.

Required:
Calculate the amount of research and development expense that Delaware should report in its 2003 income statement.

E 10–23
Multiple choice;
operational assets

The following questions dealing with operational assets are adapted from questions that appeared on recent CPA examinations. Determine the response that best completes the statements or questions.
1. Dahl Co. traded a delivery van and $5,000 cash for a newer van owned by West Corp. The following information relates to the values of the vans on the exchange date:

	Carrying Value	Fair Value
Old van	$30,000	$45,000
New van	40,000	50,000

Dahl's income tax rate is 30%. What amount should Dahl report as gain on exchange of the vans?
a. $15,000
b. $1,000
c. $700
d. $0
2. Heller Co. incurred the following costs in 2003:

Research and development services performed by Kay Corp. for Heller	$150,000
Testing for evaluation of new products	125,000
Laboratory research aimed at discovery of new knowledge	185,000

What amount should Heller report as research and development expense in its income statement for the year ended December 31, 2003?
a. $125,000
b. $150,000
c. $335,000
d. $460,000
3. During 2003, Bay Co. constructed machinery for its own use and for sale to customers. Bay Co. routinely manufactures machinery for sale. Bank loans financed these assets both during construction and after construction was complete. How much of the interest incurred should be reported as interest expense in the 2003 income statement?

	Interest Incurred for Machinery for Own Use	Interest Incurred for Machinery Held for Sale
a.	All interest incurred	All interest incurred
b.	All interest incurred	Interest incurred after completion
c.	Interest incurred after completion	Interest incurred after completion
d.	Interest incurred after completion	All interest incurred

4. Cole Co. began constructing a new building for its own use in January 2003. During 2003, Cole incurred interest of $50,000 on specific construction debt and $20,000 on other borrowings. Interest computed on the weighted-average amount of accumulated expenditures for the building during 2003 was $40,000. What amount of interest cost should Cole capitalize?
a. $20,000
b. $40,000
c. $50,000
d. $70,000

E 10–24
Concepts; terminology

Listed below are several terms and phrases associated with operational assets. Pair each item from List A (by letter) with the item from List B that is most appropriately associated with it.

List A	List B
____ 1. Depreciation	a. Exclusive right to display a word, a symbol, or an emblem.
____ 2. Depletion	b. Exclusive right to benefit from a creative work.
____ 3. Amortization	c. Operational assets that represent rights.
____ 4. Average accumulated expenditures	d. The allocation of cost for natural resources.
	e. Purchase price less fair market value of net identifiable assets.
____ 5. Revenue—donation of asset	
____ 6. Nonmonetary exchange	f. The allocation of cost for plant and equipment.
____ 7. Natural resources	g. Approximation of average amount of debt if all construction funds were borrowed.
____ 8. Intangible assets	
____ 9. Copyright	h. Account credited when assets are donated to a corporation.
____ 10. Trademark	
____ 11. Goodwill	i. The allocation of cost for intangible assets.
	j. Basic principle is to value assets acquired using fair value of assets given.
	k. Wasting assets.

E 10–25
Software development costs

Early in 2003, the Excalibur Company began developing a new software package to be marketed. The project was completed in December 2003 at a cost of $4 million. Of this amount, $3 million was spent before technological feasibility was established. Excalibur expects a useful life of five years for the new product with total revenues of $10 million. During 2004, revenue of $4 million was recognized.

Required:
1. Prepare a journal entry to record the 2003 development costs.
2. Calculate the required amortization for 2004.
3. At what amount should the computer software costs be reported in the December 31, 2004, balance sheet?

E 10–26
Full-cost and successful efforts methods compared.
(Based on Appendix 10)

The Manguino Oil Company incurred exploration costs in 2003 searching and drilling for oil as follows:

Well 101	$ 50,000
Well 102	60,000
Well 103	80,000
Wells 104–108	260,000
Total	$450,000

It was determined that Wells 104–108 were dry holes and were abandoned. Wells 101, 102, and 103 were determined to have sufficient oil reserves to be commercially successful.

Required:
1. Prepare a summary journal entry to record the indicated costs assuming that the company uses the full-cost method of accounting for exploration costs. All of the exploration costs were paid in cash.
2. Prepare a summary journal entry to record the indicated costs assuming that the company uses the successful efforts method of accounting for exploration costs. All of the exploration costs were paid in cash.

PROBLEMS

P 10–1
Acquisition costs

Tristar Production Company began operations on September 1, 2003. Listed below are a number of transactions that occurred during its first four months of operations.
1. On September 1, the company acquired five acres of land with a building that will be used as a warehouse. Tristar paid $100,000 in cash for the property. According to appraisals, the land had a fair market value of $75,000 and the building had a fair market value of $45,000.
2. On September 1, Tristar entered into a five-payment noninterest-bearing installment contract to purchase equipment. The first annual $9,000 payment was made on the date of purchase. Assume that 8% is a reasonable interest rate.

3. On September 15, the president of the company donated a truck to the corporation. Similar trucks were selling for $2,500.
4. On September 18, the company paid its lawyer $3,000 for organizing the corporation.
5. On October 10, Tristar purchased machinery for cash. The purchase price was $15,000 and $500 in freight charges also were paid.
6. On December 2, Tristar acquired various items of office equipment. The company was short of cash and could not pay the $5,500 normal cash price. The supplier agreed to accept 200 shares of the company's nopar common stock in exchange for the equipment. The market value of the stock is not readily determinable.
7. On December 10, the company acquired a tract of land at a cost of $20,000. It paid $2,000 down and signed a 10% note with both principal and interest due in one year. Ten percent is an appropriate rate of interest for this note.

Required:
Prepare journal entries to record each of the above transactions.

P 10–2
Acquisition costs; land and building

On January 1, 2003, the Blackstone Corporation purchased a tract of land (site number 11) with a building for $600,000. Additionally, Blackstone paid a real estate broker's commission of $36,000, legal fees of $6,000, and title insurance of $18,000. The closing statement indicated that the land value was $500,000 and the building value was $100,000. Shortly after acquisition, the building was razed at a cost of $75,000.

Blackstone entered into a $3,000,000 fixed-price contract with Barnett Builders, Inc., on March 1, 2003, for the construction of an office building on land site 11. The building was completed and occupied on September 30, 2004. Additional construction costs were incurred as follows:

Plans, specifications, and blueprints	$12,000
Architects' fees for design and supervision	95,000

To finance the construction cost, Blackstone borrowed $3,000,000 on March 1, 2003. The loan is payable in 10 annual installments of $300,000 plus interest at the rate of 14%. Blackstone's average amounts of accumulated building construction expenditures were as follows:

For the period March 1 to December 31, 2003	$ 900,000
For the period January 1 to September 30, 2004	2,300,000

Required:
1. Prepare a schedule that discloses the individual costs making up the balance in the land account in respect of land site 11 as of September 30, 2004.
2. Prepare a schedule that discloses the individual costs that should be capitalized in the office building account as of September 30, 2004.

(AICPA adapted)

P 10–3
Acquisition costs

The plant asset and accumulated depreciation accounts of Pell Corporation had the following balances at December 31, 2002:

	Plant Asset	Accumulated Depreciation
Land	$ 350,000	$ —
Land improvements	180,000	45,000
Building	1,500,000	350,000
Machinery and equipment	1,158,000	405,000
Automobiles	150,000	112,000

Transactions during 2003 were as follows:
a. On January 2, 2003, machinery and equipment were purchased at a total invoice cost of $260,000, which included a $5,500 charge for freight. Installation costs of $27,000 were incurred.
b. On March 31, 2003, a machine purchased for $58,000 in 1999 was sold for $36,500. Depreciation recorded through the date of sale totaled $24,650.
c. On May 1, 2003, expenditures of $50,000 were made to repave parking lots at Pell's plant location. The work was necessitated by damage caused by severe winter weather.
d. On November 1, 2003, Pell acquired a tract of land with an existing building in exchange for 10,000 shares of Pell's common stock that had a market price of $38 per share. Pell paid legal fees and title insurance totaling $23,000. Shortly after acquisition, the building was razed at a cost of $35,000 in anticipation of new building construction in 2004.

e.   On December 31, 2003, Pell purchased a new automobile for $15,250 cash and trade-in of an old automobile purchased for $18,000 in 1999. Depreciation on the old automobile recorded through December 31, 2003, totaled $13,500. The market value of the old automobile was $3,750.

Required:
1.   Prepare a schedule analyzing the changes in each of the plant assets during 2003, with detailed supporting computations.
2.   Prepare a schedule showing the gain or loss from each asset disposal that would be recognized in Pell's income statement for the year ended December 31, 2003.

(AICPA adapted)

P 10–4
Intangibles

The Horstmeyer Corporation commenced operations early in 2003. A number of expenditures were made during 2003 that were debited to one account called *intangible asset*. A recap of the $644,000 balance in this account at the end of 2003 is as follows:

Date	Transaction	Amount
2/3/03	State incorporation fees and legal costs related to organizing the corporation	$ 7,000
3/1/03	Fire insurance premium for three-year period	6,000
3/15/03	Purchased a copyright	20,000
4/30/03	Research and development costs	40,000
6/15/03	Legal fees for filing a patent on a new product resulting from an R&D project	3,000
9/30/03	Legal fee for successful defense of patent developed above	12,000
10/13/03	Entered into a 10-year franchise agreement with franchisor	40,000
Various	Advertising costs	16,000
11/30/03	Purchase of all of the outstanding common stock of Stiltz Corp.	500,000
	Total	$644,000

The total purchase price of the Stiltz Corp. stock was debited to this account. The market value of Stiltz Corp.'s assets and liabilities on the date of the purchase were as follows:

Receivables	$100,000
Equipment	350,000
Patent	150,000
Total assets	600,000
Note payable assumed	(220,000)
Market value of net assets	$380,000

Required:
Prepare the necessary journal entries to clear the intangible asset account and to set up accounts for separate intangibles, other types of assets, and expenses indicated by the transactions.

P 10–5
Acquisition costs;
journal entries

Consider each of the transactions below. All of the expenditures were made in cash.
1.   The Edison Company spent $12,000 during the year for experimental purposes in connection with the development of a new product.
2.   In April, the Marshall Company lost a patent infringement suit and paid the plaintiff $7,500.
3.   In March, the Cleanway Laundromat bought equipment on an installment note. The contract price was $24,000, payable $6,000 down, and $2,000 a month for the next nine months. The cash price for this equipment was $23,000.
4.   On June 1, the Jamsen Corporation installed a sprinkler system throughout the building at a cost of $28,000.
5.   The Mayer Company, plaintiff, paid $12,000 in legal fees in November, in connection with a successful infringement suit on its patent.
6.   The Johnson Company traded its old machine with an original cost of $7,400 and a net book value of $3,000 plus cash of $8,000 for a new one that had a fair value of $10,000.

Required:
Prepare journal entries to record each of the above transactions.

P 10–6
Nonmonetary
exchange; similar assets

Southern Company owns a building that it leases. The building's fair value is $1,400,000 and its book value is $800,000 (original cost of $2,000,000 less accumulated depreciation of $1,200,000). Southern exchanges this for another building owned by the Eastern Company. The building's book value on Eastern's books is $950,000 (original cost of $1,600,000 less accumulated depreciation of $650,000). Eastern also gives Southern $140,000 to complete the exchange.

Required:

Prepare the journal entries to record the exchange on the books of both Southern and Eastern assuming that the buildings are considered to be *similar* assets by both companies.

P 10–7

Nonmonetary exchange; dissimilar assets

[This is a variation of the previous problem modified to focus on the exchange of dissimilar assets.]

Southern Company owns a building that it leases. The building's fair value is $1,400,000 and its book value is $800,000 (original cost of $2,000,000 less accumulated depreciation of $1,200,000). Southern exchanges this for another building owned by the Eastern Company. The building's book value on Eastern's books is $950,000 (original cost of $1,600,000 less accumulated depreciation of $650,000). Eastern also gives Southern $140,000 to complete the exchange.

Required:

Prepare the journal entries to record the exchange on the books of both Southern and Eastern assuming that the buildings are considered to be *dissimilar* assets by both companies.

P 10–8

Nonmonetary exchange

On September 3, 2003, the Robers Company exchanged operational assets with Phifer Corporation. The facts of the exchange are as follows:

	Robers' Asset	Phifer's Asset
Original cost	$120,000	$140,000
Accumulated depreciation	55,000	63,000
Fair value	75,000	70,000

To equalize the exchange, Phifer paid Robers $5,000 in cash.

Required:

1. Assuming that the assets exchanged are considered *dissimilar* for both companies, record the exchange for both Robers and Phifer.
2. Assuming that the assets exchanged are considered *similar* for both companies, record the exchange for both Robers and Phifer.

P 10–9

Interest capitalization; specific interest method

On January 1, 2003, the Mason Manufacturing Company began construction of a building to be used as its office headquarters. The building was completed on September 30, 2004.

Expenditures on the project were as follows:

January 3, 2003	$1,000,000
March 1, 2003	600,000
June 30, 2003	800,000
October 1, 2003	600,000
January 31, 2004	270,000
April 30, 2004	585,000
August 31, 2004	900,000

On January 2, 2003, the company obtained a $3 million construction loan with a 10% interest rate. The loan was outstanding all of 2003 and 2004. The company's other interest-bearing debt included two long-term notes of $4,000,000 and $6,000,000 with interest rates of 6% and 8%, respectively. Both notes were outstanding during all of 2003 and 2004. The company's fiscal year-end is December 31.

Required:

1. Calculate the amount of interest that Mason should capitalize in 2003 and 2004 using the specific interest method.
2. What is the total cost of the building?
3. Calculate the amount of interest expense that will appear in the 2003 and 2004 income statements.

P 10–10

Interest capitalization; weighted-average method

[This is a variation of the previous problem, modified to focus on the weighted-average interest method.]

Required:

Refer to the facts in Problem 10–9 and answer the following questions:

1. Calculate the amount of interest that Mason should capitalize in 2003 and 2004 using the weighted-average method.
2. What is the total cost of the building?
3. Calculate the amount of interest expense that will appear in the 2003 and 2004 income statements.

P 10–11
Research and development

In 2003, Starsearch Corporation began work on three research and development projects. One of the projects was completed and commercial production of the developed product began in December. The company's fiscal year-end is December 31. All of the following 2003 expenditures were included in the R&D expense account:

Salaries and wages for:	
Lab research	$ 300,000
Design and construction of preproduction prototype	160,000
Quality control during commercial production	20,000
Materials and supplies consumed for:	
Lab research	60,000
Construction of preproduction prototype	30,000
Purchase of equipment	600,000
Patent filing and legal fees for completed project	40,000
Payments to others for research	120,000
Total	$1,330,000

$200,000 of equipment was purchased solely for use in one of the projects. After the project is completed, the equipment will be abandoned. The remaining $400,000 in equipment will be used on future R&D projects. The useful life of equipment is five years. Assume that all of the equipment was acquired at the beginning of the year.

Required:
Prepare journal entries to reflect the appropriate treatment of the expenditures.

BROADEN YOUR PERSPECTIVE

Apply your critical-thinking ability to the knowledge you've gained. These cases will provide you an opportunity to develop your research, analysis, judgment, and communication skills. You also will work with other students, integrate what you've learned, apply it in real world situations, and consider its global and ethical ramifications. This practice will broaden your knowledge and further develop your decision-making abilities.

Judgment Case 10–1
Acquisition costs

A company may acquire operational assets for cash, in exchange for a deferred payment contract, by exchanging other operational assets, or by a combination of these methods.

Required:
1. Identify six types of costs that should be capitalized as the cost of a parcel of land. For your answer, assume that the land has an existing building that is to be removed in the immediate future in order that a new building can be constructed on the site.
2. At what amount should a company record an operational asset acquired in exchange for a deferred payment contract?
3. In general, at what amount should operational assets received in exchange for other nonmonetary assets be valued? Specifically, at what amount should a company value a new machine acquired by exchanging an older, similar machine and paying cash?

(AICPA adapted)

Research Case 10–2
Locate and extract relevant information and cite authoritative support for a financial reporting issue; restoration costs; asset retirement obligation

Your client, Hazelton Mining, recently entered into an agreement to obtain the rights to operate a coal mine in West Virginia for $15 million. Hazelton incurred development costs of $6 million in preparing the mine for extraction, which began on July 1, 2003. The contract requires Hazelton to restore the land and surrounding area to its original condition after extraction is complete in three years.

The company controller, Alice Cushing, is not sure how to account for the restoration costs and has asked your advice. Alice is aware of a recent accounting pronouncement addressing this issue, but is not sure of its provisions. She has narrowed down the possible cash outflows for the restoration costs to four possibilities:

Cash Outflow	Probability
$3 million	20%
4 million	30%
5 million	25%
6 million	25%

Alice also informs you that the company's credit-adjusted risk-free interest rate is 9%. Before responding to Alice, you need to research the issue.

Required:

1. Obtain the original FASB Standard on accounting for asset retirement obligations. You might gain access through FARS, the FASB Financial Accounting Research System, from your school library, or some other source. Explain the basic treatment of asset retirement obligations.
2. Determine the capitalized cost of the coal mine.
3. Prepare a summary journal entry to record the acquisition costs of the mine.
4. How much interest expense will the company record in its income statement for the fiscal year ended December 31, 2003, related to this transaction?
5. Explain to Alice how Hazelton would account for the restoration if the restoration costs differed from the recorded liability in three years. By way of explanation, prepare the journal entry to record the payment of the retirement obligation in three years assuming that the actual restoration costs were $4.7 million.
6. Describe to Alice the necessary disclosure requirements for the obligation.

Judgment Case 10–3
Self-constructed assets

Chilton Peripherals manufactures printers, scanners, and other computer peripheral equipment. In the past, the company purchased equipment used in manufacturing from an outside vendor. In March 2003, Chilton decided to design and build equipment to replace some obsolete equipment. A section of the manufacturing plant was set aside to develop and produce the equipment. Additional personnel were hired for the project. The equipment was completed and ready for use in September.

Required:

1. In general, what costs should be capitalized for a self-constructed asset?
2. Discuss two alternatives for the inclusion of overhead costs in the cost of the equipment constructed by Chilton. Which alternative is generally accepted for financial reporting purposes?
3. Under what circumstance(s) would interest be included in the cost of the equipment?

Judgment Case 10–4
Interest capitalization

SFAS 34 provides guidelines for the inclusion of interest in the initial cost of an operational asset.

Required:

1. What assets qualify for interest capitalization? What assets do not qualify for interest capitalization?
2. Over what period should interest be capitalized?
3. Explain average accumulated expenditures.
4. Explain the two methods that could be used to determine the appropriate interest rate(s) to be used in capitalizing interest.
5. Describe the three steps used to determine the amount of interest capitalized during a reporting period.

Research Case 10–5
Goodwill

Accounting for purchased goodwill has been a controversial issue for many years. In the United States, the amount of purchased goodwill is capitalized and not amortized. Globally, the treatment of goodwill varies significantly, with some countries not recognizing goodwill as an asset. Professors Johnson and Petrone, in "Is Goodwill an Asset," discuss this issue.

Required:

1. In your library or from some other source, locate the indicated article in *Accounting Horizons*, September 1998.
2. Does goodwill meet the FASB's definition of an asset?
3. What are the key concerns of those that believe goodwill is not an asset?

Real World Case 10–6
Property, plant, and equipment; intangibles

The Coca-Cola Company reported the following amounts in the asset section of its balance sheets for the years ended December 31, 2000 and 1999:

	($ in millions)	
	2000	**1999**
Property, plant, and equipment, net	$4,168	$4,267
Intangible assets, net	1,917	1,960

In addition, the 2000 statement of cash flows reported the following items ($ in millions):

Depreciation and amortization	$773
Additions to property and equipment	733
Proceeds from sale of equipment	45

Required:
Assuming that no new intangible assets were acquired or sold during 2000, what was the gain or loss recognized in 2000 from the sale of property, plant, and equipment?

Judgment Case 10–7
Goodwill

The Athena Paper Corporation acquired for cash 100% of the outstanding common stock of Georgia, Inc., a supplier of wood pulp. The purchase price of $4,500,000 was significantly higher than the book value of Georgia's net assets (assets less liabilities) of $2,800,000. The Athena controller recorded the difference of $1,700,000 as an asset, goodwill.

Required:
1. Discuss the meaning of the term *goodwill*.
2. In what situation would the Athena controller be correct in her valuation of goodwill?

Judgment Case 10–8
Research and development

Prior to 1974, accepted practice was for companies to either expense or capitalize R&D costs. In 1974, the FASB issued *SFAS 2* which now requires all research and development costs to be charged to expense when incurred. This was a controversial standard, opposed by many companies who preferred delaying the recognition of these expenses until later years when presumably the expenditures bear fruit.

Several research studies have been conducted to determine if the standard had any impact on the behavior of companies. One interesting finding was that, prior to *SFAS 2,* companies that expensed R&D costs were significantly larger than those companies that capitalized R&D costs.

Required:
1. Explain the FASB's logic in deciding to require all companies to expense R&D costs in the period incurred.
2. Identify possible reasons to explain why, prior to *SFAS 2,* companies that expensed R&D costs were significantly larger than those companies that capitalized R&D costs.

Judgment Case 10–9
Research and development

Clonal, Inc., a biotechnology company, developed and patented a diagnostic product called Trouver. Clonal purchased some research equipment to be used exclusively for Trouver and subsequent research projects. Clonal defeated a legal challenge to its Trouver patent, and began production and marketing operations for the project.

Corporate headquarters' costs were allocated to Clonal's research division as a percentage of the division's salaries.

Required:
1. How should the equipment purchased for Trouver be reported in Clonal's income statements and statements of financial position?
2. a.   Describe the matching principle.
   b.   Describe the accounting treatment of research and development costs and consider whether this is consistent with the matching principle. What is the justification for the accounting treatment of research and development costs?
3. How should corporate headquarters' costs allocated to the research division be classified in Clonal's income statements? Why?
4. How should the legal expenses incurred in defending Trouver's patent be reported in Clonal's financial statements?

(AICPA adapted)

Communication Case 10–10
Research and development

The focus of this case is the situation described in Case 10–9. What is the appropriate accounting for R&D costs? Do you believe that (1) capitalization is the correct treatment of R&D costs, (2) expensing is the correct treatment of R&D costs, or (3) that companies should be allowed to choose between expensing and capitalizing R&D costs?

Required:
1. Develop a list of arguments in support of your view prior to the class session for which the case is assigned. Do not be influenced by the method required by the FASB. Base your opinion on the conceptual merit of the options.
2. In class, your instructor will pair you (and everyone else) with a classmate who also has independently developed a position.

a. You will be given three minutes to argue your view to your partner. Your partner likewise will be given three minutes to argue his or her view to you. During these three-minute presentations, the listening partner is not permitted to speak.

b. Then after each person has had a turn attempting to convince his or her partner, the two partners will have a three-minute discussion in which they will decide which alternative is more convincing and arguments will be merged into a single view for each pair.

3. After the allotted time, a spokesperson for each of the three alternatives will be selected by the instructor. Each spokesperson will field arguments from the class as to the appropriate alternative. The class will then discuss the merits of the alternatives and attempt to reach a consensus view, though a consensus is not necessary.

Trueblood Accounting

The following Trueblood case is recommended for use with this chapter. The case provides an excellent opportunity for class discussion, group projects, and writing assignments. The case, along with Professor's Discussion Material, can be obtained from the Deloitte Foundation at its website: **www. deloitte.com/more/DTF/cases_subj.htm.**

Case 10–11
Accounting for an R&D arrangement

Case 00-9: *Hi-Ho, Hi-Ho, It's Off to Market We Go!*

This case concerns the issues related to a proposed arrangement between two companies to create a third company for the purpose of developing a new drug.

Communication Case 10–12
Research and development

The Thomas Plastics Company is in the process of developing a revolutionary new plastic valve. A new division of the company was formed to develop, manufacture, and market this new product. As of year-end (December 31, 2003), the new product has not been manufactured for sale; however, prototype units were built and are in operation.

Throughout 2003, the new division incurred a variety of costs. These costs included expenses (including salaries of administrative personnel) and market research costs. In addition, approximately $500,000 in equipment (estimated useful life of 10 years) was purchased for use in developing and manufacturing the new valve. Approximately $200,000 of this equipment was built specifically for developing the design of the new product; the remaining $300,000 of the equipment was used to manufacture the preproduction prototypes and will be used to manufacture the new product once it is in commercial production.

The president of the company, Sally Rogers, has been told that research and development costs must be expensed as incurred, but she does not understand this treatment. She believes the research will lead to a profitable product and to increased future revenues. Also, she wonders how to account for the $500,000 of equipment purchased by the new division. "I thought I understood accounting," she growled. "Explain to me why expenditures that benefit our future revenues are expensed rather than capitalized!"

Required:
Write a one- to two-page report to Sally Rogers explaining the generally accepted accounting principles relevant to this issue. The report should also address the treatment of the equipment purchases.

(AICPA adapted)

Ethics Case 10–13
Research and development

Mayer Biotechnical, Inc., develops, manufactures, and sells pharmaceuticals. Significant research and development (R&D) expenditures are made for the development of new drugs and the improvement of existing drugs. During 2003, $220 million was spent on R&D. Of this amount, $30 million was spent on the purchase of equipment to be used in a research project involving the development of a new antibiotic.

The controller, Alice Cooper, is considering capitalizing the equipment and depreciating it over the five-year useful life of the equipment at $6 million per year, even though the equipment likely will be used on only one project. The company president has asked Alice to make every effort to increase 2003 earnings because in 2004 the company will be seeking significant new financing from both debt and equity sources. "I guess we might use the equipment in other projects later," Alice wondered to herself.

Required:
1. Assuming that the equipment was purchased at the beginning of 2003, by how much would Alice's treatment of the equipment increase before tax earnings as opposed to expensing the equipment cost?
2. Discuss the ethical dilemma Alice faces in determining the treatment of the $30 million equipment purchase.

Heineken, based in Amsterdam, is one of the world's largest international beverage companies, selling its products in some 150 countries. Operational asset disclosures accompanying a recent annual report are reproduced below.

Intangible assets (in part)
Goodwill, the difference between the acquisition price and the valuation—calculated in accordance with the Heineken accounting policies—of newly acquired companies is charged to shareholders' equity. Costs of other intangible assets, including brands, patents, licenses, software, research and development, are charged directly to the statement of income.

Fixed assets (in part)
Tangible fixed assets are valued at replacement cost and, with the exception of land, less accumulated depreciation. The replacement cost is based on valuations made by internal and external experts, taking technical and economic developments into account and supported by the experience gained in the construction of breweries throughout the world.

Required:
On the basis of the information the disclosures provide, compare operational asset valuation in the Netherlands with that in the United States.

National Semiconductor Corporation, headquartered in Santa Clara, California, is a global semiconductor manufacturer. The company's 2001 fixed-asset turnover ratio, using the average book value of property, plant, and equipment (PP&E) as the denominator, was approximately 2.61. Additional information taken from the company's 2001 annual report is as follows:

	($ in millions)
Book value of PP&E—beginning of 2001	$804
Purchases of PP&E during 2001	228
Depreciation of PP&E for 2001	216

There were no dispositions of PP&E during 2001.

Required:
1. How is the fixed-asset turnover ratio computed? How would you interpret National's ratio of 2.61?
2. Use the data to determine National's net sales for 2001.
3. Obtain annual reports from three corporations in the same primary industry as National (Intel Corporation and Advanced Micro Devices are two well-known competitors) and compare the management of each company's investment in property, plant, and equipment.

Note: You can obtain copies of annual reports from your library, from friends who are shareholders, from the investor relations department of the corporations, from a friendly stockbroker, or from EDGAR (Electronic Data Gathering, Analysis, and Retrieval) on the Internet (**www.sec.gov** or through Edgarscan at **edgarscan.pwcglobal.com**).

The Elegant Software Company recently completed the development and testing of a new software program that provides the ability to transfer data from among a variety of operating systems. The company believes this product will be quite successful and capitalized all of the costs of designing, developing, coding, and testing the software. These costs will be amortized over the expected useful life of the software on a straight-line basis.

Required:
1. Was Elegant correct in its treatment of the software development costs? Why?
2. Explain the appropriate method for determining the amount of periodic amortization for any capitalized software development costs.

EDGAR, the Electronic Data Gathering, Analysis, and Retrieval system, performs automated collection, validation, indexing, and forwarding of submissions by companies and others who are required by law to file forms with the U.S. Securities and Exchange Commission (SEC). All publicly traded domestic companies use EDGAR to make the majority of their filings. (Some foreign companies file voluntarily.) Form 10-K or 10-KSB, which includes the annual report, is required to be filed on EDGAR. The SEC makes this information available on the Internet.

Required:

1. Access EDGAR on the Internet. The web address is **www.sec.gov**. Edgarscan (**edgarscan.pwcglobal.com**) from PricewaterhouseCoopers makes the process of accessing data from EDGAR easier.
2. Search for Home Depot, Inc. Access the 10-K filing for the most recent fiscal year. Search or scroll to find the financial statements and related notes.
3. Answer the following questions related to the company's operational assets:
   a. Name the different types of operational assets the company lists in its balance sheet under property, plant, and equipment.
   b. How much cash was used for the acquisition of property, plant, and equipment during the year?
   c. What was the amount of interest capitalized during the year?
   d. Compute the fixed-asset turnover ratio for the fiscal year.

Analysis Case 10–18
Reporting operational assets

FedEx Corporation

Refer to the financial statements and related disclosure notes of FedEx Corporation in the Appendix to Chapter 1.

Required:

1. What categories of operational assets does FedEx report in its 2001 balance sheet?
2. How much interest did FedEx capitalize in 2001?
3. How much cash was used in 2001 to purchase property and equipment? How does this compare with purchases in previous years?
4. The fixed-asset turnover ratio for United Parcel Service, FedEx's chief competitor, for the year ended December 31, 2001, is 2.38. How does this compare with FedEx's ratio? What is the ratio intended to measure?

11

Operational Assets: Utilization and Impairment

CHAPTER

OVERVIEW

This chapter completes our discussion of accounting for operational assets. We address the allocation of the cost of these assets to the periods benefited by their use. The usefulness of most operational assets is consumed as the assets are applied to the production of goods or services. Cost allocation corresponding to this consumption of usefulness is known as *depreciation* for plant and equipment, *depletion* for natural resources, and *amortization* for intangibles.

We also consider the treatment of expenditures incurred subsequent to acquisition and the impairment of operational assets.

LEARNING OBJECTIVES

After studying the chapter you should be able to:

LO1 Explain the concept of cost allocation as it pertains to operational assets.

LO2 Determine periodic depreciation using both time-based and activity-based methods.

LO3 Calculate the periodic depletion of a natural resource.

LO4 Calculate the periodic amortization of an intangible asset.

LO5 Explain the appropriate accounting treatment required when a change is made in the service life or residual value of an operational asset.

LO6 Explain the appropriate accounting treatment required when a change in depreciation method is made.

LO7 Explain the appropriate treatment required when an error in accounting for an operational asset is discovered.

LO8 Identify situations that involve a significant impairment of the value of operational assets and describe the required accounting procedures.

LO9 Discuss the accounting treatment of repairs and maintenance, additions, improvements, and rearrangements to operational assets.

What's in a Name?

"I don't understand this at all," your friend Penny Lane moaned. "Depreciation, depletion, amortization; what's the difference? Aren't they all the same thing?" Penny and you are part of a class team working on a case involving Boise Cascade Corporation. "Look at these disclosure notes. The notes use all of those terms." Penny showed you a disclosure note from the annual report of Boise Cascade Corporation.

Property (in part)

Most of our paper and wood products manufacturing facilities determine depreciation by the units-of-production method; other operations use the straight-line method.

Depletion of the cost of company timber harvested and amortization of logging roads are determined on the basis of the annual amount of timber cut in relation to the total amount of recoverable timber.

> By the time you finish this chapter, you should be able to respond appropriately to the questions posed in this case. Compare your response to the solution provided at the end of the chapter.

QUESTIONS

1. Is Penny correct? Do the terms depreciation, depletion, and amortization all mean the same thing? (page 520)

2. What is the units-of-production method? How is it used by Boise Cascade? (page 525)

DEPRECIATION, DEPLETION, AND AMORTIZATION

Cost Allocation—an Overview

LO1

Operational assets are purchased with the expectation that they will provide future benefits, usually for several years. Specifically, they are acquired to be used as part of the revenue-generating operations. Logically, then, the costs of acquiring the assets should be allocated to expense during the reporting periods benefited by their use. That is, their costs are matched with the revenues they help generate.

Let's suppose that a company purchases a used delivery truck for $8,200 to be used to deliver product to customers. The company estimates that five years from the acquisition date the truck will be sold for $2,200. The cost of using the truck during the five-year period is $6,000 ($8,200 − 2,200). The situation is portrayed in Graphic 11–1.

GRAPHIC 11–1
Cost Allocation for an Operational Asset

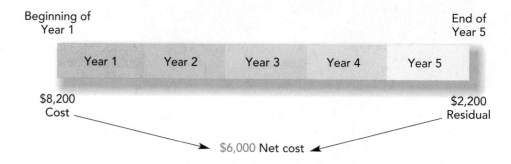

Theoretically, the matching principle requires that the $6,000 be allocated to the five individual years of asset use in direct proportion to the role the asset played in revenue production. However, very seldom is there a clear-cut relationship between the use of operational assets and revenue production. In other words, we can't tell precisely the portion of the total benefits of the asset that was consumed in any particular period. As a consequence, we must resort to arbitrary allocation methods to approximate a matching of expense with revenue. Contrast this situation with the $24,000 prepayment of two years' rent on an office building at $2,000 per month. In that case, we know precisely that the benefits of the asset, prepaid rent, are consumed at a rate of $2,000 per month.

Cost allocation for operational assets is known as **depreciation** for plant and equipment, **depletion** for natural resources, and **amortization** for intangibles. The process often is confused with measuring a decline in fair value of an asset. For example, let's say our delivery truck purchased for $8,200 can be sold for $5,000 at the end of one year but we intend to keep it for the full five-year estimated life. It has experienced a decline in value of $3,200 ($8,200 − 5,000). However, *depreciation is a process of cost allocation, not valuation.* We would not record depreciation expense of $3,200 for year one of the truck's life. Instead, we would distribute the cost of the asset, less any anticipated residual value, over the estimated useful life in a systematic and rational manner that attempts to match revenues with the *use* of the asset, not the decline in its value. After all, the truck is purchased to be used in operations, not to be sold.

The specific accounting treatment depends on the intended use of the asset. For assets used in the manufacture of a product, for example, depreciation, depletion, or amortization is considered a product cost to be included as part of the cost of inventory. Eventually, when the product is sold, it becomes part of the cost of goods sold. For assets *not* used in production, primarily plant and equipment and certain intangibles used in the selling and administrative functions of the company, periodic depreciation or amortization is reported as expense in the income statement. You might recognize this distinction as the difference

FINANCIAL REPORTING CASE

Q1, p. 519

Depreciation, depletion, and amortization are processes that attempt to satisfy the matching principle.

Depreciation, depletion, and amortization for an asset used to manufacture a product is an overhead cost included in the cost of inventory.

between a product cost and a period cost. When a product cost is reported as an expense (cost of goods sold) depends on when the product is sold; when a period cost is reported as an expense depends on the reporting period in which it is incurred.

CHECK WITH THE **COACH**

It's almost halftime in your intermediate accounting studies. Check with the Coach to finish the half on a high note. In Chapter 11 of Coach, you will find experts talking about the practical side of depreciation. The Coach explains why companies make changes in depreciation methods, how these changes affect financial statements, and how they are disclosed. The Coach also offers you a review of the accounting treatment for impairment of operational assets. ■

Measuring Cost Allocation

The process of cost allocation for operational assets requires that three factors be established at the time the asset is put into use. These factors are:

1. **Service life**—the estimated use that the company expects to receive from the asset.
2. **Allocation base**—the value of the usefulness that is expected to be consumed.
3. **Allocation method**—the pattern in which the usefulness is expected to be consumed.

Let's consider these one at a time.

SERVICE LIFE

The **service life**, or **useful life**, of an operational asset is the amount of use that the company expects to obtain from the asset before disposing of it. This use can be expressed in units of time, or in units of activity. For example, the estimated service life of a delivery truck could be expressed in terms of years or in terms of the number of miles that the company expects the truck to be driven before disposition. We use the terms service life and useful life interchangeably throughout the chapter.

Physical life provides the upper bound for service life of tangible operational assets. Physical life will vary according to the purpose for which the asset is acquired and the environment in which it is operated. For example, a diesel powered electric generator may last for many years if it is used only as an emergency backup or for only a few years if it is used regularly.

The service life of a tangible operational asset may be less than physical life for a variety of reasons. For example, the expected rate of technological change may shorten service life. If suppliers are expected to develop new technologies that are more efficient, the company may keep an asset for a period of time much shorter than physical life. Likewise, if the company sells its product in a market that frequently demands new products, the machinery and equipment used to produce products may be useful only for as long as its output can be sold. Similarly, a mineral deposit might be projected to contain 4 million tons of a mineral, but it may be economically feasible with existing extraction methods to mine only 2 million tons. For intangible assets, legal or contractual life often is a limiting factor. For instance, a patent might be capable of providing enhanced profitability for 50 years, but the legal life of a patent is only 20 years.

Management intent also may shorten the period of an asset's usefulness below its physical, legal, or contractual life. For example, a company may have a policy of using its delivery trucks for a three-year period and then trading the trucks for new models.

Companies quite often disclose the range of service lives for different categories of operational assets. For example, Graphic 11–2 shows how Ford Motor Company disclosed its service lives in a note accompanying recent financial statements.

ALLOCATION BASE

The total amount of cost to be allocated over an asset's service life is called its **allocation base.** The amount is the difference between the initial value of the asset at its acquisition (its

> The *service life*, or *useful life*, of an operational asset can be expressed in units of time or in units of activity.

> Expected obsolescence can shorten service life below physical life.

GRAPHIC 11–2
Service Life
Disclosure—Ford
Motor Company

Note 4. Net Property and Depreciation (in part)
On average, buildings and land improvements are depreciated based on a 30-year life. Furniture, fixtures, and equipment are depreciated based on lives ranging from 8 to 14 years.

Allocation base is the difference between the cost of the asset and its anticipated *residual value*.

cost) and its **residual value.** Residual or salvage value is the amount the company expects to receive for the asset at the end of its service life less any anticipated disposal costs. In our delivery truck example above, the allocation base is $6,000 ($8,200 cost less $2,200 anticipated residual value).

In certain situations, residual value can be estimated by referring to a company's prior experience or to publicly available information concerning resale values of various types of assets. For example, if a company intends to trade its delivery trucks in three years for the new model, approximations of the three-year residual value for that type of truck can be obtained from used truck blue books.

However, estimating residual value for many operational assets can be very difficult due to the uncertainty about the future. For this reason, along with the fact that residual values often are immaterial, many companies simply assume a residual value of zero. Companies usually do not disclose estimated residual values.

ALLOCATION METHOD

The *allocation method* used should be systematic and rational and correspond to the pattern of asset use.

In determining how much cost to allocate to periods of an asset's use, a method should be selected that corresponds to the pattern of the loss of the asset's usefulness. *ARB 43* states that the chosen method should allocate the asset's cost "as equitably as possible to the periods during which services are obtained from [its] use." The bulletin further specifies that the method should produce a cost allocation in a "systematic and rational manner."[1] The objective is to try to allocate cost to the period in an amount that is proportional to the amount of benefits generated by the asset during the period relative to the total benefits provided by the asset during its life.

In practice, there are two general approaches that attempt to obtain this systematic and rational allocation. The first approach allocates the cost base according to the *passage of time.* Methods following this approach are referred to as **time-based** methods. The second approach allocates an asset's cost base using a measure of the asset's *input* or *output.* This is an **activity-based** method. We compare these approaches first in the context of depreciation. Later we see that depletion of natural resources typically follows an activity-based approach and the amortization of intangibles typically follows a time-based approach.

Depreciation of Operational Assets

To demonstrate and compare the most common depreciation methods, we refer to the situation described in Illustration 11–1.

TIME-BASED DEPRECIATION METHODS

The *straight-line depreciation method* allocates an equal amount of depreciable base to each year of the asset's service life.

Straight-Line Method.   By far the most easily understood and widely used depreciation method is **straight line.** By this approach, an equal amount of depreciable base is allocated to each year of the asset's service life. The depreciable base is simply divided by the number of years in the asset's life to determine annual depreciation. In our illustration, the straight-line annual depreciation is $42,000, calculated as follows:

$$\frac{\$250,000 - 40,000}{5 \text{ years}} = \$42,000 \text{ per year}$$

---

[1]"Restatement and Revision of Accounting Research Bulletins," *Accounting Research Bulletin No. 43* (New York: AICPA, 1953), ch. 9.

	ILLUSTRATION 11–1
The Hogan Manufacturing Company purchased a machine for $250,000. The company expects the service life of the machine to be five years. During that time, it is expected that the machine will produce 140,000 units. The anticipated residual value is $40,000. The machine was disposed of after five years of use. Actual production during the five years of the asset's life was:	Depreciation Methods

Year	Units Produced
1	24,000
2	36,000
3	46,000
4	8,000
5	16,000
Total	130,000

Accelerated Methods.   Using the straight-line method implicitly assumes that the benefits derived from the use of the asset are the same each year. In some situations it might be more appropriate to assume that the asset will provide greater benefits in the early years of its life than in the later years. In these cases, a more appropriate matching of depreciation with revenues is achieved with a declining pattern of depreciation, with higher depreciation in the early years of the asset's life and lower depreciation in later years. An accelerated depreciation method also would be appropriate when benefits derived from the asset are approximately equal over the asset's life, but repair and maintenance costs increase significantly in later years. The early years incur higher depreciation and lower repairs and maintenance expense, while the later years have lower depreciation and higher repairs and maintenance. Two commonly used ways to achieve such a declining pattern are the sum-of-the-years'-digits method and declining balance methods.

Accelerated depreciation methods are appropriate when the asset is more useful in its earlier years.

Sum-of-the-years'-digits method.   The **sum-of-the-years'-digits (SYD) method** has no logical foundation other than the fact that it accomplishes the objective of accelerating depreciation in a systematic manner. This is achieved by multiplying the depreciable base by a fraction that declines each year and results in depreciation that decreases by the same amount each year. The denominator of the fraction remains constant and is the sum of the digits from one to n, where n is the number of years in the asset's service life. For example, if there are five years in the service life, the denominator is the sum of 1, 2, 3, 4, and 5, which equals 15.[2] The numerator decreases each year; it begins with the value of n in the first year and decreases by one each year until it equals one in the final year of the asset's estimated service life. The annual fractions for an asset with a five-year life are: $\frac{5}{15}$, $\frac{4}{15}$, $\frac{3}{15}$, $\frac{2}{15}$, and $\frac{1}{15}$. We calculate depreciation for the five years of the machine's life using the sum-of-the-years'-digits method in Illustration 11–1A.

The SYD method multiplies depreciable base by a declining fraction.

Declining balance methods.   As an alternative, an accelerated depreciation pattern can be achieved by various declining balance methods. Rather than multiplying a constant balance by a declining fraction as we do in SYD depreciation, we multiply a constant fraction by a declining balance each year. Specifically, we multiply a constant percentage rate times the decreasing book value (cost less accumulated depreciation) of the asset (*not depreciable base*) at the beginning of the year. Because the rate remains constant while the book value declines, annual depreciation is less each year.

Declining balance depreciation methods multiply beginning-of-year book value, not depreciable base, by an annual rate that is a multiple of the straight-line rate.

The rates used are multiples of the straight-line rate. The straight-line rate is simply one, divided by the number of years in the asset's service life. For example, the straight-line rate

---

[2]A formula useful when calculating the denominator is $n(n + 1)/2$.

ILLUSTRATION 11–1A	Year	Depreciable Base	×	Depreciation Rate per Year	=	Depreciation	Book Value End of Year
Sum-of-the-Years'-Digits Depreciation	1	$210,000		$5/15$*		$ 70,000	$180,000
	2	210,000		$4/15$		56,000	124,000
	3	210,000		$3/15$		42,000	82,000
	4	210,000		$2/15$		28,000	54,000
	5	210,000		$1/15$		14,000	40,000
	Totals			$15/15$		$210,000	

$$\frac{*n(n+1)}{2} = \frac{5(5+1)}{2} = 15$$

for an asset with a five-year life is one-fifth, or 20%. Various multiples used in practice are 125%, 150%, or 200% of the straight-line rate. When 200% is used as the multiplier, the method is known as the **double-declining-balance (DDB) method** because the rate used is twice the straight-line rate.

In our illustration, the double-declining-balance rate would be 40% (two times the straight-line rate of 20%). Depreciation is calculated in Illustration 11–1B for the five years of the machine's life using the double-declining-balance method.

ILLUSTRATION 11–1B	Year	Book Value Beginning of Year	×	Depreciation Rate per Year	=	Depreciation	Book Value End of Year
Double-Declining-Balance Depreciation	1	$250,000		40%		$100,000	$150,000
	2	150,000		40		60,000	90,000
	3	90,000		40		36,000	54,000
	4	54,000				14,000*	40,000
	5	40,000				—	40,000
	Total					$210,000	

*Amount necessary to reduce book value to residual value.

Notice that in the fourth year depreciation expense is a plug amount that reduces book value to the expected residual value (book value beginning of year, $54,000, minus expected residual value, $40,000, = $14,000). There is no depreciation expense in year 5 since book value has already been reduced to the expected residual value. Declining balance methods often allocate the asset's depreciable base over fewer years than the expected service life.

It is not uncommon for a company to switch from accelerated to straight line approximately halfway through an asset's useful life.

Switch from Accelerated to Straight Line. The result of applying the double-declining-balance method in our illustration produces an awkward result in the later years of the asset's life. By using the double-declining-balance method in our illustration, no depreciation expense is recorded in year 5 even though the asset is still producing benefits. In practice, many companies switch to the straight-line method approximately halfway through an asset's useful life.

In our illustration, the company would switch to straight line in either year 3 or year 4. Assuming the switch is made at the beginning of year 4, because the book value at the beginning of that year is $54,000, an additional $14,000 ($54,000 − 40,000 in residual value) of depreciation must be recorded. Applying the straight-line concept, $7,000 ($14,000 divided by two remaining years) in depreciation is recorded in both year 4 and year 5.

It should be noted that this switch to straight line is not a change in depreciation method requiring reporting as a change in an accounting principle. The switch is part of the company's planned depreciation approach.

ACTIVITY-BASED DEPRECIATION METHODS

The most logical way to allocate an asset's cost to periods of an asset's use is to measure the usefulness of the asset in terms of its productivity. For example, we could measure the service life of a machine in terms of its *output* (for example, the estimated number of units it will produce) or in terms of its *input* (for example, the number of hours it will operate). We have already mentioned that one way to measure the service life of a vehicle is to estimate the number of miles it will operate. The most common activity-based method is called the **units-of-production method.**

The measure of output used is the estimated number of units (pounds, items, barrels, etc.) to be produced by the machine. We could also use a measure of input such as the number of hours the machine is expected to operate. By the units-of-production method, we first compute the average depreciation rate per unit by dividing the depreciable base by the number of units expected to be produced. This per unit rate is then multiplied by the number of units produced each period. In our illustration, the depreciation rate per unit is $1.50, computed as follows:

$$\frac{\$250,000 - 40,000}{140,000 \text{ units}} = \$1.50 \text{ per unit}$$

Each unit produced will require an additional $1.50 of depreciation to be recorded. As we are estimating service life based on units produced rather than in years, depreciation is not constrained by time. However, total depreciation is constrained by the asset's cost and the anticipated residual value. In our illustration, suppose the company intended to dispose of the asset at the end of five years. Depreciation for year five must be modified. Depreciation expense would be a residual amount necessary to bring the book value of the asset down to residual value. Depreciation for the five years is determined in Illustration 11–1C using the units-of-production method. Notice that the last year's depreciation expense is a plug amount that reduces book value to the expected residual value.

> *Activity-based depreciation methods estimate service life in terms of some measure of productivity.*

> **FINANCIAL REPORTING CASE**
> Q2, p. 519

> The *units-of-production method* computes a depreciation rate per measure of activity and then multiplies this rate by actual activity to determine periodic depreciation.

Year	Units Produced	×	Depreciation Rate per Unit	=	Depreciation	Book Value End of Year
1	24,000		$1.50		$ 36,000	$214,000
2	36,000		1.50		54,000	160,000
3	46,000		1.50		69,000	91,000
4	8,000		1.50		12,000	79,000
5	16,000				39,000*	40,000
Totals	130,000				$210,000	

ILLUSTRATION 11–1C

Units-of-Production Depreciation

*Amount necessary to reduce book value to residual value.

DECISION MAKERS' PERSPECTIVE—Selecting a Depreciation Method

Illustration 11–1D compares periodic depreciation calculated using each of the alternatives we discussed and illustrated.

Theoretically, using an activity-based depreciation method provides a better matching of revenues and expenses. Clearly, the productivity of a plant asset is more closely associated with the benefits provided by that asset than the mere passage of time. Also, these methods allow for random patterns of depreciation to correspond with the random patterns of asset use.

ILLUSTRATION
11–1D

Comparison of
Various Depreciation
Methods

All methods provide
the same total
depreciation over an
asset's life.

Year	Straight Line	Sum-of-the-Years' Digits	Double-Declining Balance	Units of Production
1	$ 42,000	$ 70,000	$100,000	$ 36,000
2	42,000	56,000	60,000	54,000
3	42,000	42,000	36,000	69,000
4	42,000	28,000	14,000	12,000
5	42,000	14,000	0	39,000
Total	$210,000	$210,000	$210,000	$210,000

Activity-based methods
are theoretically
superior to time-based
methods but often are
impractical to apply in
practice.

However, activity-based methods quite often are either infeasible or too costly to use. For example, buildings don't have an identifiable measure of productivity. Even for machinery, there may be an identifiable measure of productivity such as machine hours or units produced, but it frequently is more costly to determine each period than it is to simply measure the passage of time. For these reasons, most companies use time-based depreciation methods.

Graphic 11–3 shows the results of a recent survey of depreciation methods used by large public companies.[3]

GRAPHIC 11–3
Use of Various
Depreciation Methods

Depreciation Method	Number of Companies
Straight line	576
Declining balance	22
Sum-of-the-years'-digits	7
Accelerated method—not specified	53
Units of production	34
Other	10

Why do so many companies use the straight-line method as opposed to other time-based methods? Many companies perhaps consider the benefits derived from the majority of plant assets to be realized approximately evenly over these assets' useful lives. Certainly a contributing factor is that straight line is the easiest method to understand and apply.

Another motivation is the positive effect on reported income. Straight-line depreciation produces a higher net income than accelerated methods in the early years of an asset's life. In Chapter 8 we pointed out that reported net income can affect bonuses paid to management or debt agreements with lenders.

A company does not
have to use the same
depreciation method
for both financial
reporting and income
tax purposes.

Conflicting with the desire to report higher profits is the desire to reduce taxes by reducing taxable income. An accelerated method serves this objective by reducing taxable income more in the early years of an asset's life than straight line. You probably recall a similar discussion from Chapter 8 in which the benefits were described of using the LIFO inventory method during periods of increasing costs. However, remember that the LIFO conformity rule requires companies using LIFO for income tax reporting to also use LIFO for financial reporting. *No such conformity rule exists for depreciation methods.* Income tax regulations allow firms to use different approaches to computing depreciation in their tax returns and in their financial statements. The method used for tax purposes is therefore not a constraint in the choice of depreciation methods for financial reporting. As a result, most companies use the straight-line method for financial reporting and the Internal Revenue Service's prescribed

[3]*Accounting Trends and Techniques—2001* (New York: AICPA, 2001).

accelerated method (discussed in Appendix 11A) for income tax purposes. For example, Graphic 11–4 shows Merck & Co.'s depreciation policy as reported in a disclosure note accompanying recent financial statements.

Summary of Accounting Policies (in part):

Depreciation

Depreciation is provided over the estimated useful lives of the assets, principally using the straight-line method. For tax purposes, accelerated methods are used.

GRAPHIC 11–4
Depreciation Method Disclosure—Merck & Co.

GLOBAL   PERSPECTIVE

In the United States, income tax regulations allow firms to use different approaches to computing depreciation in their tax returns and financial statements. Internationally, in a number of countries, such as Japan and Germany, depreciation rates for financial reporting must be the same as those used for income tax purposes.

It is not unusual for a company to use different depreciation methods for different classes of assets. For example, Graphic 11–5 illustrates the International Paper Company depreciation policy disclosure contained in a note accompanying recent financial statements. ■

Summary of Accounting Policies (in part):

Plants, Properties, and Equipment

Plants, properties, and equipment are stated at cost, less accumulated depreciation. For financial reporting purposes, the units-of-production method of depreciation is used for major pulp and paper mills and certain wood products facilities, and the straight-line method for other plants and equipment.

GRAPHIC 11–5
Depreciation Method Disclosure— International Paper Company

CONCEPT REVIEW EXERCISE

The Sprague Company purchased a fabricating machine on January 1, 2003, at a net cost of $130,000. At the end of its four-year useful life, the company estimates that the machine will be worth $30,000. Sprague also estimates that the machine will run for 25,000 hours during its four-year life. The company's fiscal year ends on December 31.

Depreciation Methods

Required:
Compute depreciation for 2003 through 2006 using each of the following methods:
1. Straight line.
2. Sum-of-the-years'-digits.
3. Double-declining balance.
4. Units of production (using machine hours). Actual production was as follows:

Year	Machine Hours
2003	6,000
2004	8,000
2005	5,000
2006	7,000

SOLUTION

1. Straight line.

$$\frac{\$130,000 - 30,000}{4 \text{ years}} = \$25,000 \text{ per year}$$

2. Sum-of-the-years'-digits.

Year	Depreciable Base	×	Depreciation Rate per Year	=	Depreciation
2003	$100,000		$4/10$		$ 40,000
2004	100,000		$3/10$		30,000
2005	100,000		$2/10$		20,000
2006	100,000		$1/10$		10,000
Total					$100,000

3. Double-declining balance.

Year	Book Value Beginning of Year	×	Depreciation Rate per Year	=	Depreciation	Book Value End of Year
2003	$130,000		50%		$ 65,000	$65,000
2004	65,000		50		32,500	32,500
2005	32,500				2,500*	30,000
2006	30,000				—	30,000
Total					$100,000	

*Amount necessary to reduce book value to residual value.

4. Units of production (using machine hours).

Year	Machine Hours	×	Depreciation Rate per Hour	=	Depreciation	Book Value End of Year
2003	6,000		$4*		$ 24,000	$106,000
2004	8,000		4		32,000	74,000
2005	5,000		4		20,000	54,000
2006	7,000				24,000†	30,000
Total					$100,000	

*($130,000 − 30,000)/25,000 hours = $4 per hour.
†Amount necessary to reduce book value to residual value.

Group and Composite Depreciation Methods

Group and composite depreciation methods aggregate assets to reduce the recordkeeping costs of determining periodic depreciation.

As you might imagine, depreciation records could become quite cumbersome and costly if a company has hundreds, or maybe thousands, of depreciable assets. However, the burden can be lessened if the company uses the group or composite method to depreciate assets collectively rather than individually. The two methods are the same except for the way the collection of assets is aggregated for depreciation. The **group depreciation method** defines the collection as depreciable assets that share similar service lives and other attributes. For example, group depreciation could be used for fleets of vehicles or collections of machinery. The **composite depreciation method** is used when assets are physically dissimilar but are aggregated anyway to gain the convenience of group depreciation. For instance, composite depreciation can be used for all of the depreciable assets in one manufacturing plant, even though individual assets in the composite may have widely diverse service lives.

Both approaches are similar in that they involve applying a single straight-line rate based on the average service lives of the assets in the group or composite.[4] The process is demonstrated using Illustration 11–2.

---

[4]A declining balance method could also be used with either the group or composite method by applying a multiple (e.g., 200%) to the straight-line group or composite rate.

The Express Delivery Company began operations in 2003. It will depreciate its fleet of delivery vehicles using the group method. The cost of vehicles purchased early in 2003, along with residual values, estimated lives, and straight-line depreciation per year by type of vehicle, are as follows:

ILLUSTRATION 11–2

Group Depreciation

Asset	Cost	Residual Value	Depreciable Base	Estimated Life (yrs.)	Depreciation per Year (straight line)
Vans	$150,000	$30,000	$120,000	6	$20,000
Trucks	120,000	16,000	104,000	5	20,800
Wagons	60,000	12,000	48,000	4	12,000
Totals	$330,000	$58,000	$272,000		$52,800

The *group depreciation* rate is determined by dividing the depreciation per year by the total cost. The group's *average service* life is calculated by dividing the depreciable base by the depreciation per year:

$$\text{Group depreciation rate} = \frac{\$52,800}{\$330,000} = 16\%$$

$$\text{Average service life} = \frac{\$272,000}{\$52,800} = 5.15 \text{ years (rounded)}$$

If there are no changes in the assets contained in the group, depreciation of $52,800 per year (16% × $330,000) will be recorded for 5.15 years. This means the depreciation in the sixth year will be $7,920 (.15 of a full year's depreciation = 15% × $52,800), which depreciates the cost of the group down to its estimated residual value. In other words, the group will be depreciated over the average service life of the assets in the group.

In practice, there very likely will be changes in the assets constituting the group as new assets are added and others are retired or sold. Additions are recorded by increasing the group asset account for the cost of the addition. Depreciation is determined by multiplying the group rate by the total cost of assets in the group for that period. Once the group or composite rate and the average service life are determined, they normally are continued despite the addition and disposition of individual assets. This implicitly assumes that the service lives of new assets approximate those of individual assets they replace.

Because depreciation records are not kept on an individual asset basis, dispositions are recorded under the assumption that the book value of the disposed item exactly equals any proceeds received and no gain or loss is recorded. For example, if a delivery truck in the above illustration that cost $15,000 is sold for $3,000 in the year 2006, the following journal entry is recorded:

Cash.	3,000	
Accumulated depreciation (difference)	12,000	
Vehicles		15,000

Any actual gain or loss is included in the accumulated depreciation account. This practice generally will not distort income as the unrecorded gains tend to offset unrecorded losses.

The group and composite methods simplify the recordkeeping of depreciable assets. This simplification justifies any immaterial errors in income determination. Graphic 11–6 shows a disclosure note accompanying recent financial statements of the El Paso Corporation describing the use of the group depreciation method for its regulated property.

Additional group-based depreciation methods, the retirement and replacement methods, are discussed in Appendix 11B.

The depreciation rate is applied to the total cost of the group or composite for the period.

No gain or loss is recorded when a group or composite asset is retired or sold.

Property, Plant, and Equipment (in part)
When applicable, we use the group method to depreciate regulated property, plant, and equipment. Assets with similar lives and other characteristics are grouped and depreciated as one asset. We apply the depreciation rate, approved in our rates, to the total cost of the group, until its net book value equals its salvage value. Currently, our depreciation rates vary from 1 to 33 percent. These rates depreciate the related assets over 2 to 36 years.

When we retire regulated property, plant, and equipment, we charge accumulated depreciation and amortization for the original cost, plus the cost of retirement, less its salvage value. We do not recognize a gain or loss unless we sell an entire operating unit.

Depletion of Natural Resources

Allocation of the cost of natural resources is called **depletion.** Because the usefulness of natural resources generally is directly related to the amount of the resources extracted, the activity-based units-of-production method is widely used to calculate periodic depletion. Service life is therefore the estimated amount of natural resource to be extracted (for example, tons of mineral or barrels of oil).

Depletion base is cost less any anticipated residual value. Residual value could be significant if cost includes land that has a value after the natural resource has been extracted.

The example in Illustration 11–3 was first introduced in Chapter 10.

ILLUSTRATION 11–3	The Jackson Mining Company paid $1,000,000 for the right to explore for a coal deposit on 500 acres of land in Pennsylvania. Costs of exploring for the coal deposit totaled $800,000 and intangible development costs incurred in digging and erecting the mine shaft were $500,000. In addition, Jackson purchased new excavation equipment for the project at a cost of $600,000. After the coal is removed from the site, the equipment will be sold for an anticipated residual value of $60,000.
Depletion of Natural Resources	The company geologist estimates that 1 million tons of coal will be extracted over the three-year period. During 2003, 300,000 tons were extracted. Jackson is required by its contract to restore the land to a condition suitable for recreational use after it extracts the coal.

In Chapter 10 on page 468 we determined that the capitalized cost of the natural resource, coal deposit, including the restoration costs, is $2,768,360. Since there is no residual value to the land, the depletion base equals cost and the depletion rate per ton is calculated as follows:

Depletion of the cost of natural resources usually is determined using the units-of-production method.

$$\text{Depletion per ton} = \frac{\text{Depletion base}}{\text{Estimated extractable tons}}$$

$$\text{Depletion per ton} = \frac{\$2,768,360}{1,000,000 \text{ tons}} = \$2.76836 \text{ per ton}$$

For each ton of coal extracted, $2.768360 in depletion is recorded. In 2003, the following journal entry records depletion.

Depletion ($2.76836 × 300,000 tons).	830,508	
Coal deposit		830,508

Notice that the credit is to the asset, coal deposit, rather than to a contra account, accumulated depletion. Although this approach is traditional, the use of a contra account is acceptable.

Depletion is a product cost and is included in the cost of the inventory of coal, just as the depreciation on manufacturing equipment is included in inventory cost. The depletion is then included in cost of goods sold in the income statement when the coal is sold.

What about depreciation on the $600,000 cost of excavation equipment? If the equipment can be moved from the site and used on future projects, the equipment's depreciable base should be allocated over its useful life. If the asset is not movable, as in our illustration, then it should be depreciated over its useful life or the life of the natural resource, whichever is shorter.

Quite often, companies use the units-of-production method to calculate depreciation on assets used in the extraction of natural resources. The activity base used is the same as that used to calculate depletion, the estimated recoverable natural resource. In our illustration, the depreciation rate would be $.54 per ton, calculated as follows.

$$\text{Depreciation per ton} = \frac{\$600,000 - 60,000}{1,000,000 \text{ tons}} = \$.54 \text{ per ton}$$

The units-of-production method often is used to determine depreciation on assets used in the extraction of natural resources.

In 2003, $162,000 in depreciation ($.54 × 300,000 tons) is recorded and also included as part of the cost of the coal inventory.

The property, plant, and equipment disclosure accompanying recent financial statements of the Coastal Corporation shown in Graphic 11–7 provides a good summary of depletion and depreciation for natural resource properties.

Summary of Accounting Policies (in part):

Plants, Properties, and Equipment

Depreciation, depletion, and amortization ("DD&A") of gas and oil properties are provided on the unit-of-production basis whereby the unit rate for DD&A is determined by dividing the total unrecovered carrying value of gas and oil properties plus estimated future development costs by the estimated proved reserves included therein, as estimated by company engineers and reviewed by independent engineers.

GRAPHIC 11–7
Depletion Method Disclosure—Coastal Corporation

ADDITIONAL CONSIDERATION

Percentage Depletion

Depletion of cost less residual value required by GAAP should not be confused with percentage depletion (also called *statutory depletion*) allowable for income tax purposes for oil, gas, and most mineral natural resources. Under these tax provisions, a producer is allowed to deduct a fixed percentage of gross income as depletion expense without regard to the cost of the natural resource. Over the life of the asset, percentage depletion could exceed the asset's cost. The percentage allowed varies according to the type of natural resource.

Because percentage depletion usually differs from cost depletion, a difference between taxable income and financial reporting income before tax results. These differences are discussed in Chapter 16.

Amortization of Intangible Assets

Let's turn now to a third type of long-lived asset—intangible assets. As for most other operational assets, we allocate the cost of an intangible asset over its service or useful life. However, for the few intangible assets with indefinite useful lives, amortization is inappropriate.

LO4

INTANGIBLE ASSETS SUBJECT TO AMORTIZATION

Allocating the cost of intangible assets is called **amortization**. For an intangible asset with a finite useful life, we allocate its capitalized cost less any estimated residual value to periods in which the asset is expected to contribute to the company's revenue-generating activities.

The cost of an intangible asset with a finite useful life is amortized.

This requires that we determine the asset's useful life, its amortization base (cost less estimated residual value), and the appropriate allocation method, similar to our depreciating tangible assets.

Useful Life. Legal, regulatory, or contractual provisions often limit the useful life of an intangible asset. On the other hand, useful life might sometimes be less than the asset's legal or contractual life. For example, the useful life of a patent would be considerably less than its legal life of 20 years if obsolescence were expected to limit the longevity of a protected product.

Residual Value. We discussed the cost of intangible assets in Chapter 10. The expected residual value of an intangible asset usually is zero. This might not be the case, though, if at the end of its useful life to the reporting entity the asset will benefit another entity. For example, if Quadra Corp. has a commitment from another company to purchase one of Quadra's patents at the end of its useful life at a determinable price, we use that price as the patent's residual value.

Allocation Method. The method of amortization should reflect the pattern of use of the asset in generating benefits. Most companies use the straight-line method. We discussed and illustrated a unique approach to determining the periodic amortization of software development costs in Chapter 10. Recall that the periodic amortization percentage for software development costs is the *greater* of (1) the ratio of current revenues to current and anticipated revenues (percentage of revenue method), or (2) the straight-line percentage over the useful life of the asset.

Adobe Systems, Inc. reported several intangible assets in a recent balance sheet. A note, shown in Graphic 11–8, disclosed the range of estimated useful lives and the use of the straight-line method of allocation.

GRAPHIC 11–8
Intangible Asset Useful
Life Disclosure—
Adobe Systems, Inc.

Summary of Significant Accounting Policies (in part):

Other Assets
Purchased technology and certain other intangible assets are stated at cost less accumulated amortization. Amortization is provided on the straight-line method over the estimated useful lives of the respective assets, generally three to seven years.

Like depletion, amortization expense traditionally is credited to the asset account itself rather than to accumulated amortization. However, the use of a contra account is acceptable. Let's look at an example in Illustration 11–4.

Similar to depreciation, amortization is either a product cost or a period cost depending on the use of the asset. For intangibles used in the manufacture of a product, amortization is a product cost and is included in the cost of inventory (and doesn't become an expense until the inventory is sold). For intangible assets not used in production, such as the franchise cost in our illustration, periodic amortization is expensed in the period incurred.

INTANGIBLE ASSETS NOT SUBJECT TO AMORTIZATION

The cost of an
intangible asset with an
indefinite useful life is
not amortized

An intangible asset that is determined to have an indefinite useful life is not subject to periodic amortization. Useful life is considered indefinite if there is no foreseeable limit on the period of time over which the asset is expected to contribute to the cash flows of the entity.[5]

Indefinite does not necessarily mean permanent. For example, suppose Collins Corporation acquired a trademark in conjunction with the acquisition of a tire company. Collins

---

[5]"Goodwill and Other Intangible Assets," *Statement of Financial Accounting Standards* No. 142 (Norwalk, Conn.: FASB, 2001), par. B45.

Hollins Corporation began operations in 2003. Early in January, the company purchased a franchise from Ajax Industries for $200,000. The franchise agreement is for a period of 10 years. In addition, Hollins purchased a patent for $50,000. The remaining legal life of the patent is 13 years. However, due to expected technological obsolescence, the company estimates that the useful life of the patent is only 8 years. Hollins uses the straight-line amortization method for all intangible assets. The company's fiscal year-end is December 31.

The journal entries to record a full year of amortization for these intangibles are as follows:

Amortization expense ($200,000 ÷ 10 years).	20,000	
Franchise		20,000
To record amortization of franchise.		
Amortization expense ($50,000 ÷ 8 years)	6,250	
Patent		6,250
To record amortization of patent.		

ILLUSTRATION 11–4

Amortization of Intangibles

plans to continue to produce the line of tires marketed under the acquired company's trademark. Recall from our discussion in Chapter 10 that trademarks have a legal life of 10 years, but the registration can be renewed for an indefinite number of 10-year periods. The life of the purchased trademark is initially considered to be indefinite and the cost of the trademark is not amortized. However, if after several years management decides to phase out production of the tire line over the next three years, Collins would amortize the remaining book value over a three-year period.

Goodwill is the most common intangible asset with an indefinite useful life. Recall that goodwill is measured as the difference between the purchase price of a company and the fair value of all of the identifiable net assets (tangible and intangible assets minus the fair value of liabilities assumed). Does this mean that goodwill and other intangible assets with indefinite useful lives will remain in a company's balance sheet at their original capitalized values indefinitely? Not necessarily. Like other operational assets, intangibles are subject to the impairment of value rules we discuss in a subsequent section of this chapter. In fact, indefinite life intangibles must be tested for impairment annually, or more frequently if events or circumstances indicate that the asset might be impaired.

Goodwill is an intangible asset whose cost is *not* expensed through periodic amortization.

ADDITIONAL ISSUES

In this part of the chapter, we discuss the following issues related to cost allocation:

1. Partial periods
2. Changes in estimates
3. Change in depreciation method
4. Error correction
5. Impairment of value

PART

b

Partial Periods

Only in textbooks are operational assets purchased and disposed of at the very beginning or very end of a company's fiscal year. When acquisition and disposal occur at other times, a company theoretically must determine how much depreciation, depletion, and amortization to record for the part of the year that each asset actually is used.

Let's repeat the Hogan Manufacturing Company illustration used earlier in the chapter but modify it in Illustration 11–5 to assume that the asset was acquired *during* the company's fiscal year.

ILLUSTRATION 11–5	On April 1, 2003, the Hogan Manufacturing Company purchased a machine for $250,000. The company expects the service life of the machine to be five years and the anticipated residual value is $40,000. The machine was disposed of after five years of use. The company's fiscal year-end is December 31. Partial-year depreciation is recorded based on the number of months the asset is in service.
Depreciation Methods—Partial Year	

Notice that no information is provided on the estimated output of the machine. Partial-year depreciation presents a problem only when time-based depreciation methods are used. In an activity-based method, the rate per unit of output simply is multiplied by the actual output for the period, regardless of the length of that period.

Depreciation per year of the asset's life calculated earlier in the chapter for the various time-based depreciation methods is shown in Illustration 11–5A.

ILLUSTRATION 11–5A	Year	Straight Line	Sum-of-the-Years'-Digits	Double-Declining Balance
Yearly Depreciation	1	$ 42,000	$ 70,000	$100,000
	2	42,000	56,000	60,000
	3	42,000	42,000	36,000
	4	42,000	28,000	14,000
	5	42,000	14,000	0
	Total	$210,000	$210,000	$210,000

Illustration 11–5B shows how Hogan would depreciate the machinery by these three methods assuming an April 1 acquisition date.

ILLUSTRATION 11–5B

Partial-Year Depreciation

Year	Straight Line	Sum-of-the-Years'-Digits	Double-Declining Balance
2003	$42,000 × 3/4 = $ 31,500	$70,000 × 3/4 = $ 52,500	$100,000 × 3/4 = $ 75,000
2004	$ 42,000	$70,000 × 1/4 = $ 17,500	$100,000 × 1/4 = $ 25,000
		+56,000 × 3/4 = 42,000	+60,000 × 3/4 = 45,000
		$ 59,500	$ 70,000*
2005	$ 42,000	$56,000 × 1/4 = $ 14,000	$60,000 × 1/4 = $ 15,000
		+42,000 × 3/4 = 31,500	+36,000 × 3/4 = 27,000
		$ 45,500	$ 42,000
2006	$ 42,000	$42,000 × 1/4 = $ 10,500	$36,000 × 1/4 = $9,000
		+28,000 × 3/4 = 21,000	+14,000 × 3/4 = 10,500
		$ 31,500	$ 19,500
2007	$ 42,000	$28,000 × 1/4 = $ 7,000	$14,000 × 1/4 = $ 3,500
		+14,000 × 3/4 = 10,500	
		$ 17,500	
2008	$42,000 × 1/4 = $ 10,500	$14,000 × 1/4 = $ 3,500	
	Totals $210,000	$210,000	$210,000

*Could also be determined by multiplying the book value at the beginning of the year by twice the straight-line rate: ($250,000 − $75,000) × 40% = $70,000.

Notice that 2003 depreciation is three-quarters of the full year's depreciation for the first year of the asset's life, because the asset was used nine months, or 3/4 of the year. The remaining one-quarter of the first year's depreciation is included in 2004's depreciation along with 3/4 of the depreciation for the second year of the asset's life. This calculation is not necessary for the straight-line method because a full year's depreciation is the same for each year of the asset's life.

Usually, the above procedure is impractical or at least cumbersome. As a result, most companies adopt a simplifying assumption, or convention, for computing partial year's depreciation and use it consistently. A common convention is to record one-half of a full year's depreciation in the year of acquisition and another half year in the year of disposal. This is known as the **half-year convention.**[6]

CONCEPT **REVIEW** EXERCISE

Depletion and Amortization

Part A:

On March 29, 2003, the Horizon Energy Corporation purchased the mineral rights to a coal deposit in New Mexico for $2 million. Development costs and the present value of estimated land restoration costs totaled an additional $3.4 million. The company removed 200,000 tons of coal during 2003 and estimated that an additional 1,600,000 tons would be removed over the next 15 months.

Required:
Compute depletion on the mine for 2003.

SOLUTION

Cost of coal mine:	($ in millions)
Purchase price of mineral rights	$2.0
Development and restoration costs	3.4
	$5.4

Depletion:

$$\text{Depletion per ton} = \frac{\$5.4 \text{ million}}{1.8 \text{ million tons}^*} = \$3 \text{ per ton}$$

*200,000 + 1,600,000

$$2003 \text{ depletion} = \$3 \times 200,000 \text{ tons} = \$600,000$$

Part B:

On October 1, 2003, Advanced Micro Circuits, Inc., completed the purchase of Zotec Corporation for $200 million. Included in the allocation of the purchase price were the following identifiable intangible assets ($ in millions), along with the allocated amounts and estimated useful lives:

Intangible asset	Allocated amount	Useful life (in years)
Patent	$10	5
Developed technology	50	4
Customer list	10	2

In addition, $100 million was allocated to tangible assets and $30 million to goodwill. Straight-line amortization is used for all purchased intangibles.

During 2003, Advanced finished work on a software development project. Development costs incurred after technological feasibility was achieved and before the product release date totaled $2 million. The software was available for release to the general public on September 29, 2003. During the last three months of the year, revenue from the sale of the software was $4 million. The company estimates that the software will generate an additional $36 million in revenue over the next 45 months.

---

[6]Another common method is the modified half-year convention. This method records a full year's depreciation when the asset is acquired in the first half of the year or sold in the second half. No depreciation is recorded if the asset is acquired in the second half of the year or sold in the first half. These half-year conventions are simple and, in most cases, will not result in material differences from a more precise calculation.

Required:

Compute amortization for purchased intangibles and software development costs for 2003.

SOLUTION

Amortization of Purchased Intangibles:

Patent	$10 million / 5 = $2 million × 3/12 year = $.5 million
Developed technology	$50 million / 4 = $12.5 million × 3/12 year = $3.125 million
Customer list	$10 million / 2 = $5 million × 3/12 year = $1.25 million
Goodwill	The cost of goodwill is not amortized.

Amortization of Software Development Costs:

(1) Percentage-of-revenue method:

$$\frac{\$4 \text{ million}}{(\$4 \text{ million} + 36 \text{ million})} = 10\% \times \$2 \text{ million} = \$200,000$$

(2) Straight-line:

$$\frac{3 \text{ months}}{48 \text{ months}} \text{ or } 6.25\% \times \$2 \text{ million} = \$125,000$$

Advanced will use the percentage-of-revenue method since it produces the greater amortization, $200,000.

Changes in Estimates

A change in estimate should be reflected in the financial statements of the current period and future periods.

The calculation of depreciation, depletion, or amortization requires estimates of both service life and residual value. It's inevitable that at least some estimates will prove incorrect. Chapter 4 introduced the topic of changes in estimates along with coverage of changes in accounting principles and the correction of errors. Here and in subsequent sections of this chapter, we provide overviews of the accounting treatment and disclosures required for these changes and errors when they involve operational assets.

Changes in estimates are accounted for prospectively. When a company revises a previous estimate based on new information, prior financial statements are not restated. Instead, the company merely incorporates the new estimate in any related accounting determinations from then on. So, it usually will affect some aspects of both the balance sheet and the income statement in the current and future periods. And a disclosure note should describe the effect of a change in estimate on income before extraordinary items, net income, and related per-share amounts for the current period.

Consider the example in Illustration 11–6.

The asset's book value is depreciated down to the anticipated residual value of $22,000 at the end of the revised eight-year service life. In addition, a note discloses the effect of the change in estimate on income, if material. The before-tax effect is an increase in income of $18,000 (depreciation of $42,000 if the change had not been made, less $24,000 depreciation after the change). Pepsi Bottling Group, Inc. recently revised the service lives for certain depreciable assets. Graphic 11–9 shows the note that disclosed the change.

Change in Depreciation Method

A change in depreciation method is accounted for as a change in accounting principle. The cumulative after-tax effect on prior years' income is reported in the income statement in the year of the change. The cumulative effect is the difference between retained earnings at the beginning of the year of the change as reported, and the beginning-of-year retained earnings that would have resulted if the new accounting method had been used in all prior years.

In addition, the effect of the change on income before extraordinary items, net income, and related per-share amounts, if material, should be reported for the current period and on a pro forma basis for the financial statements of all prior periods included with the current

ILLUSTRATION 11–6

Change in
Accounting Estimate

On January 1, 2001, the Hogan Manufacturing Company purchased a machine for $250,000. The company expects the service life of the machine to be five years and its anticipated residual value to be $40,000. The company's fiscal year-end is December 31 and the straight-line depreciation method is used for all depreciable assets. During 2003, the company revised its estimate of service life from five to eight years and also revised estimated residual value to $22,000.

For 2001 and 2002, depreciation is $42,000 per year [($250,000 − 40,000) ÷ 5 years] or $84,000 for the two years. However, with the revised estimate, depreciation for 2003 and subsequent years is determined by allocating the book value remaining at the beginning of 2003 less the revised residual value equally over the remaining service life of six years (8 − 2). The remaining book value at the beginning of 2003 is $166,000 ($250,000 − 84,000) and depreciation for 2003 and subsequent years is recorded as follows:

Depreciation expense (below)	24,000	
Accumulated depreciation		24,000

	$250,000	Cost
$42,000		Old annual depreciation ($210,000 ÷ 5 years)
× 2 years	84,000	Depreciation to date (2001–2002)
	166,000	Book value as of 1/1/03
	22,000	Less revised residual value
	144,000	Revised depreciable base
	÷ 6	Estimated remaining life (8 years − 2 years)
	$ 24,000	New annual depreciation

GRAPHIC 11–9
Change in Estimate
Disclosure—Pepsi
Bottling Group, Inc.

Note 3—Comparability of Results (in part):

Asset Lives
At the beginning of fiscal year 2000, we changed the estimated useful lives of certain categories of assets primarily to reflect the success of our preventive maintenance programs in extending the useful lives of these assets. The changes, which are detailed in the table below, lowered total depreciation expense by approximately $69 million, equivalent to $0.26 per diluted share.

	Estimated Useful Lives (in years)	
	2000	**1999**
Manufacturing equipment	15	10
Heavy fleet	10	8
Fountain dispensing equipment	7	5
Small specialty coolers and marketing equipment	3	5 to 7

financial statements. These disclosures allow for comparisons between periods using both the old and new accounting method. Consider the example in Illustration 11–7.

The $76,000 before-tax increase in retained earnings caused by switching from DDB to straight line would be reported, net of tax, in the income statement as a cumulative effect of an accounting change. The journal entry to record the change, ignoring income tax considerations, is:

Accumulated depreciation (determined on next page)	76,000	
Cumulative effect of accounting change.		76,000

ILLUSTRATION 11–7

Change in
Depreciation Method

On January 1, 2001, the Hogan Manufacturing Company purchased a machine for $250,000. The company expects the service life of the machine to be five years and its anticipated residual value is $40,000. The company's fiscal year-end is December 31 and the double-declining-balance (DDB) depreciation method is used. During 2003, the company switched from the DDB to the straight-line method.

Cumulative Effect of the Change:

	($ in 000s)	
	DDB	**Straight Line**
2001 depreciation	$100 ($250 × 40%)	$42 ($210 ÷ 5)
2002 depreciation	60 ($150 × 40%)	42 ($210 ÷ 5)
Accumulated depreciation and 2001–02 reduction in income	$160	$84

difference
$76

The effect of the change on 2003 income before extraordinary items, net income, and related earnings per share figures for the current year, along with the nature and justification for the change, should be described in a disclosure note. Depreciation for 2003 using DDB would have been $36,000. Compared to straight-line depreciation of $42,000, the effect of the switch is to *decrease* before-tax income by $6,000.

Also, because the company's 2003 financial statements will probably include 2002's statements for comparative purposes, 2002's income numbers must be presented, in the supplementary pro forma disclosures, as if the straight-line method had been used to calculate depreciation.

Frequently, when a company changes depreciation methods, the change will be effective only for assets placed in service after that date. Of course, that means there would be no cumulative effect on prior years' earnings because the change doesn't affect assets depreciated in prior periods. Graphic 11–10 provides an example of this type of change in depreciation method made by Dow Chemical.

GRAPHIC 11–10

Change in
Depreciation Method
for Newly Acquired
Assets—The Dow
Chemical Company

Note B: Accounting Change (in part)
For property released to operations at the beginning of the current fiscal year, the Company changed from an accelerated method to the straight-line method of depreciation. The change reflects the Company's engineering and maintenance practices which result in property not being subject to high maintenance costs or substantially reduced productivity in the later years of its useful life. In addition, the change to the straight-line method conforms to predominant industry practice. This change did not have a material effect on current year's income.

Error Correction

Errors involving operational assets include computational errors in the calculation of depreciation, depletion, or amortization and mistakes made in determining whether expenditures should be capitalized or expensed. These errors can affect many years. For example, let's say a major addition to an operational asset should be capitalized but incorrectly is expensed. Not only is income in the year of the error understated, but subsequent years' income is overstated because depreciation is omitted.

Recall from our discussion of inventory errors in Chapter 9 that if a material error is discovered in an accounting period subsequent to the period in which the error is made, any previous years' financial statements that were incorrect as a result of the error are retroactively restated to reflect the correction. Any account balances that are incorrect as a result of the error are corrected by journal entry. If retained earnings is one of the incorrect accounts, the correction is reported as a *prior period adjustment* to the beginning balance in the statement of shareholders' equity.[7] In addition, a disclosure note is needed to describe the nature of the error and the impact of its correction on net income, income before extraordinary items, and earnings per share.

Here is a summary of the treatment of material errors occurring in a previous year:

- Previous years' financial statements are retroactively restated.
- Account balances are corrected.
- If retained earnings requires correction, the correction is reported as a prior period adjustment.
- A note describes the nature of the error and the impact of the correction on income.

Consider Illustration 11–8. The 2001 and 2002 financial statements that were incorrect as a result of the error are *retroactively restated* to report the addition to the patent and to reflect the correct amount of amortization expense, assuming both statements are reported again for comparative purposes in the 2003 annual report.

In 2003, the controller of the Hathaway Corporation discovered an error in recording $300,000 in legal fees to successfully defend a patent infringement suit in 2001. The $300,000 was charged to legal fee expense but should have been capitalized and amortized over the five-year remaining life of the patent. Straight-line amortization is used by Hathaway for all intangibles.

ILLUSTRATION 11–8

Error Correction

Analysis

($ in thousands)

		Correct (Should Have Been Recorded)			Incorrect (As Recorded)	
2001	Patent........	300		Expense	300	
	Cash		300	Cash.............		300
2001	Expense	60		Amortization entry omitted		
	Patent......		60			
2002	Expense	60		Amortization entry omitted		
	Patent......		60			

During the two-year period, amortization expense was *understated* by $120 thousand, but other expenses were *overstated* by $300 thousand, so net income during the period was *understated* by $180 thousand (ignoring income taxes). This means retained earnings is currently *understated* by that amount.

Patent is understated by $180 thousand.

	($ in thousands)	
Patent	180	
Retained earnings		180

To correct incorrect accounts.

Sometimes, the analysis is easier if you re-create the entries actually recorded incorrectly and those that would have been recorded if the error hadn't occurred, and then compare them.

Because retained earnings is one of the accounts incorrect as a result of the error, a correction to that account of $180,000 is reported as a prior period adjustment to the 2003

---

[7]The prior period adjustment is applied to beginning retained earnings for the year following the error, or for the earliest year being reported in the comparative financial statements when the error occurs prior to the earliest year presented. The retained earnings balances in years after the first year also are adjusted to what those balances would be if the error had not occurred, but a company may choose not to explicitly report those adjustments as separate line items.

beginning retained earnings balance in Hathaway's comparative statements of shareholders' equity. Assuming that 2002 is included with 2003 in the comparative statements, a correction would be made to the 2002 beginning retained earnings balance as well. That prior period adjustment, though, would be for the pre-2002 difference: $300,000 − 60,000 = $240,000.

Also, a disclosure note accompanying Hathaway's 2003 financial statements should describe the nature of the error and the impact of its correction on each year's net income (understated by $240,000 in 2001 and overstated by $60,000 in 2002), income before extraordinary items (same as net income), and earnings per share.

Chapter 21 provides in-depth coverage of changes in estimates and methods, and of accounting errors. We cover the tax effect of these changes and errors in that chapter.

Impairment of Value

Depreciation, depletion, and amortization reflect a gradual consumption of the benefits inherent in an operational asset. An implicit assumption in allocating the cost of an asset over its useful life is that there has been no significant reduction in the anticipated total benefits or service potential of the asset. Situations can arise, however, that cause a significant decline or impairment of those benefits or service potentials. An extreme case would be the destruction of a plant asset—say a building destroyed by fire—before the asset is fully depreciated. The remaining carrying value of the asset in that case should be written off as a loss. Sometimes, though, the impairment of future value is more subtle.

The way we recognize and measure an impairment loss differs depending on whether the operational assets are to be held and used or are being held to be sold. Accounting is different, too, for operational assets with finite lives and those with indefinite lives. We consider those differences now.

OPERATIONAL ASSETS TO BE HELD AND USED

An increasingly common occurrence in practice is the partial write-down of operational assets that remain in use. For example, in the second quarter of 2001, American Airlines reduced the carrying value (book value) of certain aircraft by $685 million. The write-down reflected the significant reduction in demand for air travel that occurred even before the September 11, 2001, terrorist attacks on the World Trade Center and the Pentagon.

Conceptually, there is considerable merit for a policy requiring the write-down of an operational asset when there has been a significant decline in value. A write-down can provide important information about the future cash flows that a company can generate from using the asset. However, in practice, this process is very subjective. Even if it appears certain that significant impairment of value has occurred, it often is difficult to measure the amount of the required write-down.

For example, let's say a company purchased $2,000,000 of equipment to be used in the production of a new type of laser printer. Depreciation is determined using the straight-line method over a useful life of six years and the residual value is estimated at $200,000. At the beginning of year 3, the machine's book value has been reduced by accumulated depreciation to $1,400,000 [$2,000,000 − ($300,000 × 2)]. At that time, new technology is developed causing a significant reduction in the selling price of the new laser printer as well as a reduction in anticipated demand for the product. Management estimates that the equipment will be useful for only two more years and will have no significant residual value.

This situation is not simply a matter of a change in the estimates of useful life and residual value. Management must decide if the events occurring in year 3 warrant a write-down of the asset below $1,400,000. A write-down would be appropriate if the company decided that it would be unable to fully recover this amount through future use.

For operational assets to be held and used, different guidelines apply to (1) tangible operational assets and intangible operational assets with finite useful lives (subject to depreciation, depletion, or amortization) and (2) intangible operational assets with indefinite useful lives (not subject to amortization).

An operational asset held for use should be written down if there has been a significant impairment of value.

Tangible Operational Assets and Finite Life Intangibles.   *SFAS No. 144*[8] provides guidelines for when to recognize and how to measure impairment losses of long-lived tangible assets and intangible assets with finite useful lives. For purposes of this recognition and measurement, assets are grouped at the lowest level for which identifiable cash flows are largely independent of the cash flows of other assets.

Recognition.   It would be impractical to test all assets or asset groups for impairment at the end of every reporting period. *SFAS 144* requires investigation of possible impairment only if events or changes in circumstances indicate that the book value of the asset or asset group may not be recoverable. This might happen from:

> Tangible operational assets and finite life intangibles are tested for impairment only when events or changes in circumstances indicate book value may not be recoverable.

  a. A significant decrease in market price.
  b. A significant adverse change in how the asset is being used or in its physical condition.
  c. A significant adverse change in legal factors or in the business climate.
  d. An accumulation of costs significantly higher than the amount originally expected for the acquisition or construction of an asset.
  e. A current-period loss combined with a history of losses or a projection of continuing losses associated with the asset.
  f. A realization that the asset will be disposed of significantly before the end of its estimated useful life.[9]

Measurement.   Determining whether to record an impairment loss and actually recording the loss is a two-step process. The first step is a recoverability test—an impairment loss is required only when the undiscounted sum of estimated future cash flows from an asset is less than the asset's book value. The measurement of impairment loss—step 2—is the difference between the asset's book value and its fair value. If an impairment loss is recognized, the written-down book value becomes the new cost base for future cost allocation. Later recovery of an impairment loss is prohibited.

> STEP 1—An impairment loss is required only when the undiscounted sum of future cash flows is less than book value.

Let's look closer at the measurement process (step two). Fair value is the amount at which the asset could be bought or sold in a current transaction between willing parties. Quoted market prices could be used if they're available. If fair value is not determinable, it must be estimated.

> STEP 2—The impairment loss is the excess of book value over fair value.

The process is best described by an example. Consider Illustration 11–9.

Because the fair value of the factory assets was not readily available to Dakota in Illustration 11–9, the $135 million had to be estimated. One method that can be used to estimate fair value is to compute the discounted present value of future cash flows expected from the asset. Keep in mind that we use *undiscounted* estimates of cash flows in step one to determine whether an impairment loss is indicated, but *discounted* estimates of cash flows to determine the amount of the loss. In calculating present value, either a traditional approach or an expected cash flow approach can be used. The traditional approach is to incorporate risk and uncertainty into the discount rate. Recall from discussions in previous chapters that the expected cash flow approach incorporates risk and uncertainty instead into a determination of a probability-weighted cash flow expectation, and then discounts this expected cash flow using a risk-free interest rate. We discussed and illustrated the expected cash flow approach in previous chapters.

> The present value of future cash flows often is used as a measure of fair value.

A disclosure note is needed to describe the impairment loss. The note should include a description of the impaired asset or asset group, the facts and circumstances leading to the impairment, the amount of the loss if not separately disclosed on the face of the income statement, and the method used to determine fair value.

---

[8]"Accounting for the Impairment of Long-Lived Assets and for Long-Lived Assets to Be Disposed Of," *Statement of Financial Accounting Standards* No. 144 (Norwalk, Conn.: FASB, 2001). This standard retains the fundamental provisions of its predecessor, SFAS No. 121.
[9]Ibid., par. 8.

ILLUSTRATION 11–9 Impairment Loss— Tangible Operational Asset	The Dakota Corporation operates several factories that manufacture medical equipment. Near the end of the company's 2003 fiscal year, a change in business climate related to a competitor's innovative products indicated to management that the $170 million book value of the assets of one of Dakota's factories may not be recoverable. Management is able to identify cash flows from this factory and estimates that future cash flows over the remaining useful life of the factory will be $150 million. The fair value of the factory's assets is not readily available but is estimated to be $135 million. **Change in circumstances.** The change in business climate related to a competitor's innovative products requires investigation of possible impairment. **Step 1. Recoverability.** Because book value of $170 million exceeds undiscounted future cash flows of $150 million, an impairment loss is indicated. **Step 2. Measurement of impairment loss.** The impairment loss is $35 million, determined as follows:

Book value	$170 million
Fair value	135 million
Impairment loss	$ 35 million

The loss normally is reported in the income statement as a separate item included in operating expenses.

Intangible assets with indefinite useful lives should be tested for impairment at least annually.

If book value exceeds fair value, an impairment loss is recognized for the difference.

Indefinite Life Intangible Assets Other than Goodwill.   Intangible assets with indefinite useful lives should be tested for impairment annually, or more frequently if events or changes in circumstances indicate that the asset may be impaired. The measurement of an impairment loss for indefinite life intangibles other than goodwill is a one-step process. We compare the fair value of the asset with its book value. If book value exceeds fair value, an impairment loss is recognized for the difference. Notice that we omit the recoverability test with these assets. Because we anticipate cash flows to continue indefinitely, recoverability is not a good indicator of impairment.

Similar to tangible operational assets and finite life intangibles, if an impairment loss is recognized, the written-down book value becomes the new cost base for future cost allocation. Recovery of the impairment loss is prohibited. Disclosure requirements also are similar.

Goodwill.   Recall that goodwill is a unique intangible asset. Unlike other assets, its cost (a) can't be directly associated with any specific identifiable right and (b) is not separable from the company as a whole. Because of these unique characteristics, we can't measure the impairment of goodwill the same way as other operational assets. *SFAS No. 142*[10] provides guidelines for impairment, which while similar to general impairment guidelines, are specific to goodwill. Let's compare the two-step process for measuring goodwill impairment with the two-step process for measuring impairment for tangible operational assets and finite-life intangibles.

STEP 1—A goodwill impairment loss is indicated when the fair value of the *reporting* unit is less than its book value.

In Step 1, for all classifications of operational assets, we decide whether a write-down due to impairment is required by determining whether the value of an asset has fallen below its book value. However, in this comparison, the value of assets for tangible operational assets and finite-life intangibles is considered to be value in use as measured by the sum of undiscounted cash flows expected from the asset. But due to its unique characteristics, the value of goodwill is not associated with any specific cash flows and must be measured in a unique way. By its very nature, goodwill is inseparable from a particular *reporting unit.* So, for this step, we compare the value of the reporting unit itself with its book value. If the fair value of the reporting unit is less than its book value, an impairment loss is indicated. A reporting unit

---

[10]"Goodwill and Other Intangible Assets," *Statement of Financial Accounting Standards* No. 142 (Norwalk, Conn.: FASB, 2001).

is an operating segment of a company or a component of an operating segment for which discrete financial information is available and segment management regularly reviews the operating results of that component.

If goodwill is tested for impairment at the same time as other operational assets of the reporting unit, the other assets must be tested first and any impairment loss and asset write-down recorded prior to testing goodwill.

In Step 2, for all classifications of operational assets, if impairment is indicated from step 1, we measure the amount of impairment as the excess of the book value of the asset over its fair value. However, unlike for most other operational assets, the fair value of goodwill cannot be measured directly (market value, present value of associated cash flows, etc.) and so must be "implied" from the fair value of the reporting unit that acquired the goodwill.

The implied fair value of goodwill is calculated in the same way that goodwill is determined in a business combination. That is, it's a residual amount measured by subtracting the fair value of all identifiable net assets from the purchase price using the unit's previously determined fair value as the purchase price.[11] An example is provided in Illustration 11–10.

STEP 2—A goodwill impairment loss is measured as the excess of the book value of the goodwill over its "implied" fair value.

In 2002, the Upjane Corporation acquired Pharmacopia Corporation for $500 million. Upjane recorded $100 million in goodwill related to this acquisition because the fair value of the net assets of Pharmacopia was $400 million. After the acquisition, Pharmacopia continues to operate as a separate company and is considered a reporting unit.

Upjane performs a goodwill impairment test at the end of every fiscal year. At the end of 2003, the book value of Pharmacopia's net assets is $440 million, including the $100 million in goodwill. On that date, the fair value of Pharmacopia has dropped to $350 million and the fair value of all of its identifiable tangible and intangible assets, excluding goodwill, is $325 million.

Step 1. Recoverability. Because book value of the net assets of $440 million exceeds fair value of the reporting unit of $350 million, an impairment loss is indicated.

Step 2. Measurement of impairment loss. The impairment loss is $75 million, determined as follows:

Determination of implied goodwill:

Fair value of Pharmacopia	$350 million
Fair value of Pharmacopia's net assets (excluding goodwill)	325 million
Implied value of goodwill	$ 25 million

Measurement of impairment loss:

Book value of goodwill	$100 million
Implied value of goodwill	25 million
Impairment loss	$ 75 million

ILLUSTRATION 11–10

Impairment Loss—Goodwill

Similar to other intangible assets with indefinite useful lives, goodwill should be tested for impairment on an annual basis and in between annual test dates if events or circumstances indicate that the fair value of the reporting unit is below its book value.

The acquiring company in a business combination often pays for the acquisition using its own stock. In the late 1990s, the stock prices of many companies were unusually high. These often-inflated stock prices meant high purchase prices for many acquisitions and, in many cases, incredibly high values allocated to goodwill. When stock prices retreated in 2000 and 2001, it became obvious that the book value of goodwill for many companies would never be recovered. Some examples of multi-billion dollar goodwill impairment losses are shown in Graphic 11–11.

Goodwill should be tested for impairment at least annually.

---

[11]The impairment loss recognized cannot exceed the book value of goodwill.

Company	Goodwill Impairment Loss
AOL Time Warner	$54 billion
JDS Uniphase	50 billion
Nortel Networks	12 billion
Lucent Technologies	4 billion
Vivendi Universal SA	15 billion (Euro dollars)

OPERATIONAL ASSETS TO BE SOLD

We have been discussing the recognition and measurement for the impairment of value of assets to be held and used. We also test for impairment of operational assets held for sale. These are operational assets management has actively committed to sell immediately in their present condition and for which sale is probable.

An operational asset or group of assets classified as held for sale is measured at the lower of its book value or fair value less cost to sell. An impairment loss is recognized for any write-down to fair value less cost to sell.[12] Except for including the cost to sell, notice the similarity to impairment of assets to be held and used. We don't depreciate or amortize these assets while classified as held for sale and report them separately in the balance sheet. Recall from our discussion of discontinued operations in Chapter 4 that similar rules apply for a component of an entity that is classified as held for sale.[13]

Graphic 11–12 summarizes the guidelines for the recognition and measurement of impairment of losses.

> For operational assets held for sale, if book value exceeds fair value, an impairment loss is recognized for the difference.

Type of Operational Asset	When to Test for Impairment	Impairment Test
To Be Held and Used:		
Tangible and finite-life intangibles	When events or circumstances indicate book value may not be recoverable	Step 1—An impairment loss is required only when book value is not recoverable (undiscounted sum of estimated future cash flows less than book value). Step 2—The impairment loss is the excess of book value over fair value.
Indefinite life intangibles (other than goodwill)	At least annually, or more frequently if indicated	If book value exceeds fair value, an impairment loss is recognized for the difference.
Goodwill	At least annually, or more frequently if indicated	Step 1—A loss is indicated when the fair value of the reporting unit is less than its book value. Step 2—An impairment loss is measured as the excess of book value over implied fair value.
To Be Sold	When considered held for sale	If book value exceeds fair value, an impairment loss is recognized for the difference.

[12]If the asset is unsold at the end of a subsequent reporting period, a gain is recognized for any increase in fair value less cost to sell, but not in excess of the loss previously recognized.

[13]A component of an entity comprises operations and cash flows that can be clearly distinguished, operationally and for financial reporting purposes, from the rest of the entity. One objective of *SFAS No. 144* is to establish a single accounting model, based on the framework developed in *SFAS No. 121*, for long-lived assets to be disposed of by sale.

IMPAIRMENT LOSSES AND EARNINGS QUALITY

What do in-process research and development expenditures, losses from the write-down of inventory, and restructuring costs have in common? The presence of any of these items in a corporate income statement presents a challenge to an analyst trying to determine a company's permanent earnings—those likely to continue in the future. We discussed each of these issues in prior chapters.

An analyst must decide whether to consider asset impairment losses as transitory in nature or as a part of permanent earnings.

We now can add asset impairment losses to the list of "big bath" accounting techniques some companies use to manipulate earnings. By writing off large amounts of operational assets, companies significantly reduce earnings in the year of the write-off but are able to increase future earnings by lowering future depreciation, depletion, or amortization. Here's how. We measure the impairment loss as the difference between an asset's book value and its fair value. However, in most cases, fair value must be estimated, and the estimation process usually involves a forecast of future net cash flows the company expects to generate from the asset's use. If a company underestimates future net cash flows, fair value is understated. This has two effects: (1) current year's income is unrealistically low due to the impairment loss being overstated and (2) future income is unrealistically high because depreciation, depletion, and amortization are based on understated asset values.

SUBSEQUENT EXPENDITURES

PART

C

Now that we have acquired and measured operational assets, we can address accounting issues incurred subsequent to their acquisition. This part of the chapter deals with the treatment of expenditures made over the life of these assets to maintain and/or improve them.

GLOBAL PERSPECTIVE

In the United States, accounting for operational assets subsequent to initial acquisition is based on the historical cost of the asset, and revaluations to reflect changes in market values, other than in asset impairment situations, generally are not permitted. Internationally, the International Accounting Standards Committee has issued *IAS 16,* "Accounting for Property, Plant and Equipment." The requirements of *IAS 16* conform to U.S. GAAP except that a revaluation of property, plant, and equipment is permitted. Countries such as Germany, Canada, and Japan adhere strictly to historical cost valuation. However, other countries, including Australia, France, and the United Kingdom, allow the periodic revaluation of property, plant, and equipment to current market value.

Expenditures Subsequent to Acquisition

Many operational assets require expenditures to repair, maintain, or improve them. These expenditures can present accounting problems if they are material. In general, a choice must be made between capitalizing the expenditures by either increasing the asset's book value or creating a new asset, or expensing them in the period in which they are incurred. Conceptually, we can refer to the matching principle that requires the capitalization of expenditures that are expected to produce benefits beyond the current fiscal year. Expenditures that simply maintain a given level of benefits are expensed in the period they are incurred.

Expenditures related to operational assets can increase future benefits in the following ways:

1. An extension of the *useful life* of the asset.
2. An increase in the *operating efficiency* of the asset resulting in either an increase in the quantity of goods or services produced or a decrease in future operating costs.
3. An increase in the *quality* of the goods or services produced by the asset.

Theoretically, expenditures that cause any of these results should be capitalized initially and then expensed in future periods through depreciation, depletion, or amortization. This permits the matching of the expenditure with the future benefits. Of course, materiality is an important factor in the practical application of this approach.

For expediency, many companies set materiality thresholds for the capitalization of any expenditure. For example, a company might decide to expense all expenditures under $200 regardless of whether or not future benefits are increased. Judgment is required to determine the appropriate materiality threshold as well as the appropriate treatment of expenditures over $200. There often are practical problems in capitalizing these expenditures. For example, even if future benefits are increased by the expenditure, it may be difficult to determine how long the benefits will last. It's important for a company to establish a policy for treating these expenditures and apply it consistently.

We classify subsequent expenditures as (1) repairs and maintenance, (2) additions, (3) improvements, or (4) rearrangements.

> Many companies do not capitalize any expenditure unless it exceeds a predetermined amount that is considered material.

REPAIRS AND MAINTENANCE

> Expenditures for *repairs and maintenance* generally are expensed when incurred.

These expenditures are made to *maintain* a given level of benefits provided by the asset and do not *increase* future benefits. For example, the cost of an engine tune-up or the repair of an engine part for a delivery truck allows the truck to continue its productive activity. If the maintenance is not performed, the truck will not provide the benefits originally anticipated. In that sense, future benefits are provided; without the repair, the truck will no longer operate. The key, though, is that future benefits are not provided *beyond those originally anticipated.* Expenditures for these activities should be expensed in the period incurred.

ADDITIONAL CONSIDERATION

If repairs and maintenance costs are seasonal, interim financial statements may be misstated. For example, suppose annual maintenance is performed on a company's fleet of delivery trucks. The annual income statement correctly includes one year's maintenance expense. However, for interim reporting purposes, if the entire expenditure is made in one quarter, should that quarter's income statement include as expense the entire cost of the annual maintenance? If these expenditures can be anticipated, they should be accrued evenly throughout the year by crediting an allowance account. The allowance account is then debited when the maintenance is performed.

ADDITIONS

> The costs of *additions* usually are capitalized.

As the term implies, **additions** involve adding a new major component to an existing asset and should be capitalized because future benefits are increased. For example, adding a refrigeration unit to a delivery truck increases the capability of the truck, thus increasing its future benefits. Other examples include the construction of a new wing on a building and the addition of a security system to an existing building.

The capitalized cost includes all necessary expenditures to bring the addition to a condition and location for use. For a building addition, this might include the costs of tearing down and removing a wall of the existing building. The capitalized cost of additions are depreciated over the remaining useful life of the original asset or its own useful life, whichever is shorter.

IMPROVEMENTS

> The costs of *improvements* usually are capitalized.

Expenditures classified as **improvements** involve the replacement of a major component of an operational asset. The replacement can be a new component with the same characteristics as the old component or a new component with enhanced operating capabilities. For example, an existing refrigeration unit in a delivery truck could be replaced with a new but similar unit or with a new and improved refrigeration unit. In either case, the cost of the improvement usually increases future benefits and should be capitalized by increasing the book value of the related asset (the delivery truck) and depreciated over the useful life of the improved asset. There are three methods used to record the cost of improvements.

1. *Substitution.* The improvement can be recorded as both (1) a disposition of the old component and (2) the acquisition of the new component. This approach is conceptually appealing but it is practical only if the original cost and accumulated depreciation of the old component can be separately identified.
2. *Capitalization of new cost.* Another way to record an improvement is to include the cost of the improvement (net of any consideration received from the disposition of the old component) as a debit to the related asset account, without removing the original cost and accumulated depreciation of the original component. This approach is acceptable only if the book value of the original component has been reduced to an immaterial amount through prior depreciation.
3. *Reduction of accumulated depreciation.* Another way to increase an asset's book value is to leave the asset account unaltered but decrease its related accumulated depreciation. The argument for this method is that many improvements extend the useful life of an asset and are equivalent to a partial recovery of previously recorded depreciation. This approach produces the same book value as the capitalization of cost to the asset account. Cost and accumulated depreciation will differ under the two methods.

The three methods are compared in Illustration 11–11.

				ILLUSTRATION 11–11
The Palmer Corporation replaced the air conditioning system in one of its office buildings that it leases to tenants. The cost of the old air conditioning system, $200,000, is included in the cost of the building. However, the company has separately depreciated the air conditioning system. Depreciation recorded up to the date of replacement totaled $160,000. The old system was removed and the new system installed at a cost of $230,000, which was paid in cash. Parts from the old system were sold for $12,000. Accounting for the improvement differs depending on the alternative chosen.				Improvements
Cash..................................	12,000			*Substitution*
Accumulated depreciation—buildings	160,000			1. Disposition of old
Loss on disposal (difference)	28,000			component.
Buildings		200,000		
Buildings	230,000			2. Acquisition of new
Cash..		230,000		component.
Buildings	218,000			*Capitalization of*
Cash ($230,000 − 12,000)................................		218,000		*new cost*
Accumulated depreciation − buildings	218,000			*Reduction of*
Cash ($230,000 − 12,000)................................		218,000		*accumulated depreciation*

REARRANGEMENTS

Expenditures made to restructure an asset without addition, replacement, or improvement are termed **rearrangements.** The objective is to create a new capability for the asset and not necessarily to extend its useful life. Examples include the rearrangement of machinery on the production line to increase operational efficiency and the relocation of a company's operating plant or office building. If these expenditures are material and they clearly increase future benefits, they should be capitalized and expensed in the future periods benefited. If the expenditures are not material or if it's not certain that future benefits have increased, they should be expensed in the period incurred.

The costs of material *rearrangements* should be capitalized if they clearly increase future benefits.

Graphic 11–13 provides a summary of the accounting treatment for the various types of expenditures related to tangible operational assets.

GRAPHIC 11–13
Expenditures
Subsequent to
Acquisition

Type of Expenditure	Definition	Usual Accounting Treatment
Repairs and maintenance	Expenditures to maintain a given level of benefits	Expense in the period incurred
Additions	The addition of a new major component to an existing asset	Capitalize and depreciate over the remaining useful life of the original asset or its own useful life, whichever is shorter
Improvements	The replacement of a major component	Capitalize and depreciate over the useful life of the improved asset
Rearrangements	Expenditures to restructure an asset without addition, replacement, or improvement	If expenditures are material and clearly increase future benefits, capitalize and depreciate over the future periods benefited

COSTS OF DEFENDING INTANGIBLE RIGHTS

The costs incurred to *successfully* defend an intangible right should be capitalized.

Repairs, additions, improvements, and rearrangements generally relate to tangible operational assets. A possible significant expenditure incurred subsequent to the acquisition of intangible assets is the cost of defending the right that gives the asset its value. If an intangible right is *successfully* defended, the litigation costs should be capitalized and amortized over the remaining useful life of the related intangible. This is the appropriate treatment of these expenditures even if the intangible asset was originally developed rather than purchased.

The costs incurred to *unsuccessfully* defend an intangible right should be expensed.

If the defense of an intangible right is *unsuccessful*, then the litigation costs should be expensed as incurred because they provide no future benefit. In addition, the book value of any intangible asset should be reduced to realizable value. For example, if a company is unsuccessful in defending a patent infringement suit, the patent's value may be eliminated. The book value of the patent should be written off as a loss.

FINANCIAL REPORTING CASE **SOLUTION**

1. **Is Penny correct? Do the terms depreciation, depletion, and amortization all mean the same thing?** *(p. 520)* Penny is correct. Each of these terms refers to the cost allocation of operational assets over their service lives. The term depreciation is used for plant and equipment, depletion for natural resources, and amortization for intangibles.

2. **What is the units-of-production method? How is it used by Boise Cascade?** *(p. 525)* The units-of-production method is an activity-based method that computes a depreciation (or depletion or amortization) rate per measure of activity and then multiplies this rate by actual activity to determine periodic cost allocation. Boise Cascade uses this method to (1) depreciate its paper and wood products manufacturing facilities, (2) measure depletion of the cost of timber harvested, and (3) measure amortization of the cost of logging roads. The cost of logging roads is an intangible asset because the company does not own the roads. Boise Cascade has incurred costs to upgrade the roads to make them serviceable and has the right to use them in its timber operations. ■

THE BOTTOM LINE

1. The use of operational assets represents a consumption of benefits, or service potentials, inherent in the assets. The matching principle requires that the cost of these inherent benefits or service potentials that were consumed be recognized as an expense. As there

very seldom is a direct relationship between the use of operational assets and revenue production, accounting resorts to arbitrary allocation methods to achieve a matching of expenses with revenues.

2. The allocation process for plant and equipment is called *depreciation*. Time-based depreciation methods estimate service life in years and then allocate depreciable base, cost less estimated residual value, using either a straight-line or accelerated pattern. Activity-based depreciation methods allocate the depreciable base by estimating service life according to some measure of productivity.

3. The allocation process for natural resources is called *depletion*. The activity-based method called units-of-production usually is used to determine periodic depletion.

4. The allocation process for intangible assets is called *amortization*. For an intangible asset with a finite useful life, the capitalized cost less any estimated residual value must be allocated to periods in which the asset is expected to contribute to the company's revenue-generating activities. An intangible asset that is determined to have an indefinite useful life is not subject to periodic amortization. Goodwill is perhaps the most typical intangible asset with an indefinite useful life.

5. A change in either the service life or residual value of an operational asset should be reflected in the financial statements of the current period and future periods by recalculating periodic depreciation, depletion, or amortization.

6. A change in depreciation method is considered a change in accounting principle that requires the cumulative effect of the change to be reported in the income statement in the year of the change.

7. A material error in accounting for an operational asset that is discovered in a year subsequent to the year of the error requires that previous years' financial statements that were incorrect as a result of the error are retroactively restated to reflect the correction. Any account balances that are incorrect as a result of the error are corrected by journal entry. If retained earnings is one of the incorrect accounts, the correction is reported as a prior period adjustment to the beginning balance in the statement of shareholders' equity. In addition, a disclosure note is needed to describe the nature of the error and the impact of its correction on income.

8. Conceptually, there is considerable merit for a policy requiring the write-down of an operational asset when there has been a *significant* decline in value below carrying value (book value). The write-down provides important information about the future cash flows to be generated from the use of the asset. However, in practice this policy is very subjective. *SFAS 144* establishes guidance for when to recognize and how to measure impairment losses of tangible operational assets and intangible operational assets that have finite useful lives. *SFAS 142* provides additional guidance for the recognition and measurement of impairment for indefinite life intangibles and goodwill.

9. Expenditures for repairs and maintenance generally are expensed when incurred. The costs of additions and improvements usually are capitalized. The costs of material rearrangements should be capitalized if they clearly increase future benefits. ∎

COMPARISON WITH MACRS (TAX DEPRECIATION)

APPENDIX

11A

Depreciation for financial reporting purposes is an attempt to distribute the cost of the asset, less any anticipated residual value, over the estimated useful life in a systematic and rational manner that attempts to match revenues with the use of the asset. Depreciation for income tax purposes is influenced by the revenue needs of government as well as the desire to influence economic behavior. For example, accelerated depreciation schedules currently allowed are intended to provide incentive for companies to expand and modernize their facilities thus stimulating economic growth.

The federal income tax code allows taxpayers to compute depreciation for their tax returns on assets acquired after 1986 using the **modified accelerated cost recovery system**

(MACRS).[14] Key differences between the calculation of depreciation for financial reporting and the calculation using MACRS are:

1. Estimated useful lives and residual values are not used in MACRS.
2. Firms can't choose among various accelerated methods under MACRS.
3. A half-year convention is used in determining the MACRS depreciation rates.

Under MACRS, each asset is placed within a recovery period category. The six categories for personal property are 3, 5, 7, 10, 15, and 20 years. For example, the 5-year category includes most machinery and equipment, automobiles, and light trucks.

Depending on the category, fixed percentage rates are applied to the original cost of the asset. The rates for the 5-year asset category are as follows:

Year	Rate
1	20.00%
2	32.00
3	19.20
4	11.52
5	11.52
6	5.76
Total	100.00%

These rates are equivalent to applying the double-declining-balance method with a switch to straight-line in the year straight line yields an equal or higher deduction than DDB. In most cases, the half-year convention is used regardless of when the asset is placed in service.[15] The first-year rate of 20% for the five-year category is one-half of the DDB rate for an asset with a five-year life ($2 \times 20\%$). The sixth year rate of 5.76% is one-half of the straight-line rate established in year 4, the year straight-line depreciation exceeds DDB depreciation.

Companies have the option to use the straight-line method for the entire tax life of the asset, applying the half-year convention, rather than using MACRS depreciation schedules. Because of the differences discussed above, tax depreciation for a given year will likely be different from GAAP depreciation.

RETIREMENT AND REPLACEMENT METHODS OF DEPRECIATION

APPENDIX

11B

Retirement and replacement depreciation methods occasionally are used to depreciate relatively low-valued assets with short service lives. Under either approach, an aggregate asset account that represents a group of similar assets is increased at the time the initial collection is acquired.

Retirement Method

The *retirement depreciation method* records depreciation when assets are disposed of and measures depreciation as the difference between the proceeds received and cost.

Using the **retirement depreciation method,** the asset account also is increased for the cost of subsequent expenditures. When an item is disposed of, the asset account is credited for its cost, and depreciation expense is recorded for the difference between cost and proceeds received, if any. No other entries are made for depreciation. As a consequence, one or more periods may pass without any expense recorded. For example, the following entry records the purchase of 100 handheld calculators at $50 acquisition cost each:

---

[14]For assets acquired between 1981 and 1986, tax depreciation is calculated using the accelerated cost recovery system (ACRS), which is similar to MACRS. For assets acquired before 1981, tax depreciation can be calculated using any of the depreciation methods discussed in the chapter. Residual values are used in the calculation of depreciation for pre-1981 assets.
[15]In certain situations, mid-quarter and mid-month conventions are used.

Calculators (100 × $50)..	5,000	
Cash......		5,000
To record the acquisition of calculators.		

If 20 new calculators are acquired at $45 each, the asset account is increased.

Calculators (20 × $45)..	900	
Cash........		900
To record additional calculator acquisitions.		

Thirty calculators are disposed of (retired) by selling them secondhand to a bookkeeping firm for $5 each. The following entry reflects the retirement method:

Cash (30 × $5)...	150	
Depreciation expense (difference)..........................	1,350	
Calculators (30 × $50)................................		1,500
To record the sale/depreciation of calculators.		

Notice that the retirement system assumes a FIFO cost flow approach in determining the cost of assets, $50 each, that were disposed.

Replacement Method

By the **replacement depreciation method,** the initial acquisition of assets is recorded the same way as by the retirement method; that is, the aggregate cost is increased. However, depreciation expense is the amount paid for new or replacement assets. Any proceeds received from asset dispositions reduces depreciation expense. For our example, the acquisition of 20 new calculators at $45 each is recorded as depreciation as follows:

> By the *replacement method,* depreciation is recorded when assets are replaced.

Depreciation expense (20 × $45).........................	900	
Cash...........		900
To record the replacement/depreciation of calculators.		

The sale of the old calculators is recorded as a reduction of depreciation:

Cash (30 × $5)............................	150	
Depreciation expense..............		150
To record the sale of calculators.		

The asset account balance remains the same throughout the life of the aggregate collection of assets.

Because these methods are likely to produce aggregate expense measurements that differ from individual calculations, retirement and replacement methods are acceptable only in situations where the distortion in depreciation expense does not have a material effect on income. These methods occasionally are encountered in regulated industries such as utilities. ■

QUESTIONS FOR REVIEW OF KEY TOPICS

Q 11–1   Explain the similarities in and differences among depreciation, depletion, and amortization.

Q 11–2   Depreciation is a process of cost allocation, not valuation. Explain this statement.

Q 11–3   Identify and define the three characteristics of an asset that must be established to determine periodic depreciation, depletion, or amortization.

Q 11–4   Discuss the factors that influence the estimation of service life for a depreciable asset.

Q 11–5   What is meant by depreciable base? How is it determined?

Q 11–6   Briefly differentiate between activity-based and time-based allocation methods.

Q 11–7   Briefly differentiate between the straight-line depreciation method and accelerated depreciation methods.

Q 11–8   Why are time-based depreciation methods used more frequently than activity-based methods?

Q 11–9   What are some factors that could explain the predominant use of the straight-line depreciation method?

Q 11–10   Briefly explain the differences and similarities between the group approach and composite approach to depreciating aggregate assets.

Q 11–11   Define depletion and compare it with depreciation.

Q 11–12   Compare and contrast amortization of intangible assets with depreciation and depletion.

Q 11–13   What are some of the simplifying conventions a company can use to calculate depreciation for partial years?

Q 11–14   Explain the accounting treatment required when a change is made to the estimated service life of a machine.

Q 11–15   Explain the accounting treatment and disclosures required when a change is made in depreciation method.

Q 11–16   Explain the steps required to correct an error in accounting for an operational asset that is discovered in a year subsequent to the year the error was made.

Q 11–17   Explain what is meant by the impairment value of an operational asset. How should these impairments be accounted for?

Q 11–18   Explain the differences in the accounting treatment of repairs and maintenance, additions, improvements, and rearrangements.

EXERCISES

E 11–1
Depreciation methods

On January 1, 2003, the Excel Delivery Company purchased a delivery van for $22,000. At the end of its five-year service life, it is estimated that the van will be worth $2,000. During the five-year period, the company expects to drive the van 100,000 miles.

Required:
Calculate annual depreciation for the five-year life of the van using each of the following methods. Round all computations to the nearest dollar.
1.   Straight line.
2.   Sum-of-the-years' digits.
3.   Double-declining balance.
4.   Units of production using miles driven as a measure of output, and the following actual mileage:

Year	Miles
2003	22,000
2004	24,000
2005	15,000
2006	20,000
2007	21,000

E 11–2
Depreciation methods

On January 1, 2003, the Allegheny Corporation purchased machinery for $115,000. The estimated service life of the machinery is 10 years and the estimated residual value is $5,000. The machine is expected to produce 220,000 units during its life.

Required:
Calculate depreciation for 2003 and 2004 using each of the following methods. Round all computations to the nearest dollar.
1.   Straight line.
2.   Sum-of-the-years' digits.
3.   Double-declining balance.
4.   One hundred fifty percent declining balance.
5.   Units of production (units produced in 2003, 30,000; units produced in 2004, 25,000).

E 11–3
Depreciation methods; partial years

[This is a variation of the previous exercise modified to focus on depreciation for partial years.]

On October 1, 2003, the Allegheny Corporation purchased machinery for $115,000. The estimated service life of the machinery is 10 years and the estimated residual value is $5,000. The machine is expected to produce 220,000 units during its life.

Required:
Calculate depreciation for 2003 and 2004 using each of the following methods. Partial-year depreciation is calculated based on the number of months the asset is in service. Round all computations to the nearest dollar.
1. Straight line.
2. Sum-of-the-years' digits.
3. Double-declining balance.
4. One hundred fifty percent declining balance.
5. Units of production (units produced in 2003, 10,000; units produced in 2004, 25,000).

E 11–4
Depreciation methods; asset addition

The Funseth Company purchased a five-story office building on January 1, 2001, at a cost of $4,400,000. The building has a residual value of $200,000 and a 30-year life. The straight-line depreciation method is used. On June 30, 2003, construction of a sixth floor was completed at a cost of $1,100,000.

Required:
Calculate the depreciation on the building and building addition for 2003 and 2004 assuming that the addition did not change the life or residual value of the building.

E 11–5
Depreciation methods; solving for unknowns

For each of the following depreciable assets, determine the missing amount (?). Abbreviations for depreciation methods are SL for straight line, SYD for sum-of-the-years' digits, and DDB for double-declining balance.

Asset	Cost	Residual Value	Service Life (Years)	Depreciation Method	Depreciation (Year 2)
A	?	$20,000	5	DDB	$24,000
B	$ 40,000	?	8	SYD	7,000
C	65,000	5,000	?	SL	6,000
D	230,000	10,000	10	?	22,000
E	200,000	20,000	8	150%DB	?

E 11–6
Multiple choice; cost allocation

The following questions dealing with depreciation, depletion, and amortization are adapted from questions that appeared on recent CPA examinations. Determine the response that best completes the statements or questions.

1. In January 2003, Vorst Co. purchased a mineral mine for $2,640,000 with removable ore estimated at 1,200,000 tons. After it has extracted all the ore, Vorst will be required by law to restore the land to its original condition. The present value of the estimated restoration expenditures is $180,000. Vorst believes it will be able to sell the property afterwards for $300,000. During 2003, Vorst incurred $360,000 of development costs preparing the mine for production and removed and sold 60,000 tons of ore. In its 2003 income statement, what amount should Vorst report as depletion?
   a. $135,000
   b. $144,000
   c. $150,000
   d. $159,000

2. South Co. purchased a machine that was installed and placed in service on January 1, 2003, at a cost of $240,000. Salvage value was estimated at $40,000. The machine is being depreciated over 10 years by the double-declining-balance method. For the year ended December 31, 2004, what amount should South report as depreciation expense?
   a. $48,000
   b. $38,400
   c. $32,000
   d. $21,600

3. A machine with a five-year estimated service life and an estimated 10% residual value was acquired on January 1, 2001. On December 31, 2004, accumulated depreciation, using the sum-of-the-years'-digits method, would be
   a. (Original cost less residual value) multiplied by 1/15.
   b. (Original cost less residual value) multiplied by 14/15.
   c. Original cost multiplied by 14/15.
   d. Original cost multiplied by 1/15.

4. Mark Co. bought a franchise from Fred Co. on January 1, 2003, for $204,000. An independent consultant retained by Mark estimated that the remaining life of the franchise was 40 years. Its unamortized cost on Fred's books at January 1, 2003, was $68,000. What amount should be amortized for the year ended December 31, 2003?
   a. $5,100
   b. $4,080
   c. $4,000
   d. $1,700

E 11–7
Group depreciation

Highsmith Rental Company purchased an apartment building early in 2003. There are 20 apartments in the building and each is furnished with major kitchen appliances. The company has decided to use the group depreciation method for the appliances. The following data is available:

Appliance	Cost	Residual Value	Service Life (in Years)
Stoves	$15,000	$3,000	6
Refrigerators	10,000	1,000	5
Dishwashers	8,000	500	4

In 2006, three new refrigerators costing $2,700 were purchased for cash. The old refrigerators, which originally cost $1,500, were sold for $200.

Required:
1. Calculate the group depreciation rate, group life, and depreciation for 2003.
2. Prepare the journal entries to record the purchase of the new refrigerators and the sale of the old refrigerators.

E 11–8
Double-declining-balance method; switch to straight line

On January 2, 2003, the Jackson Company purchased equipment to be used in its manufacturing process. The equipment has an estimated life of eight years and an estimated residual value of $30,000. The expenditures made to acquire the asset were as follows:

Purchase price	$135,000
Freight charges	1,000
Installation charges	4,000

Jackson uses the double-declining-balance (DDB) method of depreciation in the early years of the equipment's life and then switches to straight line halfway through the equipment's life.

Required:
1. Calculate depreciation for each year of the asset's eight-year life.
2. Discuss the accounting treatment of the depreciation on the equipment.

E 11–9
Depletion

On April 17, 2003, the Loadstone Mining Company purchased the rights to a coal mine. The purchase price plus additional costs necessary to prepare the mine for extraction of the coal totaled $3,600,000. The company expects to extract 900,000 tons of coal during a four-year period. During 2003, 220,000 tons were extracted and sold immediately.

Required:
1. Calculate depletion for 2003.
2. Discuss the accounting treatment of the depletion calculated in requirement 1.

E 11–10
Cost of a natural resource; depletion and depreciation; Chapters 10 and 11

[This exercise is a continuation of Exercise 10-3 in Chapter 10 focusing on depletion and depreciation.]

The Jackpot Mining Company operates a copper mine in central Montana. The company paid $1,000,000 in 2003 for the mining site and spent an additional $500,000 to prepare the mine for extraction of the copper. After the copper is extracted in approximately four years, the company is required to restore the land to its original condition, including repaving of roads and replacing a greenbelt. The company has provided the following three cash flow possibilities for the restoration costs:

	Cash Outflow	Probability
1	$300,000	25%
2	400,000	40%
3	500,000	35%

To aid extraction, Jackpot purchased some new equipment on July 1, 2003, for $120,000. After the copper is removed from this mine, the equipment will be sold for an estimated residual amount of

$20,000. There will be no residual value for the copper mine. The credit-adjusted risk-free rate of interest is 10%.

The company expects to extract 10 million pounds of copper from the mine. Actual production was 1.6 million pounds in 2003 and 3 million pounds in 2004.

Required:
1. Compute depletion and depreciation on the mine and mining equipment for 2003 and 2004. The units-of-production method is used to calculate depreciation.
2. Discuss the accounting treatment of the depletion and depreciation on the mine and mining equipment.

E 11–11
Amortization

The Janes Company provided the following information on intangible assets:
a. A patent was purchased from the Lou Company for $600,000 on January 1, 2001. Janes estimated the remaining useful life of the patent to be 10 years. The patent was carried on Lou's accounting records at a net book value of $350,000 when Lou sold it to Janes.
b. During 2003, a franchise was purchased from the Rink Company for $500,000. The contractual life of the franchise is 10 years and Janes records a full year of amortization in the year of purchase.
c. Janes incurred research and development costs in 2003 as follows:

Materials and supplies	$140,000
Personnel	180,000
Indirect costs	60,000
Total	$380,000

d. Effective January 1, 2003, based on new events that have occurred, Janes estimates that the remaining life of the patent purchased from Lou is only five more years.

Required:
1. Prepare the entries necessary in 2001 and 2003 to reflect the above information.
2. Prepare a schedule showing the intangible asset section of Janes' December 31, 2003, balance sheet.

E 11–12
Patent amortization

On January 2, 2003, David Corporation purchased a patent for $500,000. The remaining legal life is 12 years, but the company estimated that the patent will be useful only for eight years. In January 2005, the company incurred legal fees of $45,000 in successfully defending a patent infringement suit. The successful defense did not change the company's estimate of useful life.

Required:
Prepare journal entries related to the patent for 2003, 2004, and 2005.

E 11–13
Change in estimate; useful life of patent

Van Frank Telecommunications has a patent on a cellular transmission process. The company has amortized the patent on a straight-line basis since 1999, when it was acquired at a cost of $18 million at the beginning of that year. Due to rapid technological advances in the industry, management decided that the patent would benefit the company over a total of six years rather than the nine-year life being used to amortize its cost. The decision was made at the end of 2003 (before adjusting and closing entries).

Required:
Prepare the appropriate adjusting entry for patent amortization in 2003 to reflect the revised estimate.

E 11–14
Change in estimate; useful life and residual value of equipment

Wardell Company purchased a minicomputer on January 1, 2001, at a cost of $40,000. The computer was depreciated using the straight-line method over an estimated five-year life with an estimated residual value of $4,000. On January 1, 2003, the estimate of useful life was changed to a total of 10 years, and the estimate of residual value was changed to $900.

Required:
1. Prepare the appropriate adjusting entry for depreciation in 2003 to reflect the revised estimate.
2. Repeat requirement 1 assuming that the company uses the sum-of-the-years'-digits method instead of the straight-line method.

E 11–15
Change in principle; change in depreciation methods

The Alteran Corporation purchased a machine for $1.2 million in 2000. The machine is being depreciated over a 10-year life using the sum-of-the-years'-digits method. The residual value is expected to be $200,000. At the beginning of 2003, Alteran decided to change to the straight-line depreciation method for this machine.

Required:
Prepare all appropriate journal entries relating to the machine for 2003. (Ignore income tax effects.)

E 11–16
Change in principle; change in depreciation methods

Clinton Poultry Farms has used the declining-balance method of depreciation for conveyor equipment acquired at the beginning of 2000. At the beginning of 2003 for financial reporting, Clinton decides to change to the straight-line method. There is no change in the method used for tax reporting. Clinton's tax rate is 40%.

The effect of this change on depreciation for each year is as follows:

($ in 000s)

Year	Straight Line	Declining Balance	Difference
2000	$ 400	$ 640	$240
2001	400	550	150
2002	400	460	60
	$1,200	$1,650	$450

Required:
1. Prepare the journal entry to record the change in principle. (Ignore income tax effects.)
2. Briefly describe any other steps Clinton should take to report this accounting change in the 2002–2003 comparative financial statements.

E 11–17
Error correction

In 2003, internal auditors discovered that PKE Displays, Inc., had debited an expense account for the $350,000 cost of a machine purchased on January 1, 2000. The machine's life was expected to be five years with no residual value. Straight-line depreciation is used by PKE.

Required:
1. Prepare the appropriate correcting entry assuming the error was discovered in 2003 before the adjusting and closing entries. (Ignore income taxes.)
2. Assume the error was discovered in 2004 before the adjusting and closing entries. Prepare the appropriate correcting entry.

E 11–18
Impairment; tangible operational assets

Chadwick Enterprises, Inc., operates several restaurants throughout the Midwest. Three of its restaurants located in the center of a large urban area have experienced declining profits due to declining population. The company's management has decided to test the operational assets of the restaurants for possible impairment. The relevant information for these assets is presented below.

Book value	$6.2 million
Estimated undiscounted sum of future cash flows	4.0 million
Fair value	3.5 million

Required:
1. Determine the amount of the impairment loss.
2. Repeat requirement 1 assuming that the estimated undiscounted sum of future cash flows is $6.5 million and fair value is $5 million.

E 11–19
Impairment; goodwill

In 2001, Alliant Corporation acquired Centerpoint, Inc. for $300 million, of which $50 million was allocated to goodwill. Alliant tests for goodwill impairment at the end of each year. At the end of 2003, management has provided the following information:

Fair value of Centerpoint, Inc.	$220 million
Fair value of Centerpoint's net assets (excluding goodwill)	200 million
Book value of Centerpoint's net assets (including goodwill)	250 million

Required:
1. Determine the amount of the impairment loss.
2. Repeat requirement 1 assuming that the fair value of Centerpoint is $270 million.

E 11–20
Subsequent expenditures

The Belltone Company made the following expenditures related to its 10-year-old manufacturing facility:
1. The heating system was replaced at a cost of $300,000. The cost of the old system was not known. The company accounts for improvements as reductions of accumulated depreciation.
2. A new wing was added at a cost of $750,000. The new wing substantially increases the productive capacity of the plant.
3. Annual building maintenance was performed at a cost of $12,000.
4. All of the machinery on the assembly line in the plant was rearranged at a cost of $50,000. The rearrangement clearly increases the productive capacity of the plant.

Required:
Prepare journal entries to record each of the above expenditures.

E 11–21
Depreciation methods; disposal of operational asset; Chapters 10 and 11

Howarth Manufacturing Company purchased a lathe on June 30, 1999, at a cost of $80,000. The residual value of the lathe was estimated to be $5,000 at the end of a five-year life. The lathe was sold on March 31, 2003, for $17,000. Howarth uses the straight-line depreciation method for all of its plant and equipment. Partial-year depreciation is calculated based on the number of months the asset is in service.

Required:
1. Prepare the journal entry to record the sale.
2. Assuming that Howarth had instead used the sum-of-the-years'-digits depreciation method, prepare the journal entry to record the sale.

E 11–22
Multiple choice; operational assets

The following questions involving operational assets are adapted from questions that appeared on recent CPA examinations. Determine the response that best completes the statements or questions.
1. In January 2001, Winn Corp. purchased equipment at a cost of $500,000. The equipment had an estimated residual value of $100,000, an estimated eight-year useful life, and was being depreciated by the straight-line method. Two years later, it became apparent to Winn that this equipment suffered a permanent impairment of value. In January 2003, management determined the carrying amount should be only $175,000, with a two-year remaining useful life, and the residual value should be reduced to $25,000. In Winn's December 31, 2003, balance sheet, the equipment should be reported at a carrying amount of
   a. $350,000
   b. $175,000
   c. $150,000
   d. $100,000
2. On January 1, 2000, Lane, Inc., acquired equipment for $100,000 with an estimated 10-year useful life. Lane estimated a $10,000 residual value and used the straight-line method of depreciation. During 2004, after its 2003 financial statements had been issued, Lane determined that, due to obsolescence, this equipment's remaining useful life was only four years and its residual value would be $4,000. In Lane's December 31, 2004, balance sheet, what was the carrying amount of this asset?
   a. $51,500
   b. $49,000
   c. $41,500
   d. $39,000
3. On January 1, 2000, Taft Co. purchased a patent for $714,000. The patent is being amortized over its remaining legal life of 15 years expiring on January 1, 2015. During 2003, Taft determined that the economic benefits of the patent would not last longer than 10 years from the date of acquisition. What amount should be reported in the balance sheet for the patent, net of accumulated amortization, at December 31, 2003?
   a. $428,400
   b. $489,600
   c. $504,000
   d. $523,600
4. During 2002, Yvo Corp. installed a production assembly line to manufacture furniture. In 2003, Yvo purchased a new machine and rearranged the assembly line to install this machine. The rearrangement did not significantly increase the estimated useful life of the assembly line, but it did result in significantly more efficient production. The following expenditures were incurred in connection with this project:

Machine	$75,000
Labor to install machine	14,000
Parts added in rearranging the assembly line to provide future benefits	40,000
Labor and overhead to rearrange the assembly line	18,000

What amount of the above expenditures should be capitalized in 2003?
   a. $147,000
   b. $107,000

c. $89,000
d. $75,000

E 11–23
Concepts; terminology

Listed below are several items and phrases associated with depreciation, depletion, and amortization. Pair each item from List A (by letter) with the item from List B that is most appropriately associated with it.

List A	List B
____ 1. Depreciation	a. Cost allocation for natural resource.
____ 2. Service life	b. Accounted for prospectively.
____ 3. Depreciable base	c. When there has been a significant decline in value.
____ 4. Activity-based methods	d. The amount of use expected from an operational asset.
____ 5. Time-based methods	e. Estimates service life in units of output.
____ 6. Double-declining balance	f. Cost less residual value.
____ 7. Group method	g. Cost allocation for plant and equipment.
____ 8. Composite method	h. Does not subtract residual value from cost.
____ 9. Depletion	i. Requires the cumulative effect to be reported in the income statement.
____ 10. Amortization	j. Aggregates assets that are similar.
____ 11. Change in useful life	k. Aggregates assets that are physically unified.
____ 12. Change in depreciation method	l. Cost allocation for an intangible asset.
____ 13. Write-down of asset	m. Estimates service life in years.

E 11–24
Retirement and replacement depreciation
(Based on Appendix 11B)

The Cadillac Construction Company uses the retirement method to determine depreciation on its small tools. During 2001, the first year of the company's operations, tools were purchased at a cost of $8,000. In 2003, tools originally costing $2,000 were sold for $250 and replaced with new tools costing $2,500.

Required:
1. Prepare journal entries to record each of the above transactions.
2. Repeat requirement 1 assuming that the company uses the replacement depreciation method instead of the retirement method.

PROBLEMS

P 11–1
Depreciation methods; change in methods

The fact that generally accepted accounting principles allow companies flexibility in choosing between certain allocation methods can make it difficult for a financial analyst to compare periodic performance from firm to firm.

   Suppose you were a financial analyst trying to compare the performance of two companies. Company A uses the double-declining-balance depreciation method. Company B uses the straight-line method. You have the following information taken from the 12/31/03 year-end financial statements for Company B:

Income Statement

Depreciation expense	$ 10,000

Balance Sheet

Assets:	
Plant and equipment, at cost	$200,000
Less: Accumulated depreciation	(40,000)
Net	$160,000

   You also determine that all of the assets constituting the plant and equipment of Company B were acquired at the same time, and that all of the $200,000 represents depreciable assets. Also, all of the depreciable assets have the same useful life and residual values are zero.

Required:
1. In order to compare performance with Company A, estimate what B's depreciation expense would have been for 2003 if the double-declining-balance depreciation method had been used by Company B since acquisition of the depreciable assets.

2. If Company B decided to switch depreciation methods in 2003 from the straight line to the double-declining-balance method, prepare the journal entry to record the cumulative effect of the switch. Ignore income taxes.

P 11–2
Comprehensive
problem; Chapters 10
and 11

At December 31, 2002, Cord Company's plant asset and accumulated depreciation and amortization accounts had balances as follows:

Category	Plant Asset	Accumulated Depreciation and Amortization
Land	$ 175,000	$ —
Buildings	1,500,000	328,900
Machinery and equipment	1,125,000	317,500
Automobiles and trucks	172,000	100,325
Leasehold improvements	216,000	108,000
Land improvements	—	—

Depreciation methods and useful lives:
Buildings—150% declining balance; 25 years.
Machinery and equipment—Straight line; 10 years.
Automobiles and trucks—150% declining balance; 5 years, all acquired after 1999.
Leasehold improvements—Straight line.
Land improvements—Straight line.

Depreciation is computed to the nearest month and residual values are immaterial.
Transactions during 2003 and other information:

a. On January 6, 2003, a plant facility consisting of land and building was acquired from King Corp. in exchange for 25,000 shares of Cord's common stock. On this date, Cord's stock had a market price of $50 a share. Current assessed values of land and building for property tax purposes are $187,500 and $562,500, respectively.

b. On March 25, 2003, new parking lots, streets, and sidewalks at the acquired plant facility were completed at a total cost of $192,000. These expenditures had an estimated useful life of 12 years.

c. The leasehold improvements were completed on December 31, 1999, and had an estimated useful life of eight years. The related lease, which would terminate on December 31, 2005, was renewable for an additional four-year term. On April 29, 2003, Cord exercised the renewal option.

d. On July 1, 2003, machinery and equipment were purchased at a total invoice cost of $325,000. Additional costs of $10,000 for delivery and $50,000 for installation were incurred.

e. On August 30, 2003, Cord purchased a new automobile for $12,500.

f. On September 30, 2003, a truck with a cost of $24,000 and a carrying amount of $9,100 on date of sale was sold for $11,500. Depreciation for the nine months ended September 30, 2003, was $2,650.

g. On November 4, 2003, Cord purchased for $350,000 a tract of land as a potential future building site.

h. On December 20, 2003, a machine with a cost of $17,000 and a carrying amount of $2,975 at date of disposition was scrapped without cash recovery.

Required:
1. Prepare a schedule analyzing the changes in each of the plant asset accounts during 2003. This schedule should include columns for beginning balance, increase, decrease, and ending balance for each of the plant asset accounts. Do not analyze changes in accumulated depreciation and amortization.

2. For each asset category, prepare a schedule showing depreciation or amortization expense for the year ended December 31, 2003. Round computations to the nearest whole dollar.

(AICPA adapted)

P 11–3
Depreciation methods

[This problem is a continuation of Problem 10–3 in Chapter 10 focusing on depreciation.]

Required:
For each asset classification, prepare a schedule showing depreciation expense for the year ended December 31, 2003, using the following depreciation methods and useful lives:

Land improvements—Straight line; 15 years.
Building—150% declining balance; 20 years.
Machinery and equipment—Straight line; 10 years.
Automobiles—150% declining balance; 3 years.

Depreciation is computed to the nearest month and no residual values are used.

(AICPA adapted)

P 11–4
Partial-year
depreciation; asset
addition; increase in
useful life

On April 1, 2001, the KB Toy Company purchased equipment to be used in its manufacturing process. The equipment cost $48,000, has an eight-year useful life, and has no residual value. The company uses the straight-line depreciation method for all manufacturing equipment.

On January 4, 2003, $12,350 was spent to repair the equipment and to add a feature that increased its operating efficiency. Of the total expenditure, $2,000 represented ordinary repairs and annual maintenance and $10,350 represented the cost of the new feature. In addition to increasing operating efficiency, the total useful life of the equipment was extended to 10 years.

Required:
Prepare journal entries for the following:
1. Depreciation for 2001 and 2002.
2. The 2003 expenditure.
3. Depreciation for 2003.

P 11–5
Operational assets;
comprehensive

The Thompson Corporation, a manufacturer of steel products, began operations on October 1, 2001. The accounting department of Thompson has started the fixed-asset and depreciation schedule presented below. You have been asked to assist in completing this schedule. In addition to ascertaining that the data already on the schedule are correct, you have obtained the following information from the company's records and personnel:

a. Depreciation is computed from the first of the month of acquisition to the first of the month of disposition.
b. Land A and Building A were acquired from a predecessor corporation. Thompson paid $812,500 for the land and building together. At the time of acquisition, the land had an appraised value of $72,000 and the building had an appraised value of $828,000.
c. Land B was acquired on October 2, 2001, in exchange for 3,000 newly issued shares of Thompson's common stock. At the date of acquisition, the stock had a par value of $5 per share and a fair market value of $25 per share. During October 2001, Thompson paid $10,400 to demolish an existing building on this land so it could construct a new building.
d. Construction of Building B on the newly acquired land began on October 1, 2002. By September 30, 2003, Thompson had paid $210,000 of the estimated total construction costs of $300,000. Estimated completion and occupancy are July 2004.
e. Certain equipment was donated to the corporation by the city. An independent appraisal of the equipment when donated placed the fair value at $16,000 and the residual value at $2,000.
f. Machine A's total cost of $110,000 includes installation charges of $550 and normal repairs and maintenance of $11,000. Residual value is estimated at $5,500. Machine A was sold on February 1, 2003.
g. On October 1, 2002, Machine B was acquired with a down payment of $4,000 and the remaining payments to be made in 10 annual installments of $4,000 each beginning October 1, 2003. The prevailing interest rate was 8%.

THOMPSON CORPORATION
Fixed Asset and Depreciation Schedule
For Fiscal Years Ended September 30, 2002, and September 30, 2003

Assets	Acquisition Date	Cost	Residual	Depreciation Method	Estimated Life in Years	Depreciation for Year Ended 9/30 2002	2003
Land A	10/1/01	65,000 $(1)	N/A	N/A	N/A	N/A	N/A
Building A	10/1/01	747,500 (2)	$47,500	SL	(3) 50	$14,000	$(4) 14,000
Land B	10/2/01	85,400 (5)	N/A	N/A	N/A	N/A	N/A
Building B	Under construction	210,000 to date	—	SL	30	—	Nø (6)
Donated Equipment	10/2/01	16,000 (7)	2,000	150% Declining balance	10	(8) 2,400	(9) 2,040
Machine A	10/2/01	99,000 (10)	5,500	Sum-of-the-years'-digits	10	(11) 17,000	(12)
Machine B	10/1/02	(13)		SL	15	—	(14)

N/A = not applicable

P 11–6
Depreciation methods; partial-year depreciation; sale of assets

On March 31, 2003, the Herzog Company purchased a factory complete with machinery and equipment. The allocation of the total purchase price of $1,000,000 to the various types of assets along with estimated useful lives and residual values are as follows:

Asset	Cost	Estimated Residual Value	Estimated Useful Life in Years
Land	$ 100,000	N/A	N/A
Building	500,000	none	25
Machinery	240,000	10% of cost	8
Equipment	160,000	$13,000	6
Total	$1,000,000		

On June 29, 2004, machinery included in the March 31, 2003, purchase that cost $100,000 was sold for $80,000. Herzog uses the straight-line depreciation method for buildings and machinery and the sum-of-the-years'-digits method for equipment. Partial-year depreciation is calculated based on the number of months an asset is in service.

Required:
1. Compute depreciation expense on the building, machinery, and equipment for 2003.
2. Prepare the journal entries to record (1) depreciation on the machinery sold on June 29, 2004, and (2) the sale of machinery.
3. Compute depreciation expense on the building, remaining machinery, and equipment for 2004.

P 11–7
Depletion; change in estimate

In 2003, the Marion Company purchased land containing a mineral mine for $1,600,000. Additional costs of $600,000 were incurred to develop the mine. Geologists estimated that 400,000 tons of ore would be extracted. After the ore is removed, the land will have a resale value of $100,000.

To aid in the extraction, Marion built various structures and small storage buildings on the site at a cost of $150,000. These structures have a useful life of 10 years. The structures cannot be moved after the ore has been removed and will be left at the site. In addition, new equipment costing $80,000 was purchased and installed at the site. Marion does not plan to move the equipment to another site, but estimates that it can be sold at auction for $4,000 after the mining project is completed.

In 2003, 50,000 tons of ore were extracted and sold. In 2004, the estimate of total tons of ore in the mine was revised from 400,000 to 487,500. During 2004, 80,000 tons were extracted, of which 60,000 tons were sold.

Required:
1. Compute depletion and depreciation of the mine and the mining facilities and equipment for 2003 and 2004. Marion uses the units-of-production method to determine depreciation on mining facilities and equipment.
2. Compute the book value of the mineral mine, structures, and equipment as of December 31, 2004.
3. Discuss the accounting treatment of the depletion and depreciation on the mine and mining facilities and equipment.

P 11–8
Amortization

The following information concerns the intangible assets of Epstein Corporation:
a. On June 30, 2003, Epstein completed the purchase of the Johnstone Corporation for $2,000,000 in cash. The fair value of the net identifiable assets of Johnstone was $1,700,000.
b. Included in the assets purchased from Johnstone was a patent that was valued at $80,000. The remaining legal life of the patent was 13 years, but Epstein believes that the patent will only be useful for another eight years.
c. Epstein acquired a franchise on October 1, 2003, by paying an initial franchise fee of $200,000. The contractual life of the franchise is 10 years.

Required:
1. Prepare year-end adjusting journal entries to record amortization expense on the intangibles at December 31, 2003.
2. Prepare the intangible asset section of the December 31, 2003, balance sheet.

P 11–9
Straight-line depreciation; change in useful life and residual value

The property, plant, and equipment section of the Jasper Company's December 31, 2002, balance sheet contained the following:

Property, plant, and equipment:		
Land		$120,000
Building	$840,000	
Less: Accumulated depreciation	(200,000)	640,000
Equipment	180,000	
Less: Accumulated depreciation	?	?
Total property, plant, and equipment		?

The land and building were purchased at the beginning of 1998. Straight-line depreciation is used and a residual value of $40,000 for the building is anticipated.

The equipment is comprised of the following three machines:

Machine	Cost	Date Acquired	Residual Value	Life in Years
101	$70,000	1/1/00	$7,000	10
102	80,000	6/30/01	8,000	8
103	30,000	9/1/02	3,000	9

The straight-line method is used to determine depreciation on the equipment. On March 31, 2003, Machine 102 was sold for $52,500. Early in 2003, the useful life of machine 101 was revised to seven years in total, and the residual value was revised to zero.

Required:
1. Calculate the accumulated depreciation on the equipment at December 31, 2002.
2. Prepare the journal entry to record the sale of machine 102. Also prepare the journal entry to record 2003 depreciation on machine 102 up to the date of sale.
3. Prepare the 2003 year-end adjusting journal entries to record depreciation on the building and equipment.

P 11–10
Accounting changes; three accounting situations

Described below are three independent and unrelated situations involving accounting changes. Each change occurs during 2003 before any adjusting entries or closing entries are prepared.

a. On December 30, 1999, Rival Industries acquired its office building at a cost of $1,000,000. It has been depreciated on a straight-line basis assuming a useful life of 40 years and no residual value. However, plans were finalized in 2003 to relocate the company headquarters at the end of 2008. The vacated office building will have a residual value at that time of $700,000.

b. At the beginning of 1999, the Hoffman Group purchased office equipment at a cost of $330,000. Its useful life was estimated to be 10 years with no residual value. The equipment has been depreciated by the sum-of-the-years'-digits method. On January 1, 2003, the company changed to the straight-line method.

c. At the beginning of 2003, Jantzen Specialties, which uses the sum-of-the-years'-digits method, changed to the straight-line method for newly acquired buildings and equipment. The change increased current year net income by $445,000.

Required:
For each situation:
1. Identify the type of change.
2. Prepare any journal entry necessary as a direct result of the change as well as any adjusting entry for 2003 related to the situation described. (Ignore income tax effects.)
3. Briefly describe any other steps that should be taken to appropriately report the situation.

P 11–11
Error correction; change in depreciation method

The Collins Corporation purchased office equipment at the beginning of 2001 and capitalized a cost of $2,000,000. This cost figure included the following expenditures:

Purchase price	$1,850,000
Freight charges	30,000
Installation charges	20,000
Annual maintenance charge	100,000
Total	$2,000,000

The company estimated an eight-year useful life for the equipment. No residual value is anticipated. The double-declining-balance method was used to determine depreciation expense for 2001 and 2002.

In 2003, after the 2002 financial statements were issued, the company decided to switch to the straight-line depreciation method for this equipment. At that time, the company's controller discovered that the original cost of the equipment incorrectly included one year of annual maintenance charges for the equipment.

Required:
1. Ignoring income taxes, prepare the appropriate correcting entry for the equipment capitalization error discovered in 2003.
2. Ignoring income taxes, prepare the journal entry to record the cumulative effect of the change in depreciation methods.
3. Ignoring income taxes, what is the effect of the change in methods on 2003 income before the cumulative effect?

P 11–12
Depreciation and amortization; impairment of operational assets

At the beginning of 2001, Metatec, Inc. acquired Ellison Technology Corporation for $600 million. In addition to cash, receivables, and inventory, the following allocations were made:

Plant and equipment (depreciable assets)	$150 million
Patent	40 million
Goodwill	100 million

The plant and equipment are depreciated over a 10-year useful life on a straight-line basis. There is no estimated residual value. The patent is estimated to have a 5-year useful life, no residual value, and is amortized using the straight-line method.

At the end of 2003, a change in business climate indicated to management that the operational assets of Ellison might be impaired. The following amounts have been determined:

Plant and equipment:	
Undiscounted sum of future cash flows	$ 80 million
Fair value	60 million
Patent:	
Undiscounted sum of future cash flows	$ 20 million
Fair value	13 million
Goodwill:	
Fair value of Ellison Technology	$450 million
Fair value of Ellison's net assets (excluding goodwill)	390 million
Book value of Ellison's net assets (including goodwill)	470 million*

*After first recording any impairment losses on plant and equipment and the patent.

Required:
1. Compute the book value of the plant and equipment and patent at the end of 2003.
2. When should the plant and equipment and the patent be tested for impairment?
3. When should goodwill be tested for impairment?
4. Determine the amount of any impairment loss to be recorded, if any, for the three assets.

BROADEN YOUR PERSPECTIVE

Apply your critical-thinking ability to the knowledge you've gained. These cases will provide you an opportunity to develop your research, analysis, judgment, and communication skills. You also will work with other students, integrate what you've learned, apply it in real world situations, and consider its global and ethical ramifications. This practice will broaden your knowledge and further develop your decision-making abilities.

Analysis Case 11–1
Depreciation, depletion, and amortization

The terms depreciation, depletion, and amortization all refer to the process of allocating the cost of an operational asset to the periods the asset is used.

Required:
Discuss the differences between depreciation, depletion, and amortization as the terms are used in accounting for operational assets.

Communication Case 11–2
Depreciation

At a recent luncheon, you were seated next to Mr. Hopkins, the president of a local company that manufactures bicycle parts. He heard that you were a CPA and made the following comments to you:

Why is it that I am forced to recognize depreciation expense in my company's income statement when I know that I could sell many of my operational assets for more than I paid for them? I thought that the purpose of the balance sheet was to reflect the value of my business and that the purpose of the income statement was to report the net change in value or wealth of a company. It just doesn't make sense to penalize my profits when there hasn't been any loss in value from using the operational assets.

At the conclusion of the luncheon, you promised to send him a short explanation of the rationale for current depreciation practices.

Required:
Prepare a letter to Mr. Hopkins. Explain the accounting concept of depreciation and include a brief example in your explanation showing that over the life of the asset the change in value approach to depreciation and the allocation of cost approach will result in the same total effect on income.

Judgment Case 11–3
Straight-line method; composite depreciation

Portland Co. uses the straight-line depreciation method for depreciable assets. All assets are depreciated individually except manufacturing machinery, which is depreciated by the composite method.

Required:
1. What factors should have influenced Portland's selection of the straight-line depreciation method?
2. a. What benefits should derive from using the composite method rather than the individual basis for manufacturing machinery?
   b. How should Portland have calculated the manufacturing machinery's annual depreciation in its first year of operation?

(AICPA adapted)

Judgment Case 11–4
Depreciation

At the beginning of the year, Patrick Company acquired a computer to be used in its operations. The computer was delivered by the supplier, installed by Patrick, and placed into operation. The estimated useful life of the computer is five years, and its estimated residual value is significant.

Required:
1. a. What costs should Patrick capitalize for the computer?
   b. What is the objective of depreciation accounting?
2. What is the rationale for using accelerated depreciation methods?

(AICPA adapted)

Judgment Case 11–5
Capitalize or expense; materiality

Redline Publishers, Inc., produces various manuals ranging from computer software instructional booklets to manuals explaining the installation and use of large pieces of industrial equipment. At the end of 2003, the company's balance sheet reported total assets of $62 million and total liabilities of $40 million. The income statement for 2003 reported net income of $1.1 million, which represents an approximate 3% increase from the prior year. The company's effective income tax rate is 30%.

Near the end of 2003, a variety of expenditures were made to overhaul the company's manufacturing equipment. None of these expenditures exceeded $750, the materiality threshold the company has set for the capitalization of any such expenditure. Even though the overhauls extended the service life of the equipment, the expenditures were expensed, not capitalized.

John Henderson, the company's controller, is worried about the treatment of the overhaul expenditures. Even though no individual expenditure exceeded the $750 materiality threshold, total expenditures were $70,000.

Required:
Should the overhaul expenditures be capitalized or expensed?

Communication Case 11–6
Capitalize or expense; materiality

The focus of the case is the situation described in the previous case. Your instructor will divide the class into from two to six groups depending on the size of the class. The mission of your group is to determine the treatment of the overhaul expenditures.

Required:
1. Each group member should deliberate the situation independently and draft a tentative argument prior to the class session for which the case is assigned.
2. In class, each group will meet for 10 to 15 minutes in different areas of the classroom. During the meeting, group members will take turns sharing their suggestions for the purpose of arriving at a single group treatment.
3. After the allotted time, a spokesperson for each group (selected during the group meetings) will share the group's solution with the class. The goal of the class is to incorporate the views of each group into a consensus approach to the situation.

Integrating Case 11–7
Errors; change in estimate; change in principle; inventory and operational assets

Whaley Distributors is a wholesale distributor of electronic components. Financial statements for the year ended December 31, 2003, reported the following amounts and subtotals ($ in millions):

	Assets	Liabilities	Shareholders' Equity	Net Income	Expenses
2002	$640	$330	$310	$210	$150
2003	$820	$400	$420	$230	$175

In 2004 the following situations occurred or came to light:

a. Internal auditors discovered that ending inventories reported in the financial statements the two previous years were misstated due to faulty internal controls. The errors were in the following amounts:

2002 inventory	Overstated by $12 million
2003 inventory	Understated by $10 million

b. A patent costing $18 million at the beginning of 2002, expected to benefit operations for a total of six years, has not been amortized since acquired.

c. Whaley's conveyer equipment has been depreciated by the sum-of-the-years'-digits (SYD) method since constructed at the beginning of 2002 at a cost of $30 million. It has an expected useful life of five years and no expected residual value. At the beginning of 2004, Whaley decided to switch to straight-line depreciation.

Required:
For each situation:
1. Prepare any journal entry necessary as a direct result of the change or error correction as well as any adjusting entry for 2004 related to the situation described. (Ignore tax effects.)
2. Determine the amounts to be reported for each of the items shown above from the 2002 and 2003 financial statements when those amounts are reported again in the 2004, 2003, and 2002 comparative financial statements.

Judgment Case 11–8
Accounting changes

There are various types of accounting changes, each of which is required to be reported differently.

Required:
1. What type of accounting change is a change from the sum-of-the-years'-digits method of depreciation to the straight-line method for previously recorded assets? Under what circumstances does this type of accounting change occur?
2. What type of accounting change is a change in the expected service life of an asset arising because of more experience with the asset? Under what circumstances does this type of accounting change occur?
3. With respect to a change in accounting principle,
   a. How should a company calculate the effect?
   b. How should a company report the effect? (Do not discuss earnings per share requirements.)

(AICPA adapted)

Research Case 11–9
Asset impairment

The text discusses the issue of impairment of asset value. There are those who feel that the costs of complying with asset impairment standards outweigh the benefits. Professor Kimberly Smith in "Asset Impairment Disclosures" explores the costs and benefits of providing asset impairment information.

Required:
1. In your library or from some other source, locate the indicated article in the *Journal of Accountancy,* December 1994.
2. Professor Smith discusses a process referred to as *postauditing*. Describe how postauditing is used by industrial companies.
3. How does Professor Smith recommend that postauditing be used in determining asset impairments?

Research Case 11–10
Locate and extract relevant information and cite authoritative support for a financial reporting issue; impairment of operational assets

The company controller, Barry Melrose, has asked for your help in interpreting accounting standards for the recognition and measurement of impairment losses for operational assets. "We have a significant amount of goodwill on our books from last year's acquisition of Comcast Corporation. Also, I think we may have a problem with the assets of some of our factories out West. And one of our divisions is currently considering disposing of a large group of depreciable assets."

Your task as assistant controller is to research the issue.

Required:

1. Obtain the original FASB Standards on accounting for the impairment of operational assets. You might gain access through FARS, the FASB Financial Accounting Research System, from your school library, or some other source.
2. When should operational assets be tested for impairment?
3. Explain the processes for measuring an impairment loss for operational assets to be held and used.
4. What are the specific criteria that must be met for an asset or asset group to be classified as held for sale?
5. Explain the processes for measuring an impairment loss for operational assets classified as held for sale.

Ethics Case 11–11
Asset impairment

At the beginning of 2001, the Healthy Life Food Company purchased equipment for $42 million to be used in the manufacture of a new line of gourmet frozen foods. The equipment was estimated to have a 10-year service life and no residual value. The straight-line depreciation method was used to measure depreciation for 2001 and 2002.

Late in 2003, it became apparent that sales of the new frozen food line were significantly below expectations. The company decided to continue production for two more years (2004 and 2005) and then discontinue the line. At that time, the equipment will be sold for minimal scrap values.

The controller, Heather Meyer, was asked by Harvey Dent, the company's chief executive officer (CEO), to determine the appropriate treatment of the change in service life of the equipment. Heather determined that there has been an impairment of value requiring an immediate write-down of the equipment of $12,900,000. The remaining book value would then be depreciated over the equipment's revised service life.

The CEO does not like Heather's conclusion because of the effect it would have on 2003 income. "Looks like a simple revision in service life from 10 years to 5 years to me," Dent concluded. "Let's go with it that way, Heather."

Required:

1. What is the difference in before-tax income between the CEO's and Heather's treatment of the situation?
2. Discuss Heather Meyer's ethical dilemma.

Judgment Case 11–12
Earnings management and operational assets

Companies often are under pressure to meet or beat Wall Street earnings projections in order to increase stock prices and also to increase the value of stock options. Some resort to earnings management practices to artificially create desired results.

Required:

1. How can a company manage earnings by changing its depreciation method? Is this an effective technique to manage earnings?
2. How can a company manage earnings by changing the estimated useful lives of depreciable assets? Is this an effective technique to manage earnings?
3. Using a fictitious example and numbers you make up, describe in your own words how asset impairment losses could be used to manage earnings. How might that benefit the company?

Judgment Case 11–13
Subsequent expenditures

The Cummings Company charged various expenditures made during 2003 to an account called repairs and maintenance expense. You have been asked by your supervisor in the company's internal audit department to review the expenditures to determine if they were appropriately recorded. The amount of each of the transactions included in the account is considered material.

1. Engine tune-up and oil change on the company's 12 delivery trucks—$1,300.
2. Rearrangement of machinery on the main production line—$5,500. It is not evident that the rearrangement will increase operational efficiency.
3. Installation of aluminum siding on the manufacturing plant—$32,000.
4. Replacement of the old air conditioning system in the manufacturing plant with a new system—$120,000.
5. Replacement of broken parts on three machines—$1,500.
6. Annual painting of the manufacturing plant—$11,000.
7. Purchase of new forklift to move finished product to the loading dock—$6,000.
8. Patching leaks in the roof of the manufacturing plant—$6,500. The repair work did not extend the useful life of the roof.

Required:

For each of the transactions listed above, indicate whether the expenditure is appropriately charged to the repair and maintenance expense account, and if not, indicate the proper account to be charged.

**Real World Case
11–14
Disposition and
depreciation**

International Business Machines Corporation (IBM) reported the following in the asset section of its balance sheets for the years ended December 31, 2000 and 1999.

	2000	1999
(Dollars in millions)		
Plant, rental machines, and other property	$38,455	$39,616
Less: Accumulated depreciation	21,741	22,026
Plant, rental machines, and other property—net	$16,714	$17,590

The following note was included as a part of the Significant Accounting Policies disclosure note in IBM's 2000 financial statements:

> **Depreciation**
> Plant, rental machines, and other property are carried at cost, and depreciated over their estimated useful lives using the straight-line method.

Also, Note G disclosed that the total cost of plant, rental machines, and other property included $896 and $1,026 ($ in millions) in land and land improvements at the end of 2000 and 1999, respectively. In addition, the statement of cash flows for the year ended December 31, 2000, reported the following as cash flows from investing activities:

(Dollars in millions)	
Payments for plant, rental machines, and other property	$(5,616)
Proceeds from disposition of plant, rental machines, and other property	1,619

The statement of cash flows also reported 2000 depreciation of $4,513 (dollars in millions).

Required:

1. Assume that all plant, rental machines, and other property acquired during 2000 were purchased for cash. Determine the amount of gain or loss from dispositions of plant, rental machines, and other property recognized during 2000.
2. Assume that the entire amount reported in Note G as land and land improvements represents assets that are not depreciated. What is the approximate average service life of IBM's depreciable assets?

**Real World Case
11–15
Depreciation and
depletion method;
asset impairment;
subsequent
expenditures**

EDGAR, the Electronic Data Gathering, Analysis, and Retrieval system, performs automated collection, validation, indexing, and forwarding of submissions by companies and others who are required by law to file forms with the U.S. Securities and Exchange Commission (SEC). All publicly traded domestic companies use EDGAR to make the majority of their filings. (Some foreign companies file voluntarily.) Form 10-K or 10-KSB, which include the annual report, is required to be filed on EDGAR. The SEC makes this information available on the Internet.

Required:

1. Access EDGAR on the Internet. The web address is **www.sec.gov**. Edgarscan (**edgarscan. pwcglobal.com**) from PricewaterhouseCoopers makes the process of accessing data from EDGAR easier.
2. Search for Phillips Petroleum Company. Access the 10-K filing for the fiscal year ended December 31, 2000. Search or scroll to find the financial statements and related notes.
3. Answer the following questions related to the company's operational assets:
   a. Describe the company's depreciation and depletion policies.
   b. What is the amount of the impairment write-downs recorded in 2000? What asset(s) were written down?
   c. Describe the company's policy for subsequent expenditures made for operational assets.

**Analysis Case 11–16
Depreciation and
amortization**

Refer to the financial statements and related disclosure notes of FedEx Corporation in the appendix to Chapter 1.

Required:

1. What amount of depreciation and amortization did the company report in 2001?
2. What depreciation method is used for financial reporting purposes and what are the service lives and residual values of depreciable assets? What depreciation method is used for income tax purposes?

FedEx Corporation

Financial Instruments

3

12

Investments

OVERVIEW

In this chapter, you will learn that investments that companies make in the stock and debt securities of other companies are accounted for differently depending on the nature of the investments. For instance, you'll see that investment securities categorized as securities held-to-maturity are reported at amortized cost, while securities available-for-sale and trading securities are reported at their fair values.

We also discuss the equity method— a completely different way to record and report investments in stock when specific characteristics indicate that the investor can significantly influence the operating and financial policies of the investee.

LEARNING OBJECTIVES

After studying this chapter, you should be able to:

LO1 Explain how to identify and account for investments classified for reporting purposes as held to maturity.

LO2 Explain how to identify and account for investments classified for reporting purposes as available for sale.

LO3 Explain how to identify and account for investments classified for reporting purposes as trading securities.

LO4 Explain what constitutes significant influence by the investor over the operating and financial policies of the investee.

LO5 Understand the way investments are recorded and reported by the equity method.

LO6 Explain the adjustments made in the equity method when the fair value of the net assets underlying an investment exceeds their book value at acquisition.

FINANCIAL REPORTING CASE

A Case of Coke

You are the lone accounting major in your five-member group in your Business Policy class. A part of the case your group is working on is the analysis of the financial statements of the Coca-Cola Company.

The marketing major in the group is confused by the following disclosure note from Coca-Cola's 2000 annual report:

Note 8: Financial Instruments (in part)
CERTAIN DEBT AND MARKETABLE EQUITY SECURITIES

Investments in debt and marketable equity securities, other than investments accounted for by the equity method, are categorized as either trading, available-for-sale or held-to-maturity. On December 31, 2000 and 1999, we had no trading securities. Securities categorized as available-for-sale are stated at fair value, with unrealized gains and losses, net of deferred income taxes, reported as a component of accumulated other comprehensive income. Debt securities categorized as held-to-maturity are stated at amortized cost.

On December 31, 2000 and 1999, available-for-sale and held-to-maturity securities consisted of the following (in millions)

December 31, 2000	Cost	Unrealized Gains	Unrealized Losses	Fair Value
Available-for-sale securities				
Equity securities	$ 248	$57	$(90)	$ 215
Collateralized mortgage obligations	25	–	(2)	23
Other debt securities	15	–	–	15
	$ 288	$57	$(92)	$ 253
Held-to-maturity securities				
Bank and corporate debt	$1,115	$ –	$ –	$1,115
	$1,115	$ –	$ –	$1,115

"They say unrealized gains and losses are reported as part of comprehensive income? I don't see these gains and losses on the income statement," he complained. "Maybe comprehensive income is something else altogether. And held-to-maturity securities—why are they treated differently?"

> By the time you finish this chapter, you should be able to respond appropriately to the questions posed in this case. Compare your response to the solution provided at the end of the chapter.

QUESTIONS

1. How should you respond? Why are held-to-maturity securities treated differently from other investment securities? (page 576)

2. Why are unrealized gains and losses not reported on the income statement? (page 579)

3. What is comprehensive income? (page 579)

4. Anticipate his next question and explain why Coke accounts for some of its investments by the equity method and what that means. (page 587)

Most companies invest in financial instruments issued by other companies. For some investors, these investments represent ongoing affiliations with the companies whose securities are acquired. For instance, in 2002 Hewlett-Packard acquired all the common stock of Compaq Computer to become the world's largest maker of computers and printers. Microsoft, in 1999, invested $600 million in nationwide wireless phone company Nextel Communications Inc., gaining access to wireless Internet users. Some investments, though, are made not to obtain a favorable business relationship with another firm but simply to earn a return from the dividends or interest the securities pay or from increases in the market prices of the securities—the same prospective rewards that might motivate you to buy stocks, bonds, or other investment securities. With such diversity in investment objectives, it's understandable that no single accounting method is adequate to report every investment. As you'll discover when reading this chapter, investments are accounted for in six ways, depending on the nature of the investment relationship. Before we discuss these in detail, see the quick overview of the six approaches in Graphic 12–1.

GRAPHIC 12–1
Reporting Categories
for Investments

Characteristics of the Investment	Reporting Method
The investor *controls* the investee:	
The investor owns *more than 50% of the voting stock* of the investee	**Consolidation**—financial statements are combined as if a single company
The investor can *"significantly influence"* the operating and financial policies of the investee:	
Typically the investor owns *between 20% and 50% of the voting stock* of the investee	**Equity method**—cost adjusted for subsequent growth of the investee
The investor *cannot* "significantly influence" the operating and financial policies of the investee:	
Investments in debt securities for which the investor has the "positive intent and ability" to *hold to maturity*	**Held-to-maturity**—investment reported at amortized cost
Investments *not* held in active trading account for immediate resale nor to be held to maturity	**Securities available-for-sale**—investment reported at fair value (with unrealized gains and losses excluded from earnings and reported in shareholders' equity)
Investments held in *active trading account* for immediate resale	**Trading securities**—investment reported at fair value (with unrealized gains and losses included in earnings)
Fair value of the investments *not* determinable	**Cost method**—investment reported at cost

We discuss the first four categories in Part A of the chapter. The equity method is described in Part B, as well as an abbreviated discussion of consolidated statements.

PART

a

ACCOUNTING FOR INVESTMENT SECURITIES

To finance its operations and often the expansion of those operations, a corporation raises funds by selling equity securities (common and preferred stock) and debt securities (bonds and notes). These securities are purchased as investments by individual investors, mutual funds, and also by other corporations. In later chapters we discuss equity and debt securities from the perspective of the issuing company. Our focus in this chapter is on the corporations that invest in securities issued by other corporations as well as those issued by governmental units (bonds, Treasury bills, and Treasury bonds).

For reporting purposes, all investments in *debt* securities and investments in *equity* securities that have readily determinable fair values (except those for which the equity method or consolidation is appropriate) are classified in one of three categories and accounted for differently depending on the classification as shown in Graphic 12–2.[1]

GRAPHIC 12–2
Reporting Categories for Investments in Marketable Securities

Reporting Category	Classification Criteria
Held-to-maturity	Debt securities for which the investor has the positive intent and ability to hold to maturity
Securities available-for-sale	Debt or equity securities not classified as either securities held-to-maturity or trading securities (typically securities whose sale depends on market factors and financial conditions of the company)
Trading securities	Debt or equity securities held for immediate resale

For all three categories, we include in the determination of earnings *realized* gains and losses, those that arise when securities are sold. Similarly, we include in the determination of earnings dividend and interest income for all three categories. The differences in accounting treatment among the categories of securities arise only with respect to *unrealized* gains and losses, those that arise from holding securities during a period when their market values change.

As you know, the purpose of accounting is to provide information useful in making decisions. What's most relevant for that purpose is not necessarily the same for each investment a company might make. For example, day-to-day changes in market value are less descriptive of investment success for an investment in corporate bonds that management *fully intends to hold until the bonds mature* than for an investment in the common stock of another corporation *acquired with the hope of profiting from market price changes*. Let's examine the three reporting classifications, one by one.

CHECK WITH THE **COACH**

Accounting for a company's investments in securities of other firms has been debated for decades. This topic has been the "hot button" for advocates of a fair market value approach to financial reporting. The debate led to a complex set of new measurement and disclosure rules. Let the Coach help you understand these rules. In Coach, you will find animated illustrations and experts' discussions of accounting for investments. ■

Securities to Be Held to Maturity

Unlike a share of stock, a bond or other debt security has a specified date on which it matures. On its maturity date, the "face amount" is paid to investors. In the meantime, interest equal to a specified percentage of the face amount is paid to investors on specified interest dates. However, even though the maturity amount is fixed and interest payments are fixed, this doesn't mean the market value of the security doesn't change. On the contrary, if "market" rates of interest *rise* after a fixed-rate security is purchased, the value of the now-below-market, fixed-interest payments declines. So, the market value of the investment falls. Conversely, if "market" rates of interest *fall* after a fixed-rate security is purchased, the fixed interest payments become relatively attractive, so the market value of the investment rises.

LO1

The market value of a fixed-rate investment moves in the opposite direction of market rates of interest.

---

[1]"Accounting for Certain Investments in Debt and Equity Securities," *Statement of Financial Accounting Standards No. 115* (Norwalk, Conn.: FASB, 1993).

Are these movements in market price relevant? Not if the investor has no intention of selling the investment before maturity. Increases and decreases in the market value between the time a debt security is acquired and the day it matures to a prearranged maturity value are less important if sale before maturity isn't an alternative. For this reason, if an investor has the "positive intent and ability" to hold the securities to maturity, investments in debt securities are classified as "held-to-maturity" and reported at amortized *cost* in the balance sheet.

A debt security is *not* classified as held-to-maturity if the investor might sell it in response to changes in market prices or interest rates, to meet the investor's liquidity needs, or similar factors. For instance, an investment would not be classified as held-to-maturity if the investor might sell it to achieve favorable tax treatment. An investment in securities to be "held to maturity" by the investor is demonstrated in Illustration 12–1.

> **Changes in market value are less relevant to an investor who will hold a security to its maturity regardless of those changes.**

> The Board (FASB) deliberately chose to make the held-to-maturity category restrictive because it believes that the use of amortized cost must be justified for each investment in a debt security. At acquisition, an entity should establish the positive intent and ability to hold a security to maturity, which is distinct from the mere absence of intent to sell.[2]

ILLUSTRATION 12–1	On January 1, 2003, United Intergroup, Inc. purchased as an investment $700,000 of 12% bonds. Because the 12% stated rate was less than the rate paid by other companies on similar bonds, say 14%, United was able to buy the securities at a "discounted" price of $666,633. Interest of $42,000 ($700,000 × [12% ÷ 2]) is receivable semiannually on June 30 and December 31.
Held-to-Maturity Securities	

Purchase of Investment. The journal entry to record the *purchase* of investment securities is:

> All investment securities are initially recorded at cost.

January 1
Investment in bonds (face amount)	700,000	
Discount on bond investment (difference).		33,367
Cash (price paid for the bonds).		666,633

Investment Revenue. Interest accrues on bonds, or any other interest-bearing security for that matter, at a *constant percentage* of the investment each period. Of course, under the concept of *accrual accounting,* the periodic effective interest is unaffected by when the cash interest actually is received. Recording interest each period as the *effective market rate of interest multiplied by the outstanding balance of the investment* (during the interest period) is referred to as the effective interest method. This simply is an application of the accrual concept, consistent with accruing all revenues as they are earned, regardless of when cash is received.

> The effective interest on debt is the market rate of interest multiplied by the outstanding balance of the debt.

Continuing our example, the initial investment is $666,633. Since the effective interest rate is 14%, interest recorded as *revenue* to the investor for the first six-month interest period is $46,664:

$$\underset{\text{Outstanding balance}}{\$666,633} \times \underset{\text{Effective rate}}{[14\% \div 2]} = \underset{\text{Effective interest}}{\$46,664}$$

> The "unreceived" portion of the effective interest increases the existing investment.

However, the bond security calls for semiannual interest payments of only $42,000—the *stated* rate (6%) times the *face amount* ($700,000). As always, when only a portion of revenue is received, the remainder becomes an asset—in this case an addition to the existing investment. So the difference, $4,664, increases the investment and is reflected as a reduction

---

[2]Ibid., par. 46.

in the discount (a valuation account). The journal entry to record the interest received for the first six months as *investment revenue* is:

June 30

Case (stated rate × face amount)	42,000	
Discount on bond investment (difference).	4,664	
Investment revenue (market rate × outstanding balance).		46,664

Dividend and interest income from all investment securities is included in earnings.

The amortized cost of the investment now is $700,000 − ($33,367 − 4,664) = $671,297, which is higher than the original investment. Because the balance of the investment increases each period, the dollar amount of interest revenue (market rate × outstanding balance) also will increase each period.

Reporting Investments in Securities to Be Held to Maturity.   Securities to be held to maturity are recorded at cost as illustrated above, and holding gains or losses from market price changes are ignored. So if the market value of the investment were to increase from $666,633 at January 1 to, say, $680,000 at June 30, we would ignore that holding gain and report the investment in a balance sheet at that date at its amortized cost of $671,297 as determined above:

Investment in bonds	$700,000
Less: Discount on bond investment	28,703
Book value (amortized cost)	$671,297

We will revisit our discussion of investments in debt securities to be "held to maturity" in Chapter 14, "Bonds and Long-Term Notes." This way we can more readily see that accounting by the company that issues bonds and by the company that invests in those bonds is opposite but parallel; that is, each side of the transaction is the mirror image of the other. When we resume our discussion of bond investments at that point, be sure to notice that we continue the same numerical illustration we began in this chapter.

Let's turn our attention now to accounting and reporting for investments referred to as "securities available-for-sale" and "trading securities." These include investments in *debt* securities that are not classified as held-to-maturity and *equity* securities that have *readily determinable fair values.* You'll notice that, unlike held-to-maturity securities, we report investments in the other two categories at their fair market values.

Graphic 12–3 provides a description from a recent annual report of how United Community Financial Corporation accounts for its investments in each of the three reporting categories.

Note (in part): Investment and Mortgage-Backed Securities
Securities are classified as available for sale, held to maturity, or trading upon their acquisition. Securities classified as available for sale are carried at an estimated fair value with the unrealized holding gain or loss reflected as a component of equity, net of taxes. Securities classified as held to maturity are carried at amortized cost. Securities classified as trading are carried at estimated fair value with the market value adjustment reflected in the income statement. . . . Realized gains and losses on the sale of debt securities are recorded based on the amortized cost of the securities sold.

GRAPHIC 12–3
Investments in Securities to Be Held to Maturity—United Community Financial Corporation

Obviously, not all investments are intended to be held to maturity. When an investment is acquired to be held for an *unspecified period of time,* we classify the investment as either (a) "securities available-for-sale" or (b) "trading securities." The trading securities category concerns primarily banks and other financial institutions who frequently buy and sell securities expecting to earn profits on short-term changes in price. On the other hand, securities available for sale is a more general classification that includes all investments other than trading securities or securities to be held to maturity. So, we'll discuss the less restrictive securities available for sale category first.

Securities Available-for-Sale

When you or I buy stock in a corporation, say Coca-Cola, we hope the market value will rise before we sell it. We also might look forward to the cash dividends Coca-Cola pays its shareholders every three months. We may even have fairly defined criteria for when we plan to sell the stock, or we may intend to wait and see what happens to market prices. In either case, our investment is available to sell given the right combination of market factors and our own cash situation. So it often is, too, with companies who invest in the securities of other corporations or governmental entities. When a company acquires an investment, not for an active trading account (as a financial institution might) or to be held to maturity (which of course couldn't be stock because it has no maturity date), the company classifies its investment as "securities available-for-sale." Because these securities are not expressly intended to be held to some scheduled maturity date, the investment is reported in a balance sheet at the *fair market value* of the investment securities on the reporting date. Just like any investment, regardless of how we classify it, the investment is initially recorded at its cost—that is, the total amount paid for the securities including any brokerage fees. But then, when a balance sheet is prepared, this type of investment is written up or down to its fair value, or "marked to market."

Be sure to notice that mark-to-market accounting is a departure from historical costs, which is the way most assets are reported in balance sheets. Why the difference? For these investments, fair value information is more relevant than for other assets intended primarily to be used in company operations, like buildings, land and equipment, or for investments to be *held to maturity.*[4] For instance, consider an investment in debt. As interest rates rise or fall, the fair value of the investment will decrease or increase. Movements in fair values are less relevant if the investment is to be held to maturity; the investor receives the same contracted interest payments and principal at maturity, regardless of changes in fair value. This is similar to changes in the fair values of operational assets, typically intended to be held throughout their productive lives.

> The Board concluded that fair value information is more relevant than amortized cost information, in part because it reflects the effects of a management decision to buy a financial asset at a specific time and then continue to hold it for an unspecified period of time.[3]

Investments in securities to be held for an unspecified period of time are reported at their fair values.

FINANCIAL REPORTING CASE

Q1, p. 598

Fair values are less relevant for investments to be held to maturity.

ADDITIONAL CONSIDERATION

No More Cherry Picking

One motivation of the FASB when deciding to move to mark-to-market accounting for investments was to curtail what it perceived as (and the SEC insisted was) a common practice at the time—"cherry picking." This refers to a company carefully choosing when and which of its securities to sell. Specifically, it means selling a security that had risen in value in order to realize a gain or not selling a security that had declined in value in order not to realize a loss, or even choosing to realize a loss in good years in order to "smooth" income.

As just argued, market values and changes in market value are less relevant to an investor who will hold a security to its maturity regardless of value changes. On the other hand, for investments of unspecified length, changes in market values, and thus market returns, provide an indication of management's success in deciding when to acquire the investment,

---

[3]Ibid., par. 51.
[4]Investment to be held to maturity, of course, include only debt securities.

when to sell it, whether to invest in fixed-rate or variable-rate securities, and whether to invest in long-term or short-term securities. Accounting for securities available for sale is demonstrated in Illustration 12–2.

ILLUSTRATION 12–2

Investment in Securities Available-for-Sale

American Capital buys and sells both debt and equity securities of other companies as investments. The following transactions during 2003 pertain to the investment portfolio. Assume American Capital buys securities, *not* intending to profit from short-term changes in price and *not* intending to hold debt securities to maturity. The securities are properly classified as available-for-sale. The company's fiscal year-end is December 31.

June	1	Purchased ABM Corporation 10% bonds for $40 million (face amount).
November	30	Received cash interest of $2 million on the investment in ABM Corporation bonds, calculated as $40 million × 10% × ½ year.
December	1	Sold the ABM Corporation bonds for $43 million.
December	21	Acquired two new investments costing:

Millington-Frazier common shares	$30 million
Bartlett Corporation common shares	20 million

December	31	The market prices of the investments are:

Millington-Frazier common shares	$35 million
Bartlett Corporation common shares	19 million

Purchase of Investments.   The journal entry to record the purchase of investment securities is:

June 1	**($ in millions)**	
Investment in ABM Corporation bonds	40	
Cash (price paid including brokerage fees)		40

All investment securities are initially recorded at cost.

Investment Revenue.   The journal entry to record the cash interest is:

November 30	**($ in millions)**	
Cash ($40 million × 10% × ½ year)	2	
Investment revenue		2

Dividend and interest income is included in earnings.

Sale of Investments.   The journal entry to record the sale of the ABM Corporation bonds is:

December 1	**($ in millions)**	
Cash.	43	
Investment in ABM Corporation bonds		40
Gain on sale of investments		3

Realized gains and losses are included in earnings.

Purchase of Investments.   The journal entry to record the purchase of investment securities is:

December 21	**($ in millions)**	
Investment in Millington-Frazier shares	30	
Investment in Bartlett Corporation shares	20	
Cash.		50

All investment securities are initially recorded at cost.

Adjusting Investments to Fair Value.   Reporting investments at their fair values means adjusting their carrying amounts for changes in fair value after their acquisition (or since the last reporting date if they were held at that time). These changes are called "unrealized holding gains and losses" because they haven't yet been realized through the sale of the securities. They must be recorded (or updated) any time financial statements are prepared for external use. The journal entry to adjust the investments in our illustration to fair market value at year-end is:

All investment securities (except those held to maturity) are adjusted to their fair values on each reporting date.

December 31	($ in millions)	
Investment in Millington-Frazier shares[5]	5	
Unrealized holding gain on investments ($35 − 30)		5
Unrealized holding loss on investments ($19 − 20).	1	
Investment in Bartlett Corporation shares		1

ADDITIONAL CONSIDERATION

When the Fair Value Isn't Readily Determinable
The fair value of equity securities is considered "readily determinable" if selling prices are currently available on a securities exchange.

If the fair value of an equity security is *not* readily determinable, an investment in that security is carried and reported at cost (except when the equity method described in Part B of this chapter is appropriate). Any dividends received would be recognized as investment revenue, and a gain or loss would be reported only when actually realized, which is when the investment is sold.

Having a readily determinable fair value is not a requirement for *debt* securities to be reported at fair value. Even though some debt securities don't trade regularly, their fair values can be reasonably estimated by determining the discounted present value of their interest and principal payments. You learned how to do this in Chapter 6 and will gain considerably more exposure to the process in Chapter 14.

After the transactions, these are the account balances:

($ in millions)

ASSETS

Investment in ABM Corp. Bonds

Cost	40		
Sale	40		
Balance	0		

Investment in Millington-Frazier Shares

Cost	30	
FV adj.	5	
Balance	35	

Investment in Bartlett Corp. Shares

Cost	20		
FV adj.		1	
Balance	19		

INCOME STATEMENT

Investment Revenue

	2	Interest
	2	Balance

Gain on Sale of Investments

	3	Sale
	3	Balance

SHAREHOLDERS' EQUITY
(other comprehensive income)

Unrealized Holding Gain on Investments

	5	FV adj.
	5	Balance

Unrealized Holding Loss on Investments

FV adj.	1	
Balance	1	

---

[5]An acceptable alternative to increasing (or decreasing) an investment to fair value *directly* as we're doing here is to debit (or credit) an asset valuation account to adjust the investment account *indirectly*. This, in fact, would be desirable when adjusting a *debt* security, like an investment in bonds, classified as available for sale, so we can amortize its cost separately from fair market value adjustments.

Reporting Investments in Securities Available-for-Sale.   Investments in securities *available-for-sale* are reported in a balance sheet at fair value. Holding gains and losses from retaining securities during periods of price change are *not* included in the determination of income for the period. Instead, they are accumulated and reported as a separate component of shareholders' equity, as part of Other Comprehensive Income. That is, an unrealized holding gain would increase shareholders' equity; an unrealized holding loss would decrease shareholders' equity.

FINANCIAL REPORTING CASE

Q2, p. 598

By definition, these securities are *not* acquired for the purpose of profiting from short-term market price changes, so gains and losses from holding these securities while prices change are not considered relevant performance measures to be included in earnings. This, in fact, is the argument made by the FASB. A by-product of this treatment is the avoidance of earnings volatility that would come from adjusting earnings for gains and losses as they occur. Opponents of this view argue that this amounts to a form of "income smoothing" that lessens earnings quality. This counterargument suggests that periodic gains and losses from holding securities during periods of changes in market value are, indeed, relevant measures of the performance of management that can, at its discretion, choose whether or not to realize the gains and losses by selling the securities.

On the 2003 balance sheet, investments available-for-sale are reported at the *fair value* of the investment securities ($35 + 19 = \$54$ million), but the *net* unrealized holding gain ($5 - 1 = \$4$ million) is not reported in the income statement. Instead, it's reported as a separate component of shareholders' equity, specifically as part of *other comprehensive income.*

Comprehensive income, as you may recall from Chapter 4, is a more expansive view of the change in shareholders' equity than traditional net income. In fact, it encompasses all changes in equity *other than from transactions with owners.*[6] So, in addition to net income, comprehensive income includes up to four other changes in equity as indicated in Graphic 12–4.

FINANCIAL REPORTING CASE

Q3, p. 598

	($ millions)		
Net income		$xxx	
Other comprehensive income			
Foreign currency translation adjustments*	$xx		
Net unrealized holding gains (losses) on investments†	4		
Minimum pension liability adjustment‡	(x)		
Deferred gain or loss from derivatives§	xx	xx	
Less: aggregate income tax expense (or benefit)		(xx)	xx
Comprehensive income		$xxx	

GRAPHIC 12–4
Comprehensive Income

Comprehensive income is the total nonowner change in equity for a reporting period.

*Gains or losses from changes in foreign currency exchange rates. The amount could be an addition to or reduction of shareholders' equity. (This item is discussed elsewhere in your accounting curriculum.)
†Changes in the market value of securities available-for-sale.
‡Reporting a pension liability sometimes requires a reduction in the shareholders' equity (described in Chapter 17).
§When a derivative designated as a cash flow hedge is adjusted to fair value, the gain or loss is deferred as a component of comprehensive income and included in earnings later, at the same time as earnings are affected by the hedged transaction (described in the text Addendum).

To communicate the relationship between the two measures, companies must report both net income and comprehensive income and reconcile the difference between the two.[7] On the next page we see the impact on financial statements of the transactions in Illustration 12–2:

---

[6]Transactions with owners primarily include dividends and the sale or purchase of shares of the company's stock.
[7]*Statement of Financial Accounting Standards No. 130,* "Reporting Comprehensive Income," (Norwalk, Conn.: FASB, 1997).

ILLUSTRATION 12–2

BALANCE SHEET

	($ in millions)
Assets	
Cash and cash equivalents	$xx
Short-term investments* at fair value (cost $50)	54
Accounts receivable	xx
◆	◆
◆	◆
Shareholders' Equity	
◆	◆
◆	◆
Other Comprehensive Income:	
Net unrealized holding gain on investments†	4
◆	◆

Securities available-for-sale are reported at fair value.

Net unrealized holding gains or losses are reported as a separate component of shareholders' equity.

INCOME STATEMENT

Other Income (expense)	
◆	◆
Investment revenue	2
Gain on sale of investments	3
◆	◆

Only realized gains and losses are reported in the income statement.

STATEMENT OF CASH FLOWS

Operating Activities	
◆	◆
Investment revenue	2
Investing Activities	
◆	◆
Purchase of investment securities	90
Sale of investment securities	43
◆	◆

Cash flows from buying and selling securities available-for-sale are classified as investing activities.

*Assumes both securities are intended to be held less than one year; otherwise long-term investments.
†Many companies choose to combine the various components of Other Comprehensive Income into Accumulated Other Comprehensive Income when reporting in a balance sheet.

Individual securities available for sale are classified as either current or noncurrent assets, depending on how long they're likely to be held. An example from the 2001 annual report of Cisco Systems is shown in Graphic 12–5 on the next page.

ADDITIONAL CONSIDERATION

Be sure to note that the effect on *total* shareholders' equity is precisely the same as if the holding gains and losses had been included in earnings. The difference is that, if included in earnings, the impact would be an increase or decrease in retained earnings rather than a separate component of shareholders' equity.

Selling Securities Previously Adjusted to Fair Value. To see how to record the sale of a security that was previously adjusted to fair value, let's assume the Millington-Frazier shares are sold on January 9, 2004, for $36 million. The fair value of the shares has risen $6 million since the investment was acquired for $30 million. Five million dollars of that rise occurred in 2003 but wasn't recognized in 2003 earnings because it wasn't yet realized by selling the investment. Now, the entire $6 million gain is recognized in 2004 when it is actually realized:

GRAPHIC 12–5
Investments in
Securities Available-for-
Sale—Cisco Systems

2: Summary of Significant Accounting Policies (in part)

The Company's investments comprise U.S., state, and municipal government obligations; corporate debt securities; and public corporate equity securities. Investments with maturities of less than one year are considered short-term and are carried at fair value. At July 29, 2000 and July 31, 1999, substantially all of the Company's investments were classified as available for sale. Unrealized gains and losses on these investments are included as a separate component of shareholders' equity, net of any related tax effect.

5: Investments (in part)

The following table summarizes the Company's investment in securities (in millions):

July 29, 2000	Amortized Cost	Gross Unrealized Gains	Gross Unrealized Losses	Fair Value
U.S. government notes and bonds	$ 2,317	$ —	$ (32)	$ 2,285
State, municipal, and county government notes and bonds	3,592	13	(41)	3,564
Corporate notes and bonds	3,222	1	(19)	3,204
Corporate equity securities	641	5,621	(37)	6,225
Mandatorily redeemable convertible preferred stock	987	—	—	987
Total	$10,759	$5,635	$(129)	$16,265
Reported as:				
Short-term investments				$ 1,291
Investments				13,688
Restricted investments				1,286
Total				$16,265

January 9, 2004	($ in millions)	
Cash.	36	
Unrealized holding gain on investments (balance)	5	
Investment in Millington-Frazier bonds ($30 + 5)		35
Gain on sale of investments (to balance)		6

Holding gains and losses from securities available-for-sale are included in earnings when they are realized by selling the securities.

Now suppose the market value of the Bartlett Corporation common shares has risen by $1 million to the original price American Capital paid for the investment ($20 million), and the shares are sold on February 13. Because the investment is sold at cost, the holding loss in 2003 is offset by a subsequent holding gain during 2004. As a result, no gain or loss is realized:

February 13, 2004	($ in millions)	
Cash.	20	
Unrealized holding loss on investments (to balance)		1
Investment in Bartlett Corporation shares ($20 − 1).		19

Unrealized holding gains or losses often are offset by subsequent holding losses or gains.

Impairment of Investments.   Occasionally, the fair value of a security will decline for a specific reason that's judged to be "other than temporary." For instance, a bankruptcy filing might indicate a degradation in the creditworthiness of the issuer of bonds. An investor holding the bonds as an investment might conclude that a drop in the market price of the bonds is an other-than-temporary impairment. In that case, when the investment is written down to its fair value, the amount of the write-down should be treated as though it were a realized loss (meaning it's included in income for the period). After the other-than-temporary write-down, the normal treatment of unrealized gains or losses is resumed; that is, changes in fair

A loss inherent in an "other-than-temporary" impairment is recognized in earnings even though the security hasn't been sold.

value are reported as a separate component of shareholders' equity. In the 2000 fourth quarter, Sprint Corporation recorded a $48 million write-down of investment securities due to a decline in market value the company considered other than temporary.

Trading Securities

Trading securities are actively managed in a trading account for the purpose of profiting from short-term price changes.

Some companies—primarily financial institutions—actively and frequently buy and sell securities expecting to earn profits on short-term differences in price. Investments in debt or equity securities acquired principally for the purpose of selling them in the near term are classified as **trading securities.** The holding period for trading securities generally is measured in hours and days rather than months or years. By definition, these are short-term investments to be reported among the investor's current assets.

The approach used to account for trading securities differs from how we account for securities available-for-sale in one major respect. Specifically, we report unrealized holding gains or losses on trading securities in the income statement as if they actually had been realized. Keep in mind as you study this section that relatively few investments are classified this way because, typically, only banks and other financial operations invest in securities in the manner and for the purpose necessary to be categorized as trading securities.

ADDITIONAL CONSIDERATION

Bankers' Objections

Perhaps the strongest objections to mark-to-market accounting when *SFAS No. 115* was being proposed came from the banking and insurance industries. Their concern was the volatile impact on earnings from reporting unrealized gains and losses on assets (trading securities) while not being permitted to mark liabilities to market as well. These objections were (and are) not merely self-interested urgings; there is an ongoing academic debate concerning this apparent inconsistency.

Holding gains and losses for trading securities are *included in earnings.*

When securities are actively managed, as trading securities are, with the expressed intent of profiting from short-term market price changes, the gains and losses that result from holding securities during market price changes are appropriate measures of success or lack of success in that endeavor. For that reason, it's appropriate to report these holding gains and losses in earnings for the period of change, even if they haven't yet been realized through the sale of the securities. To see how, let's modify our illustration to assume the investment securities we considered earlier are trading securities, rather than securities available-for-sale. Consider Illustration 12–3:

ILLUSTRATION 12–3 Investments in Trading Securities	American Capital buys and sells both debt and equity securities of other companies as investments. The following transactions during 2003 pertain to the investment portfolio. Assume American Capital frequently and actively buys and sells both debt and equity securities, intending to profit from short-term differences in price. The company's fiscal year-end is December 31.

December 21	Acquired two new investments costing:	
	Millington-Frazier common shares	$30 million
	Bartlett Corporation common shares	20 million
December 31	The market prices of the investments are:	
	Millington-Frazier common shares	$35 million
	Bartlett Corporation common shares	19 million

Purchase of Investments.   The purchase of the investment securities is recorded in precisely the same way for trading securities as for investments classified as available-for-sale. The journal entry to record the purchase is:

December 21	**($ in millions)**	
Investment in Millington-Frazier shares	30	
Investment in Bartlett Corporation shares	20	
Cash.		50

All investment securities are initially recorded at cost.

Adjusting Investments to Fair Value.   Likewise, the adjustments to fair value are recorded in precisely the same way for trading securities as for investments classified as available for sale. Only the way the holding gains and losses are reported in financial statements differs. The journal entry to adjust the investments in our illustration to fair value at year-end is:

December 31	**($ in millions)**	
Investment in Millington-Frazier shares	5	
Unrealized holding gain on investments ($35 − 30)		5
Unrealized holding loss on investments ($19 − 20).	1	
Investment in Bartlett Corporation shares		1

All investment securities (except those held to maturity) are adjusted to their fair values on each reporting date.

Reporting Investments in Trading Securities.   For *trading securities,* unrealized holding gains and losses are included in earnings of the period the changes in value occur. In the 2003 balance sheet, the investments in our illustration are reported at the *fair value* of the investment securities ($35 million + $19 = $54 million), and the *net* unrealized holding gain, ($5 − 1 = $4 million) is reported on the income statement:

BALANCE SHEET

	($ in millions)
Assets	
Cash and cash equivalents	$xx
Short-term investments at fair value (cost $50)	54
Accounts receivable	xx
◆	◆
◆	◆

Trading securities are reported at fair value.

INCOME STATEMENT

Other Income (expense)	
◆	◆
Gain on sale of investments	3
Net unrealized holding gain on investments	4
◆	◆

Unrealized holding gains and losses are included in earnings for trading securities only.

STATEMENT OF CASH FLOWS

Operating Activities	
◆	◆
Purchase of investment securities*	50
◆	◆

Cash flows from buying and selling trading securities are classified as operating activities.

*Inflows and outflows of cash from buying and selling trading securities typically are considered operating activities because financial institutions that routinely transact in trading securities consider them an appropriate part of their normal operations.

Transfers between Reporting Categories

At acquisition, an investor assigns debt and equity securities to one of the three reporting classifications—held-to-maturity, available-for-sale, or trading. At each reporting date, the appropriateness of the classification is reassessed. For instance, if the investor no longer has the ability to hold certain securities to maturity and will now hold them for resale, those securities would be reclassified. When a security is reclassified between two reporting categories, the security is transferred at its fair value on the date of transfer. Any unrealized

A transfer of a security between reporting categories is accounted for at fair value and in accordance with the new reporting classification.

holding gain or loss at reclassification should be accounted for *in a manner consistent with the classification into which the security is being transferred.* A summary is provided in Graphic 12–6.

Transfer from:	To:	Unrealized Gain or Loss from Transfer at Fair Market Value
Either of the other	Trading	Include in current earnings
Trading	Either of the other	There is none (already recognized in earnings)
Held-to-maturity	Available-for-sale	Report as a separate component of shareholders' equity (in Other Comprehensive Income)
Available-for-sale	Held-to-maturity	Don't write off any existing unrealized holding gain or loss, but amortize it to earnings over the remaining life of the security (fair value amount becomes the security's amortized cost basis).

Reclassifications are quite unusual, so when they occur, disclosure notes should describe the circumstances that resulted in the transfers. Other footnote disclosures are described in a later section.

CONCEPT REVIEW EXERCISE

Various Investment Securities

Diversified Services, Inc., offers a variety of business services, including financial services through its escrow division. Diversified entered into the following investment activities during the last month of 2003 and the first week of 2004. Diversified's fiscal year ends on December 31. The only securities held by Diversified at December 1 were 12 million common shares of Shelby Laminations, Inc., purchased in November for $48 million.

2003

Dec.	1	Purchased $30 million of 12% bonds of Vince-Gill Amusement Corporation and $24 million of 10% bonds of Eastern Waste Disposal Corporation, both at face value and both to be held until they mature. Interest on each bond issue is payable semiannually on November 30 and May 31.
	9	Sold one-half of the Shelby Laminations common shares for $25 million.
	29	Received cash dividends of $1.5 million from the Shelby Laminations common shares.
	30	Purchased U.S. Treasury bonds for $5.8 million as trading securities hoping to earn profits on short-term differences in prices.
	31	Recorded the necessary adjusting entry(s) relating to the investments.

The year-end market price of the Shelby Laminations common stock was $4.25 per share. The fair values of the bond investments were $32 million for Vince-Gill Amusement Corporation and $20 million for Eastern Waste Disposal Corporation. A sharp rise in short-term interest rates on the last day of the year caused the fair value of the Treasury bonds to fall to $5.7 million.

2004

Jan.	7	Sold the remaining Shelby Laminations common shares for $26 million.

Required:
Prepare the appropriate journal entry for each transaction or event and show the amounts that would be reported in the company's 2003 income statement relative to these investments.

2003   SOLUTION

Dec.   1   Purchased $30 million of 12% bonds of Vince-Gill Amusement Corpora-
tion and $24 million of 10% bonds of Eastern Waste Disposal Corpora-
tion, both at face value and both to be held until they mature. Interest on
each bond issue is payable semiannually on November 30 and May 31.

	($ in millions)	
Investment in Vince-Gill Amusement bonds....................	30	
Investment in Eastern Waste Disposal bonds..................	24	
Cash...		54

Dec.   9   Sold one-half of the Shelby Laminations common shares for $25 million.

	($ in millions)	
Cash (selling price).......................................	25	
Investment in Shelby Laminations common shares ($48 × ½)....		24
Gain on sale of investments (difference)		1

Dec.   29   Received cash dividends of $1.5 million from the Shelby Laminations
common shares.

	($ in millions)	
Cash...	1.5	
Investment revenue....................................		1.5

Dec.   30   Purchased U.S. Treasury bonds for $5.8 million as trading securities, hop-
ing to earn profits on short-term differences in prices.

	($ in millions)	
Investment in U.S. Treasury bonds	5.8	
Cash...		5.8

Dec.   31   Recorded the necessary adjusting entry(s) relating to the investments.

Accrued Interest (one month)	($ in millions)	
Investment revenue receivable—Vince-Gill Amusement		
($30 million × 12% × $\frac{1}{12}$)................................	0.3	
Investment revenue receivable—Eastern Waste Disposal		
($24 million × 10% × $\frac{1}{12}$)................................	0.2	
Investment revenue....................................		0.5
Fair Value Adjustments		
Unrealized holding loss on investments ($5.7 − 5.8 million)	0.1	
Investment in U.S. Treasury bonds		0.1
Investment in Shelby Laminations common shares	1.5	
Unrealized holding gain on investments		
([12 million shares × ½ × $4.25] − [$48 million × ½])		1.5

Note: Securities held-to-maturity are not adjusted to fair value.

Reported in the 2003 Income Statement:	($ in millions)
Investment revenue ($1.5 + 0.5)	$2.0
Gain on sale of investments (Shelby)	1.0
Unrealized holding loss on investments (Treasury bonds)	(0.1)

Note: The unrealized holding gain for the Shelby Laminations common shares is not included in income because it
pertains to securities available for sale rather than trading securities.

2004

Jan.   7   Sold the remaining Shelby Laminations common shares for $26 million.

	($ in millions)
Cash (selling price)	26.0
Unrealized holding gain on investments (balance after adjusting entry)	1.5
Investment in Shelby Laminations common shares (balance after adjusting entry)	25.5
Gain on sale of investments (difference)	2.0

Financial Statement Presentation and Disclosure

Trading securities are current assets by definition. Held-to-maturity and available-for-sale securities are either current or noncurrent depending on when they are expected to mature or to be sold. However, it's not necessary that a company report individual amounts for the three categories of investments—held-to-maturity, available-for-sale, or trading—on the face of the balance sheet as long as that information is presented in the disclosure notes.[8]

On the statement of cash flows, inflows and outflows of cash from buying and selling trading securities typically are considered operating activities because for companies that routinely transact in trading securities (financial institutions), trading in those securities constitutes an appropriate part of the companies' normal operations. But because held-to-maturity and available-for-sale securities are not purchased and held principally to be sold in the near term, cash flows from the purchase, sale, and maturity of these securities are considered investing activities.

Investors should disclose the following in the disclosure notes for each year presented:

- Aggregate fair value.
- Gross realized and unrealized holding gains.
- Gross realized and unrealized holding losses.
- Change in net unrealized holding gains and losses.
- Amortized cost basis by major security type.

Information about maturities should be reported for debt securities by disclosing the fair value and cost for at least four maturity groupings: (a) within 1 year, (b) after 1 year through 5 years, (c) after 5 years through 10 years, and (d) after 10 years.[9] A disclosure note from Microsoft's 2000 annual report (Graphic 12–7) provides us an example.

GRAPHIC 12–7
Disclosures of Investment Securities—Microsoft Corporation

	Cost Basis	Unrealized Gains	Unrealized Losses	Recorded Basis (FV)
Debt securities recorded at market, maturing:				
Within one year	$ 498	$ 27	$ —	$ 525
Between 2 and 10 years	388	11	(3)	396
Between 10 and 15 years	775	14	(93)	696
Beyond 15 years	4,745	—	(933)	3,812
Debt securities recorded at market	6,406	52	(1,029)	5,429
Common stock and warrants	5,815	5,655	(1,697)	9,773
Preferred stock	2,319	—	—	2,319
Other investments	205	—	—	205
Equity and other investments	$14,745	$5,707	($2,726)	$17,726

---

[8]*Statement of Financial Accounting Standards No. 115* "Accounting for Certain Investments in Debt and Equity Securities," (Norwalk, Conn.: FASB, 1993), par. 18.
[9]Ibid., par. 20.

THE EQUITY METHOD

When a company invests in the equity securities (primarily common stock) of another company, the investor can benefit either (a) *directly* through dividends and/or market price appreciation or (b) *indirectly* through the creation of desirable operating relationships with the investee. The way we report a company's investment in the stock of another company depends on the nature of the relationship between the investor and the investee.

For reporting purposes, we classify the investment relationship in one of three ways, and account for the investment differently depending on the classification, as shown in Graphic 12–8:

Classification	Reporting Method
The investor *cannot* significantly influence the investee (usually <20% equity ownership)	Varies by reporting category (see Part A of this chapter)
The investor can significantly influence the operating and financial policies of the investee (usually 20%–50% equity ownership)	Equity method
The investor controls the investee (usually >50% equity ownership)	Consolidation

GRAPHIC 12–8
Reporting Classifications for Investment Relationships

The *equity method* is used when an investor can't control, but can significantly influence, the investee.

FINANCIAL REPORTING CASE

Q4, p. 598

We focused on the first classification in Part A of this chapter. Now, let's turn our attention to the second classification—the **equity method.** A detailed discussion of the third classification—consolidated financial statements—is beyond the scope of this book. That discussion often is a major focus of the advanced accounting course or is taught as a separate consolidations course. In this chapter, we'll briefly overview the subject only to provide perspective to aspects of the equity method that purposely mimic some effects of consolidation. Let's do that now, before addressing the specifics of the equity method.

How the Equity Method Relates to Consolidated Financial Statements

If a company acquires more than 50% of the voting stock of another company, it's said to have a controlling interest because by voting those shares, the investor actually can control the company acquired. The investor is referred to as the *parent;* the investee is termed the *subsidiary.* For reporting purposes (although not legally), the parent and subsidiary are considered to be a single reporting entity, and their financial statements are *consolidated.* Both companies continue to operate as separate legal entities and therefore report separate financial statements. However, because of the controlling interest, the parent company also reports consolidated financial statements. So, the parent prepares two sets of financial statements—one as a separate entity and another as a consolidated entity.

Consolidated financial statements combine the separate financial statements of the parent and the subsidiary each period into a single aggregate set of financial statements as if there were only one company. This entails an item-by-item combination of the parent and subsidiary statements (after first eliminating any amounts that are shared by the separate financial statements).[10] For instance, if the parent has $8 million cash and the subsidiary has $3 million cash, the consolidated balance sheet would report $11 million cash.

Two aspects of the consolidation process are of particular interest to us in understanding the equity method. First, in consolidated financial statements, the acquired company's assets

Consolidated financial statements combine the individual elements of the parent and subsidiary statements.

The acquired company's assets are included in consolidated financial statements at their fair values and the difference between the acquisition price and fair value of the acquired net assets is recorded as goodwill.

---

[10]This avoids double counting those amounts in the consolidated statements. For example, amounts owed by one company to the other are represented by accounts payable in one set of financial statements and accounts receivable in the other. These amounts are not included in the statements of the consolidated entity because a company can't "owe itself."

are included in the financial statements at their fair values rather than their book values. Second, if the acquisition price is more than the fair value of the acquired net assets (assets less liabilities), that difference is recorded as an intangible asset—goodwill.[11] We'll return to the discussion of these two aspects when we reach the point in our discussion of the equity method where their influence is felt. As we'll see, the equity method is in many ways a partial consolidation.

We use the equity method when the investor can't control the investee but can exercise significant influence over the operating and financial policies of an investee.

What Is Significant Influence?

Usually an investor can exercise *significant influence* over the investee when it owns between 20% and 50% of the investee's voting shares.

When effective control is absent, the investor still may be able to exercise significant influence over the operating and financial policies of the investee. This would be the case if the investor owns a large percentage of the outstanding shares relative to other shareholders. By voting those shares as a block, decisions often can be swayed in the direction the investor desires. When significant influence exists, the investment should be accounted for by the equity method. It should be presumed, in the absence of evidence to the contrary, that the investor exercises **significant influence** over the investee when it owns between 20% and 50% of the investee's voting shares.[12]

ADDITIONAL CONSIDERATION

It's possible that a company that owns over 20% of the voting shares cannot exercise significant influence over the investee. If, for instance, another company or a small group of shareholders owns 51% or more of the shares, that company controls the investee regardless of how other investors vote their shares. *FASB Interpretation No. 35* provides this and other examples of indications that an investor may be unable to exercise significant influence:

- The investee challenges the investor's ability to exercise significant influence (through litigation or complaints to regulators).
- The investor surrenders significant shareholder rights in a signed agreement.
- The investor is unable to acquire sufficient information about the investee to apply the equity method.
- The investor tries and fails to obtain representation on the board of directors of the investee.[13]

In such cases, the equity method would be inappropriate.

Conversely, it's also possible that a company that owns *less than* 20% of the voting shares *is* able to exercise significant influence over the investee. Ability to exercise significant influence with less than 20% ownership might be indicated, for example, by having an officer of the investor corporation on the board of directors of the investee corporation or by having, say, 18% of the voting shares while no other investor owns more than ½%. In such cases the equity method would be appropriate. Amazon.com provided the following example in a recent disclosure note:

---

[11]This is the usual case because most companies are worth more than the sum of the values of individual components of the company due to reputation, longevity, managerial expertise, customer loyalty, or a host of other possibilities.
[12]Shareholders are the owners of the corporation. By voting their shares, it is they who determine the makeup of the board of directors—who, in turn, appoint officers—who, in turn, manage the company. Common stock usually is the class of shares given voting privileges. However, a corporation can create classes of preferred shares that also have voting rights. This is discussed at greater length in Chapter 19.
[13]"Criteria for Applying the Equity Method of Accounting for Investments in Common Stock," *FASB Interpretation No. 35* (Stamford, Conn.: FASB, 1981).

Note 6—Investments

At December 31, 2000, the Company's equity-method investees and the Company's approximate ownership interest in each investee, based on outstanding shares, were as follows:

Company	Percentage Ownership
Basis Technology	11%
Drugstore.com	21
Eziba.com	20
Greenlight.com	5
Kozmo.com	16

Although the Company's ownership percentage for Basis Technology, Greenlight.com and Kozmo.com is below 20%, the Company's representation on the investees' Board of Directors and the impact of commercial arrangements result in the Company having significant influence over the operations of each investee.

A Single Entity Concept

Much like consolidation, the equity method views the investor and investee collectively as a special type of single entity (as if the two companies were one company). However, using the equity method, the investor doesn't include separate financial statement items of the investee on an item-by-item basis as in consolidation. Instead, the investor reports its equity interest in the investee as a single investment account.

Under the equity method, the investor recognizes investment income equal to its percentage share (based on stock ownership) of the net income earned by the investee rather than the portion of that net income received as cash dividends. The rationale for this approach is the presumption of the equity method that the fortunes of the investor and investee are sufficiently intertwined that as the investee prospers, the investor prospers proportionately. Stated differently, as the investee earns additional net assets, the investor's share of those net assets increases.

Initially, the investment is recorded at cost. The carrying amount of this investment subsequently is:

- Increased by the investor's percentage share of the investee's net income (or decreased by its share of a loss).
- Decreased by dividends paid.

Let's look at the example in Illustration 12–4 on the next page.

The investor's ownership interest in individual assets and liabilities of the investee is represented by a single investment account.

The investment account is adjusted to reflect the investor's share of both increases and decreases in the investee's net assets.

Further Adjustments

When the investor's expenditure to acquire an investment exceeds the book value of the underlying net assets acquired, additional adjustments to both the investment account and investment revenue might be needed. The purpose is to approximate the effects of consolidation, without actually consolidating financial statements. More specifically, both the investment account and investment revenue are adjusted for differences between net income reported by the investee and what that amount would have been if consolidation procedures had been followed. Let's look closer at what that means.

As mentioned earlier, consolidated financial statements report (a) the acquired company's assets at their fair market values rather than their book values and (b) goodwill for the excess of the acquisition price over the fair value of the identifiable net assets acquired.

The first of these two consequences of the consolidation process usually has an effect on income, and it's the income effect that we're interested in when applying the equity method. First, increasing asset balances to their fair values usually will result in higher expenses. For instance, if buildings, equipment, or other depreciable assets are written up to higher values,

ILLUSTRATION 12–4 Equity Method	On January 2, 2003, American Capital Corporation purchased 25% of the outstanding common shares of Embassy Message Corporation for $200 million. The following information is available regarding Embassy Message Corporation during 2003:

<table>
<tr><td></td><td align="right">**($ in millions)**</td></tr>
<tr><td>Net assets at acquisition:*</td><td></td></tr>
<tr><td>   Fair value</td><td align="right">$600</td></tr>
<tr><td>   Book value</td><td align="right">480</td></tr>
<tr><td>2003 net income</td><td align="right">100</td></tr>
<tr><td>2003 dividends declared and paid</td><td align="right">24</td></tr>
</table>

When a company invests in shares of another corporation, the asset initially is recorded at cost. In accordance with the cost principal, the recorded amount includes any brokerage fees or commissions paid to acquire the shares.

The *cost principal* governs the acquisition of assets.

Initial Acquisition   **($ in millions)**

Investment in equity securities (cost of shares)	200	
Cash		200

Following the acquisition, the investment account is adjusted for the investor's percentage share of net income reported by the investee.[†]

As the investee earns additional net assets, the investment in those net assets increases.

Investee Net Income

Investment in equity securities	25	
Investment revenue (25% share of $100 million earned)		25

As the investee prospers, the investor prospers proportionately.

Adjusting the investment account reflects the equity method's presumption that as the investee earns additional net assets, the investor's equity interest in those net assets increases proportionately. This reasoning also supports recognizing investment revenue as the investee earns net income, not when those earnings actually are distributed as dividends.

In fact, when the investor actually receives dividends, the investment account is *reduced* accordingly:

As the investee distributes net assets as dividends, the investment in those net assets declines.

Dividends

Cash (25% share of $24 million dividends paid)	6	
Investment in equity securities		6

Because investment revenue is recognized as it is earned by the investee, it would be inappropriate to recognize revenue again as earnings are distributed as dividends. Instead, we view the dividend distribution as a *reduction of the investee's net assets,* indicating that the investor's equity interest in those net assets declines proportionately.

*Recall that net assets are equivalent to shareholders' equity. Each is what's left over after creditor claims have been subtracted from assets: <u>Assets − Liabilities</u> = Shareholders' equity

                    Net assets

[†]If any portion of the investee's net income was reported by the investee as an extraordinary item, the investor also would report the same proportion of its share as an extraordinary item. In this illustration, for instance, if $4 million, or 4%, of Embassy Message Corporation's income had been reported as an extraordinary gain, then American Capital Corporation would report 4% of its $25 million share, or $1 million, as an extraordinary gain as well.

depreciation expense will be higher during their remaining useful lives. Likewise, if the recorded amount of inventory is increased, cost of goods sold will be higher when the inventory is sold. However, if it's land that's increased, there is no income effect because we don't depreciate land.

On the other hand, recording goodwill will not result in higher expenses. Goodwill is an intangible asset, but one whose cost usually is not charged to earnings.[14] As a consequence, then,

---

[14]Beginning in 2002, goodwill is not amortized periodically to expense. Only if the asset's value is subsequently judged to be impaired is all or a portion of the recorded amount charged against earnings. "Goodwill and Other Intangible Assets," *Statement of Financial Accounting Standards No. 141* (Norwalk, Conn.: FASB, 2001). The Standard became effective in July 2001.

of increasing asset balances to fair value but not of recording goodwill, expenses will rise and income will fall. It is this negative effect on income that the equity method seeks to imitate.

Recall that our illustration provides the following information regarding Embassy Message Corporation's net assets at the time American Capital Corporation pays $200 million for a 25% interest in the company:

Net Assets at Acquisition:	($ in millions)
Fair value	$600
Book value	480

Let's assume that (a) two-thirds of the difference between the book value of the net assets and their fair market value is attributable to depreciable assets having a fair market value in excess of their undepreciated cost and (b) the remaining third is attributable to land having a fair market value in excess of its cost. We can determine the portion of these differences that American Capital purchased with its $200 million investment and, therefore, any additional amounts to be expensed as shown in Graphic 12–9.

	($ in millions)		
	Investee Net Assets ↓	**Net Assets Purchased** ↓	**Difference Attributed to:** ↓
Cost		$200	
			Goodwill: $50
Fair value	$600 × 25% =	$150	
			Undervaluation of:
			Depreciable assets (⅔) $20
			Land (⅓) $10
Book value	$480 × 25%=	$120	

GRAPHIC 12–9
Source of Differences between the Investment and the Book Value of Net Assets Acquired

Notice in Graphic 12–9 that American Capital paid $200 million for identifiable net assets worth $150 million, and the $50 million difference is attributable to goodwill. Similarly, the identifiable net assets worth $150 million have a book value of only $120 million, and we assumed the $30 million difference is attributable to undervalued depreciable assets ($20 million) and land ($10 million).

Amortization of Additional Depreciation.   Remember, we assumed that two-thirds of the difference between the book value of the net assets and their fair market value is attributable to depreciable assets having a fair market value in excess of their undepreciated cost, or ($150 − 120 million) × ⅔ = $20 million. Let's also assume that these depreciable assets have an average remaining useful life of 10 years, and are being depreciated by the straight-line method. Investment revenue and the investment both would be reduced by the negative income effect of the "extra depreciation" the higher fair value would cause:

Additional Depreciation	($ in millions)
Investment revenue ($20 million ÷ 10 years)	2
Investment in equity shares.	2

We would need to record this adjustment in each of the next nine years as well, since the average remaining useful life is 10 years.[15]

---

[15]If the $20 million difference between fair value and book value had been attributable to undervalued inventory rather than undervalued depreciable assets, we would adjust Investment revenue and the Investment in equity securities by the entire $20 million the first year. The reasoning is that inventory usually is sold within a year—unlike buildings and equipment that last several years. So, if inventory is increased by $20 million, cost of goods sold will be $20 million higher the first year.

No Amortization of Land.   On the contrary, the remaining $10 million difference between the book value of the net assets and their fair market value has no effect on earnings. Unlike buildings and equipment, land is not an asset we depreciate. As a result, writing up the land from book value to fair value (as would occur in consolidation) would not cause higher expenses, so as we mimic consolidation here in the equity method, we have no need to adjust Investment revenue or the Investment in equity securities.

No Amortization of Goodwill.   Recall from Chapter 11 that goodwill, unlike most other intangible assets, should not be amortized. In that sense, goodwill resembles land. Expenses are unaffected by whether goodwill is recorded or not. So acquiring goodwill ($30 million in our example) will not cause higher expenses, so we have no need to adjust Investment revenue or the Investment in equity securities.

Reporting the Investment

The market value of the investment shares at the end of the reporting period is not reported when using the equity method. The investment account is reported at its original cost, increased by the investor's share of the investee's net income (adjusted for additional expenses like depreciation), and decreased by the portion of those earnings actually received as dividends. In other words, the investment account represents the investor's share of the investee's net assets initially acquired, adjusted for the investor's share of the subsequent increase in the investee's net assets (net assets earned and not yet distributed as dividends).

Investment in Equity Securities
($ in millions)

Cost	200		
Share of income	25		
		6	Dividends
		2	Depreciation
Balance	217		

> The carrying amount of the investment is its initial cost plus the investor's equity in the undistributed earnings of the investee.

When the Investee Reports a Net Loss.   Our illustration assumed the investee earned net income. If the investee reports a *net loss* instead, the investment account would be *decreased* by the investor's share of the investee's net loss (adjusted for additional expenses).

When the Investment Is Acquired in Mid-Year.   Obviously, we've simplified the illustration by assuming the investment was acquired at the beginning of 2003, entailing a full year's income, dividends, and amortization. In the more likely event that an investment is acquired sometime after the beginning of the year, the application of the equity method is easily modified to include the appropriate fraction of each of those amounts. For example, if the investment in our illustration had been acquired on October 1 rather than January 2, we would simply record income, dividends, and amortization for three months, or $\frac{3}{12}$ of the year. This would result in the following adjustments to the investment account:

Investment in Equity Securities
($ in millions)

Cost	200.00		
Share of income ($\frac{3}{12} \times$ $25)	6.25		
		1.50 ($\frac{3}{12} \times$ $6) Dividends*	
		.50 ($\frac{3}{12} \times$ $2) Depreciation	
Balance	204.25		

> Changes in the investment account the first year are adjusted for the fraction of the year the investor has owned the investment.

*This example assumes quarterly dividends and that the dividend was declared for the October 1–December 31 quarter. Investors receive the entire amount of any dividends declared while they own stock, regardless of how long they have held the shares.

ADDITIONAL CONSIDERATION

It's possible that the investor's proportionate share of investee losses could exceed the carrying amount of the investment. If this happens, the investor should discontinue applying the equity method until the investor's share of subsequent investee earnings has equaled losses not recognized during the time the equity method was discontinued. This avoids reducing the investment account below zero.

Microsoft Corporation reported its investments in affiliated companies for which it exercised significant influence using the equity method as shown in Graphic 12–10.

In millions June 30	1998	1997
Total current assets	$15,889	$10,373
Property and equipment	1,505	1,465
Equity investments	4,703	2,346
Other assets	260	203
Total assets	$22,357	$14,387

GRAPHIC 12–10
Equity Method—
Microsoft Corporation

WHAT IF CONDITIONS CHANGE?

A Change from the Equity Method to Another Method.   When the investor's level of influence changes, it may be necessary to change from the equity method to another method. This could happen, for instance, if a sale of shares causes the investor's ownership interest to fall from, say, 25% to 15%, resulting in the equity method no longer being appropriate.[16] Another example is provided by Sprint, which in February 2001 agreed to end its exclusive alliance with EarthLink and relinquished its seats on EarthLink's board of directors. As a result, Sprint discontinued using the equity method for its investment in EarthLink. When this situation happens, *no adjustment* is made to the remaining carrying amount of the investment. Instead, the equity method is simply discontinued and the new method applied from then on. The balance in the investment account when the equity method is discontinued would serve as the new cost basis for writing the investment up or down to market value on the next set of financial statements.

A Change from Another Method to the Equity Method.   On the other hand, when a change *to* the equity method is appropriate, because the investor's ownership interest rises from 15% to 25%, the investment account should be retroactively adjusted to the balance that would have existed if the equity method always had been used. As income also would have been different, retained earnings would be adjusted as well. For example, assume it's determined that an investor's share of investee net income, reduced by dividends, was $4 million during a period when the equity method was not used, but additional purchases of shares cause the equity method to be appropriate now. The following journal entry would record the change:

	($ in millions)	
Investment in equity securities	4	
Retained earnings (investment revenue from the equity method) . .		4

Both the investment and retained earnings would be increased by the investor's share of the undistributed earnings in years prior to a change to the equity method.

[16]When a portion of an equity method investment is sold, the investor removes from the investment account the appropriate proportion of the carrying value and records a gain or loss for the difference between that amount and the selling price.

In addition to the adjustment of account balances, financial statements would be restated to the equity method for each year reported in the annual report for comparative purposes. Also, the income effect for years prior to those shown in the comparative statements is reported on the statement of retained earnings as an adjustment to beginning retained earnings of the earliest year reported. A disclosure note also should describe the change. Reporting accounting changes is described in more detail in Chapter 21.

ADDITIONAL CONSIDERATION

Effect on Deferred Income Taxes

Investment revenue is recorded by the equity method when income is earned by the investee, but that revenue is not taxed until it's actually received as cash dividends. This creates a temporary difference between book income and taxable income. You will learn in Chapter 16 that the investor must report a deferred tax liability for the income tax that ultimately will be paid when the income eventually is received as dividends.

IF AN EQUITY METHOD INVESTMENT IS SOLD

When an investment being reported by the equity method is sold, a gain or loss is recognized if the selling price is more or less than the carrying amount (book value) of the investment. For example, let's continue our illustration and assume American Capital Corporation sells its investment in Embassy Message Corporation at the end of 2003 for $234 million. A journal entry would record a gain as follows:

> When an equity method investment is sold, a gain or loss is recognized for the difference between its selling price and its carrying amount.

	($ in millions)	
Cash (proceeds from sale).	234	
Investment in equity securities (balance)		217
Gain on sale of investment (difference)		17

CONCEPT REVIEW EXERCISE

CRE The Equity Method

Delta Apparatus bought 40% of Clay Crating Corp.'s outstanding common shares on January 2, 2003, for $540 million. The carrying amount of Clay Crating's net assets (shareholders' equity) at the purchase date totaled $900 million. Book values and fair values were the same for all financial statement items except for inventory and buildings, for which fair values exceeded book values by $25 million and $225 million, respectively. All inventory on hand at the acquisition date was sold during 2003. The buildings have average remaining useful lives of 18 years. During 2003, Clay Crating reported net income of $220 million and paid an $80 million cash dividend.

Required:
1. Prepare the appropriate journal entries during 2003 for the investment.
2. Determine the amounts relating to the investment that Delta Apparatus should report in the 2003 financial statements:
   a. As an investment in the balance sheet.
   b. As investment revenue in the income statement.
   c. Among investing activities in the statement of cash flows.

SOLUTION

1. Prepare the appropriate journal entries during 2003 for the investment.

Purchase	**($ in millions)**	
Investment in Clay Crating shares.	540	
Cash.		540

Net income

Investment in Clay Crating shares (40% × $220 million)	88	
Investment revenue.		88

Dividends

Cash (40% × $80 million)	32	
Investment in Clay Crating shares.		32

Inventory

Investment revenue (higher cost of goods sold during 2000 if beginning inventory had been adjusted to fair value)	10	
Investment in Clay Crating shares (40% × $25 million)		10

Buildings

Investment revenue ([$225 million × 40%] ÷ 18 years).	5	
Investment in Clay Crating shares.		5

	Investee Net Assets $\downarrow$	Net Assets Purchased $\downarrow$	Difference Attributed to $\downarrow$	
Cost		$540 ⎱		
			Goodwill:	$80 [difference]
Fair value	$1,150† × 40% =	$460 ⎱	Undervaluation of inventory	$10 [$25 × 40%]
Book value	$ 900 × 40% =		Undervaluation of buildings	$90 [$225 × 40%]
†($900 + 25 + 225)		$360 ⎰		

2. Determine the amounts that Delta Apparatus should report in the 2003 financial statements:

   a. As an investment in the balance sheet:

   Investment in Clay Crating shares
   ($ in millions)

Cost	540		
Share of income	88		
		32	Dividends
		10	Inventory
		5	Buildings
Balance	581		

   b. As investment revenue in the income statement:

   $$\underset{\text{(share of income)}}{\$88 \text{ million}} - \underset{\text{(adjustments)}}{[\$10 + 5] \text{ million}} = \underline{\$73 \text{ million}}$$

   c. In the statement of cash flows:
   - Among investing activities: <u>$540 million cash outflow</u>
   - Among operating activities: <u>$32 million cash inflow</u>

DECISION MAKERS' PERSPECTIVE

The way we account for investments has considerable impact on both the valuation of corporate assets and income determination. Consequently, it is critical that both managers and external decision makers clearly understand those impacts and make decisions accordingly.

Managerial decisions concerning investments in other corporations are motivated by a variety of factors. Short-term investments in actively traded securities are common among banks, insurance companies, and other financial institutions. Manufacturing, merchandising,

Corporations invest in other corporations for a variety of reasons.

and nonfinancial service firms are more likely to make short-term investments to optimize the use of temporarily idle cash. Substantial portfolios of long-term securities are prominent among financial institutions who must keep large amounts of funds invested for long periods. Other firms, though, invest long term to derive any number of operating benefits such as creating desirable relationships with suppliers or customers. The way we report a company's investment in the stock of another company depends on the nature of the relationship between the investor and the investee. That is, the choice is dictated by the situation; it's not a discretionary matter.

By and large, the way we account for an investment has little effect on a company's cash flows. On the other hand, profits companies report often are significantly impacted by methods used to account for investments. For example, suppose Investor Company owns 20% of Investee Company. Investee's net income is $1 million. Suppose also that Investee distributes one-half its earnings as dividends. (Thus, Investor receives 20% × $1 million × ½ = $100,000.) Also assume the fair value of Investor's investment in Investee's common stock increased by $250,000 during the year. The investment revenue Investor includes on its income statement varies greatly depending on whether the investment is reported as a trading security, a security held for sale, or an investment accounted for by the equity method. The variation is shown in Graphic 12–11.

> The way an investment is accounted for impacts reported income as well as various financial ratios.

GRAPHIC 12–11
Variation in Earnings by Method Used to Account for Investments

Which accounting method causes reported income to be highest?

	Accounting Method Used		
	Trading Security	**Security Held for Sale**	**Equity Method**
Share of Investee income*	$100,000	$100,000	$200,000
Increase in Investee's fair value†	250,000	0	0
Investor's investment income	$350,000	$100,000	$200,000

*Recognized whether received as dividends or not by the equity method; only if received as dividends otherwise.
†Reported in income for trading securities, component of shareholders' equity for securities available for sale, and not recognized at all for equity-method investments.

Thus, despite the lack of real impact on cash flows, the accounting method affects net income, including calculations of earnings per share and any rate of return ratios. When analyzing a company's profitability, lenders and investors should be alert to the way accounting methods affect reported net income. Clearly, managerial intent plays a crucial role in classifying securities. This discretion introduces the possibility of earnings management (manipulation of income) which has obvious implications for earnings quality. As an analyst, you would want to be particularly wary if the method changes from one year to the next. Companies have been known to adjust their ownership percentage, and therefore their method of accounting, suspiciously in concert with the prosperity of an investee.

Actually, the equity method was designed in part to prevent the manipulation of income that would be possible if investing corporations recognized income only when received as dividends, even when they have significant influence over investees. This would create the possibility that an investing corporation can dictate when and if dividends are paid, effectively manipulating the timing of income recognition. The equity method limits that potential method of managing earnings but given the discretion management has in classifying investments, creates other potential abuses. ■

> Accounting methods intended to limit the opportunities for income manipulation sometimes actually create other opportunities.

Financial Instruments and Investments Derivatives

This is the first of eight chapters that deal with financial instruments. A **financial instrument** is defined as:

No other country reports its investments exactly like we do in the United States. Most countries report short-term investments at lower of cost or market. Some, including Argentina and Israel, report at fair value.

Most countries report noncurrent investments (other than equity method investees) at some variation of cost, but methods vary widely, ranging from unadjusted historical cost (China) to fair market value (New Zealand).

- Cash,
- Evidence of an *ownership interest* in an entity,[17]
- A contract that (a) imposes on one entity an obligation to *deliver* cash (say accounts payable) or another financial instrument and (b) conveys to the second entity a right to *receive* cash (say accounts receivable) or another financial instrument, or
- A contract that (a) imposes on one entity an obligation to *exchange* financial instruments on potentially unfavorable terms (say the issuer of a stock option) and (b) conveys to a second entity a right to *exchange* other financial instruments on potentially favorable terms (say the holder of a stock option).[18]

An entirely new class of financial instruments has emerged in recent years in response to the desire of firms to manage risks. In fact, these financial instruments would not exist in their own right, but have been created solely to hedge against risks created by other financial instruments or by transactions that have yet to occur but are anticipated. Financial futures, interest rate swaps, forward contracts, and options have become commonplace.[19] These financial instruments often are called **derivatives** because they "derive" their values or contractually required cash flows from some other security or index. For instance, an option to buy an asset in the future at a preset price has a value that is dependent on, or derived from, the value of the underlying asset. Their rapid acceptance as indispensable components of the corporate capital structure has left the accounting profession scrambling to keep pace.

Derivatives are financial instruments that "derive" their values from some other security or index.

The urgency to establish accounting standards for financial instruments has been accelerated by headline stories in the financial press reporting multimillion-dollar losses on exotic derivatives by Enron Corporation, Procter & Gamble, Orange County (California), Piper Jaffrey, and Gibson Greetings, to mention a few. The headlines have tended to focus attention on the misuse of these financial instruments rather than their legitimate use in managing risk. So maligned in the press have been derivatives that, in a recent conference, James Leisenring, then the FASB's vice chairman, facetiously defined a derivative as "any investment that lost money this year."

Actually, the FASB has been involved since 1986 in a project to provide a consistent framework for resolving financial instrument accounting issues, including those related to derivatives and other "off-balance-sheet" instruments. The financial instruments project has three separate but related parts: disclosure, recognition and measurement, and distinguishing between liabilities and equities. Unfortunately, issues to be resolved are extremely complex and will likely require several years to resolve. To help fill the disclosure gap in the meantime, the FASB has offered a series of temporary, "patchwork" solutions. These are primarily in the form of additional disclosures for financial instruments. More recently, the FASB has tackled the issues of recognition and measurement. We discuss these requirements in an Addendum to this text after we've spent some time with the measurement issues necessary to understand accounting for derivatives.

The FASB's ongoing financial instruments project is expected to lead to a consistent framework for accounting for all financial instruments.

---

[17]This category includes not just shares of stock, but also partnership agreements and stock options.

[18]"Disclosure of Information about Financial Instruments with Off-Balance-Sheet Risk and Financial Instruments with Concentrations of Credit Risk," *Statement of Financial Accounting Standards No. 105*, (Stamford, Conn.: FASB, 1990), par. 6.

[19]Interest rate futures were traded for the first time in 1975 on the Chicago Board of Trade. Interest rate swaps were invented in the early 1980s. They now comprise over 70% of derivatives in use.

FINANCIAL REPORTING CASE **SOLUTION**

1. **How should you respond?** *(p. 576)* You should explain that if an investor has the positive intent and ability to hold the securities to maturity, investments in debt securities are classified as held-to-maturity and reported at amortized cost in the balance sheet. Increases and decreases in market value are not reported in the financial statements. The reasoning is that the changes are irrelevant to an investor who will hold a security to its maturity regardless of those changes. Changes in the market value between the time a debt security is acquired and the day it matures to a prearranged maturity value aren't important if sale before maturity isn't an alternative.

2. **Why are unrealized gains and losses not reported on the income statement?** *(p. 579)* Available-for-sale securities are *not* acquired for the purpose of profiting from short-term market price changes, so the argument made by the FASB is that gains and losses from holding these securities while prices change are not considered relevant performance measures to be included in earnings.

3. **What is comprehensive income?** *(p. 579)* Comprehensive income is a more expansive view of the change in shareholders' equity than traditional net income. In fact, it encompasses all changes in equity other than from transactions with owners. In addition to net income, comprehensive income includes up to four other changes in equity.

4. **Anticipate his next question and explain why Coke accounts for some of its investments by the equity method and what that means.** *(p. 587)* When an investor does not have "control," but still is able to exercise *significant influence* over the operating and financial policies of the investee, the investment should be accounted for by the equity method. Apparently Coke owns between 20% and 50% of the voting shares of some of the companies it invests in. By the equity method, Coke recognizes investment income in an amount equal to its percentage share of the net income earned by those companies, instead of the amount of that net income it receives as cash dividends. The rationale is that as the investee earns additional net assets, Coke's share of those net assets increases. ∎

THE BOTTOM LINE

1. Investment securities are classified for reporting purposes as held-to-maturity, available-for-sale, or trading securities. If an investor has the positive intent and ability to hold the securities to maturity, investments in debt securities are classified as held-to-maturity and reported at amortized cost in the balance sheet. These investments are recorded at cost, and holding gains or losses from market price changes are ignored.

2. Investments in debt and equity securities that don't fit the definitions of the other reporting categories are classified as available-for-sale. They are reported at their fair values. Holding gains and losses from retaining securities during periods of price change are not included in the determination of income for the period; they are reported as a separate component of shareholders' equity.

3. Investments in debt or equity securities acquired principally for the purpose of selling them in the near term are classified as trading securities. They are reported at their fair values. Holding gains and losses for trading securities are included in earnings.

4. When an investor is able to exercise significant influence over the operating and financial policies of the investee, the investment should be accounted for by the equity method. Usually an investor can exercise significant influence when it owns between 20% and 50% of the investee's voting shares.

5. By the equity method, the investor recognizes investment income equal to its percentage share (based on share ownership) of the net income earned by the investee, rather than the portion of that net income received as cash dividends. The investment account is adjusted

for the investor's percentage share of net income reported by the investee. When the investor actually receives dividends, the investment account is reduced accordingly.

6. When the cost of an investment exceeds the book value of the underlying net assets acquired, both the investment account and investment revenue are adjusted for differences between net income reported by the investee and what that amount would have been if consolidation procedures had been followed. ■

OTHER INVESTMENTS (SPECIAL PURPOSE FUNDS, INVESTMENTS IN LIFE INSURANCE POLICIES)

Special Purpose Funds

It's often convenient for companies to set aside money to be used for specific purposes. You learned about one such special purpose fund in Chapter 7 when we discussed petty cash funds. Recall that a petty cash fund is money set aside to conveniently make small expenditures using currency rather than having to follow the time-consuming, formal procedures normally used to process checks. Similar funds sometimes are used to pay interest, payroll, or other short-term needs. Like petty cash, these short-term special purpose funds are reported as current assets.

Some special purchase funds—like petty cash—are current assets.

Special purpose funds also are sometimes established to serve longer term needs. It's common, for instance, to periodically set aside cash into a fund designated to repay bonds and other long-term debt. Such funds usually accumulate cash over the debt's term to maturity and are composed of the company's periodic contributions plus interest or dividends from investing the money in various return-generating investments. In fact, some debt contracts require the borrower to establish such a fund to repay the debt. In similar fashion, management might voluntarily choose to establish a fund to accumulate money to expand facilities, provide for unexpected losses, to buy back shares of stock, or any other special purpose that might benefit from an accumulation of funds. Of course, these funds that won't be used within the upcoming operating cycle are noncurrent assets. They are reported as part of investments and funds. The same criteria for classifying securities into reporting categories that we discussed previously should be used to classify securities in which funds are invested. Any investment revenue from these funds is reported as such on the income statement.

A special purchase fund can be established for virtually any purpose.

Noncurrent special purchase funds are reported within the category *investments and funds*.

Investments in Life Insurance Policies

Companies frequently buy life insurance policies on the lives of their key officers. Under normal circumstances, the company pays the premium for the policy and as beneficiary, receives the proceeds when the officer dies. Of course, the objective is to compensate the company for the untimely loss of a valuable resource in the event the officer dies. However, some types of life insurance policies can be surrendered while the insured is still alive in exchange for a determinable amount of money, called the **cash surrender value.** In effect, a portion of each premium payment is not used by the insurance company to pay for life insurance coverage, but instead is invested on behalf of the insured company in a fixed-income investment. Accordingly, the cash surrender value increases each year by the portion of premiums invested plus interest on the previous amount invested. This is simply a characteristic of whole life insurance, unlike term insurance whose lower premiums provide death benefits only.

Certain life insurance policies can be surrendered while the insured is still alive in exchange for its *cash surrender value*.

From an accounting standpoint, the periodic insurance premium should not be expensed in its entirety. Rather, part of each premium payment, the investment portion, is recorded as an asset. Illustration 12A–1 on the next page provides an example. ■

Part of each insurance premium represents an increase in the cash surrender value.

ILLUSTRATION 12A–1	Several years ago, American Capital acquired a $1 million insurance policy on the life of its chief executive officer, naming American Capital as beneficiary. Annual premiums are $18,000, payable at the beginning of each year. In 2003, the cash surrender value of the policy increased according to the contract from $5,000 to $7,000. The CEO died at the end of 2003.
Cash Surrender Value	

ILLUSTRATION 12A–1

Cash Surrender Value

Several years ago, American Capital acquired a $1 million insurance policy on the life of its chief executive officer, naming American Capital as beneficiary. Annual premiums are $18,000, payable at the beginning of each year. In 2003, the cash surrender value of the policy increased according to the contract from $5,000 to $7,000. The CEO died at the end of 2003.

Part of the annual premium represents a build-up in the cash surrender value.

Insurance expense (difference)	16,000	
Cash surrender value of life insurance ($7,000 − 5,000)	2,000	
Cash (2003 premium)		18,000

To record insurance expense and the increase in the investment.

The cash surrender value is considered to be a noncurrent investment and would be reported in the investments and funds section of the balance sheet. Of course when the insured officer dies, the corporation receives the death benefit of the insurance policy, and the cash surrender value ceases to exist because canceling the policy no longer is an option. The corporation recognizes a gain for the amount of the death benefit less the cash surrender value:

When the death benefit is paid, the cash surrender value becomes null and void.

Cash (death benefit)	1,000,000	
Cash surrender value of life insurance (balance)		7,000
Gain on life insurance settlement (difference)		993,000

To record the proceeds at death.

APPENDIX

12B

IMPAIRMENT OF A RECEIVABLE DUE TO A TROUBLED DEBT RESTRUCTURING

When a creditor's receivable becomes impaired due to a troubled debt restructuring or for any other reason, the receivable is remeasured based on the discounted present value of currently expected cash flows at the loan's original effective rate (regardless of the extent to which expected cash receipts have been reduced).

When the original terms of a debt agreement are changed as a result of financial difficulties experienced by the debtor (borrower), the new arrangement is referred to as a **troubled debt restructuring.** We discuss troubled debt restructurings in much more detail in Chapter 14. The essential point here is that such an arrangement involves some concessions on the part of the creditor (lender), resulting in the impairment of the creditor's asset: the investment in a receivable.

WHEN THE RECEIVABLE IS SETTLED OUTRIGHT

Sometimes a receivable in a troubled debt restructuring is actually settled at the time of the restructuring with the receipt of cash (or a noncash asset), or even shares of the debtor's stock. In that case, the creditor simply records a loss for the difference between the carrying amount of the receivable and the fair value of the asset(s) or equity securities received. Illustration 12B–1 provides an example.

ILLUSTRATION 12B–1

Debt Settled at the Time of a Restructuring

First Prudent Bank is owed $30 million by Brillard Properties under a 10% note with two years remaining to maturity. Due to financial difficulties of the developer, the previous year's interest ($3 million) was not received. The bank agrees to settle the receivable (and accrued interest receivable) in exchange for property having a fair market value of $20 million.

The carrying amount of the receivable is $33 million

	($ in millions)	
Land (fair market value)	20	
Loss on troubled debt restructuring	13	
Accrued interest receivable (10% × $30 million)		3
Note receivable (balance)		30

For most active lenders, a troubled debt restructuring unfortunately is not both unusual and infrequent; so usually the loss is not reported as an extraordinary loss.

WHEN THE RECEIVABLE IS CONTINUED, BUT WITH MODIFIED TERMS

In the previous example we assumed that First Prudent Bank agreed to accept property in full settlement of the receivable. In a troubled debt restructuring, it is more likely that the bank would allow the receivable to continue but with the terms of the debt agreement modified to make it easier for the debtor to comply. The lender might agree to reduce or delay the scheduled interest payments. Or, it may agree to reduce or delay the maturity amount. Often a troubled debt restructuring will call for some combination of these concessions.

As one of many possibilities, suppose the bank agrees to (1) forgive the interest accrued from last year, (2) reduce the two remaining interest payments from $3 million each to $2 million each, and (3) reduce the face amount from $30 million to $25 million. Clearly, the bank's investment in the receivable has been impaired. The extent of impairment is the difference between the $33 million carrying amount of the receivable (the present value of the receivable's cash flows prior to the restructuring) and the present value of the revised cash flows discounted at the loan's original effective rate (10%). See Illustration 12B–2 for a demonstration.

After restructuring, the lender still records interest annually at the 10% effective rate. ■

				ILLUSTRATION 12B–2
Brillard Properties owes First Prudent Bank $30 million under a 10% note with two years remaining to maturity. Due to financial difficulties of the developer, the previous year's interest ($3 million) was not paid. First Prudent Bank agrees to:				**Receivable Impaired by Troubled Debt Restructuring—Terms Modified**

1. Forgive the interest accrued from last year.
2. Reduce the remaining two interest payments to $2 million each.
3. Reduce the principal to $25 million.

Analysis

Previous Value				The discounted present value of the cash flows prior to the restructuring was the same as the receivable's carrying amount.
Accrued interest	(10% × $30,000,000)	$ 3,000,000		
Principal		30,000,000		
Carrying amount of the receivable			$33,000,000	
New Value				
Interest	$ 2 million × 1.73554* =	$ 3,471,080		
Principal	$25 million × 0.82645† =	20,661,250		The discounted present value of the cash flows after the restructuring is less.
Present value of the receivable			(24,132,330)	
Loss			$ 8,867,670	

*Present value of an ordinary annuity of $1: n = 2, i = 10%
†Present value of $1: n = 2, i = 10%

Journal Entry

Loss on troubled debt restructuring (to balance)	8,867,670	
Accrued interest receivable (10% × $30,000,000)		3,000,000
Note receivable ($30,000,000 − 24,132,330)		5,867,670

The difference is a loss.

QUESTIONS FOR REVIEW OF KEY TOPICS

Q 12–1   All investments in *debt* securities and investments in *equity* securities that have readily determinable fair values (except those for which the equity method or consolidation is appropriate) are classified for reporting purposes in one of three categories and accounted for differently depending on the classification. What are these three categories?

Q 12–2   When market rates of interest *rise* after a fixed-rate security is purchased, the value of the now-below-market, fixed-interest payments declines, so the market value of the investment falls. On the other hand, if market rates of interest *fall* after a fixed-rate security is purchased, the fixed-interest payments become relatively attractive, and the market value of the investment rises. How are these price changes reflected in the investment account for a security classified as held-to-maturity?

Q 12–3   When is the fair value of an equity security considered to be readily determinable? How is an investment in an equity security reported if its fair value is *not* readily determinable?

Q 12–4   When an investment is acquired to be held for an unspecified period of time as opposed to being held to maturity, it is reported at the fair value of the investment securities on the reporting date. Why?

Q 12–5   Reporting an investment at its fair value means adjusting its carrying amount for changes in fair value after its acquisition (or since the last reporting date if it was held at that time). Such changes are called unrealized holding gains and losses because they haven't yet been realized through the sale of the security. If the security is classified as available-for-sale, how are unrealized holding gains and losses reported?

Q 12–6   What is "comprehensive income"? Its composition varies from company to company but may include which financial items?

Q 12–7   Why are holding gains and losses treated differently for trading securities and securities available-for-sale?

Q 12–8   The market value of Helig Forestry and Mining Corporation common stock dropped 6⅛ points when the federal government passed new legislation banning one of the company's primary techniques for extracting ore. Harris Corporation owns shares of Helig and classifies its investment as securities available-for-sale. How should the decline in market value be handled by Harris?

Q 12–9   Western Die-Casting Company holds an investment in unsecured bonds of LGB Heating Equipment, Inc. When the investment was acquired, management's intention was to hold the bonds for resale. Now management has the positive intent and ability to hold the bonds to maturity. How should the reclassification of the investment be accounted for?

Q 12–10   Is it necessary for an investor to report individual amounts for the three categories of investments—held-to-maturity, available-for-sale, or trading—in the financial statements? What information should be disclosed about these investments?

Q 12–11   Under what circumstances is the equity method used to account for an investment in stock?

Q 12–12   The equity method has been referred to as a *one-line consolidation*. What might prompt this description?

Q 12–13   In the application of the equity method, how should dividends from the investee be accounted for? Why?

Q 12–14   The fair value of depreciable assets of Penner Packaging Company exceeds their book value by $12 million. The assets' average remaining useful life is 10 years. They are being depreciated by the straight-line method. Finest Foods Industries buys 40% of Penner's common shares. When adjusting investment revenue and the investment by the equity method, how will the situation described affect those two accounts?

Q 12–15   Superior Company owns 40% of the outstanding stock of Bernard Company. During 2003, Bernard paid a $100,000 cash dividend on its common shares. What effect did this dividend have on Superior's 2003 financial statements?

Q 12–16   Sometimes an investor's level of influence changes, making it necessary to change from the equity method to another method. How should the investor account for this change in accounting method?

Q 12–17   Define a financial instrument. Provide three examples of current liabilities that represent financial instruments.

Q 12–18   Some financial instruments are called derivatives. Why?

Q 12–19   (Based on Appendix 12A) Northwest Carburetor Company established a fund in 2000 to accumulate money for a new plant scheduled for construction in 2003. How should this special purpose fund be reported in Northwest's balance sheet?

Q 12–20   (Based on Appendix 12A) Whole-life insurance policies typically can be surrendered while the insured is still alive in exchange for a determinable amount of money called the *cash surrender value*. When a company buys a life insurance policy on the life of a key officer to protect the company against the untimely loss of a valuable resource in the event the officer dies, how should the company account for the cash surrender value?

Q 12–21   (Based on Appendix 12B) Marshall Companies, Inc., holds a note receivable from a former subsidiary. Due to financial difficulties, the former subsidiary has been unable to pay the previous year's interest on the note. Marshall agreed to restructure the debt by both delaying and reducing remaining cash payments. The concessions impair the creditor's investment in the receivable. How is this impairment recorded?

EXERCISES

E 12–1
Securities held-to-maturity; bond investment; effective interest

Tanner-UNF Corporation acquired as a long-term investment $240 million of 6% bonds, dated July 1, on July 1 2003. Company management has the positive intent and ability to hold the bonds until maturity. The market interest rate (yield) was 8% for bonds of similar risk and maturity. Tanner-UNF paid $200 million for the bonds. The company will receive interest semiannually on June 30 and December 31. As a result of changing market conditions, the fair value of the bonds at December 31, 2003, was $210 million.

Required:
1. Prepare the journal entry to record Tanner-UNF's investment in the bonds on July 1, 2003.
2. Prepare the journal entries by Tanner-UNF to record interest on December 31, 2003, at the effective (market) rate.
3. At what amount will Tanner-UNF report its investment in the December 31, 2003, balance sheet? Why?
4. Suppose Moody's bond rating agency downgraded the risk rating of the bonds motivating Tanner-UNF to sell the investment on January 2, 2004 for $190 million. Prepare the journal entry to record the sale.

E 12–2
Securities held-to-maturity

FF&T Corporation is a confectionery wholesaler that frequently buys and sells securities to meet various investment objectives. The following selected transactions relate to FF&T's investment activities during the last two months of 2003. At November 1, FF&T held $48 million of 20-year, 10% bonds of Convenience, Inc., purchased May 1, 2003, at face value. Management has the positive intent and ability to hold the bonds until maturity. FF&T's fiscal year ends on December 31.

Nov. 1   Received semiannual interest of $2.4 million from the Convenience, Inc., bonds.
Dec. 1   Purchased 12% bonds of Facsimile Enterprises at their $30 million face value, to be held until they mature in 2016. Semiannual interest is payable May 31 and November 30.
     31   Purchased U.S. Treasury bills that mature in two months for $8.9 million.
     31   Recorded any necessary adjusting entry(s) relating to the investments.

The fair values of the investments at December 31 were:
Convenience bonds $44.7 million
Facsimile Enterprises bonds   30.9 million
U.S. Treasury bills   8.9 million

Required:
Prepare the appropriate journal entry for each transaction or event.

E 12–3
Purchase and sale of investment securities

Shott Farm Supplies Corporation purchased 800 shares of General Motors stock at $50 per share and paid a brokerage fee of $1,200. Two months later, the shares were sold for $53 per share. The brokerage fee on the sale was $1,300.

Required:
Prepare entries for the purchase and the sale.

E 12–4
Securities available-for-sale; adjusting entries

Loreal-American Corporation purchased several marketable securities during 2003. At December 31, 2003, the company had the investments in common stock listed below. None was held at the last reporting date, and all are considered securities available-for-sale.

	Cost	Fair Value	Unrealized Holding Gain (Loss)
Short term:			
Blair, Inc.	$ 480,000	$ 405,000	$(75,000)
ANC Corporation	450,000	480,000	30,000
Totals	$ 930,000	$ 885,000	$(45,000)
Long term:			
Drake Corporation	$ 480,000	$ 560,000	$ 80,000
Aaron Industries	720,000	660,000	(60,000)
Totals	$1,200,000	$1,220,000	$ 20,000

Required:
1. Prepare appropriate adjusting entries at December 31, 2003.

2. What amounts would be reported in the income statement at December 31, 2003, as a result of these adjusting entries?

E 12–5
Classification of securities; adjusting entries

On February 18, 2003, Union Corporation purchased 10,000 shares of IBM common stock as a long-term investment at $60 per share. On December 31, 2003, and December 31, 2004, the market value of IBM stock is $58 and $61 per share, respectively.

Required:
1. What is the appropriate reporting category for this investment? Why?
2. Prepare the adjusting entry for December 31, 2003.
3. Prepare the adjusting entry for December 31, 2004.

E 12–6
Various transactions related to securities available-for-sale

Construction Forms Corporation buys securities to be available for sale when circumstances warrant, not to profit from short-term differences in price and not necessarily to hold debt securities to maturity. The following selected transactions relate to investment activities of Construction Forms whose fiscal year ends on December 31. No investments were held by Construction Forms at the beginning of the year.

2003

Mar.	2	Purchased 1 million Platinum Gauges, Inc., common shares for $31 million, including brokerage fees and commissions.
Apr.	12	Purchased $20 million of 10% bonds at face value from Zenith Wholesale Corporation.
July	18	Received cash dividends of $2 million on the investment in Platinum Gauges, Inc., common shares.
Oct.	15	Received semiannual interest of $1 million on the investment in Zenith bonds.
	16	Sold the Zenith bonds for $21 million.
Nov.	1	Purchased 500,000 LTD International preferred shares for $40 million, including brokerage fees and commissions.
Dec.	31	Recorded the necessary adjusting entry(s) relating to the investments. The market prices of the investments are $32 per share for Platinum Gauges, Inc., and $74 per share for LTD International preferred shares.

2004

Jan.	23	Sold half the Platinum Gauges, Inc., shares for $32 per share.
Mar.	1	Sold the LTD International preferred shares for $76 per share.

Required:
1. Prepare the appropriate journal entry for each transaction or event.
2. Show the amounts that would be reported in the company's 2003 income statement relative to these investments.

E 12–7
Securities available-for-sale; journal entries

On January 2, 2003, Sanborn Tobacco, Inc. bought 5% of Jackson Industry's capital stock for $90 million as a temporary investment. Sanborn classified the securities acquired as available-for-sale. Jackson Industry's net income for the year ended December 31, 2003, was $120 million. The fair value of the shares held by Sanborn was $98 million at December 31, 2003. During 2003, Jackson declared a dividend of $60 million.

Required:
1. Prepare all appropriate journal entries related to the investment during 2003.
2. Indicate the effect of this investment on 2003 income before taxes.

E 12–8
Various transactions relating to trading securities

Rantzow-Lear Company buys and sells securities expecting to earn profits on short-term differences in price. The company's fiscal year ends on December 31. The following selected transactions relating to Rantzow-Lear's trading account occurred during December 2003 and the first week of 2004.

2003

Dec.	17	Purchased 100,000 Grocers' Supply Corporation preferred shares for $350,000.
	28	Received cash dividends of $2,000 from the Grocers' Supply Corporation preferred shares.
	31	Recorded any necessary adjusting entry relating to the Grocers' Supply Corporation preferred shares. The market price of the stock was $4 per share.

2004

Jan.	5	Sold the Grocers' Supply Corporation preferred shares for $395,000.

Required:
1. Prepare the appropriate journal entry for each transaction.
2. Indicate any amounts that Rantzow-Lear Company would report in its 2003 balance sheet and income statement as a result of these investments.

E 12–9
Various investment securities

At December 31, 2003, Hull-Meyers Corp. had the following investments that were purchased during 2003, its first year of operations:

	Cost	Fair Value
Trading Securities:		
Security A	$ 900,000	$ 910,000
Security B	105,000	100,000
Totals	$1,005,000	$1,010,000
Securities Available-for-Sale:		
Security C	$ 700,000	$ 780,000
Security D	900,000	915,000
Totals	$1,600,000	$1,695,000
Securities to Be Held-to-Maturity:		
Security E	$ 490,000	$ 500,000
Security F	615,000	610,000
Totals	$1,105,000	$1,110,000

No investments were sold during 2003. All securities except Security D and Security F are considered short-term investments. None of the market changes is considered permanent.

Required:
Determine the following amounts at December 31, 2003.
1. Investments reported as current assets.
2. Investments reported as noncurrent assets.
3. Unrealized gain (or loss) component of income before taxes.
4. Unrealized gain (or loss) component of shareholders' equity.

E 12–10
Securities available-for-sale; adjusting entries

The accounting records of Jamaican Importers, Inc., at January 1, 2003, included the following:

Assets:	
Investment in Yucatan Growers common shares	$1,200,000
Shareholders' Equity:	
Unrealized holding loss on investment in Yucatan Growers common shares	$ 145,000

No changes occurred during 2003 in the investment portfolio.

Required:
Prepare appropriate adjusting entry(s) at December 31, 2003, assuming the market value of the Yucatan Growers common shares was:
1. $1,175,000.
2. $1,275,000.
3. $1,375,000.

E 12–11
Multiple choice; investment securities

The following questions dealing with investments are adapted from questions that appeared in recent CPA examinations. Determine the response that best completes the statements or questions.
1. Nola Co. has adopted *Statement of Financial Accounting Standards No. 115*, "Accounting for Certain Investments in Debt and Equity Securities." Nola has a portfolio of marketable equity securities that it does not intend to sell in the near term. How should Nola classify these securities, and how should it report unrealized gains and losses from these securities?

Classify as	Report as a
a. Trading securities	Component of income from continuing operations
b. Available-for-sale	Separate component shareholders' equity
c. Trading securities	Separate component of shareholders' equity
d. Available-for-sale	Component of income from continuing operations

2. Kale Co. has adopted *Statement of Financial Accounting Standards No. 115,* "Accounting for Certain Investments in Debt and Equity Securities." Kale purchased bonds at a discount on the open market as an investment and intends to hold these bonds to maturity. Kale should account for these bonds at:
   a. Cost
   b. Amortized cost
   c. Fair value
   d. Lower of cost or market

E 12–12
Investment securities and equity method investments compared

As a long-term investment, Painters' Equipment Company purchased 20% of AMC Supplies, Inc.'s 400,000 shares for $480,000 at the beginning of the fiscal year of both companies. On the purchase date, the fair value and book value of AMC's net assets were equal. During the year, AMC earned net income of $250,000 and distributed cash dividends of 25 cents per share. At year-end, the fair value of the shares is $505,000.

Required:
1. Assume no significant influence was acquired. Prepare the appropriate journal entries from the purchase through the end of the year.
2. Assume significant influence was acquired. Prepare the appropriate journal entries from the purchase through the end of the year.

E 12–13
Equity method; purchase; investee income; dividends

As a long-term investment at the beginning of the fiscal year, Florists International purchased 30% of Nursery Supplies, Inc.'s 8 million shares for $56 million. The fair value and book value of the shares were the same at that time. During the year, Nursery Supplies earned net income of $40 million and distributed cash dividends of $1.25 per share. At the end of the year, the fair value of the shares is $52 million.

Required:
Prepare the appropriate journal entries from the purchase through the end of the year.

E 12–14
Change in principle; change to the equity method

The Trump Companies, Inc. has ownership interests in several public companies. At the beginning of 2003, the company's ownership interest in the common stock of Milken Properties increased to the point that it became appropriate to begin using the equity method of accounting for the investment. The balance in the investment account was $31 million at the time of the change. Accountants working with company records determined that the balance would have been $48 million if the account had been adjusted for investee net income and dividends as prescribed by the equity method.

Required:
1. Prepare the journal entry to record the change in principle.
2. Briefly describe other steps Trump should take to report the change.
3. Suppose Trump is changing *from* the equity method rather than *to* the equity method. How would your answers to requirements 1 and 2 differ?

E 12–15
Error corrections; investment

Exercise 21–22 deals with the correction of an error in recording investments.

E 12–16
Equity method; adjustment for depreciation

Fizer Pharmaceutical paid $68 million on January 2, 2003, for 4 million shares of Carne Cosmetics common stock. The investment represents a 25% interest in the net assets of Carne and gave Fizer the ability to exercise significant influence over Carne's operations. Fizer received dividends of $1 per share on December 21, 2003, and Carne reported net income of $40 million for the year ended December 31, 2003. The market value of Carne's common stock at December 31, 2003, was $18.50 per share.
• The book value of Carne's net assets was $192 million.
• The fair market value of Carne's depreciable assets exceeded their book value by $32 million. These assets had an average remaining useful life of eight years.
• The remainder of the excess of the cost of the investment over the book value of net assets purchased was attributable to goodwill.

Required:
Prepare all appropriate journal entries related to the investment during 2003.

E 12–17
Equity method

On January 1, 2003, Cameron, Inc. bought 20% of the outstanding common stock of Lake Construction Company for $300 million cash. At the date of acquisition of the stock, Lake's net assets had a fair value of $900 million. Their book value was $800 million. the difference was attributable to the fair value of Lake's buildings and its land exceeding book value, each accounting for one-half of the difference. Lake's net income for the year ended December 31, 2003, was $150 million. During 2003, Lake declared and paid cash dividends of $30 million. The buildings have a remaining life of 10 years.

Required:
1. Prepare all appropriate journal entries related to the investment during December 31, 2003, assuming Cameron accounts for this investment by the equity method.
2. Determine the amounts to be reported by Cameron:
    a. As an investment in Cameron's 2003 balance sheet.
    b. As investment revenue in the income statement.
    c. Among investing activities in the statement of cash flows.

E 12–18
Multiple choice; equity method

The following questions dealing with the equity method are adapted from questions that appeared on recent CPA examinations. Determine the response that best completes the statements or questions. Questions 1–3 are based on the following information.

   Grant, Inc. acquired 30% of South Co's voting stock for $200,000 on January 2, 2003. Grant's 30% interest in South gave Grant the ability to exercise significant influence over South's operating and financial policies. During 2003, South earned $80,000 and paid dividends of $50,000. South reported earnings of $100,000 for the six months ended June 30, 2004, and $200,000 for the year ended December 31, 2004. On July 1, 2004, Grant sold half of its stock in South for $150,000 cash. South paid dividends of $60,000 on October 1, 2004.

1. Before income taxes, what amount should Grant include in its 2003 income statement as a result of the investment?
    a. $15,000
    b. $24,000
    c. $50,000
    d. $80,000
2. In Grant's December 31, 2003, balance sheet, what should be the carrying amount of this investment?
    a. $200,000
    b. $209,000
    c. $224,000
    d. $230,000
3. In its 2004 income statement, what amount should Grant report as gain from the sale of half of its investment?
    a. $24,500
    b. $30,500
    c. $35,000
    d. $45,500

E 12–19
Life insurance policy (Based on Appendix 12A)

Edible Chemicals Corporation owns a $4 million whole life insurance policy on the life of its CEO, naming Edible Chemicals as beneficiary. The annual premiums are $70,000 and are payable at the beginning of each year. The cash surrender value of the policy was $21,000 at the beginning of 2003.

Required:
1. Prepare the appropriate 2003 journal entry to record insurance expense and the increase in the investment assuming the cash surrender value of the policy increased according to the contract to $27,000.
2. The CEO died at the end of 2003. Prepare the appropriate journal entry.

E 12–20
Life insurance policy (Based on Appendix 12A)

Below are two unrelated situations relating to life insurance.

Required:
Prepare the appropriate journal entry for each situation.
1. Ford Corporation owns a whole life insurance policy on the life of its president. Ford Corporation is the beneficiary. The insurance premium is $25,000. The cash surrender value increased during the year from $2,500 to $4,600.
2. Petroleum Corporation received a $250,000 life insurance settlement when its CEO died. At that time, the cash surrender value was $16,000.

E 12–21
Impairment of securities available-for-sale; troubled debt restructuring (Based on Appendix 12B)

At January 1, 2003, Clayton Hoists, Inc. owed Third BancCorp $12 million, under a 10% note due December 31, 2004. Interest was paid last on December 31, 2001. Clayton was experiencing severe financial difficulties and asked Third BancCorp to modify the terms of the debt agreement. After negotiation Third BancCorp agreed to:
• Forgive the interest accrued for the year just ended.
• Reduce the remaining two years' interest payments to $1 million each.
• Reduce the principal amount to $11 million.

Required:
Prepare the journal entries by Third BancCorp necessitated by the restructuring of the debt at
1. January 1, 2003.
2. December 31, 2003.
3. December 31, 2004.

E 12–22
Impairment of securities available-for-sale; troubled debt restructuring (Based on Appendix 12B)

At January 1, 2003, NCI Industries, Inc. was indebted to First Federal Bank under a $240,000, 10% unsecured note. The note was signed January 1, 1999, and was due December 31, 2004. Annual interest was last paid on December 31, 2001. NCI was experiencing severe financial difficulties and negotiated a restructuring of the terms of the debt agreement. First Federal agreed to reduce last year's interest and the remaining two years' interest payments to $11,555 each and delay all payments until December 31, 2004, the maturity date.

Required:
Prepare the journal entries by First Federal Bank necessitated by the restructuring of the debt at
1. January 1, 2003.
2. December 31, 2003.
3. December 31, 2004.

PROBLEMS

P 12–1
Securities held-to-maturity; bond investment; effective interest

Fuzzy Monkey Technologies, Inc. purchased as a long-term investment $80 million of 8% bonds, dated January 1, on January 1, 2003. Management has the positive intent and ability to hold the bonds until maturity. For bonds of similar risk and maturity the market yield was 10%. The price paid for the bonds was $66 million. Interest is received semiannually on June 30 and December 31. Due to changing market conditions, the fair value of the bonds at December 31, 2003, was $70 million.

Required:
1. Prepare the journal entry to record Fuzzy Monkey's investment on January 1, 2003.
2. Prepare the journal entry by Fuzzy Monkey to record interest on June 30, 2003 (at the effective rate).
3. Prepare the journal entries by Fuzzy Monkey to record interest on December 31, 2003 (at the effective rate).
4. At what amount will Fuzzy Monkey report its investment in the December 31, 2003, balance sheet? Why?

P 12–2
Securities available-for-sale; bond investment; effective interest

(Note: This problem is a variation of the preceding problem, modified to cause the investment to be in securities available-for-sale.)

Fuzzy Monkey Technologies, Inc. purchased as a long-term investment $80 million of 8% bonds, dated January 1, on January 1, 2003. Management intends to have the investment available for sale when circumstances warrant. For bonds of similar risk and maturity the market yield was 10%. The price paid for the bonds was $66 million. Interest is received semiannually on June 30 and December 31. Due to changing market conditions, the fair value of the bonds at December 31, 2003, was $70 million.

Required:
1. Prepare the journal entry to record Fuzzy Monkey's investment on January 1, 2003.
2. Prepare the journal entry by Fuzzy Monkey to record interest on June 30, 2003 (at the effective rate).
3. Prepare the journal entries by Fuzzy Monkey to record interest on December 31, 2003 (at the effective rate).
4. At what amount will Fuzzy Monkey report its investment in the December 31, 2003, balance sheet? Why? Prepare any entry necessary to achieve this reporting objective.

P 12–3
Various transactions related to securities available-for-sale

The following selected transactions relate to investment activities of Ornamental Insulation Corporation. The company buys securities, *not* intending to profit from short-term differences in price and *not* necessarily to hold debt securities to maturity, but to have them available for sale when circumstances warrant. Ornamental's fiscal year ends on December 31. No investments were held by Ornamental on December 31, 2003.

2003
Feb. 21   Acquired Distribution Transformers Corporation common shares costing $400,000.
Mar. 18   Received cash dividends of $8,000 on the investment in Distribution Transformers common shares.

2003

Sep. 1   Acquired $900,000 of American Instruments' 10% bonds at face value.
Oct. 20   Sold the Distribution Transformers shares for $425,000.
Nov. 1   Purchased M&D Corporation common shares costing $1,400,000.
Dec. 31   Recorded any necessary adjusting entry(s) and closing entries relating to the investments. The market prices of the investments are:

American Instruments bonds	$ 850,000
M&D Corporation shares	$1,460,000

(Hint: Interest must be accrued for the American Instruments' bonds.)

2004

Jan. 20   Sold the M&D Corporation shares for $1,485,000.
Mar. 1   Received semiannual interest of $45,000 on the investment in American Instruments bonds.

Required:
1. Prepare the appropriate journal entry for each transaction or event during 2003.
2. Indicate any amounts that Ornamental Insulation would report in its 2003 balance sheet and income statement as a result of these investments.
3. Prepare the appropriate journal entry for each transaction or event during 2004.

P 12–4
Various transactions relating to trading securities

American Surety and Fidelity buys and sells securities expecting to earn profits on short-term differences in price. For the first 11 months of the year, gains from selling trading securities totaled $8 million, losses were $11 million, and the company had earned $5 million in investment revenue. The following selected transactions relate to American's trading account during December, 2003, and the first week of 2004. The company's fiscal year ends on December 31. No trading securities were held by American on December 1, 2003.

2003

Dec. 12   Purchased FF&G Corporation bonds for $12 million.
13   Purchased 2 million Ferry Intercommunications common shares for $22 million.
15   Sold the FF&G Corporation bonds for $12.1 million.
22   Purchased U.S. Treasury bills for $56 million and Treasury bonds for $65 million.
23   Sold half the Ferry Intercommunications common shares for $10 million.
26   Sold the U.S. Treasury bills for $57 million.
27   Sold the Treasury bonds for $63 million.
28   Received cash dividends of $200,000 from the Ferry Intercommunications common shares.
31   Recorded any necessary adjusting entry(s) and closing entries relating to the investments. The market price of the Ferry Intercommunications stock was $10 per share.

2004

Jan. 2   Sold the remaining Ferry Intercommunications common shares for $10.2 million.
5   Purchased Warehouse Designs Corporation bonds for $34 million.

Required:
1. Prepare the appropriate journal entry for each transaction or event during 2003.
2. Indicate any amounts that American would report in its 2003 balance sheet and income statement as a result of these investments.
3. Prepare the appropriate journal entry for each transaction or event during 2004.

P 12–5
Securities held-to-maturity, securities available for sale, and trading securities

Amalgamated General Corporation is a consulting firm that also offers financial services through its credit division. From time to time the company buys and sells securities intending to earn profits on short-term differences in price. The following selected transactions relate to Amalgamated's investment activities during the last quarter of 2003 and the first month of 2004. The only securities held by Amalgamated at October 1 were $30 million of 10% bonds of Kansas Abstractors, Inc. purchased on May 1 at face value. The company's fiscal year ends on December 31.

2003

Oct. 18   Purchased 2 million preferred shares of Millwork Ventures Company for $58 million as a speculative investment to be sold under suitable circumstances.
31   Received semiannual interest of $1.5 million from the Kansas Abstractors bonds.

2003

Nov.   1   Purchased 10% bonds of Holistic Entertainment Enterprises at their $18 million face value, to be held until they mature in 2010. Semiannual interest is payable April 30 and October 31.

1   Sold the Kansas Abstractors bonds for $28 million because rising interest rates are expected to cause their fair value to continue to fall.

Dec.   1   Purchased 12% bonds of Household Plastics Corporation at their $60 million face value, to be held until they mature in 2023. Semiannual interest is payable May 31 and November 30.

20   Purchased U. S. Treasury bonds for $5.6 million as trading securities, hoping to earn profits on short-term differences in prices.

21   Purchased 4 million common shares of NXS Corporation for $44 million as trading securities, hoping to earn profits on short-term differences in prices.

23   Sold the Treasury bonds for $5.7 million.

29   Received cash dividends of $3 million from the Millwork Ventures Company preferred shares.

31   Recorded any necessary adjusting entry(s) and closing entries relating to the investments. The market price of the Millwork Ventures Company preferred stock was $27.50 per share and $11.50 per share for the NXS Corporation common. The fair values of the bond investments were $58.7 million for Household Plastics Corporation and $16.7 million for Holistic Entertainment Enterprises.

2004

Jan.   7   Sold the NXS Corporation common shares for $43 million.

Required:

Prepare the appropriate journal entry for each transaction or event.

P 12–6

Investment securities and equity method investments compared

On January 4, 2003, Runyan Bakery paid $324 million for 10 million shares of Lavery Labeling Company common stock. The investment represents a 30% interest in the net assets of Lavery and gave Runyan the ability to exercise significant influence over Lavery's operations. Runyan received dividends of $2.00 per share on December 15, 2003, and Lavery reported net income of $160 million for the year ended December 31, 2003. The market value of Lavery's common stock at December 31, 2003, was $31 per share. On the purchase date, the book value of Lavery's net assets was $800 million and:

a.   The fair market value of Lavery's depreciable assets, with an average remaining useful life of six years, exceeded their book value by $80 million.

b.   The remainder of the excess of the cost of the investment over the book value of net assets purchased was attributable to goodwill.

Required:

1.   Prepare all appropriate journal entries related to the investment during 2003, assuming Runyan accounts for this investment by the equity method.

2.   Prepare the journal entries required by Runyan, assuming that the 10 million shares represents a 10% interest in the net assets of Lavery rather than a 30% interest.

P 12–7

Equity method

Northwest Paperboard Company, a paper and allied products manufacturer, was seeking to gain a foothold in Canada. Toward that end, the company bought 40% of the outstanding common shares of Vancouver Timber and Milling, Inc. on January 2, 2003, for $400 million.

At the date of purchase, the book value of Vancouver's net assets was $775 million. The book values and fair values for all balance sheet items were the same except for inventory and plant facilities. The fair value exceeded book value by $5 million for the inventory and by $20 million for the plant facilities.

The estimated useful life of the plant facilities is 16 years. All inventory acquired was sold during 2003.

Vancouver reported net income of $140 million for the year ended December 31, 2003. Vancouver paid a cash dividend of $30 million.

Required:

1.   Prepare all appropriate journal entries related to the investment during 2003.

2.   What amount should Northwest report as its income from its investment in Vancouver for the year ended December 31, 2003?

3.   What amount should Northwest report in its balance sheet as its investment in Vancouver?

4.   What should Northwest report in its statement of cash flows regarding its investment in Vancouver?

P 12–8
Equity method

On January 2, 2003, Miller Properties paid $19 million for 1 million shares of Marlon Company's 6 million outstanding common shares. Miller's CEO became a member of Marlon's board of directors during the first quarter of 2003.

The carrying amount of the Marlon's net assets was $66 million. Miller estimated the fair value of those net assets to be the same except for a patent valued at $24 million over cost. The remaining amortization period for the patent is 10 years.

Marlon reported earnings of $12 million and paid dividends of $6 million during 2003. On December 31, 2003, Marlon's common stock was trading on the NYSE at $18.50 per share.

Required:
1. When considering whether to account for its investment in Marlon under the equity method, what criteria should Miller's management apply?
2. Assume Miller accounts for its investment in Marlon using the equity method. Ignoring income taxes, determine the amounts related to the investment to be reported in its 2003:
   a. Income statement.
   b. Balance sheet.
   c. Statement of cash flows.

P 12–9
Classifying investments

Indicate (by letter) the way each of the investments listed below most likely should be accounted for based on the information provided.

Item	Reporting Category
____ 1. 35% of the nonvoting preferred stock of American Aircraft Company.	T. Trading securities
____ 2. Treasury bills to be held to maturity.	M. Securities held-to-maturity
____ 3. Two-year note receivable from affiliate.	A. Securities available-for-sale
____ 4. Accounts receivable.	E. Equity method
____ 5. Treasury bond maturing in one week.	C. Consolidation
____ 6. Common stock held in trading account for immediate resale.	N. None of these
____ 7. Bonds acquired to profit from short-term differences in price.	
____ 8. 35% of the voting common stock of Computer Storage Devices Company.	
____ 9. 90% of the voting common stock of Affiliated Peripherals, Inc.	
____ 10. Corporate bonds of Primary Smelting Company to be sold if interest rates fall ½%.	
____ 11. 25% of the voting common stock of Smith Foundries Corporation: 51% family-owned by Smith family; fair value determinable.	
____ 12. 17% of the voting common stock of Shipping Barrels Corporation: Investor's CEO on the board of directors of Shipping Barrels Corporation.	

P 12–10
Impairment of securities available-for-sale; troubled debt restructuring (Based on Appendix 12B)

At January 1, 2003, Rothschild Chair Company, Inc. was indebted to First Lincoln Bank under a $20 million, 10% unsecured note. The note was signed January 1, 1997, and was due December 31, 2006. Annual interest was last paid on December 31, 2001. Rothschild Chair Company was experiencing severe financial difficulties and negotiated a restructuring of the terms of the debt agreement.

Required:
Prepare all journal entries by First Lincoln Bank to record the restructuring and any remaining transactions relating to the debt under each of the independent circumstances below:
1. First Lincoln Bank agreed to settle the debt in exchange for land having a fair market value of $16 million but carried on Rothschild Chair Company's books at $13 million.
2. First Lincoln Bank agreed to (a) forgive the interest accrued from last year, (b) reduce the remaining four interest payments to $1 million each, and (c) reduce the principal to $15 million.
3. First Lincoln Bank agreed to defer all payments (including accrued interest) until the maturity date and accept $27,775,000 at that time in settlement of the debt.

BROADEN YOUR PERSPECTIVE

Apply your critical-thinking ability to the knowledge you've gained. These cases will provide you an opportunity to develop your research, analysis, judgment, and communication skills. You also will work with other students, integrate what you've learned, apply it in real world situations, and consider its global and ethical ramifications. This practice will broaden your knowledge and further develop your decision-making abilities.

Real World Case 12–1
Sprint's investments

The following disclosure note appeared in the 1993 annual report of the Sprint Corporation. This was the year *SFAS 115* became effective.

Investments in Securities (in part)

The cost of investments in securities was $13 million at year-end 2000 and $154 million at year-end 1999. Gross unrealized holding gains were $53 million at year-end 2000 and $310 million at year-end 1999.

The accumulated unrealized gains on investments in securities, net of income taxes and the impact of the related debt instruments, were $33 million at year-end 2000 and $84 million at year-end 1999 and are included in "Accumulated other comprehensive income" in the Spring Consolidated Balance Sheets.

During 1999, Spring sold available-for-sale securities with a cost basis of $14 million for $104 million. The $90 million gain was included in "Other income (expense), net" in Sprint's Consolidated Statements of Operations.

Required:

1. From the information provided by the disclosure note, determine the amount at which Sprint reported its investment in common stock in its 2000 balance sheet.
2. What would have been Sprint's journal entry to reflect the 2000 fair value of the investments? Ignore taxes.
3. The note indicates that Sprint sold available-for-sale securities with a cost basis of $14 million for $104 million, producing a $90 million gain. Does this imply that the securities involved had not previously been written up above the original $14 million cost? Why? What would have been the journal entry to record the sale of the investments if we assume their fair value had been $100 million at the beginning of 1999?

Research Case 12–2
Reporting securities available-for-sale; obtain and critically evaluate an annual report

Investments in common stocks potentially affect each of the various financial statements as well as the disclosure notes that accompany those statements.

Required:

1. Locate a recent annual report of a public company that includes a footnote that describes an investment in securities available-for-sale. You can use EdgarScan at edgarscan.pwcglobal.com.
2. Under what caption are the investments reported in the comparative balance sheets? Are they reported as current or noncurrent assets?
3. Are realized gains or losses reported in the comparative income statements?
4. Are unrealized gains or losses reported in the comparative statements and shareholders' equity?
5. Are unrealized gains or losses identifiable in the comparative balance sheets? If so, under what caption? Why are unrealized gains or losses reported here rather than in the income statements?
6. Are cash flow effects of these investments reflected in the company's comparative statements of cash flows? If so, what information is provided by this disclosure?
7. Does the footnote provide information not available in the financial statements?

Integrating Case 12–3
How was the adoption of *SFAS 115* an exception to the usual method of accounting for changes in accounting principle?

In Chapter 3 you learned that most changes in accounting principle require reporting the cumulative income effect of the change as part of earnings in the year of the change, but that a few exceptions require retroactive restatement of prior years' financial statements. Also, some changes mandated by new FASB accounting standards require neither of those approaches, and instead require or permit *prospective* application of the new standard. An example of this exception is *SFAS 115*, "Accounting for Certain Investments in Debt and Equity Securities." Recall that the standard requires that certain investments that previously were reported at lower of cost or market were required by the new standard to be reported instead at their fair values.

Required:

Explain how *SFAS 115* is an exception to the general method of accounting for changes in accounting principle.

Trueblood Accounting Case 12–4
Impairment charge for unrealized holding loss

The following Trueblood case is recommended for use with this chapter. The case provides an excellent opportunity for class discussion, group projects, and writing assignments. The case, along with Professor's Discussion Material, can be obtained from the Deloitte Foundation at its website: www.deloitte.com/more/DTF/cases_subj.htm.

Case 01–1: *The Tale of Stable Mable's Unstable Investment*

This case provides students the opportunity to discuss whether or not an impairment charge should be recognized for an investment in available for sale securities that have reported an unrealized holding gain for a long period of time.

International Case 12–5
Comparison of investment accounting in France and the United States

Renault is the largest automobile manufacturer in France. The investment disclosures accompanying financial statements in Renault's 1999 annual report are reproduced below:

Accounting Policies (in part)
N. Securities
Equity securities
Equity investments in non-consolidated companies are carried in the balance sheet at acquisition cost less any provisions. The corresponding dividends are recorded in the year of distribution.

Provisions are established when the value in use of the investments falls below acquisition cost. The value in use is determined on the basis of profitability prospects, the commercial outlets the investment represents for the Group, and the share in net assets.

Debt securities
Debt securities consist entirely of fixed-rate securities acquired to be held on a long-term basis, usually until maturity. They are hedged by interest rate futures for durable protection against foreign exchange exposure, or by long-term financing to ensure they can be held until maturity.

Discounts and premiums are spread over the remaining life of the security on a straight-line basis. Provisions for amortization are established when the issuer is likely to default.

Marketable securities
Marketable securities are valued at acquisition cost excluding related expenses and accrued interest for bonds, or at market value if this is lower.

Required:

On the basis of the information the disclosures provide, compare accounting for investments in France with that in the United States.

Research Case 12–6
Researching the way investments are reported; retrieving information from the Internet

All publicly traded domestic companies use EDGAR, the Electronic Data Gathering, Analysis, and Retrieval system, to make the majority of their filings with the SEC. You can access EDGAR on the Internet at www.sec.gov, or you can use EdgarScan at edgarscan.pwcglobal.com.

Required:

1. Search for a public company with which you are familiar. Access its most recent 10-K filing. Search or scroll to find financial statements and related notes.
2. Answer the following questions. (If the chosen company does not report investments in the securities of other companies, choose another company.)
   a. What is the amount and classification of any investment securities reported in the balance sheet? Are unrealized gains or losses reported in the shareholders' equity section?
   b. Are any investments reported by the equity method?
   c. What amounts from these investments are reported in the comparative income statements? Has that income increased or decreased over the years reported?
   d. Are any acquisitions or disposals of investments reported in the statement of cash flows?

Real World Case 12–7
Delta's investments

Corporations frequently invest in securities issued by other corporations. Some investments are acquired to secure a favorable business relationship with another company. On the other hand, others are intended only to earn an investment return from the dividends or interest the securities pay or from increases in the market prices of the securities—the same motivations that might cause you to invest in stocks, bonds, or other securities. This diversity in investment objectives means no single accounting method is adequate to report every investment.

Delta Airlines invests in securities of other companies. Access the most recent financial statements of Delta using EdgarScan (**edgarscan.pwcglobal.com/**).

Required:

1. What is the amount and classification of any investment securities reported on the balance sheet? In which two current and which two noncurrent asset categories are investments reported by Delta? What criteria are used to determine the classification?
2. How are unrealized gains or losses reported? realized gains and losses?
3. Are any investments reported by the equity method?
4. What amounts from these investments are reported in the comparative income statements?
5. Are cash flow effects of these investments reflected in the company's comparative statements of cash flows? If so, what information is provided by this disclosure?

Real World Case 12–8
Comprehensive
income—Microsoft

As required by SFAS No. 115, Microsoft Corporation reports its investments available for sale at the *fair value* of the investment securities. The *net* unrealized holding gain is not reported in the income statement. Instead, it's reported as part of Other comprehensive income in shareholders' equity.

Comprehensive income is a broader view of the change in shareholders' equity than traditional net income, encompassing all changes in equity from nonowner transactions. Microsoft chose to report its Other comprehensive income as a separate statement in a disclosure note in its 2000 annual report.

Other Comprehensive Income
The changes in the components of other comprehensive income are as follows: ($ in millions)

Year Ended June 30	1998	1999	2000
Net unrealized investment gains/(losses):			
Unrealized holding gains, net of tax effect of $355 in 1998, $772 in 1999, and $248 in 2000	$660	$1,432	$531
Reclassification adjustment for gains included in net income, net of tax effect of $(18) in 1998, $(205) in 1999, and $(420) in 2000	(33)	(380)	(814)
Net unrealized investment gains/(losses)	627	1,052	(283)
Translation adjustments and other	(124)	69	23
Other comprehensive income/(loss)	$503	$1,121	$(260)

Required:

1. The note indicates Unrealized holding gains during 2000 in the amount of $531 million. Is this the amount Microsoft would include as a separate component of shareholders' equity? Explain.
2. What might Microsoft mean by the term, "Reclassification adjustment for gains included in net income"?
3. Besides Unrealized holding gains, Microsoft's disclosure note refers to "Translation adjustments and other." What might the "other" components of Other comprehensive income be?

13

CHAPTER

Current Liabilities and Contingencies

OVERVIEW

With the discussion of investments in Chapter 12, we concluded our six-chapter coverage of assets that began in Chapter 7. This is the first of six chapters devoted to liabilities. Here we focus on short-term liabilities. Bonds and long-term notes are discussed in Chapter 14. Obligations relating to leases, income taxes, pensions, and other postretirement benefits are the subjects of the following four chapters. In Part A of this chapter, we discuss liabilities that are classified appropriately as current. In Part B we turn our attention to situations in which there is uncertainty as to whether an obligation really exists. These are designated as loss contingencies.

LEARNING OBJECTIVES

After studying this chapter, you should be able to:

LO1 Define liabilities and distinguish between current and long-term liabilities.

LO2 Account for the issuance and payment of various forms of notes and record the interest on the notes.

LO3 Characterize accrued liabilities and liabilities from advance collection and describe when and how they should be recorded.

LO4 Determine when a liability can be classified as a noncurrent obligation.

LO5 Identify situations that constitute contingencies and the circumstances under which they should be accrued.

LO6 Describe the appropriate accounting treatment for contingencies, including unasserted claims and assessments.

Dinstuhl's Dad

"My dad is confused," your friend Buzz Dinstuhl proclaimed at the office one morning. "You see, we're competing against each other in that investment game I told you about, and one of his hot investments is Syntel Microsystems. When he got their annual report yesterday afternoon, he started analyzing it, you know, really studying it closely. Then he asked me about this part here." Buzz pointed to the current liability section of the balance sheet and related disclosure note:

SYNTEL MICROSYSTEMS, INC.
Balance Sheet
December 31, 2003 and 2002
($ in millions)

Current Liabilities	2003	2002
Accounts payable	$233.5	$241.6
Short-term borrowings (Note 3)	187.0	176.8
Accrued liabilities	65.3	117.2
Accrued loss contingency	76.9	—
Other current liabilities	34.6	45.2
Current portion of long-term debt	44.1	40.3
Total current liabilities	$641.4	$621.1

Note 3: Short-Term Borrowings (in part)
The components of short-term borrowings and their respective weighted average interest rates at the end of the period are as follows:

$ in millions

	2003		2002	
	Amount	Average Interest Rate	Amount	Average Interest Rate
Commercial paper	$ 34.0	5.2%	$ 27.1	5.3%
Bank loans	218.0	5.5	227.7	5.6
Amount reclassified to long-term liabilities	(65.0)	—	(78.0)	—
Total short-term borrowings	$187.0		$176.8	

The Company maintains bank credit lines sufficient to cover outstanding short-term borrowings. As of December 31, 2003, the Company had $200.0 million fee-paid lines available.

At December 31, 2003 and 2002, the Company classified $65.0 million and $78.0 million, respectively, of commercial paper and bank notes as long-term debt. The Company has the intent and ability, through formal renewal agreements, to renew these obligations into future periods.

(continued)

(concluded)

Note 6: Contingencies (in part)

Between 2001 and 2002, the Company manufactured cable leads that, the Company has learned, contribute to corrosion of linked components with which they are installed. At December 31, 2003, the Company accrued $132.0 million in anticipation of remediation and claims settlement deemed probable, of which $76.9 million is considered a current liability.

"So, what's the problem?" you asked.

"Well, he thinks I'm some sort of financial wizard because I'm in the business."

"And because you tell him so all the time," you interrupted.

"Maybe so, but he's been told that current liabilities are riskier than long-term liabilities, and now he's focusing on that. He can't see why some long-term debt is reported here in the current section. And it also looks like some is reported the other way around; some current liabilities reported as long term. Plus, the contingency amount seems like it's not even a contractual liability. Then he wants to know what some of those terms mean. Lucky for me, I had to leave before I had to admit I didn't know the answers. You're the accounting graduate; help me out."

By the time you finish this chapter, you should be able to respond appropriately to the questions posed in this case. Compare your response to the solution provided at the end of the chapter.

QUESTIONS

1. What are accrued liabilities? What is commercial paper? (page 624)

2. Why did Syntel Microsystems include some long-term debt in the current liability section? (page 627)

3. Did they also report some current amounts as long-term debt? Explain. (page 627)

4. Must obligations be known contractual debts in order to be reported as liabilities? (page 630)

5. Is it true that current liabilities are riskier than long-term liabilities? (page 641)

CURRENT LIABILITIES

Before a business can invest in an asset it first must acquire the money to pay for it. This can happen in either of two ways—funds can be provided by owners or the funds must be borrowed. You may recognize this as a description of the basic accounting equation: liabilities and owners' equity on the right-hand side of the equation represent the two basic sources of the assets on the left-hand side. You studied assets in the chapters leading to this one and you will study owners' equity later. This chapter and the next four describe the various liabilities that constitute creditors' claims on a company's assets.

Characteristics of Liabilities

You already know what liabilities are. You encounter them every day. The multibillion dollar national debt we hear discussed almost daily is a liability of all of us. Our creditors are the individuals and institutions that have bought debt securities from (loaned money to) our government. Similarly, when businesses issue notes and bonds, their creditors are the banks, individuals, and organizations that exchange cash for those securities. If you are paying for a car or a home with monthly payments, you have a personal liability. Each of these obligations represents the most common type of liability—one to be paid in cash and for which the amount and timing are specified by a legally enforceable contract.

Entities routinely incur most liabilities to acquire the funds, goods, and services they need to operate and just as routinely settle the liabilities they incur.[1]

Most liabilities obligate the debtor to pay cash at specified times and result from legally enforceable agreements.

---

[1]"Elements of Financial Statements," *Statement of Financial Accounting Concepts No. 6,* (Stamford, Conn.: FASB, 1985), par. 38.

However, to be reported as a **liability,** an obligation need not be payable in cash. Instead, it may require the company to transfer other assets or to provide services. It also need not be represented by a written agreement nor be legally enforceable. Even the amount and timing of repayment need not be precisely known. From a financial reporting perspective, a liability has three essential characteristics. Liabilities:

1. Are *probable, future* sacrifices of economic benefits.
2. Arise from *present* obligations (to transfer goods or provide services) to other entities.
3. Result from *past* transactions or events.[2]

Notice that the definition of a liability involves the present, the future, and the past. It is a present responsibility to sacrifice assets in the future because of a transaction or other event that already has happened.

Later in the chapter we'll discuss several liabilities that possess these characteristics but have elements of uncertainty regarding the amount and timing of payments and sometimes even their existence.

What Is a Current Liability?

In a classified balance sheet, liabilities are categorized as either **current liabilities** or long-term liabilities. Listing financial statement elements by classification provides additional clarification concerning the nature of those elements. In the case of liabilities, the additional information provided by the classification relates to their relative riskiness. Will payment require the use of current assets and reduce the amount of liquid funds available for other uses? If so, are sufficient liquid funds available to pay currently maturing obligations in addition to meeting current operating needs? Or is the due date comfortably in the future, permitting resources to be used for other purposes without risking default or without compromising operating efficiency? Classifying liabilities as either current or long term helps investors and creditors assess the riskiness of a business's obligations in this regard. In this chapter, we focus on current liabilities. The next three chapters address liabilities classified as long term.

We often characterize current liabilities as obligations payable within one year or within the firm's operating cycle, whichever is longer. This general definition usually applies. However, a more discriminating definition identifies current liabilities as those expected to be satisfied with *current assets* or by the creation of other *current liabilities.*[3]

As you study the liabilities discussed in this chapter, you should be aware that a practical expediency usually affects the way current liabilities are reported on the balance sheet. Conceptually, liabilities should be recorded at their present values. In other words, the amount recorded is the present value of all anticipated future cash payments resulting from the debt (specifically, principal and interest payments). This is due to the time value of money.[4] However, in practice, liabilities payable within one year ordinarily are recorded instead at their maturity amounts.[5] The inconsistency usually is inconsequential because the relatively short-term maturity of current liabilities makes the interest or time value component immaterial.

The most common obligations reported as current liabilities are accounts payable, notes payable, commercial paper, income tax liability, accrued liabilities, and contingencies. Liabilities related to income taxes are the subject of Chapter 16. We discuss the others here.

Before we examine specific current liabilities, let's use the current liability section of the balance sheet of General Mills, Inc., and related disclosure notes to overview the chapter and to provide perspective on the liabilities we discuss (Graphic 13–1 on the next page).

---

[2]Ibid.

[3]Committee on Accounting Procedure, American Institute of CPAs, *Accounting Research and Terminology Bulletin, Final Edition* (New York: AICPA, August 1961), p. 21.

[4]You learned the concept of the time value of money and the mechanics of present value calculations in Chapter 6.

[5]In fact, those arising in connection with suppliers in the normal course of business and due within a year are specifically exempted from present value reporting by "Interest on Receivables and Payables," *Accounting Principles Board Opinion No. 21* (New York: AICPA, August 1971), par. 3.

GRAPHIC 13–1
Current Liabilities—
General Mills

In practice, there is little uniformity regarding precise captions used to describe current liabilities or in the extent to which accounts are combined into summary captions. These are representative and fairly typical.

Amounts reported on the face of the balance sheet seldom are sufficient to adequately describe current liabilities. Additional descriptions are provided in disclosure notes.

GENERAL MILLS, INC.
Excerpt from Balance Sheet ($ in millions)
May 27, 2001 and May 28, 2000

Liabilities

Current Liabilities:	2001	2000
Accounts payable	$ 619.1	$ 641.5
Current portion of long-term debt	349.4	413.5
Notes payable	857.9	1,085.8
Accrued taxes	111.1	104.9
Accrued payroll	141.7	142.4
Other current liabilities	129.6	141.0
Total current liabilities	$2,208.8	$2,529.1

8. Notes Payable

The components of notes payable and their respective weighted average interest rates at the end of the period are as follows:

	2001		2000	
Dollars in millions:	Note Payable	Weighted Average Interest Rate	Note Payable	Weighted Average Interest Rate
U.S. commercial paper	$ 733.1	4.4%	$1,043.2	6.3%
Canadian commercial paper	26.8	4.6	23.4	5.5
Euro commercial paper	768.0	4.9	43.0	4.2
Financial institutions	330.0	4.4	456.2	6.3
Amount reclassified to long-term debt	(1,000.0)	—	(480.0)	—
Total notes payable	$ 857.9		$1,085.8	

    To ensure availability of funds, we maintain bank credit lines sufficient to cover our outstanding short-term borrowings. As of May 27, 2001, we had $2 billion fee-paid lines and $12.9 million uncommitted, no-fee lines available in the U.S. and Canada.

    We have a revolving credit agreement expiring in January 2006 covering the fee-paid credit lines that provides us with the ability to refinance short-term borrowings on a long-term basis; accordingly, a portion of our notes payable has been reclassified to long-term debt.

    You may want to refer back to portions of Graphic 13–1 as corresponding liabilities are described later in the chapter. We discuss accounts payable and notes payable first.

Open Accounts and Notes

Many businesses buy merchandise or supplies on credit. Most also find it desirable to borrow cash from time to time to finance their activities. In this section we discuss the liabilities these borrowing activities create: namely, trade accounts and trade notes, bank loans, and commercial paper.

ACCOUNTS PAYABLE AND TRADE NOTES PAYABLE

Buying merchandise on account in the ordinary course of business creates *accounts payable*.

Accounts payable are obligations to suppliers of merchandise or of services purchased on *open account*. Most trade credit is offered on open account. This means that the only formal credit instrument is the invoice. Because the time until payment usually is short (often 30, 45, or 60 days), these liabilities typically are noninterest-bearing and are reported at their face amounts. As shown in Graphic 13–1, General Mills's second largest current liability in

2001 was accounts payable, $619.1 million. The key accounting considerations relating to accounts payable are determining their existence and ensuring that they are recorded in the appropriate accounting period. You studied these issues and learned how cash discounts are handled during your study of inventories in Chapter 8.

Trade notes payable differ from accounts payable in that they are formally recognized by a written promissory note. Often these are of a somewhat longer term than open accounts and sometimes they bear interest.

> About 30% of General Mills's current liabilities are in the form of trade credit.

SHORT-TERM NOTES PAYABLE

The most common way for a corporation to obtain temporary financing is to arrange a short-term bank loan. When a company borrows cash from a bank and signs a promissory note (essentially an IOU), the firm's liability is reported as *notes payable* (sometimes *bank loans* or *short-term borrowings*). About two-thirds of bank loans are short term, but because many are routinely renewed, some tend to resemble long-term debt. In fact, in some cases we report them as long-term financing (as you'll see later in the chapter).

Very often, smaller firms are unable to tap into the major sources of long-term financing to the extent necessary to provide for their capital needs. So they must rely heavily on short-term financing. Even large companies typically utilize short-term debt as a significant and indispensable component of their capital structure. One reason is that short-term funds usually offer lower interest rates than long-term debt. Perhaps most importantly, corporations desire flexibility. As a rule, managers want as many financing alternatives as possible.

Credit Lines.   Usually short-term bank loans are arranged under an existing **line of credit** with a bank or group of banks. These can be noncommitted or committed lines of credit. A *noncommitted* line of credit is an informal agreement that permits a company to borrow up to a prearranged limit without having to follow formal loan procedures and paperwork. Banks sometimes require the company to maintain a compensating balance on deposit with the bank, say, 5% of the line of credit.[6] The 2000 annual report of Campbell Soup Company illustrates a noncommitted line of credit (Graphic 13–2).

> A *line of credit* allows a company to borrow cash without having to follow formal loan procedures and paperwork.

Note 17: Notes Payable and Long-Term Debt (in part) ($ in millions)
The Company has total short-term lines of credit of $1,800 at July 30, 2000. These lines of credit remain unused at July 30, 2000 and include a $1,500 facility which supports commercial paper borrowings. These lines of credit are unconditional for a period of one to two years.

> GRAPHIC 13–2
> Disclosure of Short-Term Borrowings—Campbell Soup Company

A *committed* line of credit is a more formal agreement that usually requires the firm to pay a commitment fee to the bank. A typical annual commitment fee is ¼% of the total committed funds. Banks often require smaller firms to keep compensating balances in the bank. A recent disclosure note of the Black & Decker Corporation describes a committed line of credit as shown in Graphic 13–3.

> A *committed* line of credit is a formal arrangement usually requiring a commitment fee and sometimes a compensating balance.

> GRAPHIC 13–3
> Disclosure of Committed Line of Credit—Black and Decker Corporation

---

Note 5: Short-Term Borrowings (in part)
The Corporation also has a revolving credit facility in the amount of $90,000,000 with several commercial banks. This facility is at various interest rates at the Corporation's option based on the prime London interbank borrowing, certificates of deposit, bankers' acceptance, or other negotiated rates; and it also can be used to support the issuance of commercial paper in the United States and in European markets through dealers at the best available open market rates. Commitment fees are .25% on the unused balance during the availability period.

---

[6]A compensating balance is a deposit kept by a company in a low-interest or noninterest-bearing account at the bank. The required deposit usually is some percentage of the committed amount or the amount used (say, 2% to 5%). The effect of the compensating balance is to increase the borrower's effective interest rate and the bank's effective rate of return.

General Mills's disclosure notes that we looked at in Graphic 13–1 indicate that the company has both noncommitted and committed lines of credit.

Interest. When a company borrows money, it pays the lender interest in return for using the lender's money during the term of the loan. You might think of the interest as the "rent" paid for using money. Interest is stated in terms of a percentage rate to be applied to the face amount of the loan. Because the stated rate typically is an annual rate, when calculating interest for a short-term note we must adjust for the fraction of the annual period the loan spans. Interest on notes is calculated as:

$$\text{Face amount} \times \text{Annual rate} \times \text{Time to maturity}$$

This is demonstrated in Illustration 13–1.

ILLUSTRATION 13–1	On May 1, 2003, Affiliated Technologies, Inc., a consumer electronics firm borrowed $700,000 cash from First BancCorp under a noncommitted short-term line of credit arrangement and issued a six-month, 12% promissory note. Interest was payable at maturity.		
Note Issued for Cash			
	May 1, 2003		
LO2	Cash..	700,000	
	Notes payable		700,000
Interest on notes is calculated as:	**November 1, 2003**		
Face × Annual × Time to amount rate maturity	Interest expense ($700,000 × 12% × ⁶⁄₁₂)).....................	42,000	
	Notes payable........................	700,000	
	Cash ($700,000 + 42,000).............................		742,000

Sometimes a bank loan assumes the form of a so-called **noninterest-bearing note.** Obviously, though, no bank will lend money without interest. Noninterest-bearing loans actually do bear interest, but the interest is deducted (or discounted) from the face amount to determine the cash proceeds made available to the borrower at the outset. For example, the preceding note could be packaged as a $700,000 noninterest-bearing note, with a 12% discount rate. In that case, the $42,000 interest would be discounted at the outset, rather than explicitly stated:[7]

The proceeds of the note are reduced by the interest in a noninterest-bearing note.

May 1, 2003		
Cash (difference)	658,000	
Discount on notes payable ($700,000 × 12% × ⁶⁄₁₂)).............	42,000	
Notes payable (face amount)		700,000
November 1, 2003		
Interest expense	42,000	
Discount on notes payable		42,000
Notes payable (face amount)...............................	700,000	
Cash..		700,000

---

[7]Be sure to understand that we are actually recording the note at $658,000, not $700,000, but are recording the interest portion separately in a contra-liability account, discount on notes payable. The entries shown reflect the gross method. By the net method, the interest component is netted against the face amount of the note as follows:

May 1, 2003		
Cash	658,000	
Notes payable		658,000
November 1, 2003		
Interest expense ($700,000 × 12% × ⁶⁄₁₂)	42,000	
Notes payable	658,000	
Cash		700,000

Notice that the amount borrowed under this arrangement is only $658,000, but the interest is calculated as the discount rate times the $700,000 face amount. This causes the *effective* interest rate to be higher than the 12% stated rate:

$$\frac{\$42,000 \text{ Interest for 6 months}}{\$658,000 \text{ Amount borrowed}} = 6.38\% \text{ Rate for 6 months}$$

To annualize:

$$6.38\% \times {}^{12}\!/_{6} = 12.76\% \text{ Effective interest rate}$$

We studied short-term notes from the perspective of the lender (note receivable) in Chapter 7.

> When interest is discounted from the face amount of a note, the effective interest rate is higher than the stated discount rate.

Secured Loans.   Sometimes short-term loans are *secured,* meaning a specified asset of the borrower is pledged as collateral or security for the loan. Although many kinds of assets can be pledged, the secured loans most frequently encountered in practice are secured by inventory or accounts receivable. For example, Collins Industries, Inc., which sells vehicle chassis to major vehicle manufacturers, disclosed the secured notes described in Graphic 13–4.

> Inventory or accounts receivable often are pledged as security for short-term loans.

Note 4: Chassis Floorplan Notes Payable (in part)
Chassis floorplan notes are payable to a financing subsidiary of a chassis manufacturer. These notes are secured by the related chassis and are payable upon the earlier of the date the Company sells the chassis or 180 days from the date of the note.

> **GRAPHIC 13–4**
> Disclosure of Notes Secured by Inventory—Collins Industries, Inc.

When accounts receivable serve as collateral, we refer to the arrangement as *pledging* accounts receivable. Sometimes, the receivables actually are sold outright to a finance company as a means of short-term financing. This is called *factoring* receivables.[8]

GLOBAL   PERSPECTIVE

The financial market is becoming increasingly multinational. World markets have grown dramatically in the last decade. The commercial unification of European countries, the introduction of the Euro, and the fall of communism in portions of Europe and Asia are both causes and symptoms of the heightened globalization of the capital marketplace.

Companies wishing to reduce their exposure to risk and to widen their choices of funding sources are taking advantage of the broader opportunities the global environment provides. Increasingly, U.S. corporate debt is displaying a multinational dimension, with statements of financial position often reporting short-term to intermediate-term loans in several different countries. Loans from foreign banks that are denominated in dollars are called Eurodollar loans. Also, foreign loans frequently are denominated in the currency of the lender (Swiss franc, Euro, and so on). When loans must be repaid in foreign currencies a new element of risk is introduced. This is because if exchange rates change, the number of dollars representing the foreign currency that must be repaid differs from the number of dollars representing the foreign currency borrowed. We discuss hedging against this risk exposure in the next chapter.[9]

> Corporations often have loans from banks in many different countries.

---

[8]Both methods of accounts receivable financing were discussed in Chapter 7, "Cash and Receivables."
[9]Elsewhere in your accounting curriculum, often in advanced accounting, you will learn how foreign-currency-denominated loans are translated into dollars in U.S. financial statements.

Large, highly rated firms sometimes sell *commercial paper* to borrow funds at a lower rate than through a bank loan.

FINANCIAL REPORTING CASE
Q1, p. 618

COMMERCIAL PAPER

Some large corporations obtain temporary financing by issuing **commercial paper,** often purchased by other companies as a short-term investment. Commercial paper refers to unsecured notes sold in minimum denominations of $25,000 with maturities ranging from 30 to 270 days (beyond 270 days the firm would be required to file a registration statement with the SEC). Interest often is discounted at the issuance of the note. Usually commercial paper is issued directly to the buyer (lender) and is backed by a line of credit with a bank (see the Black & Decker disclosure note in Graphic 13–3). This allows the interest rate to be lower than in a bank loan. Commercial paper has become an increasingly popular way for large companies to raise funds, the total amount having expanded over fivefold in the last decade.

The name *commercial paper* refers to the fact that a paper certificate traditionally is issued to the lender to signify the obligation, although there is a trend toward total computerization of paper sold directly to the lender so that no paper is created. Since commercial paper is a form of notes payable, recording its issuance and payment is exactly the same as our earlier illustration.

In a statement of cash flows, the cash a company receives from using notes to borrow funds as well as the cash it uses to repay the notes are reported among cash flows from financing activities. Most of the other liabilities we study in this chapter are integrally related to a company's primary operations and thus are part of operating activities. We discuss long-term notes in the next chapter.

Accrued Liabilities

Accrued liabilities represent expenses already incurred but not yet paid (accrued expenses). These liabilities are recorded by adjusting entries at the end of the reporting period, prior to preparing financial statements. You learned how to record accrued liabilities in your study of introductory accounting and you reinforced your understanding in Chapter 2. Common examples are salaries and wages payable, income taxes payable, and interest payable.

ACCRUED INTEREST PAYABLE

Liabilities accrue for expenses that are incurred but not yet paid.

Accrued interest payable arises in connection with notes like those discussed earlier in this chapter (as well as other forms of debt). For example, to continue Illustration 13–1, let's assume the fiscal period for Affiliated Technologies ends on June 30, two months after the six-month note is issued. The issuance of the note, intervening adjusting entry, and note payment would be recorded as shown in Illustration 13–1A.

ILLUSTRATION 13–1A

ILLUSTRATION 13–1A

Note with Accrued Interest

At June 30, two months' interest has accrued and is recorded to avoid misstating expenses and liabilities on the June 30 financial statements.

Issuance of Note on May 1, 2003		
Cash.	700,000	
Note payable.		700,000
Accrual of Interest on June 30, 2003		
Interest expense ($700,000 × 12% × 2/12).	14,000	
Interest payable.		14,000
Note Payment on November 1, 2003		
Interest expense ($700,000 × 12% × 4/12).	28,000	
Interest payable (from adjusting entry).	14,000	
Note payable.	700,000	
Cash ($700,000 + 42,000).		742,000

SALARIES, COMMISSIONS, AND BONUSES

Compensation for employee services can be in the form of hourly wages, salary, commissions, bonuses, stock compensation plans, or pensions.[10] Accrued liabilities arise in

---

[10]Pensions are discussed in Chapter 17, and stock-based compensation plans, compensated absences, and bonuses are discussed in Chapter 18.

connection with compensation expense when employee services have been performed as of a financial statement date, but employees have yet to be paid. These accrued expenses/accrued liabilities are recorded by adjusting entries at the end of the reporting period, prior to preparing financial statements.

Liabilities from Advance Collections

Liabilities are created when amounts are received that will be returned or remitted to others. Deposits and advances from customers and collections for third parties are cases in point.

DEPOSITS AND ADVANCES FROM CUSTOMERS

Collecting cash from a customer as a refundable deposit or as an advance payment for products or services creates a liability to return the deposit or to supply the products or services.[11]

Refundable Deposits.   In some businesses it's typical to require customers to pay cash as a deposit that will be refunded when a specified event occurs. You probably have encountered such situations. When apartments are rented, security or damage deposits often are collected. Utility companies frequently collect deposits when service is begun. Similarly, deposits sometimes are required on returnable containers, to be refunded when the containers are returned. The situation is demonstrated in Illustration 13–2.

Rancor Chemical Company sells combustible chemicals in expensive, reusable containers. Customers are charged a deposit for each container delivered and receive a refund when the container is returned. Deposits collected on containers delivered in 2003 were $300,000. Deposits are forfeited if containers are not returned within one year. Ninety percent of the containers were returned within the allotted time. Deposits charged are twice the actual cost of containers. The inventory of containers remains on the company's books until deposits are forfeited.		**ILLUSTRATION 13–2** Refundable Deposits

When Deposits Are Collected		
Cash.	300,000	
Liability—refundable deposits.		300,000
When Containers Are Returned*		
Liability—refundable deposits	270,000	
Cash.		270,000
When Deposits Are Forfeited*		
Liability—refundable deposits	30,000	
Revenue—sale of containers.		30,000
Cost of goods sold	15,000	
Inventory of containers		15,000

When a deposit becomes nonrefundable, inventory should be reduced to reflect the fact that the containers won't be returned.

*Of course, not all containers are returned at the same time, nor does the allotted return period expire at the same time for all containers not returned. These entries summarize the several individual returns and forfeitures.

Advances from Customers.   At times, businesses require advance payments from customers that will be applied to the purchase price when goods are delivered or services provided. Gift certificates, magazine subscriptions, layaway deposits, special order deposits, and airline tickets are examples. These customer advances represent liabilities until the related product or service is provided. For instance, one of the largest liabilities reported by Readers Digest Association, Inc., is deferred revenue from the sale of magazine subscriptions ($289.4 million in 2000). Advances are demonstrated in Illustration 13–3.

---

[11]*SFAC 6* specifically identifies customer advances and deposits as liabilities under the definition provided in that statement. "Elements of Financial Statements," *Statement of Financial Accounting Concepts No. 6* (Stamford, CT: FASB, 1985), par. 197.

ILLUSTRATION 13–3
Customer Advance

Tomorrow Publications collects magazine subscriptions from customers at the time subscriptions are sold. Subscription revenue is recognized over the term of the subscription. Tomorrow collected $20 million in subscription sales during 2003, its first year of operations. At December 31, 2003, the average subscription was one-fourth expired.

($ in millions)

A customer advance produces an obligation that is satisfied when the product or service is provided.

When Advance Is Collected

Cash.	20	
Unearned subscriptions revenue.		20

When Product Is Delivered

Unearned subscriptions revenue.	5	
Subscriptions revenue		5

The New York Times Company described its recognition of revenue from newspaper subscriptions in the disclosure note shown in Graphic 13–5.

GRAPHIC 13–5
Disclosure of Advances from Customers—The New York Times Company

Note 1: Summary of Significant Accounting Policies (in part)
Proceeds from subscriptions are deferred at the times of sale as unexpired subscriptions and are included in revenues on a pro rata basis over the terms of the subscriptions.

Like refundable deposits, customer advances forfeited (for instance, gift certificates not redeemed) create revenue when they are deemed forfeited. Liability accounts produced by customer deposits and advances are classified as current or long-term liabilities depending on when the obligation is expected to be satisfied.

COLLECTIONS FOR THIRD PARTIES

Companies often make collections for third parties from customers or from employees and periodically remit these amounts to the appropriate governmental (or other) units. Amounts collected this way represent liabilities until remitted.

An example is sales taxes. For illustration, assume a state sales tax rate of 4% and local sales tax rate of 3%. Adding the tax to a $100 sale creates a $7 liability until the tax is paid:

Sales taxes collected from customers represent liabilities until remitted.

Cash (or accounts receivable)	107	
Sales revenue.		100
Sales taxes payable ([4% + 3%] × $100)		7

Amounts collected from employees in connection with payroll also represent liabilities until remitted.

Payroll-related deductions such as withholding taxes, Social Security taxes, employee insurance, employee contributions to retirement plans, and union dues also create current liabilities until the amounts collected are paid to appropriate parties. These payroll-related liabilities are explored further in the appendix to this chapter.

Although recorded in separate liability accounts, accrued liabilities usually are combined and reported under a single caption or perhaps two accrued liability captions in the balance sheet.

CHECK WITH THE **COACH**

Beginning in this chapter, we shift our focus to the right-hand side of the balance sheet. Specifically, you will learn about the diverse nature of liabilities and their financial reporting consequences. Check with the Coach to nail down the key factors we consider to account appropriately for liabilities. Learn practical aspects of liability reporting from the expert viewpoint of managers, lenders, and financial analysts. ■

A Closer Look at the Current and Noncurrent Classification

Given a choice, do you suppose management would prefer to report an obligation as a current liability or as a noncurrent liability? Other things being equal, most would choose the noncurrent classification. The reason is that in most settings outsiders (like banks, bondholders, and shareholders) consider debt that is payable currently to be riskier than debt that need not be paid for some time. Relatedly, the long-term classification enables the company to report higher working capital (current assets minus current liabilities) and a higher current ratio (current assets/current liabilities). Working capital and the current ratio often are explicitly restricted in loan contracts. As you study this section, you should view the classification choice from this perspective. That is, the question is not so much "What amount should be reported as a current liability?" but rather "What amount can be excluded from classification as a current liability?"

CURRENT MATURITIES OF LONG-TERM DEBT

Long-term obligations (bonds, notes, lease liabilities, deferred tax liabilities) usually are reclassified and reported as current liabilities when they become payable within the upcoming year (or operating cycle, if longer than a year). For example, a 20-year bond issue is reported as a long-term liability for 19 years but normally is reported as a current liability on the balance sheet prepared during the 20th year of its term to maturity.[12] General Mills reported $349.4 million of its long-term debt as a current liability in 2001 (see Graphic 13–1, page 620).

OBLIGATIONS CALLABLE BY THE CREDITOR

The requirement to classify currently maturing debt as a current liability includes debt that is *callable* (in other words, due on demand) *by the creditor* in the upcoming year (or operating cycle, if longer), even if the debt is not expected to be called. The current liability classification also is intended to include situations in which the creditor has the right to demand payment because an *existing violation* of a provision of the debt agreement makes it callable (say, working capital has fallen below a contractual minimum). This also includes situations in which debt is not yet callable but will be callable within the year if an existing violation is not corrected within a specified grace period (unless it's probable the violation will be corrected within the grace period or waived by the creditor).[13]

WHEN SHORT-TERM OBLIGATIONS ARE EXPECTED TO BE REFINANCED

Reconsider the 20-year bond issue we discussed earlier. Normally we would reclassify it as a current liability on the balance sheet prepared during its 20th year. But suppose a second 20-year bond issue is sold specifically to refund the first issue when it matures. Do we have a long-term liability for 19 years, a current liability for a year, and then another long-term liability? Or, do we have a single 40-year, long-term liability? If we look beyond the outward form of the transactions, the substance of the events obviously supports a single, continuing, noncurrent obligation. The concept of substance over form influences the classification of obligations expected to be refinanced.

Short-term obligations (including the callable obligations we discussed in the previous section) that are expected to be refinanced on a long-term basis can be reported as noncurrent, rather than current, liabilities only if two conditions are met. The firm (1) must intend to refinance on a long-term basis and (2) must actually have demonstrated the ability to do so. Ability to refinance on a long-term basis can be demonstrated by either an existing refinancing agreement or by actual financing prior to the issuance of the financial statements.[14] An example will provide perspective (Illustration 13–4 on the next page).

FINANCIAL REPORTING CASE

Q2, p. 618

The currently maturing portion of a long-term debt must be reported as a current liability.

Long-term liabilities that are due on demand—by terms of the contract or violation of contract covenants—must be reported as current liabilities.

FINANCIAL REPORTING CASE

Q3, p. 618

Short-term obligations can be reported as noncurrent liabilities if the company (a) *intends* to refinance on a long-term basis and (b) demonstrates the *ability* to do so by a refinancing agreement or by actual financing.

---

[12]Debt to be refinanced is an exception we discuss later.

[13]"Classification of Obligations That Are Callable by the Creditor," *Statement of Financial Accounting Standards No. 78* (Stamford, Conn.: FASB, 1983).

[14]"Classification of Obligations Expected to Be Refinanced," *Statement of Financial Accounting Standards No. 6* (Stamford, Conn.: FASB, 1975).

ILLUSTRATION 13–4	Brahm Bros. Ice Cream had $12 million of notes that mature in May 2004 and also had $4 million of bonds issued in 1978 that mature in February 2004. On December 31, 2003, the company's fiscal year-end, management intended to refinance both on a long-term basis.
Short-Term Obligations That Are Expected to Be Refinanced on a Long-Term Basis	On February 7, 2004, the company issued $4 million of 20-year bonds, applying the proceeds to repay the bond issue that matured that month. In early March, prior to the actual issuance of the 2003 financial statements, Brahm Bros. negotiated a line of credit with a commercial bank for up to $7 million any time during 2004. Any borrowings will mature two years from the date of borrowing. Interest is at the prime London interbank borrowing rate.*

	December 31, 2003
Classification	($ in 000s)
Current Liabilities	
Notes payable	$5,000
Long-Term Liabilities	
Notes payable	$7,000
Bonds payable	4,000

Management's ability to refinance the bonds on a long-term basis was demonstrated by actual financing prior to the issuance of the financial statements. Ability to refinance $7 million of the notes is demonstrated by a refinancing agreement. The remaining $5 million must be reported as a current liability.

*This is a widely available rate often used as a basis for establishing interest rates on lines of credit.

If shares of stock had been issued to refinance the bonds in the illustration, the bonds still would be excluded from classification as a current liability. The specific form of the long-term refinancing (bonds, bank loans, equity securities) is irrelevant when determining the appropriate classification. Requiring companies to actually demonstrate the ability to refinance on a long-term basis in addition to merely intending to do so avoids intentional or unintentional understatements of current liabilities.

It's important to remember that several weeks usually pass between the end of a company's fiscal year and the date the financial statements for that year actually are issued. Events occurring during that period can be used to clarify the nature of financial statement elements at the reporting date. Here we consider refinancing agreements and actual securities transactions to support a company's ability to refinance on a long-term basis. Later in the chapter we use information that becomes available during this period to decide how loss contingencies are reported.

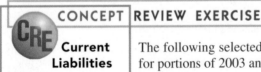

CONCEPT REVIEW EXERCISE

Current Liabilities

The following selected transactions relate to liabilities of Southern Communications, Inc., for portions of 2003 and 2004. Southern's fiscal year ends on December 31.

Required:
Prepare the appropriate journal entries for these transactions.

2003

July	1	Arranged an uncommitted short-term line of credit with First City Bank amounting to $25,000,000 at the bank's prime rate (11.5% in July). The company will pay no commitment fees for this arrangement.
Aug.	9	Received a $30,000 refundable deposit from a major customer for copper-lined mailing containers used to transport communications equipment.
Oct.	7	Received most of the mailing containers covered by the refundable deposit and a letter stating that the customer will retain containers represented by $2,000 of the deposit and forfeits that amount. The cost of the forfeited containers was $1,500.

Nov.   1   Borrowed $7 million cash from First City Bank under the line of credit arranged in July and issued a nine-month promissory note. Interest at the prime rate of 12% was payable at maturity.

Dec.   31   Recorded appropriate adjusting entries for the liabilities described above.

2004

Feb.   12   Using the unused portion of the credit line as support, issued $9 million of commercial paper and issued a six-month promissory note. Interest was discounted at issuance at a 10% discount rate.

Aug.   1   Paid the 12% note at maturity.

    12   Paid the commercial paper at maturity.

2003

SOLUTION

July 1

No entry is made for a line of credit until a loan actually is made. The existence and terms of the line would be described in a disclosure note.

August 9

Cash.	30,000	
Liability—refundable deposits.		30,000

October 7

Liability—refundable deposits	30,000	
Cash.		28,000
Revenue—sale of containers		2,000
Cost of goods sold	1,500	
Inventory of containers		1,500

November 1

Cash.	7,000,000	
Notes payable		7,000,000

December 31

Interest expense ($7,000,000 $\times$ 12% $\times$ $^2/_{12}$)	140,000	
Interest payable.		140,000

2004

February 12

Cash ($9,000,000 − [$9,000,000 $\times$ 10% $\times$ $^6/_{12}$]).	8,550,000	
Discount on notes payable (difference).	450,000	
Note payable.		9,000,000

Note that the effective interest rate is [($9,000,000 $\times$ 10% $\times$ $^6/_{12}$) $\div$ $8,550,000] $\times$ $^{12}/_6$ = $450,000 $\div$ $8,550,000 $\times$ 2 = 10.53%.

August 1

Interest expense ($7,000,000 $\times$ 12% $\times$ $^7/_{12}$)	490,000	
Interest payable (from adjusting entry).	140,000	
Note payable (face amount).	7,000,000	
Cash ($7,000,000 + $630,000)		7,630,000

August 12

Interest expense ($9,000,000 $\times$ 10% $\times$ $^6/_{12}$)	450,000	
Discount on notes payable		450,000
Note payable (face amount).	9,000,000	
Cash ($8,550,000 + $450,000)		9,000,000

CONTINGENCIES

The feature that distinguishes the contingencies we discuss in this part of the chapter from the liabilities we discussed previously is uncertainty as to whether an obligation really exists. The existing uncertainty will be resolved only when some future event occurs (or doesn't occur). We will discuss gain contingencies, too, because of their similarity to loss contingencies.

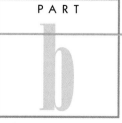

PART

b

Loss Contingencies

Ford Motor Company's financial statements recently indicated potential obligations from pending lawsuits (shown in Graphic 13–6).

GRAPHIC 13–6
Disclosure of Pending
Litigation—Ford Motor
Company

Note 12: Litigation and Claims (in part)
Various legal actions, governmental investigations and proceedings and claims are pending or may be instituted or asserted in the future against the company and its subsidiaries, including those arising out of alleged defects in the company's products, governmental regulations relating to safety, emissions and fuel economy, financial services, intellectual property rights, product warranties and environmental matters. Certain of the pending legal actions are, or purport to be, class actions. Some of the foregoing matters involve or may involve compensatory, punitive, or antitrust or other treble damage claims in very large amounts, or demands for recall campaigns, environmental remediation programs, sanctions, or other relief which, if granted, would require very large expenditures.

The disclosure indicates that if certain events occur, "very large expenditures" would result. Do these contingencies represent liabilities of Ford? Certainly the liabilities *may* exist on the date of the financial statements. But how likely is an unfavorable outcome? Also, precise amounts of any obligations Ford may have are unknown. But can the amounts be estimated? These are the key questions addressed by accounting standards for loss contingencies.

A loss contingency is an existing, uncertain situation involving potential loss depending on whether some future event occurs. Whether a contingency is accrued and reported as a liability depends on (a) the likelihood that the confirming event will occur and (b) what can be determined about the amount of loss. Consider an IRS assessment of additional income taxes for prior years, pending at year-end, for which the outcome will not be known until after the financial statements are issued. We must assess the likelihood that the company will pay the back taxes and if so, how much they will pay.

> A *loss contingency* involves an existing uncertainty as to whether a loss really exists, where the uncertainty will be resolved only when some future event occurs.

Note that the cause of the uncertainty must occur before the statement date. In this case, the prior years' operations for which the tax liability is questioned occurred before the current accounting period ended. Otherwise, regardless of the likelihood of the eventual outcome, no liability could have existed at the statement date. Recall that one of the essential characteristics of a liability is that it results "from past transactions or events."

Accounting standards require that the likelihood that the future event(s) will confirm the incurrence of the liability be (somewhat arbitrarily) categorized as probable, reasonably possible, or remote:[15]

> **FINANCIAL REPORTING** CASE
>
> Q4, p. 618
>
> *Likelihood That a Liability Exists*

Probable—Confirming event is likely to occur.
Reasonably possible—The chance the confirming event will occur is more than remote but less than likely.
Remote—The chance the confirming event will occur is slight.

Also key to reporting a contingent liability is its dollar amount. The amount of the potential loss is classified as either known, reasonably estimable, or not reasonably estimable. A liability is accrued if it is both probable that the confirming event will occur and the amount can be at least reasonably estimated. A general depiction of the accrual of a loss contingency is:

> *Accrual of a Loss Contingency—Liability*

Loss (or expense)	x,xxx	
Liability		x,xxx

---

[15]"Accounting for Contingencies," *Statement of Financial Accounting Standards No. 5* (Stamford, Conn.: FASB, 1975).

ADDITIONAL CONSIDERATION

If one amount within a range of possible loss appears better than other amounts within the range, that amount is accrued. When no amount within the range appears more likely than others, the *minimum* amount should be *recorded* and the possible *additional loss* should be *disclosed.*[16]

In a recent annual report (Graphic 13–7), Union Pacific reported a loss contingency it had accrued for a claim against it by government agencies for which the company deemed payment was both probable and reasonably estimable.

GRAPHIC 13–7
Accrual of Loss Contingency—Union Pacific

12. Commitments and Contingencies (in part)
The Corporation is also subject to federal, state and local environmental laws and regulations, pursuant to which it is currently participating in the investigation and remediation of numerous sites. For environmental sites where remediation costs can be reasonably determined, and where such remediation is probable, the Corporation has recorded a liability. At December 31, 2000, the Corporation had accrued $177 million for estimated future environmental costs.

It's important to note that some loss contingencies don't involve liabilities at all. Some contingencies when resolved cause a noncash asset to be impaired, so accruing it means reducing the related asset rather than recording a liability:

Accrual of a Loss Contingency—Asset Impairment

Loss (or expense)	x,xxx	
Asset (or valuation account)		x,xxx

The most common loss contingency of this type is an uncollectible receivable. You have recorded these before without knowing you were accruing a loss contingency (*Debit:* bad debt expense; *Credit:* allowance for uncollectible accounts).

If one or both of these criteria is not met, but there is at least a reasonable possibility that the loss will occur, a disclosure note should describe the contingency. It also should provide an estimate of the possible loss or range of loss, if possible. If an estimate cannot be made, a statement to that effect is needed.

Varian Medical Systems, Inc. designs and manufactures cancer therapy systems. VMS felt that the loss contingency from an investment was reasonably possible and accordingly did not accrue a liability but provided the information noted in Graphic 13–8.

A loss contingency is disclosed in notes to the financial statements if there is at least a reasonable possibility that the loss will occur.

GRAPHIC 13–8
Disclosure of Loss Contingency—VMS, Inc.

Note 9 (in part)
. . . we agreed to invest $5 million in a consortium to participate in the acquisition of a minority interest in dpiX LLC ("dpiX"), which supplies us with amorphous silicon based thin-film transistor arrays. Based on information provided by dpiX, management currently believes it is reasonably possible that we will recognize a loss of up to $5 million on this investment beginning in the fourth quarter of fiscal year 2001 and continuing through fiscal year 2002.

Graphic 13–9 on the next page highlights appropriate accounting treatment for each possible combination of (a) the likelihood of an obligation's being confirmed and (b) the determinability of its dollar amount.

---

[16]"Reasonable Estimation of the Amount of the Loss," *FASB Interpretation No. 14* (Stamford, Conn.: FASB, 1976).

A loss contingency is
accrued only if a loss is
probable and the
amount can reasonably
be estimated.

	Dollar Amount of Potential Loss		
Likelihood	Known	Reasonably Estimable	Not Reasonably Estimable
Probable	Liability accrued and disclosure note	Liability accrued and disclosure note	Disclosure note only
Reasonably possible	Disclosure note only	Disclosure note only	Disclosure note only
Remote	No disclosure required*	No disclosure required*	No disclosure required*

*Except for certain guarantees and other specified off-balance-sheet risk situations discussed in the next chapter.

PRODUCT WARRANTIES AND GUARANTEES

Manufacturer's Original Warranty.   Satisfaction guaranteed! Your money back if not satisfied! If anything goes wrong in the first five years or 50,000 miles . . . ! Three-year guarantee! These and similar promises accompany most consumer goods. The reason—to boost sales. It follows, then, that any costs of making good on such guarantees should be recorded as expenses in the same accounting period the products are sold (matching principle). The obstacle is that much of the cost usually occurs later, sometimes years later. This is a loss contingency. There may be a future sacrifice of economic benefits (cost of satisfying the guarantee) due to an existing circumstance (the guaranteed products have been sold) that depends on an uncertain future event (customer claim).

Most consumer
products are
accompanied by a
guarantee.

    As you might expect, meeting the accrual criteria is more likely for some types of loss contingencies than for others. For instance, the outcome of pending litigation is particularly difficult to predict. On the other hand, the criteria for accrual almost always are met for some types of loss contingencies. Product warranties (or product guarantees) inevitably entail costs. And while we usually can't predict the liability associated with an individual sale, reasonably accurate estimates of the *total* liability for a period usually are possible, based on prior experience. So the contingent liability for warranties and guarantees usually is accrued. The estimated warranty (guarantee) liability is credited and warranty (guarantee) expense is debited in the reporting period in which the product under warranty is sold. This is demonstrated in Illustration 13–5.

The contingent liability
for product warranties
almost always is
accrued.

ILLUSTRATION 13–5 Product Warranty	Caldor Health, a supplier of in-home health care products, introduced a new therapeutic chair carrying a two-year warranty against defects. Estimates based on industry experience indicate warranty costs of 3% of sales during the first 12 months following the sale and 4% the next 12 months. During December 2003, its first month of availability, Caldor sold $2 million of the chairs.

During December

Cash (and accounts receivable).............................	2,000,000	
Sales revenue...		2,000,000

December 31, 2003 (adjusting entry)

The costs of satisfying
guarantees should be
recorded as expenses
in the same
accounting period the
products are sold.

Warranty expense ([3% + 4%] × $2,000,000)...................	140,000	
Estimated warranty liability...............................		140,000

    When customer claims are made and costs are incurred to satisfy those claims, the liability is reduced (let's say $61,000 in 2004):

Estimated warranty liability.................................	61,000	
Cash, wages payable, parts and supplies, etc.		61,000

Estimates of warranty costs cannot be expected to be precise. However, if the estimating method is monitored and revised when necessary, overestimates and underestimates should cancel each other over time. The estimated liability may be classified as current or as part current and part long-term, depending on when costs are expected to be incurred.

Expected Cash Flow Approach.   In Chapter 6, you learned of a framework for using future cash flows as the basis for measuring assets and liabilities, introduced by the FASB in 2000 with *Statement of Financial Accounting Concepts No. 7*, "Using Cash Flow Information and Present Value in Accounting Measurements."[17] The approach described in the Concept Statement offers a way to take into account *any uncertainty concerning the amounts and timing of the cash flows*. Although future cash flows in many instances are contractual and certain, the amounts and timing of cash flows are less certain in other situations, such as warranty obligations.

SFAC No. 7 provides a framework for using future cash flows in accounting measurements.

As demonstrated in Illustration 13–5, the traditional way of measuring a warranty obligation is to report the "best estimate" of future cash flows, ignoring the time value of money on the basis of immateriality. However, when the warranty obligation spans more than one year and we can associate probabilities with possible cash flow outcomes, the approach described by *SFAC No. 7* offers a more plausible estimate of the warranty obligation. This new "expected cash flow approach" incorporates specific probabilities of cash flows into the analysis. In Chapter 6, we discussed the expected cash flow approach to determining present value. Illustration 13–6 on the next page provides an example.

Extended Warranty Contracts.   It's difficult these days to buy a CD player, a digital camera, a car, or almost any durable consumer product without being asked to buy an extended warranty agreement. An extended warranty provides warranty protection beyond the manufacturer's original warranty. Because an extended warranty is priced and sold separately from the warranted product, it essentially constitutes a separate sales transaction. The accounting question is "when should the revenue from the sale be recognized?"

By the accrual concept, revenue is recognized when earned, not necessarily when cash is received. Because the earning process for an extended warranty continues during the contract period, revenue should be recognized over the same period. So, revenue from separately priced extended warranty contracts is deferred as a liability at the time of sale and recognized on a straight-line basis over the contract period. Notice that this is similar to an advance payment for products or services that, as we discussed earlier, creates a liability to supply the products or services. We demonstrate accounting for extended warranties in Illustration 13–7 on the next page.

Remember that the costs incurred to satisfy customer claims under the extended warranties also will be recorded during the same three-year period, achieving a proper matching of revenues and expenses. If sufficient historical evidence indicates that the costs of satisfying customer claims will be incurred on other than a straight-line basis, revenue should be recognized by the same pattern (proportional to the costs).[18]

PREMIUMS

Cash rebates have become commonplace. Cash register receipts, bar codes, rebate coupons, or other proofs of purchase often can be mailed to the manufacturer for cash rebates. Sometimes promotional offers promise premiums other than cash (like toys, dishes, and utensils) to buyers of certain products. Of course the purpose of these premium offers is to stimulate sales. So it follows that the estimated amount of the cash rebates or the cost of noncash premiums estimated to be given out represents both an expense and an estimated liability in the

---

[17]"Using Cash Flow Information and Present Value in Accounting Measurements," *Statement of Financial Accounting Concepts No. 7* (Norwalk, Conn.: FASB, 2000). Recall that Concept Statements do not directly prescribe GAAP, but instead provide structure and direction to financial accounting.

[18]"Accounting for Separately Priced Extended Warranty and Product Maintenance Contracts," *FASB Technical Bulletin 90-1,* 1990.

ILLUSTRATION 13–6 Product Warranty	Caldor Health, a supplier of in-home health care products, introduced a new therapeutic chair carrying a two-year warranty against defects. During December of 2003, its first month of availability, Caldor sold $2 million of the chairs. Industry experience indicates the following probability distribution for the potential warranty costs:

Warranty costs	Probability
2004	
$50,000	20%
$60,000	50%
$70,000	30%
2005	
$70,000	20%
$80,000	50%
$90,000	30%

Probabilities are associated with possible cash outcomes.

An arrangement with a service firm requires that costs for the two-year warranty period be settled at the end of 2004 and 2005. The risk-free rate of interest is 5%. Applying the estimated cash flow approach, at the end of the 2003 fiscal year, Caldor would record a warranty liability (and expense) of $122,040, calculated as follows:

The probability-weighted cash outcomes provide the expected cash flows.

$50,000 × 20% =	$10,000	
60,000 × 50% =	30,000	
70,000 × 30% =	21,000	
	$61,000	
	× .95238*	$ 58,095
$70,000 × 20% =	$14,000	
80,000 × 50% =	40,000	
90,000 × 30% =	27,000	
	$81,000	
	× .90703†	73,469
		$131,564

The present value of the expected cash flows is the estimated liability.

*Present value of $1, n = 1, i = 5% (from Table 6A–2)
†Present value of $1, n = 2, i = 5% (from Table 6A–2)

December 31, 2003 (adjusting entry)

Warranty expense	131,564	
Estimated warranty liability (calculated above).		131,564

ILLUSTRATION 13–7 Extended Warranty	Brand Name Appliances sells major appliances that carry a one-year manufacturer's warranty. Customers are offered the opportunity at the time of purchase to also buy a three-year extended warranty for an additional charge. On January 3, 2003, Brand Name sold a $60 extended warranty.

The manufacturer's warranty covers 2003. Revenue from the extended warranty is recognized during the three years of the contract period.

January 3, 2003

Cash (or accounts receivable)	60	
Unearned revenue—extended warranties		60

December 31, 2004, 2005, 2006 (adjusting entries)

Unearned revenue—extended warranties	20	
Revenue—extended warranties ($60 ÷ 3)		20

reporting period the product is sold. Like a manufacturer's warranty, this loss contingency almost always meets accrual criteria. Premiums are illustrated in Illustration 13–8.

CMX Corporation offered $2 cash rebates on a particular model of hand-held hair dryers. To receive the rebate, customers must mail in a rebate certificate enclosed in the package plus the cash register receipt. Previous experience indicates that 30% of coupons will be redeemed. One million hair dryers were sold in 2003 and total payments to customers were $225,000.		**ILLUSTRATION 13–8** Premiums
Promotional expense (30% × $2 × 1,000,000) 600,000		
Estimated premium liability.............................	600,000	The costs of promotional offers should be recorded as expenses in the same accounting period the products are sold.
To record the estimated liability for premiums.		
Estimated premium liability............................. 225,000		
Cash..	225,000	
To record payments to retailers for coupons.		

The remaining liability of $375,000 is reported in the 2003 balance sheet and is reduced as future rebates are paid. The liability should be classified as current or long term depending on when future rebates are expected to be paid.

Of course, if premiums actually are included in packages of products sold, no contingent liability is created. For example, the costs of toys in Cracker Jack boxes and cereal boxes, and phone cards and compact discs in drink cartons are simply expenses of the period the product is sold, for which the amount is readily determinable.

ADDITIONAL CONSIDERATION

Cents-off coupons are a popular marketing tool. Coupons clipped from newspapers, from mail offers, or included in packages are redeemable for cash discounts at the time promoted items are purchased. Issuing the coupons creates a contingent liability to be recorded in the period the coupons are issued. However, because the hoped-for sales don't materialize until later, a question arises as to when the related expense should be recognized. Logically, since the purpose of coupon offers is to stimulate sales, the expense properly should be deferred until the coupons are redeemed (when the sales occur).

Illustration

On December 18, 2003, Craft Foods distributed coupons in newspaper inserts offering 50 cents off the purchase price of one of its cereal brands when coupons are presented to retailers. Retailers are reimbursed by Craft for the face amount of coupons plus 10% for handling. Previous experience indicates that 20% of coupons will be redeemed. Coupons issued had a total face amount of $1,000,000 and total payments to retailers in 2003 were $50,000. Retailers were paid $170,000 in 2004.

Promotional expense (redeemed in 2003)	50,000	
Cash...		50,000
To record payments to retailers for coupons in 2003.		
Deferred promotional expense (an asset)	170,000	
Estimated coupon liability		
([20% × $1,000,000 × 1.10] − $50,000)....................		170,000
To record the estimated liability for coupons in 2003.		
Estimated coupon liability..............................	170,000	
Cash...		170,000

| Promotional expense (redeemed in 2004) . . . . | 170,000 | |
| Deferred promotional expense . . . . | | 170,000 |

To record payments to retailers for coupons in 2004.

This situation, though prevalent, is not addressed by promulgated accounting standards. In practice, most firms either (a) recognize the entire expense with the liability in the period the coupons are issued, like we record premiums, or (b) recognize no liability in the period the coupons are issued, recording the expense when reimbursements are made. One reason is that the same coupons are reissued periodically, making it difficult to associate specific reimbursements with specific offers. Another reason is that the time lag between the time a merchant receives a coupon from customers and the time it's presented to the manufacturer for reimbursement prevents appropriate apportionment of the expense.

LITIGATION CLAIMS

Pending litigation similar to that disclosed by Ford in Graphic 13–6 on page 630 is not unusual. In fact, the majority of medium and large corporations annually report loss contingencies due to litigation. By far the most common disclosure is nonspecific regarding the actual litigation but uses wording similar to this contingency disclosure from an annual report of Sun Microsystems. (Graphic 13–10).

GRAPHIC 13–10
Disclosure of Litigation Contingencies—Sun Microsystems, Inc.

Note 10: Commitments and Contingencies (in part)
From time to time and in the ordinary course of business, the Company may be subject to various claims, charges, and litigation. In the opinion of management, final judgments from such pending claims, charges, and litigation, if any, against the Company would not have a material adverse effect on its consolidated financial position, results of operations, or cash flows.

In practice, accrual of a loss from pending or ongoing litigation is rare. Imagine why. Suppose you are chief financial officer of Feinz Foods. Feinz is the defendant in a $44 million class action suit. The company's legal counsel informally advises you that chances that the company will emerge victorious in the lawsuit are quite doubtful. Counsel feels the company might lose $30 million. Now suppose you decide to accrue a $30 million loss in your financial statements. Later, in the courtroom, your disclosure that Feinz management feels it is probable that the company will lose $30 million would be welcome ammunition for the opposing legal counsel. Understanding this, most companies rely on the knowledge that in today's legal environment the outcome of litigation is highly uncertain, making likelihood predictions difficult. Companies usually do not record a loss until after the ultimate settlement has been reached or negotiations for settlement are substantially completed. Instead, disclosure notes typically describe the specifics of the litigation along with whether management feels an adverse outcome would materially affect the financial position of the company. As you can see in Graphic 13–11, ExxonMobil Corporation, in a recent quarterly

GRAPHIC 13–11
Disclosure of a Lawsuit—ExxonMobil

17. Litigation and Other Contingencies (in part)
On May 22, 2001, a state court jury in New Orleans, Louisiana, returned a verdict against the corporation and three other entities in a case brought by a landowner claiming damage to his property. The jury awarded the plaintiff $56 million in compensatory damages and $1 billion in punitive damages. The award has been affirmed by the trial court, and the corporation is in the process of taking an appeal to the Louisiana Fourth Circuit Court of Appeals. The ultimate outcome is not expected to have a materially adverse effect upon the corporation's operations or financial condition.

report, disclosed but did not accrue damages from a lawsuit it lost, even after the award was affirmed by trial court, because the company was appealing the verdict.

SUBSEQUENT EVENTS

It's important to remember several weeks usually pass between the end of a company's fiscal year and the date the financial statements for that year actually are issued. Events occurring during this period can be used to clarify the nature of financial statement elements at the report date. This situation can be represented by the following time line:

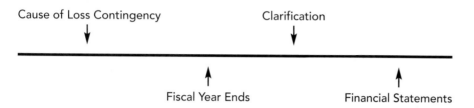

When the cause of a loss contingency occurs before the year-end, a clarifying event before financial statements are issued can be used to determine how the contingency is reported.

For instance, if information becomes available that sheds light on a claim that existed when the fiscal year ended, that information should be used in determining the probability of a loss contingency materializing and in estimating the amount of the loss. The settlement of a lawsuit after the December 31 report date of PeopleSoft, Inc. apparently influenced its accrual of a loss contingency (Graphic 13–12).

> **Notes: Legal Proceedings (in part)**
> On February 16, 2001, PeopleSoft agreed to a tentative settlement of the litigation, which would result in the dismissal of all claims against the defendants in exchange for a payment of $15 million. An insurance receivable and a settlement accrual of $15 million has been included in Other current assets and Accrued liabilities, respectively, in the accompanying consolidated balance sheet as of December 31, 2000.

GRAPHIC 13–12
Accrual of Litigation Contingency—
PeopleSoft, Inc.

For a loss contingency to be accrued, the cause of the lawsuit must have occurred before the accounting period ended. It's not necessary that the lawsuit actually was filed during that reporting period.

Sometimes, the cause of a loss contingency occurs after the end of the year but before the financial statements are issued:

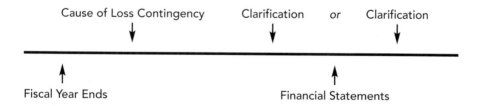

If an event giving rise to a contingency occurs after the year-end, a liability should not be accrued.

When a contingency comes into existence after the year-end, a liability cannot be accrued because it didn't exist at the end of the year. However, if the failure to disclose the possible loss would cause the financial statements to be misleading, the situation should be described in a disclosure note, including the effect of the possible loss on key accounting numbers affected.[19]

In fact, *any* event occurring after the fiscal year-end but before the financial statements are issued that has a material effect on the company's financial position must be disclosed in

---

[19]"Accounting for Contingencies," *Statement of Financial Accounting Standards No. 5* (Stamford, Conn.: FASB, 1975), par. 11.

a subsequent events disclosure note. Examples are an issuance of debt or equity securities, a business combination, and discontinued operations.

A disclosure note of the Dow Chemical Company from its 2000 annual report is shown in Graphic 13–13 and describes an event that will occur in the first quarter of fiscal 2001.

GRAPHIC 13–13
Subsequent Events—
Dow Chemical
Company

S. Merger with Union Carbide Corporation
On February 6, 2001, the Company completed its merger with Union Carbide in a tax-free, stock-for-stock transaction. Dow issued 1.611 shares of common stock for each share of Union Carbide common stock outstanding, or approximately 219 million shares.

UNASSERTED CLAIMS AND ASSESSMENTS

It must be probable that an unasserted claim or assessment or an unfiled lawsuit will occur before considering whether and how to report the possible loss.

Even if a claim has yet to be made when the financial statements are issued, a contingency may warrant accrual or disclosure. However, an unfiled lawsuit or an unasserted claim or assessment need not be disclosed unless it is *probable that the suit, claim, or assessment will occur.* If it is probable, then the likelihood of an unfavorable outcome and the feasibility of estimating a dollar amount should be considered in deciding whether and how to report the possible loss.

For example, the IRS may be in the process of auditing a company's tax returns but has not proposed a deficiency assessment. If management feels an assessment is probable, the possible tax assessment might need to be reported. An estimated loss and contingent liability would be accrued if an unfavorable outcome is probable and the amount can be reasonably estimated. However, note disclosure alone would be appropriate if an unfavorable settlement is only reasonably possible, and no action is needed if chances of that outcome are remote. Notice that when the claim or assessment is unasserted as yet, a two-step process is involved in deciding how it should be reported:

1. Is a claim or assessment probable? (If the answer to this question is no, no disclosure is needed; skip step 2.)
2. Only if a claim or assessment is probable should we evaluate (a) the likelihood of an unfavorable outcome and (b) whether the dollar amount can be estimated.

If the conclusion of step 1 is that the claim or assessment *is not* probable, no further action is required. If the conclusion of step 1 is that the claim or assessment *is* probable, the decision as to whether or not a liability is accrued or disclosed is precisely the same as when the claim or assessment already has been asserted.

As described in a recent disclosure note (see Graphic 13–14), Union Pacific felt that some unasserted claims meet the criteria for accrual under this two-step decision process.

GRAPHIC 13–14
Unasserted Claims—
Union Pacific
Corporation

12. Commitments and Contingencies (in part)
The Corporation and its subsidiaries periodically enter into financial and other commitments in connection with their businesses. It is not possible at this time for the Corporation to determine fully the effect of all unasserted claims on its consolidated financial condition, results of operations or liquidity; however, to the extent possible, where unasserted claims can be estimated and where such claims are considered probable, the Corporation has recorded a liability.

Accrued loss contingencies meet the SFAC 6 definition of liabilities.

Notice that the treatment of contingent liabilities is consistent with the accepted definition of liabilities as (a) probable, future sacrifices of economic benefits (b) that arise from present obligations to other entities and (c) that result from past transactions or events.[20] The

---

[20]"Elements of Financial Statements," *Statement of Financial Accounting Concepts No. 6* (Stamford, Conn.: FASB, 1985).

inherent uncertainty involved with contingent liabilities means additional care is required to determine whether future sacrifices of economic benefits are probable and whether the amount of the sacrifices can be quantified.

Gain Contingencies

A gain contingency is an uncertain situation that might result in a gain. For example, in a pending lawsuit, one side—the defendant—faces a loss contingency; the other side—the plaintiff—has a gain contingency. As we discussed earlier, loss contingencies are accrued when the event confirming the obligation is probable and the amount can reasonably be estimated. However, gain contingencies are not accrued. The nonparallel treatment of gain contingencies follows the same conservative reasoning that motivates reporting some assets at lower of cost or market. Specifically, it's desirable to anticipate losses, but recognizing gains should await their realization.

> **Gain contingencies are not accrued.**

Though gain contingencies are not recorded in the accounts, they are disclosed in notes to the financial statements. Care should be taken that the disclosure note not give "misleading implications as to the likelihood of realization."[21]

CONCEPT **REVIEW** EXERCISE

Contingencies

Hanover Industries manufactures and sells food products and food processing machinery. While preparing the December 31, 2003, financial statements for Hanover, the following information was discovered relating to contingencies and possible adjustments to liabilities. Hanover's 2003 financial statements were issued on April 1, 2004.

a. On November 12, 2003, a former employee filed a lawsuit against Hanover alleging age discrimination and asking for damages of $750,000. At December 31, 2003, Hanover's attorney indicated that the likelihood of losing the lawsuit was possible but not probable. On March 5, 2004, Hanover agreed to pay the former employee $125,000 in return for withdrawing the lawsuit.

b. After a tax audit of the 2002 return, the IRS has questioned some expenses paid to a major stockholder. At April, 2004, the IRS has not yet made an assessment of additional taxes, but Hanover feels it will. Hanover's accountants and legal counsel believe the deductions were appropriate but that if an assessment is made, there is a reasonable possibility that subsequent court action would result in an additional tax liability of $55,000.

c. Hanover grants a one-year warranty for each processing machine sold. Past experience indicates that the costs of satisfying warranties are approximately 2% of sales. During 2003, sales of processing machines totaled $21,300,000. 2003 expenditures for warranty repair costs were $178,000 related to 2003 sales and $220,000 related to 2002 sales. The January 1, 2003, balance of the warranty liability account was $250,000.

d. Hanover is the plaintiff in a $600,000 lawsuit filed in 2002 against Ansdale Farms for failing to deliver on contracts for produce. The suit is in final appeal. Legal counsel advises that it is probable that Hanover will prevail and will be awarded $300,000.

e. Included with certain food items sold in 2003 were coupons redeemable for a kitchen appliance at the rate of five coupons per appliance. During 2003, 30,000 coupons were issued and 5,000 coupons were redeemed. Although this is the first such promotion in years, past experience indicates that 60% of coupons are never redeemed. An inventory of kitchen appliances is maintained, and a count shows that 1,000 are on hand at December 31, 2003, with a normal retail value of $20,000 and a cost to Hanover of $8,000.

---

[21]"Accounting For Contingencies," *Statement of Financial Accounting Standards No. 5* (Stamford, Conn.: FASB, 1975), par. 17.

Required:
1. Determine the appropriate means of reporting each situation. Briefly explain your reasoning.
2. Prepare any necessary journal entries and state whether a disclosure note is needed.

SOLUTION

a. This is a loss contingency. Hanover can use the information occurring after the end of the year in determining appropriate disclosure. The cause for the suit existed at the end of the year. Hanover should accrue the $125,000 loss because an agreement has been reached confirming the loss and the amount is known.

Loss—litigation	125,000	
Liability—litigation.....................................		125,000

A disclosure note also is appropriate.

b. At the time financial statements are issued, an IRS claim is as yet unasserted. However, an assessment is probable. Thus, (a) the likelihood of an unfavorable outcome and (b) whether the dollar amount can be estimated are considered. No accrual is necessary because an unfavorable outcome is not probable. But because an unfavorable outcome is reasonably possible, a disclosure note is appropriate.

   Note: If the likelihood of a claim being asserted is not probable, disclosure is not required even if an unfavorable outcome is thought to be probable in the event of an assessment and the amount is estimable.

c. The contingency for warranties should be accrued because it is probable that expenditures will be made and the amount can be estimated from past experience. When customer claims are made and costs are incurred to satisfy those claims the liability is reduced.

Warranty expense (2% × $21,300,000)	426,000	
Estimated warranty liability		426,000
Estimated warranty liability ($178,000 + 220,000)...............	398,000	
Cash, wages payable, parts and supplies, etc.		398,000

The liability at December 31, 2003, would be reported as $278,000:

Warranty Liability
(in 000s)

		250	Balance, Jan. 1
		426	2003 expense
2003 expenditures	398		
		278	Balance, Dec. 31

A disclosure note also is appropriate.

d. This is a gain contingency. Gain contingencies cannot be accrued even if the gain is probable and reasonably estimable. The gain should be recognized only when realized. It can be disclosed, but care should be taken to avoid misleading language regarding the realizability of the gain.

e. The contingency for premiums should be accrued because it is probable that coupons will be redeemed and the amount can be estimated from past experience. When coupons are redeemed and appliances are issued, the liability is reduced.

Promotional expense (40% × [30,000 ÷ 5] × $8*)...............	19,200	
Estimated premium liability...............................		19,200
Estimated premium liability ([5,000 ÷ 5] × $8*).................	8,000	
Inventory of premiums....................................		8,000

*$8,000 ÷ 1,000 = $8

The liability at December 31, 2003, would be reported as $11,200:

		Premium Liability	
		19,200	2003 expense
2003 expenditures	8,000		
		11,200	Balance, Dec. 31

A disclosure note also is appropriate.

DECISION MAKERS' PERSPECTIVE

Current liabilities impact a company's liquidity. Liquidity refers to a company's cash position and overall ability to obtain cash in the normal course of business. A company is said to be liquid if it has sufficient cash (or other assets convertible to cash in a relatively short time) to pay currently maturing debts. Because the lack of liquidity can cause the demise of an otherwise healthy company, it is critical that managers as well as outside investors and creditors maintain close scrutiny of this aspect of a company's well-being.

> An analyst of risk should be concerned with a company's ability to meet its short-term obligations.

> **FINANCIAL REPORTING** CASE
> Q5, p. 618

Keeping track of the current ratio is one of the most common ways of doing this. The current ratio is intended as a measure of short-term solvency and is determined by dividing current assets by current liabilities.

When we compare liabilities that must be satisfied in the near term with assets that either are cash or will be converted to cash in the near term, we get a useful measure of a company's liquidity. A ratio of 1 to 1 or higher often is considered a rule-of-thumb standard, but like other ratios, acceptability should be evaluated in the context of the industry in which the company operates and other specific circumstances. Keep in mind, though, that industry averages are only one indication of adequacy and that the current ratio is but one indication of liquidity.

We can adjust for the implicit assumption of the current ratio that all current assets are equally liquid. The acid-test, or quick, ratio is similar to the current ratio but is based on a more conservative measure of assets available to pay current liabilities. Specifically, the numerator, quick assets, includes only cash and cash equivalents, short-term investments, and accounts receivable. By eliminating current assets such as inventories and prepaid expenses that are less readily convertible into cash, the acid-test ratio provides a more rigorous indication of a company's short-term solvency than does the current ratio.

> A manager should actively monitor a company's liquidity.

If either of these liquidity ratios is less than that of the industry as a whole, does that mean that liquidity is a problem? Perhaps; perhaps not. It does, though, raise a red flag that suggests caution when assessing other areas. It's important to remember that each ratio is but one piece of the puzzle. For example, profitability is probably the best long-run indication of liquidity. Also, management may be very efficient in managing current assets so that some current assets—receivables or inventory—are more liquid than they otherwise would be and more readily available to satisfy liabilities. The turnover ratios discussed in earlier chapters help measure the efficiency of asset management in this regard.

> A liquidity ratio is but one indication of a company's liquidity.

Given the actual and perceived importance of a company's liquidity in the minds of analysts, it's not difficult to adopt a management perspective and imagine efforts to manipulate the ratios that measure liquidity. For instance, a company might use its economic muscle or persuasive powers to influence the timing of accounts payable recognition by asking suppliers to change their delivery schedules. Because accounts payable is included in the denominator in most measures of liquidity, such as the current ratio, the timing of their recognition could mean the difference between an unacceptable ratio and an acceptable one, or between violating a debt covenant and compliance. For example, suppose a company with a current ratio of 1.25 (current assets of $5 million and current liabilities of $4 million) is in violation of a debt covenant requiring a minimum current ratio of 1.3. By delaying the delivery of $1 million of inventory, the ratio would increase to 1.33 (current assets of $4 million and current liability of $3 million).

> Analysts should be alert for efforts to manipulate measures of liquidity.

It is important for creditors and analysts to be attentive for evidence of activities that would indicate timing strategies, such as unusual variations in accounts payable levels. You might notice that such timing strategies are similar to earnings management techniques we discussed previously—specifically, manipulating the timing of revenue and expense recognition in order to "smooth" income over time.

In the next chapter, we continue our discussion of liabilities. Our focus will shift from current liabilities to long-term liabilities in the form of bonds and long-term notes. ■

FINANCIAL REPORTING CASE **SOLUTION**

1. **What are accrued liabilities? What is commercial paper?** *(p. 624)* Accrued liabilities are reported for expenses already incurred but not yet paid (accrued expenses). These include salaries and wages payable, income taxes payable, and interest payable. Commercial paper is a form of notes payable sometimes used by large corporations to obtain temporary financing. It is sold to other companies as a short-term investment. It represents unsecured notes sold in minimum denominations of $25,000 with maturities ranging from 30 to 270 days. Typically, commercial paper is issued directly to the buyer (lender) and is backed by a line of credit with a bank.

2. **Why did Syntel Microsystems include some long-term debt in the current liability section?** *(p. 627)* Syntel Microsystems did include some long-term debt in the current liability section. The currently maturing portion of a long-term debt must be reported as a current liability. Amounts are reclassified and reported as current liabilities when they become payable within the upcoming year.

3. **Did they also report some current amounts as long-term debt? Explain.** *(p. 627)* Yes they did. It is permissible to report short-term obligations as noncurrent liabilities if the company (a) intends to refinance on a long-term basis and (b) demonstrates the ability to do so by a refinancing agreement or by actual financing. As the disclosure note explains, this is the case for a portion of Syntel's currently payable debt.

4. **Must obligations be known contractual debts in order to be reported as liabilities?** *(p. 630)* No. From an accounting perspective, it is not necessary that obligations be known, legally enforceable debts to be reported as liabilities. They must only be probable and the dollar amount reasonably estimable.

5. **Is it true that current liabilities are riskier than long-term liabilities?** *(p. 641)* Other things being equal, current liabilities generally are considered riskier than long-term liabilities. For that reason, management usually would rather report a debt as long term. Current debt, though, is not necessarily risky. The liquidity ratios we discussed in the chapter attempt to measure liquidity. Remember, any such measure must be assessed in the context of other factors: industry standards, profitability, turnover ratios, and risk management activities, to name a few. ■

THE BOTTOM LINE

1. Liabilities are present obligations to sacrifice assets in the future because of something that already has occurred. Current liabilities are expected to require current assets (or the creation of other current liabilities) and usually are payable within one year.

2. Short-term bank loans usually are arranged under an existing line of credit with a bank or group of banks. When interest is discounted from the face amount of a note (a so-called noninterest-bearing note), the effective interest rate is higher than the stated discount rate. Large, highly rated firms sometimes sell commercial paper directly to the buyer (lender) to borrow funds at a lower rate than through a bank loan.

3. Accrued liabilities are recorded by adjusting entries for expenses already incurred, but for which cash has yet to be paid (accrued expenses). Familiar examples are salaries and wages payable, income taxes payable, and interest payable.

4. Short-term obligations can be reported as noncurrent liabilities if the company (a) intends to refinance on a long-term basis and (b) demonstrates the ability to do so by actual financing or a formal agreement to do so.

5. A loss contingency is an existing, uncertain situation involving potential loss depending on whether some future event occurs. Whether a contingency is accrued and reported as a liability depends on (a) the likelihood that the confirming event will occur and (b) what can be determined about the amount of loss. It is accrued if it is both probable that the confirming event will occur and the amount can be at least reasonably estimated.

6. A clarifying event before financial statements are issued, but after the year-end, can be used to determine how the contingency is reported. An unasserted suit, claim, or assessment warrants accrual or disclosure if it is probable it will be asserted. A gain contingency is a contingency that might result in a gain. A gain contingency is not recognized until it actually is realized. ▪

PAYROLL-RELATED LIABILITIES

All firms incur liabilities in connection with their payrolls. These arise primarily from legal requirements to withhold taxes from employees' paychecks and from payroll taxes on the firms themselves. Some payroll-related liabilities result from voluntary payroll deductions of amounts payable to third parties.

EMPLOYEES' WITHHOLDING TAXES

Employers are required by law to withhold federal (sometimes state) income taxes and Social Security taxes from employees' paychecks and remit these to the Internal Revenue Service. The amount withheld for federal income taxes is determined by a tax table furnished by the IRS and varies according to the amount earned and the number of exemptions claimed by the employee. Also, the Federal Insurance Contributions Act (FICA) requires employers to withhold a percentage of each employee's earnings up to a specified maximum. Both the percentage and the maximum are changed intermittently. As this text went to print, the deduction for Social Security was 6.2% of the first $80,400 an employee earns. Additionally, a deduction for Medicare tax was 1.45% with no limit on the base amount. The employer also must pay an equal (matching) amount on behalf of the employee.

VOLUNTARY DEDUCTIONS

Besides the required deductions for income taxes and Social Security taxes, employees often authorize their employers to deduct other amounts from their paychecks. These deductions might include union dues, contributions to savings or retirement plans, and insurance premiums. Amounts deducted this way represent liabilities until paid to the appropriate organizations.

EMPLOYERS' PAYROLL TAXES

One payroll tax mentioned earlier is the employer's matching amount of FICA taxes. The employer also must pay federal and state unemployment taxes on behalf of its employees. The Federal Unemployment Tax Act (FUTA) requires a tax of 6.2% of the first $7,000 earned by each employee. This amount is reduced by a 5.4% (maximum) credit for contributions to state unemployment programs, so the net federal rate often is .8%.[22] In many states the state rate is 5.4% but may be reduced by merit ratings affected by the employer's employment experience.

FRINGE BENEFITS

In addition to salaries and wages, withholding taxes, and payroll taxes, many companies provide employees a variety of fringe benefits. Most commonly, employers pay all or part of employees' insurance premiums and/or contributions to retirement income plans.

---

[22]All states presently have unemployment tax programs.

Representative payroll-related liabilities are presented in Illustration 13A–1.

ILLUSTRATION 13A–1 **Payroll-Related Liabilities**	Crescent Lighting and Fixtures' payroll for the second week in January was $100,000. The following deductions, fringe benefits, and taxes apply:	
	Federal income taxes to be withheld	$20,000
	State income taxes to be withheld	3,000
	Medical insurance premiums (Blue Cross)— 70% paid by employer	1,000
	Employee contribution to voluntary retirement plan (Fidelity Investments)—contributions matched by employer	4,000
	Union dues (Local No. 222)—paid by employees	100
	Life insurance premiums (Prudential Life)— 100% paid by employer	200
	Social Security tax rate	6.2%
	Medicare tax rate	1.45%
	Federal unemployment tax rate (after state deduction)	0.80%
	State unemployment tax rate	5.40%

Amounts withheld from paychecks represent liabilities until remitted to third parties.	Salaries and wages expense (total amount earned)	100,000	
	Withholding taxes payable (federal income tax)		20,000
	Withholding taxes payable (state income tax)		3,000
	Social Security taxes payable (6.2%)		6,200
	Medicare taxes payable (1.45%)		1,450
	Payable to Blue Cross (insurance premiums—30%)		300
The employer's share of FICA and unemployment taxes constitute the employer's payroll tax expense.	Payable to Fidelity Investments (employees' investment)		4,000
	Payable to Local No. 222 (union dues)		100
	Salaries and wages payable (net pay)		64,950
	Payroll tax expense (total)	13,850	
	Social Security taxes payable (employer's matching amount)		6,200
	Medicare taxes payable (employer's matching amount)		1,450
	FUTA payable (federal unemployment tax: .8%)		800
Fringe benefits are part of salaries and wages expense and represent liabilities until remitted to third parties.	State unemployment tax payable (5.4%)		5,400
	Salaries and wages expense (fringe benefits)	4,900	
	Payable to Blue Cross (insurance premiums—70%)		700
	Payable to Fidelity Investments (matching amount)		4,000
	Payable to Prudential Life (insurance premiums)		200

As you study the illustration, you should note the similarity among all payroll-related liabilities. Amounts withheld—voluntarily or involuntarily—from paychecks are liabilities until turned over to appropriate third parties. Payroll taxes and expenses for fringe benefits are incurred as a result of services performed by employees and also are liabilities until paid to appropriate third parties. ■

QUESTIONS FOR REVIEW OF KEY TOPICS

Q 13–1   What are the essential characteristics of liabilities for purposes of financial reporting?

Q 13–2   What distinguishes current liabilities from long-term liabilities?

Q 13–3   Bronson Distributors owes a supplier $100,000 on open account. The amount is payable in three months. What is the theoretically correct way to measure the reportable amount for this liability? In practice, how will it likely be reported? Why?

Q 13–4   Bank loans often are arranged under existing lines of credit. What is a line of credit? How does a non-committed line of credit differ from a committed line?

Q 13–5   Banks sometimes loan cash under noninterest-bearing notes. Is it true that banks lend money without interest?

Q 13–6   How does commercial paper differ from a bank loan? Why is the interest rate often less for commercial paper?

Q 13–7   Salaries of $5,000 have been earned by employees by the end of the period but will not be paid to employees until the following period. How should the expense and related liability be recorded? Why?

Q 13–8   How are refundable deposits and customer advances similar? How do they differ?

Q 13–9   Amounts collected for third parties represent liabilities until remitted. Provide several examples of this kind of collection.

Q 13–10   Consider the following liabilities of Future Brands, Inc., at December 31, 2003, the company's fiscal year-end. Should they be reported as current liabilities or long-term liabilities?

1. $77 million of 8% notes are due on May 31, 2007. The notes are callable by the Company's bank, beginning March 1, 2004.

2. $102 million of 8% notes are due on May 31, 2008. A debt covenant requires Future to maintain a current ratio (ratio of current assets to current liabilities) of at least 2 to 1. Future is in violation of this requirement but has obtained a waiver from the bank until May 2004, since both companies feel Future will correct the situation during the first half of 2004.

Q 13–11   Long-term obligations usually are reclassified and reported as current liabilities when they become payable within the upcoming year (or operating cycle, if longer than a year). So, a 25-year bond issue is reported as a long-term liability for 24 years but normally is reported as a current liability on the balance sheet prepared during the 25th year of its term to maturity. Name a situation in which this would not be the case.

Q 13–12   Define a loss contingency. Provide three examples.

Q 13–13   List and briefly describe the three categories of likelihood that a future event(s) will confirm the incurrence of the liability for a loss contingency.

Q 13–14   Under what circumstances should a loss contingency be accrued?

Q 13–15   Suppose the analysis of a loss contingency indicates that an obligation is not probable. What accounting treatment if any is warranted?

Q 13–16   Name two loss contingencies that almost always are accrued.

Q 13–17   Distinguish between the accounting treatment of a manufacturer's warranty and an extended warranty. Why the difference?

Q 13–18   At December 31, the end of the reporting period, the analysis of a loss contingency indicates that an obligation is only reasonably possible, though its dollar amount is readily estimable. During February, before the financial statements are issued, new information indicates the loss is probable. What accounting treatment is warranted?

Q 13–19   After the end of the reporting period, a contingency comes into existence. Under what circumstances, if any, should the contingency be reported in the financial statements for the period ended?

Q 13–20   Suppose the Environmental Protection Agency is in the process of investigating Ozone Ruination Limited for possible environmental damage but has not proposed a penalty as of December 31, 2003, the company's fiscal year-end. Describe the two-step process involved in deciding how this unasserted assessment should be reported.

Q 13–21   You are the plaintiff in a lawsuit. Your legal counsel advises that your eventual victory is inevitable. "You will be awarded $12 million," your attorney confidently asserts. Describe the appropriate accounting treatment.

EXERCISES

E 13–1
Bank loan; accrued interest

On November 1, 2003, Quantum Technology, a geothermal energy supplier, borrowed $8 million cash to fund a geological survey. The loan was made by Nevada BancCorp under a noncommitted short-term line of credit arrangement. Quantum issued a nine-month, 12% promissory note. Interest was payable at maturity. Quantum's fiscal period is the calendar year.

Required:
1. Prepare the journal entry for the issuance of the note by Quantum Technology.
2. Prepare the appropriate adjusting entry for the note by Quantum on December 31, 2003.
3. Prepare the journal entry for the payment of the note at maturity.

E 13–2
Determining accrued
interest in various
situations

On July 1, 2003, Ross-Livermore Industries issued nine-month notes in the amount of $200 million. Interest is payable at maturity.

Required:
Determine the amount of interest expense that should be recorded in a year-end adjusting entry under each of the following independent assumptions:

	Interest Rate	Fiscal Year-End
1.	12%	December 31
2.	10%	September 30
3.	9%	October 31
4.	6%	January 31

E 13–3
Multiple choice;
current liabilities

The following questions dealing with current liabilities are adapted from questions that appeared on recent CPA examinations. Determine the response that best completes the statements or questions.

1. Black Co. requires advance payments with special orders for machinery constructed to customer specifications. These advances are nonrefundable. Information for 2003 is as follows:

Customer advances—balance 12/31/02	$118,000
Advances received with orders in 2003	184,000
Advances applied to orders shipped in 2003	164,000
Advances applicable to orders canceled in 2003	50,000

In Black's December 31, 2003, balance sheet, what amount should be reported as a current liability for advances from customer?
a. $0.
b. $88,000.
c. $138,000.
d. $148,000.

2. Which of the following is generally associated with payables classified as accounts payable?

	Periodic Payment of Interest	Secured by Collateral
a.	No	No
b.	No	Yes
c.	Yes	No
d.	Yes	Yes

E 13–4
Short-term notes

The following selected transactions relate to liabilities of United Insulation Corporation. United's fiscal year ends on December 31.

Required:
Prepare the appropriate journal entries through the maturity of each liability.

2003

Jan. 13 Negotiated a revolving credit agreement with Parish Bank that can be renewed annually upon bank approval. The amount available under the line of credit is $20,000,000 at the bank's prime rate.

Feb. 1 Arranged a three-month bank loan of $5 million with Parish Bank under the line of credit agreement. Interest at the prime rate of 10% was payable at maturity.

May 1 Paid the 10% note at maturity.

Dec. 1 Supported by the credit line, issued $10 million of commercial paper on a nine-month note. Interest was discounted at issuance at a 9% discount rate.

31 Recorded any necessary adjusting entry(s).

2004

Sept. 1 Paid the commercial paper at maturity.

E 13–5
Customer advances;
sales taxes

Bavarian Bar and Grill opened for business in November 2003. During its first two months of operation, the restaurant sold gift certificates in various amounts totaling $5,200, mostly as Christmas presents. They are redeemable for meals within two years of the purchase date, although experience within the industry indicates that 80% of gift certificates are redeemed within one year. Certificates totaling $1,300 were presented for redemption during 2003 for meals having a total price of $2,100. The sales tax rate on restaurant sales is 4%, assessed at the time meals (not gift certificates) are purchased. Sales taxes will be remitted in January.

Required:

1. Prepare the appropriate journal entries (in summary form) for the gift certificates during 2003 (keeping in mind that, in actuality, each sale of a gift certificate or a meal would be recorded individually).
2. Determine the liability for gift certificates to be reported on the December 31, 2003, balance sheet.
3. What is the appropriate classification (current or noncurrent) of the liabilities at December 31, 2003? Why?

E 13–6
Customer deposits

Diversified Semiconductors sells perishable electronic components. Some must be shipped and stored in reusable protective containers. Customers pay a deposit for each container received. The deposit is equal to the container's cost. They receive a refund when the container is returned. During 2003, deposits collected on containers shipped were $850,000.

Deposits are forfeited if containers are not returned within 18 months. Containers held by customers at January 1, 2003, represented deposits of $530,000. In 2003, $790,000 was refunded and deposits forfeited were $35,000.

Required:

1. Prepare the appropriate journal entries for the deposits received and returned during 2003.
2. Determine the liability for refundable deposits to be reported on the December 31, 2003, balance sheet.

E 13–7
Various transactions involving advance collections

The following selected transactions relate to liabilities of Interstate Farm Implements for December of 2003. Interstate's fiscal year ends on December 31.

Required:
Prepare the appropriate journal entries for these transactions.

1. On December 15, received $7,500 from Bradley Farms toward the purchase of a $98,000 tractor to be delivered on January 6, 2004.
2. During December, received $25,500 of refundable deposits relating to containers used to transport equipment parts.
3. During December, credit sales totaled $800,000. The state sales tax rate is 5% and the local sales tax rate is 2%. (This is a summary journal entry for the many individual sales transactions for the period.)

E 13–8
Current—noncurrent classification of debt

A recent annual report of Sprint Corporation contained a rather lengthy narrative entitled "Review of Segmental Results of Operation." The narrative noted that short-term notes payable and commercial paper outstanding at the end of the year aggregated $756 million and that during the following year "This entire balance will be replaced by the issuance of long-term debt or will continue to be refinanced under existing long-term credit facilities."

Required:
How did Sprint report the debt in its balance sheet? Why?

E 13–9
Current—noncurrent classification of debt

At December 31, 2003, Newman Engineering's liabilities include the following:

1. $10 million of 9% bonds were issued for $10 million on May 31, 1982. The bonds mature on May 31, 2014, but bondholders have the option of calling (demanding payment on) the bonds on May 31, 2004. However, the option to call is not expected to be exercised, given prevailing market conditions.
2. $14 million of 8% notes are due on May 31, 2007. A debt covenant requires Newman to maintain current assets at least equal to 175% of its current liabilities. On December 31, 2003, Newman is in violation of this covenant. Newman obtained a waiver from National City Bank until June 2004, having convinced the bank that the company's normal 2 to 1 ratio of current assets to current liabilities will be reestablished during the first half of 2004.
3. $7 million of 11% bonds were issued for $7 million on August 31, 1972. The bonds mature on July 31, 2004. Sufficient cash is expected to be available to retire the bonds at maturity.

Required:
What portion of the debt can be excluded from classification as a current liability (that is, reported as a noncurrent liability)? Explain.

E 13–10
Warranties

Cupola Awning Corporation introduced a new line of commercial awnings in 2003 that carry a two-year warranty against manufacturer's defects. Based on their experience with previous product introductions, warranty costs are expected to approximate 3% of sales. Sales and actual warranty expenditures for the first year of selling the product were:

Sales	Actual Warranty Expenditures
$5,000,000	$37,500

Required:
1. Does this situation represent a loss contingency? Why or why not? How should Cupola account for it?
2. Prepare journal entries that summarize sales of the awnings (assume all credit sales) and any aspects of the warranty that should be recorded during 2003.
3. What amount should Cupola report as a liability at December 31, 2003?

E 13–11
Extended warranties

Carnes Electronics sells consumer electronics that carry a 90-day manufacturer's warranty. At the time of purchase, customers are offered the opportunity to also buy a two-year extended warranty for an additional charge. During 2003, Carnes received $412,000 for these extended warranties (approximately evenly throughout the year).

Required:
1. Does this situation represent a loss contingency? Why or why not? How should it be accounted for?
2. Prepare journal entries that summarize sales of the extended warranties (assume all credit sales) and any aspects of the warranty that should be recorded during 2003.

E 13–12
Contingency; product recall

Sound Audio manufactures and sells audio equipment for automobiles. Engineers notified management in December 2003 of a circuit flaw in an amplifier that poses a potential fire hazard. An intense investigation indicated that a product recall is virtually certain, estimated to cost the company $2 million. The fiscal year ends on December 31.

Required:
1. Should this loss contingency be accrued, disclosed only, or neither? Explain.
2. What loss, if any, should Sound Audio report in its 2003 income statement?
3. What liability, if any, should Sound Audio report in its 2003 balance sheet?
4. Prepare any journal entry needed.

E 13–13
Impairment of accounts receivable

The Manda Panda Company uses the allowance method to account for bad debts. At the beginning of 2003, the allowance account had a credit balance of $75,000. Credit sales for 2003 totaled $2,400,000 and the year-end accounts receivable balance was $490,000. During this year, $73,000 in receivables were determined to be uncollectible. Manda Panda anticipates that 3% of all credit sales will ultimately become uncollectible. The fiscal year ends on December 31.

Required:
1. Does this situation describe a loss contingency? Explain.
2. What is the bad debt expense that Manda Panda should report in its 2003 income statement?
3. Prepare the appropriate journal entry to record the contingency.
4. What is the net realizable value (book value) Manda Panda should report in its 2003 balance sheet?

E 13–14
Premiums

Drew-Richards iMusic is a regional music media reseller. As a promotion, it offered $5 cash rebates on specific CDs. Customers must mail in a proof-of-purchase seal from the package plus the cash register receipt to receive the rebate. Experience suggests that 70% of the rebates will be claimed. Twenty thousand of the CDs were sold in 2003. Total rebates to customers in 2003 were $22,000 and were recorded as promotional expense when paid. The fiscal year ends on December 31.

Required:
1. What is the promotional expense that Drew-Richards should report in its 2003 income statement?
2. What is the premium liability that Drew-Richards should report in its 2003 balance sheet?
3. Prepare the appropriate journal entry to record the contingency.

E 13–15
Unasserted assessment

At April 1, 2004, the IRS is in the process of auditing the tax returns of Shu Lamination, Inc. for 2004–2006, but has not proposed a deficiency assessment. Shu's fiscal year ends on December 31, 2003. The company's financial statements are published in April 2004.

Required:
For each of the following scenarios, determine the appropriate way to report the situation. Explain your reasoning and prepare any necessary journal entry.
1. Management feels an assessment is *reasonably possible,* and if an assessment is made an unfavorable settlement of $13 million is *reasonably possible.*
2. Management feels an assessment is *reasonably possible,* and if an assessment is made an unfavorable settlement of $13 million is *probable.*
3. Management feels an assessment is *probable,* and if an assessment is made an unfavorable settlement of $13 million is *reasonably possible.*
4. Management feels an assessment is *probable,* and if an assessment is made an unfavorable settlement of $13 million is *probable.*

E 13–16
Various transactions
involving contingencies

The following selected transactions relate to contingencies of Classical Tool Makers, Inc., which began operations in July 2003. Classical's fiscal year ends on December 31. Financial statements are published in April 2004.

Required:
Prepare the appropriate journal entries to record any amounts that should be recorded as a result of each of these contingencies.

1. Classical's products carry a one-year warranty against manufacturer's defects. Based on previous experience, warranty costs are expected to approximate 4% of sales. Sales were $2 million (all credit) for 2003. Actual warranty expenditures were $30,800 and were recorded as warranty expense when incurred.
2. Although no customer accounts have been shown to be uncollectible, Classical estimates that 2% of credit sales will eventually prove uncollectible.
3. In December 2003, the State of Tennessee filed suit against Classical, seeking penalties for violations of clean air laws. On January 23, 2004, Classical reached a settlement with state authorities to pay $1.5 million in penalties.
4. Classical is the plaintiff in a $4 million lawsuit filed against a supplier. The suit is in final appeal and attorneys advise that it is virtually certain that Classical will win the case and be awarded $2.5 million.
5. In November 2003, Classical became aware of a design flaw in an industrial saw that poses a potential electrical hazard. A product recall appears unavoidable. Such an action would likely cost the company $500,000.
6. Classical offered $25 cash rebates on a new model of jigsaw. Customers must mail in a proof-of-purchase seal from the package plus the cash register receipt to receive the rebate. Experience suggests that 60% of the rebates will be claimed. Ten thousand of the jigsaws were sold in 2003. Total rebates to customers in 2003 were $105,000 and were recorded as promotional expense when paid.

E 13–17
Multiple choice;
contingencies

The following questions dealing with current liabilities are adapted from questions that appeared on recent CPA examinations. Determine the response that best completes the statements or questions.

1. During 2003, Smith Co. filed suit against West, Inc., seeking damages for patent infringement. At December 31, 2003, Smith's legal counsel believed that it was probable that Smith would be successful against West for an estimated amount in the range of $75,000 to $150,000, with all amounts in the range considered equally likely. In March 2004, Smith was awarded $100,000 and received full payment thereof. In its 2003 financial statements, issued in February 2004, how should this award be reported?
   a. As a receivable and revenue of $100,000.
   b. As a receivable and deferred revenue of $100,000.
   c. As a disclosure of a contingent gain of $100,000.
   d. As a disclosure of a contingent gain of an undetermined amount in the range of $75,000 to $150,000.
2. Vadis Co. sells appliances that include a three-year warranty. Service calls under the warranty are performed by an independent mechanic under a contract with Vadis. Based on experience, warranty costs are estimated at $30 for each machine sold. When should Vadis recognize these warranty costs?
   a. Evenly over the life of the warranty.
   b. When the service calls are performed.
   c. When payments are made to the mechanic.
   d. When the machines are sold.
3. Management can estimate the amount of loss that will occur if a foreign government expropriates some company assets. If expropriation is reasonably possible, a loss contingency should be
   a. Disclosed but not accrued as a liability.
   b. Disclosed and accrued as a liability.
   c. Accrued as liability but not disclosed.
   d. Neither accrued as a liability nor disclosed.
4. In December 2003, Mill Co. began including one coupon in each package of candy that it sells and offering a toy in exchange for 50 cents and five coupons. The toys cost Mill 80 cents each. Eventually 60% of the coupons will be redeemed. During December, Mill sold 110,000 packages of candy and no coupons were redeemed. In its December 31, 2003, balance sheet, what amount should Mill report as estimated liability for coupons?

a. $3,960
b. $10,560
c. $19,800
d. $52,800

E 13–18
Disclosures of liabilities

Indicate (by letter) the way each of the items listed below should be reported on a balance sheet at December 31, 2003.

Item	Reporting Method
____ 1. Commercial paper.	N. Not reported
____ 2. Noncommitted line of credit.	C. Current liability
____ 3. Customer advances.	L. Long-term liability
____ 4. Estimated warranty cost.	D. Disclosure note only
____ 5. Accounts payable.	A. Asset
____ 6. Long-term bonds that will be callable by the creditor in the upcoming year unless an existing violation is not corrected (there is a reasonable possibility the violation will be corrected within the grace period).	
____ 7. Note due March 3, 2004.	
____ 8. Interest accrued on note, Dec. 31, 2003.	
____ 9. Short-term bank loan to be paid with proceeds of sale of common stock.	
____ 10. A determinable gain that is contingent on a future event that appears extremely likely to occur in three months.	
____ 11. Unasserted assessment of back taxes that probably will be asserted, in which case there would probably be a loss in six months.	
____ 12. Unasserted assessment of back taxes with a reasonable possibility of being asserted, in which case there would probably be a loss in 13 months.	
____ 13. A determinable loss from a past event that is contingent on a future event that appears extremely likely to occur in three months.	
____ 14. Bond sinking fund.	
____ 15. Long-term bonds callable by the creditor in the upcoming year that are not expected to be called.	

E 13–19
Change in accounting estimate

Exercise 21–12 deals with a change in estimated warranty expense.

E 13–20
Change in accounting estimate

The Commonwealth of Virginia filed suit in October 2001 against Northern Timber Corporation, seeking civil penalties and injunctive relief for violations of environmental laws regulating forest conservation. When the financial statements were issued in 2002, Northern had not reached a settlement with state authorities, but legal counsel advised Northern Timber that it was probable the ultimate settlement would be $1,000,000 in penalties. The following entry was recorded:

Loss—litigation	1,000,000	
Liability—litigation		1,000,000

Late in 2003, a settlement was reached with state authorities to pay a total of $600,000 to cover the cost of violations.

Required:
1. Prepare any journal entries related to the change.
2. Briefly describe other steps Northern should take to report the change.

E 13–21
Contingency; Dow Chemical Company disclosure

The Dow Chemical Company provides chemical, plastic, and agricultural products and services to various consumer markets. The following excerpt is taken from the disclosure notes of Dow's 2000 annual report ($ in millions):

> The Company had accrued obligations of $325 at December 31, 2000, for environmental matters, including $9 for the remediation of Superfund sites. This is management's best estimate of the costs for remediation and restoration with respect to environmental matters for which the Company has accrued liabilities, although the ultimate cost with respect to these particular matters could range up to twice that amount. Inherent uncertainties exist in these estimates primarily due to unknown conditions, changing governmental regulations and legal standards regarding liability, and evolving technologies for handling site remediation and restoration. It is the opinion of the Company's management that the possibility is remote that costs in excess of those accrued or disclosed will have a material adverse impact on the Company's consolidated financial statements.

Required:

Does the excerpt describe a loss contingency? Under what conditions would Dow accrue such a contingency? What journal entry did Dow use to record the provision (loss)?

E 13–22
Payroll-related liabilities (Based on Appendix 13)

Lee Financial Services pays employees monthly. Payroll information is listed below for January 2003, the first month of Lee's fiscal year. Assume that none of the employees exceeded any relevant wage base.

Salaries	$500,000
Federal income taxes to be withheld	100,000
Federal unemployment tax rate	0.80%
State unemployment tax rate (after FUTA deduction)	5.40%
Social Security (FICA) tax rate	7.65%

Required:

Prepare the appropriate journal entries to record salaries and wages expense and payroll tax expense for the January 2003 pay period.

PROBLEMS

P 13–1
Bank loan; accrued interest

Blanton Plastics, a household plastic product manufacturer, borrowed $14 million cash on October 1, 2003, to provide working capital for year-end production. Blanton issued a four-month, 12% promissory note to N,C&I Bank under a prearranged short-term line of credit. Interest on the note was payable at maturity. Each firm's fiscal period is the calendar year.

Required:

1. Prepare the journal entries to record (a) the issuance of the note by Blanton Plastics and (b) N,C&I Bank's receivable on October 1, 2003.
2. Prepare the journal entries by both firms to record all subsequent events related to the note through January 31, 2004.
3. Suppose the face amount of the note was adjusted to include interest (a noninterest-bearing note) and 12% is the bank's stated discount rate. Prepare the journal entries to record the issuance of the noninterest-bearing note by Blanton Plastics on October 1, 2003, the adjusting entry at December 31, and payment of the note at maturity. What would be the effective interest rate?

P 13–2
Various transactions involving liabilities

Camden Biotechnology began operations in September 2003. The following selected transactions relate to liabilities of the company for September 2003 through March 2004. Camden's fiscal year ends on December 31. Its financial statements are issued in April.

2003
a. On September 5, opened checking accounts at Second Commercial Bank and negotiated a short-term line of credit of up to $15,000,000 at the bank's prime rate (10.5% at the time). The company will pay no commitment fees.
b. On October 1, borrowed $12 million cash from Second Commercial Bank under the line of credit and issued a five-month promissory note. Interest at the prime rate of 10% was payable at maturity. Management planned to issue 10-year bonds in February to repay the note.
c. Received $2,600 of refundable deposits in December for reusable containers used to transport and store chemical-based products.

d.   For the September–December period, sales totaled $4,100,000. The state sales tax rate is 3% and the local sales tax rate is 3%. (This is a summary journal entry for the many individual sales transactions for the period.)

e.   Recorded the adjusting entry for accrued interest.

2004

f.   In February, issued $10 million of 10-year bonds at face value and paid the bank loan on the March 1 due date.

g.   Half of the storage containers covered by refundable deposits were returned in March. The remaining containers are expected to be returned during the next six months.

Required:

1.   Prepare the appropriate journal entries for these transactions.

2.   Prepare the current and long-term liability sections of the December 31, 2003, balance sheet. Trade accounts payable on that date were $252,000.

P 13–3
Current—noncurrent
classification of debt

The balance sheet at December 31, 2003, for Nevada Harvester Corporation includes the liabilities listed below:

a.   11% bonds with a face amount of $40 million were issued for $40 million on October 31, 1994. The bonds mature on October 31, 2014. Bondholders have the option of calling (demanding payment on) the bonds on October 31, 2004, at a redemption price of $40 million. Market conditions are such that the call is not expected to be exercised.

b.   Management intended to refinance $6 million of notes that mature in May 2004. In early March, prior to the actual issuance of the 2003 financial statements, Nevada Harvester negotiated a line of credit with a commercial bank for up to $5 million any time during 2004. Any borrowings will mature two years from the date of borrowing.

c.   Noncallable 12% bonds with a face amount of $20 million were issued for $20 million on September 30, 1982. The bonds mature on September 30, 2004. Sufficient cash is expected to be available to retire the bonds at maturity.

d.   A $12 million 9% bank loan is payable on October 31, 2009. The bank has the right to demand payment after any fiscal year-end in which Nevada Harvester's ratio of current assets to current liabilities falls below a contractual minimum of 1.7 to 1 and remains so for six months. That ratio was 1.45 on December 31, 2003, due primarily to an intentional temporary decline in inventory levels. Normal inventory levels will be reestablished during the first quarter of 2004.

Required:

1.   Determine the amount that can be excluded from classification as a current liability (that is, reported as a noncurrent liability) for each. Explain the reasoning behind your classifications.

2.   Prepare the liability section of a classified balance sheet and any necessary footnote disclosure for Nevada Harvester at December 31, 2003. Accounts payable and accruals are $22 million.

P 13–4
Various liabilities

The unadjusted trial balance of the Manufacturing Equitable at December 31, 2003, the end of its fiscal year, included the following account balances. Manufacturing's 2003 financial statements were issued on April 1, 2004.

Accounts receivable	$ 92,500
Accounts payable	35,000
Bank notes payable	600,000
Mortgage note payable	1,200,000

Other information:

a.   The bank notes, issued August 1, 2003, are due on July 31, 2004, and pay interest at a rate of 10%, payable at maturity.

b.   The mortgage note is due on March 1, 2004. Interest at 9% has been paid up to December 31 (assume 9% is a realistic rate). Manufacturing intended at December 31, 2003, to refinance the note on its due date with a new 10-year mortgage note. In fact, on March 1, Manufacturing paid $250,000 in cash on the principal balance and refinanced the remaining $950,000.

c.   Included in the accounts receivable balance at December 31, 2003, were two subsidiary accounts that had been overpaid and had credit balances totaling $18,000. The accounts were of two major customers who were expected to order more merchandise from Manufacturing and apply the overpayments to those future purchases.

d.   On November 1, 2003, Manufacturing rented a portion of its factory to a tenant for $30,000 per year, payable in advance. The payment for the 12 months ended October 31, 2004, was received as required and was credited to rent revenue.

Required:
1. Prepare any necessary adjusting journal entries at December 31, 2003, pertaining to each item of other information (a–d).
2. Prepare the current and long-term liability sections of the December 31, 2003, balance sheet.

P 13–5 ✓

Various contingencies

Eastern Manufacturing is involved with several situations that possibly involve contingencies. Each is described below. Eastern's fiscal year ends December 31, and the 2003 financial statements are issued on March 15, 2004.

a. Eastern is involved in a lawsuit resulting from a dispute with a supplier. On February 3, 2004, judgment was rendered against Eastern in the amount of $107 million plus interest, a total of $122 million. Eastern plans to appeal the judgment and is unable to predict its outcome though it is not expected to have a material adverse effect on the company.

b. In November, 2002, the State of Nevada filed suit against Eastern, seeking civil penalties and injunctive relief for violations of environmental laws regulating hazardous waste. On January 12, 2004, Eastern reached a settlement with state authorities. Based upon discussions with legal counsel, the Company feels it is probable that $140 million will be required to cover the cost of violations. Eastern believes that the ultimate settlement of this claim will not have a material adverse effect on the company.

c. Eastern is the plaintiff in a $200 million lawsuit filed against United Steel for damages due to lost profits from rejected contracts and for unpaid receivables. The case is in final appeal and legal counsel advises that it is probable that Eastern will prevail and be awarded $100 million.

d. At March 15, 2004, the IRS is in the process of auditing Eastern's tax returns for 2001–2003, but has not proposed a deficiency assessment. Management feels an assessment is reasonably possible, and if an assessment is made an unfavorable settlement of up to $33 million is reasonably possible.

Required:
1. Determine the appropriate means of reporting each situation. Explain your reasoning.
2. Prepare any necessary journal entries and disclosure notes.

P 13–6 ╱

Frequent flyer program

Northeast Airlines operates a frequent flyer marketing program under which mileage credits are earned by flying on Northeast. The program was designed to retain and increase the business of frequent travelers by offering incentives for their continued patronage. Awards are issued to members at the 20,000 miles level. All awards have an expiration date three years from the date earned. Experience indicates that 25% of free travel earned will actually be redeemed. Northeast accounts for its frequent flyer obligation on the accrual basis using the incremental cost method. The incremental costs include food, beverage, and an additional cost per passenger that is based on engineering formulas to determine the average fuel cost per pound per hour. Northeast's liability for free travel at the beginning of 2003 was $25 million. The incremental cost of free travel taken (redeemed) in 2003 was $8 million. The costs of free travel earned for miles traveled in 2003 are estimated to be $40 million. The fiscal year ends on December 31.

Required:
1. Is it appropriate for Northeast to account for its frequent flyer program on the accrual basis? Why?
2. What is the expense that Northeast should report in its 2003 income statement?
3. What is the liability that Northeast should report in its 2003 balance sheet?
4. Prepare the appropriate journal entry to record the year-end accrual of the 2003 expense.

P 13–7

Expected cash flow approach; product recall

The Heinrich Tire Company recalled a tire in its subcompact line in December 2003. Costs associated with the recall were originally thought to approximate $50 million. Now, though, while management feels it is probable the company will incur substantial costs, all discussions indicate that $50 million is an excessive amount. Based on prior recalls in the industry, management has provided the following probability distribution for the potential loss:

Loss Amount	Probability
$40 million	20%
$30 million	50%
$20 million	30%

An arrangement with a consortium of distributors requires that all recall costs be settled at the end of 2004. The risk-free rate of interest is 5%.

Required:
1. Applying the estimated cash flow approach of SFAC No. 7, estimate Heinrich's liability at the end of the 2003 fiscal year.

2. Prepare the journal entry to record the contingent liability (and loss).
3. Prepare the journal entry to accrue interest on the liability at the end of 2004.
4. Prepare the journal entry to pay the liability at the end of 2004, assuming the actual cost is $30 million. Heinrich records an additional loss if the actual costs are higher or a gain if the costs are lower.

P 13–8
Subsequent events

Lincoln Chemicals became involved in investigations by the U.S. Environmental Protection Agency in regard to damages connected to waste disposal sites. Below are four possibilities regarding the timing of (A) the alleged damage caused by Lincoln, (B) an investigation by the EPA, (C) the EPA assessment of penalties, and (D) ultimate settlement. In each case, assume that Lincoln is unaware of any problem until an investigation is begun. Also assume that once the EPA investigation begins, it is probable that a damage assessment will ensue and that once an assessment is made by the EPA, it is reasonably possible that a determinable amount will be paid by Lincoln.

Required:

For each case, decide whether (a) a loss should be accrued in the financial statements with an explanatory note, (b) a disclosure note only should be provided, or (c) no disclosure is necessary.

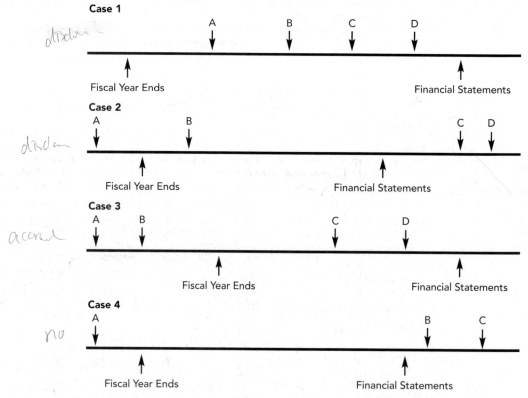

P 13–9
Concepts; terminology

Listed below are several terms and phrases associated with current liabilities. Pair each item from List A (by letter) with the item from List B that is most appropriately associated with it.

List A	List B
____ 1. Face amount × Interest rate × Time.	a. Informal agreement
____ 2. Payable with current assets.	b. Secured loan
____ 3. Short-term debt to be refinanced with common stock.	c. Refinancing prior to the issuance of the financial statements
____ 4. Present value of interest plus present value of principal.	d. Accounts payable
____ 5. Noninterest-bearing.	e. Accrued liabilities
____ 6. Noncommitted line of credit.	f. Commercial paper
____ 7. Pledged accounts receivable.	g. Current liabilities
____ 8. Reclassification of debt.	h. Long-term liability
____ 9. Purchased by other corporations.	i. Usual valuation of liabilities
____ 10. Expenses not yet paid.	j. Interest on debt
____ 11. Liability until refunded.	k. Customer advances
____ 12. Applied against purchase price.	l. Customer deposits

P 13–10
Payroll-related
liabilities
(Based on
Appendix 13)

Alamar Petroleum Company offers its employees the option of contributing up to 5% of their wages or salaries, with the contribution being matched by Alamar. The company also pays 80% of medical and life insurance premiums. Deductions relating to these plans and other payroll information for the first biweekly payroll period of February are listed below.

Wages and salaries	$2,000,000
Employee contribution to voluntary retirement plan	84,000
Medical insurance premiums	42,000
Life insurance premiums	9,000
Federal income taxes to be withheld	400,000
Local income taxes to be withheld	53,000
Payroll taxes:	
Federal unemployment tax rate	0.80%
State unemployment tax rate (after FUTA deduction)	5.40%
Social Security tax rate	6.2%
Medicare tax rate	1.45%

Required:
Prepare the appropriate journal entries to record salaries and wages expense and payroll tax expense for the biweekly pay period. Assume that no employee's cumulative wages exceed the relevant wage bases.

BROADEN YOUR PERSPECTIVE

Apply your critical-thinking ability to the knowledge you've gained. These cases will provide you an opportunity to develop your research, analysis, judgment, and communication skills. You also will work with other students, integrate what you've learned, apply it in real world situations, and consider its global and ethical ramifications. This practice will broaden your knowledge and further develop your decision-making abilities.

Research Case 13–1
Bank loan; accrued
interest

A fellow accountant has solicited your opinion regarding the classification of short-term obligations repaid prior to being replaced by a long-term security. Cheshire Foods, Inc., issued $5,000,000 of short-term commercial paper during 2002 to finance construction of a plant. At September 30, 2003, Cheshire's fiscal year-end, the company intends to refinance the commercial paper by issuing long-term bonds. However, because Cheshire temporarily has excess cash, in November 2003 it liquidates $2,000,000 of the commercial paper as the paper matures. In December 2003, the company completes a $10,000,000 long-term bond issue. Later during December, it issues its September 30, 2003 financial statements. The proceeds of the long-term bond issue are to be used to replenish $2,000,000 in working capital, to pay $3,000,000 of commercial paper as it matures in January 2004, and to pay $5,000,000 of construction costs expected to be incurred later that year to complete the plant.

You initially are hesitant because you don't recall encountering a situation in which short-term obligations were repaid prior to being replaced by a long-term security. However, you are encouraged by remembering that this general topic is covered by an FASB pronouncement to which you have access: "Classification of Obligations Expected to Be Refinanced," *Statement of Financial Accounting Standards No. 6* (Stamford, Conn.: FASB, 1975). Also, "Classification of Obligation Repaid Prior to Being Replaced by a Long-Term Security," *FASB Interpretation No. 8*, addresses this situation specifically.

Required:
Determine how the $5,000,000 of commercial paper should be classified by consulting the FASB standard. Before doing so, formulate your own opinion on the proper treatment.

Real World Case 13–2
Returnable containers

The Zoo Doo Compost Company processes a premium organic fertilizer made with the help of the animals at the Memphis Zoo. Zoo Doo is sold in a specially designed plastic pail that may be kept and used for household chores or returned to the seller. The fertilizer is sold for $12.50 per two-gallon pail (including the $1.76 cost of the pail). For each pail returned, Zoo Doo donates $1 to the Memphis Zoo and the pail is used again.[23]

---

[23]Case based on Kay McCullen, "Take The Zoo Home With You!" *Head Lions*, July 1991 and a conversation with the Zoo Doo Compost Company president, Pierce Ledbetter.

Required:

The founder and president of this start-up firm has asked your opinion on how to account for the donations to be made when fertilizer pails are returned. (Ignore any tax implications.)

Research Case 13–3
Relationship of liabilities to assets and owners' equity

SFAC No. 6 states that "an entity's assets, liabilities, and equity (net assets) all pertain to the same set of probable future economic benefits." Explain this statement.

Ethics Case 13–4
Outdoors R Us

Outdoors R Us owns several membership-based campground resorts throughout the Southwest. The company sells campground sites to new members, usually during a get-acquainted visit and tour. The campgrounds offer a wider array of on-site facilities than most. New members sign a multiyear contract, pay a down payment, and make monthly installment payments. Because no credit check is made and many memberships originate on a spur-of-the-moment basis, cancellations are not uncommon.

Business has been brisk during its first three years of operations, and since going public in 1998, the market value of its stock has tripled. The first sign of trouble came in 2003 when the new sales dipped sharply.

One afternoon, two weeks before the end of the fiscal year, Diane Rice, CEO, and Gene Sun, controller, were having an active discussion in Sun's office.

Sun: I've thought more about our discussion yesterday. Maybe something can be done about profits.

Rice: I hope so. Our bonuses and stock value are riding on this period's performance.

Sun: We've been recording unearned revenues when new members sign up. Rather than recording liabilities at the time memberships are sold, I think we can justify reporting sales revenue for all memberships sold.

Rice: What will be the effect on profits?

Sun: I haven't run the numbers yet, but let's just say very favorable.

Required:
1. Why do you think liabilities had been recorded previously?
2. Is the proposal ethical?
3. Who would be affected if the proposal is implemented?

Trueblood Accounting Case 13–5
Evaluation of a loss contingency

The following Trueblood case is recommended for use with this chapter. The case provides an excellent opportunity for class discussion, group projects, and writing assignments. The case, along with Professor's Discussion Material, can be obtained from the Deloitte Foundation at its website: **www.deloitte.com/more/DTF/cases_subj.htm.**

Case 00–7: *Up In Smoke*

This case gives students the opportunity to use their judgment related to the evaluation of a loss contingency.

Communication Case 13–6
Exceptions to the general classification guideline; group interaction

Domestic Transfer and Storage is a large trucking company headquartered in the Midwest. Rapid expansion in recent years has been financed in large part by debt in a variety of forms. In preparing the financial statements for 2004, questions have arisen regarding the way certain of the liabilities are to be classified in the company's classified balance sheet.

A meeting of several members of the accounting area is scheduled for tomorrow, April 8, 2004. You are confident that that meeting will include the topic of debt classification. You want to appear knowledgeable at the meeting, but realizing it's been a few years since you have dealt with classification issues, you have sought out information you think relevant. Questionable liabilities at the company's fiscal year-end (January 31, 2004) include the following:

a. $15 million of 9% commercial paper is due on July 31, 2004. Management intends to refinance the paper on a long-term basis. In early April, 2004, Domestic negotiated a credit agreement with a commercial bank for up to $12 million any time during the next three years, any borrowings from which will mature two years from the date of borrowing.

b. $17 million of 11% notes were issued on June 30, 2001. The notes are due on November 30, 2004. The company has investments of $20 million classified as "available for sale."

c. $25 million of 10% notes were due on February 28, 2004. On February 21, 2004, the company issued 30-year, 9.4% bonds in a private placement to institutional investors.

d.   Recently, company management has considered reducing debt in favor of a greater proportion of equity financing. $20 million of 12% bonds mature on July 31, 2004. Discussions with underwriters, which began on January 4, 2004, resulted in a contractual arrangement on March 15 under which new common shares will be sold in July for approximately $20 million.

In order to make notes to yourself in preparation for the meeting concerning the classification of these items, you decide to discuss them with a colleague. Specifically, you want to know what portion of the debt can be excluded from classification as a current liability (that is, reported as a noncurrent liability) and why.

Required:

1.   What is the appropriate classification of each liability? Develop a list of arguments in support of your view prior to the class session for which the case is assigned.

2.   In class, your instructor will pair you (and everyone else) with a classmate (who also has independently developed a position). You will be given three minutes to argue your view to your partner. Your partner likewise will be given three minutes to argue his or her view to you. During these three-minute presentations, the listening partner is not permitted to speak.

3.   Then after each person has had a turn attempting to convince his or her partner, the two partners will have a three-minute discussion to decide which classifications are more convincing. Arguments will be merged into a single view for each pair.

4.   After the allotted time, a spokesperson for each of the four liabilities will be selected by the instructor. Each spokesperson will field arguments from the class as to the appropriate classification. The class then will discuss the merits of the classification and attempt to reach a consensus view, though a consensus is not necessary.

Communication Case 13–7
Various contingencies

"I see an all-nighter coming on," Gayle grumbled. "Why did Mitch just now give us this assignment?" Your client, Western Manufacturing is involved with several situations that possibly involve contingencies. The assignment Gayle refers to is to draft appropriate accounting treatment for each situation described below in time for tomorrow's meeting of the audit group. Western's fiscal year is the calendar year 2003, and the 2003 financial statements are issued on March 15, 2004.

1.   During 2003, Western experienced labor disputes at three of its plants. Management hopes an agreement will soon be reached. However negotiations between the Company and the unions have not produced an acceptable settlement and, as a result, strikes are ongoing at these facilities since March 1, 2004. It is virtually certain that material costs will be incurred but the amount of possible costs cannot be reasonably ascertained.

2.   In accordance with a 2001 contractual agreement with A. J. Conner Company, Western is entitled to $37 million for certain fees and expense reimbursements. These were written off as bad debts in 2002. A. J. Conner has filed for bankruptcy. The bankruptcy court on February 4, 2004, ordered A. J. Conner to pay $23 million immediately upon consummation of a proposed merger with Garner Holding Group.

3.   Western warrants most products it sells against defects in materials and workmanship for a period of a year. Based on their experience with previous product introductions, warranty costs are expected to approximate 2% of sales. A warranty liability of $39 million was reported at December 31, 2002. Sales of warranted products during 2003 were $2,100 million and actual warranty expenditures were $40 million. Expenditures in excess of the existing liability were debited to warranty expense.

4.   Western is involved in a suit filed in January 2004 by Crump Holdings seeking $88 million, as an adjustment to the purchase price in connection with the Company's sale of its textile business in 2003. The suit alleges that Western misstated the assets and liabilities used to calculate the purchase price for the textile division. Legal counsel advises that it is reasonably possible that Western could end up losing an indeterminable but material amount not expected to have a material adverse effect on the Company's financial position.

Required:

1.   Determine the appropriate means of reporting each situation.

2.   In a memo to the audit manager, Mitch Riley, explain your reasoning. Include any necessary journal entries and drafts of appropriate disclosure notes.

Judgment Case 13–8
Loss contingency and full disclosure

In the March 2004 meeting of Valleck Corporation's board of directors, a question arose as to the way a possible obligation should be disclosed in the forthcoming financial statements for the year ended December 31. A veteran board member brought to the meeting a draft of a disclosure note that had been prepared by the controller's office for inclusion in the annual report. Here is the note:

On May 9, 2003, the United States Environmental Protection Agency (EPA) issued a Notice of Violation (NOV) to Valleck alleging violations of the Clean Air Act. Subsequently, in June 2003, the EPA commenced a civil action with respect to the foregoing violation seeking civil penalties of approximately $853,000. The EPA alleges that Valleck exceeded applicable volatile organic substance emission limits. The Company estimates that the cost to achieve compliance will be $190,000; in addition the Company expects to settle the EPA lawsuit for a civil penalty of $205,000 which will be paid in 2006.

"Where did we get the $205,000 figure?" he asked. On being informed that this is the amount negotiated last month by company attorneys with the EPA, the director inquires, "Aren't we supposed to report a liability for that in addition to the note?"

Required:
Explain whether Valleck should report a liability in addition to the note. Why or why not? For full disclosure, should anything be added to the disclosure note itself?

Communication Case 13–9
Change in loss contingency; write a memo

Communication Case 21–5 deals with a change in a loss contingency.

Research Case 13–10
Researching the way contingencies are reported; retrieving information from the Internet

EDGAR (Electronic Data Gathering, Analysis, and Retrieval system) performs automated collection, validation, indexing, acceptance, and forwarding of submissions by companies and others who are required by law to file forms with the U.S. Securities and Exchange Commission (SEC). All publicly traded domestic companies use EDGAR to make the majority of their filings. Form 10-K, which includes the annual report, is required to be filed on EDGAR. The SEC makes this information available on the Internet.

Required:
1. Access EDGAR on the Internet using EdgarScan at: edgarscan.pwcglobal.com.
2. Search for a public company with which you are familiar. Access its most recent 10-K filing. Search or scroll to find the financial statements and related notes.
3. Specifically, look for any contingency(s) reported in the disclosure notes. Identify the nature of the contingency(s) described and explain the reason(s) the loss or losses was or was not accrued.
4. Repeat requirements 2 and 3 for two additional companies.

Communication Case 13–11
Accounting changes

Kevin Brantly is a new hire in the controller's office of Fleming Home Products. Two events occurred in late 2003 that the company had not previously encountered. The events appear to affect two of the company's liabilities, but there is some disagreement concerning whether they also affect financial statements of prior years. Each change occurred during 2003 before any adjusting entries or closing entries were prepared. The tax rate for Fleming is 40% in all years.

• Fleming Home Products introduced a new line of commercial awnings in 2002 that carry a one-year warranty against manufacturer's defects. Based on industry experience, warranty costs were expected to approximate 3% of sales. Sales of the awnings in 2002 were $3,500,000. Accordingly, warranty expense and a warranty liability of $105,000 were recorded in 2002. In late 2003, the company's claims experience was evaluated and it was determined that claims were far fewer than expected—2% of sales rather than 3%. Sales of the awnings in 2003 were $4,000,000 and warranty expenditures in 2003 totaled $91,000.

• In November 2001, the State of Minnesota filed suit against the company, seeking penalties for violations of clean air laws. When the financial statements were issued in 2002, Fleming had not reached a settlement with state authorities, but legal counsel advised Fleming that it was probable the company would have to pay $200,000 in penalties. Accordingly, the following entry was recorded:

Loss—litigation	200,000	
Liability—litigation		200,000

Late in 2003, a settlement was reached with state authorities to pay a total of $350,000 in penalties.

Required:

Kevin's supervisor, perhaps unsure of the answer, perhaps wanting to test Kevin's knowledge, e-mails the message, "Kevin, send me a memo on how we should handle our awning warranty and that clean air suit." Wanting to be accurate, Kevin consults his reference materials. What will he find? Prepare the memo requested.

**Real World Case
13–12
Frequent flyer miles**

Most airlines offer a frequent flyer program under which passengers can earn free travel. Northwest Airlines Corporation described its program in a recent annual report:

Frequent Flyer Program (in part)

Northwest operates a frequent flyer marketing program known as "WorldPerks" under which mileage credits are earned by flying on Northwest or its alliance partners and by using the services of participating bank credit cards, hotels, long-distance companies, car rental firms and other non-airline partners. The program was designed to retain and increase the business of frequent travelers by offering incentives for their continued patronage.

Under the WorldPerks program, miles earned are accumulated in an account for each member and do not expire. Mileage credits can be redeemed for free or upgraded travel on Northwest and other participating airlines or for other travel industry awards.

Northwest accounts for its frequent flyer obligation on the accrual basis using the incremental cost method. Northwest includes food and beverage, fuel, insurance, security, miscellaneous claims and WorldPerks service center expense in its incremental cost calculation. The incremental costs do not include any contribution to overhead or profit. Food, beverage and other costs are based on average cost per passenger for the current twelve-month period. The incremental fuel unit cost per passenger is based on engineering formulas that determine the average fuel cost per pound carried. Average fuel prices and estimated average weight of each added onboard passenger and luggage are factored into the incremental cost computation and converted to a rate per passenger per award.

The number of estimated travel awards outstanding at December 31, 2000, 1999 and 1998 was approximately 7,162,000, 6,520,000 and 6,147,000 awards, respectively. The estimated liability excludes accounts that have never attained the average travel award level and awards that are expected to be redeemed for upgrades or are not expected to be redeemed at all, and includes an estimate for partially earned awards on accounts that previously earned an award. Northwest has recorded a liability for these estimated awards of $115 million, $107 million and $100 million at December 31, 2000, 1999 and 1998, respectively. The number of travel awards used for travel on Northwest during the years ended December 31, 2000, 1999 and 1998 was approximately 1,263,000, 1,295,000 and 1,159,000, respectively. These awards represented an estimated 6.6%, 6.1% and 6.8% of Northwest's total RPMs for each such year, respectively.

	($ in millions)	
Current liabilities	**2000**	**1999**
Air traffic liability	$1,307	$1,422
Accounts payable	592	494
Accrued compensation and benefits	549	523
Accrued aircraft rent	229	222
Accrued commissions	106	95
Current maturities of long-term debt	482	449
Current obligations under capital leases	191	312
Short-term borrowings	62	60
	3,518	3,577

Required:
1. Why does Northwest's frequent flyer program produce a liability?
2. Is incremental cost the appropriate measure of the liability? Why?
3. Is the liability current, long-term, or both?
4. Prepare journal entries appropriate to recognize Northwest's expense and liability making the following additional assumptions:

a. The entire liability is considered current and 80% of the Air Traffic Liability pertains to the frequent flyer program.
b. Revenue received for travel sold to companions of award recipients is recognized when the transportation is provided.
c. In 2000, Northwest provided $200 million of travel under its frequent flyer program of which $40 million was travel sold to companions of award recipients.

Real World Case 13–13
Breast implant liability

In the early 1990s, major manufacturers of silicone breast implants faced extensive litigation regarding health risks associated with the devices. Most of the leading makers, defendants in a class action lawsuit, entered into a global settlement agreement. In 1994, Bristol-Myers Squibb Company, maker of health and personal care products, reported the following information pertaining to its involvement in the suit:

Note 2: Special Charge (in part)

As described in Note 18, the company is party to a settlement concerning pending and future breast implant product liability claims (related to a previously discontinued business of a subsidiary) brought against it, its Medical Engineering Corporation subsidiary, certain other subsidiaries. In the fourth quarter of 1993, the company recorded a special charge of $500 million before taxes, $310 million after taxes, or $.60 per share. The charge consisted of $1.5 billion in anticipation of its share of the pending settlement and costs of the litigation ($1.4 billion recorded as a long-term liability in Product Liability and $100 million recorded as a current liability in Accrued Expenses), offset by $1 billion of expected insurance proceeds (recorded as Insurance Recoverable). Although the company is currently engaged in coverage litigation with certain of its insurers, expected insurance proceeds represent the amount of insurance which the company considers appropriate to record as recoverable at this time. The company believes that ultimately it will obtain substantial additional amounts of insurance proceeds.

Required:
1. From an accounting perspective, what necessitated the special charge?
2. Bristol-Myers Squibb did not report the charge as an extraordinary item on its income statement. Which of the amounts mentioned in the note is the appropriate income statement line item? Why?
3. Relying on the information provided by the disclosure note, re-create the journal entry Bristol-Myers Squibb recorded to accrue the charge.

Ethics Case 13–14
Profits guaranteed

This was Joel Craig's first visit to the controller's corner office since being recruited for the senior accountant position in May. Because he'd been directed to bring with him his preliminary report on year-end adjustments, Craig presumed he'd done something wrong in preparing the report. That he had not was Craig's first surprise. His second surprise was his boss's request to reconsider one of the estimated expenses.

S & G Fasteners was a new company, specializing in plastic industrial fasteners. All products carry a generous long-term warranty against manufacturer's defects. "Don't you think 4% of sales is a little high for our warranty expense estimate?" his boss wondered. "After all, we're new at this. We have little experience with product introductions. I just got off the phone with Blanchard (the company president). He thinks we'll have trouble renewing our credit line with the profits we're projecting. The pressure's on."

Required:
1. Should Craig follow his boss's suggestion?
2. Does revising the warranty estimate pose an ethical dilemma?
3. Who would be affected if the suggestion is followed?

International Case 13–15
Accounting for current liabilities and contingencies in other countries

The International Accounting Standards Board (IASB) seeks to narrow worldwide differences in accounting practices and the presentation of financial information. The IASB has worked toward uniformity since 1973, but harmonization has by no means been achieved. In the area of accounting for current liabilities and contingencies, significant differences exist from country to country. The differences impact the financial position and the ability of analysts to assess risk in countries where these benefits are significant.

Required:

Choose a country other than the United States and:

1. Locate a recent annual report of a non-U.S. company.
2. Determine the way that country reports current liabilities on its balance sheet. Include in your analysis:
   a. Whether they are reported as a separate classification of liabilities or whether they are netted against current assets.
   b. Whether and how details are reported in disclosure notes.
3. Determine the way that country reports contingencies. Include in your analysis:
   a. Under what conditions are loss contingencies accrued.
   b. Whether gain contingencies can be accrued or reported in disclosure notes.

Note: You can obtain copies of annual reports by contacting the investor relations department of the corporation, from a friendly stockbroker, from EDGAR, the Electronic Data Gathering and Retrieval service of the SEC, through EdgarScan at edgarscan.pwcglobal.com/, or often from the company's website.

Analysis Case 13–16
Analyzing financial
statements; liquidity
ratios

IGF Foods Company is a large, primarily domestic, consumer foods company involved in the manufacture, distribution and sale of a variety of food products. Industry averages are derived from Troy's *The Almanac of Business and Industrial Financial Ratios.* Following are the 2003 and 2002 comparative balance sheets for IGF. (The financial data we use are from actual financial statements of a well-known corporation, but the company name used is fictitious and the numbers and dates have been modified slightly.)

IGF FOODS COMPANY
Comparative Balance Sheets
Years Ended December 31, 2003 and 2002
($ in millions)

	2003	2002
Assets		
Current assets:		
Cash	$ 48	$ 142
Accounts receivable	347	320
Marketable securities	358	—
Inventories	914	874
Prepaid expenses	212	154
Total current assets	$1,879	$1,490
Property, plant, and equipment (net)	2,592	2,291
Intangibles (net)	800	843
Other assets	74	60
Total assets	$5,345	$4,684
Liabilities and Shareholders' Equity		
Current liabilities:		
Accounts payable	$ 254	$ 276
Accrued liabilities	493	496
Notes payable	518	115
Current portion of long-term debt	208	54
Total current liabilities	$1,473	$ 941
Long-term debt	534	728
Deferred income taxes	407	344
Total liabilities	$2,414	$2,013
Shareholders' equity:		
Common stock	180	180
Additional paid-in capital	21	63
Retained earnings	2,730	2,428
Total shareholders' equity	$2,931	$2,671
Total liabilities and shareholders' equity	$5,345	$4,684

Liquidity refers to a company's cash position and overall ability to obtain cash in the normal course of business. A company is said to be liquid if it has sufficient cash or is capable of converting its other assets to cash in a relatively short period of time so that currently maturing debts can be paid.

Required:
1. Calculate the current ratio for IGF for 2003. The average ratio for the stocks listed on the New York Stock Exchange in a comparable time period was 1.5. What information does your calculation provide an investor?
2. Calculate IGF's acid-test or quick ratio for 2003. The ratio for the stocks listed on the New York Stock Exchange in a comparable time period was .80. What does your calculation indicate about IGF's liquidity?

Analysis Case 13–17
Reporting current liabilities; liquidity

Refer to the financial statements and related disclosure notes of FedEx Corporation in the appendix to Chapter 1. At the end of its 2001 fiscal year, FedEx reported current liabilities of $3.2 billion on its balance sheet.

Required:
1. What are the four components of current liabilities?
2. Are current assets sufficient to cover current liabilities? What is the current ratio for 2001? How does the ratio compare with 2000?

FedEx Corporation
3. FedEx reported accrued expenses among its current liabilities. What were the two largest accrued expenses in 2001? What are accrued expenses and when does FedEx record them?

14

Bonds and Long-Term Notes

OVERVIEW

This chapter continues the presentation of liabilities. Specifically, the discussion focuses on the accounting treatment of long-term liabilities. Long-term notes and bonds are discussed, as well as the extinguishment of debt and debt convertible into stock.

LEARNING OBJECTIVES

After studying this chapter, you should be able to:

LO1 Identify the underlying characteristics of debt instruments and describe the basic approach to accounting for debt.

LO2 Account for bonds issued at par, at a discount, or at a premium, recording interest at the effective rate or by the straight-line method.

LO3 Characterize the accounting treatment of notes, including installment notes, issued for cash or for noncash consideration.

LO4 Describe the disclosures appropriate to long-term debt in its various forms.

LO5 Record the early extinguishment of debt and its conversion into equity securities.

Service Leader, Inc.

The mood is both upbeat and focused on this cool October morning. Executives and board members of Service Leader, Inc., are meeting with underwriters and attorneys to discuss the company's first bond offering in its 20-year history. You are attending in the capacity of company controller and two-year member of the board of directors. The closely held corporation has been financed entirely by equity, internally generated funds, and short-term bank borrowings.

Bank rates of interest, though, have risen recently and the company's unexpectedly rapid, but welcome, growth has prompted the need to look elsewhere for new financing. Under consideration are 15-year, 6.25% first mortgage bonds with a principal amount of $70 million. The bonds would be callable at 103 any time after June 30, 2008, and convertible into Service Leader common stock at the rate of 45 shares per $1,000 bond.

Other financing vehicles have been discussed over the last two months, including the sale of additional stock, nonconvertible bonds, and unsecured notes. This morning *The Wall Street Journal* indicated that market rates of interest for debt similar to the bonds under consideration are about 6.5%.

> By the time you finish this chapter, you should be able to respond appropriately to the questions posed in this case. Compare your response to the solution provided at the end of the chapter.

QUESTIONS

1. What does it mean that the bonds are "first mortgage" bonds? What effect does that have on financing? (page 667)

2. From Service Leader's perspective, why are the bonds callable? What does that mean? (page 667)

3. How will it be possible to sell bonds paying investors 6.25% when other, similar investments will provide the investors a return of 6.5%? (page 669)

4. Would accounting differ if the debt were designated as notes rather than bonds? (page 679)

5. Why might the company choose to make the bonds convertible into common stock? (page 689)

The Nature of Long-Term Debt

● LO1

A company must raise funds to finance its operations and often the expansion of those operations. Presumably, at least some of the necessary funding can be provided by the company's own operations, though some funds must be provided by external sources. Ordinarily, external financing includes some combination of equity and debt funding. We explore debt financing first.

In the present chapter, we focus on debt in the form of bonds and notes. The following four chapters deal with liabilities also, namely those arising in connection with leases (Chapter 15), deferred income taxes (Chapter 16), pensions (Chapter 17), and employee benefits (Chapter 18). Some employee benefits create equity rather than debt, which also are discussed in Chapter 18. Then, in Chapter 19, we examine shareholders' interest arising from external *equity* financing. In Chapter 22, we see that cash flows from both debt and equity financing are reported together in a statement of cash flows as "cash flows from financing activities."

Liabilities signify *creditors' interest* in a company's assets.

As you read this chapter, you will find the focus to be on the liability side of the transactions we examine. Realize, though, that the mirror image of a liability is an asset (bonds payable/investment in bonds, note payable/note receivable, etc.). So as we discuss accounting for debts from the viewpoint of the issuers of the debt instruments, we also will take the opportunity to see how the lender deals with the corresponding asset. Studying the two sides of the same transaction in tandem will emphasize their inherent similarities.

A note payable and a note receivable are two sides of the same coin.

Accounting for a liability is a relatively straightforward concept. This is not to say that all debt instruments are unchallenging, "plain vanilla" loan agreements. Quite the contrary, the financial community continuously devises increasingly exotic ways to flavor financial instruments in the attempt to satisfy the diverse and evolving tastes of both debtors and creditors.

Periodic interest is the effective interest rate times the amount of the debt outstanding during the interest period.

Packaging aside, a liability requires the future payment of cash in specified (or estimated) amounts, at specified (or projected) dates. As time passes, interest accrues on debt. As a general rule, the periodic interest is the effective interest rate times the amount of the debt outstanding during the period. This same principle applies regardless of the specific form of the liability—note payable, bonds payable, lease liability, pension obligation, or other debt instruments. Also, as a general rule, long-term liabilities are reported at their present values. The present value of a liability is the present value of its related cash flows (principal and/or interest payments), discounted at the effective rate of interest at issuance.

We begin our study of long-term liabilities by examining accounting for bonds. We follow that section with a discussion of debt in the form of notes in Part B. It's important to note that, although particulars of the two forms of debt differ, the basic approach to accounting for each type is precisely the same. In Part C, we look at various ways bonds and notes are retired or converted into other securities.

PART

A bond issue divides a large liability into many smaller liabilities.

BONDS

A company can borrow cash from a bank or other financial institution by signing a promissory note. We discuss notes payable later in the chapter. Medium- and large-sized corporations often choose to borrow cash by issuing bonds. In fact, the most common form of corporate debt is bonds. A bond issue, in effect, breaks down a large debt (large corporations often borrow hundreds of millions of dollars at a time) into manageable parts—usually $1,000 or $5,000 units. This avoids the necessity of finding a single lender who is both willing and able to loan a large amount of money at a reasonable interest rate. So rather than signing a $400 million note to borrow cash from a financial institution, a company may find it more economical to sell 400,000 $1,000 bonds to many lenders—theoretically up to 400,000 lenders.

Bonds obligate the issuing corporation to repay a stated amount (variously referred to as the *principal, par value, face amount,* or *maturity value*) at a specified *maturity date*. Maturities for bonds typically range from 10 to 40 years. In return for the use of the money borrowed, the company also agrees to pay *interest* to bondholders between the issue date and maturity. The periodic interest is a stated percentage of face amount (variously referred to as the *stated rate, coupon rate,* or *nominal rate*). Ordinarily, interest is paid semiannually on designated interest dates beginning six months after the day the bonds are "dated."

The Bond Indenture

The specific promises made to bondholders are described in a document called a **bond indenture**. Because it would be impractical for the corporation to enter into a direct agreement with each of the many bondholders, the bond indenture is held by a trustee, usually a commercial bank or other financial institution, appointed by the issuing firm to represent the rights of the bondholders. If the company fails to live up to the terms of the bond indenture, the trustee may bring legal action against the company on behalf of the bondholders.

Most corporate bonds are debenture bonds. A **debenture bond** is secured only by the "full faith and credit" of the issuing corporation. No specific assets are pledged as security. Investors in debentures usually have the same standing as the firm's other general creditors. So in case of bankruptcy, debenture holders and other general creditors would be treated equally. An exception is the **subordinated debenture**, which as the name implies, is not entitled to receive any liquidation payments until the claims of other specified debt issues are satisfied.

A **mortgage bond**, on the other hand, is backed by a lien on specified real estate owned by the issuer. Because a mortgage bond is considered less risky than debentures, it typically will command a lower interest rate.

Today most corporate bonds are registered bonds. Interest checks are mailed directly to the owner of the bond, whose name is registered with the issuing company. Years ago, it was typical for bonds to be structured as **coupon bonds** (sometimes called *bearer bonds*). The name of the owner of a coupon bond was not registered. Instead, to collect interest on a coupon bond the holder actually clipped an attached coupon and redeemed it in accordance with instructions in the indenture. A carryover effect of this practice is that we still often see the term *coupon rate* in reference to the stated interest rate on bonds.

Bonds are not always retired by a single-sum payment at a specific maturity date. The bond indenture also might provide for their redemption through a call feature, by serial payments, through sinking fund provisions, or by conversion.

Most corporate bonds are **callable** (or redeemable). The call feature allows the issuing company to buy back, or call, outstanding bonds from bondholders before their scheduled maturity date. This feature affords the company some protection against being stuck with relatively high-cost debt in the event interest rates fall during the period to maturity. The call price must be prespecified and often exceeds the bond's face amount (a call premium), sometimes declining as maturity is approached.

For example, recent financial statements of Emhart Corporation included this footnote disclosure:

> The Company's 9¼% (9.65% effective interest rate, after discount) sinking fund debentures are callable at prices decreasing from 105% of face amount currently to 100% in 2006.

"No call" provisions usually prohibit calls during the first few years of a bond's life. Very often, calls are mandatory. That is, the corporation may be required to redeem the bonds on a prespecified, year-by-year basis. Bonds requiring such sinking fund redemptions often are labeled *sinking fund debentures*. Emhart's disclosures regarding its sinking fund debentures also included:

> . . . sinking fund redemptions are required in the amount of $8.0 million each year.

Corporations issuing bonds are obligated to repay a stated amount at a specified maturity date *and periodic* interest *between the issue date and maturity.*

A bond indenture *describes the specific promises made to bondholders.*

Liquidation rights affect a bond issue's effective interest rate.

FINANCIAL REPORTING CASE

Q1, p. 665

FINANCIAL REPORTING CASE

Q2, p. 665

Mandatory sinking fund redemptions retire a bond issue gradually over its term to maturity.

The **sinking fund** typically is administered by a trustee who repurchases bonds in the open market. If insufficient willing sellers are found, the trustee must exercise the bonds' call feature to buy the required amount of bonds, using a lottery approach to select bonds for call from among existing bondholders.

Serial bonds provide a more structured (and less popular) way to retire bonds on a piece-meal basis. Serial bonds are retired in installments during all or part of the life of the issue. Each bond has its own specified maturity date. So for a typical 30-year serial issue, 25 to 30 separate maturity dates might be assigned to specific portions of the bond issue.

Convertible bonds are retired as a consequence of bondholders choosing to convert them into shares of stock. We look closer at convertible bonds a little later in the chapter.

CHECK WITH THE **COACH**

Although you hear a lot about the stock market in the media, many investors invest significantly in bonds and other debt securities. Check with the Coach to understand better how these securities are priced and the implications for financial reporting. Many students find these complexities challenging to master. The Coach's animated illustrations of accounting for bonds and long-term notes will help you to do so. ∎

Recording Bonds at Issuance

Bonds represent a liability to the corporation that issues the bonds and an asset to a company that buys the bonds as an investment. Each side of the transaction is the mirror image of the other.[1] This is demonstrated in Illustration 14–1.

ILLUSTRATION 14–1	On January 1, 2003, Masterwear Industries issued $700,000 of 12% bonds. Interest of $42,000 is payable semiannually on June 30 and December 31. The bonds mature in three years (an unrealistically short maturity to shorten the illustration). The entire bond issue was sold in a private placement to United Intergroup, Inc., at the face amount.
Bonds Sold at Face Amount	

At Issuance (January 1)		
Masterwear (Issuer)		
Cash..	700,000	
Bonds payable (face amount)............................		700,000
United (Investor)		
Investment in bonds (face amount).........................	700,000	
Cash..		700,000

BONDS ISSUED BETWEEN INTEREST DATES

We assumed that the bonds in the previous example were sold on the day they were dated (date printed in the indenture contract). But suppose a weak market caused a delay in selling the bonds until two months after that date (four months before semiannual interest was to be paid). In that case, the buyer would be asked to pay the seller **accrued interest** for two months in addition to the price of the bonds. For illustration, assume Masterwear was unable to sell the bonds in the previous example until March 1—two months after they are dated. This variation is shown in Illustration 14–1A. United would pay the price of the bonds ($700,000) plus $14,000 accrued interest:

All bonds sell at their price plus any interest that has accrued since the last interest date.

---

[1]You should recall from Chapter 12 that investments in bonds that are to be held to maturity by the investor are reported at amortized cost, which is the method described here. However, also remember that investments in debt securities *not* to be held to maturity are reported at the fair value of the securities held, as described in Chapter 12.

$$\underset{\substack{\text{Face} \\ \text{amount}}}{\$700{,}000} \times \underset{\substack{\text{Annual} \\ \text{rate}}}{12\%} \times \underset{\substack{\text{Fraction of the} \\ \text{annual period}}}{\tfrac{2}{12}} = \underset{\substack{\text{Accrued} \\ \text{interest}}}{\$14{,}000}$$

At Issuance (March 1)		
Masterwear (Issuer)		
Cash (price plus accrued interest)............................	714,000	
Bonds payable (face amount).............................		700,000
Interest payable (accrued interest determined above)		14,000
United (Investor)		
Investment in bonds (face amount)	700,000	
Interest receivable (accrued interest determined above)	14,000	
Cash (price plus accrued interest)		714,000

ILLUSTRATION 14–1A

Bonds Sold at Face Amount between Interest Dates

When Masterwear pays semiannual interest on June 30, a full six months' interest is paid. But having received two months' accrued interest in advance, Masterwear's *net* interest expense will be four months' interest, for the four months the bonds have been outstanding at that time. Likewise, when United receives six months' interest—after holding the bonds for only four months—United will net only the four months' interest to which it is entitled:

Since the investor will hold the bonds for only four months before receiving six months' interest, two months' accrued interest must be added to the price paid.

At the First Interest Date (June 30)		
Masterwear (Issuer)		
Interest expense (6 mo. − 2 mo. = 4 mo.)..................	28,000	
Interest payable[2] (accrued interest determined above)...........	14,000	
Cash (stated rate × face amount)		42,000
United (Investor)		
Cash (stated rate × face amount)........................	42,000	
Interest receivable (accrued interest determined above).........		14,000
Interest revenue (6 mo. − 2 mo. = 4 mo.)		28,000

The issuer incurs interest expense, and the investor earns interest revenue, for only the four months the bonds are outstanding.

DETERMINING THE SELLING PRICE

The price of a bond issue at any particular time is not necessarily equal to its face amount. The $700,000, 12% bond issue in the previous illustration, for example, may sell for more than face amount (at a **premium**) or less than face amount (at a **discount**), depending on how the 12% *stated* interest rate compares with the prevailing *market* or *effective rate* of interest (for securities of similar risk and maturity). For instance, if the 12% bonds are competing in a market in which similar bonds are providing a 14% return, the bonds could be sold only at a price less than $700,000. On the other hand, if the market rate is only 10%, the 12% stated rate would seem relatively attractive and the bonds would sell at a premium over face amount. The reason the stated rate often differs from the market rate, resulting in a discount or premium, is the inevitable delay between the date the terms of the issue are established and the date the issue comes to market.

FINANCIAL REPORTING CASE

Q3, p. 665

---

[2]Some accountants prefer to credit interest expense, rather than interest payable, when the bonds are sold. When that is done, this entry would require simply a debit to interest expense and a credit to cash for $42,000. The interest expense account would then reflect the same *net* debit of four months' interest ($42,000 − $14,000).

Interest Expense	
	2 months
6 months	
4 months	

Similarly, the investor could debit interest revenue, rather than interest receivable when buying the bonds.

Other things being equal, the lower the perceived riskiness of the corporation issuing bonds, the higher the price those bonds will command.

In addition to the characteristic terms of a bond agreement as specified in the indenture, the market rate for a specific bond issue is influenced by the creditworthiness of the company issuing the bonds. To evaluate the risk and quality of an individual bond issue, investors rely heavily on bond ratings provided by Standard & Poor's Corporation and by Moody's Investors Service, Inc. See the bond ratings in Graphic 14–1.

GRAPHIC 14–1
Bond Ratings*

	S&P	Moody's
Investment Grades:		
Highest	AAA	Aaa
High	AA	Aa
Medium	A	A
Minimum investment grade	BBB	Baa
"Junk" Ratings:		
Speculative	BB	Ba
Very speculative	B	B
Default or near default	CCC	Caa
	CC	Ca
	C	C
	D	

*Adapted from *Bond Record* (New York: Moody's Investor Service, monthly) and *Bond Guide* (New York: Standard & Poor's Corporation, monthly).

A bond issue will be priced by the marketplace to yield the market rate of interest for securities of similar risk and maturity.

Forces of supply and demand cause a bond issue to be *priced to yield the market rate.* In other words, an investor paying that price will earn an effective rate of return on the investment equal to the market rate. The price is calculated as the present value of all the cash flows required of the bonds, where the discount rate used in the present value calculation is the market rate. Specifically, the price will be the present value of the periodic cash interest payments (face amount × stated rate) plus the present value of the principal payable at maturity, both discounted at the market rate.

Bonds priced at a discount are described in Illustration 14–2.

ILLUSTRATION 14–2

Bonds Sold at a Discount

Because interest is paid semiannually, the present value calculations use:

a. one-half the stated rate (6%),

b. one-half the market rate (7%), and

c. 6 (3 × 2) semiannual periods.

On January 1, 2003, Masterwear Industries issued $700,000 of 12% bonds, dated January 1. Interest of $42,000 is payable semiannually on June 30 and December 31. The bonds mature in three years. The market yield for bonds of similar risk and maturity is 14%. The entire bond issue was purchased by United Intergroup, Inc.

Calculation of the Price of the Bonds

			Present Values
Interest	$ 42,000 × 4.76654*	=	$200,195
Principal	$700,000 × 0.66634†	=	466,438
Present value (price) of the bonds			$666,633

*Present value of an ordinary annuity of $1: $n = 6$, $i = 7\%$ (Table 6A–4).
†Present value of $1: $n = 6$, $i = 7\%$ (Table 6A–2).

The calculation is illustrated in Graphic 14–2.

Although the cash flows total $952,000, the present value of those future cash flows as of January 1, 2003, is only $666,633. This is due to the time value of money.

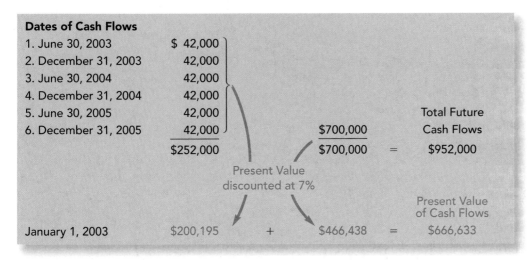

GRAPHIC 14–2
Cash Flows from a Bond Issue

Because of the time value of money, the present value of the future cash flows is less than $952,000.

Journal Entries at Issuance—Bonds Sold at a Discount

Masterwear (Issuer)		
Cash (price calculated above)	666,633	
Discount on bonds payable (difference)	33,367	
Bonds payable (face amount)		700,000
United (Investor)		
Investment in bonds (face amount)	700,000	
Discount on bond investment (difference)		33,367
Cash (price calculated above)		666,633

When bond prices are quoted in financial media, they typically are stated in terms of a percentage of face amount. Thus, a price quote of 98 means a $1,000 bond will sell for $980; a bond priced at 101 will sell for $1,010.

Determining Interest—Effective Interest Method

The *effective interest on debt is the market rate of interest multiplied by the outstanding balance of the debt.*

Interest accrues on an outstanding debt at a constant percentage of the debt each period. Of course, under the concept of accrual accounting, the periodic effective interest is not affected by the time at which the cash interest actually is paid. Recording interest each period as the *effective market rate of interest multiplied by the outstanding balance of the debt* (during the interest period) is referred to as the **effective interest method.** Although giving this a label—the effective interest method—implies some specialized procedure, this simply is an application of the accrual concept, consistent with accruing all expenses as they are incurred.

Continuing our example, we determined that the amount of debt when the bonds are issued is $666,633. Since the effective interest rate is 14%, interest recorded (as expense to the issuer and revenue to the investor) for the first six-month interest period is $46,664:

$$\underset{\text{Outstanding balance}}{\$666,633} \times \underset{\text{Effective rate}}{[14\% \div 2]} = \underset{\text{Effective interest}}{\$46,664}$$

However, the bond indenture calls for semiannual interest payments of only $42,000—the *stated* rate (6%) times the *face amount* ($700,000). As always, when only a portion of an expense is paid, the remainder becomes a liability—in this case an addition to the already outstanding liability. So the difference, $4,664, increases the liability and is reflected as a reduction in the discount (a valuation account). This is illustrated in Graphic 14–3.

Interest accrues on the outstanding debt at the effective rate. Interest paid is the amount specified in the bond indenture—the stated rate times the face amount. These amounts and the change in the outstanding debt are recorded as follows:

GRAPHIC 14–3
Change in Debt When Effective Interest Exceeds Cash Paid

The unpaid portion of the effective interest increases the existing liability.

	Account Balances				
	Outstanding Balance		Bonds Payable (face amount)		Discount on Bonds Payable
January 1	$666,633	=	$700,000	less	$33,367
Interest accrued at 7%	46,664				
Portion of interest paid	(42,000)				(4,664)
June 30	$671,297	=	$700,000	less	$28,703

Journal Entries—The Interest Method

The effective interest is calculated each period as the market rate times the amount of the debt outstanding during the interest period.

At the First Interest Date (June 30)

Masterwear (Issuer)
Interest expense (market rate × outstanding balance)	46,664	
Discount on bonds payable (difference).		4,664
Cash (stated rate × face amount)		42,000

United (Investor)
Cash (stated rate × face amount)	42,000	
Discount on bond investment (difference).	4,664	
Interest revenue (market rate × outstanding balance)		46,664

Because the balance of the debt changes each period, the dollar amount of interest (balance × rate) also will change each period. To keep up with the changing amounts, it usually is convenient to prepare a schedule that reflects the changes in the debt over its term to maturity. An amortization schedule for the situation under discussion is shown in Graphic 14–4.

GRAPHIC 14–4
Amortization Schedule—Discount

Since less cash is paid each period than the effective interest, the unpaid difference increases the outstanding balance of the debt.

	Cash Interest	Effective Interest	Increase in Balance	Outstanding Balance
	(6% × Face amount)	(7% × Outstanding balance)	(Discount reduction)	
1/1/03				666,633
6/30/03	42,000	.07 (666,633) = 46,664	4,664	671,297
12/31/03	42,000	.07 (671,297) = 46,991	4,991	676,288
6/30/04	42,000	.07 (676,288) = 47,340	5,340	681,628
12/31/04	42,000	.07 (681,628) = 47,714	5,714	687,342
6/30/05	42,000	.07 (687,342) = 48,114	6,114	693,456
12/31/05	42,000	.07 (693,456) = 48,544*	6,544	700,000
	252,000	285,367	33,367	

*Rounded.

Amounts for the journal entries each interest date are found in the first three columns of the schedule. Traditionally, this schedule has been referred to as an **amortization schedule**—a reference to alleged amortization of the discount.[3] This is an apparent carryover from earlier days when the discount was considered to be an asset to be amortized. To the contrary, the discount is a valuation account, having no existence apart from the related debt. As you learned in the previous paragraphs, changes in its balance are the derived result of

---

[3]You learned in earlier chapters that amortization is the accounting process of reducing an asset or liability by periodic write-downs or payments [*SFAC 6*, par. 142].

Terms such as *unamortized or deferred discount or premium* and *to amortize discount or premium* are carryovers from the days when debt discount was considered to be an amortizable asset and do not describe accurately either the assets or liabilities and events involved or the interest method of accounting for them.[5]

changes in the outstanding debt, when portions of periodic accrued interest go unpaid.[4]

However, because this terminology is so prevalent in practice, we too will use the label *amortization schedule.* Be sure to realize, though, that this label is a misnomer—nothing is being amortized. The essential point to remember is that the effective interest method is a straightforward application of the accrual concept, whereby interest expense (or revenue) is accrued periodically at the effective rate. It involves neither deferring expenses (or revenues) nor amortizing deferrals.

Determining interest in this manner has a convenient side effect. It results in reporting the liability at the present value of future cash payments—the appropriate valuation method for any liability.[6] This is obvious at issuance; we actually calculated the present value to be $666,633. What perhaps is not quite as obvious is that the outstanding amount of debt each subsequent period (shown in the right-hand column of the amortization schedule) is still the present value of the remaining cash flows, discounted at the original rate.

A liability should be reported at its present value.

ADDITIONAL CONSIDERATION

Although the reported amount each period is the **present value** of the bonds, at any date after issuance this amount is not necessarily equal to the **market value** of the bonds. This is because the **market** rate of interest will not necessarily remain the same as the rate implicit in the original issue price (the effective rate). Of course, for negotiable financial instruments, the issue price is the market price at any given time. Differences between market values and present values based on the original rate are holding gains and losses. If we were to use the market rate to revalue bonds on each reporting date—that is, recalculate the present value using the market rate—the reported amount always would be the market value. Some accountants contend that reporting market values and resultant holding gains and losses would provide more meaningful information than reporting debt at its present value, discounted at the original rate. Reporting debt at market values is not presently permitted by GAAP except in certain specialized industries like the mutual fund and insurance industries. Certainly the market value of existing debt is information considered by management in refinancing decisions.

ZERO-COUPON BONDS

A zero-coupon bond pays no interest. Instead, it offers a return in the form of a "deep discount" from the face amount. For illustration, let's look at the zero-coupon issue offered by Hewlett-Packard Company in 1997. One billion, eight hundred million dollars face amount of the 20-year securities sold for $968 million. As the amortization schedule in Graphic 14–5 on the next page demonstrates, they were priced to yield 3.15%.

Zero-coupon bonds provide us a convenient opportunity to reinforce a key concept we just learned: that we accrue the interest expense (or revenue) each period at the effective rate regardless of how much cash interest actually is paid (zero in this case). An advantage of issuing zero-coupon bonds or notes is that the corporation can deduct for tax purposes the annual interest expense (see schedule) but has no related cash outflow until the bonds mature. However, the reverse is true for investors in zeros. Investors receive no periodic cash interest, even

[4]Or as we see later, the debt changes when periodic interest is overpaid. This occurs when debt is sold at a premium, rather than at a discount.
[5]"Elements of Financial Statements," *Statement of Financial Accounting Concepts No. 6,* par. 36 (Stamford, Conn.: FASB, 1985), par. 239.
[6]"Interest on Receivables and Payables," *APB Opinion No. 21* (New York: AICPA, 1971).

GRAPHIC 14–5
Zero-Coupon
Securities—Hewlett-
Packard Company

($ in millions) Dec. 31	Cash Interest	Effective Interest	Increase in Balance	Outstanding Balance*
	(0% × Face amount)	(3.15% × Outstanding debt)	(Discount reduction)	
				968
1997	0	.0315 (968) = 30	30	999
1998	0	.0315 (999) = 31	31	1,030
1999	0	.0315 (1,030) = 32	32	1,062
◆	◆	◆	◆	◆
◆	◆	◆	◆	◆
◆	◆	◆	◆	◆
2016	0	.0315 (1,692) = 53	53	1,745
2017	0	.0315 (1,745) = 55	55	1,800
		832	832	

*Some numbers appear not to total because the underlying calculations are not rounded.

though annual interest revenue is reportable for tax purposes. So those who invest in zero-coupon bonds usually have tax-deferred or tax-exempt status, such as pension funds, individual retirement accounts (IRAs), and charitable organizations. Zero-coupon bonds and notes are gaining popularity but still constitute a relatively small proportion of corporate debt.

BONDS SOLD AT A PREMIUM

In Illustration 14–2, Masterwear Industries sold the bonds at a price that would yield an effective rate higher than the stated rate. The result was a discount. On the other hand, if the 12% bonds had been issued when the market yield for bonds of similar risk and maturity was *lower* than the stated rate, say 10%, the issue would have been priced at a *premium*. Because the 12% rate would seem relatively attractive in a 10% market, the bonds would command an issue price of more than $700,000, calculated in Illustration 14–3.

ILLUSTRATION 14–3

Bonds Sold at a
Premium

Because interest is
paid *semiannually*, the
present value
calculations use:

a. one-half the stated
rate (6%),

b. one-half the market
rate (5%), and

c. 6 (3 × 2) semiannual
periods.

On January 1, 2003, Masterwear Industries issued $700,000 of 12% bonds, dated January 1. Interest of $42,000 is payable semiannually on June 30 and December 31. The bonds mature in three years. The market yield for bonds of similar risk and maturity is 10%. The entire bond issue was purchased by United Intergroup, Inc.

Calculation of the Price of the Bonds

			Present Values
Interest	$42,000 × 5.07569*	=	$213,179
Principal	$700,000 × 0.74622†	=	522,354
Present value (price) of the bonds			$735,533

*Present value of an ordinary annuity of $1: n = 6, i = 5%.
†Present value of $1: n = 6, i = 5%.

*Journal Entries at
Issuance—Bonds Sold
at Premium*

Masterwear (Issuer)

Cash (price calculated above)	735,533	
Bonds payable (face amount)		700,000
Premium on bonds payable (difference)		35,533

United (Investor)

Investment in bonds (face amount)	700,000	
Premium on bond investment (difference)	35,533	
Cash (price calculated above)		735,533

Interest on bonds sold at a premium is determined in precisely the same manner as on bonds sold at a discount. Again, interest is the effective interest rate applied to the debt outstanding during each period (balance at the end of the previous interest period), and the cash paid is the stated rate times the face amount, as shown in Graphic 14–6:

Date 1	Cash Interest	Effective Interest	Decrease in Balance	Outstanding Balance
	(6% × Face amount)	(5% × Outstanding balance)	(Premium reduction)	
1/1/03				735,533
6/30/03	42,000	.05 (735,533) = 36,777	5,223	730,310
12/31/03	42,000	.05 (730,310) = 36,516	5,484	724,826
6/30/04	42,000	.05 (724,826) = 36,241	5,759	719,067
12/31/04	42,000	.05 (719,067) = 35,953	6,047	713,020
6/30/05	42,000	.05 (713,020) = 35,651	6,349	706,671
12/31/05	42,000	.05 (706,671) = 35,329*	6,671	700,000
	252,000	216,467	35,533	

GRAPHIC 14–6
Amortization Schedule—Premium

Since *more* cash is paid each period than the effective interest, the debt outstanding is reduced by the overpayment.

*Rounded.

Notice that the debt declines each period. This is because the effective interest each period is less than the cash interest paid. The overpayments each period reduce the amount owed. Remember, this is precisely the opposite of when debt is sold at a discount, when the effective interest each period is more than the cash paid, and the underpayment of interest adds to the amount owed.

ADDITIONAL CONSIDERATION

The preceding illustrations describe bonds sold at a discount and at a premium. The same concepts apply to bonds sold at face amount. But some of the procedures would be unnecessary. For instance, calculating the present value of the interest and the principal always will give us the face amount when the effective rate and the stated rate are the same:

Calculation of the Price of the Bonds

			Present Values
Interest	$42,000 × 4.91732*	=	$206,528
Principal	$700,000 × 0.70496†	=	493,472
Present value (price) of the bonds			$700,000

*Present value of an ordinary annuity of $1: n = 6, i = 6%.
†Present value of $1: n = 6, i = 6%.

WHEN FINANCIAL STATEMENTS ARE PREPARED BETWEEN INTEREST DATES

When an accounting period ends between interest dates, it is necessary to record interest that has accrued since the last interest date. As an example, refer again to Illustration 14–2 on page 670. If the fiscal years of Masterwear and United end on October 31 and interest was last paid and recorded on June 30, four months' interest must be accrued in a year-end adjusting entry. Because interest is recorded for only a portion of a semiannual period, amounts recorded are simply the amounts shown in the amortization schedule (Graphic 14–4, p. 672) times the appropriate fraction of the semiannual period (in this case ⁴⁄₆).

Any interest that has accrued since the last interest date must be recorded by an adjusting entry prior to preparing financial statements.

*Adjusting Entries—To
Accrue Interest*

*To avoid understating
interest in the financial
statements, four
months' interest is
recorded at the end of
the reporting period.*

At October 31

Masterwear (Issuer)		
Interest expense ($\frac{4}{6}$ × 46,991)	31,327	
Discount on bonds payable ($\frac{4}{6}$ × 4,991)		3,327
Interest payable ($\frac{4}{6}$ × 42,000)		28,000
United (Investor)		
Interest receivable ($\frac{4}{6}$ × 42,000)	28,000	
Discount on bond investment ($\frac{4}{6}$ × 4,991)	3,327	
Interest revenue ($\frac{4}{6}$ × 46,991)		31,327

Two months later, when semiannual interest is paid next, the remainder of the semiannual interest is allocated to the first two months of the next accounting year—November and December:

At the December 31 Interest Date

Masterwear (Issuer)		
Interest expense ($\frac{2}{6}$ × 46,991)	15,664	
Interest payable (from adjusting entry)	28,000	
Discount on bonds payable ($\frac{2}{6}$ × 4,991)		1,664
Cash (stated rate × face amount)		42,000
United (Investor)		
Cash (stated rate × face amount)	42,000	
Discount on bond investment ($\frac{2}{6}$ × 4,991)	1,664	
Interest receivable (from adjusting entry)		28,000
Interest revenue ($\frac{2}{6}$ × 46,991)		15,664

*Of the six-months'
interest paid December
31, only the November
and December interest
is expensed in the new
fiscal year.*

The Straight-Line Method—A Practical Expediency

In some circumstances the profession permits an exception to the conceptually appropriate method of determining interest for bond issues. A company is allowed to determine interest indirectly by allocating a discount or a premium equally to each period over the term to maturity—if doing so produces results that are not materially different from the usual (and preferable) interest method.[7] The decision should be guided by whether the **straight-line method** would tend to mislead investors and creditors in the particular circumstance.

By the straight-line method, the discount in Illustration 14–2 and Graphic 14–4 would be allocated equally to the six semiannual periods (three years):

$$\$33,367 \div 6 \text{ periods} = \$5,561 \text{ per period}$$

*Journal Entries—
Straight-Line Method*

At Each of the Six Interest Dates

Masterwear (Issuer)		
Interest expense (to balance)	47,561	
Discount on bonds payable (discount ÷ 6 periods)		5,561
Cash (stated rate × face amount)		42,000
United (Investor)		
Cash (stated rate × face amount)	42,000	
Discount on bond investment (discount ÷ 6 periods)	5,561	
Interest revenue (to balance)		47,561

*By the straight-line
method, interest
(expense and revenue)
is a plug figure,
resulting from
calculating the amount
of discount reduction.*

Allocating the discount or premium equally over the life of the bonds by the straight-line method results in a constant dollar amount of interest each period. An amortization schedule,

---

[7]Ibid.

then, would serve little purpose. For example, if we prepared one for the straight-line method in this situation, it would provide the same amounts each period as shown in Graphic 14–7.

	Cash Interest	Recorded Interest	Increase in Balance	Outstanding Balance
	(6% × Face amount)	(Cash + Discount reduction)	($33,367 ÷ 6)	
1/1/03				666,633
6/30/03	42,000	(42,000 + 5,561) = 47,561	5,561	672,194
12/31/03	42,000	(42,000 + 5,561) = 47,561	5,561	677,755
6/30/04	42,000	(42,000 + 5,561) = 47,561	5,561	683,316
12/31/04	42,000	(42,000 + 5,561) = 47,561	5,561	688,877
6/30/05	42,000	(42,000 + 5,561) = 47,561	5,561	694,438
12/31/05	42,000	(42,000 + 5,561) = 47,561	5,561	700,000*
	252,000	285,366	33,366	

GRAPHIC 14–7
Amortization Schedule—Straight-Line Method

By the straight-line method, the amount of the discount to be reduced periodically is calculated, and the recorded interest is the plug figure.

*Rounded.

Remember, constant dollar amounts are not produced when the effective interest method is used. By that method, the dollar amounts of interest vary over the term to maturity because the percentage rate of interest remains constant but is applied to a changing debt balance.

Also, be sure to realize that the straight-line method is not an alternative method of determining interest in a conceptual sense. Instead, it is an application of the materiality concept, by which an appropriate application of GAAP (e.g., the effective interest method) can be bypassed for reasons of practical expediency in situations when doing so has no material effect on the results. Based on the frequency with which the straight-line method is used in practice, we can infer that managers very frequently conclude that its use has no material impact on investors' decisions.

Determining interest by allocating the discount (or premium) on a straight-line basis is a practical expediency permitted in some situations by the materiality concept.

CONCEPT REVIEW EXERCISE

Issuing Bonds and Recording Interest

On January 1, 2003, the Meade Group issued $8,000,000 of 11% bonds, dated January 1. Interest is payable semiannually on June 30 and December 31. The bonds mature in four years. The market yield for bonds of similar risk and maturity is 10%.

Required:
1. Determine the price these bonds sold for to yield the 10% market rate and record their issuance by the Meade Group.
2. Prepare an amortization schedule that determines interest at the effective rate and record interest on the first interest date, June 30, 2003.

1. Determine the price these bonds sold for to yield the 10% market rate and record their issuance by the Meade Group.

SOLUTION

Calculation of the Price of the Bonds

There are eight semiannual periods and one-half the market rate is 5%.

Interest	$440,000 × 6.46321* =	$2,843,812
Principal	$8,000,000 × 0.67684† =	5,414,720
Present value (price) of the bonds		$8,258,532

*Present value of an ordinary annuity of $1: $n = 8$, $i = 5\%$.
†Present value of $1: $n = 8$, $i = 5\%$.

Cash (price calculated above)	8,258,532	
Bonds payable (face amount)		8,000,000
Premium on bonds payable (difference)		258,532

2. Prepare an amortization schedule that determines interest at the effective rate and record interest on the first interest date, June 30, 2003.

Amortization Schedule

Date	Cash Interest	Effective Interest		Decrease in Balance	Outstanding Balance
	(5.5% × Face amount)	(5% × Outstanding balance)		(Premium reduction)	
1/1/03					8,258,532
6/30/03	440,000	.05 (8,258,532) =	412,927	27,073	8,231,459
12/31/03	440,000	.05 (8,231,459) =	411,573	28,427	8,203,032
6/30/04	440,000	.05 (8,203 032) =	410,152	29,848	8,173,184
12/31/04	440,000	.05 (8,173,184) =	408,659	31,341	8,141,843
6/30/05	440,000	.05 (8,141,843) =	407,092	32,908	8,108,935
12/31/05	440,000	.05 (8,108,935) =	405,447	34,553	8,074,382
6/30/06	440.000	.05 (8,074,382) =	403,719	36,281	8,038,101
12/31/06	440,000	.05 (8,038,101) =	401,899*	38,101	8,000,000
	3,520,000		3,261,468	258,532	

*Rounded.

Interest expense (5% × $8,258,532)	412,927	
Premium on bonds payable (difference)	27,073	
Cash (5.5% × $8,000,000)		440,000

To record interest

Debt Issue Costs

Rather than sell bonds directly to the public, corporations usually sell an entire issue to an underwriter who then resells them to other security dealers and the public. By committing to purchase bonds at a set price, an investment house such as Salomon Smith Barney, Goldman Sachs, and Merrill Lynch is said to underwrite any risks associated with a new issue. The underwriting fee is the spread between the price the underwriter pays and the resale price.

Alternatively, the issuing company may choose to sell the debt securities directly to a single investor (as we assumed in previous illustrations)—often a pension fund or an insurance company. This is referred to as *private placement.* Issue costs are less because privately placed securities are not subject to the costly and lengthy process of registering with the SEC that is required of public offerings. Underwriting fees also are avoided.

With either publicly or privately sold debt, the issuing company will incur costs in connection with issuing bonds or notes, such as legal and accounting fees and printing costs, in addition to registration and underwriting fees. These **debt issue costs** are recorded *separately* and are amortized over the term of the related debt. GAAP requires a debit to an asset account—debt issue costs. The asset is allocated to expense, usually on a straight-line basis.

For example, let's assume issue costs in Illustration 14–3 had been $12,000. The entries for the issuance of the bonds would include a separate asset account for the issue costs:

Cash (price minus issue costs)	723,533	
Debt issue costs	12,000	
Bonds payable (face amount)		700,000
Premium on bonds payable (price minus face amount)		35,533

Semiannual amortization of the asset would be:

Debt issue expense ($12,000 ÷ 6)........................	2,000	
Debt issue costs......................................		2,000

The corporate bond is the basic long-term debt instrument for most large companies. But for many small and medium-sized firms, the debt instrument often used is a *note*. We discuss notes next.

LONG-TERM NOTES

When a company borrows cash from a bank and signs a promissory note (essentially an IOU), the firm's liability is reported as a *note payable*. Or a note might be issued in exchange for a noncash asset—perhaps to purchase equipment on credit. In concept, notes are accounted for in precisely the same way as bonds. In fact, we could properly substitute notes payable for bonds payable in each of our previous illustrations.

Note Issued for Cash

The interest rate stated in a note is likely to be equal to the market rate because the rate usually is negotiated at the time of the loan. So discounts and premiums are less likely than on bonds. Accounting for a note issued for cash is demonstrated in Illustration 14–4.

PART

LO3

FINANCIAL REPORTING CASE

Q4, p. 665

On January 1, 2003, Skill Graphics, Inc., a product-labeling and graphics firm, borrowed $700,000 cash from First BancCorp and issued a three-year, $700,000 promissory note. Interest of $42,000 was payable semiannually on June 30 and December 31.

ILLUSTRATION 14–4

Note Issued for Cash

[8]When the same amortization method is used for both, net income is unaffected by whether the cost is amortized as a separate debt issue expense or is reflected in a higher interest expense.

ILLUSTRATION 14–4		

At Issuance

Skill Graphics (Borrower)

Cash.	700,000	
Notes payable (face amount)		700,000

First BancCorp (Lender)

Notes receivable (face amount)	700,000	
Cash.		700,000

At Each of the Six Interest Dates

Skill Graphics (Borrower)

Interest expense	42,000	
Cash (stated rate × face amount)		42,000

First BancCorp (Lender)

Cash (stated rate × face amount)	42,000	
Interest revenue.		42,000

At Maturity

Skill Graphics (Borrower)

Notes payable.	700,000	
Cash (face amount)		700,000

First BancCorp (Lender)

Cash (face amount).	700,000	
Notes receivable		700,000

Note Exchanged for Assets or Services

Occasionally the *stated* interest rate is not indicative of the *market* rate at the time a note is negotiated. The value of the asset (cash or noncash) or service exchanged for the note establishes the market rate.[9] For example, let's assume Skill Graphics purchased a package-labeling machine from Hughes–Barker Corporation by issuing a 12%, $700,000, three-year note that requires interest to be paid semiannually. Let's also assume that the machine could have been purchased at a cash price of $666,633. You probably recognize this numerical situation as the one used earlier to illustrate bonds sold at a discount (Illustration 14–2). Reference to the earlier example will confirm that exchanging this $700,000 note for a machine with a cash price of $666,633 implies an annual market rate of interest of 14%. That is, 7% is one-half the discount rate that yields a present value of $666,633 for the note's cash flows (interest plus principal):

			Present Values
Interest	$ 42,000 × 4.76654*	=	$200,195
Principal	$700,000 × 0.66634†	=	466,438
Present value of the note			$666,633

*Present value of an ordinary annuity of $1: $n = 6$, $i = 7\%$.
†Present value of $1: $n = 6$, $i = 7\%$.

This is referred to as the **implicit rate of interest**—the rate implicit in the agreement. It may be that the implicit rate is not apparent. Sometimes the value of the asset (or service) is not readily determinable, but the interest rate stated in the transaction is unrealistic relative to the rate that would be expected in a similar transaction under similar circumstances. Deciding what the appropriate rate should be is called *imputing* an interest rate.

---

[9]If the debt instrument is negotiable and a dependable exchange price is readily available, the market value of the debt may be better evidence of the value of the transaction than the value of a noncash asset, particularly if it has no established cash selling price. The value of the asset or the debt, whichever is considered more reliable, should be used to record the transaction (*APB 21*).

For example, suppose the machine exchanged for the 12% note is custom-made for Skill Graphics so that no customary cash price is available with which to work backwards to find the implicit rate. In that case, the appropriate rate would have to be found externally. It might be determined, for instance, that a more realistic interest rate for a transaction of this type, at this time, would be 14%. Then it would be apparent that Skill Graphics actually paid less than $700,000 for the machine and that part of the face amount of the note in effect makes up for the lower than normal interest rate. You learned early in your study of accounting that the economic essence of a transaction should prevail over its outward appearance. In keeping with this basic precept, the accountant should look beyond the *form* of this transaction and record its *substance*. The amount actually paid for the machine is the present value of the cash flows called for by the loan agreement, discounted at the market rate—imputed in this case to be 14%. So both the asset acquired and the liability used to purchase it should be recorded at the real cost, $666,633.

A basic concept of accounting is substance over form.

ADDITIONAL CONSIDERATION

For another example, let's assume the more realistic interest rate for a transaction of this type is, say, 16%. In that case we would calculate the real cost of the machine by finding the present value of both the interest and the principal, discounted at half the 16% rate:

			Present Values
Interest	$42,000 × 4.62288*	=	$194,161
Principal	$700,000 × 0.63017†	=	441,119
Present value of the note			$635,280

*Present value of an ordinary annuity of $1: $n = 6$, $i = 8\%$.
†Present value of $1: $n = 6$, $i = 8\%$.

Both the asset acquired and the liability used to purchase it would be recorded at $635,280.

The accounting treatment is the same whether the amount is determined directly from the market value of the machine (and thus the note) or indirectly as the present value of the note (and thus the value of the asset):[10]

Journal Entries at Issuance—Note with Unrealistic Interest Rate

Skill Graphics (Buyer/Issuer)
Machinery (cash price)	666,633	
Discount on note payable (difference)	33,367	
Notes payable (face amount)		700,000

Hughes–Barker (Seller/Lender)
Notes receivable (face amount)	700,000	
Discount on note payable (difference)		33,367
Sales revenue (cash price)		666,633

---

[10]The method shown is the *gross method*. Alternatively, the *net method* can be used as follows:

Skill Graphics (Buyer/Issuer)
Machinery (cash price)	666,633	
Notes payable (face amount)		666,633

Hughes–Barker (Seller/Lender)
Notes receivable (face amount)	666,633	
Sales revenue (cash price)		666,633

Under the gross method the note is recorded at the face amount and a contra account, called *discount on note payable,* is recorded for the difference between face value and present value. This discount represents the interest to be recognized over the term of the loan. As payments are made, the note is reduced by the full amount of the payment. Interest revenue (and interest expense) are recognized by a reduction in the discount on note and a credit to interest revenue (debit to interest expense). After the last payment, the discount and note accounts both will be zero. Over the term of the note, the note is shown net of the discount in the balance sheet.

Likewise, whether the effective interest rate is determined as the rate implicit in the agreement, given the asset's market value, or whether the effective rate is imputed as the appropriate interest rate if the asset's value is unknown, both parties to the transaction should record periodic interest (interest expense to the borrower, interest revenue to the lender) at the effective rate, rather than the stated rate.

Journal Entries—The Interest Method

The effective interest (expense to the issuer; revenue to the investor) is calculated each period as the effective rate times the amount of the debt outstanding during the interest period.

At the First Interest Date (June 30)

Skill Graphics (Borrower)

Interest expense (effective rate × outstanding balance)...........	46,664	
Discount on notes payable (difference).....................		4,664
Cash (stated rate × face amount)........................		42,000

Hughes–Barker (Seller/Lender)

Cash (stated rate × face amount)...........................	42,000	
Discount on notes receivable (difference).....................	4,664	
Interest revenue (effective rate × outstanding balance).........		46,664

The interest expense (interest revenue for the lender) varies as the balance of the note changes over time. See the amortization schedule in Graphic 14–8.[11]

GRAPHIC 14–8
Amortization
Schedule—Note

Since less cash is paid each period than the effective interest, the unpaid difference (the discount reduction) increases the outstanding balance of the debt.

	Cash Interest	Effective Interest		Increase in Balance	Outstanding Balance
	(6% × Face amount)	(7% × Outstanding balance)		(Discount reduction)	
1/1/03					666,633
6/30/03	42,000	.07 (666,633) =	46,664	4,664	671,297
12/31/03	42,000	.07 (671,297) =	46,991	4,991	676,288
6/30/04	42,000	.07 (676,288) =	47,340	5,340	681,628
12/31/04	42,000	.07 (681,628) =	47,714	5,714	687,342
6/30/05	42,000	.07 (687,342) =	48,114	6,114	693,456
12/31/05	42,000	.07 (693,456) =	48,544*	6,544	700,000
	252,000		285,367	33,367	

*Rounded.

Installment Notes

You may have recently purchased a car, or maybe a house. If so, unless you paid cash, you signed a note promising to pay the purchase price over, say, four years for the car, or 30 years for the house. Car and house notes usually call for payment in monthly installments rather than by a single amount at maturity. Corporations, too, often borrow using installment notes. Typically, installment payments are equal amounts each period. Each payment includes both an amount that represents interest and an amount that represents a reduction of the outstanding balance. The periodic reduction of the balance is sufficient that at maturity the note is completely paid. This amount is easily calculated by dividing the amount of the loan by the appropriate discount factor for the present value of an annuity. The installment payment amount that would pay the note above is:

$$\underset{\text{Amount of loan}}{\$666{,}633} \div \underset{\substack{\text{(from Table 6A–4}\\ n = 6,\, i = 7.0\%)}}{4.76654} = \underset{\text{Installment payment}}{\$139{,}857}$$

[11]The creation of amortization schedules is simplified by an electronic spreadsheet such as Microsoft Excel.

Consider Graphic 14–9.

Date	Cash Payment	Effective Interest	Decrease in Debt	Outstanding Balance
		(7% × Outstanding balance)		
1/ 1/03				666,633
6/30/03	139,857	.07 (666,633) = 46,664	93,193	573,440
12/31/03	139,857	.07 (573,440) = 40,141	99,716	473,724
6/30/04	139,857	.07 (473,724) = 33,161	106,696	367,028
12/31/04	139,857	.07 (367,028) = 25,692	114,165	252,863
6/30/05	139,857	.07 (252,863) = 17,700	122,157	130,706
12/31/05	139,857	.07 (130,706) = 9,151*	130,706	0
	839,142	172,509	666,633	

GRAPHIC 14–9
Amortization Schedule—Installment Note

Each installment payment includes interest on the outstanding debt at the effective rate. The remainder of each payment reduces the outstanding balance.

*Rounded.

The procedure is the same as for a note whose principal is paid at maturity, but the periodic cash payments are larger and there is no lump-sum payment at maturity. We calculated the amount of the payments so that after covering the interest on the existing debt each period, the excess would exactly amortize the debt to zero at maturity (rather than to a designated maturity amount).

For installment notes, the outstanding balance of the note does not eventually become its face amount as it does for notes with designated maturity amounts. Instead, at the maturity date the balance is zero. Consequently, the significance is lost of maintaining separate balances for the face amount (in a note account) and the discount (or premium). So an installment note typically is recorded at its net carrying amount in a single note payable (or receivable) account:

Journal Entries at Issuance—Installment Note

Skill Graphics (Buyer/Issuer)
Machinery	666,633	
Note payable		666,633

Hughes–Barker (Seller/Lender)
Note receivable	666,633	
Sales revenue		666,633

At the First Interest Date (June 30)

Skill Graphics (Borrower)
Interest expense (effective rate × outstanding balance)	46,664	
Note payable (difference)	93,193	
Cash (installment payment calculated above)		139,857

Hughes–Barker (Seller/Lender)
Cash (installment payment calculated above)	139,857	
Note receivable (difference)		93,193
Interest revenue (effective rate × outstanding balance)		46,664

Each payment includes both an amount that represents interest and an amount that represents a reduction of principal.

ADDITIONAL CONSIDERATION

You will learn in the next chapter that the liability associated with a capital lease is accounted for the same way as this installment note. In fact, if the asset described above had been leased rather than purchased, the cash payments would be designated lease payments rather than installment loan payments, and a virtually identical amortization schedule would apply.

The reason for the similarity is that we view a capital lease as being, in substance, equivalent to an installment purchase/sale. Naturally, then, accounting treatment of the two essentially identical transactions should be consistent. Be sure to notice the parallel treatment as you study leases in the next chapter.

Financial Statement Disclosures

In the balance sheet, long-term debt (liability for the debtor; asset for the creditor) typically is reported as a single amount, net of any discount or increased by any premium, rather than at its face amount accompanied by a separate valuation account for the discount or premium. Any portion of the debt to be paid (received) during the upcoming year, or operating cycle if longer, should be reported as a current amount.

Supplemental disclosure is required of the fair value of bonds, notes, and other financial instruments.

The fair value of financial instruments must be disclosed either in the body of the financial statements or in disclosure notes.[12] These fair values are available for bonds and other securities traded on market exchanges in the form of quoted market prices. On the other hand, financial instruments not traded on market exchanges require other evidence of market value. For example, the market value of a note payable might be approximated by the present value of principal and interest payments using a current discount rate commensurate with the risks involved.

For all long-term borrowings, disclosures also should include the aggregate amounts maturing and sinking fund requirements (if any) for each of the next five years.[13] To comply, Procter & Gamble's 2000 annual report stated:

The fair value and scheduled amounts should be disclosed for the next five years.

> **($ in millions)**
> The fair value of the long-term debt was $8,929 and $6,517 June 30, 2000 and 1999, respectively. Long-term debt maturities during the next five years are as follows:
>
> 2001—$283; 2002—$472; 2003—$534; 2004—$1,139 and 2005—$973.

Borrowing is a financing activity; lending is an investing activity.

In a statement of cash flows, issuing bonds or notes are reported as cash flows from financing activities by the issuer (borrower) and cash flows from investing activities by the investor (lender). Similarly, when the debt is repaid, the issuer (borrower) reports the cash outflow as a financing activity while the investor (lender) reports it as a cash inflow from investing activities. However, because both interest expense and interest revenue are components of the income statement, both parties to the transaction report cash payments for interest among operating activities.

Paying or receiving interest is an operating activity.

DECISION MAKERS' PERSPECTIVE

Business decisions involve risk. Failure to properly consider risk in those decisions is one of the most costly, yet one of the most common, mistakes investors and creditors can make. Long-term debt is one of the first places decision makers should look when trying to get a handle on risk.

---

[12]"Disclosures About Fair Values of Financial Instruments," *Statement of Financial Accounting Standards No. 107* (Norwalk, Conn.: FASB, 1991).

[13]"Disclosure of Long-Term Obligations," *Statement of Financial Accounting Standards No. 47* (Stamford, Conn.: FASB, 1981), par. 10b.

In general, debt increases risk. As an owner, debt would place you in a subordinate position relative to creditors because the claims of creditors must be satisfied first in case of liquidation. In addition, debt requires payment, usually on specific dates. Failure to pay debt interest and principal on a timely basis may result in default and perhaps even bankruptcy. The debt to equity ratio, total liabilities/shareholders' equity, often is calculated to measure the degree of risk. Other things being equal, the higher the debt to equity ratio, the higher the risk. The type of risk this ratio measures is called *default risk* because it presumably indicates the likelihood a company will default on its obligations.

Debt also can be an advantage. It can be used to enhance the return to shareholders. This concept, known as leverage, was described and illustrated in Chapter 3. If a company earns a return on borrowed funds in excess of the cost of borrowing the funds, shareholders are provided with a total return greater than what could have been earned with equity funds alone. This desirable situation is called *favorable financial leverage*. Unfortunately, leverage is not always favorable. Sometimes the cost of borrowing the funds exceeds the returns they generate. This illustrates the typical risk-return trade-off faced by shareholders.

Creditors demand interest payments as compensation for the use of their capital. Failure to pay interest as scheduled may cause several adverse consequences, including bankruptcy. Therefore, another way to measure a company's ability to pay its obligations is by comparing interest payments with income available to pay those charges. The times interest earned ratio does this by dividing income before subtracting interest expense or income tax expense by interest expense.

Two points about this ratio are important. First, because interest is deductible for income tax purposes, income before interest and taxes is a better indication of a company's ability to pay interest than is income after interest and taxes (i.e., net income). Second, income before interest and taxes is a rough approximation for cash flow generated from operations. The primary concern of decision makers is, of course, the cash available to make interest payments. In fact, this ratio often is computed by dividing cash flow generated from operations by interest payments.

For illustration, let's compare the ratios for Coca-Cola and PepsiCo. Graphic 14–10 on the next page provides condensed financial statements adapted from recent annual reports of those companies.

The debt to equity ratio is higher for PepsiCo:

$$\text{Debt to equity ratio} = \frac{\text{Total liabilities}}{\text{Shareholders' equity}}$$

$$\text{Coca-Cola} = \frac{\$2,304.4}{\$144.9 + 2,476.9 - 904.7} = 1.34$$

$$\text{PepsiCo} = \frac{\$3,035.2}{\$335.0 + 1,601.9 - 964.1} = 3.12$$

Remember, that's not necessarily a positive or a negative. Let's look closer. When the return on shareholders' equity is greater than the return on assets, management is using debt funds to enhance the earnings for shareholders. Both firms do this. We calculate return on assets as follows:

$$\text{Rate of return on assets} = \frac{\text{Net income}}{\text{Total assets}}$$

$$\text{Coca-Cola} = \frac{\$593.8}{\$4,021.5} = 14.8\%$$

$$\text{PepsiCo} = \frac{\$424.6}{\$4,008.0} = 10.6\%$$

Generally speaking, debt increases risk.

To evaluate a firm's risk, you might start by calculating its debt to equity ratio.

As a manager, you would try to create favorable financial leverage to earn a return on borrowed funds in excess of the cost of borrowing the funds.

As an external analyst or a manager, you are concerned with a company's ability to repay debt.

The debt to equity ratio indicates the extent of trading on the equity, or financial leverage.

The rate of return on assets indicates profitability without regard to how resources are financed.

Balance Sheets

($ in millions)

	Coca-Cola	PepsiCo
Assets		
Current assets	$1,203.0	$1,478.7
Property, plant, and equipment (net)	2,608.2	2,064.6
Intangibles and other assets	210.3	464.7
Total assets	$4,021.5	$4,008.0
Liabilities and Shareholders' Equity		
Current liabilities	$1,280.2	$1,787.1
Long-term liabilities	1,024.2	1,248.1
Total liabilities	$2,304.4	$3,035.2
Common stock (par and additional paid-in capital)	144.9	335.0
Retained earnings	2,476.9	1,601.9
Less: Treasury stock	(904.7)	(964.1)
Total liabilities and shareholders' equity	$4,021.5	$4,008.0
Income Statements		
Net sales	$5,698.0	$7,768.2
Cost of goods sold	(2,909.0)	(4,481.7)
Gross profit	$2,789.0	$3,286.5
Operating expenses	(1,743.7)	(2,539.2)
Interest expense	(56.8)	(46.6)
Income before taxes	$ 988.5	$ 700.7
Tax expense	(394.7)	(276.1)
Net income	$ 593.8	$ 424.6

The return on assets indicates a company's overall profitability, ignoring specific sources of financing. In this regard, Coca-Cola's profitability exceeds that of PepsiCo. That advantage shifts when we compare return to shareholders:

$$\frac{\text{Rate of return on}}{\text{shareholders' equity}} = \frac{\text{Net income}}{\text{Shareholders' equity}}$$

$$\text{Coca-Cola} = \frac{\$593.8}{\$144.9 + 2,476.9 - 904.7} = 34.6\%$$

$$\text{PepsiCo} = \frac{\$424.6}{\$335.0 + 1,601.9 - 964.1} = 43.6\%$$

PepsiCo's higher leverage has been used to provide a higher return to shareholders than Coca-Cola, even though its return on assets is less. PepsiCo increased its return to shareholders 4.11 times (43.6%/10.6%) the return on assets. Coca-Cola increased its return to shareholders 2.34 times (34.6%/14.8%) the return on assets. Interpret this with caution, though. PepsiCo's higher leverage means higher risk as well. In down times, PepsiCo's return to shareholders will suffer proportionally more than will Coca-Cola's.

GLOBAL PERSPECTIVE

Capital markets are operating more and more as a global marketplace. Firms competing for international resources, such as debt funding, include domestic corporations, multi-national corporations, as well as foreign corporations and joint ventures. This poses several problems for lenders and other resource providers attempting to evaluate alternatives across international boundaries.

One persistent problem is the lack of uniformity in accounting standards used to produce the financial statements being compared. The gap has narrowed in recent years, but analysts must be aware of differences in accounting methods from country to country. Other considerations are being familiar with the accounting consequences of translating results from abroad into dollars, institutional, political, cultural, and tax differences, and identifying appropriate international industry standards for comparison.

From the perspective of a creditor, we might look at which company offers the most comfortable margin of safety in terms of its ability to pay fixed interest charges:

$$\text{Times interest earned ratio} = \frac{\text{Net income plus interest plus taxes}}{\text{Interest}}$$

$$\text{Coca-Cola} = \frac{\$593.8 + 56.8 + 394.7}{\$56.8} = 18.4 \text{ times}$$

The times interest earned ratio indicates the margin of safety provided to creditors.

$$\text{PepsiCo} = \frac{\$424.6 + 46.6 + 276.1}{\$46.6} = 16.0 \text{ times}$$

In this regard, both firms provide an adequate margin of safety. The interest coverage ratios seem to indicate an ample safety cushion for creditors, particularly when considered in conjunction with their debt-equity ratios.

Liabilities also can have misleading effects on the income statement. Decision makers should look carefully at gains and losses produced by early extinguishment of debt. These have nothing to do with a company's normal operating activities. Unchecked, corporate management can be tempted to schedule debt buybacks to provide discretionary income in down years or even losses in up years to smooth income over time.

Decision makers should be alert to gains and losses that have nothing to do with a company's normal operating activities.

Alert investors and lenders also look outside the financial statements for risks associated with "off-balance-sheet" financing and other commitments that don't show up on the face of financial statements but nevertheless expose a company to risk. Relatedly, most companies attempt to actively manage the risk associated with these and other obligations. It is important for top management to understand and closely monitor risk management strategies. Some of the financial losses that have grabbed headlines in recent years, were permitted by a lack of oversight and scrutiny by senior management of companies involved. It is similarly important for investors and creditors to become informed about risks companies face and how well-equipped those companies are in managing that risk. The supplemental disclosures designed to communicate the degree of risk associated with the financial instruments we discuss in this chapter contribute to that understanding. We examine the significance of lease commitments in the next chapter. ■

Outside analysts as well as managers should actively monitor risk management activities.

CONCEPT REVIEW EXERCISE

Note with an Unrealistic Interest Rate

Cameron-Brown, Inc., constructed for Harmon Distributors a warehouse that was completed and ready for occupancy on January 2, 2003. Harmon paid for the warehouse by issuing a $900,000, four-year note that required 7% interest to be paid on December 31 of each year. The warehouse was custom-built for Harmon, so its cash price was not known. By comparison with similar transactions, it was determined that an appropriate interest rate was 10%.

Required:
1. Prepare the journal entry for Harmon's purchase of the warehouse on January 2, 2003.
2. Prepare (a) an amortization schedule for the four-year term of the note and (b) the journal entry for Harmon's first interest payment on December 31, 2003.
3. Suppose Harmon's note had been an installment note to be paid in four equal payments. What would be the amount of each installment if payable (a) at the end of each year, beginning December 31, 2003? or (b) at the beginning of each year, beginning on January 2, 2003?

SOLUTION

1. Prepare the journal entry for Harmon's purchase of the warehouse on January 2, 2003.

			Present Values
Interest	$63,000 × 3.16987*	=	$199,702
Principal	$900,000 × 0.68301†	=	614,709
Present value of the note			$814,411

*Present value of an ordinary annuity of $1: $n = 4$, $i = 10\%$.
†Present value of $1: $n = 4$, $i = 10\%$.

Warehouse (price determined above).	814,411	
Discount on notes payable (difference)	85,589	
Notes payable (face amount)		900,000

2. Prepare (a) an amortization schedule for the four-year term of the note and (b) the journal entry for Harmon's first interest payment on December 31, 2003.

a.

Dec. 31	Cash Interest	Effective Interest	Increase in Balance	Outstanding Balance
	(7% × Face amount)	(10% × Outstanding balance)	(Discount reduction)	
				814,411
2003	63,000	.10 (814,411) = 81,441	18,441	832,852
2004	63,000	.10 (832,852) = 83,285	20,285	853,137
2005	63,000	.10 (853,137) = 85,314	22,314	875,451
2006	63,000	.10 (875,451) = 87,549*	24,549	900,000
	252,000	337,589	85,589	

*Rounded.

> Each period the unpaid interest increases the outstanding balance of the debt.

b.

> The effective interest is the market rate times the amount of the debt outstanding during the year.

Interest expense (effective rate × outstanding balance).	81,441	
Discount on notes payable (difference)		18,441
Cash (stated rate × face amount)		63,000

3. Suppose Harmon's note had been an installment note to be paid in four equal payments. What would be the amount of each installment if payable (a) at the end of each year, beginning December 31, 2003? or (b) at the beginning of each year, beginning on January 2, 2003?

> Because money has a time value, installment payments delayed until the end of each period must be higher than if the payments are made at the beginning of each period.

a. $\dfrac{\$814,411}{\text{Amount of loan}} \div \begin{array}{c} 3.16987 \\ \text{(from Table 6A–4} \\ n = 4, i = 10\%) \end{array} = \begin{array}{c} \$256,923 \\ \text{Installment payment} \end{array}$

b. $\dfrac{\$814,411}{\text{Amount of loan}} \div \begin{array}{c} 3.48685 \\ \text{(from Table 6A–6} \\ n = 4, i = 10\%) \end{array} = \begin{array}{c} \$233,566 \\ \text{Installment payment} \end{array}$

DEBT RETIRED EARLY, CONVERTIBLE INTO STOCK, OR PROVIDING AN OPTION TO BUY STOCK

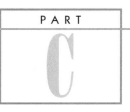

Early Extinguishment of Debt

LO5

As the previous illustration demonstrated, debt paid in installments is systematically retired over the term to maturity so that at the designated maturity date the outstanding balance is zero. When a maturity amount is specified as in our earlier illustrations, any discount or premium has been systematically reduced to zero as of the maturity date and the debt is retired simply by paying the maturity amount. However, a gain or a loss may result when debt is retired before its scheduled maturity.

Earlier we noted that a call feature accompanies most bonds to protect the issuer against declining interest rates. Even when bonds are not callable, the issuing company can retire bonds early by purchasing them on the open market. Regardless of the method, when debt of any type is retired prior to its scheduled maturity date, the transaction is referred to as **early extinguishment of debt.**

To record the extinguishment, the account balances pertinent to the debt obviously must be removed from the books. Of course cash is credited for the amount paid—the call price or market price. The difference between the carrying amount of the debt and the reacquisition price represents either a gain or a loss on the early extinguishment of debt. Let's continue an earlier example to illustrate the retirement of debt prior to its scheduled maturity (Illustration 14–5):

> **Any difference between the outstanding debt and the amount paid to retire that debt represents either a gain or a loss.**

On January 1, 2004, Masterwear Industries called its $700,000, 12% bonds when their carrying amount was $676,288. The indenture specified a call price of $685,000. The bonds were issued previously at a price to yield 14%.

Bonds payable (face amount).	700,000	
Loss on early extinguishment[14] ($685,000 − $676,288).	8,712	
Discount on bonds payable ($700,000 − $676,288).		23,712
Cash (call price)		685,000

ILLUSTRATION 14–5

Early Extinguishment of Debt

Convertible Bonds

Sometimes corporations include a convertible feature as part of a bond offering. **Convertible bonds** can be converted into (that is, exchanged for) shares of stock at the option of the bondholder. Among the reasons for issuing convertible bonds rather than straight debt are (a) to sell the bonds at a higher price (which means a lower effective interest cost),[15] (b) to use as a medium of exchange in mergers and acquisitions, and (c) to enable smaller firms or debt-heavy companies to obtain access to the bond market. Sometimes convertible bonds serve as an indirect way to issue stock when there is shareholder resistance to direct issuance of additional equity.

Central to each of these reasons for issuing convertible debt is that the conversion feature is attractive to investors. This hybrid security has features of both debt and equity. The owner has a fixed-income security that can become common stock if and when the firm's prosperity

FINANCIAL REPORTING CASE

Q5, p. 665

Convertible bonds can be exchanged for shares of stock at the option of the investor.

Convertible bonds have features of both debt and equity.

---

[14] For several years the FASB required companies to report gains and losses from early extinguishment of debt as extraordinary items, but no longer. Now, these gains and losses are subject to the same criteria as other gains and losses for such treatment; namely, that they be both (a) unusual and (b) infrequent. *Statement of Financial Accounting Standards No. 145,* "Rescission of FASB Statements No. 4, 44, and 64, Amendment of FASB Statement No. 13, and Technical Corrections" (Norwalk, Conn.: FASB, 2002).

[15] Remember, there is an inverse relationship between bond prices and interest rates. When the price is higher, the rate (yield) is lower, and vice versa.

makes that feasible. This increases the investor's upside potential while limiting the downside risk. The conversion feature has monetary value. Just how valuable it is depends on both the conversion terms and market conditions. But from an accounting perspective the question raised is how to account for its value. To evaluate the question, consider Illustration 14–6.

ILLUSTRATION 14–6	On January 1, 2003, HTL Manufacturers issued $100 million of 8% convertible debentures
Convertible Bonds	due 2013 at 103 (103% of face value). The bonds are convertible at the option of the holder into $1 par common stock at a conversion ratio of 40 shares per $1,000 bond. HTL recently issued nonconvertible, 20-year, 8% debentures at 98.

Because of the inseparability of their debt and equity features, the entire issue price of convertible bonds is recorded as debt, as if they are nonconvertible bonds.

It would appear that the conversion feature is valued by the market at $5 million—the difference between the market value of the convertible bonds, $103 million, and the market value of the nonconvertible bonds, $98 million. Some accountants argue that we should record the value of the conversion option in a shareholders' equity account ($5 million in this case) and the debt value in the bond accounts ($100 million bonds payable less $2 million discount).[16] However, the currently accepted practice is to record the entire issue price as debt in precisely the same way as for nonconvertible bonds.[17] This approach is supported by the view that the two features of the security, the debt and the conversion option, are physically inseparable—the option cannot be exercised without surrendering the debt. Treating the features as two inseparable parts of a single security also avoids the practical difficulty of trying to measure the separate values of the debt and the conversion option. We sidestepped this difficulty in our illustration by assuming that HTL had recently issued nonconvertible bonds that were otherwise similar to the convertible bonds.

Journal Entry at Issuance—Convertible Bonds

The value of the conversion feature is not separately recorded.

	($ in millions)	
Cash (103% × $100 million)	103	
Convertible bonds payable (face amount)		100
Premium on bonds payable (difference)		3

Since we make no provision for the separate value of the conversion option, all subsequent entries, including the periodic reduction of the premium, are exactly the same as if these were nonconvertible bonds. So the illustrations and examples of bond accounting we discussed earlier would pertain equally to nonconvertible or convertible bonds.

WHEN THE CONVERSION OPTION IS EXERCISED

If and when the bondholder exercises his or her option to convert the bonds into shares of stock, the bonds are removed from the accounting records and the new shares issued are recorded at the same amount (in other words, at the book value of the bonds). To illustrate, assume that half the convertible bonds issued by HTL Manufacturers are converted at a time when the remaining unamortized premium is $2 million:

Journal Entry at Conversion

The 2 million shares issued are recorded at the $51 million book value of the bonds retired.

	($ in millions)	
Convertible bonds payable (½ the account balance)	50	
Premium on bonds payable (½ the account balance)	1	
Common stock [(50,000 bonds × 40 shares) × $1 par]		2
Paid-in capital—excess of par (to balance)		49

---

[16]These arguments are summarized in the FASB *Discussion Memorandum,* "Distinguishing between Liability and Equity Instruments and Accounting for Instruments with Characteristics of Both," 1990.

[17]"Accounting for Convertible Debt and Debt Issued with Stock Purchase Warrants," *Accounting Principles Board Opinion No. 14* (New York: APB, 1969).

ADDITIONAL CONSIDERATION

The method just described is referred to as the *book value method,* since the new shares are recorded at the book value of the bonds being redeemed. It is by far the most popular method in practice. Another acceptable approach, the *market value method,* records the new shares at the market value of the shares themselves or of the bonds, whichever is more determinable. Because the market value most likely will differ from the book value of the bonds, a gain or loss on conversion will result. Assume for illustration that the market value of HTL's stock is $30 per share at the time of the conversion:

	($ in millions)	
Convertible bonds payable (½ the account balance).............	50	
Premium on bonds payable (½ the account balance)	1	
Loss on conversion of bonds (to balance)	9	
Common stock [(50,000 bonds × 40 shares) × $1 par]..........		2
Paid-in capital in excess of par [(50,000 × 40 shares) × $29].....		58

If a single investor had purchased the 50,000 bonds being converted, that company would record the conversion as follows:

	($ in millions)	
Investment in common stock	51	
Investment in convertible bonds (account balance)............		50
Premium on bond investment (account balance).............		1

INDUCED CONVERSION

Investors often are reluctant to convert bonds to stock, even when share prices have risen significantly since the convertible bonds were purchased. This is because the market price of the convertible bonds will rise along with market prices of the stock. So companies sometimes try to induce conversion. The motivation might be to reduce debt and become a better risk to potential lenders or achieve a lower debt-to-equity ratio.

One way is through the call provision. As we noted earlier, most corporate bonds are callable by the issuing corporation. When the specified call price is less than the conversion value of the bonds (the market value of the shares), calling the convertible bonds provides bondholders with incentive to convert. Bondholders will choose the shares rather than the lower call price.

Occasionally, corporations may try to encourage voluntary conversion by offering an added inducement in the form of cash, stock warrants, or a more attractive conversion ratio. When additional consideration is provided to induce conversion, the fair value of that consideration is considered an expense incurred to bring about the conversion.[18]

> Any additional consideration provided to induce conversion of convertible debt is recorded as an expense of the period.

Bonds with Detachable Warrants

Another (less common) way to sweeten a bond issue is to include **detachable stock purchase warrants** as part of the security issue. A stock warrant gives the investor an option to purchase a stated number of shares of common stock at a specified *option price,* often within a given period of time. Like a conversion feature, warrants usually mean a lower interest rate and often enable a company to issue debt when borrowing would not be feasible otherwise.

However, unlike a conversion feature, warrants can be separated from the bonds. This means they can be exercised independently or traded in the market separately from bonds, having their own market price. In essence, two different securities—the bonds and the warrants—are sold as a package for a single issue price. Accordingly, the issue price is allocated between the two different securities on the basis of their market values. If the

> The issue price of bonds with detachable warrants is allocated between the two different securities on the basis of their market values.

---

[18]"Induced Conversions of Convertible Debt," *Statement of Financial Accounting Standards No. 84* (Stamford, Conn.: FASB, 1985).

independent market value of only one of the two securities is reliably determinable, that value establishes the allocation. This is demonstrated in Illustration 14–7.

ILLUSTRATION 14–7 Bonds with Detachable Warrants	On January 1, 2003, HTL Manufacturers issued $100 million of 8% debentures due 2010 at 103 (103% of face value). Accompanying each bond were 20 warrants. Each warrant permitted the holder to buy one share of $1 par common stock at $25 per share. Shortly after issuance, the warrants were listed on the exchange at $3 per warrant.

	($ in millions)	
Cash (103% × $100 million)	103	
Discount on bonds payable (difference)	3	
Bonds payable (face amount)		100
Paid-in capital—stock warrants outstanding*		
(100,000 bonds × 20 warrants × $3)		6

*Reported as part of shareholders' equity rather than as a liability.

ADDITIONAL CONSIDERATION

Market imperfections may cause the separate market values not to sum to the issue price of the package. In this event, allocation is achieved on the basis of the **relative market values** of the two securities. Let's say the bonds have a separate market price of $940 per bond (priced at 94):

Market Values

Bonds (100,000 bonds × $940)	$ 94	94%
Warrants (100,000 bonds × 20 warrants × $3)	6	6
Total	$100	100%

Proportion of Issue Price Allocated to Bonds:

$103 million × 94% = $96,820,000

Proportion of Issue Price Allocated to Warrants:

$103 million × 6% = $6,180,000

	($ in millions)	
Cash (103% × $100 million)	103.00	
Discount on bonds payable ($100 million − $96.82 million)	3.18	
Bonds payable (face amount)		100.00
Paid-in capital—stock warrants outstanding		6.18

Notice that this is the same approach we used in Chapter 10 to allocate a single purchase price to two or more assets bought for that single price. We also will allocate the total selling price of two equity securities sold for a single issue in proportion to their relative market values in Chapter 19.

If one-half of the warrants (1 million) are exercised when the market value of HTL's common stock is $30 per share, 1 million shares would be issued for one warrant each plus the exercise price of $25 per share.

Journal Entry at Exercise of Detachable Warrants	

	($ in millions)	
Cash (1,000,000 warrants × $25)	25	
Paid-in capital—stock warrants outstanding		
(1,000,000 warrants × $3)	3	
Common stock (1,000,000 shares × $1 par per share)		1
Paid-in capital—excess of par (to balance)		27

The $30 market value at the date of exercise is not used in valuing the additional shares issued. The new shares are recorded at the total of the previously measured values of both the warrants and the shares.

CONCEPT REVIEW | EXERCISE

Issuance and Early Extinguishment of Debt

The disclosure notes to the 2002 financial statements of the Champion National Corporation included the following:

> **Note 11: 14% Subordinated Debentures**
> On October 3, 2000, the Corporation sold debentures with an aggregate principal amount of $250,000,000 bearing a 14% interest rate. The debentures will mature on September 15, 2010 and are unsecured subordinated obligations of the Corporation. Interest is payable semiannually on March 15 and September 15. The Corporation may redeem the debentures at any time beginning September 15, 2000, as a whole or from time to time in part, through maturity, at specified redemption prices ranging from 113.0% of principal in declining percentages of principal amount through 2007 when the percentage is set at 100% of principal amount. The cost of issuing the debentures, totaling $5,505,000, and the discount of $2,500,000 are being amortized over the life of the debentures, using the straight-line method and the interest method, respectively. Amortization of these items for the year ended January 31, 2002, was $480,000 and $126,000, respectively, and $172,000 and $37,000, respectively, for the year ended January 31, 2001.
>
> During the year ended January 31, 2002, the Corporation repurchased, in open market transactions, $100,050,000 in face amount of the debentures for $111,998,000, including accrued interest. The unamortized cost of issuing these debentures and the unamortized discount, $1,987,000 and $946,000, respectively, and the redemption premium paid have been expensed in the current period.

From the information provided by the Champion National Corporation in Note 11, you should be able to recreate some of the journal entries the company recorded in connection with this bond issue.

Required:
1. Prepare the journal entry for the issuance of these bonds on October 3, 2000. (Be sure to include accrued interest for the half-month period between September 15 and October 3.)
2. Prepare the journal entry for the repurchase of these bonds, assuming the date of repurchase was November 15, 2001. The accrued interest for the two-month period between September 15 and November 15 would be $100,050,000 \times 14\% \times \frac{2}{12} = $2,335,000 (rounded). Assume the entry to record accrued interest was recorded separately, so the cash paid to repurchase the bonds was $109,663,000 [$111,998,000 (amount given) − $2,335,000].

1. Prepare the journal entry for the issuance of these bonds on October 3, 2000.   SOLUTION

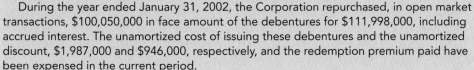

	($ in 000s)	
Cash (to balance)	243,453	
Bond issue costs (given in note)	5,505	
Discount on bonds payable (given in note)	2,500	
Bonds payable (face amount—given in note)		250,000
Interest payable (accrued interest—see below)		1,458
Accrued interest: $250,000 \times 14\% \times \frac{0.5}{12} = $1,458		

2. Prepare the journal entry for the repurchase of these bonds, assuming the date of repurchase was November 15, 2001.

	($ in 000s)	
Bonds payable (face amount repurchased).....................	100,050	
Loss on early extinguishment (to balance).....................	12,546	
Discount on bonds payable (given in note)		946
Bond issue costs (given in note)...........................		1,987
Cash (given in note)		109,663

FINANCIAL REPORTING CASE **SOLUTION**

1. **What does it mean that the bonds are first mortgage bonds? What effect does that have on financing?** *(p. 667)*   A mortgage bond is backed by a lien on specified real estate owned by the issuer. This makes it less risky than unsecured debt, so Service Leader can expect to be able to sell the bonds at a higher price (lower interest rate).

2. **From Service Leader's perspective, why are the bonds callable? What does that mean?** *(p. 667)*   The call feature gives Service Leader some protection against being stuck with relatively high-cost debt in case interest rates fall during the 15 years to maturity. Service Leader can buy back, or call, the bonds from bondholders before the 15-year maturity date, after June 30, 2008. The call price is prespecified at 103 percent of the face value—$1,030 per $1,000 bond.

3. **How will it be possible to sell bonds paying investors 6.25% when other, similar investments will provide the investors a return of 6.5%?** *(p. 669)*   Service Leader will be able to sell its 6.25% bonds in a 6.5% market only by selling them at a discounted price, below face amount. Bonds are priced by the marketplace to yield the market rate of interest for securities of similar risk and maturity. The price will be the present value of all the periodic cash interest payments (face amount × stated rate) plus the present value of the principal payable at maturity, both discounted at the market rate.

4. **Would accounting differ if the debt were designated as notes rather than bonds?** *(p. 679)*   No. Other things being equal, whether they're called bonds, notes, or some other form of debt, the same accounting principles apply. They will be recorded at present value and interest will be recorded at the market rate over the term to maturity.

5. **Why might the company choose to make the bonds convertible into common stock?** *(p. 689)*   Convertible bonds can be converted at the option of the bondholders into shares of stock. Sometimes the motivation for issuing convertible bonds rather than straight debt is to use the bonds as a medium of exchange in mergers and acquisitions, as a way for smaller firms or debt-heavy companies to obtain access to the bond market, or as an indirect way to issue stock when there is shareholder resistance to direct issuance of additional equity. None of these seems pertinent to Service Leader. The most likely reason is to sell at a higher price. The conversion feature is attractive to investors. Investors have a fixed-income security that can become common stock if circumstances make that attractive. The investor has additional possibilities for higher returns, with downside risk limited by the underlying debt. ■

THE BOTTOM LINE

1. A liability requires the future payment of cash in specified amounts at specified dates. As time passes, interest accrues on debt at the effective interest rate times the amount of the debt outstanding during the period. This same principle applies regardless of the specific form of the liability.

2. Forces of supply and demand cause a bond to be priced to yield the market rate, calculated as the present value of all the cash flows required, where the discount rate is the market rate. Interest accrues at the effective market rate of interest multiplied by the outstanding balance (during the interest period). A company is permitted to allocate a discount or a premium equally to each period over the term to maturity if doing so produces results that are not materially different from the interest method.

3. In concept, notes are accounted for in precisely the same way as bonds. When a note is issued with an unrealistic interest rate, the effective market rate is used both to determine the amount recorded in the transaction and to record periodic interest thereafter.

4. On the balance sheet, disclosure should include, for all long-term borrowings, the aggregate amounts maturing and sinking fund requirements (if any) for each of the next five years. Supplemental disclosures are needed for (a) off-balance-sheet credit or market risk, (b) concentrations of credit risk, and (c) the fair value of financial instruments.

5. A gain or loss on early extinguishment of debt should be recorded for the difference between the reacquisition price and the carrying amount of the debt. Convertible bonds are accounted for as straight debt, but the value of the equity feature is recorded separately for bonds issued with detachable warrants. ▪

TROUBLED DEBT RESTRUCTURING

APPENDIX

14

A respected real estate developer, Brillard Properties, was very successful developing and managing a number of properties in the southeastern United States. To finance these investments, the developer had borrowed hundreds of millions of dollars from several regional banks. For years, events occurred as planned. The investments prospered. Cash flow was high. Interest payments on the debt were timely and individual loans were repaid as they matured.

Almost suddenly, however, the real estate climate in the region soured. Investments that had provided handsome profits now did not provide the cash flow necessary to service the debt. Bankers who had loaned substantial funds to Brillard now faced a dilemma. Because contractual interest payments were unpaid, the bankers had the legal right to demand payment, which would force the developer to liquidate all or a major part of the properties to raise the cash. Sound business practice? Not necessarily.

If creditors force liquidation, they then must share among themselves the cash raised from selling the properties—at forced sale prices. Believing the developer's financial difficulties were caused by temporary market forces, not by bad management, the bankers felt they could minimize their losses by *restructuring* the debt agreements, rather than by forcing liquidation.

When changing the original terms of a debt agreement is motivated by financial difficulties experienced by the debtor (borrower), the new arrangement is referred to as a **troubled debt restructuring.** By definition, a troubled debt restructuring involves some concessions on the part of the creditor (lender). A troubled debt restructuring may be achieved in either of two ways:

1. The debt may be *settled* at the time of the restructuring.
2. The debt may be *continued,* but with *modified terms.*

DEBT IS SETTLED

In the situation described above, one choice the bankers had was to try to actually settle the debt outright at the time of the troubled debt restructuring. For instance, a bank holding a $30 million note from the developer might agree to accept a property valued at, let's say, $20 million as final settlement of the debt. In that case, the developer has a $10 million gain equal to the difference between the carrying amount of the debt and the fair value of the property transferred. The debtor may need to adjust the carrying amount of an asset to its fair value prior to recording its exchange for a debt. The developer in our example, for instance, would need to change the recorded amount for the property specified in the exchange agreement if it is carried at an amount other than its $20 million fair market value. In such an instance, an ordinary gain or loss on disposition of assets should be recorded as shown in Illustration 14A–1 on the next page.

The payment to settle a debt in a troubled debt restructuring might be cash, or a noncash asset (as in the example here), or even shares of the debtor's stock. An example of shares of

In all areas of accounting, a noncash transaction is recorded at fair value.

		($ in millions)
ILLUSTRATION 14A–1 **Debt Settled**	First Prudent Bank agrees to settle Brillard's $30 million debt in exchange for property having a fair market value of $20 million. The carrying amount of the property on Brillard's books is $17 million:	
	Land ($20 million minus $17 million)	3
An asset is adjusted to fair value prior to recording its exchange for a debt.	Gain on disposition of assets.	3
	Note payable (carrying amount).	30
	Gain on troubled debt restructuring	10
	Land (fair value)	20

stock being given in exchange for debt forgiveness is the celebrated reorganization of TWA in 1992 (since acquired by American Airlines), when creditors received a 55% stake in the company's common shares in return for forgiving about $1 billion of the airline's $1.5 billion debt. In any case, the debtor's gain is the difference between the carrying amount of the debt and the fair value of the asset(s) or equity securities transferred.

DEBT IS CONTINUED, BUT WITH MODIFIED TERMS

We assumed in the previous example that First Prudent Bank agreed to accept property in full settlement of the debt. A more likely occurrence would be that the bank allows the debt to continue, but modifies the terms of the debt agreement to make it easier for the debtor to comply. The bank might agree to reduce or delay the scheduled *interest payments.* Or, it may agree to reduce or delay the *maturity amount.* Often a troubled debt restructuring will call for some combination of these concessions.

> The carrying amount of a debt is the current balance of the primary debt plus any accrued (unpaid) interest.

Let's say the stated interest rate on the note in question is 10% and annual interest payments of $3 million (10% × $30 million) are payable in December of each of two remaining years to maturity. Also assume that the developer was unable to pay the $3 million interest payment for the year just ended. This means that the amount owed—the carrying amount (or book value) of the debt—is $33 million ($30 million plus one year's accrued interest).

> Two quite different situations are created when the terms of a debt are modified, depending on whether the cash payments are reduced to the extent that interest is eliminated.

According to generally accepted accounting principles, the way the debtor accounts for the restructuring depends on the extent of the reduction in cash payments called for by the restructured arrangement. More specifically, the accounting procedure depends on whether, under the new agreement, total cash payments (a) are *less than* the carrying amount of the debt or (b) still *exceed* the carrying amount of the debt.

When Total Cash Payments Are Less than the Carrying Amount of the Debt.

By the original agreement, the debtor was to pay at maturity the $30 million loaned, plus enough periodic interest to provide a 10% effective rate of return. If the new agreement calls for less cash than the $33 million now owed, interest is presumed to have been eliminated.

As one of many possibilities, suppose the bank agrees to (1) forgive the interest accrued from last year, (2) reduce the two remaining interest payments from $3 million each to $2 million each, and (3) reduce the face amount from $30 million to $25 million. Clearly, the debtor will pay less by the new agreement than by the original one. In fact, if we add up the total payments called for by the new agreement, the total [($2 million × 2) plus $25 million] is less than the $33 million carrying amount. Because the $29 million does not exceed the amount owed, the restructured debt agreement no longer provides interest on the debt. Actually, the new payments are $4 million short of covering the debt itself. So, after the debt restructuring, no interest expense is recorded. All subsequent cash payments are considered to be payment of the debt itself. Consider Illustration 14A–2 on the next page.

When the total future cash payments are less than the carrying amount of the debt, the difference is recorded as a gain at the date of restructure. No interest should be recorded thereafter. That is, all subsequent cash payments result in reductions of principal.

Brillard Properties owes First Prudent Bank $30 million under a 10% note with two years remaining to maturity. Due to financial difficulties of the developer, the previous year's interest ($3 million) was not paid. First Prudent Bank agrees to:
1. Forgive the interest accrued from last year.
2. Reduce the remaining two interest payments to $2 million each.
3. Reduce the principal to $25 million.

Analysis:

Carrying amount	$30 million + $3 million =	$33 million
Future payments	($2 million × 2) + $25 million =	29 million
Gain		$ 4 million

	($ in millions)
Accrued interest payable (10% × $30 million).................	3
Note payable ($30 million − $29 million).....................	1
Gain on debt restructuring	4

Carrying Amount

Before Restr.	Adj.	After Restr.
$30	(1)	$29
3	(3)	0
$33	(4)	$29

At Each of the Two Interest Dates

	($ in millions)
Note payable.......................................	2
Cash (revised "interest" amount)........................	2

At Maturity

Note payable.......................................	25
Cash (revised principal amount)........................	25

After restructuring, no interest expense is recorded. All cash payments are considered to be payment of the note itself.

The $25 million payment at maturity reduces the note to zero.

When Total Cash Payments Exceed the Carrying Amount of the Debt. Let's modify the example in the previous section. Now suppose the bank agrees to delay the due date for all cash payments until maturity and accept $34,333,200 at that time in full settlement of the debt. Rather than just reducing the cash payments as in the previous illustration, the payments are delayed. It is not the nature of the change that creates the need to account differently for this situation, but the amount of the total cash payments under the agreement relative to the carrying amount of the debt. This situation is demonstrated in Illustration 14A–3.

Now the total payments called for by the new agreement, $34,333,200, exceed the $33 million carrying amount. Because the payments exceed the amount owed, the restructured debt agreement still provides interest on the debt—but less than before the agreement was revised. No longer is the effective rate 10%. The accounting objective now is to determine what the new effective rate is and *record interest for the remaining term of the loan at that new, lower rate,* as shown in Illustration 14A–3.

As long as cash payments exceed the amount owed there will be interest—although at a lower effective rate.

Brillard Properties owes First Prudent Bank $30 million under a 10% note with two years remaining to maturity. Due to Brillard's financial difficulties, the previous year's interest ($3 million) was not paid. First Prudent Bank agrees to:
1. Delay the due date for all cash payments until maturity.
2. Accept $34,333,200 at that time in full settlement of the debt.

Analysis:

Future payments		$34,333,200
Carrying amount	$30 million + $3 million =	33,000,000
Interest		$ 1,333,200

Calculation of the New Effective Interest Rate
* $33,000,000 ÷ $34,333,200 = .9612, the Table 6A–2 value for n = 2, i = ?
*   In row 2 of Table 6A–2, the number .9612 is in the 2% column. So, this is the new effective interest rate.

The discount rate that equates the present value on the debt ($33 million) and its future value ($34,333,200) is the effective rate of interest.

Unpaid interest is accrued at the effective rate times the carrying amount of the note.

Because the total future cash payments are not less than the carrying amount of the debt, no reduction of the existing debt is necessary and no entry is required at the time of the debt restructuring. Even though no cash is paid until maturity under the restructured debt agreement, interest expense still is recorded annually—but at the new rate.

The carrying amount of the debt is increased by the unpaid interest from the previous year.

At the End of the First Year

Interest expense [2% × ($30,000,000 + 3,000,000)]	660,000	
Accrued interest payable		660,000

At the End of the Second Year

Interest expense [2% × ($30,000,000 + 3,660,0000)]	673,200	
Accrued interest payable		673,200

The total of the accrued interest account plus the note account is equal to the amount scheduled to be paid at maturity.

At Maturity (End of the Second Year)

Note payable	30,000,000	
Accrued interest payable ($3,000,000 + 660,000 + 673,200)	4,333,200	
Cash (required by new agreement)		34,333,200

ADDITIONAL CONSIDERATION

To keep up with the changing amounts, it may be convenient to prepare an amortization schedule for the debt.

Year	Cash Interest	Effective Interest	Increase in Balance	Outstanding Balance
		(2% × Outstanding balance)		
				33,000,000
1	0	.02 (33,000,000) = 660,000	660,000	33,660,000
2	0	.02 (33,660,000) = 673,200	673,200	34,333,200
	0	1,333,200	1,333,200	

An amortization schedule is particularly helpful if there are several remaining years to maturity.

In our example, the restructured debt agreement called for a single cash payment at maturity ($34,333,200). If more than one cash payment is required (as in the agreement in our earlier example), calculating the new effective rate is more difficult. The concept would remain straightforward: (1) determine the interest rate that provides a present value of all future cash payments that is equal to the current carrying amount and (2) record the interest at that rate thereafter. Mechanically, though, the computation by hand would be cumbersome, requiring a time-consuming trial-and-error calculation. Since our primary interest is understanding the concepts involved, we will avoid the mathematical complexities of such a situation.

You also should be aware that when a restructuring involves modification of terms, accounting for a liability by the debtor, as described in this section, and accounting for a receivable by the creditor, which was described in Chapter 12, are inconsistent. You may recall that when a creditor's investment in a receivable becomes impaired, due to a troubled debt restructuring or for any other reason, the receivable is remeasured based on the discounted present value of currently expected cash flows at the loan's original effective rate (regardless of the extent to which expected cash receipts have been reduced). For ease of comparison, the example in this chapter (Illustration 14A–3) describes the same situation as the example in Chapter 12 (Illustration 12B–2). There is no conceptual justification for the asymmetry between debtors' and creditors' accounting for troubled debt restructurings. The FASB will likely reconsider debtors' accounting in the future.[19] ■

---

[19]"Accounting by Creditors for Impairment of a Loan," *Statement of Financial Accounting Standards No. 114* (Norwalk, Conn.: FASB, 1993), par. 63.

QUESTIONS FOR REVIEW OF KEY TOPICS

Q 14–1   How is periodic interest determined for outstanding liabilities? For outstanding receivables? How does the approach compare from one form of debt instrument (say bonds payable) to another (say notes payable)?

Q 14–2   As a general rule, how should long-term liabilities be reported on the debtor's balance sheet?

Q 14–3   How are bonds and notes the same? How do they differ?

Q 14–4   What information is contained in a bond indenture? What purpose does it serve?

Q 14–5   Why will bonds always sell at their price plus any interest that has accrued since the last interest date?

Q 14–6   On January 1, 2003, Brandon Electronics issued $85 million of 11.5% bonds, dated January 1. The market yield for bonds of maturity issued by similar firms in terms of riskiness is 12.25%. How can Brandon sell debt paying only 11.5% in a 12.25% market?

Q 14–7   How is the price determined for a bond (or bond issue)?

Q 14–8   A zero-coupon bond pays no interest. Explain.

Q 14–9   When bonds are issued at a premium the debt declines each period. Explain.

Q 14–10   Compare the two commonly used methods of determining interest on bonds.

Q 14–11   *APB Opinion No. 21* requires that debt issue costs be recorded separately and amortized over the term of the related debt. Describe a logical alternative to this accounting treatment.

Q 14–12   When a note's stated rate of interest is unrealistic relative to the market rate, the concept of substance over form should be employed. Explain.

Q 14–13   How does an installment note differ from a note for which the principal is paid as a single amount at maturity?

Q 14–14   Long-term debt can be reported either (a) as a single amount, net of any discount or increased by any premium or (b) at its face amount accompanied by a separate valuation account for the discount or premium. Any portion of the debt to be paid during the upcoming year, or operating cycle if longer, should be reported as a current amount. Regarding amounts to be paid in the future, what additional disclosures should be made in connection with long-term debt?

Q 14–15   Early extinguishment of debt often produces a gain or a loss. How is the gain or loss determined?

Q 14–16   What criteria are used to classify a gain or loss on early extinguishment of debt as an extraordinary item in the income statement?

Q 14–17   Both convertible bonds and bonds issued with detachable warrants have features of both debt and equity. How does the accounting treatment differ for the two hybrid securities? Why is the accounting treatment different?

Q 14–18   At times, companies try to induce voluntary conversion by offering an added incentive—maybe cash, stock warrants, or a more favorable conversion ratio. How is such an inducement accounted for? How is it measured?

Q 14–19   (Based on Appendix 14) When the original terms of a debt agreement are changed because of financial difficulties experienced by the debtor (borrower), the new arrangement is referred to as a *troubled debt restructuring*. Such a restructuring can take a variety of forms. For accounting purposes, these possibilities are categorized. What are the accounting classifications of troubled debt restructurings?

Q 14–20   (Based on Appendix 14) Pratt Industries owes First National Bank $5 million but, due to financial difficulties, is unable to comply with the original terms of the loan. The bank agrees to settle the debt in exchange for land having a fair market value of $3 million. The carrying amount of the property on Pratt's books is $2 million. For the reporting period in which the debt is settled, what amount(s) will Pratt report on its income statement in connection with the troubled debt restructuring?

Q 14–21   (Based on Appendix 14) The way a debtor accounts for the restructuring depends on the extent of the reduction in cash payments called for by the restructured arrangement. Describe, in general, the accounting procedure for the two basic cases: when, under the new agreement, total cash payments (a) are less than the carrying amount of the debt or (b) still exceed the carrying amount of the debt.

EXERCISES

E 14–1
Accrued interest

On March 1, 2003, Brown-Ferring Corporation issued $100 million of 12% bonds, dated January 1, 2003, for $99 million (plus accrued interest). The bonds mature on December 31, 2022, and pay interest semiannually on June 30 and December 31. Brown-Ferring's fiscal period is the calendar year.

Required:
1. Determine the amount of accrued interest that was included in the proceeds received from the bond sale.
2. Prepare the journal entry for the issuance of the bonds by Brown-Ferring.

E 14–2
Bond valuation

Your investment department has researched possible investments in corporate debt securities. Among the available investments are the following $100 million bond issues, each dated January 1, 2003. Prices were determined by underwriters at different times during the last few weeks.

	Company	Bond Price	Stated Rate
1.	BB Corp.	$109 million	11%
2.	DD Corp.	$100 million	10%
3.	GG Corp.	$ 91 million	9%

Each of the bond issues matures on December 31, 2022, and pays interest semiannually on June 30 and December 31. For bonds of similar risk and maturity, the market yield at January 1, 2003, is 10%.

Required:
Other things being equal, which of the bond issues offers the most attractive investment opportunity at the prices stated? the least attractive? Why?

E 14–3
Determine the price of bonds in various situations

Determine the price of a $1 million bond issue under each of the following independent assumptions:

	Maturity	Interest Paid	Stated Rate	Effective (market) Rate
1.	10 years	annually	10%	12%
2.	10 years	semiannually	10%	12%
3.	10 years	semiannually	12%	10%
4.	20 years	semiannually	12%	10%
5.	20 years	semiannually	12%	12%

E 14–4
Determine the price of bonds; issuance; effective interest; no amortization schedule

The Bradford Company issued 10% bonds, dated January 1, with a face amount of $80 million on January 1, 2003. The bonds mature in 2012 (10 years). For bonds of similar risk and maturity, the market yield is 12%. Interest is paid semiannually on June 30 and December 31.

Required:
1. Determine the price of the bonds at January 1, 2003.
2. Prepare the journal entry to record their issuance by The Bradford Company on January 1, 2003.
3. Prepare the journal entry to record interest on June 30, 2003 (at the effective rate). (Do not prepare an amortization schedule.)
4. Prepare the journal entry to record interest on December 31, 2003 (at the effective rate). (Do not prepare an amortization schedule.)

E 14–5
Investor; effective interest; no amortization schedule

The Bradford Company sold the entire bond issue described in the previous exercise to Saxton-Bose Corporation.

Required:
1. Prepare the journal entry to record the purchase of the bonds by Saxton-Bose on January 1, 2003.
2. Prepare the journal entry to record interest revenue on June 30, 2003 (at the effective rate). (Do not prepare an amortization schedule.)
3. Prepare the journal entry to record interest revenue on December 31, 2003 (at the effective rate). (Do not prepare an amortization schedule.)

E 14–6
Determine the price of bonds; issuance; effective interest; financial statement effects

Myriad Solutions, Inc. issued 10% bonds, dated January 1, with a face amount of $320 million on January 1, 2003. The bonds mature in 2013 (10 years). For bonds of similar risk and maturity the market yield is 12%. Interest is paid semiannually on June 30 and December 31.

Required:
1. Determine the price of the bonds at January 1, 2003.
2. What would be the net amount of the liability Myriad would report in its balance sheet at December 31, 2003?
3. What would be the amount related to the bonds that Myriad would report in its income statement for the year ended December 31, 2003?
4. What would be the amount related to the bonds that Myriad would report in its statement of cash flows for the year ended December 31, 2003?

E 14–7
Determine the price of bonds; issuance; effective interest; no amortization schedule

The Gorman Group issued $900,000 of 13% bonds on June 30, 2003. The bonds were dated on June 30 and mature on June 30, 2023 (20 years). The market yield for bonds of similar risk and maturity is 12%. Interest is paid semiannually on December 31 and June 30.

Required:
1. Determine the price of the bonds at June 30, 2003.
2. Prepare the journal entry to record their issuance by The Gorman Group on June 30, 2003.
3. Prepare the journal entry to record interest on December 31, 2003 (at the effective rate). (Do not prepare an amortization schedule.)
4. Prepare the journal entry to record interest on June 30, 2004 (at the effective rate). (Do not prepare an amortization schedule.)

E 14–8
Determine the price of bonds; issuance; straight-line method

Universal Foods issued 10% bonds, dated January 1, with a face amount of $150 million on January 1, 2003. The bonds mature on December 31, 2017 (15 years). The market rate of interest for similar issues was 12%. Interest is paid semiannually on June 30 and December 31. Universal uses the straight-line method.

Required:
1. Determine the price of the bonds at January 1, 2003.
2. Prepare the journal entry to record their issuance by Universal Foods on January 1, 2003.
3. Prepare the journal entry to record interest on June 30, 2003.
4. Prepare the journal entry to record interest on December 31, 2010.

E 14–9
Investor; straight-line method

Universal Foods sold the entire bond issue described in the previous exercise to Wang Communications.

Required:
1. Prepare the journal entry to record the purchase of the bonds by Wang Communications on January 1, 2003.
2. Prepare the journal entry to record interest revenue on June 30, 2003.
3. Prepare the journal entry to record interest revenue on December 31, 2010.

E 14–10
Issuance of bonds; effective interest; no amortization schedule

Federal Semiconductors issued 11% bonds, dated January 1, with a face amount of $800 million on January 1, 2003. The bonds sold for $739,814,813 and mature in 2022 (20 years). For bonds of similar risk and maturity the market yield was 12%. Interest is paid semiannually on June 30 and December 31.

Required:
1. Prepare the journal entry to record their issuance by Federal on January 1, 2003.
2. Prepare the journal entry to record interest on June 30, 2003 (at the effective rate). (Do not prepare an amortization schedule.)
3. Prepare the journal entry to record interest on December 31, 2003 (at the effective rate). (Do not prepare an amortization schedule.)

E 14–11
Issuance of bonds; effective interest; amortization schedule

National Orthopedics Co. issued 9% bonds, dated January 1, with a face amount of $500,000 on January 1, 2003. The bonds mature in 2006 (4 years). For bonds of similar risk and maturity the market yield was 10%. Interest is paid semiannually on June 30 and December 31.

Required:
1. Determine the price of the bonds at January 1, 2003.
2. Prepare the journal entry to record their issuance by National on January 1, 2003.
3. Prepare an amortization schedule that determines interest at the effective rate each period.
4. Prepare the journal entry to record interest on June 30, 2003.
5. Prepare the appropriate journal entries at maturity on December 31, 2006.

E 14–12
Bonds; effective interest; no amortization schedule; adjusting entry

On February 1, 2003, Strauss-Lombardi issued 9% bonds, dated February 1, with a face amount of $800,000. The bonds sold for $731,364 and mature on January 31, 2023 (20 years). The market yield for bonds of similar risk and maturity was 10%. Interest is paid semiannually on July 31 and January 31. Strauss-Lombardi's fiscal year ends December 31.

Required:
1. Prepare the journal entry to record their issuance by Strauss-Lombardi on February 1, 2003.
2. Prepare the journal entry to record interest on July 31, 2003 (at the effective rate). (Do not prepare an amortization schedule.)
3. Prepare the adjusting entry to accrue interest on December 31, 2003.
4. Prepare the journal entry to record interest on January 31, 2004.

E 14–13
Bonds; straight-line method; adjusting entry

On March 1, 2003, Stratford Lighting issued 14% bonds, dated March 1, with a face amount of $300,000. The bonds sold for $294,000 and mature on February 28, 2023 (20 years). Interest is paid semiannually on August 31 and February 28. Stratford uses the straight-line method and its fiscal year ends December 31.

Required:
1. Prepare the journal entry to record the issuance of the bonds by Stratford Lighting on March 1, 2003.
2. Prepare the journal entry to record interest on August 31, 2003.
3. Prepare the journal entry to accrue interest on December 31, 2003.
4. Prepare the journal entry to record interest on February 28, 2004.

E 14–14
Multiple choice; bonds

The following questions dealing with bonds are adapted from recent CPA examinations. Determine the response that best completes the statements or questions.
1. On January 1, 2004, Oak Co. issued 400 of its 8%, $1,000 bonds at 97 plus accrued interest. The bonds are dated October 1, 2003, and mature on October 1, 2009. Interest is payable semiannually on April 1 and October 1. Accrued interest for the period October 1, 2003, to January 1, 2004, amounted to $8,000. On January 1, 2004, what amount should Oak report as bonds payable, net of discount?
   a. $380,000
   b. $388,000
   c. $388,300
   d. $392,000
2. On December 31, 2003, Moss Co. issued $1,000,000 of 11% bonds at 109. Each $1,000 bond was issued with 50 detachable stock warrants, each of which entitled the bondholder to purchase one share of $5 par common stock for $25. Immediately after issuance, the market value of each warrant was $4. On December 31, 2003, what amount should Moss record as discount or premium for issuance of bonds?
   a. $40,000 premium
   b. $90,000 premium
   c. $110,000 discount
   d. $200,000 discount
3. A bond issued on June 1, 2003, has interest payment dates of April 1 and October 1. Bond interest expense for the year ended December 31, 2003, is for a period of
   a. Three months
   b. Four months
   c. Six months
   d. Seven months

E 14–15
Note with unrealistic interest rate

Amber Mining and Milling, Inc., contracted with Truax Corporation to have constructed a custom-made lathe. The machine was completed and ready for use on January 1, 2003. Amber paid for the lathe by issuing a $600,000, three-year note that specified 4% interest, payable annually on December 31 of each year. The cash market price of the lathe was unknown. It was determined by comparison with similar transactions that 12% was a reasonable rate of interest.
Required:
1. Prepare the journal entry on January 1, 2003, for Amber Mining and Milling's purchase of the lathe.
2. Prepare an amortization schedule for the three-year term of the note.
3. Prepare the journal entries to record (a) interest for each of the three years and (b) payment of the note at maturity.

E 14–16
Installment note

American Food Services, Inc., acquired a packaging machine from Barton and Barton Corporation. Barton and Barton completed construction of the machine on January 1, 2003. In payment for the $4 million machine, American Food Services issued a four-year installment note to be paid in four equal payments at the end of each year. The payments include interest at the rate of 10%.
Required:
1. Prepare the journal entry for American Food Services' purchase of the machine on January 1, 2003.
2. Prepare an amortization schedule for the four-year term of the installment note.
3. Prepare the journal entry for the first installment payment on December 31, 2003.
4. Prepare the journal entry for the third installment payment on December 31, 2005.

E 14–17
Early extinguishment

The balance sheet of Indian River Electronics Corporation as of December 31, 2002, included 12.25% bonds having a face amount of $90 million. The bonds had been issued in 1995 and had a remaining discount of $3 million at December 31, 2002. On January 1, 2003, Indian River Electronics called the bonds before their scheduled maturity at the call price of 102.
Required:
Prepare the journal entry by Indian River Electronics to record the redemption of the bonds at January 1, 2003.

E 14–18
Convertible bonds

On January 1, 2003, Gless Textiles issued $12 million of 9%, 10-year convertible bonds at 101. The bonds pay interest on June 30 and December 31. Each $1,000 bond is convertible into 40 shares of Gless's $1 par common stock. Century Services purchased 10% of the issue as an investment.

Required:
1. Prepare the journal entries for the issuance of the bonds by Gless and the purchase of the bond investment by Century.
2. Prepare the journal entries for the June 30, 2007, interest payment by both Gless and Century assuming both use the straight-line method.
3. On July 1, 2008, when Gless's common stock had a market price of $33 per share, Century converted the bonds it held. Prepare the journal entries by both Gless and Century for the conversion of the bonds (book value method).

E 14–19
Bonds with detachable warrants

On August 1, 2003, Limbaugh Communications issued $30 million of 10% nonconvertible bonds at 104. The bonds are due on July 31, 2023. Each $1,000 bond was issued with 20 detachable stock warrants, each of which entitled the bondholder to purchase, for $60, one share of Limbaugh Communications' $10 par common stock. Interstate Containers purchased 20% of the bond issue. On August 1, 2003, the market value of the common stock was $58 per share and the market value of each warrant was $8.

In February, 2014, when Limbaugh's common stock had a market price of $72 per share and the unamortized premium balance was $1 million, Interstate Containers exercised the warrants it held.

Required:
1. Prepare the journal entries on August 1, 2003, to record (a) the issuance of the bonds by Limbaugh and (b) the investment by Interstate.
2. Prepare the journal entries for both Limbaugh and Interstate in February, 2014, to record the exercise of the warrants.

E 14–20
New debt issues; offerings announcements

When companies offer new debt security issues, they publicize the offerings in the financial press and on internet sites. Assume the following were among the debt offerings reported in December 2003:

New Securities Issues

Corporate

National Equipment Transfer Corporation—$200 million bonds via lead managers Second Tennessee Bank N.A. and Morgan, Dunavant & Co., according to a syndicate official. Terms: maturity, Dec. 15, 2006; coupon 7.46%; issue price, par; yield, 7.46%; noncallable, debt ratings: Ba-1 (Moody's Investor's Service, Inc.), BBB+ (Standard & Poor's).

IgWig Inc.—$350 million of notes via lead manager Stanley Brothers, Inc., according to a syndicate official. Terms: maturity, Dec. 1, 2008; coupon, 6.46%; Issue price, 99; yield, 6.56%; call date, NC; debt ratings: Baa-1 (Moody's Investor's Service, Inc.), A (Standard & Poor's).

Required:
1. Prepare the appropriate journal entries to record the sale of both issues to underwriters. Ignore share issue costs and assume no accrued interest.
2. Prepare the appropriate journal entries to record the first semiannual interest payment for both issues.

E 14–21
Error in amortization schedule

Exercise 21–23 deals with correcting an error in an amortization schedule.

E 14–22
Error correction; accrued interest on bonds

At the end of 2002, Majors Furniture Company failed to accrue $61,000 of interest expense that accrued during the last five months of 2002 on bonds payable. The bonds mature in 2016. The discount on the bonds is amortized by the straight-line method. The following entry was recorded on February 1, 2003, when the semiannual interest was paid:

Interest expense	73,200	
Discount on bonds payable.		1,200
Cash.		72,000

Required:

Prepare any journal entry necessary to correct the error as well as any adjusting entry for 2003 related to the situation described. (Ignore income taxes.)

E 14–23
Troubled debt restructuring; debt settled
(Based on Appendix 14)

At January 1, 2003, Transit Developments owed First City Bank Group $600,000, under an 11% note with three years remaining to maturity. Due to financial difficulties, Transit was unable to pay the previous year's interest.

First City Bank Group agreed to settle Transit's debt in exchange for land having a fair market value of $450,000. Transit purchased the land in 1999 for $325,000.

Required:

Prepare the journal entry(s) to record the restructuring of the debt by Transit Developments.

E 14–24
Troubled debt restructuring; modification of terms
(Based on Appendix 14)

At January 1, 2003, Brainard Industries, Inc., owed Second BancCorp $12 million under a 10% note due December 31, 2004. Interest was paid last on December 31, 2001. Brainard was experiencing severe financial difficulties and asked Second BancCorp to modify the terms of the debt agreement. After negotiation Second BancCorp agreed to:
a. Forgive the interest accrued for the year just ended.
b. Reduce the remaining two years' interest payments to $1 million each and delay the first payment until December 31, 2004.
c. Reduce the unpaid principal amount to $11 million.

Required:

Prepare the journal entries by Brainard Industries, Inc., necessitated by the restructuring of the debt at (1) January 1, 2003, (2) December 31, 2004, and (3) December 31, 2005.

E 14–25
Troubled debt restructuring; modification of terms
(Based on Appendix 14)

At January 1, 2003, NCI Industries, Inc., was indebted to First Federal Bank under a $240,000, 10% unsecured note. The note was signed January 1, 1999, and was due December 31, 2004. Annual interest was last paid on December 31, 2001. NCI was experiencing severe financial difficulties and negotiated a restructuring of the terms of the debt agreement. First Federal agreed to reduce last year's interest and the remaining two years' interest payments to $11,555 each and delay all payments until December 31, 2004, the maturity date.

Required:

Prepare the journal entries by NCI Industries, Inc., necessitated by the restructuring of the debt at (1) January 1, 2003, (2) December 31, 2003, and (3) December 31, 2004.

PROBLEMS

P 14–1
Determining the price of bonds; discount and premium; issuer and investor

On January 1, 2003, Instaform, Inc., issued 10% bonds with a face amount of $50 million, dated January 1. The bonds mature in 2022 (20 years). The market yield for bonds of similar risk and maturity is 12%. Interest is paid semiannually.

Required:
1. Determine the price of the bonds at January 1, 2003, and prepare the journal entry to record their issuance by Instaform.
2. Assume the market rate was 9%. Determine the price of the bonds at January 1, 2003, and prepare the journal entry to record their issuance by Instaform.
3. Assume Broadcourt Electronics purchased the entire issue in a private placement of the bonds. Using the data in requirement 2, prepare the journal entry to record their purchase by Broadcourt.

P 14–2
Accrued interest; effective interest; financial statement effects

On March 1, 2003, Baddour, Inc. issued 10% bonds, dated January 1, with a face amount of $160 million. The bonds were priced at $140 million (plus accrued interest) to yield 12%. Interest is paid semiannually on June 30 and December 31. Baddour's fiscal year ends September 30.

Required:
1. What amount(s) related to the bonds would Baddour report in its balance sheet at September 30, 2003?
2. What amount(s) related to the bonds would Baddour report in its income statement for the year ended September 30, 2003?
3. What amount(s) related to the bonds would Baddour report in its statement of cash flows for the year ended September 30, 2003?

P 14–3
Straight-line and
effective interest
compared

On January 1, 2003, Bradley Recreational Products issued $100,000, 9%, four-year bonds. Interest is paid semiannually on June 30 and December 31. The bonds were issued at $96,768 to yield an annual return of 10%.

Required:
1.   Prepare an amortization schedule that determines interest at the effective interest rate.
2.   Prepare an amortization schedule by the straight-line method.
3.   Prepare the journal entries to record interest expense on June 30, 2005, by each of the two approaches.
4.   Explain why the pattern of interest differs between the two methods.
5.   Assuming the market rate is still 10%, what price would a second investor pay the first investor on June 30, 2005, for $10,000 of the bonds?

P 14–4
Bond amortization
schedule

On January 1, 2003, Tennessee Harvester Corporation issued debenture bonds that pay interest semi-annually on June 30 and December 31. Portions of the bond amortization schedule appear below:

Payment	Cash Interest	Effective Interest	Increase in Balance	Outstanding Balance
				6,627,273
1	320,000	331,364	11,364	6,638,637
2	320,000	331,932	11,932	6,650,569
3	320,000	332,528	12,528	6,663,097
4	320.000	333,155	13,155	6,676,252
5	320,000	333,813	13,813	6,690,065
6	320,000	334,503	14,503	6,704,568
~	~	~	~	~
~	~	~	~	~
~	~	~	~	~
38	320,000	389,107	69,107	7,851,247
39	320,000	392,562	72,562	7,923,809
40	320,000	396,191	76,191	8,000,000

Required:
1.   What is the face amount of the bonds?
2.   What is the initial selling price of the bonds? 8
3.   What is the term to maturity in years? n=20
4.   Interest is determined by what approach?
5.   What is the stated annual interest rate? 8%
6.   What is the effective annual interest rate? 10%
7.   What is the total cash interest paid over the term to maturity? $12,800,000
8.   What is the total effective interest expense recorded over the term to maturity? $1,372,727+12,800000

P 14–5
Issuer and investor;
effective interest;
amortization schedule;
adjusting entries

On February 1, 2003, Cromley Motor Products issued 9% bonds, dated February 1, with a face amount of $80 million. The bonds mature on January 31, 2007 (4 years). The market yield for bonds of similar risk and maturity was 10%. Interest is paid semiannually on July 31 and January 31. Barnwell Industries acquired $80,000 of the bonds as a long-term investment. The fiscal years of both firms end December 31.

Required:
1.   Determine the price of the bonds issued on February 1, 2003.
2.   Prepare amortization schedules that indicate (a) Cromley's effective interest expense and (b) Barnwell's effective interest revenue for each interest period during the term to maturity.
3.   Prepare the journal entries to record (a) the issuance of the bonds by Cromley and (b) Barnwell's investment on February 1, 2003.
4.   Prepare the journal entries by both firms to record all subsequent events related to the bonds through January 31, 2005.

P 14–6
Issuer and investor;
straight-line method;
adjusting entries

On April 1, 2003, Western Communications, Inc., issued 12% bonds, dated March 1, 2003, with face amount of $30 million. The bonds sold for $29.3 million and mature on February 28, 2006. Interest is paid semiannually on August 31 and February 28. Stillworth Corporation acquired $30,000 of the bonds as a long-term investment. The fiscal years of both firms end December 31, and both firms use the straight-line method.

Required:
1. Prepare the journal entries to record (a) issuance of the bonds by Western and (b) Stillworth's investment on April 1, 2003.
2. Prepare the journal entries by both firms to record all subsequent events related to the bonds through maturity.

P 14–7

Issuer and investor; effective interest; no amortization schedule

McWherter Instruments sold $400 million of 8% bonds, dated January 1, on January 1, 2003. The bonds mature on December 31, 2022 (20 years). For bonds of similar risk and maturity, the market yield was 10%. Interest is paid semiannually on June 30 and December 31. Blanton Technologies, Inc., purchased $400,000 of the bonds as a long-term investment.

Required:
1. Determine the price of the bonds issued on January 1, 2003.
2. Prepare the journal entries to record (a) their issuance by McWherter and (b) Blanton's investment on January 1, 2003.
3. Prepare the journal entries by (a) McWherter and (b) Blanton to record interest on June 30, 2003 (at the effective rate). (Do not prepare an amortization schedule.)
4. Prepare the journal entries by (a) McWherter and (b) Blanton to record interest on December 31, 2003 (at the effective rate). (Do not prepare an amortization schedule.)

P 14–8

Zero-coupon bonds

On January 1, 2003, Darnell Window and Pane issued $18 million of 10-year, zero-coupon bonds for $5,795,518.

Required:
1. Prepare the journal entry to record the bond issue.
2. Determine the effective rate of interest.
3. Prepare the journal entry to record annual interest expense at December 31, 2003.
4. Prepare the journal entry to record annual interest expense at December 31, 2004.
5. Prepare the journal entry to record the extinguishment at maturity.

P 14–9

Notes exchanged for assets

At the beginning of the year, Lambert Motors issued the three notes described below.
1. The company issued a two-year, 12%, $600,000 note in exchange for a tract of land. The current market rate of interest is 12%.
2. Lambert acquired some office equipment with a fair market value of $94,643 by issuing a one-year, $100,000 note. The stated interest on the note is 6%.
3. The company purchased a building by issuing a three-year installment note. The note is to be repaid in equal installments of $1 million per year beginning one year hence. The current market rate of interest is 12%.

Required:
Prepare the journal entries to record each of the three transactions and the interest expense at the end of the first year for each.

P 14–10

Note with unrealistic interest rate

At January 1, 2003, Brant Cargo acquired equipment by issuing a five-year, $150,000 (payable at maturity), 4% note. The market rate of interest for notes of similar risk is 10%.

Required:
1. Prepare the journal entry for Brant Cargo to record the purchase of the equipment.
2. Prepare the journal entry for Brant Cargo to record the interest at December 31, 2003.
3. Prepare the journal entry for Brant Cargo to record the interest at December 31, 2004.

P 14–11

Noninterest-bearing installment note

At the beginning of 2003, VHF Industries acquired a machine with a fair market value of $6,074,700 by issuing a four-year, noninterest-bearing note in the face amount of $8 million. The note is payable in four annual installments of $2 million at the end of each year.

Required:
1. What is the effective rate of interest implicit in the agreement?
2. Prepare the journal entry to record the purchase of the machine.
3. Prepare the journal entry to record the first installment payment at December 31, 2003.
4. Prepare the journal entry to record the second installment payment at December 31, 2004.
5. Suppose the market value of the machine was unknown at the time of purchase, but the market rate of interest for notes of similar risk was 11%. Prepare the journal entry to record the purchase of the machine.

P 14–12

Note and installment note with unrealistic interest rate

Braxton Technologies, Inc., constructed a conveyor for A&G Warehousers that was completed and ready for use on January 1, 2003. A&G paid for the conveyor by issuing a $100,000, four-year note that specified 5% interest to be paid on December 31 of each year. The conveyor was custom-built for

A&G, so its cash price was unknown. By comparison with similar transactions it was determined that a reasonable interest rate was 10%.

Required:
1. Prepare the journal entry for A&G's purchase of the conveyor on January 1, 2003.
2. Prepare an amortization schedule for the four-year term of the note.
3. Prepare the journal entry for A&G's third interest payment on December 31, 2005.
4. If A&G's note had been an installment note to be paid in four equal payments at the end of each year beginning December 31, 2003, what would be the amount of each installment?
5. Prepare an amortization schedule for the four-year term of the installment note.
6. Prepare the journal entry for A&G's third installment payment on December 31, 2005.

P 14–13
Early extinguishment of debt

Three years ago American Insulation Corporation issued 10 percent, $800,000, 10-year bonds for $770,000. Debt issue costs were $3,000. American Insulation exercised its call privilege and retired the bonds for $790,000. The corporation uses the straight-line method both to determine interest and to amortize debt issue costs.

Required:
Prepare the journal entry to record the call of the bonds.

P 14–14
Early extinguishment; effective interest

The long-term liability section of Twin Digital Corporation's balance sheet as of December 31, 2002, included 12% bonds having a face amount of $20 million and a remaining discount of $1 million. Disclosure notes indicate the bonds were issued to yield 14%.

Interest is recorded at the effective interest rate and paid on January 1 and July 1 of each year. On July 1, 2003, Twin Digital retired the bonds at 102 ($20.4 million) before their scheduled maturity.

Required:
1. Prepare the journal entry by Twin Digital to record the semiannual interest on July 1, 2003.
2. Prepare the journal entry by Twin Digital to record the redemption of the bonds on July 1, 2003.

P 14–15
Investments in bonds; accrued interest; sale

The following transactions relate to bond investments of Livermore Laboratories. The company's fiscal year ends on December 31. Livermore uses the straight-line method to determine interest.

2003

July	1	Purchased $16 million of Bracecourt Corporation 10% debentures, due in 20 years (June 30, 2023), for $15.7 million. Interest is payable on January 1 and July 1 of each year.
Oct.	1	Purchased $30 million of 12% Framm Pharmaceuticals debentures, due May 31, 2013, for $31,160,000 plus accrued interest. Interest is payable on June 1 and December 1 of each year.
Dec.	1	Received interest on the Framm bonds.
	31	Accrued interest.

2004

Jan.	1	Received interest on the Bracecourt bonds.
June	1	Received interest on the Framm bonds.
July	1	Received interest on the Bracecourt bonds.
Sept.	1	Sold $15 million of the Framm bonds at 101 plus accrued interest.
Dec.	1	Received interest on the remaining Framm bonds.
	31	Accrued interest.

2005

Jan.	1	Received interest on the Bracecourt bonds.
Feb.	28	Sold the remainder of the Framm bonds at 102 plus accrued interest.
Dec.	31	Accrued interest.

Required:
Prepare the appropriate journal entries for these long-term bond investments.

P 14–16
Debt issue costs; issuance; expensing; early extinguishment

Cupola Fan Corporation issued 10%, $400,000, 10-year bonds for $385,000 on June 30, 2003. Debt issue costs were $1,500. Interest is paid semiannually on December 31 and June 30. One year from the issue date (July 1, 2004), the corporation exercised its call privilege and retired the bonds for $395,000. The corporation uses the straight-line method both to determine interest and to amortize debt issue costs.

Required:
1. Prepare the journal entry to record the issuance of the bonds.
2. Prepare the journal entries to record the payment of interest and amortization of debt issue costs on December 31, 2003.

3. Prepare the journal entries to record the payment of interest and amortization of debt issue costs on June 30, 2004.
4. Prepare the journal entries to record the call of the bonds.

P 14–17
Concepts; terminology

Listed below are several terms and phrases associated with long-term debt. Pair each item from List A (by letter) with the item from List B that is most appropriately associated with it.

List A	List B
____ 1. Effective rate times balance	a. Straight-line method
____ 2. Promises made to bondholders	b. Discount
____ 3. Present value of interest plus present value of principal	c. Liquidation payments after other claims satisfied
____ 4. Call feature	d. Name of owner not registered
____ 5. Debt issue costs	e. Premium
____ 6. Market rate higher than stated rate	f. Checks are mailed directly
____ 7. Coupon bonds	g. No specific assets pledged
____ 8. Convertible bonds	h. Bond indenture
____ 9. Market rate less than stated rate	i. Backed by a lien
____ 10. Stated rate times face amount	j. Interest expense
____ 11. Registered bonds	k. May become stock
____ 12. Debenture bond	l. Legal, accounting, printing
____ 13. Mortgage bond	m. Protection against falling rates
____ 14. Materiality concept	n. Periodic cash payments
____ 15. Subordinated debenture	o. Bond price

P 14–18
Early extinguishment

The long-term liability section of Eastern Post Corporation's balance sheet as of December 31, 2002, included 10% bonds having a face amount of $40 million and a remaining premium of $6 million. On January 1, 2003, Eastern Post retired some of the bonds before their scheduled maturity.

Required:
Prepare the journal entry by Eastern Post to record the redemption of the bonds under each of the independent circumstances below:
1. Eastern Post called half the bonds at the call price of 102 (102% of face amount).
2. Eastern Post repurchased $10 million of the bonds on the open market at their market price of $10.5 million.

P 14–19
Convertible bonds; induced conversion; bonds with detachable warrants

Bradley-Link's December 31, 2003, balance sheet included the following items:

Long-Term Liabilities	($ in millions)
9.6% convertible bonds, callable at 101 beginning in 2004, due 2010 (net of unamortized discount of $2) [note 8]	$198
10.4% registered bonds callable at 104 beginning in 2013, due 2020 (net of unamortized discount of $1) [note 8]	49
Shareholders' Equity	
Paid-in capital—stock warrants outstanding	4

Note 8: Bonds (in part)
The 9.6% bonds were issued in 1990 at 97.5 to yield 10%. Interest is paid semiannually on June 30 and December 31. Each $1,000 bond is convertible into 40 shares of the Company's $1 par common stock.

The 10.4% bonds were issued in 1994 at 102 to yield 10%. Interest is paid semiannually on June 30 and December 31. Each $1,000 bond was issued with 40 detachable stock warrants, each of which entities the holder to purchase one share of the Company's $1 par common stock for $25, beginning 2004.

On January 3, 2004, when Bradley-Link's common stock had a market price of $32 per share, Bradley-Link called the convertible bonds to force conversion. 90% were converted; the remainder were acquired at the call price. When the common stock price reached an all-time high of $37 in December of 2004, 40% of the warrants were exercised.

Required:

1. Show the journal entries that were recorded when each of the two bond issues was originally sold in 1990 and 1994.
2. Prepare the journal entry to record (book value method) the conversion of 90% of the convertible bonds in January 2004 and the retirement of the remainder.
3. Assume Bradley-Link induced conversion by offering $150 cash for each bond converted. Prepare the journal entry to record (book value method) the conversion of 90% of the convertible bonds in January 2004.
4. Assume Bradley-Link induced conversion by modifying the conversion ratio to exchange 45 shares for each bond rather than the 40 shares provided in the contract. Prepare the journal entry to record (book value method) the conversion of 90% of the convertible bonds in January 2004.
5. Prepare the journal entry to record the exercise of the warrants in December 2004.

P 14–20
Troubled debt restructuring (Based on Appendix 14)

At January 1, 2003, Rothschild Chair Company, Inc., was indebted to First Lincoln Bank under a $20 million, 10% unsecured note. The note was signed January 1, 1997, and was due December 31, 2006. Annual interest was last paid on December 31, 2001. Rothschild Chair Company was experiencing severe financial difficulties and negotiated a restructuring of the terms of the debt agreement.

Required:

Prepare all journal entries by Rothschild Chair Company, Inc., to record the restructuring and any remaining transactions relating to the debt under each of the independent circumstances below:

1. First Lincoln Bank agreed to settle the debt in exchange for land having a fair market value of $16 million but carried on Rothschild Chair Company's books at $13 million.
2. First Lincoln Bank agreed to (a) forgive the interest accrued from last year, (b) reduce the remaining four interest payments to $1 million each, and (c) reduce the principal to $15 million.
3. First Lincoln Bank agreed to defer all payments (including accrued interest) until the maturity date and accept $27,775,000 at that time in settlement of the debt.

BROADEN YOUR PERSPECTIVE

Apply your critical-thinking ability to the knowledge you've gained. These cases will provide you an opportunity to develop your research, analysis, judgment, and communication skills. You also will work with other students, integrate what you've learned, apply it in real world situations, and consider its global and ethical ramifications. This practice will broaden your knowledge and further develop your decision-making abilities.

Communication Case 14–1
Convertible securities and warrants; concepts

It is not unusual to issue long-term debt in conjunction with an arrangement under which lenders receive an option to buy common stock during all or a portion of the time the debt is outstanding. Sometimes the vehicle is convertible bonds; sometimes warrants to buy stock accompany the bonds and are separable. Interstate Chemical is considering these options in conjunction with a planned debt issue.

"You mean we have to report $7 million more in liabilities if we go with convertible bonds? Makes no sense to me," your CFO said. "Both ways seem pretty much the same transaction. Explain it to me, will you?"

Required:

Write a memo. Include in your explanation each of the following:

1. The differences in accounting for proceeds from the issuance of convertible bonds and of debt instruments with separate warrants to purchase common stock.
2. The underlying rationale for the differences.
3. Arguments that could be presented for the alternative accounting treatment.

Research Case 14–2
Alternative ways to measure interest income; research article in Accounting Horizons

As described in Chapter 12, *SFAS 115* requires that certain investment securities be reported on the balance sheet at fair value.[20] Nevertheless, the required approach is to continue to measure interest income as the original effective rate times the unadjusted outstanding balance, as described in this chapter. That is, the new fair value is ignored. Professor Means, in "Effective Interest . . . on What Basis?," compares this approach with two alternatives and suggests a theoretically correct solution.

---

[20] "Accounting for Certain Investments in Debt and Equity Securities," *Statement of Financial Accounting Standards No. 115* (Norwalk, Conn.: FASB, 1993). The standard became effective in 1994.

Required:

1. In your library or from some other source, locate the indicated article in *Accounting Horizons,* June 1994.
2. What are the two alternative ways to measure interest income described in the article?
3. What is the author's conclusion as to the theoretically correct alternative?
4. What is the primary reason for her conclusion?

Communication Case 14–3
Is convertible debt a liability or is it shareholders' equity?
Group Interaction

Some financial instruments can be considered compound instruments in that they have features of both debt and shareholders' equity. The most common example encountered in practice is convertible debt—bonds or notes convertible by the investor into common stock. A topic of debate for several years has been whether:

View 1: Issuers should account for an instrument with both liability and equity characteristics entirely as a liability or entirely as an equity instrument depending on which characteristic governs.

View 2: Issuers should account for an instrument as consisting of a liability component and an equity component that should be accounted for separately.

In considering this question, you should disregard what you know about the current position of the FASB on the issue. Instead, focus on conceptual issues regarding the practicable and theoretically appropriate treatment, unconstrained by GAAP. Also, focus your deliberations on convertible bonds as the instrument with both liability and equity characteristics.

Required:

1. Which view do you favor? Develop a list of arguments in support of your view prior to the class session for which the case is assigned.
2. In class, your instructor will pair you (and everyone else) with a classmate (who also has independently developed an argument).
   a. You will be given three minutes to argue your view to your partner. Your partner likewise will be given three minutes to argue his or her view to you. During these three-minute presentations, the listening partner is not permitted to speak.
   b. After each person has had a turn attempting to convince his or her partner, the two partners will have a three-minute discussion in which they will decide which view is more convincing. Arguments will be merged into a single view for each pair.
3. After the allotted time, a spokesperson for each of the two views will be selected by the instructor. Each spokesperson will field arguments from the class in support of that view's position and list the arguments on the board. The class then will discuss the merits of the two lists of arguments and attempt to reach a consensus view, though a consensus is not necessary.

Analysis Case 14–4
Issuance of bonds

The following appeared in the October 15, 2002, issue of the *Financial World Journal*:

This announcement is not an offer of securities for sale or an offer to buy securities.

New Issue   October 15, 2002

$750,000,000
CRAFT FOODS, INC.
7.75% Debentures Due October 1, 2012
Price 99.57%
plus accrued interest if any from date of issuance

Copies of the prospectus and the related prospectus supplement may be obtained from such of the undersigned as may legally offer these securities under applicable securities laws.

Keegan Morgan & Co. Inc.

Coldwell Bros. & Co.

Robert Stacks & Co.

Sherwin-William & Co.

Required:

1. Explain what is being described by the announcement.
2. Can you think of a psychological reason for the securities to be priced as they are?
3. What are the accounting considerations for Craft Foods, Inc.? Describe how Craft recorded the sale.

Judgment Case 14–5
Noninterest-bearing debt

While reading a recent issue of *Health & Fitness,* a trade journal, Brandon Wilde noticed an ad for equipment he had been seeking for use in his business. The ad offered oxygen therapy equipment under the following terms:

> Model BL 44582
> $204,000 zero interest loan
> Quarterly payments of $17,000 for only 3 years

The ad captured Wilde's attention, in part because he recently had been concerned that the interest charges incurred by his business were getting out of line. The price, though, was somewhat higher than prices for this model he had seen elsewhere.

Required:

Advise Mr. Wilde on the purchase he is considering.

Judgment Case 14–6
Noninterest-bearing note exchanged for cash and other privileges

The Jaecke Group, Inc., manufactures various kinds of hydraulic pumps. In June 2003, the company signed a four-year purchase agreement with one of its main parts suppliers, Hydraulics, Inc. Over the four-year period, Jaecke has agreed to purchase 100,000 units of a key component used in the manufacture of its pumps. The agreement allows Jaecke to purchase the component at a price lower than the prevailing market price at the time of purchase. As part of the agreement, Jaecke will lend Hydraulics $200,000 to be repaid after four years with no stated interest (the prevailing market rate of interest for a loan of this type is 10%).

Jaecke's chief accountant has proposed recording the note receivable at $200,000. The parts inventory purchase from Hydraulics over the next four years will then be recorded at the actual prices paid.

Required:

Do you agree with the accountant's valuation of the note and his intention to value the parts inventory acquired over the four-year period of the agreement at actual prices paid? If not, how would you account for the initial transaction and the subsequent inventory purchases?

Communication Case 14–7
Note receivable exchanged for cash and other services

The Pastel Paint Company recently loaned $300,000 to KIX 96, a local radio station. The radio station signed a noninterest-bearing note requiring the $300,000 to be repaid in three years. As part of the agreement, the radio station will provide Pastel with a specified amount of free radio advertising over the three-year term of the note.

The focus of this case is the valuation of the note receivable by Pastel Paint Company and the treatment of the "free" advertising provided by the radio station. Your instructor will divide the class into from two to six groups depending on the size of the class. The mission of your group is to reach consensus on the appropriate note valuation and accounting treatment of the free advertising.

Required:

1. Each group member should deliberate the situation independently and draft a tentative argument prior to the class session for which the case is assigned.
2. In class, each group will meet for 10 to 15 minutes in different areas of the classroom. During that meeting, group members will take turns sharing their suggestions for the purpose of arriving at a single group treatment.
3. After the allotted time, a spokesperson for each group (selected during the group meetings) will share the group's solution with the class. The goal of the class is to incorporate the views of each group into a consensus approach to the situation.

Analysis Case 14–8
Issuance, extinguishment, and conversion of bonds

On January 1, 2002, Brewster Company issued 2,000 of its five-year, $1,000 face amount, 11% bonds dated January 1 at an effective annual interest rate (yield) of 9%. Brewster uses the effective interest method of amortization. On December 31, 2003, the 2,000 bonds were extinguished early through acquisition in the open market by Brewster for $1,980,000. On July 1, 2002, Brewster issued 5,000 of its six-year, $1,000 face amount, 10% convertible bonds dated July 1 at an effective annual interest rate (yield) of 12%. The convertible bonds are convertible at the option of the investor into Brewster's common stock at a ratio of 10 shares of common stock for each bond. Brewster used the effective interest method of amortization. On July 1, 2003, an investor in Brewster's convertible bonds tendered 1,500 bonds for conversion into 15,000 shares of Brewster's common stock which had a market value of $105 per share at the date of the conversion.

Required:

1. a. Were the 11% bonds issued at par, at a discount, or at a premium? Why?
   b. Would the amount of interest expense for the 11% bonds using the effective interest method of amortization be higher in the first or second year of the life of the bonds issue? Why?
2. a. How should gain or loss on early extinguishment of debt be determined? Does the early extinguishment of the 11% bonds result in a gain or loss? Why?
   b. How should Brewster report the early extinguishment of the 11% bonds on the 2003 income statement?

3. a. Would recording the conversion of the 10% convertible bonds into common stock under the book value method affect net income? What is the rationale for the book value method?
   b. Would recording the conversion of the 10% convertible bonds into common stock under the market value affect net income? What is the rationale for the market value method?

(AICPA adapted)

Ethics Case 14–9
Debt for equity swaps; have your cake and eat it too

The cloudy afternoon mirrored the mood of the conference of division managers. Claude Meyer, assistant to the controller for Hunt Manufacturing, wore one of the gloomy faces that was just emerging from the conference room. "Wow, I knew it was bad, but not that bad," Claude thought to himself. "I don't look forward to sharing those numbers with shareholders."

The numbers he discussed with himself were fourth quarter losses which more than offset the profits of the first three quarters. Everyone had known for some time that poor sales forecasts and production delays had wreaked havoc on the bottom line, but most were caught off guard by the severity of damage.

Later that night he sat alone in his office, scanning and rescanning the preliminary financial statements on his computer monitor. Suddenly his mood brightened. "This may work," he said aloud, though no one could hear. Fifteen minutes later he congratulated himself, "Yes!"

The next day he eagerly explained his plan to Susan Barr, controller of Hunt for the last six years. The plan involved $300 million in convertible bonds issued three years earlier.

> *Meyer:* By swapping stock for the bonds, we can eliminate a substantial liability from the balance sheet, wipe out most of our interest expense, and reduce our loss. In fact, the book value of the bonds is significantly less than the market value of the stock we'd issue. I think we can produce a profit.
>
> *Barr:* But Claude, our bondholders are not inclined to convert the bonds.
>
> *Meyer:* Right. But, the bonds are callable. As of this year, we can call the bonds at a call premium of 1%. Given the choice of accepting that redemption price or converting to stock, they'll all convert. We won't have to pay a cent. And, since no cash will be paid, we won't pay taxes either.

Required:
Do you perceive an ethical dilemma? What would be the impact of following up on Claude's plan? Who would benefit? Who would be injured?

Judgment Case 14–10
Analyzing financial statements; financial leverage; interest coverage

IGF Foods Company is a large, primarily domestic, consumer foods company involved in the manufacture, distribution, and sale of a variety of food products. Industry averages are derived from Troy's *The Almanac of Business and Industrial Financial Ratios*. Following are the 2003 and 2002 comparative income statements and balance sheets for IGF. (The financial data we use are from actual financial statements of a well-known corporation, but the company name is fictitious and the numbers and dates have been modified slightly to disguise the company's identity.)

IGF FOODS COMPANY
Years Ended December 31, 2003 and 2002
($ in millions)

Comparative Income Statements	2003	2002
Net sales	$6,440	$5,800
Cost of goods sold	(3,667)	(3,389)
Gross profit	2,773	2,411
Operating expenses	(1,916)	(1,629)
Operating income	857	782
Interest expense	(54)	(53)
Income from operations before tax	803	729
Income taxes	(316)	(287)
Net income	$ 487	$ 442

Comparative Balance Sheets

Assets		
Total current assets	$1,879	$1,490
Property, plant, and equipment (net)	2,592	2,291
Intangibles (net)	800	843
Other assets	74	60
Total assets	$5,345	$4,684

Liabilities and Shareholders' Equity

Total current liabilities	$1,473	$ 941
Long-term debt	534	728
Deferred income taxes	407	344
Total liabilities	2,414	2,013
Shareholders' equity:		
Common stock	180	180
Additional paid-in capital	21	63
Retained earnings	2,730	2,428
Total shareholders' equity	2,931	2,671
Total liabilities and shareholders' equity	$5,345	$4,684

Long-term solvency refers to a company's ability to pay its long-term obligations. Financing ratios provide investors and creditors with an indication of this element of risk.

Required:

1. Calculate the debt to equity ratio for IGF for 2003. The average ratio for the stocks listed on the New York Stock Exchange in a comparable time period was 1.0. What information does your calculation provide an investor?
2. Is IGF experiencing favorable or unfavorable financial leverage?
3. Calculate IGF's times interest earned ratio for 2003. The coverage for the stocks listed on the New York Stock Exchange in a comparable time period was 5.1. What does your calculation indicate about IGF's risk?

Real World Case 14–11
Researching the way long-term debt is reported; retrieving information from the Internet

EDGAR, the Electronic Data Gathering. Analysis, and Retrieval system, performs automated collection, validation, indexing, acceptance and forwarding of submissions by companies and others who are required by law to file forms with the U.S. Securities and Exchange Commission (SEC). All publicly traded domestic companies use EDGAR to make the majority of their filings. (Some foreign companies do so voluntarily.) Form 10-K, including the annual report, is required to be filed on EDGAR. The SEC makes this information available on the Internet.

Required:

1. Access EDGAR on the Internet using EdgarScan at: edgarscan.pwcglobal.com.
2. Search for Procter & Gamble. Access its most recent 10-K filing. Search or scroll to find the financial statements and related notes.
3. What is the total debt (including current liabilities and deferred taxes) reported on the balance sheet? How has that amount changed over the most recent two years?
4. Compare the total liabilities (including current liabilities and deferred taxes) with the shareholders' equity and calculate the debt to equity ratio for the most recent two years. Has the proportion of debt financing and equity financing changed recently?
5. Does P&G obtain more financing through notes, bonds, or commercial paper? Are required debt payments increasing or decreasing over time? Is any long-term debt classified as short-term or vice versa? Why?

15

Leases

CHAPTER

OVERVIEW

In the previous chapter, we saw how companies account for their long-term debt. The focus of that discussion was *bonds* and *notes*. In this chapter we continue our discussion of debt, but we now turn our attention to liabilities arising in connection with *leases*. Leases that produce such debtor/creditor relationships are referred to as *capital* leases by the lessee and as either *direct financing* or *sales-type* leases by the lessor. We also will see that some leases do not produce debtor/creditor relationships, but instead are accounted for as rental agreements. These are designated *operating* leases.

It's a Hit!

"Don't get too comfortable with those big numbers," said Aaron Sanchez, controller for your new employer. "It's likely our revenues will take a hit over the next couple of years as more of our customers lease our machines rather than buy them."

You've just finished your first look at Higher Graphics' third quarter earnings report. Like most companies in your industry, HG leases its labeling machines to some customers and sells them to others. Eager to understand the implications of your new supervisor's concerns, you pull out your old intermediate accounting book and turn to the leases chapter.

> By the time you finish this chapter, you should be able to respond appropriately to the questions posed in this case. Compare your response to the solution provided at the end of the chapter.

QUESTIONS

1. How would HG's revenues "take a hit" as a result of more customers leasing rather than buying labeling machines? (page 721)
2. Under what kind of leasing arrangements would the "hit" not occur? (page 730)

PART

a

An apartment lease is a typical rental agreement referred to as an *operating lease.*

ACCOUNTING BY THE LESSOR AND LESSEE

We all are familiar with leases. If you ever have leased an apartment, you know that a lease is a contractual arrangement by which a **lessor** (owner) provides a **lessee** (user) the right to use an asset for a specified period of time. In return for this right, the lessee agrees to make stipulated, periodic cash payments during the term of the lease. An apartment lease is a typical rental agreement in which the fundamental rights and responsibilities of ownership are retained by the lessor; the lessee merely uses the asset temporarily. Businesses, too, lease assets under similar arrangements. These are referred to as **operating leases.** Many contracts, though, are formulated outwardly as leases, but in reality are installment purchases/sales. These are called **capital leases (direct financing** or **sales-type leases** to the lessor). Graphic 15–1 compares the possibilities.

GRAPHIC 15–1
Basic Lease
Classifications

Lessee	Lessor
Operating lease	Operating lease
Capital lease	Direct financing lease
	Sales-type lease

After looking at some of the possible advantages of leasing assets rather than buying them in certain circumstances, we will explore differences in leases further.

LO1

Leasing can facilitate asset acquisition.

DECISION MAKERS' PERSPECTIVE—Advantages of Leasing

When a young entrepreneur started a computer training center a few years ago, she had no idea how fast her business would grow. Now, while she knows she needs computers, she doesn't know how many. Just starting out, she also has little cash with which to buy them.

The mutual funds department of a large investment firm often needs new computers and peripherals—fast. The department manager knows he can't afford to wait up to a year, the time it sometimes takes, to go through company channels to obtain purchase approval.

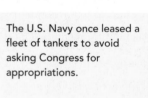

The U.S. Navy once leased a fleet of tankers to avoid asking Congress for appropriations.

An established computer software publisher recently began developing a new line of business software. The senior programmer has to be certain he's testing the company's products on the latest versions of computer hardware. And yet he views large expenditures on equipment subject to rapid technological change and obsolescence as risky business.

Each of these individuals is faced with different predicaments and concerns. The entrepreneur is faced with uncertainty and cash flow problems, the department manager with time constraints and bureaucratic control systems, the programmer with fear of obsolescence. Though their specific concerns differ, these individuals have all met their firms' information technology needs with the same solution: each has decided to lease the computers rather than buy them.

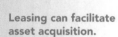

The number one method of external financing by U.S. businesses is leasing.

Computers are by no means the only assets obtained through leasing arrangements. To the contrary, leasing has grown to be the most popular method of external financing of corporate assets in America. The airplane in which you last flew probably was leased, as was the gate from which it departed. Your favorite retail outlet at the local shopping mall likely leases the space it operates. Many companies actually exist for the sole purpose of acquiring assets and leasing them to others. And, leasing often is a primary method of "selling" a firm's products. IBM and Boeing are familiar examples.

In light of its popularity, you may be surprised that leasing usually is more expensive than buying. Of course, the higher apparent cost of leasing is because the lessor usually shoulders at least some of the financial and risk burdens that a purchaser normally would assume. So, why the popularity?

The lease decisions described above are motivated by operational incentives. Tax and market considerations also motivate firms to lease. Sometimes leasing offers tax saving advantages over outright purchases. For instance, a company with little or no taxable income—maybe a business just getting started, or one experiencing an economic downturn—will get little benefit from depreciation deductions. But the company can benefit *indirectly* by leasing assets rather than buying. By allowing the *lessor* to retain ownership and thus benefit from depreciation deductions, the lessee often can negotiate lower lease payments. Lessees with sufficient taxable income to take advantage of the depreciation deductions, but still in lower tax brackets than lessors, also can achieve similar indirect tax benefits.

The desire to obtain "off-balance-sheet financing" also is sometimes a leasing stimulus. When funds are borrowed to purchase an asset, the liability has a detrimental effect on the company's debt-equity ratio and other quantifiable indicators of riskiness. Similarly, the purchased asset increases total assets and correspondingly lowers calculations of the rate of return on assets. Despite research that indicates otherwise, management actions continue to reflect a belief that the financial market is naive, and is fooled by off-balance-sheet financing.[1] Managers continue to avoid reporting assets and liabilities by leasing rather than buying and by constructing lease agreements in such a way that capitalizing the assets and liabilities is not required.[2]

Whether or not there is any real effect on security prices, sometimes off-balance-sheet financing helps a firm avoid exceeding contractual limits on designated financial ratios (like the debt to equity ratio, for instance).[3] When the operational, tax, and financial market advantages are considered, the *net* cost of leasing often is less than the cost of purchasing. ■

> **Tax incentives often motivate leasing.**
>
> **Leasing sometimes is used as a means of off-balance-sheet financing.**
>
> **Operational, tax, and financial market incentives often make leasing an attractive alternative to purchasing.**

CHECK WITH THE **COACH**

Leasing is a popular vehicle for individuals and companies to finance the use of assets. In the business world, leases take many forms and can be motivated by a wide variety of credit conditions. Let the Coach explain to you some of the key aspects of lease accounting and disclosure. At exam time, you will be glad you did. ■

Capital Leases and Installment Notes Compared

You learned in the previous chapter how to account for an installment note. To a great extent, then, you already have learned how to account for a capital lease. To illustrate, let's recall the situation described in the previous chapter. We assumed that Skill Graphics purchased a package-labeling machine from Hughes–Barker Corporation by issuing a three-year installment note that required six semiannual installment payments of $139,857 each. That arrangement provided for the purchase of the $666,633 machine as well as interest at an

---

[1]A comprehensive research study commissioned by the FASB offers strong evidence that managers try to structure leases as operating leases to avoid balance sheet effects, but also that the securities market behaves as if it sees through these attempts. That is, leases have the same effect on the market whether they are reflected as assets and liabilities on the balance sheet or are merely reported in the disclosure notes. These are conclusions of A. Rashad Abdel-khalik, "The Economic Effects on Leases of FASB *Statement No. 13,* Accounting for Leases," *Research Report* (Stamford, Conn.: FASB, 1981).

[2]You will learn later in the chapter that accounting standards are designed to identify lease arrangements that, despite their outward appearance, are in reality purchases of assets. Assets acquired by these arrangements, *capital leases,* are required to be recorded as well as the related lease liability. Managers often structure lease terms so that capitalization requirements are avoided.

[3]It is common for debt agreements, particularly long-term ones, to include restrictions on the debtor as a way to provide some degree of protection to the creditor. Sometimes a minimum level is specified for current assets relative to current liabilities, net assets, debt as a ratio of equity, or many other financial ratios. Often a restriction is placed on dividend payments, share repurchases, or other activities that might impede the debtor's ability to repay the debt. Typically, the debt becomes due on demand when the debtor becomes in violation of such a debt covenant, often after a specified grace period.

annual rate of 14% (7% twice each year). Remember, too, that each installment payment consisted of part interest (7% times the outstanding balance) and part payment for the machine (the remainder of each payment).

Now let's suppose that Skill Graphics instead acquired the package-labeling machine from Hughes–Barker Corporation under a three-year *lease* that required six semiannual rental payments of $139,857 each. Obviously, the fundamental nature of the transaction remains the same regardless of whether it is negotiated as an installment purchase or as a lease. So, it would be inconsistent to account for this lease in a fundamentally different way than for an installment purchase:

Comparison of a Note and Capital Lease

In keeping with the basic accounting concept of substance over form, accounting for a capital lease parallels that for an installment purchase.

	At Inception (January 1)	
Installment Note		
Machinery	666,633	
Note payable.		666,633
Capital Lease		
Leased machinery	666,633	
Lease payable		666,633

Consistent with the nature of the transaction, interest expense accrues each period at the effective rate times the outstanding balance:

Interest Compared for a Note and Capital Lease

Each payment includes both an amount that represents interest and an amount that represents a reduction of principal.

	At the First Semiannual Payment Date (June 30)	
Installment Note		
Interest expense (7% × $666,633)	46,664	
Note payable (difference)	93,193	
Cash (installment payment)		139,857
Capital Lease		
Interest expense (7% × $666,633)	46,664	
Lease payable (difference)	93,193	
Cash (rental payment)		139,857

Because the lease payable balance declines with each payment, the interest becomes less each period. An amortization schedule is convenient to track the changing amounts as shown in Graphic 15–2.

GRAPHIC 15–2
Lease Amortization Schedule

Each rental payment includes interest on the outstanding balance at the effective rate. The remainder of each payment reduces the outstanding balance.

Date	Payments	Effective Interest	Decrease in Balance	Outstanding Balance
		(7% × Outstanding balance)		
				666,633
1	139,857	.07(666,633) = 46,664	93,193	573,440
2	139,857	.07(573,440) = 40,141	99,716	473,724
3	139,857	.07(473,724) = 33,161	106,696	367,028
4	139,857	.07(367,028) = 25,692	114,165	252,863
5	139,857	.07(252,863) = 17,700	122,157	130,706
6	139,857	.07(130,706) = 9,151*	130,706	0
	839,142	172,509	666,633	

*Rounded.

You should recognize this as essentially the same amortization schedule we used in the previous chapter in connection with our installment note example. The reason for the similarity is that we view a capital lease as being, in substance, equivalent to an installment purchase. So naturally the accounting treatment of the two essentially identical transactions should be consistent.

Lease Classification

A lease is accounted for as either a rental agreement or a purchase/sale accompanied by debt financing. The choice of accounting method hinges on the nature of the leasing arrangement.

Capital leases are agreements that we identify as being formulated outwardly as leases, but which are in reality installment purchases. Sometimes the true nature of an arrangement is obvious. For example, a 10-year noncancelable lease of a computer with a 10-year useful life, by which title passes to the lessee at the end of the lease term, obviously more nearly represents a purchase than a rental agreement. But what if the terms of the contract do not transfer title, and the lease term is for only seven years of the asset's 10-year life? Suppose contractual terms permit the lessee to obtain title under certain prearranged conditions? What if compensation provided by the lease contract is nearly equal to the value of the asset under lease? These situations are less clear-cut.

> A basic concept of accounting is substance over form.

Professional judgment is needed to differentiate between leases that represent rental agreements and those that in reality are installment purchases/sales. The essential question is whether the usual risks and rewards of ownership have been transferred to the lessee. But judgment alone is likely to lead to inconsistencies in practice. The desire to encourage consistency in practice motivated the FASB to provide guidance for distinguishing between the two fundamental types of leases.[4] As you study the classification criteria in the following paragraphs, keep in mind that some leases clearly fit the classifications we give them, but others fall in a gray area somewhere between the two extremes. For those, we end up forcing them into one category or the other by somewhat arbitrary criteria.

> Accounting for leases attempts to see through the legal form of the agreements to determine their economic substance.

CLASSIFICATION CRITERIA

A lessee should classify a lease transaction as a capital lease if it includes a noncancelable lease term and one or more of the four criteria listed in Graphic 15–3 are met.[5] Otherwise, it is an operating lease.

LO3

1. The agreement specifies that ownership of the asset transfers to the lessee.
2. The agreement contains a bargain purchase option.
3. The noncancelable lease term is equal to 75% or more of the expected economic life of the asset.
4. The present value of the minimum lease payments is equal to or greater than 90% of the fair value of the asset.

> **GRAPHIC 15–3**
> Criteria for Classification as a Capital Lease

Let's look closer at these criteria.

Since our objective is to determine when the risks and rewards of ownership have been transferred to the lessee, the first criterion is self-evident. If legal title passes to the lessee during, or at the end of, the lease term, obviously ownership attributes are transferred.

> Criterion 1: Transfer of ownership.

A bargain purchase option (BPO) is a provision in the lease contract that gives the lessee the option of purchasing the leased property at a bargain price. This is defined as a price sufficiently lower than the expected fair value of the property (when the option becomes exercisable) that the exercise of the option appears reasonably assured at the inception of the lease. Because exercise of the option appears reasonably assured, transfer of ownership is expected. So the logic of the second criterion is similar to that of the first.

> Criterion 2: Bargain purchase option.

[4]"Accounting for Leases," *Statement of Financial Accounting Standards No. 13* (Stamford, Conn.: FASB, 1980), par. 7.
[5]Noncancelable in this context does not preclude the agreement from specifying that the lease is cancelable after a designated noncancelable lease term. If no portion of the lease term is noncancelable, it is an operating lease. Later in this section, we discuss treatment of any cancelable portion of the lease term.

Applying criterion 2 in practice, though, often is more difficult because it is necessary to make a judgment now about whether a future option price will be a bargain.

If an asset is leased for most of its useful life, then most of the benefits and responsibilities of ownership are transferred to the lessee. We presume, quite arbitrarily, that 75% or more of the **expected economic life** of the asset is an appropriate threshold point for this purpose.

Although the intent of this criterion is fairly straightforward, implementation sometimes is troublesome. First, the lease term may be uncertain. It may be renewable beyond its initial term. Or the lease may be cancelable after a designated noncancelable period. When either is an issue, we ordinarily consider the lease term to be the noncancelable[6] term of the lease plus any periods covered by **bargain renewal options.**[7] A bargain renewal option gives the lessee the option to renew the lease at a bargain rate. That is, the rental payment is sufficiently lower than the expected fair rental of the property at the date the option becomes exercisable that exercise of the option appears reasonably assured.

ADDITIONAL CONSIDERATION

Periods covered by bargain renewal options are not included in the lease term if a **bargain purchase option** is present. This is because the lease term should not extend beyond the date a bargain purchase option becomes exercisable. For example, assume a BPO allows a lessee to buy a leased delivery truck at the end of the noncancelable five-year lease term. Even if an option to renew the lease beyond that date is considered to be a bargain renewal option, that extra period would not be included as part of the lease term. Remember, we presume the BPO will be exercised after the initial five-year term, making the renewal option irrelevant.

Another implementation issue is estimating the economic life of the leased property. This is the estimated remaining time the property is expected to be economically usable for its intended purpose, with normal maintenance and repairs, at the inception of the lease. Estimates of the economic life of leased property are subject to the same uncertainty limitations of most estimates. This uncertainty presents the opportunity to arrive at estimates that cause this third criterion not to be met.

Finally, if the inception of the lease occurs during the last 25% of an asset's economic life, this third criterion does not apply. This is consistent with the basic premise of this criterion that most of the risks and rewards of ownership occur during the first 75% of an asset's life.

If the lease payments required by a lease contract substantially pay for a leased asset, it is logical to identify the arrangement as a lease equivalent to an installment purchase. This situation is considered to exist when the present value of the minimum lease payments is equal to or greater than 90% of the fair value of the asset at the inception of the lease. In general, minimum lease payments are payments the lessee is required to make in connection with the lease. We look closer at the make-up of minimum lease payments later in the chapter.

The 90% recovery criterion often is the decisive one. As mentioned earlier, lessees often try to avoid writing a lease agreement that will require recording an asset and liability. When this is an objective, it usually is relatively easy to avoid meeting the first three criteria. How-

---

[6]Noncancelable in this context is a lease that is cancelable only by (a) the occurrence of some remote contingency, (b) permission of the lessor, (c) a new lease with the same lessor, or (d) payment by the lessee of a penalty in an amount such that continuation of the lease appears, at inception, reasonably assured. "Accounting for Leases: Sale and Leaseback Transactions Involving Real Estate, Sales-Type Leases of Real Estate, Definition of the Lease Term, Initial Direct Costs of Direct Financing Leases," *Statement of Financial Accounting Standards No. 98* (Stamford, Conn.: FASB, 1988), par. 22.

[7]If applicable, the lease term also should include (a) periods for which failure to renew the lease imposes a penalty on the lessee in an amount such that renewal appears reasonably assured, (b) periods covered by ordinary renewal options during which a guarantee by the lessee of the lessor's debt directly or indirectly related to the leased property is expected to be in effect or a loan from the lessee to the lessor directly or indirectly related to the leased property is expected to be outstanding, (c) periods covered by ordinary renewal options preceding the date that a bargain purchase option is exercisable, or (d) periods representing renewals or extensions of the lease at the lessor's option. "Accounting for Leases: Sale and Leaseback Transactions Involving Real Estate, Sales-Type Leases of Real Estate, Definition of the Lease Term, Initial Direct Costs of Direct Financing Leases," *Statement of Financial Accounting Standards No. 98* (Stamford, Conn.: FASB, 1988), par. 22.

ever, when the underlying motive for the lease agreement is that the lessee substantively acquire the asset, it is more difficult to avoid meeting the 90% recovery criterion without defeating that motive. New ways, though, continually are being devised to structure leases to avoid meeting this criterion. Later we will look at some popular devices that are used.

Again consistent with the basic premise that most of the risks and rewards of ownership occur during the first 75% of an asset's life, this fourth criterion does not apply if the inception of the lease occurs during the last 25% of an asset's economic life.

ADDITIONAL LESSOR CONDITIONS

As we saw in the previous section, the lessee accounts for a capital lease as if an asset were purchased—records both an asset and a liability at the inception of the lease. Consistency would suggest that the lessor in the same lease transaction should record the sale of an asset. Indeed, consistency is a goal of the FASB's lease accounting standards. The four classification criteria discussed in the previous section apply to both parties to the transaction, lessees and lessors. However, a fundamental difference is that for a lessor to record the sale side of the transaction, it is necessary also to satisfy the conditions of the realization principle we discussed in Chapter 5. In particular, the FASB specifies that for the lessor to record a lease as a direct financing lease or a sales-type lease, two conditions must be met in addition to one of the four classification criteria. These are listed in Graphic 15–4.

> 1. The collectibility of the lease payments must be reasonably predictable.
> 2. If any costs to the lessor have yet to be incurred, they are reasonably predictable. (Performance by the lessor is substantially complete.)

GRAPHIC 15–4
Additional Conditions for Classification as a Nonoperating Lease by the Lessor

In the case of a sales-type lease (discussed later in Part A of this chapter) in which the lessor recognizes sales revenue, the reason for these additional conditions is apparent; collectibility of payments and substantial completion of the earnings process are conditions of the revenue realization principle. This logic is extended to agreements classified as direct financing leases. Although sales revenue is not recorded in a direct financing lease, the leased asset is removed from the lessor's books and is replaced by a receivable.

Although uniformity of classification is a goal of lease accounting standards, it is obvious that the additional conditions allow inconsistencies.[8] Indeed, in lease negotiations an objective of the parties involved often is to devise terms that will result in a sale by the lessor but an operating lease by the lessee.[9]

In the remaining sections of Part A of this chapter we consider, in order, operating leases, direct financing leases (capital leases to the lessee), and sales-type leases (capital leases to the lessee).

> Additional lessor conditions for classification as a nonoperating lease are consistent with criteria of the revenue realization principle.

Operating Leases

If a lease does not meet any of the criteria for a capital lease it is considered to be more in the nature of a rental agreement and is referred to as an operating lease.[10] We assume that the fundamental rights and responsibilities of ownership are retained by the lessor and that the lessee merely is using the asset temporarily. In keeping with that presumption, a sale is not recorded by the lessor; a purchase is not recorded by the lessee. Instead, the periodic rental payments are accounted for merely as rent by both parties to the transaction—rent revenue by the lessor, rent expense by the lessee.

FINANCIAL REPORTING CASE

Q1, p. 715

---

[8]"Accounting for Leases," *Statement of Financial Accounting Standards No. 13* (Stamford, Conn.: FASB, 1980).

[9]Later in the chapter we discuss ways this is done.

[10]The term *operating lease* got its name long ago when a lessee routinely received from the lessor an operator along with leased equipment.

Let's look at an example that illustrates the relatively straightforward accounting for operating leases. The earlier example comparing a capital lease to an installment purchase assumed rental payments at the *end* of each period. A more typical leasing arrangement requires rental payments at the *beginning* of each period. This more realistic payment schedule is assumed Illustration 15–1.

ILLUSTRATION 15–1	On January 1, 2003, Sans Serif Publishers, Inc., a computer services and printing firm, leased a color copier from CompuDec Corporation.
Application of Classification Criteria	The lease agreement specifies four annual payments of $100,000 beginning January 1, 2003, the inception of the lease, and at each January 1 through 2006. The useful life of the copier is estimated to be six years.

On January 1, 2003, Sans Serif Publishers, Inc., a computer services and printing firm, leased a color copier from CompuDec Corporation.

The lease agreement specifies four annual payments of $100,000 beginning January 1, 2003, the inception of the lease, and at each January 1 through 2006. The useful life of the copier is estimated to be six years.

Before deciding to lease, Sans Serif considered purchasing the copier for its cash price of $479,079. If funds were borrowed to buy the copier, the interest rate would have been 10%.

How should this lease be classified? We apply the four classification criteria:

1. Does the agreement specify that ownership of the asset transfers to the lessee? **No**
2. Does this agreement contain a bargain purchase option? **No**
3. Is the lease term equal to 75% or more of the expected economic life of the asset? **No** (4 yrs < 75% of 6 yrs)
4. Is the present value of the minimum lease payments equal to or greater than 90% of the fair value of the asset? **No** ($348,685 < 90% of $479,079)

$100,000 × 3.48685* = $348,685

| Lease payments | Present value |

Since none of the four classification criteria is met, this is an operating lease.

*Present value of an annuity due of $1: $n = 4$, $i = 10\%$. Recall from Chapter 6 that we refer to periodic payments at the beginning of each period as an *annuity due*.

Journal entries for Illustration 15–1 are shown in Illustration 15–1A.

ILLUSTRATION 15–1A	The operating lease described in Illustration 15–1 is recorded as follows:
Journal Entries for an Operating Lease	**At Each of the Four Payment Dates**

At Each of the Four Payment Dates

Sans Serif Publishers, Inc. (Lessee)

Prepaid rent.	100,000	
Cash.		100,000

At the beginning of the year, the rent payments are prepaid rent to the lessee and unearned rent to the lessor.

CompuDec Corporation (Lessor)

Cash.	100,000	
Unearned rent revenue		100,000

At the End of Each Year

Sans Serif Publishers, Inc. (Lessee)

Rent expense	100,000	
Prepaid rent.		100,000

The lessor retains the asset on its books, and accordingly records depreciation on the asset.

CompuDec Corporation (Lessor)

Unearned rent revenue.	100,000	
Rent revenue		100,000
Depreciation expense.	x,xxx	
Accumulated depreciation		x,xxx

In an operating lease, rent is recognized on a straight-line basis unless another systematic method more clearly reflects the benefits of the asset's use. So, if rental payments are uneven—for instance, if rent increases are scheduled—the total scheduled payments ordinarily would be expensed equally (straight-line basis) over the lease term.[11]

ADVANCE PAYMENTS

Often lease agreements call for advance payments to be made at the inception of the lease that represent prepaid rent. For instance, it is common for a lessee to pay a bonus in return for negotiating more favorable lease terms. Such payments are recorded as prepaid rent and allocated (normally on a straight-line basis) to rent expense/rent revenue over the lease term. So the rent that is periodically reported in those cases consists of the periodic rent payments themselves plus an allocated portion of prepaid rent. This is demonstrated in Illustration 15–1B.

Assume Sans Serif paid a $40,000 bonus (advance payment) at the inception of the lease described in Illustration 15–1 in return for lower periodic payments—$90,000 each.		
At the Inception of the Lease		
Sans Serif Publishers, Inc. (Lessee)		
Prepaid rent (bonus payment)	40,000	
Cash		40,000
CompuDec Corporation (Lessor)		
Cash	40,000	
Unearned rent revenue (bonus payment)		40,000
At Each of the Four Payment Dates		
Sans Serif Publishers, Inc. (Lessee)		
Prepaid rent (annual rent payment)	90,000	
Cash		90,000
CompuDec Corporation (Lessor)		
Cash	90,000	
Unearned rent revenue (annual rent payment)		90,000
At the End of Each Year		
Sans Serif Publishers, Inc. (Lessee)		
Rent expense (annual rent)	90,000	
Prepaid rent		90,000
Rent expense (bonus allocation)	10,000	
Prepaid rent ($40,000 ÷ 4)		10,000
CompuDec Corporation (Lessor)		
Unearned rent revenue	90,000	
Rent revenue (annual rent)		90,000
Unearned rent revenue ($40,000 ÷ 4)	10,000	
Rent revenue (bonus allocation)		10,000
Depreciation expense	x,xxx	
Accumulated depreciation		x,xxx

ILLUSTRATION 15–1B

Journal Entries— Operating Lease with Advance Payment

Advance payments in operating leases are deferred and allocated to rent over the lease term.

Rent comprises the periodic rent payments plus an allocated portion of the advance payment.

Sometimes advance payments include security deposits that are refundable at the expiration of the lease or prepayments of the last period's rent. A refundable security deposit is recorded as a long-term receivable (by the lessee) and liability (by the lessor) unless it is not expected to be returned. A prepayment of the last period's rent is recorded as prepaid rent and allocated to rent expense/rent revenue during the last period of the lease term.

---

[11]"Accounting for Operating Leases With Scheduled Rent Increases," *FASB Technical Bulletin 85-3* (Stamford, Conn.: FASB, 1985), par. 1.

At times, lease agreements call for uneven rent payments during the term of the lease. One way this can occur is when the initial payment (or maybe several payments) is waived. This is called a **rent abatement.**

Alternatively, rent payments may be scheduled to increase periodically over the lease term. In any event, the total rent over the term of the lease is allocated to individual periods on a straight-line basis. This means the (temporarily) unpaid portion of rent expense must be credited to deferred rent expense payable until later in the lease term when rent payments exceed rent expense.

LEASEHOLD IMPROVEMENTS

The cost of a leasehold improvement is depreciated over its useful life to the lessee.

Sometimes a lessee will make improvements to leased property that reverts back to the lessor at the end of the lease. If a lessee constructs a new building or makes modifications to existing structures, that cost represents an asset just like any other capital expenditure. Like other assets, its cost is allocated as depreciation expense over its useful life to the lessee, which will be the shorter of the physical life of the asset or the lease term.[12] Theoretically, such assets can be recorded in accounts descriptive of their nature, such as buildings or plant. In practice, the traditional account title used is **leasehold improvements.**[13] In any case, the undepreciated cost usually is reported in the balance sheet under the caption *property, plant, and equipment.* Movable assets like office furniture and equipment that are not attached to the leased property are not considered leasehold improvements.

Let's turn our attention now to accounting for leases that meet the criteria and conditions for classification as nonoperating leases by both the lessee and the lessor.

Nonoperating Leases—Lessee and Lessor

LO5

In the operating lease illustration, we assumed Sans Serif leased a copier directly from its manufacturer. Now let's assume a financial intermediary provided financing by acquiring the copier and leasing it to the user. And to temporarily avoid unnecessary confusion that adjusting entries might create, the example in Illustration 15–2 on the next page assumes that the inception of the lease, as well as subsequent rental payments, are made at the end of both companies' fiscal years.[15]

A lease that transfers substantially all of the benefits and risks incident to ownership of property should be accounted for as the acquisition of an asset and the incurrence of an obligation by the lessee and as a sale or financing by the lessor.[14]

Traditionally, the lessee uses the **net method** to record leases, and the lessor uses the **gross method.**[16] As you study the entries in Illustration 15–2, keep in mind that both methods achieve the same result, and theoretically either method could be used.

A leased asset is recorded by the lessee at the present value of the minimum lease payments or the asset's fair value, whichever is lower.

The amount recorded (capitalized) by the lessee is the present value of the **minimum lease payments.** However, if the fair value of the asset is lower than this amount, the recorded value of the asset should be limited to fair value. Unless the lessor is a manufacturer or dealer, the fair value typically will be the lessor's cost ($479,079 in this case). However, if considerable time has elapsed between the purchase of the property by the lessor and the inception of the lease, the fair value might be different. When the lessor is a manufacturer or dealer, the fair value of the property at the inception of the lease ordinarily will be its normal selling price (reduced by any volume or trade discounts). We study this situation (a

---

[12]If the agreement contains an option to renew, and the likelihood of renewal is uncertain, the renewal period is ignored.

[13]Also, traditionally, depreciation sometimes is labeled amortization when in connection with leased assets and leasehold improvements. This is of little consequence. Remember, both depreciation and amortization refer to the process of allocating an asset's cost over its useful life.

[14]"Accounting for Leases," *Statement of Financial Accounting Standards No. 13* (Stamford, Conn.: FASB, 1980).

[15]We relax this assumption and consider accrued interest in a later section.

[16]*SFAS 13* does not specifically mandate the methods to be used, but illustrations provided in the Standard portray the net method for the lessee and the gross method for the lessor. As indicated later in the chapter, both the lessee and the lessor must report in disclosure notes *both* the gross and net amounts of the lease.

On December 31, 2002, Sans Serif Publishers, Inc., leased a copier from First LeaseCorp. First LeaseCorp purchased the equipment from CompuDec Corporation at a cost of $479,079.

The lease agreement specifies annual payments beginning December 31, 2002, the inception of the lease, and at each December 31 through 2007. The six-year lease term is equal to the estimated useful life of the copier.

First LeaseCorp routinely acquires electronic equipment for lease to other firms. The interest rate in these financing arrangements is 10%.

Since the lease term is equal to the expected useful life of the copier (>75%), the transaction must be recorded by the lessee as a **capital lease.**[17] If we assume also that collectibility of the lease payments and any costs to the lessor that are yet to be incurred are reasonably predictable, this qualifies also as a **direct financing lease** to First LeaseCorp. To achieve its objectives, First LeaseCorp must (a) recover its $479,079 investment as well as (b) earn interest revenue at a rate of 10%. So, the lessor determined that annual rental payments would be $100,000:

$$\$479,079 \div 4.79079^* = \$100,000$$

Lessor's	Rental
cost	payments

*Present value of an annuity due of $1: $n = 6$, $i = 10\%$.

Of course, Sans Serif Publishers, Inc., views the transaction from the other side. The price the lessee pays for the copier is the present value of the rental payments:

$$\$100,000 \times 4.79079^* = \$479,079$$

Rental	Lessee's
payments	cost

*Present value of an annuity due of $1: $n = 6$, $i = 10\%$.

Direct Financing Lease (December 31, 2002)*

Sans Serif Publishers, Inc. (Lessee)

Leased equipment (present value of lease payments)	479,079	
Lease payable (present value of lease payments)		479,079

First LeaseCorp (Lessor)

Lease receivable (gross sum of lease payments)*	600,000	
Unearned interest revenue (difference)		120,921
Inventory of equipment (lessor's cost)		479,079

First Lease Payment (December 31, 2002)†

Sans Serif Publishers, Inc. (Lessee)

Lease payable	100,000	
Cash		100,000

First LeaseCorp (Lessor)

Cash	100,000	
Lease receivable		100,000

ILLUSTRATION 15–2
Nonoperating Leases

Rental payments are calculated such that their present value is equal to the lessor's cost.

Journal Entries at Inception—Direct Financing Lease

LESSEE

Net Payable
$479,079

LESSOR

Gross Rec'ble	Unearned Interest	Net Rec'ble
$600,000	(120,921)	$479,079

LESSEE

Net Payable
$479,079
(100,000)
$379,079

LESSOR

Gross Rec'ble	Unearned Interest	Net Rec'ble
$600,000	(120,921)	$479,079
(100,000)	0	(100,000)
$500,000	(120,921)	$379,079

*In the disclosure notes, the lease receivable is reported as the lessor's gross investment in the lease.
†Of course, the entries to record the lease and the first payment could be combined into a single entry since they occur at the same time.

sales-type lease) later. In unusual cases, market conditions may cause fair value to be less than the normal selling price.

Be sure to note that the entire $100,000 first rental payment is applied to principal reduction.[18] Because it occurred at the inception of the lease, no interest had yet accrued. Subsequent

Interest is a function of time. It accrues at the effective rate on the balance outstanding during the period.

[17]The fourth criterion also is met. The present value of lease payments ($479,079) is 100% (>90%) of the fair value of the copier ($479,079). Meeting any one of the four criteria is sufficient.

[18]Another way to view this is to think of the first $100,000 as a down payment with the remaining $379,079 financed by 5 (i.e., $6 - 1$) *year-end* lease payments.

~~rental payments include interest on the outstanding balance as well as a residual portion that re-duces that outstanding balance.~~ As of the second rental payment date, one year's interest has accrued on the $379,079 balance outstanding during 2003, recorded as in Illustration 15–2A.

<table>
<tr><td rowspan="2">**ILLUSTRATION 15–2A**

Journal Entries for the Second Lease Payment</td><td colspan="2">**Second Lease Payment (December 31, 2003)**</td></tr>
<tr><td colspan="2">**Sans Serif Publishers, Inc. (Lessee)**</td></tr>
</table>

ILLUSTRATION 15–2A

Journal Entries for the Second Lease Payment

LESSEE

	Net Payable
	$479,079
	(100,000)
	$379,079
	(62,092)
	$316,987

LESSOR

Gross Rec'ble	Unearned Interest	Net Rec'ble
$600,000	(120,921)	$479,079
(100,000)	0	(100,000)
$500,000	(120,921)	$379,079
(100,000)	37,908	(62,092)
$400,000	(83,013)	$316,987

Second Lease Payment (December 31, 2003)

Sans Serif Publishers, Inc. (Lessee)

Interest expense [10% × ($479,079 − 100,000)]................	37,908	
Lease payable (difference)...........................	62,092	
Cash (rental payment)............................		100,000

First LeaseCorp (Lessor)

Cash (rental payment)............................	100,000	
Lease receivable		100,000
Unearned interest revenue	37,908	
Interest revenue [10% × ($600,000 − 120,921 − 100,000)].......		37,908

Notice that by either the net method (lessee) or the gross method (lessor), the outstanding balance is reduced by $62,092—the portion of the $100,000 payment remaining after interest is covered. The lease liability is reduced directly; the reduction in the net receivable is the combined effect of reducing the gross receivable by $100,000 and unearned interest revenue, a valuation (contra) account, by $37,908.[19]

The amortization schedule in Graphic 15–5 shows how the lease balance and the effective interest change over the six-year lease term.

GRAPHIC 15–5

Lease Amortization Schedule

The first rental payment includes no interest.

The total of the cash payments ($600,000) provides for:

1. Payment for the copier ($479,079).

2. Interest ($120,921) at an effective rate of 10%.

Dec. 31	Payments	Effective Interest	Decrease in Balance	Outstanding Balance
		(10% × Outstanding balance)		
2002				479,079
2002	100,000		100,000	379,079
2003	100,000	.10 (379,079) = 37,908	62,092	316,987
2004	100,000	.10 (316,987) = 31,699	68,301	248,686
2005	100,000	.10 (248,686) = 24,869	75,131	173,555
2006	100,000	.10 (173,555) = 17,355	82,645	90,910
2007	100,000	.10 (90,910) = 9,090*	90,910	0
	600,000	120,921*	479,079	

*Adjusted for rounding of other numbers in the schedule.

Each rental payment after the first includes both an amount that represents interest and an amount that represents a reduction of principal. The periodic reduction of principal is sufficient that, at the end of the lease term, the outstanding balance is zero.

An interesting aspect of the amortization schedule that you may want to note at this point relates to a disclosure requirement that we discuss at the end of the chapter. Among other things, the lessee and lessor must report separately the current and noncurrent portions of the outstanding lease balance. Both amounts are provided by the amortization schedule. For example, if we want the amounts to report on the 2003 balance sheet, refer to the next row of

---

[19]Note that unearned interest revenue is not a liability, as you might assume from the account title. Unlike other unearned revenue accounts for which the cash is received in advance of the revenue being earned (and thus a liability), this account represents interest revenue that will be both received and earned periodically over the lease term. The account is analogous to the discount on notes receivable or on bond investment when those investments are recorded by the gross method.

the schedule. The portion of the 2004 payment that represents principal ($68,301) is the *current* (as of December 31, 2003) balance. The *noncurrent* amount is the balance outstanding after the 2004 reduction ($248,686). These amounts are the current and noncurrent lease liability for the lessee and the current and noncurrent net investment for the lessor.

DEPRECIATION

Depreciation is recorded for leased assets in a manner consistent with the lessee's usual policy for depreciating its operational assets.

End of Each Year		
Sans Serif Publishers, Inc. (Lessee)		
Depreciation expense ($479,079 ÷ 6 years*)	79,847	
Accumulated depreciation		79,847

*If the lessee depreciates assets by the straight-line method.

> Because a capital lease assumes the lessee purchased the asset, the lessee depreciates its cost.

Depreciation Period. The lessee normally should depreciate a leased asset over the term of the lease. However, if ownership transfers or a bargain purchase option is present (i.e., either of the first two classification criteria is met), the asset should be depreciated over its useful life. This means depreciation is recorded over the useful life of the asset to the lessee.

> The depreciation period is restricted to the lease term unless the lease provides for transfer of title or a BPO.

A description of leased assets and related depreciation provided in a recent disclosure note (Graphic 15–6) of Fruit of the Loom, Inc., is representative of leased asset disclosures.

> **GRAPHIC 15–6**
> Disclosure of Leased Assets—Fruit of the Loom, Inc.

Lease Commitments (in part)

Assets recorded under capital leases are included in Property, Plant, and Equipment as follows (in thousands of dollars):

	Dec. 30, 2000	Jan. 1, 2000
Land	$ 7,100	$ 7,200
Buildings, structures and improvements	15,600	21,700
Machinery and equipment	700	3,800
	23,400	32,700
Less accumulated depreciation	(8,600)	(17,200)
	$14,800	$15,500

Rental expense for operating leases amounted to $25,300,000, $46,100,000, and $38,100,000 in 2000, 1999, and 1998, respectively.

ACCRUED INTEREST

If a company's reporting period ends at any time between payment dates, it is necessary to record (as an adjusting entry) any interest that has accrued since interest was last recorded. We purposely avoided this step in the previous illustration by assuming that the lease agreement specified rental payments on December 31—the end of the reporting period. But if payments were made on another date, or if the company's fiscal year ended on a date other than December 31, accrued interest would be recorded prior to preparing financial statements. For example, if the inception of the lease had been a day later (January 1, 2003) and rental payments were made on January 1 of each year, the effective interest amounts shown in the lease amortization schedule still would be appropriate but would be recorded one day prior to the actual rental payment. For instance, the second cash payment of $100,000 would occur on January 1, 2003, but the interest component of that payment ($37,908) would be accrued a day earlier as shown in Illustration 15–2B on the next page.

> At each financial statement date, any interest that has accrued since interest was last recorded must be accrued for all liabilities and receivables, including those relating to leases.

ILLUSTRATION 15–2B

Journal Entries When Interest Is Accrued Prior to the Lease Payment

LESSEE

	Net Payable
	$479,079
	(100,000)
	$379,079
	(62,092)
	$316,987

LESSOR

Gross Rec'ble	Unearned Interest	Net Rec'ble
$600,000	(120,921)	$479,079
(100,000)	0	(100,000)
$500,000	(120,921)	$379,079
(100,000)	37,908	(62,092)
$400,000	(83,013)	$316,987

December 31, 2003 (to accrue interest)		
Sans Serif Publishers, Inc. (Lessee)		
Interest expense [10% × ($479,079 − 100,000)]...............	37,908	
Interest payable...		37,908
First LeaseCorp (Lessor)		
Unearned interest revenue...............................	37,908	
Interest revenue [10% × ($479,079 − 100,000)]...............		37,908
Second Lease Payment (January 1, 2004)		
Sans Serif Publishers, Inc. (Lessee)		
Interest payable (from adjusting entry above).................	37,908	
Lease payable (difference)................................	62,092	
Cash (rental payment).................................		100,000
First LeaseCorp (Lessor)		
Cash (rental payment)...................................	100,000	
Lease receivable......................................		100,000

Notice that this is consistent with recording accrued interest on any debt, whether in the form of a note, a bond, or a lease.

We assumed in this illustration that First LeaseCorp bought the copier for $479,079 and then leased it for the same price. There was no profit on the "sale" itself. The only income derived by the lessor was interest revenue earned over the lease term. In effect, First Lease-Corp financed the purchase of the copier by Sans Serif Publishers. This type of lease is a direct financing lease. This kind of leasing is a thriving industry. It is a profitable part of operations for banks and other financial institutions (Citicorp is one of the largest). Some leasing companies do nothing else. Often leasing companies, like IBM Credit Corporation, are subsidiaries of larger corporations, formed for the sole purpose of conducting financing activities for their parent corporations.

CONCEPT REVIEW EXERCISE

Direct Financing Lease

United Cellular Systems leased a satellite transmission device from Pinnacle Leasing Services on January 1, 2004. Pinnacle paid $625,483 for the transmission device. Its fair market value is $625,483.

Terms of the Lease Agreement and Related Information:

Lease term	3 years (6 semiannual periods)
Semiannual rental payments	$120,000 − beginning of each period
Economic life of asset	3 years
Interest rate	12%

Required:

1. Prepare the appropriate entries for both United Cellular Systems and Pinnacle Leasing Services on January 1, the inception of the lease.
2. Prepare an amortization schedule that shows the pattern of interest expense for United Cellular Systems and interest revenue for Pinnacle Leasing Services over the lease term.
3. Prepare the appropriate entries to record the second lease payment on July 1, 2004, and adjusting entries on December 31, 2004 (the end of both companies' fiscal years).

SOLUTION

Calculation of the present value of minimum lease payments.

1. Prepare the appropriate entries for both United Cellular Systems and Pinnacle Leasing Services on January 1, the inception of the lease.
   Present value of periodic rental payments:

$$(\$120,000 \times 5.21236^*) = \$625,483$$

*Present value of an annuity due of $1: $n = 6$, $i = 6\%$.

January 1, 2004

United Cellular Systems (Lessee)

Leased equipment (calculated above)	625,483	
Lease payable (calculated above)		625,483
Lease payable	120,000	
Cash (rental payment)		120,000

Pinnacle Leasing Services (Lessor)

Lease receivable ($120,000 × 6)	720,000	
Unearned interest revenue ($720,000 − 625,483)		94,517
Inventory of equipment (lessor's cost)		625,483
Cash (rental payment)	120,000	
Lease receivable		120,000

2. Prepare an amortization schedule that shows the pattern of interest expense for United Cellular Systems and interest revenue for Pinnacle Leasing Services over the lease term.

	Payments	Effective Interest	Decrease in Balance	Outstanding Balance
		(6% × Outstanding balance)		
1/1/04				625,483
1/1/04	120,000		120,000	505,483
7/1/04	120,000	.06 (505,483) = 30,329	89,671	415,812
1/1/05	120,000	.06 (415,812) = 24,949	95,051	320,761
7/1/05	120,000	.06 (320,761) = 19,246	100,754	220,007
1/1/06	120,000	.06 (220,007) = 13,200	106,800	113,207
7/1/06	120,000	.06 (113,207) = 6,793*	113,207	0
	720,000	94,517	625,483	

*Adjusted for rounding of other numbers in the schedule.

3. Prepare the appropriate entries to record the second lease payment on July 1, 2004, and adjusting entries on December 31, 2004 (the end of both companies' fiscal years).

July 1, 2004

United Cellular Systems (Lessee)

Interest expense [6% × ($625,483 − 120,000)]	30,329	
Lease payable (difference)	89,671	
Cash (rental payment)		120,000

Pinnacle Leasing Services (Lessor)

Cash (rental payment)	120,000	
Lease receivable (rental payment)		120,000
Unearned interest revenue	30,329	
Interest revenue [6% × ($625,483 − 120,000)]		30,329

December 31, 2004

United Cellular Systems (Lessee)

Interest expense (6% × $415,812: from schedule)	24,949	
Interest payable		24,949
Depreciation expense ($625,483 ÷ 3 years)	208,494	
Accumulated depreciation		208,494

Pinnacle Leasing Services (Lessor)

Unearned interest revenue	24,949	
Interest revenue (6% × $415,812: from schedule)		24,949

Let's turn our attention now to situations in which the lessors are manufacturers or retailers and use lease arrangements as a means of selling their products.

Sales-Type Leases

A sales-type lease differs from a direct financing lease in only one respect. In addition to interest revenue earned over the lease term, the lessor receives a manufacturer's or dealer's profit on the "sale" of the asset.[20] This additional profit exists when the fair value of the asset (usually the present value of the minimum lease payments, or "selling price") exceeds the cost or carrying value of the asset sold. Accounting for a sales-type lease is the same as for a direct financing lease except for recognizing the profit at the inception of the lease.[21]

To illustrate, let's modify our previous illustration. Assume all facts are the same except Sans Serif Publishers leased the copier directly from CompuDec Corporation, rather than through the financing intermediary. Also assume CompuDec's cost of the copier was $300,000. If you recall that the lease payments (their present value) provide a selling price of $479,079, you see that CompuDec receives a gross profit on the sale of $479,079 − 300,000 = $179,079. This sales-type lease is demonstrated in Illustration 15–3.

ILLUSTRATION 15–3 **Sales-Type Lease**	On December 31, 2002, Sans Serif Publishers, Inc., leased a copier from CompuDec Corporation at a price of $479,079. The lease agreement specifies annual payments of $100,000 beginning December 31, 2002, the inception of the lease, and at each December 31 through 2007. The six-year lease term is equal to the estimated useful life of the copier. CompuDec manufactured the copier at a cost of $300,000. CompuDec's interest rate for financing the transaction is 10%.

Sales-Type Lease*

CompuDec Corporation (Lessor)

		Sales revenue	$479,079
Lease receivable ($100,000 × 6)	600,000	
Cost of goods sold (lessor's cost)	300,000	
Sales revenue (present value of the minimum lease payments)		479,079
Unearned interest revenue ($600,000 − 479,079)		120,921
Inventory of equipment (lessor's cost)		300,000

Sales revenue $479,079
− COGS 300,000
───────────
Dealer's profit $179,079

Remember, no interest has accrued when the first payment is made at the inception of the lease.

First Lease Payment*

CompuDec Corporation (Lessor)

Cash	100,000	
Lease receivable		100,000

Recording a sales-type lease is similar to recording a sale of merchandise on account:

A/R .... {price}
  Sales rev. .... {price}
COGS .... {cost}
  Inventory ... {cost}

*Of course, the entries to record the lease and the first payment could be combined into a single entry:

Lease receivable ($600,000 − $100,000)	500,000	
Cost of goods sold	300,000	
Cash	100,000	
Unearned interest revenue		120,921
Sales revenue		479,079
Inventory of equipment		300,000

You should recognize the similarity between recording both the revenue and cost components of this sale by lease and recording the same components of other sales transactions. As in the sale of any product, gross profit is the difference between sales revenue and cost of goods sold.

All entries other than the entry at the inception of the lease, which includes the gross profit on the sale, are the same for a sales-type lease and a direct financing lease.

Accounting by the lessee is not affected by how the lessor classifies the lease. All lessee entries are precisely the same as in the previous illustration of a direct financing lease.

---

[20]A lessor need not be a manufacturer or a dealer for the arrangement to qualify as a sales-type lease. The existence of a profit (or loss) on the sale is the distinguishing factor.

[21]It is possible that the asset's carrying value will exceed its fair value, in which case a dealer's loss should be recorded.

Graphic 15–7 shows the relationships among various lease components, using dollar amounts from the previous illustration.

Lessor: **SALES-TYPE LEASE** **Gross Investment in Lease***	**$600,000**	Lessee: **CAPITAL LEASE** **Minimum Lease Payments**
	Less: Interest during lease term ($120,921)	
Selling Price (present value of payments)	Equals: **$479,079**	**Purchase Price** (present value of payments)
	Less: Profit on sale† ($179,079)	
Cost to Lessor	Equals: **$300,000**	**(irrelevant to lessee)**

GRAPHIC 15–7
Lease Payment Relationships

The difference between the total payments and their present value (selling price of the asset) represents interest.

If the price is higher than the cost to the lessor, the lessor realizes a profit on the sale.

*The lessor's gross investment in the lease also would include any *unguaranteed* residual value in addition to the minimum lease payments. Also, any residual value guaranteed by the lessee is included in the minimum lease payments (both companies). We address these issues later in the chapter.
†If profit is zero, this would be a direct financing lease.

RESIDUAL VALUE AND BARGAIN PURCHASE OPTIONS

PART

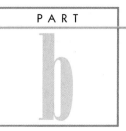

Residual Value

The **residual value** of leased property is an estimate of what its commercial value will be at the end of the lease term. In our previous examples of nonoperating leases, we assumed that the residual value was negligible. But now let's consider the economic effect of a leased asset that does have a residual value and how that will affect the way both the lessee and the lessor account for the lease agreement.

Suppose the copier leased in Illustration 15–3 was expected to be worth $60,000 at the end of the six-year lease term. Should this influence the lessor's (CompuDec) calculation of periodic rental payments? Other than the possible influence on rental payments, should the lessee (Sans Serif Publishers) be concerned with the residual value of the leased assets? The answer to both questions is maybe. We'll use modified Illustration 15–4 to see why.

In deciding whether the residual value affects how the lease is recorded, the first question that influences the answer is "Who gets the residual value?"

ILLUSTRATION 15–4	On December 31, 2002, Sans Serif Publishers, Inc., leased a color copier from CompuDec
Residual Value	Corporation at a price of $479,079. The lease agreement specifies annual payments begin-ning December 31, 2002, the inception of the lease, and at each December 31 through 2007. The estimated useful life of the copier is seven years. At the end of the six-year lease term the copier is expected to be worth $60,000.
	CompuDec manufactured the copier at a cost of $300,000.*
	CompuDec's interest rate for financing the transaction is 10%.

*This provision is to be consistent with Illustration 15–3 which described a sales-type lease. However, our discussion of the effect of a residual value would be precisely the same if our illustration were of a direct financing lease (for instance, if the lessor's cost were $479,079) except that, of course, neither sales revenue nor cost of goods sold would be recorded in a direct financing lease.

WHO GETS THE RESIDUAL VALUE?

If the *lessee* obtains title, the lessor's computation of rental payments is unaffected by any residual value.

Lessee Obtains Title.   Consider CompuDec (the lessor) first. Suppose Sans Serif will own the copier at the end of the lease term—by transfer of title or by the expected exercise of a bargain purchase option. In that case, it is Sans Serif, not CompuDec, who will benefit by the residual value. So the lessor can't count on the $60,000 residual value to help recover its $479,079 investment. The lessor's computation of rental payments of $100,000 therefore is unaffected by the residual value.

On the other side of the transaction, the residual value influences the lessee only by the fact that depreciation calculations reflect a reduced depreciable amount. However, in deter-mining the amount to capitalize as a leased asset and to record as a lease liability, the resid-ual value is ignored. The capitalized amount is simply the present value of the minimum lease payments.

If the lessor retains title, the amount to be recovered through periodic lease payments is reduced by the present value of the residual amount.

Lessor Retains Title.   On the other hand, if CompuDec retains title to the asset, then it would anticipate receiving the $60,000 residual value at the conclusion of the lease term. That amount would contribute to the total amount to be recovered by the lessor and would reduce the amount needed to be recovered from the lessee through periodic rental payments. The amount of each payment would be reduced from $100,000 to $92,931, calculated in Il-lustration 15–4A.

ILLUSTRATION 15–4A	Amount to be recovered (fair market value)	$479,079
	Less: Present value of the residual value ($60,000 × .56447*)	(33,868)
Lessor's Calculation of Rental Payments When Lessor Retains Residual Value	Amount to be recovered through periodic rental payments	$445,211
	Rental payments at the beginning of each of the next six years: ($445,211 ÷ 4.79079†)	$ 92,931

*Present value of $1: $n = 6$, $i = 10\%$.
†Present value of an annuity due of $1: $n = 6$, $i = 10\%$.

On the other side of the transaction, the lessee (Sans Serif Publishers) considers the pur-chase price of the copier to include, at a minimum, the present value of the periodic rental payments ($445,211):

$$\$92,931 \times 4.79079^* = \$445,211^†$$
$$\text{Rental} \qquad\qquad \text{Present}$$
$$\text{payments} \qquad\qquad \text{value}$$

*Present value of an annuity due of $1: $n = 6$, $i = 10\%$.
†The multiplication actually produces $445,212.9. We use $445,211 to be consistent with the lessor's calculation ($445,211 ÷ 4.79079 = $92,931). The difference is due to rounding.

Whether or not the lessee's cost also includes an amount due to the residual value depends on whether the residual value is viewed as an additional "payment" by the lessee. It is viewed as an additional payment when the lessee *guarantees* the residual value to be a particular amount at the end of the lease term.

WHEN THE RESIDUAL VALUE IS GUARANTEED BY THE LESSEE

Sometimes the lease agreement includes a guarantee by the lessee that the lessor will recover a specified residual value when custody of the asset reverts back to the lessor at the end of the lease term. This not only reduces the lessor's risk but also provides incentive to the lessee to exercise a higher degree of care in maintaining the leased asset than it otherwise might. The lessee promises to return not only the property but also sufficient cash to provide the lessor with a minimum combined value. In effect, the guaranteed residual value is an additional lease payment that is to be paid in property, or cash, or both. As such, it is included in the minimum lease payments and affects the amount the lessee records as both a leased asset and a lease liability, as shown in Illustration 15–4B.

Present value of periodic rental payments ($92,931 × 4.79079*)	$445,211	**ILLUSTRATION 15–4B**
Plus: Present value of the residual value ($60,000 × .56447)†	33,868	Lessee's Calculation of the Present Value of Minimum Lease Payments Including a Guaranteed Residual Value
Present value of minimum lease payments (Recorded as a leased asset and a lease liability)	$479,079	

*Present value of an annuity due of $1: $n = 6$, $i = 10\%$.
†Present value of $1: $n = 6$, $i = 10\%$.

You should notice that the lessee's calculation of the amount to capitalize is precisely the reverse of the lessor's calculation of periodic rental payments. This is because when the residual value is guaranteed, both view it as an additional lease payment. In accordance with *SFAS 13*, the guaranteed residual value is a component of the minimum lease payments for both the lessor and lessee.[22] We see in Graphic 15–8 how this affects the accounting for the lease as reflected in the lease amortization schedule for CompuDec and Sans Serif.

Dec. 31	Payments	Effective Interest	Decrease in Balance	Outstanding Balance
		(10% × Outstanding balance)		
2002				479,079
2002	92,931		92,931	386,148
2003	92,931	.10 (386,148) = 38,615	54,316	331,832
2004	92,931	.10 (331,832) = 33,183	59,748	272,084
2005	92,931	.10 (272,084) = 27,208	65,723	206,361
2006	92,931	.10 (206,361) = 20,636	72,295	134,066
2007	92,931	.10 (134,066) = 13,407	79,524	54,542
2008	60,000	.10 (54,542) = 5,458*	54,542	0
	617,586	138,507	479,079	

GRAPHIC 15–8

Amortization Schedule with Residual Value

As long as the asset (and its residual value) revert back to the lessor, the lessor views the residual value as an additional component of its investment in the lease.

The lessee views it as an additional payment only if the residual value is guaranteed by the lessee.

*Adjusted for rounding of other numbers in the schedule.

[22]Later you will see that when the residual value is *not* guaranteed, it is *not* considered a component of minimum lease payments for either the lessor or the lessee; but it still is considered a part of the lessor's gross investment in the lease and affects the amount of periodic lease payments.

Be aware of several points the amortization schedule reveals. First, the six periodic cash payments are now $92,931 as we calculated previously. Notice also that we now include the $60,000 residual value as an additional lease payment. Despite the different composition of the minimum lease payments, their present value ($479,079) is the same as when we assumed $100,000 periodic payments and no residual value. However, the effective interest that will be recorded over the lease term (as interest expense by the lessee and interest revenue by the lessor) now is more: $138,507. (It was $120,921 before.) The higher interest reflects the fact that payments are farther in the future, causing the outstanding lease balances (and interest on those balances) to be higher during the lease term. Also, note that the total of the lease payments now is more: $617,586. (It was $600,000 before.) This total is referred to as the lessor's **gross investment in the lease** and, as shown in Illustration 15–4C, initially is recorded by the lessor as the lease receivable:[23]

> The lessor's *gross investment in the lease* is the total of periodic rental payments and any residual value.

ILLUSTRATION 15–4C	Sales-Type Lease, December 31, 2002		
Sales-Type Lease with Guaranteed Residual Value	**Sans Serif Publishers, Inc. (Lessee)**		
	Leased equipment (present value of lease payments)............	479,079	
	Lease payable (present value of lease payments)		479,079
Sales revenue $479,079	**CompuDec Corporation (Lessor)**		
−COGS 300,000	Lease receivable [($92,931 × 6) + $60,000]..................	617,586	
	Cost of goods sold (lessor's cost)........................	300,000	
Dealer's profit $179,079	Sales revenue (present value of minimum lease payments*)		479,079
	Unearned interest revenue ($617,586 − 479,079).............		138,507
	Inventory of equipment (lessor's cost)		300,000
	First Lease Payment, December 31, 2002		
	Sans Serif Publishers, Inc. (Lessee)		
	Lease payable	92,931	
	Cash...		92,931
	CompuDec Corporation (Lessor)		
	Cash...	92,931	
	Lease receivable		92,931

*Minimum lease payments include the residual value because it's guaranteed.

Notice, too, that the timing of the $60,000 payment is December 31, 2008, the end of the lease term. Remember, the final periodic cash payment on December 31, 2007, is at the beginning of the final year. The journal entries that accompany this final cash payment are shown in Illustration 15–4D on the next page.

At December 31, 2008, the lessee's book value of the fully depreciated copier is its $60,000 estimated residual value. If we assume that the actual residual value also is at least $60,000, then the lessee is not obligated to pay cash in addition to returning the copier to the lessor (demonstrated on the next page in Illustration 15–4E).[24]

However, if we assume that the actual residual value at December 31, 2008, is only $25,000, then the lessee is required to pay $35,000 cash to the lessor in addition to returning the copier. The lessee records this payment as a loss.[25]

---

[23]Under the net method, the net investment in the lease ($479,079) would be recorded as the lessor's lease receivable.

[24]If the actual value is *more* than the estimated residual value, the lessor may realize a gain if and when the asset subsequently is sold, but the potential gain does not affect the entries at the end of the lease term.

[25]Sometimes by mutual agreement the lessee will sell the leased asset at the end of the lease term and remit the proceeds (plus any deficiency under the guarantee) to the lessor.

December 31, 2007		
Sans Serif Publishers, Inc. (Lessee)		
Depreciation expense [($479,079 − 60,000)* ÷ 6 years]	69,847	
Accumulated depreciation		69,847
Interest expense (10% × outstanding balance)	13,407	
Lease payable (difference)	79,524	
Cash (rental payment)		92,931
CompuDec Corporation (Lessor)		
Cash (rental payment)	92,931	
Lease receivable		92,931
Unearned interest revenue	13,407	
Interest revenue (10% × outstanding balance)		13,407

ILLUSTRATION 15–4D

Entries to Accompany Final Periodic Payment

The residual value reduces the asset's depreciable cost to $419,079.

As the outstanding balance becomes less toward the end of the lease term, the portion of each payment that represents interest also becomes less.

*The depreciable cost is reduced by the lessee-guaranteed residual value.

December 31, 2008		
Sans Serif Publishers, Inc. (Lessee)		
Depreciation expense [($479,079 − 60,000)* ÷ 6 years]	69,847	
Accumulated depreciation		69,847
Interest expense (10% × outstanding balance)	5,458	
Lease payable (difference)	54,542	
Accumulated depreciation (account balance)	419,079	
Leased equipment (account balance)		479,079
CompuDec Corporation (Lessor)		
Inventory of equipment (residual value)	60,000	
Lease receivable (account balance)		60,000
Unearned interest revenue (account balance)	5,458	
Interest revenue (10% × outstanding balance)		5,458

ILLUSTRATION 15–4E

End of Lease Term—Actual Residual Value Equals the Guaranteed Amount

The sixth and final depreciation charge increases the balance in accumulated depreciation to $419,079.

The copier is reinstated on the books of the lessor at its fair value at the end of the lease term.

*The depreciable cost is reduced by the lessee-guaranteed residual value.

WHEN THE RESIDUAL VALUE IS NOT GUARANTEED

The previous example demonstrates that when the residual value is guaranteed, both the lessor and lessee view it as a component of minimum lease payments. But what if the lessee does *not* guarantee the residual value? In that case, the lessee is not obligated to make any payments other than the periodic rental payments. As a result, the present value of the minimum lease payments—recorded as a leased asset and a lease liability—is simply the present value of periodic rental payments ($445,211). The same is true when the residual value is guaranteed by a third-party guarantor. (Insurance companies sometimes assume this role.)

From the lessor's perspective, the residual value is a component of minimum lease payments only if it is guaranteed (by either the lessee or a third-party guarantor). Yet, even if it is not guaranteed, the residual value is viewed as a component of the lessor's gross investment in the lease. So, if we modify the previous illustration to assume the residual value is not guaranteed, the lessor's gross investment still is $617,586 [($92,931 × 6) + $60,000], but the sales revenue is only $445,211—the present value of the minimum lease payments. In other words, sales revenue includes the present value only of the periodic rental payments, not the unguaranteed residual value. Cost of goods sold is similarly reduced by the present value of the unguaranteed residual value, as shown in Illustration 15–4F on the next page.

Sales revenue does not include the unguaranteed residual value because the revenue to be recovered from the lessee is lease payments only. The remainder of the lessor's gross investment is to be recovered—not from payment by the lessee (as is presumed when the

If the lessee doesn't guarantee the residual value, the asset and liability are recorded as the PV of periodic rental payments only.

The lessor's minimum lease payments include a residual value only if it is guaranteed (by either the lessee or a third party guarantor).

Sales-Type Lease

Sans Serif Publishers, Inc. (Lessee)

Leased equipment (present value of lease payments).	445,211	
Lease payable (present value of lease payments)		445,211

CompuDec Corporation (Lessor)

Lease receivable [($92,931 × 6) + $60,000].	617,586	
Cost of goods sold ($300,000 − 33,868)	266,132	
Sales revenue ($479,079 − 33,868)*.		445,211
Unearned interest revenue ($617,586 − 479,079)		138,507
Inventory of equipment (lessor's cost)		300,000

First Lease Payment

Sans Serif Publishers, Inc. (Lessee)

Lease payable	92,931	
Cash.		92,931

CompuDec Corporation (Lessor)

Cash.	92,931	
Lease receivable		92,931

*Also can be calculated as the present value of the lessor's minimum lease payments, which do not include
the unguaranteed residual value.

residual value is guaranteed), but by selling, re-leasing, or otherwise obtaining value from
the asset when it reverts back to the lessor. You might want to view the situation this way:
The portion of the asset sold is the portion not represented by the unguaranteed residual
value. So, both the asset's cost and its selling price are reduced by the present value of the
portion not sold.

The lessor's net lease receivable is $479,079, as described in an earlier amortization
schedule, even when the residual value is not guaranteed. However, the lessee's lease liability would be only $445,211 at the inception of the lease and would become zero with the fi-
nal payment at the beginning of the final year, with reductions occurring in accordance with
the pattern described by the schedule in Graphic 15–9.

Dec. 31	Payments	Effective Interest	Decrease in Balance	Outstanding Balance
		(10% × Outstanding balance)		
2002				445,211
2002	92,931		92,931	352,280
2003	92,931	.10 (352,280) = 35,228	57,703	294,577
2004	92,931	.10 (294,577) = 29,458	63,473	231,104
2005	92,931	.10 (231,104) = 23,110	69,821	161,283
2006	92,931	.10 (161,283) = 16,128	76,803	84,480
2007	92,931	.10 (84,480) = 8,451*	84,480	0
	557,586	112,375*	445,211*	

*Adjusted for rounding of other numbers in the schedule.

When the residual value is not guaranteed, the lessor bears any loss that results from the
actual residual value of the leased asset being less than the original estimate.

Graphic 15–10 summarizes the effect of the residual value of a leased asset for each of the
various possibilities regarding the nature of the residual value.

Is the **residual value** of a leased asset included in:

	the Lessor's		the Lessee's
	(a) **Gross Investment** **in Lease** *Computation* *of Payments*	**(b)** **Minimum** **Lease Payments** *Sales* *Revenue*	**(c)** **Minimum** **Lease Payments** *Asset &* *Liability*
Lessee gets the residual value (by transfer of title or the expected exercise of a bargain purchase option)	No	No	No
Lessor gets the residual value (title does *not* transfer; *no* bargain purchase option)			
• Residual value is not guaranteed	Yes	No	No
• Residual value is guaranteed by the lessee.	Yes	Yes	Yes
• Residual value is guaranteed by a third party guarantor.	Yes	Yes	No

(a) if included in the lessor's gross investment in the lease, the residual value is part of the computation by the **lessor** of the amount of the periodic rental payments
(b) the present value of the lessor's minimum lease payments is sales revenue in a sales-type lease
(c) the present value of the lessee's minimum lease payments is the amount to be capitalized as an asset and a liability

Bargain Purchase Options

We mentioned earlier that a **bargain purchase option (BPO)** is a provision of some lease contracts that gives the lessee the option of purchasing the leased property at a bargain price. We discussed BPOs in the context of how they affect the classification of leases, but none of our earlier illustrations included a situation in which a BPO was present. You should have noted that a bargain price is defined in such a way that an additional cash payment is expected when a BPO is included in the agreement. Remember, a bargain price is one that is sufficiently below the property's expected fair value that the exercise of the option appears reasonably assured. Because exercise of the option appears at the inception of the lease to be reasonably assured, payment of the option price is expected to occur when the option becomes exercisable.

The logic applied to lessee-guaranteed residual values in the previous section applies here too. The expectation that the option price will be paid effectively adds an additional cash flow to the lease for both the lessee and the lessor. That additional payment is included as a component of minimum lease payments for both the lessor and the lessee. It therefore (a) reduces the amount of the periodic rent payments the *lessor* must receive from the lessee and (b) is included in the computation of the amount to be capitalized (as an asset and liability) by the *lessee*. In fact, the way a BPO is included in these calculations is precisely the same way that a lessee-guaranteed residual value is included. This is demonstrated in Graphic 15–11.

LO8

When a BPO is present, both the lessor and the lessee view the option price as an additional lease payment.

✔ The **lessor,** when computing periodic rental payments, *subtracts* the present value of the BPO from the amount to be recovered (fair market value) to determine the amount that must be recovered from the lessee through the periodic rent payments.

✔ The **lessee** *adds* the present value of the BPO price to the present value of periodic payments when computing the amount to be recorded as a leased asset and a lease liability.

To emphasize the similarity in the way a lessee-guaranteed[26] residual value and a BPO affect the calculations, let's assume the $60,000 in our last illustration is an option price that could be paid by Sans Serif at the conclusion of the lease to purchase the copier. To make this a "bargain" purchase option let's say the residual value at the same time is expected now to be $75,000. This situation is assumed in Illustration 15–5.

ILLUSTRATION 15–5 Bargain Purchase Option	On December 31, 2002, Sans Serif Publishers, Inc., leased a color copier from CompuDec Corporation at a price of $479,079. The lease agreement specifies annual payments beginning December 31, 2002, the inception of the lease, and at each December 31 through 2007. The estimated useful life of the copier is seven years. At the end of the six-year lease term the copier is expected to be worth $75,000 and Sans Serif has the option to purchase it for $60,000 on that date. The residual value after seven years is zero.[27]

The lessor's selling price is reduced by the present value of the BPO price to determine the amount that must be recovered from the periodic rental payments.	CompuDec manufactured the copier at a cost of $300,000.

CompuDec's interest rate for financing the transaction is 10%.

Amount to be recovered (fair market value)	$479,079
Less: Present value of the BPO price ($60,000 × .56447*)	(33,868)
Amount to be recovered through periodic rental payments	$445,211
Rental payments at the beginning of each of the next six years: ($445,211 ÷ 4.79079†)	$ 92,931

*Present value of $1: $n = 6$, $i = 10\%$.
†Present value of an annuity due of $1: $n = 6$, $i = 10\%$.

When you compare the way the *BPO* affected the lessor's (CompuDec's) calculation with the way the lessee-guaranteed residual value affected the calculation earlier, you see that they are exactly the same. That's the case also for the lessee (Sans Serif Publishers) as shown in Illustration 15–5A.

ILLUSTRATION 15–5A Lessee's Calculation of the Present Value of Minimum Lease Payments When a BPO Is Present	Present value of periodic rental payments ($92,931 × 4.79079*)	$445,211
	Plus: Present value of the BPO price ($60,000 × .56447†)	33,868
	Present value of minimum lease payments (recorded as a leased asset and a lease liability)	$479,079

*Present value of an annuity due of $1: $n = 6$, $i = 10\%$.
†Present value of $1: $n = 6$, $i = 10\%$.

Because a BPO is expected to be exercised, its exercise price is viewed as one more cash payment. **When a BPO is present, the residual value becomes irrelevant.**	You should recognize this as the same calculation we used when there was no BPO but the residual value was guaranteed and so was considered an additional lease payment. A question you might have at this point is: Why are we now ignoring the residual value? Earlier it was considered an additional lease payment. Yet, now we view the BPO price as an additional lease payment but ignore the residual value. The reason is obvious when you recall an essential characteristic of a BPO—it's expected to be exercised. So, when it is exercised,

---

[26]The lessee-guaranteed qualification here refers to what you learned in the previous section: a residual value is part of the lessee's minimum lease payments only when guaranteed by the lessee; the lessor includes in its computation of rent payments any residual values that revert to the lessor—guaranteed or not.

[27]Our discussion of the effect of a bargain purchase option would be precisely the same if our illustration were of a direct financing lease (for instance, if the lessor's cost were $479,079) except that, of course, neither sales revenue nor cost of goods sold would be recorded in a direct financing lease.

title to the leased asset passes to the lessee and with title, any residual value. And remember, when the lessee gets the residual value it is ignored by both parties to the lease.

The lease amortization schedule for CompuDec and Sans Serif when a BPO is included in the lease agreement (Graphic 15–12) should look familiar to you also.

Dec. 31	Payments	Effective Interest	Decrease in Balance	Outstanding Balance
		(10% × Outstanding balance)		
2002				479,079
2002	92,931		92,931	386,148
2003	92,931	.10 (386,148) = 38,615	54,316	331,832
2004	92,931	.10 (331,832) = 33,183	59,748	272,084
2005	92,931	.10 (272,084) = 27,208	65,723	206,361
2006	92,931	.10 (206,361) = 20,636	72,295	134,066
2007	92,931	.10 (134,066) = 13,407	79,524	54,542
2008	60,000	.10 (54,542) = 5,458*	54,542	0
	617,586	138,507	479,079	

GRAPHIC 15–12
Amortization Schedule—with BPO

Both the lessor and lessee view the BPO price ($60,000) as an additional cash payment.

*Adjusted for rounding of other numbers in the schedule.

Recording the exercise of the option is similar to recording the periodic rent payments. That is, a portion of the payment covers interest for the year, and the remaining portion reduces the outstanding balance (to zero with this last payment), as shown in Illustration 15–5B.

December 31, 2008		
Sans Serif Publishers, Inc. (Lessee)		
Depreciation expense ($479,079* ÷ 7 years)	68,440	
Accumulated depreciation		68,440
Interest expense (10% × $54,542)	5,458	
Lease payable (difference)	54,542	
Cash (BPO price)		60,000
CompuDec Corporation (Lessor)		
Cash (BPO price)	60,000	
Lease receivable (account balance)		60,000
Unearned interest revenue (account balance)	5,458	
Interest revenue (10% × outstanding balance)		5,458

ILLUSTRATION 15–5B

Journal Entries—with BPO

The depreciation entries reflect the fact that the lessee anticipates using the copier for its full seven-year life.

*The residual value is zero after the full seven-year useful life.

Note that depreciation also is affected by the BPO. As pointed out earlier, the lessee normally depreciates a leased asset over the term of the lease. But if ownership transfers by contract or by the expected exercise of a bargain purchase option, the asset should be depreciated over the asset's useful life. This reflects the fact that the lessee anticipates using the leased asset for its full useful life. In this illustration, the copier is expected to be useful for seven years, so depreciation is $68,440 ($479,079 ÷ 7 years).

The cash payment expected when the BPO is exercised represents part interest, part principal just like the other cash payments.

WHEN A BPO IS EXERCISABLE BEFORE THE END OF THE LEASE TERM

We assumed in this example that the BPO was exercisable on December 31, 2008—the end of the lease term. This assumption was convenient to illustrate the similarity between how a

---

ETHICAL DILEMMA

"I know we had discussed that they're supposed to be worth $24,000 when our purchase option becomes exercisable," Ferris insisted. "That's why we agreed to the lease terms. But, Jenkins, you know how fast computers become dated. We can make a good case that they'll be worth only $10,000 in three years."

The computers to which Ferris referred were acquired by lease. The lease meets none of the criteria for classification as a capital lease except that it contains an apparent bargain purchase option. Under the lease option, the computers can be purchased for $10,000 after three years.

"We could avoid running up our debt that way," Jenkins agreed.

How could debt be avoided?

Do you perceive an ethical problem?

---

residual value and a BPO are dealt with when accounting for leases. It also is a very realistic assumption. Sometimes, though, the lease contract specifies that a BPO becomes exercisable before the designated lease term ends. Since a BPO is expected to be exercised, the lease term ends for accounting purposes when the option becomes exercisable. For example, let's say the BPO in the previous example could be exercised a year earlier—at the end of the fifth year. The effect this would have on accounting for the lease is to change the lease term from six years to five. All calculations would be modified accordingly. Stated differently, minimum lease payments include only the periodic cash payments specified in the agreement that occur prior to the date a BPO becomes exercisable. (We assume the option is exercised at that time and the lease ends.)

> The length of the lease term is limited to the time up to when a bargain purchase option becomes exercisable.

We have seen how minimum lease payments are affected by a residual value and by a bargain purchase option. Let's now consider how maintenance, insurance, taxes, and other costs usually associated with ownership (called *executory costs*) affect minimum lease payments.

PART

C

LO9

OTHER LEASE ACCOUNTING ISSUES

Executory Costs

One of the responsibilities of ownership that is transferred to the lessee in a capital lease is the responsibility to pay for maintenance, insurance, taxes, and any other costs usually associated with ownership. These are referred to as **executory costs.** Lease agreements usually are written in such a way that these costs are borne by the lessee. These expenditures simply are expensed by the lessee as incurred: repair expense, insurance expense, property tax expense, and so on. Let's return, for example, to Illustration 15–2. Now, suppose that a $2,000 per year maintenance agreement was arranged with an outside service for the leased copier. Sans Serif (the lessee) would expense this fee each year as incurred:

> The lessee simply expenses executory costs as incurred.

Maintenance expense	2,000	
Cash (annual fee)		2,000

The lessor is unaffected by executory costs paid by the lessee.

> Any portion of rental payments that represents maintenance, insurance, taxes, or other executory costs is not considered part of minimum lease payments.

Sometimes, as an expediency, a lease contract will specify that the lessor is to pay executory costs, but that the lessee will reimburse the lessor through higher rental payments. When rental payments are inflated for this reason, these executory costs are excluded in determining the minimum lease payments. They still are expensed by the lessee, even though paid through the lessor. For demonstration, let's modify Illustration 15–2 to assume the periodic rental payments were increased to $102,000 with the provision the lessor (First LeaseCorp) pays the maintenance fee. We do this in Illustration 15–6.

ILLUSTRATION 15–6

Rental Payments Including Executory Costs Paid by the Lessor

On December 31, 2002, Sans Serif Publishers, Inc., leased a copier from First LeaseCorp. First LeaseCorp purchased the equipment from CompuDec Corporation at a cost of $479,079.
- Six annual payments of $102,000 beginning December 31, 2002.
- Payments include $2,000 which First LeaseCorp will use to pay an annual maintenance fee.
- The interest rate in these financing arrangements is 10%.
- Capital lease to Sans Serif.
- Direct financing lease to First LeaseCorp.
- Interest-rate: 10%.

Second Payment (December 31, 2003)

Sans Serif Publishers, Inc. (Lessee)

Maintenance expense (2003 fee)	2,000	
Prepaid maintenance (paid in 2002)		2,000
Interest expense [10% × ($479,079 − 100,000)]	37,908	
Lease payable (difference)	62,092	
Prepaid maintenance (2004 fee)	2,000	
Cash (rental payment)		102,000
First LeaseCorp (Lessor)		
Cash (rental payment)	102,000	
Lease receivable		100,000
Maintenance fee payable*		2,000
Unearned interest revenue	37,908	
Interest revenue [10% × ($600,000 − 120,921 − 100,000)]		37,908

Executory costs that are included in periodic rental payments to be paid by the lessor are, in effect, indirectly paid by the lessee—and expensed by the lessee.

Amounts recorded for periodic interest and the periodic reduction of principal are unaffected by executory costs.

*This assumes the $2,000 maintenance fee has not yet been paid to the outside maintenance service.

Discount Rate

An important factor in the overall lease equation that we've glossed over until now is the discount rate used in present value calculations. Because lease payments occur in future periods, we must consider the time value of money when evaluating their present value. The rate is important because it influences virtually every amount reported in connection with the lease by both the lessor and the lessee.

One rate is implicit in the lease agreement. This is the effective interest rate the lease payments provide the lessor over and above the price at which the asset is sold under the lease. It is the desired rate of return the lessor has in mind when deciding the size of the rental payments. (Refer to our earlier calculations of the periodic rental payments.) Usually the lessee is aware of the lessor's implicit rate or can infer it from the asset's fair market value.[28] When the lessor's implicit rate is unknown, the lessee should use its own incremental borrowing rate. This is the rate the lessee would expect to pay a bank if funds were borrowed to buy the asset. When the lessor's implicit rate *is* known, the lessee should use the lower of the two rates.[29]

> The lessee uses the lower of the interest rate implicit in the lease or the lessee's own incremental borrowing rate.

WHEN THE LESSEE'S INCREMENTAL BORROWING RATE IS LESS THAN THE LESSOR'S IMPLICIT RATE

Instances are few in which the lessee actually would use its incremental borrowing rate. Here's why. We noted earlier that, like any other asset, a leased asset should not be recorded

---

[28]The corporation laws of some states, Florida for instance, actually require the interest rate to be expressly stated in the lease agreement.

[29]*Incremental borrowing rate* refers to the fact that lending institutions tend to view debt as being increasingly risky as the level of debt increases. Thus, additional (i.e., incremental) debt is likely to be loaned at a higher interest rate than existing debt, other things being equal.

at more than its fair market value. Look what happens to the present value payments if Sans Serif uses a discount rate less than the 10% rate implicit in Illustration 15–6 (let's say 9%):

$$\$100,000 \times 4.88965^* = \$488,965$$

Rental	Lessee's
payments	cost

*Present value of an annuity due of $1: $n = 6$, $i = 9\%$.

But remember, the fair market value of the copier was $479,079. The $100,000 amount for the rental payments was derived by the lessor, contemplating a market value of $479,079 and a desired interest rate of return (implicit rate) of 10%. So, using a discount rate lower than the lessor's implicit rate usually would result in the present value of minimum lease payments being more than the fair market value.

This conclusion does not hold when the leased asset has an unguaranteed residual value. You will recall that the lessor's determinations always include any residual value that accrues to the lessor; but when the lessee doesn't guarantee the residual value, it is *not* included in the lessee's present value calculations. Combining two previous examples, let's modify our demonstration of an unguaranteed residual value (Illustration 15–6) to assume the lessee's incremental borrowing rate was 9%. Because the residual value was expected to contribute to the lessor's recovery of the $479,079 fair market value, the rental payments were only $92,931. But, the lessee would ignore the unguaranteed residual value and calculate its cost of the leased asset to be $454,400.

$$\$92,931 \times 4.88965^* = \$454,400$$

Rental	Lessee's
payments	cost

*Present value of an annuity due of $1: $n = 6$, $i = 9\%$.

In this case, the present value of minimum lease payments would be *less than* the fair market value even though a lower discount rate is used. But again, if there is no residual value, or if the lessee guarantees the residual value, or if the unguaranteed residual value is relatively small, a discount rate lower than the lessor's implicit rate will result in the present value of minimum lease payments being more than the fair market value.

WHEN THE LESSOR'S IMPLICIT RATE IS UNKNOWN

What if the lessee is unaware of the lessor's implicit rate? This is a logical question in light of the rule that says the lessee should use its own incremental borrowing rate when the lessor's implicit rate is unknown to the lessee. But in practice the lessor's implicit rate usually is known. Even if the lessor chooses not to explicitly disclose the rate, the lessee usually can deduce the rate using information he knows about the value of the leased asset and the lease payments. After all, in making the decision to lease rather than buy, the lessee typically becomes quite knowledgeable about the asset.

Even so, it is possible that a lessee might be unable to derive the lessor's implicit rate. This might happen, for example, if the leased asset has a relatively high residual value. Remember, a residual value (guaranteed or not) is an ingredient in the lessor's calculation of the rental payments. Sometimes it may be hard for the lessee to identify the residual value estimated by the lessor if the lessor chooses not to make it known.[30] The longer the lease term or the more risk of obsolescence the leased asset is subject to, the less of a factor the residual value typically is.

---

[30]Disclosure requirements provide that the lessor company must disclose the components of its investments in nonoperating leases, which would include any estimated residual values. But the disclosures are aggregate amounts, not amounts of individual leased assets.

ADDITIONAL CONSIDERATION

As pointed out earlier, the management of a lessee company sometimes will try to structure a lease to avoid the criteria that would cause the lease to be classified as a capital lease in order to gain the questionable advantages of off-balance-sheet financing. On the other hand, a *lessor* normally would prefer recording a **nonoperating** lease, other things being equal. Two ways sometimes used to structure a lease to qualify as an operating lease by the lessee, but as a nonoperating lease by the lessor are: (1) cause the two parties to use different interest rates and (2) avoid including the residual value in the lessee's minimum lease payments. Let's see how they work:

1. Cause the Two Parties to Use Different Interest Rates.

It was pointed out earlier that a lessee sometimes can claim to be unable to determine the lessor's implicit rate. Not knowing the lessor's implicit rate would permit the lessee to use its own incremental borrowing rate. If higher than the lessor's implicit rate, the present value it produces may cause the 90% of fair value criterion **not** to be met for the lessee (thus an operating lease) even though the criterion is met for the lessor (thus a nonoperating lease).

2. Avoid Including the Residual Value in the Lessee's Minimum Lease Payments.

The residual value, if guaranteed by the lessee or by a third party guarantor, is included in the minimum lease payments by the lessor when applying the 90% of fair value criterion and thus increases the likelihood that it is met. However, when the residual value is guaranteed by a third-party guarantor and not by the lessee, it is **not** included in the lessee's minimum lease payments. So, if a residual value is sufficiently large and guaranteed by a third-party guarantor, it may cause the 90% of fair value criterion to be met by the lessor, but not by the lessee.

Both schemes are unintentionally encouraged by lease accounting rules. As long as arbitrary cutoff points are used (90% of fair value in this case), maneuvers will be devised to circumvent them.

Lessor's Initial Direct Costs

The costs incurred by the lessor that are associated directly with originating a lease and are essential to acquire that lease are referred to as **initial direct costs**. They include legal fees, commissions, evaluating the prospective lessee's financial condition, and preparing and processing lease documents. The method of accounting for initial direct costs depends on the nature of the lease. Remember, a lessor can classify a lease as (1) an operating lease, (2) a direct financing lease, or (3) a sales-type lease. The accounting treatment for initial direct costs by each of the three possible lease types is summarized below.

1. For *operating leases,* initial direct costs are recorded as assets and amortized over the term of the lease. Since the only revenue an operating lease produces is rental revenue, and that revenue is recognized over the lease term, initial direct costs also are automatically recognized over the lease term to match these costs with the rent revenues they help generate.

2. In *direct financing leases,* interest revenue is earned over the lease term, so initial direct costs are matched with the interest revenues they help generate. Therefore, initial direct costs are not expensed at the outset but are deferred and recognized over the lease term. This can be accomplished by reducing the lessor's *unearned interest revenue* by the total of initial direct costs. Then, as unearned interest revenue is

recognized over the lease term at a constant effective rate, the initial direct costs are recognized at the same rate (that is, proportionally).

3. For *sales-type leases,* initial direct costs are expensed at the inception of the lease. Since the usual reason for a sales-type lease is for a manufacturer or a dealer to sell its product, it's reasonable to recognize the costs of creating the transaction as a selling expense in the period of the sale.

Contingent Rentals

Sometimes rental payments may be increased (or decreased) at some future time during the lease term, depending on whether or not some specified event occurs. Usually the contingency is related to revenues or profitability above some designated level. For example, a recent annual report of Kmart Corporation included the note re-created in Graphic 15–13.

GRAPHIC 15–13
Disclosure of
Contingent Rentals—
Kmart

Note L (in part): Leases
. . . Certain leases provide for additional rental payments based on a percentage of sales in excess of a specified base. . . .

Contingent rentals are *not* included in the minimum lease payments because they are not determinable at the inception of the lease. Instead, they are included as components of income when (and if) they occur. Increases or decreases in rental payments that are dependent only on the passage of time are not contingent rentals; these are part of minimum lease payments.

Although contingent rentals are not included in minimum lease payments, they are reported in disclosure notes by both the lessor and lessee.

A Brief Summary

Leasing arrangements often are complex. In studying this chapter you've encountered several features of lease agreements that alter the way we make several of the calculations needed to account for leases. Graphic 15–14 on the next page provides a concise review of the essential lease accounting components, using calculations from a hypothetical lease situation to provide a numerical perspective.

Lease Disclosures

Lease disclosure requirements are quite extensive for both the lessor and lessee. Virtually all aspects of the lease agreement must be disclosed. For *all* leases (a) a general description of the leasing arrangement is required as well as (b) minimum future payments, in the aggregate and for each of the five succeeding fiscal years. Other required disclosures are specific to the type of lease and include: residual values, contingent rentals, unearned interest, sublease rentals, and executory costs. Some representative examples are shown in Graphics 15–15 (lessor) and 15–16 (lessee) on page 746.

IBM is a manufacturer that relies heavily on leasing as a means of selling its products. Its disclosure of sales-type leases is shown in Graphic 15–15.

Wal-Mart Stores leases facilities under both operating and capital leases. Its long-term obligations under these lease agreements are disclosed in a note to its financial statements (see Graphic 15–16).

GRAPHIC 15–14   Lease Terms and Concepts: A Summary

Lease Situation for Calculations

($ in 000s)			
Lease term (years)	4	Lessor's cost	$300
Asset's useful life (years)	5	Residual value:	
Lessor's implicit rate (known by lessee)	12%	Guaranteed by lessee	$8
Lessee's incremental borrowing rate	13%	Guaranteed by third party[a]	$6
Rental payments (including executory		Unguaranteed	$5
costs) at the beginning of each year	$102	Executory costs paid annually by lessor	$2
		Bargain purchase option	none
		Initial direct costs	3

Amount	Description	Calculation
Lessor's:		
Gross investment in the lease[b]	Total of periodic rental payments[c] plus any residual value that reverts to the lessor (guaranteed or not) or plus BPO price[d]	($100 × 4) + ($8 + 6 + 5) = $419
Net investment in the lease	Present value of the gross investment (discounted at lessor's rate) plus any initial direct costs in a direct financing lease	($100 × 3.40183[e]) + ($19 × .63552[f]) = $352[g]
Unearned interest revenue	Gross investment − Net investment	$419 − 352 = $67
Minimum lease payments	Total of periodic rental payments[c] plus residual value guaranteed to the lessor (by lessee and/or by third party) or plus BPO price[d]	($100 × 4) + ($8 + 6) = $414
Sales revenue	Present value of lessor's minimum lease payments; also, net investment − present value of unguaranteed residual value	($100 × 3.40183[e]) + ($14 × .63552[f]) = $349; also: $352 − ($5 × .63552) = $349
Cost of goods sold	Lessor's cost − Present value of unguaranteed residual value	$300 − ($5 × .63552[f]) = $297
Dealer's profit	Sales revenue − Cost of goods sold; also, Net investment − Lessor's cost	$349 − 297 = $52; also, $352 − 300 = $52
Lessee's:		
Minimum lease payments	Total of periodic rental payments[c] plus residual value guaranteed by lessee or plus BPO price[d]	($100 × 4) + $8 = $408
Leased asset	Present value of minimum lease payments (using lower of lessor's rate and lessee's incremental borrowing rate); cannot exceed fair value	($100 × 3.40183[e]) + ($8 × .63552[f]) = $345
Lease liability at inception	Same as leased asset	($100 × 3.40183[e]) + ($8 × .63552[f]) = $345

[a]Beyond any amount guaranteed by the lessee (amount guaranteed is $8 + 6 minus any amount paid by the lessee).
[b]This is the amount to be recovered by the lessor and therefore is used in the calculation of periodic lease payments. It also is the lease receivable at the inception of lease.
[c]Any portion of rental payments that represents maintenance, insurance, taxes, or other executory costs is not considered part of minimum lease payments. In this case, rentals are reduced as follows: $102 − 2 = $100.
[d]In this context, a residual value and a BPO price are mutually exclusive: if a BPO exists, any residual value is expected to remain with the lessee and is not considered an additional payment.
[e]Present value of annuity due of $1: n = 4, i = 12%.
[f]Present value of $1: n = 4, i = 12%.
[g]Since this is a sales-type lease ($352 − 300 = $52 dealer's profit), initial direct costs are expensed at the lease's inception and do not increase the net investment in the lease.

F: Financing Receivables (in part)

	($ in millions)	
	2000	**1999**
Short term:		
Commercial financing receivables	$ 6,851	$ 6,062
Customer loan receivables	4,065	3,764
Installment payment receivables	1,221	1,110
Net investment in sales-type leases	6,568	6,220
Total short-term financing receivables	$18,705	$17,156
Long term:		
Commercial financing receivables	$ 779	$ 30
Customer loan receivables	4,359	4,219
Installment payment receivables	574	848
Net investment in sales-type leases	7,596	7,981
Total long-term financing receivables	$13,308	$13,078

Net investment in sales-type leases is for leases that relate principally to IBM equipment and is generally for terms ranging from two to five years. Net investment in sales-type leases includes unguaranteed residual values of approximately $751 million and $737 million at December 31, 2000 and 1999, respectively, and is reflected net of unearned income at those dates of approximately $1,500 million and $1,600 million, respectively.

Note 8: Commitments and Contingencies (in part)

The Company and certain of its subsidiaries have long-term leases for stores and equipment. Rentals (including, for certain leases, amounts applicable to taxes, insurance, maintenance, other operating expenses, and contingent rentals) under all operating leases were $1,043 million, $893 million, and $762 million in 2002, 2001, and 2000, respectively. Aggregate minimum annual rentals at January 31, 2002, under noncancelable leases are as follows (in millions):

Fiscal Years	Operating Leases	Capital Leases
2003	$ 623	$ 425
2004	602	424
2005	586	423
2006	565	419
2007	547	409
Thereafter	5,131	3,414
Total minimum rentals	$8,054	$5,514
Less estimated executory costs		63
Net minimum lease payments		5,451
Less imputed interest at rates ranging from 6.1% to 14.0%		2,258
Present value of net minimum lease payments		$3,193

Certain of the leases provide for contingent additional rentals based on percentage of sales. Such additional rentals amounted to $63 million, $56 million, and $51 million in 2002, 2001, and 2000, respectively. Substantially all of the store leases have renewal options for additional terms from 5 to 80 years at comparable rentals.

DECISION MAKERS' PERSPECTIVE—Financial Statement Impact

As indicated in the Decision Makers' Perspective at the beginning of the chapter, leasing can allow a firm to conserve assets, to avoid some risks of owning assets, and to obtain favorable tax benefits. These advantages are desirable. It also was pointed out earlier that some firms try to obscure the realities of their financial position through off-balance-sheet financing or by avoiding violating terms of contracts that limit the amount of debt a company can have. Accounting guidelines are designed to limit the ability of firms to hide financial realities. Nevertheless, investors and creditors should be alert to the impact leases can have on a company's financial position and on its risk. ■

Leasing sometimes is used as a means of off-balance-sheet financing.

BALANCE SHEET AND INCOME STATEMENT

Lease transactions identified as nonoperating impact several of a firm's financial ratios. Because we record liabilities for capital leases, the debt-equity ratio (liabilities divided by shareholders' equity) is immediately impacted. Because we also record leased assets, the immediate impact on the rate of return on assets (net income divided by assets) is negative, but the lasting effect depends on how leased assets are utilized to enhance future net income. As illustrated in this chapter, the financial statement impact of a capital lease is no different from that of an installment purchase.

Lease liabilities affect the debt-equity ratio and the rate of return on assets.

Even operating leases, though, can significantly affect risk. Operating leases represent long-term commitments that can become a problem if business declines and cash inflows drop off. For example, long-term lease commitments became a big problem for Businessland in the early 1990s. The company's revenues declined but it was saddled with lease commitments for numerous facilities the company no longer occupied. Its stock's market price declined from $11.88 to $.88 in one year.

Do operating leases create long-term commitments equivalent to liabilities?

Whether leases are capitalized or treated as operating leases affects the income statement as well as the balance sheet. However, the impact generally is not significant. Over the life of a lease, total expenses are equal regardless of the accounting treatment of a lease. If the lease is capitalized, total expenses comprise interest and depreciation. The total of these equals the total amount of rental payments, which would constitute rent expense if not capitalized. There is, however, a timing difference between lease capitalization and operating lease treatment, but the timing difference usually isn't great.

The net income difference between treating a lease as a capital lease versus an operating lease generally is not significant.

The more significant difference between capital leases and operating leases is the impact on the balance sheet. As mentioned above, a capital lease adds to both the asset and liability side of the balance sheet; operating leases do not affect the balance sheet at all. How can external financial statement users adjust their analysis to incorporate the balance sheet differences between capital and operating leases? A frequently offered suggestion is to capitalize all noncancelable lease commitments, including those related to operating leases. Some financial analysts, in fact, do this on their own to get a better feel for a company's actual debt position.

The difference in impact on the balance sheet between capital leases and operating leases is significant.

To illustrate, refer to Graphic 15–16 (p. 746), which reveals the operating lease commitments disclosed by Wal-Mart Stores. If these lease arrangements were considered nonoperating, these payments would be capitalized (reported at the present value of all future payments). By making some reasonable assumptions, we can estimate the present value of all future payments to be made on existing operating leases. For example, the interest rates used by Wal-Mart to discount rental payments on capital leases range from 6.1% to 14.0%. If we use the approximate average rate of 10%, and make certain other assumptions, we can determine the debt equivalent of the operating lease commitments as shown in Graphic 15–17 on the next page.

If capitalized, these operating lease commitments would add $4,210 million to Wal-Mart's liabilities and approximately $4,210 to the company's assets.[31] Let's look at the impact this

---

[31]If these operating leases were capitalized, both assets and liabilities would increase by the same amount at inception of the lease. However, in later years, the leased asset account balance and the lease liability account will, generally, not be equal. The leased asset account is reduced by depreciation and the lease liability account is reduced (amortized) down to zero using the effective interest method.

Capitalized Value or Debt Equivalent of Wal-Mart's Operating Leases

Fiscal Years	Operating Leases	PV Factor 10%	Present Value
2003	$ 623	.909	$ 566
2004	602	.826	497
2005	586	.751	440
2006	565	.683	386
2007	547	.621	340
Thereafter	5,131	.386*	1,981
Total minimum rentals	$8,054		$4,210

*This is the PV factor for $i = 10\%$, $n = 10$, which treats payments after 2007 as occurring in 2012, an assumption due to not knowing precise dates of specific payments after 2007.

would have on the company's debt to equity ratio and its return on assets ratio using selected financial statement information taken from Wal-Mart's annual report for the fiscal year ending January 31, 2002, shown below:

	($ in millions)
Total assets	$83,451
Total liabilities	48,349
Total shareholders' equity	35,102
Net income	6,671

The debt to equity and return on assets ratios are calculated in Graphic 15–18 without considering the capitalization of operating leases and then again after adding $4,210 million to both total assets and total liabilities. In the calculation of return on assets, we use only the year-end total assets rather than the average total assets for the year. Also, we assume no impact on income.

	($ in millions)	
	Without Capitalization	**With Capitalization**
Debt to equity ratio	$\dfrac{\$48,349}{\$35,102} = 1.38$	$\dfrac{\$52,559}{\$31,343} = 1.68$
Return on assets	$\dfrac{\$6,671}{\$83,451} = 8.0\%$	$\dfrac{\$6,671}{\$86,355} = 7.7\%$

The debt to equity ratio rises from 1.38 to 1.68, and the return on assets ratio declines from 8.0% to 7.7%.

STATEMENT OF CASH FLOW IMPACT

Operating Leases.   Remember, lease payments for operating leases represent rent—expense to the lessee, revenue for the lessor. These amounts are included in net income, so both the lessee and lessor report cash payments for operating leases in a statement of cash flows as cash flows from operating activities.

Capital Leases and Direct Financing Leases.   You've learned in this chapter that capital leases are agreements that we identify as being formulated outwardly as leases, but which are in reality installment purchases, so we account for them as such. Each rental payment (except the first if paid at inception) includes both an amount that represents interest and an amount that represents a reduction of principal. In a statement of cash flows, then, the lessee reports the interest portion as a cash outflow from operating activities and the principal portion as a cash flow from financing activities. On the other side of the transaction, the lessor in a direct financing lease reports the interest portion as a cash inflow from operating activities and the principal portion as a cash inflow from investing activities. Both the lessee and lessor report the lease at its inception as a noncash investing/financing activity.

> The interest portion of a capital lease payment is a cash flow from operating activities and the principal portion is a cash flow from financing activities.

Sales-Type Leases.   A sales-type lease differs from a direct-financing lease for the lessor in that we assume the lessor is actually selling its product. Consistent with reporting sales of products under installment sales agreements rather than lease agreements, the lessor reports cash receipts from a sales-type lease as cash inflows from operating activities.

> Cash receipts from a sales-type lease are cash flows from operating activities.

CONCEPT **REVIEW** EXERCISE

Various Lease Accounting Issues

(This is an extension of the previous Concept Review Exercise.)
United Cellular Systems leased a satellite transmission device from Satellite Technology Corporation on January 1, 2004. Satellite Technology paid $500,000 for the transmission device. Its retail value is $653,681.

Terms of the Lease Agreement and Related Information:

Lease term	3 years (6 semiannual periods)
Semiannual rental payments	$123,000—beginning of each period
Economic life of asset	4 years
Implicit interest rate	12%
(Also lessee's incremental borrowing rate)	
Unguaranteed residual value	$40,000
Regulatory fees paid by lessor	$3,000/twice each year (included in rentals)
Lessor's initial direct costs	$4,500
Contingent rental payments	Additional $4,000 if revenues exceed a specified base

Required:
1. Prepare an amortization schedule that describes the pattern of interest expense over the lease term for United Cellular Systems.
2. Prepare an amortization schedule that describes the pattern of interest revenue over the lease term for Satellite Technology.
3. Prepare the appropriate entries for both United Cellular Systems and Satellite Technology on January 1 and June 30, 2004.
4. Prepare the appropriate entries for both United Cellular Systems and Satellite Technology on December 31, 2006 (the end of the lease term), assuming the device is returned to the lessor and its actual residual value is $14,000 on that date.

SOLUTION

1. Prepare an amortization schedule that describes the pattern of interest expense over the lease term for United Cellular Systems.

Calculation of the Present Value of Minimum Lease Payments:
Present value of periodic rental payments excluding executory costs of $3,000:

$$(\$120,000 \times 5.21236^*) = \$625,483$$

*Present value of an annuity due of $1: $n = 6$, $i = 6\%$.
Note: The *unguaranteed* residual value is excluded from minimum lease payments for both the lessee and lessor.

	Payments	Effective Interest	Decrease in Balance	Outstanding Balance
		(6% × Outstanding balance)		
1/1/04				625,483
1/1/04	120,000		120,000	505,483
6/30/04	120,000	.06 (505,483) = 30,329	89,671	415,812
1/1/05	120,000	.06 (415,812) = 24,949	95,051	320,761
6/30/05	120,000	.06 (320,761) = 19,246	100,754	220,007
1/1/06	120,000	.06 (220,007) = 13,200	106,800	113,207
6/30/06	120,000	.06 (113,207) = 6,793*	113,207	0
	720,000	94,517	625,483	

*Adjusted for rounding of other numbers in the schedule.

2. Prepare an amortization schedule that describes the pattern of interest revenue over the lease term for Satellite Technology.

Calculation of the Lessor's Net Investment:

Present value of periodic rental payments excluding executory costs of $3,000 ($120,000 × 5.21236*)	$625,483
Plus: Present value of the unguaranteed residual value ($40,000 × .70496[†])	28,198
Lessor's net investment in lease	$653,681

*Present value of an annuity due of $1: n = 6, i = 6%.
[†]Present value of $1: n = 6, i = 6%.
Note: The unguaranteed residual value is excluded from minimum lease payments, but is part of the lessor's gross and net investment in the lease.

	Payments	Effective Interest	Decrease in Balance	Outstanding Balance
		(6% × Outstanding balance)		
1/1/04				653,681
1/1/04	120,000		120,000	533,681
6/30/04	120,000	.06 (533,681) = 32,021	87,979	445,702
1/1/05	120,000	.06 (445,702) = 26,742	93,258	352,444
6/30/05	120,000	.06 (352,444) = 21,147	98,853	253,591
1/1/06	120,000	.06 (253,591) = 15,215	104,785	148,806
6/30/06	120,000	.06 (148,806) = 8,928	111,072	37,734
12/31/06	40,000	.06 (37,734) = 2,266*	37,734	0
	760,000	106,319	653,681	

*Adjusted for rounding of other numbers in the schedule.

3. Prepare the appropriate entries for both United Cellular Systems and Satellite Technology on January 1 and June 30, 2004.

January 1, 2004

United Cellular Systems (Lessee)

Leased equipment (calculated above)	625,483	
Lease payable (calculated above)		625,483
Lease payable (payment less executory costs)	120,000	
Regulatory fees expense (executory costs)	3,000	
Cash (rental payment)		123,000

Satellite Technology (Lessor)

Lease receivable [($120,000 × 6) + $40,000[a]]	760,000	
Cost of goods sold [$500,000 − ($40,000[a] × .70496)]	471,802	
Sales revenue (present value of minimum lease payments[b])		625,483
Unearned interest revenue ($760,000 − 653,681)		106,319
Inventory of equipment (lessor's cost)		500,000
Selling expense	4,500	
Cash (initial direct costs)		4,500
Cash (rental payment)	123,000	
Regulatory fees payable (or cash)		3,000
Lease receivable (payment less executory costs)		120,000

[a]This is the unguaranteed residual value.
[b]Also, $653,681 − ($40,000[a] × .70496).

June 30, 2004

United Cellular Systems (Lessee)

Interest expense [6% × ($625,483 − 120,000)]	30,329	
Lease payable (difference)	89,671	
Regulatory fees expense (annual fee)	3,000	
Cash (rental payment)		123,000

Satellite Technology (Lessor)

Cash (lease payment)	123,000	
Regulatory fees payable (or cash)		3,000
Lease receivable (payment less executory costs)		120,000
Unearned interest revenue	32,021	
Interest revenue [6% × ($653,681 − 120,000)]		32,021

4. Prepare the appropriate entries for both United Cellular Systems and Satellite Technology on December 31, 2006 (the end of the lease term), assuming the device is returned to the lessor and its actual residual value is $14,000 on that date.

December 31, 2006

United Cellular Systems (Lessee)

Depreciation expense ($625,483 ÷ 3 years)	208,494	
Accumulated depreciation		208,494
Accumulated depreciation (account balance)	625,483	
Leased equipment (account balance)		625,483

Satellite Technology (Lessor)

Inventory of equipment (actual residual value)	14,000	
Loss on leased assets ($40,000 − 14,000)	26,000	
Lease receivable (account balance)		40,000
Unearned interest revenue (account balance)	2,266	
Interest revenue (6% × $37,734: from schedule)		2,266

SPECIAL LEASING ARRANGEMENTS

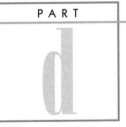

P A R T

Sale-Leaseback Arrangements

In a sale-leaseback transaction, the owner of an asset sells it and immediately leases it back from the new owner. Sound strange? Maybe, but this arrangement is common. In a sale-leaseback transaction two things happen:

1. The seller-lessee receives cash from the sale of the asset.
2. The seller-lessee pays periodic rent payments to the buyer-lessor to retain the use of the asset.

What motivates this kind of arrangement? The two most common reasons are: (1) If the asset had been financed originally with debt and interest rates have fallen, the sale-leaseback transaction can be used to effectively refinance at a lower rate. (2) The most likely motivation for a sale-leaseback transaction is to generate cash.

CAPITAL LEASES

Illustration 15–7 on the next page demonstrates a sale-leaseback involving a capital lease.

The sale and simultaneous leaseback of the warehouses should be viewed as a single borrowing transaction. Although there appear to be two separate transactions, look closer at the substance of the agreement. Teledyne still retains the use of the warehouses that it had prior

ILLUSTRATION 15–7 Sale-Leaseback	Teledyne Distribution Center was in need of cash. Its solution: sell its four warehouses for $900,000, then lease back the warehouses to obtain their continued use. The warehouses had a carrying value on Teledyne's books of $600,000 (original cost $950,000). Other information: 1. The sale date is December 31, 2003. 2. The noncancelable lease term is 10 years and requires annual payments of $133,155 beginning December 31, 2003. The estimated remaining useful life of the warehouses is 10 years. 3. The annual rental payments (present value $900,000) provides the lessor with a 10% rate of return on the financing arrangement.* Teledyne's incremental borrowing rate is 10%. 4. Teledyne depreciates its warehouses on a straight-line basis.

*$133,155 ×   6.75902   = $900,000   ($899,997.30 rounded)
  Rent   (from Table 6A-6)   Present
payments $n = 10, i = 10\%$ value

Recording a sale-leaseback transaction follows the basic accounting concept of substance over form.

to the sale-leaseback. What is different? Teledyne has $900,000 cash and a noncancelable obligation to make annual payments of $133,155. In substance, Teledyne simply has borrowed $900,000 to be repaid over 10 years along with 10% interest. From the perspective of substance over form, we do not immediately recognize the $300,000 gain on the sale of the warehouses but defer the gain to be recognized over the term of the lease (or the useful life of the asset if title is expected to transfer outright or by the exercise of a BPO), demonstrated in Illustration 15–7A.

ILLUSTRATION 15–7A Recording a Sale-Leaseback **The gain on sale-leaseback is deferred and recognized over the lease term as a reduction of depreciation expense.**	**December 31, 2003**	
	Cash.	900,000	
	Accumulated depreciation ($950,000 − 600,000)	350,000	
	Warehouses (cost)		950,000
	Deferred gain on sale-leaseback (difference).		300,000
	Leased warehouses (present value of lease payments).	900,000	
	Lease payable (present value of lease payments)		900,000
	Lease payable	133,155	
	Cash.		133,155
	December 31, 2004	
	Interest expense [10% × ($900,000 − 133,155)].	76,684	
	Lease payable (difference)	56,471	
	Cash (rental payment).		133,155
	Depreciation expense ($900,000 ÷ 10 years).	90,000	
	Accumulated depreciation		90,000
	Deferred gain on sale-leaseback ($300,000 ÷ 10 years)	30,000	
	Depreciation expense		30,000

Since the lease term is equal to the expected useful life of the warehouses (>75%), the leaseback must be recorded by the lessee as a capital lease.[32] There typically is an interdependency between the lease terms and the price at which the asset is sold. The earnings process is not complete at the time of sale but is completed over the term of the lease. So, viewing the sale and the leaseback as a single transaction is consistent with the realization principle. Look closely at the 2003 entries to see the net effect of recording the sale leaseback this way. Amortizing the deferred gain over the lease term as a reduction of depreciation expense decreases depreciation each year to $60,000.[33] Interest expense is $76,684. If Teledyne

---

[32]The fourth criterion also is met. The present value of lease payments ($900,000) is 100% (>90%) of the fair value of the warehouses ($900,000). Meeting any one of the four criteria is sufficient.

[33]If depreciation is over the useful life of the leased asset rather than the lease term because ownership is expected to transfer to the lessee, amortization of the deferred gain also would be over the useful life. If a leaseback of land is a capital lease, the amortization of the deferred gain is recorded as revenue.

had *not* sold the warehouses ($600,000 carrying value) and had borrowed $900,000 cash by issuing an installment note, the 2003 effect would have been virtually identical:

December 31, 2004		
Interest expense [10% × ($900,000 − 133,155)].	76,684	
Note payable (difference)	56,471	
Cash (installment payment).		133,155
Depreciation expense ($600,000 ÷ 10 years).	60,000	
Accumulated depreciation		60,000

> Depreciating the carrying value of the warehouses over their remaining useful life produces depreciation equal to the net depreciation recorded in a sale-leaseback.

The deferred gain is reported on the balance sheet as a valuation (contra) account, offsetting the leased asset. The 2004 balance sheet effect of the sale-leaseback transaction and a $900,000 installment note are compared in Graphic 15–19. Once again, the effect is virtually identical.

	Sale-Leaseback	Retain Asset; Borrow Cash
Assets		
Leased asset	$900,000	$950,000
Less: Accumulated depreciation	(90,000)	(410,000)
Less: Deferred gain ($300,000 − 30,000)	(270,000)	
	$540,000	$540,000
Liabilities		
Lease payable ($900,000 − 133,155 − 56,471)	$710,374	
Note payable ($900,000 − 133,155 − 56,471)		$710,374

> **GRAPHIC 15–19**
> Comparison of a Sale-Leaseback and a Purchase

Accounting by the buyer/lessor is no different in a sale-leaseback transaction than another lease transaction. That is, it records a lease in accordance with the usual lease guidelines.

OPERATING LEASES

If the leaseback portion of the previous sale-leaseback transaction were classified as an operating lease, the gain still would be deferred but would be recognized as a reduction of rent expense rather than depreciation. There is no leased asset to depreciate.[34]

December 31, 2004		
Deferred gain on sale-leaseback ($300,000 ÷ 10 years)	30,000	
Rent expense.		30,000

Those of you with a healthy sense of skepticism will question whether the leaseback portion of our sale-leaseback situation could qualify as an operating lease. After all, the 10-year lease term is equal to the 10-year remaining useful life. But when you remember that neither the third (75% of economic life) nor the fourth (90% recovery) classification criterion applies if the inception of the lease occurs during the last 25% of an asset's economic life, you see the possibility of an operating lease. Suppose, for instance, that the original useful life of the warehouses was 40 years. In that case, the current lease term would occur during the last 25% of an asset's economic life and we would have an operating lease.

LOSSES ON SALE-LEASEBACKS

In a sale-leaseback, any gain on the sale of the asset is deferred and amortized. However, a real loss on the sale of the property is recognized immediately—not deferred. A real loss means the fair value is less than the carrying amount of the asset. On the other hand, if the

---

[34]The deferred gain would be reported as a deferred liability since it could not be offset against a leased asset.

fair value exceeds the carrying amount, but the asset is sold to the buyer/lessor for less than the carrying amount, an artificial loss is produced that is probably in substance a prepayment of rent and should be deferred and amortized.

Real Estate Leases

Some leases involve land—exclusively or in part. The concepts we discussed in the chapter also relate to real estate leases. But the fact that land has an unlimited life causes us to modify how we account for some leases involving real estate.

LEASES OF LAND ONLY

Only the first (title transfers) and second (BPO) classification criteria apply in a land lease.

Because the useful life of land is indefinite, the risks and rewards of ownership cannot be presumed transferred from the lessor to the lessee unless title to the land is expected to transfer—outright or by the expected exercise of a bargain purchase option (criterion 1 or criterion 2). Since the useful life is undefined, the third and fourth criteria are not applicable. Relatedly, because the leased asset is land, depreciation is inappropriate.

LEASES OF LAND AND BUILDING

When (a) the leased property includes both land and a building, (b) neither of the first two criteria is met, and (c) the fair value of the land is 25% or more of the combined fair value, both the lessee and the lessor treat the land as an operating lease and the building as any other lease.

When the leased property includes both land and a building and the lease transfers ownership or is expected to by exercise of a BPO, the lessee should record each leased asset separately. The present value of the minimum lease payments is allocated between the leased land and leased building accounts on the basis of their relative market values.

When neither of the first two criteria is met, the question arises as to whether the third and fourth criteria apply. Because they logically should apply to the building (because its life is limited) but not to the land (because its life is unlimited), the profession employs an arbitrary guideline. If the fair value of the land is less than 25% of the combined fair value, it is in effect ignored and both the lessee and the lessor treat the land and building as a single unit. The single leased asset is depreciated as if land were not involved. If the fair value of the land is 25% or more of the combined fair value, both the lessee and the lessor treat the land and building as two separate leases. Thus, the land lease is an operating lease, and the building lease is classified and accounted for in the manner described in the chapter.

LEASES OF ONLY PART OF A BUILDING

Usual lease accounting procedures apply to leases that involve only part of a building, although extra effort may be needed to arrive at reasonable estimates of cost and fair value.

Some of the most common of leases involve leasing only part of a building. For instance, businesses frequently lease space in an office building or individual stores in a shopping mall. Practical difficulties arise when applying lease accounting procedures in these situations. What is the cost of the third shop from the entrance in a $14 million mall? What is the fair value of a sixth floor office suite in a 40-floor office complex? Despite practical difficulties, usual lease accounting treatment applies. It may, however, be necessary to employ real estate appraisals or replacement cost information to arrive at reasonable estimates of cost or fair value.

Leveraged Leases

A *leveraged lease* involves significant long-term, nonrecourse financing by a third-party creditor.

In a **leveraged lease,** a third-party, long-term creditor provides nonrecourse financing for a lease agreement between a lessor and lessee. The term *leveraged* refers to the fact that the lessor acquires title to the asset after borrowing a large part of the investment.

From the lessee's perspective, accounting for a leveraged lease is not distinguishable from accounting for a nonleveraged lease. Accounting for leveraged leases by the lessor is similar to that for nonleveraged leases. A lessor records its investment (receivable) net of the nonrecourse debt. The lessor's liability to the lender should be offset against its lease receivable from the lessee because its role is in substance that of a mortgage broker. That is, the lessor earns income by serving as an agent for a firm wishing to acquire property and a lender seeking an investment. The lessor borrows enough cash from the lender to acquire the property, which is in turn leased to the lessee under a capital lease. Payments from the lessee are applied to the note held by the lender. The note may be assumed by the lessee *without recourse* such that the lessor is absolved of responsibility for its payment. In order to qualify for favorable treatment under the tax code, the lessor must maintain at least a minimum percentage of equity position in the asset. Also, the lessor should report income from the lease only in those years when the receivable exceeds the liability.

A lessor records its investment (receivable) net of the nonrecourse debt and reports income from the lease only in those years when the receivable exceeds the liability.

FINANCIAL REPORTING CASE **SOLUTION**

1. **How would HG's revenues "take a hit" as a result of more customers leasing than buying mainframes?** *(p. 721)*   When HG leases machines under operating leases, it reports revenue as it collects "rent" over the lease term. When HG sells machines, on the other hand, it recognizes revenue "up front" in the year of sales. Actually, total revenues are not necessarily less with a lease, but are spread out over the several years of the lease term. This delays the recognition of revenues, creating the "hit" in the reporting periods in which a shift to leasing occurs.

2. **Under what kind of leasing arrangements would the "hit" not occur?** *(p. 730)*   The hit will not occur when HG leases its machines under sales-type leases. In those cases, despite the fact that the contract specifies a lease, in effect, HG actually sells its machines under the arrangement. Consequently, HG will recognize sales revenue (and cost of goods sold) at the inception of the lease. The amount recognized is roughly the same as if customers actually buy the machines. As a result, the income statement will not receive the hit created by the substitution of operating leases for outright sales. ∎

THE BOTTOM LINE

1. Leasing is used as a means of off-balance-sheet financing and to achieve operational and tax objectives.
2. In keeping with the concept of substance over form, a lease is accounted for as either a rental agreement or a purchase/sale accompanied by debt financing.
3. A lessee should classify a lease transaction as a capital lease if it is noncancelable and if one or more of four classification criteria are met. Otherwise, it is an operating lease. A lessor records a lease as a direct financing lease or a sales-type lease only if two conditions relating to revenue realization are met in addition to one of the four classification criteria.
4. In an operating lease a sale is not recorded by the lessor; a purchase is not recorded by the lessee. Instead, the periodic rental payments are accounted for merely as rent revenue by the lessor, rent expense by the lessee.
5. In a capital lease the lessee records a leased asset at the present value of the minimum lease payments. A nonoperating lease is recorded by the lessor as a sales-type lease or direct financing lease, depending on whether the lease provides the lessor a dealer's profit.
6. A sales-type lease requires recording sales revenue and cost of goods sold by the lessor at the inception of the lease. All other entries are the same as in a direct financing lease.
7. A lessee-guaranteed residual value is included as a component of minimum lease payments for both the lessor and the lessee. An unguaranteed residual value is not (but is part of the lessor's gross investment in the lease).
8. A bargain purchase option is included as a component of minimum lease payments for both the lessor and the lessee. The lease term effectively ends when the BPO is exercisable.
9. Executory costs (maintenance, insurance, taxes, and any other costs usually associated with ownership) are expenses of the lessee. Any costs incurred by the lessor that are associated directly with originating a lease and are essential to acquire that lease are called *initial direct costs* and are expensed in accordance with the matching principle. To find the present value of minimum lease payments to capitalize as an asset and liability, the lessee

usually uses a discount rate equal to the lower of the rate implicit in the lease agreement and its own incremental borrowing rate. Contingent rentals are *not* included in the minimum lease payments because they are not determinable at the inception of the lease.

10. A gain on the sale of an asset in a sale leaseback arrangement is deferred and amortized over the lease term (or asset life if title is expected to transfer to the lessee). The lease portion of the transaction is evaluated and accounted for like any lease. ■

QUESTIONS FOR REVIEW OF KEY TOPICS

Q 15–1   The basic concept of "substance over form" influences lease accounting. Explain.

Q 15–2   How is interest determined in a nonoperating lease transaction. How does the approach compare to other forms of debt (say bonds payable or notes payable)?

Q 15–3   How are leases and installment notes the same? How do they differ?

Q 15–4   A lessee should classify a lease transaction as a capital lease if it is noncancelable and one or more of four classification criteria are met. Otherwise, it is an operating lease. What are these criteria?

Q 15–5   What is a bargain purchase option? How does it differ from other purchase options?

Q 15–6   Lukawitz Industries leased equipment to Seminole Corporation for a four-year period, at which time possession of the leased asset will revert back to Lukawitz. The equipment cost Lukawitz $4 million and has an expected useful life of six years. Its normal sales price is $5.6 million. The present value of the minimum lease payments for both the lessor and lessee is $5.2 million. The first payment was made at the inception of the lease. Collectibility of the remaining lease payments is reasonably assured, and Lukawitz has no material cost uncertainties. How should this lease be classified (a) by Lukawitz Industries (the lessor) and (b) by Seminole Corporation (the lessee)? Why?

Q 15–7   Can the present value of minimum lease payments differ between the lessor and lessee? If so, how?

Q 15–8   Compare the way a bargain purchase option and a residual value are treated by the lessee when determining minimum lease payments.

Q 15–9   What are executory costs? How are they accounted for by the lessee in a capital lease when paid by the lessee? When paid by the lessor? Explain.

Q 15–10   The discount rate influences virtually every amount reported in connection with a lease by both the lessor and the lessee. What is the lessor's discount rate when determining the present value of minimum lease payments? What is the lessee's discount rate?

Q 15–11   A lease might specify that rental payments may be increased (or decreased) at some future time during the lease term depending on whether or not some specified event occurs such as revenues or profits exceeding some designated level. Under what circumstances are contingent rentals included or excluded from minimum lease payments? If excluded, how are they recognized in income determination?

Q 15–12   The lessor's initial direct costs often are substantial. What are initial direct costs?

Q 15–13   When are initial direct costs recognized in an operating lease? In a direct financing lease? In a sales-type lease? Why?

Q 15–14   In a sale-leaseback transaction the owner of an asset sells it and immediately leases it back from the new owner. This dual transaction should be viewed as a single borrowing transaction. Why?

Q 15–15   Explain how the general classification criteria are applied to leases that involve land.

Q 15–16   What are the guidelines for determining when a material amount of land is involved in a lease?

Q 15–17   How does a leveraged lease differ from a nonleveraged lease?

EXERCISES

E 15–1
Operating lease

On January 1, 2003, Nath-Langstrom Services, Inc., a computer software training firm, leased several computers from ComputerWorld Corporation under a two-year operating lease agreement. The contract calls for four rent payments of $10,000 each, payable semiannually on June 30 and December 31 each year. The computers were acquired by ComputerWorld at a cost of $90,000 and were expected to have a useful life of six years with no residual value.

Required:
Prepare the appropriate entries for both (a) the lessee and (b) the lessor from the inception of the lease through the end of 2003. (Use straight-line depreciation.)

E 15–2
Operating lease;
advance payment;
leasehold improvement

On January 1, 2003, Winn Heat Transfer leased office space under a three-year operating lease agreement. The arrangement specified three annual rent payments of $80,000 each, beginning January 1, 2003, the inception of the lease, and at each January 1 through 2005. Winn also paid a $96,000 advance payment at the inception of the lease in addition to the first $80,000 rent payment. With permission of the owner, Winn made structural modifications to the building before occupying the space at a cost of $180,000. The useful life of the building and the structural modifications were estimated to be 30 years with no residual value.

Required:
Prepare the appropriate entries for Winn Heat Transfer from the inception of the lease through the end of 2003. Winn's fiscal year is the calendar year. Winn uses straight-line depreciation.

E 15–3
Multiple choice;
operating leases

The following questions dealing with various topics in this chapter are adapted from previous CPA examinations. Determine the response that best completes the statements or questions.

1. On January 2, 2002, Ral Co. leased land and building from an unrelated lessor for a 10-year term. The lease has a renewal option for an additional 10 years, but Ral has not reached a decision with regard to the renewal option. In early January 2002, Ral completed the following improvements to the property:

Description	Estimated Life	Cost
Sales office	10 years	$47,000
Warehouse	25 years	$75,000
Parking lot	15 years	$18,000

Amortization of leasehold improvements for 2003 should be
   a. $7,000
   b. $8,900
   c. $12,200
   d. $14,000

2. As an inducement to enter a lease, Graf Co., a lessor, granted Zep, Inc., a lessee, 12 months of free rent under a five-year operating lease. The lease was effective on January 1, 2003, and provides for monthly rental payments to begin January 1, 2004. Zep made the first rental payment on December 30, 2003. In its 2003 income statement, Graf should report rental revenue in an amount equal to
   a. Zero.
   b. Cash received during 2003.
   c. One-fourth of the total cash to be received over the life of the lease.
   d. One-fifth of the total cash to be received over the life of the lease.

(Note: Exercises 4, 5, and 6 are three variations of the same basic situation.)

E 15–4
Capital lease; lessee

Manufacturers Southern leased high-tech electronic equipment from Edison Leasing on January 1, 2003. Edison purchased the equipment from International Machines at a cost of $112,080.

Related Information:

Lease term	2 years (8 quarterly periods)
Quarterly rental payments	$15,000—beginning of each period
Economic life of asset	2 years
Fair value of asset	$112,080
Implicit interest rate	8%
(Also lessee's incremental borrowing rate)	

Required:
Prepare a lease amortization schedule and appropriate entries for Manufacturers Southern from the inception of the lease through January 1, 2004. Depreciation is recorded at the end of each fiscal year (December 31) on a straight-line basis.

E 15–5
Direct financing lease;
lessor

Edison Leasing leased high-tech electronic equipment to Manufacturers Southern on January 1, 2003. Edison purchased the equipment from International Machines at a cost of $112,080.

Related Information:

Lease term	2 years (8 quarterly periods)
Quarterly rental payments	$15,000—beginning of each period
Economic life of asset	2 years
Fair value of asset	$112,080
Implicit interest rate	8%
(Also lessee's incremental borrowing rate)	

Required:

Prepare a lease amortization schedule and appropriate entries for Edison Leasing from the inception of the lease through January 1, 2004. Edison's fiscal year ends December 31.

E 15–6
Sales-type lease; lessor

Manufacturers Southern leased high-tech electronic equipment from International Machines on January 1, 2003. International Machines manufactured the equipment at a cost of $85,000.

Related Information:

Lease term	2 years (8 quarterly periods)
Quarterly rental payments	$15,000—beginning of each period
Economic life of asset	2 years
Fair value of asset	$112,080
Implicit interest rate	8%
(Also lessee's incremental borrowing rate)	

Required:

1. Show how International Machines determined the $15,000 quarterly rental payments.
2. Prepare appropriate entries for International Machines to record the lease at its inception, January 1, 2003, and the second rental payment on April 1, 2003.

E 15–7
Capital lease

American Food Services, Inc., leased a packaging machine from Barton and Barton Corporation. Barton and Barton completed construction of the machine on January 1, 2003. The lease agreement for the $4 million (fair market value) machine specified four equal payments at the end of each year. The useful life of the machine was expected to be four years with no residual value. Barton and Barton's implicit interest rate was 10% (also American Food Services' incremental borrowing rate).

Required:

1. Prepare the journal entry for American Food Services at the inception of the lease on January 1, 2003.
2. Prepare an amortization schedule for the four-year term of the lease.
3. Prepare the journal entry for the first lease payment on December 31, 2003.
4. Prepare the journal entry for the third lease payment on December 31, 2005.

(Note: You may wish to compare your solution to this exercise with that of Exercise 14–16 which deals with a parallel situation in which the packaging machine was acquired with an installment note.)

(Note: Exercise 8, 9, and 10 are three variations of the same situation.)

E 15–8
Capital lease; lessee; balance sheet and income statement effects

On June 30, 2003, Georgia-Atlantic, Inc. leased a warehouse facility from IC Leasing Corporation. The lease agreement calls for Georgia-Atlantic to make semiannual lease payments of $562,907 over a three-year lease term, payable each June 30 and December 31, with the first payment at June 30, 2003. Georgia-Atlantic's incremental borrowing rate is 10%, the same rate IC uses to calculate lease payment amounts. Depreciation is recorded on a straight-line basis at the end of each fiscal year. The fair value of the warehouse is $3 million.

Required:

1. Determine the present value of the lease payments at June 30, 2003 (to the nearest $000) that Georgia-Atlantic uses to record the leased asset and lease liability.
2. What pretax amounts related to the lease would Georgia-Atlantic report in its balance sheet at December 31, 2003?
3. What pretax amounts related to the lease would Georgia-Atlantic report in its income statement for the year ended December 31, 2003?

E 15–9
Direct financing lease; lessor; balance sheet and income statement effects

On June 30, 2003, Georgia-Atlantic, Inc. leased a warehouse facility from IC Leasing Corporation. The lease agreement calls for Georgia-Atlantic to make semiannual lease payments of $562,907 over a three-year lease term, payable each June 30 and December 31, with the first payment at June 30, 2003. Georgia-Atlantic's incremental borrowing rate is 10%, the same rate IC used to calculate lease payment amounts. IC purchased the warehouse from Builders, Inc. at a cost of $3 million.

Required:

1. What pretax amounts related to the lease would IC report in its balance sheet at December 31, 2003?
2. What pretax amounts related to the lease would IC report in its income statement for the year ended December 31, 2003?

E 15–10
Sales-type lease; lessor; balance sheet and income statement effects

On June 30, 2003, Georgia-Atlantic, Inc. leased a warehouse facility from Builders, Inc. The lease agreement calls for Georgia-Atlantic to make semiannual lease payments of $562,907 over a three-year lease term, payable each June 30 and December 31, with the first payment at June 30, 2003. Georgia-Atlantic's incremental borrowing rate is 10%, the same rate Builders used to calculate lease payment amounts. Builders constructed the warehouse at a cost of $2.5 million.

Required:
1. Determine the price at which Builders is "selling" the equipment (present value of the lease payments) at June 30, 2003 (to the nearest $000).
2. What pretax amounts related to the lease would Builders report in its balance sheet at December 31, 2003?
3. What pretax amounts related to the lease would Builders report in its income statement for the year ended December 31, 2003?

E 15–11
Lessor calculation of annual rental payments; lessee calculation of asset and liability

Each of the three independent situations below describes a nonoperating lease in which annual rental payments are payable at the beginning of each year. The lessee is aware of the lessor's implicit rate of return.

	Situation		
	1	**2**	**3**
Lease term (years)	10	20	4
Lessor's rate of return	11%	9%	12%
Lessee's incremental borrowing rate	12%	10%	11%
Fair market value of leased asset	$600,000	$980,000	$185,000

Required:
For each situation, determine:
a. The amount of the annual rental payments as calculated by the lessor.
b. The amount the lessee would record as a leased asset and a lease liability.

E 15–12
Lessor calculation of annual rental payments; lessee calculation of asset and liability

(Note: This is a variation of the previous exercise modified to assume rental payments are at the end of each period.)
Each of the three independent situations below describes a nonoperating lease in which annual rental payments are payable at the *end* of each year. The lessee is aware of the lessor's implicit rate of return.

	Situation		
	1	**2**	**3**
Lease term (years)	10	20	4
Lessor's rate of return	11%	9%	12%
Lessee's incremental borrowing rate	12%	10%	11%
Fair market value of leased asset	$600,000	$980,000	$185,000

Required:
For each situation, determine:
a. The amount of the annual rental payments as calculated by the lessor.
b. The amount the lessee would record as a leased asset and a lease liability.

E 15–13
Calculation of annual lease payments; residual value

Each of the four independent situations below describes a nonoperating lease in which annual rental payments are payable at the beginning of each year. Determine the annual rental payments for each:

	Situation			
	1	**2**	**3**	**4**
Lease term (years)	4	7	5	8
Lessor's rate of return	10%	11%	9%	12%
Fair market value of leased asset	$50,000	$350,000	$75,000	$465,000
Lessor's cost of leased asset	$50,000	$350,000	$45,000	$465,000
Residual value:				
Guaranteed by lessee	0	$ 50,000	0	$ 30,000
Unguaranteed	0	0	$ 7,000	$ 15,000

E 15–14
Lease concepts; direct financing leases; guaranteed and unguaranteed residual value

Each of the four independent situations below describes a direct financing lease in which annual rental payments of $100,000 are payable at the beginning of each year. Each is a capital lease for the lessee. Determine the following amounts at the inception of the lease:
A. The lessor's:
  1. Minimum lease payments
  2. Gross investment in the lease
  3. Net investment in the lease
  4. Unearned interest revenue

B. The lessee's:
   5.   Minimum lease payments
   6.   Leased asset
   7.   Lease liability

	Situation			
	1	**2**	**3**	**4**
Lease term (years)	7	7	8	8
Lessor's and lessee's discount rate	9%	11%	10%	12%
Residual value:				
Guaranteed by lessee	0	$50,000	0	$40,000
Unguaranteed	0	0	$50,000	$60,000

E 15–15
Calculation of annual
lease payments; BPO

For each of the three independent situations below determine the amount of the annual rental payments. Each describes a nonoperating lease in which annual rental payments are payable at the beginning of each year. Each lease agreement contains an option that permits the lessee to acquire the leased asset at an option price sufficiently lower than the expected market value that the exercise of the option appears reasonably certain.

	Situation		
	1	**2**	**3**
Lease term (years)	5	12	4
Lessor's rate of return	12%	11%	9%
Fair market value of leased asset	$60,000	$420,000	$185,000
Lessor's cost of leased asset	$50,000	$420,000	$145,000
Bargain purchase option:			
Option price	$10,000	$ 50,000	$ 22,000
Exercisable at end of year:	5	5	3

E 15–16
Capital lease; bargain
purchase option; lessee

Federated Fabrications leased a tooling machine on December 31, 2002, for a three-year period. The lease agreement specified annual payments of $36,000 beginning with the first payment at the inception of the lease, and each December 31 through 2004. The company had the option to purchase the machine on December 30, 2005, for $45,000 when its fair value was expected to be $60,000. The machine's estimated useful life was six years with no salvage value. Federated depreciates assets by the straight-line method. The company was aware that the lessor's implicit rate of return was 12%, which was less than Federated's incremental borrowing rate.

Required:
1. Calculate the amount Federated should record as a leased asset and lease liability for this capital lease.
2. Prepare an amortization schedule that describes the pattern of interest expense for Federated over the lease term.
3. Prepare the appropriate entries for Federated from the inception of the lease through the end of the lease term.

E 15–17
Bargain purchase
option; lessor; direct
financing lease

Universal Leasing leases electronic equipment to a variety of businesses. The company's primary service is providing alternate financing by acquiring equipment and leasing it to customers under long-term direct financing leases. Universal earns interest under these arrangements at a 10% annual rate.

The company leased an electronic typesetting machine purchased for $30,900 to a local publisher, Desktop Inc., on December 31, 2002. The lease contract specified annual payments of $8,000 beginning December 31, 2002, the inception of the lease, and each December 31 through 2004 (three-year lease term). The publisher had the option to purchase the machine on December 30, 2005, for $12,000 when it was expected to have a residual value of $16,000.

Required:
1. Show how Universal calculated the $8,000 annual rental payments for this direct financing lease.
2. Prepare an amortization schedule that describes the pattern of interest revenue for Universal Leasing over the lease term.
3. Prepare the appropriate entries for Universal Leasing from the inception of the lease through the end of the lease term.

E 15–18
Executory costs; lessor and lessee

On December 31, 2002, NRC Credit Corporation leased equipment to Brand Services under a direct financing lease designed to earn NRC a 12% rate of return for providing long-term financing. The lease agreement specified:

a. 10 annual payments of $55,000 (including executory costs) beginning December 31, 2002, the inception of the lease.

b. The estimated useful life of the leased equipment is 10 years with no residual value. Its cost to NRC was $316,412.

c. The lease qualifies as a capital lease to Brand.

d. A 10-year service agreement with Quality Maintenance Company was negotiated to provide maintenance of the equipment as required. Payments of $5,000 per year are specified, beginning December 31, 2002. NRC was to pay this executory cost as incurred, but lease payments reflect this expenditure.

e. A partial amortization schedule, appropriate for both the lessee and lessor, follows:

Dec. 31	Payments	Effective Interest	Decrease in Balance	Outstanding Balance
		(12% × Outstanding balance)		
				316,412
2002	50,000		50,000	266,412
2003	50,000	.12 (266,412) = 31,969	18,031	248,381
2004	50,000	.12 (248,381) = 29,806	20,194	228,187

Required:
Prepare the appropriate entries for both the lessee and lessor to record:
1. The lease at its inception.
2. The second lease payment and depreciation (straight line) on December 31, 2003.

E 15–19
Executory costs plus management fee; lessor and lessee

Refer to the lease agreement described in the previous exercise. Assume the contract specified that NRC (the lessor) was to pay, not only the $5,000 maintenance fees, but also insurance of $700 per year, and was to receive a $250 management fee for facilitating service and paying executory costs. The lessee's rental payments were increased to include an amount sufficient to reimburse executory costs plus NRC's fee.

Required:
Prepare the appropriate entries for both the lessee and lessor to record the **second** lease payment, executory costs, and depreciation (straight line) on December 31, 2003.

E 15–20
Multiple choice; nonoperating leases

The following questions dealing with various topics in this chapter are adapted from recent CPA examinations. Determine the response that best completes the statements or questions.

1. On December 31, 2002, Roe Co. leased a machine from Colt for a five-year period. Equal annual payments under the lease are $105,000 (including $5,000 annual executory costs) and are due on December 31 of each year. The first payment was made on December 31, 2002, and the second payment was made on December 31, 2003. The five lease payments are discounted at 10% over the lease term. The present value of minimum lease payments at the inception of the lease and before the first annual payment was $417,000. The lease is appropriately accounted for as a capital lease by Roe. In its December 31, 2003, balance sheet, Roe should report a lease liability of
    a. $317,000
    b. $315,000
    c. $285,300
    d. $248,700

2. Winn Co. manufactures equipment that is sold or leased. On December 31, 2003, Winn leased equipment to Bart for a five-year period ending December 31, 2008, at which date ownership of the leased asset will be transferred to Bart. Equal payments under the lease are $22,000 (including $2,000 executory costs) and are due on December 31 of each year. The first payment was made on December 31, 2003. Collectibility of the remaining lease payments is reasonably assured, and Winn has no material cost uncertainties. The normal sales price of the equipment is $77,000, and cost is $60,000. For the year ended December 31, 2003, what amount of income should Winn realize from the lease transaction?
    a. $17,000
    b. $22,000
    c. $23,000
    d. $33,000

3. At the inception of a capital lease, the guaranteed residual value should be
    a. Included as part of minimum lease payments at present value.
    b. Included as part of minimum lease payments at future value.
    c. Included as part of minimum lease payments only to the extent that guaranteed residual value is expected to exceed estimated residual value.
    d. Excluded from minimum lease payments.

E 15–21

Lessor's initial direct costs; operating, direct financing and sales-type leases

Terms of a lease agreement and related facts were:
a. Leased asset had a retail cash selling price of $100,000. Its useful life was six years with no residual value (straight-line depreciation).
b. Annual rental payments at the beginning of each year were $20,873, beginning January 1.
c. Lessor's implicit rate when calculating annual rental payments was 10%.
d. Costs of negotiating and consummating the completed lease transaction incurred by the lessor were $2,062.
e. Collectibility of the rent payments by the lessor was reasonably predictable and there were no costs to the lessor that were yet to be incurred.

Required:
Prepare the appropriate entries for the lessor to record the lease, the initial payment at its inception, and at the December 31 fiscal year-end under each of the following three independent assumptions:
1. The lease term is three years and the lessor paid $100,000 to acquire the asset (operating lease).
2. The lease term is six years and the lessor paid $100,000 to acquire the asset (direct financing lease). Also assume that adjusting the net investment by initial direct costs reduces the effective rate of interest to 9%.
3. The lease term is six years and the lessor paid $85,000 to acquire the asset (sales-type lease).

E 15–22

Lessor's initial direct costs; operating lease

The following relate to an operating lease agreement:
a. The lease term is 3 years, beginning January 1, 2003.
b. The leased asset cost the lessor $800,000 and had a useful life of eight years with no residual value. The lessor uses straight-line depreciation for its depreciable assets.
c. Annual rental payments at the beginning of each year were $137,000.
d. Costs of negotiating and consummating the completed lease transaction incurred by the lessor were $2,400.

Required:
Prepare the appropriate entries for the lessor from the inception of the lease through the end of the lease term.

E 15–23

Lessor's initial direct costs; direct financing lease

Terms of a lease agreement and related facts were:
a. Costs of negotiating and consummating the completed lease transaction incurred by the lessor were $4,242.
b. The retail cash selling price of the leased asset was $500,000. Its useful life was three years with no residual value.
c. Collectibility of the rent payments by the lessor was reasonably predictable and there were no costs to the lessor that were yet to be incurred.
d. The lease term is three years and the lessor paid $500,000 to acquire the asset (direct financing lease).
e. Annual rental payments at the beginning of each year were $184,330.
f. Lessor's implicit rate when calculating annual rental payments was 11%.

Required:
1. Prepare the appropriate entries for the lessor to record the lease and related payments at its inception, January 1, 2003.
2. Calculate the effective rate of interest revenue after adjusting the net investment by initial direct costs.
3. Record any entry(s) necessary at December 31, 2003, the fiscal year-end.

E 15–24

Lessor's initial direct costs; sales-type lease

The lease agreement and related facts indicate the following:
a. Leased equipment had a retail cash selling price of $300,000. Its useful life was five years with no residual value.

b. Collectibility of the rent payments by the lessor was reasonably predictable and there were no costs to the lessor that were yet to be incurred.
c. The lease term is five years and the lessor paid $265,000 to acquire the equipment (sales-type lease).
d. Lessor's implicit rate when calculating annual rental payments was 8%.
e. Annual rental payments beginning January 1, 2003, the inception of the lease, were $69,571.
f. Costs of negotiating and consummating the completed lease transaction incurred by the lessor were $7,500.

Required:
Prepare the appropriate entries for the lessor to record:
1. The lease and the initial payment at its inception.
2. Any entry(s) necessary at December 31, 2003, the fiscal year-end.

E 15–25
Sale-leaseback; capital lease

To raise operating funds, Signal Aviation sold an airplane on January 1, 2003, to a finance company for $770,000. Signal immediately leased the plane back for a 13-year period, at which time ownership of the airplane will transfer to Signal. The airplane has a fair value of $800,000. Its cost and its carrying value were $620,000. Its useful life is estimated to be 15 years. The lease requires Signal to make payments of $102,771 to the finance company each January 1. Signal depreciates assets on a straight-line basis. The lease has an implicit rate of 11%.

Required:
Prepare the appropriate entries for Signal on:
1. January 1, 2003, to record the sale-leaseback.
2. December 31, 2003, to record necessary adjustments.

E 15–26
Sale-leaseback; operating lease

To raise operating funds, National Distribution Center sold its office building to an insurance company on January 1, 2003, for $800,000 and immediately leased the building back. The operating lease is for the final 12 years of the building's estimated 50-year useful life. The building has a fair value of $800,000 and a carrying amount of $650,000 (its original cost was $1,000,000). The rental payments of $100,000 are payable to the insurance company each December 31. The lease has an implicit rate of 9%.

Required:
Prepare the appropriate entries for National Distribution Center on:
1. January 1, 2003, to record the sale-leaseback.
2. December 31, 2003, to record necessary adjustments.

E 15–27
Multiple choice; other lease accounting issues

The following questions dealing with various topics in this chapter are adapted from recent CPA examinations. Determine the response that best completes the statements or questions.
1. Able sold its headquarters building at a gain and simultaneously leased back the building. The lease was reported as a capital lease. At the time of sale, the gain should be reported as
    a. Operating income.
    b. An extraordinary item, net of income tax.
    c. A separate component of shareholders' equity.
    d. An asset valuation allowance.
2. On January 1, 2003, Wren Co. leased a building to Brill under an operating lease for 10 years at $50,000 per year, payable the first day of each lease year. Wren paid $15,000 to a real estate broker as a finder's fee. The building is depreciated $12,000 per year. For 2003, Wren incurred insurance and property tax expense totaling $9,000. Wren's net rental income for 2003 should be
    a. $27,500
    b. $29,000
    c. $35,000
    d. $36,500

E 15–28
Concepts; terminology

Listed below are several terms and phrases associated with leases. Pair each item from List A (by letter) with the item from List B that is most appropriately associated with it.

List A	List B
___ 1. Effective rate times balance.	a. PV of BPO price.
___ 2. Realization principle.	b. Lessor's net investment.
___ 3. Minimum lease payments plus unguaranteed residual value.	c. Lessor's gross investment.
	d. Operating lease.
___ 4. Periodic rent payments plus lessee-guaranteed residual value.	e. Depreciable assets.
	f. Loss to lessee.
___ 5. PV of minimum lease payments plus PV of unguaranteed residual value.	g. Executory costs.
	h. Depreciation longer than lease term.
___ 6. Initial direct costs.	i. Disclosure only.
___ 7. Rent revenue.	j. Interest expense.
___ 8. Bargain purchase option.	k. Additional lessor conditions.
___ 9. Leasehold improvements.	l. Lessee's minimum lease payments.
___ 10. Cash to satisfy residual value guarantee.	m. Purchase price less than fair market value.
___ 11. Capital lease expense.	n. Sales-type lease selling expense.
___ 12. Deducted in lessor's computation of rental payments.	o. Lessor's minimum lease payments.
___ 13. Title transfers to lessee.	
___ 14. Contingent rentals.	
___ 15. Rent payments plus lessee-guaranteed and third-party-guaranteed residual value.	

E 15–29
Real estate lease; land and building

On January 1, 2003, Cook Textiles leased a building with two acres of land from Peck Development. The lease is for 10 years at which time Cook has an option to purchase the property for $100,000. The building has an estimated life of 20 years with a residual value of $150,000. The lease calls for Cook to assume all costs of ownership and to make annual payments of $200,000 due at the beginning of each year. On January 1, 2003, the estimated value of the land was $400,000. Cook uses the straight-line method of depreciation and pays 10% interest on borrowed money. Peck's implicit rate is unknown.

Required:
Prepare Cook Company's journal entries related to the lease in 2003.

PROBLEMS

P 15–1
Operating lease; scheduled rent increases

On January 1, 2003, Sweetwater Furniture Company leased office space under a 21-year operating lease agreement. The contract calls for annual rent payments on December 31 of each year. The payments are $10,000 the first year and increase by $500 per year. Benefits expected from using the office space are expected to remain constant over the lease term.

Required:
Record Sweetwater's rent payment at December 31, 2007 (the fifth rent payment) and December 31, 2017 (the 15th rent payment).

P 15–2
Lease amortization schedule

On January 1, 2003, National Insulation Corporation (NIC) leased office space under a capital lease. Rental payments are made annually. Title does not transfer to the lessee and there is no bargain purchase option. Portions of the lessee's lease amortization schedule appear below:

Jan. 1	Payments	Effective Interest	Decrease in Balance	Outstanding Balance
2003				192,501
2003	20,000		20,000	172,501
2004	20,000	17,250	2,750	169,751
2005	20,000	16,975	3,025	166,726
2006	20,000	16,673	3,327	163,399
2007	20,000	16,340	3,660	159,739
2008	20,000	15,974	4,026	155,713
—	—	—	—	—
—	—	—	—	—
—	—	—	—	—
2020	20,000	7,364	12,636	61,006
2021	20,000	6,101	13,899	47,107
2022	20,000	4,711	15,289	31,818
2023	35,000	3,182	31,818	0

Required:
1. What is NIC's lease liability at the inception of the lease (after the first payment)?
2. What amount would NIC record as a leased asset?
3. What is the lease term in years?
4. What is the asset's residual value expected at the end of the lease term?
5. How much of the residual value is guaranteed by the lessee?
6. What is the effective annual interest rate?
7. What is the total amount of minimum lease payments?
8. What is the total effective interest expense recorded over the term of the lease?

P 15–3

Direct financing and sales-type lease; lessee and lessor

Rand Medical manufactures lithotripters. Lithotripsy uses shock waves instead of surgery to eliminate kidney stones. Physicians' Leasing purchased a lithotripter from Rand for $2,000,000 and leased it to Mid-South Urologists Group, Inc., on January 1, 2003.

Lease Description:

Quarterly rental payments	$130,516—beginning of each period
Lease term	5 years (20 quarters)
No residual value; no BPO	
Economic life of lithotripter	5 years
Implicit interest rate and lessee's incremental borrowing rate	12%
Fair value of asset	$2,000,000

Collectibility of the rental payments is reasonably assured, and there are no lessor costs yet to be incurred.

Required:
1. How should this lease be classified by Mid-South Urologists Group and by Physicians' Leasing?
2. Prepare appropriate entries for both Mid-South Urologists Group and Physicians' Leasing from the inception of the lease through the second rental payment on April 1, 2003. Depreciation is recorded at the end of each fiscal year (December 31).
3. Assume Mid-South Urologists Group leased the lithotripter directly from the manufacturer, Rand Medical, which produced the machine at a cost of $1,700,000. Prepare appropriate entries for Rand Medical from the inception of the lease through the second rental payment on April 1, 2003.

P 15–4

Capital lease

At the beginning of 2003, VHF Industries acquired a machine with a fair market value of $6,074,700 by signing a four-year lease. Rentals are payable in four annual payments of $2 million at the end of each year.

Required:
1. What is the effective rate of interest implicit in the agreement?
2. Prepare the lessee's journal entry at the inception of the lease.
3. Prepare the journal entry to record the first lease payment at December 31, 2003.
4. Prepare the journal entry to record the second lease payment at December 31, 2004.
5. Suppose the market value of the machine and the lessor's implicit rate were unknown at the time of the lease, but that the lessee's incremental borrowing rate of interest for notes of similar risk was 11%. Prepare the lessee's entry at the inception of the lease.

(Note: You may wish to compare your solution to this problem with that of Problem 14–11, which deals with a parallel situation in which the machine was acquired with an installment note.)

(Note: Problems 5, 6, and 7 are three variations of the same basic situation.)

P 15–5

Capital lease; lessee; financial statement effects

Werner Chemical, Inc. leased a protein analyzer on September 30, 2003. The five-year lease agreement calls for Werner to make quarterly lease payments of $391,548, payable each September 30, December 31, March 31, June 30, with the first payment at September 30, 2003. Werner's incremental borrowing rate is 12%. Depreciation is recorded on a straight-line basis at the end of each fiscal year. The useful life of the equipment is five years.

Required:
1. Determine the present value of the lease payments at September 30, 2003 (to the nearest $000).
2. What pretax amounts related to the lease would Werner report in its balance sheet at December 31, 2003?
3. What pretax amounts related to the lease would Werner report in its income statement for the year ended December 31, 2003?
4. What pretax amounts related to the lease would Werner report in its statement of cash flows for the year ended December 31, 2003?

P 15–6
Direct financing lease; lessor; financial statement effects

Abbott Equipment leased a protein analyzer to Werner Chemical, Inc. on September 30, 2003. Abbott purchased the machine from NutraLabs, Inc. at a cost of $6 million. The five-year lease agreement calls for Werner to make quarterly lease payments of $391,548, payable each September 30, December 31, March 31, June 30, with the first payment at September 30, 2003. Abbot's implicit interest rate is 12%.

Required:
1. What pretax amounts related to the lease would Abbott report in its balance sheet at December 31, 2003?
2. What pretax amounts related to the lease would Abbott report in its income statement for the year ended December 31, 2003?
3. What pretax amounts related to the lease would Abbott report in its statement of cash flows for the year ended December 31, 2003?

P 15–7
Sales-type lease; lessor; financial statement effects

NutraLabs, Inc. leased a protein analyzer to Werner Chemical, Inc. on September 30, 2003. NutraLabs manufactured the machine at a cost of $5 million. The five-year lease agreement calls for Werner to make quarterly lease payments of $391,548, payable each September 30, December 31, March 31, June 30, with the first payment at September 30, 2003. NutraLabs' implicit interest rate is 12%.

Required:
1. Determine the price at which NutraLabs is "selling" the equipment (present value of the lease payments) at September 30, 2003 (to the nearest $000).
2. What pretax amounts related to the lease would NutraLabs report in its balance sheet at December 31, 2003?
3. What pretax amounts related to the lease would NutraLabs report in its income statement for the year ended December 31, 2003?
4. What pretax amounts related to the lease would NutraLabs report in its statement of cash flows for the year ended December 31, 2003?

(Note: Problems 8, 9, and 10 are three variations of the same basic situation.)

P 15–8
Guaranteed residual value; direct financing lease

On December 31, 2003, Rhone-Metro Industries leased equipment to Western Soya Co. for a four-year period ending December 31, 2007, at which time possession of the leased asset will revert back to Rhone-Metro. The equipment cost Rhone-Metro $365,760 and has an expected useful life of six years. Its normal sales price is $365,760. The lessee-guaranteed residual value at December 31, 2007, is $25,000. Equal payments under the lease are $100,000 and are due on December 31 of each year. The first payment was made on December 31, 2003. Collectibility of the remaining lease payments is reasonably assured, and Rhone-Metro has no material cost uncertainties. Western Soya's incremental borrowing rate is 12%. Western Soya knows the interest rate implicit in the lease payments is 10%. Both companies use straight-line depreciation.

Required:
1. Show how Rhone-Metro calculated the $100,000 annual rental payments.
2. How should this lease be classified (a) by Western Soya Co. (the lessee) and (b) by Rhone-Metro Industries (the lessor)? Why?
3. Prepare the appropriate entries for both Western Soya Co. and Rhone-Metro on December 31, 2003.
4. Prepare an amortization schedule(s) describing the pattern of interest over the lease term for the lessee and the lessor.
5. Prepare all appropriate entries for both Western Soya and Rhone-Metro on December 31, 2004 (the second rent payment and depreciation).
6. Prepare the appropriate entries for both Western Soya and Rhone-Metro on December 31, 2007 assuming the equipment is returned to Rhone-Metro and the actual residual value on that date is $1,500.

P 15–9
Unguaranteed residual value; executory costs; sales-type lease

Rhone-Metro Industries manufactures equipment that is sold or leased. On December 31, 2003, Rhone-Metro leased equipment to Western Soya Co. for a four-year period ending December 31, 2007, at which time possession of the leased asset will revert back to Rhone-Metro. The equipment cost $300,000 to manufacture and has an expected useful life of six years. Its normal sales price is $365,760. The expected residual value of $25,000 at December 31, 2007, is not guaranteed. Equal payments under the lease are $104,000 (including $4,000 executory costs) and are due on December 31 of each year. The first payment was made on December 31, 2003. Collectibility of the remaining lease payments is reasonably assured, and Rhone-Metro has no material cost uncertainties. Western Soya's incremental borrowing rate is 12%. Western Soya knows the interest rate implicit in the lease payments is 10%. Both companies use straight-line depreciation.

Required:

1. Show how Rhone-Metro calculated the $104,000 annual rental payments.
2. How should this lease be classified (a) by Western Soya Co. (the lessee) and (b) by Rhone-Metro Industries (the lessor)? Why?
3. Prepare the appropriate entries for both Western Soya Co. and Rhone-Metro on December 31, 2003.
4. Prepare an amortization schedule(s) describing the pattern of interest over the lease term for the lessee and the lessor.
5. Prepare the appropriate entries for both Western Soya and Rhone-Metro on December 31, 2004 (the second rent payment and depreciation).
6. Prepare the appropriate entries for both Western Soya and Rhone-Metro on December 31, 2007, assuming the equipment is returned to Rhone-Metro and the actual residual value on that date is $1,500.

P 15–10

Bargain purchase option exercisable before lease term ends; executory costs; sales-type lease

Rhone-Metro Industries manufactures equipment that is sold or leased. On December 31, 2003, Rhone-Metro leased equipment to Western Soya Co. for a noncancelable stated lease term of four years ending December 31, 2007, at which time possession of the leased asset will revert back to Rhone-Metro. The equipment cost $300,000 to manufacture and has an expected useful life of six years. Its normal sales price is $365,760. The expected residual value of $25,000 at December 31, 2007, is not guaranteed. Western Soya Co. can exercise a bargain purchase option on December 30, 2006, at an option price of $10,000. Equal payments under the lease are $134,960 (including $4,000 annual executory costs) and are due on December 31 of each year. The first payment was made on December 31, 2003. Collectibility of the remaining lease payments is reasonably assured, and Rhone-Metro has no material cost uncertainties. Western Soya's incremental borrowing rate is 12%. Western Soya knows the interest rate implicit in the lease payments is 10%. Both companies use straight-line depreciation.

   Hint: A lease term ends for accounting purposes when an option becomes exercisable if it's expected to be exercised (i.e., a BPO).

Required:

1. Show how Rhone-Metro calculated the $134,960 annual rental payments.
2. How should this lease be classified (a) by Western Soya Co. (the lessee) and (b) by Rhone-Metro Industries (the lessor)? Why?
3. Prepare the appropriate entries for both Western Soya Co. and Rhone-Metro on December 31, 2003.
4. Prepare an amortization schedule(s) describing the pattern of interest over the lease term for the lessee and the lessor.
5. Prepare the appropriate entries for both Western Soya and Rhone-Metro on December 31, 2004 (the second rent payment and depreciation).
6. Prepare the appropriate entries for both Western Soya and Rhone-Metro on December 30, 2006, assuming the BPO is exercised on that date.

P 15–11

Operating lease to lessee—nonoperating lease to lessor

Allied Industries manufactures high performance conveyers that often are leased to industrial customers. On December 31, 2003, Allied leased a conveyer to Poole Carrier Corporation for a three-year period ending December 31, 2006, at which time possession of the leased asset will revert back to Allied. Equal payments under the lease are $200,000 and are due on December 31 of each year. The first payment was made on December 31, 2003. Collectibility of the remaining lease payments is reasonably assured, and Allied has no material cost uncertainties. The conveyer cost $450,000 to manufacture and has an expected useful life of six years. Its normal sales price is $659,805. The expected residual value of $150,000 at December 31, 2006, is guaranteed by United Assurance Group. Poole Carrier's incremental borrowing rate and the interest rate implicit in the lease payments are 10%.

Required:

1. Show how Allied Industries calculated the $200,000 annual rental payments.
2. How should this lease be classified (a) by Allied (the lessor) and (b) by Poole (the lessee)? Why?
3. Prepare the appropriate entries for both Poole and Allied on December 31, 2003.
4. Prepare an amortization schedule(s) describing the pattern of interest over the lease term.
5. Prepare the appropriate entries for both Poole and Allied on December 31, 2004, 2005, and 2006, assuming the conveyer is returned to Allied at the end of the lease and the actual residual value on that date is $105,000.

P 15–12

Lease concepts; direct financing leases; guaranteed and unguaranteed residual value

Each of the four independent situations below describes a direct financing lease in which annual rental payments of $10,000 are payable at the beginning of each year. Each is a capital lease for the lessee. Determine the following amounts at the inception of the lease:

A. The lessor's:
   1. Minimum lease payments
   2. Gross investment in the lease
   3. Net investment in the lease
   4. Unearned interest revenue
B. The lessee's:
   5. Minimum lease payments
   6. Leased asset
   7. Lease liability

	Situation			
	1	**2**	**3**	**4**
Lease term (years)	4	4	4	4
Asset's useful life (years)	4	5	5	5
Lessor's implicit rate (known by lessee)	11%	11%	11%	11%
Lessee's incremental borrowing rate	11%	12%	11%	12%
Residual value:				
Guaranteed by lessee	0	$4,000	0	0
Guaranteed by third party	0	0	$4,000	0
Unguaranteed	0	0	0	$4,000

P 15–13

Lease concepts

Four independent situations are described below. For each, annual rental payments of $100,000 (not including any executory costs paid by lessor) are payable at the beginning of each year. Each is a nonoperating lease for both the lessor and lessee. Determine the following amounts at the inception of the lease:

A. The lessor's:
   1. Minimum lease payments
   2. Gross investment in the lease
   3. Net investment in the lease
   4. Unearned interest revenue
   5. Sales revenue
   6. Cost of goods sold
   7. Dealer's profit
B. The lessee's:
   8. Minimum lease payments
   9. Leased asset
   10. Lease liability

	Situation			
	1	**2**	**3**	**4**
Lease term (years)	4	5	6	4
Lessor's cost	$369,175	$433,809	$500,000	$400,000
Asset's useful life (years)	6	7	7	5
Lessor's implicit rate (known by lessee)	10%	12%	9%	10%
Lessee's incremental borrowing rate	9%	10%	11%	12%
Residual value:				
Guaranteed by lessee	0	$ 53,000	$ 40,000	$ 60,000
Guaranteed by third party*	0	0	0	$ 50,000
Unguaranteed	$ 30,000	0	$ 35,000	$ 40,000
Executory costs paid annually by lessor	$ 1,000	$ 8,000	$ 5,000	$ 10,000

*Over and above any amount guaranteed by the lessee (after a deductible equal to any amount guaranteed by the lessee).

P 15–14

Executory costs; lessor and lessee

Branif Leasing leases mechanical equipment to industrial consumers under direct financing leases that earn Branif a 10% rate of return for providing long-term financing. A lease agreement with Branson Construction specified 20 annual payments of $100,000 beginning December 31, 2002, the inception of the lease. The estimated useful life of the leased equipment is 20 years with no residual value. Its cost to Branif was $936,500. The lease qualifies as a capital lease to Branson. Maintenance of the equipment was contracted for through a 20-year service agreement with Midway Service Company requiring 20 annual payments of $3,000 beginning December 31, 2002. Both companies use straight-line depreciation.

Required:

Prepare the appropriate entries for both the lessee and lessor to record the second lease payment and depreciation on December 31, 2003, under each of three independent assumptions:

1. The lessee pays executory costs as incurred.
2. The contract specifies that the lessor pays executory costs as incurred. The lessee's rental payments were increased to $103,000 to include an amount sufficient to reimburse these costs.
3. The contract specifies that the lessor pays executory costs as incurred. The lessee's rental payments were increased to $103,300 to include an amount sufficient to reimburse these costs plus a 10% management fee for Branif.

P 15–15
Sales-type lease;
bargain purchase
option exercisable
before lease term
ends; lessor and lessee

Mid-South Auto Leasing leases vehicles to consumers. The attraction to customers is that the company can offer competitive prices due to volume buying and requires an interest rate implicit in the lease that is one percent below alternate methods of financing. On September 30, 2003, the company leased a delivery truck to a local florist, Anything Grows.

The lease agreement specified quarterly payments of $3,000 beginning September 30, 2003, the inception of the lease, and each quarter (December 31, March 31, and June 30) through June 30, 2006 (three-year lease term). The florist had the option to purchase the truck on September 29, 2005, for $6,000 when it was expected to have a residual value of $10,000. The estimated useful life of the truck is four years. Mid-South Auto Leasing's quarterly interest rate for determining payments was 3% (approximately 12% annually). Mid-South paid $25,000 for the truck. Both companies use straight-line depreciation. Anything Grows' incremental interest rate is 12%.

Hint: A lease term ends for accounting purposes when an option becomes exercisable if it's expected to be exercised (i.e., a BPO).

Required:

1. Calculate the amount of dealer's profit that Mid-South would recognize in this sales-type lease. (Be careful to note that, although payments occur on the last calendar day of each quarter, since the first payment was at the inception of the lease, payments represent an annuity due.)
2. Prepare the appropriate entries for Anything Grows and Mid-South on September 30, 2003.
3. Prepare an amortization schedule(s) describing the pattern of interest expense for Anything Grows and interest revenue for Mid-South Auto Leasing over the lease term.
4. Prepare the appropriate entries for Anything Grows and Mid-South Auto Leasing on December 31, 2003.
5. Prepare the appropriate entries for Anything Grows and Mid-South on September 29, 2005, assuming the bargain purchase option was exercised on that date.

P 15–16
Lessee-guaranteed
residual value; third-
party-guaranteed
residual value;
unguaranteed residual
value; executory costs;
different interest rates
for lessor and lessee

On December 31, 2002, Yard Art Landscaping leased a delivery truck from Branch Motors. Branch paid $40,000 for the truck. Its retail value is $45,114.

The lease agreement specified annual payments of $11,000 beginning December 31, 2002, the inception of the lease, and at each December 31 through 2005. Branch Motors' interest rate for determining payments was 10%. At the end of the four-year lease term (December 31, 2006) the truck was expected to be worth $15,000. The estimated useful life of the truck is five years with no salvage value. Both companies use straight-line depreciation.

Yard Art guaranteed a residual value of $6,000. Guarantor Assurance Corporation was engaged to guarantee a residual value of $11,000, but with a deductible equal to any amount paid by the lessee ($11,000 reduced by any amount paid by the lessee). Yard Art's incremental borrowing rate is 9%.

A $1,000 per year maintenance agreement was arranged for the truck with an outside service firm. As an expediency, Branch Motors agreed to pay this fee. It is, however, reflected in the $11,000 rental payments.

Collectibility of the rent payments by Yard Arts is reasonably predictable and there are no costs to the lessor that are yet to be incurred.

Required:

1. How should this lease be classified by Yard Art Landscaping (the lessee)? Why?
2. Calculate the amount Yard Arts Landscaping would record as a leased asset and a lease liability.
3. How should this lease be classified by Branch Motors (the lessor)? Why?
4. Show how Branch Motors calculated the $11,000 annual rental payments.
5. Calculate the amount Branch Motors would record as sales revenue.
6. Prepare the appropriate entries for both Yard Arts and Branch Motors on December 31, 2002.
7. Prepare an amortization schedule that describes the pattern of interest expense over the lease term for Yard Arts.
8. Prepare an amortization schedule that describes the pattern of interest revenue over the lease term for Branch Motors.

9. Prepare the appropriate entries for both Yard Arts and Branch Motors on December 31, 2003.
10. Prepare the appropriate entries for both Yard Arts and Branch Motors on December 31, 2005 (the final rent payment).
11. Prepare the appropriate entries for both Yard Arts and Branch Motors on December 31, 2006 (the end of the lease term), assuming the truck is returned to the lessor and the actual residual value of the truck was $4,000 on that date.

P 15–17
Initial direct costs;
direct financing lease

Bidwell Leasing purchased a single-engine plane for its fair market value of $645,526 and leased it to Red Baron Flying Club on December 31, 2002.

Terms of the lease agreement and related facts were:

a. Eight annual payments of $110,000 beginning December 31, 2002, the inception of the lease, and at each December 31 through 2009. Bidwell Leasing's implicit interest rate was 10%. The estimated useful life of the plane is eight years. Payments were calculated as follows:

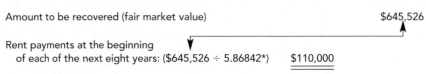

Amount to be recovered (fair market value) $645,526

Rent payments at the beginning
   of each of the next eight years: ($645,526 ÷ 5.86842*) $110,000

*Present value of an annuity due of $1: n = 8, i = 10%.

b. Red Baron's incremental borrowing rate is 11%.
c. Costs of negotiating and consummating the completed lease transaction incurred by Bidwell Leasing were $18,099.
d. Collectibility of the rent payments by Bidwell Leasing is reasonably predictable and there are no costs to the lessor that are yet to be incurred.

Required:
1. How should this lease be classified (a) by Bidwell Leasing (the lessor) and (b) by Red Baron (the lessee)?
2. Prepare the appropriate entries for both Red Baron Flying Club and Bidwell Leasing on December 31, 2002.
3. Prepare an amortization schedule that describes the pattern of interest expense over the lease term for Red Baron Flying Club.
4. Determine the effective rate of interest for Bidwell Leasing for the purpose of recognizing interest revenue over the lease term.
5. Prepare an amortization schedule that describes the pattern of interest revenue over the lease term for Bidwell Leasing.
6. Prepare the appropriate entries for both Red Baron and Bidwell Leasing on December 31, 2003 (the second rent payment). Both companies use straight-line depreciation.
7. Prepare the appropriate entries for both Red Baron and Bidwell Leasing on December 31, 2009 (the final rent payment).

P 15–18
Initial direct costs;
sales-type lease

(Note: This problem is a variation of the preceding problem, modified to cause the lease to be a sales-type lease.)

Bidwell Leasing purchased a single-engine plane for $400,000 and leased it to Red Baron Flying Club for its fair market value of $645,526 on December 31, 2002.

Terms of the lease agreement and related facts were:

a. Eight annual payments of $110,000 beginning December 31, 2002, the inception of the lease, and at each December 31 through 2009. Bidwell Leasing's implicit interest rate was 10%. The estimated useful life of the plane is eight years. Payments were calculated as follows:

Amount to be recovered (fair market value) $645,526

Rent payments at the beginning
   of each of the next eight years: ($645,526 ÷ 5.86842*) $110,000

*Present value of an annuity due of $1: n = 8, i = 10%.

b. Red Baron's incremental borrowing rate is 11%.
c. Costs of negotiating and consummating the completed lease transaction incurred by Bidwell Leasing were $18,099.
d. Collectibility of the rent payments by Bidwell Leasing is reasonably predictable and there are no costs to the lessor that are yet to be incurred.

Required:
1. How should this lease be classified (a) by Bidwell Leasing (the lessor) and (b) by Red Baron (the lessee)?
2. Prepare the appropriate entries for both Red Baron Flying Club and Bidwell Leasing on December 31, 2002.
3. Prepare an amortization schedule that describes the pattern of interest expense over the lease term for Red Baron Flying Club.
4. Prepare the appropriate entries for both Red Baron and Bidwell Leasing on December 31, 2003 (the second rent payment). Both companies use straight-line depreciation.
5. Prepare the appropriate entries for both Red Baron and Bidwell Leasing on December 31, 2009 (the final rent payment).

P 15–19
Sale-leaseback

To raise operating funds, North American Courier Corporation sold its building on January 1, 2003, to an insurance company for $500,000 and immediately leased the building back. The lease is for a 10-year period ending December 31, 2012, at which time ownership of the building will revert to North American Courier. The building has a carrying amount of $400,000 (original cost $1,000,000). The lease requires North American to make payments of $88,492 to the insurance company each December 31. The building had a total original useful life of 30 years with no residual value and is being depreciated on a straight-line basis. The lease has an implicit rate of 12%.

Required:
1. Prepare the appropriate entries for North American on (a) January 1, 2003, to record the sale-leaseback and (b) December 31, 2003, to record necessary adjustments.
2. Show how North American's December 31, 2003, balance sheet and income statement would reflect the sale-leaseback.

P 15–20
Real estate lease; land and building

On January 1, 2003, Cook Textiles leased a building with two acres of land from Peck Development. The lease is for 10 years. No purchase option exists and the property will revert to Peck at the end of the lease. The building and land combined have a fair market value on January 1, 2003, of $1,450,000 and the building has an estimated life of 20 years with a residual value of $150,000. The lease calls for Cook to assume all costs of ownership and to make annual payments of $200,000 due at the beginning of each year. On January 1, 2003, the estimated value of the land was $400,000. Cook uses the straight-line method of depreciation and pays 10% interest on borrowed money. Peck's implicit rate is unknown.

Required:
1. Prepare journal entries for Cook Textiles for 2003. Assume the land could be rented without the building for $59,000 each year.
2. Assuming the land had a fair market value on January 1, 2003, of $200,000 and could be rented alone for $30,000, prepare journal entries for Cook Textiles for 2003.

BROADEN YOUR PERSPECTIVE

Apply your critical-thinking ability to the knowledge you've gained. These cases will provide you an opportunity to develop your research, analysis, judgment, and communication skills. You also will work with other students, integrate what you've learned, apply it in real world situations, and consider its global and ethical ramifications. This practice will broaden your knowledge and further develop your decision-making abilities.

Analysis Case 15–1
Reporting leases; off-balance-sheet financing

FedEx Corporation

Refer to the financial statements and related disclosure notes of FedEx Corporation in the appendix to Chapter 1. Management's Discussion and Analysis states that "Generally, management's practice in recent years with respect to funding new aircraft acquisitions has been to finance such aircraft through long-term lease transactions that qualify as off-balance-sheet operating leases under applicable accounting rules."

Required:
1. What does FedEx's management mean when it says some leases "qualify as off-balance-sheet" financing?
2. See Note 5 in the disclosure notes. What is FedEx's capital lease liability?

3. If the operating leases were capitalized, approximately how much would that increase the capital lease liability?
4. What effect would that have on the company's debt-equity ratio?

Research Case 15–2
Locate and extract relevant information and authoritative support for a financial reporting issue; capital lease; sublease of a leased asset

"I don't see that in my intermediate accounting text I saved from college," you explain to another member of the accounting division of Dowell Chemical Corporation. "This will take some research." Your comments pertain to the appropriate accounting treatment of a proposed sublease of warehouses Dowell has used for product storage.

Dowell leased the warehouses one year ago on December 31. The five-year lease agreement called for Dowell to make quarterly lease payments of $2,398,303, payable each December 31, March 31, June 30, and September 30, with the first payment at the lease's inception. As a capital lease, Dowell had recorded the leased asset and liability at $40 million, the present value of the lease payments at 8%. Dowell records depreciation on a straight-line basis at the end of each fiscal year.

Today, Jason True, Dowell's controller, explained a proposal to sublease the underused warehouses to American Tankers, Inc. for the remaining four years of the lease term. American Tankers would be substituted as lessee under the original lease agreement. As the new lessee, it would become the primary obligor under the agreement, but Dowell would be secondarily liable for fulfilling the obligations under the lease agreement. Indications are that it would be reasonably possible, though not likely, that American Tankers would default and Dowell would be required to fulfill those obligations. "Check on how we would need to account for this and get back to me," he had said.

Required:
1. After the first full year under the warehouse lease, what is the balance in Dowell's lease liability? An amortization schedule will be helpful in determining this amount.
2. After the first full year under the warehouse lease, what is the carrying amount (after accumulated depreciation) of Dowell's leased warehouses?
3. Obtain the original FASB Standard on accounting for leases. You might gain access through FARS, the FASB Financial Accounting Research System, from your school library, or some other source. Determine the appropriate accounting treatment for the proposed sublease. What is the specific citation that Dowell would rely on in applying that accounting treatment?
4. What, if any, journal entry would Dowell record in connection with the sublease?
5. What, if any, disclosure would Dowell provide in its financial statements in connection with the sublease? Why?

Communication Case 15–3
Classification issues; lessee accounting; group interaction

Interstate Automobiles Corporation leased 40 vans to VIP Transport under a four-year noncancelable lease on December 30, 2002. Information concerning the lease and the vans follows:

a. Equal annual lease payments of $300,000 are due on December 31 each year. The first payment was made December 31, 2002. Interstate's implicit interest rate is 10% and known by VIP.
b. VIP has the option to purchase all of the vans at the end of the lease for a total of $290,000. The vans' estimated residual value is $300,000 at the end of the lease term and $50,000 at the end of 7 years, the estimated life of each van.
c. VIP estimates the fair value of the vans to be $1,240,000. Interstate's cost was $1,050,000.
d. VIP's incremental borrowing rate is 11%.
e. VIP will pay the executory costs (maintenance, insurance, and other fees not included in the annual lease payments) of $1,000 per year. The depreciation method is straight-line.
f. The collectibility of the lease payments is reasonably predictable, and there are no important cost uncertainties.

Your instructor will divide the class into from two to six groups depending on the size of the class. The mission of your group is to assess the proper recording and reporting of the lease described.

Required:
1. Each group member should deliberate the situation independently and draft a tentative argument prior to the class session for which the case is assigned.
2. In class, each group will meet for 10 to 15 minutes in different areas of the classroom. During that meeting, group members will take turns sharing their suggestions for the purpose of arriving at a single group treatment.
3. After the allotted time, a spokesperson for each group (selected during the group meetings) will share the group's solution with the class. The goal of the class is to incorporate the views of each group into a consensus approach to the situation.
   Specifically, you should address:
   a. Identify potential advantages to VIP of leasing the vans rather than purchasing them.
   b. How should the lease be classified by VIP? by Interstate?

c.   Regardless of your response to previous requirements, suppose VIP recorded the lease on December 31, 2002, as a capital lease in the amount of $1,100,000. What would be the appropriate journal entries related to the capital lease for the second lease payment on December 31, 2003?

International Case 15–4
Comparison of lease accounting in the U.K. and the United States

One of the world's largest petroleum and petrochemical groups is the British Petroleum Company p.l.c. (BP), based in London. Lease disclosures accompanying BP's 1993 financial statements are reproduced below:

Accounting Policies (in part)
Leases

Assets held under leases which result in group companies receiving substantially all risks and rewards of ownership (finance leases) are capitalized as tangible fixed assets at the estimated present value of underlying lease payments. The corresponding finance lease obligation is included with borrowings. Rentals under operating leases are charged against income as incurred.

Note 24: Finance Debt (in part)	(£ million)	
Obligations under Finance Leases	**1993**	**1992**
Minimum future lease payments payable within:		
1 year	99	81
2 to 5 years	491	487
Thereafter	3,286	3,591
	3,876	4,159
Less finance charges	2,581	2,836
Net obligations	1,295	1,323

Required:
On the basis of the information the disclosures provide, compare lessee accounting for leases in the United Kingdom with that in the United States.

Judgment Case 15–5
Debt equivalent of operating leases

At December 31, 2000, American Airlines had 201 jet aircraft under operating leases and 65 aircraft under capital leases. Lease disclosures accompanying American's 2000 financial statements are reproduced below:

---

5. Leases

American leases various types of equipment and property, including aircraft, passenger terminals, equipment and various other facilities. The future minimum lease payments required under capital leases, together with the present value of net minimum lease payments, and future minimum lease payments required under operating leases that have initial or remaining noncancelable lease terms in excess of one year as of December 31, 2000, were (in millions):

Year Ending Dec. 31	Capital Leases	Operating Leases
2001	$ 280	$ 950
2002	236	898
2003	154	910
2004	206	893
2005	135	880
2006 and subsequent	835	11,268
	1,846[1]	$15,799[2]
Less amount representing interest	482	
Present value of net minimum lease payments	$1,364	

(1) Future minimum payments required under capital leases include $191 million guaranteed by AMR relating to special facility revenue bonds issued by municipalities.
(2) Future minimum payments required under operating leases include $6.4 billion guaranteed by AMR relating to special facility revenue bonds issued by municipalities.

American's capital lease liability is reported among other debt on the balance sheet. The company's debt to equity ratio is 2.6, calculated as $16,726/$6,435. Some analysts might consider operating lease commitments as equivalent to debt when assessing financial risk. If American's operating leases were considered capital leases, lease payments would be capitalized at the present value of all future payments.

Required:

1. If the interest rate used by American to discount rental payments on capital leases is 12% and rentals after 2005 are payable approximately evenly over the following 13 years (approximated as $11,268 ÷ $880), what is the debt equivalent of the operating lease commitments?
2. If operating lease commitments are considered equivalent to debt, what is American's debt to equity ratio?

Real World Case 15–6
Lease concepts

Safeway, Inc., is one of the world's largest food retailers, operating 1,688 stores in the United States and Canada. Approximately two-thirds of the premises that the company occupies are leased. 2000 financial statements and disclosure notes revealed the following information:

Balance Sheet
($ in millions)

	2000	1999
Assets		
Property:		
Property under capital lease	$586.5	$591.4
Less: Accumulated amortization	(132.2)	(132.3)
Liabilities		
Current liabilities:		
Current obligations under capital leases	47.0	41.8
Long-term debt:		
Obligation under capital leases	415.8	435.4

Amortization expense for property under capital leases was $43.9 million in 2000.

Required:

1. Discuss some possible reasons why Safeway leases rather than purchases most of its premises.
2. The net asset "property under capital lease" has a 2000 balance of $454.3 million ($586.5 − 132.2). Liabilities for capital leases total $462.8 ($47.0 + 415.8). Why do the asset and liability amounts differ?
3. Prepare a 2001 summary entry to record its $95.6 million in rental payments.
4. Assuming that all property under capital lease is depreciated over the life of the lease, what is the average life of Safeway's capital leases?
5. What is the approximate average interest rate on Safeway's capital leases?

Ethics Case 15–7
Leasehold
improvements

American Movieplex, a large movie theater chain, leases most of its theater facilities. In conjunction with recent operating leases, the company spent $28 million for seats and carpeting. The question being discussed over breakfast on Wednesday morning was the length of the depreciation period for these leasehold improvements. The company controller, Sarah Keene, was surprised by the suggestion of Larry Person, her new assistant.

Keene: Why 25 years? We've never depreciated leasehold improvements for such a long period.
Person: I noticed that in my review of back records. But during our expansion to the Midwest, we don't need expenses to be any higher than necessary.
Keene: But isn't that a pretty rosy estimate of these assets' actual life? Trade publications show an average depreciation period of 12 years.

Required:

1. How would increasing the depreciation period affect American Movieplex's income?
2. Does revising the estimate pose an ethical dilemma?
3. Who would be affected if Person's suggestion is followed?

Research Case 15–8
Researching lease
disclosures; retrieving
information from the
Internet

EDGAR, the Electronic Data Gathering, Analysis, and Retrieval system, performs automated collection, validation, indexing, acceptance, and forwarding of submissions by companies and others who are required by law to file forms with the U.S. Securities and Exchange Commission (SEC). All publicly traded domestic companies use EDGAR to make the majority of their filings. (Some foreign companies do so voluntarily.) Form 10-K which includes the annual report, is required to be filed on EDGAR. The SEC makes this information available on the Internet.

Required:

1. Access EDGAR on the Internet using EdgarScan at: **edgarscan.pwcglobal.com**.
2. Search for a company with which you are familiar and which you believe leases some of its facilities. (Retail firms and airlines are good candidates). Access the company's most recent 10-K filing. Search or scroll to find the financial statements and related notes.
3. From the disclosure notes, determine the total capital lease obligation of the firm. What percentage does this represent of total liabilities (including current liabilities and deferred taxes) reported on the balance sheet?
4. Compare the company's rental commitments over the next five years and beyond five years for capital leases and operating leases. If operating leases were capitalized, would the company's reported debt change significantly?
5. Repeat steps 2–4 for another firm in the same industry. Are leasing practices similar between the two firms?

Real World Case 15–9
Sale-leaseback; FedEx

FedEx Corporation, the world's largest express transportation company, leases much of its aircraft, land, facilities, and equipment. A portion of those leases are part of sale and leaseback arrangements. An excerpt from FedEx's 2001 disclosure notes describes the company's handling of gains from those arrangements:

> **Deferred Gains.** Gains on the sale and leaseback of aircraft and other property and equipment are deferred and amortized ratably over the life of the lease as a reduction of rent expense. Included in other liabilities at May 31, 2001 and 2000 were deferred gains of $511,932,000 and $533,371,000, respectively.

Required:

1. Why should companies defer gains from sale-leaseback arrangements?
2. Based on the information provided in the disclosure note, determine whether the leases in the leaseback portion of the arrangements are considered by FedEx to be capital leases or operating leases. Explain.

Communication Case 15–10
Where's the gain?

General Tools is seeking ways to maintain and improve cash balances. As company controller, you have proposed the sale and leaseback of much of the company's equipment. As seller-lessee, General Tools would retain the right to essentially all of the remaining use of the equipment. The term of the lease would be six years. A gain would result on the sale portion of the transaction. The lease portion would be classified appropriately as a capital lease.

You previously convinced your CFO of the cash flow benefits of the arrangement, but now he doesn't understand the way you will account for the transaction. "I really had counted on that gain to bolster this period's earnings. What gives?" he wondered. "Put it in a memo, will you? I'm having trouble following what you're saying to me."

Required:
Write a memo to your CFO. Include discussion of each of these points:

1. How the sale portion of the sale-leaseback transaction should be accounted for at the lease's inception.
2. How the gain on the sale portion of the sale-leaseback transaction should be accounted for during the lease.
3. How the leaseback portion of the sale-leaseback transaction should be accounted for at the lease's inception.
4. The conceptual basis for capitalizing certain long-term leases.

Trueblood Case 15–11
Lease incentives

The following Trueblood case is recommended for use with this chapter. The case provides an excellent opportunity for class discussion, group projects, and writing assignments. The case, along with Professor's Discussion Material, can be obtained from the Deloitte Foundation at its website: **www.deloitte.com/more/DTF/cases_subj.htm**.

Case 00-6: *Who's Paying the Rent?*
This case gives students the opportunity to use their judgment in evaluating lease accounting alternatives when retailers receive lease incentives from a lessor.

16

Accounting for Income Taxes

CHAPTER

OVERVIEW

In this chapter we explore the financial accounting and reporting standards for the effects of income taxes. The discussion defines and illustrates temporary differences, which are the basis for recognizing deferred tax assets and deferred tax liabilities, as well as nontemporary differences, which have no deferred tax consequences. You will learn how to adjust deferred tax assets and deferred tax liabilities when tax laws or rates change. We also discuss accounting for operating loss carrybacks and carryforwards and intraperiod tax allocation.

LEARNING OBJECTIVES

After studying this chapter, you should be able to:

LO1 Describe the types of temporary differences that cause deferred tax liabilities and determine the amounts needed to record periodic income taxes.

LO2 Identify and describe the types of temporary differences that cause deferred tax assets.

LO3 Describe when and how a valuation allowance is recorded for deferred tax assets.

LO4 Explain why nontemporary differences have no deferred tax consequences.

LO5 Explain how a change in tax rates affects the measurement of deferred tax amounts.

LO6 Determine income tax amounts when multiple temporary differences exist.

LO7 Describe when and how an operating loss carryforward and an operating loss carryback are recognized in the financial statements.

LO8 Explain how deferred tax assets and deferred tax liabilities are classified and reported in a classified balance sheet and describe related disclosures.

LO9 Explain intraperiod tax allocation.

What's the Difference?

The board of directors for Times-Lehrer Industries is meeting for the first time since Laura Lynn was asked to join the board. Laura was the director of the regional office of United Charities. Although she has broad experience with the tax advantages of charitable giving and the vast array of investment vehicles available to donors, her 30 years of experience with not-for-profit organizations has not exposed her to the issues involved with corporate taxation. This gap in her considerable business knowledge causes her to turn to you, Times-Lehrer's CFO and long-time friend, who recommended Laura for appointment to the board.

"I must say," Laura confided, "I've looked long and hard at these statements, and I can't quite grasp why the amount reported for income tax expense is not the same as the amount of income taxes we paid. What's the difference?"

> By the time you finish this chapter, you should be able to respond appropriately to the questions posed in this case. Compare your response to the solution provided at the end of the chapter.

QUESTIONS

1. What's the difference? Explain to Laura how differences between financial reporting standards and income tax rules might cause the two tax amounts to differ. (page 778)

2. What is the conceptual advantage of determining income tax expense as we do? (page 778)

3. Are there differences between financial reporting standards and income tax rules that will not contribute to the difference between income tax expense and the amount of income taxes paid? (page 790)

PART

a

FINANCIAL REPORTING CASE

Q1, p. 777

DEFERRED TAX ASSETS AND DEFERRED TAX LIABILITIES

A manufacturer of leather accessories in the Midwest is obligated to pay the Internal Revenue Service $24 million in income taxes as determined by its 2003 income tax return. Another $9 million in income taxes also is attributable to 2003 activities. Conveniently, though, tax laws permit the company to defer paying the additional $9 million until subsequent tax years by reporting certain revenues and expenses on the tax return in years other than when reported on the income statement. Does the company have only a current income tax liability of $24 million? Or does it also have a deferred income tax liability for the other $9 million? To phrase the question differently: Should the company report a 2003 income tax expense of the $24 million tax payable for the current year, or $33 million to include the future tax effects of events already recognized? For perspective on this question, we should look closer at the circumstances that might create the situation. Such circumstances are called *temporary differences*.

Conceptual Underpinning

FINANCIAL REPORTING CASE

Q2, p. 777

The goals of financial accounting and tax accounting are not the same.

When a company prepares its tax return for a particular year, the revenues and expenses (and losses) included on the return are, by and large, the same as those reported on the company's income statement for the same year. However, in some instances tax laws and financial accounting standards differ. The reason they differ is that the fundamental objectives of financial reporting and those of taxing authorities are not the same. Financial accounting standards are established to provide useful information to investors and creditors. Congress, through the Internal Revenue Service, on the other hand, is primarily concerned with raising public revenues in a socially acceptable manner and, frequently, with influencing the behavior of taxpayers. In pursuing the latter objective, Congress uses tax laws to encourage activities it deems desirable, such as investment in productive assets, and to discourage activities it deems undesirable, such as violations of law.

Accounting for income taxes is consistent with the accrual concept of accounting.

A consequence of differences between GAAP and tax rules is that tax payments frequently occur in years different from when the revenues and expenses that cause the taxes are generated. The financial reporting issue is *when* the tax expense should be recognized. The issue has generated considerable controversy for decades. In 1967 the profession, through *APB 11*, embraced the concept of reporting income tax expense in the same period as events that give rise to the expense, regardless of when the tax actually is paid.[1] You may recognize this approach as being consistent with the accrual concept of accounting. The primary focus of that pronouncement was the matching principle. Income tax expense was calculated on the basis of pretax income reported on the income statement. Differences between the expense and the tax currently paid were reported on the balance sheet not as deferred tax liabilities (or assets) but as nebulous deferred credits (or debits).[2]

APB 11 focused on the income statement and the matching principle.

APB 11 was replaced in 1987 by *SFAS 96*, which reiterated the objective of reporting deferred taxes but redirected the focus to an asset-liability approach.[3] This balance sheet focus emphasizes reporting the future tax sacrifice or benefit attributable to temporary differences between the reported amount of an asset or liability in the financial statements and its tax basis.[4] Plagued by implementation complexities, *SFAS 96* was delayed three times and then replaced in 1992 with *SFAS 109* before ever becoming mandatory.[5] The current standard modified some of the more troublesome measurement and recognition requirements but retained the essential flavor of *SFAS 96*. That is, the objective of accounting for income taxes is to recognize a deferred tax liability or deferred tax asset for the tax consequences of amounts that will become taxable or deductible in future years as a result of transactions or

SFAS 109 focuses on the balance sheet and the recognition of liabilities and assets.

---

[1]"Accounting for Income Taxes," *Accounting Principles Board Opinion No. 11* (New York: AICPA, 1967).
[2]Some critics at the time referred to these amounts as "UGOs: Unidentified Growing Objects."
[3]"Accounting for Income Taxes," *Statement of Financial Accounting Standards No. 96,* (Stamford, Conn.: FASB, 1987).
[4]Research supports the notion that deferred tax liabilities are, in fact, viewed by investors as real liabilities.
[5]"Accounting for Income Taxes," *Statement of Financial Accounting Standards No. 109* (Norwalk, Conn.: FASB, 1992).

events that already have occurred. Future taxable amounts and future deductible amounts arise as a result of temporary differences. We discuss those now.

Temporary Differences

The differences in the rules for computing taxable income and those for financial reporting often cause amounts to be included in taxable income in a year later—or earlier—than the year in which they are recognized for financial reporting purposes, or not to be included in taxable income at all. For example, you learned in Chapter 4 that income from selling properties on an installment basis is reported for financial reporting purposes in the year of the sale. But tax laws permit installment income to be reported on the tax return as it actually is received (by the installment method). This means taxable income might be less than accounting income in the year of an installment sale but higher than accounting income in later years when installment income is collected.

LO1

The situation just described creates what's referred to as a **temporary difference** between pretax *accounting* income and *taxable* income and, consequently, between the reported amount of an asset or liability in the financial statements and its tax basis. In our example, the asset for which the temporary difference exists is the installment receivable that's recognized for financial reporting purposes, but not for tax purposes.

CHECK WITH THE **COACH**

Merging the worlds of income taxation and financial reporting raises conceptual and practical problems for accountants and accounting students. One of the challenging topics for intermediate accounting students is accounting for deferred income taxes. In studying this chapter, check with the Coach to see some animated illustrations of deferred income tax situations. This should boost your confidence when tackling this complex topic. ■

Deferred Tax Liabilities

It's important to understand that a temporary difference *originates* in one period and *reverses,* or turns around, in one or more subsequent periods. The temporary difference described above originates in the year the installment sales are made and are reported on the *income statement* and then reverses when the installments are collected and income is reported on the *tax return.* An example is provided in Illustration 16–1.

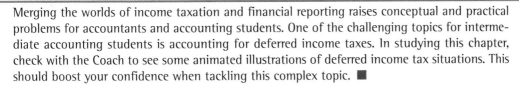

Kent Land Management reported pretax income in 2003, 2004, and 2005 of $100 million, plus additional 2003 income of $40 million from installment sales of property. However, the installment sales income is reported on the tax return when collected, in 2004 ($10 million) and 2005 ($30 million).* The enacted tax rate is 40% each year.[†]

($ in millions)

| | Temporary Difference | | | |
| | Originates | Reverses | | |
	2003	**2004**	**2005**	**Total**
Accounting income	$140	$100	$100	$340
Installment sale income on the income statement	(40)	0	0	(40)
Installment sale income on the tax return	0	10	30	40
Taxable income	$100	$110	$130	$340

ILLUSTRATION 16–1

Revenue Reported on the Tax Return after the Income Statement

In 2003, taxable income is less than accounting income because income from installment sales is not reported on the tax return until 2004–2005.

*The installment method is not available to accrual method taxpayers. H.R. 1180, sec. 536, 1999.
[†]The enacted rate refers to the tax rate indicated by currently enacted tax legislation (as distinguished from anticipated legislation). This is discussed later in the chapter.

Notice that accounting income and taxable income total the same amount over the three-year period but are different in each individual year. In 2003, taxable income is $40 million *less* than accounting income because it does not include income from installment sales. The difference is temporary, though. That situation reverses over the next two years. In 2004 and 2005 taxable income is *more* than accounting income because income on the installment sales, reported on the income statement in 2003, becomes taxable during the next two years as installments are collected.

Because tax laws permit the company to delay reporting this income as part of taxable income, the company is able to defer paying the tax on that income. The tax is not avoided, just deferred. In the meantime, the company has a liability for the income tax deferred. The liability originates in 2003 and is paid over the next two years as follows:

Deferred Tax Liability

($ in millions)			
		16	2003 ($40 × 40%)
2004 ($10 × 40%)	4		
2005 ($30 × 40%)	12		
		0	Balance after 3 years

<table>
<tr><td></td><td>Deferred Tax Liability</td></tr>
</table>

The 2003 tax liability is paid in the next two years.

At the end of 2003, financial and taxable income for 2004 and 2005 are, of course, not yet known. We assumed knowledge of that information above so we could compare the three-year effect of the temporary difference, but seeing the future is unnecessary to determine amounts needed to record income taxes in 2003. This is demonstrated in Illustration 16–1A.

ILLUSTRATION 16–1A

Determining and Recording Income Taxes—2003

($ in millions)

	Current Year 2003	Future Taxable Amounts 2004	Future Taxable Amounts 2005	Future Taxable Amounts (total)
Accounting income	$140			
Temporary difference:				
Installment income	(40)	$10	$30	$40
Taxable income	$100			
Enacted tax rate	40%			40%
Tax payable currently	$ 40			
Deferred tax liability				$16

Deferred Tax Liability

Desired ending balance	$16
Less: Beginning balance	0
Change in balance	$16

Journal Entry at the End of 2003

Income tax expense (to balance)	56	
Income tax payable (determined above)		40
Deferred tax liability (determined above)		16

With future taxable amounts of $40 million, taxable at 40%, a $16 million deferred tax liability is indicated. Since no previous balance exists, this amount is added to the liability.

Each year, income tax expense comprises both the current and the deferred tax consequences of events and transactions already recognized. This means we:

1. Calculate the income tax that is payable currently.
2. Separately calculate the change in the deferred tax liability (or asset).
3. Combine the two to get the income tax expense.

Using the 2004 and 2005 income numbers, the journal entries to record income taxes those years would be:

2004	($ in millions)	
Income tax expense (to balance)	40	
Deferred tax liability [($30 million × 40%) − 16 million]	4	
Income tax payable ($110 million × 40%).		44
2005		
Income tax expense (to balance)	40	
Deferred tax liability ($0 million − 12 million)	12	
Income tax payable ($130 million × 40%).		52

At the end of 2004, the deferred tax liability should have a balance of $12 million. Because the balance from 2003 is $16 million, we reduce it by $4 million.

At the end of 2005, the deferred tax liability should have a balance of zero. So, we eliminate the $12 million balance.

THE FASB'S BALANCE SHEET APPROACH

Our perspective in this example so far has centered around the income effects of the install-ment sales and thus on the changes in the deferred tax liability as the temporary difference reverses. Another perspective is to consider the balance sheet effect. From this viewpoint, we regard a deferred tax liability (or asset) to be the tax effect of the temporary difference be-tween the *financial statement carrying amount* of an asset or liability and its *tax basis*. The tax basis of an asset or liability is its original value for tax purposes reduced by any amounts included to date on tax returns. In our example, a temporary book-tax difference exists for a receivable from installment sales that's recognized for financial reporting purposes but not for tax purposes. When a company sells something on an installment basis, it reports a re-ceivable. From a tax perspective, though, there is no receivable because a "taxable sale" doesn't occur until installments are collected. This is shown in Illustration 16–1B.

An installment receivable has no tax basis.

	December 31 ($ in millions)					
	2003		**2004**		**2005**	
Receivable from installment sales:						
Accounting basis	$40	$40	$(10)	$30	$(30)	$0
Tax basis	(0)	(0)	(0)	(0)	(0)	(0)
Temporary difference	$40	$40	$(10)	$30	$(30)	$0
Tax rate	↑	× 40%	↑	× 40%	↑	× 40%
Deferred tax liability		$16		$12		$0
	Originating Difference		Reversing Differences			

ILLUSTRATION 16–1B

Balance Sheet Perspective

The deferred tax liability each year is the tax rate times the temporary difference between the financial statement carrying amount of the receivable and its tax basis.

Of course, the income statement view and the balance sheet view are two different per-spectives on the very same event. In this example, we derive the same deferred tax liability whether we view it as a result of a temporary difference (a) between accounting and taxable income or (b) between the financial statement carrying amount of an installment receivable and its tax basis. Conceptually, though, the balance sheet approach strives to establish de-ferred tax assets and liabilities that meet the definitions of assets and liabilities provided by the FASB's conceptual framework. As specified by *SFAC 6*, assets represent "probable fu-ture economic benefits obtained or controlled by a particular entity as a result of past trans-actions or events," and liabilities are "probable future sacrifices of economic benefits as a result of past transactions or events."[6] In our example, the probable future sacrifices of eco-nomic benefits are the payments of $4 million in 2004 and $12 million in 2005. The past transactions or events resulting in the future tax payments are the installment sales in 2003.

SFAS 109 takes a balance sheet approach to establishing deferred tax assets and liabilities that meet the definitions of assets and liabilities provided by the FASB's conceptual framework.

---

[6]"Elements of Financial Statements," *Statement of Financial Accounting Concepts No. 6* (Stamford, Conn.: FASB, 1985), par. 25, 35.

TYPES OF TEMPORARY DIFFERENCES

Examples of temporary differences are provided in Graphic 16–1.

GRAPHIC 16–1
Types of Temporary
Differences

	Revenues (or gains)	**Expenses (or losses)**
Items reported on the tax return *after* the income statement	• Installment sales of property (installment method for taxes). • Unrealized gain from recording investments at fair value (taxable when asset is sold).	• Estimated expenses and losses (tax deductible when paid). • Unrealized loss from recording investments at fair value or inventory at LCM (tax deductible when asset is sold).
Items reported on the tax return *before* the income statement	• Rent collected in advance. • Subscriptions collected in advance. • Other revenue collected in advance.	• Accelerated depreciation on tax return (straight-line depreciation in the income statement). • Prepaid expenses (tax deductible when paid).

- The temporary differences shown in the diagonal purple areas create *deferred tax liabilities* because they result in *taxable* amounts in some future year(s) when the related assets are recovered or the related liabilities are settled (when the temporary differences reverse).
- The temporary differences in the opposite diagonal (blue) areas create *deferred tax assets* because they result in *deductible* amounts in some future year(s) when the related assets are recovered or the related liabilities are settled (when the temporary differences reverse).

ADDITIONAL CONSIDERATION

Temporary differences between the reported amount of an asset or liability in the financial statements and its tax basis are primarily caused by revenues, expenses, gains, and losses being included in taxable income in a year earlier or later than the year in which they are recognized for financial reporting purposes as illustrated in Graphic 16–1. Other events also can cause temporary differences between the reported amount of an asset or liability in the financial statements and its tax basis. Three other such events that are beyond the scope of this textbook are briefly described in "Accounting for Income Taxes," *Statement of Financial Accounting Standards No. 109* (Norwalk, Conn.: FASB, 1992), par. 11 e–h. Our discussions in this chapter focus on temporary differences caused by the timing of revenue and expense recognition, but it's important to realize that the concept of temporary differences embraces all differences that will result in taxable or deductible amounts in future years.

Be sure to notice that deferred tax liabilities can arise from either (a) a revenue being reported on the tax return after the income statement or (b) an expense being reported on the tax return before the income statement. Our previous illustration was of the first type. We look at the second in Illustration 16–2 at the top of page 783.

Notice, too, that this temporary difference originates during more than a single year before it begins to reverse. This usually is true when depreciation is the cause of the temporary difference. Tax laws typically permit the cost of a depreciable asset to be deducted on the tax return sooner than it is reported as depreciation on the income statement.[7] This means tax-

---

[7]Presently, the accelerated depreciation method prescribed by the tax code is the modified accelerated cost recovery system (MACRS). The method is described in Chapter 11.

Woods Temporary Services reported pretax income in 2003, 2004, 2005, and 2006 of $100 million. In 2003, an asset was acquired for $100 million. The asset is depreciated for financial reporting purposes over four years on a straight-line basis (no residual value). For tax purposes the asset's cost is deducted (by MACRS) over 2003–2006 as follows: $33 million, $44 million, $15 million, and $8 million. No other depreciable assets were acquired. The enacted tax rate is 40% each year.

| ($ in millions) | Temporary Difference | | | | |
| | Originates | | Reverses | | |
	2003	2004	2005	2006	Total
Accounting income	$100	$100	$100	$100	$400
Depreciation on the income statement	25	25	25	25	100
Depreciation on the tax return	(33)	(44)	(15)	(8)	(100)
Taxable income	$ 92	$ 81	$110	$117	$400

ILLUSTRATION 16–2

Expense Reported on the Tax Return before the Income Statement

To determine taxable income, we add back to accounting income the actual depreciation taken in the income statement and then subtract the depreciation deduction allowed on the tax return.

able income will be less than accounting income during the years the tax deduction is higher than income statement depreciation, but higher than accounting income in later years when the situation reverses.

2003 income taxes would be recorded as follows in Illustration 16–2A:

| ($ in millions) | Current Year 2003 | Future Taxable Amounts | | | Future Taxable Amounts (total) |
		2004	2005	2006	
Accounting income	$100				
Temporary difference:					
Depreciation	(8)	$(19)	$10	$17	$8
Taxable income	$ 92				
Enacted tax rate	40%				40%
Tax payable currently	$36.8				
Deferred tax liability					$3.2
Deferred Tax Liability					
Ending balance					$3.2
Less: Beginning balance					0.0
Change in balance					$3.2

Journal Entry at the End of 2003

Income tax expense (to balance)	40	
Income tax payable (determined above)		36.8
Deferred tax liability (determined above)		3.2

ILLUSTRATION 16–2A

Determining and Recording Income Taxes—2003

Taxable income is $8 million less than accounting income because that much more depreciation is deducted on the 2003 tax return ($33 million) than is reported on the income statement ($25 million).

Income tax expense is comprised of two components: the amount payable now and the amount deferred until later.

Let's follow the determination of income taxes for this illustration all the way through the complete reversal of the temporary difference. We assume accounting income is $100 million each year and that the only difference between accounting and taxable income is caused by depreciation. 2004 income taxes would be determined as shown in Illustration 16–2B.

Notice that each year the appropriate balance is determined for the deferred tax liability. That amount is compared with any existing balance to determine whether the account must be either increased or decreased.

($ in millions)

	2003	Current Year 2004	Future Taxable Amounts 2005	2006	Future Taxable Amounts (total)
Accounting income		$100			
Temporary difference:					
Depreciation	$(8)	(19)	$10	$17	$27
Taxable income		81			
Enacted tax rate		40%			40%
Tax payable currently		$32.4			
Deferred tax liability					$10.8

Deferred Tax Liability

Ending balance	$10.8
Less: Beginning balance	(3.2)
Change in balance	$7.6

Journal Entry at the End of 2004

Income tax expense (to balance)	40	
Income tax payable (determined above)		32.4
Deferred tax liability (determined above)		7.6

Income taxes for 2005 would be recorded as shown in Illustration 16–2C.

($ in millions)

	2003	2004	Current Year 2005	Future Taxable Amounts 2006	Future Taxable Amounts (total)
Accounting income			$100		
Temporary difference:					
Depreciation	$(8)	$(19)	10	$17	$17
Taxable income			$110		
Enacted tax rate			40%		40%
Tax payable currently			$44		
Deferred tax liability					$ 6.8

Deferred Tax Liability

Ending balance	$ 6.8
Less: Beginning balance	(10.8)
Change in balance	$ (4.0)

Journal Entry at the End of 2005

Income tax expense (to balance)	40	
Deferred tax liability (determined above)	4	
Income tax payable (determined above)		44

Income taxes for 2006 would be recorded as shown in Illustration 16–2D. Notice there that the deferred tax liability is increased in 2003–2004 and decreased in 2005–2006.

Deferred Tax Liability

($ in millions)			
		3.2	2003 ($ 8 × 40%)
		7.6	2004 ($19 × 40%)
2005 ($10 × 40%)	4.0		
2006 ($17 × 40%)	6.8		
		0	Balance after 4 years

The deferred tax liability increases the first two years and is paid over the next two years.

($ in millions)				Current Year	Future Taxable Amounts
	2003	**2004**	**2005**	**2006**	**(total)**
Accounting income				$100	
Temporary difference:					
Depreciation	$(8)	$(19)	$10	17	$ 0
Taxable income				$117	
Enacted tax rate				40%	40%
Tax payable currently				$46.8	
Deferred tax liability					$ 0.0
		Deferred Tax Liability			
Ending balance					$ 0.0
Less: Beginning balance					(6.8)
Change in balance					$(6.8)

Journal Entry at the End of 2006

Income tax expense (to balance)	40.0	
Deferred tax liability (determined above).	6.8	
Income tax payable (determined above)		46.8

ILLUSTRATION 16–2D

Determining and Recording Income Taxes—2006

Because the entire temporary difference has now reversed, there is a zero cumulative temporary difference, and the balance in the deferred tax liability should be zero.

Since a credit balance of $6.8 million exists, that amount must be deducted (debited).

The final portion of the tax deferred from 2003 and 2004 is paid in 2006.

We can see this result from the alternate perspective of looking at the temporary book–tax difference that exists for the depreciable asset. Its carrying amount is its cost minus accumulated straight-line depreciation. Its tax basis is cost minus the accumulated cost recovery for tax purposes:

($ in millions)		December 31							
		2003		**2004**		**2005**		**2006**	
Depreciable asset:									
Accounting basis	$100	$(25)	$ 75	$(25)	$ 50	$(25)	$ 25	$(25)	$ 0
Tax basis	100	(33)	67	(44)	23	(15)	8	(8)	0
Temporary difference		$ 8	$ 8	$ 19	$ 27	$(10)	$ 17	$(17)	$ 0
Enacted tax rate			40%		40%		40%		40%
Deferred tax liability			$3.2		$10.8		$6.8		$ 0

Originating Differences   Reversing Differences

A balance sheet perspective focuses on the difference between the carrying amount at the tax basis.

Deferred Tax Assets

The temporary differences illustrated to this point produce future taxable amounts when the temporary differences reverse. Future taxable amounts mean taxable income will be

Deferred tax assets are recognized for the future tax benefits of temporary differences that create future deductible amounts.

increased relative to accounting income in one or more future years. Sometimes, though, the future tax consequence of a temporary difference will be to decrease taxable income relative to accounting income. Such situations produce what's referred to as *future deductible amounts*. These have favorable tax consequences that are recognized as deferred tax assets.

Two examples indicated in Graphic 16–1 are (1) estimated expenses that are recognized on income statements when incurred but deducted on tax returns in later years when actually paid and (2) revenues that are taxed when collected but recognized on income statements in later years when actually earned. An example of the first type is provided in Illustration 16–3.

ILLUSTRATION 16–3

Expense Reported on the Tax Return *after* the Income Statement

In 2003, taxable income is more than accounting income because the warranty expense is not deducted on the tax return until paid.

Lane Electronics reported pretax income in 2003, 2004, and 2005 of $70 million, $100 million, and $100 million, respectively. The 2003 income statement includes a $30 million warranty expense that is deducted for tax purposes when paid in 2004 ($15 million) and 2005 ($15 million).* The income tax rate is 40% each year.

($ in millions)	Temporary Difference			
	Originates	Reverses		
	2003	2004	2005	Total
Accounting income	$ 70	$100	$100	$270
Warranty expense on the income statement	30			30
Warranty expense on the tax return		(15)	(15)	(30)
Taxable income	$100	$ 85	$ 85	$270

*Remember from Chapter 13 that warranty expense is estimated for the period the products are sold even though the actual cost isn't incurred until later periods.

At the end of 2003, the amounts needed to record income tax for 2003 would be determined as shown in Illustration 16–3A.

ILLUSTRATION 16–3A

Determining and Recording Income Taxes—2003

Because the warranty expense was subtracted on the 2003 income statement but isn't deductible on the 2003 tax return, it is added back to accounting income to find taxable income.

The amounts deductible in 2004 and 2005 will produce tax benefits that are recognized now as a deferred tax asset.

($ in millions)	Current Year 2003	Future Deductible Amounts		Future Deductible Amounts (total)
		2004	2005	
Accounting income	$ 70			
Temporary difference:				
Warranty expense	30	$(15)	$(15)	$(30)
Taxable income	$100		(30)	
Enacted tax rate	40%			40%
Tax payable currently	$ 40			
Deferred tax asset				$(12)

Deferred Tax Asset ↓

Ending balance	$ 12
Less: Beginning balance	0
Change in balance	$ 12

Journal Entry at the End of 2003

Income tax expense (to balance)	28	
Deferred tax asset (determined above)	12	
Income tax payable (determined above)		40

At the end of 2003 and 2004, the company reports a deferred tax asset for future income tax benefits.

Deferred Tax Asset

		($ in millions)	
2003 ($30 × 40%)	12		
		6	2004 ($15 × 40%)
		6	2005 ($15 × 40%)
Balance after 3 years	0		

Income taxes payable in 2004 and 2005 are less than otherwise payable because of the taxes "prepaid" in 2003.

If we continue the assumption of $85 million taxable income in each of 2004 and 2005, income tax those years would be recorded this way:

2004
Income tax expense (to balance) 40
  Deferred tax asset ($15 million × 40%) 6
  Income tax payable ($85 million × 40%) 34
2005
Income tax expense (to balance) 40
  Deferred tax asset ($15 million × 40%) 6
  Income tax payable ($85 million × 40%) 34

The deferred tax asset represents the future tax benefit from the reversal of a temporary difference between the financial statement carrying amount of the warranty liability and its tax basis.

($ in millions)	December 31					
	2003		**2004**		**2005**	
Warranty liability:						
Accounting basis	$30	$30	$(15)	$15	$(15)	$0
Tax basis	(0)	(0)	(0)	(0)	(0)	(0)
Temporary difference	$30	$30	$(15)	$15	$(15)	$0
Tax rate		× 40%		× 40%		× 40%
Deferred tax asset		$12		$ 6		$0
	Originating Difference		Reversing Differences			

A liability is recognized for financial reporting purposes when the guaranteed product is sold:
2003 Warr. exp 30
      Liability   30
and reduced when the expense is paid:
2004 Liability 15
      Cash   15
2005 Liability 15
      Cash   15
From a tax perspective, there is no liability.

The preceding was an illustration of an estimated expense that is reported on the income statement when incurred but deducted on tax returns in later years when actually paid. A second type of temporary difference that gives rise to a deferred tax asset is a *revenue* that is taxed when collected but recognized on income statements in later years when actually earned. Illustration 16–4 on the next page demonstrates this second type.

Notice that this temporary difference produces future *deductible* amounts. In 2003, taxable income is $20 million *more* than accounting income because it includes the unearned subscriptions revenue not yet reported on the income statement. However, in 2004 and 2005 taxable income is *less* than accounting income because the subscription revenue is earned and reported on the income statements but not on the tax returns of those two years.

In effect, tax laws require the company to prepay the income tax on this revenue, which is a sacrifice now but will benefit the company later when it avoids paying the taxes when the revenue is earned. In the meantime, the company has an asset representing this future income tax benefit.

A deferred tax asset is recognized when an existing temporary difference will produce future deductible amounts.

ILLUSTRATION 16–4	Tomorrow Publications reported pretax income in 2003, 2004, and 2005 of $80 million, $115 million, and $105 million, respectively. The 2003 income statement does *not* include $20 million of magazine subscriptions received that year for one- and two-year subscriptions. The subscription revenue is reported for tax purposes in 2003. The revenue will be earned in 2004 ($15 million) and 2005 ($5 million). The income tax rate is 40% each year.
Revenue Reported on the Tax Return *before* the Income Statement	

($ in millions)		Temporary Difference			
		Originates	**Reverses**		
		2003	**2004**	**2005**	**Total**
Accounting income		$ 80	$115	$105	$300
Subscription revenue on the income statement			(15)	(5)	(20)
Subscription revenue on the tax return		20	0	0	20
Taxable income		$100	$100	$100	$300

In 2003, taxable income is more than accounting income because subscription revenue is not reported on the income statement until 2004–2005.

ILLUSTRATION 16–4A

Determining and Recording Income Taxes—2003

($ in millions)	Current Year 2003	Future Deductible Amounts		Future Deductible Amounts (total)
		2004	2005	
Accounting income	$ 80			
Temporary difference:				
Subscription revenue	20	$(15)	$(5)	$(20)
Taxable income	$100			
Enacted tax rate	40%			40%
Tax payable currently	$ 40			
Deferred tax asset				$(8)

Deferred Tax Asset

Ending balance	$8
Less: Beginning balance	0
Change in balance	$8

Journal Entry at the End of 2003

Income tax expense (to balance).............................	32	
Deferred tax asset (determined above)	8	
Income tax payable (determined above)		40

At the end of 2003, the amounts needed to record income tax for 2003 would be determined as shown in Illustration 16–4A.

At the end of 2003 and 2004, the company reports a deferred tax asset for future tax benefits.

Income taxes payable in 2004 and 2005 are less than otherwise payable because of the taxes prepaid in 2003.

Deferred Tax Asset

				($ in millions)
2003 ($20 × 40%)	8			
		6	2004 ($15 × 40%)	
		2	2005 ($ 5 × 40%)	
Balance after 3 years	0			

Again, we could also determine the deferred tax asset as the future tax benefit from the reversal of a temporary difference between the financial statement carrying amount of the subscription liability and its tax basis.[8]

($ in millions)	December 31					
	2003		**2004**		**2005**	
Liability—subscriptions:						
Accounting basis	$20	$20	$(15)	$ 5	$(5)	$ 0
Tax basis	(0)	(0)	(0)	(0)	(0)	(0)
Temporary difference	$20	$20	$(15)	$ 5	$(5)	$ 0
Tax rate		× 40%		× 40%		× 40%
Deferred tax asset		$ 8		$ 2		$ 0

Originating Difference — Reversing Differences

> A liability is recognized for financial reporting purposes when the cash is received:
> 2003 Cash   20
>   Liability   20
> and reduced when the revenue is earned:
> 2004 Liability   15
>   Revenue   15
> 2005 Liability   5
>   Revenue   5
> From a tax perspective, there is no liability.

Valuation Allowance

Deferred tax assets are recognized for all deductible temporary differences. However, a deferred tax asset is then reduced by a valuation allowance if it is "more likely than not" that some portion or all of the deferred tax asset will not be realized.[9] Remember, a future deductible amount reduces taxable income and saves taxes only if there is taxable income to be reduced when the future deduction is available. So, a valuation allowance is needed if taxable income is anticipated to be insufficient to realize the tax benefit.

For example, let's say that in the previous illustration management determines that it's more likely than not that $3 million of the deferred tax asset will not ultimately be realized. The deferred tax asset would be reduced by the creation of a valuation allowance as follows:

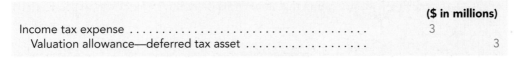

	($ in millions)	
Income tax expense	3	
Valuation allowance—deferred tax asset		3

> A valuation allowance is needed if it is more likely than not that some portion or all of a deferred tax asset will not be realized.

The effect is to increase the income tax expense as a result of reduced expectations of future tax savings. On the 2003 balance sheet, the deferred tax asset would be reported at its estimated net realizable value:

Deferred tax asset	$8
Less: Valuation allowance—deferred tax asset	(3)
	$5

> A deferred tax asset is reported at its estimated net realizable value.

ADDITIONAL CONSIDERATION

The decision as to whether a valuation allowance is needed should be based on the weight of all available evidence. The real question is whether or not there will be sufficient taxable income in future years for the anticipated tax benefit to be realized. The benefit of future deductible amounts can be realized only if future income is at least

---

[8]It is less intuitive to view an unearned revenue (Illustration 16–4) as producing future deductible amounts when the unearned revenue liability is settled than it is to view the future deductibility of an estimated expense (Illustration 16–3) as a future deductible amount. Nevertheless, the recognition of deferred tax assets for the future tax benefits of unearned revenue liability temporary differences is consistent with the asset/liability approach of *SFAS 109* because these unearned revenue liabilities are reported as if they represent future refundable amounts and therefore future deductible amounts. This point is argued persuasively by Hugo Nurnberg, "Deferred Tax Assets under FASB *Statement No. 96*," *Accounting Horizons,* December 1989.
[9]"More likely than not" means a likelihood of more than 50%, "Accounting for Income Taxes," *Statement of Financial Accounting Standards No. 109* (Norwalk, Conn.: FASB, 1992), par. 17.

equal to the deferred deductions. After all, a deduction reduces taxes only if it reduces taxable income.

All evidence—both positive and negative—should be considered. For instance, operating losses in recent years or anticipated circumstances that would adversely affect future operations would constitute negative evidence. On the other hand, a strong history of profitable operations or sizable, existing contracts would constitute positive evidence of sufficient taxable income to be able to realize the deferred tax asset.

Managerial actions that could be taken to reduce or eliminate a valuation allowance when deferred tax assets are not otherwise expected to be realized must be considered. These tax-planning strategies include any prudent and feasible actions management might take to realize a tax benefit while it is available.

This having been said, it should be clear that the decision as to whether or not a valuation allowance is used, as well as how large the allowance should be, rests squarely on managerial judgment. Because that decision directly impacts the amount of income tax expense and therefore reported income, it has obvious implications for earnings quality assessment from an analyst's perspective.

At the end of each reporting period, the valuation allowance is reevaluated. The appropriate balance is decided on and the balance is adjusted—up or down—to create that balance. For instance, let's say that at the end of the following year, 2004, available evidence indicates that $500,000 of the deferred tax asset at the end of 2004 will not be realized. We would adjust the valuation allowance to reflect the indicated amount:

Each period, the valuation allowance is adjusted to reflect the appropriate balance at the time.

	($ in millions)	
Valuation allowance—deferred tax asset ($3 million − 0.5 million) . .	2.5	
Income tax expense.		2.5

The disclosure note shown in Graphic 16–2 accompanied the 2000 annual report of Unigene Laboratories, Inc., indicating that none of its deferred tax asset was expected to be realized:

GRAPHIC 16–2
Valuation Allowance—
Unigene Laboratories,
Inc.

> Given the Company's past history of incurring operating losses, any deferred tax assets that are recognizable under *SFAS 109* have been fully reserved. As of December 31, 2000 and 1999, the Company had deferred tax assets of approximately $29,000,000 and $26,000,000, respectively, subject to a valuation allowance of $21,000,000 and $26,000,000, respectively.

LO4

Nontemporary Differences

FINANCIAL REPORTING CASE

Q3, p. 777

So far, we've dealt with temporary differences between the reported amount of an asset or liability in the financial statements and its tax basis. You learned that temporary differences result in future taxable or deductible amounts when the related asset or liability is recovered or settled. However, some differences are caused by transactions and events that under existing tax law will never affect taxable income or taxes payable. Interest received from investments in bonds issued by state and municipal governments, for instance, is exempt from taxation. Interest revenue of this type is, of course, reported as revenue on the recipient's income statement but not on its tax return—not now, not later. Accounting income exceeds taxable income. This situation will not reverse in a later year. Taxable income in a later year will not exceed accounting income because the tax-free income will never be reported on the tax return.

Permanent differences are disregarded when determining both the tax payable currently and the deferred tax asset or liability.

These permanent differences are disregarded when determining the tax payable currently, the deferred tax effect, and therefore the income tax expense.[10] This is why we adjust

---

[10]The term permanent difference was used in *APB 11* to describe differences with no deferred tax consequences. Although the term itself is not used in more recent pronouncements (*SFAS 96* and *SFAS 109*), it still is useful to describe nontemporary differences.

GLOBAL PERSPECTIVE

The extent of differences between accounting income and taxable income varies widely from country to country. In fact, in France and Germany financial accounting and tax accounting must coincide. There also is little uniformity as to how to handle these differences. In many countries, income taxes are not deferred. Instead, tax expense is simply the actual tax paid.

accounting income in the illustrations that follow to eliminate any permanent differences from taxable income. Graphic 16–3 provides examples of differences with no deferred tax consequences.

GRAPHIC 16–3
Differences without Deferred Tax Consequences

Provisions of the tax laws, in some instances, dictate that the amount of a revenue that is taxable or expense that is deductible permanently differs from the amount reported on the income statement.

- Interest received from investments in bonds issued by state and municipal governments (not taxable).
- Investment expenses incurred to obtain tax-exempt income (not tax deductible).
- Life insurance proceeds on the death of an insured executive (not taxable).
- Premiums paid for life insurance policies when the payer is the beneficiary (not tax deductible).
- Compensation expense pertaining to some employee stock option plans (not tax deductible).
- Expenses due to violations of the law (not tax deductible).
- Portion of dividends received from U.S. corporations that is not taxable due to the dividends received deduction.[11]
- Tax deduction for depletion of natural resources (percentage depletion) that permanently exceeds the income statement depletion expense (cost depletion).[12]
- Tax deduction for goodwill amortization over 15 years (goodwill is not amortized for financial reporting purposes.)[13]

To compare temporary and nontemporary differences, we can modify Illustration 16–1 to include nontaxable income in Kent Land Management's 2004 pretax accounting income. We do this in Illustration 16–5 on the next page. Note that the existence of an amount that causes a permanent difference has no effect on income taxes payable, deferred taxes, or income tax expense.

To this point, we've seen that our objective in accounting for income taxes is to recognize the tax consequences of amounts that will become taxable or deductible in future years as a result of transactions or events that already have occurred. To achieve the objective, we record a deferred tax liability or deferred tax asset for future taxable amounts or future deductible amounts that arise as a result of temporary differences. Permanent differences, on the other hand, do not create future taxable amounts and future deductible amounts and therefore have no tax consequences.

[11]When a corporation owns shares of another U.S. corporation, a percentage of the dividends from those shares is exempt from taxation due to the dividends received deduction. The percentage is 70% if the investor owns less than 20% of the investee's shares, 80% for 20% to 80% ownership, and 100% for more than 80% ownership.

[12]The cost of natural resources is reported as depletion expense over their extraction period for financial reporting purposes; but tax rules prescribe sometimes different percentages of cost to be deducted for tax purposes. There usually is a difference between the cost depletion and percentage depletion that doesn't eventually reverse.

[13]Recall, though, that goodwill might become "impaired," at which time all or a portion of it will be subtracted from earnings. Because this amount would impact the income statement in a period different from the one in which it is deducted on the tax return, it would represent a temporary difference.

ILLUSTRATION 16–5
Temporary and Permanent Differences

Because interest on municipal bonds is tax exempt, it is reported only in the income statement. This difference between accounting income and taxable income does not reverse later.

Kent Land Management reported pretax income in 2003 of $100 million except for additional income of $40 million from installment sales of property and $5 million interest from investments in municipal bonds in 2003. The installment sales income is reported for tax purposes in 2004 ($10 million) and 2005 ($30 million). The enacted tax rate is 40% each year.

($ in millions)	Current Year 2003	Future Taxable Amounts 2004	Future Taxable Amounts 2005	Future Taxable Amounts (total)
Accounting income	$145			
Permanent difference:				
Municipal bond interest	(5)			
Temporary difference:				
Installment income	(40)	$10	$30	$40
Taxable income	$100			
Enacted tax rate	40%			40%
Tax payable currently	$ 40			
Deferred tax liability				$16

Deferred Tax Liability

Ending balance				$16
Less: Beginning balance				0
Change in balance				$16

Journal Entry at the End of 2003

Income tax expense (to balance).............................	56	
Income tax payable (determined above)		40
Deferred tax liability (determined above).....................		16

Permanent differences affect a company's effective tax rate.

You might notice here that because of the permanent difference, Kent's "effective" tax rate is less than its 40% statutory rate. The effective rate is the total tax to be paid (eventually), $56 million, divided by accounting income, $145 million, or 38.6%. Without the $5 million municipal bond interest, the effective rate would have been $56 million divided by $140 million, or 40%. Nontaxable revenues and gains, as we have for Kent, cause the effective rate to be *lower* than the statutory rate; whereas, nondeductible expenses and losses would cause the effective rate to be *higher* than the statutory rate. Companies report a comparison of their effective and statutory tax rates in disclosure notes, as in Graphic 16–4's example from FedEx's 2001 financial statements.

GRAPHIC 16–4
Effective Tax Rate—FedEx Corporation

Note 9: Income Taxes (in part)

A reconciliation of the statutory federal income tax rate to FedEx's effective income tax rate for the years ended May 31 is as follows:

	2001	2000	1999
Statutory U.S. income tax rate	35.0%	35.0%	35.0%
Increase (decrease) resulting from:			
State income taxes, net of federal benefit	2.8	2.8	2.8
Other, net	(0.8)	1.7	2.7
Effective tax rate	37.0%	39.5%	40.5%

Temporary and Permanent Differences

Mid-South Cellular Systems began operations in 2003. That year the company reported pre-tax accounting income of $70 million, which included the following amounts:

1. Compensation expense of $3 million related to employee stock option plans granted to organizers was reported on the 2003 income statement. This expense is not deductible for tax purposes.
2. An asset with a four-year useful life was acquired last year. It is depreciated by the straight-line method on the income statement. MACRS is used on the tax return, causing deductions for depreciation to be more than straight-line depreciation the first two years but less than straight-line depreciation the next two years ($ in millions):

	Depreciation		
	Income Statement	**Tax Return**	**Difference**
2003	$150	$198	$ (48)
2004	150	264	(114)
2005	150	90	60
2006	150	48	102
	$600	$600	$ 0

The enacted tax rate is 40%.

Required:
Prepare the journal entry to record Mid-South Cellular's income taxes for 2003.

($ in millions)	Current Year 2003	Future Taxable Amounts			Future Taxable Amounts (total)
		2004	**2005**	**2006**	
Accounting income	$70				
Permanent difference:					
Compensation expense	3				
Temporary difference:					
Depreciation	(48)	$(114)	$60	$102	$ 48
Taxable income	$25				
Enacted tax rate	40%				40%
Tax payable	$10				
Deferred tax liability					$19.2
	Deferred Tax Liability				↓
Ending balance					$19.2
Less: Beginning balance					0.0
Change in balance					$19.2

SOLUTION

Because the compensation expense is not tax deductible, taxable income does not include that $3 million deduction and is higher by that amount than accounting income.

Journal Entry at the End of 2003
Income tax expense (to balance)	29.2	
Income tax payable (determined above)		10.0
Deferred tax liability (determined above).		19.2

Income tax expense is composed of: (1) the tax payable now and (2) the tax deferred until later.

PART

LO5

OTHER TAX ACCOUNTING ISSUES

Tax Rate Considerations

To measure the deferred tax liability or asset, we multiply the temporary difference by the currently *enacted* tax rate that will be effective in the year(s) the temporary difference reverses.[14] We do not base calculations on *anticipated* legislation that would alter the company's tax rate. A conceptual case can be made that expected rate changes should be anticipated when measuring the deferred tax liability or asset. However, this is one of many examples of the frequent trade-off between relevance and reliability. In this case, the FASB chose to favor reliability by waiting until an anticipated change actually is enacted into law before recognizing its tax consequences.

WHEN ENACTED TAX RATES DIFFER

A deferred tax liability (or asset) is based on enacted tax rates and laws.

Existing tax laws may call for enacted tax rates to be different in two or more future years in which a temporary difference is expected to reverse. When a phased-in change in rates is scheduled to occur, the specific tax rates of each future year are multiplied by the amounts reversing in each of those years. The total is the deferred tax liability or asset.

To illustrate, let's again modify our Kent Land Management illustration, this time to assume a scheduled change in tax rates. See Illustration 16–6.

ILLUSTRATION 16–6	Kent Land Management reported pretax income in 2003 of $100 million except for additional

ILLUSTRATION 16–6

Scheduled Change in Tax Rates

Kent Land Management reported pretax income in 2003 of $100 million except for additional income of $40 million from installment sales of property and $5 million interest from investments in municipal bonds in 2003. The installment sales income is reported for tax purposes in 2004 ($10 million) and 2002 ($30 million). The enacted tax rates are 40% for 2003 and 2004, and 35% for 2005.

($ in millions)	Current Year 2003	Future Taxable Amounts		(total)
		2004	**2005**	
Accounting income	$145			
Permanent difference:				
Municipal bond interest	(5)			
Temporary difference:				
Installment income	(40)	$10	$ 30	
Taxable income	$100			
Enacted tax rate	40%	40%	35%	
Tax payable currently	$ 40			
Deferred tax liability		$ 4	$10.5	$14.5

The tax effects of the future taxable amounts depend on the tax rates at which those amounts will be taxed.

Deferred Tax Liability

Ending balance	$14.5
Less: Beginning balance	0.0
Change in balance	$14.5

Journal Entry at the End of 2003

Income tax expense (to balance)	54.5	
Income tax payable (determined above)		40.0
Deferred tax liability (determined above)		14.5

---

[14]The current U.S. corporate tax rate is 34%, or 35% for corporations with taxable income over $75,000. Most states tax corporate income at rates less than 10%. We use 40% in most of our illustrations to simplify calculations.

Be sure to note that the 2004 rate (40%) as well as the 2005 rate (35%) already is enacted into law as of 2003 when the deferred tax liability is established. In the next section we discuss how to handle a change resulting from new legislation.

CHANGES IN TAX LAWS OR RATES

> As a result of a change [in tax law or rate] deferred tax consequences become larger or smaller.[15]

Tax laws sometimes change. If a change in a tax law or rate occurs, the deferred tax liability or asset must be adjusted. Remember, the deferred tax liability or asset is meant to reflect the amount to be paid or recovered in the future. When legislation changes that amount, the deferred tax liability or asset also should change. The effect is reflected in operating income in the year of the enactment of the change in the tax law or rate.

For clarification, reconsider the previous illustration. Without a change in tax rates and assuming that accounting income in 2004 is $100 million (with no additional temporary or permanent differences), the 2004 income tax amounts would be determined as shown in Illustration 16–6A.

($ in millions)	2003	Current Year 2004	Future Taxable Amount 2005
Accounting income		$100	
Temporary difference:			
Installment income	(40)	10	$ 30
Taxable income		$110	
Enacted tax rate		40%	35%
Tax payable currently		$ 44	
Deferred tax liability			$10.5 $10.5

Deferred Tax Liability

Ending balance	$10.5
Less: Beginning balance	(14.5)
Change in balance	$(4.0)

Journal Entry at the End of 2004

Income tax expense (to balance)	40	
Deferred tax liability (determined above).	4	
Income tax payable (determined above)		44

ILLUSTRATION 16–6A

Reversal of Temporary Difference *without* a Tax Rate Change

The 40% 2004 rate and the 35% 2005 rate are established by previously enacted legislation.

Now assume Congress passed a new tax law in 2004 that will cause the 2005 tax rate to be 30% instead of the previously scheduled 35% rate. Because a deferred tax liability was established in 2003 with the expectation that the 2005 taxable amount would be taxed at 35%, it would now be adjusted to reflect taxation at 30%, instead. This is demonstrated in Illustration 16–6B on the next page.

Notice that the methods used to determine the deferred tax liability and the change in that balance are the same as without the rate change—the calculation merely uses the new rate (30%) rather than the old rate (35%). So recalculating the desired balance in the deferred tax

---

[15]"Accounting for Income Taxes," *Statement of Financial Accounting Standards No. 109* (Norwalk, Conn.: FASB, 1992), par. 112.

ILLUSTRATION 16–6B	($ in millions)		Current Year	Future Taxable Amount
		2003	**2004**	**2005**

Reversal of Temporary Difference *with* a Tax Rate Change

($ in millions)	2003	Current Year 2004	Future Taxable Amount 2005
Accounting income		$100	
Temporary difference:			
Installment income	(40)	10	$30
Taxable income		$110	
Enacted tax rate		40%	30%*
Tax payable currently		$ 44	
Deferred tax liability		$ 9	$ 9.0

The deferred tax liability would have been $10.5 million (30 million × 35%) if the tax rate had not changed.

*2005 rate enacted into law in 2004.

Deferred Tax Liability

Ending balance	$ 9.0
Less: Beginning balance	(14.5)
Change in balance	$ (5.5)

Journal Entry at the End of 2004

Income tax expense (to balance)...............................	38.5	
Deferred tax liability (determined above)......................	5.5	
Income tax payable (determined above)		44.0

When a tax rate changes, the deferred tax liability or asset should be adjusted with the effect reflected in operating income in the year of the change.

liability each period and comparing that amount with any previously existing balance automatically takes into account tax rate changes.

Also notice that the income tax expense ($38.5 million) is $1.5 million less than it would have been without the tax rate change ($40 million). The effect of the change is included in income tax expense. In fact, this is highlighted if we separate the previous entry into its component parts: (1) record the income tax expense without the tax rate change and (2) separately record the adjustment of the deferred tax liability for the change:

Journal Entries at the End of 2004	($ in millions)	
Income tax expense	40	
Deferred tax liability	4	
Income tax payable.....................................		44
Deferred tax liability [$30 million × (35% − 30%)]	1.5	
Income tax expense....................................		1.5

The tax consequence of a change in a tax law or rate is recognized in the period the change is enacted. In this case, the consequence of a lower tax rate is a reduced deferred tax liability, recognized as a reduction in income tax expense in 2004 when the change occurs.

Multiple Temporary Differences

It would be unusual for any but a very small company to have only a single temporary difference in any given year. Having multiple temporary differences, though, doesn't change any of the principles you've learned so far in connection with single differences. All that's necessary is to categorize all temporary differences according to whether they create (a) future taxable amounts or (b) future deductible amounts. The total of the future taxable amounts is multiplied by the future tax rate to determine the appropriate balance for the deferred tax liability, and the total of the future deductible amounts is multiplied by the future tax rate to determine the appropriate balance for the deferred tax asset. This is demonstrated in Illustration 16–7.

2003

During 2003, its first year of operations, Eli-Wallace Distributors reported pretax accounting income of $200 million which included the following amounts:

1. Income from installment sales of warehouses in 2003 of $9 million to be reported for tax purposes in 2004 ($5 million) and 2005 ($4 million).
2. Depreciation is reported by the straight-line method on an asset with a four-year useful life. On the tax return, deductions for depreciation will be more than straight-line depreciation the first two years but less than straight-line depreciation the next two years ($ in millions):

ILLUSTRATION 16–7

Multiple Temporary
Differences

	Income Statement	Tax Return	Difference
2003	$ 50	$ 66	$(16)
2004	50	88	(38)
2005	50	30	20
2006	50	16	34
	$200	$200	$ 0

3. Estimated warranty expense that will be deductible on the tax return when actually paid during the next two years. Estimated deductions are as follows ($ in millions):

	Income Statement	Tax Return	Difference
2003	$7		$7
2004		$4	(4)
2005		3	(3)
	$7	$7	$0

2004

During 2004, pretax accounting income of $200 million included an estimated loss of $1 million from having accrued a loss contingency. The loss is expected to be paid in 2006 at which time it will be tax deductible.

The enacted tax rate is 40% each year.

Look at Illustration 16–7 on the next page to see how Eli-Wallace determines the income tax amounts for 2003. Then turn to Illustration 16–7B on page 799 to see how those amounts are determined for 2004.

After the journal entry at the end of 2004, the balances of both the deferred tax asset and the deferred tax liability reflect the desired amounts as follows ($ in millions):

Deferred Tax Asset			Deferred Tax Liability	
2.8		2003 balance		10.0
	1.2	Adjustment		13.2
1.6		2004 balance		23.2

The deferred tax asset declines and the deferred tax liability increases during 2004.

Of course, if a phased-in change in rates is scheduled to occur, it would be necessary to determine the total of the future taxable amounts and the total of the future deductible amounts for each future year as outlined previously. Then the specific tax rates of each future year would be multiplied by the two totals in each of those years. Those annual tax effects would then be summed to get the deferred tax liability and the deferred tax asset.

Net Operating Losses

A **net operating loss** is negative taxable income: tax-deductible expenses exceed taxable revenues. Of course, there is no tax payable for the year an operating loss occurs because there's no taxable income. In addition, tax laws permit the operating loss to be used to reduce

ILLUSTRATION 16–7A

Multiple Temporary Differences—2003

Temporary differences are grouped according to whether they create future *taxable* amounts or future *deductible* amounts.

The desired balances in the deferred tax liability and the deferred tax asset are separately determined.

Income tax expense is composed of three components: (1) the tax payable now plus (2) the tax deferred until later, reduced by (3) the deferred tax benefit.

($ in millions)	Current Year 2003	Future Taxable (Deductible) Amounts			Future Taxable Amounts (total)	Future Deductible Amounts (total)
		2004	2005	2006		
Accounting income	$ 200					
Temporary differences:						
Installment sales	(9)	$ 5	$ 4		$ 9	
Depreciation	(16)	(38)	20	$34	16	
Warranty expense	7	(4)	(3)			$(7)
Taxable income	$ 182				$25	(7)
Enacted tax rate	40%				40%	40%
Tax payable currently	$72.8					
Deferred tax liability					$10	
Deferred tax asset						$(2.8)
					↓	↓
					Deferred Tax Liability	Deferred Tax Asset
Ending balances:					$10	$2.8
Less: Beginning balances:					0	(0.0)
Change in balances					$10	$2.8

Journal Entry at the End of 2003

Income tax expense (to balance)	80.0	
Deferred tax asset (determined above)	2.8	
Deferred tax liability (determined above).		10.0
Income tax payable (determined above)		72.8

taxable income in other, profitable years. Offsetting operating profits with operating losses is achieved by either a carryback of the loss to prior years or a carryforward of the loss to later years, or both. In essence, the tax deductible expenses that can't be deducted this year because they exceed taxable revenues can be deducted in other years. Specifically, the operating loss can be carried back 2 years and forward for up to 20 years:

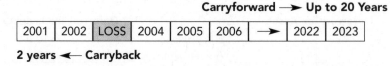

Carryforward ⟶ Up to 20 Years

| 2001 | 2002 | LOSS | 2004 | 2005 | 2006 | ⟶ | 2022 | 2023 |

2 years ◄— Carryback

Tax laws permit a choice. A company can elect an **operating loss carryback** if taxable income was reported in either of the two previous years. By reducing taxable income of a previous year, the company can receive an immediate refund of taxes paid that year.

If taxable income was not reported in either of the two previous years or higher tax rates are anticipated in the future, a company might elect to forgo the operating loss carryback and carry the loss forward for up to 20 years to offset taxable income of those years. Even if a loss carryback is elected, any loss that remains after the two-year carryback can be carried forward. The carryback election is a choice that must be made in the year of the operating loss and the choice is irrevocable. It usually is advantageous to carry back losses because by filing an amended tax return to get a refund, a company can realize the benefit much sooner than if the loss is carried forward.

The accounting question is: *When* should the tax benefit created by an operating loss be recognized on the income statement? The answer is: In the year the loss occurs.

($ millions)	2003	Current Year 2004	Future Taxable (Deductible) Amounts 2005	Future Taxable (Deductible) Amounts 2006	Future Taxable Amounts (total)*	Future Deductible Amounts (total)*
Accounting income		$200				
Temporary differences:						
Installment sales	$ (9)	$ 5	$ 4		$ 4	
Depreciation	(16)	(38)	20	$34	54	
Warranty expense	7	(4)	(3)			$(3)
Estimated loss		1		(1)		(1)
Taxable income		$164			$58	$(4)
Enacted tax rate		40%			40%	40%
Tax payable currently		$ 65.6				
Deferred tax liability					$23.2	
Deferred tax asset						$(1.6)
					↓	↓
					Deferred Tax Liability	**Deferred Tax Asset**
Ending balances:					$23.2	$ 1.6
Less: Beginning balances:					(10.0)	(2.8)
Change in balances					$13.2	$(1.2)

Journal Entry at the End of 2004

Income tax expense (to balance).	80.0	
Deferred tax asset (determined above)		1.2
Deferred tax liability (determined above).		13.2
Income tax payable (determined above)		65.6

ILLUSTRATION 16–7B

Multiple Temporary Differences—2004

The future taxable amount of installment sales ($4 million) is equal to the cumulative temporary difference ($9 million − 5 million).

Similarly, the total of other future taxable and deductible amounts are equal to the cumulative temporary differences in the related assets and liabilities.

Analysis indicates that the deferred tax liability should be increased further and the deferred tax asset should be reduced.

*Total future taxable and deductible amounts also are equal to the cumulative temporary differences in the related assets and liabilities.

OPERATING LOSS CARRYFORWARD

First consider a loss carryforward. You have learned in this chapter that a deferred tax asset is recognized for the future tax benefit of temporary differences that create future deductible amounts. An operating loss carryforward also creates future deductible amounts. Logically, then, a deferred tax asset is recognized for an operating loss carryforward also. This is demonstrated on the next page in Illustration 16–8.

The income tax benefit of an operating loss carryforward is recognized for accounting purposes in the year the operating loss occurs. The net after-tax operating loss reflects the future tax savings that the operating loss is expected to create:

Income Statement (partial)

	($ in millions)
Operating loss before income taxes	$125
Less: Income tax benefit—operating loss	(50)
Net operating loss	$ 75

The income tax benefit of an operating loss carryforward is recognized in the year the operating loss occurs.

Valuation Allowance.   Just as for all deductible temporary differences, deferred tax assets are recognized for any operating loss without regard to the likelihood of having taxable income in future years sufficient to absorb future deductible amounts. However, the deferred tax asset is then reduced by a valuation allowance if it is more likely than not that some

During 2003, its first year of operations, American Laminating Corporation reported an operating loss of $125 million for financial reporting and tax purposes. The enacted tax rate is 40%.

($ in millions)	Current Year 2003	Future Deductible Amounts (total)
Operating loss	$(125)	
Loss carryforward	125	$(125)
	$ 0	
Enacted tax rate	40%	40%
Tax payable	$ 0	
Deferred tax asset		$ (50)

Deferred Tax Asset

Ending balance	$50
Less: Beginning balance	0
Change in balance	$50

Journal Entry at the End of 2003

Deferred tax asset (determined above)	50	
Income tax benefit—operating loss (to balance)		50

portion or all of the deferred tax asset will not be realized. Remember, a valuation allowance both reduces the net deferred tax asset and increases the income tax expense just as if that portion of the deferred tax asset had not been recognized.

OPERATING LOSS CARRYBACK

To compare the treatment of an operating loss carryback, let's modify the illustration to assume that there was taxable income in the two years prior to the operating loss and that American Laminating elected a loss carryback (see Illustration 16–9). Note that the operating loss must be applied to the earlier year first and then brought forward to the next year. If any of the loss remains after reducing taxable income to zero in the two previous years, the remainder is carried forward to future years as an operating loss carryforward.

The income tax benefit of both an operating loss carryback and an operating loss carryforward is recognized for accounting purposes in the year the operating loss occurs. The net after-tax operating loss reflects the reduction of past taxes from the loss carryback and future tax savings that the loss carryforward is expected to create:

	($ in millions)	
Operating loss before income taxes		$125
Less: Income tax benefit:		
Tax refund from loss carryback	$29	
Future tax savings from loss carryforward	20	49
Net operating loss		$ 76

Notice that the income tax benefit ($49 million) is less than it was when we assumed a carryforward only ($50 million). This is because the tax rate in one of the carryback years (2001) was lower than the carryforward rate (40%).

Let's carry the illustration forward one year (see Illustration 16–9A) and assume a performance turnaround in 2004 resulted in pretax accounting income of $15 million.

During 2003, American Laminating Corporation reported an operating loss of $125 million for financial reporting and tax purposes. The enacted tax rate is 40% for 2003. Taxable income, tax rates, and income taxes paid in the two previous years were as follows:

	Taxable Income	Taxable Rates	Income Taxes Paid
2001	$20 million	35%	$ 7 million
2002	55 million	40%	22 million

Here's how the income tax benefit of the operating loss carryback and the operating loss carryforward is determined:

($ in millions)	Prior Years		Current Year	Future Deductible Amounts
	2001	**2002**	**2003**	**(total)**
Operating loss			$(125)	
Loss carryback	$(20)	$(55)	75	
Loss carryforward			50	$(50)
			$ 0	
Enacted tax rate	35%	40%	40%	40%
Tax payable (refundable)	$ (7)	$(22)	$ 0	
Deferred tax asset				$(20)
Deferred Tax Asset				↓
Ending balance				$ 20
Less: Beginning balance				0
Change in balance				$ 20

Journal Entry at the End of 2003

Receivable—income tax refund ($7 + 22).	29	
Deferred tax asset (determined above)	20	
Income tax benefit—operating loss (to balance)		49

ILLUSTRATION 16–9

Operating Loss Carryback and Carryforward

An operating loss carryback can be deducted from taxable income in the two prior years, creating a refund of taxes paid those years.

The portion of an operating loss that remains after a carryback is carried forward.

The income tax benefit of an operating loss carryback, like a carryforward, is recognized in the year the operating loss occurs.

($ in millions)		Current Year	Future Deductible Amounts
	2003	**2004**	**(total)**
Accounting income		$15	
Temporary difference:			
Loss carryforward	$50	(15)	$ (35)
Taxable income		$ 0	
Enacted tax rate		40%	40%
Tax payable currently		$ 0	
Deferred tax asset			$ (14)
Deferred Tax Asset			↓
Ending balance			$ 14.0
Less: Beginning balance			(20.0)
Change in balance			$ (6.0)

Journal Entry at the End of 2004

Income tax expense (to balance)	6	
Deferred tax asset (determined above)		6

ILLUSTRATION 16–9A

Determining and Recording Income Taxes—2004

$15 million of the carryforward can be used to offset 2004 income. The remaining $35 million is carried forward up to 19 more years.

The $20 million deferred tax asset is reduced to $14 million.

Financial Statement Presentation

BALANCE SHEET CLASSIFICATION

In a classified balance sheet, deferred tax assets and deferred tax liabilities are classified as either current or noncurrent according to how the related assets or liabilities are classified for financial reporting. For instance, a deferred tax liability arising from different depreciation methods being used for tax and book purposes would be classified as noncurrent because depreciable assets are reported as noncurrent. A deferred tax asset or deferred tax liability is considered to be related to an asset or liability if reduction (including amortization) of that asset or liability will cause the temporary difference to reverse.

A net current amount and a net noncurrent amount are reported as either an asset or a liability.

Most companies will have several different types of temporary differences that give rise to deferred tax amounts. The several deferred tax assets and liabilities should not be reported individually but combined instead into two summary amounts. Current deferred tax assets and liabilities should be offset (netted together). The resulting *net current* amount is then reported as either a current asset (if deferred tax assets exceed deferred tax liabilities) or current liability (if deferred tax liabilities exceed deferred tax assets). Similarly, a single *net noncurrent* amount should be reported as a net noncurrent asset or a net noncurrent liability. This is demonstrated in Illustration 16–10.

ILLUSTRATION 16–10 Balance Sheet Classification and Presentation **The current or noncurrent classification of deferred tax assets and deferred tax liabilities is the same as that of the related assets or liabilities.**	Warren Properties, Inc. had future taxable amounts and future deductible amounts relating to temporary differences between the tax bases of the assets and liabilities indicated below and their financial reporting amounts:

Related Balance Sheet Account	Classification Current—C Noncurrent—N	Future Taxable (Deductible) Amounts	Tax Rate	Deferred Tax (Asset) Liability C	N
Receivable—installment sales of land	C	$ 10	× 40%	$ 4	
Receivable—installment sales of land	N	5	× 40%		$ 2
Depreciable assets	N	105	× 40%		42
Allowance—uncollectible accounts	C	(15)	× 40%	(6)	
Liability—subscriptions received	C	(20)	× 40%	(8)	
Estimated warranty liability	C	(30)	× 40%	(12)	
Net current liability (asset)				$(22)	
Net noncurrent liability (asset)					$44

($ in millions)

Balance Sheet Presentation

Current Assets:
  Deferred tax asset $22

Long-Term Liabilities:
  Deferred tax liability $44

Note: Before offsetting assets and liabilities within the current and noncurrent categories, the **total** of deferred tax assets is $26 ($6 + 8 + 12) and the **total** of deferred tax liabilities is $48 ($4 + 2 + 42).

Deferred Tax Amount Not Related to a Specific Asset or Liability.   Sometimes, a deferred tax asset or a deferred tax liability cannot be identified with a specific asset or liability. When that's the case, it should be classified according to when the underlying temporary difference is expected to reverse. For instance, some organization costs are recognized as expenses for financial reporting purposes when incurred, but are deducted for tax purposes in later years. When such expenditures are made, an expense is recorded, but no asset or liability is recognized on the balance sheet. The deferred tax asset recognized for the future deductible amounts is classified as a current asset for the tax effect of the deduction expected next year, and as a noncurrent asset for the tax effect of the deductions expected in later years. Operating loss carryforwards also are unrelated to a specific asset or liability and so are classified as current or noncurrent according to when future income is expected to be sufficient to realize the benefit of the carryforward.

> A deferred tax asset or liability that is not related to a specific asset or liability should be classified according to when the underlying temporary difference is expected to reverse.

Valuation Allowance.   Any valuation allowance for deferred tax assets should be allocated between the current and noncurrent amount in proportion to the amounts of deferred tax assets that are classified as current and noncurrent. In our illustration, all three deferred tax assets were classified as current, so any valuation allowance would be reported with the net current deferred tax asset.

> A valuation allowance is allocated between current and noncurrent on a pro rata basis.

DISCLOSURE NOTES

Deferred Tax Assets and Deferred Tax Liabilities.   Additional disclosures are required pertaining to amounts reported on the balance sheet. Disclosure notes should reveal the:

- Total of all deferred tax liabilities ($48 million in our Illustration 16–10 Note).
- Total of all deferred tax assets ($26 million in our Illustration 16–10 Note).
- Total valuation allowance recognized for deferred tax assets.
- Net change in the valuation allowance.
- Approximate tax effect of each type of temporary difference (and carryforward).

In its 2000 balance sheet, the Procter & Gamble Company reported current deferred tax assets of $309 million and net noncurrent deferred tax liabilities of $625 million. The composition of these amounts was provided in the disclosure note shown in Graphic 16–5.

Note 10: Income Taxes (in part)

Deferred Income Tax Assets and Liabilities

	($ in millions)	
June 30	2000	1999
Current deferred tax assets:	$ 309	$ 621
Noncurrent deferred tax assets (liabilities):		
Depreciation	(951)	(979)
Postretirement benefits	273	392
Loss carryforwards	332	206
Other	(279)	19
	$(625)	$(362)

Included in the above are total valuation allowances of $207 and $140 in 2000 and 1999, respectively.

GRAPHIC 16–5
Disclosure of Deferred Taxes—Procter & Gamble

Operating Loss Carryforwards.   In addition, the amounts and expiration dates should be revealed for any operating loss carryforwards. Remember, operating losses can be carried forward for reduction of future taxable income for 20 years. This potential tax benefit can foreshadow desirable cash savings for the company if earnings sufficient to absorb the loss carryforwards are anticipated before their expiration date. The presence of large operating loss carryforwards also can make an unprofitable company an attractive target for acquisition by a company that could use those loss carryforwards to shelter its own earnings from taxes with that loss deduction. If the IRS determines that an acquisition is made solely to obtain the tax benefits of operating loss carryforwards, the deductions will not be allowed. However, motivation is difficult to determine, so it is not uncommon for companies to purchase operating loss carryforwards.

Income Tax Expense. Disclosures also are required pertaining to the income tax expense reported on the income statement. Disclosure notes should reveal the:

- Current portion of the tax expense (or tax benefit).
- Deferred portion of the tax expense (or tax benefit), with separate disclosure of amounts attributable to:
  - Portion that does not include the effect of the following separately disclosed amounts.
  - Operating loss carryforwards.
  - Adjustments due to changes in tax laws or rates.
  - Adjustments to the beginning-of-the-year valuation allowance due to revised estimates.
  - Tax credits.

Intraperiod Tax Allocation

You should recall that an income statement reports certain items separately from income (or loss) from continuing operations when such items are present. Specifically, (a) discontinued operations, (b) extraordinary items, and (c) changes in accounting principle are given a place of their own on the income statement to better allow the user of the statement to isolate irregular components of net income from those that represent ordinary, recurring business operations. Presumably, this permits the user to more accurately project future operations without neglecting events that affect current performance.[16] Following this logic, each component of net income should reflect the income tax effect directly associated with that component.

Consequently, the total income tax expense for a reporting period should be allocated among the financial statement items that gave rise to it. Each of the following items should be reported net of its respective income tax effects:

- Income (or loss) from continuing operations.
- Discontinued operations.
- Extraordinary items.
- Changes in accounting principle.
- Prior period adjustments (to the beginning retained earnings balance).

The related tax effect can be either a tax expense or a tax benefit. For example, an extraordinary gain adds to a company's tax expense, while an extraordinary loss produces a tax reduction because it reduces taxable income and therefore reduces income taxes. So a company with a tax rate of 40% would report $100 million pretax income that includes a $10 million extraordinary gain this way:

	($ in millions)
Income before tax and extraordinary item ($100 − 10)	$90
Less: Income tax expense ($90 × 40%)	(36)
Income before extraordinary item	54
Extraordinary gain (net of $4 income tax)	6
Net income	$60

A gain causes an increase in taxes.

---

[16]This was discussed in Chapter 3.

If the $100 million pretax income included a $10 million extraordinary loss rather than an extraordinary gain, the loss would be reported net of associated tax savings:

	($ in millions)
Income before tax and extraordinary item ($100 + 10)	$110
Less: Income tax expense ($110 × 40%)	(44)
Income before extraordinary item	66
Extraordinary loss (net of $4 income tax benefit)	(6)
Net income	$ 60

A loss causes a reduction in taxes.

ADDITIONAL CONSIDERATION

If the extraordinary gain in the earlier example had been of a type taxable at a capital gains tax rate of 30%, it would have been reported net of the specific tax associated with that gain:

Extraordinary gain (net of $3 income tax) $7

Allocating income taxes among financial statement components in this way within a particular reporting period is referred to as *intraperiod tax allocation.* You should recognize the contrast with *inter*period tax allocation—terminology sometimes used to describe allocating income taxes between two or more reporting periods by recognizing deferred tax assets and liabilities. While interperiod tax allocation is challenging and controversial, intraperiod tax allocation is relatively straightforward and substantially free from controversy.

Allocating income taxes within a particular reporting period is intraperiod tax allocation.

Conceptual Concerns

Some accountants disagree with the FASB's approach to accounting for income taxes. Some of the most persistent objections are outlined below.

Should Deferred Taxes Not Be Recognized?   Some feel the income tax expense for a reporting period should be the income tax actually payable currently. Reasons often cited include the contentions that the legal liability for taxes is determined only by the tax return and that taxes are based on aggregate taxable income, not individual components of the aggregate amount. The FASB counters that it is not only possible, but desirable, to separate the tax consequences of individual components of income from the financial reporting of those events. If tax laws permit a company to defer paying tax on a particular event, it is only when, not whether, the tax will be paid that is impacted. Recognizing the tax effect when the event occurs, regardless of when the tax will be paid is consistent with accounting on an accrual rather than a cash basis.

Should Deferred Taxes Be Recognized for Only Some Items?   Critics sometimes argue that the tax liability for certain recurring events will never be paid and therefore do not represent a liability.[17] An example often cited is the temporary difference due to depreciation. Because the temporary difference recurs frequently (as new assets are acquired), new originating differences more than offset reversing differences causing the balance in the deferred tax liability account to continually get larger. The contention is that no future tax payment will be required, so no liability should be recorded. The FASB's counter argument is that, although the aggregate amount of depreciation differences may get larger, the deferred tax liability for a particular depreciable asset usually does require payment. This is analogous to

---

[17]For example, see Paul Chaney and Debra Jeter, "Accounting for Deferred Taxes: Simplicity? Usefulness?" *Accounting Horizons,* June 1989, pp. 7–8.

specific accounts payable requiring payment even though the total balance of accounts payable may grow larger year by year.

Should Deferred Taxes Be Discounted?   Some accountants contend that deferred tax assets and liabilities should reflect the time value of money by determining those amounts on a discounted (present value) basis.[18] For some deferred tax amounts such as operating loss carryforwards that might be realized after perhaps 20 years in some cases, the time value might be significant. Practical considerations weighed heavily in the FASB's decision not to permit discounting. Discounting usually would require detailed scheduling of the reversals of all differences reversing in the future, and the selection of appropriate discount rates would pose practical difficulties.

Should Classification Be Based on the Timing of Temporary Difference Reversals?   Some feel that deferred tax assets and liabilities should be classified in a balance sheet as current or noncurrent according to the timing of the reversal of the temporary differences that gave rise to them. By this view, those deferred tax assets and liabilities related to temporary differences that will reverse within the coming year should be classified as current, others as noncurrent. Advocates of this view consider it to be consistent with the asset-liability perspective on deferred tax amounts. Again, practical considerations are reflected in the FASB's requirement that a deferred tax asset or deferred tax liability should be classified in a balance sheet as current or noncurrent according to the classification of the asset or liability to which it is related. Classifying a deferred tax liability related to depreciation as noncurrent because the depreciable asset is classified as noncurrent, for example, does not require detailed scheduling of the year-by-year originations and reversals of temporary differences related to depreciation.

DECISION MAKERS' PERSPECTIVE

Income taxes represent one of the largest expenditures that many firms incur. When state, local, and foreign taxes are considered along with federal taxes, the total bite can easily consume 40% of income. A key factor, then, in any decision that managers make should be the impact on taxes. Decision makers must constantly be alert to options that minimize or delay taxes. During the course of this chapter, we encountered situations that avoid taxes (for example, interest on municipal bonds) and those that delay taxes (for example, using accelerated depreciation on the tax return). Astute managers make investment decisions that consider the tax effect of available alternatives. Similarly, outside analysts should consider how effectively management has managed its tax exposure and monitor the current and prospective impact of taxes on their interests in the company.

Investment patterns and other disclosures can indicate potential tax expenditures.

Consider an example. Large, capital-intensive companies with significant investments in buildings and equipment often have sizable deferred tax liabilities from temporary differences in depreciation. If new investments cause the level of depreciable assets to at least remain the same over time, the deferred tax liability can be effectively delayed indefinitely. Investors and creditors should be watchful for situations that might cause material paydowns of that deferred tax liability, such as impending plant closings or investment patterns that suggest declining levels of depreciable assets. Unexpected additional tax expenditures can severely diminish an otherwise attractive prospective rate of return.

Operating loss carryforwards can indicate significant future tax savings.

You also learned in the chapter that deferred tax assets represent future tax benefits. One such deferred tax asset that often reflects sizable future tax deductions is an operating loss carryforward. When a company has a large operating loss carryforward, a large amount of future income can be earned tax free. This tax shelter can be a huge advantage, not to be overlooked by careful analysts.

---

[18]For example, see Harry Wolk, Dale Martin, and Virginia Nichols, "*Statement of Financial Standards No. 96:* Some Theoretical Problems," *Accounting Horizons,* June 1989, p. 4.

Managers and outsiders are aware that increasing debt increases risk. Deferred tax liabilities increase reported debt. As discussed and demonstrated in the previous chapter, financial risk often is measured by the debt-to-equity ratio, total liabilities divided by shareholders' equity. Other things being equal, the higher the debt-to-equity ratio, the higher the risk. Should the deferred tax liability be included in the computation of this ratio? Some analysts will argue that it should be excluded, observing that in many cases the deferred tax liability account remains the same or continually grows larger. Their contention is that no future tax payment will be required. Others, though, contend that is no different from the common situation in which long-term borrowings tend to remain the same or continually grow larger. Research supports the notion that deferred tax liabilities are, in fact, viewed by investors as real liabilities and they appear to discount them according to the timing and likelihood of the liabilities' settlement.[19]

> Deferred tax liabilities increase risk as measured by the debt-to-equity ratio.

Anytime managerial discretion can materially impact reported earnings, analysts should be wary of the implications for earnings quality assessment. We indicated earlier that the decision as to whether or not a valuation allowance is used, as well as the size of the allowance, is largely discretionary. Alert investors should not overlook the potential for "earnings management" here.

In short, managers who make decisions based on estimated pretax cash flows and outside investors and creditors who make decisions based on pretax income numbers are perilously ignoring one of the most important aspects of those decisions. Taxes should be a primary consideration in any business decision. ■

CONCEPT REVIEW EXERCISE

Multiple Differences and Operating Loss

Mid-South Cellular Systems began operations in 2003. That year the company reported taxable income of $25 million. In 2004, its second year of operations, pretax accounting income was $88 million, which included the following amounts:

1. Insurance expense of $14 million, representing one-third of a $42 million, three-year casualty and liability insurance policy that is deducted for tax purposes entirely in 2004.
2. Insurance expense for a $1 million premium on a life insurance policy for the company president. This is not deductible for tax purposes.
3. An asset with a four-year useful life was acquired last year. It is depreciated by the straight-line method on the income statement. MACRS is used on the tax return, causing deductions for depreciation to be more than straight-line depreciation the first two years but less than straight-line depreciation the next two years ($ in millions):

	Income Statement	Tax Return	Difference
2003	$150	$198	$ (48)
2004	150	264	(114)
2005	150	90	60
2006	150	48	102
	$600	$600	0

4. Equipment rental revenue of $80 million, which does not include an additional $20 million of advance payment for 2005 rent. $100 million of rental revenue is reported on the 2004 income tax return.

The enacted tax rate is 40%.

[19]See Dan Givoly and Carla Hayn, "The Valuation of the Deferred Tax Liability: Evidence from the Stock Market," *The Accounting Review,* April 1992, pp. 394–410.

Required:

1. Prepare the journal entry to record Mid-South Cellular's income taxes for 2004.
2. What is Mid-South Cellular's 2004 net income?
3. Show how any deferred tax amount(s) should be reported on the 2004 balance sheet. Assume taxable income is expected in 2005 sufficient to absorb any deductible amounts carried forward from 2004.

SOLUTION

1. Prepare the journal entry to record Mid-South Cellular's income taxes for 2004.

($ in millions)

	2003	Current Year 2004	Future Taxable Deductible Amounts 2005	Future Taxable Deductible Amounts 2006	Future Taxable Amounts (total)	Future Deductible Amounts (total)
Accounting income		$ 88				
Permanent difference:						
Life insurance premium		1				
Temporary differences:						
Prepaid insurance		(28)	$ 14	$ 14	$ 28	
Depreciation	$(48)	(114)	60	102	162	
Advance rent		20	(20)			$(20)
Operating loss		$ (33)				
Loss carryback	(25)	25				
Loss carryforward		8				(8)
		$ 0			$190	$(28)
Enacted tax rate	40%	40%			40%	40%
Tax payable (refundable)	$(10)	$ 0				
Deferred tax liability					$76.0	
Deferred tax asset						$(11.2)

	Deferred Tax Liability	Deferred Tax Asset
Ending balances:	$76.0	$11.2
Less: Beginning balance ($48* × 40%)	(19.2)	(0.0)
Change in balances	$56.8	$11.2

*2003's only temporary difference.

Differences in tax reporting and financial reporting of both the prepaid insurance and the depreciation create future taxable amounts.

Both the advance rent and the operating loss carryforward create future deductible amounts.

Journal Entry at the End of 2004

Income tax expense (to balance)	35.6	
Receivable—income tax refund (determined above)	10.0	
Deferred tax asset (determined above)	11.2	
Deferred tax liability (determined above)		56.8

Income tax expense is composed of three components: (1) the tax deferred until later, reduced by (2) the deferred tax benefit and (3) the refund of 2003 taxes paid.

Note: Adjusting accounting income by the nontemporary difference and the three temporary differences creates a negative taxable income, which is a net operating loss.

2. What is Mid-South Cellular's 2004 net income?

Pretax accounting income	$88.0
Income tax expense	(35.6)
Net income	$52.4

3. Show how any deferred tax amount(s) should be reported on the 2004 balance sheet. Assume taxable income is expected in 2005 sufficient to absorb any deductible amounts carried forward from 2004.

	($ in millions)				
Related Balance Sheet Account	**Classification Current—C Noncurrent—N**	**Future Taxable (Deductible) Amounts**	**Tax Rate**	**Deferred Tax (Asset) Liability** C	N
Prepaid insurance	C	28	× 40%	11.2	
Depreciable assets	N	162	× 40%		64.8
Liability—rent received in advance	C	(20)	× 40%	(8.0)	
Unrelated to Any Balance Sheet Account					
Operating loss carryforward	C*	(8)	× 40%	(3.2)	___
Net **current** liability (asset)				0.0	
Net **noncurrent** liability (asset)					64.8

*Deferred tax asset classified entirely as current because 2005 income is expected to be sufficient to realize the benefit of the carryforward.

No net current amount
Long-term liabilities:
Deferred tax liability $64.8

Note: These net amounts ($0.0 + 64.8 = $64.8) sum to the net **total** deferred tax liabilities and deferred tax assets from requirement 1 ($76.0 − 11.2 = $64.8).

FINANCIAL REPORTING CASE **SOLUTION**

1. **What's the difference? Explain to Laura how differences between financial reporting standards and income tax rules might cause the two tax amounts to differ.** *(p. 778)*   The differences in the rules for computing taxable income and those for financial reporting often cause amounts to be included in taxable income a different year(s) from the year in which they are recognized for financial reporting purposes. Temporary differences result in future taxable or deductible amounts when the temporary differences reverse. As a result, tax payments frequently occur in years different from the years in which the revenues and expenses that cause the taxes are generated.

2. **What is the conceptual advantage of determining income tax expense as we do?** *(p. 778)* Income tax expense is the combination of the current tax effect and the deferred tax consequences of the period's activities. Under the asset-liability approach, the objective of accounting for income taxes is to recognize a deferred tax liability or deferred tax asset for the tax consequences of amounts that will become taxable or deductible in future years as a result of transactions or events that already have occurred. A result is to recognize both the current and the deferred tax consequences of the operations of a reporting period.

3. **Are there differences between financial reporting standards and income tax rules that will not contribute to the difference between income tax expense and amount of income taxes paid?** *(p. 790)*   Yes. Some differences between accounting income and taxable income are caused by transactions and events that will never affect taxable income or taxes payable. These differences between accounting income and taxable income do not reverse later. These are permanent differences which are disregarded when determining (a) the tax payable currently, (b) the deferred tax effect, and therefore (c) the income tax expense. ■

THE BOTTOM LINE

1. Temporary differences produce future taxable amounts when the taxable income will be increased relative to accounting income in one or more future years. These produce deferred tax liabilities for the taxes to be paid on the future taxable amounts. Income tax expense for the year includes an amount for which payment (or receipt) is deferred in addition to the amount for which payment is due currently. The deferred amount is the change in the tax liability (or asset).

2. When the future tax consequence of a temporary difference will be to decrease taxable income relative to accounting income, future deductible amounts are created. These have favorable tax consequences that are recognized as deferred tax assets.

3. Deferred tax assets are recognized for all deductible temporary differences. However, a deferred tax asset is then reduced by a valuation allowance if it is more likely than not that some portion or all of the deferred tax asset will not be realized.

4. Nontemporary differences between the reported amount of an asset or liability in the financial statements and its tax basis are those caused by transactions and events that under existing tax law will never affect taxable income or taxes payable. These are disregarded when determining both the tax payable currently and the deferred tax effect.

5. The deferred tax liability (or asset) for which payment (or receipt) is deferred is based on enacted tax rates applied to the taxable or deductible amounts. If a change in a tax law or rate occurs, the deferred tax liability or asset is adjusted to reflect the change in the amount to be paid or recovered. That effect is reflected in operating income in the year of the enactment of the change in the tax law or rate.

6. When multiple temporary differences exist, the total of the future **taxable** amounts is multiplied by the future tax rate to determine the appropriate balance for the deferred tax liability, and the total of the future **deductible** amounts is multiplied by the future tax rate to determine the appropriate balance for the deferred tax asset.

7. Tax laws permit an operating loss to be used to reduce taxable income in other, profitable years by either a carryback of the loss to prior years (2) or a carryforward of the loss to later years (up to 20). The tax benefit of an operating loss carryback or an operating loss carryforward is recognized in the year of the loss.

8. Deferred tax assets and deferred tax liabilities are classified as either current or noncurrent according to how the related assets or liabilities are classified for financial reporting. Disclosure notes should reveal additional relevant information needed for full disclosure pertaining to deferred tax amounts reported on the balance sheet, the components of income tax expense, and available operating loss carryforwards.

9. Through intraperiod tax allocation, the total income tax expense for a reporting period is allocated among the financial statement items that gave rise to it; specifically, income (or loss) from continuing operations, discontinued operations, extraordinary items, changes in accounting principle, and prior period adjustments (to the beginning retained earnings balance). ▪

QUESTIONS FOR REVIEW OF KEY TOPICS

Q 16–1 A member of the board of directors is concerned that the company's income statement reports income tax expense of $12.3 million, but the income tax obligation to the government for the year is only $7.9 million. How might the corporate controller explain this apparent discrepancy?

Q 16–2 A deferred tax liability (or asset) is described as the tax effect of the temporary difference between the financial statement carrying amount of an asset or liability and its tax basis. Explain this tax effect of the temporary difference. How might it produce a deferred tax liability? A deferred tax asset?

Q 16–3 Sometimes a temporary difference will produce future deductible amounts. Explain what is meant by future deductible amounts. Describe two general situations that have this effect. How are such situations recognized in the financial statements?

Q 16–4 The benefit of future deductible amounts can be achieved only if future income is sufficient to take advantage of the deferred deductions. For that reason, not all deferred tax assets will ultimately be realized. How is this possibility reflected in the way we recognize deferred tax assets?

Q 16–5 Temporary differences result in future taxable or deductible amounts when the related asset or liability is recovered or settled. Some differences, though, are not temporary. What events create nontemporary or permanent differences? What effect do these have on the determination of income taxes payable? Of deferred income taxes?

Q 16–6 Identify three examples of differences with no deferred tax consequences.

Q 16–7   The income tax rate for Hudson Refinery has been 35% for each of its 12 years of operation. Company forecasters expect a much-debated tax reform bill to be passed by Congress early next year. The new tax measure would increase Hudson's tax rate to 42%. When measuring this year's deferred tax liability, which rate should Hudson use?

Q 16–8   Suppose a tax reform bill is enacted that causes the corporate tax rate to change from 34% to 36%. How would this affect an existing deferred tax liability? How would the change be reflected in income?

Q 16–9   An operating loss occurs when tax-deductible expenses exceed taxable revenues. Tax laws permit the operating loss to be used to reduce taxable income in other, profitable years by either a carryback of the loss to prior years or a carryforward of the loss to later years. How are loss carrybacks and loss carryforwards recognized for financial reporting purposes?

Q 16–10 How are deferred tax assets and deferred tax liabilities reported in a classified balance sheet?

Q 16–11 Additional disclosures are required pertaining to deferred tax amounts reported on the balance sheet. What are the needed disclosures?

Q 16–12 Additional disclosures are required pertaining to the income tax expense reported on the income statement. What are the needed disclosures?

Q 16–13 What is intraperiod tax allocation?

Q 16–14 Some accountants believe that deferred taxes should be recognized only for some temporary differences. What is the conceptual basis for this argument? What is the counter argument that serves as the basis for the FASB's requirement that deferred taxes should be recognized for all temporary differences?

EXERCISES

E 16–1
Single temporary difference; taxable income given

Alvis Corporation reports *pretax accounting income* of $400,000, but due to a single temporary difference, *taxable income* is only $250,000. At the beginning of the year, no temporary differences existed.

Required:
Assuming a tax rate of 35%, prepare the appropriate journal entry to record Alvis's income taxes.

E 16–2
Single temporary difference; income tax payable given

In 2003, Alworth Corporation collected rent revenue for 2004 tenant occupancy. For income tax reporting, the rent is taxed when collected. For financial statement reporting, the rent is recognized as income in the period earned. The unearned portion of the rent collected in 2003 amounted to $300,000 at December 31, 2003. Alworth had no temporary differences at the beginning of the year.

Required:
Assuming an income tax rate of 40% and 2003 income tax payable of $950,000, prepare the journal entry to record income taxes for 2003.

E 16–3
Single temporary difference; future deductible amounts; taxable income given

Lance Lawn Services reports bad debt expense using the allowance method. For tax purposes, the expense is deducted when accounts prove uncollectible (the direct write-off method). At December 31, 2003, Lance has accounts receivable and an allowance for uncollectible accounts of $20 million and $1 million, respectively, and taxable income of $75 million. At December 31, 2002, Lance reported a deferred tax asset of $435,000 related to this difference in reporting bad debts, its only temporary difference. The enacted tax rate is 40% each year.

Required:
Prepare the appropriate journal entry to record Lance's income tax provision for 2003.

E 16–4
Deferred tax asset; income tax payable given; valuation allowance

At the end of 2002, Payne Industries had a deferred tax asset account with a balance of $30 million attributable to a temporary book–tax difference of $75 million in a liability for estimated expenses. At the end of 2003, the temporary difference is $70 million. Payne has no other temporary differences and no valuation allowance for the deferred tax asset. Taxable income for 2003 is $180 million and the tax rate is 40%.

Required:
1. Prepare the journal entry(s) to record Payne's income taxes for 2003, assuming it is more likely than not that the deferred tax asset will be realized.
2. Prepare the journal entry(s) to record Payne's income taxes for 2003, assuming it is more likely than not that one-half of the deferred tax asset will not ultimately be realized.

E 16–5
Deferred tax asset;
income tax payable
given; previous balance
in valuation allowance

(This is a variation of the previous exercise, modified to assume a previous balance in the valuation allowance.)

At the end of 2002, Payne Industries had a deferred tax asset account with a balance of $30 million attributable to a temporary book-tax difference of $75 million in a liability for estimated expenses. At the end of 2003, the temporary difference is $70 million. Payne has no other temporary differences. Taxable income for 2003 is $180 million and the tax rate is 40%.

Payne has a valuation allowance of $10 million for the deferred tax asset at the beginning of 2003.

Required:
1. Prepare the journal entry(s) to record Payne's income taxes for 2003, assuming it is more likely than not that the deferred tax asset will be realized.
2. Prepare the journal entry(s) to record Payne's income taxes for 2003, assuming it is more likely than not that one-half of the deferred tax asset will not ultimately be realized.

E 16–6
Single temporary
difference; determine
taxable income;
determine prior year
deferred tax amount

On January 1, 2000, Ameen Company purchased a building for $36 million. Ameen uses straight-line depreciation for financial statement reporting and MACRS for income tax reporting. At December 31, 2002, the carrying value of the building was $30 million and its tax basis was $20 million. At December 31, 2003, the carrying value of the building was $28 million and its tax basis was $13 million. There were no other temporary differences and no nontemporary differences. Pretax accounting income for 2003 was $20 million.

Required:
1. Prepare the appropriate journal entry to record Ameen's 2003 income taxes. Assume an income tax rate of 40%.
2. What is Ameen's 2003 net income?

E 16–7
Multiple choice;
determining deferred
tax amounts

The following questions dealing with various topics in this chapter are adapted from recent CPA examinations. Determine the response that best completes the statements or questions.
1. Because Jab Co. uses different methods to depreciate equipment for financial statement and income tax purposes, Jab has temporary differences that will reverse during the next year and add to taxable income. Deferred income taxes that are based on these temporary differences should be classified in Jab's balance sheet as a
   a. Contra account to current assets.
   b. Contra account to noncurrent assets.
   c. Current liability.
   d. Noncurrent liability.

Items 2 and 3 are based on the following:
Kent, Inc.'s, reconciliation between financial statement and taxable income for 2003 follows:

Pretax financial income	$150,000
Permanent difference	(12,000)
	138,000
Temporary difference—depreciation	(9,000)
Taxable income	$129,000

Additional information:

	At	
	12/31/02	**12/31/03**
Cumulative temporary differences (future taxable amounts)	$11,000	$20,000

The enacted tax rate was 34% for 2002, and 40% for 2003 and years thereafter.
2. In its December 31, 2003, balance sheet, what amount should Kent report as deferred income tax liability?
   a. $3,600
   b. $6,800
   c. $7,340
   d. $8,000
3. In its 2003 income statement, what amount should Kent report as current portion of income tax expense?

a. $51,600
b. $55,200
c. $55,860
d. $60,000

4. Mobe Co. reported the following operating income (loss) for its first three years of operations:

2001	$ 300,000
2002	(700,000)
2003	1,200,000

For each year, there were no deferred income taxes, and Mobe's effective income tax rate was 30%. In its 2002 income tax return, Mobe elected to carry back the maximum amount of loss possible. In its 2003 income statement, what amount should Mobe report as total income tax expense?

a. $120,000
b. $150,000
c. $240,000
d. $360,000

E 16–8
Single temporary
difference; taxable
income given; calculate
deferred tax liability

Ayres Services acquired an asset for $80 million in 2003. The asset is depreciated for financial reporting purposes over four years on a straight-line basis (no residual value). For tax purposes the asset's cost is depreciated by MACRS. The enacted tax rate is 40%. Amounts for pretax accounting income, depreciation, and taxable income in 2003, 2004, 2005, and 2006 are as follows:

	($ in millions)			
	2003	**2004**	**2005**	**2006**
Accounting income	$330	$350	$365	$400
Depreciation on the income statement	20	20	20	20
Depreciation on the tax return	(25)	(33)	(15)	(7)
Taxable income	$325	$337	$370	$413

Required:
For December 31 of each year, determine (a) the temporary book–tax difference for the depreciable asset and (b) the balance to be reported in the deferred tax liability account.

E 16–9
Identifying future
taxable amounts and
future deductible
amounts

Listed below are 10 causes of temporary differences. For each temporary difference, indicate (by letter) whether it will create future deductible amounts (D) or future taxable amounts (T).

Temporary Difference

_____ 1. Accrual of loss contingency, tax-deductible when paid.
_____ 2. Newspaper subscriptions; taxable when received, recognized for financial reporting when earned.
_____ 3. Prepaid rent, tax-deductible when paid.
_____ 4. Accrued bond interest expense, tax-deductible when paid.
_____ 5. Prepaid insurance, tax-deductible when paid.
_____ 6. Unrealized loss from recording investments available for sale at fair market value (tax-deductible when investments are sold).
_____ 7. Bad debt expense; allowance method for financial reporting; direct write-off for tax purposes.
_____ 8. Advance rent receipts on an operating lease (as the lessor), taxable when received.
_____ 9. Straight-line depreciation for financial reporting; accelerated depreciation for tax purposes.
_____ 10. Accrued expense for employee postretirement benefits, tax-deductible when subsequent payments are made.

E 16–10
Identifying future
taxable amounts and
future deductible
amounts

(This is a variation of the previous exercise, modified to focus on the balance sheet accounts related to the deferred tax amounts.)

Listed below are 10 causes of temporary differences. For each temporary difference indicate the balance sheet account for which the situation creates a temporary difference.

Temporary Difference

1. Accrual of loss contingency, tax-deductible when paid.
2. Newspaper subscriptions; taxable when received, recognized for financial reporting when earned.
3. Prepaid rent, tax-deductible when paid.
4. Accrued bond interest expense, tax-deductible when paid.
5. Prepaid insurance, tax-deductible when paid.

6. Unrealized loss from recording investments available for sale at fair market (tax-deductible when investments are sold).
7. Bad debt expense; allowance method for financial reporting; direct write-off for tax purposes.
8. Advance rent receipts on an operating lease (as the lessor), taxable when received.
9. Straight-line depreciation for financial reporting; accelerated depreciation for tax purposes.
10. Accrued expense for employee postretirement benefits, tax-deductible when subsequent payments are made.

E 16–11
Single temporary difference; nontemporary difference; calculate taxable income

Southern Atlantic Distributors began operations in January 2003 and purchased a delivery truck for $40,000. Southern Atlantic plans to use straight-line depreciation over a four-year expected useful life for financial reporting purposes. For tax purposes, the deduction is 50% of cost in 2003, 30% in 2004, and 20% in 2005. Pretax accounting income for 2003 was $300,000, which includes interest revenue of $40,000 from municipal bonds. The enacted tax rate is 40%.

Required:
Assuming no differences between accounting income and taxable income other than those described above:
1. Prepare the journal entry to record income taxes in 2003.
2. What is Southern Atlantic's 2003 net income?

E16–12
Single temporary difference; non-temporary difference (goodwill); calculate taxable income

Peridot Developers, Inc. began operations in December 2003. Peridot sells plots of land for industrial development. Peridot recognizes income for financial reporting purposes in the year it sells the plots. For some of the plots sold, Peridot recognizes the income for tax purposes when collected. Income Peridot recognized for financial reporting purposes in 2003 for plots sold this way was $40 million. The company expected to collect this amount over the next two years as follows:

2004	$24 million
2005	16 million
	$40 million

Peridot's pretax *accounting* income for 2003 was $63 million. On its tax return, Peridot is amortizing $45 million of goodwill over the 15-year period permitted by tax laws. Goodwill is not amortizable for financial reporting purposes and thus is not reflected in pretax accounting income. The enacted tax rate is 40 percent.

Required:
1. Assuming no differences between accounting income and taxable income other than those described above, prepare the journal entry to record income taxes in 2003.
2. What is Peridot's 2003 net income?

E 16–13
Single temporary difference; multiple tax rates

Allmond Corporation, organized on January 3, 2003, had pretax accounting income of $14 million and taxable income of $20 million for the year ended December 31, 2003. The 2003 tax rate is 35%. The only difference between accounting income and taxable income is estimated product warranty costs. Expected payments and scheduled tax rates (based on recent tax legislation) are as follows:

2004	$2 million	30%
2005	1 million	30%
2006	1 million	30%
2007	2 million	25%

Required:
1. Determine the amounts necessary to record Allmond's income taxes for 2003 and prepare the appropriate journal entry.
2. What is Allmond's 2003 net income?

E 16–14
Change in tax rates; calculate taxable income

Arnold Industries has pretax accounting income of $33 million for the year ended December 31, 2003. The tax rate is 40%. The only difference between accounting income and taxable income relates to an operating lease in which Arnold is the lessee. The inception of the lease was December 28, 2003. An $8 million advance rent payment at the inception of the lease is tax-deductible in 2003 but, for financial reporting purposes, represents prepaid rent expense to be recognized equally over the four-year lease term.

Required:
1. Determine the amounts necessary to record Arnold's income taxes for 2003 and prepare the appropriate journal entry.

2. Determine the amounts necessary to record Arnold's income taxes for 2004 and prepare the appropriate journal entry. Pretax accounting income was $50 million for the year ended December 31, 2004.
3. Assume a new tax law is enacted in 2004 that causes the tax rate to change from 40% to 30% beginning in 2005. Determine the amounts necessary to record Arnold's income taxes for 2004 and prepare the appropriate journal entry.
4. Why is Arnold's 2004 income tax expense different when the tax rate change occurs from what it would be without the change?

E 16–15

Deferred taxes; change in tax rates

Bronson Industries reported a deferred tax liability of $8 million for the year ended December 31, 2002, related to a temporary difference of $20 million. The tax rate was 40%. The temporary difference is expected to reverse in 2004 at which time the deferred tax liability will become payable. There are no other temporary differences in 2002–2004. Assume a new tax law is enacted in 2003 that causes the tax rate to change from 40% to 30% beginning in 2004. (The rate remains 40% for 2003 taxes.) Taxable income in 2003 is $30 million.

Required:

Determine the effect of the change and prepare the appropriate journal entry to record Bronson's income tax expense in 2003. What adjustment, if any, is needed to revise retained earnings as a result of the change?

E 16–16

Multiple temporary differences; record income taxes

The information that follows pertains to Esther Food Products:

a. At December 31, 2003, temporary differences were associated with the following future taxable (deductible) amounts:

Depreciation	$60,000
Prepaid expenses	17,000
Warranty expenses	(12,000)

b. No temporary differences existed at the beginning of 2003.
c. Pretax accounting income was $80,000 and taxable income was $15,000 for the year ended December 31, 2003.
d. The tax rate is 40%.

Required:

Determine the amounts necessary to record income taxes for 2003 and prepare the appropriate journal entry.

E 16–17

Multiple temporary differences; record income taxes

The information that follows pertains to Richards Refrigeration, Inc.:

a. At December 31, 2003, temporary differences existed between the financial statement carrying amounts and the tax bases of the following:

	($ in millions)		
	Carrying Amount	Tax Basis	Future Taxable (Deductible) Amount
Buildings and equipment (net of accumulated depreciation)	$120	$90	$30
Prepaid insurance	50	0	50
Liability—loss contingency	25	0	(25)

b. No temporary differences existed at the beginning of 2003.
c. Pretax accounting income was $200 million and taxable income was $145 million for the year ended December 31, 2003. The tax rate is 40%.

Required:

1. Determine the amounts necessary to record income taxes for 2003 and prepare the appropriate journal entry.
2. What is the 2003 net income?

E 16–18

Calculate income tax amounts under various circumstances

Four independent situations are described below. Each involves future deductible amounts and/or future taxable amounts produced by temporary differences:

	($ in thousands) Situation			
	1	**2**	**3**	**4**
Taxable income	$85	$215	$195	$260
Future deductible amounts	15		20	20
Future taxable amounts		15	15	30
Balance(s) at beginning of the year:				
Deferred tax asset	2		9	4
Deferred tax liability		2	2	

The enacted tax rate is 40%.

Required:

For each situation, determine the:

a.   Income tax payable currently.
b.   Deferred tax asset—balance.
c.   Deferred tax asset—change (dr) cr.
d.   Deferred tax liability—balance.
e.   Deferred tax liability—change (dr) cr.
f.   Income tax expense.

E 16–19
Determine taxable income

Eight independent situations are described below. Each involves future deductible amounts and/or future taxable amounts produced by:

($ in millions)
Temporary Differences Reported First on:

	The Income Statement		The Tax Return	
	Revenue	**Expense**	**Revenue**	**Expense**
1.		$20		
2.	$20			
3.			$20	
4.				$20
5.	15	20		
6.		20	15	
7.	15	20		10
8.	15	20	5	10

Required:

For each situation, determine taxable income assuming pretax accounting income is $100 million.

E 16–20
Two temporary differences; nontemporary difference

For the year ended December 31, 2003, Fidelity Engineering reported pretax accounting income of $977,000. Selected information for 2003 from Fidelity's records follows:

Interest income on municipal bonds	$32,000
Depreciation claimed on the 2003 tax return in excess of depreciation on the income statement	55,000
Carrying amount of depreciable assets in excess of their tax basis at year-end	85,000
Warranty expense reported on the income statement	26,000
Actual warranty expenditures in 2003	16,000

Fidelity's income tax rate is 40%. At January 1, 2003, Fidelity's records indicated balances of zero and $12,000 in its deferred tax asset and deferred tax liability accounts, respectively.

Required:

1.   Determine the amounts necessary to record income taxes for 2003 and prepare the appropriate journal entry.
2.   What is Fidelity's 2003 net income?

E 16–21
Operating loss carryforward

During 2003, its first year of operations, Baginski Steel Corporation reported an operating loss of $375,000 for financial reporting and tax purposes. The enacted tax rate is 40%.

Required:

1.   Prepare the journal entry to recognize the income tax benefit of the operating loss. Assume the weight of available evidence suggests future taxable income sufficient to benefit from future deductible amounts from the operating loss carryforward.

2. Show the lower portion of the 2003 income statement that reports the income tax benefit of the operating loss.

E 16–22
Operating loss carryback

Wynn Sheet Metal reported an operating loss of $100,000 for financial reporting and tax purposes in 2003. The enacted tax rate is 40%. Taxable income, tax rates, and income taxes paid in Wynn's first four years of operation were as follows:

	Taxable Income	Tax Rates	Income Taxes Paid
1999	$60,000	30%	$18,000
2000	70,000	30	21,000
2001	80,000	40	32,000
2002	60,000	45	27,000

Required:
1. Prepare the journal entry to recognize the income tax benefit of the operating loss. Wynn elects the carryback option.
2. Show the lower portion of the 2003 income statement that reports the income tax benefit of the operating loss.

E 16–23
Operating loss carryback and carryforward

(This exercise is based on the situation described in the previous exercise, modified to include a carryforward in addition to a carryback.)

Wynn Sheet Metal reported an operating loss of $160,000 for financial reporting and tax purposes in 2003. The enacted tax rate is 40%. Taxable income, tax rates, and income taxes paid in Wynn's first four years of operation were as follows:

	Taxable Income	Tax Rates	Income Taxes Paid
1999	$60,000	30%	$18,000
2000	70,000	30	21,000
2001	80,000	40	32,000
2002	60,000	45	27,000

Required:
1. Prepare the journal entry to recognize the income tax benefit of the operating loss. Wynn elects the carryback option.
2. Show the lower portion of the 2003 income statement that reports the income tax benefit of the operating loss.

E 16–24
Balance sheet classification

At December 31, 2003, DePaul Corporation had a $16 million balance in its deferred tax asset account and a $68 million balance in its deferred tax liability account. The balances were due to the following cumulative temporary differences:
1. Estimated warranty expense, $15 million: expense recorded in the year of the sale; tax-deductible when paid (one-year warranty).
2. Depreciation expense, $120 million: straight-line on the income statement; MACRS on the tax return.
3. Income from installment sales of properties, $50 million: income recorded in the year of the sale; taxable when received equally over the next five years.
4. Bad debt expense, $25 million: allowance method for accounting; direct write-off for tax purposes.

Required:
Show how any deferred tax amounts should be classified and reported on the 2003 balance sheet. The tax rate is 40%.

E 16–25
Single temporary difference; nontemporary difference; multiple tax rates; balance sheet classification

Case Development began operations in December 2003. When property is sold on an installment basis, Case recognizes installment income for financial reporting purposes in the year of the sale. For tax purposes, installment income is reported by the installment method. 2003 installment income was $600,000 and will be collected over the next three years. Scheduled collections and enacted tax rates for 2004–2006 are as follows:

2004	$150,000	30%
2005	250,000	40
2006	200,000	40

Pretax accounting income for 2003 was $810,000, which includes interest revenue of $10,000 from municipal bonds. The enacted tax rate for 2003 is 30%.

Required:

1. Assuming no differences between accounting income and taxable income other than those described above, prepare the appropriate journal entry to record Case's 2003 income taxes.
2. What is Case's 2003 net income?
3. How should the deferred tax amount be classified in a classified balance sheet?

E 16–26
Two temporary differences; nontemporary difference; multiple tax rates; balance sheet classification

(This exercise is a variation of the previous exercise, modified to include a second temporary difference.)

Case Development began operations in December 2003. When property is sold on an installment basis, Case recognizes installment income for financial reporting purposes in the year of the sale. For tax purposes, installment income is reported by the installment method. 2003 installment income was $600,000 and will be collected over the next three years. Scheduled collections and enacted tax rates for 2004–2006 are as follows:

2004	$150,000	30%
2005	250,000	40
2006	200,000	40

Case also had product warranty costs of $80,000 expensed for financial reporting purposes in 2003. For tax purposes, only the $20,000 of warranty costs actually paid in 2003 was deducted. The remaining $60,000 will be deducted for tax purposes when paid over the next three years as follows:

2004	$20,000
2005	25,000
2006	15,000

Pretax *accounting* income for 2003 was $810,000, which includes interest revenue of $10,000 from municipal bonds. The enacted tax rate for 2003 is 30%.

Required:

1. Assuming no differences between accounting income and taxable income other than those described above, prepare the appropriate journal entry to record Case's 2003 income taxes.
2. What is Case's 2003 net income?
3. How should the deferred tax amounts be classified in a classified balance sheet?

E 16–27
Identifying income tax deferrals

Listed below are ten independent situations. For each situation indicate (by letter) whether it will create a deferred tax asset (A), a deferred tax liability (L), or neither (N).

Situation

_____ 1. Advance payments on an operating lease deductible when paid.
_____ 2. Estimated warranty costs, tax deductible when paid.
_____ 3. Rent revenue collected in advance; cash basis for tax purposes.
_____ 4. Interest received from investments in municipal bonds.
_____ 5. Prepaid expenses tax deductible when paid.
_____ 6. Operating loss carryforward.
_____ 7. Operating loss carryback.
_____ 8. Bad debt expense; allowance method for accounting; direct write-off for tax.
_____ 9. Organization costs expensed when incurred, tax deductible over 15 years.
_____ 10. Life insurance proceeds received upon the death of the company president.

E 16–28
Concepts; terminology

Listed below are several terms and phrases associated with accounting for income taxes. Pair each item from List A (by letter) with the item from List B that is most appropriately associated with it.

List A	List B
_____ 1. No tax consequences.	a. Deferred tax liability.
_____ 2. Originates, then reverses.	b. Deferred tax asset.
_____ 3. Revise deferred tax amounts.	c. 2 years.
_____ 4. Operating loss.	d. Current and deferred tax consequence combined.
_____ 5. Future tax effect of prepaid expenses tax deductible when paid.	e. Temporary difference.
	f. Specific tax rates times amounts reversing each year.
_____ 6. Loss carryback.	g. Nontemporary differences.
_____ 7. Future tax effect of estimated warranty expense.	h. When enacted tax rate changes.
	i. Same as related asset or liability.

_____ 8. Valuation allowance.
_____ 9. Phased-in change in rates.
_____ 10. Balance sheet classifications.
_____ 11. Individual tax consequences of
    financial statement components.
_____ 12. Income tax expense.

j. "More likely than not" test.
k. Intraperiod tax allocation.
l. Negative taxable income.

E 16–29
Intraperiod tax
allocation

The following income statement does not reflect intraperiod tax allocation.

Required:
Recast the income statement to reflect intraperiod tax allocation.

INCOME STATEMENT
For the Fiscal Year Ended March 31, 2003
($ in millions)

Revenues	$830
Cost of goods sold	(350)
Gross profit	480
Operating expenses	(180)
Income tax expense	(86)
Income before extraordinary item and cumulative effect of accounting change	214
Extraordinary casualty loss	(10)
Cumulative effect of change in depreciation methods	(75)
Net income	$129

The company's tax rate is 40%.

PROBLEMS

P 16–1
Determine deferred tax
assets and liabilities

Corning-Howell reported taxable income in 2003 of $120 million. At December 31, 2003, the reported amount of some assets and liabilities in the financial statements differed from their tax bases as indicated below:

	Carrying Amount	Tax Basis
Assets		
Current		
Accounts receivable (net of allowance)	$ 10 million	$ 12 million
Prepaid insurance	20 million	0
Prepaid rent expense (operating lease)	6 million	0
Noncurrent		
Buildings and equipment (net)	360 million	280 million
Liabilities		
Current		
Liability—subscriptions received	14 million	0
Long-term		
Liability—postretirement benefits	594 million	0
Shareholders' Equity		
Unrealized gain from recording investments available for sale at fair market value*	4 million	0

*Taxable when investments are sold.

The total deferred tax asset and deferred tax liability amounts at January 1, 2003, were $250 million and $40 million, respectively. The enacted tax rate is 40% each year.

Required:
1. Determine the total deferred tax asset and deferred tax liability amounts at December 31, 2003.
2. Determine the increase (decrease) in the deferred tax asset and deferred tax liability accounts at December 31, 2003.
3. Determine the income tax payable currently for the year ended December 31, 2003.

4. Prepare the journal entry to record income taxes for 2003.
5. Show how the deferred tax amounts should be classified and reported in the 2003 balance sheet.

P 16–2
Temporary difference; determine deferred tax amount for three years; balance sheet classification

Times-Roman Publishing Company reports the following amounts in its first three years of operation:

($ in 000s)	2003	2004	2005
Pretax accounting income	$250	$240	$230
Taxable income	290	220	260

The difference between pretax accounting income and taxable income is due to subscription revenue for one-year magazine subscriptions being reported for tax purposes in the year received, but reported on the income statement in later years when earned. The income tax rate is 40% each year. Times-Roman anticipates profitable operations in the future.

Required:
1. What is the balance sheet account for which a temporary difference is created by this situation?
2. For each year, indicate the cumulative amount of the temporary difference at year-end.
3. Determine the balance in the related deferred tax account at the end of each year. Is it a deferred tax asset or a deferred tax liability?
4. How should the deferred tax amount be classified and reported on the balance sheet?

P 16–3
Change in tax rate; single temporary difference

Dixon Development began operations in December 2003. When lots for industrial development are sold, Dixon recognizes income for financial reporting purposes in the year of the sale. For some lots, Dixon recognizes income for tax purposes when collected. Income recognized for financial reporting purposes in 2003 for lots sold this way was $12 million, which will be collected over the next three years. Scheduled collections for 2004–2006 are as follows:

2004	$ 4 million
2005	5 million
2006	3 million
	$12 million

Pretax accounting income for 2003 was $16 million. The enacted tax rate is 40%.

Required:
1. Assuming no differences between accounting income and taxable income other than those described above, prepare the journal entry to record income taxes in 2003.
2. Suppose a new tax law, revising the tax rate from 40% to 35%, beginning in 2005, is enacted in 2004, when pretax accounting income was $15 million. Prepare the appropriate journal entry to record income taxes in 2004.
3. If the new tax rate had not been enacted, what would have been the appropriate balance in the deferred tax liability account at the end of 2004? Why?

P 16–4
Change in tax rate; record taxes for four years

Zekany Corporation would have had identical income before taxes on both its income tax returns and income statements for the years 2003 through 2006 except for differences in depreciation on an operational asset. The asset cost $120,000 and is depreciated for income tax purposes in the following amounts:

2003	$39,600
2004	52,800
2005	18,000
2006	9,600

The operational asset has a four-year life and no residual value. The straight-line method is used for financial reporting purposes.

Income amounts before depreciation expense and income taxes for each of the four years were as follows.

	2003	2004	2005	2006
Accounting income before taxes and depreciation	$60,000	$80,000	$70,000	$70,000

Assume the average and marginal income tax rate for 2003 and 2004 was 30%; however, during 2004 tax legislation was passed to raise the tax rate to 40% beginning in 2005. The 40% rate remained in effect through the years 2005 and 2006. Both the accounting and income tax periods end December 31.

Required:

Prepare the journal entries to record income taxes for the years 2003 through 2006.

P 16–5

Change in tax rate; permanent and temporary differences; record taxes for four years

The DeVille Company reported pretax accounting income on its income statement as follows:

2003	$350,000
2004	270,000
2005	340,000
2006	380,000

Included in the income of 2003 was an installment sale of property in the amount of $50,000. However, for tax purposes, DeVille reported the income in the year cash was collected. Cash collected on the installment sale was $20,000 in 2004, $25,000 in 2005, and $5,000 in 2006.

Included in the 2005 income was $15,000 interest from investments in municipal bonds.

The enacted tax rate for 2003 and 2004 was 30%, but during 2004 new tax legislation was passed reducing the tax rate to 25% for the years 2005 and beyond.

Required:

Prepare the year-end journal entries to record income taxes for the years 2003–2006.

P 16–6

Multiple temporary differences; multiple tax rates; balance sheet classification

The following information relates to Barry Transport Company:

a. Pretax accounting income was $41 million and taxable income was $8 million for the year ended December 31, 2003.

b. Temporary differences at December 31, 2003, were related to:

	Future Taxable (Deductible) Amounts	
Depreciation	2004	($60 million)
	2005	50 million
	2006	40 million
		$30 million
Prepaid insurance, 2004 coverage		9 million
Loss contingency, to be paid in 2005		(6 million)

c. No temporary differences existed at the beginning of 2003.

d. The tax rate is 40%.

Required:

1. Determine the amounts necessary to record income taxes for 2003 and prepare the appropriate journal entry.

2. How should the deferred tax amounts be classified in a classified balance sheet?

3. Assume the enacted federal income tax law specifies that the tax rate will change from 40% to 35% as of 2005. Determine the amounts necessary to record income taxes for 2003 and prepare the appropriate journal entry.

P 16–7

Multiple temporary differences; nontemporary difference; calculate taxable income; balance sheet classification

Sherrod, Inc., reported pretax accounting income of $76 million for 2003. The following information relates to differences between pretax accounting income and taxable income:

a. Income from installment sales of properties included in pretax accounting income in 2003 exceeded that reported for tax purposes by $3 million. The installment receivable account at year-end had a balance of $4 million (representing portions of 2002 and 2003 installment sales), expected to be collected equally in 2004 and 2005.

b. Sherrod was assessed a penalty of $2 million by the Environmental Protection Agency for violation of a federal law in 2003. The fine is to be paid in equal amounts in 2003 and 2004.

c. Sherrod rents its operating facilities but owns one asset acquired in 2002 at a cost of $80 million. Depreciation is reported by the straight-line method assuming a four-year useful life. On the tax return, deductions for depreciation will be more than straight-line depreciation the first two years but less than straight-line depreciation the next two years ($ in millions):

	Income Statement	Tax Return	Difference
2002	$20	$26	$ (6)
2003	20	35	(15)
2004	20	12	8
2005	20	7	13
	$80	$80	$ 0

d. Bad debt expense is reported using the allowance method, $3 million in 2003. For tax purposes, the expense is deducted when accounts prove uncollectible (the direct write-off method), $2 million in 2003. At December 31, 2003, the allowance for uncollectible accounts was $2 million (after adjusting entries). The balance was $1 million at the end of 2002.

e. In 2003, Sherrod accrued an expense and related liability for estimated paid future absences of $7 million relating to the company's new paid vacation program. Future compensation will be deductible on the tax return when actually paid during the next two years ($4 million in 2004; $3 million in 2005).

f. During 2002, accounting income included an estimated loss of $2 million from having accrued a loss contingency. The loss is paid in 2003 at which time it is tax deductible.

   Balances in the deferred tax asset and deferred tax liability accounts at January 1, 2003, were $1.2 million and $2.8 million, respectively. The enacted tax rate is 40% each year.

Required:
1. Determine the amounts necessary to record income taxes for 2003 and prepare the appropriate journal entry.
2. What is the 2003 net income?
3. Show how any deferred tax amounts should be classified and reported on the 2003 balance sheet.

P 16–8
Multiple temporary differences; nontemporary difference; taxable income given; two years; balance sheet classification

Arndt, Inc., reported the following for 2002 and 2003 ($ in millions):

	2002	2003
Revenues	$888	$983
Expenses	760	800
Pretax accounting income (income statement)	$128	$183
Taxable income (tax return)	$120	$200
Tax rate: 40%		

a. Expenses each year include $30 million from a two-year casualty insurance policy purchased in 2002 for $60 million. The cost is tax-deductible in 2002.

b. Expenses include $2 million insurance premiums each year for life insurance on key executives.

c. Arndt sells one-year subscriptions to a weekly journal. Subscription sales collected and taxable in 2002 and 2003 were $33 million and $35 million, respectively. Subscriptions included in 2002 and 2003 financial reporting revenues were $25 million ($10 million collected in 2001 but not earned until 2002) and $33 million, respectively. Hint: View this as two temporary differences—one reversing in 2002; one originating in 2002.

d. 2002 expenses included a $17 million unrealized loss from reducing investments (classified as trading securities) to fair value. The investments were sold in 2003.

e. During 2001, accounting income included an estimated loss of $5 million from having accrued a loss contingency. The loss was paid in 2002 at which time it is tax deductible.

f. At January 1, 2002, Arndt had a deferred tax asset of $6 million and no deferred tax liability.

Required:
1. Which of the five differences described are temporary and which are nontemporary differences? Why?
2. Prepare a schedule that (a) reconciles the difference between pretax accounting income and taxable income and (b) determines the amounts necessary to record income taxes for 2002. Prepare the appropriate journal entry.
3. Show how any 2002 deferred tax amounts should be classified and reported on the 2002 balance sheet.
4. Prepare a schedule that (a) reconciles the difference between pretax accounting income and taxable income and (b) determines the amounts necessary to record income taxes for 2003. Prepare the appropriate journal entry.
5. Explain how any 2003 deferred tax amounts should be classified and reported on the 2003 balance sheet.

P 16–9
Single temporary difference originates each year for four years

Alsup Consulting sometimes performs services for which it receives payment at the conclusion of the engagement, up to six months after services commence. Alsup recognizes service revenue for financial reporting purposes when the services are performed. For tax purposes, revenue is reported when fees are collected. Service revenue, collections, and pretax accounting income for 2002–2005 are as follows:

	Service Revenue	Collections	Pretax Accounting Income
2002	$650,000	$620,000	$186,000
2003	750,000	770,000	250,000
2004	715,000	700,000	220,000
2005	700,000	720,000	200,000

There are no differences between accounting income and taxable income other than the temporary difference described above. The enacted tax rate for each year is 40%.

Required:
1. Prepare the appropriate journal entry to record Alsup's 2003 income taxes.
2. Prepare the appropriate journal entry to record Alsup's 2004 income taxes.
3. Prepare the appropriate journal entry to record Alsup's 2005 income taxes.
(Hint: You may find it helpful to prepare a schedule that shows the balances in service revenue receivable at December 31, 2002–2005.)

P 16–10
Operating loss carryback and carryforward; temporary difference; nontemporary difference

Fores Construction Company reported a pretax operating loss of $135 million for financial reporting purposes in 2003. Contributing to the loss were (a) a penalty of $5 million assessed by the Environmental Protection Agency for violation of a federal law and paid in 2003 and (b) an estimated loss of $10 million from accruing a loss contingency. The loss will be tax deductible when paid in 2004.

The enacted tax rate is 40%. There were no temporary differences at the beginning of the year and none originating in 2003 other than those described above. Taxable income in Fores's two previous years of operation was as follows:

2001	$75 million
2002	30 million

Required:
1. Prepare the journal entry to recognize the income tax benefit of the operating loss in 2003. Fores elects the carryback option.
2. Show the lower portion of the 2003 income statement that reports the income tax benefit of the operating loss.
3. Prepare the journal entry to record income taxes in 2004 assuming pretax accounting income is $60 million. No additional temporary differences originate in 2004.

P 16–11
Integrating problem—bonds, leases, taxes

Ex

The following is the long-term liabilities section of Tempo Co.'s December 31, 2002, balance sheet:

Long-Term Liabilities:

Note payable—bank; 15 principal payments of $5,000, plus 10% interest due annually on September 30	$75,000	
Less current portion	(5,000)	$ 70,000
Capital lease obligation—16 payments of $9,000 due annually on January 1	$76,600	
Less current portion	(1,340)	75,260
Deferred income tax liability		15,750
Total long-term liabilities		$161,010

a. Tempo's incremental borrowing rate on the date of the lease was 11% and the lessor's implicit rate, which was known by Tempo, was 10%.
b. The only difference between Tempo's taxable income and pretax accounting income is depreciation on a machine acquired on January 1, 2002, for $250,000. The machine's estimated useful life is five years, with no salvage value. Depreciation is computed using the straight-line method for financial reporting purposes and the MACRS method for tax purposes. Depreciation expense for tax and financial reporting purposes for 2003 through 2006 is as follows:

Year	Tax Depreciation	Financial Depreciation	Tax Depreciation Over (Under) Financial Depreciation
2003	$80,000	$50,000	$ 30,000
2004	40,000	50,000	(10,000)
2005	35,000	50,000	(15,000)
2006	30,000	50,000	(20,000)

The enacted federal income tax rates are 30% for 2002 and 2003, and 35% for 2004 through 2006.

c. Included in Tempo's December 2002 balance sheet was a deferred tax asset of $9,000.

d. For the year ended December 31, 2003, Tempo's income before income taxes was $430,000.

e. On July 1, 2003, Tempo received proceeds of $459,725 from a $500,000 bond issuance. The bonds mature in 30 years and interest of 11% is payable each January 1 and July 1. The bonds were issued at a price to yield the investors 12%. Tempo uses the effective interest method to amortize the bond discount.

Required:

1. Prepare a schedule showing Tempo's income before income taxes, current income tax expense, deferred income tax expense, and net income for 2003. Show supporting calculations for current and deferred income tax amounts.

2. Prepare a schedule showing the calculations of Tempo's interest expense for the year ended December 31, 2003.

3. Prepare the long-term liabilities section of Tempo's December 31, 2003, balance sheet. Show supporting calculations.

(AICPA adapted)

BROADEN YOUR PERSPECTIVE

Apply your critical-thinking ability to the knowledge you've gained. These cases will provide you an opportunity to develop your research, analysis, judgment, and communication skills. You also will work with other students, integrate what you've learned, apply it in real world situations, and consider its global and ethical ramifications. This practice will broaden your knowledge and further develop your decision-making abilities.

Analysis Case 16–1
Basic concepts

One of the longest debates in accounting history is the issue of deferred taxes. The controversy began in the 1940s and has continued, even after the FASB issued *Statement of Financial Accounting Standards No. 109* in 1992. At issue is the appropriate treatment of tax consequences of economic events that occur in years other than that of the events themselves.

Required:

1. Distinguish between temporary differences and permanent differences. Provide an example of each.

2. Distinguish between intraperiod tax allocation and interperiod tax allocation (deferred tax accounting). Provide an example of each.

3. How are deferred tax assets and deferred tax liabilities classified and reported in the financial statements?

Integrating Case 16–2
Postretirement benefits

Statement of Financial Accounting Standards No. 106 establishes accounting standards for postretirement benefits other than pensions, most notably postretirement health care benefits. Essentially, the standard requires companies to accrue compensation expense each year employees perform services, for the expected cost of providing future postretirement benefits that can be attributed to that service. Typically, companies do not prefund these costs for two reasons: (a) unlike pension liabilities, no federal law requires companies to fund nonpension postretirement benefits and (b) funding contributions, again unlike for pension liabilities, are not tax deductible. (The costs aren't tax deductible until paid to, or on behalf of, employees.)

Required:

1. As a result of being required to record the periodic postretirement expense and related liability, most companies now report lower earnings and higher liabilities. How might many companies also report higher assets as a result of *SFAS 106?*

2. One objection to *SFAS 109,* "Accounting for Income Taxes," as cited in the chapter is the omission of requirements to discount deferred tax amounts to their present values. This objection is inappropriate in the context of deferred tax amounts necessitated by accounting for postretirement benefits. Why?

Judgment Case 16–3
Intraperiod tax allocation

Russell-James Corporation is a diversified consumer products company. During 2003, Russell-James discontinued its line of cosmetics, which constituted discontinued operations for financial reporting purposes. As vice president of the food products division, you are interested in the effect of the discontinuance on the company's profitability. One item of information you requested was an income statement. The income statement you received was labeled *preliminary* and *unaudited:*

RUSSELL-JAMES CORPORATION
Income Statement
For the Year Ended December 31, 2003
($ in millions, except per share amounts)

Revenues		$300
Cost of goods sold		90
Gross profit		210
Selling and administrative expenses		(60)
Income from continuing operations before income taxes		150
Income taxes		(24)
Income from continuing operations		126
Discontinued operations:		
Loss from operations of cosmetics division	$(100)	
Gain from disposal of cosmetics division	15	(85)
Income before extraordinary item and cumulative effect of accounting change		41
Extraordinary loss from earthquake		(10)
Cumulative effect of change in inventory costing		5
Net income		$ 36
Per Share of Common Stock (100 million shares):		
Income from continuing operations		$1.26
Loss from operations of cosmetics division		(1.00)
Gain from disposal of cosmetics division		.15
Income before extraordinary item and cumulative effect of accounting change		.41
Extraordinary loss from earthquake		(.10)
Cumulative effect of change in inventory costing		.05
Net income		$ .36

You are somewhat surprised at the magnitude of the loss incurred by the cosmetics division prior to its disposal. Another item that draws your attention is the apparently low tax rate indicated by the statement ($24 ÷ 150 = 16\%$). Upon further investigation you are told the company's tax rate is 40%.

Required:
1. Recast the income statement to reflect intraperiod tax allocation.
2. How would you reconcile the income tax expense shown on the statement above with the amount your recast statement reports?

International Case 16–4
Accounting for income taxes in other countries

The primary objective of the International Accounting Standards Committee (IASC) is to narrow worldwide differences in accounting practices and the presentation of financial information. Although the IASC has worked toward uniformity since 1973, harmonization has by no means been achieved. In the area of accounting for income taxes, significant differences exist from country to country that impact reported earnings and financial position.

Required:
Choose a country other than the United States and:
1. Locate a recent annual report of a company located in that country.
2. Determine the way that country accounts for income taxes. Include in your analysis:
   a. The extent of variations between accounting income and taxable income.
   b. Whether these differences create deferred taxes.
   c. Whether tax deferral depends on expectations as to when differences are expected to reverse.
3. Prepare a short report highlighting the similarities and differences between the United States and your chosen country in the way income taxes are accounted for.

Note: You can obtain copies of annual reports from the company's website, a friendly stockbroker, Public Register's Annual Report Service at www.PRARS.com or from EDGAR, the Electronic Data Gathering and Retrieval service of the SEC, from EdgarScan at: **edgarscan.pwcglobal.com/**.

Judgment Case 16–5
Analyzing the effect of
deferred tax liabilities
on firm risk; Hewlett-
Packard Company

The following disclosure note appeared in the 2001 annual report of the Hewlett-Packard Company.

Note 11: Taxes on Earnings (in part)

The significant components of deferred tax assets and deferred tax liabilities were as follows at October 31:

	2001		2000	
	Deferred Tax Assets	Deferred Tax Liabilities	Deferred Tax Assets	Deferred Tax Liabilities
($ in millions)				
Inventory	$ 281	$ –	$ 632	$ 2
Fixed assets	138	7	101	2
Warranty	291	–	382	–
Employee and retiree benefits	474	160	490	84
Intracompany sales	2,248	–	1,433	–
Unremitted earnings of foreign subsidiaries	–	874	–	347
Credits and net operating loss carryforwards	1,160	–	–	–
Other	490	90	258	99
Gross deferred tax assets and liabilities	5,082	1,131	3,296	534
Valuation allowance	(74)	–	–	–
Total deferred tax assets and liabilities	$5,008	$1,131	$3,296	$534

The current portion of the deferred tax asset, which is included in other current assets, was $3,073 million at October 31, 2001 and $2,607 million at October 31, 2000.

HP's debt-to-equity ratio was 1.34, calculated as $18,631 ÷ $13,953. Some analysts argue that long-term deferred tax liabilities should be excluded from liabilities when computing the debt-to-equity ratio.

Required:

1. What is the rationale for the argument that long-term deferred tax liabilities should be excluded from liabilities when computing the debt-to-equity ratio?
2. What would be the effect on HP's debt-to-equity ratio of excluding deferred tax liabilities from its calculation? What would be the percentage change?
3. What might be the rationale for not excluding long-term deferred tax liabilities from liabilities when computing the debt-to-equity ratio?

Integrating Case 16–6
Income taxes and
investment securities

The Wrigley Company is the world's largest manufacturer of chewing gum. The following disclosure note appeared in Wrigley's 2001 annual report.

Investments in Debt and Equity Securities (in part, $ in 000s)

The Company's investments in marketable equity securities are held for an indefinite period. Application of *Statement of Financial Accounting Standards (SFAS) No. 115,* "Accounting for Certain Investments in Debt and Equity Securities," resulted in unrealized holding gains of $21,912 at December 31, 2001, and $26,644 at December 31, 2000. Unrealized holding gains, net of the related tax effect, of $14,274 and $17,351 at December 31, 2001 and 2000, respectively, are included as components of Accumulated Other Comprehensive Income in stockholders' equity.

Required:

1. From the information provided by the disclosure note, determine the amount at which Wrigley would have reported its investment in marketable equity securities in its 2001 balance sheet. Explain how investment securities available for sale are accounted for.
2. What would have been Wrigley's journal entry to reflect the 2001 fair value of the investments?

Communication Case 16–7

Notes, leases, bonds

Chris Green, CPA, is auditing Rayne Co.'s 2003 financial statements. The controller, Ben Dunn, has provided Green with the following information:

a. At December 31, 2002, Rayne had a note payable to Federal Bank with a balance of $90,000. The annual principal payment of $10,000, plus 8% interest on the unpaid balance, was paid when due on March 31, 2003.

b. On January 2, 2003, Rayne leased two automobiles for executive use under a capital lease. Five annual lease payments of $15,000 are due beginning January 3, 2003. Rayne's incremental borrowing rate on the date of the lease was 11% and the lessor's implicit rate, which was known by Rayne, was 10%. The lease was properly recorded at $62,500, before the first payment was made.

c. On July 1, 2003, Rayne received proceeds of $538,000 from a $500,000 bond issuance. The bonds mature in 15 years and interest of 11% is payable semiannually on June 30 and December 31. The bonds were issued at a price to yield investors 10%. Rayne uses the effective interest method to amortize bond premium.

d. For the year ended December 31, 2003, Rayne has adopted *Statement of Financial Accounting Standards No. 109*, "Accounting for Income Taxes." Dunn has prepared a schedule of all differences between financial statement and income tax return income. Dunn believes that as a result of pending legislation, the enacted tax rate at December 31, 2003, will be increased for 2004. Dunn is uncertain which differences to include and which rates to apply in computing deferred taxes under *SFAS 109*. Dunn has requested an overview of *SFAS 109* from Green.

Required:

1. Prepare a schedule of interest expense for the year ended December 31, 2003.
2. Prepare a brief memo to Dunn from Green:
    a. Identifying the objectives of accounting for income taxes.
    b. Defining temporary differences.
    c. Explaining how to measure deferred tax assets and liabilities.
    d. Explaining how to measure deferred income tax expense or benefit.

(AICPA adapted)

Research Case 16–8

Valuation allowance; research an article in *Accounting Horizons*

SFAS 109 requires companies to recognize deferred tax assets for *all* deductible temporary differences and then reduce a deferred tax asset by a valuation allowance if it is more likely than not that some portion or all of the deferred tax asset will not be realized. This is referred to in the *Standard* as the impairment approach. The Board rejected an alternative affirmative approach, under which a firm would start at zero and then adjust the deferred tax asset upward as warranted by positive evidence about reliability, but suggested that either approach would likely lead to the same net deferred tax asset if a more likely than not realization criterion is used. Professors Heiman-Hoffman and Patton, in "An Experimental Investigation of Deferred Tax Asset Judgments under *SFAS 109*," conducted an empirical test of whether the two approaches lead to the same result.

Required:

1. In your library or from some other source, locate the indicated article in *Accounting Horizons*, March 1994.
2. What is the authors' conclusion as to whether the two approaches lead to the same net deferred tax asset?
3. On what evidence do they base their conclusion?

Integrating Case 16–9

Accounting changes and error correction; six situations; tax effects considered

Williams-Santana, Inc., is a manufacturer of high-tech industrial parts that was started in 1991 by two talented engineers with little business training. In 2003, the company was acquired by one of its major customers. As part of an internal audit, the following facts were discovered. The audit occurred during 2003 before any adjusting entries or closing entries were prepared. The income tax rate is 40% for all years.

a. A five-year casualty insurance policy was purchased at the beginning of 2001 for $35,000. The full amount was debited to insurance expense at the time.

b. On December 31, 2002, merchandise inventory was overstated by $25,000 due to a mistake in the physical inventory count using the periodic inventory system.

c. The company changed inventory cost methods to FIFO from LIFO at the end of 2003 for both financial statement and income tax purposes. The change will cause a $960,000 increase in the beginning inventory at January 1, 2002.

d. At the end of 2002, the company failed to accrue $15,500 of sales commissions earned by employees during 2002. The expense was recorded when the commissions were paid in early 2003.

e. At the beginning of 2001, the company purchased a machine at a cost of $720,000. Its useful life was estimated to be 10 years with no salvage value. The machine has been depreciated by the double-declining-balance method. Its carrying amount on December 31, 2002, was $460,800. On January 1, 2003, the company changed retroactively to the straight-line method.

f. Additional industrial robots were acquired at the beginning of 2000 and added to the company's assembly process. The $1,000,000 cost of the equipment was inadvertently recorded as repair expense. Robots have 10-year useful lives and no material salvage value. This class of equipment is depreciated by the straight-line method for both financial reporting and income tax reporting.

Required:

For each situation:

1. Identify whether it represents an accounting change or an error. If an accounting change, identify the type of change.
2. Prepare any journal entry necessary as a direct result of the change or error correction as well as any adjusting entry for 2003 related to the situation described. Any tax effects should be adjusted for through the deferred tax liability account.
3. Briefly describe any other steps that should be taken to appropriately report the situation.

Real World Case 16–10
Disclosure issues; balance sheet classifications

The income tax disclosure note accompanying the 2001 financial statements of the Walgreen Company is reproduced below:

Income Taxes

The provision for income taxes consists of the following (in millions):

	2001	2000	1999
Current provision			
Federal	$417.1	$400.9	$350.5
State	73.1	64.5	62.1
	490.2	465.4	412.6
Deferred provision			
Federal	47.1	17.7	(8.0)
State	(.2)	3.3	(1.4)
	46.9	21.0	(9.4)
	$537.1	$486.4	$403.2

The components of the deferred provision were (in millions):

	2001	2000	1999
Accelerated depreciation	$49.7	$51.5	$ 9.7
Inventory	18.6	(2.3)	11.1
Insurance	(15.7)	(11.0)	(2.7)
Employee benefit plans	(11.1)	(17.7)	(12.2)
Accrued rent	2.2	(5.2)	(8.7)
Other	3.2	5.7	(6.6)
	$46.9	$21.0	$(9.4)

The deferred tax assets and liabilities included in the Consolidated Balance Sheets consist of the following (in millions):

	2001	2000
Deferred tax assets:		
Employee benefit plans	$146.3	$135.4
Accrued rent	52.7	54.9
Insurance	68.3	52.6
Inventory	28.1	23.6
Other	39.0	38.9
	334.4	305.4

Deferred tax liabilities:		
Accelerated depreciation	341.7	292.0
Inventory	92.9	69.8
Other	16.1	13.0
	450.7	374.8
Net deferred tax liabilities	$116.3	$ 69.4

Income taxes paid were $432.1 million, $398.4 million, and $377.3 million during the fiscal years ended August 31, 2001, 2000, and 1999, respectively. The difference between the statutory income tax rate and the effective tax rate is principally due to state income tax provisions.

Required:
1. On its 2001 balance sheet, Walgreens reported as a noncurrent liability, "Deferred income taxes" of $137 million. Why is this different from the $116.3 million "net deferred tax liability" reported in the disclosure note?
2. Re-create the journal entry that summarizes the entries Walgreens used to record its 2001 income taxes.

International Case 16–11
Comparison of deferred tax accounting in the U.K. and the United States

The British Petroleum Company p.l.c. (BP), based in London, is one of the world's largest petroleum and petro-chemical groups. The income tax disclosures accompanying BP's 2000 financial statements are reproduced below:

Accounting Policies (in part)
Deferred Taxation
Deferred taxation is calculated, using the liability method, in respect to timing differences arising primarily from the different accounting and tax treatment both of depreciation and petroleum revenue tax. Provision is made or recovery anticipated where timing differences are expected to reverse in the foreseeable future.

Balance Sheets (partial) at December 31	Note	2000	1999
Total assets less current liabilities		106,791	66,286
Creditors—amounts falling due after more than one year:			
Finance debt	24	14,772	9,644
Other creditors	25	5,223	2,245
Provision for liabilities and charges:			
Deferred taxation	11	1,822	1,783
Other provisions	26	10,973	8,272
Net assets		74,001	44,342

Note 11: Taxation (in part)

	Provisions		millions Gross Potential Liability	
Analysis of Provision	2000	1999	2000	1999
Depreciation	2,641	2,567	13,008	10,279
Petroleum revenue tax	(337)	(332)	(337)	(332)
Other timing differences	(482)	(452)	(2,987)	(2,808)
	1,822	1,783	9,684	7,139

Required:
On the basis of the information the disclosures provide, compare accounting for income taxes in the U.K. with that in the United States.

Research Case 16–12
Researching the way tax deductions are reported on a corporation tax return; retrieving a tax form from the Internet

The U.S. Treasury maintains an information site on the Internet. As part of this site the Internal Revenue Service provides tax information and services. Among those services is a server for publications and forms which allows a visitor to download a variety of IRS forms and publications.

Required:

1. Access the Treasury site on the Internet. The web address is **www.ustreas.gov**. After exploring the information available there, navigate to the IRS server for forms and publications via the IRS home page.
2. Download the corporation tax return, Form 1120.
3. Note the specific deductions listed that are deductible from total income to arrive at taxable income. Are any deductions listed that might not also be included among expenses on the income statement?
4. One of the deductions indicated is "net operating loss deduction." Under what circumstances might a company report an amount for this item?
5. Based on how taxable income is determined, how might temporary differences be created between taxable income and pretax income on the income statement?

Analysis Case 16–13
Reporting deferred taxes

FedEx Corporation

Refer to the financial statements and related disclosure notes of FedEx Corporation in the appendix to Chapter 1. On FedEx's balance sheet, deferred income taxes are reported as both an asset ($435.4 million in 2001) and a liability ($455.6 million in 2001).

Required:

1. Explain why deferred income taxes can be reported as both an asset and a liability. Why is the deferred tax asset reported as current and the deferred tax liability as long term?
2. Note 9 in the disclosure notes indicates that deferred tax assets are $1,013.1 million in 2001 and deferred tax liabilities are $1,033.3 million. How can that be explained in light of the two amounts reported in the balance sheet?
3. Does FedEx feel the need to record a valuation allowance for its deferred tax assets?

Analysis Case 16–14
Consult financial statements; analyze tax disclosures; recreate journal entry

Kroger Co. is the largest retail food company in the United States as measured by total annual sales. Kroger operates 2,300 food stores under 23 names across 31 states, and 787 convenience stores under six logos in 15 states. Food stores are its primary business and account for over 93% of total company sales. Its convenience stores and 34 manufacturing facilities contribute the remainder of total sales.

Like most corporations, Kroger has significant deferred tax assets and liabilities resulting from accounting for income taxes in accordance with *SFAS 109*. Using EdgarScan, (**edgarscan. pwcglobal.com/**) check the company's annual report for the year ended February 2, 2002.

Required:

1. From the income statement, determine the income tax expense for the year. What is the current portion and the deferred portion of the expense? (See the "Income Taxes" note in the Notes to Consolidated Financial Statements.) Why is the income tax expense from the income statement different from the "provision for income taxes in the disclosure note"?
2. How are the deferred taxes classified on Kroger's balance sheet? (See the "Income Taxes" note in the Notes to Consolidated Financial Statements.) What amounts are reported among current assets or liabilities and among noncurrent assets or liabilities? Why?
3. What was the amount of the extraordinary loss for the year ended at February 3, 2001, without considering the tax savings from being able to deduct the loss? Why is the tax effect of the loss not reported with the primary income tax expense?

17

Pensions

CHAPTER

OVERVIEW

Employee compensation comes in many forms. Salaries and wages, of course, provide direct and current payment for services provided. However, it's commonplace for compensation also to include benefits payable after retirement. We discuss pension benefits in this chapter. Accounting for pension benefits recognizes that they represent deferred compensation for current service. Accordingly, the cost of these benefits is recognized on an accrual basis during the years that employees earn the benefits.

LEARNING OBJECTIVES

After studying this chapter, you should be able to:

LO1 Explain the fundamental differences between a defined contribution pension plan and a defined benefit pension plan.

LO2 Distinguish among the vested benefit obligation, the accumulated benefit obligation, and the projected benefit obligation.

LO3 Describe the five events that might change the balance of the PBO.

LO4 Explain how plan assets accumulate to provide retiree benefits and understand the role of the trustee in administering the fund.

LO5 Describe how pension expense is a composite of periodic changes that occur in both the pension obligation and the plan assets.

LO6 Understand the interrelationships among the elements that constitute a defined benefit pension plan.

LO7 Describe how pension disclosures fill a reporting gap left by the minimal disclosures in the primary financial statements.

United Dynamics

You read yesterday that many companies in the United States have pension plans that are severely underfunded. This caught your attention in part because you have your office interview tomorrow with United Dynamics. You hadn't really thought that much about the pension plan of your potential future employer, in part because your current employer has a defined contribution 401K plan, for which funding is not a concern. However, United Dynamics is an older firm with a defined benefit plan, for which funding is the employer's responsibility.

To prepare for your interview, you obtained a copy of United Dynamics' financial statements. Unfortunately, the financial statements themselves are of little help. You are unable to find any pension liability on the balance sheet, but the statement does report a relatively small "prepaid pension asset." The income statement reports pension expense for each of the years reported. For help, you search the disclosure notes. In part, the pension disclosure note reads as follows:

Note 7: Pension Plan

United Dynamics has a defined benefit pension plan covering substantially all of its employees. Plan benefits are based on years of service and the employee's compensation during the last three years of employment. The company's funding policy is consistent with the funding requirements of federal law and regulations. The net periodic pension expense for the company included the following components. The company's pension expense was as follows ($ in millions):

	2003	2002	2001
Current service costs	$ 43	$ 47	$ 42
Interest cost on projected benefit obligation	178	164	152
Return on assets	(213)	(194)	(187)
Amortization of prior service cost	43	43	43
Amortization of net gain	(2)	(1)	—
Net pension costs	$ 49	$ 59	$ 50

The following table describes the change in projected benefit obligation for the plan years ended December 31, 2003, and December 31, 2002 ($ in millions):

	2003	2002
Projected benefit obligation at beginning of year	$2,194	$2,121
Service cost	43	53
Interest cost	178	164
Actuarial (gain) loss	319	(46)
Benefits paid	(106)	(98)
Projected benefit obligation at end of year	$2,628	$2,194

(continued)

The weighted average discount rate and rate of increase in future compensation levels used in determining the actuarial present value of the projected benefit obligations in the above table was 8.1% and 4.3%, respectively, at December 31, 2003, and 7.73% and 4.7%, respectively, at December 31, 2002. The expected long-term rate of return on assets was 9.1% at December 31, 2003 and 2002.

The following table describes the change in the fair value of plan assets for the plan years ended December 31, 2003 and 2002 ($ in millions):

	2003	2002
Fair value of plan assets at beginning of year	$2,340	$2,133
Actual return on plan assets	215	178
Employer contributions	358	127
Benefits paid	(106)	(98)
Fair value of plan assets at end of year	$2,807	$2,340

"Ouch! I can't believe how much of my accounting I forgot," you complain to yourself. "I'd better get out my old intermediate accounting book."

> By the time you finish this chapter, you should be able to respond appropriately to the questions posed in this case. Compare your response to the solution provided at the end of the chapter.

QUESTIONS

1. Why is underfunding not a concern in your present employment? (page 837)

2. Were you correct that the pension liability is not reported on the balance sheet? What is the liability? (page 839)

3. What is the amount of the plan assets available to pay benefits? What are the factors that can cause that amount to change? (page 846)

4. How is the pension expense influenced by changes in the pension liability and plan assets? (page 848)

5. Are you interviewing with a company whose pension plan is severely underfunded? (page 856)

PART	THE NATURE OF PENSION PLANS

a

Over 60 million American workers are covered by pension plans. The United States' pension funds tripled in size during the previous two decades and now are roughly the size of Japan's gross national product. This powerful investment base now controls about one-fourth of the stock market. At the company level, the enormous size of pension funds is reflected in a periodic pension cost that constitutes one of the largest expenses many companies report. The corporate liability for providing pension benefits, though largely off-balance-sheet, is huge. Obviously, then, the financial reporting responsibility for pensions has important social and economic implications.

Pension plans are designed to provide income to individuals during their retirement years. This is accomplished by setting aside funds during an employee's working years so that at retirement the accumulated funds plus earnings from investing those funds are available to replace wages. Actually, an individual who periodically invests in stocks, bonds, certificates of deposit (CDs), or other investments for the purpose of saving for retirement is establishing a personal pension fund. Often, such individual plans take the form of individual retirement accounts (IRAs) to take advantage of tax breaks offered by that arrangement. In employer plans, some or all of the periodic contributions to the retirement fund often are provided by the employer.

Corporations establish pension plans for a variety of reasons. Sponsorship of pension plans provides employees with a degree of retirement security and fulfills a moral obligation felt by many employers. This security also can induce a degree of job satisfaction and perhaps loyalty that might enhance productivity and reduce turnover. Motivation to sponsor a

Pension plans often enhance productivity, reduce turnover, satisfy union demands, and allow employers to compete in the labor market.

plan sometimes comes from union demands and often relates to being competitive in the labor market.

ADDITIONAL CONSIDERATION

When established according to tight guidelines, a pension plan gains important tax advantages. Such arrangements are called *qualified plans* because they qualify for favorable tax treatment. In a qualified plan, the employer is permitted an immediate tax deduction for amounts paid into the pension fund (within specified limits). The employees, on the other hand, are not taxed at the time employer contributions are made—only when retirement benefits are received. Moreover, earnings on the funds set aside by the employer are not taxed while in the pension fund, so the earnings accumulate tax free. If you are familiar with the tax advantages of IRAs, you probably recognize the similarity between those individual plans and corporate pension arrangements.

> Qualified pension plans offer important tax benefits.

For a pension plan to be qualified for special tax treatment it must meet these general requirements.

1. It must cover at least 70% of employees.
2. It cannot discriminate in favor of highly compensated employees.
3. It must be funded in advance of retirement through contributions to an irrevocable trust fund.
4. Benefits must vest after a specified period of service, commonly five years. (We discuss this in more detail later.)
5. It complies with specific restrictions on the timing and amount of contributions and benefits.

Sometimes, employers agree to annually contribute a specific (defined) amount to a pension fund on behalf of employees but make no commitment regarding benefit amounts at retirement. In other arrangements, employers don't specify the amount of annual contributions but promise to provide determinable (defined) amounts at retirement. These two arrangements describe defined contribution pension plans and defined benefit pension plans, respectively:

- **Defined contribution pension plans** promise fixed annual contributions to a pension fund (say, 5% of the employees' pay). Employees choose (from designated options) where funds are invested—usually stocks or fixed-income securities. Retirement pay depends on the size of the fund at retirement.
- **Defined benefit pension plans** promise fixed retirement benefits defined by a designated formula. Typically, the pension formula bases retirement pay on the employees' (a) years of service, (b) annual compensation (often final pay or an average for the last few years), and sometimes (c) age. Employers are responsible for ensuring that sufficient funds are available to provide promised benefits.

Today, more than two-thirds of workers covered by pension plans are covered by defined contribution plans, fewer than one-third by defined benefit plans. This represents a radical shift from previous years when the traditional defined benefit plan was far more common. However, very few new pension plans are of the defined benefit variety. In fact, many companies are terminating long-standing defined benefit plans and substituting defined contribution plans. Why the shift? There are three main reasons:

> Virtually all new pension plans are defined contribution plans.

1. Government regulations make defined benefit plans cumbersome and costly to administer.
2. Employers are increasingly unwilling to bear the risk of defined benefit plans; with defined contribution plans, the company's obligation ends when contributions are made.
3. There has been a shift among many employers from trying to "buy long-term loyalty" (with defined benefit plans) to trying to attract new talent (with more mobile defined contribution plans).

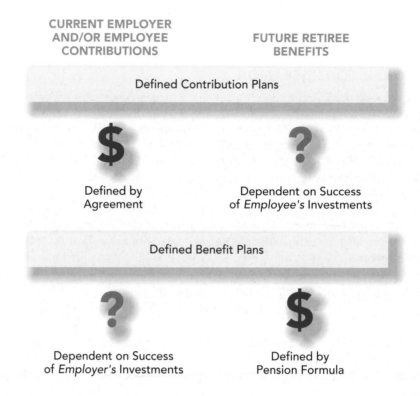

The two categories of pension plans are depicted in Graphic 17–1.

Both types of plans have a common goal: to provide income to employees during their retirement years. Still, the two types of plans differ regarding who bears the risk—the employer or the employees—for whether the retirement objectives are achieved. The two types of plans also have entirely different implications for accounting and financial reporting. Our discussion of defined contribution plans will be brief. Although these are now the most popular type of corporate pension plan, their relative simplicity permits a rather straightforward accounting treatment that requires little explanation. On the other hand, defined benefit plans require considerably more complex accounting treatment and constitute the primary focus of this chapter.

Defined Contribution Pension Plans

Defined contribution pension plans are becoming increasingly popular vehicles for employers to provide retirement income without the paperwork, cost, and risk generated by the more traditional defined benefit plans. Defined contribution plans promise fixed periodic contributions to a pension fund. Retirement income depends on the size of the fund at retirement. No further commitment is made by the employer regarding benefit amounts at retirement.

Defined contribution plans promise defined periodic contributions to a pension fund, without further commitment regarding benefit amounts at retirement.

These plans have several variations. In money purchase plans, employers contribute a fixed percentage of employees' salaries. Thrift plans, savings plans, and 401(k) plans (named after the Tax Code section that specifies the conditions for the favorable tax treatment of these plans) permit voluntary contributions by employees. These contributions typically are matched to a specified extent by employers. Over 30 million employees participate in 401(k) plans. More than a trillion dollars are invested in these plans.

When plans link the amount of contributions to company performance, labels include profit-sharing plans, incentive savings plans, 401(k) profit-sharing plans, and similar titles. When employees make contributions to the plan in addition to employer contributions, it's called a *contributory* plan. Sometimes the amount the employer contributes is tied to the amount of the employee contribution.[1] Variations are seemingly endless. Two examples from recent annual reports of Eli Lilly and Cisco Systems are re-created in Graphics 17–2 and 17–3.

GRAPHIC 17–2
Defined Contribution Plans—Eli Lilly and Company

Note 9: Retirement Benefits (in part)
The Company has defined contribution savings plans that cover its eligible employees worldwide. The purpose of these defined contribution plans is generally to provide additional financial security during retirement by providing employees with an incentive to make regular savings. Company contributions to the plans are based on employee contributions and the level of company match.

GRAPHIC 17–3
Defined Contribution Plans—Cisco Systems

Note 9: Employee Benefit Plans (in part)
Employee 401(k) Plans The Company sponsors the Cisco Systems, Inc., 401(k) Plan ("the Plan") to provide retirement benefits for its employees. As allowed under Section 401(k) of the Internal Revenue Code, the Plan provides tax-deferred salary deductions for eligible employees. Employees may contribute from 1% to 15% of their annual compensation to the Plan, limited to a maximum annual amount as set periodically by the Internal Revenue Service. The Company matches employee contributions dollar for dollar up to a maximum of $1,500 per year per person. All matching contributions vest immediately. Company matching contributions to the Plan totaled $34 million, $20 million, and $15 million in fiscal 2000, 1999, and 1998, respectively.

Accounting for these plans is quite easy. Each year, the employer simply records pension expense equal to the amount of the annual contribution. Suppose a plan promises an annual contribution equal to 3% of an employee's salary. If an employee's salary is $110,000 in a particular year, the employer would simply recognize compensation expense in the amount of the contribution:

FINANCIAL REPORTING CASE
Q1, p. 834

Pension expense...	3,300	
Cash ($110,000 × 3%)		3,300

> For defined contribution plans, the employer simply records pension expense equal to the cash contribution.

The employee's retirement benefits are totally dependent upon how well investments perform. Who bears the risk (or reward) of that uncertainty? The employee would bear the risk of uncertain investment returns and, potentially, settle for far less at retirement than at first expected.[2] On the other hand, the employer would be free of any further obligation. Because the actual investments are held by an independent investment firm, the employer is free of that recordkeeping responsibility as well.

Risk is reversed in a defined benefit plan. Because specific benefits are promised at retirement, the employer would be responsible for making up the difference when investment performance is less than expected. We look at defined benefit plans next.

CHECK WITH THE **COACH**

This is the first of two chapters on employment benefits, both of which deal with some of the more difficult subject matter in intermediate accounting. The Coach is ready to help you meet the challenge of learning this material. Coach has animated illustrations to review the key concepts of pension accounting and demonstrate a structured approach for analyzing the required reporting for pension obligations. ■

---

[1]One popular way for employer companies to provide contributions is with shares of its own common stock. If so, the arrangements usually are designed to comply with government requirements to be designated an employee stock ownership plan (ESOP).
[2]Of course this is not entirely unappealing to the employee. Defined contribution plans allow an employee to select investments in line with his or her own risk preferences and often provide greater retirement benefits than defined benefit plans.

Defined Benefit Pension Plans

Defined benefit plans promise fixed retirement benefits defined by a designated formula.

When setting aside cash to fund a pension plan, the uncertainty surrounding the rate of return on plan assets is but one of several uncertainties inherent in a defined benefit plan. Employee turnover affects the number of employees who ultimately will become eligible for retirement benefits. The age at which employees will choose to retire as well as life expectancies will impact both the length of the retirement period and the amount of the benefits. Inflation, future compensation levels, and interest rates also have obvious influence on eventual benefits.

Uncertainties complicate determining how much to set aside each year to ensure that sufficient funds are available to provide promised benefits.

This is particularly true when pension benefits are defined by a pension formula, as usually is the case. A typical formula might specify that a retiree will receive annual retirement benefits based on the employee's years of service and annual pay at retirement (say, pay level in the final year, highest pay achieved, or average pay in last two or more years). For example, a pension formula might define annual retirement benefits as:

$$1\tfrac{1}{2}\% \times \text{Years of service} \times \text{Final year's salary}$$

A pension formula typically defines retirement pay based on the employees' (a) years of service, (b) annual compensation, and sometimes (c) age.

By this formula, the annual benefits to an employee who retires after 30 years of service, with a final salary of $100,000, would be:

$$1\tfrac{1}{2}\% \times 30 \text{ years} \times \$100,000 = \$45,000$$

Typically, a firm will hire an **actuary,** a professional trained in a particular branch of statistics and mathematics, to assess the various uncertainties (employee turnover, salary levels, mortality, etc.) and to estimate the company's obligation to employees in connection with its pension plan. Such estimates are inherently subjective, so regardless of the skill of the actuary, estimates invariably deviate from the actual outcome to one degree or another.[3]

Pension gains and losses occur when the return on plan assets is higher or lower than expected.

For instance, the return on assets can turn out to be more or less than expected. These deviations are referred to as *gains* and *losses* on pension assets. When it's necessary to revise estimates related to the pension obligation because it's determined to be more or less than previously thought, these revisions are referred to as *losses* and *gains,* respectively, on the pension liability. Later, we will discuss the accounting treatment of gains and losses from either source. The point here is that the risk of the pension obligation changing unexpectedly or the pension funds being inadequate to meet the obligation is borne by the employer with a defined benefit pension plan.

Pension gains and losses occur when the pension obligation is lower or higher than expected.

The key elements of a defined benefit pension plan are:

1. The *employer's obligation* to pay retirement benefits in the future.
2. The *plan assets* set aside by the employer from which to pay the retirement benefits in the future.
3. The *periodic expense* of having a pension plan.

Neither the pension obligation nor the plan assets are reported in the balance sheet.

As you will learn in this chapter, the first two of these elements are not reported directly in the financial statements. This may seem confusing at first because it is inconsistent with the way you're accustomed to treating assets and liabilities. Even though they are not recorded in the formal accounts, it's critical that you understand the composition of both the pension obligation and the plan assets because (a) they affect amounts that actually are reported on the balance sheet, and (b) their balances are reported in disclosure notes. And, importantly, the pension expense reported on the income statement is a direct composite of periodic changes that occur in both the pension obligation and the plan assets.

> In applying accrual accounting to pensions, this *Statement (87)* retains three fundamental aspects of past pension accounting: *delayed recognition* of certain events, reporting *net cost,* and *offsetting* liabilities and assets. Those three features of practice have shaped financial reporting for many years . . . and they conflict in some respects with accounting principles applied elsewhere.[4]

---

[3]We discuss changes in more detail in Chapter 21.

[4]"Employers' Accounting for Pensions," *Statement of Financial Accounting Standards No. 87* (Stamford, Conn.: FASB, 1985).

For this reason, we will devote a considerable portion of our early discussion to understanding the composition of the pension obligation and the plan assets before focusing on the derivation of pension expense and required financial statement disclosures. We will begin with a quick overview of how periodic changes that occur in both the pension obligation and the plan assets affect pension expense. Next we will explore how those changes occur, beginning with changes in the pension obligation followed by changes in plan assets. We'll then return to pension expense for a closer look at how those changes influence its calculation. After that, we will bring together the separate but related parts by using a simple spreadsheet to demonstrate how each element of the pension plan articulates with the other elements.

Pension Expense—An Overview

The annual pension expense reflects changes in both the pension obligation and the plan assets. Graphic 17–4 provides a brief overview of how these changes are included in pension expense. After the overview, we'll look closer at each of the components.

> The pension expense is a direct composite of periodic changes that occur in both the pension obligation and the plan assets.

Next we explore each of these pension expense components in the context of its being a part of either (a) the pension obligation or (b) the plan assets. After you learn how the expense components relate to these elements of the pension plan, we'll return to explore further how they are included in the pension expense.

Components of Pension Expense

+	**Service cost** ascribed to employee service during the period	
+	**Interest** accrued on the pension liability	
−	**Return** on the plan assets*	
	Amortized portion of:	
+	**Prior service cost** attributed to employee service before an amendment to the pension plan	
+ or (−)	**Losses or (gains)** from revisions in the pension liability or from investing plan assets	
=	**Pension expense**	

> **GRAPHIC 17–4**
> Components of Pension Expense
>
> Interest and investment return are financing aspects of the pension cost.
>
> The recognition of some elements of the pension expense is delayed.

*The actual return is adjusted for any difference between actual and expected return, resulting in the *expected* return being reflected in pension expense. This loss or gain from investing plan assets is combined with losses and gains from revisions in the pension liability for deferred inclusion in pension expense. (See the last component of pension expense.)

THE PENSION OBLIGATION AND PLAN ASSETS

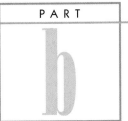

PART

b

The Pension Obligation

Now we consider more precisely what is meant by the pension obligation. Unfortunately, there's not just one definition, nor is there uniformity concerning which definition is most appropriate for pension accounting. Actually, three different ways to measure the pension obligation have meaning in pension accounting, as shown in Graphic 17–5 on the next page.

Later you will learn that an accumulated benefits approach is used to determine the minimum pension liability that a company must report, and the projected benefits obligation is the basis for some elements of the periodic pension expense. Remember, there is but one obligation; these are three ways to measure it. The relationship among the three is depicted in Graphic 17–6 on the next page.

Now let's look closer at how the obligation is measured in each of these three ways. Keep in mind, though, that it's not the accountant's responsibility to actually derive the measurement; a professional actuary provides these numbers. However, for the accountant to effectively use the numbers provided, she or he must understand their derivation.

> **FINANCIAL REPORTING CASE**
> Q2, p. 834

LO2

GRAPHIC 17–5
Ways to Measure the
Pension Obligation

1. **Accumulated benefit obligation (ABO)** The actuary's estimate of the total retirement benefits (at their discounted present value) earned so far by employees, applying the pension formula using existing compensation levels.
2. **Vested benefit obligation (VBO)** The portion of the accumulated benefit obligation that plan participants are entitled to receive regardless of their continued employment.
3. **Projected benefit obligation (PBO)** The actuary's estimate of the total retirement benefits (at their discounted present value) earned so far by employees, applying the pension formula using estimated future compensation levels. (If the pension formula does not include future compensation levels, the PBO and the ABO are the same.)

GRAPHIC 17–6
Alternative Measures
of the Pension
Obligation

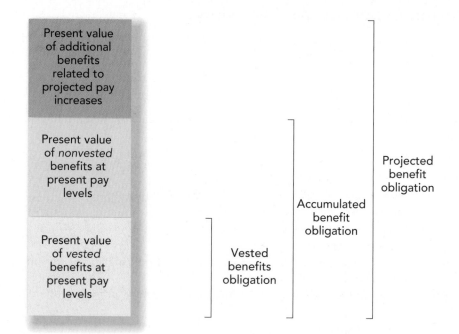

VESTED BENEFIT OBLIGATION

Suppose an employee leaves the company to take another job. Will she still get earned benefits at retirement? The answer depends on whether the benefits are vested under the terms of this particular pension plan. If benefits are fully vested—yes. **Vested benefits** are those that employees have the right to receive even if their employment were to cease today.

Pension plans typically require some minimum period of employment before benefits vest. Before the Employee Retirement Income Security Act (ERISA) was passed in 1974, horror stories relating to lost benefits were commonplace. It was possible, for example, for an employee to be dismissed a week before retirement and be left with no pension benefits. Vesting requirements were tightened drastically to protect employees. These requirements have been changed periodically since then. Beginning in 1989, benefits must vest (a) fully within five years or (b) 20% within three years with another 20% vesting each subsequent year until fully vested after seven years. Five-year vesting is most common. ERISA also established the Pension Benefit Guaranty Corporation (PBGC) to impose liens on corporate assets for unfunded pension liabilities in certain instances and to administer terminated pension plans. The PBGC is financed by premiums from employers equal to specified amounts for each covered employee. It makes retirement payments for terminated plans and guarantees basic vested benefits when pension liabilities exceed assets.

The benefits of most pension plans vest after five years.

ACCUMULATED BENEFIT OBLIGATION

The **accumulated benefit obligation (ABO)** is an estimate of the discounted present value of the retirement benefits earned so far by employees, applying the plan's pension formula using existing compensation levels. When we look at a detailed calculation of the projected benefit obligation below, keep in mind that simply substituting the employee's existing compensation in the pension formula for her projected salary at retirement would give us the accumulated benefit obligation.

> The *accumulated benefit obligation* ignores possible pay increases in the future.

PROJECTED BENEFIT OBLIGATION

As described earlier, when the ABO is estimated, the most recent salary is included in the pension formula to estimate future benefits, even if the pension formula specifies the final year's salary. No attempt is made to forecast what that salary would be the year before retirement. Of course, the most recent salary certainly offers an objective number to measure the obligation, but is it realistic? Since it's unlikely that there will be no salary increases between now and retirement, a more meaningful measurement should include a projection of what the salary might be at retirement.[5] Measured this way, the liability is referred to as the **projected benefit obligation (PBO)**. The PBO measurement may be less reliable than the ABO but is more relevant and representationally faithful.

> The *PBO* estimates retirement benefits by applying the pension formula using projected future compensation levels.

To understand the concepts involved, it's helpful to look at a numerical example. We'll simplify the example (Illustration 17–1) by looking at how pension amounts would be determined for a single employee. Keep in mind though, that in actuality, calculations would be made (by the actuary) for the entire employee pool rather than on an individual-by-individual basis.

Jessica Farrow was hired by Global Communications in 1992. The company has a defined benefit pension plan that specifies annual retirement benefits equal to:

$$1.5\% \times \text{Service years} \times \text{Final year's salary}$$

Farrow is expected to retire in 2031 after 40 years service. Her retirement period is expected to be 20 years. At the end of 2001, 10 years after being hired, her salary is $100,000. The interest rate is 6%. The company's actuary projects Farrow's salary to be $400,000 at retirement.*

What is the company's projected benefit obligation with respect to Jessica Farrow?

Steps to calculate the projected benefit obligation:
1. Use the pension formula (including a projection of future salary levels) to determine the retirement benefits earned to date.
2. Find the present value of the retirement benefits as of the retirement date.
3. Find the present value of retirement benefits as of the current date.

3. Present value ($n = 30$, $i = 6\%$ of retirement benefits at 2001 is $688,195 \times .17411 =$ **$119,822 (PBO)**

1. Actuary estimates employee has earned (as of 2001) retirement benefits of $1.5\% \times 10 \text{ years} \times \$400,000 =$ **$60,000 per year**

```
1992        2001              2031                2051
  |          ↓                                      |
  |----------+----------------|--------------------|
   10 years      30 years       ↑     20 years
  Service period               Retirement
```

2. Present value ($n = 20$, $i = 6\%$) of the retirement annuity at the retirement date is $60,000 \times 11.46992 =$ **$688,195**

> **ILLUSTRATION 17–1**
> Projected Benefit Obligation

> The actuary includes projected salaries in the pension formula. The projected benefit obligation is the present value of those benefits.

> The lump-sum equivalent at retirement of annuity payments during the retirement period is the present value of those payments.

---

*This salary reflects an estimated compound rate of increase of about 5% and should take into account expectations concerning inflation, promotions, productivity gains, and other factors that might influence salary levels.

---

[5]To project future salaries for a group of employees, actuaries usually assume some percentage rate of increase in compensation levels in upcoming years. Recent estimates of the rate of compensation increase have ranged from 4.5% to 11% with 4.5% being the most commonly reported expectation (AICPA, *Accounting Trends and Techniques,* 2001).

If the actuary's estimate of the final salary hasn't changed, the PBO a year later at the end of 2002 would be $139,715 as demonstrated in Illustration 17–1A.

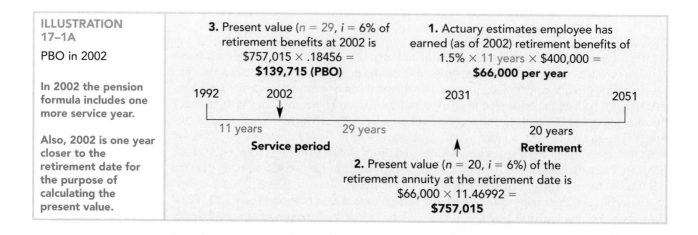

ILLUSTRATION 17–1A	
PBO in 2002	

ILLUSTRATION 17–1A

PBO in 2002

In 2002 the pension formula includes one more service year.

Also, 2002 is one year closer to the retirement date for the purpose of calculating the present value.

3. Present value ($n = 29$, $i = 6\%$ of retirement benefits at 2002 is $757,015 \times .18456 =$ **$139,715 (PBO)**

1. Actuary estimates employee has earned (as of 2002) retirement benefits of $1.5\% \times 11$ years $\times$ $400,000 =$ **$66,000 per year**

1992   2002   2031   2051

11 years   29 years   20 years
Service period   **Retirement**

2. Present value ($n = 20$, $i = 6\%$) of the retirement annuity at the retirement date is $66,000 \times 11.46992 =$ **$757,015**

Changes in the PBO. Notice that the PBO increased during 2002 (Illustration 17–1A) from $119,822 to $139,715 for two reasons:

1. One more service year is included in the pension formula calculation (service cost).
2. The employee is one year closer to retirement, causing the present value of benefits to increase due to the time value of future benefits (interest cost).

These represent two of the events that might possibly cause the balance of the PBO to change. Let's elaborate on these and the three other events that might change the balance of the PBO. The five events are (1) service cost, (2) interest cost, (3) prior service cost, (4) gains and losses, and (5) payments to retired employees.

Each year's service adds to the obligation to pay benefits.

1. Service cost. As we just witnessed in the illustration, the PBO increases each year by the amount of that year's **service cost**. This represents the increase in the projected benefit obligation attributable to employee service performed during the period. As we explain later, it also is the primary component of the annual pension expense.

Interest accrues on the PBO each year.

2. Interest cost. The second reason the PBO increases is called the **interest cost.** Even though the projected benefit obligation is not formally recognized as a liability in the company's balance sheet, it is a liability nevertheless. And, as with other liabilities, interest accrues on its balance as time passes. The amount can be calculated directly as the assumed discount rate multiplied by the projected benefit obligation at the beginning of the year.[6]

ADDITIONAL CONSIDERATION

We can verify the increase in the PBO as being caused by the service cost and interest cost as follows:

PBO at the beginning of 2002 (end of 2001)				$119,822
Service cost: $(1.5\% \times 1$ yr. $\times$ $400,000)$	$\times$ 11.46992	$\times$ .18456		12,701
Annual retirement benefits from 2002 service	To discount to 2031*	To discount to 2002†		
Interest cost: $119,822 \times 6\%$				7,189

---

[6]Assumed discount rates should reflect rates used currently in annuity contracts. Discount rates recently reported have ranged from 5% to 8.5%, with 7% being the most commonly assumed rate (AICPA, *Accounting Trends and Techniques,* 2001).

PBO at the end of 2002	$139,712[‡]

*Present value of an ordinary annuity of $1: $n = 20$, $i = 6\%$.
[†]Present value of $1: $n = 29$, $i = 6\%$.
[‡]Differs from $139,715 due to rounding.

3. Prior service cost. Another reason the PBO might change is when the pension plan itself is *amended* to revise the way benefits are determined. For example, Global Communications in our illustration might choose to revise the pension formula by which benefits are calculated. Let's back up and assume the formula's salary percentage is increased in 2002 from 1.5% to 1.7%:

1.7% × Service years × Final year's salary
(revised pension formula)

Obviously, the annual service cost from this date forward will be higher than it would have been without the amendment. This will cause a more rapid future expansion of the PBO. But it also might cause an immediate increase in the PBO as well. Here's why.

Suppose the amendment becomes effective for future years' service only, without consideration of employee service to date. As you might imagine, the morale and dedication of long-time employees of the company could be expected to suffer. So, for economic as well as ethical reasons, most companies choose to make amendments retroactive to prior years. In other words, the more beneficial terms of the revised pension formula are not applied just to future service years, but benefits attributable to all prior service years also are recomputed under the more favorable terms. Obviously, this decision is not without cost to the company. Making the amendment retroactive to prior years adds an extra layer of retirement benefits, increasing the company's benefit obligation. The increase in the PBO attributable to making a plan amendment retroactive is referred to as **prior service cost**.[7] For instance, Graphic 17–7 presents an excerpt from a recent annual report of Ecolab, Inc., describes the increase in its PBO as a result of making an amendment retroactive:

> When a pension plan is amended, credit often is given for employee service rendered in prior years. The cost of doing so is called *prior service cost.*

Note 1: Retirement Plans (in part)
. . . The Company amended its U.S. pension plan to change the formula for pension benefits and to provide a more rapid vesting schedule. The plan amendments resulted in a $6 million increase in the projected benefits obligation.

> **GRAPHIC 17–7**
> Prior Service Cost—
> Ecolab, Inc.

Let's put prior service cost in the context of our illustration.

At the end of 2001, and therefore the beginning of 2002, the PBO is $119,822. If the plan is amended on January 3, 2002, the PBO could be recomputed as:

PBO *without* Amendment		PBO *with* Amendment	
1. 1.5% × 10 yrs. × $400,000	= $ 60,000	1.7% × 10 yrs. × $400,000	= $ 68,000
2. $60,000 × 11.46992	= 688,195	$68,000 × 11.46992	= 779,955
3. $688,195 × .17411	= 119,822	$779,955 × .17411	= 135,798

> Retroactive benefits from an amendment add additional costs, increasing the company's PBO. This increase is the prior service cost.

$15,976
Prior service cost

---

[7]Prior service cost also is created if a defined benefit pension plan is initially adopted by a company that previously did not have one, and the plan itself is made retroactive to give credit for prior years' service. Prior service cost is created by plan amendments far more often than by plan adoptions because most companies already have pension plans, and new pension plans in recent years have predominantly been defined contribution plans.

The $15,976 increase in the PBO attributable to applying the more generous terms of the amendment to prior service years is the prior service cost. And, because we assumed the amendment occurred at the beginning of 2002, both the 2002 service cost and the 2002 interest cost would change as a result of the prior service cost. This is how:

Prior service cost increased the PBO at the beginning of the year.

PBO at the beginning of 2002 (end of 2001)	$119,822
Prior service cost (determined above)	15,976
PBO including prior service cost at the beginning of 2002	135,798
Service cost: (1.7% × 1 yr. × $400,000) × 11.46992 × .18456	14,395

$$\underset{\substack{\text{Annual retirement benefits}\\\text{from 2002 service}}}{} \quad \underset{\substack{\text{To discount}\\\text{to 2031*}}}{} \quad \underset{\substack{\text{To discount}\\\text{to 2002}^\dagger}}{}$$

Interest cost: $135,798‡ × 6%	8,148
PBO at the end of 2002	$158,341

*Present value of an ordinary annuity of $1: $n = 20$, $i = 6\%$.
†Present value of $1: $n = 29$, $i = 6\%$.
‡Includes the beginning balance plus the prior service cost because the amendment occurred at the beginning of the year.

The pension formula reflects the plan amendment.

ADDITIONAL CONSIDERATION

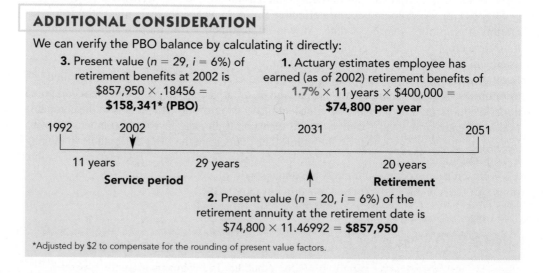

We can verify the PBO balance by calculating it directly:

3. Present value ($n = 29$, $i = 6\%$) of retirement benefits at 2002 is $857,950 × .18456 = **$158,341* (PBO)**

1. Actuary estimates employee has earned (as of 2002) retirement benefits of 1.7% × 11 years × $400,000 = **$74,800 per year**

```
1992        2002                     2031                     2051
            |_____|_____|
   11 years          29 years                  20 years
  Service period                              Retirement
```

2. Present value ($n = 20$, $i = 6\%$) of the retirement annuity at the retirement date is $74,800 × 11.46992 = **$857,950**

*Adjusted by $2 to compensate for the rounding of present value factors.

The plan amendment would affect not only the year in which it occurs, but also each subsequent year because the revised pension formula determines each year's service cost. Continuing our illustration to 2003 demonstrates this:

During 2003, the PBO increased as a result of service cost and interest cost.

PBO at the beginning of 2003 (end of 2002)	$158,341
Service cost: (1.7% × 1 yr. × $400,000) × 11.46992 × .19563	15,258

$$\underset{\substack{\text{Annual retirement benefits}\\\text{from 2003 service}}}{} \quad \underset{\substack{\text{To discount}\\\text{to 2031*}}}{} \quad \underset{\substack{\text{To discount}\\\text{to 2003}^\dagger}}{}$$

Interest cost: $158,341 × 6%	9,500
PBO at the end of 2003	$183,099

*Present value of an ordinary annuity of $1: $n = 20$, $i = 6\%$.
†Present value of $1: $n = 28$, $i = 6\%$.

Decreases and increases in estimates of the PBO because of periodic reevaluation of uncertainties are called gains and losses.

4. Gain or loss on the PBO. We mentioned earlier that a number of estimates are necessary to derive the PBO. When one or more of these estimates requires revision, the estimate of the PBO also will require revision. The resulting decrease or increase in the PBO is referred to as a *gain* or *loss,* respectively. Let's modify our illustration to imitate the effect of revising one of the several possible estimates involved. Suppose, for instance, that new information at the end of 2003 about inflation and compensation trends suggests that the estimate of Farrow's final salary should be increased by 5% to $420,000. This would affect the estimate of the PBO as follows:

PBO *without* Revised Estimate			PBO *with* Revised Estimate			
1. 1.7% × 12 yrs. × $400,000	=	$ 81,600	1.7% × 12 yrs. × **$420,000**	=	$ 85,680	*Changing the final salary estimate changes the PBO.*
2. $81,600 × 11.46992	=	935,945	$85,680 × 11.46992	=	982,743	
3. $935,945 × .19563	=	183,099	$982,743 × .19563	=	192,254	

$9,155
Loss on PBO

The difference of $9,155 represents a loss on the PBO because the obligation turned out to be higher than previously expected. Now there would be three elements of the increase in the PBO during 2003.[8]

PBO at the beginning of 2003	$158,341
Service cost (calculated above)	15,258
Interest cost (calculated above)	9,500
Loss on PBO (calculated above)	9,155
PBO at the end of 2003	$192,254

The revised estimate caused the PBO to increase.

If a revised estimate causes the PBO to be lower than previously expected, a gain would be indicated. Consider how a few of the other possible estimate changes would affect the PBO:

- A change in life expectancies might cause the retirement period to be estimated as 21 years rather than 20 years. Calculation of the present value of the retirement annuity would use $n = 21$, rather than $n = 20$. The estimate of the PBO would increase.
- The expectation that retirement will occur two years earlier than previously thought would cause the retirement period to be estimated as 22 years rather than 20 years and the service period to be estimated as 28 years rather than 30 years. The new expectation would probably also cause the final salary estimate to change. The net effect on the PBO would depend on the circumstances.
- A change in the assumed discount rate would affect the present value calculations. A lower rate would increase the estimate of the PBO. A higher rate would decrease the estimate of the PBO.

5. Payment of retirement benefits.   We've seen how the PBO will change due to the accumulation of service cost from year to year, the accrual of interest as time passes, making plan amendments retroactive to prior years, and periodic adjustments when estimates change. Another change in the PBO occurs when the obligation is reduced as benefits actually are paid to retired employees.

Payment of retirement benefits reduces the PBO.

The payment of such benefits is not applicable in our present illustration because we've limited the situation to calculations concerning an individual employee who is several years from retirement. Remember, though, in reality the actuary would make these calculations for the entire pool of employees covered by the pension plan. But the concepts involved would be the same. Graphic 17–8 on the next page summarizes the five ways the PBO can change.

ILLUSTRATION EXPANDED TO CONSIDER THE ENTIRE EMPLOYEE POOL

For our single employee, the PBO at the end of 2003 is $192,254. Let's say now that Global Communications has 2,000 active employees covered by the pension plan and 100 retired employees receiving retirement benefits. Illustration 17–2 on the next page expands the numbers to represent all covered employees.

We remind you that the PBO is not formally recognized as a liability in the balance sheet. It is, however, actively monitored in the employer's informal pension records because its

The PBO is not formally recognized in the balance sheet.

---

[8]The increase in the PBO due to amending the pension formula (prior service cost) occurred in 2002.

GRAPHIC 17–8
Components of
Change in the PBO

The Projected Benefits Obligation Changes as a Result of:		
Cause	**Effect**	**Frequency**
Service cost	+	Each period
Interest cost	+	Each period (except the first period of the plan, when no obligation exists to accrue interest)
Prior service cost	+	Only if the plan is amended (or initiated) that period
Loss or gain on PBO	+ or −	Whenever revisions are made in the pension liability estimate
Retiree benefits paid	−	Each period (unless no employees have yet retired under the plan)

balance must be reported in disclosure notes to the financial statements. Also, as mentioned earlier and explained later, some of the changes in its balance are included in the calculation of the periodic pension expense.

ILLUSTRATION 17–2

The PBO Expanded
to Include All
Employees

The changes in the PBO for Global Communications during 2003 were as follows:

	($ in millions)*
PBO at the beginning of 2003† (amount assumed)	$400
Service cost, 2003 (amount assumed)	41
Interest cost: $400 × 6%	24
Loss (gain) on PBO (amount assumed)	23
Less: Retiree benefits paid (amount assumed)	(38)
PBO at the end of 2003	$450

*Of course, these expanded amounts are not simply the amounts for Jessica Farrow multiplied by 2,000 employees because her years of service, expected retirement date, and salary are not necessarily representative of other employees. Also, the expanded amounts take into account expected employee turnover and current retirees.
†Includes the prior service cost that increased the PBO when the plan was amended in 2002.

Pension Plan Assets

So far our focus has been on the employer's obligation to provide retirement benefits in the future. We turn our attention now to the resources with which the company will satisfy that obligation—the **pension plan assets.** Like the PBO, the pension plan assets are not formally recognized on the balance sheet but are actively monitored in the employer's informal records. Its balance, too, must be reported in disclosure notes to the financial statements, and as explained below, the return on these assets is included in the calculation of the periodic pension expense.

**FINANCIAL
REPORTING CASE**

Q3, p. 834

*A trustee manages
pension plan assets.*

We assumed in the previous section that Global Communications' obligation is $450 million for service performed to date. When employees retire, will there be sufficient funds to provide the anticipated benefits? To ensure sufficient funding, Global will contribute cash each year to a pension fund.

The assets of a pension fund must be held by a trustee. A trustee accepts employer contributions, invests the contributions, accumulates the earnings on the investments, and pays benefits from the plan assets to retired employees or their beneficiaries. The trustee can be an individual, a bank, or a trust company. Plan assets are invested in stocks, bonds, and other income-producing assets. The accumulated balance of the annual employer contributions plus the return on the investments (dividends, interest, market price appreciation) must be sufficient to pay benefits as they come due.

When an employer estimates how much it must set aside each year to accumulate sufficient funds to pay retirement benefits as they come due, it's necessary to estimate the return those investments will produce. This is the **expected return on plan assets.** The higher the return, the less the employer must actually contribute. On the other hand, a relatively low return means the difference must be made up by higher contributions. In practice, recent estimates of the rate of return have ranged from 6% to 11.5%, with 9% being the most commonly reported expectation.[9] In Illustration 17–3, we shift the focus of our numerical illustration to emphasize Global's pension plan assets.

ILLUSTRATION 17–3

How Plan Assets Change

A trustee accepts employer contributions, invests the contributions, accumulates the earnings on the investments, and pays benefits from the plan assets.

Global Communications funds its defined benefit pension plan by contributing each year the year's service cost plus a portion of the prior service cost. Cash of $48 million was contributed to the pension fund at the end of 2003.

Plan assets at the beginning of 2003 were valued at $300 million. The expected rate of return on the investment of those assets was 9%, but the actual return in 2003 was 10%. Retirement benefits of $38 million were paid at the end of 2003 to retired employees.

What is the value of the company's pension plan assets at the end of 2003?

	($ in millions)
Plan assets at the beginning of 2003	$300
Return on plan assets (10% × $300)	30
Cash contributions	48
Less: Retiree benefits paid	(38)
Plan assets at the end of 2003	$340

Recall that Global's PBO at the end of 2003 is $450 million. Because the plan assets are only $340 million, the pension plan is said to be *underfunded*. One reason is that we assumed Global incurred a $60 million prior service cost from amending the pension plan at the beginning of 2002, and that cost is being funded over several years. Another factor is the loss from increasing the PBO due to the estimate revision, since funding has been based on the previous estimate. Later, we'll assume earlier revisions also have increased the PBO. Of course, actual performance of the investments also impacts a plan's funded status.

An *underfunded* pension plan means the PBO exceeds plan assets.

It is not unusual for pension plans today to be underfunded. Historically the funded status of pension plans has varied considerably. Prior to the Employee Retirement Income Security Act (ERISA) in 1974, many plans were grossly underfunded. The new law established minimum funding standards among other matters designed to protect plan participants. The new standards brought most plans closer to full funding. Then the stock market boom of the 1980s caused the value of plan assets for many pension funds to swell to well over their projected benefit obligations. More than 80% of pension plans were overfunded. As a result, managers explored ways to divert funds to other areas of operations. Today a majority of plans again are underfunded. Many of the underfunded plans are with troubled companies, placing employees at risk. The PBGC guarantees are limited to about $3,400 per month, often less than promised pension benefits.

An *overfunded* pension plan means plan assets exceed the PBO.

We mentioned earlier that the return on plan assets affects not only the value of the plan assets but also the calculation of the amount annually recorded as pension expense. Also, we mentioned earlier that the annual increases in the PBO due to service cost and interest affect the calculation of pension expense, too. Now, let's look at all the ways that changes in the pension liability and the pension plan assets affect pension expense.

[9]AICPA, *Accounting Trends and Techniques,* 2001.

DETERMINING PENSION EXPENSE

The Relationship between Pension Expense and Changes in the PBO and Plan Assets

LO5

The matching principle and the time period assumption dictate that the costs be allocated to the periods the services are performed.

Like wages, salaries, commissions, and other and forms of pay, pension expense is part of a company's compensation for employee services each year. Accordingly, the accounting objective is to achieve a matching of the costs of providing this form of compensation with the benefits of the services performed. However, the fact that this form of compensation actually is paid to employees many years after the service is performed means that other elements in addition to the annual service cost will affect the ultimate pension cost. These other elements are related to changes that occur over time in both the pension liability and the pension plan assets. Graphic 17–9 provides a summary of how some of these changes influence pension expense.

GRAPHIC 17–9
Components of the Periodic Pension Expense

FINANCIAL REPORTING CASE

Q4, p. 834

The pension expense reported in the income statement is a composite of periodic changes that occur in both the pension obligation and the plan assets.

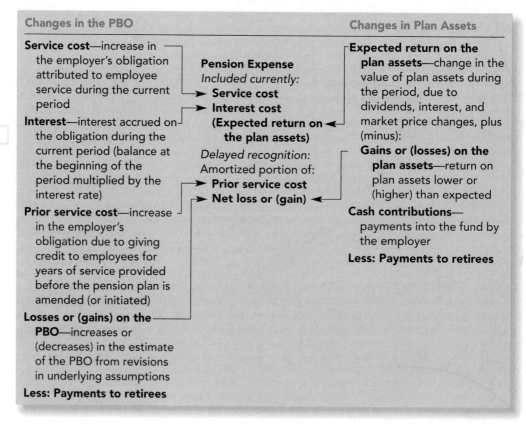

We've examined each of the components of pension expense from the viewpoint of its effect on the PBO or on plan assets, using the Global Communications illustration to demonstrate that effect. Now, let's expand the same illustration to see how these changes affect *pension expense*. Illustration 17–4 provides this expanded example.

COMPONENTS OF PENSION EXPENSE

Illustration 17–4 demonstrates the relationship between some of the changes in the PBO and in plan assets and the components of pension expense: service cost, interest cost, the return on plan assets, prior service cost amortization, and net gain or loss amortization. Let's look at these five components of pension expense one at a time.

ILLUSTRATION 17–4

Pension Expense

Reports from the actuary and the trustee of plan assets indicate the following changes during 2003 in the PBO and plan assets of Global Communications:

($ in millions)	PBO		Plan Assets
Beginning of 2003	$400	Beginning of 2003	$300
Service cost	41	Return on plan assets,*	
Interest cost, 6%	24	10% (9% expected)	30
Loss (gain) on PBO	23	Cash contributions	48
Less: Retiree benefits	(38)	Less: Retiree benefits	(38)
End of 2003	$450	End of 2003	$340

These are the changes in the PBO and in the plan assets we previously discussed (Illustration 17–2 and Illustration 17–3).

Informal records also indicate a prior service cost incurred at the beginning of the previous year (2002) of $60 million due to a plan amendment increasing the PBO at that time. At the beginning of 2003 Global had an unrecognized net loss of $55 million (previous losses exceeded previous gains). The average remaining service life of the employee group is 15 years in both 2002 and 2003.

Global's 2003 Pension Expense Is Determined as Follows:		($ in millions)
Service cost (from PBO above)		$41
Interest cost (from PBO above)		24
Actual return on the plan assets (from plan assets above)	$(30)	
Adjusted for gain on the plan assets [(10% − 9%) × $300]	3	
Expected return on the plan assets		(27)
Amortization of prior service cost (calculated later)		4
Amortization of the net loss (calculated later)		1
Pension expense		$43

2003 Pension Expense

*Expected rates of return anticipate the performance of various investments of plan assets. This is not necessarily the same as the discount rate used by the actuary to estimate the pension obligation. Assumed rates of return recently reported have ranged from 4.5% to 11%, with 9% being the most commonly assumed rate (AICPA, *Accounting Trends and Techniques*, 2001).

1. Service Cost.   The $41 million service cost represents the increase in the projected benefit obligation attributable to employee service performed during 2003 (benefits earned by employees during the year). Each year this is the first component of the pension expense.

2. Interest Cost.   The interest cost is calculated as the interest rate (actuary's discount rate) multiplied by the projected benefit obligation at the beginning of the year. In 2003, this is 6% times $400 million, or $24 million.

Interest cost is the discount rate times the PBO balance at the beginning of the year.

The PBO is not formally recognized as a liability in the company's balance sheet, but it is a liability nevertheless. The interest expense that accrues on its balance is not separately reported on the income statement but is instead combined with the service cost (and other amounts) as the second component of the annual pension expense.

3. Return on Plan Assets.   Remember, plan assets comprise funds invested in stocks, bonds, and other securities that presumably will generate dividends, interest, and capital gains. Each year these earnings represent the return on plan assets during that year. When accounting for the return, we need to differentiate between its two modes: the *expected* return and the *actual* return.

The return earned on investment securities increases the plan asset balance.

Actual versus expected return.   We've assumed Global's expected rate of return is 9%, so its expected return on plan assets in 2003 was 9% times $300 million, or $27 million. But, as previously indicated the actual rate of return in 2003 was 10%, producing an actual return on plan assets of 10% times $300 million, or $30 million.

Obviously, investing plan assets in income-producing assets lessens the amounts employers must contribute to the fund. So, the return on plan assets reduces the net cost of having a pension plan. Accordingly, the return on plan assets each year *reduces* the amount recorded as pension expense. Just as the interest expense that accrues on the PBO is included as a component of pension expense rather than being separately reported, the investment revenue on plan assets is not separately reported either. In actuality, both the interest and return-on-assets components of pension expense do not directly represent employee compensation. Instead, they are financial items created only because the pension payment is delayed while the obligation is funded currently.

Adjustment for loss or gain. A controversial question is *when* differences between the actual and expected return should be recognized in pension expense. It seems logical that since the net cost of having a pension plan is reduced by the actual return on plan assets, the periodic reduction in pension expense should be the actual return on plan assets. However, the FASB concluded that the actual return should first be adjusted by any difference between that return and what the return had been expected to be. That difference is a loss or gain on plan assets and its recognition as part of pension expense is delayed. We will discuss later the circumstances that determine whether and when these amounts are recognized. At this point, note that by adjusting the actual return for any loss or gain, it is actually the *expected* return that is included in the calculation of pension expense. In our illustration, Global's pension expense is reduced by the expected return of $27 million.

4. Amortization of Prior Service Cost.
Recall that the increase in Global's PBO attributable to making its plan amendment retroactive is referred to as the prior service cost. Obviously, prior service cost adds to the cost of having a pension plan. But when should this cost be recognized as pension expense?

Amending a pension plan, and especially choosing to make that amendment retroactive, typically is done with the idea that future operations will benefit from those choices. For that reason, the cost is not recognized as pension expense entirely in the year the plan is amended. Instead, it is recognized as pension expense over the time that the employees who benefited from the retroactive amendment will work for the company in the future. Presumably, this future service period is when the company will receive the benefits of its actions.

In our illustration, the amendment occurred in 2002, increasing the PBO at that time. For the individual employee, Jessica Farrow, the prior service cost was calculated to be $15,976. Our illustration assumes that, for all plan participants, the prior service cost was $60 million at the beginning of 2002. The unrecognized prior service cost at the beginning of 2003 is $56 million. The following section explains how this amount was computed.

One assumption in our illustration is that the average remaining service life of the active employee group is 15 years. To recognize the $60 million prior service cost in equal annual amounts over this period, the amount amortized as an increase in pension expense each year is $4 million:[10]

Amortization of Prior Service Cost	($ in millions)	
Service cost		$41
Interest cost		24
Actual return on the plan assets	$(30)	
Adjusted for gain on the plan assets	3	(27)
Amortization of prior service cost ($60 million ÷ 15 years)		4
Amortization of net loss		1
Pension expense		$43

[10]An alternative to this straight line approach, called the *service method,* attempts to allocate the prior service cost to each year in proportion to the fraction of the total remaining service years worked in each of those years. This method is described in the chapter appendix.

Since the amendment occurred at the beginning of 2002, this amount was amortized in 2002 as part of the 2002 pension expense. That's why, at the beginning of 2003, the unrecognized prior service cost is $56 million. Another $4 million is included in the 2003 pension expense as well as in the pension expense of each of the next 13 years.

Be sure to note that the prior service cost is not formally recognized as a separate account in the company's records. Its balance is monitored in the informal records, though, to recognize the cost gradually over the 15-year period. Actually, it represents a deferred expense that arose when the cost of making the amendment retroactive increased the employer's obligation to pay retirement benefits (the PBO) but wasn't immediately recognized as an expense.[11] One way to view it is that if we did formally record the prior service cost, we would debit the asset *unrecognized prior service cost* and credit the liability *projected benefit obligation*. In fact, both of these balances are increased, we just don't formally record the increases but informally track those balances instead.

The informal records would show the balance in the unrecognized prior service cost declining by $4 million each year.

Unamortized Prior Service Cost	($ in millions)
Unamortized prior service cost at the beginning of 2003	$56
Less: 2003 amortization	(4)
Unamortized prior service cost at the end of 2003	$52

Note: The balance in this memorandum "account" is not recognized in the financial statements.

5. Amortization of Deferred Net Loss or Net Gain.

You learned previously that gains and losses can occur when expectations are revised concerning either the PBO or the return on plan assets. Graphic 17–10 summarizes the possibilities.

We noted earlier that neither a loss (gain) on the PBO nor a loss (gain) on plan assets is immediately recognized in pension expense. There is no conceptual justification for this. After all, these increases and decreases in either the PBO or plan assets immediately impact the net cost of providing a pension plan and, conceptually, should be recognized as they occur. Nevertheless, *SFAS 87* requires that recognition of gains and losses from either source be delayed. Why?—for practical reasons.

	Projected Benefits Obligation	Return on Plan Assets
Higher than Expected	Loss	Gain
Lower than Expected	Gain	Loss

INCOME SMOOTHING

The FASB acknowledged the conceptual shortcoming of delaying the recognition of a gain or a loss while opting for this more politically acceptable approach. Delayed recognition was favored by a dominant segment of corporate America that was concerned with the effect of allowing gains and losses to immediately impact reported earnings.

[11]The FASB proposed recognizing prior service cost as an intangible asset in its Preliminary Views document, but didn't follow this approach in the final document: FASB, "Employers' Accounting for Pension and Other Postemployment Benefits," *Preliminary Views,* November 1982, par. 15b.

The practical justification for delayed recognition is that, over time, gains and losses might cancel one another out. Given this possibility, why create unnecessary fluctuations in reported income by letting temporary gains and losses decrease and increase (respectively) pension expense? Of course, as years pass there may be more gains than losses, or vice versa, preventing their offsetting one another completely. So, if a net gain or a net loss gets "too large," pension expense must be adjusted.

> The Board believes that it would be conceptually appropriate and preferable to [have] . . . no delay in recognition of gains and losses, or perhaps [to have] . . . gains and losses reported currently in comprehensive income but not in earnings. However, it concluded that those approaches would be too great a change from past practice to be adopted at the present time.[12]

SFAS 87 defines too large rather arbitrarily as being when a net gain or a net loss at the beginning of a year exceeds an amount equal to 10% of the PBO, or 10% of plan assets, whichever is higher.[14] *SFAS 87* refers to this threshold amount as the "corridor." When the corridor is exceeded, the excess is not charged to pension expense all at once. Instead, as a further concession to income smoothing, only a portion of the excess is included in pension expense. The minimum amount that should be included is the excess divided by the average remaining service period of active employees expected to receive benefits under the plan.[15]

> A net gain or a net loss affects pension expense only if it exceeds an amount equal to 10% of the PBO, or 10% of plan assets, whichever is higher.

In our illustration, we're assuming that at the beginning of 2003 an unrecognized net loss of $55 million is revealed by Global's informal records. Also recall that the PBO and plan assets are $400 million and $300 million, respectively, at that time. The amount amortized to 2003 pension expense is $1 million, calculated as follows:

> The Board acknowledges that the delayed recognition included in this Statement results in excluding the most current and most relevant information.[13]

Determining Net Loss Amortization—2003	($ in millions)
Net loss (previous losses exceeded previous gains)	$55
10% of $400 ($400 is greater than $300): the "corridor"	(40)
Excess at the beginning of the year	$15
Average remaining service period	÷ 15 years
Amount amortized to 2003 pension expense	$ 1

> Because the net loss exceeds an amount equal to the greater of 10% of the PBO or 10% of plan assets, part of the excess is amortized to pension expense.

The pension expense is increased because a net loss is being amortized. If a net *gain* were being amortized, the amount would be *deducted* from pension expense because a gain would indicate that the net cost of providing the pension plan had decreased.

Amortization of Net Loss		($ in millions)
Service cost		$41
Interest cost		24
Actual return on the plan assets	($30)	
Adjusted for gain on the plan assets	3	(27)
Amortization of prior service cost		4
Amortization of net loss		1
Pension expense		$43

> Amortization of a net gain would decrease pension expense.

> Amortization of a net loss increases pension expense.

---

[12]Ibid., par. 107.

[13]Ibid., par. 88.

[14]For this purpose the FASB specifies the market-related value of plan assets. This can be either the fair market value or a weighted-average fair market value over a period not to exceed five years. We will uniformly assume fair market value in this chapter.

[15]Companies are permitted to amortize the entire unrecognized loss (or gain) rather than just the excess, but few choose that option. (*SFAS 87*, par. 33.)

This amortization reduces the unrecognized net loss in 2003 by $1 million. Also recall that (a) Global incurred a 2003 $23 million loss from revising estimates relating to the PBO and (b) a $3 million gain when the 2003 return on plan assets was higher than expected. These three changes affected the unrecognized net loss in 2003 as follows:

Unamortized Net Loss	($ in millions)
Unamortized net loss at the beginning of 2003	$55
Less: 2003 amortization	(1)
Plus: 2003 loss on PBO	23
Less: 2003 gain on plan assets	(3)
Unamortized net loss at the end of 2003	$74

The unamortized net loss or gain is not formally recognized as a separate account in the company's records.

Note: the balance in this memorandum account is not recognized in the financial statements.

ADDITIONAL CONSIDERATION

The $74 million balance at the end of 2003 would be the beginning balance in 2004. It would be compared with the 2004 beginning balances in the PBO and plan assets to determine whether amortization would be necessary in 2004. If you were to look back to our analyses of the changes in those two balances, you would see the 2004 beginning balances in the PBO and plan assets to be $450 million and $340 million, respectively. The amount amortized to 2004 pension expense will be $1.93 million, calculated as follows:

	($ in millions)
Net loss (previous losses exceeded previous gains)	$74
10% of $450 ($450 is greater than $340)	(45)
Excess at the beginning of the year	$29
Average remaining service period	÷ 15 years*
Amount amortized to 2004 pension expense	**$1.93**

*Assumes the average remaining service period of active employees is still 15 years in 2004 due to new employees joining the firm.

Recording the Periodic Expense and Periodic Funding

By combining its five components in the preceding sections, we determined that Global's pension expense in 2003 is $43 million. Also, recall that Global contributed $48 million cash to the pension fund at the end of 2003. It is not unusual for the cash contribution to differ from that year's pension expense. After all, the determination of the periodic pension expense and the funding of the pension plan are two separate processes. Pension expense is an *accounting* decision. How much to contribute each year is a *financing* decision affected by cash flow and tax considerations, as well as minimum funding requirements of ERISA. Subject to these considerations, cash contributions are actuarially determined with the objective of accumulating (along with investment returns) sufficient funds to provide promised retirement benefits.

The following journal entry would be made by Global in 2003 to record both the annual pension expense and the annual contribution to the pension fund. This is the only journal entry normally required in pension accounting.[16]

---

[16]An exception is when the situation requires an additional liability to be recorded as described in a later section of this chapter.

GLOBAL PERSPECTIVE

Most large companies in Japan sponsor pension plans that are funded through financial institutions. Contributions to pension funds are tax deductible. Because the taxes levied by the government are reported as income tax expense on the income statement, most Japanese companies report annual pension expense equal to cash contributions to the pension fund.

In other countries, such as France, Belgium, Finland, India, and New Zealand, pension costs are not covered by accounting standards. In still other countries pension accounting is irrelevant because the occurrence of pension plans is rare (Korea, Argentina, and Brazil, for example).

To Record Pension Expense and Pension Funding	($ in millions)
Pension expense (calculated on previous page)	43
Prepaid (accrued) pension cost (difference)	5
Cash (contribution to fund)	48

> **A debit balance in prepaid (accrued) pension cost is reported as an asset; a credit balance is reported as a liability.**

Notice that in this particular situation, the contribution exceeds the expense. Consistent with other situations when an expense is overpaid, the excess payment represents an asset—prepaid pension cost. Very often, though, the cash payment is less than the expense. In those instances, the underpayment represents a liability. Either way, the difference between the pension expense and the cash contribution is debited or credited, depending on the situation, to a single account: prepaid (accrued) pension cost. When the account has a *debit* balance it represents a cumulative overpayment and is reported as an asset—prepaid pension cost. When it has a *credit* balance it represents a cumulative underpayment and is reported as a liability—accrued pension cost.

The pension expense is, of course, reported on the income statement. In addition, the composition of that amount must be reported in disclosure notes. For instance, Northwest Air Lines described the composition of its pension expense in the following disclosure note in its 2000 annual report:

> **GRAPHIC 17–11**
> Disclosure of Pension Expense—Northwest Air Lines
>
> The components of pension expense are itemized in the disclosure note.

Note 10: Pension and Other Postretirement Health Care Benefits

The components of net periodic cost of defined benefit plans included the following (in millions):

	2000	1999	1998
Service cost	$ 149	$ 167	$ 133
Interest cost	397	363	310
Expected return on plan assets	(468)	(403)	(357)
Amortization of prior service cost	55	46	20
Recognized net actuarial loss	1	21	30
Net periodic benefit cost	$ 134	$ 194	$ 136

> **PART**
>
> **d**

REPORTING ISSUES

Putting the Pieces Together

In preceding sections, we've discussed (1) the projected benefit obligation (including changes due to periodic service cost, accrued interest, revised estimates, plan amendments, and the payment of benefits); (2) the plan assets (including changes due to investment returns, employer contributions, and the payment of benefits); (3) the periodic pension expense (comprising components of each of these); and (4) the periodic journal entry. These elements of a pension plan are interrelated. It's helpful to see how each element relates to the others. One way is to bring each part together in a pension spreadsheet. We do this for our 2003 Global illustration in Graphic 17–12.

LO6

GRAPHIC 17–12
Pension Spreadsheet

($ in millions)	Informal Records*				Formal Records		
	PBO	Plan Assets	Prior Service Cost	Net Loss	Pension Expense	Cash	Prepaid (Accrued) Cost
Balance, Jan. 1, 2003	$(400)	$300	$56	$55			$11
Service cost	(41)				$41		
Interest cost, 6%	(24)				24		
Actual return on assets		30			(30)		
Gain on assets†				(3)	3		
Amortization of:							
Prior service cost			(4)		4		
Net loss				(1)	1		
Loss on PBO†	(23)			23			
Contributions to fund		48				$(48)	
Retiree benefits paid	38	(38)					
2003 journal entry					$43	$(48)	5
Balance, Dec. 31, 2003	$(450)	$340	$52	$74			$16

The debit balance in the prepaid (accrued) pension cost account is increased to $16 million.

Note: ( )s indicate credits; debits otherwise
*Balances in these memorandum accounts are not recognized in the financial statements.
†Deferred for later recognition.

You should spend several minutes studying this spreadsheet, focusing on the relationships among the elements that constitute a defined benefit pension plan. Notice that the first numerical column simply repeats the actuary's report of how the PBO changed during the year, as explained previously (Illustration 17–2). Likewise, the second column reproduces the changes in plan assets we discussed earlier (Illustration 17–3). We've also previously noted the changes in the unrecognized prior service cost (page 851) and the unrecognized net loss (page 853) that are duplicated in the third and fourth columns.

The last three columns represent the amounts that are formally recognized in the accounts: (1) the 2003 pension expense determined earlier (page 849), (2) the cash contribution, and (3) the prepaid (accrued) pension cost. These are the three accounts that comprise the journal entry that records the 2003 pension expense and pension funding.

Reconciliation of Funded Status with the Amount Recognized in the Balance Sheet

Another point to notice is that the four off-balance-sheet asset and liability amounts combine to account for the balance in the one pension account that is reported on the balance sheet—the prepaid (accrued) pension cost. This always will be true. The relationship is demonstrated below for both the beginning and ending balances from the spreadsheet:

Reconciliation of Pension Amounts

	($ in millions)	
	2003 Beginning Balances	**2003 Ending Balances**
Projected benefit obligation	$(400)	$(450)
Plan assets	300	340
Funded status	(100)	(110)
Unamortized prior service cost	56	52
Unamortized net loss	55	74
Prepaid (accrued) pension cost	$ 11	$ 16

The net total of all the memorandum accounts equals the prepaid (accrued) pension cost balance.

A pension plan is underfunded when the PBO exceeds the plan assets and overfunded when the opposite is the case.

Here's why this relationship holds. The difference between the employer's obligation (PBO) and the resources available to satisfy that obligation (plan assets) is referred to as the **funded status** of the pension plan. Global's pension plan is underfunded by $100 million at the beginning of 2003 and $110 million at the end of the year. If all the changes in the PBO and plan assets were immediately recognized in pension expense, the balance in the prepaid (accrued) pension cost would report the funded status because that balance is the cumulative difference between what's been expensed and the cash contributions. But remember, not all the changes in the PBO and plan assets are immediately recognized in pension expense. Recognition is delayed for both gains and losses and the prior service cost. So the unrecognized (unamortized) portions of each of these are reflected in the funded status but not yet in the prepaid (accrued) pension cost. As a result, the difference between the funded status and the amount recognized in the balance sheet as prepaid (accrued) pension cost can be reconciled by the unrecognized prior service cost and the unrecognized net loss. In fact, this reconciliation must be disclosed in the financial statements.

FINANCIAL REPORTING CASE

Q5, p. 834

Minimum Liability

The FASB faced two very controversial decisions in *SFAS 87* concerning the pension liability: (1) should the pension liability be measured as the vested, accumulated, or projected benefit obligation, and (2) should the pension liability (however measured) be reported separately or offset against plan assets? On both issues, the decisions appear to reflect compromises between the Board's conceptual preferences and political considerations.

MEASUREMENT

On the measurement issue, disagreement among Board members is evident in the minority opinions of dissenting members as stated in *SFAS 87*. In a 4 to 3 vote for approval, one dissenter based his dissent on the use of the PBO measure in determining the pension expense.[17] Another based his dissent on *not* using the PBO as the reported measure of the pension liability.

As a theoretical preference, however, the majority view appears to favor measurement of the liability as the projected benefit obligation (see the quotation at the right). However, while this may be the best estimate of an employer's liability related to its pension plan, the PBO is not reported on the balance sheet. The balance sheet reports either an *accrued* pension cost as a liability or a *prepaid* pension cost as an asset, depending on whether the prepaid (accrued) pension cost account has a credit or a debit balance. This balance represents the difference

... the Board concluded that estimated future compensation levels should be considered in measuring the service cost component and the projected benefit obligation if the plan's benefit formula incorporates them.[18]

Conceptually, the pension liability is best measured by the projected benefit obligation.

---

[17]It's interesting to note that the FASB now requires 5 "for" votes to promulgate a new standard.
[18]"Employers' Accounting for Pensions," *Statement of Financial Accounting Standards No. 87* (Stamford, Conn.: FASB, 1985), par. 143.

between the PBO and the plan assets when there are no elements of either that haven't yet been recognized in pension expense (unrecognized prior service cost, unrecognized net loss or net gain). However, when elements of delayed recognition exist, the balance is not easily interpreted.

The Board concluded that this reported amount is insufficient when the employer's obligation is underfunded (assets less than liability). In that case, any pension balance on the books should be increased to reflect a minimum liability equal to that underfunded amount. Importantly, though, when measuring the underfunded liability, it is the accumulated benefit obligation, ABO (rather than the PBO), that is required as the measure of the pension liability. In other words, an employer must report a pension liability at least equal to the amount by which its ABO exceeds its plan assets.

> The minimum pension liability is the excess of the accumulated benefit obligation over the plan assets.

It is not clear why the *SFAS 87* specifies the ABO as the appropriate measurement for this purpose, since the PBO is specified for determining the service cost and interest cost components of the pension expense and since the PBO is apparently the Board's conceptual preference to represent the liability. The motivation appears to be political acceptability—the ABO results in reporting a lower pension liability.

OFFSETTING

Regarding the offsetting of the pension liability and pension plan assets when determining the minimum liability, *SFAS 87* requires offsetting despite an apparent conceptual preference by the Board for recognizing the pension liability and plan assets as separate elements of the balance sheet. The FASB acknowledged that this requirement is made "even though the liability has not been settled, the assets may still be largely controlled, and substantial risks and rewards associated with both of those amounts are clearly borne by the employer."[19] Empirical research supports the FASB's *conceptual* position, not *SFAS 87,* on this point. A study of stock prices indicates that investors apparently view the pension liability and pension plan assets separately.[20]

> Offsetting of the pension liability and pension plan assets is inconsistent with the way assets and liabilities in other areas are reported.

ADDITIONAL LIABILITY

The numerical example in Illustration 17–5 on the next page will clarify the implementation of the minimum liability provision.

The fact that a minimum liability is indicated, as in this situation, doesn't necessarily mean action is required. It might be that the minimum liability requirement already is satisfied by a liability balance already recorded. Remember, though, that the only journal entry recorded in pension accounting (unless the additional liability described next is required) is the following:

```
Pension expense (calculated each year) . . . . . . . . . . . . . . . . . . . . . .    xxx
Prepaid (accrued) pension cost (difference) . . . . . . . . . . . . . . . . . .    {debit or credit}
   Cash (annual contribution)  . . . . . . . . . . . . . . . . . . . . . . . . . . . . . .          xxx
```

As described earlier, this process produces a liability only when the prepaid (accrued) pension cost account has a credit balance. If the account has a debit balance, an asset exists instead.

In our present illustration, is the balance in the prepaid (accrued) pension cost account sufficient to satisfy this minimum liability requirement? No, not in this case.

If the account had a credit balance of at least $30 million, no additional liability would be required. Reporting the accrued pension cost credit balance as a pension liability would be sufficient. If the account had a credit balance of less than $30 million, an additional liability

> Sometimes a credit balance in the prepaid (accrued) pension cost account is sufficient to satisfy the minimum liability requirement.

---

[19]"Employers' Accounting for Pensions," *Statement of Financial Accounting Standards No. 87* (Stamford, Conn.: FASB, 1985), par. 87.
[20]Wayne Landsman, "An Empirical Investigation of Pension and Property Rights," *The Accounting Review,* October 1986, pp. 662–92.

ILLUSTRATION 17–5

Determining the Minimum Liability

Recall from our earlier illustration that Global Communications informal and formal records revealed the following balances at the end of 2002 (beginning of 2003): December 31, 2002 balances:

December 31, 2002, balances:

PBO	$(400)
Plan assets	300
Prepaid pension cost—debit	11

Now, let's also assume an accumulated benefit obligation of $330 million:

ABO	330

If the plan assets exceed the ABO, there is no minimum liability the company must report. A minimum liability must be reported only to the extent that the accumulated benefit obligation (ABO) exceeds the fair value of plan assets. So, in this instance, the minimum liability that must be reported is:

ABO	$(330)
Plan assets	300
Minimum liability	$ (30)

There is no minimum liability unless the ABO exceeds the fair value of plan assets.

would be required for the difference. The sum of the prepaid (accrued) pension cost and the additional liability would be reported as a single pension liability on the balance sheet.

In our present illustration, the prepaid (accrued) pension cost account has a *debit* balance ($11 million), normally reported as an asset. However, since an underfunded ABO exists, this is unacceptable. An additional liability account must be established to combine with the prepaid (accrued) pension cost account balance to reflect the minimum liability. To progress from a debit balance of $11 million to a credit amount of $30 million, a provision must be made for an additional liability of $41 million.

Sometimes an additional liability is needed to combine with the prepaid (accrued) pension cost balance to provide the minimum liability.

Minimum liability	$(30)
Less: prepaid pension cost	11
Additional liability	$(41)

We are assuming that there is no balance already in the additional liability account from the previous year. An additional liability must be recorded:

Recording an additional liability creates an intangible asset.

	($ in millions)	
Intangible pension asset	41	
Additional liability		41

The journal entry to record the additional liability includes a debit to an intangible asset. Here's why. Presumably, an employer undertakes a pension obligation with the expectation of future economic benefits. When a portion of the liability is recognized in the accounts, a commensurate amount of the associated asset also is recognized.

Recording the additional liability achieves the objective of providing for a minimum liability of $30 million:

The net total of the prepaid (accrued) pension cost and the additional liability must equal the minimum liability.

Additional liability—credit balance	$(41)
Prepaid (accrued) pension cost—debit balance	11
Pension liability (reported as a single amount on the balance sheet)	$(30)

ADDITIONAL CONSIDERATION

If the intangible asset balance exceeds the unrecognized prior service cost ($56 million in our illustration), the excess should be debited to a shareholders' equity account entitled "minimum pension liability adjustment." An underfunded pension obligation usually is due primarily to prior service cost not yet funded. Because the minimum pension liability adjustment can be thought of as an asset not formally recognized, recording an intangible asset to the extent of this amount is appropriate. However, the portion of an underfunded pension obligation that is due to unrecognized net losses rather than prior service cost is more appropriately represented by a contra equity account.

To illustrate, if prior service cost had been $36 million, rather than $56 million, the journal entry to record the additional liability would have been as follows:

	($ in millions)	
Intangible pension asset	36	
Minimum pension liability adjustment (contra equity account) . . .	5	
Additional liability		41

An additional liability is recorded at year-end only for the purpose of reporting the appropriate minimum liability on the balance sheet. It has no effect whatsoever on pension expense or any other amounts we've discussed to this point. Each year, the necessity of a minimum liability is reassessed, and if necessary, an adjustment is made. For instance, if we move forward a year, taking the December 31, 2003, balances from our earlier example (Graphic 17–12), and assume an accumulated benefit obligation of $350 million on that date, we have the situation depicted in Illustration 17–6.

The need for a minimum liability is reevaluated each year.

	($ in millions)	ILLUSTRATION 17–6
December 31, 2003, balances:		Reassessing the Minimum Liability
PBO	$(450)	
ABO	350	
Plan assets	340	
Prepaid pension cost (debit)	16	
Additional liability (credit)	(41)	
Intangible pension asset	41	
The minimum liability that must be reported is:		
ABO	$(350)	
Plan assets	340	
Minimum liability	$ (10)	
So, an additional liability balance of only $26 million is needed:		
Minimum liability	$ (10)	
Less: prepaid (accrued) pension cost	16	
Additional liability	$ (26)	

Because the additional liability balance already is $41 million from the previous year, the following adjustment is made:

	($ in millions)	
Additional liability ($41 million − 26 million)	15	
Intangible pension asset		15

The balances in both the additional liability and the intangible pension asset accounts are reduced to $26 million.

Pension Disclosures—A Compromise

You learned in the previous sections of this chapter that the pension information actually reported in the financial statements falls short of the conceptual ideal and even shy of the FASB's own preferences. The Board acknowledged that *SFAS 87* represents a political compromise. The "Basis for Conclusions" portion of the *Statement* indicates that its requirements "represent a worthwhile improvement," but that some of the Board's conceptual preferences "would be too great a change from past practice to be adopted at this time."[21]

The pension items that are included in the income statement and balance sheet are indicated in Graphic 17–13. Where appropriate for demonstration, amounts from the chapter illustrations (2003) are indicated.

GRAPHIC 17–13
Financial Statement
Disclosures

Income Statement	($ in millions)
Pension expense	$43
Balance Sheet	
Assets:	
Intangible pension asset	$26
Liabilities:	
Pension liability {$16 + (26)}	$(10)
Stockholders' equity (other comprehensive income):	
Unrealized pension cost	none

Pension amounts
reported in the
disclosure notes fill a
reporting gap left by
the minimal disclosures
in the primary financial
statements.

DECISION MAKERS' PERSPECTIVE

Although financial statement items are casualties of the political compromises of *SFAS 87*, information provided in the disclosure notes fortunately makes up for some of the deficiencies. *SFAS 132*, which became effective in 1998, revised the pension disclosure requirements.[22] Foremost among the useful disclosures are changes in the projected benefit obligation, changes in the fair value of plan assets, and a breakdown of the components of the annual pension expense. Other information also is made available to make it possible for interested analysts to reconstruct the financial statements with pension assets and liabilities included. The items shown in Graphic 17–14 are required to be provided in the disclosure notes (with 2003 amounts from the chapter illustrations where appropriate).

Investors and creditors must be cautious of the nontraditional treatment of pension information when developing financial ratios as part of an analysis of financial statements. The various elements of pensions that are not reported separately on the balance sheet (PBO, plan assets, net gains and losses, prior service cost) can be included in ratios such as the debt-to-equity ratio or return on assets, but only by deliberately obtaining those numbers from the disclosure notes and adjusting the computation of the ratios. Similarly, without adjustment, profitability ratios and the times interest earned ratio will be distorted because pension expense includes the financial components of interest and return on assets.

Earnings quality (as defined in Chapter 4 and discussed in other chapters) also can be influenced by amounts reported in pension disclosures. Companies with relatively sizeable unrecognized pension costs (prior service cost, net gain or loss) can be expected to exhibit a relatively high "transitory" earnings component. Recall that transitory earnings are expected to be less predictive of future earnings than the "permanent" earnings component. ■

---

[21]"Employers' Accounting for Pensions," *Statement of Financial Accounting Standards No. 87* (Stamford, Conn.: FASB, 1985), par. 107.
[22]"Employers' Disclosures about Pensions and Other Postretirement Benefits," *Statement of Financial Accounting Standards No. 132* (Stamford, Conn.: FASB, 1998).

1.	Changes in the benefit obligation	($ in millions)
	PBO at the *beginning* of 2003	$ 400
	Service cost, 2003	41
	Interest cost	24
	Loss (gain) on PBO	23
	Less: Retiree benefits paid	(38)
	PBO at the *end* of 2003	$ 450

The benefit obligation, though not reported on the balance sheet, is reported in the disclosure notes.

2. The discount rate (6%), the assumed rate of compensation increase used to measure the PBO (not given), and the expected long-term rate of return on plan assets (9%)

Actuarial assumptions used to measure the PBO and plan assets are disclosed.

3.	Changes in the plan assets	
	Plan assets at the *beginning* of 2003	$ 300
	Return on plan assets	30
	Cash contributions	48
	Less: Retiree benefits paid	(38)
	Plan assets at the *end* of 2003	$ 340

The fair value of plan assets, though not reported on the balance sheet, is reported in the disclosure notes.

4.	Composition of *pension expense*	
	Service cost	$ 41
	Interest cost	24
	Return on plan assets	
	[actual return, $30, less $3 gain, equals expected return]	(27)
	Amortization of prior service cost	4
	Amortization of net loss	1
		$ 43

The components of pension expense are itemized.

5.	Reconciliation schedule—relating *funded status* and balance sheet amounts:	
	Projected benefit obligation	$(450)
	Fair value of plan assets	340
	Underfunded amount	(110)
	Unrecognized prior service cost	52
	Unrecognized net loss (gain)	74
	Prepaid (accrued) pension cost	$ 16

The difference between the funded status and the prepaid (accrued) pension cost can be reconciled by the unrecognized prior service cost and net loss or gain.

Settlement or Curtailment of Pension Plans

You learned earlier that many companies are deciding to terminate long-standing defined benefit plans to cut down on cumbersome paperwork and to lessen their exposure to the risk posed by defined benefit plans. Many are substituting defined contribution plans.

Sometimes the motivation to terminate a plan is to take advantage of the excess funding position of many plans that was created by the stock market boom of the 1980s and 1990s and to divert these assets to another purpose. This trend was given impetus in 1982 when Tengelmann Group took over ailing A&P and used the acquired company's excess pension plan assets to finance its turnaround. Since then, so-called reversion assets have been used, not only in takeovers, but by existing management as well. Exxon (now ExxonMobil), for instance, used $1.6 billion from its $5.6 billion pension fund to bolster operations during a period of depressed oil prices in 1986. Asset reversions are not as common now as in the 1980s, largely because of excise taxes on amounts recovered when plans are terminated and other restrictive legislation taken by Congress to limit terminations.

Companies sometimes terminate defined benefit plans to reduce costs and lessen risk.

Companies sometimes terminate defined benefit plans to siphon off excess pension fund assets for other purposes.

When a plan is terminated, *SFAS 88* requires a gain or loss to be reported at that time.[23] For instance, Melville Corporation described the termination of its pension plan in the following disclosure note:

GRAPHIC 17–15
Gain on the Termination of a Defined Benefit Plan— Melville Corporation

Retirement Plans (in part)
. . . As a result of the termination of the defined benefit plans, and after the settlement of the liability to plan participants through the purchase of nonparticipating annuity contracts or lump-sum rollovers into the new 401(k) Profit Sharing Plan, the Company recorded a non-recurring gain of approximately $4,000,000 which was the amount of plan assets that reverted to the Company. This was accounted for in accordance with *Statement of Financial Accounting Standards No. 88,* "Employers' Accounting for Settlements and Curtailments of Defined Benefit Pension Plans and for Termination Benefits."

CONCEPT REVIEW EXERCISE

Pension Plans

Allied Services, Inc. has a noncontributory, defined benefit pension plan. Pension plan assets had a fair market value of $900 million at December 31, 2002.

On January 1, 2003, Allied amended the pension formula to increase benefits for each service year. By making the amendment retroactive to prior years, Allied incurred a prior service cost of $75 million, adding to the previous projected benefit obligation of $875 million. The prior service cost is to be amortized (expensed) over 15 years. The service cost is $31 million for 2003. Both the actuary's discount rate and the expected rate of return on plan assets were 8%. The actual rate of return on plan assets was 10%.

At December 31, $16 million was contributed to the pension fund and $22 million was paid to retired employees. Also, at that time, the actuary revised a previous assumption, increasing the PBO estimate by $10 million. The unrecognized net loss at the beginning of the year was $13 million.

Required:
Determine each of the following amounts as of December 31, 2003, the fiscal year-end for Allied:

1. Projected benefit obligation
2. Plan assets
3. Pension expense

SOLUTION

($ in millions)	Projected Benefit Obligation	Plan Assets	Pension Expense
Balances at Jan. 1	$ 875	$900	$ 0
Prior service cost	75		
Service cost	31		31
Interest cost [($875 + 75)* × 8%]	76		76
Return on plan assets:			
Actual ($900 × 10%)		90	
Expected ($900 × 8%)			(72)
Amortization of prior service cost ($75 ÷ 15)			5
Amortization of unrecognized net loss			0†
Loss on PBO	10		

---

[23]"Employers' Accounting for Settlements and Curtailments of Defined Benefit Pension Plans and for Termination Benefits," *Statement of Financial Accounting Standards No. 88* (Stamford, Conn.: FASB, 1985).

Cash contribution		16	
Retirement payments	(22)	(22)	
Balance at Dec. 31	$1,045	$984	$40

Note: The $18 million gain on plan assets ($90 − 72 million) is not recognized yet; it is carried forward to be combined with previous and future gains and losses, which will be recognized only if the net gain or net loss exceeds 10% of the higher of the PBO or plan assets.
*Since the plan was amended at the beginning of the year, the prior service cost increased the PBO at that time.
†Since the unrecognized net loss ($13) does not exceed 10% of $900 (higher than $875), no amortization is required for 2003.

FINANCIAL REPORTING CASE **SOLUTION**

1. **Why is underfunding not a concern in your present employment?** *(p. 837)*   In a defined contribution plan, the employer is not obliged to provide benefits beyond the annual contribution to the employees' plan. No liability is created. Unlike retirement benefits paid in a defined benefit plan, the employee's retirement benefits in a defined contribution plan are totally dependent on how well invested assets perform in the marketplace.

2. **Were you correct that the pension liability is not reported on the balance sheet? What is the liability?** *(p. 839)*   Yes. The pension liability is measured (in three ways) and tracked informally, but not reported on the balance sheet. It is disclosed, however, in the notes. For United Dynamics, the PBO in 2003 is $2,628 million.

3. **What is the amount of the plan assets available to pay benefits? What are the factors that can cause that amount to change?** *(p. 846)*   The plan assets at the end of 2003 total $2,807 million. A trustee accepts employer contributions, invests the contributions, accumulates the earnings on the investments, and pays benefits from the plan assets. So the amount is increased each year by employer cash contributions and (hopefully) a return on assets invested. It is decreased by amounts paid out to retired employees.

4. **How is the pension expense influenced by changes in the pension liability and plan assets?** *(p. 848)*   The pension expense reported on the income statement is a composite of periodic changes that occur in both the pension obligation and the plan assets. For United Dynamics in 2003, the pension expense included the service cost and interest cost, which are changes in the PBO, and the return on plan assets. It also included an amortized portion of prior service costs (a previous change in the PBO) and of net gains (gains and losses result from changes in both the PBO and plan assets).

5. **Are you interviewing with a company whose pension plan is severely underfunded?** *(p. 856)*   No. United Dynamics' plan assets exceed the pension obligation in each year presented. ■

THE BOTTOM LINE

1. Pension plans are arrangements designed to provide income to individuals during their retirement years. *Defined contribution* plans promise fixed annual contributions to a pension fund, without further commitment regarding benefit amounts at retirement. *Defined benefit* plans promise fixed retirement benefits defined by a designated formula. The employer sets aside cash each year to provide sufficient funds to pay promised benefits.

2. The *accumulated benefit obligation* is an estimate of the discounted present value of the retirement benefits earned so far by employees, applying the plan's pension formula to *existing* compensation levels. The vested benefit obligation is the portion of the accumulated benefit obligation that plan participants are entitled to receive regardless of their continued employment. The *projected benefit obligation* estimates retirement benefits by applying the pension formula to *projected future* compensation levels.

3. The PBO can change due to the accumulation of *service cost* from year to year, the accrual of *interest* as time passes, making plan amendments retroactive to prior years (prior service cost), and periodic adjustments when estimates change (gains and losses). The obligation is reduced as benefits actually are paid to retired employees.

4. The plan assets consist of the accumulated balance of the annual employer contributions plus the return on the investments (dividends, interest, market price appreciation) less benefits paid to retirees.

5. The pension expense is a composite of periodic changes in both the pension obligation and the plan assets. Service cost is the increase in the PBO attributable to employee service and is the primary component of pension expense. The interest and return-on-assets components are financial items created only because the pension payment is delayed and the obligation is funded currently. Prior service cost is recognized over employees' future service period. Also, neither a loss (gain) on the PBO nor a loss (gain) on plan assets is immediately recognized in pension expense; they are recognized on a delayed basis to achieve income smoothing.

6. The difference between pension expense and the cash contribution to plan assets is debited or credited to a single account: prepaid (accrued) pension cost. A debit balance in this account is reported as an asset; a credit balance is reported as a liability. This amount equals the net sum of the elements that constitute a defined benefit pension plan that aren't formally recognized in the accounts: the PBO, the plan assets, the unrecognized prior service cost, and the unrecognized net loss (or gain).

7. Pension amounts reported in the disclosure notes fill a reporting gap left by the minimal disclosures in the primary financial statements. Disclosures include a breakdown of the components of the annual pension expense, changes in the projected benefit obligation, changes in plan assets, and other information to make it possible for interested analysts to reconstruct the financial statements with pension assets and liabilities included. ■

SERVICE METHOD OF ALLOCATING PRIOR SERVICE COST

APPENDIX

17

When amortizing prior service cost, our objective is to match the cost with employee service. The straight-line method described in this chapter allocates an equal amount of the prior service cost to each year of the 15-year average service period of affected employees. But consider this: fewer of the affected employees will be working for the company toward the end of that period than at the beginning. Some probably will retire or quit in each year following the amendment.

An allocation approach that reflects the declining service pattern is called the **service method.** This method allocates the prior service cost to each year in proportion to the fraction of the total remaining service years worked in each of those years. To do this, it's necessary to estimate how many of the 2,000 employees working at the beginning of 2002 when the amendment is made will still be employed in each year after the amendment.

Let's suppose, for example, that the actuary estimates that a declining number of these employees still will be employed in each of the next 28 years as indicated in the abbreviated schedule below. The portion of the prior service cost amortized to pension expense each year is $60 million times a declining fraction. Each year's fraction is that year's service divided by the 28-year total (30,000). This is demonstrated in Graphic 17A–1.

The service method amortized an equal amount per employee each year.

Conceptually, the service method achieves a better matching of the cost and benefits. In fact, this is the FASB's recommended approach. However, *SFAS 87* permits the consistent use of any method that amortizes the prior service cost at least as quickly.[24] The straight-line method meets this condition and is the approach most often used in practice. In our illustration, the cost is completely amortized over 15 years rather than the 28 years required by the service method. The 15-year average service life is simply the total estimated service years divided by the total number of employees in the group:

30,000 years	÷	2,000	=	15 years
Total number of service years		Total number of employees		Average service years ■

---

[24]"Employers' Accounting for Pensions," *Statement of Financial Accounting Standards No. 87* (Stamford, Conn.: FASB, 1985), par. 26.

				($ in millions)		
Year	Number of Employees Still Employed (assumed for the illustration)	Fraction of Total Service Years		Prior Service Cost		Amount Amortized
2002	2,000	$2{,}000/30{,}000$	×	$60	=	$ 4.0
2003	2,000	$2{,}000/30{,}000$	×	60	=	4.0
2004	1,850	$1{,}850/30{,}000$	×	60	=	3.7
2005	1,700	$1{,}700/30{,}000$	×	60	=	3.4
2006	1,550	$1{,}550/30{,}000$	×	60	=	3.1
—	—	—		—		—
2027	400	$400/30{,}000$	×	60	=	.8
2028	250	$250/30{,}000$	×	60	=	.5
2029	100	$100/30{,}000$	×	60	=	.2
Totals	30,000	$30{,}000/30{,}000$				$60.0
	Total number of service years					Total amount amortized

GRAPHIC 17A-1
Service Method of Amortizing Prior Service Cost

By the service method, prior service cost is recognized each year in proportion to the fraction of the total remaining service years worked that year.

QUESTIONS FOR REVIEW OF KEY TOPICS

Q 17–1 What is a pension plan? What motivates a corporation to offer a pension plan for its employees?

Q 17–2 Qualified pension plans offer important tax benefits. What is the special tax treatment and what qualifies a pension plan for these benefits?

Q 17–3 Lamont Corporation has a pension plan in which the corporation makes all contributions and employees receive benefits at retirement based on the balance in their accumulated pension fund. What type of pension plan does Lamont have?

Q 17–4 What is the vested benefit obligation?

Q 17–5 Differentiate between the accumulated benefit obligation and the projected benefit obligation.

Q 17–6 Name five events that might change the balance of the PBO.

Q 17–7 Name three events that might change the balance of the plan assets.

Q 17–8 What are the components that might be included in the calculation of net pension cost recognized for a period by an employer sponsoring a defined benefit pension plan?

Q 17–9 Define the service cost component of the periodic pension expense.

Q 17–10 Define the interest cost component of the periodic pension expense.

Q 17–11 The return on plan assets is the increase in plan assets (at fair value), adjusted for contributions to the plan and benefits paid during the period. How is the return included in the calculation of the periodic pension expense?

Q 17–12 Define prior service cost. How is it included in pension expense?

Q 17–13 How should gains or losses related to pension plan assets be recognized? How does this treatment compare to that for gains or losses related to the pension obligation?

Q 17–14 Name four pension-related balances that can be described as off-balance-sheet asset and liability amounts.

Q 17–15 What two components of pension expense may be negative (i.e. reduce pension expense)?

Q 17–16 Which are the components of pension expense that involve delayed recognition?

Q 17–17 Evaluate this statement: The excess of the actual return on plan assets over the expected return decreases the employer's pension cost.

Q 17–18 When accounting for pension costs, how should any difference between net periodic pension expense and the payment into the pension fund be reported?

Q 17–19 Compare the way the pension obligation is reported in the balance sheet with the FASB's apparent conceptual preference for reporting that obligation.

Q 17–20   A pension plan is underfunded when the employer's obligation (PBO) exceeds the resources available to satisfy that obligation (plan assets) and overfunded when the opposite is the case. Explain how this funded status can be reconciled with the balance in the prepaid (accrued) pension cost that is reported on the balance sheet.

Q 17–21   Assuming a zero balance in the prepaid (accrued) pension cost account, when must an additional minimum pension liability be recorded? What if the account has a credit balance? A debit balance?

EXERCISES

E 17–1
Changes in the PBO

Indicate by letter whether each of the events listed below increases (**I**), decreases (**D**), or has no effect (**N**) on an employer's projected benefits obligation.

Events

____ 1. Interest cost.
____ 2. Amortization of prior service cost.
____ 3. A decrease in the average life expectancy of employees.
____ 4. An increase in the average life expectancy of employees.
____ 5. A plan amendment that increases benefits is made retroactive to prior years.
____ 6. An increase in the actuary's assumed discount rate.
____ 7. Cash contributions to the pension fund by the employer.
____ 8. Benefits are paid to retired employees.
____ 9. Service cost.
____ 10. Return on plan assets during the year are lower than expected.
____ 11. Return on plan assets during the year are higher than expected.

E 17–2
Determine the projected benefit obligation

On January 1, 2003, Burleson Corporation's projected benefit obligation was $30 million. During 2003 pension benefits paid by the trustee were $4 million. Service cost for 2003 is $12 million. Pension plan assets (at fair value) increased during 2003 by $6 million as expected. At the end of 2003, there were no unrecognized pension costs. The actuary's discount rate was 10%.

Required:
Determine the amount of the projected benefit obligation at December 31, 2003.

E 17–3
Components of pension expense

Indicate by letter whether each of the events listed below increases (**I**), decreases (**D**), or has no effect (**N**) on an employer's periodic pension expense in the year the event occurs.

Events

____ 1. Interest cost.
____ 2. Amortization of prior service cost.
____ 3. Excess of the expected return on plan assets over the actual return.
____ 4. Expected return on plan assets.
____ 5. A plan amendment that increases benefits is made retroactive to prior years.
____ 6. Actuary's estimate of the PBO is increased.
____ 7. Cash contributions to the pension fund by the employer.
____ 8. Benefits are paid to retired employees.
____ 9. Service cost.
____ 10. Excess of the actual return on plan assets over the expected return.
____ 11. Amortization of unrecognized net loss.
____ 12. Amortization of unrecognized net gain.

E 17–4
Recording pension expense

Harrison Forklift determined its pension expense to be $14 million in 2003.

Required:
Prepare the appropriate general journal entries to record Harrison's pension expense and funding in each of the following independent situations:
1.   Harrison contributed $14 million to the pension fund at the end of 2003.
2.   Harrison contributed $11 million to the pension fund at the end of 2003.
3.   Harrison contributed $16 million to the pension fund at the end of 2003.

E 17–5
Determine pension plan assets

The following data relates to Voltaire Company's defined benefit pension plan during 2003:

	($ in millions)
Plan assets at fair value, January 1	$600
Expected return on plan assets	60
Actual return on plan assets	48
Contributions to the pension fund (end of year)	100
Amortization of unrecognized loss	10
Pension benefits paid (end of year)	11
Pension expense	72

Required:
Determine the amount of pension plan assets at fair value on December 31, 2003.

E 17–6
Changes in the pension obligation; determine service cost

Pension data for Millington Enterprises includes the following:

	($ in millions)
Discount rate, 10%	
Projected benefit obligation, January 1, 2003	$360
Projected benefit obligation, December 31, 2003	465
Accumulated benefit obligation, January 1, 2003	300
Accumulated benefit obligation, December 31, 2003	415
Cash contributions to pension fund, December 31, 2003	150
Benefit payments to retirees, December 31, 2003	54

Required:
Assuming no change in actuarial assumptions and estimates, determine the service cost component of pension expense for 2003.

E 17–7
Changes in plan assets; determine cash contributions

Pension data for Fahy Transportation, Inc. includes the following:

	($ in millions)
Discount rate, 7%	
Expected return on plan assets, 10%	
Actual return on plan assets, 11%	
Projected benefit obligation, January 1, 2003	$730
Plan assets (fair market value), January 1, 2003	700
Plan assets (fair market value), December 31, 2003	750
Benefit payments to retirees, December 31, 2003	66

Required:
Assuming cash contributions were made at the end of the year, what was the amount of those contributions for 2003?

E 17–8
Components of pension expense

Pension data for Sterling Properties includes the following:

	($ in 000s)
Service cost, 2003	$112
Projected benefit obligation, January 1, 2003	850
Plan assets (fair market value), January 1, 2003	900
Unrecognized prior service cost, (2003 amortization, $8)	80
Unrecognized net loss, (2003 amortization, $1)	101
Discount rate, 6%	
Expected return on plan assets, 10%	
Actual return on plan assets, 11%	

Required:
Determine pension expense for 2003.

E 17–9
Determine pension expense

Abbott and Abbott has a noncontributory, defined benefit pension plan. At December 31, 2003, Abbott and Abbott received the following information:

Projected Benefit Obligation	($ in millions)
Balance, January 1	$120
Service cost	20
Interest cost	12
Benefits paid	(9)
Balance, December 31	$143

[handwritten: 4 80 × 10% = 8]

Plan Assets

Balance, January 1	$80
Actual return on plan assets	9
Contributions 2003	20
Benefits paid	(9)
Balance, December 31	$100

[handwritten: not on the P/L of comp. on the b/sheet]

The expected long-term rate of return on plan assets was 10%. There was no unrecognized prior service cost or gains and losses on January 1, 2003.

Required:

1. Determine Abbott and Abbott's pension expense for 2003.
2. Prepare the journal entry to record Abbott and Abbott's pension expense and funding for 2003.

E 17–10
Components of pension expense; journal entry

[handwritten: Compare ending balance when looking for the minimum liab.]

Pension data for Barry Financial Services, Inc. include the following:

	($ in 000s)
[handwritten: when looking]	
Discount rate, 7%	
Expected return on plan assets, 10%	
Actual return on plan assets, 9%	
Service cost, 2003	$ 310
January 1, 2003:	
Projected benefit obligation	2,300
Accumulated benefit obligation	2,000
Plan assets (fair market value)	2,400
Unrecognized prior service cost, (2003 amortization, $25)	325
Unrecognized net gain, (2003 amortization, $6)	330
December 31, 2003:	
Cash contributions to pension fund, December 31, 2003	245
Benefit payments to retirees, December 31, 2003	270

Required:

1. Determine pension expense for 2003.
2. Prepare the journal entry to record pension expense and funding for 2003.

E 17–11
PBO calculations; ABO calculations; present value concepts

Clark Industries has a defined benefit pension plan that specifies annual retirement benefits equal to:

$$1.2\% \times \text{Service years} \times \text{Final year's salary}$$

Stanley Mills was hired by Clark at the beginning of 1983. Mills is expected to retire at the end of 2028 after 45 years service. His retirement is expected to span 15 years. At the end of 2003, 20 years after being hired, his salary is $80,000. The company's actuary projects Mills's salary to be $270,000 at retirement. The actuary's discount rate is 7%.

Required:

1. Estimate the amount of Stanley Mills's annual retirement payments for the 15 retirement years earned as of the end of 2003.
2. Suppose Clark's pension plan permits a lump-sum payment at retirement in lieu of annuity payments. Determine the lump-sum equivalent as the present value as of the retirement date of annuity payments during the retirement period.
3. What is the company's projected benefit obligation at the end of 2003 with respect to Stanley Mills?
4. What is the company's accumulated benefit obligation at the end of 2003 with respect to Stanley Mills?
5. If we assume no estimates change in the meantime, what is the company's projected benefit obligation at the end of 2004 with respect to Stanley Mills?
6. What portion of the 2004 increase in the PBO is attributable to 2004 service (the service cost component of pension expense) and to accrued interest (the interest cost component of pension expense)?

E 17–12
Determining the
amortization of
unrecognized net gain

Hicks Cable Company has a defined benefit pension plan. Three alternative possibilities for pension-related data at January 1, 2003, are shown below:

	($ in 000s)		
	Case 1	**Case 2**	**Case 3**
Unrecognized net loss (gain), Jan. 1	$ 320	$ (330)	$ 260
2003 loss (gain) on plan assets	(11)	(8)	2
2003 loss (gain) on PBO	(23)	16	(265)
Accumulated benefit obligation, Jan. 1	(2,950)	(2,550)	(1,450)
Projected benefit obligation, Jan. 1	(3,310)	(2,670)	(1,700)
Fair value of plan assets, Jan. 1	2,800	2,700	1,550
Average remaining service period of active employees (years)	12	15	10

Required:
1. For each independent case, calculate any amortization of the net loss or gain that should be included as a component of net pension expense for 2003.
2. Determine the unrecognized net loss or gain as of January 1, 2004.

E 17–13
Pension spreadsheet

A partially completed pension spreadsheet, showing the relationships among the elements that comprise the defined benefit pension plan of Universal Products, is given below. The actuary's discount rate is 5%. At the end of 2001, the pension formula was amended, creating a prior service cost of $120,000. The expected rate of return on assets was 8%, and the average remaining service life of the active employee group is 20 years in the current year as well as the previous two years.

	Informal Records				**Formal Records**		
($ in 000s)	PBO	Plan Assets	Prior Service Cost	Net Loss	Pension Expense	Cash	Prepaid (Accrued) Cost
Balance, Jan. 1, 2003	$(800)	$600	$114	$ 80			$(6)
Service cost					$ 84		
Interest cost, 5%	(40)						
Actual return on assets					(42)		
Loss on assets				6			
Amortization of:							
Prior service cost							
Net loss							
Gain on PBO				(12)			
Contributions to fund						$(48)	
Retiree benefits paid						————	
2003 journal entry	————			————	════	════	(34)
Balance, Dec. 31, 2003	$(862)		$108				

Note: ( )s indicate credits; debits otherwise.

Required:
Copy the incomplete spreadsheet and fill in the missing amounts.

E 17–14
Minimum liability

Willis-Chambers Company has a noncontributory, defined benefit pension plan. On December 31, 2003, the following pension-related data were available:

	($ in millions)
Projected benefit obligation	$25
Accumulated benefit obligation	22
Plan assets (fair value)	20
Accrued pension cost (credit balance)	3

Required:
1. Determine Willis-Chambers' minimum pension liability to be reported on the 2003 balance sheet and prepare any journal entry necessary to achieve that reporting objective.
2. Suppose Willis-Chambers had a prepaid pension cost of $3 (debit balance), instead of a credit balance. Prepare any journal entry necessary to achieve that reporting objective.

E 17–15
Minimum liability

Norsouth Corporation has a defined benefit pension plan. Norsouth's policy is to fund the plan annually, cash payments being made at the end of each year. Data relating to the pension plan for 2003 are as follows:

	($ in millions)
Prepaid (accrued) pension cost at the beginning of the year—debit balance	$ 8
Net pension expense for 2003	40
Unrecognized prior service cost at year-end	30
Accumulated benefit obligation at year-end	117
Projected benefit obligation at year-end	140
Fair value of plan assets at year-end	105
Payment to trustee at year-end	38

Required:
Determine Norsouth's pension liability to be reported on the 2003 balance sheet and prepare any journal entry necessary to achieve that reporting objective.

E 17–16
Concepts; terminology

Listed below are several terms and phrases associated with pensions. Pair each item from List A (by letter) with the item from List B that is most appropriately associated with it.

List A	List B
____ 1. Future compensation levels estimated.	a. Additional minimum liability
____ 2. All funding provided by the employer.	b. Prepaid pension cost
____ 3. Cumulative employer's contributions in excess of recognized pension.	c. Vested benefit obligation
____ 4. Retirement benefits specified by formula.	d. Projected benefit obligation
____ 5. Trade-off between relevance and reliability.	e. Choice between PBO and ABO
____ 6. Causes a debit to an intangible asset.	f. Noncontributory pension plan
____ 7. Current pay levels implicitly assumed.	g. Accumulated benefit obligation
____ 8. Created by the passage of time.	h. Plan assets
____ 9. Not contingent on future employment.	i. Interest cost
____ 10. Risk borne by employee.	j. Delayed recognition
____ 11. Increased by employer contributions.	k. Defined contribution plan
____ 12. Caused by plan amendment.	l. Defined benefit plan
____ 13. Gain on plan assets.	m. Prior service cost
____ 14. Excess over 10% of plan assets or PBO.	n. Amortize unrecognized net loss

E 17–17
Determine pension expense; minimum liability; prior service cost; unrecognized net loss

Beale Management has a noncontributory, defined benefit pension plan. On December 31, 2003 (the end of Beale's fiscal year), the following pension-related data were available:

Projected Benefit Obligation	($ in millions)
Balance, January 1, 2003	$480
Service cost	82
Interest cost, discount rate, 10%	24
Gain due to changes in actuarial assumptions in 2003	(10)
Pension benefits paid	(40)
Balance, December 31, 2003	$536

Plan Assets	
Balance, January 1, 2003	$500
Actual return on plan assets	40
(Expected return on plan assets, $45)	
Contributions	70
Pension benefits paid	(40)
Balance, December 31, 2003	$570

Accumulated Benefits Obligation, Dec. 31, 2003	$490

January 1, 2003, balances:	
Prepaid (accrued) pension cost (credit balance)	$ (12)
Unrecognized prior service cost (amortization $8 per year)	48
Unrecognized net gain (any amortization over 15 years)	80
Intangible pension asset	none

Required:
1. Prepare the 2003 journal entry to record pension expense and funding.
2. Prepare the 2003 journal entry to record any necessary additional pension liability.
3. Suppose that at December 31, 2003, the minimum liability is calculated to be $15 million. Prepare the 2003 journal entry to record any necessary additional pension liability.

E 17–18
Additional minimum liability; multiple years

Goode Corporation established a noncontributory, defined benefit pension plan for its employees at the company's inception in 1987. The plan was amended in 2003. Prior to 2003, Goode had not found it necessary to record an additional minimum pension liability. The following information is available for the reporting years ended December 31:

	($ in 000s)		
	2003	**2004**	**2005**
Projected benefit obligation	$1,100	$1,500	$2,000
Accumulated benefit obligation	900	1,050	1,200
Plan assets at fair value	800	975	1,100
(Accrued)/prepaid pension cost	(30)	(25)	5
Unrecognized prior service cost (to be amortized over five years beginning in 2004)	40		

Required:
1. Compute the required additional minimum liability for each year, 2003 through 2005.
2. Prepare the journal entry to recognize the additional minimum liability for each year, 2003 through 2005.

E 17–19
Multiple choice

The following questions dealing with pensions are adapted from questions that appeared on recent CPA examinations. Determine the response that best completes the statements or questions.
1. The following information pertains to Lee Corp.'s defined benefit pension plan for 2003:

Service cost	$160,000 S
Actual and expected return on plan assets	35,000 R
Unexpected loss on plan assets related to a 2003 disposal of a subsidiary	40,000
Amortization of unrecognized prior service cost	5,000 P
Annual interest on pension obligation	50,000 I

What amount should Lee report as pension expense in its 2003 income statement?
   a. $250,000
   b. $220,000
   c. $210,000
   d. $180,000
2. Interest cost included in the net pension cost recognized by an employer sponsoring a defined benefit pension plan represents the
   a. Amortization of the discount on unrecognized prior service costs.
   b. Increase in the fair value of plan assets due to the passage of time.
   c. Increase in the projected benefit obligation due to the passage of time.
   d. Shortage between the expected and actual returns on plan assets.
3. Webb Co. implemented a defined benefit pension plan for its employees on January 1, 2000. During 2000 and 2001, Webb's contributions fully funded the plan. The following data are provided for 2003 and 2002:

	2003 Estimated	2002 Actual
Projected benefit obligation, December 31	$750,000	$700,000
Accumulated benefit obligation, December 31	520,000	500,000
Plan assets at fair value, December 31	675,000	600,000
Projected benefit obligation in excess of plan assets	75,000	100,000
Pension expense	90,000	75,000
Employer's contribution	?	50,000

What amount should Webb contribute in order to report an accrued pension liability of $15,000 in its December 31, 2003, balance sheet?

see the note book

a. $50,000
b. $60,000
c. $75,000
d. $100,000

4. Payne, Inc., implemented a defined-benefit pension plan for its employees on January 2, 2003. The following data are provided for 2003, as of December 31, 2003:

Accumulated benefit obligation	$103,000
Plan assets at fair value	78,000
Net periodic pension cost	90,000
Employer's contribution	70,000

What amount should Payne record as additional minimum pension liability at December 31, 2003?

a. $0
b. $5,000
c. $20,000
d. $45,000

E 17–20
Classifying accounting
changes and errors

Indicate with the appropriate letter the nature of each adjustment described below:

Type of Adjustment

A. Change in principle (general)
B. Change in principle (exception reported retroactively)
C. Change in principle (exception reported prospectively)
D. Change in estimate
E. Correction of an error
N. Neither an accounting change nor an error

___ 1. Change in actuarial assumptions for a defined benefit pension plan.
___ 2. Determination that the accumulated benefits obligation under a pension plan exceeded the fair value of plan assets at the end of the previous year by $17,000. The only pension-related amount on the balance sheet was prepaid pension costs of $30,000.
___ 3. Pension plan assets for a defined benefit pension plan achieving a rate of return in excess of the amount anticipated.
___ 4. Instituting a pension plan for the first time and adopting *Statement of Financial Accounting Standards No. 87,* "Employers' Accounting for Pensions."

E 17–21
Prior service cost;
service method;
straight-line method
(Based on Appendix)

Frazier Refrigeration amended its defined benefit pension plan on December 31, 2003, to increase retirement benefits earned with each service year. The consulting actuary estimated the prior service cost incurred by making the amendment retroactive to prior years to be $110,000. Frazier's 100 present employees are expected to retire at the rate of approximately 10 each year at the end of each of the next 10 years.

Required:
1. Using the service method, calculate the amount of prior service cost to be amortized to pension expense in each of the next 10 years.
2. Using the straight-line method, calculate the amount of prior service cost to be amortized to pension expense in each of the next 10 years.

PROBLEMS

(Note: Problems 1–5 are variations of the same situation, designed to focus on different elements of the pension plan.)

P 17–1
ABO calculations;
present value concepts

Sachs Brands' defined benefit pension plan specifies annual retirement benefits equal to: 1.6% × service years × final year's salary, payable at the end of each year. Angela Davenport was hired by Sachs at the beginning of 1989 and is expected to retire at the end of 2023 after 35 years service. Her retirement is expected to span 18 years. Davenport's salary is $90,000 at the end of 2003 and the company's actuary projects her salary to be $240,000 at retirement. The actuary's discount rate is 7%.

Required:
1. Draw a time line that depicts Davenport's expected service period, retirement period, and a 2003 measurement date for the pension obligation.

2. Estimate by the accumulated benefits approach the amount of Davenport's annual retirement payments earned as of the end of 2003.
3. What is the company's accumulated benefit obligation at the end of 2003 with respect to Davenport?
4. If no estimates are changed in the meantime, what will be the accumulated benefit obligation at the end of 2006 (three years later) when Davenport's salary is $100,000?

P 17–2
PBO calculations; present value concepts

Sachs Brands' defined benefit pension plan specifies annual retirement benefits equal to: 1.6% × service years × final year's salary, payable at the end of each year. Angela Davenport was hired by Sachs at the beginning of 1989 and is expected to retire at the end of 2023 after 35 years service. Her retirement is expected to span 18 years. Davenport's salary is $90,000 at the end of 2003 and the company's actuary projects her salary to be $240,000 at retirement. The actuary's discount rate is 7%.

Required:
1. Draw a time line that depicts Davenport's expected service period, retirement period, and a 2003 measurement date for the pension obligation.
2. Estimate by the projected benefits approach the amount of Davenport's annual retirement payments earned as of the end of 2003.
3. What is the company's projected benefit obligation at the end of 2003 with respect to Davenport?
4. If no estimates are changed in the meantime, what will be the company's projected benefit obligation at the end of 2006 (three years later) with respect to Davenport?

P 17–3
Service cost, interest, and PBO calculations; present value concepts

Sachs Brands' defined benefit pension plan specifies annual retirement benefits equal to: 1.6% × service cost × final year's salary, payable at the end of each year. Angela Davenport was hired by Sachs at the beginning of 1989 and is expected to retire at the end of 2023 after 35 years service. Her retirement is expected to span 18 years. Davenport's salary is $90,000 at the end of 2003 and the company's actuary projects her salary to be $240,000 at retirement. The actuary's discount rate is 7%.

Required:
1. What is the company's projected benefit obligation at the beginning of 2003 (after 14 years' service) with respect to Davenport?
2. Estimate by the projected benefits approach the portion of Davenport's annual retirement payments attributable to 2003 service.
3. What is the company's service cost for 2003 with respect to Davenport?
4. What is the company's interest cost for 2003 with respect to Davenport?
5. Combine your answers to requirements 1, 3, and 4 to determine the company's projected benefit obligation at the end of 2003 (after 15 years' service) with respect to Davenport.

P 17–4
Prior service cost; components of pension expense; present value concepts

Sachs Brands' defined benefit pension plan specifies annual retirement benefits equal to: 1.6% × service years × final year's salary, payable at the end of each year. Angela Davenport was hired by Sachs at the beginning of 1989 and is expected to retire at the end of 2023 after 35 years service. Her retirement is expected to span 18 years. Davenport's salary is $90,000 at the end of 2003 and the company's actuary projects her salary to be $240,000 at retirement. The actuary's discount rate is 7%.

At the beginning of 2004, the pension formula was amended to:

$$1.75\% \times \text{Service years} \times \text{Final year's salary}$$

The amendment was made retroactive to apply the increased benefits to prior service years.

Required:
1. What is the company's prior service cost at the beginning of 2004 with respect to Davenport after the amendment described above?
2. Since the amendment occurred at the *beginning* of 2004, amortization of the prior service cost begins in 2004. What is the prior service cost amortization that would be included in pension expense?
3. What is the service cost for 2004 with respect to Davenport?
4. What is the interest cost for 2004 with respect to Davenport?
5. Calculate pension expense for 2004 with respect to Davenport, assuming plan assets attributable to her of $150,000 and a rate of return (actual and expected) of 10%.

P 17–5
Gain on PBO; present value concepts

Sachs Brands' defined benefit pension plan specifies annual retirement benefits equal to: 1.6% × service years × final year's salary, payable at the end of each year. Angela Davenport was hired by Sachs at the beginning of 1989 and is expected to retire at the end of 2023 after 35 years service. Her retirement is expected to span 18 years. Davenport's salary is $90,000 at the end of 2003 and the company's actuary projects her salary to be $240,000 at retirement. The actuary's discount rate is 7%.

At the beginning of 2004, changing economic conditions caused the actuary to reassess the applicable discount rate. It was decided that 8% is the appropriate rate.

Required:
Calculate the effect of the change in the assumed discount rate on the PBO at the beginning of 2004 with respect to Davenport.

P 17–6
Determine the PBO; plan assets, pension expense; two years

Stanley-Morgan Industries adopted a defined benefit pension plan on April 12, 2003. The provisions of the plan were not made retroactive to prior years. A local bank, engaged as trustee for the plan assets, expects plan assets to earn a 10% rate of return. A consulting firm, engaged as actuary, recommends 6% as the appropriate discount rate. The service cost is $150,000 for 2003 and $200,000 for 2004. Year-end funding is $160,000 for 2003 and $170,000 for 2004. No assumptions or estimates were revised during 2003.

Required:
Calculate each of the following amounts as of both December 31, 2003, and December 31, 2004:
1.   Projected benefit obligation
2.   Plan assets
3.   Pension expense
4.   Prepaid (accrued) pension cost

P 17–7
Determining the amortization of unrecognized net gain

Herring Wholesale Company has a defined benefit pension plan. On January 1, 2003, the following pension-related data were available:

	($ in 000s)
Unrecognized net gain	$ 170
Accumulated benefit obligation	1,170
Projected benefit obligation	1,400
Fair value of plan assets	1,100
Average remaining service period of active employees (expected to remain constant for the next several years)	15 years

The rate of return on plan assets during 2003 was 9%, although it was expected to be 10%. The actuary revised assumptions regarding the PBO at the end of the year, resulting in a $23,000 decrease in the estimate of that obligation.

Required:
1.   Calculate any amortization of the net gain that should be included as a component of net pension expense for 2003.
2.   Assume the net pension expense for 2003, not including the amortization of the net gain component, is $325,000. What is pension expense for the year?
3.   Determine the unrecognized net loss or gain as of January 1, 2004.

P 17–8
Pension spreadsheet; journal entry; reconciliation schedule

A partially completed pension spreadsheet showing the relationships among the elements that constitute Winston, Inc.'s defined benefit pension plan follows. At the end of 2000, the pension formula was amended, creating a prior service cost of $30 million. The expected rate of return on assets was 8%, and the average remaining service life of the active employee group is 15 years in the current year as well as the previous three years. The actuary's discount rate is 7%.

	Informal Records				Formal Records		
($ in millions)	PBO	Plan Assets	Prior Service Cost	Net (gain) Loss	Pension Expense	Cash	Prepaid (Accrued) Cost
Balance, Jan. 1, 2003	$(600)	$800	?	$(95)			?
Service cost	?				$65		
Interest cost	?				?		
Actual return on assets		?			(72)		
Gain (loss) on assets				?	?		
Amortization of:							
Prior service cost			(2)		?		
Net gain				?	?		
Loss on PBO	(4)			?			
Contributions to fund		?				?	

Retiree benefits paid	?	(52)					
2003 journal entry					?	$(30)	?
Balance, Dec. 31, 2003	$(659)	$850	$24	$(98)			$117

Note: ( )s indicate credits; debits otherwise.

Required:
1. Copy the incomplete spreadsheet and fill in the missing amounts.
2. Prepare the journal entry to record pension expense and funding for 2003.
3. Prepare a schedule that reconciles the funded status of the plan with the amount recorded on the balance sheet at December 31, 2003.

P 17–9

Determine pension expense; prepaid (accrued) pension cost; PBO; plan assets

U.S. Metallurgical, Inc. reported the following balances in its financial statements and disclosure notes at December 31, 2002.

Plan assets	$ 400,000
Projected benefit obligation	(320,000)
Prepaid (accrued) pension cost	$ 80,000

U.S.M.'s actuary determined that 2003 service cost is $60,000. Both the expected and actual rate of return on plan assets are 9%. The interest (discount) rate is 5%. U.S.M. contributed $120,000 to the pension fund at the end of 2003, and retirees were paid $44,000 from plan assets.

Required:
Determine the following amounts at the end of 2003.
1. Pension expense
2. Prepaid (accrued) pension cost
3. Projected benefit obligation
4. Plan assets

P 17–10

Determine pension expense, PBO, and plan assets; journal entries; two years

The Kollar Company has a defined benefit pension plan. Pension information concerning the fiscal years 2003 and 2004 are presented below ($ in millions):

Information Provided by Pension Plan Actuary:
a. Projected benefit obligation as of December 31, 2002 = $1,800.
b. Prior service cost from plan amendment on January 2, 2003 = $400 (straight-line amortization for 10-year average remaining service period).
c. Service cost for 2003 = $520.
d. Service cost for 2004 = $570.
e. Discount rate used by actuary on projected benefit obligation for 2003 and 2004 = 10%.
f. Payments to retirees in 2003 = $400.
g. Payments to retirees in 2004 = $450.
h. No changes in actuarial assumptions or estimates.

Information Provided by Pension Fund Trustee:
a. Plan asset balance at fair value on January 1, 2003 = $1,600.
b. 2003 contributions = $540.
c. 2004 contributions = $590.
d. Expected long-term rate of return on plan assets = 12%.
e. 2003 actual return on plan assets = $180.
f. 2004 actual return on plan assets = $210.
g. Unrecognized net gain from prior years on January 1, 2003 = $230.
h. Unrecognized gains and losses are amortized for 10 years for 2003 and 2004.

Required:
1. Compute pension expense for 2003 and 2004.
2. Prepare the journal entries for 2003 and 2004 pension expense.

P 17–11

Determine the PBO, plan assets, pension expense; prior service cost

Lewis Industries adopted a defined benefit pension plan on January 1, 2003. By making the provisions of the plan retroactive to prior years, Lewis incurred a prior service cost of $2 million. The prior service cost was funded immediately by a $2 million cash payment to the fund trustee on January 2, 2003. However, the cost is to be amortized (expensed) over 10 years. The service cost—$250,000 for 2003—is fully funded at the end of each year. Both the actuary's discount rate and the expected rate of return on plan assets were 9%. The actual rate of return on plan assets was 11%. At December 31, the trustee paid $16,000 to an employee who retired during 2003.

Required:

Determine each of the following amounts as of December 31, 2003, the fiscal year-end for Lewis:
1. Projected benefit obligation
2. Plan assets
3. Pension expense

P 17–12
Relationship among pension elements

Reconciliation schedules, reconciling the funded status of Hilton Paneling, Inc.'s defined benefit pension plan and the amount recognized in its balance sheet as prepaid (accrued) pension cost, are given below.

	($ in 000s)	
	2003 **Beginning Balances**	**2003** **Ending Balances**
Projected benefit obligation	$(2,300)	$(2,501)
Plan assets	2,400	2,591
Funded status	100	90
Unamortized prior service cost	325	300
Unamortized net gain	(330)	(300)
Prepaid (accrued) pension cost	$ 95	$ 90

Retirees were paid $270,000 and the employer contribution to the pension fund was $245,000 at the end of 2003. The expected rate of return on plan assets was 10%, and the actuary's discount rate is 7%. There were no changes in actuarial estimates and assumptions regarding the PBO.

Required:
Determine the following amounts for 2003:
1. Actual return on plan assets
2. Loss or gain on plan assets
3. Service cost
4. Pension expense
5. Average remaining service life of active employees (used to determine amortization of the unrecognized net gain)

P 17–13
Determine pension expense; minimum liability; prior service cost; unrecognized net loss

Musseli Transport has a noncontributory, defined benefit pension plan. On December 31, 2003 (the end of the fiscal period), the following pension-related data were available:

Projected Benefit Obligation	**($ in 000s)**
Balance, January 1, 2003	$2,000
Service cost	410
Interest cost, discount rate, 10%	200
Losses (gains) due to changes in actuarial assumptions in 2003	0
Pension benefits paid	(210)
Balance, December 31, 2003	$2,400

Plan Assets	
Balance, January 1, 2003	$1,500
Actual return on plan assets	150
(Expected return on plan assets, $135)	
Contributions	500
Pension benefits paid	(210)
Balance, December 31, 2003	$1,940

Accumulated Benefits Obligation, Dec. 31, 2003	$2,100

January 1, 2003, balances:	
Prepaid (accrued) pension cost (credit balance)	$ (30)
Unrecognized prior service cost (amortization $40 per year)	240.
Unrecognized net loss (any amortization over 15 years)	230
Intangible pension asset	none

Required:

1. Prepare the 2003 journal entry to record pension expense and funding.
2. Prepare the 2003 journal entry to record any necessary additional pension liability.
3. Suppose that at December 31, 2004, the minimum liability is calculated to be $170,000 and the prepaid (accrued) pension cost has a debit balance of $10,000. Prepare the 2004 journal entry to record any necessary additional pension liability.

P 17–14
Comprehensive—
pension elements

The following pension-related data pertain to Metro Recreation's noncontributory, defined benefit pension plan for 2003:

	($ in 000s)	
	Jan. 1	Dec. 31
Projected benefit obligation	$4,100	$4,380
Accumulated benefits obligation	3,715	3,950
Plan assets (fair value)	4,530	4,975
Interest (discount) rate, 7%		
Expected return on plan assets, 10%		
Unrecognized prior service cost (from Dec. 31, 2002, amendment)	840	
Unrecognized net loss	477	
Average remaining service life: 12 years		
Gain due to changes in actuarial assumptions		44
Contributions to pension fund (end of year)		340
Pension benefits paid (end of year)		295

Required:

Prepare a pension spreadsheet that shows the relationships among the various pension balances, shows the changes in those balances, and computes pension expense for 2003.

BROADEN YOUR PERSPECTIVE

Apply your critical-thinking ability to the knowledge you've gained. These cases will provide you an opportunity to develop your research, analysis, judgment, and communication skills. You also will work with other students, integrate what you've learned, apply it in real world situations, and consider its global and ethical ramifications. This practice will broaden your knowledge and further develop your decision-making abilities.

Communication Case 17–1
Pension concepts

Noel Zoeller is the newly hired assistant controller of Kemp Industries, a regional supplier of hardwood derivative products. The company sponsors a defined benefit pension plan that covers its 420 employees. On reviewing last year's financial statements, Zoeller was concerned about some items reported in the disclosure notes relating to the pension plan. Portions of the relevant note follow:

Note 8: Pensions

The company has a defined benefit pension plan covering substantially all of its employees. Pension benefits are based on employee service years and the employee's compensation during the last two years of employment. The company contributes annually the maximum amount permitted by the federal tax code. Plan contributions provide for benefits expected to be earned in the future as well as those earned to date. The following reconciles the plan's funded status and amount recognized in the balance sheet at December 31, 2003 ($ in 000s).

Actuarial Present Value Benefit Obligations:

Accumulated benefit obligation (including vested benefits of $318)	$(1,305)
Projected benefit obligation	(1,800)
Plan assets at fair value	1,575
Projected benefit obligation in excess of plan assets	$ (225)

Kemp's comparative income statements reported net periodic pension expense of $108,000 in 2003 and $86,520 in 2002. Since employment has remained fairly constant in recent years, Zoeller expressed concern over the increase in the pension expense. He expressed his concern to you, a three-year senior accountant at Kemp. "I'm also interested in the differences in these liability measurements," he mentioned.

Required:

Write a memo to Zoeller. In the memo:

1. Explain to Zoeller how the composition of the net periodic pension expense can create the situation he sees. Briefly describe the components of pension expense. The transition amount has been completely amortized, so you need not discuss that element.
2. Briefly explain how pension gains and losses are recognized in earnings.
3. Describe for him the differences and similarities between the accumulated benefit obligation and the projected benefit obligation.
4. Explain the circumstances that would require Kemp to recognize an additional minimum liability.

Judgment Case 17–2
Barlow's Wife; relationship among pension elements

LGD Consulting is a medium-sized provider of environmental engineering services. The corporation sponsors a noncontributory, defined benefit pension plan. Alan Barlow, a new employee and participant in the pension plan, obtained a copy of the 2003 financial statements, partly to obtain additional information about his new employer's obligation under the plan. In part, the pension footnote reads as follows:

Note 8: Retirement Benefits

The Company has a defined benefit pension plan covering substantially all of its employees. The benefits are based on years of service and the employee's compensation during the last two years of employment. The company's funding policy is consistent with the funding requirements of federal law and regulations. Generally, pension costs accrued are funded. Plan assets consist primarily of stocks, bonds, commingled trust funds, and cash.

The change in projected benefit obligation for the plan years ended December 31, 2003, and December 31, 2002:

($ in 000s)	2003	2002
Projected benefit obligation at beginning of year	$3,786	$3,715
Service cost	103	94
Interest cost	287	284
Actuarial (gain) loss	302	(23)
Benefits paid	(324)	(284)
Projected benefit obligation at end of year	$4,154	$3,786

The weighted average discount rate and rate of increase in future compensation levels used in determining the actuarial present value of the projected benefit obligations in the above table was 7.0% and 4.3%, respectively, at December 31, 2003, and 7.75% and 4.7%, respectively, at December 31, 2002. The expected long-term rate of return on assets was 10.0% at December 31, 2003 and 2002.

The change in the fair value of plan assets for the plan years ended December 31, 2003 and 2002:

($ in 000s)	2003	2002
Fair value of plan assets at beginning of year	$3,756	$3,616
Actual return on plan assets	1,101	372
Employer contributions	27	52
Benefits paid	(324)	(284)
Fair value of plan assets at end of year	$4,560	$3,756

The accrued pension cost recognized in the Consolidated Balance Sheets is computed as follows:

($ in 000s)	2003	2002
Funded status	$ 405	$ (30)
Unrecognized net actuarial gain	(620)	(165)
Unrecognized prior service cost	44	46
Accrued pension cost recognized in the Consolidated Balance Sheets	$(171)	$(149)

Net periodic defined benefit pension cost for fiscal 2003, 2002 and 2001 included the following components:

($ in 000s)	2003	2002	2001
Service cost	$ 103	$ 94	$ 112
Interest cost	287	284	263
Expected return on plan assets	(342)	(326)	(296)
Amortization of prior service cost	2	2	1
Recognized net actuarial (gain) loss	(2)	2	4
Net periodic pension cost	$ 48	$ 56	$ 84

In attempting to reconcile amounts reported in the footnote with amounts reported in the income statement and balance sheet, Barlow became confused. He was able to find the pension expense on the income statement but was unable to make sense of the balance sheet amounts. Expressing his frustration to his wife, Barlow said, "It appears to me that the company has calculated pension expense as if they have the pension liability and pension assets they include in the footnote, but I can't seem to find those amounts in the balance sheet. In fact, there are several amounts here I can't seem to account for. They also say they've made some assumptions about interest rates, pay increases, and profits on invested assets. I wonder what difference it would make if they assumed other numbers,"

Barlow's wife took accounting courses in college and remembers most of what she learned about pension accounting. She attempts to clear up her husband's confusion.

Required:
Assume the role of Barlow's wife. Answer the following questions for your husband.
1. Is Barlow's observation correct that the company has calculated pension expense on the basis of amounts not reported in the balance sheet?
2. What amount would the company report as a pension liability on the balance sheet?
3. What amount would the company report as a pension asset on the balance sheet?
4. Which of the other amounts reported in the disclosure note would the company report on the balance sheet?
5. The disclosure note reports an unrecognized net actuarial gain as well as an actuarial loss. How are these related? What do the amounts mean?
6. Which components of the pension expense represent deferred recognition of previously unrecognized amounts?

Communication Case 17–3
Barlow's Wife; relationship among pension elements

The focus of this case is question 1 in the previous case. Your instructor will divide the class into from two to six groups, depending on the size of the class. The mission of your group is to assess the correctness of Barlow's observation and to suggest the appropriate treatment of the pension obligation. The suggested treatment need not be that required by *SFAS 87*.

Required:
1. Each group member should deliberate the situation independently and draft a tentative argument prior to the class session for which the case is assigned.
2. In class, each group will meet for 10 to 15 minutes in different areas of the classroom. During that meeting, group members will take turns sharing their suggestions for the purpose of arriving at a single group treatment.
3. After the allotted time, a spokesperson for each group (selected during the group meetings) will share the group's solution with the class. The goal of the class is to incorporate the views of each group into a consensus approach to the situation.

The following Trueblood case is recommended for use with this chapter. The case provides an excellent opportunity for class discussion, group projects, and writing assignments. The case, along with Professor's Discussion Material, can be obtained from the Deloitte Foundation at its website: **www.deloitte.com/more/DTF/cases_subj.htm**.

Case 01-4: *Bag-Phones-R-Us*

This case gives students the opportunity to determine the accounting for termination benefits and whether a termination benefit should be recorded under termination contracts.

Since its inception in 1973, the primary objective of the International Accounting Standards Committee (IASC) has been to narrow differences worldwide in accounting practices and the presentation of financial information. While progress has been made, the goal is far from having been met. Significant differences exist from country to country in the area of accounting for pensions. These differences impact on reported earnings and financial position in countries where these benefits are significant.

Required:

Choose a country other than the United States and:

1. Locate a recent annual report of a company from that country.
2. Determine the way that country accounts for pensions. Include in your analysis:
   a. Whether and how the cost of providing pension benefits is reported in disclosure notes.
   b. Whether the obligation for the pension benefits is accrued in the balance sheet.
   c. The impact on the income statement, if any.
3. Prepare a short report highlighting the similarities and differences between the United States and your chosen country in the way pension benefits are accounted for.

Note: You can obtain copies of annual reports from the company's website, a friendly stockbroker, or EDGAR, the Electronic Data Gathering and Retrieval service of the SEC, at **www.sec.gov**, or you can use EdgarScan at **edgarscan.pwcglobal.com**.

You are in your third year as internal auditor with VXI International, manufacturer of parts and supplies for jet aircraft. VXI began a defined contribution pension plan in 2001. The plan is a so-called 401(k) plan (named after the Tax Code section that specifies the conditions for the favorable tax treatment of these plans) that permits voluntary contributions by employees. Employees' contributions are matched with one dollar of employer contribution for every two dollars of employee contribution. Approximately $500,000 of contributions are deducted from employee paychecks each month for investment in one of three employer-sponsored mutual funds.

While performing some preliminary audit tests you happen to notice that employee contributions to these plans usually do not show up on mutual fund statements for up to two months following the end of pay periods from which the deductions are drawn. On further investigation, you discover that when the plan was first begun, contributions were invested within one week of receipt of the funds. When you question the firm's investment manager about the apparent change in the timing of investments, you are told, "Last year Mr. Maxwell (the CFO) directed me to initially deposit the contributions in the corporate investment account. At the close of each quarter, we add the employer matching contribution and deposit the combined amount in specific employee mutual funds."

Required:

1. What is Mr. Maxwell's apparent motivation for the change in the way contributions are handled?
2. Do you perceive an ethical dilemma?

All publicly traded domestic companies use EDGAR, the Electronic Data Gathering, Analysis, and Retrieval system, to make the majority of their filings with the SEC. You can access EDGAR on the Internet at **www.sec.gov**, or you can use EdgarScan at **edgarscan.pwcglobal.com**.

Required:

1. Search for a company with which you are familiar and which you believe is likely to have a pension plan. (Older, established firms are good candidates.) Access the company's most recent 10-K filing. Search or scroll to find the financial statements and related notes.
2. From the disclosure notes, determine the type of pension plan(s) the company has.
3. For any defined contribution plans, determine the contributions the company made to the plans on behalf of employees during the most recent three years.
4. For any defined benefit plans, determine the projected benefit obligation for the most recent year. Compare this obligation with the company's total long-term debt. What interest rate was used in estimating the PBO?
5. Repeat steps 2 through 4 for a second firm. Compare and contrast the types of pension plans offered. Are actuarial assumptions the same for defined benefit plans?

Financial Analysis Case 17–8
Pension disclosures

FedEx Corporation

Refer to the financial statements and related disclosure notes of FedEx Corporation in the appendix to Chapter 1. FedEx sponsors pension plans covering substantially all employees. The largest plan covers U.S. domestic employees age 21 and over, with at least one year of service, and provides benefits based on average earnings and years of service. The plans are described in Note 10.

Required:
1. Are FedEx's pension plans overfunded or underfunded?
2. What amounts related to the pension plans are reported by FedEx in the balance sheets for 2001 and 2000?
3. FedEx reports three actuarial assumptions used in its pension calculations. Did the reported changes in those assumptions from 2000 to 2001 increase or decrease the projected benefit obligation? Why?

Real World Case 17–9
Pension amendment

Charles Rubin is a 30-year employee of General Motors. Charles was pleased with recent negotiations between his employer and the United Auto Workers. Among other favorable provisions of the new agreement, the pact also includes a 13% increase in pension payments for workers under 62 with 30 years of service who retire during the agreement. Although the elimination of a cap on outside income earned by retirees has been generally viewed as an incentive for older workers to retire, Charles sees promise for his dream of becoming a part-time engineering consultant after retirement. What has caught Charles's attention is the following excerpt from an article in *the financial press:*

> **General Motors Corp.** will record a $170 million charge due to increases in retirement benefits for hourly United Auto Workers employees.
>
> The charge stems from GM's new tentative labor contract with the UAW. According to a filing with the Securities and Exchange Commission, the charge amounts to 22 cents a share and is tied to the earnings of GM's Hughes Electronics unit.
>
> The company warned that its "unfunded pension obligation and pension expense are expected to be unfavorably impacted as a result of the recently completed labor negotiations."

Taking advantage of an employee stock purchase plan, Charles has become an active GM stockholder as well as employee. His stockholder side is moderately concerned by the article's reference to the unfavorable impact of the recently completed labor negotiations.

Required:
1. When a company modifies its pension benefits the way General Motors did, what name do we give the added cost? How is it accounted for?
2. What does GM mean when it says its "unfunded pension obligation and pension expense are expected to be unfavorably impacted as a result of the recently completed labor negotiations"?

Real World Case 17–10
Effect of pensions on earnings; Quest Communications International

While doing some online research concerning a possible investment in Qwest Communications International you spot a January 24, 2001, news release that indicates results that meet or exceed expectations. Your enthusiasm is dampened somewhat when you access Qwest's 2000 annual report and notice a net loss for the year of $81 million. This prompts you to dig deeper for what might have contributed to the reported numbers. You come across an article that mentions in passing that a representative of Morgan Stanley had indicated that Qwest's pension plan had benefited its reported earnings. Curiosity piqued, you search further.

Required:
1. Can the net periodic pension "cost" cause a company's reported earnings to increase?
2. Access EDGAR on the Internet at **www.sec.gov**, or through EdgarScan at **edgarscan.pwcglobal. com**. Find Qwest's 2000 annual report and look at the income statement. What if anything is indicated concerning the effect of pensions on earnings?
3. Look at the disclosure notes. What effect of the pension plan on earnings does the note on employee benefits indicate? What is the major contributor to this effect?
4. Companies must report the actuarial assumptions used to make estimates concerning pension plans. Do any of the changes reported by Qwest impact the effect of the pension plan on reported earnings? Explain.

18

Employee Benefit Plans

CHAPTER

OVERVIEW

Employee benefits commonly include *postretirement* benefits other than pensions, like retiree health care, as well as compensation plans provided *during* employment. Accounting for both benefit types is the *same* in that their costs are recognized during the years that employees earn the benefits. The accounting is *different* in that postretirement benefits create liabilities while stock-based compensation plans create shareholders' equity in some instances, but liabilities in others. This is a transition chapter between the liability chapters (13–17) and shareholders' equity (19).

LEARNING OBJECTIVES

After studying this chapter, you should be able to:

LO1 Describe the nature of postretirement benefit plans other than pensions and identify the similarities and differences in accounting for those plans and pensions.

LO2 Explain how the obligation for postretirement benefits is measured and how the obligation changes.

LO3 Determine the components of postretirement benefit expense.

LO4 Explain and implement the elective fair value approach for stock compensation plans.

LO5 Explain and implement the alternate intrinsic value approach to accounting for stock compensation plans.

LO6 Explain and implement the accounting for stock appreciation rights and differentiate between those that create liabilities and those that create equity.

LO7 Identify other preretirement compensation plans and the accounting treatment of those plans.

Proper Motivation?

The coffee room discussion Thursday morning was particularly lively. Yesterday's press release describing National Electronic Ventures' choice of Sandra Veres as its president and chief operating officer was today's hot topic in all the company's departments. The press release noted that Ms. Veres's compensation package includes elements beyond salary that are intended to not only motivate her to accept the offer, but also to remain with the company and work to increase shareholder value. Excerpts from the release follow:

> National Electronic Ventures, Inc. today announced it had attracted G. Sandra Veres, respected executive from the wireless communications industry to succeed chairman Walter Kovac. Veres will assume the new role as CEO on Jan. 1, 2003. Ms. Veres will receive a compensation package at NEV of more than $1 million in salary, stock options to buy more than 800,000 shares and a grant of restricted stock.
>
> *Press release, November 12, 2002*

> By the time you finish this chapter, you should be able to respond appropriately to the questions posed in this case. Compare your response to the solution provided at the end of the chapter.

QUESTIONS:

1. Besides the compensation mentioned in the press release, what other types of compensation do you think Ms. Veres might receive for her services? (page 884)

2. How can a compensation package such as this serve as an incentive to Ms. Veres? (page 898)

3. Ms. Veres received a "grant of restricted stock." How should NEV account for the grant? (page 898)

4. Included were stock options to buy more than 800,000 shares. How will the options affect NEV's compensation expense? (page 900)

As indicated in the previous chapter, most companies have pension plans that provide for the future payment of retirement benefits to compensate employees for their current services. Many companies also furnish *other postretirement* benefits such as postretirement health care and life insurance benefits. In addition, companies often provide nonsalary benefits prior to retirement. These preretirement benefits frequently involve compensation plans in which the amount of compensation is in some way tied to the market value of the employer's common stock. We refer to these as stock-based compensation plans. Still other forms of compensation are tied to performance measures other than stock values.

This chapter is divided into three parts. Postretirement benefit plans other than pensions are described in Part a. Stock-based compensation plans are discussed in Part b. Then in Part c we discuss other compensation prior to retirement.

POSTRETIREMENT BENEFITS OTHER THAN PENSIONS

PART

FINANCIAL REPORTING CASE

Q1, p. 883

Postretirement benefit costs must be accrued.

LO1

Postretirement benefits encompass all types of retiree health and welfare benefits other than pensions. These may include medical coverage, dental coverage, life insurance, group legal services, and other benefits. By far the most common is health care benefits. One of every three U.S. workers in medium- and large-size companies participates in health care plans that provide for coverage that continues into retirement. The aggregate impact is considerable; the total obligation for all U.S. corporations is about $500 billion.

Prior to 1993, employers accounted for postretirement benefit costs on a pay-as-you-go basis, meaning the expense each year was simply the amount of insurance premiums or medical claims paid, depending on the way the company provided health care benefits. *SFAS 106* requires a completely different approach. The expected future health care costs for retirees now must be recognized as an expense over the years necessary for employees to become entitled to the benefits.[1] This is the accrual basis that also is the basis for pension accounting.

In fact, accounting for postretirement benefits is similar in most respects to accounting for pension benefits. This is because the two forms of benefits are fundamentally similar. Each is a form of deferred compensation earned during the employee's service life and each can be estimated as the present value of the cost of providing the expected future benefits. General Motors described its plan as shown in Graphic 18–1.

GRAPHIC 18–1
Disclosures—General Motors

> **Note 5: Other Postretirement Benefits (in part)**
> The Corporation and certain of its domestic subsidiaries maintain hourly and salaried benefit plans that provide postretirement medical, dental, vision, and life insurance to retirees and eligible dependents. These benefits are funded as incurred from the general assets of the Corporation. Effective January 1, 1992, the Corporation adopted *SFAS No. 106*, Employers Accounting for Postretirement Benefits Other Than Pensions. This Statement requires that the cost of such benefits be recognized in the financial statements during the period employees provide service to the Corporation.

Despite the similarities, though, there are a few differences in the characteristics of the benefits that necessitate differences in accounting treatment. Because accounting for the two types of retiree benefits is so nearly the same, our discussion in this chapter will emphasize the differences. This will allow you to use what you learned in the previous chapter regarding pension accounting as a foundation for learning how to account for other postretirement benefits, supplementing that common base only when necessary. Focusing on the differences also will reinforce your understanding of pension accounting.

---

[1]"Employers' Accounting for Postretirement Benefits Other Than Pensions," *Statement of Financial Accounting Standards No. 106* (Norwalk, Conn.: FASB, 1990). The Standard became effective (with some exceptions) in 1993.

CHECK WITH THE **COACH**

Now that you've studied pension accounting, you are ready to tackle other compensation accounting issues. Check with the Coach and see some animated illustrations of accounting for nonpension retirement benefits and stock options. These are two of the more controversial issues the FASB has addressed. Let the Coach help you experience the controversy and understand the issues. ∎

What Is a Postretirement Benefit Plan?

Before addressing the accounting ramifications, let's look at a typical retiree health care plan.[2] First, it's important to distinguish retiree health care benefits from health care benefits provided during an employee's working years. The annual cost of providing *preretirement* benefits is simply part of the annual compensation expense. However, most companies offer coverage that continues into retirement. It is the deferred aspect of these *postretirement* benefits that creates an accounting issue.

Usually a plan promises benefits in exchange for services performed over a designated number of years, or reaching a particular age, or both. For instance, a plan might specify that employees are eligible for postretirement benefits after both working 20 years and reaching age 62 while in service. Eligibility requirements and the nature of benefits usually are specified by a written plan, or sometimes only by company practice.

Eligibility usually is based on age and/or years of service.

POSTRETIREMENT HEALTH BENEFITS AND PENSION BENEFITS COMPARED

Keep in mind that retiree health benefits differ fundamentally from pension benefits in some important respects:

1. The amount of *pension* benefits generally is based on the number of years an employee works for the company so that the longer the employee works, the higher are the benefits. On the other hand, the amount of *postretirement health care* benefits typically is unrelated to service. It's usually an all-or-nothing plan in which a certain level of coverage is promised upon retirement, independent of the length of service beyond that necessary for eligibility.
2. Although coverage might be identical, the cost of providing the coverage might vary significantly from retiree to retiree and from year to year because of differing medical needs.
3. Postretirement health care plans often require the retiree to share in the cost of coverage through monthly contribution payments. For instance, a company might pay 80% of insurance premiums, with the retiree paying 20%. The net cost of providing coverage is reduced by these contributions as well as by any portion of the cost paid by Medicare or other insurance.
4. Coverage often is provided to spouses and eligible dependents.

DETERMINING THE NET COST OF BENEFITS

To determine the postretirement benefit obligation and the postretirement benefit expense, the company's actuary first must make estimates of what the postretirement benefit costs will be for current employees. Then, as illustrated in Graphic 18–2 on the next page, contributions to those costs by employees are deducted, as well as Medicare's share of the costs (for retirement years when the retiree will be 65 or older), to determine the estimated net cost of benefits to the employer:

Remember, postretirement health care benefits are anticipated actual costs of providing the promised health care, rather than an amount estimated by a defined benefit formula. This makes these estimates inherently more intricate, particularly because health care costs in

---

[2]For convenience, our discussion focuses on health care benefits because these are by far the most common type of postretirement benefits other than pensions. But, the concepts we discuss apply equally to other forms of postretirement benefits.

GRAPHIC 18–2
Estimating the Net Cost of Benefits

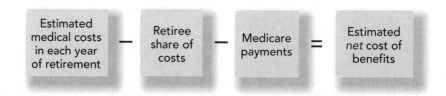

general are notoriously difficult to forecast. And, since postretirement health care benefits are partially paid by the retiree and by Medicare, these cost-sharing amounts must be estimated as well.

On the other hand, estimating postretirement benefits costs is similar in many ways to estimating pension costs. Both estimates entail a variety of assumptions to be made by the company's actuary. Many of these assumptions are the same; for instance both require estimates of:

> **Many of the assumptions needed to estimate postretirement health care benefits are the same as those needed to estimate pension benefits.**

1. A discount rate.
2. Expected return on plan assets (if the plan is funded).
3. Employee turnover.
4. Expected retirement age.
5. Expected compensation increases (if the plan is pay-related).
6. Expected age of death.
7. Number and ages of beneficiaries and dependents.

Of course, the relative importance of some estimates is different from that for pension plans. Dependency status, turnover, and retirement age, for example, take on much greater significance. Also, additional assumptions become necessary as a result of differences between pension plans and other postretirement benefit plans. Specifically, it's necessary to estimate:

> **Some additional assumptions are needed to estimate postretirement health care benefits besides those needed to estimate pension benefits.**

1. The current cost of providing health care benefits at each age that participants might receive benefits.
2. Demographic characteristics of plan participants that might affect the amount and timing of benefits.
3. Benefit coverage provided by Medicare, other insurance, or other sources that will reduce the net cost of employer-provided benefits.
4. The expected health care cost trend rate.[3]

> **The postretirement benefit obligation is the discounted present value of the benefits during retirement.**

Taking these assumptions into account, the company's actuary estimates what the net cost of postretirement benefits will be for current employees in each year of their expected retirement. The discounted present value of those costs is the expected **postretirement benefit obligation.**

Postretirement Benefit Obligation

There are two related obligation amounts. As indicated in Graphic 18–3, one measures the total obligation and the other refers to a specific portion of the total:

GRAPHIC 18–3
Two Views of the Obligation for Postretirement Benefits Other Than Pensions

1. **Expected postretirement benefit obligation (EPBO):** The actuary's estimate of the *total* postretirement benefits (at their discounted present value) expected to be received by plan participants.
2. **Accumulated postretirement benefit obligation (APBO):** The portion of the EPBO attributed to employee service to date.

---

[3]Health care cost trend rates recently reported have ranged from 5.5% to 14%, with 7% being the most commonly assumed rate. AICPA, *Accounting Trends and Techniques*, 2001.

The accumulated postretirement benefit obligation (APBO) is analogous to the projected benefit obligation (PBO) for pensions. Like the PBO, the APBO is an off-balance-sheet obligation, reported only in the disclosure notes.

MEASURING THE OBLIGATION

To illustrate, assume the actuary estimates that the net cost of providing health care benefits to Jessica Farrow (our illustration employee from the previous chapter) during her retirement years has a present value of $10,842 as of the end of 2001. This is the EPBO. If the benefits (and therefore the costs) relate to an estimated 35 years of service[4] and 10 of those years have been completed, the APBO would be:

$$\underset{\text{EPBO}}{\$10,842} \quad \times \quad \underset{\substack{\text{Fraction attributed} \\ \text{to service to date}}}{{}^{10}\!/_{35}} \quad = \quad \underset{\text{APBO}}{\$3,098}$$

$3,098 represents the portion of the EPBO related to the first 10 years of the 35-year service period.

If the assumed discount rate is 6%, a year later the EPBO will have grown to $11,492 simply because of a year's interest accruing at that rate ($10,842 × 1.06 = $11,492). Notice that there is no increase in the EPBO for service because, unlike the obligation in most pension plans, the total obligation is not increased by an additional year's service.

The APBO, however, is the portion of the EPBO related to service up to a particular date. Consequently, the APBO will have increased both because of interest and because the service fraction will be higher (service cost):

$$\underset{\text{EPBO}}{\$11,492} \quad \times \quad \underset{\substack{\text{Fraction attributed} \\ \text{to service to date}}}{{}^{11}\!/_{35}} \quad = \quad \underset{\text{APBO}}{\$3,612}$$

$3,612 represents the portion of the EPBO related to the first 11 years of the 35-year service period.

The two elements of the increase in 2002 can be separated as follows:

APBO at the beginning of the year	$3,098
Interest cost: $3,098 × 6%	186
Service cost: ($11,492 × ⅟₃₅) portion of EPBO attributed to the year	328
APBO at the end of the year	$3,612

The APBO increases each year due to (a) interest accrued on the APBO and (b) the portion of the EPBO attributed to that year.

ATTRIBUTION

Attribution is the process of assigning the cost of benefits to the years during which those benefits are assumed to be earned by employees. The approach required by *SFAS 106* is to assign an equal fraction of the EPBO to each year of service from the employee's date of hire to the employee's full eligibility date.[5] This is the date the employee has performed all the service necessary to have earned all the retiree benefits estimated to be received by that employee.[6] In our earlier example, we assumed the attribution period was 35 years and accordingly accrued ⅟₃₅ of the EPBO each year. The amount accrued each year increases both the APBO and the postretirement benefit expense. In Illustration 18–1 on the next page we see how the 35-year attribution (accrual) period was determined.

The cost of benefits is attributed to the years during which those benefits are assumed to be earned by employees.

Some critics of *SFAS 106* feel there is a fundamental inconsistency between the way we measure the benefits and the way we assign the benefits to specific service periods. The benefits (EPBO) are measured with the concession that the employee may work beyond the full eligibility date; however, the attribution period does not include years of service after that date. The counter argument is the fact that at the full eligibility date the employee will have earned the right to receive the full benefits expected under the plan and the amount of the benefits will not increase with service beyond that date.[7]

The attribution period does not include years of service beyond the full eligibility date even if the employee is expected to work after that date.

---

[4]Assigning the costs to particular service years is referred to as the *attribution* of the costs to the years the benefits are assumed earned. We discuss attribution in the next section.

[5]If the plan specifically grants credit only for service from a date after employee's date of hire, the beginning of the attribution period is considered to be the beginning of that credited service period, rather than the employee's date of hire.

[6]Or any beneficiaries and covered dependents.

[7]"Employers' Accounting for Postretirement Benefits Other Than Pensions," *Statement of Financial Accounting Standards No. 106* (Norwalk, Conn.: FASB, 1990), par. 219–239.

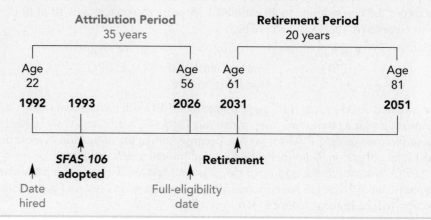

ILLUSTRATION 18–1

Determining the Attribution Period

The attribution period spans each year of service from the employee's date of hire to the employee's full eligibility date.

Jessica Farrow was hired by Global Communications at age 22 at the beginning of 1992 and is expected to retire at the end of 2031 at age 61. The retirement period is estimated to be 20 years.*

Global's employees are eligible for postretirement health care benefits after both reaching age 56 while in service and having worked 20 years.

Since Farrow becomes fully eligible at age 56 (the end of 2026), retiree benefits are attributed to the 35-year period from her date of hire through that date. Graphically, the situation can be described as follows:

*You probably recognize this as the situation used in the previous chapter to illustrate pension accounting.

Postretirement Benefit Expense

LO3

Similar to pension expense, there are six potential components of postretirement benefit expense. Graphic 18–4 lists the six components, comparing each with its counterpart in pension accounting.

GRAPHIC 18–4

Comparison of the Components of Postretirement Benefit Expense and of Pension Expense

The components of postretirement benefit expense are quite similar to the components of pension expense.

Component	Pension Expense	Postretirement Benefit Expense
Service cost	Portion of the PBO earned in the current period	Portion of the EPBO attributed to the current period
Interest cost	Increase in PBO due to the passage of time	Increase in APBO due to the passage of time
Return on plan assets	Earnings on plan investments	Same, if the postretirement benefit plan is funded
Prior service cost	Amortization of compensation cost from amending the plan	Same, but a negative amendment occurs more often in postretirement benefit plans
Losses or gains	Amortization of unexpected changes in either the obligation or plan assets	Same, and more frequent due to greater difficulty in making health benefit predictions
Transition obligation	Amortization of the pension obligation (or asset) existing when *SFAS 87* was adopted (presently fully amortized by most companies)*	Amortization of the APBO existing when *SFAS 106* was adopted

SFAS 87 became effective in 1985. Companies were to amortize the transition amount over the average remaining service life of their employees at that time. Because the amount is mostly or fully amortized by now, we did not discuss the transition amount for pensions in the previous chapter.

RECORDING THE EXPENSE

Recording the postretirement benefit expense is similar to recording pension expense. For illustration, assume the components of the expense combine to indicate a postretirement benefit expense of $12 million and that $2 million cash is paid to present retirees. The following journal entry would be appropriate:

	($ in millions)	
Postretirement benefit expense (given)	12	
Accrued postretirement benefit cost (difference)		10
Cash (retiree benefits paid[8])		2
To record postretirement benefit expense and payment of benefits.		

The fact that the cash payment is less than the expense is typical. Unlike for pension benefits, the cash paid usually is the amount necessary to pay only the current year's medical costs, rather than an amount to anticipate future years' needs. This is because there are few tax incentives to encourage prefunding of retiree health care benefits like those for pension plans, and these benefits are not subject to the stringent funding requirements relating to pensions under ERISA. As a result, there typically is a cumulative underpayment reported as a liability—accrued postretirement benefit cost.

COMPONENTS OF THE EXPENSE

As indicated in Graphic 18–4, the components of the postretirement benefit expense are substantially the same as the components of pension expense. Some differences, though, deserve note.

Service Cost.   It's important to understand that the service cost for pensions reflects additional benefits employees earn from an additional year's service. The service cost for retiree health care plans, on the other hand, is simply an allocation to the current year of a portion of a fixed total cost.

Interest Cost.   As with other liabilities, interest accrues on the accumulated postretirement benefit obligation as time passes. As demonstrated earlier, this amount can be calculated as the assumed discount rate multiplied by the APBO at the beginning of the year. In comparison with pensions, this is analogous to the interest on a pension's projected benefit obligation.

Return on Plan Assets.   Unlike pension plans, many postretirement benefit plans are not funded currently. Those that are funded often are greatly underfunded. However, when these plans are funded, investing plan assets in income-producing assets lessens the amounts employers must eventually contribute to the fund. So, the return on plan assets reduces the net cost of having a postretirement benefit plan. Therefore, similar to pension expense, the return on plan assets each year reduces the amount recorded as postretirement benefit expense. As in the case of pensions, both the interest and return-on-assets components of the postretirement benefit expense do not directly represent employee compensation. Instead, they are financial items created only because the compensation is delayed and the obligation is funded currently.

> Most retiree health plans are not prefunded the way pension plans are.

Amortization of Prior Service Cost.   One difference regarding delayed recognition is that prior service cost is attributed to the service of active employees from the date of the amendment to the full eligibility date, not the expected retirement date.[9] Remember that

---

[8]Because we're assuming this plan is not funded, retiree benefits are being paid from company funds rather than from plan assets. If the plan were funded, the company's cash payment would have been its contribution to the plan's fund instead of payments to retirees.

[9]If substantially all employees already are fully eligible for benefits when the amendment occurs, prior service cost would be amortized over the life expectancy of eligible employees instead.

prior service cost increases or reduces (if a negative plan amendment) the postretirement benefit cost. Since that cost is attributed to service up until the full eligibility date, it's consistent to attribute changes in that amount to a similar period. As with pensions, the pattern of attribution can follow the service method or the straight-line approach.

A negative plan amendment is one that reduces, rather than increases, the accumulated postretirement benefit obligation. This is not a rare occurrence. During the first two years following the adoption of *SFAS 106,* 79% of employers changed retiree medical plans in an effort to control costs. Of those, 78% increased retirees' share of costs; 1% eliminated coverage altogether.[10] The effect of a negative amendment should first be offset against any unrecognized prior service cost and, second, against any unrecognized transition obligation. If an excess remains after offsetting, it is amortized the same way as prior service cost (over the period to full eligibility).

> A negative plan amendment creates negative prior service cost.

Amortization of Deferred Net Losses or Net Gains.

As with pensions, gains and losses can occur when expectations are revised concerning either the obligation (APBO) or the return on plan assets. Accounting for losses or gains from revising expectations regarding postretirement benefits is precisely the same as for losses or gains on pensions. That is, neither a loss (gain) on the APBO nor a loss (gain) on plan assets is immediately recognized in postretirement benefit expense. Instead, losses and gains from either source are deferred as a means of smoothing income. The conceptual shortcomings and practical justification are described in more detail in the previous chapter. Here is a brief summary of that process.

Over time, deferred gains and losses tend to cancel one another out. As years pass there may be more gains than losses, or vice versa, preventing their offsetting one another completely. Only if a net gain or a net loss gets too large, must postretirement benefit expense be adjusted. *SFAS 106* defines too large as a net gain or a net loss at the beginning of a year that exceeds an amount equal to 10% of the APBO, or 10% of plan assets, whichever is higher. When this corridor is exceeded, the excess is amortized over the average remaining service period of active employees expected to receive benefits under the plan.

> A net gain or a net loss affects postretirement benefit expense only if it exceeds an amount equal to 10% of the APBO, or 10% of plan assets, whichever is higher.

For illustration, assume that at the beginning of 2003, a company has an unrecognized net gain of $110 million. Also assume the APBO and plan assets are $800 million and $120 million, respectively, at that time. The average remaining service period of active employees expected to receive benefits under the plan is 15 years. The amount amortized to 2003 postretirement benefit expense is $2 million, calculated as follows:

Determining Net Gain Amortization—2003	($ in millions)
Net gain (previous gains exceeded previous losses)	$110
10% of $800 ($800 is greater than $120): the corridor	(80)
Excess at the beginning of the year	$ 30
Average remaining service period	÷ 15 years
Amount amortized to 2003 pension expense	$ 2

> Since the net gain exceeds an amount equal to the greater of 10% of the APBO or 10% of plan assets, part of the excess is amortized to postretirement benefit expense.

The amortization of a net gain *reduces* postretirement benefit expense; the amortization of a net loss *increases* postretirement benefit expense. Although losses and gains on other postretirement benefits are accounted for the same as losses and gains on pensions, they actually occur more frequently due to greater difficulty in making health benefit predictions.

Amortization of the Transition Obligation.

The unfunded accumulated postretirement benefit obligation existing when *SFAS 106* was adopted (1993 for most companies) is called the *transition obligation.* It, too, is recognized as part of the postretirement benefit expense. Depending on which of the two permitted methods is used, an employer can choose to recognize either:

> The transition obligation is the unfunded APBO that existed when *SFAS 106* was first implemented.

---

[10]Ron Coddington, "USA Snapshots," Hewitt Associates Survey of 992 Large Employers, *USA Today,* November 8, 1994.

1. The entire transition obligation immediately.[11]
2. The transition obligation on a straight-line basis over the plan participants' future service periods (optionally over a 20-year period if that's longer).[12]

The transition obligation can be expensed either immediately or over a period of years.

When we first demonstrated the calculation of the APBO on page 887, it was for the first 10 years of Jessica Farrow's service. If, instead, we had calculated the APBO at the end of 1992, for her first year of service and prior to the adoption of *SFAS 106,* the APBO existing at that time would have been the transition obligation pertaining to this single employee. For the entire employee pool, let's say the transition obligation at that time was $12 million.

If recognized on a delayed basis over 20 years, postretirement benefit expense would include as one of its components $600,000 each year ($12 million ÷ 20) over the 20-year period. The amortized portion of the transition obligation becomes one of the several components of the annual expense, along with other components including service cost, interest cost, return on plan assets, and amortized portions of unrecognized gains and losses and unrecognized prior service cost.

On the other hand, some companies chose to recognize the entire transition obligation immediately upon adopting *SFAS 106.* Then, the effect was to reduce net income in the year of the change by the total amount by which net income would have been reduced over many years if accrual of the postretirement benefit cost had been required prior to 1993. You should recognize this as the general approach to reporting a change in accounting principle, which the change to *SFAS 106* is. For our previous illustration and assuming a 40% tax rate, the journal entry would be:

	($ in millions)	
Cumulative effect of accounting change (net effect)	7.2	
Deferred tax asset ($12 million × 40%)	4.8	
Accrued postretirement benefit cost[13]		12.0
To immediately recognize the transition liability.		

Remember that the cumulative effect of an accounting change is reported on the income statement net of its tax effect. The tax effect in this example requires explanation. First of all, the tax effect is deferred. Although for financial reporting purposes the income is reduced now, only the actual payments for retiree benefits can be deducted for tax purposes. This creates a temporary difference between financial reporting income and taxable income. For most companies, this produces a hefty deferred tax asset. Remember from Chapter 16 that temporary differences that generate future deductible amounts give rise to deferred tax assets, representing the future tax benefits from those deductible amounts. In this case, when the postretirement benefit expense (already reported on the income statement) becomes tax deductible when paid in later years, the tax deduction generates lower income taxes. That future tax savings is represented in the meantime by a deferred tax asset.

Although larger for companies that chose to recognize the entire transition obligation when *SFAS 106* was first adopted, a deferred tax asset is created also when companies gradually recognize the obligation in advance of its being paid and deducted for tax purposes.

IBM Corporation chose to recognize the cumulative effect immediately as shown in Graphic 18–5 on the next page.

Theoretically, the transition amount could be either a transition liability or a transition asset. However, virtually all plans were unfunded in 1992 and 1993 when companies began accruing postretirement benefit costs for the first time. As a result, virtually all transition amounts were transition liabilities—quite large ones, in fact.

The transition amount almost always is a transition liability because few plans were funded when *SFAS 106* was adopted.

---

[11]If recognized immediately, it is treated as the effect of an accounting change. We discuss the treatment of the adoption of new accounting standards as accounting changes in Chapter 21.

[12]The delayed recognition cannot result in less rapid recognition than accounting for the transition obligation on a pay-as-you-go basis.

[13]The accrued postretirement benefit cost account is analogous to the prepaid (accrued) pension cost account in the previous chapter that is an asset when it has a debit balance and a liability when it has a credit balance. Since the amount is always a liability when a company recognizes a transition obligation for postretirement benefits, we omit the prepaid portion of the account title.

GRAPHIC 18–5
Change to New
Accounting Standard—
IBM Corporation

Nonpension Postretirement Benefits (in part)

The company and its U.S. subsidiaries have defined benefit postretirement plans that provide medical, dental, and life insurance for retirees and eligible dependents. In 1990, the company established plan cost maximums in order to more effectively account for and control future medical costs.

Effective January 1, 1991, the company and its subsidiaries implemented on the immediate recognition basis, *Statement of Financial Accounting Standards (SFAS) 106*, "Employers' Accounting for Postretirement Benefits Other Than Pensions." This statement requires that the cost of these benefits, which are primarily for health care, be recognized in the financial statements during the employee's active working career. The company's previous practice was to accrue these costs principally at retirement.

The transition effect of adopting *SFAS 106* on the immediate recognition basis, as of January 1, 1991, resulted in a charge of $2,263 million to 1991 earnings, net of approximately $350 million of income tax effects.

The size of the unrecognized liability at transition was a major concern for many employers. For General Electric, the initial liability was $1.8 billion; for IBM it was $2.3 billion. How would shareholders react to recording such a sizable expense and liability all at once?[15] When General Motors announced in 1991 that it would take a one-time charge of $16 billion to $24 billion, the automaker's stock price dropped 4%. Or, if recognized on a delayed basis, what would be the effect of a slow degradation of earnings over a period of years? These concerns caused the decision of how the obligation should be recognized to be among the most controversial issues to face the FASB during its deliberations. Conceptually, the FASB favored requiring immediate recognition of the entire obligation. But, for practical reasons, delayed recognition was permitted as an alternative.[16] Unexpectedly, though, most companies chose to bite the bullet with a one-time charge to earnings. Many firms were experiencing down years anyway, and explaining to shareholders a further reduction due to a change in accounting method seemed preferable to having to relive the experience over several years.

> So we're talking about hits bigger than the defense budget dragging the net worth of U.S. businesses. The accounting changes don't cost companies cash, but putting their financial portraits in a withering if more realistic light could hurt their ability to raise funds.[14]

If recognized on a delayed basis, the amortization of the transition liability is one of the six potential components of the postretirement benefit expense in Graphic 18–4 (page 888).

DETERMINING THE EXPENSE

Let's return to our earlier, single-employee illustration in which we determined that the APBO increased in 2002 due to (a) the service cost attributed to that year, $328, and (b) interest accrued on the APBO, $186 (see page 887). Let's also assume the plan is unfunded, so there's no return on plan assets and that there was no prior service cost or significant net gain or loss. So, the service cost and interest cost would be the only components of the postretirement benefit expense unless the transition cost is being recognized on a delayed basis. If we assume the transition liability was $220 and is amortized over 20 years, the 2002 expense would be $525 as shown in Graphic 18–6.

Notice that, as for pensions, a single postretirement benefit expense is reported that includes three types of events that might otherwise be reported separately: (1) deferred com-

---

[14]Don Snyder of the General Accounting Office, quoted in Kevin Anderson, "Health-Care Bill," *USA Today,* December 2, 1991.
[15]Some opponents of the requirement to accrue postretirement benefit costs argued that the requirement actually would cause companies to discontinue or reduce benefits offered to employees. Empirical evidence that this did in fact occur was found by Professors Mittelstaedt, Nichols, and Regier in *"SFAS No. 106* and Benefit Reductions in Employer-Sponsored Retiree Health Care Plans," *The Accounting Review,* October 1995.
[16]"Employers' Accounting for Postretirement Benefits Other Than Pensions," *Statement of Financial Accounting Standards No. 106* (Norwalk, Conn.: FASB, 1990), par. 252.

Service cost	$328	
Interest cost	186	
Actual return on the plan assets	(none)	
Adjusted for gain or loss on the plan assets	none	
Amortization of prior service cost	none	
Amortization of net loss	none	
Amortization of transition liability ($220 ÷ 20 yrs)	11	
Postretirement benefit expense	$525	

GRAPHIC 18–6
Postretirement Benefit Expense

The situation assumes no plan assets, prior service cost, or net gain or loss.

pensation for employee service ($328), (2) interest created by the passage of time until that compensation is paid ($186), and (3) earnings from the investment of any plan assets (none in this instance).

Also as for pensions, some changes in the obligation for postretirement benefits are not recognized as they occur. Instead, any prior service cost (arising as a result of a plan amendment) or gains and losses (from changes in either the obligation or the investment of plan assets) are recognized systematically over future periods. The transition amount, too, can be recognized on a delayed basis if the employer elected not to recognize it immediately.

ETHICAL DILEMMA

Earlier this year, you were elected to the board of directors of Champion International, Inc. Champion has offered its employees postretirement health care benefits for 35 years. The practice of extending health care benefits to retirees began modestly. Most employees retired after age 65, when most benefits were covered by Medicare. Costs also were lower because life expectancies were shorter and medical care was less expensive. Because costs were so low, little attention was paid to accounting for these benefits. The company simply recorded an expense when benefits were provided to retirees. *SFAS 106* changed all that. Now, the obligation for these benefits must be anticipated and reported in the annual report. Worse yet, the magnitude of the obligation has grown enormously, almost unnoticed. Health care costs have soared in recent years. Medical technology and other factors have extended life expectancies. Of course, the value to employees of this benefit has grown parallel to the growth of the burden to the company.

Without being required to anticipate future costs, many within Champion's management were caught by surprise at the enormity of the company's obligation. Equally disconcerting was the fact that such a huge liability now must be exposed to public view. Now you find that several board members are urging the dismantling of the postretirement plan altogether.

What do you think?

A COMPREHENSIVE ILLUSTRATION

We assumed earlier that the EPBO at the end of 2001 was determined by the actuary to be $10,842. This was the present value on that date of all anticipated future benefits. Then we noted that the EPBO at the end of the next year would have grown by 6% to $11,492. This amount, too, would represent the present value of the same anticipated future benefits, but as of a year later. The APBO, remember, is the portion of the EPBO attributed to service performed to a particular date. So, we determined the APBO at the end of 2002 to be $11,492 × $^{11}/_{35}$, or $3,612. We determined the $328 service cost noted earlier for 2002 as the portion of the EPBO attributed to that year: $11,492 × $^1/_{35}$.

Now, let's review our previous discussion of how the EPBO, the APBO, and the postretirement benefit expense are determined by calculating those amounts a year later, at the end of 2003. Before doing so, however, we can anticipate (a) the ~~EPBO~~ to be $11,492 × 1.06, or $12,182, (b) the APBO to be $^{12}\!/_{35}$ of that amount or $4,177, and (c) the 2003 service cost to be $^{1}\!/_{35}$ of that amount, or $348. In Illustration 18–2 we see if our expectations are borne out by direct calculation.

ILLUSTRATION 18–2	Assume the actuary has estimated the net cost of retiree benefits in each year of Jessica Farrow's 20-year expected retirement period to be the amounts shown in the calculation below. She is fully eligible for benefits at the end of 2026 and is expected to retire at the end of 2031.

Determining the Postretirement Benefit Obligation

The EPBO is the discounted present value of the total benefits expected to be earned.

The fraction of the EPBO considered to be earned so far is the APBO.

The fraction of the ~~EPBO considered~~ to ~~be earned this year~~ is the ~~service cost~~.

Calculating the APBO and the postretirement benefit expense at the end of 2003, 12 years after being hired, begins with estimating the EPBO as follows.

Steps to calculate (a) the EPBO, (b) the APBO, and (c) the annual service cost at the end of 2003, 12 years after being hired are:

(a). Estimate the cost of retiree benefits in each year of the expected retirement period and deduct anticipated Medicare reimbursements and retiree cost-sharing to derive the net cost to the employer in each year of the expected retirement period.

Find the present value of each year's net benefit cost as of the *retirement date*.
Find the present value of the total net benefit cost as of the *current date*. This is the EPBO.

(b). Multiply the EPBO by the attribution factor, (service to date/total attribution period). This is the APBO. The service cost in any year is simply one year's worth of the EPBO.

(c). Multiply the EPBO by $^{1}\!/$total attribution period.

The steps are demonstrated in Illustration 18–2A.

ILLUSTRATION 18–2A	(a.1). Actuary estimates the net cost of benefits paid during retirement years:			(a.2). Present value [*n* = 1, 2, 3, 4, . . . 19, 20: *i* = 6%] of the net benefits as of the retirement date:

EPBO, APBO, and Service Cost in 2003

The actuary estimates the net cost to the employer in each year the retiree is expected to receive benefits.

As of the retirement date, the lump-sum equivalent of the expected yearly costs is $62,269.

Year	Age	Net Benefit	Present Value at 2031
2032	62	5,000	4,717
2033	63	5,600	4,984
2034	64	6,300	5,290
2035	65	3,000	2,376
~	~	~	~
2050	80	9,550	3,156
2051	81	10,300	3,212
			$62,269

The EPBO in 2003 is the present value of those benefits.

The APBO is the portion of the EPBO attributed to service to date.

The service cost is the portion of the EPBO attributed to a particular year's service.

Attribution Period
35 years

Retirement Period
20 years

12 years

1992   2003

1993   2026   2031   2051

SFAS 106 adopted

Retirement

Date hired

Full-eligibility date

> (a.3). Present value ($n = 28$, $i = 6\%$) of postretirement benefits at 2003 is
> $62,269 \times .19563 = \$12,182$ (EPBO)
> (b). $\$12,182 \times \frac{12}{35} = \$4,177$ (APBO)
> (c). $\$12,182 \times \frac{1}{35} = \$348$ (Service Cost)

DECISION MAKERS' PERSPECTIVE

When they analyze financial statements, investors and creditors should be wary of the non-standard way companies report other postretirement information similar to the way they report pensions. Recall that in the balance sheet, firms do not separately report many elements of postretirement benefits (APBO, plan assets, net gains and losses, prior service cost). As a result, analysts can only include these items in ratio computations (such as the debt to equity ratio or return on assets) by deliberately obtaining relevant numbers from the disclosure notes and adjusting their computation. In fact, without adjustment, profitability ratios and the times interest earned ratio will be inaccurate because postretirement benefit expense includes the financial components of interest and return on assets. Fortunately, information provided in the disclosure notes makes up for some of the deficiency in balance sheet information and makes it possible for interested analysts to modify their analysis. The disclosures required are very similar to pension disclosures.[17] For instance disclosures provide:

Postretirement benefit amounts reported in the disclosure notes fill a reporting gap left by the minimal disclosures in the primary financial statements.

- Changes in the accumulated postretirement benefit obligation.
- Changes in the plan assets (if any).
- The net periodic postretirement benefit expense and its components.
- Reconciliation of the funded status of the plan with amounts reported in the balance sheet.
- The weighted-average discount rate, rate of compensation, and expected long-term rate of return used to measure the postretirement benefit obligation.

Some additional disclosures are needed for retiree health benefit plans, specifically:

- The assumed health care cost trend rate used to measure benefit costs for the next year, plus a description of the direction and pattern of change in the assumed trend rates thereafter.
- The effect on various amounts reported of a 1% increase or decrease in the health care cost trend rate.

Walgreens provided the disclosures shown in Graphic 18–7 in its 2001 annual report. ■

Retirement Benefits (in part)

The company provides certain health and life insurance benefits for retired employees who meet eligibility requirements, including age and years of service.

The costs of these benefits are accrued over the period earned. At August 31, 2001, the unrecognized actuarial loss was $27.9 million compared to a $5.1 million loss at August 31, 2000. The actuarial loss is amortized over the future service period of employees, which approximates 20 years. The company's postretirement health and life benefit plans currently are not funded.

GRAPHIC 18–7
Postretirement Benefit Disclosures—Walgreens

---

[17]"Employers' Disclosures about Pensions and Other Postretirement Benefits," *Statement of Financial Accounting Standards No. 132* (Stamford, Conn.: FASB, 1998).

GRAPHIC 18–7
(Continued)

Components of net periodic benefit costs (in millions):

	2001	2000	1999
Service cost	$ 4.8	$ 4.7	$ 5.2
Interest cost	8.7	7.7	7.3
Amortization of actuarial loss	.3	—	.4
Total postretirement healthcare benefits costs	$13.8	$12.4	$12.9

Change in benefit obligation (in millions):

	2001	2000
Benefit obligation at September 1	$118.6	$104.6
Service cost	4.8	4.7
Interest cost	8.7	7.7
Amendments	(7.1)	—
Actuarial loss (gain)	23.1	5.7
Benefit payments	(6.3)	(4.9)
Participants contributions	.9	.8
Benefit obligation at August 31	$142.7	$118.6

The discount rate assumptions used to compute the postretirement benefit obligation at year-end were 7.5% for 2001 and 2000.

Future benefit costs were estimated assuming medical costs would increase at a 6.5% annual rate decreasing to 5% over the next 4 years and then remaining at a 5% annual growth rate thereafter. A one percentage point change in the assumed medical cost trend rate would have the following effects (in millions):

	1% Increase	1% Decrease
Effect on service and interest cost	$ 4.0	$ (3.0)
Effect on postretirement obligation	28.2	(21.6)

CONCEPT REVIEW EXERCISE

Other Post-retirement Benefits

Technology Group, Inc., has an unfunded retiree health care plan. The actuary estimates the net cost of providing health care benefits to a particular employee during his retirement years to have a present value of $24,000 as of the end of 2002 (the EPBO). The benefits and therefore the expected postretirement benefit obligation relate to an estimated 36 years of service and 12 of those years have been completed. The interest rate is 6%.

Required:
Pertaining to the one employee only:

1. What is the accumulated postretirement benefit obligation at the end of 2002?
2. What is the expected postretirement benefit obligation at the end of 2003?
3. What is service cost to be included in 2003 postretirement benefit expense?
4. What is interest cost to be included in 2003 postretirement benefit expense?
5. What is the accumulated postretirement benefit obligation at the end of 2003?
6. Show how the APBO changed during 2003 by reconciling the beginning and ending balances.
7. What is 2003 postretirement benefit expense, assuming no gains or losses, no prior service cost, and no unamortized transition cost?

1. What is the accumulated postretirement benefit obligation at the end of 2002?

$$\underset{\substack{\text{EPBO} \\ 2002}}{\$24{,}000} \quad \times \quad \underset{\substack{\text{Fraction} \\ \text{earned}}}{{}^{12}\!/_{36}} \quad = \quad \underset{\substack{\text{APBO} \\ 2002}}{\$8{,}000}$$

2. What is the expected postretirement benefit obligation at the end of 2003?

$$\underset{\substack{\text{EPBO} \\ 2002}}{\$24{,}000} \quad \times \quad \underset{\substack{\text{To accrue} \\ \text{interest}}}{1.06} \quad = \quad \underset{\substack{\text{EPBO} \\ 2003}}{\$25{,}440}$$

3. What is service cost to be included in 2003 postretirement benefit expense?

$$\underset{\substack{\text{EPBO} \\ 2003}}{\$25{,}440} \quad \times \quad \underset{\substack{\text{Earned in} \\ 2003}}{{}^{1}\!/_{36}} \quad = \quad \underset{\substack{\text{Service} \\ \text{cost}}}{\$707}$$

4. What is interest cost to be included in 2003 postretirement benefit expense?

$$\$8{,}000 \text{ (beginning APBO)} \times 6\% = \$480$$

5. What is the accumulated postretirement benefit obligation at the end of 2003?

$$\underset{\substack{\text{EPBO} \\ 2003}}{\$25{,}440} \quad \times \quad \underset{\substack{\text{Fraction} \\ \text{earned}}}{{}^{13}\!/_{36}} \quad = \quad \underset{\substack{\text{APBO} \\ 2003}}{\$9{,}187}$$

6. Show how the APBO changed during 2003 by reconciling the beginning and ending balances.

APBO at the beginning of 2003 (from req. 1)	$8,000
Service cost: (from req. 3)	707
Interest cost: (from req. 4)	480
APBO at the end of 2003 (from req. 5)	$9,187

7. What is 2003 postretirement benefit expense, assuming no gains or losses, no prior service cost, and no unamortized transition cost?

Service cost	$ 707
Interest cost	480
Actual return on the plan assets	(not funded)
Adjusted for: gain or loss on the plan assets	(not funded)
Amortization of prior service cost	none
Amortization of net gain or loss	none
Amortization of transition liability	none
Postretirement benefit expense	$1,187

GLOBAL PERSPECTIVE

In the United States, postretirement benefits are accrued in a manner similar to pensions. In the United Kingdom, accounting is similar to the United States. In most other countries, little official guidance is offered.

In many countries, postretirement benefits other than pensions are rare. In Japan, for instance, the prevalence of government-sponsored plans has encouraged most Japanese companies not to provide separate benefits.

PART

b

LO4

FINANCIAL REPORTING CASE

Q2, p. 883

The accounting objective is to record compensation expense over the periods in which related services are performed.

STOCK-BASED COMPENSATION PLANS

Employee compensation plans frequently include stock-based awards. These may be outright awards of shares, stock options, or cash payments tied to the market price of shares. Sometimes only key executives participate in a stock benefit plan. Typically, an executive compensation plan is tied to performance in a strategy that uses compensation to motivate its recipients. Some firms pay their directors entirely in shares. Actual compensation depends on the market value of the shares. Obviously, that's quite an incentive to act in the best interests of shareholders.

Although the variations of stock-based compensation plans are seemingly endless, each shares common goals. Whether the plan is a stock award plan, a stock option plan, a stock appreciation rights (SARs) plan, or one of the several similar plans, the goals are to provide compensation to designated employees, while sometimes providing those employees with some sort of performance incentive. Likewise, our goals in accounting for each of these plans are the same for each: (1) to determine the value of the compensation and (2) to expense that compensation over the periods in which participants perform services. The issue is not trivial. The median total compensation of chief executives of the 350 largest U.S. businesses, including salary, bonuses, gains from the exercise of stock options, long-term incentive payouts and the value of restricted stock at the time of grant, was $5,223,000 in 2000.

Stock Award Plans

Usually, restricted shares are subject to forfeiture if the employee doesn't remain with the company.

Executive compensation sometimes includes a grant of shares of stock. Usually, such shares are restricted in such a way as to provide some incentive to the recipient. Typically, restricted stock award plans are tied to continued employment. In a restricted stock plan, shares actually are awarded in the name of the employee, although the company might retain physical possession of the shares. The employee has all rights of a shareholder, subject to certain restrictions or forfeiture. Ordinarily, the shares are subject to forfeiture by the employee if employment is terminated within some specified number of years from the date of grant. The employee usually is not free to sell the shares during the restriction period and a statement to that effect often is inscribed on the stock certificates. These restrictions give the employee incentive to remain with the company until rights to the shares vest. Graphic 18–8 describes the restricted award plan for the Peerless Manufacturing Co.

GRAPHIC 18–8
Restricted Stock Award Plan—Peerless Manufacturing Company

Note 4: Stockholders' Equity (in part)
The Company has a restricted stock plan under which 75,000 shares of common stock were reserved for awards to employees. Restricted stock grants made under the Plan generally vest ratably over a three to five-year period. The Company awarded 3,000 shares (fair value at date of grant of $31,875), in fiscal 1998 and 6,500 shares (fair value at date of grant of $80,211) in fiscal 2000. Compensation expenses for stock grants is charged to earnings over the restriction period and amounted to $13,835, $17,416, and $25,115 in fiscal 2000, 1999 and 1998, respectively.

FINANCIAL REPORTING CASE

Q3, p. 883

The compensation associated with a share of restricted stock (or nonvested stock) is the market price at the grant date of an unrestricted share of the same stock. This amount is accrued as compensation expense over the service period for which participants receive the shares, usually from the date of grant to when restrictions are lifted (the vesting date).[18] This is demonstrated in Illustration 18–3.

---

[18]Restricted stock plans usually are designed to comply with Tax Code Section 83 to allow employee compensation to be non-taxable to the employee until the year the shares become substantially vested, which is when the restrictions are lifted. Likewise, the employer gets no tax deduction until the compensation becomes taxable to the employee.

Under its restricted stock award plan, Universal Communications grants five million of its $1 par common shares to certain key executives at January 1, 2003. The shares are subject to forfeiture if employment is terminated within four years. Shares have a current market price of $12 per share.

January 1, 2003
No entry

Calculate total compensation expense:

$12	Fair value per share
× 5 million	Shares awarded
= $60 million	Total compensation

The total compensation is to be allocated to expense over the four-year service (vesting) period: 2003–2006

$$\$60 \text{ million} \div 4 \text{ years} = \$15 \text{ million per year}$$

December 31, 2003, 2004, 2005, 2006	**($ in millions)**	
Compensation expense ($60 million ÷ 4 years)...............	15	
Paid-in capital—restricted stock		15
December 31, 2006		
Paid-in capital—restricted stock (5 million shares at $12)	60	
Common stock (5 million shares at $1 par)		5
Paid-in capital—excess of par (difference).................		55

> **ILLUSTRATION 18–3**
>
> Restricted Stock Award Plan
>
> The total compensation is the market value of the shares ($12) times five million shares.
>
> The $60 million is accrued to compensation expense over the four-year service period.
>
> When restrictions are lifted, paid-in capital—restricted stock, is replaced by common stock and paid-in capital—excess of par.

ADDITIONAL CONSIDERATION

An alternative way of accomplishing the same result is to debit deferred compensation for the full value of the restricted shares ($60 million in the illustration) on the date they are granted:

Deferred compensation (5 million shares at $12)	60	
Common stock (5 million shares at $1 par)		5
Paid-in capital—excess of par (difference)		55

If so, deferred compensation is reported as a reduction in shareholders' equity, resulting in a zero net effect on shareholders' equity. Then, deferred compensation is credited when compensation expense is debited over the service period. Just as in Illustration 18–3, the result is an increase in both compensation expense and shareholders' equity each year over the vesting period.

Once the shares vest and the restrictions are lifted, paid-in capital—restricted stock is replaced by common stock and paid-in capital—excess of par.

The amount of the compensation is measured at the date of grant—at the market price on that date. Any market price changes that might occur after that don't affect the total compensation.

If restricted stock is forfeited because, say, the employee leaves the company, related entries previously made would simply be reversed. This would result in a decrease in compensation expense in the year of forfeiture. The total compensation, adjusted for the forfeited amount, is then allocated over the remaining service period.

Stock Option Plans

More commonly, employees aren't actually awarded shares, but rather are given the option to buy shares in the future. In fact, options have become an integral part of the total compensation package for key officers of most medium and large companies.[19] As with any compensation plan, the accounting objective is to report compensation expense during the period of service for which the compensation is given.

EXPENSE—THE GREAT DEBATE

Stock option plans give employees the option to purchase (a) a specified number of shares of the firm's stock, (b) at a specified price, (c) during a specified period of time. One of the most heated controversies in standard-setting history has been the debate over the amount of compensation to be recognized as expense for stock options. At issue is how the value of stock options is measured, which for most options determines whether any expense at all is recognized.

Historically, options have been measured at their intrinsic values—the simple difference between the market price of the shares and the option price at which they can be acquired. For instance, an option that permits an employee to buy $25 stock for $10 has an intrinsic value of $15. However, plans in which the exercise price equals the market value of the underlying stock at the date of grant (which describes most executive stock option plans) have no intrinsic value and therefore result in zero compensation when measured this way, even though the fair value of the options can be quite significant. About half of the chief executives of the largest U.S. companies cashed in stock options in 2000 for a median gain of over $8.7 million. In 2000, Citigroup's chairman Sanford Weill exercised enough stock options to realize a pretax profit of $196 million from selling shares. To many, it seems counterintuitive to not recognize compensation expense for plans that routinely provide executives with a substantial part of their total compensation.

This is where the controversy ensues. In 1993, the FASB issued an Exposure Draft of a new standard that would have required companies to measure options at their *fair values* at the time they are granted and to expense that amount over the appropriate service period. To jump straight to the punch line, the FASB bowed to public pressure and agreed to withdraw the requirement before it became a standard. The FASB consented to encourage, rather than require, that fair value compensation be recognized as expense. Companies are permitted to continue accounting under *APB Opinion 25* (the intrinsic value method referred to in the previous paragraph).[20] Companies that choose to ignore the FASB's recommendation to recognize fair value compensation as expense on the income statement are required instead to provide essentially the same information in disclosure notes.[21] Before we move to the details of the two alternative approaches to accounting for stock options, it's important to look back at what led the FASB to first propose fair value accounting and later rescind that proposal.

As the 1990s began, the public was becoming increasingly aware of the enormity of executive compensation in general and compensation in the form of stock options in particular. The lack of accounting for this compensation was apparent, prompting the SEC to encourage the FASB to move forward on their stock option project. Even Congress got into the fray when, in 1992, a bill was introduced that would require firms to report compensation expense based on the fair value of options. Motivated by this encouragement, the FASB issued its exposure draft in 1993. The real disharmony began then. Opposition to the proposed standard was broad and vehement; and that perhaps is an understatement. Critics based their opposition on one or more of three objections:

1. *Options with no intrinsic value at issue have zero fair value and should not give rise to expense recognition.* The FASB, and even some critics of the proposal, were adamant that options provide valuable compensation at the grant date to recipients.
2. *It is impossible to measure the fair value of the compensation on the grant date.* The FASB argued vigorously that value can be approximated using one of several **option pricing models.** These are statistical models that use computers to incorporate

[19]In a recent survey of 600 corporations, 591 companies disclosed the existence of stock option plans (AICPA, *Accounting Trends and Techniques,* 2001).
[20]"Accounting for Stock Issued to Employees," *Opinions of the Accounting Principles Board No. 25* (New York: AICPA, 1972).
[21]"Accounting for Stock-Based Compensation," *Statement of Financial Accounting Standards No. 123* (Stamford, Conn.: FASB, 1995).

FINANCIAL REPORTING CASE

Q4, p. 883

After lengthy debate, the FASB consented to encourage, rather than require, that the fair value of options be recognized as expense.

information about a company's stock and the terms of the stock option to estimate the options' fair value. We might say the FASB position is that it's better to be approximately right than precisely wrong.

3. *The proposed standard would have unacceptable economic consequences.* Essentially, this argument asserted that requiring this popular means of compensation to be expensed would cause companies to discontinue the use of options.

There were consistent criticisms of the FASB's requirement to expense option compensation.

The opposition included corporate executives, auditors, members of Congress, and the SEC.[22] Ironically, the very groups that provided the most impetus for the rule change initially—the SEC and Congress—were among the most effective detractors in the end. The only group that offered much support at all was the academic community, and that was by-and-large nonvocal support. In reversing its decision, the FASB was not swayed by any of the specific arguments of any opposition group. Dennis Beresford, chair of the FASB at the time, indicated that it was fear of government control of the standard-setting process that prompted the Board to modify its position. The Board remained steadfast that the proposed change was appropriate.

In backing away from its original proposal, the FASB did not completely abandon its position on option accounting. Instead, it decided to encourage, rather than require, expensing of the fair value of option compensation in the income statement. Companies that choose to continue accounting under *APB Opinion 25* must still follow fair value accounting to comply with enhanced disclosure requirements. The disclosures are designed to allow investors and creditors to compare companies that choose the elective accounting approach and those that do not. Notice in Graphic 18–9 Yahoo, Inc. would have reported a sizable loss in 2000 instead of the profit it did report if the company had followed the FASB's suggested fair value accounting for its stock options.

GRAPHIC 18–9
Disclosure of Stock Options; Yahoo, Inc.

Stock Compensation (in part)
The Company accounts for stock-based compensation in accordance with the provisions of *APB 25*. Had compensation expense been determined based on the fair value at the grant dates, as prescribed in *SFAS 123*, the Company's results would have been as follows (in thousands, except per share amounts):

	Years Ended December 31,		
	2000	**1999**	**1998**
Net income (loss)			
As reported	$70,776	$47,811	$(13,641)
Pro forma	$(1,264,987)	$(269,563)	$(64,500)
Net income (loss) per share:			
As reported basic	$0.13	$0.09	$(0.03)
Pro forma basic	(2.30)	(0.52)	(0.15)
As reported diluted	0.12	0.08	(0.03)
Pro forma diluted	$(2.30)	$(0.52)	$(0.15)

The fair value of option grants is determined using the Black-Scholes model. The weighted average fair market value of an option granted during 2000, 1999, and 1998 was $55.04, $39.15, and $11.94, respectively.

Prior to 2002, only two companies—Boeing and Winn-Dixie—reported stock option compensation expense at fair value. However, in 2002 public outrage mounted amid high-profile accounting scandals at Enron, WorldCom, Tyco, and others. Some degree of

---

[22]All of the "Big Six" CPA firms lobbied against the proposal. Senator Lieberman of Connecticut introduced a bill in Congress that if passed would have forbidden the FASB from passing a requirement to expense option compensation.

consensus emerged that greed on the part of some corporate executives contributed to the fraudulent and misleading financial reporting at the time. In fact, many in the media were pointing to the proliferation of stock options as a primary form of compensation as a culprit in fueling that greed. Renewed interest surfaced in requiring stock option compensation to be reported in income statements. At least partly in response to this public sentiment, Coca-Cola in 2002 announced it would begin reporting the fair value of its stock options as an expense. Perhaps seeing the "writing on the wall," other companies soon followed suit. The next section describes the fair value approach.

RECOGNIZING THE FAIR VALUE OF OPTIONS (THE ELECTIVE FAIR VALUE APPROACH)

The fair value of a stock option can be determined by employing a recognized option pricing model.

Companies are encouraged, but not required, to estimate the fair value of stock options on the grant date. This requires the use of one of several option pricing models. These mathematical models assimilate a variety of information about a company's stock and the terms of the stock option to estimate the option's fair value. The model should take into account the:

An option pricing model takes into account several variables.

- Exercise price of the option.
- Expected term of the option.
- Current market price of the stock.
- Expected dividends.
- Expected risk-free rate of return during the term of the option.
- Expected volatility of the stock.

Option-pricing theory, on which the pricing models are based, is a topic explored in depth in finance courses and is subject to active empirical investigation and development. A simplified discussion is provided in Appendix 18A.[24]

The total compensation as estimated by the options' fair value is reported as compensation expense over the period of service for which the options are given. The service period is the vesting period in Illustration 18–4.

ILLUSTRATION 18–4	At January 1, 2003, Universal Communications grants options that permit key executives to acquire 10 million of the company's $1 par common shares within the next eight years, but not before December 31, 2006 (the vesting date). The exercise price is the market price of the shares on the date of grant, $35 per share. The fair value of the options, estimated by an appropriate option pricing model, is $8 per option.
Stock Option Plan— The Elective Fair Value Approach	

January 1, 2003
No entry

Calculate total compensation expense:

Fair value is estimated at the date of grant.

$ 8	Estimated fair value per option
× 10 million	Options granted
= $80 million	Total compensation

The total compensation is to be allocated to expense over the four-year service (vesting) period: 2003–2006

$$\$80 \text{ million} \div 4 \text{ years} = \$20 \text{ million per year}$$

The value of the award is expensed over the service period for which the compensation is provided.

December 31, 2003, 2004, 2005, 2006	**($ in millions)**	
Compensation expense ($80 million ÷ 4 years)	20	
Paid-in capital—stock options		20

[23] As quoted in "Some Firms Doing It Right Re: Options," *The Motley Fool*, August 8, 2002.
[24] An expanded discussion is provided in *SFAS 123*.

Forfeitures.   If previous experience indicates that a material number of the options will be forfeited before they vest (due to employee turnover or violation of other terms of the options), it's permissible, but not required, to adjust the fair value estimate on the grant date to reflect that expectation. For instance, if a forfeiture rate of 4% is expected, the estimated total compensation would be 96% of $80 million.

If no forfeitures had been anticipated, but material forfeitures occur later, amounts previously expensed would not be altered. Instead, paid-in capital—stock options would be reduced by the fair value of options forfeited times the fraction previously expensed. The offsetting credit is to compensation expense, resulting in a decrease in compensation expense in the year of forfeiture. Then, the remaining total compensation, adjusted for the value of forfeited options, would be allocated over the remaining service period.

> Unanticipated forfeitures are treated as a change in estimate, so the effect is a reduction in current and future expense, not previously recorded expense.

WHEN OPTIONS ARE EXERCISED

If half the options in Illustration 18–4 (five million shares) are exercised on July 11, 2009, when the market price is $50 per share, the following journal entry is recorded:

July 11, 2009	($ in millions)	
Cash ($35 exercise price × 5 million shares)	175	
Paid-in capital—stock options (½ account balance)	40	
Common stock (5 million shares at $1 par per share)		5
Paid-in capital—excess of par (to balance)		210

> Recording the exercise of options is not affected by the market price on the exercise date.

Notice that the market price at exercise is irrelevant. Changes in the market price of underlying shares do not influence the previously measured fair value of options.

WHEN UNEXERCISED OPTIONS EXPIRE

If options that have vested expire without being exercised, the following journal entry is made (assuming none of the options in our illustration was exercised):

	($ in millions)	
Paid-in capital—stock options (account balance).	80	
Paid-in capital—expiration of stock options		80

> Paid-in capital—stock options becomes paid-in capital—expiration of stock options, when options expire without being exercised.

In effect, we simply rename the paid-in capital attributable to the stock option plan. Compensation expense for the four years' service, as measured on the measurement date, is not affected.

TAX REASONS FOR HOW OPTION PLANS ARE STRUCTURED

It is common for the option price to be equal to the market price at the date of grant as it is in the preceding illustration. One important reason is the ability to avoid expensing compensation when the elective fair value approach is not chosen. Another reason is that this is one requirement for a plan to qualify as an incentive stock option plan under the Tax Code. There are other requirements, but they are unimportant to our discussion here. Under an **incentive plan,** the recipient pays no tax at the time of the grant or when the options are exercised. Instead, the tax on the difference between the exercise price and the market price at the exercise date isn't paid until any shares acquired are subsequently sold. On the other hand, the company gets no tax deduction at all. Hewlett-Packard provides an example of an incentive plan in Graphic 18–10.

> Tax treatment favors the executive in an incentive stock option plan.

Incentive Compensation Plans (in part)
The company has three principal stock option plans . . . All plans permit options granted to qualify as "Incentive Stock Options" under the Internal Revenue Code. The exercise price of a stock option is generally equal to the fair market value of the company's common stock on the date the option is granted.

> **GRAPHIC 18–10**
> Incentive Stock Option—Hewlett-Packard

Tax treatment favors the employer in a nonqualified stock option plan.

An incentive plan offers favorable tax treatment to the *executive;* but a **nonqualified plan** offers favorable tax treatment to the *employer.* With a nonqualified plan, the employee cannot delay paying tax. The tax that could be deferred until the shares are sold under an incentive plan must be paid at the exercise date under a nonqualified plan. However, the employer is permitted to deduct the difference between the exercise price and the market price at the exercise date. Since tax treatment favors the employer in a nonqualified stock option plan, why are the vast majority of options structured as incentive plans? There are two reasons:

Options usually are structured as incentive plans.

- The favorable tax treatment provided to executives by incentive plans allows companies to use the plans to attract and retain quality management personnel.
- Due to Tax Code requirements, incentive plans typically offer an exercise price equal to the market price on the grant date. The market price usually exceeds the exercise price in a nonqualified plan. This difference allows companies to elect not to report compensation expense for an incentive plan; whereas a nonqualified plan requires earnings to be reduced by compensation expense. We discuss this next.

ADDITIONAL CONSIDERATION

Tax Consequences of Stock-Based Compensation Plans

In Illustration 18–4 we ignored the tax effect. To illustrate the effect on taxes, let's assumed Universal Communications' income tax rate is 40%.

Because an incentive plan provides no tax deduction, it has no deferred tax consequences.

Case 1. Recall from our earlier discussion that with an incentive plan, the employer receives no tax deduction at all. If Universal's plan qualifies as an incentive plan, the company will receive no tax deduction upon exercise of the options and thus no tax consequences.

Case 2. On the other hand, if we assume the plan does not qualify as an incentive plan, Universal will deduct the difference between the exercise price and the market price at the exercise date. Recall from Chapter 16 that this creates a temporary difference between accounting income (for which compensation expense is recorded currently) and taxable income (for which the tax deduction is taken later upon the exercise of the options). Under *SFAS 123*, we assume the temporary difference is the cumulative amount expensed for the options. The following entries would be recorded on the dates shown:

A deferred tax asset is recognized now for the future tax savings from the tax deduction when the options are exercised.

December 31, 2003, 2004, 2005, 2006	($ in millions)	
Compensation expense ($80 million ÷ 4 years)	20	
Paid-in capital—stock options		20
Deferred tax asset (40% × $20 million)	8	
Income tax expense		8

The after-tax effect on earnings is thus $12 million each year ($20 − 8).

If all of the options (ten million shares) are exercised in April 2008:

Cash ($35 exercise price × 10 million shares)	350	
Paid-in capital—stock options (account balance)	80	
Common stock (10 million shares at $1 par per share)		10
Paid-in capital—excess of par (to balance)		420

If the eventual tax savings exceed the deferred tax asset, the difference is recognized as equity.

a. Options exercised when the tax benefit *exceeds* the deferred tax asset:
   If the market price is $50 per share:

Income taxes payable [($50 − 35) × 10 million shares × 40%] . . .	60	
Deferred tax asset (4 years × $8 million)		32
Paid-in capital—tax effect of stock options (remainder)*		28

If the eventual tax savings is less than the deferred tax asset, the difference is recognized as a reduction in either tax expense or previously recognized equity from the same source.

b. Options exercised when the tax benefit is *less than* the deferred tax assets:
   If the market price is $40 per share:

Income taxes payable [($40 − 35) × 10 million shares × 40%] . . .	20	
Income tax expense or paid-in capital—tax effect of		
stock options† (remainder)	12	
Deferred tax asset (4 years × $8 million)		32

The tax consequences of all nonqualifying stock options, including those for which companies choose to account for options in accordance with *APB Opinion 25*, as well as restricted stock plans also are accounted for in the manner demonstrated above.

*This treatment is consistent with a provision of *SFAS 109* (par. 36C) that requires the tax effect of an increase or decrease in equity (paid-in capital—stock options, in this case) be allocated to equity.
†Paid-in capital—tax effect of stock options is debited only if that account has a sufficient credit balance from previous transactions in which the tax benefit exceeded the deferred tax asset.

RECOGNIZING THE INTRINSIC VALUE OF OPTIONS (THE ALTERNATE INTRINSIC VALUE APPROACH)

As pointed out in a previous discussion, most companies are adamantly opposed to expensing the fair value of options. As you might expect, most choose *not* to adopt the elective fair value approach. These companies continue to account for options in accordance with *APB Opinion 25* issued in 1972. By this approach, the value of fixed options is measured at the grant date in an amount equal to their intrinsic values rather than their fair values. Intrinsic value is simply the difference between the market price of the shares and the exercise price at which they can be acquired. In other words, it is the benefit the holder of an option would realize by exercising the option now and immediately selling the underlying stock.

An option that permits an employee to buy $25 stock for $10 has an intrinsic value of $15.

Market Value Equals Exercise Price.   An option whose exercise price equals or exceeds the market price of the underlying stock has zero intrinsic value. This was the situation in Illustration 18–4. Under the *APB Opinion 25* alternate approach, then, no compensation would be recorded for the options described in the illustration. Although the financial statements would be unaffected by the existence of options whose exercise price equals or exceeds the market price, accompanying disclosure notes would report essentially the same information as would have been provided in the financial statements if the elective fair value approach is followed. As a result, companies opting to forgo the elective fair value approach still must make the same fair value calculations (Illustration 18–4) as companies electing that approach. In fact, one required disclosure is pro forma (as if) net income and earnings per share determined as if the elective method had been applied in the financial statements. The objective of the enhanced disclosures is to permit comparability among companies regardless of which method they choose.

An option whose exercise price equals the market price of the underlying stock has zero intrinsic value.

Market Value Exceeds Exercise Price.   Suppose the options described in Illustration 18–4 were structured so they did have intrinsic value on the grant date. This would have been the case if Universal's shares had a market value on that date of, say, $37. (Remember, the exercise price was $35.) We make that assumption in Illustration 18–5 on the next page. Compensation is recorded only to the extent of intrinsic value. However, in addition to their intrinsic value, the fair value of options also includes a time value due to the fact that (a) the holder of an option does not have to pay the exercise price until the option is exercised and (b) the market price of the underlying stock may yet rise and create additional intrinsic value. All options have time value so long as time remains before expiration. The longer the time until expiration, other things being equal, the greater the time value. As a result, all options will be undervalued by not recording their fair values. In fact, as discussed earlier, there usually is no intrinsic value (exercise price equals market price), resulting in no compensation being recorded at all.

PERFORMANCE STOCK OPTION PLANS

In the restricted stock award plans and stock option plans we discussed in the previous sections, both the number of shares employees can receive and the price they must pay to receive the shares (if any) are known when the awards are granted. For that reason, they often are referred to as *fixed plans*. Sometimes, though, compensation plans are structured in such a way that some of the terms needed to measure the compensation vary in response to some performance measure such as share price, sales, rate of return, or market share. These are known as *variable plans*.

The terms of performance options vary with some measure of performance to tie rewards to productivity.

ILLUSTRATION 18–5	At January 1, 2003, Universal Communications grants options that permit key executives to acquire 10 million of the company's $1 par common shares within the next eight years, but not before December 31, 2006 (the vesting date). The exercise price is $35 and the market price of the shares $37 per share on the date of grant.
Market Value Exceeds Exercise Price (Nonqualifying Options)	

January 1, 2003
  No entry

Calculate total compensation expense:

$37	Market value per share
(35)	Exercise price
$ 2	Intrinsic value per option
× 10 million	Options granted
= $20 million	Intrinsic value of award

The total compensation is to be allocated to expense over the four-year service (vesting) period: 2003–2006

$$\$20 \text{ million} \div 4 \text{ years} = \$5 \text{ million per year}$$

December 31, 2003, 2004, 2005, 2006   **($ in millions)**
  Compensation expense ($20 million ÷ 4 years).   5
    Paid-in capital—stock options.   5

Under the alternative intrinsic value approach, compensation is recorded only when an option's market price exceeds its exercise price.

The intrinsic value of the options is expensed over the service period for which the compensation is provided.

One example of a variable plan is a stock option plan in which the number of shares, the exercise price, or both vary with criteria related to managerial performance. For example, the criteria might be earnings per share, division revenues, rate of return on assets, or some other measure of performance. The number of shares obtainable under the option plan, for instance, might be calculated as some multiple of sales growth over the two years following the grant date. The possibilities are limitless.

To avoid recording compensation, most options have fixed rather than variable terms.

To achieve corporate objectives and maximize shareholder wealth, performance option plans are preferable to fixed plans because they directly tie management incentive to firm performance. Unfortunately, the vast majority of option plans have fixed terms. Why? The answer is simple. Unless a company opts for the FASB's elective fair value approach, fixed plans allow the company to avoid reducing earnings with compensation expense (as discussed earlier). On the other hand, in a variable plan, compensation expense usually *is* recorded whether the company chooses the elective fair value approach or not. Here's why:

1. Using the FASB's *elective fair value approach,* the fair value of the options is estimated at the grant date and accrued to expense over the service period. Even when terms vary with future performance, option-pricing models usually are capable of estimating the fair value. In cases when it is not possible to determine fair value, compensation is accrued each year based on the *intrinsic value* of the award, using option terms that would apply if the options were exercised that year.
2. Using the *alternate approach,* the intrinsic value of the options is accrued to expense over the service period. But since the terms are dependent on performance, the measurement date is delayed until compensation can be measured but the expense is estimated and recorded in the meantime. So, as long as performance measures indicate positive compensation under the terms of the options, expense is recorded.

Accounting for performance option plans under the alternate approach is similar to accounting for SARs.

The way we estimate, record, and adjust compensation for revised estimates under the alternate approach is similar to the way we account for stock appreciation rights (SARs), demonstrated in Illustration 18–6 in the next section. The difference would be that the credit entry to recognize accrued compensation is paid-in capital—stock options, rather than paid-in capital—SAR plan, or liability—SAR plan. Because performance option plans are found much less frequently in practice, we provide a detailed illustration for SARs. Just remember, the approach is the same for performance option plans.

> ## ADDITIONAL CONSIDERATION
>
> Companies that have performance plans or other variable plans may actually choose the elective fair value approach to *reduce* compensation expense. The amount of estimated compensation under a variable plan is adjusted for changes in the price of the underlying stock after the grant date. This can be avoided if the company opts to determine the total compensation as the fair value of the options on the grant date. The FASB does not permit a mix-and-match approach. If the fair value approach is chosen for performance plans, it must be used for all stock-based plans.

Stock Appreciation Rights

Stock appreciation rights (SARs) overcome a major disadvantage of stock option plans that require employees to actually buy shares when the options are exercised. Even though the options' exercise price may be significantly lower than the market value of the shares, the employee still must come up with enough cash to take advantage of the bargain. This can be quite a burden if the award is sizable. In a nonqualified stock option plan, income taxes also would have to be paid when the options are exercised.[25]

LO6

SARs offer a solution. Unlike stock options, these awards enable an employee to benefit by the amount that the market price of the company's stock rises without having to buy shares. Instead, the employee is awarded the share appreciation, which is the amount by which the market price on the exercise date exceeds a prespecified price (usually the market price at the date of grant). For instance, if the share price rises from $35 to $50, the employee receives $15 cash for each SAR held. The share appreciation usually is payable in cash or the recipient has the choice between cash and shares. A plan of this type offered by IBM is described in Graphic 18–11.

In an SAR plan, the employer pays compensation equal to the increase in share price from a specified level.

> **Long-Term Performance Plan (in part)**
> SARs offer eligible optionees the alternative of electing not to exercise the related stock option, but to receive payment in cash and/or stock, equivalent to the difference between the option price and the average market price of IBM stock on the date of exercising the right.

GRAPHIC 18–11
Stock Appreciation Rights—IBM Corporation

IS IT DEBT OR IS IT EQUITY?

In some plans, the employer chooses whether to issue shares or cash at exercise. In other plans, the choice belongs to the employee.[26] Who has the choice determines the way it's accounted for. More specifically, the accounting treatment depends on whether the award is considered an equity instrument or a liability. If the employer can elect to settle in shares of stock rather than cash, the award is considered to be equity. On the other hand, if the employee will receive cash or can elect to receive cash, the award is considered to be a liability.[27]

If an employer can elect to settle in shares of stock rather than cash, the award is considered to be equity.

The distinction between stock-based awards that are considered equity and those that are considered liabilities is based on the definition of liabilities in *SFAC 6*.[28] That statement

If an employee can elect to receive cash, the award is considered to be a liability.

---

[25]The tax treatment of stock-based plans is discussed in an earlier section.

[26]Many such plans are called tandem plans and award an employee both a cash SAR and an SAR that calls for settlement in an equivalent amount of shares. The exercise of one cancels the other.

[27]The FASB's elective accounting approach mandates the distinction between debt and equity to be whether the *employee* can choose cash or whether the *employer* can choose to settle in shares. A company not choosing to follow the elective approach decides which settlement method is most likely. The result usually is the same.

[28]"Elements of Financial Statements," *Statement of Financial Accounting Concepts No. 6* (Stamford, Conn.: FASB 1985).

classifies an instrument as a liability if it obligates the issuer to transfer its assets to the holder. A stock option is an equity instrument if it requires only the issuance of stock. A cash SAR, on the other hand, requires the transfer of assets, and therefore is a liability. This does not mean that a stock option whose issuer may later choose to settle in cash is not an equity instrument. Instead, cash settlement would be considered equivalent to repurchasing an equity instrument for cash.

SARS PAYABLE IN SHARES (EQUITY)

When an SAR is considered to be equity (because the employer can elect to settle in shares of stock rather than cash), accounting depends on whether or not the company has chosen the elective fair value approach for stock-based compensation plans:

1. Using the *elective fair value approach,* the fair value of the SARs is estimated at the grant date and accrued to expense over the service period. Normally, the fair value of an SAR is the same as the fair value of a stock option with the same terms. The fair value is determined at the grant date and accrued to compensation expense over the service period the same way as for other stock-based compensation plans. The total compensation is not revised for subsequent changes in the price of the underlying stock.

2. Using the *alternative intrinsic value approach,* the intrinsic value of the SARs is accrued to expense over the service period. But since the terms are dependent on future stock price, the eventual compensation is estimated and recorded in the meantime. This is the same method used for performance stock options discussed earlier as well as for cash SARs discussed next.

SARS PAYABLE IN CASH (LIABILITY)

When an SAR is considered to be a liability (because the employee can elect to receive cash upon settlement), accounting does *not* depend on whether or not the company has chosen the elective fair value approach for stock-based compensation plans. Instead, consistent with recording other liabilities, the amount of compensation (and related liability) is estimated each period and continually adjusted to reflect changes in the market price of stock until the compensation is finally paid.

A difficulty in accounting for cash SARs is that the amount of compensation (and eventual liability) is not known for certain until the compensation actually is paid on the date the SAR is exercised. We solve this problem the usual way—by estimating the amounts needed for periodic reporting. The amount of total compensation is estimated at the end of each period as the excess of the current market price of the shares over the prespecified price (usually the market price at the date of grant). A portion of that total compensation is attributed to employee service during each reporting period and is recorded as compensation expense.

The periodic expense (and adjustment to the liability) is the percentage of the total compensation earned to date by recipients of the SARs (based on the elapsed percentage of the service period) reduced by any amounts expensed in prior periods. For example, if the market price at the end of the period is $14 and was $10 at the grant date, the total compensation would be $40 million if 10 million SARs are expected to vest. Let's say two years of a four-year service period have elapsed, and $5 million was expensed the first year. Then, compensation expense the second year would be $15 million, calculated as ($\frac{2}{4}$ of $40 million) minus $5.

An example spanning several years is provided in Illustration 18–6.

Note that the way we treat changes in compensation estimates entails a catch-up adjustment in the period of change, inconsistent with the usual treatment of a change in estimate. For most changes in estimate, including changes in forfeiture rates and other estimates under the elective fair value approach described earlier, revisions are allocated (to compensation expense in this case) over remaining periods, rather than all at once in the period of change.

Universal Communications grants 10 million SARs to key executives at January 1, 2003. Upon exercise, the SARs entitle executives to receive cash or stock equal in value to the excess of the market price at exercise over the share price at the date of grant. The $1 par common shares have a current market price of $10 per share. The SARs vest at the end of 2006 (cannot be exercised until then) and expire at the end of 2010. The year-end share prices following the grant of the SARs are:

2003	$12
2004	14
2005	16
2006	14
2007	15

ILLUSTRATION 18–6

Stock Appreciation Rights

January 1, 2003
No entry because the intrinsic value of the SARs is zero: ($10 − 10) × 10 million shares = $0

December 31, 2003	**($ in millions)**	
Compensation expense*...	5	
Liability—SAR plan		5

When the share price rises above $10, a liability is created.

*Calculation:

($12 − $10) × 10 million	×	¼	−	$0	=	$5
Estimated total compensation		Fraction of service to date		Expensed earlier		Current expense

December 31, 2004		
Compensation expense*...	15	
Liability—SAR plan		15

In 2004, both the expense and the liability are adjusted to reflect not only another year's service but also a revised estimate of total compensation.

*Calculation:

($14 − $10) × 10 million	×	²⁄₄	−	($5 million)	=	$15
Estimated total compensation		Fraction of service to date		Expensed earlier		Current expense

December 31, 2005		
Compensation expense*...	25	
Liability—SAR plan		25

The 2005 expense is the revised total compensation to be reported to date ($45 million) less the $20 million expensed previously.

*Calculation:

($16 − $10) × 10 million	×	¾	−	($5 + 15 million)	=	$25
Estimated total compensation		Fraction of service to date		Expensed earlier		Current expense

December 31, 2006		
Liability—SAR plan	5	
Compensation expense*...		5

If the share price declines, both the liability and expense are *reduced.*

*Calculation:

($14 − $10) × 10 million	×	¼	−	($5 + 15 + 25 million)	=	$(5)
Estimated total compensation		Fraction of service to date		Expensed earlier		Current expense

The liability continues to be adjusted after the service period if the rights haven't been exercised yet.

December 31, 2007	**($ in millions)**	
Compensation expense*...	10	
Liability—SAR plan		10

Compensation expense and the liability continue to be adjusted until the SARs expire or are exercised.

*Calculation:

($15 − 10) × 10 million	×	All	−	($5 + 15 + 25 − 5 million)	=	$10
Estimated total compensation		Fraction of service to date		Expensed earlier		Current expense

Adjustment continues after the service period if the SARs have not yet been exercised.

It's necessary to continue to adjust both compensation expense and the liability until the SARs ultimately either are exercised or lapse.[29] Assume for example that the SARs are exercised on October 11, 2008, when the share price is $14.50, and executives choose to receive the market price appreciation in cash:

October 11, 2008	($ in millions)	
Liability—SAR plan	5	
Compensation expense*		5
Liability—SAR plan (balance)	45	
Cash		45

*Calculation:

$$(\$14.50 - 10) \times 10 \text{ million} \times \underset{\substack{\text{Fraction} \\ \text{of service to date}}}{\text{All}} - \underset{\substack{\text{Expensed} \\ \text{earlier}}}{(\$50 \text{ million})} = \underset{\substack{\text{Current} \\ \text{expense}}}{\$(5)}$$

$\underset{\substack{\text{Actual} \\ \text{total compensation}}}{}$

Let's look at the changes in the liability—SAR plan account during the 2003–2008 period:

The liability is adjusted each period as changes in the share price cause changes in the liability estimates.

Liability—SAR Plan

			($ in millions)	
			5	2003
			15	2004
			25	2005
2006	5			
			10	2007
2008	5			
2008	45			
			0	Balance after exercise

The form of settlement determines whether compensation expense is accrued as a liability or as paid-in capital.

As discussed earlier, if the employer had retained the choice of settling in shares rather than cash, the award would have been considered an equity instrument at the outset. In that case, unless the company uses the elective fair value approach, paid-in capital—SAR plan would replace the liability account in each of Universal's journal entries above.

Broad-Based (Noncompensatory) Plans

Sometimes long-term stock options are issued to substantially all employees rather than to certain targeted individuals. These so-called broad-based plans typically permit employees to buy shares at an exercise price equal to the stock's price on the date the options are granted, or sometimes at a slight discount.

Options of this type traditionally have been referred to as **noncompensatory plans** due to terminology used in the Tax Code. This term also is consistent with the reason most such plans exist. The plans encourage stock ownership among rank and file employees. As stakeholders, employees become more loyal and financially concerned with enhancing the value of common stock. As long as the price discount is no higher than (a) what would be reasonable in a recurring offer to shareholders or others or (b) the share issuance costs avoided by not having to finance a public offering of new stock, no entry is made when options are issued under a broad-based plan. These criteria are considered met if the discount is 5% or less.[30] If and when those options are exercised, the company simply records the sale of new shares.

---

[29]Except that the cumulative compensation expense cannot be negative; that is, the liability cannot be reduced below zero.

[30]A discount of more than 5% without recording compensation expense is permitted by *SFAS 123* if the company can justify it under criteria (a) and (b) above.

GRAPHIC 18–12   Income Statement and Balance Sheet Impact of Stock-Based Compensation Plans

Type of Plan	Elective Fair Value Approach		Alternative Intrinsic Value Approach	
	Total Compensation	**Balance Sheet**	**Total Compensation**	**Balance Sheet**
Restricted stock award	Fair value: Amount fixed at grant date, accrued over service period	Shareholders' equity: Paid-in capital—restricted stock	Same as fair value approach	Same as fair value approach
Fixed stock options	Fair value: Amount fixed at grant date, accrued over service period	Shareholders' equity: Paid-in capital—stock options	Intrinsic value: Amount fixed at grant date, accrued to service period	Shareholders' equity: Paid-in capital—stock options
Performance (variable) stock options	Fair value: Amount fixed at grant date, accrued over service period	Shareholders' equity: Paid-in capital—stock options	Intrinsic value: Amount varies until option terms are known; estimates expensed until then	Shareholders' equity: Paid-in capital—stock options
Stock appreciation rights (share payment choice of *employer*)	Fair value: Amount fixed at grant date, accrued over service period	Shareholders' equity: Paid-in capital—SAR plan	Share price appreciation: Amount varies until exercise (or lapse); estimates expensed until then	Shareholders' equity: Paid-in capital—SAR plan
Stock appreciation rights (cash payment choice of *employee*)	Share price appreciation: Amount varies until exercise (or lapse), estimates expensed until then	Liabilities: Liability—SAR plan	Same as fair value approach	Same as fair value approach
Broad-based plans (noncompensatory)	None	Shareholders' equity: (Only when shares are sold)	Same as fair value approach	Same as fair value approach

Graphic 18–12 provides a summary of the effects of each type of stock-based compensation plan we've discussed on compensation recorded and on affected balance sheet categories.

DECISION MAKERS' PERSPECTIVE

In several previous chapters, we have revisited the concept of "earnings quality" (as first defined in Chapter 4). We also have noted that one rather common practice that negatively influences earnings quality is earnings management, which refers to companies' use of one or more of several techniques designed to artificially increase (or decrease) earnings. A frequent objective of earnings management is to meet analysts' expectations regarding projections of income. The stock-based compensation plans we discuss in this chapter suggest another motive managers sometimes have to manipulate income. If a manager's personal compensation includes company stock, stock options, or other compensation based on the value of the firm's stock, it's not hard to imagine an increased desire to ensure that market expectations are met and that reported earnings have a positive effect on stock prices. In fact, as we discussed earlier, that is precisely the reaction these incentive compensation plans are designed to elicit. Investors and creditors, though, should be alert to indications of attempts to artificially manipulate income and realize that the likelihood of earnings management is probably higher for companies with generous stock-based compensation plans. ▪

Analysts should be aware of the possibility of earnings management as a way to increase managers' compensation.

P A R T

LO7

OTHER COMPENSATION PRIOR TO RETIREMENT

In stock-based plans, compensation might be quite generous—if stock prices rise, that is. On the other hand, if stock prices never rise above the prespecified base price, they're worthless. Some executives believe their performance is better measured by other criteria not tied to the unpredictable stock market. This contention has led to the increasing use of several incentive compensation programs not tied to stock prices. Such programs include annual bonuses, performance share plans, long-term cash bonuses, performance unit plans, and phantom stock plans. Regardless of the name and specific form of the plan, the accounting objective once again is to record compensation expense over the appropriate service period.

A wide variety of bonus plans provide compensation tied to performance other than stock prices.

ANNUAL BONUSES

Sometimes compensation packages include annual bonuses tied to performance objectives designed to provide incentive to executives. The most common performance measures are earnings per share, net income, and operating income, each being used by about a quarter of firms having bonus plans. Nonfinancial performance measures, such as customer satisfaction and product or service quality, also are used by about 13% of these firms.[31] In recent years, **annual bonuses** are gaining in use, not just for executives, but for nonmanagerial personnel as well. Unfortunately for employees, bonuses often take the place of annual raises. This allows a company to increase employee pay without permanently locking the increases in salaries. Bonuses are compensation expense of the period they are earned.

Bonuses sometimes take the place of permanent annual raises.

PERFORMANCE SHARE PLANS AND LONG-TERM CASH BONUSES

Performance share plans offer another way to reward employees on the basis of their productivity.[32] In these arrangements, shares are promised to key personnel, subject to the achievement of specific financial goals. For example, performance shares might represent rights to receive a certain number of shares of common stock provided the company achieves specified income goals over a four-year period.[33] The criteria might be growth in earnings per share, revenue growth or maintenance, rate of return on assets, or some other measure representative of performance. This would give executives additional incentive to see that the company's financial goals are achieved.

Performance shares give key personnel the right to receive shares if the company achieves specified financial goals.

A variation of this plan, **long-term cash bonuses,** pays cash rather than shares. This version is popular among smaller companies, particularly nonpublic companies, in which share prices are not available or issuing additional shares is undesirable.

Many variations exist. **Performance unit plans** pay cash or shares on the basis of the number of performance units employees have earned. Similar to other bonus plans, earning performance units depends on achievement of specific financial goals. The difference is that actual compensation per unit is determined after the fact by a compensation committee. This makes estimating compensation more difficult. **Phantom stock plans** employ a formula to calculate compensation based on changes in one of several possible performance measures (net assets per share, for example) designed to mimic the way stock prices might change. The objective is to approximate share price movements without actually tying compensation to the unpredictable stock market, or in the case of nonpublic companies, nonexistent stock prices.

For any of these plans, compensation expense and a related liability should be accrued annually based on the estimated eventual value of compensation, similar to variable stock-

---

[31]C. D. Ittner, D. F. Larker, and M. V. Rajan, "The Choice of Performance Measures in Annual Bonus Contracts," Working Paper, The Wharton School, University of Pennsylvania (August 1995).

[32]These sometimes are called "Restricted Performance Share Plans" (Unisys Corporation), "Stock Performance Plans" (Scott Paper Company), "Stock Incentive Compensation Plans" (Gencorp Inc.), "Incentive Compensation Plans" (Outboard Marine Corporation), and various other titles. Terminology is nonstandard, so the plan's description is more meaningful than the name it's given.

[33]When you study earnings per share in Chapter 20, you will find that "contingently issuable shares" are a factor in their calculation. Be alert when you reach that point that performance shares are an example of contingently issuable shares.

based plans (e.g., SARs). Sometimes, though, material uncertainties exist concerning how much, or even whether, compensation ultimately will be paid. Consistent with the treatment of contingent liabilities, which many of these plans represent, accrual cannot occur unless it's both probable that payment will be made and the amount can be reasonably estimated.[34] If shares will be issued rather than cash (as in a performance share plan, for instance), a shareholders' equity account is created rather than a liability.

STOCK PURCHASE PLANS

Stock purchase plans often permit all employees to buy shares directly from their company at favorable terms. The primary intent of these plans is to encourage employee ownership of the company's shares. These are quite similar to the noncompensatory stock options we discussed earlier. Presumably loyalty is enhanced among employee-shareholders. The employee also benefits because, typically, these plans allow employees to buy shares from their employer without brokerage fees and, perhaps, at a slight discount (often 5%). Some companies even encourage participation by matching or partially matching employee purchases.

Stock purchase plans permit employees to buy shares directly from the corporation.

As long as (a) substantially all employees can participate, (b) employees have no longer than one month after the price is fixed to decide whether to participate, and (c) the discount is no greater than 5% (or can be justified as reasonable), accounting is straightforward. Simply record the sale of new shares as employees buy shares. Compensation expense replaces the cash debit for any employer-paid portion.

VACATIONS, SICK DAYS, AND OTHER PAID FUTURE ABSENCES

Suppose a firm grants two weeks of paid vacation each year to nonsalaried employees. Some take their vacations during the year earned and are compensated then. Some wait. Is the compensation an expense during the year earned for only those who actually are paid that year for their absence? When you recall what you've learned about accrual accounting, you probably conclude otherwise.

An employer should accrue an expense and the related liability for employees' compensation for future absences (such as vacation pay) if the obligation meets four conditions. These conditions, all of which must be met for accrual, are listed in Graphic 18–13.

1. The obligation is attributable to employees' services already performed.
2. The paid absence can be taken in a later year—the benefit vests (will be compensated even if employment is terminated) or the benefit can be accumulated over time.
3. Payment is probable.
4. The amount can be reasonably estimated.[35]

GRAPHIC 18–13
Conditions for Accrual of Paid Future Absences

If these conditions look familiar, it's because they are simply the characteristics of a liability we discussed in Chapter 13, adapted to relate to a potential obligation for future absences of employees. Also, be sure to recognize the consistency of these conditions with accruing loss contingencies only when the obligation is both (a) probable and (b) can be reasonably estimated. The situation is demonstrated in Illustration 18–7 on the next page.

---

[34]No pronouncement specifically governs most nonstock-based plans. Because payment is contingent upon a future event, the achievement of performance objectives, the plans usually are best classified as contingent liabilities as covered by "Accounting for Contingencies," *Statement of Financial Accounting Standards No. 5* (Stamford, Conn.: FASB, 1975).

[35]"Accounting for Compensated Absences," *Statement of Financial Accounting Standards No. 43* (Stamford, Conn.: FASB, 1980).

ILLUSTRATION 18–7
Paid Future Absences

Davidson-Getty Chemicals has 8,000 employees. Each employee earns two weeks of paid vacation per year. Vacation time not taken in the year earned can be carried over to subsequent years. During 2003, 2,500 employees took both weeks' vacation, but at the end of the year, 5,500 employees had vacation time carryovers as follows:

Employees	Vacation Weeks Earned but Not Taken	Total Carryover Weeks
2,500	0	0
2,000	1	2,000
3,500	2	7,000
8,000		9,000

When the necessary conditions are met, compensated future absences are accrued in the year the compensation is earned.

During 2003, compensation averaged $600 a week per employee.

When Vacations Were Taken in 2003

Salaries and wages expense (2,500 × 2 wks. × $600) +		
(2,000 × 1 wk. × $600)	4,200,000	
Cash (or wages payable).....................................		4,200,000

December 31, 2003 (adjusting entry)

Salaries and wages expense (9,000 carryover weeks × $600)	5,400,000	
Liability—compensated future absences		5,400,000

The liability for paid absences usually is accrued at the existing wage rate rather than at a rate estimated to be in effect when absences occur.[36] So, if wage rates have risen, the difference between the accrual and the amount paid increases compensation expense that year. For example, let's assume all the carryover vacation time is taken in 2004 and the actual amount paid to employees is $5,700,000:

When Year 2003 Vacations Are Taken in 2004

Liability—compensated future absences (account balance).......	5,400,000	
Salaries and wages expense (difference)......................	300,000	
Cash (or salaries and wages payable) (given).................		5,700,000

Customary practice should be considered when deciding whether an obligation exists.

Company policy and actual practice should be considered when deciding whether the rights to payment for absences have been earned by services already rendered. Consider an illustrative situation. Suppose scientists in a private laboratory are eligible for paid sabbaticals every seven years. Should a liability be accrued at the end of a scientist's sixth year? No—if sabbatical leave is granted only to perform research beneficial to the employer. Yes—if past practice indicates that sabbatical leave is intended to provide unrestricted compensated absence for past service and other conditions are met.

Custom and practice also influence whether unused rights to paid absences expire or can be carried forward. Obviously, if rights vest (payable even if employment is terminated) they haven't expired. But holiday time, military leave, maternity leave, and jury time typically do not accumulate if unused, so a liability for those benefits usually is not accrued. On the other hand, if it's customary that a particular paid absence, say holiday time, can be carried forward—if employees work on holidays, in this case—a liability is accrued if it's probable that employees will be compensated in a future year.

Accrual of sick pay is not required, but is permitted.

Interestingly, sick pay quite often meets the conditions for accrual but is specifically excluded by *SFAS 43*, "Accounting for Compensated Absences," from mandatory accrual. Its exclusion is because future absence depends on future illness, which usually is not a certainty. However, similar to other forms of paid absences, the decision of whether to accrue

---

[36]Actually, *SFAS 43* is silent on how the liability should be measured. In practice, most companies choose the current rate because it avoids estimates and usually produces a lower expense and liability.

nonvesting sick pay should be based on actual policy and practice. If company policy or custom is that employees are paid sick pay even when their absences are not due to illness, it's appropriate to record a liability for unused sick pay. For example, some companies routinely allow unused sick pay benefits to be accumulated and paid at retirement (or to beneficiaries if death comes before retirement). If each condition is met except that the company finds it impractical to reasonably estimate the amount of compensation for future absences, a disclosure note should describe the situation.

POSTEMPLOYMENT BENEFITS

Sometimes employers provide benefits to former or inactive employees after employment but before retirement. These postemployment (rather than postretirement) benefits might include salary continuation, severance benefits, supplemental unemployment benefits, disability-related benefits, job training and counseling, and continuation of benefits such as health care benefits and life insurance coverage.

> Sometimes postemployment benefits meet the criteria for accrual as compensated absences.

Often these postemployment benefits resemble other forms of compensated absences like sick pay. If so, the accounting should be the same and employers should recognize the obligation to provide these benefits in accordance with *SFAS 43*. Recall that the liability should be accrued (debit expense; credit liability) if the four conditions of Graphic 18–13 are met. Delta Air Lines described its accrual of this expense for 2000 as shown in Graphic 18–14.

> *Postemployment Benefits*—Delta provides certain other welfare benefits to eligible former or inactive employees after employment but before retirement, primarily as part of the disability and survivorship plans. Postemployement benefit income (expense) was $51 million in 2000, $12 million in 1999, and $(29) million in 1998. We include the amount funded in excess of the liability in other noncurrent assets on our Consolidated Balance Sheets.

GRAPHIC 18–14
Postemployment Benefits—Delta Air Lines

If the postemployment benefits don't meet all four conditions, the estimated cost of those benefits should be treated as a contingency and accrued when it is probable that a liability has been incurred and the amount can be reasonably estimated in accordance with *SFAS 5*, "Accounting for Contingencies."[37]

> Otherwise, postemployment benefits should be treated as loss contingencies.

CONCEPT **REVIEW** EXERCISE

Pre-retirement Compensation Plans

Listed below are transactions dealing with various stock benefit plans of Fortune-Time Corporation during the period 2003–2005. The share prices for the $1 par common stock for various dates follow:

Jan. 1, 2003	$45
Jan. 5, 2003	44
Dec. 31, 2003	45
Dec. 31, 2004	46

a. On January 1, 2003, the company issued 10 million common shares to divisional managers under its restricted stock award plan. The shares are subject to forfeiture if employment is terminated within three years.

b. On January 1, 2003, the company granted incentive stock options to its senior management exercisable for 1.5 million common shares. The options must be exercised within five years, but not before January 1, 2005. The exercise price of the stock options is equal to the fair market value of the common stock on the date the options are granted. An option pricing model estimates the fair value of the options to be $4 per option. All recipients are expected to remain employed through the vesting date.

c. On January 5, 2003, the company granted 16 million SARs to its junior managers. The SARs entitle managers to receive their choice of cash or stock equal in value to the

---

[37]"Employers' Accounting For Postemployment Benefits," *Statement of Financial Accounting Standards No. 112* (Norwalk, Conn.: FASB, 1992) amends *SFAS No. 5* and *SFAS No. 43*.

excess of the market price at exercise over the share price at the date of grant. The SARs vest at the end of 2004 (cannot be exercised until then) and expire at the end of 2006.

d. On January 5, 2003, the company granted 3 million performance share rights to key executives. The rights entitle executives to receive 3 million of its $1 par common shares, subject to the achievement of specific financial goals over the next three years. Achievement of the goals is probable at the end of each year.

e. Recorded compensation expense on December 31, 2003.

f. A divisional manager holding 1 million of the restricted shares left the company to become CEO of a competitor on September 15, 2004, before the required service period ended.

g. Recorded compensation expense on December 31, 2004.

Required:

Prepare the journal entries that Fortune-Time recorded for each of these transactions. Assume the company opts for the elective fair value approach to accounting for stock-based plans. (Ignore any tax effects.)

SOLUTION

January 1, 2003
Restricted Stock Award Plan
No entry.
Total compensation is measured as 10 million shares at $45 = $450 million

Incentive Stock Options
No entry.
Total compensation is measured as 1.5 million shares at $4 = $6 million
(Note: No compensation would be measured unless the elective fair value approach is used.)

SARs
No entry because the SARs have no intrinsic value on the grant date (market price equals reference price).

Performance Share Plan
No entry until compensation is estimated at the end of the reporting period

December 31, 2003   **($ in millions)**

Restricted Stock

Compensation expense ($450 million ÷ 3 years)...............	150	
Paid-in capital—restricted stock		150

Incentive Options

Compensation expense ($6 million ÷ 2 years)................	3	
Paid-in capital—stock options............................		3

SARs

Compensation expense*....................................	8	
Liability—SAR plan		8

*Calculation:

($45 − 44) × 16 million	×	½	−	0	=	8
Estimated total compensation		Fraction of service to date		Expensed earlier		Current expense

Performance Share Plan

Compensation expense*....................................	45	
Paid-in capital—performance shares.......................		45

*Calculation:

$45 × 3 million	×	⅓	−	0	=	45
Estimated total compensation		Fraction of service to date		Expensed earlier		Current expense

September 15, 2004
Restricted Stock

Paid-in capital—restricted stock (10% × $150)	15	
Compensation expense....................................		15

December 31, 2004
Restricted Stock

Compensation expense [($450 − 150 − 15 million) ÷ 2 years]	142.5	
Paid-in capital—restricted stock		142.5

Incentive Options

Compensation expense ($6 million ÷ 2 years).	3	
Paid-in capital—stock options.		3

SARs

Compensation expense*.	24	
Liability SAR plan.		24

*Calculation:

($46 − $44) × 16 million	×	⅔	−	8	=	24
Estimated total compensation		Fraction of service to date		Expensed earlier		Current expense

Performance Share Plan

Compensation expense*.	47	
Paid-in capital—performance shares.		47

*Calculation:

$46 × 3 million	×	⅔	−	45	=	47
Estimated total compensation		Fraction of service to date		Expensed earlier		Current expense

FINANCIAL REPORTING CASE **SOLUTION**

1. **Besides the compensation mentioned in the press release, what types of compensation do you think Ms. Veres might receive for her services?** *(p. 884)*   Postretirement benefits might include pension benefits and others that may include medical coverage, dental coverage, life insurance, and group legal services. Regardless of whether compensation is received before or after retirement, the cost to NEV is expensed over the period of service the benefits are earned.

2. **How can a compensation package such as this serve as an incentive to Ms. Veres?** *(p. 898)* Stock-based plans like the restricted stock and stock options that Ms. Veres is receiving are designed to motivate recipients. If the shares awarded are restricted so that Ms. Veres is not free to sell the shares during the restriction period, she has an incentive to remain with the company until rights to the shares vest. Likewise, stock options can be made exercisable only after a specified period of employment. An additional incentive of stock-based plans is that the recipient has an incentive to take actions that will maximize the value of the shares.

3. **Ms. Veres received a "grant of restricted stock." How should NEV account for the grant?** *(p. 898)*   The compensation associated with restricted stock is the market price of unrestricted shares of the same stock. NEV will accrue this amount as compensation expense over the service period from the date of grant to when restrictions are lifted.

4. **Included were stock options to buy more than 800,000 shares. How will the options affect NEV's compensation expense?** *(p. 900)*   Similar to the method used for restricted stock, the value of the options is recorded as compensation over the service period, usually the vesting period. If NEV elects the FASB's fair value approach, the total compensation will be the fair value of the options at the grant date. Otherwise, it will be the intrinsic value at the grant date, which likely will be zero because the exercise price usually is made equal to the market price at the date of grant. Most companies do not elect the FASB's fair value approach. ■

THE BOTTOM LINE

1. Accounting for postretirement benefits is similar in most respects to accounting for pension benefits. Like pensions, other postretirement benefits are a form of deferred compensation. Unlike pensions, their cost is attributed to the years from the employee's date of hire to the full eligibility date.

2. The expected postretirement benefit obligation (EPBO) is the actuary's estimate of the total postretirement benefits (at their discounted present value) expected to be received by plan participants. The accumulated postretirement benefit obligation (APBO) is the portion of the EPBO attributed to employee service to date.

3. The components of postretirement benefit expense are essentially the same as those for pension expense. The transition obligation existing when *SFAS 106* was adopted can be expensed either immediately or over a period of years.

4. By the elective fair value approach, compensation is measured at the grant date using an option-pricing model that considers the exercise price and expected term of the option, the current market price of the underlying stock and its expected volatility, expected dividends, and the expected risk-free rate of return.

5. By the alternate intrinsic value approach to accounting for stock-based compensation plans, compensation is measured as the intrinsic value of the award and expensed over the service period, usually from the date of grant to the vesting date.

6. For stock appreciation rights with variable terms, the award is considered to be equity if the employer can elect to settle in shares of stock rather than cash. If the employee can elect to receive cash, the award is considered to be a liability. In either case, the amount of compensation is continually adjusted to reflect changes in the market price of stock until the compensation is finally paid unless the award is considered equity and the elective fair value approach is used. In that case, fair value is measured at the grant date.

7. Other preretirement compensation plans include annual bonuses, performance share plans, long-term cash bonuses, performance unit plans, and phantom stock plans. Regardless of the name and specific form of the plan, the accounting objective is to record compensation over the appropriate service period. ■

APPENDIX

18A

OPTION-PRICING THEORY

Option values have two essential components: (1) intrinsic value and (2) time value.

Intrinsic Value

Intrinsic value is the benefit the holder of an option would realize by exercising the option rather than buying the underlying stock directly. An option that permits an employee to buy $25 stock for $10 has an intrinsic value of $15. An option whose exercise price equals or exceeds the market price of the underlying stock has zero intrinsic value.

TIME VALUE

In addition to their intrinsic value, options also have a time value due to the fact that (a) the holder of an option does not have to pay the exercise price until the option is exercised and (b) the market price of the underlying stock may yet rise and create additional intrinsic value. All options have time value so long as time remains before expiration. The longer the time until expiration, other things being equal, the greater the time value. For instance, the option described above with an intrinsic value of $15, might have a fair value of, say, $22 if time still remains until the option expires. The $7 difference represents the time value of the option. Time value can be subdivided into two components: (1) the effects of time value of money and (2) volatility value.

TIME VALUE OF MONEY

An option's value is enhanced by the delay in paying cash for the shares.

The time value of money component arises because the holder of an option does not have to pay the exercise price until the option is exercised. Instead, the holder can invest funds elsewhere while waiting to exercise the option. For measurement purposes, the time value of money component is assumed to be the rate of return available on risk-free U.S. Treasury Securities. The higher the time value of money, the higher the value of being able to delay payment of the exercise price.

When the underlying stock pays no dividends, the time value of money component is the difference between the exercise price (a future amount) and its discounted present value.

Let's say the exercise price is $30. If the present value (discounted at the risk-free rate) is $24, the time value of money component is $6. On the other hand, if the stock pays a dividend (or is expected to during the life of the option), the time value of money component is lower. The value of being able to delay payment of the exercise price would be partially offset by the cost of foregoing the dividend in the meantime. For instance, if the stock underlying the options just described were expected to pay dividends and the discounted present value of the expected dividends were $2, the time value of money component in that example would be reduced from $6 to $4.

> The time value of money component is the difference between the exercise price and its discounted present value minus the present value of expected dividends.

VOLATILITY VALUE

The volatility value represents the possibility that the option holder might profit from market price appreciation of the underlying stock while being exposed to the loss of only the value of the option, rather than the full market value of the stock. For example, fair value of an option to buy a share at an exercise price of $30 might be measured as $7. The potential profit from market price appreciation is conceptually unlimited. And yet, the potential loss from the stock's value failing to appreciate is only $7.

A stock's volatility is the amount by which its price has fluctuated previously or is expected to fluctuate in the future. The greater a stock's volatility, the greater the potential profit. It usually is measured as one standard deviation of a statistical distribution. Statistically, if the expected annualized volatility is 25%, the probability is approximately 67% that the stock's year-end price will fall within roughly plus or minus 25% of its beginning-of-year price. Stated differently, the probability is approximately 33% that the year-end stock price will fall outside that range.

> Volatility enhances the likelihood of stock price appreciation.

Option-pricing models make assumptions about the likelihood of various future stock prices by making assumptions about the statistical distribution of future stock prices that take into account the expected volatility of the stock price. One popular option pricing model, the Black–Scholes model, for instance, assumes a log-normal distribution. This assumption posits that the stock price is as likely to fall by half as it is to double and that large price movements are less likely than small price movements. The higher a stock's volatility, the higher the probability of large increases or decreases in market price. Because the cost of large decreases is limited to the option's current value, but the profitability from large increases is unlimited, an option on a highly volatile stock has a higher probability of a large profit than does an option on a less volatile stock.

Summary

In summary, the fair value of an option is (a) its intrinsic value plus (b) its time value of money component plus (c) its volatility component. The variables that affect an option's fair value and the effect of each are indicated in Graphic 18A–1.

All Other Factors Being Equal, If the:	The Option Value Will Be:
Exercise price is higher	Lower
Term of the option is longer	Higher
Market price of the stock is higher	Higher
Dividends are higher	Lower
Risk-free rate of return is higher	Higher
Volatility of the stock is higher	Higher

GRAPHIC 18A–1
Effect of Variables on an Option's Fair Value

EMPLOYEE STOCK OWNERSHIP PLANS (ESOPS)

APPENDIX

18B

Another common form of deferred compensation is an Employee Stock Ownership Plan (ESOP). An ESOP is a legal entity separate from the sponsoring company and is created by a trust agreement. The sponsoring company contributes to the ESOP shares of stock, or cash which is used to purchase the company's stock. Employees have an ownership interest in the stock but actually receive compensation when they leave the firm, due to retirement or otherwise. The cash that employees receive is raised by the ESOP from selling shares. The sponsoring company gets a tax deduction for the cash or market value of shares contributed to the ESOP, while employees get to defer paying taxes on their compensation until they ultimately receive cash from the ESOP. A benefit to the company is that employees, as owners, have a monetary stake in the well-being of their employer.

As contributions are made to an ESOP, the sponsoring company records compensation expense. For example, if 1 million $1 par shares worth $15 million are contributed, the following entry is recorded:

	($ in millions)	
Compensation expense (fair value of contribution)	15	
Common stock (1 million shares @ $1 par)		1
Paid-in capital—excess of par (difference)		14

Note: If $15 million cash had been contributed instead of shares, cash would substitute for the stock accounts in this entry.

Sometimes, the ESOP borrows cash to buy shares from the employer company. This is called a **leveraged ESOP.** In that case, the sponsoring company records a liability, offset by a contra-equity account. For example, let's say $30 million cash is borrowed by the ESOP and 2 million $1 par shares worth $30 million are purchased from the firm with that cash. The following entries are recorded:

	($ in millions)	
Deferred compensation—ESOP plan	30	
Liability—ESOP plan (amount borrowed by the ESOP)		30
Cash (received from ESOP)	30	
Common stock (2 million shares @ $1 par)		2
Paid-in capital—excess of par (difference)		28

As the ESOP repays the debt, both the liability and deferred compensation (a contra-equity account) on the employer's books are reduced.[38] Notice that the effect of this accounting treatment is to effectively treat the ESOP's debt as company debt.

QUESTIONS FOR REVIEW OF KEY TOPICS

Q 18–1   The basis of accounting for postretirement benefits other than pensions is the substantive plan. What does this mean? When should anticipated changes be incorporated in the accounting treatment?

Q 18–2   What are the two ways to measure the obligation for postretirement benefits other than pensions? Define these measurement approaches.

Q 18–3   How are the costs of providing postretirement benefits other than pensions expensed?

Q 18–4   The APBO existing when *SFAS 106* was adopted is called the transition obligation. When is it recognized as part of compensation expense?

Q 18–5   The components of postretirement benefit expense are similar to the components of pension expense. In what fundamental way does the service cost component differ between these two expenses?

Q 18–6   The EPBO for Branch Industries at the end of 2003 was determined by the actuary to be $20,000 as it relates to employee Will Lawson. Lawson was hired at the beginning of 1989. He will be fully eligible to retire with health care benefits in 15 years but is expected to retire in 25 years. What is the APBO as it relates to Will Lawson?

Q 18–7   What is restricted stock? Describe how compensation expense is determined and recorded for a restricted stock award plan.

---

[38]"Accounting Practices for Certain Employee Stock Ownership Plans," *Statement of Position No. 76-3* (New York: AICPA, 1976).

Q 18–8   Stock option plans provide employees the option to purchase (a) a specified number of shares of the firm's stock, (b) at a specified price, (c) during a specified period of time. The most controversial and complex aspect of accounting for stock-based compensation is how the fair value of stock options should be measured. Describe the elective measurement approach suggested by the FASB.

Q 18–9   The Tax Code differentiates between qualified option plans, including incentive plans, and nonqualified plans. What are the major differences in tax treatment between incentive plans and nonqualified plans?

Q 18–10   General Electric Corporation has chosen not to use the elective fair value approach for its stock option plans. Identify the major difference between the elective fair value approach and the alternative intrinsic value approach that GE uses.

Q 18–11   Why are most stock option plans structured as incentive plans?

Q 18–12   The fair value of stock options can be considered to be composed of two main components. What are they?

Q 18–13   LTV Corporation grants SARs to key executives. Upon exercise, the SARs entitle executives to receive either cash or stock equal in value to the excess of the market price at exercise over the share price at the date of grant. How should LTV account for the awards?

Q 18–14   Performance share plans, long-term cash bonuses, performance unit plans, and phantom stock plans, among other variations, promise cash or shares to key personnel, subject to the achievement of specific financial goals. How should an employer account for such plans?

Q 18–15   Under what conditions should an employer accrue an expense and the related liability for employees' compensation for future absences? How do company custom and practice affect the accrual decision?

Q 18–16   Benevolent Corporation provides benefits to former and inactive employees after their employment but before they retire. Included in these postemployment (rather than postretirement) benefits are supplemental unemployment benefits, disability-related benefits, and continuation of health care benefits and life insurance coverage. Should Benevolent accrue a liability to provide these benefits?

Q 18–17   (Based on Appendix 18B) The Gillette Company has an Employee Stock Ownership Plan (ESOP). Its disclosure notes included the following: "The ESOP purchased Series C shares with borrowed funds. The ESOP loan and principal will be repaid on a semiannual basis over a 10-year period by Company contributions to the ESOP and by the dividends paid on the Series C shares." An effect of this is that Gillette has received $100 million cash (from the sale to the ESOP of shares) and now is responsible (indirectly) for the repayment of debt used by the ESOP to acquire the cash. Does this mean the company was able to achieve a sizable amount of off-balance-sheet financing?

EXERCISES

E 18–1
Postretirement benefits; determine the APBO and service cost

Prince Distribution, Inc., has an unfunded postretirement health care benefit plan. Medical care and life insurance benefits are provided to employees who render 10 years service and attain age 55 while in service. At the end of 2003, Jim Lukawitz is 31. He was hired by Prince at age 25 (6 years ago) and is expected to retire at age 62. The expected postretirement benefit obligation for Lukawitz at the end of 2003 is $50,000 and $54,000 at the end of 2004.

Required:
Calculate the accumulated postretirement benefit obligation at the end of 2003 and 2004 and the service cost for 2003 and 2004 as pertaining to Lukawitz.

E 18–2
Postretirement benefits; changes in the APBO

On January 1, 2003, Medical Transport Company's accumulated postretirement benefit obligation was $25 million. At the end of 2003, retiree benefits paid were $3 million. Service cost for 2003 is $7 million. At the end of 2003, there were no unrecognized postretirement benefit costs. Assumptions regarding the trend of future health care costs were revised at the end of 2003, causing the actuary to revise downward the estimate of the APBO by $1 million. The actuary's discount rate is 8%.

Required:
Determine the amount of the accumulated postretirement benefit obligation at December 31, 2003.

E 18–3
Postretirement benefits; determine APBO, EPBO

Classified Electronics has an unfunded retiree health care plan. Each of the company's three employees has been with the firm since its inception at the beginning of 2002. As of the end of 2003, the actuary estimates the total net cost of providing health care benefits to employees during their retirement years to have a present value of $72,000. Each of the employees will become fully eligible for benefits after 28 more years of service but aren't expected to retire for 35 more years. The interest rate is 6%.

Required:
1. What is the expected postretirement benefit obligation at the end of 2003?
2. What is the accumulated postretirement benefit obligation at the end of 2003?

3. What is the expected postretirement benefit obligation at the end of 2004?
4. What is the accumulated postretirement benefit obligation at the end of 2004?

E 18–4
Postretirement benefits; determine APBO, service cost, interest cost; prepare journal entry

The following data are available pertaining to Household Appliance Company's retiree health care plan for 2003:

Number of employees covered	2
Years employed as of January 1, 2003	3 [each]
Attribution period	25 years
Expected postretirement benefit obligation, Jan. 1	$50,000
Expected postretirement benefit obligation, Dec. 31	$53,000
Interest rate	6%
Funding	none

Required:
1. What is the accumulated postretirement benefit obligation at the beginning of 2003?
2. What is interest cost to be included in 2003 postretirement benefit expense?
3. What is service cost to be included in 2003 postretirement benefit expense?
4. Prepare the journal entry to record the postretirement benefit expense for 2003.

E 18–5
Postretirement benefits; determine EPBO; attribution period

Lorin Management Services has an unfunded postretirement benefit plan. On December 31, 2003, the following data were available concerning changes in the plan's accumulated postretirement benefit obligation with respect to one of Lorin's employees:

APBO at the beginning of 2003	$16,364
Interest cost: ($16,364 × 10%)	1,636
Service cost: ($44,000 × 1/22)	2,000
Portion of EPBO attributed to 2003	
APBO at the end of 2003	$20,000

Required:
1. Over how many years is the expected postretirement benefit obligation being expensed (attribution period)?
2. What is the expected postretirement benefit obligation at the *end* of 2003?
3. When was the employee hired by Lorin?
4. What is the expected postretirement benefit obligation at the *beginning* of 2003?

E 18–6
Postretirement benefits; components of postretirement benefit expense

Data pertaining to the postretirement health care benefit plan of Sterling Properties include the following for 2003:

	($ in 000s)
Service cost	$124
Accumulated postretirement benefit obligation, January 1	700
Plan assets (fair market value), January 1	50
Unrecognized prior service cost	none
Unrecognized net gain (2003 amortization, $1)	91
Unrecognized transition obligation (2003 amortization, $2)	36
Retiree benefits paid (end of year)	87
Contribution to health care benefit fund (end of year)	185
Discount rate, 7%	
Return on plan assets (actual and expected), 10%	

Required:
1. Determine the postretirement benefit expense for 2003.
2. Prepare the appropriate journal entry to record the postretirement benefit expense and funding for 2003.

E 18–7
Postretirement benefits; amortization of unrecognized net loss

Cahal-Michael Company has a postretirement health care benefit plan. On January 1, 2003, the following plan-related data were available:

	($ in 000s)
Unrecognized net loss	$ 336
Accumulated postretirement benefit obligation	2,800

	($ in 000s)
Fair value of plan assets	500
Average remaining service period to retirement	14 years (same in previous 10 yrs.)
Average remaining service period to full eligibility	12 years (same in previous 10 yrs.)

The rate of return on plan assets during 2003 was 10%, although it was expected to be 9%. The actuary revised assumptions regarding the APBO at the end of the year, resulting in a $39,000 increase in the estimate of that obligation.

Required:
1. Calculate any amortization of the net loss that should be included as a component of postretirement benefit expense for 2003.
2. Assume the postretirement benefit expense for 2003, not including the amortization of the net loss component, is $212,000. What is the expense for the year?
3. Determine the unrecognized net loss or gain as of December 31, 2003.

E 18–8
Postretirement benefits; amortization of unrecognized transition obligation and prior service cost

Gorky-Park Corporation provides postretirement health care benefits to employees who provide at least 12 years service and reach age 62 while in service. On January 1, 2003, the following plan-related data were available:

	($ in 000s)
Unrecognized transition obligation	$ 50
Accumulated postretirement benefit obligation	130
Fair value of plan assets	none
Average remaining service period to retirement	25 years (same in previous 10 yrs.)
Average remaining service period to full eligibility	20 years (same in previous 10 yrs.)

On January 1, 2003, Gorky-Park amends the plan to provide certain dental benefits in addition to previously provided medical benefits. The actuary determines that the cost of making the amendment retroactive increases the APBO by $20 million. Management chooses to amortize the prior service cost on a straight-line basis. The service cost for 2003 is $34 million. The interest rate is 8%.

Required:
Calculate the postretirement benefit expense for 2003.

E 18–9
Postretirement benefits; negative plan amendment

Southeast Technology provides postretirement health care benefits to employees. On January 1, 2003, the following plan-related data were available:

	($ in 000s)
Unrecognized prior service cost	$ 50
Accumulated postretirement benefit obligation	530
Fair value of plan assets	none
Average remaining service period to retirement	20 years (same in previous 10 yrs.)
Average remaining service period to full eligibility	15 years (same in previous 10 yrs.)

On January 1, 2003, Southeast amends the plan in response to spiraling health care costs. The amendment establishes an annual maximum of $3,000 for medical benefits that the plan will provide. The actuary determines that the effect of this amendment is to decrease the APBO by $80,000. Management amortizes prior service cost on a straight-line basis. The interest rate is 8%. The service cost for 2003 is $114,000.

Required:
1. Calculate the prior service cost amortization for 2003.
2. Calculate the postretirement benefit expense for 2003.
3. Suppose Southeast had an unrecognized transition obligation of $120,000 at January 1. Calculate the prior service cost amortization for 2003.

E 18–10
Multiple choice

The following question dealing with postretirement benefit plans appeared on a recent CPA examination. Enter the letter corresponding to the response which *best* completes the question.
1. An employer's obligation for postretirement health benefits that are expected to be provided to or for an employee must be fully accrued by the date the
   a. Employee is fully eligible for benefits.
   b. Employee retires.
   c. Benefits are utilized.
   d. Benefits are paid.

E 18–11
Restricted stock award plan

Allied Paper Products, Inc. offers a restricted stock award plan to its vice presidents. On January 1, 2003, the company granted 16 million of its $1 par common shares, subject to forfeiture if employment is terminated within two years. The common shares have a market price of $5 per share on the grant date.

Required:
1. Determine the total compensation cost pertaining to the restricted shares.
2. Prepare the appropriate journal entries related to the restricted stock through December 31, 2004.

E 18–12
Restricted stock award plan

On January 1, 2003, VKI Corporation awarded 12 million of its $1 par common shares to key personnel, subject to forfeiture if employment is terminated within three years. On the grant date, the shares have a market price of $2.50 per share.

Required:
1. Determine the total compensation cost pertaining to the restricted shares.
2. Prepare the appropriate journal entry to record the award of restricted shares on January 1, 2003.
3. Prepare the appropriate journal entry to record compensation expense on December 31, 2003.
4. Prepare the appropriate journal entry to record compensation expense on December 31, 2004.
5. Prepare the appropriate journal entry to record compensation expense on December 31, 2005.
6. Prepare the appropriate journal entry to record the lifting of restrictions on the shares at December 31, 2005.

E 18–13
Restricted stock award plan; forfeitures anticipated

Magnetic-Optical Corporation offers a variety of stock-based compensation plans to employees. Under its restricted stock award plan, the company on January 1, 2003, granted 4 million of its $1 par common shares to various division managers. The shares are subject to forfeiture if employment is terminated within three years. The common shares have a market price of $22.50 per share on the grant date.

Required:
1. Determine the total compensation cost pertaining to the restricted shares.
2. Prepare the appropriate journal entry to record the award of restricted shares on January 1, 2003.
3. Prepare the appropriate journal entry to record compensation expense on December 31, 2003.
4. Suppose Magnetic-Optical expected a 10% forfeiture rate on the restricted shares prior to vesting. Determine the total compensation cost, assuming the company chooses to follow the elective fair value approach for fixed compensation plans and chooses to anticipate forfeitures at the grant date.

E 18–14
Stock options; elective fair value approach and alternate intrinsic value approach

American Optical Corporation provides a variety of stock-based compensation plans to its employees. Under its executive stock option plan, the company granted options on January 1, 2003, that permit executives to acquire 4 million of the company's $1 par common shares within the next five years, but not before December 31, 2004 (the vesting date). The exercise price is the market price of the shares on the date of grant, $14 per share. The fair value of the 4 million options, estimated by an appropriate option pricing model, is $3 per option. No forfeitures are anticipated. Ignore taxes.

Required:
1. Determine the total compensation cost pertaining to the options, assuming the company chooses to follow the elective fair value approach for fixed compensation plans.
2. Prepare the appropriate journal entry to record the award of options on January 1, 2003.
3. Prepare the appropriate journal entry to record compensation expense on December 31, 2003.
4. Prepare the appropriate journal entry to record compensation expense on December 31, 2004.
5. Determine the total compensation cost pertaining to the options, assuming the company does not choose to follow the elective fair value approach for fixed compensation plans.

E 18–15
Stock option plan; elective fair value approach; forfeiture of options

On January 1, 2003, Adams-Meneke Corporation granted 25 million incentive stock options to division managers, each permitting holders to purchase one share of the company's $1 par common shares within the next six years, but not before December 31, 2005 (the vesting date). The exercise price is the market price of the shares on the date of grant, currently $10 per share. The fair value of the options, estimated by an appropriate option pricing model, is $3 per option. Adams-Meneke chooses to follow the elective fair value approach for fixed compensation plans.

Required:
1. Determine the total compensation cost pertaining to the options on January 1, 2003.
2. Prepare the appropriate journal entry to record compensation expense on December 31, 2003.
3. Unexpected turnover during 2004 caused the forfeiture of 6% of the stock options. Determine the adjusted compensation cost, and prepare the appropriate journal entry(s) on December 31, 2004.

E 18–16
Stock option plan; elective fair value approach; forfeitures anticipated

Walters Audio Visual, Inc. offers an incentive stock option plan to its regional managers. On January 1, 2003, options were granted for 40 million $1 par common shares. The exercise price is the market price on the grant date—$8 per share. Options cannot be exercised prior to January 1, 2005, and expire December 31, 2009. The fair value of the 40 million options, estimated by an appropriate option pricing model, is $1 per option. Walters chooses to follow the elective fair value approach for fixed compensation plans.

Required:
1. Determine the total compensation cost pertaining to the incentive stock option plan.
2. Prepare the appropriate journal entry to record compensation expense on December 31, 2003.
3. Prepare the appropriate journal entry to record compensation expense on December 31, 2004.
4. Prepare the appropriate journal entry to record the exercise of 75% of the options on March 12, 2005, when the market price is $9 per share.
5. Prepare the appropriate journal entry on December 31, 2009, when the remaining options that have vested expire without being exercised.

E 18–17
Stock option plan; market value exceeds exercise price; alternate intrinsic value approach

(Note: This is a variation of Exercise 18–16, modified to consider nonqualifying stock options.)
   Walters Audio Visual, Inc., offers a stock option plan to its regional managers. On January 1, 2003, options were granted for 40 million $1 par common shares. The exercise price is $8 per share. The market price of the shares on the date of grant is $8.50 per share. Options cannot be exercised prior to January 1, 2005, and expire December 31, 2009. Walters chooses not to follow the elective fair value approach for fixed compensation plans.

Required:
1. Determine the total compensation cost pertaining to the stock option plan at January 1, 2003.
2. Prepare the appropriate journal entry to record compensation expense on December 31, 2003.
3. Prepare the appropriate journal entry to record compensation expense on December 31, 2004.
4. Prepare the appropriate journal entry to record the exercise of 75% of the options on March 12, 2005, when the market price is $9 per share.
5. Prepare the appropriate journal entry on December 31, 2009, when the remaining options that have vested expire without being exercised.

E 18–18
Stock option plan; alternate intrinsic value approach

SSG Cycles manufactures and distributes motorcycle parts and supplies. Employees are offered a variety of stock-based compensation plans. Under its nonqualified stock option plan, SSG granted options to key officers on January 1, 2003. The options permit holders to acquire 12 million of the company's $1 par common shares for $11 within the next six years, but not before January 1, 2006 (the vesting date). The market price of the shares on the date of grant is $13 per share. The fair value of the 12 million options, estimated by an appropriate option pricing model, is $3 per option. JBL chooses not to follow the elective fair value approach for fixed compensation plans.

Required:
1. Determine the total compensation cost pertaining to the incentive stock option plan.
2. Prepare the appropriate journal entries to record compensation expense on December 31, 2003, 2004, and 2005.
3. Record the exercise of the options if all of the options are exercised on May 11, 2007, when the market price is $14 per share.

E 18–19
Stock appreciation rights; cash settlement

As part of its stock-based compensation package, International Electronics granted 24 million stock appreciation rights (SARs) to top officers on January 1, 2003. At exercise, holders of the SARs are entitled to receive cash or stock equal in value to the excess of the market price at exercise over the share price at the date of grant. The SARs cannot be exercised until the end of 2006 (vesting date) and expire at the end of 2008. The common shares have a market price of $46 per share on the grant date. All recipients are expected to remain employed through the vesting date. The year-end share prices following the grant of the SARs are:

2003	$50
2004	$49
2005	$50
2006	$51
2007	$50

Required:
1. Prepare the appropriate journal entry to record the award of SARs on January 1, 2003
2. Prepare the appropriate journal entries pertaining to the SARs on December 31, 2003–2006.

3. The SARs remain unexercised on December 31, 2007. Prepare the appropriate journal entry on that date.
4. The SARs are exercised on June 6, 2008, when the share price is $53, and executives choose to receive the market price appreciation in cash. Prepare the appropriate journal entry(s) on that date.

E 18–20
Multiple choice

The following questions dealing with stock-based compensation plans are adapted from recent CPA examinations. Enter the letter corresponding to the response that *best* completes each of the statements or questions.

1. Wolf Co.'s grant of 30,000 stock appreciation rights enables key employees to receive cash equal to the difference between $20 and the market price of the stock on the date each right is exercised. The service period is 2003 through 2005, and the rights are exercisable in 2006 and 2007. The market price of the stock was $25 and $28 at December 31, 2003 and 2004, respectively. What amount should Wolf report as the liability under the stock appreciation rights plan in its December 31, 2004, balance sheet?
    a. $0
    b. $130,000
    c. $160,000   *See note*
    d. $240,000

2. On January 2, 2003, Morey Corp. granted Dean, its president, 20,000 stock appreciation rights for past services. Those rights are exercisable immediately and expire on January 1, 2006. On exercise, Dean is entitled to receive cash for the excess of the stock's market price on the exercise date over the market price on the grant date. Dean did not exercise any of the rights during 2003. The market price of Morey's stock was $30 on January 2, 2003, and $45 on December 31, 2003. As a result of the stock appreciation rights, Morey should recognize compensation expense for 2003 of
    a. $0
    b. $100,000
    c. $300,000
    d. $600,000

3. On January 2, 2003, Farm Co. granted an employee an option to purchase 1,000 shares of Farm's stock at $40 per share. The option became exercisable on December 31, 2003, after the employee had completed one year of service, and was exercised on that date. The market prices of Farm's stock were as follows: (Farm chooses not to follow the elective fair value approach.)

January 2, 2003	$50
December 31, 2003	65

What amount should Farm recognize as compensation expense for 2003?

    a. $0
    b. $10,000
    c. $15,000
    d. $25,000

E 18–21
Paid future absences

JWS Transport Company's employees earn vacation time at the rate of 1 hour per 40-hour work period. The vacation pay vests immediately (that is, an employee is entitled to the pay even if employment terminates). During 2003, total wages paid to employees equaled $404,000, including $4,000 for vacations actually taken in 2003 but not including vacations related to 2003 that will be taken in 2004. All vacations earned before 2003 were taken before January 1, 2003. No accrual entries have been made for the vacations. No overtime premium and no bonuses were paid during the period.

Required:
Prepare the appropriate adjusting entry for vacations earned but not taken in 2003.

E 18–22
Paid future absences

On January 1, 2003, Poplar Fabricators Corporation agreed to grant its employees two weeks' vacation each year, with the stipulation that vacations earned each year can be taken the following year. For the year ended December 31, 2003, Poplar Fabricators' employees each earned an average of $900 per week. Seven hundred vacation weeks earned in 2003 were not taken during 2003.

Required:
1. Prepare the appropriate adjusting entry for vacations earned but not taken in 2003.
2. Suppose wage rates for employees have risen by an average of 5 percent by the time vacations actually are taken in 2004. Also, assume wages earned in 2004 (including vacations earned and taken in 2004) were $31,000,000. Prepare a journal entry that summarizes 2004 wages and the payment for 2003 vacations taken in 2004.

PROBLEMS

P 18–1
Postretirement
benefits; EPBO
calculations; APBO
calculations; transition
obligation; present
value concepts

Century-Fox Corporation's employees are eligible for postretirement health care benefits after both being employed at the end of the year in which age 60 is attained and having worked for Century-Fox for at least 20 years. Jason Snyder was hired at the beginning of 1981 by Century-Fox at age 34 (he turned 35 during 1981) and is expected to retire at the end of 2008 (age 62). His retirement is expected to span five years (unrealistically short to simplify calculations). The company's actuary has estimated the net cost of retiree benefits in each retirement year as shown below. The discount rate is 6%. The plan is not prefunded.

Year	Age	Expected Net Cost
2009	63	$4,000
2010	64	4,400
2011	65	2,300
2012	66	2,500
2013	67	2,800

Required:
1. Draw a time line that depicts Snyder's attribution period for retiree benefits, expected retirement period, and adoption of *SFAS 106* at the beginning of 1993.
2. Calculate the present value of the net benefits as of the expected retirement date.
3. With respect to Snyder, what is the company's expected postretirement benefit obligation at the beginning of 1993 when *SFAS 106* is adopted?
4. With respect to Snyder, what is the company's accumulated postretirement benefit obligation at the beginning of 1993 when *SFAS 106* is adopted?
5. With respect to Snyder, what is the company's transition obligation at the beginning of 1993?
6. What portion of the transition obligation would be included in 1993 postretirement benefit expense if management chooses:
   a. Immediate recognition.
   b. Recognition over future service periods.
   c. Optional recognition over a 20-year period.

P 18–2
Postretirement
benefits; EPBO
calculations; APBO
calculations;
components of
postretirement benefit
expense; present value
concepts

(Note: This is a variation of the previous problem, designed to focus on different elements of the postretirement benefit plan.)
   Century-Fox Corporation's employees are eligible for postretirement health care benefits after both being employed at the end of the year in which age 60 is attained and having worked 20 years. Jason Snyder was hired at the beginning of 1981 by Century-Fox at age 34 (he turned 35 during 1981) and is expected to retire at the end of 2008 (age 62). His retirement is expected to span five years (unrealistically short to simplify calculations). The company's actuary has estimated the net cost of retiree benefits in each retirement year as shown below. The discount rate is 6%. The plan is not prefunded.

Year	Expected Age	Net Cost
2009	63	$4,000
2010	64	4,400
2011	65	2,300
2012	66	2,500
2013	67	2,800

Required:
1. Calculate the present value of the net benefits as of the expected retirement date.
2. With respect to Snyder, what is the company's expected postretirement benefit obligation at the end of 2003?
3. With respect to Snyder, what is the company's accumulated postretirement benefit obligation at the end of 2003?
4. With respect to Snyder, what is the company's accumulated postretirement benefit obligation at the end of 2004?
5. What is the service cost to be included in 2004 postretirement benefit expense?
6. What is the interest cost to be included in 2004 postretirement benefit expense?
7. Show how the APBO changed during 2004 by reconciling the beginning and ending balances.

P 18–3
Postretirement
benefits; schedule of
postretirement benefit
costs

P 18–4
Postretirement
benefits; relationship
among elements of
postretirement benefit
plan

Stockton Labeling Company has a retiree health care plan. Employees become fully eligible for benefits after working for the company eight years. Stockton hired Misty Newburn on January 1, 2003. As of the end of 2003, the actuary estimates the total net cost of providing health care benefits to Newburn during her retirement years to have a present value of $18,000. The actuary's discount rate is 10%.

Required:
Prepare a schedule that shows the EPBO, the APBO, the service cost, the interest cost, and the postretirement benefit expense for each of the years 2003–2010.

The reconciliation schedules below pertain to the retiree health care plan of Thompson Technologies:

	($ in 000s)	
	2003 Beginning Balances	**2003 Ending Balances**
Accumulated postretirement benefit obligation	$(460)	$(485)
Plan assets	0	75
Funded status	(460)	(410)
Unamortized transition obligation	120	110
Unamortized net gain	(50)	(49)
Accrued postretirement benefit cost	$(390)	$(349)

Thompson began funding the plan in 2003 with a contribution of $127,000 to the pension fund at the end of the year. Retirees were paid $52,000. The actuary's discount rate is 5%. There were no changes in actuarial estimates and assumptions.

Required:
Determine the following amounts for 2003:
1. Service cost
2. Postretirement benefit expense

P 18–5
Postretirement
benefits;
comprehensive

Eastern Transfer and Storage has a postretirement benefit plan. The company adopted *SFAS 106* for the 1994 fiscal year. The APBO at that date was $375 million and the plan was not funded, resulting in a transition obligation of $375 million at the beginning of the year. The transition obligation is to be amortized over the 15-year average remaining service period of plan participants active at the beginning of the year. Eastern began funding at the end of 1994. The discount rate is 8%, and the expected rate of return on plan assets is 10%.

1994 service cost was $23 million, $60 million was contributed to plan assets at the end of the year, and retiree benefit payments were $20 million. Because of changes in assumptions and estimates at the end of 1994, the APBO is determined to be $92 million higher than anticipated.

Required:
1. Determine the APBO at the end of fiscal year 1994.
2. Determine postretirement benefit expense for fiscal year 1994.
3. Prepare the journal entry to record postretirement benefit expense and funding for fiscal year 1994.
4. Prepare a schedule to reconcile the funded status of the plan with the amount reported on the balance sheet for fiscal year 1994.
5. Eastern's 1995 service cost was $32 million, asset contributions were $90 million, retiree benefit payments were $55 million, and the return on plan assets was $5 million. Determine the APBO and plan assets at December 31, 1995.
6. The average remaining service period of plan participants active at the beginning of the 1995 fiscal year was 14 years. Determine the amortization of the unrecognized net loss for 1995.
7. Determine postretirement benefit expense for fiscal year 1995.
8. Prepare the journal entry to record postretirement benefit expense and funding for fiscal year 1995.
9. Prepare a schedule to reconcile the funded status of the plan with the amount reported on the balance sheet for fiscal year 1995.

P 18–6
Stock options; elective
fair value approach and
alternate intrinsic value
approach

On October 15, 2002, the board of directors of Ensor Materials Corporation approved a stock option plan for key executives. On January 1, 2003, 20 million stock options were granted, exercisable for 20 million shares of Ensor's $1 par common stock. The options are exercisable between January 1, 2005, and December 31, 2007, at 80% of the quoted market price on January 1, 2003, which was $15. The fair value of the 20 million options, estimated by an appropriate option pricing model, is $7 per option.

Two million options were forfeited when an executive resigned in 2004. All other options were exercised on July 12, 2006, when the stock's price jumped unexpectedly to $19 per share.

Required:
1. When is Ensor's stock option measurement date if the company chooses to follow the elective fair value approach for fixed compensation plans? Is it different if they choose the alternative intrinsic value approach?
2. Determine the compensation expense, if any, for the stock option plan in 2003 by each of the two approaches. (Ignore taxes.)
3. What is the effect of forfeiture of the stock options on Ensor's financial statements for 2004 by each approach? Why?

P 18–7
Stock option plan;
deferred tax effect
recognized

Walters Audio Visual, Inc. offers a stock option plan to its regional managers. On January 1, 2003, options were granted for 40 million $1 par common shares. The exercise price is the market price on the grant date, $8 per share. Options cannot be exercised prior to January 1, 2005, and expire December 31, 2009. The fair value of the options, estimated by an appropriate option pricing model, is $2 per option. Because the plan does not qualify as an incentive plan, Walters will receive a tax deduction upon exercise of the options equal to the excess of the market price at exercise over the exercise price. The income tax rate is 40%. Walters chooses to follow the elective fair value approach for fixed compensation plans.

Required:
1. Determine the total compensation cost pertaining to the stock option plan.
2. Prepare the appropriate journal entries to record compensation expense and its tax effect on December 31, 2003.
3. Prepare the appropriate journal entries to record compensation expense and its tax effect on December 31, 2004.
4. Record the exercise of the options and their tax effect if *all* of the options are exercised on March 20, 2008, when the market price is $12 per share.
5. Assume the option plan qualifies as an incentive plan. Prepare the appropriate journal entries to record compensation expense and its tax effect on December 31, 2003.
6. Assuming the option plan qualifies as an incentive plan, record the exercise of the options and their tax effect if *all* of the options are exercised on March 20, 2008, when the market price is $11 per share.

P 18–8
Stock option plan;
deferred tax effect of
a nonqualifying plan;
alternate intrinsic value
approach

JBL Aircraft manufactures and distributes aircraft parts and supplies. Employees are offered a variety of stock-based compensation plans. Under its nonqualified stock option plan, JBL granted options to key officers on January 1, 2003. The options permit holders to acquire six million of the company's $1 par common shares for $22 within the next six years, but not before January 1, 2006 (the vesting date). The market price of the shares on the date of grant is $26 per share. The fair value of the 6 million options, estimated by an appropriate option pricing model, is $6 per option. JBL chooses not to follow the elective fair value approach for fixed compensation plans. Because the plan does not qualify as an incentive plan, JBL will receive a tax deduction upon exercise of the options equal to the excess of the market price at exercise over the exercise price. The tax rate is 40%.

Required:
1. Determine the total compensation cost pertaining to the incentive stock option plan.
2. Prepare the appropriate journal entries to record compensation expense and its tax effect on December 31, 2003, 2004, and 2005.
3. Record the exercise of the options and their tax effect if *all* of the options are exercised on August 21, 2007, when the market price is $27 per share.

P 18–9
Performance share plan

LCI Cable Company grants 1 million performance share rights to key executives at January 1, 2003. The rights entitle executives to receive 1 million of TCI $1 par common shares, subject to the achievement of specific financial goals over the next four years. Attainment of these goals is considered probable initially and throughout the service period. LCI does not employ the elective fair value approach for stock-based compensation plans.

The shares have a current market price of $10 per share. The year-end share prices following the grant of the rights are:

2003	$12
2004	$14
2005	$16
2006	$14

Required:

1. Prepare the appropriate entry when the rights are awarded on January 1, 2003.
2. Prepare the appropriate entries on December 31 of each year 2003–2006.
3. Prepare the appropriate entry when the shares are awarded on January 1, 2007.
4. Suppose the performance objectives aren't met. What action should occur on January 1, 2007?

P 18–10
Bonus compensation

Sometimes compensation packages include bonuses designed to provide performance incentives to employees. The difficulty a bonus can cause accountants is not an accounting problem, but a math problem. The complication is that the bonus formula sometimes specifies that the calculation of the bonus is based in part on the bonus itself. This occurs anytime the bonus is a percentage of income because expenses are components of income, and the bonus is an expense.

Regalia Fashions has an incentive compensation plan through which a division manager receives a bonus equal to 10% of the division's net income. Division income in 2003 before the bonus and income tax was $150,000. The tax rate is 30%.

Required:

1. Express the bonus formula as one or more algebraic equation(s).*
2. Using these formulas calculate the amount of the bonus.
3. Prepare the adjusting entry to record the bonus compensation.
4. Bonus arrangements take many forms. Suppose the bonus specifies that the bonus is 10% of the division's income before tax, but after the bonus itself. Calculate the amount of the bonus.

BROADEN YOUR PERSPECTIVE

Apply your critical-thinking ability to the knowledge you've gained. These cases will provide you an opportunity to develop your research, analysis, judgment, and communication skills. You also will work with other students, integrate what you've learned, apply it in real world situations, and consider its global and ethical ramifications. This practice will broaden your knowledge and further develop your decision-making abilities.

Integrating Case 18–1
Postretirement benefits and income taxes

Complying with *SFAS 106*, "Employers' Accounting for Postretirement Benefits Other than Pensions," creates for most companies a temporary difference in connection with income taxation. The difference is due to the fact that the standard requires companies to accrue postretirement benefit expense each year employees perform services, and yet the costs aren't tax-deductible until paid in future years. The following data were available in 1993 when GRE Systems adopted *SFAS 106:*

	($ in millions)
Accumulated postretirement benefit obligation, 1/1/93	$275
Service cost for 1993	43
Interest cost for 1993	32
Benefits paid in 1993 (end of year)	10
Plan assets	0
Average remaining service period	25 years
No unrecognized gains or losses or prior service cost	
No other temporary differences	
Tax rate	40%

Required:

1. Assuming the transition liability is not recognized immediately, what is the postretirement benefit expense for 1993?
2. Indicate the appropriate journal entry to record the 1993 postretirement expense.
3. Assuming taxable income in 1993 is $400 million, indicate the appropriate journal entry to record the 1993 income tax expense.
4. Assuming the transition liability is recognized immediately, indicate the appropriate journal entries to record the 1993 postretirement expense and income tax expense.

---

*Remember when you were studying algebra, and you wondered if you would ever use it?

Integrating Case 18–2
How was the adoption of *SFAS 106* an exception to the usual method of accounting for changes in accounting principle?

In Chapter 3 you learned that most changes in accounting principle require reporting the cumulative income effect of the change as part of earnings in the year of the change. In Chapter 21, you will discover five exceptions that require retroactive restatement of prior years' financial statements. Also, a few changes mandated by new FASB accounting standards require neither of those approaches and instead require or permit prospective application of the new standard. An example of this exception is *SFAS 106,* "Employers' Accounting for Postretirement Benefits Other Than Pensions."

Required:
Explain how *SFAS 106* is an exception to the general method of accounting for changes in accounting principle.

International Case 18–3
Accounting or postretirement benefits in other countries

The primary objective of the International Accounting Standards Committee (IASC) is to narrow worldwide differences in accounting practices and the presentation of financial information. Although the IASC has worked toward uniformity since 1973, harmonization has by no means been achieved. In the area of accounting for postretirement benefits, particularly those other than pensions, significant differences exist from country to country. The differences impact reported earnings and financial position in countries where these benefits are significant.

Required:
1. Locate a recent annual report of a non-U.S. company and determine the way that country accounts for postretirement benefits other than pensions. Include in your analysis:
   a. Whether and how the cost of providing benefits is reported in disclosure notes.
   b. Whether the obligation for the benefits is accrued in the balance sheet.
   c. The impact on the income statement, if any.
2. Prepare a short report highlighting the similarities and differences between the United States and your chosen country in the way postretirement benefits are accounted for.

Research Case 18-4
Researching the way employee benefits are tested on the CPA Exam; retrieving information from the Internet

The board of examiners of the American Institute of Certified Public Accountants (AICPA) is responsible for preparing the CPA examination. The boards of accountancy of all 50 states, the District of Columbia, Guam, Puerto Rico, and the U.S. Virgin Islands use the examination as the primary way to measure the technical competence of CPA candidates. The content for each examination section is specified by the AICPA and described in outline form.

Required:
1. Access the AICPA web site on the Internet. The web address is **www.aicpa.org**.
2. Access the CPA exam section within the site. Locate the content specification portion of the section. Which topics pertaining to employee benefits are specifically listed as testable items on the exam?
3. In which of the four separately graded sections of the exam are employee benefits tested?
4. From the AICPA site, access the Board of Accounting for your state. What are the education requirements in your state to sit for the CPA exam?

Analysis Case 18–5
Reporting postretirement benefits
FedEx Corporation

Refer to the financial statements and related disclosure notes of FedEx Corporation in the appendix to Chapter 1.

Required:
1. What types of postretirement benefits other than pensions does FedEx provide its retirees? What are the eligibility requirements?
2. When FedEx adopted *SFAS 106,* did it choose to expense the transition cost immediately or over the average service life of employees?
3. Is the postretirement benefit plan funded? Explain.

Real World Case 18–6
Restricted stock plan; Dell computer

Dell Computer is the world's leading computer systems company and a provider of related products and services. Compensation to executives is provided in the form of a variety of incentive compensation plans including restricted stock award grants. The following is an excerpt from a disclosure note from Dell's 2001 annual report:

> **Restricted Stock Grants**—During fiscal years 2001, 2000, and 1999, the Company granted 1.7 million shares, 1.4 million shares, and 1 million shares, respectively, of restricted stock. For substantially all restricted stock grants, at the date of grant, the recipient has all rights of a stockholder, subject to certain restrictions on transferability and a risk of forfeiture. Restricted shares typically vest over a seven-year period beginning on the date of grant.

Required:
1. What is the "incentive" provided by Dell's restricted stock grants?
2. If the fair value of Dell's stock at dates of grant was $37.06, $40, and $28 per share granted during fiscal years 2001, 2000, and 1999, respectively, what is the compensation expense in 2001 pertaining to the three stock awards? Explain.

Trueblood Accounting Case 18–7
Stock compensation arrangements; impact of modifications

The following Trueblood case is recommended for use with this chapter. The case provides an excellent opportunity for class discussion, group projects, and writing assignments. The case, along with Professor's Discussion Material, can be obtained from the Deloitte Foundation at its website: **www.deloitte.com/more/DTF/cases_subj.htm**.

Case 00-1: *Mini-Options*

This case gives students the opportunity to evaluate the accounting impact of modifications to a stock compensation plan.

Communication Case 18–8
Stock options; basic concepts; prepare a memo

You are Assistant Controller of Stamos & Company, a medium-size manufacturer of machine parts. On October 22, 2002, the board of directors approved a stock option plan for key executives. On January 1, 2003, a specific number of stock options were granted. The options were exercisable between January 1, 2005, and December 31, 2007, at 100% of the quoted market price at the grant date. The service period is for 2003 through 2005. The board is considering opting for the elective fair value approach.

Your boss, the controller, is one of the executives to receive options. Neither he nor you have had occasion to deal with the FASB pronouncement on accounting for stock options. He and you are aware of the traditional approach that can be chosen as an alternative but do not know the newer method. Your boss understands how options might benefit him personally but wants to be aware also of how the options will be reported in the financial statements. He has asked you for a one-page synopsis of accounting for stock options under the elective fair value approach. He instructed you, "I don't care about the effect on taxes or earnings per share—just the basics, please."

Required:
Prepare such a report that includes the following:
1. At what point should the compensation cost be measured? How should it be measured?
2. How should compensation expense be measured for the stock option plan in 2003 and later?
3. If options are forfeited because an executive resigns before vesting, what is the effect of that forfeiture of the stock options on the financial statements?
4. If options are forfeited because they are allowed to lapse after vesting, what is the effect of that forfeiture of the stock options on the financial statements?
5. What is the primary difference between the elective fair value approach and the alternative intrinsic value approach?

Real World Case 18–9
Stock options; Delta Airlines

The following disclosure note appeared in the Delta Airlines' annual report for 2000.

15. Stock Options and Awards
The following table summarizes all stock option activity during 2000, 1999 and 1998:

Stock Options	2000 Shares (000)	2000 Weighted Average Exercise Price	1999 Shares (000)	1999 Weighted Average Exercise Price	1998 Shares (000)	1998 Weighted Average Exercise Price
Outstanding at beginning of year	47,859	$48	47,663	$47	31,892	$43
Granted	3,914	52	3,395	58	20,896	51
Exercised	(725)	41	(2,410)	44	(4,955)	34
Forfeited	(683)	53	(789)	49	(170)	50
Outstanding at end of year	50,365	48	47,859	48	47,663	47
Stock options exercisable at year end	46,309	$48	44,615	$47	27,557	$44

The following table summarizes information about stock options outstanding and exercisable at December 31, 2000:

	Stock Options Outstanding			Stock Options Exercisable	
Range of Exercise Prices	Number Outstanding (000)	Weighted Average Remaining Life (Years)	Weighted Average Exercise Price	Number Exercisable (000)	Weighted Average Exercise Price
$26–$34	211	4	$26	211	$26
$35–$41	7,580	6	35	7,580	35
$42–$63	42,574	7	51	38,518	51

The estimated fair values of stock options granted in 2000, 1999 and 1998 were derived using the Black-Scholes stock option pricing model. The exercise price for stock options is the fair market value of the common stock on the grant date.

The following table shows what our net income and earnings per share would have been for 2000, 1999, and 1998 had we accounted for our stock option plans under the fair value method of SFAS 123, "Accounting for Stock-Based Compensation:"

(In Millions)	2000	1999	1998
Net income:			
As reported	**$828**	**$1,208**	**$1,078**
As adjusted for the fair value method under SFAS 123	801	1,147	994
Basic earnings per share:			
As reported	**$6.58**	**$8.66**	**$7.22**
As adjusted for the fair value method under SFAS 123	6.36	8.23	6.66
Diluted earnings per share:			
As reported	**$6.28**	**$8.15**	**$6.87**
As adjusted for the fair value method under SFAS 123	6.07	7.75	6.42

Required:

1. What amount of compensation expense does Delta's income statement report related to the stock options for 3,914 shares the company granted in 2000? Why?
2. What is the most likely reason that options for 683 shares were forfeited in 2000?
3. If Delta had followed the FASB's recommended fair value approach, what amount of compensation expense would it have recorded related to stock options? Why?

Judgment Case 18–10
Paid future absences

Cates Computing Systems develops and markets commercial software for personal computers and workstations. Three situations involving compensation for possible future absences of Cates' employees are described below.

a. Cates compensates employees at their regular pay rate for time absent for military leave, maternity leave, and jury time. Employees are allowed predetermined absence periods for each type of absence.
b. Members of the new product development team are eligible for three months' paid sabbatical leave every four years. Five members of the team have just completed their fourth year of participation.
c. Company policy permits employees four paid sick days each year. Unused sick days can accumulate and can be carried forward to future years.

Required:

1. What are the conditions that require accrual of an expense and related liability for employees' compensation for future absences?
2. For each of the three situations, indicate the circumstances under which accrual of an expense and related liability is warranted.

Ethics Case 18–11
Stock options

You are in your second year as an auditor with Dantly and Regis, a regional CPA firm. One of the firm's long-time clients is Mayberry-Cleaver Industries, a national company involved in the manufacturing, marketing, and sales of hydraulic devices used in specialized manufacturing applications. Early in this year's audit you discover that Mayberry-Cleaver has changed its method of determining inventory from LIFO to FIFO. Your client's explanation is that FIFO is consistent with the method used by some other companies in the industry. Upon further investigation, you discover an executive stock option plan whose terms call for a significant increase in the shares available to executives if net income this year exceeds $44 million. Some quick calculations convince you that without the change in inventory methods, the target will not be reached; with the change, it will.

Required:

Do you perceive an ethical dilemma? What would be the likely impact of following the controller's suggestions? Who would benefit? Who would be injured?

Communication Case 18–12

Should the present two-category distinction between liabilities and equity be retained? group interaction.

The current conceptual distinction between liabilities and equity defines liabilities independently of assets and equity, with equity defined as a residual amount. The present proliferation of financial instruments that combine features of both debt and equity and the difficulty of drawing a distinction have led many to conclude that the present two-category distinction between liabilities and equity be eliminated. Two opposing viewpoints are:

View 1: The distinction should be maintained.
View 2: The distinction should be eliminated and financial instruments should instead be reported in accordance with the priority of their claims to enterprise assets.

One type of security that often is mentioned in the debate is mandatorily redeemable preferred stock. Although stock in many ways, such a security also obligates the issuer to transfer assets at a specified price and redemption date. Thus it also has features of debt. In considering this question, focus on conceptual issues regarding the practicable and theoretically appropriate treatment, unconstrained by GAAP.

Required:

1. Which view do you favor? Develop a list of arguments in support of your view prior to the class session for which the case is assigned.
2. In class, your instructor will pair you (and everyone else) with a classmate (who also has independently developed an argument).
   a. You will be given three minutes to argue your view to your partner. Your partner likewise will be given three minutes to argue his or her view to you. During these three-minute presentations, the listening partner is not permitted to speak.
   b. Then after each person has had a turn attempting to convince his or her partner, the two partners will have a three-minute discussion in which they will decide which view is more convincing and arguments will be merged into a single view for each pair.
3. After the allotted time, a spokesperson for each of the two views will be selected by the instructor. Each spokesperson will field arguments from the class in support of that view's position and list the arguments on the board. The class then will discuss the merits of the two lists of arguments and attempt to reach a consensus view, though a consensus is not necessary.

Trueblood Accounting Case 18–13

Stock options' granting at time of an IPO

The following Trueblood case is recommended for use with this chapter. The case provides an excellent opportunity for class discussion, group projects, and writing assignments. The case, along with Professor's Discussion Material, can be obtained from the Deloitte Foundation at its website: **www.deloitte.com/more/DTF/cases_subj.htm**.

Case 00-1: *Dirt Cheap*

This case gives students the opportunity to evaluate the accounting impact of granting stock options at the time of a company's initial offering of stock.

Real World Case 18–14

Stock options; Boeing Company

The Boeing Company is one of the world's major aerospace firms. The Company operates in three principal segments: commercial airplanes, military aircraft and missiles, and space and communications. The following is an excerpt from a disclosure note from Boeing's 2000 annual report:

> **Stock Options (in part)**
> ($ in millions)
> The Company's 1997 Incentive Stock Plan permits the grant of stock options, stock appreciation rights (SARs), and restricted stock awards (denominated in stock or stock units) to any employee of the Company or its subsidiaries and contract employees. Options and SARs have been granted with an exercise price equal to the fair market value of the Company's stock on the date of grant and expire ten years after the grant date.
>
> Information concerning stock options issued to directors, officers and other employees is presented in the following table.

(Shares in thousands)	2000 Shares	Weighted Average Exercise Price	1999 Shares	Weighted Average Exercise Price	1998 Shares	Weighted Average Exercise Price
Number of shares under option:						
Outstanding at beginning of year	29,228	$38.02	28,653	$36.03	27,705	$32.36
Granted	3,693	45.63	3,462	43.40	3,772	52.72
Exercised	(4,673)	28.30	(2,345)	22.03	(2,493)	20.77
Canceled or expired	(328)	46.20	(515)	39.33	(255)	46.35
Exercised as SARs	(16)	21.56	(27)	19.70	(76)	19.27
Outstanding at end of year	27,904	40.58	29,228	38.02	28,653	36.03
Exercisable at end of year	18,710	$37.32	19,749	$34.58	15,577	$29.57

The Company recognized share-based expense of $41, $35 and $31 in 2000, 1999, and 1998, respectively, attributable to stock options with an offset to additional paid-in capital.

Required:
1. For its stock options, does Boeing follow the FASB's elective fair value approach or the alternative *APB 23* approach? Explain.
2. Based on the information provided in the note, what was the average fair value of the options Boeing granted during 2000? Explain.

Research Case 18-15 Effect of accounting for stock options on firm performance; research article in *Accounting Horizons*

The FASB advocates recognizing stock options at fair value. In their article "Stock Option Expense: The Sword of Damocles Revealed," Professors Christine Botosan and Marlene Plumlee investigate the effect of stock option expense on performance measures for 100 firms.

Required:
1. In your library or from some other source, locate the indicated article in *Accounting Horizons*, December 2001.
2. Which firms did the authors choose to investigate? Why?
3. How many of the sample firms elected to record the fair value of stock option expense in their income statements?
4. In year 3 of the study, what were the median and mean percentage reductions in diluted earnings per share due to stock option expense?

19

CHAPTER

Shareholders' Equity

OVERVIEW

We turn our attention from liabilities, which represent the creditors' interests in the assets of a corporation, to the shareholders' residual interest in those assets. The discussions distinguish between the two basic sources of shareholders' equity: (1) *invested* capital and (2) *earned* capital. We explore the expansion of corporate capital through the issuance of shares and the contraction caused by the retirement of shares or the purchase of treasury shares. In our discussions of retained earnings, we examine cash dividends, property dividends, stock dividends, and stock splits.

LEARNING OBJECTIVES

After studying this chapter, you should be able to:

LO1 Describe the components of shareholders' equity and explain how they are reported.

LO2 Prepare a statement of shareholders' equity and explain its usefulness.

LO3 Record the issuance of shares when sold for cash, for noncash consideration, and by share purchase contract.

LO4 Describe what occurs when shares are retired and how the retirement is recorded.

LO5 Distinguish between accounting for retired shares and for treasury shares.

LO6 Describe retained earnings and distinguish it from paid-in capital.

LO7 Explain the basis of corporate dividends, including the similarities and differences between cash and property dividends.

LO8 Explain stock dividends and stock splits and how they are accounted for.

FINANCIAL REPORTING CASE

GE

Finally, you have some uninterrupted time to get back on the net. Earlier today you noticed on the Internet that the market price of GE's common stock was up almost $4 a share. You've been eager to look into why, but have had one meeting after another all day.

You've been a stockholder of GE since the beginning of the year and a customer of its home appliances for several years now. The dividends of 16 cents a share that you get quarterly are nice, but that's not why you bought the stock; you were convinced at the time that the stock price was poised to rise rapidly. That hasn't really happened. There has been no real news from the company since the three-for-one split of common stock back in May of last year.

A few well-placed clicks of the mouse and you come across the following news article:

FAIRFIELD, Conn—The Board of Directors of GE today raised the Company's quarterly dividend 13% to $0.18 per outstanding share of its common stock and increased its share repurchase program to $30 billion from $22 billion.

"GE has paid a dividend every year since 1899," said GE Chairman and CEO Jeff Immelt. "Today's increases, in both our dividend and our share repurchase program, signal our confidence in our ability to extend this track record of returning value to shareowners."

The dividend increase, from $0.16 per share, marks the 26th consecutive year in which GE has increased its dividend. The dividend is payable January 25, 2002, to shareowners of record on December 31, 2001. The ex-dividend date is December 27.

In the seven years since the share repurchase program was begun, GE has purchased more than 1 billion shares for $20.6 billion.

Source: "GE Raises Dividend for 26th Consecutive Year and Increases Share Repurchase Program," *Business Wire*, December 14, 2001.

> By the time you finish this chapter, you should be able to respond appropriately to the questions posed in this case. Compare your response to the solution provided at the end of the chapter.

QUESTIONS

1. Do you think the stock price increase is related to GE's share repurchase plan? (page 953)

2. What are GE's choices in accounting for the share repurchases? (page 954)

3. What effect does the quarterly cash dividend of 18 cents a share have on GE's assets? Its liabilities? Its shareholders' equity? (page 960)

4. What effect did the stock split have on GE's assets? Its liabilities? Its shareholders' equity? (page 963)

LO1

THE NATURE OF SHAREHOLDERS' EQUITY

A corporation raises money to fund its business operations by some mix of debt and equity financing. In earlier chapters, we examined debt financing in the form of notes, bonds, leases, and other liabilities. Amounts representing those liabilities denote *creditors' interest* in the company's assets. Now we focus on various forms of equity financing. Specifically, in this chapter we consider transactions that affect shareholders' equity—those accounts that represent the *ownership interests* of shareholders.

In principle, shareholders' equity is a relatively straightforward concept. Shareholders' equity is a residual amount—what's left over after creditor claims have been subtracted from assets (in other words, net assets). You probably recall the residual nature of shareholders' equity from the basic accounting equation:

Net assets equal shareholders' equity.

$$\underbrace{\text{Assets} - \text{Liabilities}}_{\text{Net Assets}} = \text{Shareholders' equity}$$

Ownership interests of shareholders arise primarily from two sources: (1) amounts *invested* by shareholders in the corporation and (2) amounts *earned* by the corporation on behalf of its shareholders. These two sources are reported as (1) paid-in capital and (2) retained earnings.

Shareholders' equity accounts denote the *ownership interests* of shareholders.

Despite being a seemingly clear-cut concept, shareholders' equity and its component accounts often are misunderstood and misinterpreted. As we explore the transactions that affect shareholders' equity and its component accounts, try not to allow yourself to be overwhelmed by unfamiliar terminology or to be overly concerned with precise account titles. Terminology pertaining to shareholders' equity accounts is notoriously diverse. To give you one example—retained earnings is reported variously as *retained income* (NACCO Industries), *reinvested earnings* (Consolidated Papers), *earnings reinvested in the business* (The New York Times Company), *earnings retained for use in the business* (Armada Corporation), *retained earnings reinvested and employed in the business* (L.S. Starret Company), and *accumulated earnings employed in the business* (Outboard Marine). Every shareholders' equity account has several aliases. Indeed, shareholders' equity itself is often referred to as *stockholders' equity, shareowners' equity, shareholders' investment,* and many other similar titles.

GAAP permits many choices in accounting for transactions affecting shareholders' equity.

Complicating matters, transactions that affect shareholders' equity are influenced by corporation laws of individual states in which companies are located. And, as we see later, generally accepted accounting principles provide companies with considerable latitude when choosing accounting methods in this area.

Keeping this perspective in mind while you study the chapter should aid you in understanding the essential concepts. At a very basic level, each transaction we examine can be viewed simply as an increase or decrease in shareholders' equity, per se, without regard to specific shareholders' equity accounts. In fact, for a business organized as a single proprietorship, all capital changes are recorded in a single owner's equity account. The same concepts apply to a corporation. But for corporations, additional considerations make it desirable to separate owners' equity into several separate shareholders' equity accounts. These additional considerations—legal requirements and disclosure objectives—are discussed in following sections of this chapter. So, as you study the separate effects of transactions on retained earnings and specific paid-in capital accounts, you may find it helpful to ask yourself frequently "What is the net effect of this transaction on shareholders' equity?" or, equivalently, "By how much are net assets (assets minus liabilities) affected by this transaction?"

Legal requirements and disclosure objectives make it preferable to separate a corporation's capital into several separate shareholders' equity accounts.

Financial Reporting Overview

Before we examine the events that underlie specific shareholders' equity accounts, let's overview how individual accounts relate to each other. The condensed balance sheet of Exposition Corporation, a hypothetical company, in Graphic 19–1 provides that perspective.

EXPOSITION CORPORATION
Balance Sheet
December 31, 2003

($ in millions)

Assets minus Liabilities *equals* Shareholders' Equity.

Assets
$3,000

Liabilities
$1,000

Shareholders' Equity

Paid-in capital:

Capital stock (par):		
Preferred stock, 10%, $10 par, cumulative, nonparticipating	$100	
Common stock, $1 par	55	
Common stock dividends distributable	5	
Additional paid-in capital:		
Paid-in capital—excess of par, common	300	
Paid-in capital—excess of par, preferred	50	
Receivable from share purchase contract	(40)	
Paid-in capital—reacquired shares	8	
Paid-in capital—conversion of bonds	7	
Paid-in capital—stock options	9	
Paid-in capital—stock award plan	5	
Paid-in capital—lapse of stock options	1	
Total paid-in capital		$ 500
Retained Earnings (Note A)		1,670
Accumulated other comprehensive income:		
Net unrealized gains (losses) on investment securities	(85)	
Minimum pension liability adjustment	(75)	
Deferred gains (losses) on derivatives*	(4)	
Foreign currency translation adjustments†	–0–	(164)
Treasury stock (at cost)		(6)
Total shareholders' equity		$2,000

The primary source of paid-in capital is the investment made by shareholders when buying preferred and common stock.

Several other events affect paid-in capital.

Retained earnings represents earned capital.

Note A: Assets represented by $300 million of retained earnings are restricted from distribution as dividends in order to facilitate expansion of manufacturing facilities.

*Gains or losses from changes in foreign currency exchange rates. This item is discussed elsewhere in your accounting curriculum. The amount could be an addition to or reduction in shareholders' equity. Also see the Global Perspective on page 940.
†When a derivative designated as a cash flow hedge is adjusted to fair value, the gain or loss is deferred as a component of comprehensive income and included in earnings later, at the same time as earnings are affected by the hedged transaction (described in the text Addendum).

Graphic 19–1 depicts a rather comprehensive situation. It's unlikely that any one company would have shareholders' equity from all of these sources at any one time. Remember that, at this point, our objective is only to get a general perspective of the items constituting shareholders' equity. You should, however, note a few aspects of the statement shown in Graphic 19–1. First, the four components of Exposition Corporation's shareholders' equity are paid-in capital, retained earnings, accumulated other comprehensive income, and treasury stock.

PAID-IN CAPITAL

Paid-in capital consists primarily of amounts invested by shareholders when they purchase shares of stock from the corporation. In addition, amounts sometimes are invested (or disinvested) by others on behalf of the shareholders. For Exposition Corporation, shareholders invested $470 million ($100 + 55 + 5 + 300 + 50 − $40). An additional $30 million

The two primary components of shareholders' equity are *paid-in capital* and *retained earnings*.

GLOBAL PERSPECTIVE

Ours is truly a global economy. Most large U.S. companies are, in fact, multinational companies that may derive only a fraction of their revenues in this country. As a result, many operations are located abroad and foreign operations frequently are denominated in the currency of the foreign country (Japanese yen, Swiss franc, Euro, and so on). When exchange rates change, the dollar equivalent of the foreign currency changes.

Currency rate changes that affect cash flows because they require settlement in a currency other than the entity's functional currency result in transaction adjustments. These are reported as gains and losses in the earnings of the period the changes occur. Those that do not require settlement and thus don't affect cash flows are translation adjustments. These are accumulated in a separate component of shareholders' equity: Foreign currency translation adjustments.

($8 + 7 + 9 + 5 + 1) of paid-in capital arose from financing activities, bringing the total to $500 million. Later in this chapter, we consider in more detail the events and transactions that affect paid-in capital.

RETAINED EARNINGS

Retained earnings is reported as a single amount, $1,670 million, but a disclosure note provides additional information about a specific restriction on dividends.

ACCUMULATED OTHER COMPREHENSIVE INCOME

Some accounts can be viewed as contra-shareholders' equity accounts.

Also notice that shareholders' equity of Exposition Corporation is adjusted for three events that are not included in net income and so don't affect retained earnings but are part of "other comprehensive income" and therefore are included as separate components of shareholders' equity.[1] **Comprehensive income** is a more expansive view of the change in shareholders' equity than traditional net income. It is the total *nonowner* change in equity for a reporting period. In fact, it encompasses all changes in equity other than those from transactions with owners. Transactions between the corporation and its shareholders primarily include dividends and the sale or purchase of shares of the company's stock. Most nonowner changes are reported in the income statement. So, the changes other than those that are part of traditional net income are the ones reported as "other comprehensive income." Two attributes of other comprehensive income are reported: (1) components of comprehensive income *created during the reporting period* and (2) the comprehensive income *accumulated* over the current and prior periods.

The first of these—components of comprehensive income *created during the reporting period*—can be reported either as (a) an additional section of the income statement, (b) part of the statement of shareholders' equity, or (c) a separate statement, usually included in the financial statements in a disclosure note. Regardless of the placement a company chooses, the presentation is similar. It will report net income, other components of comprehensive income, and total comprehensive income, similar to the presentation in Graphic 19–2 on the next page. Note that each component is reported net of its related income tax expense or income tax benefit.

The second measure—the comprehensive income *accumulated* over the current and prior periods—is reported as a separate component of shareholders' equity, similar to the presentation by Exposition Corporation in Graphic 19-1. Note that amounts reported here—accumulated other comprehensive income—represent the *cumulative* sum of the changes in each component created during each reporting period (Graphic 19–2) throughout all prior years.

TREASURY STOCK

We discuss the final component of shareholders' equity—treasury stock—later in the chapter. It indicates that some of the shares previously sold were bought back by the corporation from shareholders.

---

[1]Comprehensive income was introduced in Chapter 4.

GRAPHIC 19–2
Comprehensive income

	($ in millions)	
Net income		$xxx
Other comprehensive income:		
Net unrealized holding gains (losses) on investments (net of tax)*	$x	
Minimum pension liability adjustment (net of tax)†	(x)	
Deferred gain (loss) from derivatives (net of tax)‡	x	
Foreign currency translation adjustments (net of tax)§	x	xx
Comprehensive income		$xxx

Comprehensive income includes all changes in shareholders' equity except transactions between the corporation and its shareholders.

*Changes in the market value of securities available for sale (described in Chapter 12).
†Reporting a pension liability sometimes requires a reduction in shareholders' equity (described in Chapter 17).
‡When a derivative designated as a cash flow hedge is adjusted to fair value, the gain or loss is deferred as a component of comprehensive income and included in earnings later, at the same time as earnings are affected by the hedged transaction (described in the Derivatives Addendum to the text).
§Gains or losses from changes in foreign currency exchange rates. The amount could be an addition to or reduction in shareholders' equity. (This item is discussed elsewhere in your accounting curriculum.)

You seldom if ever will see this degree of detail reported in the presentation of paid-in capital. Instead, companies keep track of individual additional paid-in capital accounts in company records but ordinarily report these amounts as a single subtotal—additional paid-in capital. Pertinent rights and privileges of various securities outstanding such as dividend and liquidation preferences, call and conversion information, and voting rights are summarized in disclosure notes.[2] The shareholders' equity portion of the balance sheet of Gateway, Inc., shown in Graphic 19–3 is a typical presentation format.

Ordinarily, less detail is reported than is kept in company records.

GRAPHIC 19–3
Typical Presentation Format—Gateway, Inc.

GATEWAY, INC.
Balance Sheet
[Shareholders' Equity Section]
(in 000s)

	2000	1999
Stockholders'equity:		
Preferred stock, $.01 par value, 5,000 shares authorized; none issued and outstanding	—	—
Class A common stock, nonvoting, $.01 par value, 1,000 shares authorized; none issued and outstanding	—	—
Common stock, $.01 par value, 1,000,000 shares authorized; 323,955 shares and 320,016 shares issued in 2000 and 1999, respectively	$ 3,239,000	$ 3,200,000
Additional paid-in capital	741,646,000	656,870,000
Retained earnings	1,650,335,000	1,408,852,000
Accumulated other comprehensive income (loss)	7,067,000	(8,000)
Common stock in treasury, at cost, 552 shares and 730 shares in 2000 and 1999, respectively	(21,948,000)	(51,796,000)
Total stockholders' equity	$2,380,339,000	$2,017,118,000

Details of each class of stock are reported on the face of the balance sheet or in disclosure notes.

---

[2]"Disclosure of Information about Capital Structure," *Statement of Financial Accounting Standards No. 129* (Norwalk, Conn.: FASB, 1997).

The balance sheet reports annual balances of shareholders' equity accounts. However, companies also should disclose the sources of the changes in those accounts.[3] This is the purpose of the **statement of shareholders' equity.** To illustrate, Graphic 19–4 shows how Gateway, Inc. reported the changes in its shareholders' equity balances (shown in Graphic 19–3).

The changes that Gateway's statements of shareholders' equity reveal are net income and two other items of comprehensive income, the purchase of treasury stock and the issuance of common stock.

The Corporate Organization

A company may be organized in any of three ways: (1) a single proprietorship, (2) a partnership, or (3) a corporation. In your introductory accounting course, you studied each form. In this course we focus exclusively on the corporate form of organization.

Most well-known companies, such as Microsoft, IBM, and General Motors, are corporations. Also, many smaller companies—even one-owner businesses—are corporations. Although fewer in number than proprietorships and partnerships, in terms of business volume, corporations are the predominant form of business organization.

In most respects, transactions are accounted for in the same way regardless of the form of business organization. Assets and liabilities are unaffected by the way a company is organized. The exception is the method of accounting for capital, the ownership interest in the company. Rather than recording all changes in ownership interests in a single capital account for each owner, as we do for single proprietorships and partnerships, we use the several capital accounts overviewed in the previous section to record those changes for a corporation. Before discussing how we account for specific ownership changes, let's look at the characteristics of a corporation that make this form of organization distinctive and require special accounting treatment.

LIMITED LIABILITY

The owners are not personally liable for debts of a corporation. Unlike a proprietorship or a partnership, a corporation is a separate legal entity, responsible for its own debts. Shareholders' liability is limited to the amounts they invest in the company when they purchase shares (unless the shareholder also is an officer of the corporation). The limited liability of shareholders is perhaps the single most important advantage of corporate organization. In other forms of business, creditors may look to the personal assets of owners for satisfaction of business debt.

EASE OF RAISING CAPITAL

A corporation is better suited to raising capital than is a proprietorship or a partnership. All companies may raise capital by operating at a profit or by borrowing. However, attracting equity capital is easier for a corporation. Because corporations sell ownership interest in the form of shares of stock, ownership rights are easily transferred. An investor can sell his/her ownership interest at any time and without affecting the corporation or its operations.

From the viewpoint of a potential investor, another favorable aspect of investing in a corporation is the lack of mutual agency. Individual partners in a partnership have the power to bind the business to a contract. Therefore, an investor in a partnership must be careful regarding the character and business savvy of fellow co-owners. On the other hand, shareholders' participation in the affairs of a corporation is limited to voting at shareholders' meetings (unless the shareholder also is a manager). Consequently, a shareholder needn't exercise the same degree of care that partners must in selecting co-owners.

Obviously, then, a corporation offers advantages over the other forms of organization, particularly in its ability to raise investment capital. As you might guess, though, these benefits do not come without a price.

---

[3]"Omnibus Opinion," *APB Opinion No. 12* (New York: AICPA, 1967).

GRAPHIC 19–4 Changes in Shareholders' Equity—Gateway, Inc.

GATEWAY, INC.
Consolidated Statements of Changes in Shareholders' Equity and
Comprehensive Income for the Years Ended December 31, 2000, 1999, and 1998
($ in 000)

	Common Shares	Stock Amount	Additional Paid-in Capital	Treasury Stock	Retained Earnings	Accumulated Other Comprehensive Income (Loss)	Total
Balances at December 31, 1997	308,256	$3,080	$297,944	$ —	$ 634,509	$(5,489)	$ 930,044
Comprehensive income:							
Net income	—	—	—	—	346,399	—	346,399
Other comprehensive income:							
Foreign currency translation	—	—	—	—	—	1,549	1,549
Unrealized gain on available-for-sale securities	—	—	—	—	—	(145)	(145)
Comprehensive income							347,803
Stock issuances under employee plans	4,846	49	65,879	—	—	—	65,928
Stock issued to officer	36	2	598	—	—	—	600
Balances at December 31, 1998	313,138	3,131	364,421	—	980,908	(4,085)	1,344,375
Comprehensive income:							
Net income	—	—	—	—	427,944	—	427,944
Other comprehensive income:							
Foreign currency translation	—	—	—	—	—	4,941	4,941
Unrealized gain on available-for-sale securities	—	—	—	—	—	(864)	(864)
Comprehensive income							432,021
Purchase of treasury stock	—	—	—	(122,580)	—	—	(122,580)
Stock issuances under employee plans	4,153	42	92,476	70,784	—	—	163,302
Issuance of common stock	2,725	27	199,973	—	—	—	200,000
Balances at December 31, 1999	320,016	3,200	656,870	(51,796)	1,408,852	(8)	2,017,118
Comprehensive income:							
Net income	—	—	—	—	241,483	—	241,483
Other comprehensive income:							
Foreign currency translation	—	—	—	—	—	(732)	(732)
Unrealized gain on available-for-sale securities	—	—	—	—	—	7,807	7,807
Comprehensive income							248,558
Purchase of treasury stock	—	—	—	(58,992)	—	—	(58,992)
Stock issuances under employee plans	3,371	34	50,577	88,840	—	—	139,451
Issuance of common stock	568	5	34,199	—	—	—	34,204
Balances at December 31, 2000	323,955	3,239	741,646	(21,948)	1,650,335	7,067	2,380,339

DISADVANTAGES

Paperwork! To protect the rights of those who buy a corporation's stock or who loan money to a corporation, the state in which the company is incorporated and the federal government

Corporations are subject to expensive government regulation.

impose expensive reporting requirements. Primarily the required paperwork is intended to ensure adequate disclosure of information needed by investors and creditors.

You read earlier that corporations are separate legal entities. As such, they also are separate taxable entities. Often this causes what is referred to as *double taxation*. Corporations first pay income taxes on their earnings. Then, when those earnings are distributed as cash dividends, shareholders pay personal income taxes on the previously taxed earnings. Proprietorships and partnerships are not taxed at the business level; each owner's share of profits is taxed only as personal income.

Corporations create double taxation

TYPES OF CORPORATIONS

When referring to corporations in this text, we are referring to corporations formed by private individuals for the purpose of generating profits. These corporations raise capital by selling stock. There are, however, other types of corporations.

Some corporations such as churches, hospitals, universities, and charities do not sell stock and are not organized for profit. Also, some not-for-profit corporations are government-owned—the Federal Deposit Insurance Corporation (FDIC), for instance. Accounting for not-for-profit corporations is discussed elsewhere in the accounting curriculum.

Not-for-profit corporations may be owned:
1. By the public sector.
2. By a governmental unit.

Corporations organized for profit may be:
1. Publicly held and traded:
   a. On an exchange.
   b. Over-the-counter.
2. Privately held.

Corporations organized for profit may be publicly held or privately (or closely) held. The stock of publicly held corporations is available for purchase by the general public. You can buy shares of General Electric, Ford Motor Company, or ExxonMobil through a stockbroker. These shares are traded on the New York Stock Exchange. Other publicly held stock, like Intel and Microsoft, are not listed on a national exchange but are available over-the-counter from securities dealers, organized through Nasdaq (National Association of Securities Dealers Automated Quotations).

On the other hand, shares of privately held companies are owned by only a few individuals (perhaps a family) and are not available to the general public. Corporations whose stock is privately held do not need to register those shares with the Securities and Exchange Commission and are spared the voluminous, annual reporting requirements of the SEC. Of course, new sources of equity financing are limited when shares are privately held, as is the market for selling existing shares.

Privately held companies' shares are held by only a few individuals and are not available to the general public.

Frequently, companies begin as smaller, privately held corporations. Then as success broadens opportunities for expansion, the corporation goes public. For example, in 1999 UPS (United Parcel Service), competitor of Federal Express, decided to take public the privately held company. The result was one of the largest initial public offerings ever.

HYBRID ORGANIZATIONS

A corporation can elect to comply with a special set of tax rules and be designated an **S corporation.** S corporations have characteristics of both regular corporations and partnerships. Owners have the limited liability protection of a corporation, but income and expenses are passed through to the owners as in a partnership, avoiding double taxation.

Two relatively recent business structures have evolved in response to liability issues and tax treatment—limited liability companies and limited liability partnerships.

A **limited liability company** offers several advantages. Owners are not liable for the debts of the business, except to the extent of their investment. Unlike a limited partnership, all members of a limited liability company can be involved with managing the business without losing liability protection. Like an S corporation, income and expenses are passed through to the owners as in a partnership, avoiding double taxation, but there are no limitations on the number of owners as in an S corporation.

A **limited liability partnership** is similar to a limited liability company, except it doesn't offer all the liability protection available in the limited liability company structure. Partners are liable for their own actions but not entirely liable for the actions of other partners.

THE MODEL BUSINESS CORPORATION ACT

Corporations are formed in accordance with the corporation laws of individual states. State laws are not uniform, but share many similarities, thanks to the widespread adoption of the

Model Business Corporation Act.[4] This act is designed to serve as a guide to states in the development of their corporation statutes. It presently serves as the model for the majority of states.

State laws regarding the nature of shares that can be authorized, the issuance and repurchase of those shares, and conditions for distributions to shareholders obviously influence actions of corporations. Naturally, differences among state laws affect how we account for many of the shareholders' equity transactions discussed in this chapter. For that reason, we will focus on the normal case, as described by the Model Business Corporation Act, and note situations where variations in state law might require different accounting. Your goal is not to learn diverse procedures caused by peculiarities of state laws, but to understand the broad concepts of accounting for shareholders' equity that can be applied to any specific circumstance.

The process of incorporating a business is similar in all states. The **articles of incorporation** (sometimes called the *corporate charter*) describe (a) the nature of the firm's business activities, (b) the shares to be issued, and (c) the composition of the initial **board of directors.** The board of directors establishes corporate policies and appoints officers who manage the corporation.

At least some of the shares authorized by the articles of incorporation are sold at the inception of the corporation. Frequently, the initial shareholders include members of the board of directors or officers (who may be one and the same). Ultimately, it is the corporation's shareholders that control the company. Shareholders are the owners of the corporation. By voting their shares, it is they who determine the makeup of the board of directors—who in turn appoint officers, who in turn manage the company.

Shareholders' investment in a corporation ordinarily is referred to as paid-in capital. In the next section, we examine the methods normally used to maintain records of shareholders' investment and to report such paid-in capital in financial statements.

> The *Model Business Corporation Act* serves as the model for the corporation statutes of most states.

> Variations among state laws influence GAAP pertaining to shareholders' equity transactions.

PAID-IN CAPITAL

PART

b

Fundamental Share Rights

In reading the previous paragraphs, you noted that corporations raise equity funds by selling shares of the corporation. Shareholders are the owners of a corporation. If a corporation has only one class of shares, no designation of the shares is necessary, but they typically are labeled *common shares.* Ownership rights held by common shareholders, unless specifically withheld by agreement with the shareholders, are:

a. The right to vote on matters that come before the shareholders, including the election of corporate directors. Each share represents one vote.
b. The right to share in profits when dividends are declared. The percentage of shares owned by a shareholder determines his/her share of dividends distributed.
c. The right to share in the distribution of assets if the company is liquidated. The percentage of shares owned by a shareholder determines his/her share of assets after creditors and preferred shareholders are paid.

Another right sometimes given to common shareholders is the right to maintain one's percentage share of ownership when new shares are issued. This is referred to as a *preemptive right.* Each shareholder is offered the opportunity to buy a percentage of any new shares issued equal to the percentage of shares he/she owns at the time. In most states this right must be specifically granted; in others, it is presumed unless contractually excluded.

This right usually is withheld because of the inconvenience it causes corporations when they issue new shares. The exclusion of the preemptive right ordinarily is inconsequential because few shareholders own enough stock to be concerned about their ownership percentage.

> For reasons of practicality, the preemptive right usually is excluded.

---

[4]*Revised Model Business Corporation Act,* the American Bar Association, 1994.

Distinguishing Classes of Shares

It is not uncommon for a firm to have more than one, and perhaps several, classes of shares, each with different rights and limitations. To attract investors, companies have devised quite a variety of ownership securities.

If more than one class of shares is authorized by the articles of incorporation, the specific rights of each (for instance, the right to vote, residual interest in assets, and dividend rights) must be stated. Also, some designation must be given to distinguish each class.

Some of the distinguishing designations often used are:

1. Class A, class B, and so on (NACCO Industries, Inc.).
2. Preferred stock, common stock, and class B stock (Ford Motor Company).
3. Common and preferred (Witco Corporation).
4. Common stock, redeemable preferred stock, voting preference stock—first series, voting preference stock—second series, voting preference stock—third series (Pennwalt Corporation).
5. Class A common, Class B common, cumulative prior preference, and serial preferred (New York Times Company).

Terminology varies in the way companies differentiate among share types.

In your introductory study of accounting, you probably became most familiar with the common stock–preferred stock distinction. That terminology has deep roots in tradition. Early English corporate charters provided for shares that were preferred over others as to dividends and liquidation rights. These provisions were reflected in early American corporation laws. But as our economy developed, corporations increasingly felt the need for innovative ways of attracting investment capital. The result has been a gradual development of a wide range of share classifications that cannot easily be identified by these historical designations.

It often is difficult to predict the rights and privileges of shares on the basis of whether they are labeled *common* or *preferred*.

To reflect the flexibility that now exists in the creation of equity shares, the Model Business Corporation Act, and thus many state statutes, no longer mention the words common and preferred. But the influence of tradition lingers. Most corporations still designate shares as common or preferred. For consistency with practice, the illustrations you study in this chapter use those designations. As you consider the examples, keep in mind that the same concepts apply regardless of the language used to distinguish shares.

TYPICAL RIGHTS OF PREFERRED SHARES

An issue of shares with certain preferences or features that distinguish it from the class of shares customarily called common shares may be assigned any of the several labels mentioned earlier. Very often the distinguishing designation is *preferred shares*. The special rights of preferred shareholders usually include one or both of the following:

a. Preferred shareholders typically have a preference to a specified amount of dividends (stated dollar amount per share or % of par value per share). That is, if the board of directors declares dividends, preferred shareholders will receive the designated dividend before any dividends are paid to common shareholders.
b. Preferred shareholders customarily have a preference (over common shareholders) as to the distribution of assets in the event the corporation is dissolved.

Shares may be:
1. *Convertible* into a specified number of another class of shares.
2. *Redeemable* at the option of:
   a. Shareholders.
   b. The corporation.

Preferred shareholders sometimes have the **right of conversion** which allows them to exchange shares of preferred stock for common stock at a specified conversion ratio. Alternatively, a **redemption privilege** might allow preferred shareholders the option, under specified conditions, to return their shares for a predetermined redemption price. For instance, in 2001, Xerox Corporation had outstanding 8.2 million shares of convertible preferred stock. Preferred shareholders have preference over common stockholders in dividends and liquidation rights. Each preferred share is convertible into common shares or an equivalent amount of cash. Similarly, shares may be redeemable at the option of the issuing corporation (sometimes referred to as *callable*).

Preferred shares may be **cumulative** or **noncumulative.** Typically, preferred shares are cumulative, which means that if the specified dividend is not paid in a given year, the unpaid dividends (called *dividends in arrears*) accumulate and must be made up in a later dividend year before any dividends are paid on common shares.

Preferred shares may be **participating** or **nonparticipating.** A participating feature allows preferred shareholders to receive additional dividends beyond the stated amount. If the preferred shares are fully participating, the distribution of dividends to common and preferred shareholders is a pro rata allocation based on the relative par value amounts of common and preferred stock outstanding. Participating preferred stock, previously quite common, is rare today.

Remember that the designations of common and preferred imply no necessary rights, privileges, or limitations of the shares so designated. Such relative rights must be specified by the contract with shareholders. A corporation can create classes of preferred shares that are indistinguishable from common shares in voting rights and/or the right to participate in assets (distributed as dividends or distributed upon liquidation). Likewise, it is possible to devise classes of common shares that possess preferential rights, superior to those of preferred shares.

You probably also can imagine an issue of preferred shares that is almost indistinguishable from a bond issue. Let's say, for instance, that preferred shares call for annual cash dividends of 10% of the par value, dividends are cumulative, and the shares must be redeemed for cash in 10 years. Although the declaration of dividends rests in the discretion of the board of directors, the contract with preferred shareholders can be worded in such a way that directors are compelled to declare dividends each year the company is profitable. For a profitable company, it would be difficult to draw the line between this issue of preferred shares and a 10%, 10-year bond issue. Even in a more typical situation, preferred shares are somewhat hybrid securities—a cross between equity and debt.

The Concept of Par Value

Another prevalent practice (besides labeling shares as common and preferred) that has little significance other than historical is assigning a par value to shares. The concept of par value dates back as far as the concept of owning shares of a business. Par value originally indicated the real value of shares. All shares were issued at that price.

During the late 19th and early 20th centuries, many cases of selling shares for less than par value—known as *watered shares*—received a great deal of attention and were the subject of a number of lawsuits. Investors and creditors contended that they relied on the par value as the permanent investment in the corporation and therefore net assets must always be at least that amount. Not only was par value assumed to be the amount invested by shareholders, but it also was defined by early corporation laws as the amount of net assets not available for distribution to shareholders (as dividends or otherwise).

To escape some of the complexities of laws dealing with par value, in 1912 New York enacted corporate law that permitted no-par shares. Many other states followed suit. But the utility of the no-par option was restricted. One reason was that no-par shares usually were given status as an exception to the traditional par value shares, often requiring an arbitrary stated value in place of par value. More importantly, many companies were turning to par value shares with very low par values—often pennies—to escape the watered shares liability of issuing shares below an arbitrary par value and to limit the restrictions on distributions. This practice is common today.

Accountants and attorneys have been aware for decades that laws pertaining to par value and legal capital not only are bewildering but fail in their intent to safeguard creditors from payments to shareholders. A recent action by Bowne & Co., Inc., demonstrates the lack of protection afforded by par value. The company amended its articles of incorporation to reduce the par value of its shares from one dollar to one cent per share.

Actually, to the extent that creditors are led to believe that they are afforded protection, they are misled. Like the designations of common and preferred shares, the concepts of par value and legal capital have been eliminated entirely from the Model Business Corporation Act.[5]

---

[5]*Revised Model Business Corporation Act,* the American Bar Association, 1994, official comment to Section 6.21.

Many states already have adopted these provisions of the Model Act. But most established corporations issued shares prior to changes in the state statutes. Consequently, most companies have par value shares outstanding and continue to issue previously authorized par value shares. The evolution will be gradual to the simpler, more meaningful provisions of the Model Act.

In the meantime, accountants must be familiar with the outdated concepts of par value and legal capital in order to properly record and report transactions related to par value shares. For that reason, most of the discussion in this chapter centers around par value shares. Largely, this means only that proceeds from shareholders' investment is allocated between stated capital and additional paid-in capital. Be aware, though, that in the absence of archaic laws that prompted the creation of par value shares, there is no theoretical reason to do so.

Accounting for the Issuance of Shares

SHARES ISSUED FOR CASH

When shares are sold for cash, the capital stock account (usually common or preferred) is credited for the amount representing stated capital. When shares have a designated par value, that amount denotes stated capital and is credited to the stock account. Proceeds in excess of this amount are credited to paid-in capital—excess of par.

ILLUSTRATION 19–1	Dow Industrial sells 100,000 of its common shares, $1 par per share, for $10 per share:		
Shares Sold for Cash			**($ in 000s)**
	Cash (100,000 shares at $10 price per share).	1,000	
	Common stock (100,000 shares at $1 par per share).		100
	Paid-in capital—excess of par (remainder).		900
The total amount received from the sale of no-par shares is credited to the stock account.	The entire proceeds from the sale of no-par stock are deemed stated capital and recorded in the stock account. If the shares are no-par, the entry is as follows:		
	Cash (100,000 shares at $10 price per share).	1,000	
	Common stock		1,000

SHARES ISSUED ON CREDIT

Preincorporation Subscription Agreements. In times past, capital to finance new ventures ordinarily was raised by obtaining subscriptions for shares of the impending corporation. These preincorporation subscription agreements typically specified that the subscriber would purchase a certain number of shares if a specified amount of venture capital was obtained.

A difficult issue was determining what, if any, legal recourse the new company had if a subscriber defaulted. That issue seldom is encountered today. State and federal laws that require elaborate procedures for the registration of new securities make subscription agreements impractical for new ventures. Venture financing by subscription is virtually an activity of the past. Simple contracts to sell shares have replaced preincorporation subscription agreements.

Share Purchase Contracts and Stock Subscriptions. After incorporation, a subscription agreement is a contract between the subscriber and the corporation. When shares are sold by **share purchase contract,** shares ordinarily are sold in exchange for a promissory note from the subscriber. In essence, the shares are sold on credit. Recording the sale of shares is modified only by including a receivable for the portion of the selling price not yet received.

For illustration, assume the shares described in Illustration 19–1 are sold by share purchase contract, with 60% of the selling price to be received after six months.

		ILLUSTRATION 19–2
Dow Industrial sells and issues 100,000 of its common shares, $1 par per share. The shares are sold by share purchase contract for $10 per share, with 60% of the selling price to be received after six months: Shares have been issued but are restricted from being resold and from voting privileges until paid in full.		Share Purchase Contracts

	($ in 000s)	
Cash.	400	
Receivable from share purchase contract.	600	
Common stock		100
Paid-in capital—excess of par		900

A receivable is recorded for the $600,000 not yet received.

Reporting the Receivable.   How should the receivable be reported? Your initial response probably is that this account is an *asset,* similar to accounts receivable. Why should the receivable be precluded from being an asset merely because it is exchanged for shares rather than assets?

We can look to an infamous event in accounting history for a persuasive answer. For much of 2000 and the first part of 2001, Enron Corporation invested Enron stock in (and committed Enron stock to) "special purpose entities" that were created by Enron. To record these investments and commitments, Enron debited notes receivable and credited shareholders equity as described above. The problem, though, that contributed to Enron's collapse was that it then reported the result as an increase in both assets and shareholders' equity, creating a $1.2 billion asset that didn't really exist. Enron eventually restated its financial statements, referring to its actions as an "accounting error." Rules in place at the time prohibited such accounting. Instead, a receivable from issuing shares is not an asset, but should be reported as a *reduction in paid-in capital.*[7] Dow Industrial's paid-in capital, immediately after the stock subscription described in Illustration 19–2, would be reported by this approach as:

n now believes that, er generally accepted unting principles, the receivable should have presented as a ction to shareholders' ty. . . The net effect of nitial accounting entry to overstate both the receivable and eholders' equity. . .[6]

	($ in 000s)
Paid-in capital:	
Common stock, 100,000 shares at $1 par	$100
Paid-in capital—excess of par	900
Less: Receivable from share purchase contract	(600)
Total paid-in capital	$400

A receivable from issuing stock is a contra equity account until collected.

Reporting the receivable as a contra equity account results in reporting total paid-in capital only to the extent that capital actually has been contributed. This is the prevalent practice.

SHARES ISSUED FOR NONCASH CONSIDERATION

Occasionally, a company might issue its shares for consideration other than cash. It is not uncommon for a new company, yet to establish a reliable cash flow, to pay for promotional and legal services with shares rather than with cash. Similarly, shares might be given in payment for land, or for equipment, or for some other noncash asset.

---

[6]Enron's November 2001 8K filing with the SEC.
[7]This accounting treatment is specified by *EITF Issue 85-1,* "Classifying Notes Received for Capital Stock," and SEC Regulation S-X, Article 5-02.30, *Commons Stocks,* and *Staff Accounting Bulletin Topic 4-E,* "Receivables from Sale of Stock."

Shares should be issued at fair market value.

Even without a receipt of cash to establish the fair market value of the shares at the time of the exchange, the transaction still should be recorded at fair market value. Best evidence of fair market value might be:

- A quoted market price for the shares.
- A selling price established in a recent issue of shares for cash.
- The amount of cash that would have been paid in a cash purchase of the asset or service.
- An independent appraisal of the value of the asset received.
- Other available evidence.

Whichever evidence of fair market value seems more clearly evident should be used.[8]

Illustration 19–3 demonstrates a situation where the quoted market price is the best evidence of fair value.

ILLUSTRATION 19–3 Shares Sold for Noncash Consideration **The quoted market price for the shares issued might be the best evidence of fair market value.**	DuMont Chemicals issues 1 million of its common shares, $1 par per share, in exchange for a custom-built factory for which no cash price is available. Today's issue of *The Wall Street Journal* lists DuMont's stock at $10 per share: |	**($ in millions)**
Property, plant, and equipment (1 million shares at $10 per share) . .	10
Common stock (1 million shares at $1 par per share)	1
Paid-in capital—excess of par (remainder).	9	

MORE THAN ONE SECURITY ISSUED FOR A SINGLE PRICE

Although uncommon, a company might sell more than one security—perhaps common shares and preferred shares—for a single price. As you might expect, the cash received usually is the sum of the separate market values of the two securities. Of course, each is then recorded at its market value. However, if only one security's value is known, the second security's market value is inferred from the total selling price as demonstrated in Illustration 19–4.

ILLUSTRATION 19–4 More than One Security Sold for a Single Price **When only one security's value is known ($40 million), the second security's market value ($60 million) is assumed from the total selling price ($100 million).**	AP&P issues 4 million of its common shares, $1 par per share, and 4 million of its preferred shares, $10 par, for $100 million. Today's issue of *The Wall Street Journal* lists AP&P's common at $10 per share. There is no established market for the preferred shares: |	**($ in millions)**
Cash.	100
Common stock (4 million shares × $1 par)	4
Paid-in capital—excess of par, common	36
Preferred stock (4 million shares × $10 par)	40
Paid-in capital—excess of par, preferred	20	

Because the shares sell for a total of $100 million, and the market value of the common shares is known to be $40 million (4 million × $10), the preferred shares are inferred to have a market value of $60 million.

---

[8]Although stock issuances are not specifically mentioned in *APB Opinion No. 29*, this treatment is consistent with the general rule for accounting for noncash transactions as described in that pronouncement, pars. 18 and 25.

In the unlikely event that the total selling price is not equal to the sum of the two market prices (when both market values are known), the total selling price is allocated between the two securities, in proportion to their relative market values. You should note that this is the same approach we use (a) when more than one asset is purchased for a single purchase price to allocate the single price to the various assets acquired, (b) when detachable warrants and bonds are issued for a single price, and (c) in any other situation when more than one item is associated with a single purchase price or selling price.

SHARE ISSUE COSTS

When a company sells shares, it obtains the legal, promotional, and accounting services necessary to effect the sale. The cost of these services reduces the net proceeds from selling the shares. Since paid-in capital—excess of par is credited for the excess of the proceeds over the par value of the shares sold, the effect of share issue costs is to reduce the amount credited to that account. For example, on completing a public offering of 825,000 shares at a price of $17.75 per share, the Duriron Company, Inc., noted in its financial statements: "The proceeds of the offering, after deducting all associated costs, were $13,491,000 or $16.35 per newly issued share." Duriron's entry to record the sale was:

> **Share issue costs reduce the net cash proceeds from selling the shares and thus paid-in capital—excess of par.**

	($ in millions)	
Cash (825,000 shares at $16.35 net price per share)	13.49	
Common stock (825,000 shares at $1.25 par per share)		1.03
Paid-in capital—excess of par (remainder)		12.46

> **The cash proceeds is the net amount received after paying share issue costs.**

You should notice that not separately reporting issue costs differs from how *debt* issue costs are recorded. In Chapter 14 you learned that the costs associated with a debt issue are recorded in a separate debt issue costs account and amortized to expense over the life of the debt.

> **Like interest, debt issue costs are an expense of borrowing funds.**

It can be argued that share issue costs and debt issue costs are fundamentally different. That view would argue that a debt issue has a fixed maturity and, like interest expense, debt issue costs are part of the expense of borrowing funds for that period of time (even though it's recorded in a separate expense account—debt issue expense). Selling shares, on the other hand, represents a perpetual equity interest. Dividends paid on that capital investment are not an expense; neither are the costs of obtaining that capital investment (share issue costs).

> **Like dividends, share issue costs are *not* an expense.**

Although expensing debt issue costs presently is required by GAAP, the FASB has suggested in *Concept Statement 6* that those costs should be treated the same way as share issue costs. That is, the recorded amount of the debt would be reduced by the debt issue costs instead of recording the costs separately as an asset. Remember, though, that concept statements do not constitute GAAP, so until a new FASB standard is issued to supersede *APB Opinion 21*, the prescribed practice is to record debt issue costs as assets and expense the asset over the maturity of the debt.

CONCEPT REVIEW EXERCISE

Expansion of Corporate Capital

Situation: The shareholders' equity section of the balance sheet of National Foods, Inc. included the following accounts at December 31, 2001:

Shareholders' Equity	($ in millions)
Paid-in capital:	
Common stock, 120 million shares at $1 par	$ 120
Paid-in capital—excess of par	836
Retained earnings	2,449
Total shareholders' equity	$3,405

Required:
1. During 2002, several transactions affected the stock of National Foods. Prepare the appropriate entries for these events.
    a. On March 11, National Foods sold 10 million of its 9.2% preferred shares, $1 par per share, for $44 per share by share purchase contract. 50% of the selling price was received at the time of sale, a five-year note was received for the remainder. The shares were not issued but held in escrow until the note was paid.
    b. On November 22, 1 million common shares, $1 par per share, were issued in exchange for eight labeling machines. Each machine was built to custom specifications so no cash price was available. National Food's stock was listed at $10 per share.
    c. On November 23, 1 million of the common shares and 1 million preferred shares were sold for $60 million. The preferred shares had not traded since March and their market value was uncertain.
2. Prepare the shareholders' equity section of the comparative balance sheets for National Foods at December 31, 2002 and 2001. Assume that net income for 2002 was $400 million and the only other transaction affecting shareholders' equity was the payment of the 9.2% dividend on the 11 million preferred shares ($1 million).

SOLUTION

1. During 2002 several transactions affected the stock of National Foods. Prepare the appropriate entries for these events.
    a. On March 11, National Foods sold 10 million of its preferred shares, $1 par per share, for $44 per share by share purchase contract:

$220 million cash (50% × $440 million) was received at the time of sale. The remaining $220 million was to be received later.

	($ in millions)	
Cash.	220	
Receivable from share purchase contract.	220	
Preferred stock (10 million shares × $1 par per share)		10
Paid-in capital—excess of par, preferred		430

    b. On November 22, 1 million common shares, $1 par per share, were issued in exchange for 8 labeling machines:

The transaction was recorded at the fair market value of the shares exchanged for the machinery.

Machinery (fair value of shares).	10	
Common stock (1 million shares × $1 par per share).		1
Paid-in capital—excess of par, common (1 million shares × $9). . .		9

    c. On November 23, 1 million of the common shares and 1 million preferred shares were sold for $60 million:

Since the value of only the common stock was known, the preferred stock's market value ($50/share) was inferred from the total selling price.

Cash.	60	
Common stock (1 million shares × $1 par per share).		1
Paid-in capital—excess of par, common		9
Preferred stock (1 million shares × $1 par per share)		1
Paid-in capital—excess of par, preferred (to balance)		49

2. Prepare the shareholders' equity section of the comparative balance sheets for National Foods at December 31, 2002 and 2001.

NATIONAL FOODS, INC.
Balance Sheet
[Shareholders' Equity Section]

	($ in millions)	
	2002	**2001**
Shareholders' Equity		
Preferred stock, 9.2%, $1 par (2002: $10 million + 1 million)	$ 11	$ —
Common stock, $1 par (2002: $120 million + 1 million + 1 million)	122	120

	2002	2001
Paid-in capital—excess of par, preferred (2002: $430 million + 49 million)	479	—
Paid-in capital—excess of par, common (2002: $836 million + 9 million + 9 million)	854	836
Less: Receivable from share purchase contract	(220)	—
Retained earnings (2001: $2,449 million + 400 million − 1 million)	2,848	2,449
Total shareholders' equity	$4,094	$3,405

Share Buybacks

In the previous section we examined various ways stock might be issued. In this section, we look at situations in which companies reacquire shares previously sold. Most medium- and large-size companies occasionally buy back their own shares. Many have formal share repurchase plans. The motivation often is to support the market price of the shares.

DECISION MAKERS' PERSPECTIVE

When a company's management feels the market price of its stock is undervalued, it may attempt to support the price by decreasing the supply of stock in the marketplace. A Johnson & Johnson announcement that it planned to buy back up to $5 billion of its outstanding shares triggered a buying spree that pushed the stock price up by more than 3 percent.

When announcing plans to repurchase up to $1 billion of its shares, Compaq chairman and chief executive officer Michael Capellas explained, "At current price levels, we believe Compaq's stock offers a tremendous investment opportunity for the company."[9] Although clearly a company may attempt to increase net assets by buying its shares at a low price and selling them back later at a higher price, that investment is not viewed as an asset. Similarly, increases and decreases in net assets from that activity are not reported as gains and losses in the company's income statement. Instead, buying and selling its shares are transactions between the corporation and its owners, analogous to retiring shares and then selling previously unissued shares. You should note the contrast between a company's purchasing of its own shares and its purchasing of shares in another corporation as an investment.

Though not considered an investment, the repurchase of shares often is a judicious use of a company's cash. By increasing per share earnings and supporting share price, shareholders benefit. In 1998, when IBM announced its second $3.5 billion buyback of common stock that same year, Merrill Lynch & Co. commented, "I think it's a reasonable use of cash. How many investment opportunities do they have that can return cost of capital? They should be investing up to that point, and beyond that they should return cash to the shareholders."[10]

To the extent this strategy is effective, a share buyback can be viewed as a way to "distribute" company profits without paying dividends. Capital gains from any stock price increase are taxed at lower capital gains tax rates than ordinary income tax rates on dividends.

Supporting the share price is not the only motivation for a stock buyback. When relatively few shares are needed to complete a transaction, it often is more convenient for a company to reacquire outstanding shares and then transfer them than it is to issue previously unissued shares. For instance, Microsoft recently reported the policy of reacquiring its shares to distribute to employees under its stock option and share repurchase plans as shown in Graphic 19–5 on the next page. Even if new shares are distributed in such stock-based compensation plans, a buyback of shares around the same time can serve to offset that increase in shares.

Similarly, shares might be reacquired to distribute in a stock dividend, a proposed merger, or as a defense against a hostile takeover.[11]

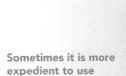

Decreasing the supply of shares in the marketplace supports the price of remaining shares.

FINANCIAL REPORTING CASE

Q1, p. 937

Unlike an investment in another firm's shares, the acquisition of a company's own shares does not create an asset.

Sometimes it is more expedient to use previously issued shares in a transaction involving the transfer of shares.

---

[9]"HP, Compaq Resume Stock Buyback," *CNET News.com*, September 17, 2001.
[10]"IBM Sets Another Big Buyback of Its Shares," *The New York Times*, October 28, 1998.
[11]A corporate takeover occurs when an individual or group of individuals acquires a majority of a company's outstanding common stock from present shareholders. Corporations that are the object of a hostile takeover attempt—a public bid for control of a company's stock against the company's wishes—often take evasive action involving the reacquisition of shares.

GRAPHIC 19–5
Disclosure of Share
Repurchase Program—
Microsoft

Repurchase Program (in part)

. . . The Company repurchases its common stock in the open market to provide shares for issuance to employees under stock option and stock repurchase plans. The Company's Board of Directors authorized continuation of this program in 1999. . . .

Whatever the reason shares are repurchased, a company has a choice of how to account for the buyback:

1. The shares can be formally retired.
2. The shares can be called treasury stock.

Unfortunately, the choice is not dictated by the nature of the buyback, but by practical motivations of the company. ■

FINANCIAL REPORTING CASE

Q2, p. 937

Reacquired shares are equivalent to authorized but unissued shares.

SHARES FORMALLY RETIRED OR VIEWED AS TREASURY STOCK

When a corporation retires its own shares, those shares assume the same status as authorized but unissued shares, just the same as if they never had been issued. We saw earlier in the chapter that when shares are sold, both cash (usually) and shareholders' equity are increased; the company becomes larger. Conversely, when cash is paid to retire stock, the effect is to decrease both cash and shareholders' equity; the size of the company literally is reduced.

Out of tradition and for practical reasons, companies usually reacquire shares of previously issued stock without formally retiring them.[12] Shares repurchased and not retired are referred to as **treasury stock.** Because reacquired shares are essentially the same as shares that never were issued at all, treasury shares have no voting rights nor do they receive dividends. Like the concepts of par value and legal capital, the concept of treasury shares no longer is recognized in most state statutes.[13] Some companies, in fact, are eliminating treasury shares from their financial statements as corporate statutes are modernized.

ACCOUNTING FOR RETIRED SHARES

When shares are formally retired, we should reduce precisely the same accounts that previously were increased when the shares were sold, namely, common (or preferred) stock and paid-in capital—excess of par. The first column of Illustration 19–5 on the next page demonstrates this. The paid-in capital—excess of par account shows a balance of $900 million while the common stock account shows a balance of $100 million. Thus the 100 million outstanding shares were originally sold for an average of $9 per share above par, or $10 per share. Consequently, when 1 million shares are retired (regardless of the retirement price), American Semiconductor should reduce its common stock account by $1 per share and its paid-in capital—excess of par by $9 per share. Another way to view the reduction is that because 1% of the shares are retired, both share account balances (common stock and paid-in capital—excess of par) are reduced by 1%.

How we treat the difference between the cash paid to buy the shares and the amount the shares originally sold for (amounts debited to common stock and paid-in capital—excess of par) depends on whether the cash paid is *less* than the original issue price (credit difference) or the cash paid is *more* than the original issue price (debit difference):

1. If a *credit* difference is created (as in Case 1 of Illustration 19–5), we credit paid-in capital—share repurchase.

---

[12]The concept of treasury shares originated long ago when new companies found they could sell shares at an unrealistically low price equal to par value to incorporators, who then donated those shares back to the company. Since these shares already had been issued (though not outstanding), they could be sold at whatever the real market price was without adjusting stated capital.

Because treasury shares are already issued, different rules apply to their purchase and resale than to unissued shares. Companies can:

  a. Issue shares without regard to preemptive rights of shareholders.

  b. Distribute shares as a dividend to shareholders even without a balance in retained earnings.

[13]The *Revised Model Business Corporation Act* eliminated the concept of treasury shares in 1984 after 1980 revisions had eliminated the concepts of par value and legal capital. Most state laws have since followed suit.

American Semiconductor's balance sheet included the following:

ILLUSTRATION 19–5

Comparison of Share Retirement and Treasury Stock Accounting—Share Buybacks

Shareholders' Equity	($ in millions)
Common stock, 100 million shares at $1 par	$ 100
Paid-in capital—excess of par	900
Paid-in capital—share repurchase	2
Retained earnings	2,000

Retirement		Treasury Stock	
Reacquired 1 million of its common shares			

Case 1: Shares repurchased at $7 per share

Common stock ($1 par × 1 million shares) . . .	1	Treasury stock (cost)	7
Paid-in capital—excess of par			
($9 per shares)	9		
Paid-in capital—share repurchase			
(difference)	3		
Cash	7	Cash	7

OR

Case 2: Shares repurchased at $13 per share

Common stock ($1 par × 1 million shares) . . .	1	Treasury stock (cost)	13
Paid-in capital—excess of par			
($9 per shares)	9		
Paid-in capital—share repurchase	2*		
Retained earnings (difference).	1		
Cash	13	Cash	13

Formally retiring shares restores the balances in both the Common stock account and Paid-in capital—excess of par to what those balances would have been if the shares never had been issued.

When we view a buyback as treasury stock the *cost* of acquiring the shares is "temporarily" debited to the treasury stock account.

*Because there is a $2 million credit balance.

2. If a *debit* difference is created (as in Case 2 of Illustration 19–5), we debit paid-in capital—share repurchase, but only if that account already has a credit balance. Otherwise, we debit retained earnings. (Reducing the account beyond its previous balance would create a negative balance.)

Why is paid-in capital credited in Case 1 and retained earnings debited in Case 2? The answer lies in the fact that the payments made by a corporation to repurchase its own shares are a distribution of corporate assets to shareholders.

In Case 1, only $7 million is distributed to shareholders to retire shares that originally provided $10 million of paid-in capital. Thus, some of the original investment ($3 million in this case) remains and is labeled *paid-in capital—share repurchase.*

In Case 2, more cash ($13 million) is distributed to shareholders to retire shares than originally was paid in. The amount paid in comprises the original investment of $10 million for the shares being retired plus $2 million of paid-in capital created by previous repurchase transactions—$12 million total. Thirteen million is returned to shareholders. The additional $1 million paid is viewed as a dividend on the shareholders' investment, and thus a reduction of retained earnings.[14]

Paid-in capital—share repurchase is debited to the extent of its credit balance before debiting retained earnings.

Payments made by a corporation to retire its own shares are viewed as a distribution of corporate assets to shareholders.

ACCOUNTING FOR TREASURY STOCK

We view the purchase of treasury stock as a temporary reduction of shareholders' equity, to be reversed later when the treasury stock is resold. The cost of acquiring the shares is "temporarily" debited to the treasury stock account (second column of Illustration 19–5).

LO5

---

[14]In the next section of this chapter, you will be reminded that dividends reduce retained earnings. (You first learned this in your introductory accounting course.)

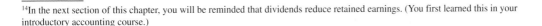

When a share repurchase is viewed as treasury stock, recording the effects on specific shareholders' equity accounts is delayed until the shares are reissued.

Recording the effects on specific shareholders' equity accounts is delayed until later when the shares are reissued. In the meantime, the shares assume the fictional status we discussed earlier of being neither unissued nor outstanding. Effectively, we consider the purchase of treasury stock and its subsequent resale to be a "single transaction."

ADDITIONAL CONSIDERATION

The approach to accounting for treasury stock we discuss in this chapter is referred to as the "cost method." Another permissible approach is the "par value method." It is essentially identical to formally retiring shares, which is why it sometimes is referred to as the *retirement method of accounting for treasury stock*. In fact, if we substitute Treasury stock for Common stock in each of the journal entries we used to account for retirement of shares in Illustrations 19–5 and 19–6, we have the par value method. Because the method has virtually disappeared from practice, we do not discuss it further in this chapter.

Balance Sheet Effect. Formally retiring shares restores the balances in both the Common stock account and Paid-in capital—excess of par to what those balances would have been if the shares never had been issued at all. As discussed above, any net increase in assets resulting from the sale and subsequent repurchase is reflected as Paid-in capital—share repurchase. On the other hand, any net decrease in assets resulting from the sale and subsequent repurchase is reflected as a reduction in retained earnings.

In contrast, when a share repurchase is viewed as treasury stock, the cost of the treasury stock is simply reported as a reduction in total shareholders' equity. Reporting under the two approaches is compared in Graphic 19–6 using the situation described above for American Semiconductor after the purchase of treasury stock in Illustration 19–5 (Case 2). Notice that either way total shareholders' equity is the same.

GRAPHIC 19–6
Reporting Share Buyback in the Balance Sheet

Retirement reduces common stock and associated shareholders' equity accounts.

Treasury stock reduces total shareholders' equity.

	($ in millions)	
	Shares Retired	**Treasury Stock**
Shareholders' Equity		
Paid-in capital:		
Common stock, 100 million shares at $1 par	$ 99	$ 100
Paid-in capital—excess of par	891	900
Paid-in capital—reacquired shares		2
Retained earnings	1,999	2,000
Less: Treasury stock, 1 million shares (at cost)		(13)
Total shareholders' equity	$2,989	$2,989

RESALE OF SHARES

When shares are retired or the par value method is used, we view any subsequent sale as the sale of new shares.

After shares are formally retired, any subsequent sale of shares is simply the sale of new, unissued shares and is accounted for accordingly. This is demonstrated in the first column of Illustration 19–6 on the next page.

The resale of treasury shares is viewed as the consummation of the single transaction begun when the treasury shares were repurchased. The effect of the single transaction of purchasing treasury stock and reselling it for more than cost (Case 2 of Illustration 19–5 and Case A of Illustration 19–6) is to *increase* both cash and shareholders' equity (by $1 million). The effect of the single transaction of purchasing treasury stock and reselling it for less than cost (Case 2 of Illustration 19–5 and Case B of Illustration 19–6) is to *decrease* both cash and shareholders' equity (by $3 million).

Allocating the cost of treasury shares occurs when the shares are resold.

American Semiconductor sold 1 million shares after reacquiring shares at $13 per share (Case 2 in Illustration 19–5).

Retirement			Treasury Stock		
Sold 1 million shares					
Case A: Shares sold at $14 per share					
Cash.........................	14		Cash.....................	14	
Common stock (par)...........		1	Treasury stock (cost)........		13
Paid-in capital—excess of par....		13	Paid-in capital—share		
			repurchase		1
OR					
Case B: Shares sold at $10 per share					
Cash.........................	10		Cash.....................	10	
Common stock (par)...........		1	Retained earnings (to balance)..		1
Paid-in capital—excess of par....		9	Paid-in capital—share		
			repurchase		2*
			Treasury stock (cost)........		13

ILLUSTRATION 19-6

Comparison of Share Retirement and Treasury Stock Accounting—Subsequent Sale of Shares

After formally retiring shares, we record a subsequent sale of shares exactly like any sale of shares.

The resale of treasury shares is viewed as the consummation of the "single transaction" begun when the treasury shares were purchased.

*Because there is a $2 million credit balance.

Note that retained earnings may be debited in a treasury stock transaction, but not credited. Also notice that transactions involving treasury stock have no impact on the income statement. This follows the reasoning discussed earlier that a corporation's buying and selling of its own shares are transactions between the corporation and its owners and not part of the earnings process.

ADDITIONAL CONSIDERATION

Treasury Shares Acquired at Different Costs
Notice that the treasury stock account always is credited for the cost of the reissued shares ($13 million in Illustration 19–6). When shares are reissued, if treasury stock on hand has been purchased at different per share prices, the cost of the shares sold must be determined using a cost flow assumption—FIFO, LIFO, or weighted average—similar to determining the cost of goods sold when inventory items are acquired at different unit costs.

Determining the cost of treasury stock sold is similar to determining the cost of goods sold.

CONCEPT REVIEW EXERCISE

Treasury Stock

Situation: The shareholders' equity section of the balance sheet of National Foods, Inc. included the following accounts at December 31, 2002.

Shareholders' Equity	($ in millions)
Paid-in capital:	
Preferred stock, 11 million shares at $1 par	$ 11
Common stock, 122 million shares at $1 par	122
Paid-in capital—excess of par, preferred	479
Paid-in capital—excess of par, common	854
Less: Receivable from share purchase contract	(220)
Retained earnings	2,848
Total shareholders' equity	$4,094

Required:

1. National Foods reacquired common shares during 2003 and sold shares in two separate transactions later that year. Prepare the entries for both the purchase and subsequent sale of shares during 2003 assuming that the shares were (a) retired and (b) considered to be treasury stock.

   a. National Foods purchased 6 million shares at $10 per share.

   b. National Foods sold 2 million shares at $12 per share.

   c. National Foods sold 2 million shares at $7 per share.

2. Prepare the shareholders' equity section of National Foods' balance sheet at December 31, 2003, assuming the shares were both (a) retired and (b) viewed as treasury stock. Net income for 2003 was $400 million, and preferred shareholders were paid $1 million cash dividends.

SOLUTION

1. National Foods reacquired common shares during 2000 and sold shares in two separate transactions later that year. Prepare the entries for both the purchase and subsequent sale of shares during 2003 assuming that the shares were (a) retired and (b) considered to be treasury stock.

   a. National Foods purchased 6 million shares at $10 per share:

Retirement ($ in millions)		Treasury Stock ($ in millions)	
Common stock (6 million shares × $1) .. 6		Treasury stock	
Paid-in capital—excess of par		(6 million shares × $10) 60	
(6 million shares × $7*)............ 42		Cash	60
Retained earnings (to balance)........ 12			
Cash	60		

*$854 million ÷ 122 million shares

   b. National Foods sold 2 million shares at $12 per share: ($ in millions)

Cash 24		Cash..................... 24	
Common stock		Treasury stock	
(2 million shares × $1)............	2	(2 million shares × $10) ..	20
Paid-in capital—excess of par	22	Paid-in capital—	
		reacquired shares.......	4

   c. National Foods sold 2 million shares at $7 per share: ($ in millions)

Cash 14		Cash..................... 14	
Common stock		Paid-in capital—	
(2 million shares × $1 par)	2	reacquired shares.........	4
Paid-in capital—excess of par	12	Retained earnings	
		(to balance)	2
		Treasury stock	
		(2 million shares × $10) ..	20

2. Prepare the shareholders' equity section of National Foods' balance sheet at December 31, 2003, assuming the shares were both (a) retired and (b) viewed as treasury stock.

NATIONAL FOODS, INC.
Balance Sheet
[Shareholders' Equity Section]
At December 31, 2003

	($ in millions)	
	Shares Retired	**Treasury Stock**
Shareholders' Equity		
Preferred stock, 11 million shares at $1 par	$ 11	$ 11
Common stock, 122 million shares at $1 par	120	122
Paid-in capital—excess of par, preferred	479	479

Paid-in capital—excess of par, common	846*	854
Less: Receivable from share purchase contract	(220)	(220)
Retained earnings	3,235†	3,245‡
Treasury stock, at cost; 2 million common shares	—	(20)
Total shareholders' equity	$4,471	$4,471

*$854 − 42 + 22 + 12
†$2,848 − 12 + 400 − 1
‡$2,848 − 2 + 400 − 1

RETAINED EARNINGS

P A R T

C

LO6

Characteristics of Retained Earnings

In the previous section we examined *invested* capital. Now we consider *earned* capital, that is, retained earnings. In general, retained earnings represents a corporation's accumulated, undistributed net income (or net loss). A more descriptive title used by some companies is reinvested earnings. A credit balance in this account indicates a dollar amount of assets previously earned by the firm but not distributed as dividends to shareholders. We refer to a debit balance in retained earnings as a **deficit.**

You saw in the previous section that the buyback of shares (as well as the resale of treasury shares in some cases) can decrease retained earnings. We examine the effect on retained earnings of dividends and stock splits in this section.

Dividends

LO7

Shareholders' initial investments in a corporation are represented by amounts reported as paid-in capital. One way a corporation provides a return to its shareholders on their investments is to pay them a **dividend,** typically cash.[15]

Dividends are distributions of assets the company has earned on behalf of its shareholders. If dividends are paid that exceed the amount of assets earned by the company, then management is, in effect, returning to shareholders a portion of their investments, rather than providing them a return on that investment. So most companies view retained earnings as the amount available for dividends.[16]

LIQUIDATING DIVIDEND

In unusual instances in which a dividend exceeds the balance in retained earnings, the excess is referred to as a **liquidating dividend** because some of the invested capital is being liquidated. This might occur when a corporation is being dissolved and assets (not subject to a superior claim by creditors) are distributed to shareholders. Any portion of a dividend not representing a distribution of earnings should be debited to additional paid-in capital rather than retained earnings.

> Any dividend not representing a distribution of earnings should be debited to paid-in capital.

RETAINED EARNINGS RESTRICTIONS

Sometimes the amount available for dividends purposely is reduced by management. A restriction of retained earnings designates a portion of the balance in retained earnings as being *unavailable for dividends.* A company might restrict retained earnings to indicate

> A restriction of retained earnings communicates management's intention to withhold assets represented by a specified portion of the retained earnings balance.

---

[15]Dividends are not the only return shareholders earn; when market prices of their shares rise, shareholders benefit also. Indeed, many companies have adopted policies of never paying dividends but reinvesting all assets they earn. The motivation is to accommodate more rapid expansion and thus, presumably, increases in the market price of the stock.

[16]Ordinarily, this is not the legal limitation. Most states permit a company to pay dividends so long as, after the dividend, its assets would not be "less than the sum of its total liabilities plus the amount that would be needed, if the corporation were to be dissolved at the time of the distribution, to satisfy the preferential rights upon dissolution of shareholders whose preferential rights are superior to those receiving the distribution." (Revised Model Business Corporation Act, American Bar Association, 1994). Thus, legally, a corporation can distribute amounts equal to total shareholders' equity less dissolution preferences of senior equity securities (usually preferred stock).

management's intention to withhold for some specific purpose the assets represented by that portion of the retained earnings balance. For example, management might anticipate the need for a specific amount of assets in upcoming years to repay a maturing debt, to cover a contingent loss, or to finance expansion of the facilities. Be sure to understand that the restriction itself does not set aside cash for the designated event but merely communicates management's intention not to distribute the stated amount as a dividend.

> **Normally a restriction of retained earnings is indicated by a disclosure note.**

A restriction of retained earnings normally is indicated by a disclosure note to the financial statements. Although instances are rare, a formal journal entry may be used to reclassify a portion of retained earnings to an "appropriated" retained earnings account.

CASH DIVIDENDS

> **FINANCIAL REPORTING CASE**
>
> Q3, p. 937

You learned in Chapter 14 that paying interest to creditors is a contractual obligation. No such legal obligation exists for paying dividends to shareholders. A liability is not recorded until a company's board of directors votes to declare a dividend. In practice, though, corporations ordinarily try to maintain a stable dividend pattern over time.

> **The name of an investor who buys shares on the ex-dividend date or later will not appear on the company's list of registered owners until after the date of record.**

When directors declare a cash dividend, we reduce retained earnings and record a liability. Before the payment actually can be made, a listing must be assembled of shareholders entitled to receive the dividend. A specific date is stated as to when the determination will be made of the recipients of the dividend. This date is called the **date of record.** Registered owners of shares of stock on this date are entitled to receive the dividend—even if they sell those shares prior to the actual cash payment. To be a registered owner of shares on the date of record, an investor must purchase the shares before the **ex-dividend date.** This date usually is two business days before the date of record. Shares purchased on or after that date are purchased ex dividend— without the right to receive the declared dividend. As a result, the market price of a share typically will decline by the amount of the dividend, other things being equal, on the ex-dividend date. Consider Illustration 19–7.

> Marriott International, Inc. today announced that its board of directors has declared a quarterly cash dividend of six and one-half cents per share of common stock. The dividend is payable Oct. 12, 2001, to shareholders of record as of September 28, 2001.[17]

ILLUSTRATION 19–7 Cash Dividends At the declaration date, retained earnings is reduced and a liability is recorded. Registered owners of shares on the date of record are entitled to receive the dividend.	On June 1, the board of directors of Craft Industries declares a cash dividend of $2 per share on its 100 million shares, payable to shareholders of record June 15, to be paid July 1:	

	($ in millions)	
June 1—Declaration Date		
Retained earnings	200	
Cash dividends payable (100 million shares at $2/share).		200
June 13—Ex-Dividend Date		
No entry		
June 15—Date of Record		
No entry		
July 1—Payment Date		
Cash dividends payable	200	
Cash.		200

A sufficient balance in retained earnings permits a dividend to be declared. Remember, though, that retained earnings is a shareholders' equity account representing a dollar claim on assets in general, but not on any specific asset in particular. Sufficient retained earnings does not ensure sufficient cash to make payment. These are two separate accounts having no necessary connection with one another. When a dividend is "paid from retained earnings,"

---

[17]*PR Newswire,* August 2, 2001.

this simply means that sufficient assets previously have been earned to pay the dividend without returning invested assets to shareholders.

PROPERTY DIVIDENDS

Because cash is the asset most easily divided and distributed to shareholders, most corporate dividends are cash dividends. In concept, though, any asset can be distributed to shareholders as a dividend. When a noncash asset is distributed, it is referred to as a **property dividend** (often called a *dividend in kind*).

In 1994, Litton Industries declared to its shareholders a property dividend in shares of Western Atlas stock that Litton was holding as an investment. Securities held as investments are the assets most often distributed in a property dividend due to the relative ease of dividing these assets among shareholders and determining their fair market values.

A property dividend should be recorded at the fair market value of the assets to be distributed. This may require revaluing the asset to fair market value prior to recording the dividend. If so, a gain or loss is recognized for the difference between book value and fair market value. This is demonstrated in Illustration 19–8.

> The *fair market value* of the assets to be distributed is the amount recorded for a property dividend.

On October 1 the board of directors of Craft Industries declares a property dividend of 2 million shares of Beaman Corporation's preferred stock that Craft had purchased in March as an investment (book value: $9 million). The investment shares have a fair market value of $5 per share, $10 million, and are payable to shareholders of record October 15, to be distributed November 1:

October 1—Declaration Date	($ in millions)	
Investment in Beaman Corporation preferred stock	1	
Gain on appreciation of investment ($10 − 9).		1
Retained earnings (2 million shares at $5 per share)	10	
Property dividends payable.		10
October 15—Date of Record		
No entry		
November 1—Payment Date		
Property dividends payable	10	
Investment in Beaman Corporation preferred stock.		10

ILLUSTRATION 19–8

Property Dividends

Before recording the property dividend, the asset first must be written up to fair market value.

Stock Dividends and Splits

STOCK DIVIDENDS

A **stock dividend** is the distribution of additional shares of stock to current shareholders of the corporation. Be sure to note the contrast between a stock dividend and either a cash or property dividend. A stock dividend affects neither the assets nor the liabilities of the firm. Also, because each shareholder receives the same percentage increase in shares, shareholders' proportional interest in (percentage ownership of) the firm remains unchanged.

The prescribed accounting treatment of a stock dividend requires that shareholders' equity items be reclassified by reducing one or more shareholders' equity accounts and simultaneously increasing one or more paid-in capital accounts. The amount reclassified depends on the size of the stock dividend. For a small stock dividend, typically less than 25%, the fair market value of the additional shares distributed is transferred from retained earnings to paid-in capital as demonstrated in Illustration 19–9 on the next page.[18]

---

[18]The Committee on Accounting Procedure prescribes this accounting treatment in "Restatement and Revision of Accounting Research Bulletins," *Accounting Research Bulletin No. 43* (New York: AICPA, 1961), chap. 7, sec. B, pars. 10–14. In this pronouncement, a small stock dividend is defined as one 20 to 25% or less. For filings with that agency, the SEC has refined the definition to comprise stock distributions of less than 25%.

ILLUSTRATION 19–9	Craft declares and distributes a 10% common stock dividend (10 million shares) when the market value of the $1 par common stock is $12 per share.		
Stock Dividend			
			($ in millions)
A small stock dividend requires reclassification to paid-in capital of retained earnings equal to the fair value of the additional shares distributed.	Retained earnings (10 million shares at $12 per share)	120	
	Common stock (10 million shares at $1 par per share)		10
	Paid-in capital—excess of par (remainder).		110

ADDITIONAL CONSIDERATION

The entry above is recorded on the declaration date. Since the additional shares are not yet issued, some accountants would prefer to credit "common stock dividends issuable" at this point, instead of common stock. In that case, when the shares are issued, common stock dividends issuable is debited and common stock credited. The choice really is inconsequential; either way the $10 million amount would be reported as part of paid-in capital on a balance sheet prepared between the declaration and distribution of the shares.

Stock Market Reaction to Stock Distributions. As a Craft shareholder owning 10 shares at the time of the 10% stock dividend, you would receive an 11th share. Since each is worth $12, would you benefit by $12 when you receive the additional share from Craft? Of course not. If the value of each share were to remain $12 when the 10 million new shares are distributed, the total market value of the company would grow by $120 million (10 million shares × $12 per share).

A corporation cannot increase its market value simply by distributing additional stock certificates. Because all shareholders receive the same percentage increase in their respective holdings, you, and all other shareholders, still would own the same percentage of the company as before the distribution. Accordingly, the per share value of your shares should decline from $12 to $10.91 so that your 11 shares would be worth $120—precisely what your 10 shares were worth prior to the stock dividend. Any failure of the stock price to actually adjust in proportion to the additional shares issued probably would be due to information other than the distribution reaching shareholders at the same time.

The market price per share will decline in proportion to the increase in the number of shares distributed in a stock dividend.

Then, what justification is there for recording the additional shares at market value? In 1941 (and reaffirmed in 1953), accounting rulemakers felt that many shareholders are deceived by small stock dividends, believing they benefit by the market value of their additional shares.[19] Furthermore they erroneously felt that these individual beliefs are collectively reflected in the stock market by per share prices that remain unchanged by stock dividends. Consequently, their prescribed accounting treatment is to reduce retained earnings by the same amount as if cash dividends were paid equal to the market value of the shares issued.

Early rulemakers felt that per share market prices do not adjust in response to an increase in the number of shares.

This obsolete reasoning is inconsistent with our earlier conclusion that the market price per share will decline in approximate proportion to the increase in the number of shares distributed. Our intuitive conclusion is supported also by formal research.[20]

Capitalizing retained earnings for a stock dividend artificially reclassifies earned capital as invested capital.

Besides being based on fallacious reasoning, accounting for stock dividends by artificially reclassifying "earned" capital as "invested" capital conflicts with the reporting objective of

---

[19]"Restatement and Revision of Accounting Research Bulletins," *Accounting Research Bulletin No. 43* (New York: AICPA, 1961), chap. 7.

[20]Foster and Vickrey, "The Information Content of Stock Dividend Announcements," *Accounting Review* (April 1978), and Spiceland and Winters, "The Market Reaction to Stock Distributions: The Effect of Market Anticipation and Cash Returns," *Accounting and Business Research* (Summer 1986).

reporting shareholders' equity by source. Despite these limitations, this outdated accounting standard still applies.

Reasons for Stock Dividends.
Since neither the corporation nor its shareholders apparently benefits from stock dividends, why do companies declare them?[21] Occasionally, a company tries to give shareholders the illusion that they are receiving a real dividend.

Another reason is merely to enable the corporation to take advantage of the accepted accounting practice of capitalizing retained earnings. Specifically, a company might wish to lower an existing balance in retained earnings—otherwise available for *cash* dividends—so it can reinvest the earned assets represented by that balance without carrying a large balance in retained earnings.

Companies sometimes declare a stock dividend in lieu of a real dividend.

Companies sometimes declare a stock dividend so they can capitalize retained earnings.

STOCK SPLITS

A frequent reason for issuing a stock dividend is actually to induce the per share market price decline that follows. For instance, after a company declares a 100% stock dividend on 100 million shares of common stock, with a per share market price of $12, it then has 200 million shares, each with an approximate market value of $6. The motivation for reducing the per share market price is to increase the stock's *marketability* by making it attractive to a larger number of potential investors.

FINANCIAL REPORTING CASE

Q4, p. 937

ADDITIONAL CONSIDERATION

No cash dividends are paid on treasury shares. Usually stock dividends aren't paid on treasury shares either. Treasury shares are essentially equivalent to shares that never have been issued. In some circumstances, though, the intended use of the repurchased shares will give reason for the treasury shares to participate in a stock dividend. For instance, if the treasury shares have been specifically designated for issuance to executives in a stock option plan or stock award plan it would be appropriate to adjust the number of shares by the stock distribution.

A stock distribution of 25% or higher, although often called a "large" stock dividend, is more often referred to as a stock split.[22] Thus, a 100% stock dividend could be labeled a 2-for-1 stock split. Conceptually, the proper accounting treatment of a stock dividend or a stock split is to make no journal entry, avoiding the reclassification of earned capital as invested capital. This, in fact, is the prescribed accounting treatment for a stock split.

Since the same common stock account balance (total par) represents twice as many shares, the par value per share should be reduced by one-half. In the previous example, if the par were $1 per share before the stock distribution, then after the 2- for-1 stock split, the par would be $.50 per share.

A large stock dividend is known as a *stock split*.

Fred's Inc. declared a 3-for-2 stock split, which will be effected as a 50% stock dividend. The new shares will be distributed on February 1, 2002, to shareholders of record on January 25, 2002.

Michael J. Hayes, CEO, said, "We believe this stock split will benefit our shareholders by increasing the Company's trading activity and liquidity."[23]

STOCK SPLITS EFFECTED IN THE FORM OF STOCK DIVIDENDS (LARGE STOCK DIVIDENDS)

If the per share par value of the shares is not changed, the stock distribution is referred to as a *stock split effected in the form of a stock dividend*, or simply a *stock dividend*. In that case, a journal entry increases the common stock account by the par value of the additional shares. To avoid reducing

---

[21]After hitting a high in the 1940s, the number of stock dividends has declined significantly. Currently, about 3% of companies declare stock dividends in any given year.

[22]"Restatement and Revision of Accounting Research Bulletins," *Accounting Research Bulletin No. 43* (New York: AICPA, 1961), chap. 7, sec. B, par. 11.

[23]Business Wire, January 15, 2002.

retained earnings in these instances, most companies reduce (debit) paid-in capital—excess of par to offset the credit to common stock (Illustration 19–10).

ILLUSTRATION 19–10

Stock Split Effected in the Form of a Stock Dividend

If the *per share* par value of the shares is *not* changed, a stock distribution is referred to as a *stock split effected in the form of a stock dividend.*

Craft declares and distributes a 2-for-1 stock split effected in the form of a 100% stock dividend (100 million shares) when the market value of the $1 par common stock is $12 per share:

	($ in millions)	
Paid-in capital—excess of par...............................	100	
Common stock (100 million shares at $1 par per share).........		100

Notice that this entry does not reclassify earned capital as invested capital. Some companies, though, choose to debit retained earnings instead.[24]

Some companies capitalize retained earnings when recording a stock split effected in the form of a stock dividend.

	($ in millions)	
Retained earnings..	100	
Common stock (100 million shares at $1 par per share).........		100

Concord EFS, Inc. described its recent stock split in its 2001 annual report as shown in Graphic 19–7.

GRAPHIC 19–7
Stock Split Disclosure—Concord EFS, Inc.

Note M—Stockholders' Equity (in part)
The Board of Directors approved a two-for-one stock split on August 30, 2001. On September 28, 2001 additional shares were distributed to shareholders of record as of September 14, 2001. All appropriate share data, earnings per share, and per share data have been restated to reflect the stock split.

ADDITIONAL CONSIDERATION

A company choosing to capitalize retained earnings when recording a stock split effected in the form of a stock dividend may elect to capitalize an amount other than par value. Accounting guidelines are vague in this regard, stating only that legal amounts are minimum requirements and do not prevent the capitalization of a larger amount per share.

Source: "Restatement and Revision of Accounting Research Bulletins," *Accounting Research Bulletin No. 43* (New York: AICPA, 1961), chap. 7, sec. B, par. 14.

Reverse Stock Split. A **reverse stock split** occurs when a company decreases, rather than increases, its outstanding shares. After a 1-for-4 reverse stock split, for example, 100 million shares, $1 par per share, would become 25 million shares, $4 par per share. No journal entry is necessary. Of course the market price per share theoretically would quadruple,

---

[24]The 1998 *Accounting Trends & Techniques* reports that 80 of its 600 sample companies reported a stock split. Of those, 23 debited additional paid-in capital, 16 debited retained earnings, and 41 made no entry. Thus all but 16 were handled as stock splits effected in the form of stock dividends.

which usually is the motivation for declaring a reverse stock split. Companies that reverse split their shares frequently are struggling companies trying to accomplish with the split what the market has been unwilling to do—increase the stock price.

Fractional Shares.   Typically, a stock dividend or stock split results in some shareholders being entitled to fractions of whole shares. For example, if a company declares a 25% stock dividend, or equivalently a 5-for-4 stock split, a shareholder owning 10 shares would be entitled to 2½ shares. Another shareholder with 15 shares would be entitled to 3¾ shares.

Cash payments usually are made to shareholders for **fractional shares.** In the situation described above, for instance, if the market price at declaration is $12 per share, the shareholder with 15 shares would receive 3 additional shares and $9 in cash ($12 × ¾).

> Cash payments usually are made when shareholders are entitled to fractions of whole shares.

CHECK WITH THE **COACH**

Your study of balance sheet topics is nearing an end. We close our discussion of shareholders' equity with a decision makers' perspective of its components. Check with the Coach to assist your study of these components. The Coach has some interesting materials to help you strengthen your grip on the accounting issues and on the way the pros view the relation between debt and equity. ■

DECISION MAKERS' PERSPECTIVE

Profitability is the key to a company's long-run survival. A summary measure of profitability often used by investors and potential investors, particularly common shareholders, is the return on shareholders' equity. This ratio measures the ability of company management to generate net income from the resources that owners provide. The ratio is computed by dividing net income by average shareholders' equity. A variation of this ratio often is used when a company has both preferred and common stock outstanding. The return to common shareholders' equity is calculated by subtracting dividends to preferred shareholders from the numerator and using average common shareholders' equity as the denominator. The modified ratio focuses on the profits generated on the assets provided by common shareholders.

> The return on shareholders' equity is a popular measure of profitability.

Although the ratio is useful when evaluating the effectiveness of management in employing resources provided by owners, analysts must be careful not to view it in isolation or without considering how the ratio is derived. Keep in mind that shareholders' equity is a measure of the book value of equity, equivalent to the book value of net assets. Book value measures quickly become out of line with market values. An asset's book value usually equals its market value on the date it's purchased; the two aren't necessarily the same after that. Equivalently, the market value of a share of stock (or of total shareholders' equity) usually is different from its book value. As a result, to supplement the return on shareholders' equity ratio, analysts often relate earnings to the market value of equity, calculating the earnings-price ratio. This ratio is simply the earnings per share divided by the market price per share.

> Book value measures have limited use in financial analysis.

To better understand the differences between the book value ratio and the market value ratio, let's consider the following condensed information reported by Sharp-Novell Industries for 2003 and 2002:

($ in 000s except per share amounts)	2003	2002
Sales	$3,500	$3,100
Net income	125	114
Current assets	$ 750	$ 720
Property, plant, and equipment (net)	900	850
Total assets	$1,650	$1,570
Current liabilities	$ 550	$ 530

	2003	**2002**
Long-term liabilities	540	520
Paid-in capital	210	210
Retained earnings	350	310
Liabilities and shareholders' equity	$1,650	$1,570
Shares outstanding	50,000	50,000
Stock price (average)	$42.50	$42.50

The 2003 return on shareholders' equity is computed by dividing net income by average shareholders' equity:

$$\$125 \div [(\$560 + 520)/2] = \underline{\underline{23.1\%}}$$

The earnings-price ratio is the earnings per share divided by the market price per share:

$$\text{Earnings per share (2003)} = \$125 \div 50 = 2.50$$
$$\text{Earnings-price ratio} = \$2.50 \div 42.50 = \underline{5.9\%}$$

Obviously, the return on the market value of equity is much lower than on the book value of equity. This points out the importance of looking at more than a single ratio when making decisions. While 23.1% may seem like a desirable return, 5.9% is not nearly so attractive. Companies often emphasize the return on shareholders' equity in their annual reports. Alert investors should not accept this measure of achievement at face value. For some companies this is a meaningful measure of performance; but for others, the market-based ratio means more, particularly for a mature firm whose book value and market value are more divergent.

Share retirement and treasury stock transactions can affect the return to owners.

Decisions managers make with regard to shareholders' equity transactions can significantly impact the return to shareholders. For example, when a company buys back shares of its own stock, the return on shareholders' equity goes up. Net income is divided by a smaller amount of shareholders' equity. On the other hand, the share buyback uses assets, reducing the resources available to earn net income in the future. So, managers as well as outside analysts must carefully consider the decision to reacquire shares in light of the current economic environment, the firm's investment opportunities, and cost of capital to decide whether such a transaction is in the long-term best interests of owners.

Dividend decisions should be evaluated in light of prevailing circumstances.

The decision to pay dividends requires similar considerations. When earnings are high, are shareholders better off receiving substantial cash dividends or having management reinvest those funds to finance future growth (and future dividends)? The answer, of course, depends on the particular circumstances involved. Dividend decisions should reflect managerial strategy concerning the mix of internal versus external financing, alternative investment opportunities, and industry conditions. High dividends often are found in mature industries and low dividends in growth industries. ■

ETHICAL DILEMMA

Interworld Distributors has paid quarterly cash dividends since 1975. The dividends have steadily increased from $.25 per share to the latest dividend declaration of $2.00 per share. The board of directors is eager to continue this trend despite the fact that revenues fell significantly during recent months as a result of worsening economic conditions and increased competition. The company founder and member of the board proposes a solution. He suggests a 5% stock dividend in lieu of a cash dividend to be accompanied by the following press announcement:

"In lieu of our regular $2.00 per share cash dividend, Interworld will distribute a 5% stock dividend on its common shares, currently trading at $40 per share. Changing the form of the dividend will permit the Company to direct available cash resources to the modernization of physical facilities in preparation for competing in the 21st century."

What do you think?

CONCEPT **REVIEW** | EXERCISE

Changes in Retained Earnings

Situation: The shareholders' equity section of the balance sheet of National Foods, Inc., included the following accounts at December 31, 2003:

Shareholders' Equity	($ in millions)
Paid-in capital:	
Preferred stock, 9.09%, 11 million shares at $1 par	$ 11
Common stock, 122 million shares at $1 par	122
Paid-in capital—excess of par, preferred	479
Paid-in capital—excess of par, common	854
Less: Receivable from share purchase contract	(220)
Retained earnings:	3,245
Treasury stock, at cost, 2 million common shares	(20)
Total shareholders' equity	$4,471

Required:

1. During 2004, several events and transactions affected the retained earnings of National Foods. Prepare the appropriate entries for these events.
   a. On March 1, the board of directors declared a cash dividend of $1 per share on its 120 million outstanding shares (122 million − 2 million treasury shares), payable on April 3 to shareholders of record March 11.
   b. On March 5, the board of directors declared a property dividend of 120 million shares of Kroger common stock that National Foods had purchased in February as an investment (book value: $900 million). The investment shares had a fair market value of $8 per share and were distributed March 30 to shareholders of record March 15.
   c. On April 13, a 3-for-2 stock split was declared and distributed. The stock split was effected in the form of a 50% stock dividend. The market value of the $1 par common stock was $20 per share.
   d. On October 13, a 10% common stock dividend was declared and distributed when the market value of the $1 par common stock was $12 per share. Fractional share rights for 1 million equivalent whole shares were paid in cash.
   e. On December 1, the board of directors declared the 9.09% cash dividend on the 11 million preferred shares, payable on December 23 to shareholders of record December 11.

2. Prepare a statement of shareholders' equity for National Foods reporting the changes in shareholders' equity accounts for 2002, 2003, and 2004. Refer to the previous two Concept Reviews in this chapter for the 2002 and 2003 changes. For 2003, assume that shares were reacquired as treasury stock. Also, look back to the statement of shareholders' equity in Graphic 19–3 for the format of the statement. Assume that net income for 2004 is $225 million.

SOLUTION

1. During 2004, several events and transactions affected the retained earnings of National Foods. Prepare the appropriate entries for these events.
   a. Cash dividend of $1 per share on its 120 million *outstanding* common shares (122 million − 2 million treasury shares), payable on April 3 to shareholders of record March 11 (Note: Dividends aren't paid on treasury shares.):

March 1—Declaration Date	($ in millions)	
Retained earnings	120	
Cash dividends payable (120 million shares at $1/share).		120
March 11—Date of Record		
No entry		
April 3—Payment Date		
Cash dividends payable	120	
Cash.		120

The declaration of a dividend reduces retained earnings and creates a liability.

b. Property dividend of 120 million shares of Kroger common stock:

<table>
<tr><td colspan="3">**March 5—Declaration Date**</td><td>**($ in millions)**</td></tr>
<tr><td colspan="3">Investment in Kroger common stock . . . .</td><td>60</td><td></td></tr>
<tr><td colspan="3">   Gain on appreciation of investment ($960 − 900) . . . .</td><td></td><td>60</td></tr>
<tr><td colspan="3">Retained earnings (fair value of asset to be distributed) . . . .</td><td>960</td><td></td></tr>
<tr><td colspan="3">   Property dividends payable. . . . .</td><td></td><td>960</td></tr>
<tr><td colspan="5">**May 15—Date of Record**</td></tr>
<tr><td colspan="5">No entry</td></tr>
<tr><td colspan="5">**May 30—Payment Date**</td></tr>
<tr><td colspan="3">Property dividends payable . . . .</td><td>960</td><td></td></tr>
<tr><td colspan="3">   Investment in Kroger common stock. . . . .</td><td></td><td>960</td></tr>
</table>

The investment first must be written up to the $960 million fair market value ($8 × 120 million shares).

The liability is satisfied when the Kroger shares are distributed to shareholders.

c. 3-for-2 stock split effected in the form of a 50% stock dividend:

<table>
<tr><td></td><td>**($ in millions)**</td></tr>
<tr><td>**April 13**</td><td></td></tr>
<tr><td>Paid-in capital—excess of par* . . . .</td><td>60</td><td></td></tr>
<tr><td>   Common stock (60 million shares at $1 par per share) . . . .</td><td></td><td>60</td></tr>
</table>

*Alternatively, retained earnings may be debited.

120 million shares times 50% equals 60 million new shares—recorded at par.

d. 10% common stock dividend—fractional share rights for 1 million equivalent whole shares:

<table>
<tr><td></td><td>**($ in millions)**</td></tr>
<tr><td>**October 13**</td><td></td></tr>
<tr><td>Retained earnings (18 million shares* at $12 per share). . . . .</td><td>216</td><td></td></tr>
<tr><td>   Common stock (17 million shares at $1 par per share) . . . .</td><td></td><td>17</td></tr>
<tr><td>   Paid-in capital—excess of par</td><td></td><td></td></tr>
<tr><td>   (17 million shares at $11 per share above par) . . . .</td><td></td><td>187</td></tr>
<tr><td>   Cash (1 million shares at $12 market price per share). . . . .</td><td></td><td>12</td></tr>
</table>

*(120 million + 60 million) × 10% = 18 million shares

The stock dividend occurs after the 3-for-2 stock split; thus 18 million shares are distributed.

The $12 fair market value of the additional shares is capitalized in this small stock dividend.

e. 9.09% cash dividend on the 11 million preferred shares, payable on December 23 to shareholders of record December 11:

<table>
<tr><td colspan="2">**December 1—Declaration Date**</td><td>**($ in millions)**</td></tr>
<tr><td colspan="2">Retained earnings . . . .</td><td>1</td><td></td></tr>
<tr><td colspan="2">   Cash dividends payable ($11 million par × 9.09%) . . . .</td><td></td><td>1</td></tr>
<tr><td colspan="4">**December 11—Date of Record**</td></tr>
<tr><td colspan="4">NO ENTRY</td></tr>
<tr><td colspan="4">**December 23—Payment Date**</td></tr>
<tr><td colspan="2">Cash dividends payable . . . .</td><td>1</td><td></td></tr>
<tr><td colspan="2">   Cash. . . . .</td><td></td><td>1</td></tr>
</table>

Preferred shareholders annually receive the designated percentage (9.09%) of the preferred's par value ($1 million), if dividends are declared.

2. Prepare a statement of shareholders' equity for National Foods reporting the changes in shareholders' equity accounts for 2002, 2003, and 2004.

NATIONAL FOODS
Statement of Shareholders' Equity
For the Years Ended December 31, 2004, 2003, and 2002

($ in millions)	Preferred Stock	Common Stock	Additional Paid-In Capital	Receivable from Share Purchase Contract	Retained Earnings	Treasury Stock (at cost)	Total Share-holder's Equity	
Balance at January 1, 2002		120	836		2,449		3,405	These are the transactions from Concept Review Exercise—Expansion of Corporate Capital.
Sale of preferred shares	10		430	(220)			220	
Issuance of common shares		1	9				10	
Issuance of common and preferred shares	1	1	58				60	
Net income					400		400	
Cash dividends, preferred	—	—	—	—	(1)	—	(1)	
Balance at December 31, 2002	11	122	1,333	(220)	2,848		4,094	
Purchase of treasury shares						(60)	(60)	These are the transactions from Concept Review Exercise—Treasury Stock.
Sale of treasury shares			4			20	24	
Sale of treasury shares			(4)		(2)	20	14	
Net income					400		400	
Cash dividends, preferred	—	—	—	—	(1)	—	(1)	
Balance at December 31, 2003	11	122	1,333	(220)	3,245	(20)	4,471	
Cash dividends, common					(120)		(120)	These are the transactions from Concept Review Exercise—Changes in Retained Earnings.
Property dividends, common					(960)		(960)	
3-for-2 split effected in the form of a stock dividend		60	(60)					
10% stock dividend		17	187		(216)		(12)	
Preferred dividends					(1)		(1)	
Net income	—	—	—	—	225	—	225	
Balance at December 31, 2004	11	199	1,460	(220)	2,173	(20)	3,603	

FINANCIAL REPORTING CASE **SOLUTION**

1. **Do you think the stock price increase is related to GE's share repurchase plan?** *(p. 953)*
The stock price increase probably is related to GE's buyback plan. The marketplace realizes that decreasing the supply of shares supports the price of remaining shares. However, the repurchase of shares is not necessarily the best use of a company's cash. Whether it is in the shareholders' best interests depends on what other opportunities the company has for the cash available.

2. **What are GE's choices in accounting for the share repurchases?** *(p. 954)* When a corporation reacquires its own shares, those shares assume the same status as authorized but unissued shares, just as if they never had been issued. However, for exactly the same transaction, companies can choose between two accounting alternatives: (a) formally retiring them or (b) accounting for the shares repurchased as treasury stock. In actuality, GE uses alternative (b).

3. **What effect does the quarterly cash dividend of 18 cents a share have on GE's assets? Its liabilities? Its shareholders' equity?** *(p. 960)* Each quarter, when directors declare a cash dividend, retained earnings is reduced and a liability is recorded. The liability is paid with cash on the payment date. So, the net effect is a decrease in GE's assets and its shareholders' equity. The effect on liabilities is temporary.

4. **What effect did the stock split have on GE's assets? Its liabilities? Its shareholders' equity?** *(p. 963)* Conceptually, the proper accounting treatment of a stock split is to make no journal entry. However, since GE refers to the stock distribution as a "stock split effected in the form of a stock dividend," a journal entry would increase the common stock account by the par value of the additional shares and would reduce paid-in capital—excess of par. This merely moves an amount from one part of shareholders' equity to another. Regardless of the accounting method, there is no change in GE's assets, liabilities, or total shareholders' equity. ■

THE BOTTOM LINE

1. Shareholders' equity is the owners' residual interest in a corporation's assets. It arises primarily from (1) amounts invested by shareholders and (2) amounts earned by the corporation on behalf of its shareholders. These are reported as (1) paid-in capital and (2) retained earnings.

2. A statement of shareholders' equity reports the sources of the changes in individual shareholders' equity accounts.

3. Shares sold by share purchase contract in essence are sold on credit. Shares sold for consideration other than cash (maybe services or a noncash asset) should be recorded at the fair market value of the shares or the noncash consideration, whichever seems more clearly evident.

4. When a corporation retires previously issued shares, those shares assume the same status as authorized but unissued shares—just the same as if they had never been issued. Payments made to retire shares are viewed as a distribution of corporate assets to shareholders.

5. When required shares are viewed as treasury stock, the cost of acquiring the shares is temporarily debited to the treasury stock account. Recording the effects on specific shareholders' equity accounts is delayed until later when the shares are reissued.

6. Retained earnings represents, in general, a corporation's accumulated, undistributed or reinvested net income (or net loss). Distributions of earned assets are dividends.

7. Most corporate dividends are paid in cash. When a noncash asset is distributed, it is referred to as a property dividend. The fair market value of the assets to be distributed is the amount recorded for a property dividend.

8. A stock dividend is the distribution of additional shares of stock to current shareholders. For a small stock dividend (25% or less), the fair value of the additional shares distributed is transferred from retained earnings to paid-in capital. For a stock distribution of 25% or higher, the par value of the additional shares is reclassified within shareholders' equity if referred to as a stock split effected in the form of a stock dividend, but if referred to merely as a stock split, no journal entry is recorded. ■

APPENDIX
19

QUASI REORGANIZATIONS

A firm undergoing financial difficulties, but with favorable future prospects, may use a **quasi reorganization** to write down inflated asset values and eliminate an accumulated deficit (debit balance in retained earnings). To effect the reorganization the following procedures are followed:

1. The firm's assets (and perhaps liabilities) are revalued (up or down) to reflect fair market values, with corresponding credits or debits to retained earnings. This process typically increases the deficit.
2. The debit balance in retained earnings (deficit) is eliminated against additional paid-in capital. If additional paid-in capital is not sufficient to absorb the entire deficit, a reduction in capital stock may be necessary (with an appropriate restating of the par amount per share).
3. Retained earnings is dated. That is, disclosure is provided to indicate the date the deficit was eliminated and when the new accumulation of earnings began.

The procedure is demonstrated in Illustration 19A–1. The shareholders approved the quasi reorganization effective January 1, 2003. The plan was to be accomplished by a reduction of inventory by $75 million, a reduction in property, plant, and equipment (net) of $175 million, and appropriate adjustments to shareholders' equity.

The Emerson-Walsch Corporation has incurred operating losses for several years. A newly elected board of directors voted to implement a quasi reorganization, subject to shareholder approval. The balance sheet, on December 31, 2002, immediately prior to the restatement, includes the data shown below.

	($ in millions)
Cash	$ 75
Receivables	200
Inventory	375
Property, plant, and equipment (net)	400
	$1,050
Liabilities	$ 400
Common stock (800 million shares at $1 par)	800
Additional paid-in capital	150
Retained earnings (deficit)	(300)
	$1,050

	($ in millions)	
To Revalue Assets:		
Retained earnings	75	
Inventory		75
Retained earnings	175	
Property, plant, and equipment		175
To Eliminate a Portion of the Deficit against Available		
Additional Paid-In Capital:		
Additional paid-in capital	150	
Retained earnings		150
To Eliminate the Remainder of the Deficit against		
Common Stock:		
Common stock	400	
Retained earnings		400

When assets are revalued to reflect fair market values, the process often increases the deficit.

The deficit, $550 ($300 + 75 + 175), can be only partially absorbed by the balance of additional paid-in capital.

The remaining deficit, $400 ($300 + 75 + 175 − 150), must be absorbed by reducing the balance in common stock.

The balance sheet immediately after the restatement would include the following:

	($ in millions)
Cash	$ 75
Receivables	200
Inventory	300
Property, plant, and equipment (net)	225
	$800
Liabilities	$400
Common stock (800 million shares at $.50 par)	400
Additional paid-in capital	0
Retained earnings (deficit)	0
	$800

Assets and liabilities reflect current values.

Because a reduced balance represents the same 800 million shares, the par amount per share must be reduced.

The deficit is eliminated.

Note A: Upon the recommendation of the board of directors and approval by shareholders a quasi reorganization was implemented January 1, 2003. The plan was accomplished by a reduction of inventory by $75 million, a reduction in property, plant, and equipment (net) of $175 million, and appropriate adjustments to shareholders' equity. The balance in retained earnings reflects the elimination of a $300 million deficit on that date.

QUESTIONS FOR REVIEW OF KEY TOPICS

Q 19–1 Identify and briefly describe the two primary sources of shareholders' equity.

Q 19–2 The balance sheet reports the balances of shareholders' equity accounts. What additional information is provided by the statement of shareholders' equity?

Q 19–3 What is comprehensive income? How does comprehensive income differ from net income? Where do companies report it in a balance sheet?

Q 19–4 Identify the three common forms of business organization and the primary difference between the way they are accounted for.

Q 19–5 Corporations offer the advantage of limited liability. Explain what is meant by that statement.

Q 19–6 Distinguish between not-for-profit and for-profit corporations.

Q 19–7 Distinguish between publicly held and privately (or closely) held corporations.

Q 19–8 How does the Model Business Corporation Act affect the way corporations operate?

Q 19–9 The owners of a corporation are its shareholders. If a corporation has only one class of shares, they typically are labeled common shares. Indicate the ownership rights held by common shareholders, unless specifically withheld by agreement.

Q 19–10 What is meant by a shareholder's preemptive right?

Q 19–11 Terminology varies in the way companies differentiate among share types. But many corporations designate shares as common or preferred. What are the two special rights usually given to preferred shareholders?

Q 19–12 Most preferred shares are cumulative. Explain what this means.

Q 19–13 The par value of shares historically indicated the real value of shares and all shares were issued at that price. The concept has changed with time. Describe the meaning of par value as it has evolved to today.

Q 19–14 When shares are sold by share purchase contract, shares ordinarily are issued in exchange for a promissory note from the subscriber and a receivable is recorded for the portion of the selling price not yet received. How is this receivable reported in financial statements?

Q 19–15 At times, companies issue their shares for consideration other than cash. What is the measurement objective in those cases?

Q 19–16 Companies occasionally sell more than one security for a single price. How is the issue price allocated among the separate securities?

Q 19–17 The costs of legal, promotional, and accounting services necessary to effect the sale of shares are referred to as share issue costs. How are these costs recorded? Compare this approach to the way debt issue costs are recorded.

Q 19–18 When a corporation acquires its own shares, those shares assume the same status as authorized but unissued shares, as if they never had been issued. Explain how this is reflected in the accounting records if the shares are formally retired.

Q 19–19 Discuss the conceptual basis for accounting for a share buyback as treasury stock.

Q 19–20 The prescribed accounting treatment for stock dividends implicitly assumes that shareholders are fooled by small stock dividends and benefit by the market value of their additional shares. Explain this statement. Is it logical?

Q 19–21 Brandon Components declares a 2-for-1 stock split. What will be the effects of the split, and how should it be recorded?

Q 19–22 What is a reverse stock split? What would be the effect of a reverse stock split on one million $1 par shares? On the accounting records?

Q 19–23 Suppose you own 80 shares of IBM common stock when the company declares a 4% stock dividend. What will you receive as a result?

Q 19–24 (based on Appendix 19) A quasi reorganization is sometimes employed by a firm undergoing financial difficulties, but with favorable future prospects. What are two objectives of this procedure? Briefly describe the procedural steps.

EXERCISES

E 19–1
Comprehensive income

The following is an excerpt from a disclosure note from the 2003 annual report of Kaufman Chemicals, Inc:

COMPREHENSIVE INCOME (LOSS)

The components of comprehensive income, net of tax, are as follows (in millions):

Years Ended December 31	2003	2002	2001
Net income	$856	$766	$594
Other comprehensive income:			
Change in net unrealized gains on available-for-sale investments, net of tax of $22, ($14), and $15 in 2003, 2002, and 2001, respectively	34	(21)	23
Other	(2)	(1)	1
Total	$888	$744	$618

Kaufman reports Accumulated other comprehensive income in its balance sheet as a component of shareholders' equity as follows:

	($ in millions)	
	2003	2002
Shareholders' equity:		
Common stock	355	355
Additional paid-in capital	8,567	8,567
Retained earnings	6,544	5,988
Accumulated other comprehensive income	107	75
Total shareholders' equity	$15,573	$14,985

Required:
1. What is comprehensive income and how does it differ from net income?
2. How is comprehensive income reported in a balance sheet?
3. Why is Kaufman's 2003 balance sheet amount different from the 2003 amount reported in the disclosure note? Explain.
4. From the information provided, determine how Kaufman calculated the $107 million Accumulated other comprehensive income in 2003.

E 19–2
Stock issued for cash;
Wright Medical Group;

The following is a news item reported by Reuters on January 29, 2002:

WASHINGTON, Jan 29 (Reuters)—Wright Medical Group, a maker of reconstructive implants for knees and hips, on Tuesday filed to sell 3 million shares of common stock.

In a filing with the U.S. Securities and Exchange Commission, it said it plans to use the proceeds from the offering for general corporate purposes, working capital, research and development, and acquisitions.

After the sale there will be about 31.5 million shares outstanding in the Arlington, Tennessee-based company, according to the SEC filing.

Wright shares closed at $17.15 on Nasdaq.

The common stock of Wright Medical Group has a par of $.01 per share.

Required:
Prepare the journal entry to record the sale of the shares assuming the price existing when the announcement was made and ignoring share issue costs.

E 19–3
Issuance of shares;
share purchase
contract

During the first year of operations, Bekon International, Inc., sold and issued 28 million of its common shares, $1 par per share. During the first year, which ended December 31, 2003, net income was $50 million and no dividends were paid.

Required:
1. Prepare the journal entry to record the sale of the shares for cash at a price of $20 per share.
2. Prepare the journal entry to record the sale of the shares if sold by share purchase contract for $20 per share, with 50% of the selling price to be received after 14 months.
3. Show how shareholders' equity would be reported in Bekon's balance sheet at December 31, 2003, assuming the shares were sold by share purchase contract.

4. Prepare the journal entry to record the collection of the receivable from the share purchase contract during the second year of operations.

5. Show how shareholders' equity would be reported in Bekon's balance sheet at December 31, 2004, assuming no additional changes to shareholders' equity other than 2004 net income of $65 million.

E 19–4
Issuance of shares; noncash consideration

During its first year of operations, Eastern Data Links Corporation entered into the following transactions relating to shareholders' equity. The articles of incorporation authorized the issue of 8 million common shares, $1 par per share, and 1 million preferred shares, $50 par per share.

Required:
Prepare the appropriate journal entries to record each transaction.

Feb. 12   Sold 2 million common shares, for $9 per share.
13   Issued 40,000 common shares to attorneys in exchange for legal services.
13   Sold 80,000 of its common shares and 4,000 preferred shares for $945,000.
Nov. 15   Issued 380,000 of its common shares in exchange for equipment for which the cash price was known to be $3,688,000.

E 19–5
Share issue costs; issuance

ICOT Industries issued 15 million of its $1 par common shares for $424 million on April 11, 2003. Legal, promotional, and accounting services necessary to effect the sale cost $2 million.

Required:
1. Prepare the journal entry to record the issuance of the shares.
2. Explain how recording the share issue costs differs from the way debt issue costs are recorded (discussed in Chapter 14).

E 19–6
Effect of cumulative, nonparticipating preferred stock on dividends—3 years

The shareholders' equity of WBL Industries includes the items shown below. The board of directors of WBL declared cash dividends of $8 million, $20 million, and $150 million in its first three years of operation—2003, 2004, and 2005, respectively.

	($ in millions)
Common stock	$100
Paid-in capital—excess of par, common	980
Preferred stock, 8%	200
Paid-in capital—excess of par, preferred	555

Required:
Determine the amount of dividends to be paid to preferred and common shareholders in each of the three years, assuming that the preferred stock is cumulative and nonparticipating.

	Preferred	Common
2003		
2004		
2005		

E 19–7
Retirement of shares

Borner Communications' articles of incorporation authorized the issuance of 130 million common shares. The transactions described below effected changes in Borner's outstanding shares. Prior to the transactions, Borner's shareholders' equity included the following:

Shareholders' Equity	($ in millions)
Common stock, 100 million shares at $1 par,	$100
Paid-in capital—excess of par	300
Retained earnings	210

Required:
Assuming that Borner Communications retires shares it reacquires (restores their status to that of authorized but unissued shares), record the appropriate journal entry for each of the following transactions:
1. On January 7, 2003, Borner reacquired 2 million shares at $5.00 per share.
2. On August 23, 2003, Borner reacquired 4 million shares at $3.50 per share.
3. On July 25, 2004, Borner sold 3 million common shares at $6 per share.

E 19–8
Retirement of shares

In 2003, Borland Semiconductors entered into the transactions described below. In 2000, Borland had issued 170 million shares of its $1 par common stock at $34 per share.

Required:
Assuming that Borland retires shares it reacquires, record the appropriate journal entry for each of the following transactions:
1.   On January 2, 2003, Borland reacquired 10 million shares at $32.50 per share.
2.   On March 3, 2003, Borland reacquired 10 million shares at $36 per share.
3.   On August 13, 2003, Borland sold 1 million shares at $42 per share.
4.   On December 15, 2003, Borland sold 2 million shares at $36 per share.

E 19–9
Treasury stock

In 2003, Western Transport Company entered into the treasury stock transactions described below. In 2001, Western Transport had issued 140 million shares of its $1 par common stock at $17 per share.

Required:
Prepare the appropriate journal entry for each of the following transactions:
1.   On January 23, 2003, Western Transport reacquired 10 million shares at $20 per share.
2.   On September 3, 2003, Western Transport sold 1 million treasury shares at $21 per share.
3.   On November 4, 2003, Western Transport sold 1 million treasury shares at $18 per share.

E 19–10
Treasury stock;
weighted-average and
FIFO cost

At December 31, 2002, the balance sheet of Meca International included the following shareholders' equity accounts:

Shareholders' Equity	($ in millions)
Common stock, 60 million shares at $1 par	$ 60
Paid-in capital—excess of par	300
Retained earnings	410

Required:
Assuming that Meca International views its share buybacks as treasury stock, record the appropriate journal entry for each of the following transactions:
1.   On February 12, 2003, Meca reacquired 1 million common shares at $13 per share.
2.   On June 9, 2004, Meca reacquired 2 million common shares at $10 per share.
3.   On May 25, 2005, Meca sold 2 million treasury shares at $15 per share—determine cost as the weighted average cost of treasury shares.
4.   For the previous transaction, assume Meca determines the cost of treasury shares by the FIFO method.

E 19–11
Reporting
shareholders' equity
after share repurchase

On two previous occasions, the management of Dennison and Company, Inc. repurchased some of its common shares. Between buyback transactions, the corporation issued common shares under its management incentive plan. Shown below is shareholders' equity following these share transactions, as reported by two different methods of accounting for reacquired shares.

	($ in millions)	
	Method A	Method B
Shareholders' Equity		
Paid-in capital:		
Preferred stock, $10 par	$ 150	$ 150
Common stock, $1 par	200	197
Additional paid-in capital	1,204	1,201
Retained earnings	2,994	2,979
Less: Treasury stock	(21)	
Total shareholders' equity	$4,527	$4,527

Required:
1.   Infer from the presentation which method of accounting for reacquired shares is represented by each of the two columns.
2.   Explain why presentation formats are different and why some account balances are different for the two methods.

E 19–12
Change from treasury
stock to retired stock

In keeping with a modernization of corporate statutes in its home state, UMC Corporation decided in 2003 to discontinue accounting for reacquired shares as treasury stock. Instead, shares repurchased will be viewed as having been retired, reassuming the status of unissued shares. As part of the change, treasury shares held were reclassified as retired stock. At December 31, 2002 UMC's balance sheet reported the following shareholders' equity:

	($ in millions)
Common stock, $1 par	$200
Paid-in capital—excess of par	800
Retained earnings	956
Treasury stock (4 million shares at cost)	(25)
Total shareholders' equity	$1,931

Required:

Identify the type of accounting change this decision represents, and prepare the journal entry to effect the reclassification of treasury shares as retired shares.

E 19–13

Multiple choice; paid-in capital

The following questions dealing with paid-in capital are adapted from recent CPA examinations. Determine the response that best completes the statements or questions.

1. East Co. issued 1,000 shares of its $5 par common stock to Howe as compensation for 1,000 hours of legal services performed. Howe usually bills $160 per hour for legal services. On the date of issuance, the stock was trading on a public exchange at $140 per share. By what amount should the additional paid-in capital account increase as a result of this transaction?
   a. $135,000
   b. $140,000
   c. $155,000
   d. $160,000

2. If a corporation sells some of its treasury stock at a price that exceeds its cost, this excess should be
   a. Reported as a gain in the income statement.
   b. Treated as a reduction in the carrying amount.
   c. Credited to additional paid-in capital.
   d. Credited to retained earnings.

E 19–14

Transactions affecting retained earnings

Shown below in T-account format are the changes affecting the retained earnings of Brenner-Jude Corporation during 2003. At January 1, 2003, the corporation had outstanding 105 million common shares, $1 par per share.

Retained Earnings ($ in millions)

		90	Beginning balance
Retirement of 5 million common shares for $22 million	2		
		88	Net income for the year
Declaration and payment of a $.33 per share cash dividend	33		
Declaration and distribution of a 4% stock dividend	20		
		123	Ending balance

Required:

1. From the information provided by the account changes you should be able to recreate the transactions that affected Brenner-Jude's retained earnings during 2003. Prepare the journal entries that Brenner-Jude must have recorded during the year for these transactions.
2. Prepare a statement of retained earnings for Brenner-Jude for the year ended 2003.

E 19–15

Stock dividend

The shareholders' equity of Core Technologies Company on June 30, 2002, included the following:

Common stock, $1 par; authorized, 8 million shares; issued and outstanding, 3 million shares	$ 3,000,000
Paid-in capital—excess of par	12,000,000
Retained earnings	14,000,000

On April 1, 2003, the board of directors of Core Technologies declared a 10% stock dividend on common shares, to be distributed on June 1. The market price of Core Technologies' common stock was $30 on April 1, 2003, and $40 on June 1, 2003.

Required:

Prepare the journal entry to record the distribution of the stock dividend on the declaration date.

E 19–16
Stock split; Concord EFS, Inc.

Concord EFS, Inc. is an electronic transaction processor, providing transaction authorization, data capture, settlement and funds transfer services to financial institutions, supermarkets, petroleum retailers, convenience stores, and other independent retailers. The company's eighth stock split was announced in the following Business Wire:

MEMPHIS, Tenn.—(BUSINESS WIRE)—Aug. 30, 2001—Concord EFS, Inc. (Nasdaq) announced today that its Board of Directors has declared a 2-for-1 stock split to be effected by a dividend payable in shares of common stock. The stock split will be distributed on September 28, 2001, to stockholders of record as of September 14, 2001.

At the time of the stock split, 243.4 million shares of common stock, $.33⅓ par per share, were outstanding.

Required:
1. Prepare the journal entry, if any, that Concord recorded at the time of the stock split.
2. What is the probable motivation for declaring the 2-for-1 stock split to be effected by a dividend payable in shares of common stock?
3. If Concord's stock price had been $28 at the time of the split, what would be its approximate value after the split (other things equal)?

E 19–17
Cash for fractional share rights

Douglas McDonald Company's balance sheet included the following shareholders' equity accounts at December 31, 2002:

	($ in millions)
Paid-in capital:	
Common stock, 900 million shares at $1 par	$ 900
Paid-in capital—excess of par	15,800
Retained earnings	14,888
Total shareholders' equity	$31,588

On March 16, 2003, a 4% common stock dividend was declared and distributed. The market value of the common stock was $21 per share. Fractional share rights represented 2 million equivalent whole shares. Cash was paid in place of the fractional share rights.

Required:
1, What is a fractional share right?
2. Prepare the appropriate entries for the declaration and distribution of the stock dividend.

E 19–18
Transactions affecting retained earnings

The balance sheet of Consolidated Paper, Inc. included the following shareholders' equity accounts at December 31, 2002:

	($ in millions)
Paid-in capital:	
Preferred stock, 8.8%, 90,000 shares at $1 par	$ 90,000
Common stock, 364,000 shares at $1 par	364,000
Paid-in capital—excess par, preferred	1,437,000
Paid-in capital—excess of par, common	2,574,000
Retained earnings	9,735,000
Treasury stock, at cost; 4,000 common shares	(44,000)
Total shareholders' equity	$14,156,000

During 2003, several events and transactions affected the retained earnings of Consolidated Paper.

Required:
1. Prepare the appropriate entries for these events:
    a. On March 3 the board of directors declared a property dividend of 240,000 shares of Leasco International common stock that Consolidated Paper had purchased in January as an investment (book value: $700,000). The investment shares had a fair market value of $3 per share and were distributed March 31 to shareholders of record March 15.
    b. On May 3 a 5-for-4 stock split was declared and distributed. The stock split was effected in the form of a 25% stock dividend. The market value of the $1 par common stock was $11 per share.

c. On July 5 a 2% common stock dividend was declared and distributed. The market value of the common stock was $11 per share.

d. On December 1 the board of directors declared the 8.8% cash dividend on the 90,000 preferred shares, payable on December 28 to shareholders of record December 20.

e. On December 1 the board of directors declared a cash dividend of $.50 per share on its common shares, payable on December 28 to shareholders of record December 20.

2. Prepare the shareholders' equity section of the balance sheet for Consolidated Paper, Inc. for the year ended at December 31, 2003. Net income for the year was $810,000.

E 19–19
Multiple choice;
retained earnings

The following questions dealing with retained earnings are adapted from recent CPA examinations. Determine the response that best completes the statements or questions.

1. At December 31, 2002, and December 31, 2003, Apex Co. had 3,000 shares of $100 par, 5% cumulative preferred stock outstanding. No dividends were in arrears as of December 31, 2001. Apex did not declare a dividend during 2002. During 2003 Apex paid a cash dividend of $10,000 on its preferred stock. Apex should report dividends in arrears in its 2003 financial statements as a (an)
   a. Accrued liability of $15,000.
   b. Disclosure of $15,000.
   c. Accrued liability of $20,000.
   d. Disclosure of $20,000.

2. On January 2, 2003, Lake Mining Co.'s board of directors declared a cash dividend of $400,000 to shareholders of record on January 18, 2003, payable on February 10, 2003. The dividend is permissible under law in Lake's state of incorporation. Selected data from Lake's December 31, 2002, balance sheet are as follows:

Accumulated depletion	$100,000
Capital stock	500,000
Additional paid-in capital	150,000
Retained earnings	300,000

The $400,000 dividend includes a liquidating dividend of
   a. $0
   b. $100,000
   c. $150,000
   d. $300,000

3. When a company declares a cash dividend, retained earnings is decreased by the amount of the dividend on the date of
   a. Declaration.
   b. Record.
   c. Payment.
   d. Declaration or record, whichever is earlier.

E 19–20
Profitability ratio

Comparative balance sheets for Softech Canvas Goods for 2003 and 2002 are shown below. Softech pays no dividends, instead reinvesting all earnings for future growth.

Comparative Balance Sheets
($ in 000s)

	December 31	
	2003	**2002**
Assets:		
Cash	$ 50	$ 40
Accounts receivable	100	120
Short-term investments	50	40
Inventory	200	140
Property, plant, and equipment (net)	600	550
	$1,000	$890
Liabilities and Shareholders' Equity:		
Current liabilities	$ 240	$210
Bonds payable	160	160
Paid-in capital	400	400
Retained earnings	200	120
	$1,000	$890

Required:

1. Determine the return on shareholders' equity for 2003.
2. What does the ratio measure?

E 19–21
New equity issues;
offerings
announcements

When companies offer new equity security issues, they publicize the offerings in the financial press and on Internet sites. Assume the following were among the equity offerings reported in December 2003:

NEW SECURITIES ISSUES

Equity

American Materials Transfer Corporation (AMTC)—7.5 million common shares, $.001 par, priced at $13.546 each through underwriters led by Second Tennessee Bank N.A. and Morgan, Dunavant & Co., according to a syndicate official.

Proactive Solutions Inc. (PSI)—Offering of nine million common shares, $.01 par, was priced at $15.20 a share via lead manager Stanley Brothers, Inc., according to a syndicate official.

Required:

Prepare the appropriate journal entries to record the sale of both issues to underwriters. Ignore share issue costs.

E 19–22
Stock buyback; Fluor
Corporation; press
announcement

The following excerpts are from an article reported in the September 20, 2001, online issue of *Yahoo Finance.*

"Fluor Announces Share Repurchase"
ALISO VIEJO, Calif., Sept. 20 /PRNewswire/—Fluor Corporation (NYSE: FLR) today announced that it has initiated a modest share repurchase program. The company's board of directors had earlier approved an authorization to repurchase up to 5 million shares.

The share repurchases will be implemented in an opportunistic fashion either on the open market or in privately negotiated transactions, based on market conditions, and will be aimed primarily at offsetting the dilution, which has occurred over the past year from the exercise of stock options.

Fluor's stock closed at $36.17, down $.14.

Fluor has not previously bought back shares. The par amount per share for Fluor common stock is $.01. Paid-in capital—excess of par is $4.31per share on average.

Required:

1. Suppose Fluor retires the 5 million shares through repurchase on the open market at the price indicated. Prepare the appropriate journal entry to record the purchase.
2. What does the company mean by saying that the buyback "will be aimed primarily at offsetting the dilution, which has occurred over the past year from the exercise of stock options"?

PROBLEMS

P 19–1
Various stock
transactions; correction
of journal entries

Part A

During its first year of operations, the McCollum Corporation entered into the following transactions relating to shareholders' equity. The corporation was authorized to issue 100 million common shares, $1 par per share.

Required:

Prepare the appropriate journal entries to record each transaction.

Jan. 9   Issued 40 million common shares for $20 per share.
Mar. 11   Issued 5,000 shares in exchange for custom-made equipment. McCollum's shares
          have traded recently on the stock exchange at $20 per share.

Part B

A new staff accountant for the McCollum Corporation recorded the following journal entries during the second year of operations. McCollum retires shares that it reacquires (restores their status to that of authorized but unissued shares).

			($ in millions)
Jan. 12	Land	2	
	Paid-in capital—donation of land.		2
Sept. 1	Common stock.	2	
	Retained earnings	48	
	Cash		50
Dec. 1	Cash	26	
	Common stock		1
	Gain on sale of previously issued shares		25

Required:

Prepare the journal entries that should have been recorded for each of the transactions.

P 19–2

Share buyback—
comparison of
retirement and treasury
stock treatment

The shareholders' equity section of the balance sheet of TNL Systems, Inc. included the following accounts at December 31, 2002:

Shareholders' Equity	($ in millions)
Common stock, 240 million shares at $1 par,	$ 240
Paid-in capital—excess of par	1,680
Paid-in capital—share repurchase	1
Retained earnings	1,100

Required:

1. During 2003, TNL Systems reacquired shares of its common stock and later sold shares in two separate transactions. Prepare the entries for both the purchase and subsequent resale of the shares assuming the shares are (a) retired and (b) viewed as treasury stock.
   a. On February 5, 2003, TNL Systems purchased 6 million shares at $10 per share.
   b. On July 9, 2003, the corporation sold 2 million shares at $12 per share.
   c. On November 14, 2005, the corporation sold 2 million shares at $7 per share.
2. Prepare the shareholders' equity section of TNL Systems' balance sheet at December 31, 2005, comparing the two approaches. Assume all net income earned in 2003–2005 was distributed to shareholders as cash dividends.

P 19–3

Reacquired shares—
comparison of retired
shares and treasury
shares

National Supply's shareholders' equity included the following accounts at December 31, 2002:

Shareholders' Equity	($ in millions)
Common stock, 6 million shares at $1 par	$ 6,000,000
Paid-in capital—excess of par	30,000,000
Retained earnings	86,500,000

Required:

1. National Supply reacquired shares of its common stock in two separate transactions and later sold shares. Prepare the entries for each of the transactions under each of two separate assumptions: the shares are (a) retired and (b) accounted for as treasury stock.

February 15, 2003	Reacquired 300,000 shares at $8 per share.
February 17, 2004	Reacquired 300,000 shares at $5.50 per share.
November 9, 2005	Sold 200,000 shares at $7 per share (assume FIFO cost).

2. Prepare the shareholders' equity section of National Supply's balance sheet at December 31, 2005, assuming the shares are (a) retired and (b) accounted for as treasury stock. Net income was $14 million in 2003, $15 million in 2004, and $16 million in 2005. No dividends were paid during the three-year period.

P 19–4

Statement of retained
earnings

Comparative statements of retained earnings for Renn-Dever Corporation were reported in its 2003 annual report as follows.

RENN-DEVER CORPORATION
Statements of Retained Earnings

For the Years Ended December 31,	2003	2002	2001
Balance at beginning of year	$6,794,292	$5,464,052	$5,624,552
Net income (loss)	3,308,700	2,240,900	(160,500)

Deductions:

Stock dividend (34,900 shares)	242,000		
Common shares retired (110,000 shares)		212,660	
Common stock cash dividends	889,950	698,000	0
Balance at end of year	**$8,971,042**	**$6,794,292**	**$5,464,052**

At December 31, 2000, common shares consisted of the following:

Common stock, 1,855,000 shares at $1 par	$1,855,000
Paid-in capital—excess of par	7,420,000

Required:

Infer from the reports the events and transactions that affected Renn-Dever Corporation's retained earnings during 2001, 2002, and 2003. Prepare the journal entries that reflect those events and transactions.

P 19–5

Shareholders' equity transactions, statement of shareholders' equity

Listed below are the transactions that affected the shareholders' equity of Branch-Rickie Corporation during the period 2003–2005. At December 31, 2002, the corporation's accounts included:

	($ in 000s)
Common stock, 105 million shares at $1 par	$105,000
Paid-in capital—excess of par	630,000
Retained earnings	970,000

a. November 1, 2003, the board of directors declared a cash dividend of $.80 per share on its common shares, payable to shareholders of record November 15, to be paid December 1.

b. On March 1, 2004, the board of directors declared a property dividend consisting of corporate bonds of Warner Corporation that Branch-Rickie was holding as an investment. The bonds had a fair market value of $1.6 million, but were purchased two years previously for $1.3 million. Because they were intended to be held to maturity, the bonds had not been previously written up. The property dividend was payable to shareholders of record March 13, to be distributed April 5.

c. On July 12, 2004, the corporation declared and distributed a 5% common stock dividend (when the market value of the common stock was $21 per share). Cash was paid for fractional share rights representing 250,000 equivalent whole shares.

d. On November 1, 2004, the board of directors declared a cash dividend of $.80 per share on its common shares, payable to shareholders of record November 15, to be paid December 1.

e. On January 15, 2005, the board of directors declared and distributed a 3-for-2 stock split effected in the form of a 50% stock dividend when the market value of the common stock was $22 per share.

f. On November 1, 2005, the board of directors declared a cash dividend of $.65 per share on its common shares, payable to shareholders of record November 15, to be paid December 1.

Required:

1. Prepare the journal entries that Branch-Rickie recorded during the three-year period for these transactions.
2. Prepare comparative statements of shareholders' equity for Branch-Rickie for the three-year period ($ in 000s). Net income was $330 million, $395 million, and $455 million for 2003, 2004, and 2005, respectively.

P 19–6

Statement of shareholders' equity

Comparative statements of shareholders' equity for Anaconda International Corporation were reported as follows for the fiscal years ending December 31, 2003, 2004, and 2005.

ANACONDA INTERNATIONAL CORPORATION
Statements of Shareholders' Equity
For the Years Ended Dec. 31, 2003, 2004, and 2005
($ in millions)

	Preferred Stock $10 par	Common Stock $1 par	Additional Paid-In Capital	Receivable from Share Purchase Contract	Retained Earnings	Total Shareholders' Equity
Balance at January 1, 2003		55	495		1,878	2,428
Sale of preferred shares	10		470	(360)		120
Sale of common shares		7	63			70
Cash dividend, preferred					(1)	(1)
Cash dividend, common					(16)	(16)

Net income					290	290
Balance at December 31, 2003	**10**	**62**	**1,028**	**(360)**	**2,151**	**2,891**
Received balance from share purchase contract				360		360
Retirement of shares		(3)	(27)		(20)	(50)
Cash dividend, preferred					(1)	(1)
Cash dividend, common					(20)	(20)
3-for-2 split effected in the form of a dividend	5		(5)			
Net income					380	380
Balance at December 31, 2004	**15**	**59**	**996**	**0**	**2,490**	**3,560**
Common stock dividend		6	59		(65)	
Cash dividend, preferred					(1)	(1)
Cash dividend, common					(22)	(22)
Net income					412	412
Balance at December 31, 2005	**15**	**65**	**1,055**	**0**	**2,814**	**3,949**

Required:

Infer from the statements the events and transactions that affected Anaconda International Corporation's shareholders' equity during 2003, 2004, and 2005. Prepare the journal entries that reflect those events and transactions.

P 19–7
Reporting shareholders' equity; comprehensive income; Hewlett-Packard

Hewlett-Packard is a leading provider of computing and imaging solutions and services for business and home. The following is the Statement of Shareholders' Equity from HP's 2001 annual report:

HEWLETT-PACKARD COMPANY AND SUBSIDIARIES
Consolidated Statement of Stockholders' Equity

($ in millions) shares in 000s	Number of Shares	Par Value	Add'l Paid-in Capital	Retained Earnings	Accum. Other Compr. Income	Total
Balance October 31, 1998	**2,030,806**	**20**	**506**	**16,393**	**—**	**16,919**
Net earnings	—	—	—	3,491	—	3,491
Issuance of common stock	40,416	—	889	—	—	889
Repurchase of common stock	(62,084)	—	(1,684)	(959)	—	(2,643)
Tax benefit on employee stock options	—	—	289	—	—	289
Dividends	—	—	—	(650)	—	(650)
Balance October 31, 1999	**2,009,138**	**20**	**—**	**18,275**	**—**	**18,295**
Net earnings	—	—	—	3,697	—	3,697
Net unrealized gain on available-for-sale securities	—	—	—	—	93	93
Comprehensive income						3,790
Issuance of common stock	35,152	—	741	—	—	741
Repurchase of common stock	(96,978)	(1)	(2,571)	(2,998)	—	(5,570)
Tax benefit on employee stock options	—	—	495	—	—	495
Initial public offering and spin-off of Agilent Technologies	—	—	1,335	(4,239)	—	(2,904)
Dividends	—	—	—	(638)	—	(638)
Balance October 31, 2000	**1,947,312**	**19**	**—**	**14,097**	**93**	**14,209**
Net earnings	—	—	—	408	—	408
Net unrealized loss on available-for-sale securities	—	—	—	—	(74)	(74)
Net unrealized gain on derivative instruments	—	—	—	—	22	22
Comprehensive income						356
Issuance of common stock	35,152	—	1,233	—	—	1,233
Repurchase of common stock	(45,036)	—	(1,049)	(191)	—	(1,240)
Tax benefit on employee stock plans	—	—	16	—	—	16
Dividends	—	—	—	(621)	—	(621)
Balance October 31, 2001	**1,937,828**	**19**	**200**	**13,693**	**41**	**13,953**

Required:
1. What is the purpose of the statement of shareholders' equity?
2. How does HP account for its share buybacks?
3. For its share buybacks in 2001, was the price HP paid for the shares repurchased more or less than the average price at which HP had sold the shares previously? (Note: The par per share is $.01, so the par of the 45 million shares repurchased rounded downward to less than $1 million, which is why no amount is reported in that column.)
4. What is comprehensive income? What is other comprehensive income?
5. What caused the change in HP's comprehensive income in 2001? What was the amount of Accumulated other comprehensive income that HP reported in its 2001 balance sheet?

P 19–8
Share issue costs; issuance; dividends; early retirement

During its first year of operations, Cupola Fan Corporation issued 30,000 of $1 par Class B shares for $385,000 on June 30, 2003. Share issue costs were $1,500. One year from the issue date (July 1, 2004), the corporation retired 10% of the shares for $39,500.

Required:
1. Prepare the journal entry to record the issuance of the shares.
2. Prepare the journal entry to record the declaration of a $2 per share dividend on December 1, 2003.
3. Prepare the journal entry to record the payment of the dividend on December 31, 2003.
4. Prepare the journal entry to record the retirement of the shares.
(Note: You may wish to compare your solution to this problem with that of Problem 14–16, which deals with parallel issues of debt issue costs and the retirement of debt.)

P 19–9
Effect of preferred stock characteristics on dividends

The shareholders' equity of Kramer Industries includes the data shown below. During 2003, cash dividends of $150 million were declared. Dividends were not declared in 2001 or 2002.

	($ in millions)
Common stock	$200
Paid-in capital—excess of par, common	800
Preferred stock, 10% nonparticipating	100
Paid-in capital—excess of par, preferred	270

Required:
Determine the amount of dividends payable to preferred shareholders and to common shareholders under each of the following two assumptions regarding the characteristics of the preferred stock.

Assumption A—The preferred stock is noncumulative.
Assumption B—The preferred stock is cumulative.

P 19–10
Transactions affecting retained earnings

Indicate by letter whether each of the transactions listed below increases (**I**), decreases (**D**), or has no effect (**N**) on retained earnings. Assume the shareholders' equity of the transacting company includes only common stock, paid-in capital—excess of par, and retained earnings at the time of each transaction.

Transactions

Example   __N__   1. Sale of common stock
_____   2. Purchase of treasury stock at a cost *less* than the original issue price
_____   3. Purchase of treasury stock at a cost *greater* than the original issue price
_____   4. Declaration of a property dividend
_____   5. Sale of treasury stock for *more* than cost
_____   6. Sale of treasury stock for *less* than cost
_____   7. Net income for the year
_____   8. Declaration of a cash dividend
_____   9. Payment of a previously declared cash dividend
_____   10. Issuance of convertible bonds for cash
_____   11. Declaration and distribution of a 5% stock dividend
_____   12. Retirement of common stock at a cost *less* than the original issue price
_____   13. Retirement of common stock at a cost *greater* than the original issue price
_____   14. A stock split effected in the form of a stock dividend
_____   15. A stock split in which the par value per share is reduced (not effected in the form of a stock dividend)
_____   16. A net loss for the year

Ellis Transport Company acquired 1.2 million shares of stock in L&K Corporation at $44 per share. They are classified by Ellis as available for sale. Ellis sold 200,000 shares at $46, received a 10% stock dividend, and then later in the year sold another 100,000 shares at $43.

Hint: There is no entry for the stock dividend, but a new investment per share must be calculated for use later when the shares are sold.

Required:
Prepare journal entries to record these transactions.

Part A

In late 2002, the Nicklaus Corporation was formed. The corporate charter authorizes the issuance of 5,000,000 shares of common stock carrying a $1 par value, and 1,000,000 shares of $5 par value, non-cumulative, nonparticipating preferred stock. On January 2, 2003, 3,000,000 shares of the common stock are issued in exchange for cash at an average price of $10 per share. Also on January 2, all 1,000,000 shares of preferred stock are issued at $20 per share.

Required:
1. Prepare journal entries to record these transactions.
2. Prepare the shareholders' equity section of the Nicklaus balance sheet as of March 31, 2003. (Assume net income for the first quarter 2003 was $1,000,000.)

Part B

During 2003, the Nicklaus Corporation participated in three treasury stock transactions:
a. On June 30, 2003, the corporation reacquires 200,000 shares for the treasury at a price of $12 per share.
b. On July 31, 2003, 50,000 treasury shares are reissued at $15 per share.
c. On September 30, 2003, 50,000 treasury shares are reissued at $10 per share.

Required:
1. Prepare journal entries to record these transactions.
2. Prepare the Nicklaus Corporation shareholders' equity section as it would appear in a balance sheet prepared at September 30, 2003. (Assume net income for the second and third quarter was $3,000,000.)

Part C

On October 1, 2003, Nicklaus Corporation receives permission to replace its $1 par value common stock (5,000,000 shares authorized, 3,000,000 shares issued, and 2,900,000 shares outstanding) with a new common stock issue having a $.50 par value. Since the new par value is one-half the amount of the old, this represents a 2-for-1 stock split. That is, the shareholders will receive two shares of the $.50 par stock in exchange for each share of the $1 par stock they own. The $1 par stock will be collected and destroyed by the issuing corporation.

On November 1, 2003, the Nicklaus Corporation declares a $.05 per share cash dividend on common stock and a $.25 per share cash dividend on preferred stock. Payment is scheduled for December 1, 2003, to shareholders of record on November 15, 2003.

On December 2, 2003, the Nicklaus Corporation declares a 1% stock dividend payable on December 28, 2003, to shareholders of record on December 14. At the date of declaration, the common stock was selling in the open market at $10 per share. The dividend will result in 58,000 (.01 × 5,800,000) additional shares being issued to shareholders.

Required:
1. Prepare journal entries to record the declaration and payment of these stock and cash dividends.
2. Prepare the December 31, 2003, shareholders' equity section of the balance sheet for the Nicklaus Corporation. (Assume net income for the fourth quarter was $2,500,000.)
3. Prepare a statement of shareholders' equity for Nicklaus Corporation for 2003.

A new CEO was hired to revive the floundering Champion Chemical Corporation. The company had endured operating losses for several years, but confidence was emerging that better times were ahead. The board of directors and shareholders approved a quasi reorganization for the corporation. The reorganization included devaluing inventory for obsolescence by $105 million and increasing land by $5 million. Immediately prior to the restatement, at December 31, 2002, Champion Chemical Corporation's balance sheet appeared as follows (in condensed form):

CHAMPION CHEMICAL CORPORATION
Balance Sheet
At December 31, 2002
($ in millions)

Cash	$ 20
Receivables	40
Inventory	230
Land	40
Buildings and equipment (net)	90
	$420
Liabilities	$240
Common stock (320 million shares at $1 par)	320
Additional paid-in capital	60
Retained earnings (deficit)	(200)
	$420

Required:

1. Prepare the journal entries appropriate to record the quasi reorganization on January 1, 2003.
2. Prepare a balance sheet as it would appear immediately after the restatement.

BROADEN YOUR PERSPECTIVE

Apply your critical-thinking ability to the knowledge you've gained. These cases will provide you an opportunity to develop your research, analysis, judgment, and communication skills. You also will work with other students, integrate what you've learned, apply it in real world situations, and consider its global and ethical ramifications. This practice will broaden your knowledge and further develop your decision-making abilities.

Real World Case 19–1
Initial public offering of common stock; Wright Medical Group

Wright Medical Technology, Inc., headquartered in Arlington, Tennessee, has been a designer, manufacturer and worldwide distributor of orthopedic implants and instrumentation for over 50 years. Wright's product offerings include large joint implants for the hip and knee; extremity implants for the shoulder, elbow, hand, wrist, and foot; and biologic products, including bone graft substitutes. On July 18, 2001, the company completed an initial public offering for 7.5 million shares of voting common stock. In connection with the sale, Wright incurred an underwriting discount of approximately $6.6 million and estimated offering expenses of approximately $2.0 million. The company used the net proceeds of this offering to repay debt.

A few months after the stock sale, IPO Home.com provided the following information at its website.

WRIGHT MEDICAL GROUP (WMGI)
Company Profile

Deal Summary

Offer Date	7/12/2001	Offer Price	$12.50
Ticker	WMGI	Shares Offered	7.50mm
Lead Underwriter	J.P. Morgan	Co-Manager	CS First Boston

Required:

1. What were the net proceeds of the sale of shares that Wright had available to retire debt?
2. The par amount of the common shares is $0.01 per share. What entry did Wright use to record the sale of the shares?

Analysis Case 19–2
Statement of shareholders' equity

The shareholders' equity portion of the balance sheet of Sessel's Department Stores, Inc., a large regional specialty retailer, is as follows:

SESSEL'S DEPARTMENT STORES, INC.
Comparative Balance Sheets
Shareholders' Equity Section

($ in 000s, except per share amounts)	Dec. 31, 2003	Dec. 31, 2002
Shareholders' Equity		
Preferred stock—$1 par value; 20,000 total shares authorized,		
Series A—600 shares authorized, issued, and outstanding,		
$50 per share liquidation preference	$ 57,700	$ —
Series B—33 shares authorized, no shares outstanding		
Common stock—$.10 par; 200,000 shares authorized,		
19,940 and 18,580 shares issued and outstanding at		
Dec. 31, 2003, and Dec. 31, 2002, respectively	1,994	1,858
Additional paid-in capital	227,992	201,430
Retained income	73,666	44,798
Total shareholders' equity	$361,352	$248,086

Disclosures elsewhere in Sessel's annual report revealed the following changes in shareholders' equity accounts for 2003, 2002, 2001:

2003:
1. The only changes in retained earnings during 2003, were preferred dividends on preferred stock of $3,388,000 and net income.
2. The preferred stock is convertible. During the year, 6,592 shares were issued. All shares were converted into 320,000 shares of common stock. No gain or loss was recorded on the conversion.
3. Common shares were issued in a public offering and upon the exercise of stock options. On the statement of shareholders' equity, Sessel's reports these two items on a single line entitled: "Issuance of shares."

2002:
1. Net income: $12,126,000.
2. Issuance of common stock: 5,580,000 shares at $112,706,000.

2001:
1. Net income: $13,494,000.
2. Issuance of common stock: 120,000 shares at $826,000.

Required:
From these disclosures, prepare comparative statements of shareholders' equity for 2003, 2002, and 2001.

Communication Case 19–3
Is a receivable for stock issued or to be issued a recognizable asset, or should it be deducted from equity?
Group interaction

An unsettled question in accounting for stock is: Should a receivable for stock issued or to be issued, such as a note receivable for stock already issued or a stock subscription receivable, be recognized as an asset, or should it be deducted from equity? The prevalent practice is reporting the receivable as a contra equity account. This results in reporting total paid-in capital only to the extent that unrestricted shares are outstanding. However, many accountants believe receivables for stock fit the definition of assets.

Two opposing viewpoints are:

View 1: Receivables for stock should be deducted from equity.
View 2: Receivables for stock should be reported as assets.

In considering this question, focus on conceptual issues regarding the practicable and theoretically appropriate treatment, unconstrained by GAAP.

Required:
1. Which view do you favor? Develop a list of arguments in support of your view prior to the class session for which the case is assigned.
2. In class, your instructor will pair you (and everyone else) with a classmate (who also has independently developed an argument).
    a. You will be given three minutes to argue your view to your partner. Your partner likewise will be given three minutes to argue his or her view to you. During these three-minute presentations, the listening partner is not permitted to speak.
    b. Then after each person has had a turn attempting to convince his or her partner, the two partners will have a three-minute discussion in which they will decide which view is more convincing and arguments will be merged into a single view for each pair.

3. After the allotted time, a spokesperson for each of the two views will be selected by the instructor. Each spokesperson will field arguments from the class in support of that view's position and list the arguments on the board. The class then will discuss the merits of the two lists of arguments and attempt to reach a consensus view, though a consensus is not necessary.

Research Case 19–4
Comprehensive income; locate and extract relevant information and authoritative support for a financial reporting issue; integrative; Cisco Systems

Titan Networking became a public company through an IPO (initial public offering) two weeks ago. You are looking forward to the challenges of being assistant controller for a publicly owned corporation. One such challenge came in the form of a memo in this morning's in-box. "We need to start reporting comprehensive income in our financials," the message from your boss said. "Do some research on that, will you? That concept didn't exist when I went to school." In response, you sought out the financial statements of Cisco Systems, the networking industry leader. The following is an excerpt from a disclosure note from Cisco's 2001 annual report:

Comprehensive Income (Loss)

The components of comprehensive income (loss), net of tax, are as follows (in millions):

Years Ended	July 28, 2001	July 29, 2000	July 31, 1999
Net income (loss)	$(1,014)	$2,668	$2,023
Other comprehensive income (loss):			
Change in net unrealized gains on investments, net of tax of ($1,953), $1,762, and $144 in fiscal 2001, 2000, and 1999, respectively	(3,812)	3,240	234
Other	7	(8)	6
Total	$(4,819)	$5,900	$2,263

Required:
1. Use EdgarScan (edgarscan.pwcglobal.com) or another method to locate the financial statements of Cisco. Search the 2001 annual report for information about how Cisco accounts for comprehensive income. What does Cisco report in its balance sheet regarding comprehensive income?
2. Consult the Summaries of FASB pronouncements at accounting.rutgers.edu/raw/fasb/st/stpg.html or from some other source. What authoritative literature does Cisco rely on when reporting comprehensive income? When did the requirement become effective?
3. What is comprehensive income? How does it differ from net income? Where is it reported in a balance sheet? Why does Cisco's 2001 balance sheet amount differ from the 2001 amount reported in the disclosure note? Explain.
4. The primary component of Other comprehensive income for Cisco is "Change in net unrealized gains on investments." What does this mean? From the information Cisco's financial statements provide, determine how the company calculated the $275 million accumulated other comprehensive loss in fiscal 2001.
5. What might be possible causes for the "Other" component of Cisco's Other comprehensive income?

Judgment Case 19–5
Treasury stock; stock split; cash dividends; Alcoa

Alcoa is the world's leading producer of primary aluminum, fabricated aluminum, and alumina. The following is a recent press release from the company:

Alcoa Announces 33% Increase in Base Dividend, 2-for-1 Stock Split
PITTSBURGH—Alcoa today announced that its Board of Directors approved a base quarterly dividend increase of 33.3%, to 25 cents per common share from 18.75 cents per share. For a full year, base dividends will now total $1.00 compared with 75 cents before the increase.

2-for-1 Stock Split
The Board declared a two-for-one split of Alcoa's common stock. The stock split is subject to approval of Alcoa shareholders who must approve an amendment to the company's articles to increase the authorized shares of common stock at Alcoa's annual meeting. Shareholders of record on May 26 will receive an additional common share for each share held, which will be distributed on June 9.

> **Commitment to Stock Repurchase Program**
> Alcoa restated its commitment to its previously authorized share repurchase program which it announced last year.

Required:
1. What are the two primary reporting alternatives Alcoa has in accounting for the repurchase of its shares? What would be the effect of the optional courses of action on total shareholders' equity? Explain. What would be the effect of the optional courses of action on how stock would be presented in Alcoa's balance sheet? If the shares are later resold for an amount greater than cost, how should Alcoa account for the sale?
2. What are the two primary courses of action Alcoa has in accounting for the stock split, and how would the choice affect Alcoa's shareholders' equity? Why?
3. How should Alcoa account for the cash dividend, and how would it affect Alcoa's balance sheet? Why?

Communication Case 19–6
Issuance of shares; share issue costs; prepare a report

You are the newest member of the staff of Brinks & Company, a medium-size investment management firm. You are supervised by Les Kramer, an employee of two years. Les has a reputation as being technically sound but has a noticeable gap in his accounting education. Knowing you are knowledgeable about accounting issues, he requested you provide him with a synopsis of accounting for share issue costs.

"I thought the cost of issuing securities is recorded separately and expensed over time," he stated in a handwritten memo. "But I don't see that for IBR's underwriting expenses. What gives?"

He apparently was referring to a disclosure note on a page of IBR's annual report, photocopied and attached to his memo. To raise funds for expansion, the company sold additional shares of its $.10 par common stock. The following disclosure note appeared in the company's most recent annual report:

> **NOTES TO CONSOLIDATED FINANCIAL STATEMENTS**
>
> **Note 10—Stock Transactions (in part)**
> In February and March, the Company sold 2,395,000 shares of Common Stock at $22.25 per share in a public offering. Net proceeds to the Company were approximately $50.2 million after the underwriting discount and offering expenses.

Required:
Write a formal memo to your supervisor. Briefly explain how share issue costs are accounted for and how that accounting differs from that of debt issue costs. To make sure your explanation is understood in context of the footnote, include in your memo the following:
a. At what total amount did the shares sell to the public? How is the difference between this amount and the $50.2 million net proceeds accounted for?
b. The appropriate journal entry to record the sale of the shares.

Analysis Case 19–7
Analyzing financial statements; price-earnings ratio; dividend payout ratio

IGF Foods Company is a large, primarily domestic, consumer foods company involved in the manufacture, distribution, and sale of a variety of food products. Industry averages are derived from Troy's *The Almanac of Business and Industrial Financial Ratios* and Dun and Bradstreet's *Industry Norms and Key Business Ratios*. Following are the 2003 and 2002 comparative income statements and balance sheets for IGF. The market price of IGF's common stock is $47 during 2003. (The financial data we use are from actual financial statements of a well-known corporation, but the company name used in our illustration is fictitious and the numbers and dates have been modified slightly to disguise the company's identity.)

IGF FOODS COMPANY
Years Ended December 31, 2003 and 2002

($ in millions)	2003	2002
Comparative Income Statements		
Net sales	$6,440	$5,800
Cost of goods sold	(3,667)	(3,389)
Gross profit	2,773	2,411

	2003	**2002**
Operating expenses	(1,916)	(1,629)
Operating income	857	782
Interest expense	(54)	(53)
Income from operations before tax	803	729
Income taxes	(316)	(287)
Net income	$ 487	$ 442
Net income per share	$2.69	$2.44
Average shares outstanding	181 million	181 million

Comparative Balance Sheets
Assets

Current assets:		
Cash	$ 48	$ 142
Accounts receivable	347	320
Marketable securities	358	—
Inventories	914	874
Prepaid expenses	212	154
Total current assets	$1,879	$1,490
Property, plant, and equipment (net)	2,592	2,291
Intangibles (net)	800	843
Other assets	74	60
Total assets	$5,345	$4,684

Liabilities and Shareholders' Equity

Current liabilities:		
Accounts payable	$ 254	$ 276
Accrued liabilities	493	496
Notes payable	518	115
Current portion of long-term debt	208	54
Total current liabilities	1,473	941
Long-term debt	534	728
Deferred income taxes	407	344
Total liabilities	2,414	2,013
Shareholders' equity:		
Common stock, $1 par	180	180
Additional paid-in capital	21	63
Retained earnings	2,730	2,428
Total shareholders' equity	2,931	2,671
Total liabilities and shareholders' equity	$5,345	$4,684

Profitability is the key to a company's long-run survival. Profitability measures focus on a company's ability to provide an adequate return relative to resources devoted to company operations.

Required:

1. Calculate the return on shareholders' equity for IGF. The average return for the stocks listed on the New York Stock Exchange in a comparable period was 18.8%. What information does your calculation provide an investor?

2. Calculate IGF's earnings per share and earnings-price ratio. The average return for the stocks listed on the New York Stock Exchange in a comparable time period was 5.4%. What does your calculation indicate about IGF's earnings?

Research Case 19–8
Preferred stock and the distinction between debt and equity; research an article in *Accounting Horizons*

A continuing debate in accounting circles is whether to maintain, modify, or eliminate the current distinction between debt and equity. For example, is preferred stock debt, or is it equity? Professor Myrtle Clark explores these issues in her article "Entity Theory, Modern Capital Structure Theory, and the Distinction between Debt and Equity." Professor Clark reviews financial economics literature to support her observations.

Required:

1. In your library or from some other source, locate the indicated article in *Accounting Horizons*, September 1993.

2. How is preferred stock classified in traditional financial statements (Exhibit 2)?
3. How is preferred stock classified in Paton's Entity Theory model (Exhibit 3)?
4. How is preferred stock classified in decision-useful financial statements (Exhibit 4)?
5. Which approach does Professor Clark prefer?
6. Does Professor Clark recommend drawing a sharp distinction between debt and equity? Why?
7. Do you agree with the author's conclusion?

International Case 19–9
Accounting for shareholders' equity in other countries

In the United States, shareholders' equity represents a residual amount: assets minus liabilities. It is reported in two primary categories: paid-in (or invested) capital and retained earnings (or earned capital). Worldwide, there is little uniformity in how capital or shareholders' equity is defined or reported on the balance sheet. Significant differences exist from country to country.

Required:
1. Choose a country other than the United States and research the way that country accounts for shareholders' equity. Include in your analysis:
   a. How shareholders' equity is defined.
   b. The categories by which it is reported in the financial statements.
   c. What if any requirements exist to separately maintain legal capital.
   d. Restrictions on dividend payments and how dividends are reported.
   e. Whether a statement of shareholders' equity, or equivalent, is reported.
2. Prepare a short report highlighting the similarities and differences between the United States and your chosen country in the way shareholders' equity is accounted for. Optionally, the report might compare (a) the degree of conservatism in the approaches taken by the two countries or (b) whether cultural differences are likely contributors to the differences observed.

Ethics Case 19–10
The Swiss label maker; value of shares issued for equipment

Bricker Graphics is a privately held company specializing in package labels. Representatives of the firm have just returned from Switzerland, where a Swiss firm is manufacturing a custom-made high speed, color labeling machine. Confidence is high that the new machine will help rescue Bricker from sharply declining profitability. Bricker's chief operating officer, Don Benson, has been under fire for not achieving the company's performance goals of achieving a rate of return on assets of at least 12%.

The afternoon of his return from Switzerland, Benson called Susan Sharp into his office. Susan is Bricker's Controller.

Benson: I wish you had been able to go. We have some accounting issues to consider.
Sharp: I wish I'd been there, too. I understand the food was marvelous. What are the accounting issues?
Benson: They discussed accepting our notes at the going rate for a face amount of $12.5 million. We also discussed financing with stock.
Sharp: I thought we agreed, debt is the way to go for us now.
Benson: Yes, but I've been thinking. We can issue shares for a total of $10 million. The labeler is custom-made and doesn't have a quoted selling price, but the domestic labelers we considered went for around $10 million. It sure would help our rate of return if we keep the asset base as low as possible.

Required:
1. How will Benson's plan affect the return measure? What accounting issue is involved?
2. Is the proposal ethical?
3. Who would be affected if the proposal is implemented?

Research Case 19–11
Researching the way shareholders' equity transactions are reported; retrieving financial statements from the Internet

EDGAR, the Electronic Data Gathering, Analysis, and Retrieval system, performs automated collection, validation, indexing, and forwarding of submissions by companies and others who are required by law to file forms with the U.S. Securities and Exchange Commission (SEC). All publicly traded domestic companies use EDGAR to make the majority of their filings. (Filings by foreign companies are not required to be filed on EDGAR, but some of these companies do so voluntarily.) Form 10-K or 10-KSB, which include the annual report, is required to be filed on EDGAR. The SEC makes this information available on the Internet.

Required:
1. Access EDGAR on the Internet at **www.sec.gov**, or through EdgarScan at **edgarscan.pwcglobal. com/**.
2. Search for a public company with which you are familiar. Access its most recent 10-K filing. Search or scroll to find the statement of shareholders' equity and related note(s). If a statement of shareholders' equity is not provided, try another company.
3. Determine from the statement the transactions that occurred during the most recent three years that affected retained earnings.

4. Determine from the statement the transactions that occurred during the most recent three years that affected common stock. Were any of these transactions identified in requirement 3 also?
5. Cross-reference your findings with amounts reported on the balance sheet. How do these two statements articulate with one another?

Real World Case 19–12
Reporting preferred shares

Stokely-Van Camp, Inc., a wholly owned subsidiary of The Quaker Oats Company, is the processor, marketer, and distributor of Gatorade thirst quencher. The following disclosure note appeared in the company's 2000 annual report.

> **Note 6: Capital Stock (in part)**
> Since October 31, 1983, all outstanding shares of the Company's common stock have been held by Quaker and the balances of common stock ($3.6 million; 3,591,381 shares issued), additional paid-in capital ($68.7 million) and treasury common stock ($20.9 million; 602,010 shares) have remained unchanged.
>
> The Company has three series of preferred stock: voting 5% Cumulative Convertible Second Preferred Stock; non-voting 5% Cumulative Prior Preference Stock; and Serial Preferred Stock. The voting 5% Cumulative Convertible Second Preferred Stock is convertible at the holder's option, on a share for share basis, into the non-voting 5% Cumulative Prior Preference Stock. As of December 31, 2000, authorized shares were 500,000 and issued and outstanding shares were 7,355 for the 5% Cumulative Convertible Second Preferred Stock. As of December 31, 2000, 1,500,000 shares were authorized, 756,789 shares were issued, 756,456 shares were outstanding and 7,355 shares were reserved for conversion for the 5% Cumulative Prior Preference Stock. Both issues are redeemable at the Company's option for $21 per share. No Serial Preferred Stock has been issued, although 500,000 shares are authorized.

Required:
1. The par amount of the preferred and preference shares is $20. What amount of dividends is paid annually to a preferred shareholder owning 100 shares?
2. If dividends are not paid in 2001 and 2002, but are paid in 2003, what dividend will the shareholder receive?
3. If Stokely chooses to redeem the shares in 2004, what amount will the investor be paid for his/her 100 shares?
4. How do you think the preferred and preference shares should be reported on Stokely's balance sheet?

Additional Topics

20

Earnings Per Share

CHAPTER

OVERVIEW

Earnings per share is the most commonly cited and reported measure of a company's performance. If a firm's capital structure includes securities that could potentially dilute (reduce) earnings per share (such as convertible securities or stock options), the company must calculate both basic and diluted earnings per share. The effect of potential common shares are considered by calculating earnings per share as if the security already had been exercised or converted into additional common shares. We discuss this calculation and other issues affecting the determination and presentation of earnings per share.

LEARNING OBJECTIVES

After studying this chapter, you should be able to:

LO1   Distinguish between a simple and a complex capital structure.

LO2   Describe what is meant by the weighted average number of common shares.

LO3   Differentiate the effect on EPS of the sale of new shares, a stock dividend or stock split, and the reacquisition of shares.

LO4   Describe how preferred dividends affect the determination of EPS.

LO5   Describe how options, rights, and warrants are incorporated in the calculation of EPS.

LO6   Describe how convertible securities are incorporated in the calculation of EPS.

LO7   Explain the way contingently issuable shares are incorporated in the calculation of EPS.

LO8   Describe the financial statement presentation of EPS.

FINANCIAL REPORTING CASE

ExxonMobil

"I guess I'll win that bet!" you announced to no one in particular.

"What bet?" Meg asked. Meg Forsythe was close enough to overhear you.

"When I bought my ExxonMobil stock last year Larry insisted it was a mistake, that they were going downhill. I bet him a Coke he was wrong. This press release says per share earnings are up 10%," you bragged. Meg was looking over your shoulder now at the article you were pointing at:

> IRVING, Texas—October 23, 2001—ExxonMobil Corporation today reported third quarter results. Excluding merger effects, third quarter 2001 earnings of $3,320 million ($0.48 per share) decreased $970 million from the record third quarter of 2000. These per share amounts reflect the two-for-one stock split implemented in June 2001.
>
> Per share earnings increased 10% reflecting higher earnings and the results of the company's share buy-back activity.
>
> ExxonMobil's Chairman Lee R. Raymond commented as follows: "During the quarter, the Corporation acquired 32.1 million shares of its common stock at a gross cost of $1,315 million to offset the dilution associated with benefit plans and to reduce common stock outstanding.
>
> Excerpt from: "ExxonMobil Corporation Announces Estimated Third Quarter 2001 Results, October 23, 2001.

"Forty-eight cents a share, huh?" Meg asked. "How many shares do you have? When do you get the check?"

> By the time you finish this chapter, you should be able to respond appropriately to the questions posed in this case. Compare your response to the solution provided at the end of the chapter.

QUESTIONS

1. Meg's questions imply that she thinks you will get cash dividends of 48 cents a share. What does earning per share really tell you? (page 996)

2. The press release says, "per share amounts reflect the two-for-one stock split implemented in June 2001." What does that mean? (page 998)

3. Chairman Raymond commented that "the Corporation acquired 32.1 million shares of its common stock." Is that reduction in shares taken into account when EPS is calculated? How? (page 999)

4. The share buyback, according to Raymond, was "to offset the dilution associated with benefit plans." You know from statements ExxonMobil mailed you that "benefit plans" likely refer to a number of stock options that company executives hold. If those options are exercised, you know the resulting increase in shares might reduce earnings per share. Is that possibility taken into account when EPS is calculated? (page 1001)

A typical corporate annual report contains four comparative financial statements, an extensive list of disclosure notes and schedules, and several pages of charts, tables, and textual descriptions. Of these myriad facts and figures, the single accounting number that is reported most frequently in the media and receives by far the most attention by investors and creditors is **earnings per share.** The reasons for the considerable attention paid to earnings per share certainly include the desire to find a way to summarize the performance of business enterprises into a single number.

> Information . . . gains greatly in usefulness if it can be compared with similar information about other enterprises and with similar information about the same enterprise for other time periods.[1]

Earnings per share is the single accounting number that receives the most media attention.

FINANCIAL REPORTING CASE

Q1, p. 995

Comparability is a qualitative characteristic of relevant accounting information (Concept Statement 2).

Summarizing performance in a way that permits comparisons is difficult because the companies that report the numbers are different from one another. And yet, the desire to condense performance to a single number has created a demand for EPS information. The profession has responded with rules designed to maximize the comparability of EPS numbers by minimizing the inconsistencies in their calculation from one company to the next.[2]

Keep in mind as you study the requirements that a primary goal is comparability. As a result, many of the rules devised to achieve consistency are unavoidably arbitrary, meaning that other choices the FASB might have made in many instances would be equally adequate.

BASIC EARNINGS PER SHARE

PART

LO1

A firm has a simple capital structure if it has no potential common shares.

Basic EPS reflects no dilution, only shares now outstanding.

A firm is said to have a **simple capital structure** if it has no outstanding securities that could potentially dilute earnings per share. In this context, to dilute means to *reduce* earnings per share. For instance, if a firm has convertible bonds outstanding and those bonds are converted, the resulting increase in common shares could decrease (or dilute) earnings per share. That is, the new shares represented by the bonds might participate in future earnings. So convertible bonds are referred to as **potential common shares.** Other potential common shares are convertible preferred stock and stock options. We will see how the potentially dilutive effects of these securities are included in the calculation of EPS in Part B of this chapter. Now, though, our focus is on the calculation of EPS for a simple capital structure—when no potential common shares are present. In these cases, the calculation is referred to as **basic EPS,** and is simply earnings available to common shareholders divided by the weighted-average number of common shares outstanding.

In the most elemental setting, earnings per share (or net loss per share) is merely a firm's net income (or net loss) divided by the number of shares of common stock outstanding throughout the year. The calculation becomes more demanding (a) when the number of shares has changed during the reporting period, (b) when the earnings available to common shareholders are diminished by dividends to preferred shareholders, or (c) when we attempt

---

[1]"Qualitative Characteristics of Accounting Information," *FASB Statement of Concepts No. 2,* FASB, 1980, par. 111.
[2]"Earnings per Share," *Statement of Financial Accounting Standards No. 128* (Norwalk, Conn.: FASB, 1977).

to take into account the impending effect of potential common shares (which we do in Part B). To illustrate the calculation of EPS in each of its dimensions, we will use only one example in this chapter. We'll start with the most basic situation and then add one new element at a time until we have considered all the principal ways the calculation can be affected. In this way you can see the effect of each component of earnings per share, not just in isolation, but in relation to the effects of other components as well. The basic calculation is shown in Illustration 20–1.

EPS expresses a firm's profitability on a per share basis.

Sovran Financial Corporation reported net income of $154 million in 2003 (tax rate 40%). Its capital structure consisted of:

Common Stock

Jan. 1   60 million common shares outstanding

(amounts in millions, except per share amount)

Basic EPS:

$$\frac{\text{Net income}}{\underset{\text{Shares}}{\underset{\text{outstanding}}{60}}} \quad \frac{\$154}{60} = \$2.57$$

ILLUSTRATION 20–1

Fundamental Calculation

In the most elemental setting, earnings per share is simply a company's earnings divided by the number of shares outstanding.

Issuance of New Shares

Because the shares discussed in Illustration 20–1 remained unchanged throughout the year, the denominator of the EPS calculation is simply the number of shares outstanding. But if the number of shares has changed, it's necessary to find the weighted average of the shares outstanding during the period the earnings were generated. For instance, if an additional 12 million shares had been issued on March 1 of the year just ended, we calculate the weighted-average number of shares to be 70 million as demonstrated in Illustration 20–2.

Sovran Financial Corporation reported net income of $154 million for 2003 (tax rate 40%). Its capital structure included:

Common Stock

Jan. 1   60 million common shares outstanding

Mar. 1   12 million new shares were sold

(amounts in millions, except per share amount)

Basic EPS:

$$\frac{\text{Net income}}{\underset{\substack{\text{Shares} \\ \text{at Jan. 1}}}{60} + \underset{\substack{\text{New} \\ \text{Shares}}}{12\,(^{10}\!/_{12})}} = \frac{\$154}{70} = \$2.20$$

ILLUSTRATION 20–2

Weighted Average

Any new shares issued are time-weighted by the fraction of the period they were outstanding and then added to the number of shares outstanding for the entire period.

Because the new shares were outstanding only 10 months, or $^{10}\!/_{12}$ of the year, we increase the 60 million shares already outstanding by the additional shares—weighted by the fraction of the year ($^{10}\!/_{12}$) they were outstanding. The weighted average is $60 + 12\,(^{10}\!/_{12}) = 60 + 10 = 70$ million shares. The reason for time-weighting the shares issued is that the resources the stock sale provides the company are available for generating income only after the date the shares are sold. So, weighting is necessary to make the shares in the fraction's denominator consistent with the income in its numerator.

LO2

Stock Dividends and Stock Splits

Recall that a stock dividend or a stock split is a distribution of additional shares to existing shareholders. But there's an important and fundamental difference between the increase in shares caused by a stock dividend and an increase from selling new shares. When new shares are sold, both assets and shareholders' equity are increased by an additional investment in the firm by shareholders. On the other hand, a stock dividend or stock split merely increases the number of shares without affecting the firm's assets. In effect, the same pie is divided into more pieces. The result is a larger number of less valuable shares.[3] This fundamental change in the nature of the shares is reflected in a calculation of EPS by simply increasing the number of shares.

In Illustration 20–3, notice that the additional shares created by the stock dividend are *not* weighted for the time period they were outstanding. Instead, the increase is treated as if it occurred at the beginning of the year.

ILLUSTRATION 20–3 Stock Dividends and Stock Splits	Sovran Financial Corporation reported net income of $154 million in 2003 (tax rate 40%). Its capital structure included: **Common Stock** Jan. 1 — 60 million common shares outstanding Mar. 1 — 12 million new shares were sold June 17 — A 10% stock dividend was distributed (amounts in millions, except per share amount) **Basic EPS:**
Shares outstanding prior to the stock dividend are retroactively restated to reflect the 10% increase in shares—that is, treated as if the distribution occurred at the beginning of the period.	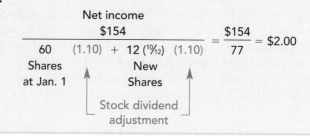

$$\frac{\text{Net income}}{\underset{\substack{\text{Shares} \\ \text{at Jan. 1}}}{60\ (1.10)} + \underset{\substack{\text{New} \\ \text{Shares}}}{12\ (^{10}\!/_{12})\ (1.10)}} = \frac{\$154}{77} = \$2.00$$

Stock dividend adjustment

 LO3

The number of shares outstanding after a 10% stock dividend is 1.10 times higher than before. This multiple is applied to both the beginning shares and the new shares sold before the stock distribution. If this had been a 25% stock dividend, the multiple would have been 1.25; a 2-for-1 stock split means a multiple of 2; and so on.

Notice that EPS without the 10% stock dividend ($2.20) is 10% more than it is with the stock distribution ($2). This is caused by the increase in the number of shares. But, unlike a sale of new shares, this should not be interpreted as a "dilution" of earnings per share. Shareholders' interests in their company's earnings have not been diluted. Instead, each shareholder's interest is represented by more—though less valuable—shares.

A simplistic but convenient way to view the effect is to think of the predistribution shares as having been "blue." After the stock dividend, the more valuable "blue" shares are gone, replaced by a larger number of, let's say, "green" shares. From now on, we compute the earnings per "green" share, whereas we previously calculated earnings per "blue" share. We restate the number of shares retroactively to reflect the stock dividend, as if the shares always had been "green." After all, our intent is to let the calculation reflect the fundamental change in the nature of the shares.

---

[3]For a more complete discussion of why the market price per share declines in proportion to the increase in the number of shares see Chapter 19.

ADDITIONAL CONSIDERATION

When last year's EPS is reported again for comparison purposes in the current year's comparative income statements, it too should reflect the increased shares from the stock dividend. For instance, suppose last year's EPS were $2.09: $115 million net income divided by 55 million weighted-average shares. When reported again for comparison purposes in the 2003 comparative income statements, that figure would be restated to reflect the 10% stock dividend [$115 ÷ (55 × 1.10) = $1.90]:

Earnings per Share:	2003	2002
	$2.00	$1.90

The EPS numbers now are comparable—both reflect the stock dividend. Otherwise we would be comparing earnings per "green" share with earnings per "blue" share; this way both are earnings per "green" share.

Reacquired Shares

If shares were reacquired during the period (either retired or as treasury stock), the weighted-average number of shares is reduced. The number of reacquired shares is time-weighted for the *fraction of the year they were **not** outstanding*, prior to being *subtracted* from the number of shares outstanding during the period. Let's modify our continuing illustration to assume 8 million shares were reacquired on October 1 as treasury stock (Illustration 20–4).

FINANCIAL REPORTING CASE

Q3, p. 995

Sovran Financial Corporation reported net income of $154 million in 2003 (tax rate 40%). Its capital structure included:

Common Stock

Jan. 1	60 million common shares outstanding
Mar. 1	12 million new shares were sold
June 17	A 10% stock dividend was distributed
Oct. 1	8 million shares were reacquired as treasury stock

(amounts in millions, except per share amounts)

Basic EPS:

$$\frac{\text{Net income} \quad \$154}{60 \,(1.10) + 12 \,(^{10}\!/_{12}) \,(1.10) - 8 \,(^{3}\!/_{12})} = \frac{\$154}{75} = \$2.05$$

60 Shares at Jan. 1 ↑ 12 New Shares ↑ 8 Treasury shares

└─ Stock dividend adjustment* ─┘

ILLUSTRATION 20–4
Reacquired Shares

The 8 million shares reacquired as treasury stock are weighted by ($^{3}\!/_{12}$) to reflect the fact they were not outstanding the last three months of the year.

*Not necessary for the treasury shares since they were reacquired after the stock dividend and thus already reflect the adjustment (that is, the shares repurchased are 8 million "new green" shares).

Compare the adjustment for treasury shares with the adjustment for new shares sold. Each is time-weighted for the fraction of the year the shares were or were not outstanding. But also notice two differences. The new shares are added, while the reacquired shares are subtracted. The second difference is that the reacquired shares are not multiplied by 1.10 to adjust for the 10% stock dividend. The reason is the shares were repurchased after the June 17 stock dividend; the reacquired shares are 8 million of the new post-distribution shares. (To

The adjustment for reacquired shares is the same as for new shares sold except the shares are deducted rather than added.

Any sales or purchases of shares that occurred before, but not after, a stock dividend or split are affected by the distribution.

use our earlier representation, these are 8 million "green" shares.) To generalize, when a stock distribution occurred during the reporting period, any sales or purchases of shares that occurred *before* the distribution are increased by the distribution. But the stock distribution does not increase the number of shares sold or purchased, if any, *after* the distribution.

Earnings Available to Common Shareholders

The denominator in an EPS calculation is the weighted average number of common shares outstanding. Logically, the numerator should similarly represent earnings available to common shareholders. This was automatic in our illustrations to this point because the only shares outstanding were common shares. But when a senior class of shareholders (like preferred stockholders) is entitled to a specified allocation of earnings (like preferred dividends), those amounts are subtracted from earnings before calculating earnings per share.[4] This is demonstrated in Illustration 20–5.

ILLUSTRATION 20–5
Preferred Dividends

Sovran Financial Corporation reported net income of $154 million in 2003 (tax rate 40%). Its capital structure included:

Common Stock

January 1	60 million common shares outstanding
March 1	12 million new shares were sold
June 17	A 10% stock dividend was distributed
October 1	8 million shares were reacquired as treasury stock

Preferred Stock, Nonconvertible

January 1–December 31   5 million 8%, $10 par, shares

(amounts in millions, except per share amount)

Preferred dividends are subtracted from net income so that "earnings available to common shareholders" is divided by the weighted-average number of common shares.

Basic EPS:

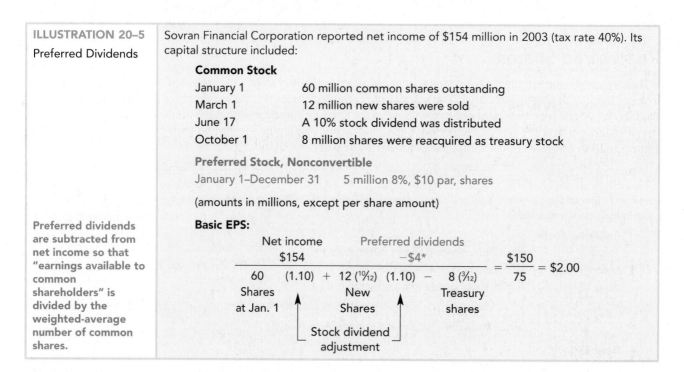

*8% × $10 par × 5 million shares.

Preferred dividends reduce earnings available to common shareholders unless the preferred stock is noncumulative and no dividends were declared that year.

Suppose no dividends were declared for the year. Should we adjust for preferred dividends? Yes, if the preferred stock is cumulative—and most preferred stock is. This means that when dividends are not declared, the unpaid dividends accumulate to be paid in a future year when (if) dividends are subsequently declared. Obviously, the presumption is that, although the year's dividend preference isn't distributed this year, it eventually will be paid.

We have encountered no potential common shares to this point in our continuing illustration. As a result, we have what is referred to as a simple capital structure. (Although, at this point, you may question this label.) For a simple capital structure, a single presentation of basic earnings per common share is appropriate. We turn our attention now to situations described as complex capital structures. In these situations, two separate presentations are required: basic EPS and diluted EPS.

---

[4]You learned in Chapter 19 that when dividends are declared, preferred shareholders have a preference (over common shareholders) to a specified amount.

CHECK WITH THE **COACH**

Earnings per share (EPS) is the most widely quoted accounting statistic. It is the "bottom line" for many managers and investors alike. For firms with complex capital structures in particular, understanding EPS can be difficult. Check with the Coach to get new insights into how and why EPS is calculated, as well as the many controversies about measuring and reporting EPS. ■

DILUTED EARNINGS PER SHARE

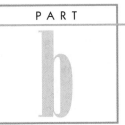

PART

b

Potential Common Shares

Imagine a situation in which convertible bonds are outstanding that will significantly increase the number of common shares if bondholders exercise their options to exchange their bonds for shares of common stock. Should these be ignored when earnings per share is calculated? After all, they haven't been converted as yet, so to assume an increase in shares for a conversion that may never occur might mislead investors and creditors. On the other hand, if conversion is imminent, not taking into account the dilutive effect of the share increase might mislead investors and creditors. The profession's solution to the dilemma is to calculate earnings per share twice.

Securities like these convertible bonds, while not being common stock, may become common stock through their exercise or conversion. Therefore, they may dilute (reduce) earnings per share and are called **potential common shares**. A firm is said to have a **complex capital structure** if potential common shares are outstanding. Besides convertible bonds, other potential common shares are convertible preferred stock, stock options, rights, or warrants, and contingently issuable securities. (We'll discuss each of these shortly.) A firm with a complex capital structure reports two EPS calculations. **Basic EPS** ignores the dilutive effect of such securities, **diluted EPS** incorporates the dilutive effect of all potential common shares.

FINANCIAL REPORTING CASE

Q4, p. 995

In a complex capital structure, a second EPS computation takes into account the assumed effect of *potential common shares,* essentially a "worst case scenario."

Options, Rights, and Warrants

Stock options, stock rights, and stock warrants are similar. Each gives its holders the right to exercise their option to purchase common stock, usually at a specified exercise price. The dilution that would result from their exercise should be reflected in the calculation of diluted EPS, but not basic EPS.

To include the dilutive effect of a security means to calculate EPS *as if* the potential increase in shares already has occurred (even though it hasn't yet). So, for a stock option (or right, or warrant), we pretend the option has been exercised. In fact, we assume the options were exercised at the beginning of the reporting period, or when the options were issued if that's later. We then assume the cash proceeds from selling the new shares at the exercise price are used to buy back as many shares as possible at the shares' average market price during the year. This is demonstrated in Illustration 20–6 on the next page.

When we simulate the exercise of the stock options, we calculate EPS as if 15 million shares were sold at the beginning of the year. This obviously increases the number of shares in the denominator by 15 million shares. But it is insufficient to simply add the additional shares without considering the accompanying consequences. Remember, if this hypothetical scenario had occurred, the company would have had $300 million cash proceeds from the exercise of the options (15 million shares × $20 exercise price per share). What would have been the effect on earnings per share? This depends on what the company would have done with the $300 million cash proceeds. Would the proceeds have been used to buy more equipment? Increase the sales force? Expand facilities? Pay dividends?

LO5

Stock options are assumed to have been exercised when calculating diluted EPS.

ILLUSTRATION 20–6 Stock Options	Sovran Financial Corporation reported net income of $154 million in 2003 (tax rate 40%). Its capital structure included:

Common Stock

Jan. 1	60 million common shares outstanding
Mar. 1	12 million new shares were sold
June 17	A 10% stock dividend was distributed
Oct. 1	8 million shares were reacquired as treasury stock

(The average market price of the common shares during 2003 was $25 per share.)

Preferred Stock, Nonconvertible

January 1–December 31   5 million 8%, $10 par, shares

Executive Stock Options

Options granted in 2001, exercisable for 15 million common shares* at an exercise price of $20 per share

(amounts in millions, except per share amounts)

> Stock options give their holders (company executives in this case) the right to purchase common stock at a specified exercise price ($20 in this case).
>
> The stock options do not affect the calculation of basic EPS.
>
> The calculation of diluted EPS assumes that the shares specified by stock options were issued at the exercise price and that the proceeds were used to buy back (as treasury stock) as many of those shares as can be purchased at the average market price during the period.

Basic EPS (unchanged)

$$\frac{\overset{\text{Net income}}{\$154} \quad \overset{\text{Preferred dividends}}{-\$4}}{\underset{\substack{\text{Shares} \\ \text{at Jan. 1}}}{60} \quad (1.10) + \underset{\substack{\text{New} \\ \text{Shares}}}{12 \, (^{10}\!/_{12})} \, (1.10) - \underset{\substack{\text{Treasury} \\ \text{shares}}}{8 \, (^{3}\!/_{12})}} = \frac{\$150}{75} = \$2$$

Stock dividend adjustment

Diluted EPS

$$\frac{\overset{\text{Net income}}{\$154} \quad \overset{\text{Preferred dividends}}{-\$4}}{\underset{\substack{\text{Shares} \\ \text{at Jan. 1}}}{60} \, (1.10) + \underset{\substack{\text{New} \\ \text{Shares}}}{12 \, (^{10}\!/_{12})} \, (1.10) - \underset{\substack{\text{Treasury} \\ \text{shares}}}{8 \, (^{3}\!/_{12})} + \underset{\substack{\text{Exercise} \\ \text{of options}}}{(15^* - 12^\dagger)}} = \frac{\$150}{78} = \$1.92$$

Stock dividend adjustment

---

*Adjusted for the stock dividend. Prior to the stock dividend, the options were exercisable for $13^{7}\!/_{11}$ million of the "old" shares which became 15 million ($13^{7}\!/_{11} \times 1.10$) of the "new" shares after the stock dividend.
†**Shares Reacquired for Diluted EPS**

	15 million shares
$\times$ $	20 (exercise price)
	$300 million
$\div$ $	25 (average market price)
	12 million shares reacquired

Obviously, there are literally hundreds of choices, and it's unlikely that any two firms would spend the $300 million exactly the same way. But remember, our objective is to create some degree of uniformity in the way firms determine earnings per share so the resulting numbers are comparable. So, standard-setters decided on a single assumption for all firms to provide some degree of comparability.

For diluted EPS, we assume the proceeds from exercise of the options were used to reacquire shares as treasury stock at the average market price of the common stock during the reporting period. Consequently, the weighted-average number of shares is increased by the difference between the shares assumed issued and those assumed reacquired—in our illustration: 15 million shares issued minus 12 million shares reacquired ($300 million ÷ $25 per share) equals 3 million net increase in shares.

The way we take into account the dilutive effect of stock options is called the *treasury stock method* because of our assumption that treasury shares are purchased with the cash proceeds of the exercise of the options. Besides providing comparability, this assumption actually is plausible because, if the options were exercised, more shares would be needed to issue to option-holders. And, as discussed in the previous chapter, many firms routinely buy back shares either to issue to option-holders or, equivalently, to offset the issuance of new shares.

ADDITIONAL CONSIDERATION

Technically, the number of shares represented by options or warrants should be determined on a quarter by quarter basis. As a result, the net increase in shares is determined for the first quarter for which the market price has been above the exercise price for 11 weeks and for each quarter thereafter (for which the effect is dilutive). Of course, the shares would be appropriately weighted for the time they are assumed outstanding. For example, let's say the $25 average market price in our illustration was the average price for the third and fourth quarters, but the average price for the first two quarters was less than the $20 exercise price. In that case, the share adjustment would have been:

$$+ (15 - 12) \left(\tfrac{2}{4}\right)$$

Convertible Securities

Sometimes corporations include a conversion feature as part of a bond offering, a note payable, or an issue of preferred stock. Convertible securities can be converted into (exchanged for) shares of stock at the option of the holder of the security. For that reason, convertible securities are potentially dilutive. EPS will be affected if and when such securities are converted and new shares of common stock are issued. In the previous section you learned that the potentially dilutive effect of stock options is reflected in diluted EPS calculations by assuming the options were exercised. Similarly, the potentially dilutive effect of convertible securities is reflected in diluted EPS calculations by assuming they were converted.

By the *if converted method* as it's called, we assume the conversion into common stock occurred at the beginning of the period (or at the time the convertible security is issued, if that's later). We increase the denominator of the EPS fraction by the additional common shares that would have been issued upon conversion. We increase the numerator by the interest (after-tax) on bonds or other debt or preferred dividends that would have been avoided if the convertible securities had not been outstanding due to having been converted.

When we assume conversion, the denominator of the EPS fraction is increased by the additional common shares that would have been issued upon conversion.

CONVERTIBLE BONDS

Now, let's return to our continuing illustration and modify it to include the existence of convertible bonds (Illustration 20–7) on the next page. We increase the denominator by the 12 million shares that would have been issued if the bonds had been converted. However, if that hypothetical conversion had occurred, the bonds would not have been outstanding during the year. What effect would the absence of the bonds have had on income? Obviously, the bond interest expense (10% × $300 million = $30 million) would have been saved, causing income to be higher. But saving the interest paid would also have meant losing a $30 million tax deduction on the income tax return. With a 40% tax rate that would mean paying $12 million more income taxes. So, to reflect in earnings the $18 million after-tax interest that would have been avoided in the event of conversion, we add back the $30 million of interest expense, but deduct 40% × $30 million for the higher tax expense.

The numerator is increased by the after-tax interest that would have been avoided.

ILLUSTRATION 20–7 Convertible Bonds	Sovran Financial Corporation reported net income of $154 million in 2003 (tax rate 40%). Its capital structure included:

Common Stock

Jan. 1	60 million common shares outstanding
Mar. 1	12 million new shares were sold
June 17	A 10% stock dividend was distributed
Oct. 1	8 million shares were reacquired as treasury stock

(The average market price of the common shares during 2003 was $25 per share.)

Preferred Stock, Nonconvertible

January 1–December 31   5 million 8%, $10 par, shares

Executive Stock Options

Options granted in 2001, exercisable for 15 million common shares* at an exercise price of $20 per share

Convertible Bonds

10%, $300 million face amount issued in 2002, convertible into 12 million common shares)*

(amounts in millions, except per share amounts)

The convertible bonds do not affect the calculation of basic EPS.

Basic EPS (unchanged)

$$\frac{\overset{\text{Net income}}{\$154} \quad \overset{\text{Preferred dividends}}{-\$4}}{\underset{\substack{\text{Shares} \\ \text{at Jan. 1}}}{60} \quad (1.10) + \underset{\substack{\text{New} \\ \text{Shares}}}{12\,(^{10}\!/_{12})} \,(1.10) - \underset{\substack{\text{Treasury} \\ \text{shares}}}{8\,(^{3}\!/_{12})}} = \frac{\$150}{75} = \$2.00$$

Stock dividend adjustment

If the bonds had been converted, 12 million more common shares would have been issued, and net income would have been higher by the interest saved (after tax) from not having the bonds outstanding.

Diluted EPS

$$\frac{\overset{\text{Net income}}{\$154} \quad \overset{\text{Preferred dividends}}{-\$4} \quad \overset{\substack{\text{After-tax} \\ \text{interest savings}}}{+\,\$30 - 40\%\,(30)}}{\underset{\substack{\text{Shares} \\ \text{at Jan. 1}}}{60} \, (1.10) + \underset{\substack{\text{New} \\ \text{Shares}}}{12\,(^{10}\!/_{12})} \,(1.10) - \underset{\substack{\text{Treasury} \\ \text{shares}}}{8\,(^{3}\!/_{12})} + \underset{\substack{\text{Exercise} \\ \text{of options}}}{(15 - 12)} \quad \underset{\substack{\text{Conversion} \\ \text{of bonds}}}{+\,12}} = \frac{\$168}{90} = \$1.87$$

Stock dividend adjustment

*Adjusted for the stock dividend, For example, prior to the stock dividend, the bonds were exercisable for $10^1\!/_{11}$ million of the "old" shares which became 12 million ($10^1\!/_{11} \times 1.10$) of the "new" shares after the stock dividend.

ADDITIONAL CONSIDERATION

The $300 million of convertible bonds in our illustration were issued at face value. Suppose the bonds had been issued for $282 million. In that case, the adjustment to earnings would be modified to include the amortization of the $18 million bond discount. Assuming straight-line amortization and a 10-year maturity, the adjustment to the diluted EPS calculation would have been:

$$\frac{+\,[\$30 + (\$18 \div 10 \text{ years})] \times (1 - 40\%)*}{+\,12}$$

to reflect the fact that the interest expense would include the $30 million stated interest plus one-tenth of the bond discount.[†]

*This is an alternative way to represent the after-tax adjustment to interest since subtracting 40% of the interest expense is the same as multiplying interest expense by 60%.

[†]See Chapter 14 if you need to refresh your memory about bond discount amortization.

Our illustration describes the treatment of convertible bonds. The same treatment pertains to other debt that is convertible into common shares such as convertible notes payable. Remember from our discussion of debt in earlier chapters that all debt is similar whether in the form of bonds, notes, or other configurations.

ADDITIONAL CONSIDERATION

Notice that we assumed the bonds were converted at the beginning of the reporting period since they were outstanding all year. However, if the convertible bonds had been issued during the reporting period, we would assume their conversion occurred on the date of issue. It would be illogical to assume they were converted before they were issued. If the convertible bonds in our illustration had been sold on September 1, for instance, the adjustment to the EPS calculation would have been:

$$\frac{+\ [\$30 - 40\%\ (\$30)]\ (\frac{4}{12})}{+\ 12\ (\frac{4}{12})}$$

to reflect the fact that the after-tax interest savings and the net increase in shares would have been effective for only four months of the year.

This is our approach not just for convertible bonds, but for any potential common shares. For example, we assumed the options in our illustration were exercised at the beginning of the reporting period so the net increase in shares was not weighted for a fraction of the year outstanding. If the options had been granted to company executives on April 1 the adjustment to the weighted-average number of shares would have been:

$$+\ (15 - 12)\ (\frac{9}{12})$$

to reflect the fact that the net increase in shares would have been effective for only nine months of the year.

> We assume convertible securities were converted (or options exercised) at the beginning of the reporting period or at the time the securities are issued, if later.

CONVERTIBLE PREFERRED STOCK

The potentially dilutive effect of convertible preferred stock is reflected in EPS calculations in much the same way as convertible debt. That is, we calculate EPS as if conversion already had occurred. Specifically, we add shares to the denominator of the EPS fraction and add back to earnings available to common shareholders the preferred dividends that would have been avoided if the preferred stock had been converted. Illustration 20–8 on the next page offers an example.

The adjustment for the conversion of the preferred stock should be applied only to diluted EPS computations. However, the existence of another issue of preferred stock also will affect the calculation of basic EPS. The effect on basic EPS is the same as the effect of the first (nonconvertible) issue of preferred stock: the numerator is reduced by the preferred dividends in order to derive earnings available to common shareholders.

This second issue of preferred stock would reduce earnings available to common shareholders by $8 million (8% × $100 million par). However, when diluted EPS is calculated, we hypothetically assume the convertible preferred stock was *not* outstanding. Accordingly, no preferred dividends on these shares would have been paid. So we add back the $8 million preferred dividends in much the same way we added back the interest saved when we assumed

ILLUSTRATION 20–8	Sovran Financial Corporation reported net income of $154 million in 2003 (tax rate 40%). Its capital structure included:
Convertible Preferred Stock	

Common Stock

Jan. 1	60 million common shares outstanding
Mar. 1	12 million new shares were sold
June 17	A 10% stock dividend was distributed
Oct. 1	8 million shares were reacquired as treasury stock

(The average market price of the common shares during 2000 was $25 per share.)

Preferred Stock, Nonconvertible

January 1–December 31   5 million 8%, $10 par, shares

Executive Stock Options

Options granted in 2001, exercisable for 15 million common shares* at an exercise price of $20 per share

Convertible Bonds

10%, $300 million face amount issued in 2002, convertible into 12 million common shares*

Preferred Stock, Convertible

10 million, 8%, cumulative, $10 par, shares issued in 1999, convertible into 5 million shares*

(amounts in millions, except per share amounts)

Basic EPS

$$\frac{\overset{\text{Net income}}{\$154} \quad \overset{\text{Preferred dividends}}{-\$4} \quad \overset{\text{Preferred dividends}}{-\$8}}{\underset{\substack{\text{Shares} \\ \text{at Jan. 1}}}{60} \; (1.10) + \underset{\substack{\text{New} \\ \text{Shares}}}{12 \, (^{10}\!/_{12})} \; (1.10) - \underset{\substack{\text{Treasury} \\ \text{shares}}}{8 \, (^3\!/_{12})}} = \frac{\$142}{75} = \$1.89$$

Stock dividend adjustment

Since diluted EPS is calculated *as if* the preferred shares had been converted, there are no dividends. Earnings available to common shareholders is increased by the dividends that otherwise would have been distributed to preferred shareholders.

Diluted EPS

$$\frac{\overset{\text{Net income}}{\$154} \; \overset{\text{Preferred dividends}}{-\$4} \; \overset{\text{Preferred dividends}}{-\$8} \; \overset{\substack{\text{After-tax} \\ \text{interest savings}}}{+\$30 - 40\%(\$30)} \; \overset{\text{Preferred dividends}}{+\$8}}{\underset{\substack{\text{Shares} \\ \text{at Jan. 1}}}{60} \; (1.10) + \underset{\substack{\text{New} \\ \text{Shares}}}{12 \, (^{10}\!/_{12})} \; (1.10) - \underset{\substack{\text{Treasury} \\ \text{shares}}}{8 \, (^3\!/_{12})} + \underset{\substack{\text{Exercise} \\ \text{of options}}}{(15 - 12)} + \underset{\substack{\text{Conversion} \\ \text{of bonds}}}{12} + \underset{\substack{\text{Conversion} \\ \text{of preferred} \\ \text{shares}}}{5}} = \frac{\$168}{95} = \$1.77$$

Stock dividend adjustment

*Adjusted for the stock dividend. For example, prior to the stock dividend, the preferred shares were convertible into $4^5\!/_{11}$ million of the "old" shares which became 5 million ($4^5\!/_{11} \times 1.10$) of the "new" shares after the stock dividend.

convertible bonds were converted. An important difference, though, is that, unlike interest expense, dividends have no tax effect. Dividends are not an expense and no income tax deduction is lost when dividends are not paid. Of course, adding back the preferred dividends that otherwise would have been deducted is equivalent to simply not deducting them in the first place.

Antidilutive Securities

At times, the effect of the conversion or exercise of potential common shares would be to increase, rather than decrease, EPS. These we refer to as **antidilutive securities.** Such securities are ignored when calculating both basic and diluted EPS.

OPTIONS, WARRANTS, RIGHTS

For illustration, recall the way we treated the stock options in our continuing illustration. In applying the treasury stock method, the number of shares assumed repurchased is fewer than the number of shares assumed sold. This is the case any time the buyback (average market) price is higher than the exercise price. Consequently, there will be a net increase in the number of shares, so earnings per share will decline.

On the other hand, when the exercise price is *higher* than the market price, to assume shares are sold at the exercise price and repurchased at the market price would mean buying back *more* shares than were sold. This would produce a net decrease in the number of shares. EPS would increase, not decrease, if we were to assume the exercise of stock options, stock warrants, or their equivalent. These would have an antidilutive effect and would not be considered exercised. In fact, a rational investor would not exercise options at an exercise price higher than the current market price anyway. Let's look at the example provided by Illustration 20–9.

> Antidilutive securities are ignored when calculating both basic and diluted EPS.

Sovran Financial Corporation reported net income of $154 million in 2003 (tax rate 40%). Its capital structure included:

ILLUSTRATION 20–9

Antidilutive Warrants

Common Stock

Jan. 1	60 million common shares outstanding
Mar. 1	12 million new shares were sold
June 17	A 10% stock dividend was distributed
Oct. 1	8 million shares were reacquired as treasury stock

(The average market price of the common shares during 2003 was $25 per share.)

Preferred Stock, Nonconvertible

January 1–December 31   5 million 8%, $10 par, shares

Executive Stock Options

Options granted in 2001, exercisable for 15 million common shares* at an exercise price of $20 per share

Convertible Bonds

10%, $300 million face amount issued in 2002, convertible into 12 million common shares*

Preferred Stock, Convertible

10 million, 8%, cumulative, $10 par, shares issued in 1999, convertible into 5 million shares*

Stock warrants

Warrants granted in 2002, exercisable for 4 million common shares* at an exercise price of $32.50 per share

Calculations:

The calculations of both basic and diluted EPS are unaffected by the warrants because the effect of exercising the warrants would be antidilutive.

> The $32.50 exercise price is higher than the market price, $25, so to assume shares are sold at the exercise price and repurchased at the market price would mean reacquiring more shares than were sold.

---

*Adjusted for the stock dividend. For example, prior to the stock dividend, the bonds were convertible into 10\%1 million of the "old" shares which became 12 million (10\%1 × 1.10) of the "new" shares after the stock dividend.

To assume 4 million shares were sold at the $32.50 exercise price and repurchased at the lower market price ($25) would mean reacquiring 5.2 million shares—more shares than were assumed sold. Because the effect would be antidilutive, we would simply ignore the warrants in the calculations.

In our continuing illustration, only the stock warrants were antidilutive. The other potential common shares caused EPS to decline when we considered them exercised or converted. In the case of the executive stock options, it was readily apparent that their effect would be dilutive because the exercise price was less than the market price, indicating that fewer shares could be repurchased (at the average market price) than were assumed issued (at the exercise price). As a result, the denominator increased. When only the denominator of a fraction increases, the fraction itself decreases. On the other hand, in the case of the warrants, it was apparent that their effect would be antidilutive because the exercise price was higher than the market price, which would have decreased the denominator and therefore increased the fraction.

When a company has a net loss, rather than net income, it reports a loss per share. In that situation, stock options that otherwise are dilutive will be antidilutive. Here's why. Suppose we have a loss per share of $2.00 calculated as ($150 million) ÷ 75 million shares = ($2.00). Now suppose stock options are outstanding that, if exercised, will increase the number of shares by 5 million. If that increase is included in the calculation, the loss per share will be $1.88 calculated as ($150 million) ÷ 80 million shares = ($1.88). The *loss* per share *declines*. This represents an *increase* in performance—not a dilution of performance. The options would be considered antidilutive, then, and not included in the calculation of the net loss per share. Any potential common shares not included in dilutive EPS because they are antidilutive should be revealed in the disclosure notes.

CONVERTIBLE SECURITIES

For convertible securities, though, it's not immediately obvious whether the effect of their conversion would be dilutive or antidilutive because the assumed conversion would affect both the numerator and the denominator of the EPS fraction. We discovered each was dilutive only after including the effect in the calculation and observing the result—a decline in EPS. But there's an easier way.

To determine whether convertible securities are dilutive and should be included in a diluted EPS calculation, we can compare the incremental effect of the conversion (expressed as a fraction) with the EPS fraction before the effect of any convertible security is considered. This, of course is our basic EPS. Recall from Illustration 20–8 that basic EPS is $1.89.

For comparison, we determine the "earnings per incremental share" of the two convertible securities:

Conversion of Bonds

The incremental effect (of conversion) of the bonds is the after-tax interest saved divided by the additional common shares from conversion.

$$\frac{\overset{\text{After-tax}}{\overset{\text{interest savings}}{+\$30 - 40\% \,(\$30)}}}{\underset{\substack{\text{Conversion} \\ \text{of bonds}}}{+12}} = \frac{\$18}{12} = \$1.50$$

Conversion of Preferred Stock

The incremental effect (of conversion) of the preferred stock is the dividends that wouldn't be paid divided by the additional common shares from conversion.

$$\frac{\overset{\substack{\text{Preferred} \\ \text{dividends}}}{+\$8}}{\underset{\substack{\text{Conversion of} \\ \text{preferred shares}}}{+5}} = \$1.60$$

If the incremental effect of a security is *higher* than basic EPS, it is antidilutive. That's not the case in our illustration.

ORDER OF ENTRY FOR MULTIPLE CONVERTIBLE SECURITIES

A convertible security might seem to be dilutive when looked at individually but, in fact, may be antidilutive when included in combination with other convertible securities. This is

GLOBAL PERSPECTIVE

Earnings per share receives more attention in the United States than in most other countries. In countries that do require EPS disclosures, requirements differ widely. For instance, earnings for the numerator of the EPS calculation are defined in the United States as earnings available for common shareholders, and separate calculations are required for ordinary income and net income when differences exist. In some countries, though, earnings is defined as continuing income from operations only (Norway, for example).

In the United States, basic and diluted EPS are reported. Other countries have similar requirements but define the two calculations differently than the United States (that is, the potential common shares included are different). Japan requires basic and diluted EPS to be reported in disclosure notes. Some countries (Spain, Switzerland, and Germany for instance) require no EPS disclosure at all, but disclosure may be provided anyway.

Some countries require disclosures not provided by U.S. companies. Japan, for instance, also discloses net assets per share.

because the *order of entry* for including their effects in the EPS calculation determines by how much, or even whether, EPS decreases as a result of their assumed conversion. Because our goal is to reveal the maximum potential dilution that might result, theoretically we should calculate diluted EPS using every possible combination of potential common shares to find the combination that yields the lowest EPS. But that's not necessary.

We can use the earnings per incremental share we calculated to determine the sequence of including securities' effects in the calculation. We include the securities in reverse order, beginning with the lowest incremental effect (that is, most dilutive), followed by the next lowest, and so on. This is, in fact, the order in which we included the securities in our continuing illustration.

ADDITIONAL CONSIDERATION

Actually, the order of inclusion made no difference in our example, but would in many instances. For example, suppose the preferred stock had been convertible into 4.3 million shares, rather than 5 million shares. The incremental effect of its conversion would have been:

Conversion of Preferred Stock:

$$\frac{\text{Preferred dividends } + \$8}{\text{Conversion of preferred shares } + 4.3} = \$1.86$$

On the surface, the effect would seem to be dilutive because $1.86 is less than $1.89, basic EPS. In fact, if this were the only convertible security, it would be dilutive. But, after the convertible bonds are assumed converted first, then the assumed conversion of the preferred stock would be *antidilutive*:

With Conversion of Bonds:

	Preferred dividends	Preferred dividends	After-tax interest savings		
Net income $154	−$4	−$8	+ $30 − 40% ($30)		
60 (1.10) +12 ($^{10}\!/_{12}$)(1.10) −	8 ($^{3}\!/_{12}$) +	(15 − 12) +	12	$= \dfrac{\$160}{90} = \$1.777$	
Shares at Jan. 1	New shares Stock dividend adjustment	Treasury shares	Exercise of options	Conversion of bonds	

Because the incremental effect of the convertible bonds ($1.50) is lower than the incremental effect of the convertible preferred stock ($1.86), it is included first.

A convertible security might seem to be dilutive when looked at individually but may be antidilutive when included in combination with other convertible securities.

With Conversion of Preferred Stock:

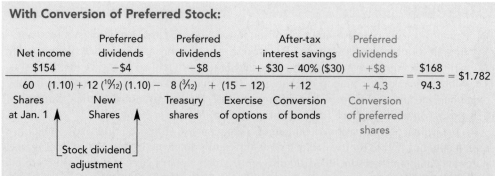

$$\frac{\underset{\$154}{\text{Net income}} \underset{-\$4}{\overset{\text{Preferred dividends}}{}} \underset{-\$8}{\overset{\text{Preferred dividends}}{}} \underset{+\ \$30 - 40\%\ (\$30)}{\overset{\text{After-tax interest savings}}{}} \underset{+\$8}{\overset{\text{Preferred dividends}}{}}}{\underset{\substack{\text{Shares} \\ \text{at Jan. 1}}}{60} \underset{\substack{\text{New} \\ \text{Shares}}}{(1.10) + 12\ (^{10}\!/_{12})\ (1.10)} - \underset{\substack{\text{Treasury} \\ \text{shares}}}{8\ (^{3}\!/_{12})} + \underset{\substack{\text{Exercise} \\ \text{of options}}}{(15 - 12)} \underset{\substack{\text{Conversion} \\ \text{of bonds}}}{+ 12} \underset{\substack{\text{Conversion} \\ \text{of preferred} \\ \text{shares}}}{+ 4.3}} = \frac{\$168}{94.3} = \$1.782$$

(Stock dividend adjustment)

Although the incremental effect of the convertible preferred stock ($1.86) is lower than basic EPS ($1.89), when included in the calculation after the convertible bonds the effect is antidilutive (EPS increases).

CONCEPT REVIEW EXERCISE

CRE **Basic and Diluted EPS**

At December 31, 2003, the financial statements of Clevenger Casting Corporation included the following:

Net income for 2003	$500 million
Common stock, $1 par:	
Shares outstanding on January 1	150 million shares
Shares retired for cash on February 1	24 million shares
Shares sold for cash on September 1	18 million shares
2-for-1 split on July 23	
Preferred stock, 10%, $60 par, cumulative, nonconvertible	$ 70 million
Preferred stock, 8%, $50 par, cumulative, convertible into 4 million shares of common stock	$100 million
Common stock warrants outstanding for 4 million shares of common stock; the exercise price is $15	
Bonds payable, 12.5%, convertible into 20 million shares of common stock	$200 million

Additional data:
The market price of the common stock averaged $20 during 2003.
The convertible preferred stock and the bonds payable had been issued at par in 2001.
The tax rate for the year was 40%.

Required:
Compute basic and diluted earnings per share for the year ended December 31, 2003.

SOLUTION

(amounts in millions, except per share amounts)

Basic EPS

$$\frac{\underset{\$500}{\text{Net income}} \underset{-\$7^a}{\overset{\text{Preferred dividends}}{}} \underset{-\$8^b}{\overset{\text{Preferred dividends}}{}}}{\underset{\substack{\text{Shares} \\ \text{at Jan. 1}}}{150}\ (2.00) - \underset{\substack{\text{Retired} \\ \text{shares}}}{24\ (^{11}\!/_{12})}\ (2.00) + \underset{\substack{\text{New} \\ \text{shares}}}{18\ (^{4}\!/_{12})}} = \frac{\$485}{262} = \$1.85$$

(Stock split adjustment*)

Diluted EPS

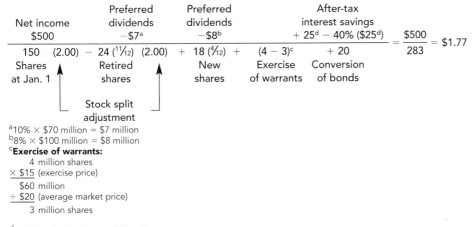

a10% × $70 million = $7 million
b8% × $100 million = $8 million
c**Exercise of warrants:**
    4 million shares
× $15 (exercise price)
    $60 million
÷ $20 (average market price)
    3 million shares

d12.5% × $200 million = $25 million

Dilution:

Conversion of Bonds	Conversion of 8% Preferred Stock

$$\frac{\text{After-tax interest savings} + \$25 - 40\%(\$25)}{+20 \atop \text{Conversion of bonds}} = \$0.75 \qquad \frac{\text{Preferred dividends} + \$8}{+4 \atop \text{Conversion of preferred shares}} = \$2.00*$$

*Because the incremental effect of conversion of the preferred stock ($2) is higher than EPS without the conversion of the preferred stock, the conversion would be *antidilutive* and is *not* considered in the calculation of diluted EPS.

ADDITIONAL EPS ISSUES

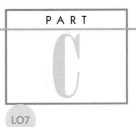

Contingently Issuable Shares

Sometimes an agreement specifies that additional shares of common stock will be issued, contingent on the occurrence of some future circumstance. For instance, in the disclosure note reproduced in Graphic 20–1, Hunt Manufacturing Co. reported contingent shares in connection with its acquisition of Feeny Manufacturing Company.

GRAPHIC 20–1
Contingently Issuable Shares—Hunt Manufacturing Company

> **Note 12: Acquisitions (in part)**
> The Company acquired Feeny Manufacturing Company of Muncie, Indiana, for 135,000 shares of restricted common stock with a value of $7.71 per share. Feeny Manufacturing Company is a manufacturer of kitchen storage products. The acquisition was accounted for as a purchase. The purchase agreement calls for the issuance of up to 135,000 additional shares of common stock in the next fiscal year based on the earnings of Feeny Manufacturing Company. . . .

At times, contingent shares are issuable to shareholders of an acquired company, certain key executives, or others in the event a certain level of performance is achieved. Contingent performance may be a desired level of income, a target stock price, or some other measurable activity level.

When calculating EPS, contingently issuable shares are considered to be outstanding in the computation of diluted EPS if the target performance level already is being met (assumed

Contingently issuable shares are considered outstanding in the computation of diluted EPS.

to remain at existing levels until the end of the contingency period). For example, if shares will be issued at a future date if a certain level of income is achieved and that level of income or more was already earned this year, those additional shares are simply added to the denominator of the diluted EPS fraction.[5]

For clarification, refer to our continuing illustration and assume 3 million additional shares will become issuable to certain executives in the following year (2004) if net income that year is $150 million or more. Recall that net income in 2003 was $154 million, so the additional shares would be considered outstanding in the computation of diluted EPS by simply adding 3 million additional shares to the denominator of the EPS fraction. Obviously, the 2004 condition ($150 million net income or more) has not been met yet since it's only year 2003. But because that level of income was achieved in 2003, the presumption is it's likely to be earned in 2004 as well.

If a level of income must be attained before the shares will be issued, and income already is that amount or more, the additional shares are simply added to the denominator.

Assumed Issuance of Contingently Issuable Shares (diluted EPS):

$$\frac{\text{No adjustment to the numerator}}{\underset{\text{Additional shares}}{+3}}$$

On the other hand, if the target income next year is $160 million, the contingent shares would simply be ignored in our calculation.

Summary of the Effect of Potential Common Shares on Earnings per Share

You have seen that under certain circumstances, securities that have the potential of reducing earnings per share by becoming common stock are assumed already to have become common stock for the purpose of calculating EPS. The table in Graphic 20–2 summarizes the circumstances under which the dilutive effect of these securities is reflected in the calculation of basic and diluted EPS.

GRAPHIC 20–2
When Potential Common Shares Are Reflected in EPS

Potential Common Shares	Is the Dilutive Effect Reflected in the Calculation of EPS?*	
	Basic EPS	**Diluted EPS**
• Stock options (or warrants, rights)	no	yes
• Convertible securities (bonds, notes, preferred stock)	no	yes
• Contingently issuable shares	no	yes[†]

*The effect is not included for any security if its effect is antidilutive.
[†]Unless shares are contingent upon some level of performance not yet achieved.

Graphic 20–3 on the next page summarizes the specific effects on the diluted EPS fraction when the dilutive effect of a potentially dilutive security is reflected in the calculation.

Actual Conversions

When calculating EPS in our example, we "pretended" the convertible bonds had been converted at the beginning of the year. What if they actually had been converted, let's say on November 1? Interestingly, diluted EPS would be precisely the same. Here's why:

---

[5]The shares should be included in both basic and diluted EPS if all conditions have actually been met so that there is no circumstance under which those shares would not be issued. In essence, these are no longer contingent shares.

GRAPHIC 20–3
How Potential
Common Shares Are
Reflected in a Diluted
EPS Calculation

Potential Common Shares	Modification to the Diluted EPS Fractions:	
	Numerator	**Denominator**
• Stock options (or warrants, rights)	None	Add the shares that would be created by their exercise,* reduced by shares repurchased at the average share price.
• Convertible bonds (or notes)	Add the interest (after-tax) that would have been avoided if the debt had been converted.	Add shares that would be created by the conversion* of the bonds (or notes).
• Convertible preferred stock	Do not deduct the dividends that would have been avoided if the preferred stock had been converted.	Add shares that would have been created by the conversion* of the preferred stock.
• Contingently issuable shares: Issuable upon the mere passage of time or Issuable when specified conditions are met, and those conditions are currently being met	None	Add shares that are issuable.
• Contingently issuable shares: Issuable when specified condition are met, and those condition are **not** currently being met	None	None

*At the beginning of the year or when potential common shares were issued, whichever is later (time-weight the increase in shares if assumed exercised or converted in midyear).

1. The actual conversion would cause an actual increase in shares of 12 million on November 1. These would be time-weighted so the denominator would increase by 12 ($\frac{2}{12}$). Also, the numerator would be higher because net income actually would be increased by the after-tax interest saved on the bonds for the last two months, [$30 − 40% ($30)] × ($\frac{2}{12}$). Be sure to note that this would not be an adjustment in the EPS calculation. Instead, net income would actually have been higher by [$30 − 40% ($30)] × ($\frac{2}{12}$) = $3. That is, reported net income would have been $157 rather than $154.

2. We would assume conversion for the period before November 1 because they were potentially dilutive during that period. The 12 million shares assumed outstanding from January 1 to November 1 would be time-weighted for that 10-month period: 12 ($\frac{10}{12}$). Also, the numerator would be increased by the after-tax interest assumed saved on the bonds for the first 10 months, [$30 − 40% ($30)] × ($\frac{10}{12}$).

Notice that the incremental effect on EPS is the same either way:

Not Actually Converted:	**Converted on November 1:**	
Assumed after-tax interest savings	Actual after-tax interest savings	Assumed after-tax interest savings

$$\frac{+\ \$30 - 40\%\ (\$30)}{+\ 12} = \frac{+[\$30 - 40\%\ (\$30)] \times (\frac{2}{12}) + [\$30 - 40\%\ (\$30)] \times (\frac{10}{12})}{+\ 12\ (\frac{2}{12}) + 12\ (\frac{10}{12})}$$

Assumed conversion of bonds	Actual conversion of bonds	Assumed conversion of bonds

EPS would be precisely the same whether convertible securities were actually converted or not.

Graphic 20–4 shows the disclosure note Clorox Company reported after the conversion of convertible notes during the year.

GRAPHIC 20–4
Conversion of Notes—
The Clorox Company

> **Note 1: Significant Accounting Policies—Earnings Per Common Share (in part)**
> A $9,000,000 note payable to Henkel Corporation was converted into 1,200,000 shares of common stock on August 1. . . . Earnings per common share and weighted-average shares outstanding reflect this conversion as if it were effective during all periods presented.

Options Outstanding for Only Part of the Period

Options outstanding for only part of the reporting period are included in the denominator on a time-weighted basis. For example, if options were issued on April 1 the denominator would include the appropriate incremental shares $\times \, \frac{9}{12}$. Likewise, if options expired on April 1 the weighted-average shares should include the appropriate incremental shares $\times \, \frac{3}{12}$.

Similarly, if options were exercised on April 1 the weighted-average shares should include the appropriate incremental shares $\times \, \frac{3}{12}$ for the period prior to actual exercise. The weighted-average shares should include the appropriate actual shares issued $\times \, \frac{9}{12}$ for the period after the exercise.

Financial Statement Presentation of Earnings Per Share Data

Recall from Chapter 4 that the income statement sometimes includes items that require separate presentation within the statement as follows:

> **Income from Continuing Operations**
> Discontinued operations
> Extraordinary items
> Cumulative effect of a change in accounting principle
> **Net income**

When the income statement includes one or more of the separately reported items, EPS data (both basic and diluted) must also be reported separately for income from continuing operations and net income. Per share amounts for discontinued operations, extraordinary items, and the cumulative effect of an accounting change would be disclosed either on the face of the income statement or in the notes to financial statements. Presentation on the face of the income statement is illustrated by the partial income statements of AK Steel from its 2000 annual report and exhibited in Graphic 20–5 on the next page.

Basic and diluted EPS data should be reported on the face of the income statement for all reporting periods presented in the comparative statements. Businesses without potential common shares present basic EPS only. Disclosure notes should provide additional disclosures including:

1. A reconciliation of the numerator and denominator used in the basic EPS computations to the numerator and the denominator used in the diluted EPS computations. An example of this is presented in Graphic 20–6 on the next page using the situation described in Illustration 20–8 on page 1006.
2. Any adjustments to the numerator for preferred dividends.
3. Any potential common shares that weren't included because they were antidilutive.
4. Any transactions that occurred after the end of the most recent period that would materially affect earnings per share.

Consolidated Statements of Income (partial)

GRAPHIC 20–5
EPS Disclosure—AK Steel

	For Years ended December 31		
	2000	**1999**	**1998**
Income from continuing operations	$132,400,000	$71,300,000	$195,800,000
Discontinued operations		7,500,000	
Income before extraordinary item and cumulative effect of a change in accounting	132,400,000	78,800,000	195,800,000
Extraordinary loss on retirement of debt, net of tax		(13,400,000)	
Cumulative effect of a change in accounting, net of tax			133,900,000
Net income	132,400,000	65,400,000	329,700,000
Other comprehensive income, net of tax	(3,200,000)	(1,400,000)	(2,800,000)
Comprehensive income	$129,200,000	$64,000,000	$326,900,000
Basic earnings per share:			
Income from continuing operations	$1.20	$0.62	$1.86
Discontinued operations		0.07	
Extraordinary loss on retirement of debt		(0.13)	
Cumulative effect of a change in accounting			1.33
Net income	$1.20	$0.56	$3.19
Diluted earnings per share:			
Income from continuing operations	$1.20	$0.62	$1.82
Discontinued operations		0.07	
Extraordinary loss on retirement of debt		(0.13)	
Cumulative effect of a change in accounting			1.24
Net income	$1.20	$0.56	$3.06

Earnings per Share Reconciliation:

GRAPHIC 20–6
Reconciliation of Basic EPS Computations to Diluted EPS Computations

	Income (Numerator)	Share (Denominator)	Per Share Amount
Net income	$154		
Preferred dividends	(12)		
Basic earnings per share	$142	75	$1.89
Stock options	None	3*	
Convertible debt	18	12	
Convertible preferred stock	8	5	
Diluted earnings per share	$168	95	$1.77

Note: Stock warrants to purchase an additional 4 million shares at $32.50 per share were outstanding throughout the year but were not included in diluted EPS because the warrants' exercise price is greater than the average market price of the common shares.

*15 million − [(15 million × $20)/$25] = 3 million net additional shares

ADDITIONAL CONSIDERATION

It is possible that potential common shares would have a dilutive effect on one component of net income but an antidilutive effect on another. When the inclusion of the potential common shares has a dilutive effect on "income from continuing operations," the effect should be included in all calculations of diluted EPS. In other words, the same number of potential common shares used in computing the diluted per-share amount for income from continuing operations is used in computing all other diluted per-share amounts, even when amounts are antidilutive to the individual per-share amounts.

DECISION MAKERS' PERSPECTIVE

We noted at the beginning of the chapter that investors and creditors pay a great deal of attention to earnings per share information. Because of the importance analysts attach to earnings announcements, companies are particularly eager to meet earnings expectations. As we first noted in Chapter 4, this desire has contributed to a relatively recent trend, especially among technology firms, to report **pro forma** earnings per share. What exactly are pro forma earnings? Unfortunately there is no answer to that question. Essentially, pro forma earnings are actual (GAAP) earnings reduced by any expenses the reporting company feels are unusual and should be excluded. Always, though, the pro forma results of a company look better than the real results. Qualcomm, Inc., a digital and wireless company, reported first quarter 2001 pro forma *earnings* of $0.29 per share. However on a GAAP basis, it actually had a *loss* of $0.31 per share. This is not an isolated example.

> Make sure you pay lots of attention to the man behind the curtain. If any earnings figure says pro forma, you should immediately look for a footnote or explanation telling you just what is and is not included in the calculation.[6]

When companies report pro forma results, they argue they are trying to help investors by giving them numbers that more accurately reflect their normal business activities, because they exclude unusual expenses. Analysts should be skeptical, though. Because of the purely discretionary nature of pro forma reporting and several noted instances of abuse, analysts should, at a minimum, find out precisely what expenses are excluded and what the actual GAAP numbers are.

Another way management might enhance the appearance of EPS numbers is by massaging the denominator of the calculation. Reducing the number of shares increases earnings *per share*. Some companies judiciously use share buyback programs to manipulate the number of shares and therefore EPS. There is nothing inherently wrong with share buybacks and, as we noted in Chapter 19, they can benefit shareholders. The motivation for buybacks, though, can sometimes be detected in the year-to-year pattern. A recent *Fortune* article asserts that, "One way Big Blue has kept the fabulous EPS growth going has been by buying back shares of its own stock. Since 1995, IBM has spent a stunning $34.1 billion to shrink shares outstanding. Indeed, $34.1 billion is more than IBM reported in net income ($31.3 billion) over the same period."[7]

One way analysts use EPS data is in connection with the price-earnings ratio. This ratio is simply the market price per share divided by the earnings per share. It measures the market's perception of the quality of a company's earnings by indicating the price multiple the capital market is willing to pay for the company's earnings. Presumably, this ratio reflects the information provided by all financial information in that the market price reflects analysts' perceptions of the company's growth potential, stability, and relative risk. The price-

---

[6]Bill Mann, "Qualcomm's Globalstar Headache," *MotleyFool.com,* January 25, 2001.
[7]"Hocus-Pocus: How IBM Grew 27% a Year," *Fortune,* Bethany McLean, June 26, 2000.

earnings ratio relates these performance measures with the external judgment of the marketplace concerning the value of the firm.

The ratio measures the quality of earnings in the sense that it represents the market's expectation of future earnings as indicated by current earnings. Caution is called for in comparing price-earnings ratios. For instance, a ratio might be low, not because earnings expectations are low, but because of abnormally elevated current earnings. On the contrary, the ratio might be high, not because earnings expectations are high, but because the company's current earnings are temporarily depressed. Similarly, an analyst should be alert to differences among accounting methods used to measure earnings from company to company when making comparisons.

Another ratio frequently calculated by shareholders and potential shareholders is the dividend payout ratio. This ratio expresses the percentage of earnings that is distributed to shareholders as dividends. The ratio is calculated by dividing dividends per common share by the earnings per share.

This ratio provides an indication of a firm's reinvestment strategy. A low payout ratio suggests that a company is retaining a large portion of earnings for reinvestment for new facilities and other operating needs. Low payouts often are found in growth industries and high payouts in mature industries. Often, though, the ratio is merely a reflection of managerial strategy concerning the mix of internal versus external financing. The ratio also is considered by investors who, for tax or other reasons, prefer current income over market price appreciation, or vice versa. ■

> The price-earnings ratio measures the quality of a company's earnings.

> The dividend payout ratio indicates the percentage of earnings that is distributed to shareholders as dividends.

CONCEPT REVIEW EXERCISE

Additional EPS Issues

At December 31, 2003, the financial statements of Bahnson General, Inc., included the following:

Net income for 2003 (including a net-of-tax extraordinary loss of $10 million)	$180 million
Common stock, $1 par:	
Shares outstanding on January 1	44 million
The share price was $25 and $28 at the beginning and end of the year, respectively.	

Additional data:

At January 1, 2003, $200 million of 10% convertible notes were outstanding. The notes were converted on April 1 into 16 million shares of common stock.

An agreement with company executives calls for the issuance of up to 12 million additional shares of common stock in 2004 and 2005 based on the Bahnson's net income in those years. Executives will receive 2 million shares at the end of each of those two years if the company's stock price is at least $26 and another 4 million shares each year if the stock price is at least $29.50.

The tax rate is 40%.

Required:

Compute basic and diluted earnings per share for the year ended December 31, 2003.

(amounts in millions, except per share amounts)   SOLUTION

Basic EPS

$$\frac{\underset{\$180}{\overset{\text{Net income}}{}}}{\underset{\substack{\text{Shares} \\ \text{at Jan. 1}}}{44} + \underset{\substack{\text{Actual} \\ \text{conversion} \\ \text{of notes}}}{16\,(\%_2)}} = \frac{\$180}{56} = \$3.21$$

Diluted EPS

$$\frac{\overset{\text{Net income}}{\$180} + \overset{\substack{\text{Assumed after-tax}\\\text{interest savings}}}{[\$20 - 40\%\,(\$20)] \times (^3\!/_{12})}}{\underset{\substack{\text{Shares}\\\text{at Jan. 1}}}{44} + \underset{\substack{\text{Actual}\\\text{conversion}\\\text{of notes}}}{16\,(^9\!/_{12})} + \underset{\substack{\text{Assumed}\\\text{conversion}\\\text{of notes}}}{16\,(^3\!/_{12})} + \underset{\substack{\text{Contingent}\\\text{shares}}}{(2 \times 2)}} = \frac{\$183}{64} = \$2.86$$

Convertible Notes: Notice that the effect on diluted EPS would be precisely the same whether the convertible notes were actually converted or not.

Converted on April 1:

$$\frac{\overset{\substack{\text{Net income including}\\\text{actual after-tax}\\\text{interest savings}}}{\$180} + \overset{\substack{\text{Assumed after-tax}\\\text{interest savings}}}{[\$20 - 40\%\,(\$20)] \times (^3\!/_{12})}}{\underset{\substack{\text{Shares}\\\text{at Jan. 1}}}{44} + \underset{\substack{\text{Actual}\\\text{conversion}\\\text{of notes}}}{16\,(^9\!/_{12})} + \underset{\substack{\text{Assumed}\\\text{conversion}\\\text{of notes}}}{16\,(^3\!/_{12})}} = \frac{\$183}{60}$$

Not Actually Converted:

$$\frac{\overset{\substack{\text{Net income without}\\\text{actual after-tax}\\\text{interest savings}}}{\$171^*} + \overset{\substack{\text{Assumed after-tax}\\\text{interest savings}}}{[\$20 - 40\%\,(\$20)]}}{\underset{\substack{\text{Shares}\\\text{at Jan. 1}}}{44} + \underset{\substack{\text{Assumed}\\\text{conversion}\\\text{of notes}}}{16}} = \frac{\$183}{60}$$

*$\$180 - \{[\$20 - 40\%\,(\$20)] \times (^9\!/_{12})\} = \$171$
After-tax interest from Apr. 1 to Dec. 31

Contingently Issuable Shares:

Because the conditions are met for issuing 4 million shares (2 million for each of two years), those shares are simply added to the denominator of diluted EPS. The current share price ($28) is projected to remain the same throughout the contingency period, so the other 8 million shares (4 million for each of two years) are excluded.

Income Statement Presentation:

To determine the per share amounts for income before extraordinary items, we substitute that amount for net income in the numerator (in this case, that means adding back the $10 million extraordinary loss):

$$\text{Basic:}\ \frac{\$180 + 10}{56} = \$3.39 \qquad \text{Diluted:}\ \frac{\$183 + 10}{64} = \$3.02$$

Earnings per Share:	Basic*	Diluted
Income before extraordinary items	$3.39	$3.02
Extraordinary loss	(.18)	(.16)
Net income	$3.21	$2.86

*Only diluted EPS is required on the face of the income statement. Basic EPS is reported in the EPS reconciliation shown in the disclosure note (below).

Disclosure Note:

Earnings per Share Reconciliation:

	Income (Numerator)	Shares (Denominator)	Per Share Amount
Basic Earnings per Share			
Income before extraordinary items	$190	56	$3.39
Extraordinary loss	(10)	56	(.18)
Net income	$180	56	$3.21
Convertible debt	3	4	
Contingently issuable shares	—	4	

Diluted Earnings per Share

Income before extraordinary items	$193	64	$3.02
Extraordinary loss	(10)	64	(.16)
Net income	$183	64	$2.86

FINANCIAL REPORTING CASE **SOLUTION**

1. **Meg's questions imply that she thinks you will get cash dividends of 48 cents a share. What does earning per share really tell you?** *(p. 996)*   Earnings per share is a way to summarize the performance of business enterprises into a single number. It is simply earnings expressed on a per share basis. It does not imply anything about cash dividends. Whether some, all, or none of the earnings are distributed depends on the company's reinvestment strategy. A dividend payout ratio expresses the percentage of earnings that is distributed to shareholders as dividends.

2. **The press release says, "per share amounts reflect the two-for-one stock split implemented in June 2001." What does that mean?** *(p. 999)*   When calculating earnings per share, shares outstanding prior to a stock split (or stock dividend) are retroactively restated to reflect the increase in shares (100% in this instance). That is, it is treated as if the June split occurred at the beginning of the period. When reported again for comparison purposes in the comparative income statements, the year earlier figure also would be restated to reflect the 2-for-1 stock split. Otherwise we would be comparing apples and oranges.

3. **Chairman Raymond commented that "the Corporation acquired 32.1 million shares of its common stock." Is that reduction in shares taken into account when EPS is calculated? How?** *(p. 999)*   If the number of shares has changed, it's necessary to find the weighted average of the shares outstanding during the period the earnings were generated. Since shares were reacquired during the period (either retired or as treasury stock), Exxon Mobil reduced the weighted-average number of shares. The company time-weighted the number of reacquired shares for the fraction of the year they were *not* outstanding, prior to subtracting from the number of shares outstanding during the period.

4. **The share buyback, according to Raymond, was "to offset the dilution associated with benefit plans." You know from statements ExxonMobil mailed you that "benefit plans" likely refer to a number of stock options that company executives hold. If those options are exercised, you know the resulting increase in shares might reduce earnings per share. Is that possibility taken into account when EPS is calculated?** *(p. 1001)*   Yes, it is. If we don't take into account the dilutive effect of the share increase we might mislead investors and creditors. So, in addition to basic EPS, we also calculate diluted EPS to include the dilutive effect of options and other potential common shares. This means to calculate EPS *as if* the potential increase in shares already has occurred (even though it hasn't yet). For Exxon Mobil's' stock options, the calculation assumes the options were exercised at the beginning of the reporting period. Then the cash proceeds from selling the new shares are used to buy back as many shares as possible at the shares' average market price during the year. ■

THE BOTTOM LINE

1. A company has a simple capital structure if it has no outstanding securities that could potentially dilute earnings per share. For such a firm, EPS is simply earnings available to common shareholders divided by the weighted average number of common shares outstanding. When potential common shares are outstanding, the company is said to have a complex capital structure. In that case, two EPS calculations are reported. Basic EPS assumes no dilution. Diluted EPS assumes maximum potential dilution.

2. EPS calculations are based on the weighted-average number of shares outstanding during the period. Any new shares issued during the period are time-weighted by the fraction of the period they were outstanding and then added to the number of shares outstanding for the period.

3. For a stock dividend or stock split, shares outstanding prior to the stock distribution are retroactively restated to reflect the increase in shares. When shares are reacquired, as treasury stock or to be retired, they are time-weighted for the fraction of the period they were not outstanding, prior to being subtracted from the number of shares outstanding during the reporting period.

4. The numerator in the EPS calculation should reflect earnings available to common shareholders. So, any dividends on preferred stock outstanding should be subtracted from reported net income. This adjustment is made for cumulative preferred stock whether or not dividends are declared that period.

5. For diluted EPS, it is assumed that stock options, rights, and warrants are exercised at the beginning of the period (or at the time the options are issued, if later) and the cash proceeds received are used to buy back (as treasury stock) as many of those shares as can be acquired at the average market price during the period.

6. To incorporate convertible securities into the calculation of diluted EPS, the conversion is assumed to have occurred at the beginning of the period (or at the time the convertible security is issued, if later). The denominator of the EPS fraction is adjusted for the additional common shares assumed and the numerator is increased by the interest (after-tax) or preferred dividends that would have been avoided in the event of conversion.

7. Contingently issuable shares are considered outstanding in the computation of diluted EPS when they will later be issued upon the mere passage of time or because of conditions that currently are met.

8. EPS data (both basic and diluted) must be reported separately for income from continuing operations and net income. Per share amounts for discontinued operations, extraordinary items, and an accounting change should be disclosed. Disclosures also should include a reconciliation of the numerator and denominator used in the computations.

QUESTIONS FOR REVIEW OF KEY TOPICS

Q 20–1 What is a simple capital structure? How is EPS determined for a company with a simple capital structure?

Q 20–2 When calculating the weighted average number of common shares, how are stock dividends and stock splits treated? Compare this treatment with that of additional shares sold for cash in midyear.

Q 20–3 Blake Distributors had 100,000 common shares outstanding at the beginning of the year, January 1. On May 13, Blake distributed a 5% stock dividend. On August 1, 1,200 shares were retired. What is the weighted average number of shares for calculating EPS?

Q 20–4 Why are preferred dividends deducted from net income when calculating EPS? Are there circumstances when this deduction is not made?

Q 20–5 Distinguish between basic and diluted EPS.

Q 20–6 The treasury stock method is used to incorporate the dilutive effect of stock options, stock warrants, and similar securities. Describe this method as it applies to diluted EPS.

Q 20–7 The potentially dilutive effect of convertible securities is reflected in EPS calculations by the if-converted method. Describe this method as it relates to convertible bonds.

Q 20–8 How is the potentially dilutive effect of convertible preferred stock reflected in EPS calculations by the if-converted method? How is this different from the way convertible bonds are considered?

Q 20–9 A convertible security may appear to be dilutive when looked at individually but might be antidilutive when included in combination with other convertible securities. How should the order be determined for inclusion of convertible securities in an EPS calculation to avoid including an antidilutive security?

Q 20–10 Wiseman Electronics has an agreement with certain of its division managers that 50,000 contingently issuable shares will be issued next year in the event operating income exceeds $2.1 million that year. In what way, if any, is the calculation of EPS affected by these contingently issuable shares assuming this year's operating income was $2.2 million? $2.0 million?

Q 20–11 Diluted EPS would be precisely the same whether convertible securities were actually converted or not. Why?

Q 20–12   When the income statement includes one or more of the separately reported items, such as discontinued operations, extraordinary items, or the cumulative effect of a change in accounting principle, which amounts require per share presentation?

Q 20–13   In addition to EPS numbers themselves, what additional disclosures should be provided concerning the EPS information?

EXERCISES

E 20–1
Shares issued; treasury shares

McDonnell-Myer Corporation reported a $741 million net income in 2003. The company had 544 million common shares outstanding at January 1, 2003, the beginning of its fiscal year. Changes in the number of shares during 2003 are shown below:

Feb. 28   36 million shares were issued as part of the consideration for the purchase of assets from Burrell Corporation.

May 2   As part of an annual share repurchase plan, 6 million shares were reacquired for $47 per share as treasury stock.

Required:
Compute McDonnell-Myer's earnings per share for the year ended December 31, 2003.

E 20–2
Shares issued; stock dividend

For the year ended December 31, 2003, Norstar Industries reported net income of $655,000. At January 1, 2003, the company had 900,000 common shares outstanding. The following changes in the number of shares occurred during 2003:

Apr. 30   Sold 60,000 shares in a public offering.
May 24   Declared and distributed a 5% stock dividend.
June 1   Issued 72,000 shares as part of the consideration for the purchase of assets from a subsidiary.

Required:
Compute Norstar's earnings per share for the year ended December 31, 2003.

E 20–3
Nonconvertible preferred stock

At December 31, 2002 and 2003, Funk & Noble Corporation had outstanding 820 million shares of common stock and 2 million shares of 8%, $100 par value cumulative preferred stock. No dividends were declared on either the preferred or common stock in 2002 or 2003. Net income for 2003 was $426 million. The income tax rate is 40%.

Required:
Compute earnings per share for the year ended December 31, 2003.

E 20–4
Stock dividend; nonconvertible preferred stock

Hardaway Fixtures' balance sheet at December 31, 2002, included the following:

Shares issued and outstanding:	
Common stock, $1 par	$800,000
Nonconvertible preferred stock, $50 par	20,000

On July 21, 2003, Hardaway issued a 25% stock dividend on its common stock. On December 12 it paid $50,000 cash dividends on the preferred stock. Net income for the year ended December 31, 2003, was $2,000,000.

Required:
Compute Hardaway's earnings per share for the year ended December 31, 2003.

E 20–5
Net loss; nonconvertible preferred stock; shares sold

At December 31, 2002, Albrecht Corporation had outstanding 373,000 shares of common stock and 8,000 shares of 9.5%, $100 par value cumulative, nonconvertible preferred stock. On May 31, 2003, Albrecht sold for cash 12,000 shares of its common stock. No cash dividends were declared for 2003. For the year ended December 31, 2003, Albrecht reported a net loss of $114,000.

Required:
Calculate Albrecht's net loss per share for the year ended December 31, 2003.

E 20–6
Treasury stock; new shares; stock dividends; two years

The Alford Group had 202,000 shares of common stock outstanding at January 1, 2003. The following activities affected common shares during the year. There are no potential common shares outstanding.

2003
Feb. 28   Purchased 6,000 shares of treasury stock.
Oct. 31   Sold the treasury shares purchased on February 28.

Nov. 30   Issued 24,000 new shares.
Dec. 31   Net income for 2003 is $400,000.

2004
Jan. 15   Declared and issued a 2-for-1 stock split.
Dec. 31   Net income for 2004 is $400,000.

Required:
1.   Determine the 2003 EPS.
2.   Determine the 2004 EPS.
3.   At what amount will the 2003 EPS be presented in the 2004 comparative financial statements?

E 20–7
Stock dividend; nonconvertible preferred stock; treasury shares; shares sold

On December 31, 2002, Berclair, Inc. had 200 million shares of common stock and 3 million shares of 9%, $100 par value cumulative preferred stock issued and outstanding. On March 1, 2003, Berclair purchased 24 million shares of its common stock as treasury stock. Berclair issued a 5% common stock dividend on July 1, 2003. Four million treasury shares were sold on October 1. Net income for the year ended December 31, 2003, was $150 million.

Required:
Compute Berclair's earnings per share for the year ended December 31, 2003.

E 20–8
Stock dividend; nonconvertible preferred stock; treasury shares; shares sold; stock options

(Note: This is a variation of the previous exercise, modified to include stock options.)
On December 31, 2002, Berclair, Inc. had 200 million shares of common stock and 3 million shares of 9%, $100 par value cumulative preferred stock issued and outstanding. Berclair issued a 5% common stock dividend on July 1, 2003. On March 1, 2003, Berclair purchased 24 million shares of its common stock as treasury stock. Four million treasury shares were sold on October 1. Net income for the year ended December 31, 2003, was $150 million.

Also outstanding at December 31, 2003, were stock options granted to key executives on September 13, 2002. The options are exercisable for 30 million common shares at an exercise price of $56 per share. During 2003, the market price of the common shares averaged $70 per share, peaking at $80 on December 31.

Required:
Compute Berclair's basic and diluted earnings per share for the year ended December 31, 2003.

E 20–9
Stock dividend; nonconvertible preferred stock; treasury shares; shares sold; stock options exercised

(Note: This is a variation of the previous exercise, modified to include the exercise of stock options.)
On December 31, 2002, Berclair, Inc. had 200 million shares of common stock and 3 million shares of 9%, $100 par value cumulative preferred stock issued and outstanding. Berclair issued a 5% common stock dividend on July 1, 2003. On March 1, 2003, Berclair purchased 24 million shares of its common stock as treasury stock. Four million treasury shares were sold on October 1. Net income for the year ended December 31, 2003, was $150 million.

Also outstanding at December 31 were stock options granted to key executives on September 13, 2002. The options are exercisable for 30 million common shares at an exercise price of $56 per share. During 2003, the market price of the common shares averaged $70 per share, peaking at $80 on December 31.

The options were exercised on September 1, 2003.

Required:
Compute Berclair's basic and diluted earnings per share for the year ended December 31, 2003.

E 20–10
Stock dividend; nonconvertible preferred stock; treasury shares; shares sold; stock options; convertible bonds

(Note: This is a variation of Exercise 20–9, modified to include convertible bonds).
On December 31, 2002, Berclair, Inc. had 200 million shares of common stock and 3 million shares of 9%, $100 par value cumulative preferred stock issued and outstanding. Berclair issued a 5% common stock dividend on July 1, 2003. On March 1, 2003, Berclair purchased 24 million shares of its common stock as treasury stock. Four million treasury shares were sold on October 1. Net income for the year ended December 31, 2003, was $150 million. The income tax rate is 40%.

Also outstanding at December 31 were stock options granted to key executives on September 13, 2002. The options are exercisable for 30 million common shares at an exercise price of $56 per share. During 2003, the market price of the common shares averaged $70 per share, peaking at $80 on December 31.

$62.5 million of 8% bonds, convertible into 6 million common shares, were issued at face value in 1999.

Required:
Compute Berclair's basic and diluted earnings per share for the year ended December 31, 2003.

E 20–11
Stock options

Stock options exercisable at $50 per share to obtain 24,000 shares of common stock were outstanding during a period when the average market price of the common stock was $60 and the ending market price was $55.

Required:
By how many shares will the assumed exercise of these options increase the weighted-average number of shares outstanding when calculating diluted earnings per share?

E 20–12
Convertible preferred stock

Ahnberg Corporation had 800,000 shares of common stock issued and outstanding at December 31, 2002. No common shares were issued during 2003. On January 1, 2003, Ahnberg issued 100,000 shares of convertible preferred stock. The preferred shares are convertible into 200,000 shares of common stock. During 2003 Ahnberg paid $60,000 cash dividends on the preferred stock. Net income for the year ended December 31, 2003, was $1,500,000.

Required:
Compute Ahnberg's basic and diluted earnings per share for the year ended December 31, 2003.

E 20–13
Convertible preferred stock; convertible bonds

Information from the financial statements of the Ames Fabricators, Inc., included the following:

	December 31	
	2003	**2002**
Common shares	100,000	100,000
Convertible preferred shares (convertible into 32,000 shares of common)	12,000	12,000
10% convertible bonds (convertible into 30,000 shares of common)	$1,000,000	$1,000,000

Ames' net income for the year ended December 31, 2003, is $500,000. The income tax rate is 40%. Ames paid dividends of $5 per share on its preferred stock during 2003.

Required:
Compute basic and diluted earnings per share for the year ended December 31, 2003.

E 20–14
Shares sold; convertible bonds

Wagnell's, Inc. had 50 million shares of common stock outstanding at January 1, 2003. On October 1, 2003, an additional 12 million shares of common stock were issued for cash. Wagnell's also had $400 million of 10% convertible bonds outstanding throughout 2003. The bonds are convertible into 10 million shares of common stock. Wagnell's net income for the year ended December 31, 2003, is $250 million. The income tax rate is 40%.

Required:
Compute basic and diluted earnings per share for the year ended December 31, 2003.

E 20–15
Shares issued; stock options

For the year ended December 31, 2003, Croft Industries reported net income of $900 million. During the year, the market price of Croft's common stock averaged $12, ending 2003 at $12.25 per share. At January 1, 2003, Croft had 191 million common shares outstanding. On May 1 Croft sold 9 million shares in a public offering. Stock options exercisable for 48 million shares at an exercise price of $11 were outstanding throughout the year. Croft's only debt consisted of $83 million of 10% short-term bank notes. The company's income tax rate is 40%.

Required:
Compute Croft's basic and diluted earnings per share for the year ended December 31, 2003.

E 20–16
Shares issued; stock options

Stanley Department Stores reported net income of $720,000 for the year ended December 31, 2003.

Additional Information:

Common shares outstanding at Jan. 1, 2003	80,000
Stock warrants outstanding throughout 2003	24,000

(Each warrant is exercisable for one common share at an exercise price of $37.50)
During the year, the market price of Stanley's common stock averaged $45, ending 2003 at $50 per share.
On Aug. 30 Stanley sold 15,000 common shares.
Stanley's only debt consisted of $50,000 of 10% short term bank notes.
The company's income tax rate is 40%.

Required:
Compute Stanley's basic and diluted earnings per share for the year ended December 31, 2003.

E 20–17
Contingently issuable shares

During its first year of operations, McCollum Tool Works entered into the following transactions relating to shareholders' equity. The corporation was authorized to issue 100 million common shares, $1 par per share.

Jan. 2 Issued 35 million common shares for cash.

3 Entered an agreement with the company president to issue up to 2 million additional shares of common stock in 2004 based on the earnings of McCollum in 2004. If net income exceeds $140 million, the president will receive 1 million shares; 2 million shares if net income exceeds $150 million.

Mar. 31 Issued 4 million shares in exchange for plant facilities.

Net income for 2003 was $148 million.

Required:
Compute basic and diluted earnings per share for the year ended December 31, 2003.

E 20–18
New shares; contingent agreements

Anderson Steel Company began 2003 with 600,000 shares of common stock outstanding. On March 31, 2003, 100,000 new shares were sold at a price of $45 per share. The market price has risen steadily since that time to a high of $50 per share at December 31. No other changes in shares occurred during 2003, and no securities are outstanding that can become common stock. However, there are two agreements with officers of the company for future issuance of common stock. Both agreements relate to compensation arrangements reached in 2002. The first agreement grants to the company president a right to 10,000 shares of stock each year the closing market price is at least $48. The agreement begins in 2004 and expires in 2007. The second agreement grants to the controller a right to 15,000 shares of stock if she is still with the firm at the end of 2011. Net income for 2003 was $2,000,000.

Required:
Compute Anderson Steel Company's basic and diluted EPS for the year ended December 31, 2003.

E 20–19
Concepts; terminology

Listed below are several terms and phrases associated with earnings per share. Pair each item from List A (by letter) with the item from List B that is most appropriately associated with it.

List A	List B
____ 1. Subtract preferred dividends.	a. Options exercised.
____ 2. Time-weighted by $\frac{5}{12}$.	b. Simple capital structure.
____ 3. Time-weighted shares assumed issued plus time-weighted actual shares	c. Basic EPS.
	d. Convertible preferred stock.
____ 4. Midyear event treated as if it occurred at the beginning of the reporting period.	e. Earnings available to common shareholders.
	f. Antidilutive.
____ 5. Preferred dividends do not reduce earnings.	g. Increased marketability.
____ 6. Single EPS presentation.	h. Extraordinary items.
____ 7. Stock split.	i. Stock dividend.
____ 8. Potentially dilutive security.	j. Add after-tax interest to numerator.
____ 9. Exercise price exceeds market price.	k. Diluted EPS.
____ 10. No dilution assumed.	l. Noncumulative, undeclared preferred dividends.
____ 11. Convertible bonds.	m. Common shares retired in August.
____ 12. Contingently issuable shares.	n. Include in diluted EPS when conditions for issuance are met.
____ 13. Maximum potential dilution.	
____ 14. Per share amounts for net income and for income from continuing operations.	

PROBLEMS

P 20–1
Net loss; stock dividend; nonconvertible preferred stock; treasury shares; shares sold; extraordinary loss

On December 31, 2002, Ainsworth, Inc. had 600 million shares of common stock outstanding. Twenty million shares of 8%, $100 par value cumulative, nonconvertible preferred stock were sold on January 2, 2003. On April 30, 2003, Ainsworth purchased 30 million shares of its common stock as treasury stock. Twelve million treasury shares were sold on August 31. Ainsworth issued a 5% common stock dividend on June 12, 2003. No cash dividends were declared in 2003. For the year ended December 31, 2003, Ainsworth reported a net loss of $140 million, including an after-tax extraordinary loss of $400 million from a litigation settlement.

Required:
1. Determine Ainsworth's net loss per share for the year ended December 31, 2003.

2. Determine the per share amount of income or loss from continuing operations for the year ended December 31, 2003.
3. Prepare an EPS presentation that would be appropriate to appear on Ainsworth's 2003 and 2002 comparative income statements. Assume EPS was reported in 2002 as $.75, based on net income (no extraordinary items) of $450 million and a weighted-average number of common shares of 600 million.

P 20–2
EPS from statement of retained earnings

(Note: Problem 20–2 is based on the same situation described in Problem 19–4 in Chapter 19, modified to focus on EPS rather than recording the events that affected retained earnings.)
Comparative Statements of Retained Earnings for Renn-Dever Corporation were reported as follows for the fiscal years ending December 31, 2001, 2002, and 2003.

RENN-DEVER CORPORATION
Statements of Retained Earnings

For the Years Ended December 31	2003	2002	2001
Balance at beginning of year	$6,794,292	$5,464,052	$5,624,552
Net income (loss)	3,308,700	2,240,900	(160,500)
Deductions:			
Stock dividend (34,900 shares)	242,000		
Common shares retired, September 30 (110,000 shares)		212,660	
Common stock cash dividends	889,950	698,000	0
Balance at end of year	$8,971,042	$6,794,292	$5,464,052

At December 31, 2000, paid-in capital consisted of the following:

Common stock, 1,855,000 shares at $1 par,	$1,855,000
Paid in capital—excess of par	7,420,000

No preferred stock or potential common shares were outstanding during any of the periods shown.

Required:
Compute Renn-Dever's earnings per share as it would have appeared in income statements for the years ended December 31, 2001, 2002, and 2003.

P 20–3
EPS from statement of shareholders' equity

Comparative Statements of Shareholders' Equity for Locke Intertechnology Corporation were reported as follows for the fiscal years ending December 31, 2001, 2002, and 2003.

LOCKE INTERTECHNOLOGY CORPORATION
Statements of Shareholders' Equity
For the Years Ended Dec. 31, 2001, 2002, and 2003
($ in millions)

	Preferred Stock, $10 par	Common Stock, $1 par	Additional Paid-In Capital	Retained Earnings	Total Shareholders' Equity
Balance at January 1, 2001		55	495	1,878	2,428
Sale of preferred shares	10		470		480
Sale of common shares, 7/1		9	81		90
Cash dividend, preferred				(1)	(1)
Cash dividend, common				(16)	(16)
Net income				290	290
Balance at December 31, 2001	10	64	1,046	2,151	3,271
Retirement of common shares, 4/1		(4)	(36)	(20)	(60)
Cash dividend, preferred				(1)	(1)
Cash dividend, common				(20)	(20)
3-for-2 split effected in the form of a common stock dividend, 8/12		30	(30)		
Net income				380	380
Balance at December 31, 2002	10	90	980	2,490	3,570
10% common stock dividend, 5/1		9	90	(99)	
Sale of common shares, 9/1		3	31		34

Cash dividend, preferred				(2)	(2)
Cash dividend, common				(22)	(22)
Net income				412	412
Balance at December 31, 2003	**10**	**102**	**1,101**	**2,779**	**3,992**

Required:

Infer from the statements the events and transactions that affected Locke Intertechnology Corporation's shareholders' equity and compute earnings per share as it would have appeared on the income statements for the years ended December 31, 2001, 2002, and 2003. No potential common shares were outstanding during any of the periods shown.

P 20–4
Nonconvertible preferred stock; treasury shares; shares sold; stock dividend

On December 31, 2002, Dow Steel Corporation had 600,000 shares of common stock and 300,000 shares of 8%, noncumulative, nonconvertible preferred stock issued and outstanding. Dow issued a 4% common stock dividend on May 15 and paid cash dividends of $400,000 and $75,000 to common and preferred shareholders, respectively, on December 15, 2003.

On February 28, 2003, Dow sold 60,000 common shares. In keeping with its long-term share repurchase plan, 2,000 shares were retired on July 1. Dow's net income for the year ended December 31, 2003, was $2,100,000. The income tax rate is 40%.

Required:
Compute Dow's earnings per share for the year ended December 31, 2003.

P 20–5
Nonconvertible preferred stock; treasury shares; shares sold; stock dividend; options

(Note: Problem 20–5 is a variation of Problem 20–4, modified to include stock options.)
On December 31, 2002, Dow Steel Corporation had 600,000 shares of common stock and 300,000 shares of 8%, noncumulative, nonconvertible preferred stock issued and outstanding. Dow issued a 4% common stock dividend on May 15 and paid cash dividends of $400,000 and $75,000 to common and preferred shareholders, respectively, on December 15, 2003.

On February 28, 2003, Dow sold 60,000 common shares. In keeping with its long-term share repurchase plan, 2,000 shares were retired on July 1. Dow's net income for the year ended December 31, 2003, was $2,100,000. The income tax rate is 40%.

As part of an incentive compensation plan, Dow granted stock options to division managers at December 31 of the current and each of the previous two years. Each option permits its holder to buy one share of common stock at an exercise price equal to market value at the date of grant. Information concerning the number of options granted and common share prices follows:

Date Granted	Options Granted	Share Price
	(adjusted for the stock dividend)	
December 31, 2001	3,000	$33
December 31, 2002	8,000	$24
December 31, 2003	6,500	$31

The market price of the common stock averaged $32 per share during 2003.

Required:
Compute Dow's earnings per share for the year ended December 31, 2003.

P 20–6
Nonconvertible preferred stock; treasury shares; shares sold; stock dividend; options; convertible bonds; contingently issuable shares

(Note: Problem 20–6 is a variation of Problem 20–5, modified to include convertible bonds and contingently issuable shares.)
On December 31, 2002, Dow Steel Corporation had 600,000 shares of common stock and 300,000 shares of 8%, noncumulative, nonconvertible preferred stock issued and outstanding. Dow issued a 4% common stock dividend on May 15 and paid cash dividends of $400,000 and $75,000 to common and preferred shareholders, respectively, on December 15, 2003.

On February 28, 2003, Dow sold 60,000 common shares. Also, as a part of a 2002 agreement for the acquisition of Merrill Cable Company, another 23,000 shares (already adjusted for the stock dividend) are to be issued to former Merrill shareholders on December 31, 2004, if Merrill's 2004 net income is at least $500,000. In 2003, Merrill's net income was $630,000.

In keeping with its long-term share repurchase plan, 2,000 shares were retired on July 1. Dow's net income for the year ended December 31, 2003, was $2,100,000. The income tax rate is 40%.

As part of an incentive compensation plan, Dow granted stock options to division managers at December 31 of the current and each of the previous two years. Each option permits its holder to buy one share of common stock at an exercise price equal to market value at the date of grant. Information concerning the number of options granted and common share prices follows:

Date Granted	Options Granted	Share Price
	(adjusted for the stock dividend)	
December 31, 2001	3,000	$33
December 31, 2002	8,000	$24
December 31, 2003	6,500	$31

The market price of the common stock averaged $32 per share during 2003.

On July 12, 2001, Dow issued $800,000 of convertible 10% debentures at face value. Each $1,000 bond is convertible into 30 common shares (adjusted for the stock dividend).

Required:

Compute Dow's basic and diluted earnings per share for the year ended December 31, 2003.

P 20–7

Antidilution

Alciatore Company earned a net income of $150,000 in 2003. The weighted-average number of common shares outstanding for 2003 was 40,000. The average stock price for 2003 was $33. Assume an income tax rate of 40%.

Required:

For each of the following independent situations, indicate whether the security is antidilutive for diluted EPS.

1. 10,000 shares of 7.7% of $100 par convertible, cumulative preferred stock. Each share may be converted into two common shares.
2. 8% convertible 10-year, $500,000 of bonds, issued at face value. The bonds are convertible to 5,000 shares of common stock.
3. Stock options exercisable at $30 per share after January 1, 2005.
4. Warrants for 1,000 common shares with an exercise price of $35 per share.
5. A contingent agreement to issue 5,000 shares of stock to the company president if net income is at least $125,000 in 2004.

P 20–8

Convertible bonds; treasury shares

At December 31, 2003, the financial statements of Hollingsworth Industries included the following:

Net income for 2003	$560 million
Bonds payable, 10%, convertible into 36 million shares of common stock	$300 million
Common stock:	
Shares outstanding on January 1	400 million
Treasury shares purchased for cash on September 1	30 million

Additional data:
The bonds payable were issued at par in 2001. The tax rate for 2003 was 40%.

Required:

Compute basic and diluted EPS for the year ended December 31, 2003.

P 20–9

Options; convertible preferred; additional shares

On January 1, 2003, Tonge Industries had outstanding 440,000 common shares (par $1) that originally sold for $20 per share, and 4,000 shares of 10% cumulative preferred stock (par $100), convertible into 40,000 common shares.

On October 1, 2003, Tonge sold and issued an additional 16,000 shares of common stock at $33. At December 31, 2003, there were common stock options outstanding, issued in 2002, and exercisable for 20,000 shares of common stock at an exercise price of $30. The market price of the common stock at year-end was $48. During the year the price of the common shares had averaged $40.

Net income was $650,000. The tax rate for the year was 40%.

Required:

Compute basic and diluted EPS for the year ended December 31, 2003.

P 20–10

Stock options; nonconvertible preferred; convertible bonds; shares sold

At January 1, 2003, Canaday Corporation had outstanding the following securities:

600 million common shares

20 million 6% cumulative preferred shares, $50 par

8% convertible bonds, $2,000 million face amount, convertible into 80 million common shares

The following additional information is available:

• On September 1, 2003, Canaday sold 72 million additional shares of common stock.

- Unexercised stock options to purchase 60 million shares of common stock at $12 per share were outstanding at the beginning and end of 2003. The average market price of Canaday 's common stock was $18 per share during 2003.
- Canaday's net income for the year ended December 31, 2003, was $1,476 million. The effective income tax rate was 40%.

Required:
1. Calculate basic earnings per common share for the year ended December 31, 2003.
2. Calculate the diluted earnings per common share for the year ended December 31, 2003.

BROADEN YOUR PERSPECTIVE

Apply your critical-thinking ability to the knowledge you've gained. These cases will provide you an opportunity to develop your research, analysis, judgment, and communication skills. You also will work with other students, integrate what you've learned, apply it in real world situations, and consider its global and ethical ramifications. This practice will broaden your knowledge and further develop your decision-making abilities.

Judgment Case 20–1
Where are the profits?

Hawkins Construction Company has experienced generally steady growth since its inception in 1950. Management is proud of its record of having maintained or increased its earnings per share in each year of its existence.

Recessionary pressures in the construction industry have led to disturbing dips in revenues the past two years. Despite concerted cost-cutting efforts, profits have actually declined in each of the two previous years. Net income in 2001, 2002, and 2003 was as follows:

2001	$145 million
2002	$134 million
2003	$ 95 million

A major shareholder has hired you to provide advice on whether to continue her present investment position or to curtail that position. Of particular concern is the declining profitability, despite the fact that earnings per share has continued a pattern of growth:

	Basic	Diluted
2001	$2.15	$1.91
2002	$2.44	$2.12
2003	$2.50	$2.50

She specifically asks you to explain this apparent paradox. During the course of your investigation you discover the following events:

- For the decade ending December 31, 2000, Hawkins had 60 million common shares and 20 million shares of 8%, $10 par nonconvertible preferred stock outstanding. Cash dividends have been paid quarterly on both.
- On July 1, 2002, half the preferred shares were retired in the open market. The remaining shares were retired on December 30, 2002.
- $55 million of 8% nonconvertible bonds were issued at the beginning of 2003 and a portion of the proceeds were used to call and retire $50 million of 10% debentures (outstanding since 1998) that were convertible into 9 million common shares.
- In 2001 management announced a share repurchase plan by which up to 24 million common shares would be retired. 12 million shares were retired on March 1 of both 2002 and 2003.
- Hawkins' income tax rate is 40% and has been for the last several years.

Required:
Explain the apparent paradox to which your client refers. Include calculations that demonstrate your explanation.

Communication Case 20–2
Dilution

"I thought I understood earnings per share," lamented Brad Dawson, "but you're telling me we need to pretend our convertible bonds have been converted! Or maybe not?"

Dawson, your boss, is the new manager of the Fabricating division of BVT Corporation. His background is engineering and he has only a basic understanding of earnings per share. Knowing you are an accounting graduate, he asks you to explain the questions he has about the calculation of the company's EPS. His reaction is to your explanation that the company's convertible bonds might be included in this year's calculation.

"Put it in a memo!" he grumbled as he left your office.

Required:
Write a memo to Dawson. Explain the effect on earnings per share of each of the following:
1. Convertible securities.
2. Antidilutive securities.

Real World Case 20–3
Reporting EPS; extraordinary item; discontinued operations; complex capital structure

Harris Corporation is an international company focused on the worldwide market for voice, data, and video communications equipment. The company provides a wide range of products and services for wireless, broadcast, network support, and government markets. Harris has sales and service facilities in nearly 90 countries. Its total revenues in fiscal 2001 were approximately $1.96 billion.

The following is an excerpt from the comparative income statements (beginning with income from continuing operations before extraordinary item) from Harris's 2001 annual report:

	For fiscal years ended June 29		
	2001	**2000**	**1999**
Income from continuing operations before extraordinary item	$21,400,000	$25,000,000	$49,900,000
Discontinued operations net of taxes		(7,000,000)	12,400,000
Income before extraordinary item	$21,400,000	$18,000,000	$62,300,000
Extraordinary loss from early retirement of debt net of taxes			(9,200,000)
Net income	$21,400,000	$18,000,000	$53,100,000

An income statement sometimes includes items that require separate presentation (net of income taxes) within the statement. The three possible "special items" are the following:

Income from continuing operations:
  Discontinued operations
  Extraordinary items
  Cumulative effect of a change in accounting principle
Net income

Harris reports two of these items. A disclosure note from Harris's 2001 annual report is shown below:

Net Income per Share
Average outstanding shares used in the computation of net income per share are summarized below:

Basic:
Weighted average shares outstanding	66.8	73.5	79.9
Contingently issuable shares	(0.2)	(0.3)	(0.5)
	66.6	73.2	79.4

Diluted:
Weighted average shares outstanding	66.8	73.5	79.9
Dilutive stock options	0.4	0.2	0.1
Contingently issuable shares	(0.2)	(0.3)	(0.3)
	67.0	73.4	79.7

Required:
1. The disclosure note shows adjustments for both "dilutive stock options" and "contingently issuable shares." Explain why and how these adjustments are made to the weighted-average shares outstanding.
2. Is it possible for stock options *not* to be dilutive? What difference does it make? Explain.
3. Based on the information provided, prepare the presentation of basic and diluted earnings per share for 2001, 2000, and 1999 that Harris reports in its 2001 annual report.

International Case 20–4
Reporting earnings per share in other countries

A key objective of the International Accounting Standards Board (IASB) is to narrow worldwide differences in accounting practices and the presentation of financial information. Although the IASB has worked toward uniformity since 1973, harmonization has by no means been achieved. Toward this end, the United States has cooperated with the IASB in developing common requirements for earnings per share. Still significant differences exist from country to country that do not choose to follow the international standards in this area.

Required:

1. Choose a country other than the United States and obtain an annual report for a company based in that country. Research the way that country reports earnings per share. Include in your analysis:
   a. The extent of variations in the definition of earnings for the numerator of the EPS calculation.
   b. Whether both basic and diluted EPS are reported in the financial statements of the non-U.S. firm.
   c. Whether additional related disclosures are provided.

2. Prepare a short report highlighting the similarities and differences between the United States and your chosen country in the way earnings per share and related amounts are reported.

Note: You can obtain copies of annual reports from the company's website, from a friendly stockbroker, from Public Register's Annual Report Service, on the Internet at www.**PRARS.com** or from EDGAR, the Electronic Data Gathering and Retrieval service of the SEC, at www.**sec.gov**.

Analysis Case 20–5
Analyzing financial statements; price–earnings ratio; dividend payout ratio

IGF Foods Company is a large, primarily domestic, consumer foods company involved in the manufacture, distribution and sale of a variety of food products. Industry averages are derived from Troy's *The Almanac of Business and Industrial Financial Ratios* and Dun and Bradstreet's *Industry Norms and Key Business Ratios*. Following are the 2003 and 2002 comparative income statements and balance sheets for IGF. The market price of IGF's common stock is $47 during 2003. (The financial data we use are from actual financial statements of a well-known corporation, but the company name used in our illustration is fictitious and the numbers and dates have been modified slightly to disguise the company's identity.)

IGF FOODS COMPANY
Years Ended December 31, 2003 and 2002

($ in millions)	2003	2002
Comparative Income Statements		
Net sales	$6,440	$5,800
Cost of goods sold	(3,667)	(3,389)
Gross profit	2,773	2,411
Operating expenses	(1,916)	(1,629)
Operating income	857	782
Interest expense	(54)	(53)
Income from operations before tax	803	729
Income taxes	(316)	(287)
Net income	$ 487	$ 442
Net income per share	$2.69	$2.44
Average shares outstanding	181 million	181 million
Comparative Balance Sheets		
Assets		
Total current assets	$1,879	$1,490
Property, plant, and equipment (net)	2,592	2,291
Intangibles (net)	800	843
Other assets	74	60
Total assets	$5,345	$4,684
Liabilities and Shareholders' Equity		
Total current liabilities	$1,473	$ 941
Long term debt	534	728
Deferred income taxes	407	344
Total liabilities	2,414	2,013
Shareholders' equity:		
Common stock	180	180
Additional paid-in capital	21	63
Retained earnings	2,730	2,428
Total shareholders' equity	2,931	2,671
Total liabilities and shareholders' equity	$5,345	$4,684

Some ratios express income, dividends, and market prices on a per share basis. As such, these ratios appeal primarily to common shareholders, particularly when weighing investment possibilities. These ratios focus less on the fundamental soundness of a company and more on its investment characteristics.

Required:
1. Earnings per share expresses a firm's profitability on a per share basis. Calculate earnings per share for IGF.
2. Calculate IGF's price-earnings ratio. The average price-earnings ratio for the stocks listed on the New York Stock Exchange in a comparable time period was 18.5. What does your calculation indicate about IGF's earnings?
3. Calculate IGF's dividend payout ratio. What information does the calculation provide an investor?

Ethics Case 20–6
International Network Solutions

International Network Solutions provides products and services related to remote access networking. The company has grown rapidly during its first 10 years of operations. As its segment of the industry has begun to mature, though, the fast growth of previous years has begun to slow. In fact, this year revenues and profits are roughly the same as last year.

One morning, nine weeks before the close of the fiscal year, Rob Mashburn, CFO, and Jessica Lane, controller, were sharing coffee and ideas in Lane's office.

Lane:	About the Board meeting Thursday. You may be right. This may be the time to suggest a share buyback program.
Mashburn:	To begin this year, you mean?
Lane:	Right! I know Barber will be lobbying to use the funds for our European expansion. She's probably right about the best use of our funds, but we can always issue more notes next year. Right now, we need a quick fix for our EPS numbers.
Mashburn:	Our shareholders are accustomed to increases every year.

Required:
1. How will a buyback of shares provide a "quick fix" for EPS?
2. Is the proposal ethical?
3. Who would be affected if the proposal is implemented?

Integrating Case 20–7
Executive stock options and EPS

Microsoft Corporation offers compensation to its employees and executives through a variety of compensation plans. One such plan is its stock option plan, which is described in the following disclosure note from its fiscal 2001 annual report:

> **Stock Option Plans**
> The Company has stock option plans for directors, officers, and employees, which provide for nonqualified and incentive stock options. Options granted prior to 1995 generally vest over four and one-half years and expire 10 years from the date of grant. Options granted between 1995 and 2000 generally vest over four and one-half years and expire seven years from the date of grant, while certain options vest either over four and one-half years or over seven and one-half years and expire after 10 years. Options granted during 2001 vest over four and one-half years and expire 10 years from the date of grant. At June 30, 2001, options for 331 million shares were vested and 550 million shares were available for future grants under the plans.

At June 30, 2001, approximately 898 million outstanding options were exercisable. The financial statements also reported 5,482 million shares of common stock used in calculating diluted earnings per share and the shares used in the basic EPS calculations were 5,025 million.

Required:
1. How might the employee stock options described in the disclosure note affect earnings per share?
2. If we assume (a) dilutive potential common shares consist entirely of stock options, and (b) the actual number of common shares and number of options did not change during the year, how could we reconcile the shares used in basic and diluted EPS calculations and the number of options outstanding?

Research Case 20–8
Determining and
comparing price-
earnings ratios;
retrieving stock prices
and earnings per share
numbers from the
Internet

Many sites on the Internet allow the retrieval of current stock price information. Among those sites are Marketwatch (cbs.marketwatch.com) and Quicken (www.quicken.com). EDGAR, the Electronic Data Gathering, Analysis, and Retrieval system, (www.sec.gov) performs automated collection, validation, indexing, acceptance, and forwarding of submissions by companies and others who are required by law to file forms with the U.S. Securities and Exchange Commission (SEC). Form 10-K which include the annual report, is required to be filed on EDGAR. The SEC makes this information available on the Internet.

Required:
1. Access any site on the Internet that permits you to get a current stock quote. Determine the current price of Microsoft Corporation's common stock (MSFT) and that of Intel Corporation (INTC).
2. Access EDGAR on the Internet using EdgarScan at: **edgarscan.pwcglobal.com**. Search for Microsoft and access its most recent 10-K or 10-Q filing. Search or scroll to find the income statement and related note(s). Determine the most recent earnings per share. Repeat this step for Intel.
3. Calculate the price-earnings ratio for each company.
4. Compare the PE ratios of Microsoft and Intel. What information might be gleaned from your comparison?

Analysis Case 20–9
Kellogg's EPS; PE ratio;
news article

While eating his Kellogg's Frosted Flakes one October morning, Fred Sparring noticed the following article in his local paper:

KELLOGG'S EPS AND CASH FLOW EXCEED EXPECTATIONS
BATTLE CREEK, Mich., Oct. 30 /PRNewswire/—Kellogg Company today reported that net earnings for the third quarter of 2001 were $150.3 million compared to last year's $181.9 million and earnings per share were $.37 compared to last year's $.45. For the first nine months of 2001, Kellogg had net sales of $6.64 billion compared to $5.40 billion in 2000, net earnings of $349 million compared to $494.5 million in 2000, and earnings per share of $.86 compared to $1.22 in 2000.

Excluding restructuring charges, integration impact, the cumulative effect of an accounting change, and extraordinary items, net earnings for the nine months were $414.5 million compared to $509.2 million in 2000 and earnings per share were $1.02 compared to $1.26 in 2000.

Kellogg declared a regular quarterly dividend of $.2525 per share on the common stock of the company, payable September 14, 2001, to share owners of record at the close of business on August 31, 2001.

PRNewswire

A quick click on a price quote service indicated that Kellogg's shares closed at $30.40 on October 30. That web page also reported Kellogg's previous year's EPS as $1.45. Fred noted that this would mean fourth quarter EPS last year must have been $1.45 − $1.22 = $.23.

Required:
1. What does the article mean when it refers to earnings per share "excluding restructuring charges, integration impact, the cumulative effect of an accounting change, and extraordinary items"? Is that the way EPS is calculated?
2. Using the numbers provided, determine the price/earnings ratio for Kellogg Company for the 12 months ending October 31, 2001. What information does this ratio impart?
3. What was the dividend payout ratio for Kellogg? What does it indicate?

Analysis Case 20–10
EPS concepts

The shareholders' equity of Proactive Solutions, Inc. included the following at December 31, 2003:

> Common stock, $ 1 par
> Paid-in capital—excess of par on common stock
> 7% cumulative convertible preferred stock, $100 par value
> Paid-in capital—excess of par on preferred stock
> Retained earnings

Additional information:
• Proactive had 7 million shares of preferred stock authorized of which 2 million were outstanding. All 2 million shares outstanding were issued in 1997 for $112 a share. The preferred stock is convertible into common stock on a two-for-one basis until December 31, 2005, after which the preferred stock no longer is convertible. None of the preferred stock has been converted into common stock at December 31, 2003. There were no dividends in arrears.

- Of the 13 million common shares authorized, there were 8 million shares outstanding at January 1, 2003. Proactive also sold 3 million shares at the beginning of September 2003 at a price of $52 a share.
- The company has an employee stock option plan where certain key employees and officers may purchase shares of common stock at the market price at the date of the option grant. All options are exercisable beginning one year after the date of the grant and expire if not exercised within five years of the grant date. On January 1, 2003, options for 2 million shares were outstanding at prices ranging from $45 to $53 a share. Options for 1 million shares were exercised at $49 a share at the end of June 2003. No options expired during 2003. Additional options for 1.5 million shares were granted at $55 a share during the year. The 2.5 million options outstanding at December 31, 2003, were exercisable at $45 to $55 a share.

The only changes in the shareholders' equity for 2003 were those described above, 2003 net income, and cash dividends paid.

Required:

Explain how each of the following amounts should be determined when computing earnings per share for presentation in the income statements. For each, be specific as to the treatment of each item.
1. Numerator for basic EPS.
2. Denominator for basic EPS.
3. Numerator for diluted EPS.
4. Denominator for diluted EPS.

Real World Case 20–11
Stock options; antidilutive securities; Cisco Systems

Cisco Systems, Inc., headquartered in San Jose, California, is the world's leading supplier of internetworking of geographically dispersed computer networks. Cisco's 2001 annual report included the following disclosure notes:

> **Computation of Net Income (Loss) per Share**
> Basic net income (loss) per share is computed using the weighted-average number of common shares outstanding during the period. Diluted net income per share is computed using the weighted-average number of common and dilutive potential common shares outstanding during the period. Diluted net loss per share is computed using the weighted-average number of common shares and excludes dilutive potential common shares outstanding, as their effect is antidilutive. Dilutive potential common shares primarily consist of employee stock options.
>
> **14. Net Income (Loss) per Share**
> The following table presents the calculation of basic and diluted net income (loss) per common share (in millions, except per-share amounts):
>
> | | July 28, 2001 | July 29, 2000 | July 31, 1999 |
> |---|---|---|---|
> | Net income (loss) | ($1,014) | $2,668 | $2,023 |
> | Weighted-average shares—basic | 7,196 | 6,917 | 6,646 |
> | Effect of dilutive securities: | | | |
> | Employee stock options | — | 521 | 416 |
> | Weighted-average shares—diluted | 7,196 | 7,438 | 7,062 |
> | Net income (loss) per share—basic | ($0.14) | 0.39 | 0.30 |
> | Net income (loss) per share—diluted | ($0.14) | 0.36 | 0.29 |
>
> The dilutive potential common shares that were antidilutive for fiscal 2001 amounted to 348 million shares.

Required:
1. The note indicates that "diluted net income per share is computed using the weighted-average number of common and dilutive potential common shares." What are dilutive potential common shares?
2. In fiscal 2000, Cisco includes 521 million dilutive potential common shares from employee stock options. Why? Without using specific numbers, describe how Cisco derived that number.
3. In fiscal 2001, Cisco does not include dilutive potential common shares from employee stock options. Why not? If Cisco had included dilutive potential common shares from employee stock options, what would have been the amount of diluted earnings per share for fiscal 2001?

21

Accounting Changes and Error Corrections

LEARNING OBJECTIVES

After studying this chapter, you should be able to:

LO1 Differentiate among the three types of accounting changes and distinguish among the retroactive, current, and prospective approaches to accounting for and reporting accounting changes.

LO2 Determine the cumulative effect of an accounting change and describe how changes in accounting principle typically are reported.

LO3 Explain how and why some changes in accounting principle are reported retroactively or prospectively.

LO4 Explain how and why changes in estimates are reported prospectively.

LO5 Describe the situations that constitute a change in reporting entity.

LO6 Understand and apply the four-step process of correcting and reporting errors, regardless of the type of error or the timing of its discovery.

OVERVIEW

Chapter 4 provided an overview of accounting changes and error correction. Later, we discussed changes encountered in connection with specific assets and liabilities as we dealt with those topics in subsequent chapters.

Here we revisit accounting changes and error correction to synthesize the way these are handled in a variety of situations that might be encountered in practice. We see that most changes in accounting principle are reported using the current approach, changes in estimates are accounted for prospectively, and both changes in reporting entities and the correction of errors are handled retroactively.

Martin's Dilemma

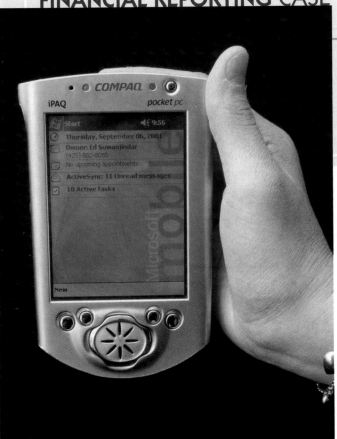

"How can an accounting change cost a company $375 million?" Martin asked as he handed you the 2001 annual report for Microsoft. He had circled a section on the comparative income statements that showed a reduction in 2001 income. The circled section was:

Cumulative Effect of Accounting Change   (375)

"I was comparing profits over the three years shown when I came across this," he continued. "When I bought Microsoft shares last month, I promised myself I would monitor things pretty closely, but it's not as easy as I thought it would be."

As an accounting graduate, you can understand Martin's confusion and proceed to answer his question.

> By the time you finish this chapter, you should be able to respond appropriately to the questions posed in this case. Compare your response to the solution provided at the end of the chapter.

QUESTIONS

1. How would you respond to Martin's question? (page 1039)
2. Are all changes in accounting method reported this way? Are there other accounting changes that are reported differently? (page 1044)

You learned early in your study of accounting that two of the qualitative characteristics of accounting information that contribute to its relevance and reliability are *consistency* and *comparability.* Though we strive to achieve and maintain these financial reporting attributes, we cannot ignore the forces of change. Ours is a dynamic business environment. The economy is increasingly a global one. Technological advances constantly transform both day-to-day operations and the flow of information about those operations. The accounting profession's response to the fluid environment often means issuing new standards that require companies to change accounting methods. Often, developments within an industry or the economy will prompt a company to voluntarily switch methods of accounting or to revise estimates or expectations. In short, change is inevitable. The question then becomes a matter of how best to address change when reporting financial information from year to year.

In the first part of this chapter, we differentiate among the various types of accounting changes that businesses face, with a focus on the most meaningful and least disruptive ways to report those changes. Then, in the second part of the chapter, we direct our attention to a closely related circumstance—the correction of errors.

PART

ACCOUNTING CHANGES

Accounting changes fall into one of three categories listed in Graphic 21–1.[1]

GRAPHIC 21–1
Types of Accounting Changes

Type of Change	Description	Examples
Change in accounting principle	Change from one generally accepted accounting principle to another.	• Change depreciation methods. • Adopt a new FASB standard. • Change methods of inventory costing. • Change from cost method to equity method, or vice versa. • Change from completed contract to percentage-of-completion, or vice versa.
Change in accounting estimate	Revision of an estimate because of new information or new experience.	• Change estimate of useful life of depreciable asset. • Change estimate of residual value of depreciable asset. • Change estimate of bad debt percentage. • Change estimate of periods benefited by intangible assets. • Change actuarial estimates pertaining to a pension plan.
Change in reporting entity	Change from reporting as one type of entity to another type of entity.	• Consolidate a subsidiary not previously included in consolidated financial statements. • Report consolidated financial statements in place of individual statements.

The correction of an error is another adjustment sometimes made to financial statements that is not actually an accounting change but is accounted for similarly. Errors occur when transactions are either recorded incorrectly or not recorded at all as shown in Graphic 21–2.

---

[1]"Accounting Changes," *Accounting Principles Board Opinion No. 20* (New York: AICPA, 1971).

Type of Change	Description	Examples
Error correction	Correction of an error caused by a transaction being recorded incorrectly or not at all.	• Mathematical mistakes. • Inaccurate physical count of inventory. • Change from the cash basis of accounting to the accrual basis. • Failure to record an adjusting entry. • Recording an asset as an expense, or vice versa. • Fraud or gross negligence.

GRAPHIC 21–2
Correction of Errors

Three approaches to reporting accounting changes and error corrections are used, depending on the situation.

LO1

1. Using the **retroactive approach,** financial statements issued in previous years are restated to reflect the impact of the change whenever those statements are presented again for comparative purposes. An advantage of this approach is that it achieves comparability among financial statements. All financial statements presented are prepared on the same basis. However, some argue that public confidence in the integrity of financial data suffers when numbers previously reported as correct are later superseded. On the other hand, proponents argue the opposite—that it's impossible to maintain public confidence unless the financial statements are comparable.

    The balance in retained earnings at the beginning of the year of the error is adjusted by the cumulative effect of the change on prior years' income, not only in the company records but also on the face of the statement of shareholders' equity (or statement of retained earnings). If the error precedes the earliest year reported in the comparative statements, the earliest year's beginning retained earnings are adjusted. Any balances other than retained earnings that would be different after the change also are adjusted as part of the same journal entry.

The retroactive approach offers consistency and comparability, perhaps at the expense of public confidence.

2. Under the **current approach,** prior years' statements are not restated. Instead, the cumulative effect of the change on prior years' income is determined and is included as a separate component of income in the year of the change. Be sure to notice that this increases or decreases retained earnings for the effect on prior years by way of the current income statement rather than by actually restating income in those prior years as in the retroactive approach.

    Certain key numbers from prior years' statements, however, are restated to reflect the impact of the change and are reported on a pro forma (as-if) basis. The amounts recast this way are income before extraordinary items, net income, and related per share amounts. The pro forma disclosure is intended to mitigate the potential confusion caused by having comparative financial statements not being prepared on the basis of the same accounting methods. Another reporting practice that helps in this regard is that the auditor's report accompanying the financial statements of the change year directs attention to the change by specifically indicating that it has occurred.

    Since prior years' financial statements are not restated under this approach, some argue that financial statement integrity is better maintained. Others argue the opposite—that the lack of consistency and comparability reduces user confidence. Certainly, reporting the entire effect in one year impacts earnings in a way contrary to the "income smoothing" objective of most managers—that is, the objective of reporting earnings that follow a smooth, regular, (and preferably upward) trend from year to year. Irregular earnings, particularly those with wide variations from year to year, tend to imply a riskier venture than earnings that follow a predictable pattern.

The cumulative effect on prior years' income is included as a separate component of income under the current approach.

Key income numbers from prior years' statements are reported on a pro forma basis.

The effects of a change are reflected in the financial statements of only the current and future years under the prospective approach.

3. The **prospective approach** requires neither a restatement of prior years' financial statements nor a current recognition of the past effect of the change. Instead, the change is merely implemented and its effects are reflected in the financial statements of the current and future years only.

Now, let's look at each type of accounting change, one at a time, focusing on the selective application of these approaches.

CHECK WITH THE **COACH**

Changes in accounting estimates and principles (methods) are a mystery to many students and users of financial statements. Because such changes often are discretionary, they create suspicion by users that management may be manipulating financial statement data and trends. Check with the Coach to gain a deeper understanding of accounting changes. You will master the accounting and disclosures required by such changes, and you will gain insights about how the marketplace reacts to them. ■

Change in Accounting Principle

LO2

Accounting is not an exact science. Professional judgment is required to apply a set of principles, concepts, and objectives to specific sets of circumstances. This means choices must be made. In your study of accounting to date, you've encountered many areas where choices are necessary. For example, management must choose whether to use accelerated or straight-line depreciation. Is FIFO, LIFO, or average cost most appropriate to measure inventories? Would the completed contract or percentage-of-completion method best reflect the performance of our construction operations? Should we adopt a new FASB standard early or wait until it's mandatory? These are but a few of the accounting choices management makes.

Although consistency and comparability are desirable, changing to a new method sometimes is appropriate.

You also probably recall that consistency and comparability are two fundamental qualitative characteristics of accounting information. To achieve these attributes of information, accounting choices, once made, should be consistently followed from year to year. This doesn't mean, though, that methods can never be changed. Changing circumstances might make a new method more appropriate. A change in economic conditions, for instance, might prompt a company to change accounting methods. The most extensive voluntary accounting change ever—a switch by hundreds of companies from FIFO to LIFO in the mid-1970s, for example—was a result of heightened inflation. Changes within a specific industry, too, can lead a company to switch methods, often to adapt to new technology or to be consistent with others in the industry. And, of course, a change might be mandated. This happens when the FASB issues a new accounting standard. In 1993, all firms were required to switch from accounting for income taxes according to *APB 11*[2] to the method prescribed by *SFAS 109*. For these reasons, it's not uncommon for a company to switch from one accounting method to another. This is called a **change in accounting principle**.

DECISION MAKERS' PERSPECTIVE—Motivation for Accounting Choices

It would be nice to think that all accounting choices are made by management in the best interest of fair and consistent financial reporting. Unfortunately, other motives influence the choices among accounting methods and whether to change methods. It has been suggested that the effect of choices on management compensation, on existing debt agreements, and on union negotiations each can affect management's selection of accounting methods.[3] For instance, research has suggested that managers of companies with bonus plans are more likely

---

[2]*SFAS 96* for those companies that voluntarily adopted that interim standard.
[3]R. L. Watts and J. L. Zimmerman, "Towards a Positive Theory of the Determination of Accounting Standards," *The Accounting Review,* January 1978, and "Positive Accounting Theory: A Ten Year Perspective," *The Accounting Review,* January 1990.

to choose accounting methods that maximize their bonuses (often those that increase net income).[4] Other research has indicated that the existence and nature of debt agreements and other aspects of a firm's capital structure can influence accounting choices.[5] Whether a company is forbidden from paying dividends if retained earnings fall below a certain level, for example, can affect the choice of accounting methods.

A financial analyst must be aware that different accounting methods used by different firms and by the same firm in different years complicate comparisons. Financial ratios, for example, will differ when different accounting methods are used, even when there are no differences in attributes being compared.

Investors and creditors also should be alert to instances in which companies change accounting methods. They must consider not only the effect on comparability but also possible hidden motivations for making the changes. Are managers trying to compensate for a downturn in actual performance with a switch to methods that artificially inflate reported earnings? Is the firm in danger of violating debt covenants or other contractual agreements regarding financial position? Are executive compensation plans tied to reported performance measures? Fortunately, the nature and effect of changes are reported in the financial statements. Although a justification for a change is provided by management, analysts should be wary of accepting the reported justification at face value without considering a possible hidden agenda.

Choices are not always those that tend to increase income. As you learned in Chapter 8, many companies use the LIFO inventory method because it reduces income and therefore reduces the amount of income taxes that must be paid currently. Also, some very large and visible companies might be reluctant to report high income that might render them vulnerable to union demands, government regulations, or higher taxes.[6]

Another reason managers sometimes choose accounting methods that don't necessarily increase earnings was mentioned earlier. Most managers tend to prefer to report earnings that follow a regular, smooth trend from year to year. The desire to "smooth" earnings means that any attempt to manipulate earnings by choosing accounting methods is not always in the direction of higher income. Instead, the choice might be to avoid irregular earnings, particularly those with wide variations from year to year, a pattern that might be interpreted by analysts as denoting a risky situation.

Obviously, any time managers make accounting choices for any of the reasons discussed here, when the motivation is an objective other than to provide useful information, earnings quality suffers. As mentioned frequently throughout this text, earnings quality refers to the ability of reported earnings (income) to predict a company's future earnings.

Let's turn our attention now to situations involving changes in methods and how we account for those changes. ■

THE CURRENT APPROACH: MOST CHANGES IN ACCOUNTING PRINCIPLE
The cumulative effect of a change in accounting principle should be reflected in the financial statements of the change year. Previous financial statements included for comparative purposes should be presented as previously reported. Recall from our earlier discussion that this is the current approach to accounting for a change.

Determining the Effect of the Change.
The cumulative effect of a change in accounting principle is the cumulative effect on the income of previous years from having used the old method rather than the new method. Stated differently, it's the difference between the

FINANCIAL REPORTING CASE
Q1, p. 1035

[4]For example, see P. M. Healy, "The Effect of Bonus Schemes on Accounting Decisions," *Journal of Accounting and Economics,* April 1985, and D. Dhaliwal, G. Salamon, and E. Smith, "The Effect of Owner versus Management Control on the Choice of Accounting Methods," *Journal of Accounting and Economics,* July 1992.
[5]R. M. Bowen., E. W. Noreen, and J. M. Lacy, "Determinants of the Corporate Decision to Capitalize Interest," *Journal of Accounting and Economics,* August 1981.
[6]This political cost motive is suggested by R. L. Watts and J. L. Zimmerman, "Positive Accounting Theory: A Ten Year Perspective," *The Accounting Review,* January 1990, and M. Zmijewski and R. Hagerman, "An Income Strategy Approach to the Positive Theory of Accounting Standard Setting/Choice," *Journal of Accounting and Economics,* August 1981.

balance in retained earnings at the beginning of the period of the change and what that balance would have been if the new method had been applied all along.

An example is provided in Illustration 21–1.

ILLUSTRATION 21–1 Change in Accounting Principle **The current approach avoids changing accounting data reported previously.**	Universal Semiconductors switched from the SYD depreciation method to straight-line depreciation in 2003. The change affects its precision equipment purchased at the beginning of 2001 at a cost of $60 million. The machinery has an expected useful life of five years and no estimated salvage value. **Cumulative Effect of the Change**

Cumulative Effect of the Change

	($ in millions)	
	SYD	**Straight Line**
2001 depreciation	$20 ($60 × 5/15)	$12 ($60 ÷ 5)
2002 depreciation	16 ($60 × 4/15)	12 ($60 ÷ 5)
Accumulated depreciation and 2001–2002 reduction in income	$36	$24

Difference
$12

1. Reporting the Cumulative Income Effect.

The cumulative income effect is reported on the income statement as a separate item of income, between extraordinary items and net income. It should be reported net of the tax effect of the change. In other words, it should be increased or decreased by the difference between income tax expense as reported in previous years and what it would have been if the new accounting method had been used in those years.[7]

If Universal's tax rate is 40%, the cumulative tax effect of the depreciation change would be $4.8 million ($12 million × 40%). This is because, the straight-line reduction of income for depreciation would be $12 million less, causing tax expense to be higher by that amount times the tax rate.[8] The higher tax expense partially offsets the lower depreciation expense when determining the net, after-tax, cumulative effect of the change. Reporting of the cumulative effect is shown here:

The cumulative after-tax effect on prior years' income is a separate item of income between extraordinary items and net income.

Reported As a Separate Component of Income:
($ in millions)

	2003	**2002**
Income before extraordinary items and accounting change	$xxx	$xxx
Extraordinary gain (loss), net of tax	xx	xx
Cumulative effect of accounting change (net of $4.8 tax)	7.2	
Net income	$xxx	$xxx

Tenneco Automotive, Inc. reported a change in accounting principle in its 2000 annual report. Notice in Graphic 21–3 that (a) the cumulative effect on prior years is reported in both in the determination of net income and in the EPS presentation, and (b) the cumulative effect is shown after both discontinued operations and extraordinary items.

---

[7]You should notice that reporting this income net of its tax effect is consistent with the way we report other special items on the income statement net of tax. Remember, extraordinary gains and losses are reported separately on the income statement, net of their tax impact, as are discontinued operations.

[8]It actually is the deferred portion of the tax expense that increases, rather than the current portion. Because the change is not made for tax purposes, neither taxable income nor the currently payable tax would change. The increase in accounting income, though, would have increased the temporary difference between accounting income and taxable income. Thus, the deferred tax liability (and therefore the deferred portion of income tax expense) would have been higher.

Statements of Income (partial)
($ in millions, except per share amounts)

	2000	1999	1998
Income (Loss) from continuing operations	($41)	($63)	$116
Income (loss) from discontinued operations, net of income tax	—	(208)	139
Income (loss) before extraordinary loss	(41)	(271)	255
Extraordinary loss, net of income tax	(1)	(18)	—
Income (loss) before cumulative effect of changes in accounting principles	(42)	(289)	255
Cumulative effect of changes in accounting principles, net of income tax.	—	(134)	—
Net income (loss)	($42)	($423)	$255

Earnings (Loss) per share:

Basic earnings (loss) per share of common stock

	2000	1999	1998
Continuing operations	($1.18)	($1.87)	$3.45
Discontinued operations	—	(6.23)	4.13
Extraordinary loss	(0.02)	(0.55)	—
Cumulative effect of changes in accounting principles	—	(3.99)	—
	($1.20)	($12.64)	$7.58

Diluted earnings (loss) per share of common stock

	2000	1999	1998
Continuing operations	($1.18)	($1.87)	$3.44
Discontinued operations	—	(6.23)	4.12
Extraordinary loss	(0.02)	(0.55)	—
Cumulative effect of changes in accounting principles	—	(3.99)	—
	($1.20)	($12.64)	$7.56

Note: Changes in Accounting Principles
Prior to January 1, 1999, we capitalized certain costs related to start-up activities, primarily pre-production design and development costs for new automobile original equipment platforms. We adopted SOP 98-5 on January 1, 1999, and recorded an after-tax charge for the cumulative effect of this change in accounting principle of $102 million (net of a $50 million tax benefit), or $3.04 per diluted common share.

   Effective January 1, 1999, we changed our method of accounting for customer acquisition costs from a deferral method to an expense-as-incurred method. We recorded an after-tax charge for the cumulative effect of this change in accounting principle of $32 million (net of a $22 million tax benefit), or $.95 per diluted common share.

2. Account Adjustment for the Change.   Besides income, other financial statement amounts usually would have been different if a new method had been applied in previous years. In our illustration, accumulated depreciation would have been less if straight-line rather than SYD depreciation had been used. The balance in this account should be adjusted to reflect the new method:

	($ in millions)	
Accumulated depreciation (cumulative effect determined in Illustration 21–1)	12.0	
Deferred tax liability ($12 × 40%)		4.8
Cumulative effect of accounting change (net effect)		7.2

Accumulated depreciation would have been $12 million *less* and net income $7.2 million *more* if straight-line rather than SYD depreciation had been used.

The reason for the credit to deferred tax liability requires some explanation. Remember from Chapter 16 that when taxable income is less than pretax accounting income because of a temporary difference, a deferred tax liability is recorded. This liability reflects the tax that eventually will be paid when the difference later reverses and taxable income is higher than pretax accounting income. In our illustration, tax depreciation would have been more than SYD depreciation during the two previous years, but the temporary difference would have been greater still if accounting income had been based on straight-line depreciation.[9] So, we need to increase the deferred tax liability from what it is now to what it would have been if straight-line depreciation had been used the two previous years. It's not necessary to know what the old or new balance is, only that the new balance should be $4.8 million higher.

ADDITIONAL CONSIDERATION

If the switch had been from straight-line to SYD depreciation, rather than from SYD to straight-line, the effects would have been reversed and the journal entry to record the effects would be:

	($ in millions)	
Cumulative effect of accounting change (net effect)............	7.2	
Deferred tax liability ($12 × 40%)	4.8	
Accumulated depreciation (cumulative effect determined above)....................................		12.0

3. Pro Forma Disclosure of Key Income Items. Remember, prior years' financial statements are *not* restated under the current approach. However, the effect of the change on certain key income numbers should be disclosed for the current period and on a "pro forma" (as-if) basis for the financial statements of all prior periods that are included for comparison with the current financial statements. Specifically, income statements should include pro forma restatement of (a) income before extraordinary items, (b) net income, and (c) earnings per share. In other words, these specific items, calculated as if the new method had been in effect in those prior years, are reported as supplemental information. For instance, after changing its method of recognizing revenue, Novell, Inc. reported in its third quarter 2001 quarterly report (Graphic 21–4) that both its net income and net income per share would have been over twice as high in fiscal 2000 if the new method had been used in prior years.

> The effect of the change on certain key income numbers is reported for the current period and on a pro forma (as-if) basis for all prior periods included.

GRAPHIC 21–4
Pro forma disclosure of effect of accounting change—Novell, Inc.

Statements of Income (partial)	**Three Months Ended July 31**	
($ in 000s, except per share amounts)	**2001**	**2000**
Net income (loss)	($19,274)	$8,572
Net income (loss) per share:		
Basic	($0.06)	$0.03
Diluted	($0.06)	$0.03
Pro forma amounts assuming the accounting change is applied retroactively		
Net income (loss)	—	$20,020
Net income (loss) per share	—	$0.06

L. Change in Accounting Principle—Revenue Recognition (in part)

The pro forma amounts presented in the unaudited consolidated statements of income were calculated assuming the accounting change was made retroactively to prior periods.

---

[9]Presently, the accelerated depreciation method prescribed by the tax code is the Modified Accelerated Cost Recovery system (MACRS). The method is described in Chapter 11. For our purposes now, recall that this method produces tax deductions higher in the first years of an asset's useful life than does straight-line (and usually SYD) depreciation. The opposite is true in the later years of the asset's useful life.

If Novell had reported an extraordinary gain or loss in its income statements, it would have reported pro forma amounts for income before extraordinary items as well.

4. Disclosure Note.   A description of the change, justification for the change, and the effect of the change on the current period's income should be provided in the disclosure notes to the financial statements. Disclosure of a recent change by Safeco Corporation provides us the example shown in Graphic 21–5.

GRAPHIC 21–5
Disclosure of an Accounting Change—Safeco Corporation

Accounting Changes
Effective March 31, 2001, SAFECO elected to change its accounting policy for assessing goodwill from one based on undiscounted cash flows to one based on a market-value method. The company believes that the market-value method is a preferable way to assess the current value of goodwill. As a result, SAFECO recorded a one-time write-off of $916.9 million after tax, or $7.17 per share.

Frequently, when a company changes depreciation methods, the change will be effective only for assets placed in service after that date. Of course, that means there would be no cumulative effect on prior years' earnings because the change doesn't affect assets depreciated in prior periods (see Graphic 21–6).

GRAPHIC 21–6
Change in Depreciation Method for Newly Acquired Assets—Rohm and Haas Company

Note 12: Land, Buildings, and Equipment, Net (in part)
The company changed its method of depreciation for newly acquired buildings and equipment to the straight-line method. The change had no cumulative effect on prior years' earnings but did increase (current year) net earnings by $9 million, or $.14 per share . . .

ADDITIONAL CONSIDERATION

Companies subject to the reporting requirements of the Securities and Exchange Commission (most public companies) must prepare quarterly financial statements in addition to their annual reports. For interim reporting, the cumulative effect of an accounting change should be reported in the *first* quarter of the fiscal year in which the change is made, even if the change actually is made in a later quarter. The reported amount is the cumulative effect on the income of previous years from using the previous method rather than the new method as of the beginning of that fiscal year. If the change occurs in an interim period other than the first, financial statement information for prechange interim periods is restated to reflect the new accounting method when those prior statements are presented again.*

*"Reporting Accounting Changes in Interim Financial Statements," *Statement of Financial Accounting Standards No. 3* (Stamford, Conn.: FASB, 1974).

THE RETROACTIVE APPROACH: CERTAIN SPECIFIED CHANGES IN ACCOUNTING PRINCIPLE

LO3

Because of their unique nature, some changes in accounting principle are more appropriately accounted for by the retroactive approach rather than the current approach. For these exceptions to the general manner of treating changes in the accounting principle, prior years' financial statements are restated to reflect the use of the new accounting method. Restatement is required for the changes indicated in Graphic 21–7 on the next page.

These exceptions receive special treatment—restating prior years for the income effect of the change, rather than reporting that effect as part of income in the year the change occurs. The predominant reason is that the effect of these changes is usually quite large. Not only would net income be distorted in the year of the change if the total effect is recognized currently, but prior statements would be rendered meaningless if not restated.

Beginning retained earnings of the earliest year reported is adjusted for any portion of the cumulative income effect attributable to years prior to those reported.

GRAPHIC 21–7
Changes in Accounting
Principle Requiring
Retroactive
Restatement

FINANCIAL REPORTING CASE

Q2, p. 1035

Prior years' statements are restated under the retroactive approach.

1. A retroactive change required by a specific accounting standard
   a. Some FASB statements require retroactive application for the initial transition to the new standards. (Prior years were restated to reflect the loss contingency provisions of *SFAS 11*. The FASB requires restatement of all prior period earnings per share data upon the adoption of the EPS provisions described in the previous chapter. *SFAS 109* states a preference for the restatement of prior years to reflect the liability method of accounting of income taxes but also permits reporting the cumulative effect instead.*)
   b. Some FASB statements and other authoritative pronouncements require retroactive application for specific changes in accounting methods. (For a change from the cost method to the equity method of accounting for long-term investments, *APB 18* requires the retroactive application of the equity method.)
2. A change from the LIFO method to another inventory valuation method.
3. A change from the percentage of completion to the completed contract method (or vice versa) in accounting for long-term construction contracts.
4. A change to or from the full cost method in the oil and gas and other extractive industries.†
5. Changes made when a closely held corporation first issues financial statements to obtain equity financing, for registering securities, or for effecting a business combination.

*"Accounting for Contingencies—Transition Method," *Statement of Financial Accounting Standards No. 11* (Stamford, Conn.: FASB, 1975); "Earnings per Share," *Statement of Financial Accounting Standards No. 128* (Norwalk, Conn.: FASB, 1997); "Accounting for Income Taxes," *Statement of Financial Accounting Standards No. 109* (Norwalk, Conn.: FASB, 1992). Pro forma amounts are not required when a company chooses to report the cumulative effect due to complexity and cost of doing so—the same reason restatement is not mandatory.
†Extensive discussion of accounting by extractive industries is beyond the scope of this text.

Financial statements are restated for each year reported for comparative purposes, and the income effect for years prior to those reported is accounted for as an adjustment to beginning retained earnings of the earliest year reported.

A Change from the LIFO Method. The change from the LIFO method to FIFO in Illustration 21–2 provides us an example of a change requiring retroactive restatement.

ILLUSTRATION 21–2

Changes in Principle Requiring Retroactive Restatement

Account balances are adjusted to what they would have been if the new method had been used in previous years.

Traci Wright Fashions had used the LIFO method of costing inventories but at the beginning of 2003 decided to change to the FIFO method. The inventory as reported at the end of 2002 using LIFO would have been $20 million higher using FIFO.

Retained earnings had been reported at the end of 2001 and 2002 as $240 million and $260 million, respectively (reflecting the LIFO method). Those amounts reflecting the FIFO method would have been $250 million and $272 million, respectively. 2002 net income had been reported at the end of 2002 as $28 million (LIFO method) but would have been $30 million using FIFO. After changing to FIFO, 2003 net income was $36 million. Dividends of $8 million were paid each year. The tax rate is 40%.

The journal entry to record the change in principle at the beginning of 2003 would be:

	($ in millions)	
Inventory (additional inventory if FIFO had been used)	20	
Retained earnings (additional net income if FIFO had been used). .		12
Deferred tax liability (40% × $20 million)		8

Retained earnings is increased by $12 million because the net income in years prior to 2003 would have been higher by that amount, and net income increases retained earnings. Changing inventory methods for financial reporting requires the same change for tax purposes. The Internal Revenue Code requires that taxes saved previously from having used another inventory method ($8 million in this case) must now be repaid (over no longer than six years). In the meantime, there is temporary book-tax difference for the inventory account, reflected in the deferred tax liability.

Net income, which was reported in 2002 as $28 million would be restated to $30 million in the 2003–2002 comparative income statements. The comparative income statements and balance sheets also would be restated to reflect the following items as if the FIFO method had been used in 2002:

> Earnings per share
> Inventory (and total assets)
> Retained earnings (and total shareholders' equity)

Prior years' financial statements are restated to reflect the use of the new accounting method.

Because the switch to FIFO occurred at the beginning of 2003, after the journal entry above, the year 2003 numbers already reflect the new method.

The change would be reflected in the 2003–2002 comparative statements of shareholders' equity by adjusting the beginning balance of retained earnings for any portion of the cumulative income effect *attributable to years prior to 2002*. The adjusted balance is then followed by any increases or decreases to retained earnings during the year (net income, dividends, etc.).

TRACI WRIGHT FASHIONS
Statement of Shareholders' Equity
For the Years Ended December 31, 2003 and 2002

($ in millions)

	Common Stock	Additional Paid-In Capital	Retained Earnings	Total Shareholders' Equity
Balance at Jan. 1, 2002			240	
Adjustment due to change from the LIFO to the FIFO method of accounting for inventories			10*	
Balance at Jan. 1 as adjusted			250	
Net income (restated to FIFO)			30†	
Cash dividends			(8)	
Balance at Dec. 31, 2002			272	
Net income (using FIFO)			36	
Cash dividends			(8)	
Balance at Dec. 31, 2003			300	

*Difference in net income *before* 2002: $250 million − 240 million
†(given)

Because it's the earlier year reported, 2002's beginning retained earnings is adjusted for the portion of the cumulative income effect attributable to years prior to those reported.

Similarly, if three-year comparative statements were provided, it would be the balance in retained earnings at the beginning of 2001 that would be adjusted for any portion of the cumulative income effect attributable to years prior to 2001. Retained earnings is adjusted for the earliest year reported in the comparative statements.

A disclosure note from an annual report of SPS Technologies, Inc. is shown in Graphic 21–8 on the next page that illustrates the footnote description of a change from the LIFO method to another inventory valuation method.

THE PROSPECTIVE APPROACH: CERTAIN SPECIFIED CHANGES IN ACCOUNTING PRINCIPLE

A Change to the LIFO Method.   When a company changes to the LIFO inventory method from another inventory method, accounting records of prior years usually are inadequate to determine the cumulative income effect of the change or to determine pro forma disclosures for prior years. It would be necessary, for instance, to make assumptions as to when specific LIFO inventory layers were created in years prior to the change. Because of the impracticality of doing so, a company changing to LIFO does not report the cumulative

It usually is impractical for a company changing to LIFO to report the cumulative income effect.

GRAPHIC 21–8
Change in Accounting
Principle: Retroactive
Approach—SPS
Technologies, Inc.

**A change from the
LIFO method to
another method of
costing inventory is a
change in principle
requiring retroactive
restatement.**

Note 2: Change in Accounting Principle
. . . the Company changed its basis of valuing inventories in the United States from the
last-in, first-out (LIFO) method to the average cost method. In 1989 and prior years, the cost
of substantially all inventories in the United States, except tools, was determined using the
LIFO method. The change to the average cost method will conform all inventories of the
Company to the same method of valuation. The Company believes that the average cost
method of inventory valuation provides a more meaningful presentation of the financial position of the Company since it reflects more recent costs in the balance sheet. Under the
current economic environment of low inflation and an expected reduction in inventories and
lower production costs, the Company believes that the average cost method also results in
a better matching of current costs with current revenues.
   The effect of the change in accounting principle was to reduce the net loss reported . . .
by $318,000, or $.06 per share. The change has been applied to prior years by retroactively
restating the financial statements as required by generally accepted accounting principles.

income effect in current income nor revise the balance in retained earnings. Instead, the base
year inventory for all future LIFO calculations is the beginning inventory in the year the
LIFO method is adopted. The only disclosure required is a footnote to the financial statements describing the nature of and justification for the change, the effect of the change on
current period earnings, and an explanation as to why the cumulative income effect was
omitted. When the Penn Central Corporation adopted the LIFO cost flow assumption for
valuing its communications wire and cable inventories, the change was reported as follows:

GRAPHIC 21–9
Disclosure of a Change
to LIFO—The Penn
Central Corporation

Note 6: Inventories (in part)
. . . the Company changed its method of valuing a significant component of its communications wire and cable inventories from the FIFO to the LIFO method. Management believes
the LIFO method results in a better matching of current costs with current revenues.
   The effect of the change . . . was to decrease net income by $16 million, or $.03 per share.
The cumulative effect of this accounting change and the pro forma effects on prior years'
earnings have not been included because such effects are not reasonably determinable.

   A related situation occurred when Kmart changed price indexes used in determining
LIFO inventories:

GRAPHIC 21–10
Disclosure of a Change
in Method of
Determining
Inventories—Kmart
Corporation

Note F: Merchandise Inventories (in part)
. . . the company changed its method of accounting for LIFO inventories in U.S. Kmart
stores. Prior to 1990, the company used the U.S. Department of Labor's Department Store
Price Index to measure inflation in retail prices. . . . the company developed and used
internal price indices to measure inflation in the retail prices of its merchandise inventories.
The company believes the use of internal indices results in a more accurate measurement
of the impact of inflation in the prices of merchandise sold in its stores. This change reduced
the LIFO charge in 1990 by $105 million net of tax, or $52 per share. The company was not
able to determine the cumulative effect of this change nor the impact on any individual year
prior to [the change].

**Some new accounting
standards require or
permit prospective
application of the new
standard.**

Mandated by New Accounting Standards.   A few changes mandated by new accounting standards require or permit prospective application of the new standard. An example is, *SFAS 106*,[10] "Employers' Accounting for Postretirement Benefits Other than
Pensions," in which the transition amount due to changing from the old standard may be

---

[10]"Employers' Accounting for Postretirement Benefits Other than Pensions," *Statement of Financial Accounting Standards No.
106* (Stamford, Conn.: FASB, 1990).

amortized to expense on a prospective basis over the average remaining service life of those employed on the transition date.[11]

Regardless of whether a change is accounted for currently, retroactively, or prospectively, the most important responsibility is to communicate to users of the financial statements that a change has occurred as well as the nature and effect of the change.

Change in Accounting Estimate

LO4

You've encountered many instances during your study of accounting in which it's necessary to make estimates of uncertain future events. Depreciation, for example, entails estimates not only of the useful lives of depreciable assets, but their anticipated salvage values as well. Anticipating uncollectible accounts receivable, predicting warranty expenses, amortizing intangible assets, and making actuarial assumptions for pension benefits are but a few of the accounting tasks that require estimates.

Accordingly, estimates are an inherent aspect of accounting. Unfortunately, though, estimates routinely turn out to be wrong. No matter how carefully known facts are considered and forecasts are prepared, new information and experience frequently force the revision of estimates.[12] Of course, if the original estimate was based on erroneous information or calculations or was not made in good faith, the revision of that estimate constitutes the correction of an error.

Revisions are viewed as a natural consequence of making estimates.

Changes in estimates are accounted for prospectively. When a company revises a previous estimate, prior financial statements are *not* restated, nor is a cumulative effect of the change included in current income. Instead, the company merely incorporates the new estimate in any related accounting determinations from then on. So, it usually will affect some aspects of both the balance sheet and the income statement in the current period and future periods. A disclosure note should describe the effect of a change in estimate on income before extraordinary items, net income, and related per share amounts for the current period.

A change in estimate is reflected in the financial statements of the current period and future periods.

When Owens-Corning Fiberglass revised estimates of the useful lives of some of its depreciable assets, the change was disclosed in its annual report as shown in Graphic 21–11.

GRAPHIC 21–11
Change in Estimate—
Owens-Corning
Fiberglass Corporation

Note 6: Depreciation of Plant and Equipment (in part)
. . . the Company completed a review of its fixed asset lives. The Company determined that as a result of actions taken to increase its preventative maintenance and programs initiated with its equipment suppliers to increase the quality of their products, actual lives for certain asset categories were generally longer than the useful lives for depreciation purposes. Therefore, the Company extended the estimated useful lives of certain categories of plant and equipment, effective . . . The effect of this change in estimate reduced depreciation expense for the year ended . . . , by $14 million and increased income before cumulative effect of accounting change by $8 million ($.19 per share).

---

[11]The transition amount is discussed in Chapter 18.
[12]The most common estimate change is a revision of estimates regarding depreciable lives. AICPA, *Accounting Trends and Techniques,* 2000.

An example of another change in estimate is provided in Illustration 21–3.

ILLUSTRATION 21–3 Change in Accounting Estimate	Universal Semiconductors estimates bad debt expense as 2% of credit sales. After a review during 2002, Universal determined that 3% of credit sales is a more realistic estimate of its collection experience. Credit sales in 2002 are $300 million. The effective income tax rate is 40%.

Neither bad debt expense nor the allowance for uncollectible accounts reported in prior years is restated. No account balances are adjusted. The cumulative effect of the estimate change is not reported in current income. Rather, in 2002 and later years, the adjusting entry to record bad debt expense simply will reflect the new percentage. In 2002, the entry would be:

	($ in millions)	
Bad debt expense (3% × $300 million)	9	
Allowance for uncollectible accounts		9

The after-tax effect of the change in estimate is $1.8 million [$300 million × (3% − 2%) = $3 million, less 40% of $3 million]. Assuming 100 million outstanding shares of common stock, the effect is described in a disclosure note to the financial statements as follows:

Note A: Accounts Receivable
In 2002, the company revised the percentage used to estimate bad debts. The change provides a better indication of collection experience. The effect of the change was to decrease 2002 net income by $1.8 million, or $.018 per share.

When it's not possible to distinguish between a change in principle and a change in estimate, the change should be treated as a change in estimate.

Sometimes, it's not easy to distinguish between a change in principle and a change in estimate. For example, if a company begins to capitalize rather than expense the cost of tools because their benefits beyond one year become apparent, the change could be construed as either a change in principle or a change in the estimated life of the asset. When the distinction is not possible, the change should be treated as a change in estimate. This treatment also is appropriate when both a change in principle and a change in estimate occur simultaneously.

ETHICAL DILEMMA

The net income of Union Carbide increased in 1980 by over $200 million, due almost entirely to three changes in accounting principle: (a) the depreciation method was changed, resulting in lower expense, (b) interest costs during construction were capitalized rather than expensed, and (c) the method for recognizing investment tax credits (not available under current tax law) was changed to a method that reduced tax expense.

What ethical question does this situation suggest?

Change in Reporting Entity

LO5

The issuance of SFAS 94 resulted in many companies consolidating previously unconsolidated subsidiaries.

A reporting entity can be a single company, or it can be a group of companies that reports a single set of financial statements. For example, the consolidated financial statements of Philip Morris Cos., Inc. report the financial position and results of operations not only for the parent tobacco company but also for its subsidiaries which include Kraft Foods and Miller Brewing Company. Sometimes, changes occur that cause the financial statements to be those of a different reporting entity. The issuance of SFAS 94, "Consolidation of All Majority-Owned Subsidiaries," resulted in hundreds of reporting entities being altered to include previously unconsolidated finance subsidiaries. For instance, General Motors' consolidated financial statements now include its finance subsidiary, GMAC, as part of the reporting entity. A

change in reporting entity occurs as a result of (1) presenting consolidated financial statements in place of statements of individual companies or (2) changing specific companies that constitute the group for which consolidated or combined statements are prepared.[13]

A change in reporting entity is reported by restating all previous periods' financial statements as if the new reporting entity existed in those periods.[14] In the first set of financial statements after the change, a disclosure note should describe the nature of the change and the reason it occurred. Also, the effect of the change on net income, income before extraordinary items, and related per share amounts should be indicated for all periods presented. These disclosures aren't necessary in subsequent financial statements. Hewlett-Packard Company changed the composition of its reporting entity in response to *SFAS 94* and described it this way:

> A change in reporting entity requires that financial statements of prior periods be retroactively restated to report the financial information for the new reporting entity in all periods.

Note 12: Accounting and Reporting Changes (in part)
The Company implemented *Statement of Financial Accounting Standards No. 94 (SFAS 94)*, "Consolidation of All Majority-Owned Subsidiaries," in fiscal 1989. With the adoption of *SFAS 94*, the company consolidated the accounts of Hewlett-Packard Finance Company (HPFC), a wholly-owned subsidiary previously accounted for under the equity method, with those of the company. The change resulted in an increase in consolidated assets and liabilities but did not have a material effect on the company's financial position. Since HPFC was previously accounted for under the equity method, the change did not affect net earnings. Prior years' consolidated financial information has been restated to reflect this change for comparative purposes.

GRAPHIC 21–12
Change in Reporting Entity—Hewlett-Packard Company

Error Correction

The correction of an error is not actually an accounting change but is accounted for similarly. In fact, it's accounted for retroactively like a change in reporting entity and like some changes in accounting principle.

More specifically, previous years' financial statements that were incorrect as a result of the error are retroactively restated to reflect the correction. And, of course, any account balances that are incorrect as a result of the error are corrected by a journal entry. If retained earnings is one of the incorrect accounts, the correction is reported as a prior period adjustment to the beginning balance in a statement of shareholders' equity (or statement of retained earnings if that's presented instead).[15] And, as for accounting changes, a disclosure note is needed to describe the nature of the error and the impact of its correction on operations. We discuss the correction of errors in more detail in Part B of this chapter. But first, let's compare the three approaches for reporting accounting changes and error corrections (Graphic 21–13).

> Previous years' financial statements are retroactively restated to reflect the correction of an error.

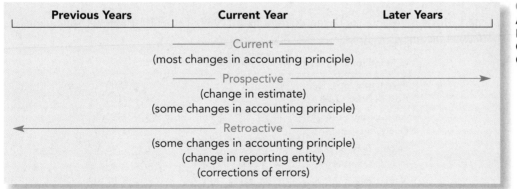

GRAPHIC 21–13
Approaches to Reporting Accounting Changes and Error Corrections

---

[13]"Consolidation of All Majority-Owned Subsidiaries," *Statement of Financial Accounting Standards No. 94*, (Stamford, Conn.: FASB, 1987).

[14]When those statements are presented again for comparative purposes.

[15]"Prior Period Adjustments," *Statement of Financial Accounting Standards No. 16* (Stamford, CT: FASB, 1977).

A comparison of accounting treatments is provided by Graphic 21–14.

GRAPHIC 21–14 Accounting Changes and Errors: A Summary

| Method of accounting | Change in Accounting Principle | | | Change in Estimate | Change in Reporting Entity | Error |
	Most Changes	Retroactive Exceptions*	Prospective Exceptions†			
	Current	Retroactive	Prospective	Prospective	Retroactive	Retroactive
• Restate prior years' statements?	No	Yes	No	No	Yes	Yes
• Pro forma disclosures of income and EPS ?	Yes	No	No	No	No	No
• Cumulative effect on prior years' income reported:	On income statement between E.O. items and net income.	As adjustment to retained earnings of earliest year reported.‡	Not reported.§	Not reported.	Not reported.	As adjustment to retained earnings of earliest year reported.‡
• Journal entry cumulative income effect and adjust affected balances to new method.	To record retained earnings and any other affected balances to the new method.	To adjust subsequent accounting is affected by the change.	None, but subsequent accounting is affected by the new estimate.	None, but consolidated financial statements discussed in other courses.	Involves any balances that are incorrect as a result of the error.	To correct
• Disclosure note?	Yes	Yes	Yes	Yes	Yes	Yes

*See Graphic 21–7 (page 1044).
†Change to LIFO and certain mandated changes.
‡On the statement of shareholders' equity or statement of retained earnings.
§Transition amount disclosed for some new standards.

CONCEPT REVIEW EXERCISE

CRE

Accounting Changes

Modern Business Machines began operations in 1997. The 2002 financial statements reported net income as follows:

($ in millions, except per share amount)	
Revenues	$500
Cost of goods sold	(180)
Gross profit	320
Operating expenses	(175)
Income before taxes	145
Income tax expense	(58)
Net income	$ 87
Earnings per common share: (100 million shares)	$0.87

In 2003, revenues were $590 million, operating expenses were $190 million, and the company realized a $10 million (before tax) extraordinary gain. The tax rate is 40% for all years. The following accounting changes affecting the company occurred during 2003:

1. MBM has a patent on a copier design. The patent has been amortized on a straight-line basis since it was acquired at a cost of $340,000 in 2000. During 2003, it was decided that the benefits from the patent would be experienced over a total of 10 years rather than the 17-year legal life now being used to amortize its cost.
2. At the beginning of 2003, MBM changed its method of valuing inventory from the FIFO cost method to the average cost method. The change is made for both financial reporting and income tax purposes. At December 31, 2002, MBM's inventories were $205 million on a FIFO cost basis. Inventories would have totaled $170 million at December 31, 2003, if determined on an average cost basis. The difference was reflected in cost of goods sold as follows:

Cost of Goods Sold
($ in millions)

	FIFO	Average Cost	Difference
1997–2001	$600	$625	$25
2002	180	190	10
2003	230	240	10
			$45

Required:
Prepare all journal entries needed in 2003 related to each change. Also, briefly describe any other measures MBM would take in connection with reporting the changes. Prepare comparative income statements for 2003 and 2002.

1. Change in estimate

	($ in 000s)	
Patent amortization expense (determined below)........	40	
Patent		40

Calculation of Annual Amortization after the Estimate Change

	$340,000	Cost
$20,000		Old annual amortization ($340,000 ÷ 17 years)
× 3 years	(60,000)	Amortization to date (2000, 2001, 2002)
	280,000	Unamortized cost
	÷ 7	Estimated remaining life (10 years − 3 years)
	$ 40,000	New annual amortization

A disclosure note should describe the effect of a change in estimate on income before extraordinary items, net income, and related per-share amounts for the current period.

2. Change in principle

	($ in millions)	
Cumulative effect of accounting change (net effect)..	21	
Income tax payable ($35 million × 40%)	14	
Inventory ($205 million − 170 million).............		35

The cumulative income effect is reported on the income statement as a separate item of income between extraordinary items and net income. It should be reported net of the $14 million tax effect of the change.

Income statements should include pro forma restatement of (a) income before extraordinary items, (b) net income, and (c) earnings per share for both income amounts. In other words, these specific items, calculated as if the new method had been in effect in those prior years, are reported as supplemental information. Also, the nature of and justification for the change should be described in the disclosure notes to the financial statements.

Comparative Income Statements

($ in millions, except per share amounts)	2003	2002
Revenues	$ 590	$ 500
Cost of goods sold	(240)	(180)
Gross profit	350	320
Operating expenses	(190)	(175)
Income before taxes	160	145
Income tax expense	(64)	(58)
Income before extraordinary item and accounting change	96	87
Extraordinary gain (net of $4 tax)	6	
Cumulative effect of accounting change (net of $14 tax benefit)	(21)	
Net Income	$ 81	$ 87
Earnings per Share		
Before extraordinary item and accounting change	$ .96	$ .87
Extraordinary gain	.06	
Cumulative effect of accounting change	(.21)	
Earnings per share	$ .81	$ .87
Pro Forma Amounts Assuming the Change Is Applied Retroactively		
Income before extraordinary items	$ 96	$ 81*
Per common share	$0.96	$0.81
Net income	$102[†]	$ 81[†]
Earnings per common share	$1.02	$0.81

*$87 million − ([$190 million − 180 million] less tax)
$87 million − ($10 million less 40% of $10 million)
$87 million − 6 million
[†]$96 million + 6 million extraordinary gain

PART

b

LO6

GRAPHIC 21–15
Steps to Correct an Error

The retroactive approach is used for the correction of errors.

The correction of an error is treated as a prior period adjustment.

CORRECTION OF ACCOUNTING ERRORS

Nobody's perfect. People make mistakes, even accountants. When errors are discovered, they should be corrected.[16] Graphic 21–15 describes the steps to be taken to correct an error, if the effect of the error is material.[17]

1. A journal entry is made to correct any account balances that are incorrect as a result of the error.
2. Previous years' financial statements that were incorrect as a result of the error are retroactively restated to reflect the correction (for all years reported for comparative purposes).
3. If retained earnings is one of the accounts incorrect as a result of the error, the correction is reported as a prior period adjustment to the beginning balance in a statement of shareholders' equity (or statement of retained earnings if that's presented instead).
4. A disclosure note should describe the nature of the error and the impact of its correction on net income.

---

[16]Interestingly, it appears that not all accounting errors are unintentional. Research has shown that firms with errors that overstate income are more likely "to have diffuse ownership, lower growth in earnings and fewer income-increasing GAAP alternatives available, and are less likely to have audit committees," suggesting that "overstatement errors are the result of managers responding to economic incentives." M. L. DeFond and J. Jiambaolvo, "Incidence and Circumstances of Accounting Errors," *The Accounting Review*, July, 1991.

[17]In practice, the vast majority of errors are not material with respect to their effect on the financial statements and are, therefore, simply corrected in the year discovered (step 1 only).

Prior Period Adjustments

Before we see these steps applied to the correction of an error, one of the steps requires elaboration. As discussed in Chapter 4, the correction of errors is the more common of only two situations that are considered to be prior period adjustments.[18] A prior period adjustment refers to an addition to or reduction in the beginning retained earnings balance in a statement of shareholders' equity (or statement of retained earnings if that's presented instead).

In an earlier chapter we saw that a statement of shareholders' equity is the most commonly used way to report the events that cause components of shareholders' equity to change during a particular reporting period. Some companies, though, choose to report the changes that occur in the balance of retained earnings separately in a statement of retained earnings. When it's discovered that the ending balance of retained earnings in the period prior to the discovery of an error was incorrect as a result of that error, the balance must be corrected when it appears as the beginning balance the following year. However, simply reporting a corrected amount might cause misunderstanding for someone familiar with the previously reported amount. Explicitly reporting a prior period adjustment on the statement itself avoids this confusion. Assume, for example, the following comparative statements of retained earnings:

STATEMENTS OF RETAINED EARNINGS
For the Years Ended December 31, 2002 and 2001

	2002	2001
Balance at beginning of year	$600,000	$450,000
Net income	400,000	350,000
Less: Dividends	(200,000)	(200,000)
Balance at end of year	$800,000	$600,000

A statement of retained earnings reports the events that cause changes in retained earnings.

Now suppose that in 2003 it's discovered that an error in 2001 caused that year's net income to be overstated by $20,000 (it should have been $330,000). This means retained earnings both years were overstated. Comparative statements the following year, when the error is discovered, would include a prior period adjustment as shown below:

STATEMENTS OF RETAINED EARNINGS
For the Years Ended December 31, 2003 and 2002

	2003	2002
Balance at beginning of year	$ 780,000	$600,000
Prior period adjustment		(20,000)
Corrected balance		$580,000
Net Income	500,000	400,000
Less: Dividends	(200,000)	(200,000)
Balance at end of year	$1,080,000	$780,000

The incorrect balance as previously reported is corrected by the prior period adjustment.

At least two years' (as in our example) and often three years' statements are reported in comparative financial statements. The prior period adjustment is applied to beginning retained earnings for the year following the error, or for the earliest year being reported in the comparative financial statements when the error occurs prior to the earliest year presented.[19]

---

[18]The other is an adjustment that results from the realization of income tax benefits of preacquisition operating loss carryforwards of purchased subsidiaries. See "Prior Period Adjustments," *Statement of Financial Accounting Standards No. 16* (Stamford, Conn.: FASB, 1977). This situation arises in connection with consolidation which is covered in many advanced accounting courses.

[19]The retained earnings balances in years after the first year also are adjusted to what those balances would be if the error had not occurred, but a company may choose not to explicitly report those adjustments as separate line items.

Error Correction Illustrated

You shouldn't try to memorize how specific errors are corrected; you should learn the *process* needed to analyze whatever errors you might encounter.

Now, let's discuss these procedures to correct errors in the context of a variety of the most common types of errors. Since there are literally thousands of possibilities, it's not practical to describe every error in every stage of its discovery. However, by applying the process to the situations described below, you should become sufficiently comfortable with the *process* that you could apply it to whatever situation you might encounter.

As you study these examples, be sure to notice that it's significantly more complicated to deal with an error if (a) it affected net income in the reporting period in which it occurred and (b) it is not discovered until a later period.

ERROR DISCOVERED IN THE SAME REPORTING PERIOD THAT IT OCCURRED

If an accounting error is made and discovered in the same accounting period, the original erroneous entry should simply be reversed and the appropriate entry recorded. The possibilities are limitless. Let's look at the one in Illustration 21–4.

ILLUSTRATION 21–4 Error Discovered in the Same Reporting Period That It Occurred	G. H. Little, Inc. paid $3 million for replacement computers and recorded the expenditure as maintenance expense. The error was discovered a week later.

To Reverse Erroneous Entry	**($ in millions)**	
Cash...	3	
Maintenance expense		3
To Record Correct Entry		
Equipment.......................................	3	
Cash...		3

Note: These entries can, of course, be combined.

ERROR AFFECTING PREVIOUS FINANCIAL STATEMENTS, BUT NOT NET INCOME

If an error did *not* affect net income in the year it occurred, it's relatively easy to correct. Examples are incorrectly recording salaries payable as accounts payable, recording a loss as an expense, or classifying a cash flow as an investing activity rather than a financing activity on the statement of cash flows.

ILLUSTRATION 21–5 Error Affecting Previous Financial Statements, but Not Net Income		MDS Transportation incorrectly recorded a $2 million note receivable as accounts receivable. The error was discovered a year later.
	Step 1	**To Correct Incorrect Accounts** **($ in millions)** Note receivable......................... 2 Accounts receivable 2
	Step 2	When reported for comparative purposes in the current year's annual report, last year's balance sheet would be restated to report the note as it should have been reported last year.
	Step 3	Since last year's net income was not affected by the error, the balance in retained earnings was not incorrect. So no prior period adjustment to that account is necessary.
	Step 4	A disclosure note would describe the nature of the error, but there would be no impact on net income, income before extraordinary items, and earnings per share to report.

ERROR AFFECTING A PRIOR YEAR'S NET INCOME

Most errors affect net income in some way. When they do, they affect the balance sheet as well. Both statements must be retroactively restated; the statement of cash flows sometimes is affected, too. As with any error, all incorrect account balances must be corrected. Because these errors affect income, one of the balances that will require correcting is retained earnings. Complicating matters, income taxes often are affected by income errors. In those cases, amended tax returns are prepared either to pay additional taxes or to claim a tax refund for taxes overpaid.

In Illustration 21–6 (except as indicated), we ignore the tax effects of the errors and their correction to allow us to focus on the errors themselves rather than their tax aspects.

In 2003, internal auditors discovered that Seidman Distribution, Inc. had debited an expense account for the $7 million cost of sorting equipment purchased at the beginning of 2001. The equipment's useful life was expected to be five years with no residual value. Straight-line depreciation is used by Seidman.

Analysis:

($ in millions)

	Correct			**Incorrect**	
	(Should have been recorded)			(As recorded)	
2001	Equipment	7.0		Expense	7.0
	Cash		7.0	Cash.		7.0
2001	Expense	1.4		Depreciation entry omitted	
	Accum. deprec.		1.4		
2002	Expense	1.4		Depreciation entry omitted	
	Accum. deprec.		1.4		

During the two-year period, depreciation expense was understated by $2.8 million, but other expenses were overstated by $7 million, so net income during the period was understated by $4.2 million. This means retained earnings is currently understated by that amount. Accumulated depreciation is understated by $2.8 million.

To Correct Incorrect Accounts	**($ in millions)**
Equipment.	7.0
Accumulated depreciation	2.8
Retained earnings	4.2

Step 1

The 2001 and 2002 financial statements that were incorrect as a result of the error are retroactively restated to report the equipment acquired and to reflect the correct amount of depreciation expense and accumulated depreciation, assuming both statements are reported again for comparative purposes in the 2003 annual report.

Because retained earnings is one of the accounts that is incorrect as a result of the error, a correction to that account of $4.2 million is reported as a prior period adjustment to the 2003 beginning retained earnings balance in Seidman's comparative statements of shareholders' equity. A correction would be made also to the 2002 beginning retained earnings balance. That prior period adjustment, though, would be for the pre-2002 difference: $7 million − 1.4 million = $5.6 million. If 2001 statements also are included in the comparative report, no adjustment would be necessary for that period because the error didn't occur until after the beginning of 2001.

Also, a disclosure note accompanying Seidman's 2003 financial statements should describe the nature of the error and the impact of its correction on each year's net income (understated by $5.6 million in 2001 and overstated by $1.4 million in 2002), income before extraordinary items (same as net income), and earnings per share.

ILLUSTRATION 21–6
Error Affecting Net Income: Recording an Asset as an Expense

Sometimes, the analysis is easier if you re-create the entries actually recorded incorrectly and those that would have been recorded if the error hadn't occurred and then compare them.

Step 2
Restate previous years' financial statements

Step 3
Prior period adjustment

Step 4
Disclosure note

The effect of most errors is different, depending on *when* the error is discovered. For example, if the error in Illustration 21–6 is not discovered until 2004, rather than 2003, accumulated depreciation would be understated by another $1.4 million, or a total of $4.2 million. If not discovered until 2007 or after, no correcting entry at all would be needed. By then, the sum of the omitted depreciation amounts ($1.4 million × 5 years) would equal the expense incorrectly recorded in 2001 ($7 million), so the retained earnings balance would be the same as if the error never had occurred. Also, the asset would have been disposed of—if the useful life estimate was correct—so neither the equipment nor accumulated depreciation would need to be recorded. Of course, any statements of prior years that were affected and are reported again in comparative statements still would be restated, and a footnote would describe the error.

Most errors, in fact, eventually self-correct. An example of an uncommon instance in which an error never self-corrects would be an expense account debited for the cost of land. Because land doesn't depreciate, the error would continue until the land is sold.

Some errors correct themselves the following year. For instance, if a company's ending inventory is incorrectly counted or otherwise misstated, the income statement would be in error for the year of the error and the following year, but the balance sheet would be incorrect only for the year the error occurs. After that, all account balances will be correct. This is demonstrated in Illustration 21–7.

> Even errors that eventually correct themselves cause financial statements to be misstated in the meantime.

ILLUSTRATION 21–7

Error Affecting Net Income: Inventory Misstated

In early 2003, Overseas Wholesale Supply discovered that $1 million of inventory had been inadvertently excluded from its 2001 ending inventory count.

Analysis:

U = Understated   O = Overstated

2001		**2002**	
Beginning inventory		Beginning inventory	U
Plus: Net purchases		Plus: Net purchases	
Less: Ending inventory	U	Less: Ending inventory	
Cost of goods sold	O	Cost of goods sold	U
Revenues		Revenues	
Less: Cost of goods sold	O	Less: Cost of goods sold	U
Less: Other expenses		Less: Other expenses	
Net income	U	Net income	O
Retained earnings	U	Retained earnings	*corrected*

> When analyzing inventory errors or other errors that affect cost of goods sold, you may find it helpful to visualize the determination of cost of goods sold, net income, and retained earnings.

Step 1

If Error Is Discovered in 2002 (before closing):   **($ in millions)**

Inventory	1	
Retained earnings		1

If Error Discovered in 2003 or Later:
No correcting entry needed

Step 2

If the error is discovered in 2002, the 2001 financial statements that were incorrect as a result of the error are retroactively restated to reflect the correct inventory amounts, cost of goods sold, and retained earnings when those statements are reported again for comparative purposes in the 2002 annual report. If the error is discovered in 2003, the 2002 financial statements also are retroactively restated to reflect the correct inventory amounts and cost of goods sold (retained earnings would not require adjustment), even though no correcting entry would be needed at that point.

Step 3

Because retained earnings is one of the accounts incorrect if the error is discovered in 2002, the correction to that account is reported as a prior period adjustment to the 2002 beginning retained earnings balance in Overseas' statement of shareholders' equity. Of course, no prior period adjustment is needed if the error isn't discovered until 2003 or later.

Step 4

Also, a disclosure note in Overseas' annual report should describe the nature of the error and the impact of its correction on each year's net income (understated by $1 million in 2001, overstated by $1 million in 2002), income before extraordinary items (same as net income), and earnings per share.

ADDITIONAL CONSIDERATION

We ignored the tax impact of the error and its correction in Illustration 21–6. To consider taxes, we need to know whether depreciation was also omitted from the tax return and the depreciation methods used for tax reporting. Let's say that depreciation was omitted from the tax return also, and that straight-line depreciation is used by Seidman for both tax and financial reporting. The tax rate is 40%.

Total operating expenses (nontax) still would have been overstated by $4.2 million over the two-year period. But that would have caused taxable income to be understated and the tax liability and income tax expense to be understated by 40% of $4.2 million, or $1.68 million. So net income and retained earnings would have been understated by only $2.52 million:

Operating expenses *overstated*	$4.20 million
Income tax expense *understated*	(1.68) million
Net income (and retained earnings) *understated*	$2.52 million

To Correct Incorrect Accounts:	**($ in millions)**	
Equipment.	7.00	
Accumulated depreciation		2.80
Income tax payable (40% × $4.2 million)		1.68
Retained earnings		2.52

If depreciation had been omitted from the income statement but not from the tax return, or if accelerated depreciation was used for tax reporting but straight-line depreciation for financial reporting, the credit to income tax payable in the correcting entry would be replaced by a credit to deferred tax liability.

Other error corrections that benefit from a similar analysis are the overstatement of ending inventory, the overstatement or understatement of beginning inventory, and errors in recording merchandise purchases (or returns).

An error also would occur if a revenue or an expense is recorded in the wrong accounting period. Illustration 21–8 on the next page offers an example.

ETHICAL DILEMMA

As a second-year accountant for McCormack Chemical Company, you were excited to be named assistant manager of the Agricultural Chemicals Division. After two weeks in your new position, you were supervising the year-end inventory count when the senior manager mentioned that two carloads of herbicides were omitted from the count and should be added. Upon checking, you confirm your understanding that the inventory in question had been deemed to be unsaleable. "Yes," your manager agreed, "but we'll write that off next year when our bottom line won't be so critical to the continued existence of the Agricultural Chemicals Division. Jobs and families depend on our division showing well this year."

Graphic 21-16 on the next page illustrates how Xerox Corporation reported in its 2000 financial statements the correction of errors involving improper business practices in Mexico, expensing items that should have been asset reductions and accounting incorrectly for leases.

The correction is reported as a **prior period adjustment** to beginning retained earnings balance in Xerox's Statement of Shareholders' Equity. The adjustment is made to the 1997 balance since that's the earliest year included in the comparative statements. The retained earnings balances in years after 1997 also are adjusted to what those balances would be if the error had not occurred.

ILLUSTRATION 21–8

Error Affecting Net Income: Failure to Record Sales Revenue

In 2003, General Paper Company discovered that $3,000 of merchandise (credit) sales the last week of 2002 were not recorded until the first week of 2003. The merchandise sold was appropriately excluded from 2002 ending inventory.

Analysis:

($ in 000s)

	Correct		**Incorrect**	
	(Should have been recorded)		(As recorded)	
2002	Accounts receivable....	3	No entry	
	Sales revenue		3	
2003	No entry		Accounts receivable	3
			Sales revenue	3

2002 sales revenue was incorrectly recorded in 2003, so 2002 net income was understated. Retained earnings is currently understated in 2003. 2003 sales revenue is overstated.

Step 1

To Correct Incorrect Accounts	**($ in 000s)**	
Sales revenue	3	
Retained earnings		3

Note: If the sales revenue had not been recorded at all, the correcting entry would include a debit to accounts receivable rather than sales revenue.

Step 2   The 2002 financial statements that were incorrect as a result of the error are retroactively restated to reflect the correct amount of sales revenue and accounts receivable when those statements are reported again for comparative purposes in the 2003 annual report.

Step 3   Because retained earnings is one of the accounts incorrect as a result of the error, the correction to that account is reported as a prior period adjustment to the 2002 beginning retained earnings balance in General Paper's comparative statements of shareholders' equity.

Step 4   Also, a disclosure note in General Paper's 2003 annual report should describe the nature of the error and the impact of its correction on each year's net income ($3,000 in 2002), income before extraordinary items ($3,000 in 2002), and earnings per share.

GRAPHIC 21–16

Disclosure of Error Correction – Xerox Corporation

2. **Restatement (in part)**

We have restated our Consolidated Financial Statements for the fiscal years ended December 31, 1999 and 1998 as a result of two separate investigations conducted by the Audit Committee of the Board of Directors.

In fiscal 2000 the Company had initially recorded charges totaling $170 ($120 after taxes) which arose from imprudent and improper business practices in Mexico that resulted in certain accounting errors and irregularities. The Company has restated its prior year Consolidated Financial Statements to reflect reductions to pre-tax income of $53 and $13 in 1999 and 1998, respectively. It is not practical to determine what portion, if any, of the approximate remaining $101 charge reflected in adjusted 2000 results of operations relates to prior years.

In connection with our acquisition of the remaining 20 percent of Xerox Limited from Rank Group, Plc in 1997, we recorded a liability of $100 for contingencies identified at the date of acquisition. During 1998, we determined that the liability was no longer required. During 1998 and 1999, we charged to the liability certain expenses incurred as part of the consolidation of our European back-office operations. This reversal should have been recorded as a reduction of Goodwill and Deferred tax assets. Therefore, we have restated our previously reported Consolidated Financial Statements to reflect decreases of $67 to Goodwill and $33 of Deferred tax assets and increases in Selling, administrative and general expenses of $76 in 1999 and $24 in 1998.

In addition to the above items, we have made adjustments in connection with certain misapplications of GAAP under *SFAS No. 13,* "Accounting for Leases." These adjustments primarily relate to the accounting for lease modifications and residual values as well as certain other items.

Retained earnings at December 31, 1997 was restated from $3,960 to $3,852 as a result of the effect of these aforementioned adjustments on years prior to 1998.

As mentioned at the outset, we've made no attempt to demonstrate the correction process for every kind of error in every stage of its discovery. However, after seeing the process applied to the few situations described, you should feel comfortable that the process is the same regardless of the specific situation you might encounter.

CONCEPT **REVIEW** | EXERCISE

Correction of Errors

In 2003, the following errors were discovered by the internal auditors of Development Technologies, Inc.

1. 2002 accrued wages of $2 million were not recognized until they were paid in 2003.
2. A $3 million purchase of merchandise in 2003 was recorded in 2002 instead. The physical inventory count at the end of 2002 was correct.

Required:
Prepare the journal entries needed in 2003 to correct each error. Also, briefly describe any other measures Development Technologies would take in connection with correcting the errors. (Ignore income taxes.)

Step 1:

SOLUTION

1. To reduce 2003 wages expense and reduce retained earnings to what it would have been if the expense had reduced net income in 2002.

	($ in millions)	
Retained earnings	2	
Wages expense		2

2. To include the $3 million in 2003 purchases and increase retained earnings to what it would have been if 2002 cost of goods sold had not included the $3 million purchases.

Analysis
U = Understated   O = Overstated

2002		**2003**	
Beginning inventory		Beginning inventory	
Purchases	O	Purchases	U
Less: Ending inventory			
Cost of goods sold	O		
Revenues			
Less: Cost of goods sold	O		
Less: Other expenses			
Net income	U		
↓			
Retained earnings	U		

	($ in millions)	
Purchases	3	
Retained earnings		3

Step 2:
The 2002 financial statements that were incorrect as a result of the errors would be *retroactively restated* to reflect the correct wages expense, cost of goods sold (income tax expense if taxes are considered), net income, and retained earnings when those statements are reported again for comparative purposes in the 2003 annual report.

Step 3:

Because retained earnings is one of the accounts incorrect, the correction to that account is reported as a *"prior period adjustment"* to the 2002 beginning retained earnings balance in the comparative Statements of Shareholders' Equity.

Step 4:

Also, a *disclosure note* should describe the nature of the error and the impact of its correction on each year's net income, income before extraordinary items, and earnings per share.

FINANCIAL REPORTING CASE **SOLUTION**

1. **How would you respond to Martin's question?** *(p. 1039)* The accounting change did not really cost Microsoft $375 million. Like the amount reported for most changes in accounting principle, this is the cumulative income effect from years prior to the change to the new accounting method. In this instance, it is the cumulative effect on the income of previous years from not having reported derivatives in the way that became mandatory with *SFAS 133*. It is reported, net of tax, on the income statement as a separate item of income between extraordinary items and net income.

2. **Are all changes in accounting method reporting this way? Are there other accounting changes that are reported differently?** *(p. 1044)* Most, but not all. There are five exceptions that are reported by retroactively adjusting prior financial statements to reflect the new method. A few allow or permit prospective application only. Besides a change in accounting principle, the two other accounting changes are changes in estimate, which are reported prospectively, and changes in reporting entity, which are reported retroactively. ■

THE BOTTOM LINE

1. Accounting changes are categorized as:
   a. Changes in *principle,*
   b. Changes in *estimates,* or
   c. Changes in *reporting entity.*
   Accounting changes can be accounted for: retroactively (prior years restated); currently (cumulative effect reported currently); or prospectively (only current and future years affected).

2. Most changes in accounting principles are recorded and reported by the "current approach." The cumulative income effect (net of the tax effect) is reported as a separate item of income between extraordinary items and net income. The effect of the change on certain key income numbers should be reported for the current period and on a pro forma (as-if) basis for the financial statements of all prior periods included, and the nature of and justification for the change, as well as the effect on current earnings, should be described in the disclosure notes.

3. Because of their unique nature, prior years' financial statements are restated to reflect some changes in accounting principle. Also, a change to LIFO and a few changes mandated by new accounting standards are accounted for prospectively.

4. Changes in estimates are accounted for prospectively. When a company revises a previous estimate, prior financial statements are not restated, nor is a cumulative effect of the change included in current income. Instead, the company merely incorporates the new estimate in any related accounting determinations from then on.

5. A change in reporting entity requires that financial statements of prior periods be retroactively restated to report the financial information for the new reporting entity in all periods.

6. When errors are discovered, they should be corrected and accounted for retroactively. Previous years' financial statements that were incorrect as a result of an error are retroactively restated, and any account balances that are incorrect are corrected by a

journal entry. If retained earnings is one of the accounts incorrect, the correction is reported as a prior period adjustment to the beginning balance in a statement of shareholders' equity. And, a disclosure note should describe the nature of the error and the impact of its correction on operations. ■

QUESTIONS FOR REVIEW OF KEY TOPICS

Q 21–1   For accounting purposes, we classify accounting changes into three categories. What are they? Provide a short description of each.

Q 21–2   There are three accounting approaches to reporting accounting changes. What are they?

Q 21–3   How we account for changes in accounting principle depends on the type of change. However, most changes in accounting principle are accounted for by the current approach. Describe this general way of recording and reporting changes in accounting principle.

Q 21–4   Lynch Corporation changes from the sum-of-the-years'-digits method of depreciation for existing assets to the straight-line method. How should the cumulative effect be reported of the change on the amount of retained earnings at the beginning of the period of the change?

Q 21–5   Sugarbaker Designs, Inc. changed from the FIFO inventory costing method to the average cost method during 2003. Which items from the 2002 financial statements should be restated on the basis of the average cost method when reported in the 2003 comparative financial statements?

Q 21–6   Most accounting principles are recorded and reported by the "current approach." But, because of their unique nature, some changes in accounting principle are more appropriately reported by the *retroactive approach* instead. For these exceptions to the general way of accounting for changes in accounting principle, prior years' financial statements are restated to reflect the use of the new accounting method. What are the exceptions for which restatement is required?

Q 21–7   Southeast Steel, Inc. changed from the FIFO inventory costing method to the LIFO method during 2002. How would this change likely be reported in the 2003 comparative financial statements?

Q 21–8   Direct Assurance Company revised the estimates of the useful life of a trademark it had acquired three years earlier. How should the change be accounted for?

Q 21–9   It's not easy sometimes to distinguish between a change in principle and a change in estimate. In these cases, how should the change be accounted for?

Q 21–10   For financial reporting, a reporting entity can be a single company, or it can be a group of companies that reports a single set of financial statements. When changes occur that cause the financial statements to be those of a different reporting entity, we account for the situation as a change in reporting entity. What are the situations deemed to constitute a change in reporting entity?

Q 21–11   The issuance of *SFAS 94,* "Consolidation of All Majority-Owned Subsidiaries," required Ford Motors to include a previously unconsolidated finance subsidiary as part of the reporting entity. How did Ford report the change?

Q 21–12   Describe the process of correcting an error when it's discovered in a subsequent reporting period.

Q 21–13   If merchandise inventory is understated at the end of 2002, and the error is not discovered, how will net income be affected in 2003?

Q 21–14   If it is discovered that an extraordinary repair in the previous year was incorrectly debited to repair expense, how will retained earnings be reported in the current year's statement of shareholders' equity?

Q 21–15   What action is required when it is discovered that a five-year insurance premium payment of $50,000 two years ago was debited to insurance expense? (Ignore taxes.)

Q 21–16   Suppose the error described in the previous question is not discovered until six years later. What action will the discovery of this error require?

EXERCISES

E 21–1
Change in principle;
change in depreciation
methods

Clinton Poultry Farms has used for financial reporting the declining balance method of depreciation for conveyor equipment acquired at the beginning of 2000. At the beginning of 2003, Clinton decides to change to the straight-line method. There is no change in the method used for tax reporting. Clinton's tax rate is 40%.

The effect of this change on depreciation for each year is as follows ($ in 000s):

Year	Straight Line	Declining Balance	Difference
2000	$ 400	$ 640	$240
2001	400	550	150
2002	400	460	60
	$1,200	$1,650	$450

Required:
1. Prepare the journal entry to record the change in principle. (All tax effects should be reflected in the deferred tax liability account.)
2. Briefly describe any other steps Clinton should take to report this accounting change in the 2002–2003 comparative financial statements.

E 21–2
Change in accounting principle; change in depreciation methods

Deere Company constructed a machine at a total cost of $35 million in 2000. The machine was being depreciated over a 10-year life using the sum-of-the-years'-digits method. The residual value is expected to be $2 million. At the beginning of 2003 Deere decided to change to the straight-line method.

Required:
Prepare all appropriate journal entry(s) relating to the machine for 2003. (Ignore income tax effects.)

E 21–3
Change in principle; change to the percentage-of-completion method

The Long Island Construction Company has used the completed contract method of accounting for construction contracts. At the beginning of 2003, the company decides to change to the percentage-of-completion method for financial reporting purposes, but will continue to use the completed contract method for tax reporting. The following table presents information concerning the change. The income tax rate for all years is 40%.

	Income before Income Tax		
	Percentage of Completion Method	Completed Contract Method	Difference
Before 2002	$15 million	$8 million	$7 million
2002	8 million	5 million	3 million
2003	10 million	9 million	1 million

Required:
1. Prepare the journal entry to record the change in principle. (All tax effects should be reflected in the deferred tax liability account.)
2. Determine the net income to be reported in the 2003–2002 comparative income statements.
3. Which other 2002 amounts would be reported differently in the 2003–2002 comparative income statements and 2003–2002 comparative balance sheets than they were reported the previous year?
4. How would the change be reflected in the 2003–2002 comparative statements of shareholders' equity? Cash dividends were $1 million each year.

E 21–4
Change in principle; change to the equity method

Exercise 12–14 deals with investments and change to the equity method.

E 21–5
Classifying accounting changes

Indicate with the appropriate letter the nature of each situation described below:

Type of Change

PC	Change in principle reported currently
PR	Change in principle reported retroactively
PP	Change in principle reported prospectively
E	Change in estimate
R	Change in reporting entity
N	Not an accounting change

____ 1. Change from declining balance depreciation to straight-line.
____ 2. Change in the estimated useful life of office equipment.
____ 3. Technological advance that renders worthless a patent with an unamortized cost of $45,000.

_____ 4. Change from determining lower of cost or market for the inventories by the individual item approach to the aggregate approach.

_____ 5. Change from LIFO inventory costing to the weighted-average inventory costing.

_____ 6. Settling a lawsuit for less than the amount accrued previously as a loss contingency.

_____ 7. Including in the consolidated financial statements a subsidiary acquired several years earlier that was appropriately not included in previous years.

_____ 8. Change by a retail store from reporting bad debt expense on a pay-as-you-go basis to the allowance method.

_____ 9. A shift of certain manufacturing overhead costs to inventory that previously were expensed as incurred to more accurately measure cost of goods sold. (Either method is generally acceptable.)

_____ 10. Pension plan assets for a defined benefit pension plan achieving a rate of return in excess of the amount anticipated.

E 21–6

Change in inventory costing methods

In 2003, the Quayle Company changed its method of valuing inventory from the FIFO method to the average cost method. At December 31, 2002, Quayle's inventories were $32 million (FIFO). Quayle's records indicated that the inventories would have totaled $23.8 million at December 31, 2002, if determined on an average cost basis.

Required:
1. Prepare the journal entry to record the adjustment. (Ignore income taxes.)
2. Briefly describe other steps Quayle should take to report the change.

E 21–7

Change from the treasury stock method to retired stock

Exercise 19–12 deals with treasury stock and a change to considering reacquired stock to be retired.

E 21–8

Multiple choice; accounting changes

The following questions dealing with accounting changes are adapted from questions that appeared on recent CPA examinations. Determine the response that best completes the statements or questions.

1. When a company changes from the straight-line method of depreciation for previously recorded assets to the double-declining balance method, which of the following should be reported?

	Cumulative Effects of Change in Accounting Principle	Pro Forma Effects of Retroactive Application
a.	No	No
b.	No	Yes
c.	Yes	Yes
d.	Yes	No

2. On January 1, 2003, Roem Corp. changed its inventory method to FIFO from LIFO for both financial and income tax reporting purposes. The change resulted in a $500,000 increase in the January 1, 2003, inventory. Assume that the income tax rate for all years is 30%. The cumulative effect of the accounting change should be reported by Roem in its 2003:
    a. Retained earnings statement as a $350,000 addition to the beginning balance.
    b. Income statement as a $350,000 cumulative effect of accounting change.
    c. Retained earnings statement as a $500,000 addition to the beginning balance.
    d. Income statement as a $500,000 cumulative effect of accounting change.

3. A company has included in its consolidated financial statements this year a subsidiary acquired several years ago that was appropriately excluded from consolidation last year. This results in:
    a. An accounting change that should be reported prospectively.
    b. An accounting change that should be reported by restating the financial statements of all prior periods presented.
    c. A correction of an error.
    d. Neither an accounting change nor a correction of an error.

E 21–9

Deferred taxes; change in tax rates

Exercise 16–15 deals with deferred taxes and a change in tax rates.

E 21–10

Book royalties

Dreighton Engineering Group receives royalties on a technical manual written by two of its engineers and sold to William B. Irving Publishing, Inc. Royalties are 10% of net sales, receivable on October 1 for sales in January through June and on April 1 for sales in July through December of the prior year. Sales of the manual began in July 2002, and Dreighton accrued royalty revenue of $31,000 at December 31, 2002, as follows:

Receivable—royalty revenue................................	31,000	
Royalty revenue..		31,000

Dreighton received royalties of $36,000 on April 1, 2003, and $40,000 on October 1, 2003. Irving indicated to Dreighton on December 31 that book sales subject to royalties for the second half of 2003 are expected to be $500,000.

Required:
1. Prepare any journal entries Dreighton should record during 2003 related to the royalty revenue.
2. What adjustments, if any, should be made to retained earnings or to the 2002 financial statements? Explain.

E 21–11
Loss contingency

Exercise 13–20 deals with a change in the estimated amount of a loss contingency.

E 21–12
Warranty expense

Woodmier Lawn Products introduced a new line of commercial sprinklers in 2002 that carry a one-year warranty against manufacturer's defects. Because this was the first product for which the company offered a warranty, trade publications were consulted to determine the experience of others in the industry. Based on that experience, warranty costs were expected to approximate 2% of sales. Sales of the sprinklers in 2002 were $2,500,000. Accordingly, the following entries relating to the contingency for warranty costs were recorded during the first year of selling the product:

Accrued liability and expense		
Warranty expense (2% × $2,500,000)	50,000	
Estimated warranty liability...............................		50,000
Actual expenditures (summary entry)		
Estimated warranty liability.................................	23,000	
Cash, wages payable, parts and supplies, etc.		23,000

In late 2003, the company's claims experience was evaluated and it was determined that claims were far more than expected—3% of sales rather than 2%.

Required:
1. Assuming sales of the sprinklers in 2003 were $3,600,000 and warranty expenditures in 2003 totaled $88,000, prepare any journal entries related to the warranty.
2. Assuming sales of the sprinklers were discontinued after 2002, prepare any journal entry(s) in 2003 related to the warranty.

E 21–13
Change in estimate; useful life of patent

Exercise 11–13 deals with a change in the estimated life of a patent.

E 21–14
Change in inventory costing methods

Exercise 9–19 deals with a change in inventory costing methods.

E 21–15
Accounting change involving machinery

Exercise 4–9 deals with an accounting change involving machinery.

E 21–16
Accounting change involving machinery

Exercise 4–10 deals with an accounting change involving machinery.

E 21–17
Change in estimate; equipment

Exercise 11–14 deals with changes in estimates involving equipment.

E 21–18
Accounting change; depreciation

Exercise 11–16 deals with a change in depreciation methods.

E 21–19
Error correction;
inventory error

During 2003, WMC Corporation discovered that its ending inventories reported on its financial statements were misstated by the following amounts:

2001	understated by	$120,000
2002	overstated by	150,000

WMC uses the periodic inventory system and the FIFO cost method.

Required:
1. Determine the effect of these errors on retained earnings at January 1, 2003, before any adjustments. Explain your answer. (Ignore income taxes.)
2. Prepare a journal entry to correct the error.
3. What other step(s) would be taken in connection with the error?

E 21–20
Error correction

DeSoto Water Works purchased a machine at the end of 2002 at a cost of $65,000 and recorded the following journal entry:

Buildings	65,000	
Cash		65,000

The error was discovered in 2003.

Required:
1. Prepare a journal entry to correct the error.
2. What other step(s) would be taken in connection with the error?

E 21–21
Error correction;
operational asset

Exercise 11–17 deals with an error related to recording an operational asset.

E 21–22
Error corrections;
investment

On December 12, 2003, an investment costing $80,000 was sold for $100,000. The total of the sale proceeds was credited to the investment account.

Required:
1. Prepare the journal entry to correct the error assuming it is discovered before the books are adjusted or closed in 2003. (Ignore income taxes.)
2. Prepare the journal entry to correct the error assuming it is not discovered until early 2004. (Ignore income taxes.)

E 21–23
Error in amortization
schedule

Wilkins Food Products, Inc. acquired a packaging machine from Lawrence Specialists Corporation. Lawrence completed construction of the machine on January 1, 2001. In payment for the machine Wilkins issued a three-year installment note to be paid in three equal payments at the end of each year. The payments include interest at the rate of 10%.

Lawrence made a conceptual error in preparing the amortization schedule which Wilkens failed to discover until 2003. The error had caused Wilkens to understate interest expense by $45,000 in 2001 and $40,000 in 2002.

Required:
1. Determine which accounts are incorrect as a result of these errors at January 1, 2003, before any adjustments. Explain your answer. (Ignore income taxes.)
2. Prepare a journal entry to correct the error.
3. What other step(s) would be taken in connection with the error?

E 21–24
Multiple choice; errors

The following questions dealing with errors are adapted from questions that appeared on recent CPA examinations. Determine the response that best completes the statements or questions.
1. During 2003, Paul Company discovered that the ending inventories reported on its financial statements were incorrect by the following amounts:

2001	$60,000	understated
2002	75,000	overstated

Paul uses the periodic inventory system to ascertain year-end quantities that are converted to dollar amounts using the FIFO cost method. Prior to any adjustments for these errors and ignoring income taxes, Paul's retained earnings at January 1, 2003, would be
a. Correct.
b. $15,000 overstated.

c. $75,000 overstated.

d. $135,000 overstated.

2. Terry, Inc. is a calendar-year corporation whose financial statements for 2001 and 2002 included errors as follows:

Year	Ending Inventory	Depreciation Expense
2001	$15,000 overstated	$12,500 overstated
2002	5,000 understated	4,000 understated

Assume that purchases were recorded correctly and that no correcting entries were made at December 31, 2001 or at December 31, 2002. Ignoring income taxes, by how much should Terry's retained earnings be retroactively adjusted at January 1, 2003?

a. $13,500 increase.

b. $3,500 decrease.

c. $1,500 decrease.

d. $1,000 decrease.

3. After the issuance of its 2002 financial statements Terry, Inc. discovered a computational error of $150,000 in the calculation of its December 31, 2002, inventory. The error resulted in a $150,000 overstatement in the cost of goods sold for the year ended December 31, 2002. In October 2003, Terry paid $500,000 in settlement of litigation instituted against it during 2002. Ignore income taxes. In the 2003 financial statements the December 31, 2002, retained earnings balance, as previously reported, should be adjusted by a

a. $150,000 credit.

b. $350,000 debit.

c. $500,000 debit.

d. $650,000 credit.

E 21–25
Error correction; accrued interest on bonds

Exercise 14–22 deals with the correction of an error in accrued interest on bonds.

E 21–26
Error correction; three errors

Below are three independent and unrelated errors.

a. On December 31, 2002, Wolfe-Bache Corporation failed to accrue office supplies expense of $1,800. In January 2003, when it received the bill from its supplier, Wolfe-Bache made the following entry:

Office supplies expense	1,800	
Cash		1,800

b. On the last day of 2002, Midwest Importers received a $90,000 prepayment from a tenant for 2003 rent of a building. Midwest recorded the receipt as rent revenue.

c. At the end of 2002, Dinkins-Lowery Corporation failed to accrue interest of $8,000 on a note receivable. At the beginning of 2003, when the company received the cash, it was recorded as interest revenue.

Required:

For each error:

1. What would be the effect of each error on the income statement and the balance sheet in the 2002 financial statements?

2. Prepare any journal entries each company should record in 2003 to correct the errors.

E 21–27
Inventory errors

Exercise 9–21 deals with inventory errors.

E 21–28
Inventory error

Exercise 9–22 deals with an inventory error.

E 21–29
Classifying accounting changes and errors

Indicate with the appropriate letter the nature of each adjustment described below:

Type of Adjustment

A. Change in principle (general)
B. Change in principle (exception reported retroactively)
C. Change in principle (exception reported prospectively)
D. Change in estimate
E. Change in reporting entity
F. Correction of an error

____ 1. Change from expensing extraordinary repairs to capitalizing the expenditures.

____ 2. Change in the residual value of machinery.

____ 3. Change from FIFO inventory costing to LIFO inventory costing.

____ 4. Change in the percentage used to determine bad debts.

____ 5. Change from LIFO inventory costing to FIFO inventory costing.

____ 6. Change from reporting pension benefits according to the provisions of *Accounting Principles Board Opinion 8* to reporting pension benefits according to the provisions of *SFAS 87* in 1987. (*SFAS 87* became generally effective in 1987.)

____ 7. Change in the composition of a group of firms reporting on a consolidated basis.

____ 8. Change from sum-of-the-years'-digits depreciation to straight-line.

____ 9. Change from the percentage-of-completion method by a company in the long-term construction industry.

____ 10. Change in actuarial assumptions for a defined benefit pension plan.

PROBLEMS

P 21–1

Change in principle; change in depreciation methods

During 2001 and 2002, Faulkner Manufacturing used the sum-of-the-years'-digits (SYD) method of depreciation for its operational assets, for both financial reporting and tax purposes. At the beginning of 2003, Faulkner decided to change to the straight-line method for both financial reporting and tax purposes. A tax rate of 40% is in effect for all years.

The effect of this change on net income for each year is as follows ($ in 000s):

Year	Straight Line	SYD	Difference	Taxes	Net Change in Income
2001	$2,000	$3,200	$1,200	$480	$ 720
2002	2,000	2,800	800	320	480
	$4,000	$6,000	$2,000	$800	$1,200

Income from continuing operations (before income tax) for 2003 and 2002 were $6 million and $5 million, respectively. There were no extraordinary items. There were 1 million common shares outstanding each year.

Required:

1. Prepare the journal entry to record the change in principle. (All tax effects should be reflected in the deferred tax liability account.)
2. Prepare the 2003–2002 comparative income statements beginning with income from continuing operations. Include per share amounts and any necessary pro forma disclosures.

P 21–2

Change in inventory costing methods; comparative income statements

Shown below are net income amounts as they would be determined by Weihrich Steel Company by each of three different inventory costing methods ($ in 000s).

	FIFO	Average Cost	LIFO
Pre-2002	$2,800	$2,540	$2,280
2002	750	600	540
	$3,550	$3,140	$2,820

Required:

1. Assume that Weihrich used FIFO before 2003, and then in 2003 decided to switch to average cost. Prepare the journal entry to record the change in principle and briefly describe any other steps Weihrich should take to appropriately report the situation. (Ignore income tax effects.)

2. Assume that Weihrich used LIFO before 2003, and then in 2003 decided to switch to average cost. Prepare the journal entry to record the change in principle and briefly describe any other steps Weihrich should take to appropriately report the situation. (Ignore income tax effects.)

3. Assume that Weihrich used FIFO before 2003, and then in 2003 decided to switch to LIFO. Prepare the journal entry to record the change in principle and briefly describe any other steps Weihrich should take to appropriately report the situation. (Ignore income tax effects.)

P 21–3

Change in inventory costing methods; comparative income statements

The Cecil-Booker Vending Company changed its method of valuing inventory from the weighted-average cost method to the FIFO cost method at the beginning of 2003. At December 31, 2002, inventories were $120,000 (average cost basis) and were $124,000 a year earlier. Cecil-Booker's accountants determined that the inventories would have totaled $155,000 at December 31, 2002, and $160,000 at December 31, 2001, if determined on a FIFO basis. A tax rate of 40% is in effect for all years.

One hundred thousand common shares were outstanding each year. Income from continuing operations was $400,000 in 2002 and $525,000 in 2003. There were no extraordinary items either year.

Required:

1. Prepare the journal entry to record the change in principle. (All tax effects should be reflected in the deferred tax liability account.)

2. Prepare the 2003–2002 comparative income statements beginning with income from continuing operations. Include per share amounts and any necessary pro forma disclosures.

P 21–4

Change in principle; change in method of accounting for long-term construction

The Pyramid Construction Company has used the completed-contract method of accounting for construction contracts during its first two years of operation, 2001 and 2002. At the beginning of 2003, Pyramid decides to change to the percentage-of-completion method for both tax and financial reporting purposes. The following table presents information concerning the change for 2001–2003. The income tax rate for all years is 40%.

	Income before Income Tax				
	Percentage of Completion Method	**Completed Contract Method**	**Difference**	**Income Tax Effect**	**Difference after Tax**
2001	$ 90,000	$60,000	$30,000	$12,000	$18,000
2002	45,000	36,000	9,000	3,600	5,400
Total	$135,000	$96,000	$39,000	$15,600	$23,400
2003	$ 51,000	$46,000	$ 5,000	$ 2,000	$ 3,000

Pyramid issued 50,000 $1 par, common shares for $230,000 when the business began, and there have been no changes in paid-in capital since then. Dividends were not paid the first year, but $10,000 cash dividends were paid in both 2002 and 2003.

Required:

1. Prepare the journal entry to record the change in principle. (All tax effects should be reflected in the deferred tax liability account.)

2. Prepare the 2003–2002 comparative income statements beginning with income before income taxes.

3. Prepare the 2003–2002 comparative statements of shareholders' equity. (Hint: The 2001 statements reported retained earnings of $36,000. This is $60,000 − [$60,000 × 40%].)

P 21–5

Accounting changes; six situations

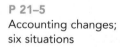

Described below are six independent and unrelated situations involving accounting changes. Each change occurs during 2003 before any adjusting entries or closing entries were prepared. Assume the tax rate for each company is 40% in all years. Any tax effects should be adjusted through the deferred tax liability account.

a. Fleming Home Products introduced a new line of commercial awnings in 2002 that carry a one-year warranty against manufacturer's defects. Based on industry experience, warranty costs were expected to approximate 3% of sales. Sales of the awnings in 2002 were $3,500,000. Accordingly, warranty expense and a warranty liability of $105,000 were recorded in 2002. In late 2003, the company's claims experience was evaluated and it was determined that claims were far fewer than expected: 2% of sales rather than 3%. Sales of the awnings in 2003 were $4,000,000 and warranty expenditures in 2003 totaled $91,000.

b. On December 30, 1999, Rival Industries acquired its office building at a cost of $1,000,000. It has been depreciated on a straight-line basis assuming a useful life of 40 years and no salvage value. However, plans were finalized in 2003 to relocate the company headquarters at the end of 2010. The vacated office building will have a salvage value at that time of $700,000.

c.　Hobbs-Barto Merchandising, Inc. changed inventory cost methods to LIFO from FIFO at the end of 2003 for both financial statement and income tax purposes. Under FIFO, the inventory at January 1, 2004, is $690,000.

d.　At the beginning of 1999, the Hoffman Group purchased office equipment at a cost of $330,000. Its useful life was estimated to be 10 years with no salvage value. The equipment has been depreciated by the sum-of-the-years'-digits method. On January 1, 2003, the company changed to the straight-line method.

e.　In November 2001, the State of Minnesota filed suit against Huggins Manufacturing Company, seeking penalties for violations of clean air laws. When the financial statements were issued in 2002, Huggins had not reached a settlement with state authorities, but legal counsel advised Huggins that it was probable the company would have to pay $200,000 in penalties. Accordingly, the following entry was recorded:

Loss—litigation	200,000	
Liability—litigation.		200,000

Late in 2003, a settlement was reached with state authorities to pay a total of $350,000 in penalties.

f.　At the beginning of 2003, Jantzen Specialties, which uses the sum-of-the-years'-digits method changed to the straight-line method for newly acquired buildings and equipment. The change increased current year net earnings by $445,000.

Required:
For each situation:
1.　Identify the type of change.
2.　Prepare any journal entry necessary as a direct result of the change as well as any adjusting entry for 2003 related to the situation described.
3.　Briefly describe any other steps that should be taken to appropriately report the situation.

P 21–6
Accounting changes; identify type and reporting approach

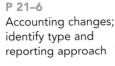

At the beginning of 2003, Wagner Implements undertook a variety of changes in accounting methods, corrected several errors, and instituted new accounting policies.

Required:
On a sheet of paper numbered from 1 to 10, indicate for each item below the type of change and the reporting approach Wagner would use.

Type of change (Choose one)	Reporting approach (Choose one)
P.　Change in accounting principle	C.　Current effect
E.　Change in accounting estimate	R.　Retroactive restatement
X.　Correction of an error	P.　Prospective approach
N.　Neither an accounting change nor an accounting error.	

Change:
1.　By acquiring additional stock, Wagner increased its investment in Wise, Inc. from a 12% interest to 25% and changed its method of accounting for the investment from an available-for-sale investment to the equity method.
2.　Wagner instituted a postretirement benefit plan for its employees in 2003 and adopted *SFAS No. 106*, "Accounting for Postretirement Benefit Plans Other than Pensions." Wagner had not previously had such a plan.
3.　Wagner changed its method of depreciating computer equipment from the SYD method to the straight-line method.
4.　Wagner determined that a liability insurance premium it both paid and expensed in 2002 covered the 2002–2004 period.
5.　Wagner custom-manufactures farming equipment on a contract basis. Wagner switched its accounting for these long-term contracts from the completed-contract method to the percentage-of-completion method.
6.　Due to an unexpected relocation, Wagner determined that its office building previously to be depreciated over 45 years should be depreciated over 18 years.
7.　Wagner offers a three-year warranty on the farming equipment it sells. Manufacturing efficiencies caused Wagner to reduce its expectation of warranty costs from 2% of sales to 1% of sales.
8.　Wagner changed from LIFO to FIFO to account for its materials and work in process inventories.
9.　Wagner changed from FIFO to average cost to account for its equipment inventory.

10. Wagner sells extended service contracts on some of its equipment sold. Wagner performs services related to these contracts over several years, so in 2003 Wagner changed from recognizing revenue from these service contracts on a cash basis to the accrual basis.

P 21–7

Error; a change in principle; operational assets

Problem 11–11 deals with the correction of an error related to recording an operational asset and a change in depreciation methods.

P 21–8

Change in inventory costing methods

Problem 9–11 deals with a change in inventory costing methods.

P 21–9

Depreciation methods; change in methods

Problem 11–1 deals with a change in depreciation methods.

P 21–10

Depletion; change in estimate

Problem 11–7 deals with a change in an estimate involving a natural resource.

P 21–11

Straight-line depreciation; change in useful life and residual value

Problem 11–9 deals with changes in the useful life and residual value of machinery.

P 21–12

Accounting changes and error correction; eight situations; tax effects ignored

Williams-Santana, Inc. is a manufacturer of high-tech industrial parts that was started in 1991 by two talented engineers with little business training. In 2003, the company was acquired by one of its major customers. As part of an internal audit, the following facts were discovered. The audit occurred during 2003 before any adjusting entries or closing entries were prepared.

a. A five-year casualty insurance policy was purchased at the beginning of 2001 for $35,000. The full amount was debited to insurance expense at the time.

b. Effective January 1, 2003, the company changed the salvage value used in calculating depreciation for its office building. The building cost $600,000 on December 29, 1992, and has been depreciated on a straight-line basis assuming a useful life of 40 years and a salvage value of $100,000. Declining real estate values in the area indicate that the salvage value will be no more than $25,000.

c. On December 31, 2002, merchandise inventory was overstated by $25,000 due to a mistake in the physical inventory count using the periodic inventory system.

d. The company changed inventory cost methods to FIFO from LIFO at the end of 2003 for both financial statement and income tax purposes. The change will cause a $960,000 increase in the beginning inventory at January 1, 2004.

e. At the end of 2002, the company failed to accrue $15,500 of sales commissions earned by employees during 2002. The expense was recorded when the commissions were paid in early 2003.

f. At the beginning of 2001, the company purchased a machine at a cost of $720,000. Its useful life was estimated to be 10 years with no salvage value. The machine has been depreciated by the double-declining balance method. Its carrying amount on December 31, 2002, was $460,800. On January 1, 2003, the company changed retroactively to the straight-line method.

g. Bad debt expense is determined each year as 1% of credit sales. Actual collection experience of recent years indicates that 0.75% is a better indication of uncollectible accounts. Management effects the change in 2003. Credit sales for 2003 are $4,000,000; in 2002 they were $3,700,000.

h. Additional industrial robots were acquired at the beginning of 2000 and added to the company's assembly process. The $1,000,000 cost of the equipment was inadvertently recorded as repair expense. Robots have 10-year useful lives and no material salvage value. This class of equipment is depreciated by the straight-line method.

Required:

For each situation:

1. Identify whether it represents an accounting change or an error. If an accounting change, identify the type of change.

2. Prepare any journal entry necessary as a direct result of the change or error correction as well as any adjusting entry for 2003 related to the situation described. (Ignore tax effects.)

3. Briefly describe any other steps that should be taken to appropriately report the situation.

P 21–13

Accounting changes
and error correction;
eight situations; tax
effects considered

(Note: This problem is a variation of the previous problem, modified to consider income tax effects.) Williams-Santana, Inc. is a manufacturer of high-tech industrial parts that was started in 1991 by two talented engineers with little business training. In 2003, the company was acquired by one of its major customers. As part of an internal audit, the following facts were discovered. The audit occurred during 2003 before any adjusting entries or closing entries were prepared. The income tax rate is 40% for all years.

a.   A five-year casualty insurance policy was purchased at the beginning of 2001 for $35,000. The full amount was debited to insurance expense at the time.

b.   Effective January 1, 2003, the company changed the salvage values used in calculating depreciation for its office building. The building cost $600,000 on December 29, 1992, and has been depreciated on a straight-line basis assuming a useful life of 40 years and a salvage value of $100,000. Declining real estate values in the area indicate that the salvage value will be no more than $25,000.

c.   On December 31, 2002, merchandise inventory was overstated by $25,000 due to a mistake in the physical inventory count using the periodic inventory system.

d.   The company changed inventory cost methods to FIFO from LIFO at the end of 2003 for both financial statement and income tax purposes. The change will cause a $960,000 increase in the beginning inventory at January 1, 2004.

e.   At the end of 2002, the company failed to accrue $15,500 of sales commissions earned by employees during 2002. The expense was recorded when the commissions were paid in early 2003.

f.   At the beginning of 2001, the company purchased a machine at a cost of $720,000. Its useful life was estimated to be ten years with no salvage value. The machine has been depreciated by the double-declining balance method. Its carrying amount on December 31, 2002, was $460,800. On January 1, 2003, the company changed retroactively to the straight-line method.

g.   Bad debt expense is determined each year as 1% of credit sales. Actual collection experience of recent years indicates that 0.75% is a better indication of uncollectible accounts. Management effects the change in 2003. Credit sales for 2003 are $4,000,000; in 2002 they were $3,700,000.

h.   Additional industrial robots were acquired at the beginning of 2000 and added to the company's assembly process. The $1,000,000 cost of the equipment was inadvertently recorded as repair expense. Robots have 10-year useful lives and no material salvage value. This class of equipment is depreciated by the straight-line method.

Required:

For each situation:

1.   Identify whether it represents an accounting change or an error. If an accounting change, identify the type of change.

2.   Prepare any journal entry necessary as a direct result of the change or error correction as well as any adjusting entry for 2003 related to the situation described. Any tax effects should be adjusted for through the deferred tax liability account.

3.   Briefly describe any other steps that should be taken to appropriately report the situation.

P 21–14

Errors; change in
estimate; change in
principle; restatement
of previous financial
statements

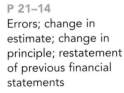

Whaley Distributors is a wholesale distributor of electronic components. Financial statements for the year ended December 31, 2002, reported the following amounts and subtotals ($ in millions):

	Assets	Liabilities	Shareholders' Equity	Net Income	Expenses
2001	$740	$330	$410	$210	$150
2002	820	400	420	230	175

In 2003 the following situations occurred or came to light:

a.   Internal auditors discovered that ending inventories reported on the financial statements the two previous years were misstated due to faulty internal controls. The errors were in the following amounts:

2001 inventory	overstated by $12 million
2002 inventory	understated by $10 million

b.   A liability was accrued in 2001 for a probable payment of $7 million in connection with a lawsuit ultimately settled in December 2003 for $4 million.

c.   A patent costing $18 million at the beginning of 2001, expected to benefit operations for a total of six years, has not been amortized since acquired.

d.   Whaley's conveyer equipment has been depreciated by the sum-of-the-years'-digits (SYD) basis since constructed at the beginning of 2001 at a cost of $30 million. It has an expected useful life of five years and no expected residual value. At the beginning of 2003, Whaley decided to switch to straight-line depreciation.

Required:

For each situation:

1.   Prepare any journal entry necessary as a direct result of the change or error correction as well as any adjusting entry for 2003 related to the situation described. (Ignore tax effects.)
2.   Determine the amounts to be reported for each of the five items shown above from the 2001 and 2002 financial statements when those amounts are reported again in the 2003, 2002, 2001 comparative financial statements.

P 21–15
Accounting changes; three situations

Problem 11–10 deals with three unrelated situations involving accounting changes related to operational assets.

P 21–16
Inventory errors

Problem 9–12 deals with inventory errors.

P 21–17
Correction of errors; six errors

Conrad Wholesale Supply underwent a restructuring in 2003. The company conducted a thorough internal audit, during which the following facts were discovered. The audit occurred during 2003 before any adjusting entries or closing entries are prepared.

a.   Additional computers were acquired at the beginning of 2001 and added to the company's office network. The $45,000 cost of the computers was inadvertently recorded as maintenance expense. Computers have five-year useful lives and no material salvage value. This class of equipment is depreciated by the straight-line method.
b.   Two weeks prior to the audit, the company paid $17,000 for assembly tools and recorded the expenditure as office supplies. The error was discovered a week later.
c.   On December 31, 2002, merchandise inventory was understated by $78,000 due to a mistake in the physical inventory count. The company uses the periodic inventory system.
d.   Two years earlier, the company recorded a 4% stock dividend (2,000 common shares, $1 par) as follows:

Retained earnings	2,000	
Common stock		2,000

The shares had a market price at the time of $12 per share.

e.   At the end of 2002, the company failed to accrue $104,000 of interest expense that accrued during the last four months of 2002 on bonds payable. The bonds which were issued at face value mature in 2007. The following entry was recorded on March 1, 2003, when the semiannual interest was paid:

Interest expense	156,000	
Cash		156,000

f.   A three-year liability insurance policy was purchased at the beginning of 2002 for $72,000. The full premium was debited to insurance expense at the time.

Required:

For each error, prepare any journal entry necessary to correct the error as well as any year-end adjusting entry for 2003 related to the situation described. (Ignore income taxes.)

BROADEN YOUR PERSPECTIVE

Apply your critical-thinking ability to the knowledge you've gained. These cases will provide you an opportunity to develop your research, analysis, judgment, and communication skills. You also will work with other students, integrate what you've learned, apply it in real world situations, and consider its global and ethical ramifications. This practice will broaden your knowledge and further develop your decision-making abilities.

Judgment Case 21–1
Accounting changes;
independent situations

Sometimes a business entity will change its method of accounting for certain items. The change may be classified as a change in accounting principle, a change in accounting estimate, or a change in reporting entity.

Listed below are three independent, unrelated sets of facts relating to accounting changes.

Situation I: A company determined that the depreciable lives of its fixed assets are presently too long to fairly match the cost of the fixed assets with the revenue produced. The company decided at the beginning of the current year to reduce the depreciable lives of all of its existing fixed assets by five years.

Situation II: On December 31, 2002, Gary Company owned 51% of Allen Company, at which time Gary reported its investment on a nonconsolidated basis due to political uncertainties in the country in which Allen was located. On January 2, 2003, the management of Gary Company was satisfied that the political uncertainties were resolved and the assets of the company were in no danger of nationalization. Accordingly, Gary will prepare consolidated financial statements for Gary and Allen for the year ended December 31, 2003.

Situation III: A company decides in January 2003 to adopt the straight-line method of depreciation for plant equipment. The straight-line method will be used for new acquisitions as well as for previously acquired plant equipment for which depreciation had been provided on an accelerated basis.

Required:
For each of the situations described above, provide the information indicated below. Complete your discussion of each situation before going on to the next situation.
1. Type of accounting change.
2. Manner of reporting the change under current generally accepted accounting principles including a discussion, where applicable, of how amounts are computed.
3. Effect of the change on the balance sheet and income statement.
4. Footnote disclosures that would be necessary.

Analysis Case 21–2
Various changes

DRS Corporation changed the way it depreciates its computers from the sum-of-the-year's-digits method to the straight-line method beginning January 1, 2003, DRS also changed its estimated residual value used in computing depreciation for its office building. At the end of 2003, DRS changed the specific subsidiaries constituting the group of companies for which its consolidated financial statements are prepared.

Required:
1. For each accounting change DRS undertook, indicate the type of change and how DRS should report the change. Be specific.
2. Why should companies disclose changes in accounting principles?

Analysis Case 21–3
Various changes

Ray Solutions decided to make the following changes in its accounting policies on January 1, 2003:
a. Changed from the cash to the accrual basis of accounting for recognizing revenue on its service contracts.
b. Adopted straight-line depreciation for all future equipment purchases, but continued to use accelerated depreciation for all equipment acquired before 2003.
c. Changed from the LIFO inventory method to the FIFO inventory method.

Required:
For each accounting change Ray undertook, indicate the type of change and how Ray should report the change. Be specific.

Integrating Case 21–4
Change to dollar-value
LIFO

Webster Products, Inc. adopted the dollar-value LIFO method of determining inventory costs for financial and income tax reporting on January 1, 2003. Webster continues to use the FIFO method for internal decision-making purposes. Webster's FIFO inventories at December 31, 2003, 2004, and 2005, were $300,000, $412,500, and $585,000, respectively. Internally generated cost indexes are used to convert FIFO inventory amounts to dollar-value LIFO amounts. Webster estimated these indexes as follows:

2003	1.00
2004	1.25
2005	1.50

Required:
1. Determine Webster's dollar-value LIFO inventory at December 31, 2004 and 2005.
2. Describe how the change should have been reported in Webster's 2003 financial statements.

Communication Case 21–5
Change in loss contingency; write a memo

Late in 2003, you and two other officers of Curbo Fabrications Corporation just returned from a meeting with officials of The City of Jackson. The meeting was unexpectedly favorable even though it culminated in a settlement with city authorities that your company pay a total of $475,000 to cover the cost of violations of city construction codes. Jackson had filed suit in November 2001 against Curbo Fabrications Corporation, seeking civil penalties and injunctive relief for violations of city construction codes regulating earthquake damage standards. Alleged violations involved several construction projects completed during the previous three years. When the financial statements were issued in 2002, Curbo had not reached a settlement with state authorities, but legal counsel had advised the company that it was probable the ultimate settlement would be $750,000 in penalties. The following entry had been recorded:

Loss—litigation	750,000	
Liability—litigation		750,000

The final settlement, therefore, was a pleasant surprise. While returning from the meeting, conversation turned to reporting the settlement in the 2003 financial statements. You drew the short straw and were selected to write a memo to Janet Zeno, the financial vice president, advising the proper course of action.

Required:
Write the memo. Include descriptions of any journal entries related to the change in amounts. Briefly describe other steps Curbo should take to report the settlement.

Analysis Case 21–6
Two wrongs make a right?

Early one Wednesday afternoon, Ken and Larry studied in the dormitory room they shared at Fogelman College. Ken, an accounting major, was advising Larry, a management major, regarding a project for Larry's Business Policy class. One aspect of the project involved analyzing the 2002 annual report of Craft Paper Company. Though not central to his business policy case, a footnote had caught Larry's attention.

Depreciation and Cost of Timber Harvested (in part)
($ in millions)

	2002	2001	2000
Depreciation of buildings, machinery and equipment	$260.9	$329.8	$322.5
Cost of timber harvested and amortization of logging roads	4.9	4.9	4.9
	$265.8	$334.7	$327.4

Beginning in 2002, the Company revised the estimated average useful lives used to compute depreciation for most of its pulp and paper mill equipment from 16 years to 20 years and for most of its finishing and converting equipment from 12 years to 15 years. These revisions were made to more properly reflect the true economic lives of the assets and to better align the Company's depreciable lives with the predominant practice in the industry. The change had the effect of increasing net income by approximately $55 million.

"If I understand this right, Ken, the company is not going back and recalculating a lower depreciation for earlier years. Instead they seem to be leaving depreciation overstated in earlier years and making up for that by understating it in current and future years," Larry mused. "Is that the way it is in accounting? Two wrongs make a right?"

Required:
What are the two wrongs to which Larry refers? Is he right?

Ethics Case 21–7
Softening the blow

Late one Thursday afternoon, Joy Martin, a veteran audit manager with a regional CPA firm, was reviewing documents for a long-time client of the firm, AMT Transport. The year-end audit was scheduled to begin Monday.

For three months, the economy had been in a down cycle and the transportation industry was particularly hard hit. As a result, Joy expected AMT's financial results would not be pleasant news to shareholders. However, what Joy saw in the preliminary statements made her sigh aloud. Results were much worse than she feared.

"Larry (the company president) already is in the doghouse with shareholders," Joy thought to herself. "When they see these numbers, they'll hang him out to dry."

"I wonder if he's considered some strategic accounting changes," she thought, after reflecting on the situation. "The bad news could be softened quite a bit by changing inventory methods from LIFO to FIFO or reconsidering some of the estimates used in other areas."

Required:
1. How would the actions contemplated contribute toward "softening" the bad news?
2. Do you perceive an ethical dilemma? What would be the likely impact of following up on Joy's thoughts? Who would benefit? Who would be injured?

Integrating Case 21–8
Error; a change in principle; change in estimate; operational assets; inventories

Case 11–7 deals with the correction of an error, a change in principle, and a change in estimate related to operational assets and inventories.

Analysis Case 21–9
Change in inventory costing methods

Case 9–6 deals with a change in inventory costing methods.

Real World Case 21–10
Change in inventory costing methods

Case 9–7 deals with a change in inventory costing methods.

Real World Case 21–11
Change in inventory costing methods

Case 9–8 deals with a change in inventory costing methods.

Judgment Case 21–12
Inventory errors

Case 9–10 deals with inventory errors.

Ethics Case 21–13
Inventory errors

Case 9–11 deals with an ethical dilemma involving inventory errors.

Judgment Case 21–14
Asset impairment

Case 11–8 deals with accounting changes.

Research Case 21–15
Researching the way changes in postretirement benefit estimates are reported; retrieving disclosures from the Internet

It's financial statements preparation time at Center Industries where you have been assistant controller for two months. Ben Huddler, the controller, seems to be pleasant but unpredictable. Today, although your schedule is filled with meetings with internal and outside auditors and two members of the board of directors, Ben made a request. "As you know, we're decreasing the rate at which we assume health care costs will rise when measuring our postretirement benefit obligation. I'd like to know how others have reported similar changes. Can you find me an example?" he asked. "I'd bet you could get one off the Internet you're always using." As a matter of fact, you often use EDGAR, the Electronic Data Gathering, Analysis, and Retrieval system (www.sec.gov) to access financial statements filed with the U.S. Securities and Exchange Commission (SEC).

Required:
1. Access EDGAR on the Internet. You might want to use one of the EDGAR retrieval sites listed at the course website. Access a recent 10-K filing of a firm you think might have a postretirement health care plan. You may need to look up several companies before you find what you're looking for. Older, established companies are most likely to have such benefit plans.
   (Note: You may be able to focus your search by searching with key words and phrases in one of the several "search engines" available on the Internet.)
2. Copy the portion of the disclosures that reports the effect of a change in health care cost trends.
3. What information is provided about the effect of the change on the company's estimated benefit obligation?

22

The Statement of Cash Flows Revisited

CHAPTER

OVERVIEW

The objective of financial reporting is to provide investors and creditors with useful information, primarily in the form of financial statements. The balance sheet and the income statement—the focus of your study in earlier chapters—do not provide all the information needed by these decision makers. Here you will learn how the statement of cash flows fills the information gap left by the other financial statements.

The statement lists all cash inflows and cash outflows, and classifies them as cash flows from (a) operating, (b) investing, or (c) financing activities. Investing and financing activities that do not directly affect cash also are reported.

LEARNING OBJECTIVES

After studying this chapter, you should be able to:

LO1 Explain the usefulness of cash flow information.

LO2 Describe the purpose of the statement of cash flows.

LO3 Relate the statement of cash flows to its historical evolution.

LO4 Define cash equivalents.

LO5 Distinguish among operating activities, investing activities, and financing activities.

LO6 Identify transactions that represent noncash investing and financing activities.

LO7 Prepare a statement of cash flows with the aid of a spreadsheet.

LO8 Reconcile net income to net cash flows from operating activities (the indirect method).

FINANCIAL REPORTING CASE

Where's the Cash?

"What do you mean you can't afford a wage increase?" union negotiator Vince Barr insisted. "We've all seen your income statement. You had record earnings this year."

This is the first day of negotiations with the company's union representatives. As company controller, you know it's going to be up to you to explain the company's position on the financial aspects of the negotiations. In fact, you've known for some time that a critical point of contention would be the moderate increase in this year's profits after three years of level or slightly declining earnings. Not helping the situation is that the company has always used accelerated depreciation on its equipment which it began replacing this year at considerably higher prices than it cost several years back.

> By the time you finish this chapter, you should be able to respond appropriately to the questions posed in this case. Compare your response to the solution provided at the end of the chapter.

QUESTIONS

1. What are the cash flow aspects of the situation that Mr. Barr may be overlooking in making his case for a wage increase? How can a company's operations generate a healthy profit and yet produce meager or even negative cash flows? (page 1083)

2. What information can a statement of cash flows provide about a company's investing activities that can be useful in decisions such as this? (page 1085)

3. What information can a statement of cash flows provide about a company's financing activities that can be useful in decisions such as this? (page 1086)

THE CONTENT AND VALUE OF THE STATEMENT OF CASH FLOWS

PART

LO1

Investors and creditors require cash flows from the corporation.

Cash flows to investors and creditors depend on the corporation generating cash flows to itself.

DECISION MAKERS' PERSPECTIVE—Usefulness of Cash Flow Information

A fund manager of a major insurance company, considering investing $8,000,000 in the common stock of The Coca-Cola Company, asks herself: "What are the prospects of future dividends and market-price appreciation? Will we get a return commensurate with the cost and risk of our investment?" A bank officer, examining an application for a business loan, asks himself: "If I approve this loan, what is the likelihood of the borrower making interest payments on time and repaying the loan when due?" Investors and creditors continually face these and similar decisions that require projections of the relative ability of a business to generate future cash flows and of the risk associated with those forecasts.

To make these projections, decision makers rely heavily on the information reported in periodic financial statements. In the final analysis, cash flows into and out of a business enterprise are the most fundamental events on which investors and creditors base their decisions. Naturally, these decisions focus on the prospects of the decision makers receiving cash returns from their dealings with the firm. However, it is the ability of the firm to generate cash flows to itself that ultimately determines the potential for cash flows from the firm to investors and creditors.

The financial statements that have been the focus of your study in earlier chapters—the income statement and the balance sheet—offer information helpful in forecasting future cash-generating ability. Some important questions, however, are not easily answered from the information these statements provide. For example, meaningful projections of a company's future profitability and risk depend on answers to such questions as:

Many decisions benefit from information about the company's underlying cash flow process.

- In what types of activities is the company investing?
- Are these activities being financed with debt? with equity? by cash generated from operations?
- Are facilities being acquired to accommodate future expansion?
- How does the amount of cash generated from operations compare with net income over time?
- Why isn't the increase in retained earnings reflected as an increase in dividends?
- What happens to the cash received from the sale of assets?
- By what means is debt being retired?

The information needed to answer these and similar questions is found in the continuous series of cash flows that the income statement and the balance sheet describe only indirectly. This underlying cash flow process is considered next. ■

Cash Inflows and Outflows

Cash continuously flows into and out of an active business. Businesses disburse cash to acquire operational assets to maintain or expand productive capacity. When no longer needed, these assets may be sold for cash. Cash is paid to produce or purchase inventory for resale, as well as to pay for the expenses of selling these goods. The ultimate outcome of these selling activities is an inflow of cash. Cash might be invested in securities of other firms. These investments provide cash inflows during the investment period in the form of dividends or interest and at the end of the investment period when the securities are sold. To raise cash to finance their operations, firms sell stock and/or acquire debt. Cash payments are made as dividends to shareholders and interest to creditors. When debt is repaid or stock repurchased, cash flows out of the firm. To help you visualize the continual process of cash receipts and cash payments, that process is diagrammed in Graphic 22–1. The diagram also previews the way we will later classify the cash flows on a statement of cash flows.

Embodied in this assortment of cash flows is a wealth of information that investors and creditors require to make educated decisions. Much of the value of the underlying

GRAPHIC 22–1
Cash Inflows and Cash
Outflows

CASH INFLOWS

Operating Activities	Investing Activities	Financing Activities
Cash received from revenues	Sale of operational assets Sale of investments in securities Collections of loans	Issuance of stock Issuance of bonds and notes

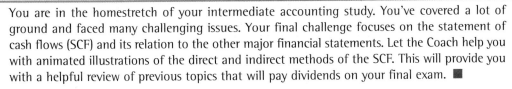

Business

Cash paid for expenses	Purchase of operational assets Purchase of investments in securities Loans to others	Payment of cash dividends Repurchase of stock Repayment of debt

CASH OUTFLOWS

information provided by the cash flows is lost when reported only indirectly by the balance sheet and the income statement. Each cash flow eventually impacts decision makers by affecting the balances of various accounts on the balance sheet. Also, many of the cash flows—those related to income-producing activities—are represented on the income statement. However, they are not necessarily reported in the period the cash flows occur because the income statement measures activities on an accrual basis. The statement of cash flows fills the information gap by reporting the cash flows directly.

CHECK WITH THE **COACH**

You are in the homestretch of your intermediate accounting study. You've covered a lot of ground and faced many challenging issues. Your final challenge focuses on the statement of cash flows (SCF) and its relation to the other major financial statements. Let the Coach help you with animated illustrations of the direct and indirect methods of the SCF. This will provide you with a helpful review of previous topics that will pay dividends on your final exam. ■

Role of the Statement of Cash Flows

A statement of cash flows is shown in Graphic 22–2 on the next page. The statement lists all cash inflows and cash outflows during the reporting period. To enhance the informational value of the presentation, the cash flows are classified according to the nature of the activities that bring about the cash flows. The three primary categories of cash flows are (1) cash flows from operating activities, (2) cash flows from investing activities, and (3) cash flows from financing activities. Classifying each cash flow by source (operating, investing, or financing activities) is more informative than simply listing the various cash flows. Notice, too, that the noncash investing and financing activities—investing and financing activities that do not directly increase or decrease cash—also are reported. *FASB Statement 95*, requiring the statement of cash flows, was issued in direct response to *FASB Concept Statement 1*, which states that the primary objective of financial reporting is to "provide information to help investors and creditors, and others assess the amounts, timing, and uncertainty of prospective net cash inflows to the related enterprise."[1]

 LO2

The statement of cash flows provides information about cash flows that is lost when reported only indirectly by the balance sheet and the income statement.

---

[1]"Objectives of Financial Reporting by Business Enterprises," *FASB Statement of Financial Accounting Concepts* No. 1, par. 37.

GRAPHIC 22–2
Statement of Cash
Flows

UNITED BRANDS CORPORATION
Statement of Cash Flows
For Year Ended December 31, 2003
($ in millions)

Cash Flows from Operating Activities

Cash inflows:

From customers	$98	
From investment revenue	3	

Cash outflows:

To suppliers of goods	(50)	*Cash paid*
To employees	(11)	
For interest	(3)	
For insurance	(4)	
For income taxes	(11)	
Net cash flows from operating activities		$22

Cash Flows from Investing Activities

Purchase of land	(30)	
Purchase of short-term investment	(12)	
Sale of land	18	
Sale of equipment	5	
Net cash flows from investing activities		(19)

Cash Flows from Financing Activities

Sale of common shares	26	
Retirement of bonds payable	(15)	
Payment of cash dividends	(5)	
Net cash flows from financing activities		6
Net increase in cash		9
Cash balance, January 1		20
Cash balance, December 31		$29

- -

Note X:

Noncash Investing and Financing Activities

Acquired $20 million of equipment by issuing a 12%, 5-year note.	$20

Reconciliation of Net Income to Cash Flows from Operating Activities:

Net income	$12
Adjustments for noncash effects:	
Gain on sale of land	(8)
Depreciation expense	3
Loss on sale of equipment	2
Changes in operating assets and liabilities:	
Increase in accounts receivable	(2)
Decrease in inventory	4
Increase in accounts payable	6
Increase in salaries payable	2
Discount on bonds payable	2
Decrease in prepaid insurance	3
Decrease in income tax payable	(2)
Net cash flows from operating activities	$22

Many companies have experienced bankruptcy because they were unable to generate sufficient cash to satisfy their obligations. Doubtless, many investors in the stock of these firms would have been spared substantial losses if the financial statements had been designed to foresee the cash flow problems the companies were experiencing. A prominent illustration is the demise of W. T. Grant during the 1970s. Grant, a general retailer in the days before malls, was a blue chip stock of its time. Grant's statement of changes in financial position (the predecessor of the statement of cash flows) reported working capital from operations of $46 million in 1972. Yet, if presented, a statement of cash flows would have reported cash flows from operating activities of negative $10 million. In fact, the unreported cash flow deficiency grew to $114 million in 1973, while working capital from operations was reported as having increased by $1 million. That year, without the benefit of cash flow information, investors were buying Grant's stock at prices that represented up to 20 times its earnings.[2]

More recently, even with cash flow information available, cash flow problems can go unnoticed. An example is the rapid growth and subsequent bankruptcy of the Wicks 'N' Sticks franchise. The company's drive for rapid growth led to a dependence on the sale of new franchises in order to generate cash flow instead of doing so in a more healthy way through its operations. As we see shortly, a statement of cash flows can indicate not just the amount of cash flows, but also whether those cash flows are coming from operations or from outside sources. Wicks 'N' Sticks was able to emerge from bankruptcy through restructuring and a new perspective on cash flow management.

The statement of cash flows for United Brands Corporation (UBC), shown in Graphic 22–2, is intended at this point in the discussion to illustrate the basic structure and composition of the statement. Later we will see how the statement of cash flows for UBC is prepared from the information typically available for this purpose. We will refer to UBC's statement of cash flows frequently throughout the chapter as the discussion becomes more specific regarding the criteria for classifying cash flows in the three primary categories and as we identify the specific cash flows to be reported on the statement. We will examine the content of the statement in more detail following a look at how this relatively recent financial statement has evolved to its present form over the course of the last several decades.

Evolution of the Statement of Cash Flows

In light of the obvious value of cash flow information, it's interesting to note that the statement of cash flows has been a required financial statement only since 1988. The relatively recent requirement completes a full-cycle movement of accounting thought back to cash flow reporting, which, in different form, was common practice several decades ago.

During the early part of this century and continuing into the mid-1930s, the preparation of financial statements on a cash basis was a widely used means of financial reporting, particularly by small and medium-sized companies. It is important to realize, however, that the cash flow reporting requirements of today are quite different from the cash flow reporting practiced during that earlier era, when emphasis was placed on cash-based income determination. The accounting profession was fully aware that accrual accounting (recognizing revenues when earned, expenses when incurred) provides a far better measure of a company's profitability. However, without official standards to ensure the general use of accrual accounting, cash-based reporting flourished. Motivated by the desire to instill the standard of accrual accounting, a concerted effort was exerted to suppress cash-based methods.

Early efforts to instill the standard of accrual accounting intentionally suppressed the widespread practice of cash flow reporting.

As cash-flow reporting abated, the need for some type of funds-flow reporting became apparent and a funds statement began to appear in the annual reports of many companies. Because the statement was not required and there was no officially prescribed format, the definition and presentation of funds varied widely among firms that issued the statement. The mounting bias against cash-based reporting certainly influenced many firms to choose alternate definitions of funds.

Prompted by increasing concerns over the lack of uniformity in the reporting of funds flow, the AICPA sponsored a 1961 research study by Perry Mason (the accountant, not the lawyer) entitled "Cash Flow Analysis and the Funds Statement." The study recommended that a funds statement be required.[3] Two years later, *APB Opinion 3* officially recommended, but did not

Early official recommendations confessed a noncash bias.

---

[2]Cheryl A. Zega, "The New Statement of Cash Flows," *Management Accounting,* September 1988.
[3]Perry Mason, "Cash Flow Analysis and the Funds Statement," *Accounting Research Study No. 2,* 1961.

require, a "Statement of Source and Application of Funds."[4] The noncash bias was evident in this opinion. It cautioned against the use of terms such as cash flow and cash earnings and defined funds generally as working capital (current assets minus current liabilities).

The first official requirement that a funds statement be included as an integral part of a complete set of financial statements was issued in 1971. *APB Opinion 19* required a statement of changes in financial position that reported funds flows classified as either sources (increases) or applications (decreases) of funds, as well as any significant nonfund investing and financing activities. Funds could be defined as either cash or working capital.[5] Although defining funds as cash was permitted, a working capital definition predominated practice until the early 1980s. This preference was influenced by the historical bias, described earlier, against cash flow reporting.

> **The statement of changes in financial position was the predecessor to the statement of cash flows.**

Financial Executives International recommended that its members report on a cash basis after being persuaded by many accounting professors and practitioners that a cash-based definition of funds is more meaningful than a working capital definition.[6] This recommendation provided the impetus for a dramatic increase in the number of firms choosing to define funds as cash in their statements of changes in financial position.[7]

The increasingly widespread acceptance of cash-flow reporting, coupled with a recommendation in 1984 of *FASB Concept Statement 5* that a full set of financial statements show cash flows during the period, virtually assured the eventual requirement of a statement of cash flows.[8] In November 1987 the FASB prescribed *SFAS 95* (to supersede *APB Opinion 19*), described in this chapter.

CASH AND CASH EQUIVALENTS

Skilled cash managers will invest temporarily idle cash in short-term investments to earn interest on those funds, rather than maintain an unnecessarily large balance in a checking account. The FASB views short-term, highly liquid investments that can be readily converted to cash, with little risk of loss, as **cash equivalents.** Amounts held as investments of this type are essentially equivalent to cash because they are quickly available for use as cash. Therefore, on the statement of cash flows there is no differentiation between amounts held as cash (e.g., currency and checking accounts) and amounts held in cash equivalent investments. So, when we refer in this chapter to cash, we are referring to the total of cash and cash equivalents.

> **There is no differentiation between amounts held as cash and amounts held in cash equivalent investments.**
>
> **Each firm's policy regarding which short-term, highly liquid investments it classifies as cash equivalents should be disclosed in the notes to the financial statements.**

Examples of cash equivalents are money market funds, treasury bills, and commercial paper. To be classified as cash equivalents, these investments must have a maturity date not longer than three months from the date of purchase. Flexibility is permitted in designating cash equivalents. Each company must establish a policy regarding which short-term, highly liquid investments it classifies as cash equivalents. The policy should be consistent with the company's customary motivation for acquiring various investments and should be disclosed in the notes to the statement.[9] A recent annual report of ExxonMobil Corporation provides this description of its cash equivalents (Graphic 22–3):

GRAPHIC 22–3
Disclosure of Cash Equivalents— ExxonMobil Corporation

> **Note 4: Cash Flow Information (in part)**
> The consolidated statement of cash flows provides information about changes in cash and cash equivalents. All short-term marketable securities, generally with original maturities of three months or less, that are readily convertible to known amounts of cash and are so near maturity that they present insignificant risk of changes in value because of changes in interest rates, are classified as cash equivalents.

---

[4]"The Statement of Source and Application of Funds," *Opinions of the Accounting Principles Board No. 3,* 1963, par. 8.
[5]"Reporting Changes in Financial Position," *Opinions of the Accounting Principles Board No. 19,* 1971.
[6]See, for example, Lloyd C. Heath, "Let's Scrap the Funds Statement," *The Journal of Accountancy,* October 1978, and Edward Swanson and Richard Vandermeersch, "Statement of Financing and Investing Activities," *The CPA Journal,* November 1981.
[7]Allen H. Seed, III, *The Funds Statement—Structure and Use,* Financial Executives Research Foundation, 1984.
[8]"Recognition and Measurement in Financial Statements of Business Enterprises," *FASB Statement of Financial Accounting Concepts No. 5,* par. 13.
[9]A change in that policy is treated as a change in accounting principle.

Transactions that involve merely transfers from cash to cash equivalents (such as the purchase of a three-month treasury bill), or from cash equivalents to cash (such as the sale of a treasury bill), should not be reported on the statement of cash flows. The total of cash and cash equivalents is not altered by such transactions.[10] The cash balance reported on the balance sheet also represents the total of cash and cash equivalents, which allows us to compare the change in that balance with the net increase or decrease in the cash flows reported on the statement of cash flows.

PRIMARY ELEMENTS OF THE STATEMENT OF CASH FLOWS

This section describes the three primary activity classifications: (1) operating activities, (2) investing activities, and (3) financing activities; and two other requirements of the statement of cash flows: (4) the reconciliation of the net increase or decrease in cash with the change in the balance of the cash account and (5) noncash investing and financing activities.

Cash Flows from Operating Activities.   The income statement reports the success of a business in generating a profit from its operations. Net income (or loss) is the result of netting together the revenues earned during the reporting period, regardless of when cash is received, and the expenses incurred in generating those revenues, regardless of when cash is paid. This is the accrual concept of accounting that has been emphasized throughout your study of accounting. Information about net income and its components, measured by the accrual concept, generally provides a better indication of current operating performance than does information about current cash receipts and payments.[11] Nevertheless, as indicated earlier, the cash effects of earning activities also provide useful information that is not directly accessible from the income statement. The first cash flow classification in the statement of cash flows reports that information.

Cash flows from operating activities are both inflows and outflows of cash that result from activities reported on the income statement. In other words, this classification of cash flows includes the elements of net income, but reported on a cash basis. The components of this section of the statement of cash flows, and their relationship with the elements of the income statement, are illustrated in Graphic 22–4.

LO5

FINANCIAL REPORTING CASE
Q1, p. 1077

The cash effects of the elements of net income are reported as cash flows from operating activities.

Income Statement	Cash Flows from Operating Activities
Revenues:	Cash inflows:
Sales and service revenue	Cash received from customers
Investment revenue	Cash revenue received (e.g., dividends, interest)
Noncash revenues and gains (e.g., gain on sale of assets)	(Not reported)
Less: Expenses:	Less: Cash outflows:
Cost of goods sold	Cash paid to suppliers of inventory
Salaries expense	Cash paid to employees
Noncash expenses and losses (e.g., depreciation, amortization, bad debts, loss on sale of assets)	(Not reported)
Interest expense	Cash paid to creditors
Other operating expenses	Cash paid to insurance companies and others
Income tax expense	Cash paid to the government
Net income	*Net cash flows from operating activities*

GRAPHIC 22–4
Relationship between the Income Statement and Cash Flows from Operating Activities (Direct Method)

---

[10]An exception is the sale of a cash equivalent at a gain or loss. This exception is described in more detail later in the chapter.
[11]*FASB Statement of Financial Accounting Concepts No. 1,* par. 44.

To see the concept applied, let's look again at the cash flows from operating activities reported by National Brands Corporation. That section of the statement of cash flows is extracted from Graphic 22–2 and reproduced in Graphic 22–5.

Cash Flows from Operating Activities:

Cash inflows:	
From customers	$98
From investment revenue	3
Cash outflows:	
To suppliers of goods	(50)
To employees	(11)
For interest	(3)
For insurance	(4)
For income taxes	(11)
Net cash flows from operating activities	$22

Cash inflows from operating activities exceeded cash outflows for expenses by $22 million. We'll see later (in Illustration 22–1) that UBC's net income from the same operating activities was only $12 million. Why did operating activities produce net cash inflows greater than net income? The reason will become apparent when we determine, in a later section, the specific amounts of these cash flows.

You also should be aware that the generalization stated earlier that cash flows from operating activities include the elements of net income reported on a cash basis is not strictly true for all elements of the income statement. Notice in Graphic 22–5 that no cash effects are reported for depreciation and amortization of operational assets, nor for gains and losses from the sale of those assets. Cash outflows occur when operational assets are acquired, and cash inflows occur when the assets are sold. However, as described later, the acquisition and subsequent resale of operational assets are classified as investing activities, rather than as operating activities.

Quite the opposite, the purchase and the sale of inventory are considered operating activities. The cash effects of these transactions—namely, (1) cash payments to suppliers and (2) cash receipts from customers—are included in the determination of cash flows from operating activities. Why are inventories and operational assets treated differently when classifying their cash effects if both are acquired for the purpose of producing revenues? The essential difference is that inventory typically is purchased for the purpose of being sold as part of the firm's current operations, while an operational asset is purchased as an investment to benefit the business over a relatively long period of time.

Direct Method or Indirect Method of Reporting Cash Flows from Operating Activities. The presentation by UBC of cash flows from operating activities illustrated in Graphic 22–2 and reproduced in Graphic 22–5 above is referred to as the *direct method*. The method is named for the fact that the cash effect of each operating activity (i.e., income statement item) is reported *directly* on the statement of cash flows. For instance, UBC reports "cash received from customers" as the cash effect of sales activities, "cash paid to suppliers" as the cash effect of cost of goods sold, and so on. Then, UBC simply omits from the presentation any income statement items that do not affect cash at all, such as depreciation expense.

Another way UBC might have reported cash flows from operating activities is by the *indirect method*. By this approach, the net cash increase or decrease from operating activities ($22 million in our example) would be derived *indirectly* by starting with reported net income and working backwards to convert that amount to a cash basis. As we see later in the chapter, UBC's net income is $12 million. Using the indirect method, UBC would replace the previous presentation of net cash flows from operating activities with the one shown in Graphic 22–6.

GRAPHIC 22–6
Indirect Method

Cash Flows from Operating Activities:		
Net income		$12
Adjustments for noncash effects:		
Gain on sale of land	(8)	
Depreciation expense	3	
Loss on sale of equipment	2	
Changes in operating assets and liabilities:		
Increase in accounts receivable	(2)	
Decrease in inventory	4	
Increase in accounts payable	6	
Increase in salaries payable	2	
Discount on bonds payable	2	
Decrease in prepaid insurance	3	
Decrease in income tax payable	(2)	
Net cash flows from operating activities		$22

By the indirect method, UBC derives the net cash increase or decrease from operating activities *indirectly*, by starting with reported net income and working backwards to convert that amount to a cash basis.

Be sure to note that the indirect method generates the same $22 million net cash flows from operating activities as did the direct method. Rather than directly reporting only the components of the income statement that *do* represent increases or decreases in cash, by the indirect method we begin with net income—which includes both cash and noncash components—and back out all amounts that *don't* reflect increases or decreases in cash. Later in the chapter, we explore the specific adjustments made to net income to achieve this result. At this point it is sufficient to realize that two alternative methods are permitted for reporting net cash flows from operating activities. Either way, we convert accrual-based income to cash flows produced by those same operating activities.

Notice also that the indirect method presentation is identical to what UBC reported earlier as the "Reconciliation of Net Income to Cash Flows from Operating Activities" in Note X of Graphic 22–2. Whether cash flows from operating activities are reported by the direct method or by the indirect method, the financial statements must reconcile the difference between net income and cash flows from operating activities. When a company uses the *direct method*, the company presents the reconciliation in a separate schedule as UBC did. That presentation is precisely the same as the presentation of net cash flows from operating activities by the indirect method. On the other hand, a company choosing to use the indirect method is not required to provide a separate reconciliation schedule because the "cash flows from operating activities" section of the statement of cash flows serves that purpose.[12]

It's important to understand, too, that regardless of which method a company chooses to report *operating* activities, that choice has no effect on the way it identifies and reports cash flows from *investing* and *financing* activities. We turn our attention now to those two sections of the statement of cash flows. Later in Part c, we'll return for a more thorough discussion of the alternative methods of reporting the operating activities section.

Cash Flows from Investing Activities.   Companies periodically invest cash to replace or expand productive facilities such as property, plant, and equipment. Investments might also be made in other assets, such as securities of other firms, with the expectation of a return on those investments. Information concerning these investing activities can provide valuable insight to decision makers regarding the nature and magnitude of operational assets being acquired for future use, as well as provide clues concerning the company's ambitions for the future.

FINANCIAL REPORTING CASE

Q2, p. 1077

---

[12]According to the *AICPA, Accounting Trends and Techniques*, 2001, a recent survey of 600 companies showed that 593 companies chose to use the indirect method, only 7 the direct method.

Cash outflows and cash inflows due to the acquisition and disposition of assets (other than inventory and assets classified as cash equivalents) are reported as cash flows from investing activities.

Cash flows from investing activities are both outflows and inflows of cash caused by the acquisition and disposition of assets. Included in this classification are cash payments to acquire (1) property, plant, and equipment and other productive assets (except inventories), (2) investments in securities (except cash equivalents and trading securities[13]), and (3) nontrade receivables.[14] When these assets later are liquidated, any cash receipts from their disposition also are classified as investing activities. For instance, cash received from the sale of the assets or from the collection of a note receivable (principal amount only) represents cash inflows from investing activities. Be sure to realize that, unlike the label might imply, any investment revenue like interest, dividends, or other cash return from these investments is not an investing activity. The reason, remember, is that investment revenue is an income statement item and therefore is an operating activity.

For illustration, notice the cash flows reported as investing activities by UBC. That section of the statement of cash flows is extracted from Graphic 22–2 and reproduced in Graphic 22–7.

GRAPHIC 22–7
Cash Flows from Investing Activities

Cash flows from investing activities include investments in assets and their subsequent sale.

Cash Flows from Investing Activities:		
Purchase of land	(30)	
Purchase of short-term investment	(12)	
Sale of land	18	
Sale of equipment	5	
Net cash flows from investing activities		(19)

UBC reports as investing activities the cash paid to purchase both land and a short-term investment. The other two investing activities reported are cash receipts for the sale of assets—equipment and land—that were acquired in earlier years. The specific transactions creating these cash flows are described in a later section of this chapter.

The purchase and sale of inventories are not considered investing activities. Inventories are purchased for the purpose of being sold as part of the firm's primary operations, so their purchase and sale are classified as operating activities.

Also, the purchase and sale of assets classified as cash equivalents are not reported as investing activities. In fact, these activities usually are not reported on the statement of cash flows. For example, when temporarily idle cash is invested in a money market fund considered to be a cash equivalent, the total of cash and cash equivalents does not change. Likewise, when the cash is later withdrawn from the money market fund, the total remains unchanged. The exception is when cash equivalents are sold at a gain or a loss. In that case, the total of cash and cash equivalents actually increases or decreases in the process of transferring from one cash equivalent account to another cash equivalent account. As a result, the change in cash would be reported as a cash flow from operating activities. This is illustrated later in the chapter.

FINANCIAL REPORTING CASE
Q3, p. 1077

Cash Flows from Financing Activities. Not only is it important for investors and creditors to be informed about how a company is investing its funds, but also how its investing activities are being financed. Hopefully, the primary operations of the firm provide a source of internal financing. Information revealed in the cash flows from operating activities section of the statement of cash flows lets statement users know the extent of available internal fi-

---

[13]Inflows and outflows of cash from buying and selling trading securities typically are considered operating activities because financial institutions that routinely transact in trading securities consider them an appropriate part of their normal operations.
[14]A nontrade receivable differs from a trade receivable in that it is not one associated with the company's normal trade; that is, it's not received from a customer. A trade receivable, or accounts receivable, is an *operating asset*. A nontrade receivable, on the other hand, might be a loan to an affiliate company or to an officer of the firm. To understand how the creation of a nontrade receivable is an *investing* activity, you might view such a loan as an investment in the receivable.

nancing. However, a major portion of financing for many companies is provided by external sources, specifically by shareholders and creditors.

Cash flows from financing activities are both inflows and outflows of cash resulting from the external financing of a business. We include in this classification cash inflows from (a) the sale of common and preferred stock and (b) the issuance of bonds and other debt securities. Subsequent transactions related to these financing transactions, such as a buyback of stock (to retire the stock or as treasury stock), the repayment of debt, and the payment of cash dividends to shareholders, also are classified as financing activities.

For illustration, refer to Graphic 22–8 excerpted from Graphic 22–2.

Cash inflows and cash outflows due to the external financing of a business are reported as cash flows from financing activities.

Cash Flows from Financing Activities		
Sale of common shares	26	
Retirement of bonds payable	(15)	
Payment of cash dividends	(5)	
Net cash flows from financing activities		6

GRAPHIC 22–8
Cash Flows from Financing Activities

Cash flows from financing activities include the sale or repurchase of shares, the issuance or repayment of debt securities, and the payment of cash dividends.

The cash received from the sale of common stock is reported as a financing activity. Since the sale of common stock is a financing activity, providing a cash return (dividend) to common shareholders also is a financing activity. Similarly, when the bonds being retired were sold in a prior year, that cash inflow was reported as a financing activity. In the current year, when the bonds are retired, the resulting cash outflow is likewise classified as a financing activity.

At first glance, it may appear inconsistent to classify the payment of cash dividends to shareholders as a financing activity when, as stated earlier, paying interest to creditors is classified as an operating activity. But remember, cash flows from operating activities should reflect the cash effects of items that enter into the determination of net income. Interest expense is a determinant of net income. A dividend, on the other hand, is a distribution of net income and not an expense.[15]

Interest, unlike dividends, is a determinant of net income and therefore an operating activity.

Reconciliation with Change in Cash Balance.
One of the first items you may have noticed about UBC's statement of cash flows is that there is a net change in cash of $9 million. Is this a significant item of information provided by the statement? The primary objective of the statement of cash flows is not to tell us that cash increased by $9 million. We can readily see the increase or decrease in cash by comparing the beginning and ending balances in the cash account in comparative balance sheets. Instead, the purpose of the statement of cash flows is to explain *why* cash increased by $9 million.

To reinforce the fact that the net amount of cash inflows and outflows explains the change in the cash balance, the statement of cash flows includes a reconciliation of the net increase (or decrease) in cash with the company's beginning and ending cash balances. Notice, for instance, that on UBC's statement of cash flows, the reconciliation appears as:

Net Increase in Cash	**$ 9**
Cash balance, January 1	20
Cash balance, December 31	$29

The net amount of cash inflows and outflows reconciles the change in the company's beginning and ending cash balances.

Noncash Investing and Financing Activities.
Suppose UBC were to borrow $20 million cash from a bank, issuing a long-term note payable for that amount. This transaction would be reported on a statement of cash flows as a financing activity. Now suppose UBC

---

[15]Not all accountants are satisfied with the FASB's distinctions among operating, investing, and financing activities. See for example, Hugo Nurnberg, "Inconsistencies and Ambiguities in Cash Flow Statements under *FASB Statement No. 95*," *Accounting Horizons*, June 1993.

used that $20 million cash to purchase new equipment. This second transaction would be reported as an investing activity.

Instead of two separate transactions, as indicated by Graphic 22–2, UBC acquired $20 million of new equipment by issuing a $20 million long-term note payable in a single transaction. Undertaking a significant investing activity and a significant financing activity as two parts of a single transaction does not diminish the value of reporting these activities. For that reason, transactions that do not increase or decrease cash, but which result in significant investing and financing activities, must be reported in related disclosures.

These noncash investing and financing activities, such as UBC's acquiring equipment (an investing activity) by issuing a long-term note payable (a financing activity), are reported in a separate disclosure schedule or note. UBC reported this transaction in the following manner:

> **Noncash Investing and Financing Activities:**
> Acquired $20 million of equipment by issuing a 12%, 5-year note.

It's convenient to report noncash investing and financing activities on the same page as the statement of cash flows as did UBC only if there are few such transactions. Otherwise, precisely the same information would be reported in disclosure notes to the financial statements.[16]

Examples of noncash transactions that would be reported in this manner are:

1. Acquiring an asset by incurring a debt payable to the seller.
2. Acquiring an asset by entering into a capital lease.
3. Converting debt into common stock or other equity securities.
4. Exchanging noncash assets or liabilities for other noncash assets or liabilities.

Noncash transactions that do not affect a company's assets or liabilities, such as the distribution of stock dividends, are not considered investing or financing activities and are not reported. Recall from Chapter 19 that stock dividends merely increase the number of shares of stock owned by existing shareholders. From an accounting standpoint, the stock dividend causes a dollar amount to be transferred from one part of shareholders' equity (retained earnings) to another part of shareholders' equity (paid-in capital). Neither assets nor liabilities are affected; therefore, no investing or financing activity has occurred.

ADDITIONAL CONSIDERATION

A transaction involving an investing and financing activity may be part cash and part noncash. For example, a company might pay cash for a part of the purchase price of new equipment and issue a long-term note for the remaining amount. In our previous illustration, UBC issued a note payable for the $20 million cost of the equipment it acquired. Suppose the equipment were purchased in the following manner:

Equipment..	20	
Cash...		6
Note payable.......................................		14

In that case, $6 million would be reported under the caption "Cash flows from investing activities," and the noncash portion of the transaction—issuing a $14 million note payable for $14 million of equipment—would be reported as a "noncash investing and financing activity." UBC's statement of cash flows, if modified by the assumption of a part cash/part noncash transaction, would report these two elements of the transaction as follows:

---

[16]"Statement of Cash Flows," *Statement of Financial Accounting Standards No. 95* (Stamford, Conn.: FASB, 1987), par. 74.

Cash Flows from Investing Activities:

Purchase of land	$(30)
Purchase of short-term investments	(12)
Sale of land	18
Sale of equipment	5
Purchase of equipment	(6)
Net cash flows from investing activities	(25)

Noncash Investing and Financing Activities:

Acquired $20 million of equipment by paying cash and issuing a 12%, 5-year note as follows:

Cost of equipment	$20 million
Cash paid	6 million
Note issued	$14 million

Preparation of the Statement of Cash Flows

The objective in preparing the statement of cash flows is to identify all transactions and events that represent operating, investing, or financing activities and to list and classify those activities in proper statement format. A difficulty in preparing a statement of cash flows is that typical accounting systems are not designed to produce the specific information we need for the statement. At the end of a reporting cycle, balances exist in accounts reported on the income statement (sales revenue, cost of goods sold, etc.) and the balance sheet (accounts receivable, common stock, etc.). However, the ledger contains no balances for cash paid to acquire equipment, or cash received from sale of land, or any other cash flow needed for the statement. As a result, it's necessary to find a way of using information that is available to reconstruct the various cash flows that occurred during the reporting period. Typically, the information available to assist the statement preparer includes an income statement for the year and balance sheets for both the current and preceding years (comparative statements). The accounting records also can provide additional information about transactions that caused changes in account balances during the year.

The typical year-end data is provided for UBC in Illustration 22–1 on the next page.

We have referred frequently to the statement of cash flows of UBC to illustrate the nature of the activities the statement reports. Now we will see how that statement is developed from the data provided in that illustration.

In situations involving relatively few transactions, it is possible to prepare the statement of cash flows by merely inspecting the available data and logically determining the reportable activities. Few real-life situations are sufficiently simple to be solved this way. Usually, it is more practical to use some systematic method of analyzing the available data to ensure that all operating, investing, and financing activities are detected. A common approach is to use either a manual or electronic spreadsheet to organize and analyze the information used to prepare the statement.[17]

Whether the statement of cash flows is prepared by an unaided inspection and analysis or with the aid of a systematic technique such as spreadsheet analysis, the analytical process is the same. To identify the activities to be reported on the statement, we use available data to reconstruct the events and transactions that involved operating, investing, and financing activities during the year. It is helpful to reproduce the journal entries that were recorded at the time of the transaction. Examining reconstructed journal entries makes it easier to visualize whether a reportable activity is involved and how that activity is to be classified.

Reconstructing the events and transactions that occurred during the period helps identify the operating, investing, and financing activities to be reported.

LO7

---

[17]The T-account method is a second systematic approach to the preparation of the statement of cash flows. This method is identical in concept and similar in application to the spreadsheet method. The T-account method is used to prepare the statement of cash flows for UBC in Appendix 22B.

ILLUSTRATION 22–1

Comparative Balance
Sheets and Income
Statement

UNITED BRANDS CORPORATION
Comparative Balance Sheets
December 31, 2003 and 2002
($ in millions)

Assets	2003	2002
Cash	$ 29	$ 20
Accounts receivable	32	30
Short-term investments	12	0
Inventory	46	50
Prepaid insurance	3	6
Land	80	60
Buildings and equipment	81	75
Less: Accumulated depreciation	(16)	(20)
	$267	$221
Liabilities		
Accounts payable	$ 26	$ 20
Salaries payable	3	1
Income tax payable	6	8
Notes payable	20	0
Bonds payable	35	50
Less: Discount on bonds	(1)	(3)
Shareholders' Equity		
Common stock	130	100
Paid-in capital—excess of par	29	20
Retained earnings	19	25
	$267	$221

UNITED BRANDS CORPORATION
Income Statement
For the Year Ended December 31, 2003
($ in millions)

Revenues		
Sales revenue	$100	
Investment revenue	3	
Gain on sale of land	8	$111
Expenses		
Cost of goods sold	60	
Salaries expense	13	
Depreciation expense	3	
Bond interest expense	5	
Insurance expense	7	
Loss on sale of equipment	2	
Income tax expense	9	99
Net income		$ 12

Additional Information from the Accounting Records

a. A portion of company land, purchased in a previous year for $10 million, was sold for $18 million.

b. Equipment that originally cost $14 million, and which was one-half depreciated, was sold for $5 million cash.

c. The common shares of Mazuma Corporation were purchased for $12 million as a short-term investment.

d. Property was purchased for $30 million cash for use as a parking lot.

e. On December 30, 2003, new equipment was acquired by issuing a 12%, five-year, $20 million note payable to the seller.

ILLUSTRATION 22–1

concluded

f. On January 1, 2003, $15 million of bonds were retired at maturity.
g. The increase in the common stock account is attributable to the issuance of a 10% stock dividend (1 million shares) and the subsequent sale of 2 million shares of common stock. The market price of the $10 par value common stock was $13 per share on the dates of both transactions.
h. Cash dividends of $5 million were paid to shareholders.

Next, in Part b, we see how a spreadsheet simplifies the process of preparing a statement of cash flows. Even if you choose not to use a spreadsheet, the summary entries described can be used to help you find the cash inflows and outflows you need to prepare a statement of cash flows. For this demonstration, we assume the direct method is used to determine and report cash flows from operating activities. Appreciation of the direct method provides the backdrop for a thorough understanding of the indirect method that we explore in Part c.

PREPARING AN SCF: THE DIRECT METHOD OF REPORTING CASH FLOWS FROM OPERATING ACTIVITIES

PART

b

Using a Spreadsheet

An important advantage gained by using a spreadsheet is that it ensures that no reportable activities are inadvertently overlooked. Spreadsheet analysis relies on the fact that, in order for cash to increase or decrease, there must be a corresponding change in a noncash account. Therefore, if we can identify the events and transactions that caused the change in each non-cash account during the year, we will have identified all the operating, investing, and financing activities that are to be included in the statement of cash flows.

The beginning and ending balances of each account are entered on the spreadsheet. Then, as journal entries are reconstructed in our analysis of the data, those entries are recorded on the spreadsheet so that the debits and credits of the spreadsheet entries explain the changes in the account balances. Only after spreadsheet entries have explained the changes in all account balances, can we feel confident that all operating, investing, and financing activities have been identified. The spreadsheet is designed in such a way that, as we record spreadsheet entries that explain account balance changes, we are simultaneously identifying and classifying the activities to be reported on the statement of cash flows.

We begin by transferring the comparative balance sheets and income statement to a blank spreadsheet. For illustration, refer to the 2003 and 2002 balances in the completed spreadsheet for UBC, shown in Illustration 22–1A on the next two pages. Notice that the amounts for elements of the income statement are ending balances resulting from accumulations during the year. Beginning balances in each of these accounts are always zero.

Following the balance sheets and income statement, we allocate space on the spreadsheet for the statement of cash flows. Although at this point we have not yet identified the specific cash flow activities shown in the completed spreadsheet, we can include headings for the major categories of activities: cash flows from operating activities, cash flows from investing activities, and cash flows from financing activities. Leaving several lines between headings allows adequate space to include the specific cash flows identified in subsequent analysis.

The spreadsheet entries shown in the two changes columns, which separate the beginning and ending balances, explain the increase or decrease in each account balance. You will see in the next section how these entries were reconstructed. Although spreadsheet entries are in the form of debits and credits like journal entries, they are entered on the spreadsheet only. They are not recorded in the formal accounting records. In effect, these entries duplicate,

There can be no cash inflow or cash outflow without a corresponding change in a noncash account.

Recording spreadsheet entries that explain account balance changes simultaneously identifies and classifies the activities to be reported on the statement of cash flows.

Spreadsheet entries duplicate the actual journal entries used to record the transactions as they occurred during the year.

ILLUSTRATION
22–1A

Spreadsheet

UNITED BRANDS CORPORATION
Spreadsheet for the Statement of Cash Flows

	Dec. 31 2002	Changes				Dec. 31 2003
		Debits		Credits		
Balance Sheet						
Assets:						
Cash	20	(19)	9			29
Accounts receivable	30	(1)	2			32
Short-term investments	0	(12)	12			12
Inventory	50			(4)	4	46
Prepaid insurance	6			(8)	3	3
Land	60	(13)	30	(3)	10	80
Buildings and equipment	75	(14)	20X	(9)	14	81
Less: Accumulated depreciation	(20)	(9)	7	(6)	3	(16)
	221					267
Liabilities:						
Accounts payable	20			(4)	6	26
Salaries payable	1			(5)	2	3
Income tax payable	8	(10)	2			6
Notes payable	0			(14)	20X	20
Bonds payable	50	(15)	15			35
Less: Discount on bonds	(3)			(7)	2	(1)
Shareholders' Equity:						
Common stock	100			(16)	10	
				(17)	20	130
Paid-in capital—excess of par	20			(16)	3	
				(17)	6	29
Retained earnings	25	(16)	13			
		(18)	5	(11)	12	19
	221					267
Income Statement						
Revenues:						
Sales revenue				(1)	100	100
Investment revenue				(2)	3	3
Gain on sale of land				(3)	8	8
Expenses:						
Cost of goods sold		(4)	60			(60)
Salaries expense		(5)	13			(13)
Depreciation expense		(6)	3			(3)
Bond interest expense		(7)	5			(5)
Insurance expense		(8)	7			(7)
Loss on sale of equipment		(9)	2			(2)
Income tax expense		(10)	9			(9)
Net income		(11)	**12**			**12**

		Changes			
	Dec. 31			**Dec. 31**	
	2002	**Debits**		**Credits**	**2003**
Statement of Cash Flows					
Operating Activities:					
Cash inflows:					
From customers		(1)	98		
From investment revenue		(2)	3		
Cash outflows:					
To suppliers of goods				(4)	50
To employees				(5)	11
To bondholders				(7)	3
For insurance expense				(8)	4
For income taxes				(10)	11
Net cash flows					22
Investing Activities:					
Sale of land		(3)	18		
Sale of equipment		(9)	5		
Purchase of S-T investment				(12)	12
Purchase of land				(13)	30
Net cash flows					(19)
Financing Activities:					
Retirement of bonds payable				(15)	15
Sale of common shares		(17)	26		
Payment of cash dividends				(18)	5
Net cash flows					6
Net increase in cash				(19)	9	9
Totals			376		376

ILLUSTRATION 22–1A

concluded

X—As explained later, the X's serve as a reminder to report this noncash transaction.

frequently in summary form, the actual journal entries used to record the transactions as they occurred during the year.

To reconstruct the journal entries, we analyze each account, one at a time, deciding at each step what transaction or event caused the change in that account. Often, the reason for the change in an account balance is readily apparent from viewing the change in conjunction with that of a related account elsewhere in the financial statements. Sometimes it is necessary to consult the accounting records for additional information to help explain the transaction that resulted in the change.

You may find it helpful to diagram in T-account format the relationship between accounts to better visualize certain changes, particularly in your initial study of the chapter. The analysis that follows is occasionally supplemented with such diagrams to emphasize *why*, rather than merely *how*, specific cash flow amounts emerge from the analysis.

Although there is no mandatory order in which to analyze the accounts, it is convenient to begin with the income statement accounts, followed by the balance sheet accounts. We analyze the accounts of UBC in that order below. Although our analysis of each account culminates in a spreadsheet entry, keep in mind that the analysis described also is appropriate to identify reportable activities when a spreadsheet is not used.[18]

INCOME STATEMENT ACCOUNTS

Amounts reported in the income statement usually are not the same as the cash effects of the items reported.

As described in an earlier section, cash flows from operating activities are inflows and outflows of cash that result from activities reported on the income statement. Thus, to identify those cash inflows and outflows, we begin by analyzing the components of the income statement. It is important to keep in mind that the amounts reported in the income statement usually do not represent the cash effects of the items reported. For example, UBC reports sales revenue of $100 million. This does not mean, however, that it collected $100 million cash from customers during the year. In fact, by referring to the beginning and ending balances in accounts receivable, we see that cash received from customers could not have been $100 million. Since accounts receivable increased during the year, some of the sales revenue earned must not yet have been collected. This is explained further in the next section.

The cash effects of other income statement elements can be similarly discerned by referring to changes in the balances of the balance sheet accounts that are directly related to those elements. So, to identify cash flows from operating activities we examine, one at a time, the elements of the income statement in conjunction with any balance sheet accounts affected by each element.

1. Sales Revenue. Accounts receivable is the balance sheet account that is affected by sales revenue. Specifically, accounts receivable is increased by credit sales and is decreased as cash is received from customers. We can compare sales and the change in accounts receivable during the year to determine the amount of cash received from customers. This relationship can be viewed in T-account format as follows:

Accounts Receivable

Beginning balance	30		
Credit sales	100	?	Cash received
(increases A/R)			(decreases A/R)
Ending balance	32		

We see from this analysis that cash received from customers must have been $98 million. Note that even if some of the year's sales were cash sales, say $40 million cash sales and $60 million credit sales, the result is the same:

Accounts Receivable

Beginning balance	30			Cash sales	$40
Credit sales	60	58	⟶	Received on account	58
Ending balance	32			Cash received	$98

Thus, cash flows from operating activities should include cash received from customers of $98 million. The net effect of sales revenue activity during the year can be summarized in the following entry.

Relating sales and the change in accounts receivable during the period helps determine the amount of cash received from customers.

	($ in millions)	
Entry (1) Cash (received from customers)	98	
Accounts receivable (given)	2	
Sales revenue ($100 − 0)		100

The entry above appears as entry (1) in the completed spreadsheet for UBC, shown in Illustration 22–1A. The entry explains the changes in two account balances—accounts

---

[18]The spreadsheet entries also are used to record the same transactions when the T-account method is used. We refer again to these entries when that method is described in Appendix 22B.

receivable and sales revenue. Since the entry affects cash, it also identifies a cash flow to be reported on the statement of cash flows. The $98 million debit to cash is therefore entered in the statement of cash flows section of the spreadsheet under the heading of cash flows from operating activities.

ADDITIONAL CONSIDERATION

The preceding discussion describes the most common situation—companies earn revenue by selling goods and services, increase accounts receivable, and then collect the cash and decrease accounts receivable later. Some companies, though, often collect the cash in advance of earning it, record unearned revenue, and then later record revenue and decrease unearned revenue. In those cases, we need to analyze any changes in the unearned revenue account for differences between revenue reported and cash collected. For instance, if UBC also had a $1 million increase in unearned revenue, the summary entry would be modified as follows:

		($ in millions)	
Entry (1)	Cash (received from customers)	99	
	Accounts receivable (given)	2	
	Unearned revenue (given).		1
	Sales revenue ($100 − 0).		100

Notice that we enter the cash portion of entry (1) as one of several cash flows on the statement of cash flows rather than as a debit to the cash account. Only after all cash inflows and outflows have been identified will the net change in cash be entered as a debit to the cash account. In fact, the entry to reconcile the $9 million increase in the cash account and the $9 million net increase in cash on the statement of cash flows will serve as a final check of the accuracy of our spreadsheet analysis.

ADDITIONAL CONSIDERATION

Notice that bad debt expense does not appear on the income statement and allowance for uncollectible accounts does not appear on the balance sheet. We have assumed that bad debts are immaterial for UBC. When this is not the case, it's necessary to consider the write-off of bad debts as we determine cash received from customers. Here's why.

When using the allowance method to account for bad debts, a company estimates the dollar amount of customer accounts that will ultimately prove uncollectible and records both bad debt expense and allowance for uncollectible accounts for that estimate.

Bad debt expense.	xxx	
Allowance for uncollectible accounts		xxx

Then, when accounts actually prove uncollectible, accounts receivable and the allowance are reduced.

Allowance for uncollectible accounts	xxx	
Accounts receivable.		xxx

In our illustration, we concluded that UBC received $2 million less cash ($98 million) than sales for the year ($100 million) because accounts receivable increased by that amount. However, if a portion of the change in accounts receivable had been due to write-offs of bad debts, that conclusion would be incorrect. Let's say, for instance, that UBC had bad debt expense of $2 million and its allowance for uncollectible accounts had increased by $1 million. Because the allowance for uncollectible accounts would be credited by $2 million in the adjusting entry for bad debts expense, necessarily there also would have been a $1 million debit to the account in order for there to have been a net increase (credit) in its balance of only $1 million. That debit would occur due to write-offs of bad debts totaling $1 million.

	($ in millions)
Allowance for uncollectible accounts	1
Accounts receivable.	1

This would indicate that a portion ($1 million credit) of the total change in accounts receivable ($2 million debit) would have been due to write-offs of bad debts, and the remaining change ($3 million debit) would have been due to cash collections being less than sales revenue. Cash received from customers would have been only $97 million in that case. We can view this in the framework of our T-account analysis as follows:

Accounts Receivable

Beginning balance	30		
Credit Sales	100	97	Cash received
		1	Bad Debt write-offs
Ending balance	32		

The effect of write-offs of bad debts can be explicitly considered by combining all the accounts related to sales and collection activities into a single summary spreadsheet entry:

		($ in millions)	
Entry (1)	Cash (received from customers)	97	
	Accounts receivable ($32 − 30).	2	
	Bad debt expense (from income statement)	2	
	Allowance for uncollectible accounts ($3 − 2)		1
	Sales revenue ($100 − 0).		100

This single entry summarizes all transactions related to sales, bad debts expense, write-offs of accounts receivable, and cash collections from sales.

The remaining spreadsheet entries are described in subsections 2 through 19. When including the entries on the spreadsheet, it is helpful to number the entries sequentially to provide a means of retracing the steps taken in the analysis if the need arises. You also may find it helpful to put a check mark (✓) to the right of the ending balance when the change in that balance has been explained. Then, once you have check marks next to every noncash account, you will know you are finished.

2. Investment Revenue.   The income statement reports investment revenue of $3 million. Before concluding that this amount was received in cash, we first refer to the balance sheets to see whether a change in an account there indicates otherwise. A change in either of two balance sheet accounts, (a) investment revenue receivable or (b) long-term investments, might indicate that cash received from investment revenue differs from the amount reported on the income statement.

Changes in related accounts might indicate that investment revenue reported on the income statement is a different amount from cash received from the investment.

a. If we observe either an increase or a decrease in an *investment revenue receivable* account (e.g., interest receivable, dividends receivable), we would conclude that the amount of cash received during the year was less than (if an increase) or more than (if a decrease) the amount of revenue reported. The analysis would be identical to that of sales revenue and accounts receivable.

b. Also, an unexplained increase in a *long-term investment* account might indicate that a portion of investment revenue has not yet been received in cash. Recall from Chapter 12 that when using the equity method to account for investments in the stock of another corporation, investment revenue is recognized as the investor's percentage share of the investee's income, whether or not the revenue is received currently as cash dividends. For example, assume the investor owns 25% of the common stock of a corporation that reports net income of $12 million and pays dividends of $4 million. This situation would have produced a $2 million increase in long-term investments, which can be demonstrated by reconstructing the journal entries for the recognition of investment and the receipt of cash dividends:

	($ in millions)	
Long-term investments.	3	
Investment revenue ($12 × 25%)		3
Cash ($4 × 25%).	1	
Long-term investments		1

A combined entry would produce the same results:

	($ in millions)	
Long-term investments	2	
Cash ($4 × 25%).	1	
Investment revenue ($12 × 25%)		3

The $2 million net increase in long-term investments would represent the investment revenue not received in cash. This would also explain why there is a $3 million increase (credit) in investment revenue. If these events had occurred, we would prepare a spreadsheet entry identical to the combined entry above. The spreadsheet entry would (a) explain the $2 million increase in long-term investments, (b) explain the $3 million increase in investment revenue, and (c) identify a $1 million cash inflow from operating activities.

However, because neither an investment revenue receivable account nor a long-term investment account appears on the comparative balance sheets, we can conclude that $3 million of investment revenue was collected in cash. Entry (2) on the spreadsheet is:

	($ in millions)	
Entry (2) Cash (received from investment revenue)	3	
Investment revenue ($3 − 0)		3

> Because no other transactions are apparent that would have caused a change in investment revenue, we can conclude that $3 million of investment revenue was collected in cash.

3. Gain on Sale of Land.
The third item reported on the income statement is an $8 million gain on the sale of land. Recall that our objective in analyzing each element of the statement is to determine the cash effect of that element. To do so, we need additional information about the transaction that caused this gain. The accounting records—item (a) in Illustration 22–1—indicate that land that originally cost $10 million was sold for $18 million. The entry recorded in the journal when the land was sold also serves as our spreadsheet entry:

	($ in millions)	
Entry (3) Cash (received from sale of land)	18	
Land (given)		10
Gain on sale of land ($8 − 0)		8

> A gain (or loss) is simply the difference between cash received in the sale of an asset and the book value of the asset—not a cash flow.

The cash effect of this transaction is a cash increase of $18 million. We therefore include the debit as a cash inflow in the statement of cash flows section of the spreadsheet. However, unlike the cash effect of the previous two spreadsheet entries, it is not reported as an operating activity. The sale of land is an *investing* activity, so this cash inflow is listed under that heading of the spreadsheet. The entry also accounts for the $8 million gain on sale of land. The $10 million credit to land does not, by itself, explain the $20 million increase in that account. As we will later discover, another transaction also affected the land account.

It is important to understand that the gain is simply the difference between cash received in the sale of land (reported as an investing activity) and the book value of the land. To report the $8 million gain as a cash flow from operating activities, in addition to reporting $18 million as a cash flow from investing activities, would be to report the $8 million twice.

4. Cost of Goods Sold. During the year UBC sold goods that had cost $60 million. This does not necessarily indicate that $60 million cash was paid to suppliers of those goods. To determine the amount of cash paid to suppliers, we look to the two current accounts affected by merchandise purchases—inventory and accounts payable. The analysis can be viewed as a two-step process.

First, we compare cost of goods sold with the change in inventory to determine the cost of goods *purchased* (not necessarily cash paid) during the year. To facilitate our analysis, we can examine the relationship in T-account format:

Inventory			
Beginning balance	50		
Cost of goods **purchased** ?		60	Cost of goods **sold**
(increases inventory)			*(decreases inventory)*
Ending balance	46		

From this analysis, we see that $56 million of goods were *purchased* during the year. It is not necessarily true, though, that $56 million cash was paid to suppliers of these goods. By looking in accounts payable, we can determine the cash paid to suppliers:

Accounts Payable			
		20	Beginning balance
Cash paid to suppliers	?	56	Cost of goods *purchased*
(decreases A/P)			*(increases A/P)*
		26	Ending Balance

We now see that cash paid to suppliers was $50 million. The spreadsheet entry that summarizes merchandise acquisitions is:

		($ in millions)
Entry (4) Cost of goods sold ($60 − 0).	60	
Inventory ($46 − 50).		4
Accounts payable ($26 − 20).		6
Cash (paid to suppliers of goods)		50

5. Salaries Expense. The balance sheet account affected by salaries expense is salaries payable. By analyzing salaries expense in relation to the change in salaries payable, we can determine the amount of cash paid to employees:

Salaries Payable			
		1	Beginning balance
Cash paid to employees	?	13	Salaries expense
(decreases salaries payable)			*(increases salaries payable)*
		3	Ending Balance

This analysis indicates that only $11 million cash was paid to employees; the remaining $2 million of salaries expense is reflected as an increase in salaries payable.

Viewing the relationship in journal entry format provides the same conclusion and also gives us the entry in our spreadsheet analysis:

		($ in millions)
Entry (5) Salaries expense ($13 − 0).	13	
Salaries payable ($3 − 1).		2
Cash (paid to employees)		11

Determining the amount of cash paid to suppliers means looking at not only the cost of goods sold, but also the changes in both inventory and accounts payable.

Although $60 million of goods were sold during the year, only $50 million cash was paid to suppliers of these goods.

Although salaries expense was $13 million, only $11 million cash was paid to employees.

6. Depreciation Expense.   The income statement reports depreciation expense of $3 million. The entry used to record depreciation, which also serves as our spreadsheet entry, is:

	($ in millions)	
Entry (6) Depreciation expense ($3 − 0)	3	
Accumulated depreciation		3

Depreciation expense does not require a current cash expenditure.

Depreciation is a noncash expense. It is merely an allocation in the current period of a prior cash expenditure (for the depreciable asset). Therefore, unlike the other entries to this point, the depreciation entry has no effect on the statement of cash flows. However, it does explain the change in the depreciation expense account and a portion of the change in accumulated depreciation.

7. Interest Expense.   Recall from Chapter 14 that bond interest expense differs from the amount of cash paid to bondholders when bonds are issued at either a premium or a discount. The difference between the two amounts is the reduction of the premium or discount. By referring to the balance sheet, we see that UBC's bonds were issued at a discount. Since we know that bond interest expense is $5 million and that $2 million of the discount was reduced in 2003, we can determine that $3 million cash was paid to bondholders by recreating the entry that summarizes the recording of bond interest expense.

	($ in millions)	
Entry (7) Bond interest expense ($5 − 0).	5	
Discount on bonds payable ($1 − 3)		2
Cash (paid to bondholders).		3

Bond interest expense is not the same as the amount of cash paid to bondholders when bonds are issued at either a premium or a discount.

Recording this entry on the spreadsheet explains the change in both the bond interest expense and discount on bonds payable accounts. It also provides us with another cash outflow from operating activities. Of course, if a premium were being reduced, rather than a discount, the cash outflow would be *greater* than the expense.

ADDITIONAL CONSIDERATION

If the balance sheet had revealed an increase or decrease in an accrued bond interest payable account, the entry calculating cash paid to bondholders would require modification. For example, if UBC had a bond interest payable account, and that account had increased (a credit) by $1 million, the entry would have been:

	($ in millions)	
Entry (7) Bond interest expense	5	
(revised) Discount on bonds payable		2
Bond interest payable.		1
Cash (paid to bondholders).		2

If the amount owed to bondholders increased by $1 million, they obviously were paid $1 million less cash than if there had been no change in the amount owed them. Similarly, if bond interest payable decreased by $1 million, the opposite would be true; that is, cash paid them would have been $1 million more.

---

8. Insurance Expense.   A decrease of $3 million in the prepaid insurance account indicates that cash paid for insurance coverage was $3 million less than the $7 million insurance expense for the year. Viewing prepaid insurance in T-account format clarifies this point.

Prepaid Insurance

Beginning balance	6		
Cash paid for insurance	?	7	Insurance expense
(increases prepaid insurance)			*(decreases prepaid insurance)*
Ending balance	3		

From this analysis, we can conclude that $4 million was paid for insurance. We reach the same conclusion by preparing the following spreadsheet entry:

	($ in millions)	
Entry (8) Insurance expense ($7 − 0)	7	
Prepaid insurance ($3 − 6)		3
Cash (paid for insurance)		4

> Since $3 million of prepaid insurance was allocated to insurance expense, only $4 million of the expense was paid in cash during the period.

The entry accounts for the change in both the insurance expense and prepaid insurance accounts and also identifies a cash outflow from operating activities.

9. Loss on Sale of Equipment. A $2 million loss on the sale of equipment is the next item reported on the income statement. To determine the cash effect of the sale of equipment, we need additional information about the transaction. The information we need is provided in item (b) of Illustration 22–1. Re-creating the journal entry for the transaction described gives us the following entry:

	($ in millions)	
Entry (9) Cash (from the sale of equipment)	5	
Loss on sale of equipment ($2 − 0)	2	
Accumulated depreciation ($14 × 50%)	7	
Buildings and equipment (given)		14

> Recreating the journal entry for the sale of equipment reveals a $5 million cash inflow from investing activities.

The $5 million cash inflow is entered in the statement of cash flows section of the spreadsheet as an investing activity. The $2 million debit to the loss on sale of equipment explains the change in that account balance. Referring to the spreadsheet, we see that a portion of the change in accumulated depreciation was accounted for in entry (6). The debit to accumulated depreciation in the entry above completes the explanation for the change in that account. However, the credit to buildings and equipment only partially justifies the change in that account. We must assume that the analysis of a subsequent transaction will account for the unexplained portion of the change.

Recognize too that the loss, like the gain in entry (3), has no cash effect in the current period. Therefore, it is not reported on the statement of cash flows.

10. Income Tax Expense. The final expense reported on the income statement is income tax expense. Since income taxes payable is the balance sheet account affected by this expense, we look to the change in that account to help determine the cash paid for income taxes. A T-account analysis can be used to find the cash effect as follows:

Income Tax Payable

		8	Beginning balance
Cash paid for income tax	?	9	Income tax expense
(decreases the liability)			
		6	Ending Balance

This analysis reveals that $11 million cash was paid for income taxes, $2 million more than the year's expense. The overpayment explains why the liability for income taxes decreased by $2 million.

The same conclusion can be reached from the following spreadsheet entry, which represents the net effect of income taxes on UBC's accounts.

		($ in millions)
Entry (10) Income tax expense ($9 − 0).....................	9	
Income tax payable ($6 − 8).....................	2	
Cash (paid for income taxes)....................		11

ADDITIONAL CONSIDERATION

Entry (10) would require modification in either of the two independent situations described below.

1. Note that UBC does not have a deferred income tax account. Recall from Chapter 16 that temporary differences between taxable income and pretax accounting income give rise to deferred taxes. If temporary differences had been present, which would be evidenced by a change in a deferred income taxes account, the calculation of cash paid for income taxes would require modification. Assume, for example, that a deferred income tax liability account had experienced a credit change of $1 million for the year. In that case, the previous spreadsheet entry would be revised as follows:

		($ in millions)
Entry (10) Income tax expense	9	
(revised) Income tax payable...........................	2	
Deferred income tax liability		1
Cash (paid for income taxes)		10

As the revised entry indicates, only $10 million cash would have been paid in this situation, rather than $11 million. The $1 million difference represents the portion of the income tax expense whose payment is deferred to a later year.

2. The spreadsheet entry also would be affected if the income statement includes either an extraordinary gain or an extraordinary loss. Recall from Chapter 3 and Chapter 16 that the income tax effect of an extraordinary item is not reflected in income tax expense, but instead is separately reported as a reduction in the extraordinary item. For example, if UBC's loss on the sale of equipment had been due to an extraordinary event, the tax savings from that loss would be reported as a reduction in the extraordinary loss rather than as a reduction in income tax expense. (Since the loss reduces taxable income by $2 million, assuming a marginal tax rate of 50%, taxes would be reduced by $1 million.) The lower portion of the income statement would have appeared as shown below, in comparison with the presentation in Illustration 22–1:

Ordinary Loss (from Illustration 22–1)		**Extraordinary Loss**		
		Income tax expense		(10)
		Income before extraordinary items		$13
Loss on sale of equipment	(2)	E.O. loss—sale of equipment	$2	
Income tax expense	(9)	Less: Tax savings	(1)	(1)
Net income	$12	Net income		$12

Without the tax savings produced by the loss, income tax expense would have been $10 million, rather than $9 million. But the tax savings still reduces the amount of cash paid for income taxes, even though it is reported separately from the income tax expense. Therefore, whether the loss is extraordinary or not, the amount of cash paid for income taxes is the same. If the loss is extraordinary, entry (10) would be modified as follows:

	($ in millions)	
Entry (10) Income tax expense (on ordinary income)	10	
(revised) Income tax payable.	2	
Income tax expense		
(savings from extraordinary loss).		1
Cash (paid for income taxes)		11

Entry (9) would be unaffected. Whether or not the loss is extraordinary, it is not reported on the statement of cash flows, and the cash inflow from the sale is reported as an investing activity.

11. Net Income. The balance in the retained earnings account at the end of the year includes an increase due to net income. If we are to account for all changes in each of the accounts, we must include the following spreadsheet entry, which represents the closing of net income to retained earnings.

This entry partially explains the change in the retained earnings account.

	($ in millions)	
Entry (11) Net income	12	
Retained earnings		12

This entry does not affect amounts reported on the statement of cash flows. We include the entry in the spreadsheet analysis only to help explain account balance changes.

BALANCE SHEET ACCOUNTS

To identify all the operating, investing, and financing activities when using a spreadsheet, we must account for the changes in each account on both the income statement and the balance sheet. Thus far, we have explained the change in each income statement account. Since the transactions that gave rise to some of those changes involved balance sheet accounts as well, some changes in balance sheet accounts have already been explained. We now reconstruct the transactions that caused changes in the remaining balances.

With the exception of the cash account, the accounts are analyzed in the order of their presentation in the balance sheet. As noted earlier, we save the entry that reconciles the change in the cash account with the net change in cash from the statement of cash flows as a final check on the accuracy of the spreadsheet.

12. Short-Term Investments. Since the change in accounts receivable was explained previously [in entry (1)], we proceed to the next asset on the balance sheet. The balance in short-term investments increased from zero to $12 million. In the absence of evidence to the contrary, we could assume that the increase is due to the purchase of short-term investments during the year. This assumption is confirmed by item (c) of Illustration 22–1.

The entry to record the investment and our spreadsheet entry is:

The $12 million increase in the short-term investments account is due to the purchase of short-term investments during the year.

	($ in millions)	
Entry (12) Short-term investment ($12 − 0).	12	
Cash (purchase of short-term investment)		12

The $12 million cash outflow is entered in the statement of cash flows section of the spreadsheet as an investing activity.

ADDITIONAL CONSIDERATION

Recall that some highly liquid, short-term investments such as money market funds, treasury bills, or commercial paper might be classified as cash equivalents. If the short-term investment above were classified as a cash equivalent, its purchase would have no effect on the total of cash and cash equivalents. In other words, since cash would include this investment, its purchase would constitute both a debit and a credit to cash. We would neither prepare a spreadsheet entry nor report the transaction on the statement of cash flows.

Likewise, a sale of a cash equivalent would not affect the total of cash and cash equivalents and would not be reported.

An exception would be if the cash equivalent investment were sold for either more or less than its acquisition cost. For example, assume a treasury bill classified as a cash equivalent were sold for $1 million more than its $2 million cost. The sale would constitute both a $3 million increase and a $2 million decrease in cash. We see the effect more clearly if we reconstruct the transaction in journal entry format:

	($ in millions)	
Cash.	3	
Gain on sale of cash equivalent.		1
Cash (cash equivalent investment).		2

The spreadsheet entry to reflect the net increase in cash would be:

Entry (X) Cash (from sale of cash equivalents).	1	
Gain on sale of cash equivalent		1

The $1 million net increase in cash and cash equivalents would be reported as a cash inflow from *operating* activities.

13. Land.   The changes in the balances of both inventory and prepaid insurance were accounted for in previous spreadsheet entries: (4) and (8). Land is the next account whose change has yet to be fully explained. We discovered in a previous transaction that a sale of land caused a $10 million reduction in the account. Yet, the account shows a net *increase* of $20 million. It would be logical to assume that the unexplained increase of $30 million was due to a purchase of land. The transaction described in item (d) of Illustration 22–1 supports that assumption and is portrayed in the following spreadsheet entry:

	($ in millions)	
Entry (13) Land (given).	30	
Cash (purchase of land).		30

A $30 million purchase of land accounts for the portion of the $20 million increase in the account that was not previously explained by the sale of land.

The $30 million payment is reported as a cash outflow from investing activities.

14. Buildings and Equipment.   When examining a previous transaction [entry (9)], we determined that the buildings and equipment account was reduced by $14 million from the sale of used equipment. And yet the account shows a net *increase* of $6 million for the year. The accounting records [item (e) of Illustration 22–1] reveal the remaining unexplained cause of the net increase. New equipment costing $20 million was purchased by issuing a $20 million note payable. Recall from the discussion in a previous section of this chapter that, although this is a noncash transaction, it represents both a significant investing activity (investing in new equipment) and a significant financing activity (financing the acquisition with long-term debt).

The journal entry used to record the transaction when the equipment was acquired also serves as our spreadsheet entry:

Investing in new equipment is a significant investing activity and financing the acquisition with long-term debt is a significant financing activity.

	($ in millions)	
Entry (14) Buildings and equipment (given).	20	
Note payable (given).		20

Remember that the statement of cash flows section of the spreadsheet will serve as the basis for our preparation of the formal statement. But the noncash entry above will not affect the cash flows section of the spreadsheet. Because we want to report this noncash investing and financing activity when we prepare the statement of cash flows, it is helpful to "mark" the spreadsheet entry as a reminder not to overlook this transaction when the statement is prepared. Crosses (X) serve this purpose on the spreadsheet in Illustration 22–1A.

ADDITIONAL CONSIDERATION

Payments on Debt

When a debt, such as the note payable above, is paid, the payment is reported on a statement of cash flows as a financing activity. However, any interest paid on the debt is reported as a cash outflow from operating activities. The reason is that interest expense is a component of net income, and the cash effects of income statement elements are reported as cash flows from operating activities. If the note is an installment note, each installment payment includes both an amount that represents interest and an amount that represents a reduction of principal. In a statement of cash flows, then, the interest portion is reported as a cash outflow from operating activities and the principal portion as a cash outflow from financing activities.

Leases

As we discussed in Chapter 15, lease arrangements vary greatly, in both their purpose and the ways we account for them. Consistent with those differences, we also report leases differently in a statement of cash flows depending on their type. Lease payments for **operating leases**, for instance, represent rent—expense to the lessee, revenue for the lessor. These amounts are included in net income, so both the lessee and lessor report cash payments for operating leases in a statement of cash flows as cash flows from operating activities. **Capital leases**, on the other hand, are agreements that we identify as being formulated outwardly as leases, but which are in reality installment purchases, so we account for them as such. Each rental payment (except the first if paid at inception) includes both an amount that represents interest and an amount that represents a reduction of principal. In a statement of cash flows, then, the lessee reports the interest portion as a cash outflow from operating activities and the principal portion as a cash outflow from financing activities. On the other side of the transaction, the lessor in a **direct financing lease** reports the interest portion as a cash inflow from operating activities and the principal portion as a cash inflow from investing activities. Both the lessee and lessor report the lease at its inception as a noncash investing/financing activity. Remember, though, that a **sales-type lease** differs from a direct financing lease for the lessor in that we assume the lessor is actually selling its product. Consistent with reporting sales of products under installment sales agreements rather than lease agreements, the lessor reports cash receipts from a sales-type lease as cash inflows from operating activities.

---

15. Bonds Payable.   The balance in the bonds payable account decreased during the year by $15 million. Illustration 22–1, item (f), reveals the cause. Cash was paid to retire $15 million face value of bonds. The spreadsheet entry that duplicates the journal entry that was recorded when the bonds were retired is:

	($ in millions)	
Entry (15) Bonds payable ($35 − 50)	15	
Cash (retirement of bonds payable)		15

The cash outflow is reported as a financing activity.

ADDITIONAL CONSIDERATION

The description of the transaction stipulated that $15 million of bonds were retired at their maturity on the first day of the year. Thus, any discount or premium on the bonds would have been completely amortized before the start of the year. If bonds are retired prior to their scheduled maturity, any unamortized discount or premium would be removed from the accounts at that time. For instance, assume that the bonds above were callable at $16 million and that $1 million of unamortized discount remained when they were retired by a call at that price. The spreadsheet entry would be revised as follows:

		($ in millions)	
Entry (15)	Bonds payable	15	
(revised)	Extraordinary loss on early extinguishment of bonds.	2	
	Discount on bonds payable		1
	Cash (retirement of bonds payable)		16

The loss, of course, would not be reported on the statement of cash flows. The amortization of the discount, however, would affect a previous spreadsheet entry. In entry (7) we concluded that the decrease in discount on bonds payable was due to the amortization of $2 million of the discount when recording bond interest expense. However, if the early retirement assumed above had occurred, that transaction would have accounted for $1 million of the $2 million decrease in the discount. Entry (7) would be modified as follows:

		($ in millions)	
Entry (7)	Bond interest expense	5	
(revised)	Discount on bonds payable		1
	Cash (paid to bondholders)		4

Remember, too, that the tax savings from the loss would be reported on the income statement as a reduction of the extraordinary loss, rather than as a reduction of the income tax expense. Therefore, the spreadsheet entry that determines the amount of cash paid for income taxes would require the modification described in subsection 10 (Additional Consideration) on pages 1101–1102.

16–17. Common Stock. The comparative balance sheets indicate that the common stock account balance increased by $30 million. We look to the accounting records—Illustration 22–1, item (g)—for an explanation. Two transactions, a stock dividend and a sale of new shares of common stock, combined to cause the increase. To create the spreadsheet entries for our analysis, we replicate the journal entries for the two transactions as described below.

Remember from Chapter 19 that to record a small stock dividend, we capitalize retained earnings for the market value of the shares distributed—in this case, 1 million shares times $13 per share, or $13 million. The entry is:

Although this transaction does not identify a cash flow, nor does it represent an investing or financing activity, we include the spreadsheet entry to help explain changes in the three account balances affected.

		($ in millions)	
Entry (16)	Retained earnings (1 million shares × $13)	13	
	Common stock (1 million shares × $10 par)		10
	Paid-in capital—excess of par (difference)		3

Also recall from the discussion of noncash investing and financing activities earlier in the chapter, that stock dividends do not represent a significant investing or financing activity. Therefore, this transaction is not reported on the statement of cash flows. We include the entry in our spreadsheet analysis only to help explain changes in the account balances affected.

The sale of 2 million shares of common stock at $13 per share is represented by the following spreadsheet entry:

The sale of common shares explains the remaining increase in the common stock account and the remaining increase in paid-in capital—excess of par.

		($ in millions)
Entry (17) Cash (from sale of common stock)	26	
Common stock ([$130 − 100] − 10)		20
Paid-in capital—excess of par ([$29 − 20] − 3)		6

The cash inflow is reported on the statement of cash flows as a financing activity.

ADDITIONAL CONSIDERATION

If cash is paid to retire outstanding shares of stock or to purchase those shares as treasury stock, the cash outflow would be reported on a statement of cash flows as a financing activity.

Together, the two entries above account for both the $30 million increase in the common stock account and the $9 million increase in paid-in capital—excess of par.

18. Retained Earnings. The stock dividend in entry (16) above includes a $13 million reduction of retained earnings. Previously, we saw in entry (11) that net income increased retained earnings by $12 million. The net reduction of $1 million accounted for by these two entries leaves $5 million of the $6 million net decrease in the account unexplained.

Retained Earnings			
		25	Beginning balance
(16) Stock dividend	13	12	Net income (11)
(18) ?	?		
		19	Ending balance

Without additional information about the $5 million decrease in retained earnings, we might assume it was due to a $5 million cash dividend. This assumption is unnecessary, though, because the cash dividend is described in Illustration 22–1, item (h).

Retained Earnings			
		25	Beginning balance
(16) Stock dividend	13	12	Net income (11)
(18) Cash dividend	5		
		19	Ending balance

The spreadsheet entry is:

The cash dividend accounts for the previously unexplained change in retained earnings.

		($ in millions)
Entry (18) Retained earnings	5	
Cash (payment of cash dividends)		5

19. Completing the Spreadsheet. In preparing the spreadsheet to this point, we have analyzed each noncash account on both the income statement and the balance sheet. Our purpose was to identify the transactions that, during the year, had affected each account. By recreating each transaction in the form of a spreadsheet entry—in effect, duplicating the journal entry that had been used to record the transaction—we were able to explain the change in the balance of each account. That is, the debits and credits in the changes columns of the spreadsheet account for the increase or decrease in each noncash account. When a transaction being entered on the spreadsheet included an operating, investing, or financing activity, we entered that portion of the entry under the corresponding heading of the statement of cash flows section of the spreadsheet. Since, as noted earlier, there can be no operating, investing, or financing activity without a corresponding change in one or more of the

---

ETHICAL DILEMMA

"We must get it," Courtney Lowell, president of Industrial Fasteners, roared. "Without it we're in big trouble." The "it" Mr. Lowell referred to is the renewal of a $14 million loan with Community First Bank. The big trouble he fears is the lack of funds necessary to repay the existing debt and few, if any, prospects for raising the funds elsewhere.

Mr. Lowell had just hung up the phone after a conversation with a bank vice-president in which it was made clear that this year's statement of cash flows must look better than last year's. Mr. Lowell knows that improvements are not on course to happen. In fact, cash flow projections were dismal.

Later that day, Tim Cratchet, assistant controller, was summoned to Mr. Lowell's office. "Cratchet," Lowell barked, "I've looked at our accounts receivable. I think we can generate quite a bit of cash by selling or factoring most of those receivables. I know it will cost us more than if we collect them ourselves, but it sure will make our cash flow picture look better."

Is there an ethical question facing Cratchet?

---

noncash accounts, we should feel confident at this point that we have identified all of the activities that should be reported on the statement of cash flows.

To check the accuracy of the analysis, we compare the change in the balance of the cash account with the net change in cash flows produced by the activities listed in the statement of cash flows section of the spreadsheet. The net increase or decrease in cash flows from each of the statement of cash flows categories is extended to the extreme right column of the spreadsheet. By reference to Illustration 22–1A, we see that net cash flows from operating, investing, and financing activities are: $22 million; ($19 million); and $6 million, respectively. Together these activities provide a net increase in cash of $9 million. This amount corresponds to the increase in the balance of the cash account from $20 million to $29 million. To complete the spreadsheet, we include the final spreadsheet entry:

> The cash flows section of the spreadsheet provides the information to be reported in the statement of cash flows.

	($ in millions)
Entry (19) Cash	9
Net increase in cash (from statement of cash flows activities)	9

As a final check of accuracy, we can confirm that the total of the debits is equal to the total of the credits in the changes columns of the spreadsheet.[19]

The spreadsheet is now complete. The statement of cash flows can now be prepared directly from the spreadsheet simply by presenting the items included in the statement of cash flows section of the spreadsheet in the appropriate format of the statement.

The statements of cash flows from an annual report of Office Depot, Inc. are shown in Graphic 22–9 on the next page. Notice that the reconciliation schedule was reported by Office Depot on the statement of cash flows itself shown above. Many companies report the schedule separately in the disclosure notes.

GLOBAL PERSPECTIVE

A statement of cash flows (or funds flow statement some places) is optional in many countries. France and some other West European countries are examples. In some countries, such as the United Kingdom, it's required only for firms listed on a stock exchange.

---

[19]The mechanical and computational aspects of the spreadsheet analysis are simplified greatly when performed on an electronic spreadsheet such as Microsoft Excel.

GRAPHIC 22–9 Statement of Cash Flows—Office Depot, Inc.

	Dec. 26, 1998	Dec. 26, 1997	Dec. 26, 1996
Cash Flows from Operating Activities:			
Cash received from customers	$8,928,519,000	$8,017,406,000	$7,193,535,000
Cash paid to suppliers	(8,137,802,000)	(7,420,731,000)	(6,924,217,000)
Interest received	23,972,000	(4,703,000)	3,914,000
Interest paid	(3,625,000)	(4,166,000)	(9,187,000)
Income taxes paid	(151,032,000)	(140,831,000)	(82,400,000)
Net cash provided by operating activities	$ 660,032,000	$ 446,975,000	$ 181,645,000
Cash Flows from Investing Activities:			
Purchase of short-term investment securities and bonds	(36,697,000)	0	(30,230,000)
Proceeds from maturities or sale of short-term investment securities and bonds	44,260,000	20,030,000	20,539,000
Purchase of remaining ownership interest in joint venture	(27,680,000)		
Capital expenditures	(254,981,000)	(165,213,000)	(234,489,000)
Proceeds from sale of property and equipment	22,364,000	4,127,000	1,741,000
Net cash used in investing activities	($ 252,734,000)	($ 141,056,000)	($ 242,439,000)
Cash Flows from Financing Activities:			
Proceeds from exercise of stock options and sale of stock under employee stock purchase plan	64,237,000	19,959,000	22,677,000
Proceeds from long- and short-term borrowings	0	0	146,652,000
Payments on long- and short-term borrowings	(2,490,000)	(151,888,000)	(107,639,000)
Net cash provided by (used in) financing activities	$ 61,747,000	($ 131,929,000)	$ 61,690,000
Effect of exchange rate changes on cash and cash equivalents	(4,381,000)	(1,939,000)	(1,020,000)
Net Increase (decrease) in Cash and Cash Equivalents	$ 464,664,000	$ 172,051,000	($124,000)
Cash and cash equivalents at beginning of period	239,877,000	67,826,000	67,950,000
Cash and cash equivalents at end of period	$ 704,541,000	$ 239,877,000	$ 67,826,000
Reconciliation of Net Earnings to Net Cash Provided by Operating Activities			
Net earnings	$ 233,196,000	$ 234,861,000	$ 196,218,000
Adjustments to reconcile net earnings to net cash provided by operating activities:			
Depreciation and amortization	140,940,000	119,476,000	99,118,000
Provision for losses on inventory and accounts receivable	81,270,000	76,919,000	49,606,000
Accreted interest on zero coupon, convertible subordinated notes	18,812,000	18,005,000	17,064,000
Contributions of common stock to employee benefit and stock purchase plans	4,501,000	3,373,000	2,780,000
Deferred income taxes	(38,244,000)	9,534,000	6,605,000
Loss (gain) on disposal of property & equipment	2,023,000	4,657,000	(430,000)
Changes in assets and liabilities:			
Increase in receivables	(88,595,000)	(147,991,000)	(61,791,000)
Decrease (increase) in merchandise inventories	106,189,000	(28,251,000)	(103,463,000)
Increase in prepaid expenses and other assets	(42,013,000)	(22,492,000)	(26,607,000)
Increase in accounts payable, accrued expenses and deferred credits	241,953,000	178,884,000	2,545,000
Total adjustments	426,836,000	212,114,000	(14,573,000)
Net cash provided by operating activities	$ 660,032,000	$ 446,975,000	$ 181,645,000

The comparative balance sheets for 2003 and 2002 and the income statement for 2003 are given below for Beneficial Drill Company. Additional information from Beneficial Drill's accounting records is provided also.

Comprehensive Review

Required:

Prepare the statement of cash flows of Beneficial Drill Company for the year ended December 31, 2003. Present cash flows from operating activities by the direct method and use a spreadsheet to assist in your analysis.

BENEFICIAL DRILL COMPANY
Comparative Balance Sheets
December 31, 2003 and 2002
($ in millions)

Assets	2003	2002
Cash	$ 20	$ 40
Accounts receivable	99	100
Less: Allowance for uncollectible accounts	(5)	(4)
Investment revenue receivable	3	2
Inventory	115	110
Prepaid insurance	2	3
Long-term investments	77	60
Land	110	80
Buildings and equipment	220	240
Less: Accumulated depreciation	(35)	(60)
Patent	15	16
	$621	$587
Liabilities		
Accounts payable	$ 23	$ 30
Salaries payable	2	5
Bond interest payable	4	2
Income tax payable	6	7
Deferred income tax liability	5	4
Notes payable	15	0
Bonds payable	150	130
Less: Discount on bonds	(9)	(10)
Shareholders' Equity		
Common stock	210	200
Paid-in capital—excess of par	44	40
Retained earnings	178	179
Less: Treasury stock (at cost)	(7)	0
	$621	$587

BENEFICIAL DRILL COMPANY
Income Statement
For Year Ended December 31, 2003
($ in millions)

Revenues

Sales revenue	$200	
Investment revenue	6	
Investment revenue—sale of treasury bills	1	$207

Expenses

Cost of goods sold		110	
Salaries expense		30	
Depreciation expense		5	
Patent amortization expense		1	
Bad debts expense		4	
Insurance expense		3	
Bond interest expense		14	
Extraordinary loss on destruction of equipment	$10		
Less: Tax savings	(5)	5	
Income tax expense		12	(184)
Net income			**$ 23**

Additional information from the accounting records:

a. During 2003, $3 million of customer accounts were written off as uncollectible.

b. Investment revenue includes Beneficial Drill Company's $3 million share of the net income of Hammer Company, an equity method investee.

c. Treasury bills were sold during 2003 at a gain of $1 million. Beneficial Drill Company classifies its investments in treasury bills as cash equivalents.

d. A machine that originally cost $60 million and was one-half depreciated, was rendered unusable by a freak bolt of lightning. Most major components of the machine were unharmed and were sold for $20 million.

e. Temporary differences between pretax accounting income and taxable income caused the deferred income tax liability to increase by $1 million.

f. The common stock of Wrench Corporation was purchased for $14 million as a long-term investment.

g. Land costing $30 million was acquired by paying $15 million cash and issuing a 13%, seven-year, $15 million note payable to the seller.

h. New equipment was purchased for $40 million cash.

i. $20 million of bonds were sold at face value.

j. On January 19, Drill issued a 5% stock dividend (1 million shares). The market price of the $10 par value common stock was $14 per share at that time.

k. Cash dividends of $10 million were paid to shareholders.

l. In November, 500,000 common shares were repurchased as treasury stock at a cost of $7 million. Drill uses the cost method to account for treasury stock.

Page references indicate the location within the chapter of discussions pertaining to the ref-   SOLUTION
erenced items.

BENEFICIAL DRILL COMPANY
Spreadsheet for the Statement of Cash Flows

	Dec. 31 2002	Changes Debits		Changes Credits		Dec. 31 2003	Page Ref.
Balance Sheet							
Assets							
Cash	40			(20)	20	20	1107
Accounts receivable	100			(1)	1	99	1094
Less: Allowance for uncollectible accounts	(4)			(1)	1	(5)	1096
Investment revenue receivable	2	(2)	1			3	1096
Inventory	110	(4)	5			115	1098
Prepaid insurance	3			(8)	1	2	1099
Long-term investments	60	(2)	3				
		(13)	14			77	1096
Land	80	(14)	30X			110	1103
Buildings and equipment	240	(15)	40	(10)	60	220	1100, 1103
Less: Accumulated depreciation	(60)	(10)	30	(6)	5	(35)	1099, 1100
Patent	16			(7)	1	15	1099
	587					621	
Liabilities							
Accounts payable	30	(4)	7			23	1098
Salaries payable	5	(5)	3			2	1098
Bond interest payable	2			(9)	2	4	1099
Income tax payable	7	(11)	1			6	1100
Deferred tax liability	4			(11)	1	5	1101
Notes payable	0			(14)	15 X	15	1103
Bonds payable	130			(16)	20	150	1104
Less: Discount	(10)			(9)	1	(9)	1105
Shareholders' Equity							
Common stock	200			(17)	10	210	1105, 1106
Paid-in capital—excess of par	40			(17)	4	44	1105, 1106
Retained earnings	179	(17)	14				
		(18)	10	(12)	23	178	1106
Less: Treasury stock	0	(19)	7			(7)	1087
	587					621	
Income Statement							
Revenues:							
Sales revenue				(1)	200	200	1094
Investment revenue				(2)	6	6	1096
Investment revenue—sale of treasury bills				(3)	1	1	1102
Expenses:							
Cost of goods sold		(4)	110			(110)	1098
Salaries expense		(5)	30			(30)	1098
Depreciation expense		(6)	5			(5)	1099
Patent amortization expense		(7)	1			(1)	1099
Bad debts expense		(1)	4			(4)	1095, 1096
Insurance expense		(8)	3			(3)	1099
Bond interest expense		(9)	14			(14)	1099
Extraordinary loss		(10)	10			(10)	1101
Less: Tax savings				(11)	5	5	1101
Income tax expense		(11)	12			(12)	1101
Net income		(12)	23			23	1102

	Dec. 31 2002	Changes		Dec. 31 2003	Page Ref.
		Debits	Credits		
Statement of Cash Flows					1083
Operating activities:					
Cash inflows:					
From customers		(1) 198			1094
From investment revenue		(2) 2			1095
From sale of treasury bills		(3) 1			1102
Cash outflows:					
To suppliers of goods			(4) 122		1098
To employees			(5) 33		1098
For insurance expense			(8) 2		1099
For bond interest expense			(9) 11		1099
For income taxes			(11) 7		1101
Net cash flows				26	
Investing activities:					1085
Sale of equipment		(10) 20			1100
Purchase of LT investments			(13) 14		1096
Purchase of land			(14) 15		1103
Purchase of equipment			(15) 40		1103
Net cash flows				(49)	
Financing activities:					1086
Sale of bonds payable		(16) 20			1104
Payment of cash dividends			(18) 10		1106
Purchase of treasury stock			(19) 7		1087
Net cash flows				3	
Net decrease in cash		(20) 20		(20)	1107
Totals		638	638		1107

BENEFICIAL DRILL COMPANY
Statement of Cash Flows
For Year Ended December 31, 2003
($ in millions)

Cash Flows from Operating Activities

Cash inflows:

From customers	$198	
From investment revenue	2	
From sale of treasury bills	1	

Cash outflows:

To suppliers of goods	(122)	
To employees	(33)	
For insurance expense	(2)	
For bond interest expense	(11)	
For income taxes	(7)	
Net cash flows from operating activities		$26

Cash Flows from Investing Activities

Sale of equipment	$20	
Purchase of long-term investments	(14)	
Purchase of land	(15)	
Purchase of equipment	(40)	
Net cash flows from investing activities		(49)

Cash Flows from Financing Activities

Sale of bonds payable	$20	
Payment of cash dividends	(10)	
Purchase of treasury stock	(7)	
Net cash flows from financing activities		3
Net decrease in cash		($20)
Cash balance, January 1		40
Cash balance, December 31		$20

Noncash Investing and Financing Activities

Acquired $30 million of land by paying cash and issuing a 13%, 7-year note as follows:

Cost of land	$30
Cash paid	15
Note issued	$15

PREPARING AN SCF: THE INDIRECT METHOD OF REPORTING CASH FLOWS FROM OPERATING ACTIVITIES

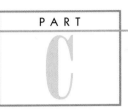

PART

LO8

Getting There through the Back Door

The presentation of cash flows from operating activities illustrated in Part b is referred to as the *direct method.* By this method, the cash effect of each operating activity (i.e., income statement item) is reported directly on the statement of cash flows. For instance, cash received from customers is reported as the cash effect of sales activities, and cash paid to suppliers is reported as the cash effect of cost of goods sold. Income statement items that have *no* cash effect, such as depreciation expense, bad debt expense, gains, and losses, are simply not reported.

As pointed out previously, a permissible alternative is the *indirect method,* by which the net cash increase or decrease from operating activities is derived indirectly by starting with reported net income and working backwards to convert that amount to a cash basis. The derivation by the indirect method of net cash flows from operating activities for UBC is shown in Illustration 22–1B. For the adjustment amounts, you may wish to refer back to UBC's balance sheets and income statement presented in Illustration 22–1.

Cash Flows from Operating Activities—Indirect Method *and* **Reconciliation of Net Income to Net Cash Flows from Operating Activities**	
Net Income	**$12**
Adjustments for noncash effects:	
Increase in accounts receivable	(2)
Gain on sale of land	(8)
Decrease in inventory	4
Increase in accounts payable	6
Increase in salaries payable	2
Depreciation expense	3
Discount on bonds payable	2
Decrease in prepaid insurance	3
Loss on sale of equipment	2
Decrease in income tax payable	(2)
Net cash flows from operating activities	**$22**

ILLUSTRATION 22–1B

Indirect Method

The indirect method derives the net cash increase or decrease from operating activities indirectly, by starting with reported net income and "working backwards" to convert that amount to a cash basis.

Notice that the indirect method yields the same $22 million net cash flows from operating activities as does the direct method. This is understandable when you consider that the indirect method simply reverses the differences between the accrual-based income statement and cash flows from operating activities. We accomplish this as described in the next two sections.

Components of Net Income that Do Not Increase or Decrease Cash

Amounts that were subtracted in determining net income but did not reduce cash are *added back* to net income to reverse the effect of their having been subtracted. For example, depreciation expense and the loss on sale of equipment are added back to net income. Other things being equal, this restores net income to what it would have been had depreciation and the loss not been subtracted at all.

Similarly, amounts that were added in determining net income but did not increase cash are subtracted from net income to reverse the effect of their having been added. For example, UBC's gain on sale of land is deducted from net income. Here's why. UBC sold for $18 million land that originally cost $10 million. Recording the sale produced a gain of $8 million, which UBC appropriately included in its income statement. But did this gain increase UBC's cash? No. Certainly selling the land increased cash—by $18 million. We therefore include the $18 million as a cash inflow in the statement of cash flows. However, the sale of land is an investing activity. The gain itself, though, is simply the difference between cash received in the sale of land (reported as an investing activity) and the original cost of the land. If UBC also reported the $8 million gain as a cash flow from operating activities, in addition to reporting $18 million as a cash flow from investing activities, UBC would report the $8 million twice. So, because UBC added the gain in determining its net income but the gain had no effect on cash, the gain must now be subtracted from net income to reverse the effect of its having been added.

Components of Net Income that Do Increase or Decrease Cash

For components of net income that increase or decrease cash, but by an amount different from that reported on the income statement, net income is adjusted for changes in the balances of related balance sheet accounts to *convert the effects of those items to a cash basis*. For example, sales of $100 million are included on the income statement as a component of net income, and yet, since accounts receivable increased by $2 million, only $98 million cash was collected from customers during the reporting period. Sales are converted to a cash basis by subtracting the $2 million increase in accounts receivable. Here's another example:

The income statement reports salaries expense as $13 million. Just because employees earned $13 million during the reporting period, though, doesn't necessarily mean UBC paid those employees $13 in cash during the same period. In fact, we see in the comparative balance sheets that salaries payable increased from $1 million to $3 million; UBC owes its employees $2 million more than before the year started. The company must not have paid the entire $13 million expense. By analyzing salaries expense in relation to the change in salaries payable, we can determine the amount of cash paid to employees:

Salaries Payable

		1	Beginning balance
Cash paid to employees	?	13	Salaries expense
(decreases salaries payable)			*(increases salaries payable)*
		3	Ending balance

This inspection indicates that UBC paid only $11 million cash to its employees; the remaining $2 million of salaries expense is reflected as an increase in salaries payable. From a cash perspective, then, by subtracting $13 million for salaries in the income statement, UBC has subtracted $2 million more than the reduction in cash. Adding back the $2 million leaves UBC in the same position as if it had deducted only the $11 million cash paid to employees.

Following a similar analysis of the cash effects of the remaining components of net income, those items are likewise converted to a cash basis by adjusting net income for increases and decreases in related accounts.

For components of net income that increase or decrease cash by an amount exactly the same as that reported on the income statement, no adjustment of net income is required. For example, investment revenue of $3 million is included in UBC's $12 million net income amount. Because $3 million also is the amount of cash received from that activity, this element of net income already represents its cash effect and needs no adjustment.[20]

Comparison with the Direct Method

The indirect method is compared with the direct method in Graphic 22–10, using the data of UBC. To better illustrate the relationship between the two methods, the adjustments to net income using the indirect method are presented parallel to the related cash inflows and cash outflows of the direct method. The income statement is included in the graphic to demonstrate that the indirect method also serves to reconcile differences between the elements of that statement and the cash flows reported by the direct method.

As a practical consideration, you might notice that the adjustments to net income using the indirect method follow a convenient pattern. *Increases* in related assets are deducted from net income (i.e., the increase in accounts receivable) when converting to cash from operating activities. Conversely, *decreases* in assets are added (inventory and prepaid insurance in this case). Changes in related liabilities are handled in just the opposite way. Increases in related liabilities are *added* to net income (i.e., the increases in accounts payable and salaries payable) while decreases in liabilities are subtracted (i.e., decrease in income tax payable).[21] Of course, these are adjustments to net income that effectively convert components of income from reported accrual amounts to a cash basis. The other adjustments to net income

GRAPHIC 22–10 Comparison of the Indirect Method and the Direct Method of Determining Cash Flows from Operating Activities

Income Statement		Cash Flows from Operating Activities			
		Indirect Method		**Direct Method**	
		Net income	$12		
		Adjustments:			
Sales	$100	Increase in accounts receivable	(2)	Cash received from customers	$98
Investment revenue	3	(No adjustment—no investment revenue receivable or			
		long-term investments)		Cash received from investments	3
Gain on sale of land	8	Gain on sale of land	(8)	(Not reported—no cash effect)	
Cost of goods sold	(60)	Decrease in inventory	4		
		Increase in accounts payable	6	Cash paid to suppliers	(50)
Salaries expense	(13)	Increase in salaries payable	2	Cash paid to employees	(11)
Depreciation expense	(3)	Depreciation expense	3	(Not reported—no cash effect)	
Interest expense	(5)	Decrease in bond discount	2	Cash paid for interest	(3)
Insurance expense	(7)	Decrease in prepaid insurance	3	Cash paid for insurance	(4)
Loss on sale of equipment	(2)	Loss on sale of equipment	2	(Not reported—no cash effect)	
Income tax expense	(9)	Decrease in income tax payable	(2)	Cash paid for income taxes	(11)
Net Income	$ 12	**Net cash flows from operating activities**	**$22**	**Net cash flows from operating activities**	**$22**

---

[20]We determined in Part b (subsection 2) that there is no evidence that cash received from investments differs from investment revenue.

[21]The adjustment for the decrease in bond discount is logically consistent with this pattern as well. Bond discount is a contra liability. It's logical, then, that an adjustment for a decrease in this account be added—the opposite of the way a decrease in a liability is treated.

(gain, depreciation, loss) as pointed out earlier are to get rid of the three income statement components that have no effect at all on cash. This pattern is summarized in Graphic 22–11.

Type of Adjustment	To Adjust for Noncash Effect
Income statement components that have *no effect* at all on cash but are *additions* to income	Deduct from net income
Income statement components that have *no effect* at all on cash but are *deductions* from income	Add to net income
Increases in assets related to an income statement component	Deduct from net income
Decreases in assets related to an income statement component	Add to net income
Increases in liabilities related to an income statement component	Add to net income
Decreases in liabilities related to an income statement component	Deduct from net income

Although either the direct method or the indirect method is permitted, the FASB strongly encourages companies to report cash flows from operating activities by the direct method. The obvious appeal of this approach is that it reports specific operating cash receipts and operating cash payments, which is consistent with the primary objective of the statement of cash flows. Investors and creditors gain additional insight into the specific sources of cash receipts and payments from operating activities revealed by this reporting method. Also, statement users can more readily interpret and understand the information presented because the direct method avoids the confusion caused by reporting noncash items and other reconciling adjustments under the caption *cash flows from operating activities.* Nonetheless, the vast majority of companies choose to use the indirect method. Reasons for this choice range from longstanding tradition to the desire to withhold as much information as possible from competitors.[22]

Reconciliation of Net Income to Cash Flows from Operating Activities

As we discussed earlier, whether cash flows from operating activities are reported by the direct method or by the indirect method, the financial statements must report a reconciliation of net income to net cash flows from operating activities. When the direct method is used, the reconciliation is presented in a separate schedule and is identical to the presentation of net cash flows from operating activities by the indirect method. In other words, Illustration 22–1B also serves as the reconciliation schedule to accompany a statement of cash flows using the direct method. Obviously, a separate reconciliation schedule is not required when using the indirect method because the cash flows from operating activities section of the statement of cash flows *is* a reconciliation of net income to net cash flows from operating activities.[23]

Remember that the direct and indirect methods are alternative approaches to deriving net cash flows from *operating* activities only. The choice of which method is used for that purpose does not affect the way cash flows from *investing* and *financing* activities are identified and reported.

The statements of cash flows from the annual report of Kroger Company, which uses the indirect method, for its fiscal year ended February are shown in Graphic 22–12.

---

[22]Strong arguments are made for the FASB requiring the direct method by Paul R. Bahnson, Paul B. W. Miller, and Bruce P. Budge in "*Nonarticulation in Cash Flow Statements and Implications for Education, Research and Practice*," *Accounting Horizons*, December 1996, and by G. V. Krishnan and J. A. Largay III in "The Predictive Ability of Direct Method Cash Flow Information," *Journal of Business Finance & Accounting*, January 2000.

[23]It is permissible to present the reconciliation in a separate schedule and to report the net cash flows from operating activities as a single line item on the statement of cash flows.

($ in millions)	2000	1999	1998
Cash Flows from Operating Activities:			
Net earnings.	$ 877	$ 613	$ 247
Adjustments to reconcile net earnings to			
net cash provided by operating activities:			
Extraordinary loss	3	10	257
Depreciation	907	847	745
Goodwill amortization	101	99	91
Non cash merger charges	286	105	109
Deferred income taxes	213	308	(49)
Other	(4)	(9)	101
Changes in operating assets and liabilities:			
Inventories	(114)	(271)	86
Receivables	(49)	(70)	(66)
Accounts payable	67	50	91
Other	(6)	(134)	226
Net cash provided by operating activities	$ 2,281	$ 1,548	$ 1,838
Cash Flows from Investing Activities:			
Capital expenditures	$(1,623)	$(1,691)	$(1,646)
Proceeds from sale of assets	127	139	96
Payments for acquisitions, net of cash acquired	(67)	(230)	(86)
Other	40	(28)	171
Net cash used by investing activities	$(1,523)	$(1,810)	$(1,465)
Cash Flows from Financing Activities:			
Proceeds from issuance of long-term debt	$ 838	$ 1,763	$ 5,307
Reductions in long-term debt	(1,339)	(1,469)	(5,089)
Debt prepayment costs	(3)	(2)	(308)
Financing charges incurred	(10)	(11)	(118)
Increase (decrease) in book overdrafts	160	(62)	(44)
Proceeds from issuance of capital stock	57	67	122
Treasury stock purchases	(581)	(6)	(122)
Other	0	0	(5)
Net cash provided (used) by financing activities	$ (878)	$ 280	$ (257)
Net (decrease) increase in cash and temporary			
cash investments	$ (120)	$ 18	$ 116
Cash and temporary cash investments:			
Beginning of year	281	263	183
End of year	$ 161	$ 281	$ 299
Disclosure of cash flow information:			
Cash paid during the year for interest	$ 691	$ 536	$ 635
Cash paid during the year for income taxes	$ 259	$ 113	$ 172
Noncash changes related to purchase acquisitions:			
Fair value of assets acquired	$ 84	$ 201	$ 2,209
Goodwill recorded	33	53	2,344
Value of stock issued	0	0	(652)
Liabilities assumed	(49)	(19)	(3,746)

GRAPHIC 22–12
Statement of Cash flows—Indirect Method; Kroger Co.

For most companies, expenditures for interest and for taxes are significant. Cash payments for interest and for taxes usually are specifically indicated when the direct method is employed as is the case for Office Depot reported earlier in Graphic 22–9 on page 1108. When the indirect method is used, those amounts aren't readily apparent and should be *separately reported* either on the face of the statement as Kroger does or in an accompanying disclosure note.

We use a spreadsheet to help prepare a statement of cash flows by the indirect method in Appendix 22A.

DECISION MAKERS' PERSPECTIVE—Cash Flow Ratios

We have emphasized the analysis of financial statements from a decision maker's perspective throughout this text. Often that analysis included the development and comparison of financial ratios. Ratios based on income statement and balance sheet amounts enjoy a long tradition of acceptance from which several standard ratios, including those described in earlier chapters, have evolved. To gain another viewpoint, some analysts supplement their investigation with cash flow ratios. Some cash flow ratios are derived by simply substituting cash flow from operations (CFFO) from the statement of cash flows in place of net income in many ratios, not to replace those ratios but to complement them. For example, the times interest earned ratio can be modified to reflect the number of times the cash outflow for interest is provided by cash inflow from operations and any of the profitability ratios can be modified to determine the cash generated from assets, shareholders' equity, sales, etc. Graphic 22–13 summarizes the calculation and usefulness of several representative cash flow ratios.

GRAPHIC 22–13
Cash Flow Ratios

	Calculation	Measures
Performance Ratios		
Cash flow to sales	$\dfrac{CFFO}{Net\ sales}$	Cash generated by each sales dollar
Cash return on assets	$\dfrac{CFFO}{Average\ total\ assets}$	Cash generated from all resources
Cash return on shareholders' equity	$\dfrac{CFFO}{Average\ shareholders'\ equity}$	Cash generated from owner-provided resources
Cash to income	$\dfrac{CFFO}{Income\ from\ continuing\ operations}$	Cash-generating ability of continuing operations
Cash flow per share	$\dfrac{CFFO - preferred\ dividends}{Weighted\text{-}average\ shares}$	Operating cash flow on a per share basis
Sufficiency Ratios		
Debt coverage	$\dfrac{Total\ liabilities}{CFFO}$	Financial risk and financial leverage
Interest coverage	$\dfrac{CFFO + interest + taxes}{Interest}$	Ability to satisfy fixed obligations
Reinvestment	$\dfrac{CFFO}{Cash\ outflow\ for\ noncurrent\ assets}$	Ability to acquire assets with operating cash flows
Debt payment	$\dfrac{CFFO}{Cash\ outflow\ for\ LT\ debt\ repayment}$	Ability to pay debts with operating cash flows
Dividend payment	$\dfrac{CFFO}{Cash\ outflow\ for\ dividends}$	Ability to pay dividends with operating cash flows
Investing and financing activity	$\dfrac{CFFO}{Cash\ outflows\ for\ investing\ and\ financing\ activities}$	Ability to acquire assets, pay debts, and make distributions to owners

Cash flow ratios have received limited acceptance to date due, in large part, to the long tradition of accrual-based ratios coupled with the relatively brief time that all companies have published statements of cash flows. A lack of consensus on cash flow ratios by which to make comparisons also has slowed their acceptance. Nevertheless, cash flow ratios offer insight in the evaluation of a company's profitability and financial strength.[24] ■

---

[24]Proposals for informative sets of cash flow ratios are offered by Charles Carslaw and John Mills, "Developing Ratios for Effective Cash Flow Analysis," *Journal of Accountancy,* November 1991; Don Giacomino and David Mielke, "Cash Flows: Another Approach to Ratio Analysis," *Journal of Accountancy,* March 1993; and John Mills and Jeanne Yamamura, "The Power of Cash Flows Ratios," *Journal of Accountancy,* October 1998.

FINANCIAL REPORTING CASE SOLUTION

1. **What are the cash flow aspects of the situation that Mr. Barr may be overlooking in making his case for a wage increase? How can a company's operations generate a healthy profit and yet produce meager or even negative cash flows?** *(p. 1083)* Positive net income does not necessarily indicate a healthy cash position. A statement of cash flows provides information about cash flows not seen when looking only at the balance sheet and the income statement. Although cash flows from operating activities result from the same activities that are reported on the income statement, the income statement reports the activities on an accrual basis. That is, revenues reported are those earned during the reporting period, regardless of when cash is received, and the expenses incurred in generating those revenues, regardless of when cash is paid. Thus, the very same operations can generate a healthy profit and yet produce meager or even negative cash flows.

2. **What information can a statement of cash flows provide about a company's investing activities that can be useful in decisions such as this?** *(p. 1085)* Cash flows from investing activities result from the acquisition and disposition of assets. Information about investing activities is useful to decision makers regarding the nature and magnitude of productive assets being acquired for future use. In the union negotiations, for instance, Mr. Barr may not be aware of the substantial investments underway to replace and update equipment and the cash requirements of those investments. Relatedly, the relatively low depreciation charges accelerated depreciation provides in the later years of assets' lives may cause profits to seem artificially high given the necessity to replace those assets at higher prices.

3. **What information can a statement of cash flows provide about a company's financing activities that can be useful in decisions such as this?** *(p. 1086)* Information about financing activities provides insights into sources of a company's external financing. Recent debt issues, for instance, might indicate a need for higher cash flows to maintain higher interest charges. Similarly, recent external financing activity may suggest that a company might be near its practical limits from external sources and, therefore, a greater reliance on internal financing through operations. ∎

THE BOTTOM LINE

1. Decision makers focus on the prospects of receiving a cash return from their dealings with a firm. But it is the ability of the firm to generate cash flows to itself that ultimately determines the potential for cash flows to investors and creditors.

2. The statement of cash flows fills an information gap left by the balance sheet and the income statement by presenting information about cash flows that the other statements either do not provide or provide only indirectly.

3. The stipulation that companies present the statement of cash flows is a relatively recent requirement. *SFAS 95* completed a full-cycle movement of accounting thought back to cash flow reporting, which, in different form, was common practice several decades ago.

4. Cash includes cash equivalents. These are short-term, highly liquid investments that can readily be converted to cash with little risk of loss.

5. Cash flows from operating activities are both inflows and outflows of cash that result from activities reported on the income statement. Cash flows from investing activities are related to the acquisition and disposition of assets, other than inventory and assets classified as cash equivalents. Cash flows from financing activities result from the external financing of a business.

6. Noncash investing and financing activities, such as acquiring equipment (an investing activity) by issuing a long-term note payable (a financing activity), are reported in a related disclosure schedule or note.

7. A spreadsheet provides a systematic method of preparing a statement of cash flows by analyzing available data to insure that all operating, investing, and financing activities are

detected. Recording spreadsheet entries that explain account balance changes simultaneously identifies and classifies the activities to be reported on the statement of cash flows.

8. Either the direct or the indirect method can be used to calculate and present the net cash increase or decrease from operating activities. Unlike the direct method, which directly lists cash inflows and outflows, the indirect method derives cash flows indirectly, by starting with reported net income and working backwards to convert that amount to a cash basis. ◼

<table>
<tr><td>APPENDIX
22A</td><td></td></tr>
</table>

SPREADSHEET FOR THE INDIRECT METHOD

A spreadsheet is equally useful in preparing a statement of cash flows whether we use the direct or the indirect method of determining cash flows from operating activities. The format of the spreadsheet differs only with respect to operating activities. The analysis of transactions for the purpose of identifying cash flows to be reported is the same. To illustrate, Illustration 22A–1 provides a spreadsheet analysis of the data for UBC.

ILLUSTRATION 22A–1
Indirect Method

UNITED BRANDS CORPORATION
Spreadsheet for the Statement of Cash Flows

	Dec. 31 2002	Debits		Credits		Dec. 31 2003
Balance Sheet						
Assets						
Cash	20	(19)	9			29
Accounts receivable	30	(5)	2			32
Short-term investments	0	(12)	12			12
Inventory	50			(6)	4	46
Prepaid insurance	6			(8)	3	3
Land	60	(13)	30	(2)	10	80
Buildings and equipment	75	(14)	20X	(3)	14	81
Less: Accumulated depreciation	(20)	(3)	7	(4)	3	(16)
	221					267
Liabilities						
Accounts payable	20			(7)	6	26
Salaries payable	1			(9)	2	3
Income tax payable	8	(11)	2			6
Notes payable	0			(14)	20X	20
Bonds payable	50	(15)	15			35
Less: Discount on bonds	(3)			(10)	2	(1)
Shareholders' Equity						
Common stock	100			(16)	10	
				(17)	20	130
Paid-in capital—excess of par	20			(16)	3	
				(17)	6	29
Retained earnings	25	(16)	13			
		(18)	5	(1)	12	19
	221					267

Statement of Cash Flows

Operating activities:

Net income	(1)	12				
Adjustments for noncash effects:						
Gain on sale of land			(2)	8		
Depreciation expense	(4)	3				
Loss on sale of equipment	(3)	2				
Increase in accounts receivable			(5)	2		
Decrease in inventory	(6)	4				
Decrease in prepaid insurance	(8)	3				
Increase in accounts payable	(7)	6				
Increase in salaries payable	(9)	2				
Decrease in income tax payable			(11)	2		
Amortization of discount	(10)	2				
Net cash flows					22	

Investing activities:

Purchase of land			(13)	30		
Purchase of S-T investment			(12)	12		
Sale of land	(2)	18				
Sale of equipment	(3)	5				
Net cash flows					(19)	

Financing activities:

Sale of common shares	(17)	26				
Retirement of bonds payable			(15)	15		
Payment of cash dividends			(18)	5		
Net cash flows					6	
Net increase in cash			(19)	9	9	
Totals		198		198		

Two differences should be noted between the spreadsheet in Illustration 22A–1 and the spreadsheet we used earlier for the direct method. First, in the statement of cash flows section of the spreadsheet, under the heading of "cash flows from operating activities," specific cash inflows and cash outflows are replaced by net income and the required adjustments for noncash effects. Second, we do not include an income statement section. This section is unnecessary because, using the indirect method, we are not interested in identifying specific operating activities that cause increases and decreases in cash. Instead, we need from the income statement only the amount of net income, which is converted to a cash basis by adjusting for any noncash amounts included in net income. The spreadsheet entries in journal entry form for the indirect method are illustrated in Illustration 22A–2 on the next page.

Remember that there is no mandatory order in which the account changes must be analyzed. However, since we determine net cash flows from operating activities by working backwards from net income when using the indirect method, it is convenient to start with the spreadsheet entry that represents the credit to retained earnings due to net income. This entry corresponds to spreadsheet entry (11) of the direct method. By entering the debit portion of the entry as the first item under the cash flows from operating activities (CFOA), we establish net income as the initial amount of cash flows from operating activities, which is then adjusted to a cash basis by subsequent entries. Entries (2)–(4) duplicate the transactions that involve noncash components of net income. Changes in current assets and current liabilities that represent differences between revenues and expenses and the cash effects of those revenues and expenses are accounted for by entries (5)–(11). Spreadsheet entries (12)–(19) explain the

ILLUSTRATION 22A–2				
Spreadsheet Entries for the Indirect Method	**Entry (1)**	Net income—CFOA.	12	
		Retained earnings.		12

Entry (1) Net income—CFOA.   12

      Retained earnings.   12

Establishes net income as the initial amount of cash flows from operating activities, to be adjusted to a cash basis by subsequent entries.

Entry (2) Cash (received from sale of land).   18

      Land   10

      Gain on sale of land—CFOA   8

Deducts the noncash gain added in determining net income, explains a portion of the change in land, and identifies a cash inflow from investing activities.

Entry (3) Cash (received from sale of equipment).   5

Loss on sale of equipment—CFOA   2

Accumulated depreciation.   7

      Buildings and equipment   14

Adds back the noncash loss subtracted in determining net income, explains portions of the changes in accumulated depreciation and buildings and equipment, and identifies a cash inflow from investing activities.

Entry (4) Depreciation expense—CFOA   3

      Accumulated depreciation.   3

Adds back the noncash expense subtracted in determining net income.

Entry (5) Accounts receivable.   2

      Increase in accounts receivable—CFOA   2

Reduces net income to reflect $98 million cash received from customers rather than $100 million sales.

Entry (6) Decrease in inventory—CFOA.   4

      Inventory.   4

Increases net income to reflect a deduction of $56 million cost of goods purchased rather than $60 million cost of goods sold.

Entry (7) Increase in accounts payable—CFOA   6

      Accounts payable.   6

Increases net income to reflect a deduction of $50 million cash paid to suppliers rather than $56 million cost of goods purchased.

Entry (8) Decrease in prepaid insurance—CFOA.   3

      Prepaid insurance.   3

Increases net income to reflect a deduction of $10 million cash paid for insurance rather than $13 million insurance expense.

Entry (9) Increase in salaries payable—CFOA   2

      Salaries payable   2

Increases net income to reflect a deduction of $11 million cash paid to employees rather than $13 million salaries expense.

Entry (10) Amortization of discount on bonds—CFOA   2

      Discount on bonds.   2

Increases net income to reflect a deduction of $3 million cash paid for bond interest rather than $5 million bond interest expense.

Entry (11) Income taxes payable   2

      Decrease in income taxes payable—CFOA.   2

Reduces net income to reflect a deduction of $11 million cash paid for income taxes rather than $9 million income tax expense.

Entry (12) Short-term investment.   12

      Cash (purchase of short-term investment)   12

Explains the increase in the short-term investment account and identifies a cash outflow from investing activities.

Entry (13) Land.   30

      Cash (purchase of land)   30

Explains a portion of the change in the land account and identifies a cash outflow from investing activities.

Entry (14)	Buildings and equipment......................	20		**ILLUSTRATION 22A–2**
	Note payable		20	concluded
	Partially explains the changes in the buildings and equipment and notes payable accounts and identifies a noncash investing and financing activity.			
Entry (15)	Bonds payable	15		
	Cash (retirement of bonds payable)		15	
	Explains the decrease in the bonds payable account and identifies a cash outflow from financing activities.			
Entry (16)	Retained earnings	13		
	Common stock.............................		10	
	Paid-in capital—excess of par		3	
	Partially explains the changes in the retained earnings, common stock, and paid-in capital—excess of par accounts.			
Entry (17)	Cash (from sale of common stock)................	26		
	Common stock.............................		20	
	Paid-in capital—excess of par		6	
	Partially explains the changes in the common stock and paid-in capital—excess of par accounts and identifies a cash inflow from financing activities.			
Entry (18)	Retained earnings	5		
	Cash (payment of cash dividends)		5	
	Partially explains the change in the retained earnings account and identifies a cash outflow from financing activities.			
Entry (19)	Cash..	9		
	Net increase in cash (from statement of cash flows activities)		9	
	Reconciles the net increase in cash from operating, investing, and financing activities to the increase in the cash balance.			

changes in the balance sheet not already accounted for by previous entries, and are identical to entries (12)–(19) recorded using the direct method.

The statement of cash flows presenting net cash flows from operating activities by the indirect method is illustrated in Illustration 22A–3.

UNITED BRANDS CORPORATION **Statement of Cash Flows** **For Year Ended December 31, 2003** **($ in millions)**			**ILLUSTRATION 22A–3** Statement of Cash Flows—Indirect Method
Cash Flows from Operating Activities			
Net income	$12		
Adjustments for noncash effects:			
Gain on sale of land	(8)		
Depreciation expense	3		**All parts of the statement of cash flows except operating activities are precisely the same as in the direct method.**
Loss on sale of equipment	2		
Increase in accounts receivable	(2)		
Decrease in inventory	4		
Decrease in prepaid insurance	3		
Increase in accounts payable	6		
Increase in salaries payable	2		
Decrease in income tax payable	(2)		
Amortization of discount on bonds	2		
Net cash flows from operating activities		$22	

Cash Flows from Investing Activities

Purchase of land	(30)	
Purchase of short-term investment	(12)	
Sale of land	18	
Sale of equipment	5	
Net cash from investing activities		(19)

Cash Flows from Financing Activities

Sale of common shares	26	
Retirement of bonds payable	(15)	
Payment of cash dividends	(5)	
Net cash flows from financing activities		6
Net increase in cash		9
Cash balance, January 1		20
Cash balance, December 31		$29

Noncash Investing and Financing Activities

Acquired $20 million of equipment by issuing a 12%, 5-year note.	$20

THE T-ACCOUNT METHOD OF PREPARING THE STATEMENT OF CASH FLOWS

This chapter demonstrates the use of a spreadsheet to prepare the statement of cash flows. A second systematic approach to the preparation of the statement is referred to as the T-account method. The two methods are identical in concept. Both approaches reconstruct the transactions that caused changes in each account balance during the year, simultaneously identifying the operating, investing, and financing activities to be reported on the statement of cash flows. The form of the two methods differs only by whether the entries for those transactions are recorded on a spreadsheet or in T-accounts. In both cases, entries are recorded until the net change in each account balance has been explained.

Some accountants feel that the T-account method is less time-consuming than preparing a spreadsheet but accomplishes precisely the same goal. Since both methods are simply analytical techniques to assist in statement preparation, the choice is a matter of personal preference.

The following five steps outline the T-account method:

1. Draw T-accounts for each income statement and balance sheet account.
2. The T-account for cash should be drawn considerably larger than other T-accounts because more space is required to accommodate the numerous debits and credits to cash. Also, the cash T-account will serve the same purpose as the statement of cash flows section of the spreadsheet in that the formal statement of cash flows is developed from the cash flows reported there. Therefore, it is convenient to partition the cash T-account with headings for "Operating Activities," "Investing Activities," and "Financing Activities" before entries are recorded.
3. Enter each account's net change on the appropriate side (debit or credit) of the uppermost portion of each T-account. These changes will serve as individual check figures for determining whether the increase or decrease in each account balance has been explained. These first three steps establish the basic work form for the T-account method.
4. Reconstruct the transactions that caused changes in each account balance during the year and record the entries for those transactions directly in the T-accounts. Again using UBC as an example, the entries we record in the T-accounts are exactly the same as the spreadsheet entries we created in the chapter when using the spreadsheet

method. The analysis we used in creating those spreadsheet entries is equally applicable to the T-account method. For that reason, that analysis is not repeated here. The complete T-account work form for UBC is presented below. Account balance changes are provided by Illustration 22–1.

BALANCE SHEET ACCOUNTS
Cash (statement of cash flows)

		9		

Operating Activities:

From customers	(1)	98	50	(4)	To suppliers of goods
From investment revenue	(2)	3	11	(5)	To employees
			3	(7)	For interest
			4	(8)	For insurance
			11	(10)	For income taxes

Investing Activities:

Sale of land	(3)	18	12	(12)	Purchase of short-term investment
Sale of equipment	(9)	5	30	(13)	Purchase of land

Financing Activities:

Sale of common stock	(17)	26	15	(15)	Retirement of bonds payable
			5	(18)	Payment of cash dividends

Accounts Receivable

	2	
(1)	2	

Short-Term Investments

	12	
(12)	12	

Inventory

	4		
	4		(4)

Prepaid Insurance

	3		
	3		(8)

Land

	20		
(13)	30	10	(3)

Buildings and Equipment

	6		
X(14)	20	14	(9)

Accumulated Depreciation

	4		
(9)	7	3	(6)

Accounts Payable

	6		
	6		(4)

Salaries Payable

	2		
	2		(5)

Income Tax Payable

	2	
(10)	2	

Notes Payable

	20		
	20		(14)**X**

Bonds Payable

	15	
(15)	15	

Discount on Bonds

	2		
	2		(7)

Common Stock

	30		
	10		(16)
	20		(17)

Paid-in Capital— excess of par

	9		
	3		(16)
	6		(17)

Retained Earnings

	6		
(16)	13		
(18)	5	12	(11)

X Noncash Investing and Financing Activity

INCOME STATEMENT ACCOUNTS

Sales Revenue		Investment Revenue		Gain on Sale of Land	
	100		3		8
	100 (1)		3 (2)		8 (3)

Cost of Goods Sold		Salaries Expense		Depreciation Expense	
60		13		3	
(4) 60		(5) 13		(6) 3	

Interest Expense		Insurance Expense		Loss of Sale of Equipment	
5		7		2	
(7) 5		(8) 7		(9) 2	

Income Tax Expense		Net Income (Income Summary)	
9		12	
(10) 9		(11) 12	

5. After all account balances have been explained by T-account entries, prepare the statement of cash flows from the cash T-account, being careful also to report noncash investing and financing activities. The statement of cash flows for UBC appears in Graphic 22–2 on page 1080.

QUESTIONS FOR REVIEW OF KEY TOPICS

Q 22–1 Effects of all cash flows affect the balances of various accounts reported on the balance sheet. Also, the activities that cause some of these cash flows are reported on the income statement. What, then, is the need for an additional financial statement that reports cash flows?

Q 22–2 The statement of cash flows has been a required financial statement only since 1988. Is cash flow reporting a totally new concept? Explain.

Q 22–3 Is an investment in treasury bills always classified as a cash equivalent? Explain.

Q 22–4 Transactions that involve merely purchases or sales of cash equivalents generally are not reported on a statement of cash flows. Describe an exception to this generalization. What is the essential characteristic of the transaction that qualifies as an exception?

Q 22–5 What are the differences between cash flows from operating activities and the elements of an income statement?

Q 22–6 Do cash flows from operating activities report all the elements of the income statement on a cash basis? Explain.

Q 22–7 Investing activities include the acquisition and disposition of assets. Provide four specific examples. Identify two exceptions.

Q 22–8 The sale of stock and the sale of bonds are reported as financing activities. Are payments of dividends to shareholders and payments of interest to bondholders also reported as financing activities? Explain.

Q 22–9 Does the statement of cash flows report only transactions that cause an increase or a decrease in cash? Explain.

Q 22–10 How would the acquisition of a building be reported on a statement of cash flows if purchased by issuing a mortgage note payable in addition to a significant cash down payment?

Q 22–11 Perhaps the most noteworthy item reported on an income statement is net income—the amount by which revenues exceed expenses. The most noteworthy item reported on a statement of cash flows is *not* the amount of net cash flows. Explain.

Q 22–12 What is the purpose of the "changes" columns of a spreadsheet to prepare a statement of cash flows?

Q 22–13 Given sales revenue of $200,000, how can it be determined whether or not $200,000 cash was received from customers?

Q 22–14 When an asset is sold at a gain, why is the gain not reported as a cash inflow from operating activities?

Q 22–15 Are ordinary losses and extraordinary losses treated alike in preparing a statement of cash flows? Explain.

Q 22–16 When determining the amount of cash paid for income taxes, what would be indicated by an increase in the deferred income tax liability account?

Q 22–17 When using the indirect method of determining net cash flows from operating activities, how is bad debt expense reported? Why? What other expenses are reported in a like manner?

Q 22–18 When using the indirect method of determining net cash flows from operating activities, how are revenues and expenses reported on the statement of cash flows if their cash effects are identical to the amounts reported on the income statement?

Q 22–19 Why does the FASB recommend the direct method over the indirect method?

Q 22–20 Compare the manner in which investing activities are reported on a statement of cash flows prepared by the direct method and by the indirect method.

EXERCISES

E 22–1
Classification of cash flows

Listed below are several transactions that typically produce either an increase or a decrease in cash. Indicate by letter whether the cash effect of each transaction is reported on a statement of cash flows as an operating (**O**), investing (**I**), or financing (**F**) activity.

	Transactions
F	1. Sale of common stock
___	2. Sale of land
___	3. Purchase of treasury stock
___	4. Merchandise sales
___	5. Issuance of a long-term note payable
___	6. Purchase of merchandise
___	7. Repayment of note payable
___	8. Employee salaries
___	9. Sale of equipment at a gain
___	10. Issuance of bonds
___	11. Acquisition of bonds of another corporation
___	12. Payment of semiannual interest on bonds payable
___	13. Payment of a cash dividend
___	14. Purchase of a building
___	15. Collection of nontrade note receivable (principal amount)
___	16. Loan to another firm
___	17. Retirement of common stock
___	18. Income taxes
___	19. Issuance of a short-term note payable
___	20. Sale of a copyright

E 22–2
Determine cash paid to suppliers of merchandise

Shown below in T-account format are the beginning and ending balances ($ in millions) of both inventory and accounts payable.

Inventory

Beginning balance	90	
Ending balance	93	

Accounts Payable

	14	Beginning balance
	16	Ending balance

Required:
1. Use a T-account analysis to determine the amount of cash paid to suppliers of merchandise during the reporting period if cost of goods sold was $300 million.
2. Prepare a summary entry that represents the net effect of merchandise purchases during the reporting period.

E 22–3
Determine cash received from customers

Determine the amount of cash received from customers for each of the six independent situations below. All dollars are in millions.

Situation	Sales Revenue	Accounts Receivable Increase (Decrease)	Bad Debt Expense	Allowance for Uncollectible Accounts Increase (Decrease)	Cash Received from Customers
1	100	-0-	-0-	-0-	?
2	100	5	-0-	-0-	?
3	100	(5)	-0-	-0-	?
4	100	5	2	2	?
5	100	(5)	2	1	?
6	100	5	2	(1)	?

E 22–4
Summary entries for cash received from customers

For each of the four independent situations below, prepare journal entries that summarize the selling and collection activities for the reporting period in order to determine the amount of cash received from customers and to explain the change in each account shown. All dollars are in millions.

Situation	Sales Revenue	Accounts Receivable Increase (Decrease)	Bad Debt Expense	Allowance for Uncollectible Accounts Increase (Decrease)	Cash Received from Customers
1	200	-0-	-0-	-0-	?
2	200	10	-0-	-0-	?
3	200	10	4	4	?
4	200	10	4	(2)	?

E 22–5
Determine cash paid to suppliers of merchandise

Determine the amount of cash paid to suppliers of merchandise for each of the nine independent situations below. All dollars are in millions.

Situation	Cost of Goods Sold	Inventory Increase (Decrease)	Accounts Payable Increase (Decrease)	Cash Paid to Suppliers
1	100	0	0	?
2	100	3	0	?
3	100	(3)	0	?
4	100	0	7	?
5	100	0	(7)	?
6	100	3	7	?
7	100	3	(7)	?
8	100	(3)	(7)	?
9	100	(3)	7	?

E 22–6
Summary entries for cash paid to suppliers of merchandise

For each of the five independent situations below, prepare a journal entry that summarizes the purchases, sales, and payments related to inventories in order to determine the amount of cash paid to suppliers and explain the change in each account shown. All dollars are in millions.

Situation	Cost of Goods Sold	Inventory Increase (Decrease)	Accounts Payable Increase (Decrease)	Cash Paid to Suppliers
1	200	0	0	?
2	200	6	0	?
3	200	0	14	?
4	200	6	14	?
5	200	(6)	(14)	?

E 22–7
Determine cash paid for bond interest

Determine the amount of cash paid to bondholders for bond interest for each of the six independent situations below. All dollars are in millions.

Situation	Bond Interest Expense	Bond Interest Payable Increase (Decrease)	Unamortized Discount Increase (Decrease)	Cash Paid for Interest
1	10	0	0	?
2	10	2	0	?
3	10	(2)	0	?
4	10	0	(3)	?
5	10	2	(3)	?
6	10	(2)	(3)	?

E 22–8
Determine cash paid for bond interest

For each of the four independent situations below, prepare a single journal entry that summarizes the recording and payment of interest in order to determine the amount of cash paid for bond interest and explain the change (if any) in each of the accounts shown. All dollars are in millions.

Situation	Bond Interest Expense	Bond Interest Payable Increase (Decrease)	Unamortized Discount Increase (Decrease)	Cash Paid for Interest
1	20	0	0	?
2	20	4	0	?
3	20	0	(6)	?
4	20	(4)	(6)	?

E 22–9
Determine cash paid for income taxes

Determine the amount of cash paid for income taxes in each of the nine independent situations below. All dollars are in millions.

Situation	Income Tax Expense	Income Tax Payable Increase (Decrease)	Deferred Tax Liability Increase (Decrease)	Cash Paid for Taxes
1	10	0	0	?
2	10	3	0	?
3	10	(3)	0	?
4	10	0	2	?
5	10	0	(2)	?
6	10	3	2	?
7	10	3	(2)	?
8	10	(3)	(2)	?
9	10	(3)	2	?

E 22–10
Summary entries for cash paid for income taxes

For each of the five independent situations below, prepare a single journal entry that summarizes the recording and payment of income taxes in order to determine the amount of cash paid for income taxes and explain the change (if any) in each of the accounts shown. All dollars are in millions.

Situation	Income Tax Expense	Income Tax Payable Increase (Decrease)	Deferred Tax Liability Increase (Decrease)	Cash Paid for Taxes
1	10	0	0	?
2	10	3	0	?
3	10	0	(2)	?
4	10	3	2	?
5	10	(3)	(2)	?

E 22–11
Bonds; statement of cash flow effects

Most Solutions, Inc. issued 10% bonds, dated January 1, with a face amount of $640 million on January 1, 2003. The bonds mature in 2013 (10 years). For bonds of similar risk and maturity the market yield is 12%. Interest is paid semiannually on June 30 and December 31. Most recorded the sale as follows:

January 1, 2003

Cash (price)	566,589,440	
Discount on bonds (difference)	73,410,560	
Bonds payable (face amount)		640,000,000

Required:

What would be the amount(s) related to the bonds that Most would report in its statement of cash flows for the year ended December 31, 2003?

E 22–12
Installment note; statement of cash flow effects

National Food Services, Inc. borrowed $4 million from its local bank on January 1, 2003, and issued a 4-year installment note to be paid in four equal payments at the end of each year. The payments include interest at the rate of 10%. Installment payments are $1,261,881 annually.

Required:

What would be the amount(s) related to the note that National would report in its statement of cash flows for the year ended December 31, 2003?

E 22–13
Identifying cash flows from investing activities and financing activities

In preparation for developing its statement of cash flows for the year ended December 31, 2003, RapidPac, Inc. collected the following information:

	($ in millions)
Fair value of shares issued in a stock dividend	$ 65
Payment for the early extinguishment of long-term bonds (carrying amount: $97 million)	102
Proceeds from the sale of treasury stock (cost: $17 million)	22
Gain on sale of land	4
Proceeds from sale of land	12
Purchase of Microsoft common stock	160
Declaration of cash dividends	44
Distribution of cash dividends declared in 2002	40

Required:

1. In RapidPac's statement of cash flows, what were net cash inflows (or outflows) from investing activities for 2003?
2. In RapidPac's statement of cash flows, what were net cash inflows (or outflows) from financing activities for 2003?

E 22–14
Identifying cash flows from investing activities and financing activities

In preparation for developing its statement of cash flows for the year ended December 31, 2003, Millennium Solutions, Inc. collected the following information ($ in millions):

Payment for the early extinguishments of long-term notes (book value: $50 million)	$ 54
Sale of common shares	176
Retirement of common shares	(122)
Loss on sale of equipment	(2)
Proceeds from sale of equipment	8
Issuance of short-term note payable for cash	10
Acquisition of building for cash	(7)
Purchase of marketable securities (not a cash equivalent)	(5)
Purchase of marketable securities (considered a cash equivalent)	(1)
Cash payment for 3-year insurance policy	(3)
Collection of note receivable with interest (principal amount, $11)	13
Declaration of cash dividends	33
Distribution of cash dividends declared in 2002	(30)

Required:

1. In Millennium's statement of cash flows, what were net cash inflows (or outflows) from investing activities for 2003?
2. In Millennium's statement of cash flows, what were net cash inflows (or outflows) from financing activities for 2003?

E 22–15
Capital lease; lessee; statement of cash flows effects

Wilson Foods Corporation leased a commercial food processor on September 30, 2003. The five-year lease agreement calls for Wilson to make quarterly lease payments of $195,774, payable each September 30, December 31, March 31, June 30, with the first payment at September 30, 2003. Wilson's incremental borrowing rate is 12%. Wilson records depreciation on a straight-line basis at the end of each fiscal year. Wilson recorded the lease as follows:

September 30, 2003

Leased equipment (calculated below)	3,000,000	
Lease payable (calculated below)		3,000,000

Lease payable	195,774	
Cash (rental payment)		195,774

Calculation of the present value of lease payments

$$\$195,774 \times 15.32380^* \quad = \quad \$3,000,000$$
$$\text{(rounded)}$$

*Present value of an annuity due of $1: n = 20, i = 3%

Required:
What would be the pretax amounts related to the lease that Wilson would report in its statement of cash flows for the year ended December 31, 2003?

E 22–16
Equity method investment; statement of cash flows effects

On January 1, 2003, Beilich Enterprises bought 20% of the outstanding common stock of Wolfe Construction Company for $600 million cash. Wolfe's net income for the year ended December 31, 2003, was $300 million. During 2003, Wolfe declared and paid cash dividends of $60 million. Beilich recorded the investment as follows:

	($ in millions)
Purchase	
Investment in Wolfe Construction shares	600
Cash	600
Net income	
Investment in Wolfe Construction shares (20% × $300 million)	60
Investment revenue	60
Dividends	
Cash (20% × $60 million)	12
Investment in Wolfe Construction shares	12

Required:
What would be the pretax amounts related to the investment that Beilich would report in its statement of cash flows for the year ended December 31, 2003?

E 22–17
Indirect method; reconciliation of net income to net cash flows from operating activities

The accounting records of EZ Company provided the data below. Prepare a reconciliation of net income to net cash flows from operating activities.

Net income	$50,000
Depreciation expense	7,000
Increase in inventory	1,500
Decrease in salaries payable	800
Decrease in accounts receivable	2,000
Amortization of patent	500
Amortization of premium on bonds	1,000
Increase in accounts payable	4,000
Cash dividends	12,000

E 22–18
Spreadsheet entries from statement of retained earnings

The statement of retained earnings of Gary Larson Publishers is presented below.

GARY LARSON PUBLISHERS
Statement of Retained Earnings
For the Year Ended December 31, 2003
($ in millions)

Retained earnings, January 1		$200
Add:	Net income	75
Deduct:	Cash dividend	(25)
	Stock dividend (1 million shares of $1 par common stock)	(16)
	Property dividend (Garfield Company preferred stock held as a short-term investment)	(12)
	Sale of treasury stock (cost $53 million)	(10)
Retained earnings, December 31		$212

Required:
For the transactions that affected Larson's retained earnings, reconstruct the journal entries for the transactions that affected retained earnings and that can be used to determine cash flows to be reported

in a statement of cash flows. Also indicate any investing and financing activities you identify from this analysis that should be reported on the statement of cash flows.

E 22–19
Relationship between the income statement and cash flows from operating activities (direct method and indirect method)

The following schedule relates the income statement with cash flows from operating activities, derived by both the direct and indirect methods, in the format illustrated by Graphic 22–10 in the chapter. The amounts for income statement elements are missing.

Cash Flows from Operating Activities

Income Statement		Indirect Method		Direct Method	
		Net income	$?		
		Adjustments:			
Sales	$?	Decrease in accounts receivable	12	Cash received from customers	$612
Cost of goods sold	?	Increase in inventory	(24)		
		Decrease in accounts payable	(36)	Cash paid to suppliers	(420)
Salaries expense	?	Increase in salaries payable	12	Cash paid to employees	(66)
Depreciation expense	?	Depreciation expense	18	(Not reported—no cash effect)	
Insurance expense	?	Decrease in prepaid insurance	18	Cash paid for insurance	(24)
Loss on sale of land	?	Loss on sale of land	12	(Not reported—no cash effect)	
Income tax expense	?	Increase in income tax payable	12	Cash paid for income taxes	(42)
Net income	$?	**Net cash flows from operating activities**	$60	**Net cash flows from operating activities**	$ 60

Required:
Deduce the missing amounts and prepare the income statement.

E 22–20
Reconciliation of net cash flows from operating activities to net income

The income statement and the cash flows from the operating activities section of the statement of cash flows are provided below for Far Side Company. The merchandise inventory account balance neither increased nor decreased during the reporting period. Far Side had no liability for either insurance, deferred income taxes, or interest at any time during the period.

FAR SIDE COMPANY
Income Statement
For the Year Ended December 31, 2003
($ in 000s)

Sales		$312
Cost of goods sold		(188)
Gross margin		124
Salaries expense	$41	
Insurance expense	22	
Depreciation expense	11	
Depletion expense	5	
Bond interest expense	10	(89)
Gains and losses:		
Gain on sale of equipment		25
Loss on sale of land		(8)
Income before tax		52
Income tax expense		(26)
Net income		$ 26

Cash Flows from Operating Activities:

Cash received from customers	$258
Cash paid to suppliers	(175)
Cash paid to employees	(37)
Cash paid for interest	(9)
Cash paid for insurance	(16)
Cash paid for income taxes	(14)
Net cash flows from operating activities	$ 7

Required:
Prepare a schedule to reconcile net income to net cash flows from operating activities.

E 22–21
Cash flows from operating activities (direct method) derived from an income statement and cash flows from operating activities (indirect method)

The income statement and a schedule reconciling cash flows from operating activities to net income are provided below ($ in 000s) for Peach Computers.

PEACH COMPUTERS Income Statement For the Year Ended December 31, 2003				Reconciliation of Net Income To Net Cash Flows from Operating Activities	
Sales		$305		Net income	$22
Cost of goods sold		(185)			
Gross margin		120		**Adjustments for Noncash Effects**	
Salaries expense	$41			Depreciation expense	11
Insurance expense	19			Loss on sale of land	5
Depreciation expense	11			Decrease in accounts receivable	6
Loss on sale of land	5	76		Increase in inventory	(13)
Income before tax		44		Decrease in accounts payable	(8)
Income tax expense		(22)		Increase in salaries payable	5
Net income		$ 22		Decrease in prepaid insurance	9
				Increase in income tax payable	20
				Net cash flows from operating activities	$57

Required:
1. Calculate each of the following amounts for Peach Computers:
   a. Cash received from customers during the reporting period.
   b. Cash paid to suppliers of goods during the reporting period.
   c. Cash paid to employees during the reporting period.
   d. Cash paid for insurance during the reporting period.
   e. Cash paid for income taxes during the reporting period.
2. Prepare the cash flows from operating activities section of the statement of cash flows (direct method).

E 22–22
Indirect method; reconciliation of net income to net cash flows from operating activities

The accounting records of EZ Company provided the data below. Prepare a reconciliation of net income to net cash flows from operating activities.

Net loss	$5,000
Depreciation expense	6,000
Increase in salaries payable	500
Decrease in accounts receivable	2,000
Increase in inventory	2,300
Amortization of patent	300
Reduction in discount on bonds	200

E 22–23
Cash flows from operating activities (direct method)— includes loss on sale of cash equivalents and extraordinary loss

Portions of the financial statements for Trapper John Company are provided below.

TRAPPER JOHN COMPANY
Income Statement
For the Year Ended December 31, 2003 ($ in millions)

Sales		$660
Cost of goods sold		(250)
Gross margin		410
Salaries expense	$110	
Depreciation expense	90	
Patent amortization expense	5	
Interest expense	20	
Loss on sale of cash equivalents	3	(228)
Income before taxes and extraordinary loss		182
Income tax expense		(91)
Income before extraordinary loss		91
Extraordinary loss (earthquake)	10	
Less: Tax savings	(5)	(5)
Net Income		$ 86

TRAPPER JOHN COMPANY
Selected Accounts from Comparative Balance Sheets
December 31, 2003 and 2002 ($ in millions)

	Year		
	2003	**2002**	**Change**
Cash	$102	$100	$ 2
Accounts receivable	220	232	(12)
Inventory	440	450	(10)
Accounts payable	140	134	6
Salaries payable	80	86	(6)
Interest payable	25	20	5
Income taxes payable	15	10	5

Required:

Prepare the cash flows from operating activities section of the statement of cash flows for Trapper John Company using the *direct method*.

E 22–24
Cash flows from operating activities (indirect method) includes loss on sale of cash equivalents and extraordinary loss

Refer to the data provided in the previous exercise for Trapper John Company.

Required:

Prepare the cash flows from operating activities section of the statement of cash flows for Trapper John Company using the *indirect method*.

E 22–25
Cash flows from operating activities (direct method)—includes loss on sale of cash equivalents and extraordinary gain

Portions of the financial statements for Radar Company are provided below.

RADAR COMPANY
Income Statement
For the Year Ended December 31, 2003 ($ in 000s)

Sales		$1,320
Cost of goods sold		(500)
Gross margin		820
Salaries expense	$220	
Depreciation expense	180	
Patent amortization expense	10	
Interest expense	40	
Loss on sale of cash equivalents	6	(456)
Income before taxes and extraordinary gain		364
Income tax expense		(182)
Income before extraordinary gain		182
Extraordinary gain (early extinguishment of debt)	20	
Less: Tax on gain	(10)	10
Net Income		$ 192

RADAR COMPANY
Selected Accounts from Comparative Balance Sheets
December 31, 2003 and 2002 ($ in 000s)

	Year		
	2003	**2002**	**Change**
Cash	$102	$100	$ 2
Accounts receivable	220	232	(12)
Inventory	440	450	(10)
Accounts payable	140	134	6
Salaries payable	80	86	(6)
Interest payable	25	20	5
Income taxes payable	15	10	5

Required:
Prepare the cash flows from operating activities section of the statement of cash flows for Radar Company using the *direct method.*

E 22–26
Cash flows from operating activities (indirect method)— includes loss on sale of cash equivalents and extraordinary gain

Refer to the data provided in the previous exercise for Radar Company.

Required:
Prepare the cash flows from operating activities section of the statement of cash flows for Radar Company using the *indirect method.*

E 22–27
Statement of cash flows; direct method

Comparative balance sheets for 2003 and 2002, a statement of income for 2003, and additional information from the accounting records of Whoops, Inc. are provided below.

WHOOPS, INC.
Comparative Balance Sheets
December 31, 2003 and 2002 ($ in millions)

	2003	2002
Assets		
Cash	$ 24	$110
Accounts receivable	178	132
Prepaid insurance	7	3
Inventory	285	175
Buildings and equipment	400	350
Less: Accumulated depreciation	(119)	(240)
	$775	$530
Liabilities		
Accounts payable	$ 87	$100
Accrued expenses payable	6	11
Notes payable	50	0
Bonds payable	160	0
Shareholders' Equity		
Common stock	400	400
Retained earnings	72	19
	$775	$530

WHOOPS, INC.
Statement of Income
For Year Ended December 31, 2003 ($ in millions)

Revenues		
Sales revenue		$2,000
Expenses		
Cost of goods sold	$1,400	
Depreciation expense	50	
Operating expenses	447	1,897
Net income		$ 103

Additional information from the accounting records:
a. During 2003, $230 million of equipment was purchased to replace $180 million of equipment (95% depreciated) sold at book value.
b. In order to maintain the usual policy of paying cash dividends of $50 million, it was necessary for Whoops to borrow $50 million from its bank.

Required:
Prepare the statement of cash flows of Whoops, Inc. for the year ended December 31, 2003. Present cash flows from operating activities by the direct method. (You may omit the schedule to reconcile net income with cash flows from operating activities.)

E 22–28
Pension plan funding

Mayer Corporation has a defined benefit pension plan. Mayer's policy is to fund the plan annually, cash payments being made at the end of each year. Data relating to the pension plan for 2003 are as follows:

	December 31 ($ in millions)	
	2003	**2002**
Prepaid (accrued) pension cost	$ 5	$ (1)
Net Pension Expense for 2003:		
Service cost	$112	
Interest cost (6% × $850)	51	
Actual return on the plan assets (11% × $900 = $99)		
Adjusted for: $9 gain on the plan assets*	(90)	
Amortization of prior service cost	8	
Amortization of net loss	1	
	$ 82	

*(11% × $900) − (10% × $900)

Required:
Re-create the journal entry used to record Mayer's 2003 pension expense in order to determine the cash paid to the pension trustee as reported on the statement of cash flows.

E 22–29
Multiple choice

The following questions dealing with cash flows are adapted from questions that appeared on recent CPA examinations. Determine the response that best completes the statements or questions.
1. The primary purpose of a statement of cash flows is to provide relevant information about
   a. Difference between net income and associated cash receipts and disbursements.
   b. An enterprise's ability to generate future positive net cash flows.
   c. The cash receipts and cash disbursements of an enterprise during a period.
   d. An enterprise's ability to meet cash operating needs.

Items 2 and 3 are based on the following:

In preparing its cash flow statement for the year ended December 31, 2003, Reve Co. collected the following data:

Gain on sale of equipment	$ (6,000)
Proceeds from sale of equipment	10,000
Purchase of A.S., Inc. bonds (par value $200,000)	(180,000)
Amortization of bond discount	2,000
Dividends declared	(45,000)
Dividends paid	(38,000)
Proceeds from sales of treasury stock (carrying amount $65,000)	75,000

In its December 31, 2003, statement of cash flows,
2. What amount should Reve report as net cash used in investing activities?
   a. $170,000
   b. $176,000
   c. $188,000
   d. $194,000
3. What amount should Reve report as net cash provided by financing activities?
   a. $20,000
   b. $27,000
   c. $30,000
   d. $37,000

E 22–30
Statement of cash flows; indirect method

Refer to the data provided in Exercise 22–27 for Whoops, Inc.

Required:
Prepare the statement of cash flows for Whoops, Inc. using the indirect method to report operating activities.

E 22–31
Statement of cash flows; T-account method (based on Appendix 22B)

Refer to the data provided in Exercise 22–27 for Whoops, Inc.

Required:
Prepare the statement of cash flows (direct method) for Whoops, Inc. Use the T-account method to assist in your analysis.

PROBLEMS

P 22–1
Classification of cash flows from investing and financing activities

Example

Listed below are transactions that might be reported as investing and/or financing activities on a statement of cash flows. Possible reporting classifications of those transactions are provided also.

Required:
Indicate the reporting classification of each transaction by entering the appropriate classification code.

Classifications

+ I	Investing activity (cash inflow)
− I	Investing activity (cash outflow)
+ F	Financing activity (cash inflow)
− F	Financing activity (cash outflow)
N	Noncash investing and financing activity
X	Not reported as an investing and/or a financing activity

Transactions

+ I   1. Sale of land.
_____ 2. Issuance of common stock for cash. +F
_____ 3. Purchase of treasury stock. −F
_____ 4. Conversion of bonds payable to common stock. N
_____ 5. Lease of equipment by capital lease. N
_____ 6. Sale of patent. I
_____ 7. Acquisition of building for cash. −I
_____ 8. Issuance of common stock for land. N
_____ 9. Collection of note receivable (principal amount). +I
_____ 10. Issuance of bonds. +F
_____ 11. Issuance of stock dividend. X
_____ 12. Payment of property dividend. N
_____ 13. Payment of cash dividends. −F
_____ 14. Issuance of short-term note payable for cash. +F
_____ 15. Issuance of long-term note payable for cash. +F
_____ 16. Purchase of marketable securities (not cash equivalent). −I
_____ 17. Payment of note payable. −F
_____ 18. Cash payment for 5-year insurance policy. X
_____ 19. Sale of equipment. +I
_____ 20. Issuance of note payable for equipment. N
_____ 21. Acquisition of common stock of another corporation. −I
_____ 22. Repayment of long-term debt by issuing common stock. N
_____ 23. Appropriation of retained earnings for plant expansion. X
_____ 24. Payment of semiannual interest on bonds payable. X
_____ 25. Retirement of preferred stock. −F
_____ 26. Loan to another firm. −I
_____ 27. Sale of inventory to customers. X
_____ 28. Purchase of marketable securities (cash equivalents). X

P 22–2
Statement of cash flows; direct method

The comparative balance sheets for 2003 and 2002 and the statement of income for 2003 are given below for U.B. Wright Company. Additional information from Wright's accounting records is provided also.

U.B. WRIGHT COMPANY
Comparative Balance Sheets
December 31, 2003 and 2002
($ in 000s)

	2003	2002
Assets		
Cash	$ 42	$ 30
Accounts receivable	73	75
Short-term investment	40	15
Inventory	75	70
Land	50	60
Buildings and equipment	550	400
Less: Accumulated depreciation	(115)	(75)
	$715	$575
Liabilities		
Accounts payable	$ 28	$ 35
Salaries payable	2	5
Interest payable	5	3
Income tax payable	9	12
Notes payable	0	30
Bonds payable	160	100
Shareholders' Equity		
Common stock	250	200
Paid-in capital—excess of par	126	100
Retained earnings	135	90
	$715	$575

U.B. WRIGHT COMPANY
Income Statement
For Year Ended December 31, 2003
($ in 000s)

Revenues		
Sales revenue		$380
Expenses		
Cost of goods sold	$130	
Salaries expense	45	
Depreciation expense	40	
Interest expense	12	
Loss on sale of land	3	
Income tax expense	70	300
Net income		$ 80

Additional information from the accounting records:

a. Land that originally cost $10,000 was sold for $7,000.
b. The common stock of I. B. Wrong Corporation was purchased for $25,000 as a short-term investment not classified as a cash equivalent.
c. New equipment was purchased for $150,000 cash.
d. A $30,000 note was paid at maturity on January 1.
e. On January 1, 2003, $60,000 of bonds were sold at face value.
f. Common stock ($50,000 par) was sold for $76,000.
g. Net income was $80,000 and cash dividends of $35,000 were paid to shareholders.

Required:
Prepare the statement of cash flows of U. B. Wright Company for the year ended December 31, 2003. Present cash flows from operating activities by the direct method. (You may omit the schedule to reconcile net income with cash flows from operating activities.)

P 22–3
Statement of cash flows; direct method

The comparative balance sheets for 2003 and 2002 and the statement of income for 2003 are given below for National Intercable Company. Additional information from NIC's accounting records is provided also.

NATIONAL INTERCABLE COMPANY
Comparative Balance Sheets
December 31, 2003 and 2002
($ in millions)

	2003	2002
Assets		
Cash	$ 72	$ 55
Accounts receivable	181	170
Less: Allowance for uncollectible accounts	(8)	(6)
Prepaid insurance	7	12
Inventory	170	165
Long-term investment	66	90
Land	150	150
Buildings and equipment	290	270
Less: Accumulated depreciation	(85)	(75)
Trademark	24	25
	$867	$856
Liabilities		
Accounts payable	$ 30	$ 45
Salaries payable	3	8
Deferred income tax liability	18	15
Lease liability	80	0
Bonds payable	145	275
Less: Discount on bonds	(22)	(25)
Shareholders' Equity		
Common stock	310	290
Paid-in capital—excess of par	95	85
Preferred stock	50	0
Retained earnings	158	163
	$867	$856

NATIONAL INTERCABLE COMPANY
Income Statement
For Year Ended December 31, 2003
($ in millions)

Revenues		
Sales revenue	$320	
Investment revenue	15	
Gain on sale of investments	5	$340
Expenses		
Cost of goods sold	125	
Salaries expense	55	
Depreciation expense	25	
Trademark amortization expense	1	
Bad debt expense	7	
Insurance expense	13	
Bond interest expense	30	(256)
Income before tax and extraordinary items		84
Income tax expense		(38)
Income before extraordinary items		46
Extraordinary loss (tornado)	42	
Less: Tax savings	(21)	(21)
Net income		$25

Additional information from the accounting records:
a.   During 2003, $5 million of customer accounts were written off as uncollectible.
b.   Investment revenue includes National Intercable Company's $6 million share of the net income of Central Fiber Optics Corporation, an equity method investee.

c. A long-term investment in bonds, originally purchased for $30 million, was sold for $35 million.
d. Pretax accounting income exceeded taxable income causing the deferred income tax liability to increase by $3 million.
e. A building that originally cost $60 million, and which was one-fourth depreciated, was destroyed by a tornado. Some undamaged parts were sold for $3 million.
f. A building was acquired by a seven-year capital lease; present value of lease payments, $80 million.
g. $130 million of bonds were retired at maturity.
h. $20 million par value of common stock was sold for $30 million, and $50 million of preferred stock was sold at par.
i. Shareholders were paid cash dividends of $30 million.

Required:

1. Prepare a spreadsheet for preparation of the statement of cash flows (direct method) of National Intercable Company for the year ended December 31, 2003.
2. Prepare the statement of cash flows. (A reconciliation schedule is not required.)

P 22–4
Statement of cash flows; direct method

The comparative balance sheets for 2003 and 2002 and the statement of income for 2003 are given below for Dux Company. Additional information from Dux's accounting records is provided also.

DUX COMPANY
Comparative Balance Sheets
December 31, 2003 and 2002
($ in 000s)

	2003	2002
Assets		
Cash	$ 33	$ 20
Accounts receivable	48	50
Less: Allowance for uncollectible accounts	(4)	(3)
Dividends receivable	3	2
Inventory	55	50
Long-term investment	15	10
Land	70	40
Buildings and equipment	225	250
Less: Accumulated depreciation	(25)	(50)
	$420	$369
Liabilities		
Accounts payable	$ 13	$ 20
Salaries payable	2	5
Interest payable	4	2
Income tax payable	7	8
Notes payable	30	0
Bonds payable	95	70
Less: Discount on bonds	(2)	(3)
Shareholders' Equity		
Common stock	210	200
Paid-in capital—excess of par	24	20
Retained earnings	45	47
Less: Treasury stock (at cost)	(8)	0
	$420	$369

DUX COMPANY
Income Statement
For the Year Ended December 31, 2003
($ in 000s)

Revenues		
Sales revenue	$200	
Dividend revenue	3	$203

Expenses

Cost of goods sold	120	
Salaries expense	25	
Depreciation expense	5	
Bad debt expense	1	
Interest expense	8	
Loss on sale of building	3	
Income tax expense	16	178
Net income		$ 25

Additional information from the accounting records:

a.   A building that originally cost $40,000, and which was three-fourths depreciated, was sold for $7,000.

b.   The common stock of Byrd Corporation was purchased for $5,000 as a long-term investment.

c.   Property was acquired by issuing a 13%, seven-year, $30,000 note payable to the seller.

d.   New equipment was purchased for $15,000 cash.

e.   On January 1, 2003, $25,000 of bonds were sold at face value.

f.   On January 19, Dux issued a 5% stock dividend (1,000 shares). The market price of the $10 par value common stock was $14 per share at that time.

g.   Cash dividends of $13,000 were paid to shareholders.

h.   On November 12, 500 shares of common stock were repurchased as treasury stock at a cost of $8,000. Dux uses the cost method to account for treasury stock.

Required:

Prepare the statement of cash flows of Dux Company for the year ended December 31, 2003. Present cash flows from operating activities by the direct method. (You may omit the schedule to reconcile net income with cash flows from operating activities.)

P 22–5

Statement of cash flows; direct method

Comparative balance sheets for 2003 and 2002 and a statement of income for 2003 are given below for Metagrobolize Industries. Additional information from the accounting records of Metagrobolize also is provided.

METAGROBOLIZE INDUSTRIES
Comparative Balance Sheets
December 31, 2003 and 2002
($ in 000s)

	2003	2002
Assets		
Cash	$ 600	$ 375
Accounts receivable	600	450
Inventory	900	525
Land	675	600
Building	900	900
Less: Accumulated depreciation	(300)	(270)
Equipment	2,850	2,250
Less: Accumulated depreciation	(525)	(480)
Patent	1,200	1,500
	$6,900	$5,850
Liabilities		
Accounts payable	$ 750	$ 450
Accrued expenses payable	300	225
Lease liability—land	150	0
Shareholders' Equity		
Common stock	3,150	3,000
Paid-in capital—excess of par	750	675
Retained earnings	1,800	1,500
	$6,900	$5,850

METAGROBOLIZE INDUSTRIES
Income Statement
For the Year Ended December 31, 2003
($ in 000s)

Revenues		
Sales revenue	$2,645	
Gain on sale of land	90	$2,735
Expenses		
Cost of goods sold	$ 600	
Depreciation expense—building	30	
Depreciation expense—equipment	315	
Loss on sale of equipment	15	
Amortization of patent	300	
Operating expenses	500	1,760
Net income		$ 975

Additional information from the accounting records:
a.   During 2003, equipment with a cost of $300,000 (90% depreciated) was sold.
b.   The statement of retained earnings reveals reductions of $225,000 and $450,000 for stock dividends and cash dividends, respectively.

Required:
Prepare the statement of cash flows of Metagrobolize for the year ended December 31, 2003. Present cash flows from operating activities by the direct method. (You may omit the schedule to reconcile net income with cash flows from operating activities.)

P 22–6
Cash flows from operating activities (direct method) derived from an income statement and cash flows from operating activities (indirect method)

The income statement and a schedule reconciling cash flows from operating activities to net income are provided below ($ in millions) for Mike Roe Computers.

MIKE ROE COMPUTERS
Income Statement
For the Year Ended December 31, 2003

Sales	$150	
Cost of goods sold	(90)	
Gross margin	60	
Salaries expense	$20	
Insurance expense	10	
Depreciation expense	5	
Bad debt expense	2	
Interest expense	6	(43)
Gains and losses:		
Gain on sale of equipment	12	
Loss on sale of land	(3)	
Income before tax	26	
Income tax expense	(13)	
Net income		$ 13

Reconciliation of Net Income
to Net Cash Flows
from Operating Activities

Net income	$13
Adjustments for noncash effects:	
Decrease in accounts receivable	3
Gain on sale of equipment	(12)
Increase in inventory	(6)
Increase in accounts payable	9
Increase in salaries payable	3
Depreciation expense	5
Increase in allowance for uncoll.	2
Decrease in bond discount	3
Decrease in prepaid insurance	2
Loss on sale of land	3
Increase in income tax payable	6
Net cash flows from operating activities	$31

Required:
1.   Calculate each of the following amounts for Mike Roe Computers:
   a.   Cash received from customers during the reporting period.
   b.   Cash paid to suppliers of goods during the reporting period.
   c.   Cash paid to employees during the reporting period.
   d.   Cash paid for interest during the reporting period.
   e.   Cash paid for insurance during the reporting period.
   f.   Cash paid for income taxes during the reporting period.
2.   Prepare the cash flows from operating activities section of the statement of cash flows (direct method).

P 22–7

Cash flows from operating activities (direct method) derived from an income statement and cash flows from operating activities (indirect method)

The income statement and a schedule reconciling cash flows from operating activities to net income are provided below for Macrosoft Corporation.

MACROSOFT CORPORATION Income Statement For the Year Ended December 31, 2003 ($ in millions)		
Sales		$310
Cost of goods sold		(120)
Gross margin		$190
Salaries expense	$40	
Insurance expense	20	
Depreciation expense	10	
Patent amortization expense	4	
Interest expense	12	(86)
Loss on sale of land		(6)
Gain on sale of cash equivalents		2
Income before taxes and extraordinary gain		100
Income tax expense		(50)
Income before extraordinary gain		50
Extraordinary gain (extinguishment of debt)	24	
Less: Tax on gain	(12)	12
Net income		**$ 62**

Reconciliation of Net Income to Net Cash Flows from Operating Activities	
Net income	$62
Adjustments for noncash effects:	
Depreciation expense	10
Patent amortization expense	4
Loss on sale of land	6
Extraordinary gain (extinguishment of debt)	(24)
Decrease in accounts receivable	6
Increase in inventory	(12)
Increase in accounts payable	18
Decrease in bond discount	1
Increase in salaries payable	6
Decrease in prepaid insurance	4
Increase in income tax payable	10
Net cash flows from operating activities	**$91**

Required:

Prepare the cash flows from operating activities section of the statement of cash flows (direct method).

P 22–8

Cash flows from operating activities (direct method and indirect method)— deferred income tax liability and amortization of bond discount

Portions of the financial statements for Parnell Company are provided below.

PARNELL COMPANY Income Statement For the Year Ended December 31, 2003 ($ in 000s)		
Sales		$800
Cost of goods sold		(300)
Gross margin		500
Salaries expense	$120	
Insurance expense	40	
Depreciation expense	123	
Interest expense	50	(333)
Gains and losses:		
Gain on sale of buildings		11
Loss on sale of machinery		(12)
Income before tax		166
Income tax expense		(78)
Net income		**$ 88**

PARNELL COMPANY
Selected Accounts from Comparative Balance Sheets
December 31, 2003 and 2002
($ in 000s)

	Year		
	2003	2002	Change
Cash	$134	$100	$ 34
Accounts receivable	324	216	108

Inventory	321	425	(104)
Prepaid insurance	66	88	(22)
Accounts payable	210	117	93
Salaries payable	102	93	9
Deferred income tax liability	60	52	8
Bond discount	190	200	(10)

Required:

1. Prepare the cash flows from operating activities section of the statement of cash flows for Parnell Company using the direct method.
2. Prepare the cash flows from operating activities section of the statement of cash flows for Parnell Company using the indirect method.

P 22–9
Cash flows from operating activities (direct method and indirect method)—gain on sale of cash equivalents and extraordinary loss

Portions of the financial statements for Hawkeye Company are provided below.

HAWKEYE COMPANY
Income Statement
For the Year Ended December 31, 2003

Sales		$900
Cost of goods sold		(350)
Gross margin		550
Salaries expense	$220	
Depreciation expense	190	
Bad debt expense	12	
Interest expense	40	
Gain on sale of cash equivalents	(4)	(458)
Income before taxes and extraordinary loss		92
Income tax expense		(46)
Income before extraordinary loss		46
Extraordinary loss (flood damage)	12	
Less: Tax savings	(6)	(6)
Net Income		$ 40

HAWKEYE COMPANY
Selected Accounts from Comparative Balance Sheets
December 31, 2003 and 2002

	Year		
	2003	**2002**	**Change**
Cash	$212	$200	$12
Accounts receivable	418	432	(14)
Allowance for uncollectibles	23	11	12
Inventory	860	850	10
Accounts payable	210	234	(24)
Salaries payable	180	188	(8)
Interest payable	55	50	5
Income taxes payable	90	104	(14)

Required:

1. Prepare the cash flows from operating activities section of the statement of cash flows for Hawkeye Company using the direct method.
2. Prepare the cash flows from operating activities section of the statement of cash flows for Hawkeye Company using the indirect method.

P 22–10
Relationship between the income statement and cash flows from operating activities (direct method and indirect method)

The following schedule relates the income statement with cash flows from operating activities, derived by both the direct and indirect methods, in the format illustrated by Graphic 22–10 in the chapter. Some elements necessary to complete the schedule are missing.

Cash Flows From Operating Activities

Income Statement			Indirect Method		Direct Method	
			Net income	$?		
			Adjustments:			
Sales	$300		Decrease in accounts receivable	6	Cash received from customers	$?
Gain on sale of			Gain on sale of equipment	(24)	(Not reported—no cash effect)	
equipment	24		Increase in inventory	(12)		
Cost of goods sold	(?)		Increase in accounts payable	18	Cash paid to suppliers	(174)
Salaries expense	(39)		? in salaries payable	6	Cash paid to employees	(33)
Depreciation expense	(9)		Depreciation expense	9	Cash paid for depreciation	?
Bad debt expense	(3)		Bad debt expense	3	(Not reported—no cash effect)	
Interest expense	(?)		Decrease in bond discount	3	Cash paid for interest	(9)
Insurance expense	(21)		Decrease in prepaid insurance	9	Cash paid for insurance	(?)
Loss on sale of land	(6)		Loss on sale of land	6	(Not reported—no cash effect)	
Income tax expense	(27)		Increase in income tax payable	?	Cash paid for income taxes	(21)
Net Income	$?		**Net cash flows from operating activities**	$57	**Net cash flows from operating activities**	$57

Required:
Complete the schedule by determining each of the following missing elements:
1. Cash received from customers
2. Cost of goods sold
3. ? in salaries payable (Increase? or decrease?)
4. Cash paid for depreciation
5. Interest expense
6. Cash paid for insurance
7. Increase in income tax payable
8. Net income

P 22–11

Prepare a statement of cash flows; direct method

The comparative balance sheets for 2003 and 2002 and the income statement for 2003 are given below for Arduous Company. Additional information from Arduous's accounting records is provided also.

ARDUOUS COMPANY
Comparative Balance Sheets
December 31, 2003 and 2002
($ in millions)

	2003	2002
Assets		
Cash	$ 116	$ 81
Accounts receivable	200	202
Less: Allowance for uncollectible accounts	(10)	(8)
Investment revenue receivable	6	4
Inventory	205	200
Prepaid insurance	4	8
Long-term investment	156	125
Land	196	150
Buildings and equipment	412	400
Less: Accumulated depreciation	(97)	(120)
Patent	30	32
	$1,218	$1,074
Liabilities		
Accounts payable	$ 50	$ 65
Salaries payable	6	11
Bond interest payable	8	4
Income tax payable	12	14
Deferred income tax liability	11	8
Notes payable	23	0
Lease liability	82	0
Bonds payable	215	275
Less: Discount on bonds	(22)	(25)

Shareholders' Equity

Common stock	430	410
Paid-in capital—excess of par	95	85
Preferred stock	75	0
Retained earnings	242	227
Less: Treasury stock (at cost)	(9)	0
	$1,218	$1,074

ARDUOUS COMPANY
Income Statement
For Year Ended December 31, 2003
($ in millions)

Revenues			
Sales revenue		$410	
Investment revenue		11	
Gain on sale of treasury bills		2	$423
Expenses			
Cost of goods sold		180	
Salaries expense		65	
Depreciation expense		12	
Patent amortization expense		2	
Bad debt expense		8	
Insurance expense		7	
Bond interest expense		28	
Extraordinary loss (flood)	$18		
Less: Tax savings	(9)	9	
Income tax expense		45	356
Net income			$ 67

Additional information from the accounting records:

a. During 2003, $6 million of customer accounts were written off as uncollectible.

b. Investment revenue includes Arduous Company's $6 million share of the net income of Demur Company, an equity method investee.

c. Treasury bills were sold during 2003 at a gain of $2 million. Arduous Company classifies its investments in treasury bills as cash equivalents.

d. A machine originally costing $70 million that was one-half depreciated was rendered unusable by a rare flood. Most major components of the machine were unharmed and were sold for $17 million.

e. Temporary differences between pretax accounting income and taxable income caused the deferred income tax liability to increase by $3 million.

f. The preferred stock of Tory Corporation was purchased for $25 million as a long-term investment.

g. Land costing $46 million was acquired by issuing $23 million cash and a 15%, four-year, $23 million note payable to the seller.

h. A building was acquired by a 15-year capital lease; present value of lease payments, $82 million.

i. $60 million of bonds were retired at maturity.

j. In February, Arduous issued a 4% stock dividend (4 million shares). The market price of the $5 par value common stock was $7.50 per share at that time.

k. In April, 1 million shares of common stock were repurchased as treasury stock at a cost of $9 million. Arduous uses the cost method to account for treasury stock.

Required:

Prepare the statement of cash flows of Arduous Company for the year ended December 31, 2003. Present cash flows from operating activities by the direct method. (A reconciliation schedule is not required.)

P 22–12
Transactions affecting retained earnings

Shown below in T-account format are the changes affecting the retained earnings of Brenner-Jude Corporation during 2003. At January 1, 2003, the corporation had outstanding 105 million common shares, $1 par per share.

Retained Earnings ($ in millions)

		90	Beginning balance
Retirement of 5 million common shares for $22 million	2		
		88	Net income for the year
Declaration and payment of a $.33 per share cash dividend	33		
Declaration and distribution of a 4% stock dividend	20		
		123	Ending balance

Required:

1. From the information provided by the account changes you should be able to re-create the transactions that affected Brenner-Jude's retained earnings during 2003. Reconstruct the journal entries which can be used as spreadsheet entries in the preparation of a statement of cash flows. Also indicate any investing and financing activities you identify from this analysis that should be reported on the statement of cash flows.
2. Prepare a statement of retained earnings for Brenner-Jude for the year ended 2003.
   (You may wish to compare your solution to this problem with the parallel situation described in Exercise 19–14.)

P 22–13
Various cash flows

Following are selected balance sheet accounts of Zach Corp. at December 31, 2003 and 2002, and the increases or decreases in each account from 2002 to 2003. Also presented is selected income statement information for the year ended December 31, 2003, and additional information.

Selected Balance Sheet Accounts	2003	2002	Increase (Decrease)
Assets			
Accounts receivable	$ 34,000	$ 24,000	$10,000
Property, plant, and equipment	277,000	247,000	30,000
Accumulated depreciation	(178,000)	(167,000)	(11,000)
Liabilities and Stockholders' Equity			
Bonds payable	49,000	46,000	3,000
Dividends payable	8,000	5,000	3,000
Common stock, $1 par	22,000	19,000	3,000
Additional paid-in capital	9,000	3,000	6,000
Retained earnings	104,000	91,000	13,000

Selected Income Statement Information for the Year Ended December 31, 2003	
Sales revenue	$155,000
Depreciation	33,000
Gain on sale of equipment	13,000
Net income	28,000

Additional information:

a. Accounts receivable relate to sales of merchandise.
b. During 2003, equipment costing $40,000 was sold for cash.
c. During 2003, $20,000 of bonds payable were issued in exchange for property, plant, and equipment. There was no amortization of bond discount or premium.

Required:

Items 1 through 5 represent activities that will be reported in Zach's statement of cash flows for the year ended December 31, 2003. The following two responses are required for each item:

- Determine the amount that should be reported in Zach's 2003 statement of cash flows.
- Using the list below, determine the category in which the amount should be reported in the statement of cash flows.
    - O. Operating activity
    - I. Investing activity
    - F. Financing activity

	Amount	Category
1. Cash collections from customers (direct method).	——	——
2. Payments for purchase of property, plant, and equipment.	——	——
3. Proceeds from sale of equipment.	——	——
4. Cash dividends paid.	——	——
5. Redemption of bonds payable.	——	——

(AICPA adapted)

P 22–14
Statement of cash flows; indirect method; limited information

The comparative balance sheets for 2003 and 2002 are given below for Surmise Company. Net income for 2003 was $50 million.

SURMISE COMPANY
Comparative Balance Sheets
December 31, 2003 and 2002
($ in millions)

	2003	2002
Assets		
Cash	$ 45	$ 40
Accounts receivable	92	96
Less: Allowance for uncollectible accounts	(12)	(4)
Prepaid expenses	8	5
Inventory	145	130
Long-term investment	80	40
Land	100	100
Buildings and equipment	411	300
Less: Accumulated depreciation	(142)	(120)
Patent	16	17
	$743	$604
Liabilities		
Accounts payable	$ 17	$ 32
Accrued liabilities	(2)	10
Notes payable	35	0
Lease liability	111	0
Bonds payable	65	125
Shareholders' Equity		
Common stock	60	50
Paid-in capital—excess of par	245	205
Retained earnings	212	182
	$743	$604

Required:
Prepare the statement of cash flows of Surmise Company for the year ended December 31, 2003. Use the indirect method to present cash flows from operating activities because you do not have sufficient information to use the direct method. You will need to make reasonable assumptions concerning the reasons for changes in some account balances. A spreadsheet or T-account analysis will be helpful.

P 22–15
Statement of cash flows; indirect method

Refer to the data provided in the Problem 22–4 for Dux Company.
Required:
Prepare the statement of cash flows for Dux Company using the *indirect method.*

P 22–16
Statement of cash flows; indirect method

Refer to the data provided in the Problem 22–5 for Metagrobolize Industries.
Required:
Prepare the statement of cash flows for Metagrobolize Industries using the *indirect method.*

P 22–17
Statement of cash flows; indirect method

Refer to the data provided in the Problem 22–11 for Arduous Company.
Required:
Prepare the statement of cash flows for Arduous Company using the *indirect method.*

(Note: The following problems use the technique learned in Appendix 22B.)

P 22–18	Refer to the data provided in the Problem 22–4 for Dux Company.
Statement of cash flows; T-account method	**Required:**
	Prepare the statement of cash flows for Dux Company. Use the T-account method to assist in your analysis.

P 22–19	Refer to the data provided in the Problem 22–5 for Metagrobolize Industries.
Statement of cash flows; T-account method	**Required:**
	Prepare the statement of cash flows for Metagrobolize Industries. Use the T-account method to assist in your analysis.

P 22–20	Refer to the data provided in the Problem 22–11 for Arduous Company.
Statement of cash flows; T-account method	**Required:**
	Prepare the statement of cash flows for Arduous Company. Use the T-account method to assist in your analysis.

BROADEN YOUR PERSPECTIVE

Apply your critical-thinking ability to the knowledge you've gained. These cases will provide you an opportunity to develop your research, analysis, judgment, and communication skills. You also will work with other students, integrate what you've learned, apply it in real world situations, and consider its global and ethical ramifications. This practice will broaden your knowledge and further develop your decision-making abilities.

Communication Case 22–1

Distinguish income and cash flows

"Why can't we pay our shareholders a dividend?" shouted your new boss. "This income statement you prepared for me says we earned $5 million in our first half-year!"

You were hired last month as the chief accountant for Enigma Corporation which was organized on July 1 of the year just ended. You recently prepared the financial statements below:

ENIGMA CORPORATION
Income Statement
For the Six Months Ended December 31, 2003
($ in millions)

Sales revenue	$75
Cost of goods sold	(30)
Depreciation expense	(5)
Remaining expenses	(35)
Net income	$ 5

ENIGMA CORPORATION
Balance Sheet
December 31, 2003 ($ in millions)

Cash	$ 1
Accounts receivable (net)	20
Merchandise inventory	15
Machinery (net)	44
Total	$80
Accounts payable	$ 2
Accrued expenses payable	7
Notes payable	36
Common stock	30
Retained earnings	5
Total	$80

You have just explained to your boss, Robert James, that although net income was $5 million, operating activities produced a net decrease in cash. Unable to understand your verbal explanation, he has asked you to prepare a written report.

Required:
Prepare a report explaining the apparent discrepancy between Enigma's profitability and its cash flows. To increase the chances of your boss's understanding the situation, include in your report a

determination of net cash flows from operating activities by both the direct and indirect methods. Your report should also include a narrative explanation of how it is possible for operating activities to simultaneously produce a positive net income and negative net cash flows.

Judgment Case 22–2
Distinguish income and cash flows

You are a loan officer for First Benevolent Bank. You have an uneasy feeling as you examine a loan application from Daring Corporation. The application included the following financial statements.

DARING CORPORATION
Income Statement
For the Year Ended December 31, 2003

Sales revenue	$100,000
Cost of goods sold	(50,000)
Depreciation expense	(5,000)
Remaining expenses	(25,000)
Net income	$ 20,000

DARING CORPORATION
Balance Sheet
December 31, 2003

Cash	$ 5,000
Accounts receivable	25,000
Inventory	20,000
Operational assets	55,000
Accumulated depreciation	(5,000)
Total	$100,000
Accounts payable	$ 10,000
Interest payable	5,000
Note payable	45,000
Common stock	20,000
Retained earnings	20,000
Total	$100,000

It is not Daring's profitability that worries you. The income statement submitted with the application shows net income of $20,000 in Daring's first year of operations. By referring to the balance sheet, you see that this net income represents a 20% rate of return on assets of $100,000. Your concern stems from the recollection that the note payable reported on Daring's balance sheet is a two-year loan you approved earlier in the year.

You also recall another promising new company that, just last year, defaulted on another of your bank's loans when it failed due to its inability to generate sufficient cash flows to meet its obligations. Before requesting additional information from Daring, you decide to test your memory of the intermediate accounting class you took in night school by attempting to prepare a statement of cash flows from the information available in the loan application.

Required:
Prepare a statement of cash flows using the direct method. Are your concerns justified?

Integrating Case 22–3
Lease transaction; lessee and lessor; financial statement effects

Advanced Equipment leased a protein analyzer to Richards Chemical, Inc. on September 30, 2003. Advanced purchased the machine from Makers, Inc. at a cost of $6 million. The five-year lease agreement calls for Richards to make quarterly lease payments of $391,548, payable each September 30, December 31, March 31, June 30, with the first payment at September 30, 2003. Advanced's implicit interest rate is 12%.

Required:
1. What pretax amounts related to the lease would *Richards* report in its statement of cash flows for the year ended December 31, 2003?
2. What pretax amounts related to the lease would *Advanced* report in its statement of cash flows for the year ended December 31, 2003?
3. Assume Makers manufactured the machine at a cost of $5 million and that Richards leased the machine directly from Makers. What pretax amounts related to the lease would *Makers* report in its statement of cash flows for the year ended December 31, 2003?

Research Case 22–4
Locate and extract relevant information and authoritative support for a financial reporting issue; integrative; Microsoft Corporation

A meeting of your accounting department is scheduled for early tomorrow morning. One topic of discussion is certain to be the appropriate adjustments to net income in your company's statement of cash flows using the indirect method of reporting operating activities. Hallway discussions have suggested some degree of uncertainty, particularly regarding unearned revenues, which are substantial for the company. Because your firm went public only seven months ago, this reporting issue is a new one for you and most other members of the department. In preparation for the meeting, you sought out the financial statements of Microsoft Corporation, knowing that it too had substantial unearned revenues. The operating activities section of the comparative statements of cash flows for Microsoft is presented below.

Cash Flows Statements (in millions)

Year Ended June 3	1999	2000	2001
Operations			
Net income	$ 7,785	$ 9,421	$ 7,346
Cumulative effect of accounting change, net of tax	—	—	375
Depreciation, amortization, and other noncash items	926	1,250	1,536
Net recognized (gains)/losses on investments	(803)	(1,732)	2,221
Stock option income tax benefits	3,107	5,535	2,066
Deferred income taxes	(650)	(425)	(420)
Unearned revenue	5,877	6,177	6,970
Recognition of unearned revenue	(4,526)	(5,600)	(6,369)
Accounts receivable	(687)	(944)	(418)
Other current assets	(235)	(775)	(482)
Other long-term assets	(117)	(864)	(330)
Other current liabilities	1,469	(617)	927
Net cash from operations	12,146	11,426	13,422

Required:

1. Use EdgarScan (**edgarscan.pwcglobal.com/**) or another method to locate the financial statements of Microsoft Corporation. Search the disclosure notes for information about how Microsoft accounts for its unearned revenues. What authoritative literature does Microsoft rely on in deciding the percentages of revenue to recognize at the time of shipment as opposed to deferring as unearned revenue?

2. Why does the statement of cash flows include "unearned revenue" as an addition to net income in the operations section? Why is "recognition of unearned revenue" included as a deduction from net income? Why do you think Microsoft reported these two items separately rather than just adjusting net income for the change in the unearned revenue account balance?

3. Which accounting change necessitated the adjustment for the "cumulative effect of accounting change"? Why is it added?

Integrating Case 22–5
Postretirement benefits and accounting for income taxes

The operating activities section of the comparative statements of cash flows from the Walgreen annual report for 1993, the year accounting for postretirement benefits changed, is reproduced below:

WALGREEN CO. AND SUBSIDIARIES
Consolidated Statements of Cash Flows
For the Years Ended August 31, 1993, 1992, and 1991
($ in 000s)

	1993	1992	1991
Cash Flows from Operating Activities:			
Net Earnings	$221,666	$220,628	$194,965
Adjustments to reconcile net earnings to net cash provided by operating activities:			
Cumulative effect of accounting changes:			
Postretirement benefits other than pensions	35,813	—	—
Income taxes	(13,190)		
Depreciation and amortization	104,660	92,109	84,346
Deferred income taxes	(12,645)	11,158	3,259
Loss on closing distribution center	—	—	4,118
Other	(1,772)	(719)	(2,745)

Changes in current assets and liabilities:			
Inventories	(99,867)	(82,173)	(83,998)
Accrued expenses and other liabilities	70,767	52,737	30,857
Trade accounts payable	15,502	46,143	17,014
Other current assets	(7,814)	(3,095)	(2,281)
Accounts receivable, net	(7,427)	(3,079)	(24,813)
Income taxes	184	4,802	(2,374)
Net cash provided by operating activities	305,877	338,511	218,348

Required:

Why are the two adjustments for accounting changes included on the statement of cash flows? Why is one added and the other subtracted?

Real World Case 22–6
Analyze cash flow activities; WorldCom, Inc.

WorldCom, Inc. is a global business telecommunications company. Operating in more than 65 countries, the company is a provider of facilities-based and fully integrated local, long distance, international, and Internet services. The common shares of WorldCom stock trade on the NASDAQ National Market (U.S.) under the symbol WCOM.

($ in millions)	1999	2000	2001
Cash Flows from Operating Activities:			
Net income (loss)	$ 4,013	$ 4,153	$ 1,501
Adjustments to reconcile net income to net cash provided by operating activities:			
Cumulative effect of accounting change	0	85	0
Minority interests	186	305	(35)
Other charges	(8)	0	0
Depreciation and amortization	4,354	4,878	5,880
Provision for deferred income taxes	2,903	1,649	1,104
Change in assets and liabilities:			
Accounts receivable, net	(875)	(1,126)	281
Other current assets	143	(797)	164
Accounts payable and other current liabilities	692	(1,050)	(1,154)
Other	(403)	(431)	253
Net cash provided by operating activities	$11,005	$ 7,666	$ 7,994
Cash Flows from Investing Activities:			
Capital expenditures	$ (8,716)	$(11,484)	$ (7,886)
Acquisitions and related costs	(1,078)	(14)	(206)
Increase in intangible assets	(743)	(938)	(694)
Decrease in other liabilities	(650)	(839)	(480)
All other investing activities	1,632	(1,110)	(424)
Net cash used in investing activities	$ (9,555)	$(14,385)	$(9,690)
Cash Flows from Financing Activities:			
Principal borrowings (repayments) on debt, net	$ (2,894)	$ 6,377	$ 3,031
Common stock issuance	886	585	124
Distributions on mandatorily redeemable preferred securities	(72)	(65)	(154)
Redemption of preferred stock	0	(190)	(200)
All other financing activities	0	(84)	(272)
Net cash provided by (used in) financing activities	$ (2,080)	$ 6,623	$ 2,529
Effect of exchange rate changes on cash	(221)	(19)	38
Net increase (decrease) in cash and cash equivalents	$ (851)	$ (115)	$ 871
Cash and cash equivalents at beginning of period	1,727	876	761
Deconsolidation of Embratel	0	0	(216)
Cash and cash equivalents at end of period	$ 876	$ 761	$ 1,416

Required:

1. In the three years reported, what were WorldCom's primary investing activities? How were these activities financed? Be specific.
2. During the most recent fiscal year, WorldCom purchased certificates of deposit. How were these purchases reported in the statement of cash flows? (Note: This is not an investing activity.)
3. How are issuances of debt securities and issuances of equity securities classified in a statement of cash flows?

4. How are payments to investors in debt securities (interest) and payments to investors in equity securities (dividends) classified in a statement of cash flows? Is this a conceptual inconsistency? Explain.

5. WorldCom's statement of cash flows reports expenditures for property and equipment. It also reports the issuance of debt securities. Suppose property and equipment had been acquired, not with cash, but by exchange for debt securities. Would such a transaction be reported? Explain.

Ethics Case 22–7
Where's the cash?

After graduating near the top of his class, Ben Naegle was hired by the local office of a Big 5 CPA firm in his hometown. Two years later, impressed with his technical skills and experience, Park Electronics, a large regional consumer electronics chain, hired Ben as assistant controller. This was last week. Now Ben's initial excitement has turned to distress.

The cause of Ben's distress is the set of financial statements he's stared at for the last four hours. For some time prior to his recruitment, he had been aware of the long trend of moderate profitability of his new employer. The reports on his desk confirm the slight, but steady, improvements in net income in recent years. The trend he was just now becoming aware of, though, was the decline in cash flows from operations.

Ben had sketched out the following comparison ($ in millions):

	2003	**2002**	**2001**	**2000**
Income from operations	$140.0	$132.0	$127.5	$127.0
Net income	38.5	35.0	34.5	29.5
Cash flow from operations	1.6	17.0	12.0	15.5

Profits? Yes. Increasing profits? Yes. The cause of his distress? The ominous trend in cash flow which is consistently lower than net income.

Upon closer review, Ben noticed three events in the last two years that, unfortunately, seemed related:

a. Park's credit policy had been loosened; credit terms were relaxed and payment periods were lengthened.

b. Accounts receivable balances had increased dramatically.

c. Several of the company's compensation arrangements, including that of the controller and the company president, were based on reported net income.

Required:
1. What is so ominous about the combination of events Ben sees?
2. What course of action, if any, should Ben take?

Research Case 22–8
Cash flow ratio analysis; research article in the *Journal of Accountancy*

The FASB requirement to prepare a statement of cash flows is a relatively recent development in the evolution of financial reporting. Partially as a result, widespread use of cash flow ratios has been slow to develop. Professors Mills and Yamamura, in "The Power of Cash Flow Ratios," propose a complete set of cash flow ratios to complement accrual-based ratios in financial statement analysis.

Required:
1. In your library, from the Internet, or from some other source, locate the indicated article in the *Journal of Accountancy,* October 1998.
2. What are the ratios proposed by the authors to test solvency?
3. What are the ratios proposed by the authors to measure financial health?
4. What are the proposed net cash free ratios?
5. What do the ratios in each category purport to measure?

Research Case 22–9
Statement of cash flows; classifying interest on borrowed funds; research article in the *Accounting Horizons*

The statement of cash flows classifies interest as an operating activity and the receipt and payment of borrowed funds as financing activities. Implementing this classification requirement has produced several methods of classifying the cash flows related to long-term debt. Professors Vent, Cowling, and Sevalstad, in "Cash Flow Comparability: Accounting for Long-Term Debt under *SFAS 95*," identify and illustrate four such methods and point out problems posed by the variation in methods used.

Required:
1. In your library, from the American Accounting Association website, or from some other source, locate the indicated article in the *Accounting Horizons,* December 1995.
2. What are four methods of classifying long-term debt identified by the authors? Are readers of financial statements usually aware of the method used?
3. What conclusions do the authors draw concerning the effect on financial statements' usefulness? What solution do they propose?

Research Case 22–10
Researching the way cash flows are reported; retrieving information from the Internet

EDGAR, the Electronic Data Gathering, Analysis, and Retrieval system, performs automated collection, validation, indexing, acceptance, and forwarding of submissions by companies and others who are required by law to file forms with the U.S. Securities and Exchange Commission (SEC). All publicly traded domestic companies use EDGAR to make the majority of their filings. (Filings by foreign companies are not required to be filed on EDGAR, but some of these companies do so voluntarily.) Form 10-K, which include the annual report, is required to be filed on EDGAR. The SEC makes this information available on the Internet.

Required:

1. Access EDGAR on the Internet. The web address is **www.sec.gov** or use **edgarscan.pwcglobal.com**.

2. Search for a public company with which you are familiar. Access its most recent 10-K filing. Search or scroll to find the statement of cash flows and related note(s).

3. Is the direct or indirect method used to report operating activities? What is the largest adjustment to net income in reconciling net income and cash flows from operations in the most recent year?

4. What are the cash payments for interest and for taxes?

5. What has been the most significant investing activity for the company in the most recent three years?

6. What has been the most significant financing activity for the company in the most recent three years?

7. Repeat requirements 2–6 for another company.

Analysis Case 22–11
Information from cash flow activities

FedEx Corporation

Refer to the financial statements and related disclosure notes of FedEx Corporation in the appendix to Chapter 1. Notice that financing activities created a sizable net reduction in cash in each of the three years reported. Investing activities have required large and increasing amounts of cash over the same period.

Required:

1. From the information provided on the statement of cash flows, explain what allows FedEx Corporation to expand its business as evidenced by the investing activities, while at the same time not raising (in fact, decreasing) cash through financing activities.

2. Describe the five activities listed under financing activities for the 2001 fiscal year. [*Hint:* FedEx's Statement of Changes in Common Stockholders' Investment (statement of shareholders' equity) will help you determine the nature of the stock activity.] What is the most notable financing activity reported?

3. What are the cash payments FedEx made for interest and for income taxes in two of the three years reported? (*Hint:* See the disclosure notes.)

Derivatives

In today's global economy and evolving financial markets, businesses are increasingly exposed to a variety of risks, which, unmanaged, can have major impacts on earnings or even threaten a company's very existence. Risk management, then, has become critical. Derivative financial instruments have become the key tools of risk management.[1]

Derivatives are financial instruments that "derive" their values or contractually required cash flows from some other security or index. For instance, a contract allowing a company to buy a particular asset (say steel, gold, or flour) at a designated future date, at a predetermined price is a financial instrument that derives its value from expected and actual changes in the price of the underlying asset. Financial futures, forward contracts, options, and interest rate swaps are the most frequently used derivatives. Derivatives are valued as tools to manage or hedge companies' increasing exposures to risk, including interest rate risk, price risk, and foreign exchange risk. The variety, complexity, and magnitude of derivatives have grown rapidly in recent years. Tens of trillions of dollars in derivative contracts are used every year. Accounting standard-setters have scrambled to keep pace.

A persistent stream of headline stories has alerted us to multimillion-dollar losses by Dell Computer, Procter & Gamble, Gibson Greetings, and Orange County (California), to name a few. Focusing on these headlines, it would be tempting to conclude that derivatives are risky business indeed. Certainly they can be quite risky, if misused, but the fact is, these financial instruments exist to lessen, not increase, risk. Properly used, they serve as a form of "insurance" against risk. In fact, if a company is exposed to a substantial risk and does not hedge that risk, it is taking a gamble. On the other hand, if a derivative is used improperly, it can be a huge gamble itself.

Derivatives are financial instruments that "derive" their values from some other security or index.

Derivatives serve as a form of "insurance" against risk.

Derivatives Used to Hedge Risk

Hedging means taking an action that is expected to produce exposure to a particular type of risk that is precisely the *opposite* of an actual risk to which the company already is exposed. For instance, the volatility of interest rates creates exposure to interest-rate risk for companies that issue debt—which, of course, includes most companies. So, a company that frequently arranges short-term loans from its bank under a floating (variable) interest rate agreement is exposed to the risk that interest rates might increase and adversely affect borrowing costs. Similarly, a company that regularly reissues commercial paper as it matures faces the possibility that new rates will be higher and cut into forecasted income. When borrowings are large, the potential cost can be substantial. So, the firm might choose to hedge its position by entering into a transaction that would produce a *gain* of roughly the same amount as the potential loss if interest rates do, in fact, increase.

Hedging is used to deal with three areas of risk exposure: fair value risk, cash flow risk, and foreign currency risk. Let's look at some of the more common derivatives.

Hedging means taking a risk position that is opposite to an actual position that is exposed to risk.

FINANCIAL FUTURES

A futures contract is an agreement between a seller and a buyer that requires the seller to deliver a particular commodity (say corn, gold, or pork bellies) at a designated future date, at a *predetermined* price. These contracts are actively traded on regulated futures exchanges. When the "commodity" is a *financial instrument,* such as a Treasury bond, Treasury bill,

A futures contract allows a firm to sell (or buy) a financial instrument at a designated future date, at today's price.

---

[1]Almost all financial institutions and over half of all nonfinancial companies use derivatives.

commercial paper, or a certificate of deposit, the agreement is referred to as a *financial futures contract*.[2]

To appreciate the way these hedges work, you need to remember that when interest rates rise, the market price of interest-bearing securities goes down. For instance, if you have an investment in a 10% bond and market interest rates go up to, say, 12%, your 10% bond is less valuable relative to other bonds paying the higher rate. Conversely, when interest rates decline, the market price of interest-bearing securities goes up. This risk that the investment's value might change is referred to as *fair value risk*. The company that issued the securities is faced with fair value risk also. If interest rates decline, the fair value of that company's debt would rise, a risk the borrower may want to hedge against. Later in this section, we'll look at an illustration of how the borrower would account for and report such a hedge.

Now let's look at the effect on a contract to sell or buy securities (or any asset for that matter) at preset prices. One who is contracted to *sell* securities at a *preset* price after their market price has fallen, benefits from the rise in interest rates. Consequently, the value of the *contract* that gives one the right to sell securities at a preset price goes up as the market price declines. The seller in a futures contract derives a gain (loss) when interest rates rise (decline).[3] Conversely, the one obligated to *buy* securities at a preset price experiences a loss. This risk of having to pay more cash or receive less cash is referred to as *cash flow risk*.

The seller in a financial futures contract realizes a gain (loss) when interest rates rise (decline).

Another example of cash flow risk would be borrowing money by issuing a variable (floating) rate note. If market interest rates rise, the borrower would have to pay more interest. Similarly, the lender (investor) in the variable (floating) rate note transaction would face cash flow risk that interest rates would decline, resulting in lower cash interest receipts.

Let's look closer at how a futures contract can mitigate cash flow risk. Consider a company in April that will replace its $10 million of 8.5% bank notes when they mature in June. The company is exposed to the risk that interest rates in June will have risen, increasing borrowing costs. To counteract that possibility, the firm might enter a contract in April to deliver (sell) bonds in June at their *current* price. Since there are no corporate bond futures contracts, the company buys Treasury bond futures, which will accomplish essentially the same purpose. In essence, the firm agrees to sell Treasury bonds in June at a price established now (April). Let's say it's April 6 and the price of Treasury bond futures on the International Monetary Market of the Chicago Mercantile Exchange is quoted as 95.24.[4] Since the trading unit of Treasury bond futures is a 15-year, $100,000, 8% Treasury bond, the company might sell 105 Treasury bond futures to hedge the June issuance of debt. This would effectively provide a hedge of $105 \times \$100,000 \times 95.24\% = \$10,000,200$.[5]

Here's what happens then. If interest rates rise, borrowing costs will go up for our example company because it will have to sell debt securities at a higher interest cost (or lower price). But that loss will be offset (approximately) by the gain produced by being in the opposite position on Treasury bond futures. Take note, though, this works both ways. If interest rates go down causing debt security prices to rise, the potential benefit of being able to issue debt at that lower interest rate (higher price) will be offset by a loss on the futures position.

A very important point about futures contracts is that the seller does not need to have actual possession of the commodity (the Treasury bonds, in this case), nor is the purchaser of the contract required to take possession of the commodity. In fact, virtually all financial futures contracts are "netted out" before the actual transaction is to take place. This is simply a matter of reversing the original position. A seller closes out his transaction with a purchase. Likewise, a purchaser would close out her transaction with a sale. After all, the objective is not to actually buy or sell Treasury bonds (or whatever the commodity might be), but to

---

[2]Note that a financial futures contract meets the definition of a financial instrument because it entails the exchange of financial instruments (cash for Treasury bonds, for instance). But, a futures contract for the sale or purchase of a nonfinancial commodity like corn or gold does not meet the definition because one of the items to be exchanged is not a financial instrument.

[3]The seller of a futures contract is obligated to sell the bonds at a future date. The buyer of a futures contract is obligated to buy the bonds at a future date. The company in our example, then, is the seller of the futures contract.

[4]Price quotes are expressed as a percentage of par.

[5]This is a simplification of the more sophisticated way financial managers determine the optimal number of futures.

incur the financial impact of movements in interest rates as reflected in changes in Treasury bond prices. Specifically, it will buy at the lower price (to reverse the original seller position) at the same time it's selling its new bond issue at that same lower price. The financial futures market is an "artificial" exchange in that its reason for existing is to provide a mechanism to transfer risk from those exposed to it to those willing to accept the risk, not to actually buy and sell the underlying financial instruments.

If the impending debt issue being hedged is a short-term issue, the company may attain a more effective hedge by selling Treasury *bill* futures since Treasury bills are 90-day securities, or maybe certificate of deposit (CD) futures that also are traded in futures markets. The object is to get the closest association between the financial effects of interest rate movements on the actual transaction and the effects on the financial instrument used as a hedge.

The effectiveness of a hedge is influenced by the closeness of the match between the item being hedged and the financial instrument chosen as a hedge.

FINANCIAL FORWARD CONTRACTS

A forward contract is similar to a futures contract but differs in three ways:

1. A forward contract calls for delivery on a specific date, whereas a futures contract permits the seller to decide later which specific day within the specified month will be the delivery date (if it gets as far as actual delivery before it is closed out).
2. Unlike a futures contract, a forward contract usually is not traded on a market exchange.
3. Unlike a futures contract, a forward contract does not call for a daily cash settlement for price changes in the underlying contract. Gains and losses on forward contracts are paid only when they are closed out.

OPTIONS

Options frequently are purchased to hedge exposure to the effects of changing interest rates. Options serve the same purpose as futures in that respect but are fundamentally different. An option on a financial instrument—say a Treasury bill—gives its holder the right either to buy or to sell the Treasury bill at a specified price and within a given time period. Importantly, though, the option holder has no obligation to exercise the option. On the other hand, the holder of a futures contract must buy or sell within a specified period unless the contract is closed out before delivery comes due.

FOREIGN CURRENCY FUTURES

Foreign loans frequently are denominated in the currency of the lender (Japanese yen, Swiss franc, Euro, and so on). When loans must be repaid in foreign currencies, a new element of risk is introduced. This is because if exchange rates change, the dollar equivalent of the foreign currency that must be repaid differs from the dollar equivalent of the foreign currency borrowed.

To hedge against "foreign exchange risk" exposure, some firms buy or sell foreign currency futures contracts. These are similar to financial futures except specific foreign currencies are specified in the futures contracts rather than specific debt instruments. They work the same way to protect against foreign exchange risk as financial futures protect against fair value or cash flow risk.

Foreign exchange risk often is hedged in the same manner as interest rate risk.

INTEREST RATE SWAPS

Over 70% of derivatives are interest rate swaps. These contracts exchange fixed interest payments for floating rate payments, or vice versa, without exchanging the underlying principal amounts. For example, suppose you owe $100,000 on a 10% fixed rate home loan. You envy your neighbor who also is paying 10% on her $100,000 mortgage, but hers is a floating rate loan, so if market rates fall, so will her loan rate. To the contrary, she is envious of your fixed rate, fearful that rates will rise, increasing her payments. A solution would be for the two of you to effectively swap interest payments using an interest rate swap agreement. The way a swap works, you both would continue to actually make your own interest payments, but would exchange the net cash difference between payments at specified intervals.

Interest rate swaps exchange fixed interest payments for floating rate payments, or vice versa, without exchanging the underlying notional amounts.

So, in this case, if market rates (and thus floating payments) increase, you would pay your neighbor; if rates fall, she pays you. The net effect is to exchange the consequences of rate changes. In other words, you have effectively converted your fixed-rate debt to floating-rate debt; your neighbor has done the opposite.

Of course, this technique is not dependent on happening into such a fortuitous pairing of two borrowers with opposite philosophies on interest rate risk. Instead, banks or other intermediaries offer, for a fee, one-sided swap agreements to companies desiring to be either fixed-rate payers or variable-rate payers. Intermediaries usually strive to maintain a balanced portfolio of matched, offsetting swap agreements.

Theoretically, the two parties to such a transaction exchange principal amounts, say the $100,000 amount above, in addition to the interest on those amounts. It makes no practical sense, though, for the companies to send each other $100,000. So, instead, the principal amount is not actually exchanged, but serves merely as the computational base for interest calculations and is called the *notional amount*. Similarly, the fixed-rate payer doesn't usually send the entire fixed interest amount (say $10\% \times \$100,000 = \$10,000$) and receive the entire variable interest amount (say $9\% \times \$100,000 = \$9,000$). Generally, only the net amount ($1,000 in this case) is exchanged. This is illustrated in Graphic A–1.

GRAPHIC A–1
Interest Rate Swap

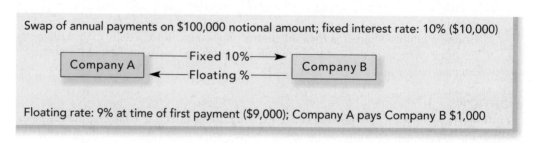

Swap of annual payments on $100,000 notional amount; fixed interest rate: 10% ($10,000)

Company A ——Fixed 10%—→ Company B
◄——Floating %——

Floating rate: 9% at time of first payment ($9,000); Company A pays Company B $1,000

From an accounting standpoint, the central issue is not the operational differences among various hedge instruments, but their similarities in functioning as hedges against risk.

Accounting for Derivatives

A key to accounting for derivatives is knowing the purpose for which a company holds them and whether the company is effective in serving that purpose. Derivatives, for instance, may be held for risk management (hedging activities). The desired effect, and often the real effect, is a reduction in risk. On the other hand, derivatives sometimes are held for speculative position taking, hoping for large profits. The effect of this activity usually is to increase risk. Perhaps more important, derivatives acquired as hedges and intended to reduce risk may, in fact, unintentionally increase risk instead.

Derivatives not serving as hedges are extremely speculative due to the high leverage inherent in such investments.

It's important to understand that, serving as investments rather than as hedges, derivatives are extremely speculative. This is due to the high leverage inherent in derivatives. Here's why. The investment outlay usually is negligible, but, the potential gain or loss on the investment usually is quite high. A small change in interest rates or another underlying event can trigger a large change in the fair value of the derivative. Because the initial investment was minimal, the change in value relative to the investment itself represents a huge percentage gain or loss. Accounting for derivatives is designed to treat differently (a) derivatives designated as hedges and those not designated as hedges as well as (b) the effective portion and the ineffective portion of gains and losses from intended hedges.

All derivatives are reported on the balance sheet at fair value.

The basic approach to accounting for derivatives is fairly straightforward, although implementation can be quite cumbersome. All derivatives, no exceptions, are carried on the balance sheet as either assets or liabilities at fair (or market) value.[6] The reasoning is that (a) derivatives create either rights or obligations that meet the definition of assets or liabilities, and (b) fair value is the most meaningful measurement.

Accounting for the gain or loss on a derivative depends on how it is used. Specifically, if the derivative is not designated as a hedging instrument, or doesn't qualify as one, any gain or loss from fair value changes is recognized immediately in earnings. On the other hand, if a derivative is used to hedge against exposure to risk, any gain or loss from fair value changes is either (a) recognized immediately in earnings along with an offsetting loss or gain on the item being hedged or (b) deferred in comprehensive income until it can be recognized in earnings at the same time as earnings are affected by a hedged transaction. Which way depends on whether the derivative is designated as a (a) fair value hedge, (b) cash flow hedge, or (c) foreign currency hedge. Let's look now at each of the three hedge designations.

FAIR VALUE HEDGES

A company can be adversely affected when a change in either prices or interest rates causes a change in the fair value of one of its assets, its liabilities, or a commitment to buy or sell assets or liabilities. If a derivative is used to hedge against the exposure to changes in the fair value of an asset or liability or a firm commitment, it can be designated as a **fair value hedge**. In that case, when the derivative is adjusted to reflect changes in fair value, the other side of the entry recognizes a gain or loss to be included *currently* in earnings. At the same time, though, the loss or gain from changes in the fair value (due to the risk being hedged)[7] of the item being hedged also is included currently in earnings. This means that, to the extent the hedge is effective in serving its purpose, the gain or loss on the derivative will be offset by the loss or gain on the item being hedged. In fact, this is precisely the concept behind the procedure.

> A gain or loss from a *fair value hedge* is recognized immediately in earnings along with the loss or gain from the item being hedged.

The reasoning is that as interest rates or other underlying events change, a hedge instrument will produce a gain approximately equal to a loss on the item being hedged (or vice versa). These income effects are interrelated and offsetting, so it would be improper to report the income effects in different periods. More critically, the intent and effect of having the hedge instrument is to *lessen* risk. And yet, recognizing gains in one period and counterbalancing losses in another period would tend to cause fluctuations in income that convey an *increase* in risk. However, to the extent that a hedge is ineffective and produces gains or losses different from the losses or gains being hedged, the ineffective portion is recognized in earnings immediately.

> The income effects of the hedge instrument and the income effects of the item being hedged should affect earnings at the same time.

Some of the more common fair value hedges use:

- An interest rate swap to synthetically convert fixed-rate debt (for which interest rate changes could change the fair value of the debt) into floating-rate debt.
- A futures contract to hedge changes in the fair value (due to price changes) of aluminum, sugar, or some other type of inventory.
- A futures contract to hedge the fair value (due to price changes) of a firm commitment to sell natural gas or some other asset.

ILLUSTRATION

Because interest rate swaps comprise over 70% of derivatives in use, we will use swaps to illustrate accounting for derivatives. Let's look at the example in Illustration A–1 on the next page.

---

[6]"Accounting for Derivative Instruments and Hedging Activities," *Statement of Financial Accounting Standards No. 133* (Norwalk, Conn.: FASB, 1998).
[7]The fair value of a hedged item might also change for reasons other than from effects of the risk being hedged. For instance, the hedged risk may be that a change in interest rates will cause the fair value of a bond to change. The bond price might also change, though, if the market perceives that the bond's default risk has changed.

ILLUSTRATION A–1 Interest Rate Swap	Wintel Semiconductors issued $1 million of 18-month, 10% bank notes on January 1, 2003. Wintel is exposed to the risk that general interest rates will decline, causing the fair value of its debt to rise. (If the fair value of Wintel's debt increases, its effective borrowing cost is higher relative to the market.) To hedge against this fair value risk, the firm entered into an 18-month interest rate swap agreement on January 1 and designated the swap as a hedge against changes in the fair value of the note. The swap calls for the company to *receive payment* based on a 10% fixed interest rate on a notional amount of $1 million and to *make payment* based on a floating interest rate tied to changes in general rates.[8] As the Illustration will show, this effectively converts Wintel's fixed-rate debt to floating-rate debt. Cash settlement of the net interest amount is made semiannually at June 30 and December 31 of each year with the net interest being the difference between the $50,000 fixed interest [$1 million × (10% × ½)] and the floating interest rate times $1 million at those dates.	

Floating (market) settlement rates were 9% at June 30, 2003, 8% at December 31, 2003, and 9% at June 30, 2004. Net interest receipts can be calculated as shown below. Fair values of both the derivative and the note resulting from those market rate changes are assumed to be quotes obtained from securities dealers.

	1/1/03	6/30/03	12/31/03	6/30/04
Fixed rate	10%	10%	10%	10%
Floating rate	10%	9%	8%	9%
Fixed payments ($1 million × [10% × ½])		$ 50,000	$ 50,000	$ 50,000
Floating payments ($1 million × ½ floating rate)		45,000	40,000	45,000
Net interest receipts		$ 5,000	$ 10,000	$ 5,000
Fair value of interest rate swap	0	$ 9,363	$ 9,615	0
Fair value of note payable	$1,000,000	$1,009,363	$1,009,615	$1,000,000

When the floating rate declined from 10% to 9%, the fair values of both the derivative (swap) and the note increased. This created an offsetting gain on the derivative and holding loss on the note. Both are recognized in earnings at the same time (at June 30, 2003).

The interest rate swap is designated as a cash flow hedge on this note at issuance.	**January 1, 2003** Cash. . . . . Notes payable . . . . *To record the issuance of the note.*	1,000,000 1,000,000
	June 30, 2003 Interest expense (10% × ½ × $1 million) . . . . Cash . . . . *To record interest.*	50,000 50,000
The swap settlement is the difference between the fixed interest (5%) and variable interest (4.5%).	Cash ($50,000—[9% × ½ × $1 million]) . . . . Interest expense . . . . *To record the net cash settlement.*	5,000 5,000
The fair value of derivatives is recognized in the balance sheet.	Interest rate swap[9] ($9,363 − 0) . . . . Holding gain—interest rate swap . . . . *To record change in fair value of the derivative.*	9,363 9,363
The hedged liability (or asset) is adjusted to fair value as well.	Holding loss—hedged note . . . . Note payable ($1,009,363 − 1,000,000). *To record change in fair value of the note due to interest rate changes.*	9,363 9,363

---

[8]A common measure for benchmarking variable interest rates is LIBOR, the London Interbank Offered Rate, a base rate at which large international banks lend funds to each other.

[9]This would be a liability rather than an investment (asset) if the fair value had declined.

The net interest settlement on June 30, 2003, is $5,000 because the fixed rate is 5% (half of the 10% annual rate) and the floating rate is 4.5% (half of the 9% annual rate).

December 31, 2003

Interest expense	50,000	
Cash (10% × ½ × $1,000,000)		50,000
To record interest.		
Cash ($50,000—[8% × ½ × $1 million])	10,000	
Interest expense		10,000
To record the net cash settlement.		
Interest rate swap ($9,615 − 9,363)	252	
Holding gain—interest rate swap		252
To record the change in fair value of the derivative.		
Holding loss—hedged note	252	
Note payable ($1,009,615 − 1,009,363)		252
To record the change in fair value of the note due to interest rate changes.		

> As with any debt, interest expense is the effective rate times the outstanding balance.
>
> The settlement is the difference between the fixed interest (5%) and variable interest (4%).
>
> The derivative is increased by the change in fair value.
>
> The note is increased by the change in fair value.

The fair value of the swap increased by $252 (from $9,363 to $9,615). Similarly, we adjust the note's carrying value by the amount necessary to increase it to fair value. This produces a holding loss on the note that exactly offsets the gain on the swap. This result is the hedging effect that motivated Wintel to enter the cash flow hedging arrangement in the first place.

At June 30, 2004, Wintel repeats the process of adjusting to fair value both the derivative investment and the note being hedged.

June 30, 2004

Interest expense	50,000	
Cash (10% × ½ × $1,000,000)		50,000
To record interest.		
Cash [$50,000—(9% × ½ × $1 million)]	5,000	
Interest expense		5,000
To record the net cash settlement.		
Holding loss—interest rate swap	9,615	
Interest rate swap ($0 − 9,615)		9,615
To record the change in fair value of the derivative.		
Note payable ($1,000,000 − 1,009,615)	9,615	
Holding gain—hedged note		9,615
To record the change in fair value of the note due to interest rate changes.		
Note payable	1,000,000	
Cash		1,000,000
To repay the loan.		

> The net interest received is the difference between the fixed interest (5%) and floating interest (4.5%).
>
> The swap's fair value now is zero.

The net interest received is the difference between the fixed rate (5%) and floating rate (4%) times $1 million. The fair value of the swap decreased by $9,615 (from $9,615 to zero).[10] That decline represents a holding *loss* that we recognize in earnings. Similarly, we record an offsetting holding *gain* on the note for the change in its fair value.

Now let's see how the carrying values changed for the swap account and the note:

---

[10]Because there are no future cash receipts from the swap arrangement at this point, the fair value of the swap is zero.

	Swap				Note
Jan. 1, 2003					1,000,000
June 30, 2003	9,363				9,363
Dec. 31, 2003	252				252
June 30, 2004			9,615	9,615	
				1,000,000	
	0				0

The income statement is affected as follows:

Income Statement + (−)

June 30, 2003	(50,000)	Interest expense—fixed payment
	5,000	Interest expense—net cash settlement
	9,363	Holding gain—interest rate swap
	(9,363)	Holding loss—hedged note
	(45,000)	Net effect—same as floating interest payment
Dec. 31, 2003	(50,000)	Interest expense—fixed payment
	10,000	Interest expense—net cash settlement
	252	Holding gain—interest rate swap
	(252)	Holding loss—hedged note
	(40,000)	Net effect—same as floating interest payment
June 30, 2004	(50,000)	Interest expense—fixed payment
	5,000	Interest expense—net cash settlement
	9,615	Holding gain—interest rate swap
	(9,615)	Holding loss—hedged note
	(45,000)	Net effect—same as floating interest payment

As this demonstrates, the swap effectively converts fixed-interest debt to floating-interest debt.

ADDITIONAL CONSIDERATION

Fair Value of the Swap

The fair value of a derivative typically is based on a quote obtained from a derivatives dealer. That fair value will approximate the present value of the expected net interest settlement receipts for the remaining term of the swap. In fact, we can actually calculate the fair value of the swap that we accepted as given in our illustration.

Since the June 30, 2003, floating rate of 9% caused the cash settlement on that date to be $5,000, it's reasonable to look at 9% as the best estimate of future floating rates and therefore assume the remaining two cash settlements also will be $5,000 each. We can then calculate at June 30, 2003, the present value of those expected net interest settlement receipts for the remaining term of the swap:

Fixed interest	10% × ½ × $1 million	$50,000
Expected floating interest	9% × ½ × $1 million	45,000
Expected cash receipts for both Dec. 31, 2003 and June 30, 2004		$ 5,000
		× 1.87267*
Present value		$ 9,363

*Present value of an ordinary annuity of $1: n = 2, i = 4.5% (½ of 9%)

Fair Value of the Notes

The fair value of the note payable will be the present value of principal and remaining interest payments discounted at the *market rate*. The market rate will vary with the designated floating rate but might differ due to changes in default (credit) risk and the term structure of interest rates. Assuming it's 9% at June 30, 2003, we can calculate the fair value (present value) of the notes:

Interest	$50,000* × 1.87267† =	$ 93,633
Principal	$1,000,000 × .91573‡ =	915,730
		$1,009,363

*½ of 10% × $1,000,000
†Present value of an ordinary annuity of $1: n = 2, i = 4.5%
‡Present value of $1: n = 2, i = 4.5%

Note: Often the cash settlement rate is "reset" as of each cash settlement date (thus the floating rate actually used at the *end* of each period to determine the payment is the floating market rate as of the *beginning* of the same period). In our illustration, for instance, there would have been no cash settlement at June 30, 2003, since we would use the beginning floating rate of 10% to determine payment. Similarly, we would have used the 9% floating rate at June 30, 2003, to determine the cash settlement six months later at December 31. In effect, each cash settlement would be delayed six months. Had this arrangement been in effect in the current illustration, there would have been one fewer cash settlement payments (two rather than three), but would not have affected the fair value calculations above because, either way, our expectation would be cash receipts of $5,000 for both Dec. 31, 2003, and June 30, 2004.

CASH FLOW HEDGES

The risk in some transactions or events is the risk of a change in cash flows, rather than a change in fair values. We noted earlier, for instance, that *fixed-rate* debt subjects a company to the risk that interest rate changes could change the fair value of the debt. On the other hand, if the obligation is *floating-rate* debt, the fair value of the debt will not change when interest rates do, but cash flows will. If a derivative is used to hedge against the exposure to changes in cash inflows or cash outflows of an asset or liability or a forecasted transaction (like a future purchase or sale), it can be designated as a **cash flow hedge.** In that case, when the derivative is adjusted to reflect changes in fair value, the other side of the entry is a gain or loss to be deferred as a **component of Other comprehensive income** and included in earnings later, at the same time as earnings are affected by the hedged transaction. Once again, the effect is matching the earnings effect of the derivative with the earnings effect of the item being hedged, precisely the concept behind hedge accounting.

> A gain or loss from a *cash flow hedge* is deferred as Other comprehensive income until it can be recognized in earnings along with the earnings effect of the item being hedged.

To understand the deferral of the gain or loss, we need to revisit the concept of comprehensive income. Comprehensive Income, as you may recall from Chapters 4 and 12, is a more expansive view of the change in shareholders' equity than traditional net income. In fact, it encompasses all changes in equity other than from transactions with owners.[11] So, in addition to net income itself, comprehensive income includes up to four other changes in equity that don't (yet) belong in net income, namely, foreign currency translation adjustments, net unrealized gains and losses on available-for-sale securities (Chapter 12), unrealized pension costs (Chapter 17), and the deferred gain or loss from derivatives designated as cash flow hedges.[12]

Some of the more commonly used cash flow hedges are:

- An interest rate swap to synthetically convert floating rate debt (for which interest rate changes could change the cash interest payments) into fixed rate debt.
- A futures contract to hedge a forecasted sale (for which price changes could change the cash receipts) of natural gas, crude oil, or some other asset.

FOREIGN CURRENCY HEDGES

Today's economy is increasingly a global one. The majority of large "U.S." companies are, in truth, multinational companies that may receive only a fraction of their revenues from U.S. operations. Many operations of those companies are located abroad. Foreign operations often are denominated in the currency of the foreign country (the Euro, Japanese yen, Russian

---

[11]Transactions with owners primarily include dividends and the sale or purchase of shares of the company's stock.
[12]"Reporting Comprehensive Income," *Statement of Financial Accounting Standards No. 130* (Norwalk, Conn.: FASB, 1997).

The possibility that foreign currency exchange rates might change exposes many companies to foreign currency risk.

rubles, and so on). Even companies without foreign operations sometimes hold investments, issue debt, or conduct other transactions denominated in foreign currencies. As exchange rates change, the dollar equivalent of the foreign currency changes. The possibility of currency rate changes exposes these companies to the risk that some transactions require settlement in a currency other than the entities' functional currency or that foreign operations will require translation adjustments to reported amounts.

A **foreign currency hedge** can be a hedge of foreign currency exposure of:

- A firm commitment—treated as a fair value hedge.
- An available-for-sale security—treated as a fair value hedge.
- A forecasted transaction—treated as a cash flow hedge.
- A company's net investment in a foreign operation—the gain or loss is reported in *other comprehensive income* as part of the cumulative translation adjustment.[13]

HEDGE EFFECTIVENESS

When a company elects to apply hedge accounting, it must establish at the inception of the hedge the method it will use to assess the effectiveness of the hedging derivative as well as the measurement approach it will use to determine the ineffective portion of the hedge.[14] The key criterion for qualifying as a hedge is that the hedging relationship must be highly effective in achieving offsetting changes in fair values or cash flows based on the hedging company's specified risk management objective and strategy.

To qualify as a hedge, the hedging relationship must be highly effective in achieving offsetting changes in fair values or cash flows.

An assessment of this effectiveness must be made at least every three months and whenever financial statements are issued. There are no precise guidelines for assessing effectiveness, but it generally means a high correlation between changes in the fair value or cash flows of the derivative and of the item being hedged, not necessarily a specific reduction in risk. Hedge accounting must be terminated for hedging relationships that no longer are highly effective.

HEDGE INEFFECTIVENESS

In Illustration A–1, the loss on the hedged note exactly offset the gain on the swap. This is because the swap in this instance was highly effective in hedging the risk due to interest rate changes. However, the loss and gain would not have exactly offset each other if the hedging arrangement had been ineffective. For instance, suppose the swap's term had been different from that of the note (say a three-year swap term compared with the 18-month term of the note) or if the notional amount of the swap differed from that of the note (say $500,000 rather than $1 million). In that case, changes in the fair value of the swap and changes in the fair value of the note would not be the same. The result would be a greater (or lesser) amount recognized in earnings for the swap than for the note. Because there would not be an exact offset, earnings would be affected, an effect resulting from hedge ineffectiveness. That is a desired effect of hedge accounting; to the extent that a hedge is effective, the earnings effect of a derivative cancels out the earnings effect of the item being hedged. However, even if a hedge is highly effective, all ineffectiveness is recognized currently in earnings.

Imperfect hedges result in part of the derivative gain or loss being included in current earnings.

FAIR VALUE CHANGES UNRELATED TO THE RISK BEING HEDGED

In Illustration A–1, the fair value of the hedged note and the fair value of the swap changed by the same amounts each year because we assumed the fair values changed only due to interest rate changes. It's also possible, though, that the note's fair value would change by an amount different from that of the swap for reasons unrelated to interest rates. Remember from our earlier discussion that the market's perception of a company's creditworthiness, and thus its ability to pay interest and principal when due, also can affect the value of debt, whether interest rates change or not. In hedge accounting, we ignore those changes. We

---

[13]This is the same treatment previously prescribed for these translation adjustments by *Statement of Financial Accounting Standards No. 52.*

[14]Remember, if a derivative is not designated as a hedge, any gains or losses from changes in its fair value are recognized immediately in earnings.

recognize only the fair value changes in the hedged item that we can attribute to the risk being hedged (interest rate risk in this case). For example, if a changing perception of default risk had caused the note's fair value to increase by an additional, say $5,000, our journal entries in Illustration A–1 would have been unaffected. Notice, then, that although we always mark a *derivative* to fair value, the reported amount of the *item being hedged* may not be its fair value. We mark a hedged item to fair value only to the extent that its fair value changed due to the risk being hedged.

Fair value changes unrelated to the risk being hedged are ignored.

Disclosure of Derivatives and Risk

To be adequately informed about the adequacy of a company's risk management, investors and creditors need information about strategies for holding derivatives and specific hedging activities. Toward that end, extensive disclosure requirements provide information that includes:

- Objectives and strategies for holding and issuing derivatives.
- A description of the items for which risks are being hedged.
- For forecasted transactions: a description, time before the transaction is expected to occur, the gains and losses accumulated in other comprehensive income, and the events that will trigger their recognition in earnings.
- Beginning balance of, changes in, and ending balance of the derivative component of other comprehensive income.
- The net amount of gain or loss reported in earnings (representing aggregate hedge ineffectiveness).
- Qualitative and quantitative information about failed hedges: canceled commitments or previously hedged forecasted transactions no longer expected to occur.

The intent is to provide information about the company's success in reducing risks and consequently about risks not managed successfully. Remember, too, that when derivatives are employed ineffectively, risks can escalate. Ample disclosures about derivatives are essential to maintain awareness of potential opportunities and problems with risk management.

Even for some traditional liabilities, the amounts reported on the face of the financial statements provide inadequate disclosure about the degree to which a company is exposed to risk of loss. To provide adequate disclosure about a company's exposure to risk, additional information must be provided about (a) concentrations of credit risk and (b) the fair value of all financial instruments.[15]

Extended Method for Interest Rate Swap Accounting

A short-cut method for accounting for an interest rate swap is permitted by *SFAS 133* when a hedge meets certain criteria. In general, the criteria are designed to see if the hedge supports the assumption of "no ineffectiveness." Illustration A–1 of a fair value hedge met those criteria, in particular, (a) the swap's notional amount matches the note's principal amount, (b) the swap's expiration date matches the note's maturity date, (c) the fair value of the swap is zero at inception, and (d) the floating payment is at the market rate.[16] Because Wintel can conclude that the swap will be highly effective in offsetting changes in the fair value of the debt, it can use the changes in the fair value of the swap to measure the offsetting changes in the fair value of the debt. That's the essence of the short-cut method used in Illustration A–1. The extended method required when the criteria are *not* met for the short-cut method is described in this section (Illustration A–2 on the next page). It produces the same effect on earnings and in the balance sheet as does the procedure shown in Illustration A–1.

---

[15]"Disclosures About Fair Values of Financial Instruments," *Statement of Financial Accounting Standards No. 107* (Norwalk, Conn.: FASB, 1991) as amended by *Statement of Financial Accounting Standards No. 133,* "Accounting for Derivative Instruments and Hedging Activities" (Norwalk, Conn.: FASB, 1998).

[16]There is no precise minimum interval, though it generally is three to six months or less. Other criteria are specified by *SFAS 133* (para. 68) in addition to the key conditions listed here.

ILLUSTRATION A–2	Wintel Semiconductors issued $1 million of 18-month, 10% bank notes on January 1, 2003. Wintel is exposed to the risk that general interest rates will decline, causing the fair value of its debt to rise. (If the fair value of Wintel's debt increases, its effective borrowing cost is higher relative to the market.) To hedge against this fair value risk, the firm entered into an 18-month interest rate swap agreement on January 1 and designated the swap as a hedge against changes in the fair value of the note. The swap calls for the company to *receive payment* based on a 10% fixed interest rate on a notional amount of $1 million and to *make payment* based on a floating interest rate tied to changes in general rates. Cash settlement of the net interest amount is made semiannually at June 30 and December 31 of each year with the net interest being the difference between the $50,000 fixed interest [$1 million $\times$ (10% $\times$ ½)] and the floating interest rate times $1 million at those dates.
Interest Rate Swap— Extended Method	

Floating (market) settlement rates were 9% at June 30, 2003, 8% at December 31, 2003, and 8% at June 30, 2004. Net interest receipts can be calculated as shown below. Fair values of both the derivative and the note resulting from those market rate changes are assumed to be quotes obtained from securities dealers.

	1/1/03	6/30/03	12/31/03	6/30/04
Fixed rate	10%	10%	10%	10%
Floating rate	10%	9%	8%	8%
Fixed payments [$1 million $\times$ (10% $\times$ ½)]		$ 50,000	$ 50,000	$ 50,000
Floating payments ($1 million $\times$ ½ floating rate)		45,000	40,000	40,000
Net interest receipts		$ 5,000	$ 10,000	$ 10,000
Fair value of interest rate swap	0	$ 9,363	$ 9,615	0
Fair value of note payable	$1,000,000	$1,009,363	$1,009,615	$1,000,000

When the floating rate declined in Illustration A–2 from 10% to 9%, the fair values of both the derivative (swap) and the note increased. This created an offsetting gain on the derivative and holding loss on the note. Both are recognized in earnings the same period (June 30, 2003).

The interest rate swap is designated as a cash flow hedge on this note at issuance.	**January 1, 2003**		
	Cash	1,000,000	
	Notes payable		1,000,000
	To record the issuance of the note.		

June 30, 2003

Interest expense (10% $\times$ ½ $\times$ $1 million)	50,000	
Cash		50,000
To record interest.		

The swap settlement is the difference between the fixed interest (5%) and variable interest (4.5%).

Cash ($50,000—[9% $\times$ ½ $\times$ $1 million])	5,000	
Interest rate swap ($9,363 − 0)	9,363	
Interest revenue (10% $\times$ ½ $\times$ $0)		0
Holding gain—interest rate swap (to balance)		14,363
To record the net cash settlement, accrued interest on the swap, and change in the fair value of the derivative.		

The fair value of derivatives is recognized in the balance sheet.

To record change in fair value of the derivative.

The hedged liability (or asset) is adjusted to fair value as well.

Holding loss—hedged note	9,363	
Notes payable ($1,009,363 − 1,000,000)		9,363
To record change in fair value of the note due to interest rate changes.		

The net interest settlement on June 30, 2003, is $5,000 because the fixed rate is 5% (half of the 10% annual rate) and the floating rate is 4.5% (half of the 9% annual rate). A holding gain ($14,363) is produced by holding the derivative security during a time when an interest rate decline caused a rise in the value of that asset. A portion ($5,000) of the gain was received in cash and another portion ($9,363) is reflected as an increase in the value of the asset.

We also have holding loss of the same amount. This is because we also held a liability during the same time period, and the interest rate change caused its fair value to increase as well.

December 31, 2003

Interest expense (9% $\times$ ½ $\times$ $1,009,363)	45,421	
Notes payable (difference)*	4,579	
Cash (10% $\times$ ½ $\times$ $1,000,000)		50,000
To record interest.		
Cash [$50,000 − (8% $\times$ ½ $\times$ $1 million)].	10,000	
Interest rate swap ($9,615 − 9,363)	252	
Interest revenue (9% $\times$ ½ $\times$ $9,363)		421
Holding gain—interest rate swap (to balance)		9,831
To record the net cash settlement, accrued interest on the swap,		
and change in the fair value of the derivative.		
Holding loss—hedged note	4,831	
Notes payable ($1,009,615 − 1,009,363 + 4,579)		4,831
To record the change in fair value of the note due to interest rate changes.		

As with any debt, interest expense is the effective rate times the outstanding balance.

The cash settlement is the difference between the fixed interest (5%) and variable interest (4%).

Interest ($421) accrues on the asset.

The note is increased by the change in fair value.

*We could use a premium on the note to adjust its carrying amount.

We determine interest on the note the same way we do for any liability, as you learned earlier—at the effective rate (9% $\times$ ½) times the outstanding balance ($1,009,363). This results in reducing the note's carrying amount for the cash interest paid in excess of the interest expense.

The fair value of the swap increased due to the interest rate decline by $252 (from $9,363 to $9,615). The holding gain we recognize in earnings consists of that increase (a) plus the $10,000 cash settlement also created by the interest rate decline and (b) minus the $421 increase that results not from the interest rate decline, but from interest accruing on the asset.[17] Similarly, we adjust the note's carrying value by the amount necessary to increase it to fair value, allowing for the $4,579 reduction in the note in the earlier entry to record interest.

At June 30, 2004, Wintel repeats the process of adjusting to fair value both the derivative investment and the note being hedged.

June 30, 2004

Interest expense (8% $\times$ ½ $\times$ $1,009,615)	40,385	
Notes payable (difference)	9,615	
Cash (10% $\times$ ½ $\times$ $1,000,000)		50,000
To record interest.		
Cash [$50,000 − (9% $\times$ ½ $\times$ $1 million)].	5,000	
Holding loss—interest rate swap (to balance)	5,000	
Interest rate swap ($0 − $9,615)		9,615
Interest revenue (8% $\times$ ½ $\times$ $9,615)		385
To record the net cash settlement, accrued interest on the swap,		
and change in the fair value of the derivative.		

Interest expense is the effective rate times the outstanding balance.

The net interest received is the difference between the fixed interest (5%) and floating interest (4.5%).

The swap's fair value now is zero.

---

[17]The investment in the interest rate swap represents the present value of expected future net interest receipts. As with other such assets, interest accrues at the effective rate times the outstanding balance. You also can think of the accrued interest mathematically as the increase in present value of the future cash flows as we get one period nearer to the dates when the cash will be received.

Notes payable ($1,000,000 − 1,009,615 + 9,615).   0
   Holding gain—hedged note.   0
To record the change in fair value of the note due to interest rate changes.

Note payable.   1,000,000
   Cash.   1,000,000
To repay the loan

The net interest received is the difference between the fixed rate (5%) and floating rate (4%) times $1 million. The fair value of the swap decreased by $9,615 (from $9,615 to zero).[18] The holding loss we recognize in earnings consists of that decline (a) minus the $5,000 portion of the decline resulting from it being realized in cash settlement and (b) plus the $385 increase that results not from the interest rate change, but from interest accruing on the asset.

Now let's see how the carrying values changed for the swap account and the note:

	Swap			Note	
Jan. 1, 2003					1,000,000
June 30, 2003	9,363				9,363
Dec. 31, 2003	252			4,579	4,831
June 30, 2004			9,615	9,615	
				1,000,000	
	0				0

The income statement is affected as follows:

	Income Statement + (−)	
June 30, 2003	(50,000)	Interest expense
	0	Interest revenue (no time has passed)
	14,363	Holding gain interest rate swap
	(9,363)	Holding loss—hedged note
	(45,000)	Net effect—same as floating interest payment
Dec. 31, 2003	(45,421)	Interest expense
	421	Interest revenue
	9,831	Holding gain—interest rate swap
	(4,831)	Holding loss—hedged note
	(40,000)	Net effect—same as floating interest payment
June 30, 2004	(40,385)	Interest expense
	385	Interest revenue
	(5,000)	Holding loss—interest rate swap
	0	Holding gain—hedged note
	(45,000)	Net effect—same as floating interest payment

As this demonstrates, the swap effectively converts Wintel's fixed-interest debt to floating-interest debt.

THE BOTTOM LINE

1. All derivatives are reported in the balance sheet at fair value.
2. *Hedging* means taking a risk position that is opposite to an actual position that is exposed to risk. For a derivative used to hedge against exposure to risk, treatment of any

---

[18]Because there are no future cash receipts or payments from the swap arrangement at this point, the fair value of the swap is zero.

gain or loss from fair value changes depends on whether the derivative is designated as (a) a fair value hedge or (b) a cash flow hedge.

3. We recognize a gain or loss from a *fair value hedge* immediately in earnings along with the loss or gain from the item being hedged. This is so the income effects of the hedge instrument and the income effects of the item being hedged will affect earnings at the same time.

4. We defer a gain or loss from a *cash flow hedge* as part of Other comprehensive income until it can be recognized in earnings along with the earnings effect of the item being hedged.

5. Imperfect hedges result in part of the derivative gain or loss being included in current earnings. We ignore market value changes unrelated to the risk being hedged.

6. Extensive disclosure requirements about derivatives are designed to provide investors and creditors information about the adequacy of a company's risk management and the company's success in reducing risks, including risks not managed successfully. ▪

QUESTIONS FOR REVIEW OF KEY TOPICS

Q A–1   Some financial instruments are called derivatives. Why?

Q A–2   Should gains and losses on a fair value hedge be recorded as they occur, or should they be recorded to coincide with losses and gains on the item being hedged?

Q A–3   Hines Moving Company held a fixed-rate debt of $2 million. The company wanted to hedge its fair value exposure with an interest rate swap. However, the only notional available at the time on the type of swap it desired was $2.5 million. What will be the effect of any gain or loss on the $500,000 notional difference?

Q A–4   What is a futures contract?

Q A–5   What is the effect on interest of an interest rate swap?

Q A–6   How are derivatives reported on the balance sheet? Why?

Q A–7   When is a gain or a loss from a cash flow hedge reported in earnings?

EXERCISES

E A–1
Derivatives—hedge classification

Indicate (by abbreviation) the type of hedge each activity described below would represent.

Hedge Type

FV	Fair value hedge
CF	Cash flow hedge
FC	Foreign currency hedge
N	Would not qualify as a hedge

Activity

_____ 1. An options contract to hedge possible future price changes of inventory.

_____ 2. A futures contract to hedge exposure to interest rate changes prior to replacing bank notes when they mature.

_____ 3. An interest rate swap to synthetically convert floating rate debt into fixed rate debt.

_____ 4. An interest rate swap to synthetically convert fixed rate debt into floating rate debt.

_____ 5. A futures contract to hedge possible future price changes of timber covered by a firm commitment to sell.

_____ 6. A futures contract to hedge possible future price changes of a forecasted sale of tin.

_____ 7. ExxonMobil's net investment in a Kuwait oil field.

_____ 8. An interest rate swap to synthetically convert floating rate interest on a stock investment into fixed rate interest.

_____ 9. An interest rate swap to synthetically convert fixed rate interest on a held-to-maturity debt investment into floating rate interest.

_____ 10. An interest rate swap to synthetically convert floating rate interest on a held-to-maturity debt investment into fixed rate interest.

_____ 11. An interest rate swap to synthetically convert fixed rate interest on a stock investment into floating rate interest.

E A–2

Derivatives; interest rate swap; fixed rate debt

On January 1, 2003, LLB Industries borrowed $200,000 from Trust Bank by issuing a 2-year, 10% note, with interest payable quarterly. LLB entered into a 2-year interest rate swap agreement on January 1, 2003, and designated the swap as a fair value hedge. Its intent was to hedge the risk that general interest rates will decline, causing the fair value of its debt to increase. The agreement called for the company to receive payment based on a 10% fixed interest rate on a notional amount of $200,000 and to pay interest based on a floating interest rate. The contract called for cash settlement of the net interest amount quarterly.

Floating (LIBOR) settlement rates were 10% at January 1, 8% at March 31, and 6% June 30, 2003. The fair values of the swap are quotes obtained from a derivatives dealer. Those quotes and the fair values of the note are as indicated below. The additional rise in the fair value of the note (higher than that of the swap) on June 30 was due to investors' perceptions that the creditworthiness of LLB was improving.

	January 1	March 31	June 30
Fair value of interest rate swap	0	$ 6,472	$ 11,394
Fair value of note payable	$200,000	$206,472	$211,394

Required:
1. Calculate the net cash settlement at June 30, 2003.
2. Prepare the journal entries on June 30, 2003, to record the issuance of the note, interest, and necessary adjustments for changes in fair value.

E A–3

Derivatives; interest rate swap; fixed rate investment

(This is a variation of Exercise A–2, modified to consider an investment in debt securities.)

On January 1, 2003, S&S Corporation invested in LLB Industries' negotiable 2-year, 10% notes, with interest receivable quarterly. The company classified the investment as a available-for-sale. S&S entered into a two-year interest rate swap agreement on January 1, 2003, and designated the swap as a a fair value hedge. Its intent was to hedge the risk that general interest rates will decline, causing the fair value of its investment to decline. The agreement called for the company to make payment based on a 10% fixed interest rate on a notional amount of $200,000 and to receive interest based on a floating interest rate. The contract called for cash settlement of the net interest amount quarterly.

Floating (LIBOR) settlement rates were 10% at January 1, 8% at March 31, and 6% June 30, 2003. The fair values of the swap are quotes obtained from a derivatives dealer. Those quotes and the fair values of the note are as follows:

	January 1	March 31	June 30
Fair value of interest rate swap	0	$ 6,472	$ 11,394
Fair value of the investment in notes	$200,000	$206,472	$211,394

Required:
1. Calculate the net cash settlement at March 31 and June 30, 2003
2. Prepare the journal entries through June 30, 2003, to record the issuance of the note, interest, and necessary adjustments for changes in fair value.

E A–4

Derivatives; interest rate swap; fixed rate debt; fair value change unrelated to hedged risk

(This is a variation of Exercise A–2, modified to consider fair value change unrelated to hedged risk.)

LLB Industries borrowed $200,000 from Trust Bank by issuing a two-year, 10% note, with interest payable quarterly. LLB entered into a two-year interest rate swap agreement on January 1, 2003 and designated the swap as a fair value hedge. Its intent was to hedge the risk that general interest rates will decline, causing the fair value of its debt to increase. The agreement called for the company to receive payment based on a 10% fixed interest rate on a notional amount of $200,000 and to pay interest based on a floating interest rate. The contract called for cash settlement of the net interest amount quarterly. The floating rate was to be rest at each cash settlement date. Thus the floating rate applied at the end of each quarter is the rate as of the beginning of the same quarter.

Floating (LIBOR) settlement rates were 10% at January 1, 8% at March 31, and 6% at June 30, 2003. The fair values of the swap are quotes obtained from a derivatives dealer. Those quotes and the fair values of the not are as indicated below. The additional rise in the fair value of the not (higher than that of the swap) on June 30 was due to investors' perceptions that the creditworthiness of LLB was improving.

	January 1	March 31	June 30
Fair value of interest rate swap	0	$ 6,472	$ 11,394
Fair value of note payable	$200,000	$206,472	$220,000

Required:

1. Calculate the net cash settlement at June 30, 2003
2. Prepare the journal entries on June 30, 2003, to record the interest and necessary adjustments for changes in fair value.

E A–5

Derivatives; interest rate swap; fixed rate debt; extended method

This is a variation of Exercise A–2, modified to consider the extended method.

On January 1, 2003, LLB Industries borrowed $200,000 from Trust Bank by issuing a two-year, 10% note, with interest payable quarterly. LLB entered into a two-year interest rate swap agreement on January 1, 2003, and designated the swap as a fair value hedge. Its intent was to hedge the risk that general interest rates will decline, causing the fair value of its debt to increase. The agreement called for the company to receive payment based on a 10% fixed interest rate on a notional amount of $200,000 and to pay interest based on a floating interest rate. The contract called for cash settlement of the net interest amount quarterly. The floating rate was to be reset at each cash settlement date. Thus the floating rate applied at the end of each quarter is the rate as of the beginning of the same quarter.

Floating (LIBOR) settlement rates were 10% at January 1, 8% at March 31, and 6% at June 30, 2003. The fair values of the swap are quotes obtained from a derivatives dealer. Those quotes and the fair values of the note are as follows:

	January 1	March 31	June 30
Fair value of interest rate swap	0	$ 6,472	$ 11,394
Fair value of note payable	$200,000	$206,472	$211,394

Required:
Prepare the journal entries through June 30, 2003, to record the issuance of the note, interest, and necessary adjustments for changes in fair value. Use the extended method demonstrated in Illustration A–2.

E A–6

Derivatives; interest rate swap; fixed-rate debt; fair value change unrelated to hedged risk; extended method

(Note: This is a variation of Exercise A–5, modified to consider fair value change unrelated to hedged risk.)

On January 1, 2003, LLB Industries borrowed $200,000 from trust Bank by issuing a 2-year, 10% note, with interest payable quarterly. LLB entered into a 2-year interest rate swap agreement on January 1, 2003, and designated the swap as a fair value hedge. Its intent was to hedge the risk that general interest rates will decline, causing the fair value of its debt to increase. The agreement called for the company to receive payment based on a 10% fixed-interest rate on a notional amount of $200,000 and to pay interest based on a floating-interest rate. The contract called for cash settlement of the net interest amount quarterly.

Floating (LIBOR) settlement rates were 10% at January 1, 8% at March 31, and 6% June 30, 2003. The fair values of the swap are quotes obtained from a derivatives dealer. Those quotes and the fair values of the note are as indicated below. The additional rise in the fair value of the note (higher than that of the swap) on June 30 was due to investors' perceptions that the creditworthiness of LLB was improving.

	January 1	March 31	June 30
Fair value of interest rate swap	0	$ 6,472	$ 11,394
Fair value of note payable	$200,000	206,472	220,000

Required:

1. Calculate the net cash settlement at June 30, 2003.
2. Prepare the journal entries on June 30, 2003, to record the interest and necessary adjustments for changes in fair value. Use the extended method demonstrated in Illustration A–2.

PROBLEMS

P A–1

Derivatives—interest rate swap

On January 1, 2003, Labtech Circuits borrowed $100,000 from First Bank by issuing a three-year, 8% note, payable on December 31, 2005. Labtech wanted to hedge the risk that general interest rates will decline, causing the fair value of its debt to increase. Therefore, Labtech entered into a three-year interest rate swap agreement on January 1, 2003, and designated the swap as a fair value hedge. The agreement called for the company to receive payment based on an 8% fixed interest rate on a notional amount of $100,000 and to pay interest based on a floating interest rate tied to LIBOR. The contract called for cash settlement of the net interest amount on December 31 of each year.

Floating (LIBOR) settlement rates were 8% at inception and 9%, 7%, and 7% at the end of 2003, 2004, and 2005, respectively. The fair values of the swap are quotes obtained from a derivatives dealer. These quotes and the fair values of the note are as follows:

| | January 1 | December 31 | | |
	2003	**2003**	**2004**	**2005**
Fair value of interest rate swap	0	$ (1,783)	$ 935	0
Fair value of note payable	$100,000	$98,217	$100,935	$100,000

Required:

1. Calculate the net cash settlement at the end of 2003, 2004, and 2005.
2. Prepare the journal entries during 2003 to record the issuance of the note, interest, and necessary adjustments for changes in fair value.
3. Prepare the journal entries during 2004 to record interest, net cash interest settlement for the interest rate swap, and necessary adjustments for changes in fair value.
4. Prepare the journal entries during 2005 to record interest, net cash interest settlement for the interest rate swap, necessary adjustments for changes in fair value, and repayment of the debt.
5. Calculate the carrying values of both the swap account and the note in each of the three years.
6. Calculate the net effect on earnings of the hedging arrangement in each of the three years. (Ignore income taxes.)
7. Suppose the fair value of the note at December 31, 2003, had been $97,000 rather than $98,217 with the additional decline in fair value due to investors' perceptions that the creditworthiness of Labtech was worsening. How would that affect your entries to record changes in the fair values?

P A–2

Derivatives; interest rate swap; comprehensive

CMOS Chips is hedging a 20-year, $10 million, 7% bond payable with a 20-year interest rate swap and has designated the swap as a fair value hedge. The agreement called for CMOS to receive payment based on a 7% fixed interest rate on a notional amount of $10 million and to pay interest based on a floating interest rate tied to LIBOR. The contract calls for cash settlement of the net interest amount on December 31 of each year.

At December 31, 2003, the fair value of the derivative and of the hedged bonds has increased by $100,000 because interest rates declined during the reporting period.

Required:

1. Does CMOS have an unrealized gain or loss on the derivative for the period? On the bonds? Will earnings increase or decrease due to the hedging arrangement? Why?
2. Suppose interest rates increased, rather than decreased, causing the fair value of both the derivative and of the hedged bonds to decrease by $100,000. Would CMOS have an unrealized gain or loss on the derivative for the period? On the bonds? Would earnings increase or decrease due to the hedging arrangement? Why?
3. Suppose the fair value of the bonds at December 31, 2003, had increased by $110,000 rather than $100,000, with the additional increase in fair value due to investors' perceptions that the creditworthiness of CMOS was improving. Would CMOS have an unrealized gain or loss on the derivative for the period? On the bonds? Would earnings increase or decrease due to the hedging arrangement? Why
4. Suppose the notional amount of the swap had been $12 million, rather than the $10 million principal amount of the bonds. As a result, at December 31, 2003, the swap's fair value had increased by $120,000 rather than $100,000. Would CMOS have an unrealized gain or loss on the derivative for the period? On the bonds? Would earnings increase or decrease due to the hedging arrangement? Why?
5. Suppose BIOS Corporation is an investor having purchased all $10 million of the bonds issued by CMOS as described in the original situation above. BIOS is hedging its investment, classified as available-for-sale, with a 20-year interest rate swap and has designated the swap as a fair value hedge. The agreement called for BIOS to make *payment* based on a 7% fixed interest rate on a notional amount of $10 million to *receive* interest based on a floating interest rate tied to LIBOR. Would BIOS have an unrealized gain or loss on the derivative for the period due to interest rates having declined? On the bonds? Would earnings increase or decrease due to the hedging arrangement? Why?

P A–3

Derivatives; interest rate swap; fixed rate debt; extended method

(Note: This is a variation of Problem A–1. modified to consider the extended method demonstrated in Illustration A–2.)

On January 1, 2003, Labtech Circuits borrowed $100,000 from First Bank by issuing a 3-year, 8% note, payable on December 31, 2005. Labtech wanted to hedge the risk that general interest rates will decline, causing the fair value of its debt to increase. Therefore, Labtech entered into a 3-year interest rate swap agreement on January 1, 2003, and designated the swap as a fair value hedge. The agreement called for the company to receive payment based on an 8% fixed interest rate on a notional amount of $100,000 and to pay interest based on a floating interest rate tied to LIBOR. The contract called for cash settlement of the net interest amount on December 31 of each year.

Floating (LIBOR) settlement rates were 8% at inception and 9%, 7%, and 7% at the end of 2003, 2004, and 2005, respectively. The fair values of the swap are quotes obtained from a derivatives dealer. Those quotes and the fair values of the note are as follows:

| | January 1 | December 31 | | |
	2003	2003	2004	2005
Fair value of interest rate swap	0	$ (1,783)	$ 935	0
Fair value of note payable	$100,000	98,217	100,935	$100,000

Required:
Use the extended method demonstrated in Illustration A–2.
1. Calculate the net cash settlement at the end of 2003, 2004, and 2005.
2. Prepare the journal entries during 2003 to record the issuance of the note, interest, and necessary adjustments for changes in fair value.
3. Prepare the journal entries during 2004 to record interest, net cash interest settlement for the interest rate swap, and necessary adjustments for changes in fair value.
4. Prepare the journal entries during 2005 to record interest, net cash interest settlement for the interest rate swap, necessary adjustments for changes in fair value, and repayment of the debt.
5. Calculate the carrying values of both the swap account and the note in each of the three years.
6. Calculate the net effect on earnings of the hedging arrangement in each of the three years. (Ignore income taxes.)
7. Suppose the fair value of the note at December 31, 2003, had been $97,000 rather than $98,217 with the additional decline in fair value due to investors' perceptions that the creditworthiness of Labtech was worsening. How would that affect your entries to record changes in the fair values?

BROADEN YOUR PERSPECTIVE

Apply your critical-thinking ability to the knowledge you've gained. These cases will provide you an opportunity to develop your research, analysis, judgment, and communication skills. You also will work with other students, integrate what you've learned, apply it in real world situations, and consider its global and ethical ramifications. This practice will broaden your knowledge and further develop your decision-making abilities.

Research Case A–1
Disclosure of derivative risk; research article in *Accounting Horizons*

Some financial instruments are derivatives related to foreign exchange transactions. Professors Goldbert, Tritschler, and Godwin, in "Financial Reporting for Foreign Exchange Derivatives," surveyed actual disclosures on foreign exchange derivatives to examine the extent and usefulness of those disclosures. Based on their survey, the authors drew conclusions regarding avoiding large derivative losses like those reported recently by Procter & Gamble and Gibson Greetings, or at least avoiding being surprised by them.

Required:
1. In your library or from some other source, locate the indicated article in *Accounting Horizons*, June 1995.
2. What are the three conclusions the authors reach regarding avoiding large derivative losses like those reported recently by Procter & Gamble and Gibson Greetings, or at least avoiding being surprised by them?

Communication Case A–2
Derivatives; hedge accounting

A conceptual question in accounting for derivatives is: Should gains and losses on a hedge instrument be recorded as they occur, or should they be recorded to coincide (match) with income effects of the item being hedged?

ABI Wholesalers plans to issue long-term notes in May that will replace its $20 million of 9.5% bonds when they mature in July. ABI is exposed to the risk that interest rates in July will have risen, increasing borrowing costs (reducing the selling price of its notes). To hedge that possibility, ABI entered a (Treasury bond) futures contract in May to deliver (sell) bonds in July at their *current* price.

As a result, if interest rates rise, borrowing costs will go up for ABI because it will sell notes at a higher interest cost (or lower price). But that loss will be offset (approximately) by the gain produced by being in the opposite position on Treasury bond futures.

Two opposing viewpoints are:

View 1: Gains and losses on instruments designed to hedge anticipated transactions should be recorded as they occur.

View 2: Gains and losses on instruments designed to hedge anticipated transactions should be recorded to coincide (match) with income effects of the item being hedged.

In considering this question, focus on conceptual issues regarding the practicable and theoretically appropriate treatment, unconstrained by GAAP. Your instructor will divide the class into from two to six groups depending on the size of the class. The mission of your group is to reach consensus on the appropriate accounting for the gains and losses on instruments designed to hedge anticipated transactions.

Required:

1. Each group member should deliberate the situation independently and draft a tentative argument prior to the class session for which the case is assigned.

2. In class, each group will meet for 10 to 15 minutes in different areas of the classroom. during that meeting, group members will take turns sharing their suggestions for the purpose of arriving at a single group treatment.

3. After the allotted time, a spokesperson for each group (selected during the group meetings) will share the group's solution with the class. the goal of the class is to incorporate the views of each group into a consensus approach to the situation.

Real World Case A–3
Researching the way interest rate futures prices are quoted on the Chicago Mercantile Exchange; retrieving information from the Internet

The Chicago Mercantile Exchange, or Merc, at 30 S. Wacker Drive in Chicago, is the world's largest financial exchange, an international marketplace enabling institutions and businesses to trade futures and options contracts including currencies, interest rates, stock indices, and agricultural commodities.

Required:

1. Access the Merc on the Internet. The web address is **www.cme.com**.
2. Access the daily settlement prices within the site. Scroll to find the 13-week Treasury bill futures.
3. What are the settlement prices for September and December futures contracts?
4. In terms of dollars, how can we interpret the settlement price?

Research Case A–4
Issue related to the derivatives standard; research an article

In an effort to keep up with the rapidly changing global financial markets, the FASB issued a standard—*SFAS 133*—on accounting for derivative financial instruments. A *Journal of Accountancy* article that discusses this standard is "The Decision on Derivatives," by Arlette C. Wilson, Gary Waters and Barry J. Bryan, November 1998.

Required:

On the Internet, go to the AICPA site at **www.aicpa.org** and find the article mentioned.

1. What are the primary problems or issues the FASB is attempting to address with the new standard?
2. In considering the issues, the FASB made four fundamental decisions that became the cornerstones of the proposed statement. What are those fundamental decisions? Which do you think is most critical to fair financial reporting?

Subject Index

Note: Page numbers followed by *n* indicate material in footnotes.

Accounting Standards Index

Note: Page numbers followed by *n* indicate material in footnotes.